W9-CTW-429

Twentieth-Century Literary Criticism

Guide to Gale Literary Criticism Series

For criticism on	Consult these Gale series
Authors now living or who died after December 31, 1959	*CONTEMPORARY LITERARY CRITICISM (CLC)*
Authors who died between 1900 and 1959	*TWENTIETH-CENTURY LITERARY CRITICISM (TCLC)*
Authors who died between 1800 and 1899	*NINETEENTH-CENTURY LITERATURE CRITICISM (NCLC)*
Authors who died between 1400 and 1799	*LITERATURE CRITICISM FROM 1400 TO 1800 (LC)* *SHAKESPEAREAN CRITICISM (SC)*
Authors who died before 1400	*CLASSICAL AND MEDIEVAL LITERATURE CRITICISM (CMLC)*
Black writers of the past two hundred years	*BLACK LITERATURE CRITICISM (BLC)*
Authors of books for children and young adults	*CHILDREN'S LITERATURE REVIEW (CLR)*
Dramatists	*DRAMA CRITICISM (DC)*
Hispanic writers of the late nineteenth and twentieth centuries	*HISPANIC LITERATURE CRITICISM (HLC)*
Native North American writers and orators of the eighteenth, nineteenth, and twentieth centuries	*NATIVE NORTH AMERICAN LITERATURE (NNAL)*
Poets	*POETRY CRITICISM (PC)*
Short story writers	*SHORT STORY CRITICISM (SSC)*
Major authors from the Renaissance to the present	*WORLD LITERATURE CRITICISM, 1500 TO THE PRESENT (WLC)*

ISSN 0276-8178

Volume 64

Twentieth-Century Literary Criticism

**Excerpts from Criticism of the
Works of Novelists, Poets, Playwrights,
Short Story Writers, and Other Creative Writers
Who Lived between 1900 and 1960,
from the First Published Critical
Appraisals to Current Evaluations**

**Nancy Dziedzic
Scot Peacock
*Editors***

**Thomas Ligotti
Brandon Trenz
*Associate Editors***

GALE

DETROIT • NEW YORK • TORONTO • LONDON

Library of Congress Catalog Card Number 76-46132
ISBN 0-7876-0778-9
ISSN 0276-8178

Printed in the United States of America
10 9 8 7 6 5 4 3 2 1

Contents

Preface vii

Acknowledgments xi

Preface

Since its inception more than fifteen years ago, *Twentieth-Century Literary Criticism* has been purchased and used by nearly 10,000 school, public, and college or university libraries. *TCLC* has covered more than 500 authors, representing 58 nationalities, and over 25,000 titles. No other reference source has surveyed the critical response to twentieth-century authors and literature as thoroughly as *TCLC*. In the words of one reviewer, "there is nothing comparable available." *TCLC* "is a gold mine of information—dates, pseudonyms, biographical information, and criticism from books and periodicals—which many libraries would have difficulty assembling on their own."

Scope of the Series

TCLC is designed to serve as an introduction to authors who died between 1900 and 1960 and to the most significant interpretations of these author's works. The great poets, novelists, short story writers, playwrights, and philosophers of this period are frequently studied in high school and college literature courses. In organizing and excerpting the vast amount of critical material written on these authors, *TCLC* helps students develop valuable insight into literary history, promotes a better understanding of the texts, and sparks ideas for papers and assignments. Each entry in *TCLC* presents a comprehensive survey of an author's career or an individual work of literature and provides the user with a multiplicity of interpretations and assessments. Such variety allows students to pursue their own interests; furthermore, it fosters an awareness that literature is dynamic and responsive to many different opinions.

Every fourth volume of *TCLC* is devoted to literary topics. These topic entries widen the focus of the series from individual authors to such broader subjects as literary movements, prominent themes in twentieth-century literature, literary reaction to political and historical events, significant eras in literary history, prominent literary anniversaries, and the literatures of cultures that are often overlooked by English-speaking readers.

TCLC is designed as a companion series to Gale's *Contemporary Literary Criticism,* which reprints commentary on authors now living or who have died since 1960. Because of the different periods under consideration, there is no duplication of material between *CLC* and *TCLC.* For additional information about *CLC* and Gale's other criticism titles, users should consult the Guide to Gale Literary Criticism Series preceding the title page in this volume.

Coverage

Each volume of *TCLC* is carefully compiled to present:

- criticism of authors, or literary topics, representing a variety of genres and nationalities

- both major and lesser-known writers and literary works of the period

- 6-12 authors or 3-6 topics per volume

- individual entries that survey critical response to each author's work or each topic in literary history, including early criticism to reflect initial reactions; later criticism to represent any rise or decline in reputation; and current retrospective analyses.

Organization of This Book

An author entry consists of the following elements: author heading, biographical and critical introduction, list of principal works, excerpts of criticism (each preceded by an annotation and a bibliographic citation), and a bibliography of further reading.

- The **Author Heading** consists of the name under which the author most commonly wrote, followed by birth and death dates. If an author wrote consistently under a pseudonym, the pseudonym will be listed in the author heading and the real name given in parentheses on the first line of the biographical and critical introduction. Also located at the beginning of the introduction to the author entry are any name variations under which an author wrote, including transliterated forms for authors whose languages use nonroman alphabets.

- The **Biographical and Critical Introduction** outlines the author's life and career, as well as the critical issues surrounding his or her work. References to past volumes of *TCLC* are provided at the beginning of the introduction. Additional sources of information in other biographical and critical reference series published by Gale, including *Short Story Criticism, Children's Literature Review, Contemporary Authors, Dictionary of Literary Biography,* and *Something about the Author,* are listed in a box at the end of the entry.

- Some *TCLC* entries include **Portraits** of the author. Entries also may contain reproductions of materials pertinent to an author's career, including manuscript pages, title pages, dust jackets, letters, and drawings, as well as photographs of important people, places, and events in an author's life.

- The **List of Principal Works** is chronological by date of first book publication and identifies the genre of each work. In the case of foreign authors with both foreign-language publications and English translations, the title and date of the first English-language edition are given in brackets. Unless otherwise indicated, dramas are dated by first performance, not first publication.

- Critical excerpts are prefaced by **Annotations** providing the reader with information about both the critic and the criticism that follows. Included are the critic's reputation, individual approach to literary criticism, and particular expertise in an author's works. Also noted are the relative importance of a work of criticism, the scope of the excerpt, and the growth of critical controversy or changes in critical trends regarding an author. In some cases, these annotations cross-reference excerpts by critics who discuss each other's commentary.

- A complete **Bibliographic Citation** designed to facilitate location of the original essay or book precedes each piece of criticism.

- **Criticism** is arranged chronologically in each author entry to provide a perspective on changes in critical evaluation over the years. All titles of works by the author featured in the entry are printed in boldface type to enable the user to easily locate discussion of particular works. Also for purposes of easier identification, the critic's name and the publication date of the essay are given at the beginning of each piece of criticism. Unsigned criticism is preceded by the title of the journal in which it appeared. Some of the excerpts in *TCLC* also contain translated material. Unless otherwise noted, translations in brackets are by the editors; translations in parentheses or continuous with the text are by the critic. Publication information (such as footnotes or page and line references to specific editions of works) have been deleted at the editor's discretion to provide smoother reading of the text.

- An annotated list of **Further Reading** appearing at the end of each author entry suggests secondary sources on the author. In some cases it includes essays for which the editors could not obtain reprint rights.

Cumulative Indexes

- Each volume of *TCLC* contains a cumulative **Author Index** listing all authors who have appeared in Gale's Literary Criticism Series, along with cross references to such biographical series as *Contemporary Authors* and *Dictionary of Literary Biography*. For readers' convenience, a complete list of Gale titles included appears on the first page of the author index. Useful for locating authors within the various series, this index is particularly valuable for those authors who are identified by a certain period but who, because of their death dates, are placed in another, or for those authors whose careers span two periods. For example, F. Scott Fitzgerald is found in *TCLC*, yet a writer often associated with him, Ernest Hemingway, is found in *CLC*.

- Each *TCLC* volume includes a cumulative **Nationality Index** which lists all authors who have appeared in *TCLC* volumes, arranged alphabetically under their respective nationalities, as well as Topics volume entries devoted to particular national literatures.

- Each new volume in Gale's Literary Criticism Series includes a cumulative **Topic Index,** which lists all literary topics treated in *NCLC, TCLC, LC 1400-1800,* and the *CLC* yearbook.

- Each new volume of *TCLC,* with the exception of the Topics volumes, includes a **Title Index** listing the titles of all literary works discussed in the volume. In response to numerous suggestions from librarians, Gale has also produced a **Special Paperbound Edition** of the *TCLC* title index. This annual cumulation lists all titles discussed in the series since its inception and is issued with the first volume of *TCLC* published each year. Additional copies of the index are available on request. Librarians and patrons will welcome this separate index; it saves shelf space, is easy to use, and is recyclable upon receipt of the following year's cumulation. Titles discussed in the Topics volume entries are not included *TCLC* cumulative index.

Citing *Twentieth-Century Literary Criticism*

When writing papers, students who quote directly from any volume in Gale's literary Criticism Series may use the following general forms to footnote reprinted criticism. The first example pertains to materials drawn from periodicals, the second to material reprinted from books.

[1]William H. Slavick, "Going to School to DuBose Heyward," *The Harlem Renaissance Re-examined,* (AMS Press, 1987); excerpted and reprinted in *Twentieth-Century Literary Criticism,* Vol. 59, ed. Jennifer Gariepy (Detroit: Gale Research, 1995), pp. 94-105.

[2]George Orwell, "Reflections on Gandhi," *Partisan Review,* 6 (Winter 1949), pp. 85-92; excerpted and reprinted in *Twentieth-Century Literary Criticism,* Vol. 59, ed. Jennifer Gariepy (Detroit: Gale Research, 1995), pp. 40-3.

Suggestions Are Welcome

In response to suggestions, several features have been added to *TCLC* since the series began, including annotations to excerpted criticism, a cumulative index to authors in all Gale literary criticism series, entries devoted to criticism on a single work by a major author, more extensive illustrations, and a title index listing all literary works discussed in the series since its inception.

Readers who wish to suggest authors or topics to appear in future volumes, or who have other suggestions, are cordially invited to write the editors.

Acknowledgments

The editors wish to thank the copyright holders of the excerpted criticism included in this volume and the permissions managers of many book and magazine publishing companies for assisting us in securing reprint rights. We are also grateful to the staffs of the Detroit Public Library, the Library of Congress, the University of Detroit Mercy Library, Wayne State University Purdy/Kresge Library Complex, and the University of Michigan Libraries for making their resources available to us. Following is a list of the copyright holders who have granted us permission to reprint material in this volume of *TCLC*. Every effort has been made to trace copyright, but if omissions have been made, please let us know.

COPYRIGHTED EXCERPTS IN *TCLC*, VOLUME 64, WERE REPRINTED FROM THE FOLLOWING PERIODICALS:

American Anthropologist, v. 72, February, 1970 for a review of "The Conflict in Modern Culture and Other Essays," by Donald N. Levine. Copyright © 1970 by the American Anthropological Association. Reproduced by permission of the American Anthropological Association and the author.—*The American Economic Review*, v. LXII, May, 1972. Copyright © 1972 by American Economic Association. Reprinted by permission of the publisher.—*American Literary Realism 1870-1910*, v. XIII, Autumn, 1980. Copyright © 1980 by the Department of English, The University of Texas at Arlington. Reprinted by permission of the publisher.—*American Literature*, v. XXXVI, March, 1964. Copyright © 1964, renewed 1992 Duke University Press, Durham, NC. Reprinted by permission of the publisher.—*American Quarterly*, v. XVII, Fall, 1965 for "The Genteel Reader and Daisy Miller" by John H. Randall III. Copyright © 1965, American Studies Association. Reprinted by permission of the publisher and the author.—*The American-Scandinavian Review*, v. XIV, April, 1926. Copyright © 1926 by The American-Scandinavian Foundation.—*Annals of Collective Economy*, v. XXXIV, October-December, 1963. Reprinted by permission of the publisher.—*The Antioch Review*, v. 41, Fall, 1983. Copyright © 1983 by the Antioch Review, Inc. Reprinted by permission of the editors.—*The Boston Public Library Quarterly*, v. X, January, 1958. Reprinted by permission of the publisher.—*The Chesterton Review*, v. 7, November, 1981. Copyright © 1981 The Chesterton Review. Reprinted by permission of the author—*Children's Literature: Annual of the Modern Language Association Seminar on Children's Literature and The Children's Literature Association*, v. 4, 1975. Copyright © 1975 by Francelia Butler. All rights reserved. Reprinted by permission of the publisher.—*Children's Literature Association Quarterly*, v. 13, Fall, 1988. Copyright © 1988 Children's Literature Association. Reprinted by permission of the publisher.—*Classical and Modern Literature*, v. 10, Fall, 1989. Copyright © 1989 CML, Inc. Reprinted by permission of the publisher. —*The Commonweal*, March 21, 1947. Copyright © 1947 Commonweal Publishing Co., Inc. Reprinted by permission of Commonweal Foundation.—*Comparative Literature Studies*, v. VI, March, 1969. Copyright © 1969 by The Pennsylvania State University. Reproduced by permission of The Pennsylvania State University Press—*English Literature in Transition: 1880-1920*, v. 20, 1977. Copyright © 1977 English Literature in Transition: 1880-1920. Reprinted by permission of the publisher.—*Henry James Review*, v. 1, Winter, 1980. Copyright © 1980 The Henry James Society. All rights reserved. Reprinted by permission of the publisher.—*The Journal of Economic Literature*, v. XVI, June, 1978 for "Some Aspects of the Development Keynes's Thought" by Richard Kahn. Copyright © 1978 by the American Economic Association. Reprinted by permission of the publisher.—*The Journal of the Midwest Modern Language Association*, v. 23, Spring, 1990 for "Pottering About in the Garden: Kenneth Grahame's Version of Pastoral in `The Wind in the Willows' " by John David Moore. Copyright © 1990 by The Midwest Modern Language Association. Reprinted by permission of the publisher and the author.—*Journal of Political Economy*, v. 82, January-February, 1974. Copyright © 1974 by the University of Chicago. All rights reserved. Reprinted by permission of The University of Chicago Press.—*The Kyoto University Economic Review*, v. XXXIX, April, 1969.— *Literature and Psychology*, v. XIX, 1969. Copyright © Editor, 1969. Reprinted by permission of the publisher.—*The Midwest Quarterly*, v. XXX, Spring, 1989. Copyright © 1989 by The Midwest Quarterly, Pittsburg State University. Reprinted by permission of the publisher.—*The New Republic*, v. 167, December 23 & 30, 1972. Copyright © 1972 The New Republic, Inc. Reprinted by permission of The New Republic.—*The New York Times Book Review*, April 29, 1923. Copyright ©

COPYRIGHTED EXCERPTS IN *TCLC*, VOLUME 64, WERE REPRINTED FROM THE FOLLOWING BOOKS:

Johan Bojer

1872-1959

Norwegian novelist, playwright, and short story writer.

INTRODUCTION

Bojer was one of the most prominent Norwegian writers of his time. His works, which gained him an international reading audience, are especially praised for their insight into human nature and sensitive depiction of working class life.

Biographical Information

Bojer was born in Orkdalsoyra, Norway. The illegitimate son of a businessman and a servant, he was raised by foster parents in a Norwegian fishing town. Bojer's experiences and observations growing up in a rugged coastal region of Norway provided the background and subject matter for many of his works. With inheritance money from his biological father, Bojer was able to complete his education, which included instruction at a business school. After graduation, he briefly held a job at an export company while at the same time pursuing a career as a playwright and fiction writer. Soon after the successful production of one of his plays, Bojer devoted himself exclusively to writing. His subsequent literary career spanned more than six decades. Bojer died in 1959.

Major Works

Bojer explored various themes and subjects during his long and prolific career. His first major work, *Et folketog,* centered on the corrupting influence of political power on a once-idealistic farmer, who manipulates and ultimately betrays the people of the town who placed him in office. Issues of public morality also figure in *Troens magt (The Power of a Lie),* wherein Bojer creates an effective psychological profile of a man who fashions a lie into an accepted truth. Bojer expressed a celebratory affirmation of life in such works as *Den store hunger (The Great Hunger), Fangen som sang (The Prisoner Who Sang),* and *Liv (Life).* Bojer's interest in what he considered a basic human need for spiritual nourishment was central to a number of his works. In *The Great Hunger,* for example, the protagonist, Peer Troen, achieves fulfillment as an individual only after he acknowledges the existence of a higher power and the importance of striving for a common good. In the nineteen twenties, when critics consider Bojer to have been at the peak of his literary power, he published *Den siste Viking (The Last of the Vikings)* and *Vor egen stamme (The Emigrants).* Together these works portrayed the vanishing way of life of Norway's farmers and fishermen, and the emigration of many of them to the United States.

PRINCIPAL WORKS

Et folketog (novel) 1896
Moder Lea (novel) 1900
En pilgrimsgang [A Pilgrimage] (novel) 1902
Troens magt [The Power of a Lie] (novel) 1903
Vort rige [Treacherous Ground] (novel) 1908
Liv [Life] (novel) 1911
Fangen som sang [The Prisoner Who Sang] (novel) 1913
Den store hunger [The Great Hunger] (novel) 1916
Verdens ansigt [The Face of the World] (novel) 1917
Dyrendal [God and Woman] (novel) 1919
Den siste Viking [The Last of the Vikings] (novel) 1921
Vor egen stamme [The Emigrants] (novel) 1924
Det nye tempel [The New Temple] (novel) 1927
Folk ved sjøen [The Everlasting Struggle] (novel) 1929
Huset og havet [The House and the Sea] (novel) 1933
Dagen og natten [By Day and By Night] (novel) 1935
Kogens karer [The King's Men] (novel) 1938

CRITICISM

Robert Morss Lovett (essay date 1919)

SOURCE: "The Great Hunger," in *The Dial,* Chicago, Vol. 66, March 22, 1919, pp. 299-300.

[*In the following essay, Lovett discusses the epic qualities of* The Great Hunger.]

The epic motive of man in warfare with nature is the first theme of **The Great Hunger,** by Johan Bojer, translated from the Norwegian by W. J. Alexander Worster and C. Archer. Peer Tröen, the hero, bursts upon us in a typical adventure. The boys were forbidden to touch the big deep-sea line because "the thing about a deep-sea line is that it may bring to the surface fish so big and so fearsome that the like has never been seen before." But as all the men of the village are off at the Lofoten fishery, Peer and his friends have carried the line across the fjord and baited the hooks. Now they are hauling in the catch: on the first hook a big cod, on the second a catfish, on the third a great shadow bearing up through the water, a gleam of white, a row of great white teeth on the underside—a Greenland Shark. "The heavy body big as a grown man was heaved in over the gunwale . . . There it lay raging, the great black beast of prey with its sharp threatening snout and wicked eyes ablaze . . . Now and again it would leap high up in the air, only to fall back again, writhing furiously, hissing and spitting and frothing at the mouth, its red eyes glaring from one to another of the terrified captors as if to say 'Come on—just a little nearer.' " Knives and gaffs were buried in the creature's back, one gaff between the eyes while another hung on the flank. Now Peer's knife flashed out and sent a stream of blood from between the shoulders, but the blow cost him his foothold—and in a moment the two bodies were rolling over and over together in the bottom of the boat. Then as the brute's jaws seized Peer's arm, Peter Rönningen dropped his oars and sent his knife straight in between the beast's eyes. The blade pierced through to the brain, and the grip of the teeth relaxed. "C-c-cursed d-d-devil!" stammered Peter, as he scrambled back to his oars.

With this auspicious beginning Peer Tröen, bastard, sets out to conquer his world. His path leads him far—to the binding of the cataracts of the Nile by barrage, and the taming of the jungles of Abyssinia by railroads. And at length this Beowulf returns to Norway, marries and has children about him, lives at ease in his great house at Loreng, full of the joy of life as he drives his stallions over the frozen lake, or comes home on ski in "the pale winter evenings, with a violet twilight over woods and fields and lake, over white snow and blue"—home to rest, and wine, and joy. But the old restlessness leads him forth to a new adventure, the harnessing of the waters of the Bresna and its lakes far up in the mountains, a struggle with rock and flood and snow, and the weakness of human wills. His success is his ruin—and once more he meets nature single-handed, forced back foot by foot along the path which he had climbed so joyously in the morning of his youth, back from the heights which he had reached to the valley whence he had started, weary, broken, but indomitable.

This is the primitive heroic theme of the Northland, recognizable enough in its modern dress of steel and power. Mingled with it is another—one of wistful, eager questioning, equally modern and northern. The meaning of this striving, this incessant urge toward conquest—is it expressed in the words of Peer's half brother?

> "You! Are you still going about feeling your own pulse and wanting to live forever? My dear fellow, *you* don't exist. There is just one person on our side—the world-will. And that includes us all. That's what I mean by 'we.' And we are working towards the day when we can make god respect us in good earnest. The spirit of man will hold a Day of Judgment, and settle accounts with Olympus—with the riddle, the almighty power beyond. It will be a great reckoning. And mark my words—that is the one single religious idea that lives and works in each and every one of us—the thing that makes us hold up our heads and walk upright, forgetting that we are slaves and things that die."

No. It is not in the great wind, or the earthquake, or the fire—powers with which man can struggle—but in the still small voice of human compassion that Peer finds his answer. Mercy, forgiveness, reconciliation with his fellow men—one act of divine charity means more in Peer's reading of the universe than all his triumphs over nature.

> I began to feel an unspeakable compassion for all men upon earth, and yet in the last resort I was

proud that I was one of them. And I knew now that what I had hungered after in my best years was neither knowledge, nor honour, nor riches; nor to be a priest or a great creator in steel; no, friend, but to build temples; not chapels for prayers or churches for wailing penitent sinners, but a temple for the human spirit in its grandeur, where we could lift up our souls in an anthem as a gift to heaven.

As he finishes planting his last bushel of corn in the field of his enemy, the slayer of his last darling child, he sees Merle, his wife, smiling: "As if she too, the stricken mother, had risen from the ocean of her suffering that here, in the daybreak, she might take her share in the creating of God."

The Great Hunger is a book of individual striving—a type made familiar in northern literature by Frenssen's *Jörn Uhl* and *Klaus Heinrich Bass.* It will also recall to readers of an older generation Mrs. Schreiner's *Story of an African Farm.* In *The Great Hunger* the northern scene—the sea on sunlighted beaches or shadowed in overhanging fiords, the lakes, pine-encircled under moonlight, the iron hills, the wind-swept uplands, and the far fields of snow—is cold and bright in color, clear and hard in atmosphere; the human figures are attenuated to epic simplicity, perfectly comprehended and defined, and incontestably real. In *The African Farm* it is the veldt which stretches to infinity like the sea—yellow under the sun, gray and violet under the stars: and the human beings who dwell upon it are held in bondage by their environment, pathetic in their subjection, vague in outline, as individuals only half disengaged from the vast blocks of subconscious human stuff. *The Great Hunger* revives the epic manner as opposed to the impressionistic, psychoanalytic realism of which *The Story of an African Farm* contained such startling premonitions. But in theme the books will call to each other across the decades and across the world—incarnating the same energy of conquest, the same passion of understanding, the same thirst for God.

Llewellyn Jones   (essay date 1920)

SOURCE: "Bojer's Works in America," in *Johan Bojer: The Man and His Works* by Carl Gad, translated by Elizabeth Jelliffe MacIntire, Moffat, Yard and Company, 1920, pp. 9-25.

[*In the following essay, Jones surveys the moral and spiritual themes in Bojer's fiction.*]

The series of English translations of Johan Bojer's novels, of which *The Power of a Lie* is the fourth, was begun by Messrs. Moffat, Yard & Co., with *The Great Hunger* in 1919. *The Face of the World* followed in the same year, *Treacherous Ground* and *The Power of a Lie* were both published early in 1920, *Life* announced for later in the year, and now this biography.

To my certain knowledge there has been nothing parallel in the last ten years, and I doubt if ever a foreign author has been acclimatized so quickly. Some English authors have made a success in this country and then their earlier works have been given us in "collected" editions, but that is not a parallel case. Here is an author practically none of us not of Norwegian birth or parentage has been able to read in the original, an author of whom few of us had even heard. He has had no advance publicity. One of his books is published; it is so successful that another is issued the same year—while the sales of the first go merrily on. A third and fourth follow, and his circle of readers enlarges steadily. He is not, like Ibanez, an already fairly well known but little read author who makes a hit by publishing a book dealing with the war, and then rides on the wave of its momentum. He is an artist who deals with the materials offered by his native country, and we read his books for no other reason than that they appeal to us on their intrinsic merits. And yet, in two years, we have so taken him into our hearts that biography is called for. It is an interest that certainly makes Bojer an American author by adoption.

How is it? I confess that the problem is almost insoluble apart from what a critic would naturally feel to be the desperate admission that the American reading public is a more intelligent, more truly feeling creature than we usually care to suppose.

For Bojer is at the opposite pole from *Pollyanna,* nor has he a single characteristic in common with Harold Bell Wright. Nor for that matter does he quite compete with them in point of sales—that would be too much like the literary millennium. But he does compete in point of sales with a great many of our native authors who are not quite so saccharine as the two above mentioned but who do write in a manner that is a compromise between art and what the ethically-minded American public believes in reading.

I think one reason for this success is the very creditable way in which American authors have expressed their own liking of Bojer's work. Just the other day, for instance, I read Zona Gale's praise of the beautiful ending of **The Great Hunger**. James Branch Cabell, Joseph Hergesheimer, and Gene Stratton-Porter have each spoken most highly of Bojer's work, and probably the words of each were hearkened to by a separate section of the reading public. Add to this the praise of John Galsworthy and of Blasco Ibanez, and it is obvious that any American reader must have been impressed beforehand with the fact that here was a novelist well worth attention.

And so we opened the pages of Bojer and began to read. It is at this point that the thing gets mysterious, for we have kept on reading, and it certainly takes more than the endorsements of other novelists to keep the public going in any one direction. Who is there that has not praised and recommended Henry James? And outside a very limited circle who is there that reads him? But we have kept on reading Bojer, and that in spite of a shock. For his books undoubtedly do shock the average American. I use the word shock, not in the sense of the sort of dismay which Cabell in playful mood produces in our too-maidenly breasts, but in the sense of that effect which a cold shower bath produces.

We read the first chapter of any book by Bojer and we see immediately that here is a novelist who deals with what we call ethical themes, with problems of conduct. *The Great Hunger*—we read. Ah! We draw a deep breath. With the perspicacity of spiritually minded people we can tell that this great hunger is a spiritual hunger, and we revel in anticipation of one more justification of the ways of God to man. Perhaps we have already read *The Inside of the Cup,* and that later novel in which Mr. Churchill justifies not so much the ways of God as the ways of the I. W. W. to man. Certainly we feel, after the first chapter, that here is a novel serious in intent and clean cut in workmanship, quite free from that horrid Russian introspective sex-pathology which we dislike so much.

As we read on we note that our aesthetic sensibilities—if we have them—are charmed and satisfied. Bojer can tell a better story with more real character, with more vividly presented backgrounds, all in 300 pages than our own realists can tell in five or seven hundred. His stories have unity and form where our own writers are often not only content to give us a "slice of life," as they say, but never even to trim the edges.

Our human sensibilities, however, do receive a shock. Bojer is utterly sincere, and he will not justify the ways of God to us—or the ways of nature if there are any readers to whom the word God is still a cause of intellectual offense—either by misrepresenting God or by assuming that he must be justified to the orthodox man or woman. Bojer strips us of all our social disguises. He knows that the way to peace, to spiritual adjustment, is through fire and travail. How many people who start to read **The Great Hunger** in optimism will willingly go all the way with its author and its hero—will, without inner protest, agree that Peer Holm did well when he found God and exchanged for him all that his youth had brought of health and strength, all the money that he had made, all his power over men, the life of his child, his assurance of daily bread. A healthy-minded, fairly well-off American, with the right amount of life insurance, would certainly be aghast at the road Peer Holm took Godward. "Found God?" he would exclaim, "why, the man is down and out!" And if one asked him if the first fact might not be worth while, even if it involved the truth of the latter, he would, if he were well enough informed, come back with "But what is pragmatism for? Doesn't pragmatism get you to God by a better way than that?" Or else he might suggest that Peer Holm should have studied "New Thought."

My surprise at the bravery with which the American public as a whole has taken to Bojer and his bracing philosophy is partly due to the fact that I have spoken to some members of the reading public to whom his lack of sentimentality was a stumbling block. They thought him cruel and unyielding. His Norwegian snows chilled them, and they did not see that it is that very snow, pure and cold, that really makes us appreciate the light of the sun that shines upon it.

Somewhere in **Treacherous Ground** Bojer has used the phrase about the fresh warmth of the oncoming summer in the northern fjords of Norway that it is like "inhaling a mixture of sunshine and snow." And that figure is an almost perfect one for the enjoyment of all art. Take away the snow, and the sunshine is too warm; let the sunshine melt the snow, and we have muddy sentimentality. Bojer hates that sentimentality in life as well as in art, and his **Treacherous Ground** is a closely observed exposition of it in life. For, on the treacherous ground of sentimentality, does Erik Evje build a foundation for his own happiness as well as for the happiness and security of others, and of course the ground gives way.

Would that our American novelists would treat us with such kindly roughness as does Bojer! Perhaps, emboldened by his success, they will try to work in the same manner. I am convinced that, to many of his readers, some of the charm of his work is that they cannot predict the course of his novels by *a priori* considerations. To illustrate, let us glance for a moment at Mr. Winston Churchill's *The Dwelling Place of Light,* in which a girl in humble circumstances gets a job in a New England woolen mill, has a love affair with the manager, joins the I. W. W., takes part in a strike, and then dies. Throughout the book the reader is always two jumps ahead of the author because he knows exactly what a serious-minded author like Mr. Churchill must and must not do. He knows that the manager's love advances to the girl will be of the sort known as "dishonorable" because American sentiment is on the whole against the obvious misalliance. He knows that the I. W. W. will be treated in such and such a way because Mr. Churchill is a liberal who will not damn it utterly, but who, wishing to retain the good will of those to whom he appeals, will not exactly take its side (of course it is the pre-war I. W. W. that figures here), and saddest of all, the reader knows that the girl is going to die. He knows that the moment he sees she cannot marry the manager—he gets killed, if I remember aright—and that she is due to give birth to a child of which he was the father. Kind people take her in, and the child is born. But no respectable American novel could harbor a young woman, unmarried, with a living to earn, and a child to keep and explain. So the girl has to die. Not of any disease or by an accident, but just by fading away. There was no artistic necessity for it, and certainly none in physiology, but Mr. Churchill was writing sentimentally to please a sentimental public.

But how differently does Bojer handle things. How unsentimental is the figure of Peer Holm finding God at the expense of everything else. What a rebuke to sentiment there is in Erik Evje paying for his private sins by doing good to people who did not ask him to come into their lives—doing them good until his good tumbles down in irretrievable disaster. And with what surgical calmness does Bojer show us the figure of Evje, himself unhurt by the catastrophe he has caused, his life and most of his land safe while other people's lives and lands have gone down together—Evje, standing over the wreckage, and lamenting, not the loss, not the dishonesty in himself that caused him to make these people a sacrifice for his own sins; but lamenting the fact that this disaster had hurt him—had robbed him of the protection that he had built against the assaults of his own conscience.

This lack of sentimentality does not imply brutality. For at the point we have mentioned the author leaves Evje, and ends his book with one of the characters, a farm work-er, who had escaped from the disaster, a lad whom Evje, in his zeal for other people's righteousness, had persuaded to marry a girl whom he had wronged. But Lars had done this in spite of the fact that he loved another woman: well, if the reader has not seen the book I will not spoil his enjoyment of it by retelling the end, but for actual beauty of human feeling, for unpretentious but real pathos, this ending is one of the most beautiful things that a novelist has done for a long time. Certainly few contemporary English-writing novelists have approached it.

It is a dangerous thing to sum up a novelist's contribution to us in terms of the philosophy he expresses. And yet the novel is the form that does, more than any other, deal with conduct and with world views. What saves Bojer's novels from being didactic and, therefore, misleading is his adherence to the great truth that there is no such thing as a science of ethics, but that there is such a thing as an art of conduct. You cannot make general rules of conduct, for every case has its not to be duplicated features. Human situations are not like the situations of geometry, infinitely repeatable. But the general "lie of the land" in the case of an author may, at least, be indicated roughly.

And in all four of these novels we see men trying this, that and the other patent medicine of conduct. They try to compound their secret sins not so much by damning those they are not inclined to as by trying to remedy their effects—as did Evje—or they rely upon the justice of their "cause"—as Wangen in **The Power of a Lie** relied upon the fact of his innocence to excuse that in them which is not just and not innocent. Or, like Doctor Mark in **The Face of the World,** they try to find peace by taking the sins of the world upon their own too weak shoulders, and find that they cannot help the world, and that they have lost the strength that might, at least, have upheld their own loved ones who suffer while they agonize over suffering that they cannot stop. Dr. Mark may well be contrasted with Evje: a good man and a bad man each trying by almost the same means to find peace.

The typical Bojer novel may be said to exhibit a modern soul tortured with moral ideas, as Rolland said of Tolstoy; "sometimes, too, pregnant with a hidden god," but always blundering toward an adjustment with the world, Blundering hopefully, but really, not finding a chart as our ethical teachers would assure us is possible, but finding that there is no chart and that we must keep on blundering until, by trial and error, we make our own adjustment to life. After all it is the method of all human advance. Science is the finding of things out by experiment, and an experiment is simply a success following a number of blunders. If the world were really what homilists try to assure us it is, science would be unnecessary because we could deduce all knowledge from *a priori* principles. And the novelists of piety have their *a priori* principles of charity and fidelity and courage and truth-telling, and, like Harold Bell Wright, begin with those abstractions and clothe them in human garments.

So Bojer shows us the futility of charts and the great perils of self-deception. We keep our souls by eternal vigilance and by feeding them upon the bread of the moment. Dr. Mark ends by embracing love and taking all that he can get from the world's stores—the philosophy of Jesus as well as the music of Beethoven. And Peer Holm sows his neighbor's field "that God may exist."

And Peter Wangen, disdaining the spiritual food of his wife's love when he is under the cloud of a false accusation, becoming self-righteous because he knows that he is innocent, overdraws his account. He asks too much from that little stock of innocency—as if thousands of men, though not falsely accused, were not just as innocent as he was. He overdraws and spends lavishly. He becomes wicked, that is to say, bankrupt of virtue, because he magnifies the virtue that is maligned by Knut Norby's accusation of forgery against him. He makes the accusation almost a true one by becoming a forger. And Norby, tortured by his conscience for his misdeed—for he had not intended to accuse Wangen of forgery until chance set the rumor going and so suggested this sin to him—Norby, so tortured as long as Wangen is a helpless adversary, is hardened in his course and relieved of remorse when Wangen begins falsely to accuse him, to ascribe to him motives for the injury that were far from his mind. Then, when public opinion lets Norby know that it is behind him, that it considers him an honest man traduced by a blackguard, Norby actually forgets he was anything but an honest man, he expands in the smiles of approval, and actually does become a better man than he had ever been before, simply because he feeds on the spiritual food that is brought to him on the winds of circumstance.

That the food was stolen, that he was not innocent, is what will shock the sentimental reader, as it has shocked Hall Caine who writes an introduction for this latest novel. That is because Hall Caine believes that life is a charted affair, that setting a certain course always brings you to a certain destination, and he cannot see how the course of evil brings Norby to the destination of good. But Bojer knows that the world as such is amoral, uncharted. Stolen money is as likely to earn a safe six per cent as money that was toiled for. Nature is not a justice of the peace, and she does not protect the Wangens because they are honest or punish the Norbys because they are dishonest. Both the Norbys and the Wangens reward or punish themselves. Wangen was weak. In his trouble he leaned on the outside fact of his innocence, just as Mark, a good man, and Evje, a bad man, tried to lean on the outside facts of Socialism and philanthropy. They all three found that outside facts are likely to fail us.

Norby was ethically in the wrong, but he did not squeal or run after sympathy. He faced his sin in his own bosom until the tactics of the innocent aroused his fighting blood. He was a scoundrel, undoubtedly, but he was not trying to live above his ethical means: he did not try to overdraw his moral account. He does not beg spiritual sympathy— and lo, it comes flooding in upon and makes him virtuous in spite of himself.

That is rather bitter teaching for our nation of well-intentioned people. It was too bitter for Mr. Hall Caine, and he frankly says so in his introduction.

But when one reflects upon the unique reception which the work of Bojer has had in America, one wonders whether we are not beginning to grow up, whether our reading public is not ceasing to be juvenile or adolescent, and becoming mature. Certainly that large proportion of it which is reading Bojer will never again be satisfied with sentimentality in fiction. They will have seen how even the most ethical aspects of life, the most pressing "problems" of conduct, may be made the subject matter of novels at once utterly sincere in their approach to life, beautifully proportioned in their massing of background, circumstances, and character, and psychologically honest and significant in their illumination of the depths of the human soul.

Carl Gad   (essay date 1920)

SOURCE: "Social Criticism" and "Politics and an Author," in *Johan Bojer: The Man and His Works*, translated by Elizabeth Jelliffe MacIntire, Moffat, Yard and Company, 1920, pp. 43-64, 65-88.

[*In the following excerpt, Gad explores Bojer's disdain for political corruption as represented in his works.*]

SOCIAL CRITICISM

The first of Johan Bojer's books that assumes a likeness of lasting worth is the novel *Et Folketog* (1896). This book is a sign manual of his right to be ranked as author, and together with his two succeeding novels, *Den Evige Krig* (1899) and *Moder Lea* (1900) it makes up, in a natural sequence the first group of his writings—novels of social criticism. All three are concerned with the antagonism of politics to labor.

Et Folketog—an amazingly mature and assured piece of work for a writer of but twenty-four years of age—pictures the political struggle in a Vestland parish, and analyses its effect upon the farmer Peter Hegge, upon his home, and upon the whole district.

Hegge himself was a well-meaning idealist who believed in the great aims of democracy, and felt a call to enter personally into the fight against all the poverty and wrong in the land. But, at the same time, he was practical enough to understand that direct work for bettering the conditions of life for the peasant was more interesting and worth while than the great platform points—universal suffrage and a separate minister for foreign affairs. He determined therefore, that when he got into Parliament, he would, first and foremost, work to bring about one achievement— free loans for farmers.

This loan, and more especially what he would accomplish in Parliament, became his constant dream. Hegge determined that he would do great and honorable acts, and gain justly a reputation as an upright, great-souled character. But, in order to be elected, it was, alas, necessary to go crooked ways and to make use of many petty means. Hegge found himself dragged into these inevitably. The nearer election day approached, and the more hotly he pursued the campaign, the more firmly he became bound by promises and pledges that he knew could never be fulfilled, and the more wretched his conscience made him.

Thus, however, Hegge made his way into Parliament. But

if he had not been a free man in his actions before, he was now forever bound. "The psychological moment" to introduce the proposal of the loan obviously never arrived, and Peter Hegge quickly learned that he must knuckle down to the "interests of the party." And what else was there really to do? His very position was at stake if he ventured to take his own way! So he gave up every thought of practical politics, and when the next election came, he talked no more about interest, free loans, timber laws, and fishing laws, but fell, like the others, into phrase-making, and spoke great words about supporting the party—for the fatherland's sake.

At the same time that Peter Hegge's character was being undermined and his personality lost in a maze of words and sterile tactics, his home affairs also went wrong.

He had no time to attend to the care of the farm, because reports and meetings filled his days. And so it came about that the political struggle was followed by a financial one. In order to stand well with people he had to sign notes for them when they wanted to borrow money from the bank of which he was director. But his opponent, Bergheimen, who was the richest man of the parish, had money out on mortgage in various farm properties, and by causing the ruin of first one and then another farmer, brought it to pass that Hegge must sell his farm in order to pay up the notes he had endorsed.

Together with the financial wreck, politics brought unhappiness into the home itself. When Peter Hegge and his wife, Gunhild, became alienated from one another it was clearly evident that the cause lay in an extrinsic circumstance. The youngest child fell sick of pneumonia and died before the doctor came. Gunhild could not forgive her husband for the fact that she had to stand alone at the child's death bed, and that even the physician could not be secured quickly enough because the father was away on political business. But the event was, in reality, only a symbol of the fact that she must be alone in everything that was to be done in the home, since he neglected all else for the sake of public interests.

This lack of family interest showed itself also upon the other children. The son Anders grew up a good-for-naught, and the daughter, Kristine, the book's one fine and bright character, was sacrificed inexorably. The father's politics and the financial difficulties he had met with, had delivered him into the clutches of the old and, in every respect, uninviting color-sergeant, Mo. He demanded, in payment of the debt, Kristine as wife, and got her—there was no other way out.

The plot's final development shows how a taint affects the whole parish, bringing about decay and disintegration, enmity, strife, estrangements because of politics extending into every relation of life. Public affairs take up a preposterous and disproportionate amount of time and thought. "The Controlling Party," says one of the few far-seeing characters in the book, Schoolmaster Trong, "is so constantly busy with seventeenth of May speeches and national hymns that they are almost ashamed to mention anything so prosaic as farming or dairy management."

The leaders went about in the parish and talked of the fatherland with their hands in their pockets. Instead of taking the lead in up-to-date methods and business-like, solid work, they subjugate everything—as Hegge with his interest-free loan—to the party and its support. All really useful matters were laid on the table and came to nothing. Thus, for instance, when a new mill was needed, which would be of inestimable value to the parish if one could only get the plans made, other things were proposed and the plans were forgotten.

The bitter mood of the book is fully expressed at last by a symbol—artistically speaking, a strained and very unsuccessful one. After a great public meeting the politicians sail away down the river to the sound of singing and music. Each believed the other was looking out for the rapids. It is Björnson, who sings: "Put your all into the nearest call."

In the meantime they drove blindly on, and only discovered the danger when it was too late. And then it appeared that no one would jump out, all wanted to row. They fought among themselves and many were injured, while the rowboat glided on—a symbol for the parish or for Norway—steadily towards the rapids.

If *Et Folketog* is a bitter book for parliamentary devotees to read, **Den Evige Krig** is so in a still higher degree.

The chief personage, the estate owner Samuel Brandt, is a character of the same sort as Peter Hegge, but from another class of society.

He began with the most upright intentions and the most ardent desire to fight for honest measures. Belief in democracy was his religion, and he threw himself into the agitation with a truly religious fervor. But things went with him as with Hegge; his character suffered in the fight.

The first time he talked at a public meeting, he was carried away by mob-feeling and felt ashamed of himself afterward as a liar, and swore never again to mount a platform. The next day he was sneered at and lashed at in the Conservative papers. He thought this right and proper, and he was angry at the comments of the radical paper, *The Future*. Afterwards, however, when he thought over the articles in the Conservative papers, he came to have a sense of injury, and, at the same time, to be better pleased with his speech. The sense of affront grew, the more he thought about it, until he finally became so bitter against the Conservatives that he made up his mind to set out on a regular speaking tour. Thus the trend of things was changed.

In the Conservative papers Samuel Brandt was persecuted, and each speech was distorted, but he was, at the same time, praised to the heavens by *The Future*. It became more and more impossible for him, in this exciting life, to maintain restraint and independence in his convictions, and little by little, he became sucked into the great, fatal whirlpool of party fanaticism.

But Brandt is constantly racked with doubt and uncertainty. He is robbed by practical politics, little by little, of all his faith in the party and its mission, and later, as minister, having pursued a hopeless fight against the spoil system and stupidity in "the practical layman's sense," he returned home to Lindegard a defeated and broken man.

While the radical Brandt was pursuing his political gods, his own estate fell into decay. In this case, too, "the human sacrifice" was not avoided; it was the sister Sarah, who—a small improbability—gave up her own chance of happiness in order to attend to her brother's home and child, while he went into politics.

That Samuel Brandt is considered the chief character in **Den Evige Krig** is only because, on account of the book's temper, he is brought somewhat more strongly forward than the others, and because he is examined more as to mental processes. But there are a number of other characters who lay claim, with perhaps equal right, to as much space and interest.

There is, first, the laborer, Jansen. He had, while apprentice, been sent to prison because, half dead from hunger, he had stolen a couple of young chickens. His parents died of shame and sorrow, the girl he loved married another man, and Jansen felt himself to be an outcast from society. After many years of sailing the sea, and when no one longer remembered him, he married, but bitterness had become rooted in his heart by this time, and he developed into a passionate and sullen agitator against the existing social system.

Then he met Samuel Brandt and his bitterness was conquered by the latter's friendliness and human sympathy. He gave up the agitations and found happiness in his home, but this did not last long. Soon he re-entered politics, because the radical leaders who had seen that he was useful, made advances and flattered him into taking a share in the party's work.

Jansen became a member of Parliament. There are long speeches made about his many excellences and his high virtue as a man. At the same time there is much talk about democracy as the party of brotherly love, which carries out "Christ's own will" both for the small and the great in society. The time seems ripe to Jansen to ease his conscience and tell of the dark blot on his childhood.

Such an instance had come to Bojer's own ears. In 1893 the laborer, Hagerup, was elected member of Parliament at Trondhjem, strongly supported by the radical press. He also had been in prison when young, and when he was naïve enough, relying on the humanity of the party, to confess to this, they threw him over completely. Bojer, who knew Hagerup, was greatly upset by the lack of generosity that was shown on all sides, and one can see the indignation still burning in this book, where he pictures the fate of Jansen.

The whole thing is treated as a party affair; it is a matter of concern that the Conservative papers shall not make capital of this to attack the party, and therefore, they hastened to be rid of him. *The Future* represented him as a cunning imposter who had deceived everyone. The scandal took on mighty dimensions, and, branded as a criminal, Jansen is driven out into wretchedness, utterly crushed. The party is the pearl without price—whatever brings stain upon it, must be sacrificed.

Unscrupulous party opportunism is personified in the editor, Sokrates Hector Snorre Kahrs. He is Bojer's "perfect type" of politician, conspicuously talented, with no other passion than ambition, and with an unusually cold-blooded scorn of mankind. Every man was, for him, either a voter or one who could influence a voter. He knew everybody in the town, their family relations, abilities, possessions, money, vices, ambitions, and he knew how they must be handled, whether flattered or threatened. He had a well-organized staff of political job hunters under him who, like subscription collectors, received little commissions for each vote they procured. But his most powerful tool was his paper. As he would make speeches on everything between heaven and earth, from poultry breeding and protective tariff to love affairs and Jesus Christ—so he treated in his paper all themes—and used them for political purposes. He was practically omnipotent in the town, and used his power without scruple. Pastor Borg understood this: to have *The Future* against one—that meant an empty church and poor collections, distractions in work, insult, and scorn. And he adjusted himself to the situation after this, and affected a reconciliation with the paper. Then—behold! the church grew full again. Thanks to newspaper publicity, the offerings increased, and the agitations were smoothed down, until the sense of his own falsity at last drove him to the fjord.

It is the paper, that is to say, Kahrs, that brought about his end, and so with one and another. The town acquired his stamp by degrees, as well as the political struggle in which he was leader.

Kahrs declared that a powerful wedge must be used to conquer the old conservative town. Platforms and things of that sort were not enough. It would be far better to bring about a little personal enmity between man and man.

Success marked the venture in the House, and at election time, which, every three years, descended on the town like a hail storm on summer flowers. A sort of epidemic of bitterness and hate was disseminated from man to man. The political difference of opinion grew to a practical burgher war in miniature. Old friendships were sundered, family divisions arose, and it came to be clenched fist against clenched fist in every sphere of action.

"The spirit of the press, with its whole and half lies, roguery, equivocal words, and its hasty, implacable enmities—more and more, like a clammy, winter blight, overlaid all true and happy community life, all fresh youth, and unqualified gladness and contentment. This smouldered between school children and teachers, it reeked from cellar to garret, it entered into business affairs, it knocked down banker and credit, it reached the pastor in the church, and took hold of the affairs of the Exchange. It breathed in every home, and even stood beside graves and cast in the first clump of earth upon the dead."

Hegge and Samuel Brandt were the tragic political figures, Jansen the martyr, and Kahrs the master.

In **Moder Lea** we meet the fool and rascal. In the two first books, politics appear chiefly as enmities, here it is seen chiefly in its public characters: its two representatives, Hakon Hakonsen and Hans Lunde, are both impressed with the idea that their *milieu* lies in public life rather than in the less strenuous pursuits of the private individual.

Already in *Et Folketog* Bojer had made an attempt to exhibit the effect of this craving for publicity on a man. The doctor tells, for example, of his own children: "One strives at art because his call goes in the direction of making sorry verses about the joy of life and freedom and the fatherland, really impossible stuff, I assure you. And the other does not finish at the technical school because he is wasting his time and money on something erudite. Is it, however, because their talent drives them? Oh no. The fact is they wish to be famous, they will not be so terribly deadly as father is. Isn't it natural this should make me bitter against the age, whose fault it is? For my two are not the only ones. There is a sickness upon the young people of today, a sickness which our public life has bred. Now, I myself, played a violin indifferently when I was a young chap, you remember that yourself. But I did it entirely in secret and because music then had the most interest for me. Now, every little aptitude must be placed on exhibition and developed into the chief business of life; people want to be famous. To create something actually worth while, to please father and mother, and sacrifice a little fame to gladden them, oh, no—don't ask that. Youth has too much talent, too many 'calls,' to work, and is ambitious, for the fatherland's sake, to unite in a peaceful and fruitful work. The young people realize that, in order to be famous, one must be either an artist or a politician in this country."

The same trend toward publicity we see in Anders Hegge with his "call" to be editor, to found an alliance of the youth of the country for the doing of something. And we see it again in Jens Nordseth, though, be it admitted, in somewhat more complicated fashion. He deserts his love because he wants to be an artist and so cannot be married to a peasant girl, and when his home is ruined and desolate, and his parents have been obliged to take a position as gate-keeper to the farm's new owners, this ruin is for him only a theme—for a painting that may make him famous.

In Hakon Hakonsen's and Hans Lunde's characters this idea is developed yet further. They both suffered from a distinct misapprehension of the difference between what they are and what they think they are, and what they strive for is not to produce something actual, which would bring them real reason for pride, but rather to make themselves a subject of public talk.

Hakon Hakonsen is the worse of the two. All his life was absorbed in winning recognition and pleasure. In his youth he had tried one thing and another; spiritual life, art, religion, anarchism, but recognition for his talent had not come, and he was at a loss to know what expedient to attempt by which to become a great man. At this juncture he discovered that politics was the way. He fastened on "Norway" and "cut his cloth according to his pattern." He worked for the peasants that they might "call their souls their own"—or he talked town projects and spoke platitudes about culture just as he might mention that the wind was blowing. All the while, he was going about pretending to say something bold and profound and looking

for recognition, but because of his merely coquettish desire to please, he rigged himself out theatrically like a peasant, in real museum clothes, and like a "man of culture" in elegant dress. He ended as a minister of the church.

Hans Lunde is somewhat more complex. He was poorly brought up, that is to say, even as a child he was allowed to follow his own inclination, which is to avoid all hard things. Not unlike Peer Gynt, he constantly allowed his thoughts to wander to something amusing instead of using to advantage the talents he had.

At the age of twenty Hans had failed three times in the grammar school examinations. His people then wanted him to go to an agricultural school, but he had a wide-awake instinct for what would suit him best, and went to an art school instead.

Like Anders Hegge he started a club in order to have a place to talk. Because he had discovered, "a person can get out of any difficulty, if only he can speak for himself," and that it was an excellent way to talk round a thing instead of really delving deep into it.

The three great experiences life brought him, led him all the farther along this same course.

The first one was that he discovered that his mother was in love with the Swedish helper on her farm. In the beginning, Hans was in doubt—did not know what to do; then he fancied himself killing the Swede and heard himself making a brilliant apologetic discourse to the judge and becoming famous. It came finally to him that he had experienced something wonderful that would develop him, perhaps make him a great writer, and bring him public applause and wide fame.

"As soon as he thought of this he sat down with pencil and note book and tried to set down his grief in a couple of verses in the national tongue." Several days later, the youth had thought of a number of plans, which he greatly admired himself for, but which he delayed putting into execution.

Then the Swede killed his father—apparently through an accident when driving—and later married his mother, and Hans, who was the only one that knew the dreadful truth, stood in Hamlet's position. He decided to devote his life to having the crime disclosed and the murderer punished. But this would occasion considerable hard work, and so he finds very soon all sorts of fine excuses for putting this off.

The two men then learn to live beside each other on the farm, each with his guilty consciousness—the Swede because of the crime he had committed, and Hans because of the accusation he could not force himself to make.

And what is it Ase says in *Peer Gynt:*

> It is ghastly to see one's evil destiny under
> one's eyes,
> And therefore will a man gladly shake off his
> sorrows
> And try his best to get away from his thoughts
> of himself.
> One tries brandy, another, lies—

So it happened in this case; the Swede took to drinking cognac (later, to religion) and Hans to fine, stirring words. Hans had to fight a constantly harder fight to keep self-accusation under. He, therefore, made speeches about eternal peace, world-revolution, newly-established Norway, and King Sverre's legacy to youth. There is nothing that so shuts one's mind to himself as talking of others. Hans became a great speaker and intoxicated himself both by his own words and by the approval that streamed toward him. Even the pastor was finally so impressed by the oratory of Hans, that he had him sent as agent on a royal commission that demanded profound wisdom in its discharge.

Then it happened that the wife of the golden-tongued speaker, who understood the situation, and once had believed in his "mission," and wished to help him to perform it, came to know to the uttermost, his equivocations and indecision; and for fear that their child should grow up like his father, she killed it. To the judge she would make no other explanation than that the father was a coward.

She is sentenced to fifteen years in prison, while Hans is too weak to try to save her by any excuse. Again comes the struggle between his "two selves"; his own judgment of himself, and other people's judgment of him. Again it happened that his evil self conquered because of people's sympathy and respect for him—due to his fine speech-making. He had thrust upon him a halo of martyrdom because of his wife's crime. It heightened wonderfully his popularity, and he rose higher and steadily higher through the humbug of people's sentimentality.

Thus Hans became a prominent person in Parliament. None could get such a sweep of the ballots as he, and obtain exactly what he wished.

> Then, if they tried to get a clear understanding of things, he blinded them with emotion; if one asked for figures and facts, he confused their minds by gripping speeches about Norway and the good wife!
>
> There began to be a smattering of Hans Lunde in every man's life. One met him in the laws, which were enacted or repealed throughout the land, he popped up in the schools, in the courts, at the University, in business, in union-politics—everywhere one could realize by the accumulated mass of words and pity that Hans Lunde had had a finger in the pie, and had made a speech about that wife of his.

POLITICS AND AN AUTHOR

If we try to bring together the thoughts on politics and its effects, which Bojer expresses in these three books, we see by his socially critical sight pictures, the political game as a source of enmities and a means of financial ruin. Small feuds are blown into big ones, new ones arise, whole parishes and hamlets are torn by ruinous animosities, and weak men are trampled heartlessly down. At the same time, politics take up the life and thought of those who should be leaders in the economic and industrial development. So, they neglect their work and have no time to start anything new. Universal stagnation and economic wretchedness are the result.

But beyond and deeper than this social consequence of the political struggle, lie the influences of politics on the individual character—there are, especially, two of these.

First, politics force men to compromise with their conscience. Peter Hegge illustrates this particularly. He wants to wash his conscience clean by great and pure acts when he first gets into Parliament. But to get there he has to make use of the voters and of the party, and, in both ways, he becomes dependent and forfeits his freedom. To attain a great and good end he has to use small and petty means, and that leaves its mark on him, so that even his abilities become dulled in the process.

Secondly, politics is the chief port that men seek to reach, when they run away from personal responsibility. Of this, Hans Lunde is the most typical expression when he shakes free from every action and grasps at a phrase instead, when he feels himself persecuted instead of responsible, when he smothers his conscience in a debauch of great words,—then is he the representative of a whole group avoiding responsibility. "Those who would meanly lie down in dirt and rags were there ever any self-excuse to find, and no powerful pressure to make them rise again. They drugged their hurts, their hidden shames for the sake of the martyr's glory, intoxicated themselves, and rejoiced in vague ideas of reform, which left them free while putting all responsibility on some remote fabulous creature, on Society, the State, the Lord, Destiny, or some other far-off thing, so long as they themselves escape."

But, in essence, the two things arc the same. Peter Hegge, who compromises with his conscience for the sake of the party and the votes, and Hans Lunde, who flies from responsibility to empty words, resemble one another in one thing: they have not strength of character enough to find their center of gravity in themselves. They are weak men, who have not strength enough to stand alone, and, without dependence on some one else, do what they feel is right. That this is so, we shall see clearly, when we examine "the dark characters" in Bojer's later books, all of whom have been endowed with the same stamp. This appears immediately from the contrasts in even these three books, where we have not yet examined the bright side. In contrast to weakness and decadence, Bojer opposes naturally the positive upbuilding work of people of will power, who take responsibility upon themselves for their own acts and are independent of others' judgment.

In *Et Folketog* the positive side is not very much in the foreground. This appears chiefly in the strong prominence of what is neglected, but, then, also, in the picture of Gunhild's loyal work, in the doctor's arguments, and in the schoolmaster, Trang, who hasn't time for politics because he is studying the ant.

But, already, in *Den Evige Krig*, it is sufficiently clear that the contrast is growing plain. Even in the beginning, when Samuel Brandt determines to go into the party struggle, he becomes a candidate against the will of his family, who are "capable, solid, conservative men, who worked and achieved results." This opposition comes to a point in the great scene with the father, to whose clear sight politics appear as opposed to honest, sterling work. "See, if everybody was a source of pride to his family," says he, "don't you understand that the country's affairs would straighten out themselves? When the estate came into my hands it was loaded with debt. Now it is paid for and I have made great additions to it. The fatherland, you say? Well, I have cleared five hundred acres of land!"

The same opposition appears in Jansen's life. In the period when he had withdrawn from politics his home began to blossom; he is full of the joy of work and one sees that his children, even as small students, understand the blessing of independent creative work.

But it is chiefly Samuel Brandt's brother, Carsten, and his friend the painter, Bratt, who in *Den Evige Krig* stand as representatives of the positive values, and it is clear even as early as in this book, that the "work" Bojer admires is of a particular sort. His workmen, so to say, are all types of "clean youth; possessed of independent ideas which are born in the brain and nourished in the heart"—and who have religious perspective.

Carsten was, at first, a theologian, but that wasn't a success, and then he became an engineer and "used his ideas of eternity in practical work." He invents a boring machine, and his life work becomes railroad construction, and the work becomes his religion. It is really the struggle between light and darkness, a new trade route, a new bank, railroad, road, steamship route, school—they are all practical applications of religion and brotherly love, and, particularly, does this hold true in respect of a mountainous country like Norway. These are the beliefs also of King Haakon himself. They will fill the land with light, and drive out the evil powers of the trolls.

Bratt is of the same way of thinking. He also believes it, in a way, religious to do creative things. He is not a painter, as he thinks of it, but a priest, and will do honor to God's will, until he finds Him, himself. There is really no difficulty in seeing the family resemblance between this engineer and this painter, and a number of Bojer's later "bright" characters—like the young Peer Holm, of *The Great Hunger,* who believes himself a sort of descendant of Prometheus.

It is true of both *Et Folketog* and *Den Evige Krig* that, viewed as problem novels, they are works of censure and their force is destructive. The positive ideal appears only in glimpses. It has no chance to live an independent life, and in reality, serves only to increase the violence of the attack.

In *Moder Lea* it is quite different. Here the contrast is sharp and clearly outlined, and the accent is laid on the constructive, not on the destructive. This appears even in the fact that it is *Moder Lea,* and not Hans Lunde, who has given the book its name.

Mother Lea and her children are, however, not alone in possessing the author's sympathy; they have to share it with Hans Lunde's wife, Inga. In seeking, however, for an absolute contrast to Hans Lunde, there appear two characters that fulfil these requirements. One is Inga. She had married Hans Lunde because she believed in his "call"— his life's great task to expose his father's murderer, and to

see justice done, and because she herself saw it as her mission to sacrifice herself in helping him to do this. Later, when she came to understand him in all his weakness, she despised him to such an extent that she could not bear the shame of having had a child by such a coward. She thought with horror of what a child might become who had such a father. To make reparation for the crime that she considered she had committed in bringing him into the world she killed the child and took her punishment with face uplifted, as one who had fulfilled a pledge.

The other character that presents itself in stern contrast with Hans Lunde the victim of the destructive force is Mother Lea. Her husband was of the same mold as Hans Lunde, and she could not imagine anything more terrible than that her children should grow up to resemble their father, who is dead when the story opens. This is the difference between her moral problem and that of Inga. The children's inheritance from their father does not seem to be more than what can be overcome by training. Inga would like to bar Hans Lunde out in order to wipe out the blot of him on their child's life, but she can only accomplish this by killing the child. Mother Lea, on the contrary, is so fortunately placed that she can accomplish the same thing by training her children to be a living protest against the entire character of their father.

The farm of Lea's father has been impoverished and all but ruined that her husband may have money to pursue his political career. Upon his death, however, Lea manages to keep the farm and begins the task of building it up again. Success crowns her efforts because she does not flinch from any trouble, and because she depends on herself alone, desiring to be independent of all other people.

Lea wants, first of all, that her children shall become efficient men, for "she understood that will power is the strongest rampart to character and that, without will, there is no safeguard, no sense of responsibility, no ability to resist. No one could preserve an individual conviction without the ability to form one. The weak lie themselves out of difficulty, the strong-willed have the strength to be upright."

The mother taught them that their proper value was no greater than what they had achieved, and every time something failed of success, there was a sense of stain upon them, until they had brought it to success. At the same time she suggested, in every case, that which had been omitted in the former instance, and opened the way for them to progress. She gave them a goal that demanded of them independent action for its attainment.

They began to work as it were in their play, but learned easily, from the beginning, to lookout for themselves and never give up half way. First they made their own toys, then their own implements, and then discovered improvements. All that they made was, in the beginning, called forth by the need of the moment; they were necessary things, whose value, in use, was immediately put to proof. Then the nursery was exchanged for the work shop and the smithy; these, in turn, for the factory and the laboratory, and the activities constantly grew in importance.

Thus these young men grew up as ideal workmen. Halvard, the eldest, farmed and, naturally, had helpers. The same principles that Mother Lea had used in bringing up her children, Halvard employed with his workmen. It seemed to him that most men went about with dead minds. They learned in school to wrap themselves in a maze of other people's thoughts, others' beliefs, others' convictions, and underneath all this haze, their own actual personal thought and nature lay like a still-born child. But he believed that "even the weakest man must have had, in his youth, an ideal to be able to be of independent value." And, quite like John Ruskin, he sought to develop this through creative work. Ruskin's central idea is, practically, that unhappiness in modern society is caused because men are not happy enough in their work, because they must work like slaves instead of creating like free persons. And a quite similar idea will one find in Bojer. "What use either of reform or religion so long as men do not love their work, which they ought to be able to put their soul into. Men must work like slaves to *create* and then the God in them will be awakened, and they will be lifted above themselves." This is the principle Halvard applied in his work, and he and his brothers succeeded in creating joyous, personally-interested workmen out of the youth of the district.

Also, the other brother, the smith Olaf, who became an engineer, the carpenter Erik, who became a sculptor, the scientific Henrik, and the sisters Johanna and Hedvig, who did weaving and embroidering—all are shown as ideal workers, who begin small and end great, and who look with a religious attitude upon their work, and are wholly absorbed in it.

Then, however, comes death into the midst of the little family group and steals away the youngest, Hedvig. And for a while it seems as though they would be beaten to the earth by that old query: "What use is there in all this, since we must die?" But they are strong enough to rise even above death. The fear of death is only the painful consciousness of life's being over, and the only remedy for this fear is an upstanding spirit. The weak and useless die— that is their penalty, but the worth-while endure and do good for that which comes after.

In *Et Folketog* there are two scenes—which particularly deserve notice because here one sees Bojer's characters in their first rather than their second cinematic form.

Bojer wishes to give as widely comprehensive a picture of the parish as possible, but this demands a picture of the fishing industry. If now such a picture were to appear in a natural manner in a realistic novel, one or other of the people concerned would oversee or take part in a concrete fishery with a definite location.

This is, however, not the method that our author uses. He paints a fishery in general terms, without definite characters, and that there is no talk of a single concrete fishery, but that the whole is quite abstract, is emphasized by the author's use of general, guarded, or hesitating expression: "*Perhaps* they were then praying for him there." "But then a steamboat might show its red eye from out the fog, or, *perhaps,* it would bear straight down upon the net."

"But, if all went well, then *we may be sure,* at dawn, they weighed anchor."

In the realistic novel the practice is, certainly, either that the author tells of a definite situation and person, and tries to present to the reader the illusion that the events have actually occurred, and the people have lived, and that he—the author—knew them. But here we see a complete break, with every device for creating illusion. We hear about indefinite characters, who at an indefinite time, possibly, may have lived, and could have done this and that.

The next stage, where the picture has become more concrete, we get in the picture of the typical poor man. And here the picture is set in the present, and the whole is more definite. It is a single peasant that is talked of, and we are told that he must sell his horse, and even must pull the seed himself in order to use it, and we see how he can not take any rest when he gets home, but must carry on the struggle, and cut wood and get tinder.

But it is not a particular peasant that is told of—it is *the* peasant. We don't hear what his name is; we don't meet him later, and he has no effect on the development of the action. He is an example; or, if one likes to call him so, an illustration. The author wants to paint the severe struggle of the peasant, and he does so by this method, putting into a single portrait all of the features to serve as a type.

From this to the next stage the distance is not far. We meet a group of characters who, quite certainly, have individual names, and dwelling places and take part in the action, but who, in reality, are only personifications—who have, as their function, to illustrate the author's ideas.

We hear, for example, in *Den Evige Krig* of the position of the church and the army in the radical party. Powerfully and mercilessly are shown how the first natural hostility ends in reconciliation and united work for mutual benefit. But, as *Den Evige Krig* is not a debate but a novel, the author cannot use really historic and recognized developments; he must clothe them in flesh and blood, and thus are born Pastor Berg and Captain Bull.

Of similar origin are Mrs. Ramm and Editor Kahrs. Instead of saying that the woman question is ludicrous, and motivating the statement with a group of examples, the author gathers all the ludicrousness and pettiness and endows a character with it who can play a rôle in a novel. And instead of, or to put it more exactly, besides portraying the influence of the press on people's lives, a personification, Editor Kahrs, is created, about whom the picture centers.

Also the laborer Jansen serves, despite the fact that he is partially drawn from a model, in a high degree, as an illustration. First he illustrates, by his development, hatred against the social system, the rising up against unfair treatment, and then the power of love and friendliness to turn a fanatic, full of hate, into a happy and useful man. And, finally, he illustrates by his fate society's—and especially that portion of society excited by party strife—brutal heartlessness for one who has been rash enough to expose himself because he took empty cant seriously. One cannot help being reminded of Victor Hugo's *Les Misérables,*

TWENTIETH-CENTURY LITERARY CRITICISM, Vol. 64

where the galley slave Jean Valjean, in quite similar manner, on account of the bishop's friendliness, is saved to society, and as Père Madeleine, becomes altogether a suitable priest, until he confesses who he is, and is heartlessly sent back to the galleys.

If one runs through Bojer's characters and attempts to find the connecting link among them, he will see that most of them are made on similar lines. The kernel in them is an idea—be it either moral or psychological—which has caught the author's attention, and which has become living for him in a human character. In so saying we do not, of course, mean to suggest anything belittling of Bojer's power to portray men. It is true of a great many of the most valuable characters in the literature of the world, that they, in similar manner, to a certain degree, can be used as illustrations. What decides their value is unquestionably the degree to which the author has had the ability *to give his characters life.*

When one compares two characters such as Peter Hegge and his son Anders, it is easy to see the difference. Their origin is assuredly the same; they can both be used as personifications, but Peter Hegge is a living thing, Anders is not. Because Anders is *nothing more than* a personification; he, literally, does not open his mouth without saying, "see who I am." We discover quickly that he is a vain fool, but besides this, we know nothing of him; there is nothing which differentiates him from any other peasant youth who believes himself born to something great, and imagines himself able to become this without doing anything. Peter Hegge, on the contrary, we have an opportunity to see from several points of view. We realize that he is not only a politician, but also a peasant and the father of a family. We see him swayed by various feelings and impulses, and besides the traits that render him typical, we learn to know others that are his alone, and that distinguish him from other peasant politicians, whose destinies perhaps are similar; and, at the same time that we see mistakes that he makes in politics, on the farm, and in his home, we realize also the difficulties that beset him, and that rise higher and higher till they overwhelm him.

This is the one method by which an author can give a character life—by making him many sided and composite, and by bringing out his connection and interaction with his environment.

This same thing can be made clear in another way. Why Berg really is plainly more living than Kahrs, is not only and not first and foremost, because he is a little more individualized, but it is, especially, because the author—and through him, the reader also—feels more strongly for him. His struggle and his wavering is not so strongly individual, but the portrayal, in its stead, has strength enough to grip us, so that the struggle and wavering emotional attitude become living for us. Somewhat similarly this is true, at times, of Jansen—especially after the great catastrophe. Bojer is too great a writer to let such moving material, with the personal indignation lying back of it, remain wholly and constantly dead under his hand. Despite the finger pointing, there are moments when one is absolutely carried away.

The difference between Kahrs and Karsten Brandt is even more characteristic. Karsten is almost as one-sidedly treated as the editor. We know nothing much more of him than that he is an engineer who believes religiously in his cultural mission. The portrait is, in nowise, individual, but the author has, to that degree, lived through his eyes and, to that degree, felt with his feelings and impulses that he makes him live, regardless of anything in the book.

One of the most conspicuous results of Bojer's disposition towards this personifying is that dimensions are easily magnified. Just because Kahrs is not a man, as has been remarked, but a constructed personification of an idea, both his abilities and his importance are overdrawn. No real editor would be able to be, to such a degree, ubiquitous as he is, and however great the power of the press, yet such an attack of nightmare in a whole parish as this, which is here told of, seems, certainly in the same way, impossible in reality. The contrast between the three periods in Pastor Berg's life—before the radicals come into power, during the struggle, and after the reconciliation—is also too glaring to be worthy of belief. And, without wanting to say anything good about feminine gossip, one must certainly admit that Mrs. Ramm is several degrees worse than real life is likely to produce.

Very strongly marked is this overdrawing in **Moder Lea**. Both she and, particularly, her sons surpass, by far, the limits of ordinary humanity. That educator of man, that engineer and artist and man of science—they are not men but heroes. And the portrayal of their development, from the time when they play their first games till their work spreads out in its influence over the whole world, is not a novel but a myth. Their energy, the extent of their ability, their success, the method by which they overcome nature and the elements, their music, their beauty—all alike are on a much higher plane than that of the average man. It is impossible to think of them as living beings in a valley amidst the Norwegian mountains; they have only one real home place—in the author's imagination.

Now there is obviously none that would want to forbid an author writing myths, or fairy tales, or stories of Utopias, but when this is introduced into a realistic novel, the framework is shattered, and there is an element of uncertainty and lack of form that impair the value of the book.

Et Folketog is the one of the three books in which this is least true. It is, by far, the most homogeneous, and constructed with the surest touch, even though, perhaps in depth, it must stand below both the others. It is uniform and single in its plan, and, with the exception of the unhappy ending, the author has, nowhere, set himself too great a task for his ability. At the heart of the book stands Peter Hegge, and, about him, are grouped the other people, so to speak, in circles which become less individualized and more typical the nearer they reach the periphery, until they become merely part of the background, like the typical poor man and the abstract fishing group already mentioned. In fact, the book's chief theme is, at least, nearly as much the parish as it is Peter Hegge. It is, first and foremost, the portrayal of a *milieu,* and for this purpose, it is well for the people seldom to be presented separately, but chiefly when engaged in joint work, or when definite occasions bring them together. The book, certainly, has a purpose, but one can see, at the same time, that the author has an evident pleasure in the picture for its own sake, and this pleasure shows itself, not least of all, in the pictures of the typical events and scenes that take up the greater part of the book. The fishermen's homecoming, the cutting of the hay, going to church, summer fairs, Christmas festivities, and, naturally, the political events, electoral meetings and voting—all these are painted quietly and in detail, without great gestures, but graphically and vividly, so that the picture of the parish and its life grows into a whole, and stand forth clearly and vividly.

In *Den Evige Krig* the descriptions are much less equally balanced. The number of people and their different destinies are assuredly and adroitly knitted together, but they become divergent to a great degree. The inhabitants of Lindegard are, nearly all, very livingly portrayed, and that part of the book which is concerned with them, is a realistic romance, written in a strongly lyrical spirit. Editor Kahrs and his circle are, however, more or less lifeless personifications, and the parts of the book in which they dominate are, practically, social-criticism essays in novel form. It cannot be denied that these parts are written with great power, and despite the more abstract and didactic flavor, are read with interest. But the different constituent parts of the book do not cohere, so that the work lacks homogeneity. In still greater degree is this same thing true of *Moder Lea*. The two contrasted parts are here, over plainly, ungermane. Lea and her sons are portrayed as ideal figures, with great lives and in mighty dimensions, but their opposite, Hans Lunde, is a little common man who is painted with great sedulousness and most minute psychological analysis. That such different sorts of beings are brought together into the same valley and united by the action of the novel is disintegrating in its effect on the book. One has the impulse to try to disentangle it into its separate strands, and this can quite easily be done. There would then be a fantasy or myth, or whatever one really wants to call it, about Lea and her sons, that could be read with profit because of the value of the idea and the power of the descriptions, and there would be a psychological novel about Hans Lunde and his wife that would take its place as Bojer's most distinguished work before *Troens Magt (The Power of a Lie)*.

James Branch Cabell   (essay date 1920)

SOURCE: "The Face of the World," in *Johan Bojer: The Man and His Works* by Carl Gad, translated by Elizabeth Jelliffe MacIntire, Moffat, Yard and Company, 1920, pp. 247-55.

[*Cabell was an American journalist and fiction writer. In the following essay, he offers a favorable review of* The Face of the World.]

I

What Johan Bojer planned to make *The Face of the World* there is no way of telling. But as the volume stands it is a very handsome piece of irony; and its main character in particular is "rendered" in such a manner that all readers of this book will (I believe) remember Harold Mark for a long while, with (I sincerely trust) unuttered sentiments.

This Harold Mark the reader encounters as a newly graduated Norwegian doctor, contentedly married, and temporarily established in Paris, where his wife, Thora, is vaguely studying "art" at the Louvre and thereabouts. And the two were happy enough until Harold fell to thinking of a world he and his fellow creatures inhabited and began extending toward his fellow creatures a great, burning sympathy.

Now, as everybody knows, when Scandinavians once begin sympathizing they go further than the philanthropists of more abstemious races, who can take pity or leave it alone. Thus this great, burning sympathy at once demolished Harold's liking for Thora's art. "Looking at Veronese's beautiful women, he thought of the number of slaves there must have been to maintain such an article of luxury." He would even embarrass his wife by voicing such high reflections quite openly before strangers.

One day Harold and Thora were standing in front of David's picture of Napoleon's coronation. Thora was for saying the proper things and for enjoying all the proper reactions; but Harold's devastating contribution to esthetic criticism was to remark that Napoleon was "one of the world's greatest criminals" and to reflect "How far along the world would have been if only he had lost the battle of Lodi!"

Thora was startled, but she exhibited commendable self-restraint by turning silently away from him to converse with a Finnish sculptor who estimated the Louvre pictures by more customary touchstones.

Then came the evening when there was a public meeting in the *Place de la République* to protest against the massacre of the Jews in Kiev, and Harold was wishful to extend to these dead Jews his great, burning sympathy by standing in the crowd and hearing M. Anatole France deliver an address.

But Thora's feeling was that for them to stand in the crowd in all that rain would do small good to the dead Jews and a great deal of harm to her best clothes. So she undressed and went to bed. "Do you come too!" she urged. "And the candle threw a yellow light over the simple bed and her pretty young face, while the slender, warm body beneath the bedclothes made its appeal to him. She was full of the joyful present and wanted him to forget everything else."

So Harold took her hands in his and pressed them. "Listen, Thora," he said, "if you'll be good and let me go to that meeting this evening I'll go with you to the Louvre tomorrow."

Thora let him go. Later she very sensibly let him go for good and all and she married the Finnish sculptor who estimated the Louvre at its true value.

II

Later still Harold Mark returned to Norway to practice medicine in Christiania. He was by this time a socialist, and, sinking gradually into yet murkier depths of mentality, became at last a prohibitionist. He spoke at labor demonstrations, wrote letters to the newspapers and (very gratifyingly) was sued and fined for his verbal assaults upon various liquor dealers in a land as yet unterrorized by an Anti-Saloon League. All this was due to Harold's continuing to think quite seriously about the world, which seemed to him in a very bad way indeed, and eminently deserving of his great, burning sympathy.

"I think," he wrote his mother, "about everything and everybody. My mind enlarges itself so as to embrace the whole world. Mankind becomes a seething ocean that rolls backwards and forwards through all my being. I grow dizzy with the feeling of infinity. Millions of cries for help rise from the hopeless confusion: I see a crowd of faces contorted with pain: arms are outstretched for help as from millions in danger of drowning. . . . Good Lord, mother! If I could only get rid of this great, burning sympathy for everything and everybody!"

In fact, that does not seem to be a pleasant way of spending one's evenings: nor, after several years of thus enlarging his mind after supper, could Harold detect that his great, burning sympathy was being of any use to any specific person. In consequence, at about the time he is appointed senior physician of the seaside hospital at his birthplace, Dr. Mark resolves to focus all his great, burning sympathy upon "one human being who is unhappy"; and casting about for a likely victim decides that Ivar Holth, a partly insane ex-convict, has received from the town what is vernacularly describable as a pretty raw deal.

So Dr. Mark makes Holth the steward of Mark's hospital, and day after day, affords the former convict the full benefit of Harold Mark's companionship and great, burning sympathy.

There may be scoffers to suggest that it was Harold Mark's society which proved the last proverbial straw to Holth's weak mind. At all events Holth presently becomes violent and sets fire to a building which unpleasantly reminds him of his past. Then the fire spreads, the whole town ignites with Scandinavian thoroughness, the hospital is destroyed and Harold Mark himself sustains severe bodily injuries.

III

Mentally, too, Harold Mark is shaken as he lies abed and continues his serious thinking. "Behold," declares Harold Mark in effect, "I have tested man as an individual and see what comes of it! I put faith in my fellow creature and he has repaid my great, burning sympathy by burning down my hospital." To which, of course, the obvious answer would be that to place a mentally unbalanced person in a position of grave responsibility is not a test of anything except the full scope of your personal muddle-headedness.

Even so, the reader is delusively encouraged as Harold Mark continues his serious thinking: "You with the bleeding world's conscience, you stretch yourself upon the cross and suffer and bleed like a fool. You help no one." For the reader begins to hope that this Mark is on the verge of discovering at least a fraction of the truth about Harold Mark, when, in the nick of need, the most gratifying up-

lifting reflections occur to the hurt dreamer concerning "the great dreamers of the past."

"A slave rises in Rome with a star on his brow: one of his disciples becomes emperor of the world. In Judæa the son of a carpenter stands with some fishermen round him and takes water out of a well. Over the Italy of the Renaissance rises a figure with a chisel in his hand; in England a poet builds a world throne. They were dreamers like you," says Harold Mark to himself with very moving modesty. "They were dreamers, and yet they are the torch bearers in the procession of mankind: and it is owing to them that there is not night over the world."

And that makes him quite happy.

Thus, finally, in wringing gladness from the reflection that, but for the strivings of dead dreamers, things might, you know, really have been much worse than they are, does Harold Mark attain to tranquil mental unison with that other eminent philosopher, Pollyanna. And the book ends with the reader comprehending that the already devastated town, and all Norway, and the face of the world at large, are doomed indefinitely to remain the objects of Dr. Mark's serious thinking and great, burning sympathy, once he is out of bed again.

IV

So much for this Dr. Harold Mark, whom Bojer has made the pivot of a big ironic book, very finely conceived and very finely executed. I have but outlined, with, it may be, improper levity, where Bojer meticulously "renders"— with, as I think, a loving malevolence—this man of average endowments who is dissatisfied with human life as it is now conducted, and as it has hitherto been conducted, and who is distrustful (having reason) of the circumambient and ambiguous universe.

"What does it all mean, and toward what is this disastrous muddle striving?—I do not know. What can I do about the incomprehensible huge mess? Why, nothing whatever: and indeed my efforts to do anything about it appear but to augment the discomfort of my fellow animalculæ. Very well, then! I will make the humiliation of my position endurable by tipsifying myself with optimistic verbiage and with uplifting drivel about what fine fellows are, at any rate, such an elect minority among mankind as Shakespeare and Christ and myself."

One cannot but think, be it repeated, that this portrait of a philanthropist has been etched with the acid of premeditated irony: though the publishers, to all appearance, would have you believe that Johan Bojer portrayed this Harold Mark with tender seriousness and whole-hearted admiration and, in a word, with the indorsement of Bojer's own "great, burning sympathy." One must respectfully question that. Yet, even should the case be such, the irony is none the less keen for being two-edged, nor is the portrait rendered a whit less impressive by any queer light thrown upon the painter. The volume as it stands may fairly be decreed a very handsome piece of irony either way.

Cecil Roberts   (essay date 1920)

SOURCE: "Treacherous Ground," in *Johan Bojer: The Man and His Works* by Carl Gad, translated by Elizabeth Jelliffe MacIntire, Moffat, Yard and Company, 1920, pp. 256-60.

[*Roberts was an English journalist, editor, poet, and novelist. In the following essay, he delineates the plot of* On Treacherous Ground *and comments on the lyricism of Bojer's writing.*]

Some years ago the first Bojer book found its way into my hands and a review resulted in a number of inquiries as to who Johan Bojer was and where he lived. It was hardly necessary to answer questions because there have been few authors of whom one feels that they write themselves into their books more than Bojer. You can trace the intellectual development of this Norwegian through intellectual revolt to romantic realism. It is no paradox to declare that he is a romantic realist. He writes of men who fail because they hold an ideal and unlike most idealists they scorn propaganda and experiment upon themselves. In **Treacherous Ground,** as in **The Great Hunger** or **The Power of a Lie** we encounter a hero who belittles himself and cultivates the luxury of despair. Erik Evje is a socialist who does everything to provoke society against him. He disgraces a girl, fails in a promise to a friend, and is never so contemptible as when filled with contrition. Faced by the man he has wronged he flies home to the mother he has neglected and takes control of the estate. There he rewards the old family laborers with plots of land on the heights of the fiord. His conscience is eased by this sacrifice of his patrimony until a candid friend, otherwise an insincere enemy, warns him that the whole settlement is threatened with a landslide. "It sometimes happens, however, that a man who jokes and laughs has a little sore place upon his foot, which hurts at every step, although he thinks about other things and walks as if nothing was the matter. Erik Evje also had a little sore place. It was a secret fear that in spite of everything, there was something wrong up at Newland."

There is no truth so hard to run down as an unestablished one. A jealous engineer predicted a landslide, Evje, his wife and his settlers cannot believe it is true, because the truth seems treacherous to the ideal of a man who sought to clear himself by self sacrifice. This is a theme such as Bojer delights in.

He stands forth among novelists because he champions the indifference of nature. An idealist builds a hospital and puts in charge of it an ex-convict who burns it down; a dreamer who has sinned against his fellows builds a new settlement and the land slides away with it. To the Socialist first God is a joke, then a joker, and the man seeking to establish himself in righteousness is walking on treacherous ground. Bojer's work is the study of the courage of men to battle long with life. Yet his work is never depressing, his heroes have the courage of despair and the consistency of the pessimist. Life cheats them by bringing them love where they were vowed to solitude, success where they predicted disaster, and hope, like a recurring decimal, pours through their sum total of things. There is no Blue

Bird necromancy in Bojer's books, but he has the genius to show the ordinary man behaving in the ordinary way, yet fighting all the world because revolt seizes upon the third and fourth generation of them that reform us. When all Evje's world tumbles down in the landslide, when the reformer's dream is shattered, when the little homes and their domestic romances sweep down to death, it is then that Bojer becomes lyrical and reveals, through a chapter of strong beauty, how one man, with a dream in his heart for long years, suddenly finds release in disaster. Stubborn, drunken Lars, like Evje, attempted to retrieve a mistake and married the woman he did not love. He toils on the landslide to find the body of the woman he loves, lightly ignoring the mother who dies in an heroic attempt to save her children. A beast, he has the faithfulness of a beast, so he is happiest when he is driving the body of his beloved through the snow to its last sleeping place. Where most of us would see only the cynic, the unfaithful husband, Bojer sees the inability of the heart to effect a compromise. It is a lyrical close to a symphony of disaster.

"He passed the houses and entered a wood white with snow, and here the little bell on the horse's chest rang out clear and melodious, like an old ballad. Presently a red full moon peeped out above the snow-white mountain tops, reminding him of the time when he wandered about alone up there on the pale moors as a goatherd, and had poured forth from his horn all that moved and sounded in his brain. And almost unconsciously, as he sat he put it all together—the recollection of the prettiest voice in the church, the slender waist, a uniform, of which nothing would ever come now, and the girl in the coffin, perhaps still silently weeping—it all seemed to grow together into a long forgotten wordless song."

Here we see the courage of a romantic realist. He finds music in disaster, out of defeat sings the human heart at war with life. It is this courage to write as life writes on the human mind which makes Bojer not only a novelist of power but a maker of books that challenge the intellect.

Julius Moritzen   (essay date 1923)

SOURCE: "Before the Mast of a North Sea Fisherman," in *The New York Times Book Review,* April 29, 1923, p. 7.

[*In the following essay, Moritzen comments on Bojer's realistic portrayal of Norwegian seafaring life in* The Last of the Vikings.]

The courage that possessed the men that went down to the sea in ships centuries ago and cut the first path across the Atlantic Ocean became the heritage of those dauntless fishermen of Norway who made the Lofoten Islands their cherished goal before steam, electricity and other motor power put sailing craft in the discard. In open boats, scarcely different in construction from those used by their Viking ancestors, Norwegian fishermen of less than a generation ago would sail the long distance north in search of the shining cod, while in constant battle with the elements. It was a struggle with wind and weather, and danger lurking in every wave that beat furiously against the boat with its complement of half a dozen men. It is these to whom Johan Bojer builds a monument in *The Last of the Vikings*.

Two great characters stand out conspicuously in modern Norwegian fiction—Isac, of Knut Hamsun's *The Growth of the Soil,* and Kristàver Myran of Bojer's last work. It is difficult to say which of these is the greatest. As *The Growth of the Soil* wrote itself down as an epic of the cultivator's labor, so assuredly *The Last of the Vikings* must be assigned a place as an epic of the sea. Side by side, Knut Hamsun and Johan Bojer are the legitimate successors to Björnstjerne Björnson and Jonas Lie as interpreters of a Norway whose sons and daughters have done their part in advancing civilization.

It is a simple story that Bojer has to tell, and yet how effective. Criticism may well think twice before declaring that it has found any vulnerable spots in the plot itself or in the manner of its telling. It is one of these books that unrolls a canvas on which the artist has employed no high colors to fascinate the eye. It is all so subdued in tone, and yet what action there is as the characters become living personalities and grip the onlooker!

> The dim, blue twilight had already fallen upon the countryside, and when the bell at Lindegaard rang to call the workers home to supper, its sound rose and fell like an angelus over fjord and mountains. . . . The farm laborers lived in the little fishermen's cottages down by the steel-gray fjord, each with a small piece of land about it. They were pledged to work many weeks of the year on the big farm, and cultivated their own land when they came home in the evening, and even then they had to resort to the sea for their principal means of subsistence. They took part in the herring fisheries in the Autumn, and in the Winter sailed hundreds of miles in open boats up to Lofoten, perhaps tempted by the hope of gain, but perhaps, too, because on the sea they were free men.

With a few strokes Bojer produces a striking contrast between peace on land and the danger of the sea. It is a peace, of course, made almost insufferable because of the difficulty for these humble folks of the Norwegian coast country to make a bare living on shore. There is Màrya Myran, the wife of one of the farm laborers, cutting the grain on the big farm, the single worker remaining on one of the large barley fields, and "though Màrya had done twice an ordinary day's work, she wanted to finish the last little bit before she went home; but she dreaded standing erect, for she was ready to drop with fatigue."

Kristàver's wife has with her in the field her baby. It is a touching picture where she finally stumbles homeward with the little one on her back. It is a household in which her boy Lars is soon to join his father on the Lofoten trip; a thing that his youthful fancy has pictured as the height of ambition.

It is not impossible that in the person of Lars, Johan Bojer tells of some of his own experiences as a Lofoten fisherman. He, too, was a poor boy, born March 6, 1872, at Orkesdaloren near Trondhjem. The greater part of his childhood was passed at Risen, on the other side of the fjord. He fished in the fjord, tended cattle in the fields in Summer, and went once a week to school, to stay two days. On Sundays he went to service with the grown-ups, and in the evenings, in front of the open fire, he heard Mother Randi tell fairy tales and stories like those that Bojer later retold under the title *Old Tales*. Mother Randi herself had seen these little queer people and believed firmly in them. All was preparatory to the time when Bojer turned to writing.

Màrya Myran had passed the seventeen years of her married life on the coast, but had lived her earlier life in a valley, among the forests and mountains, and was now as little reconciled to her life by the sea as she had been on the first day of it. Her husband, Kristàver, was still the handsomest man in the district, but he was out on the sea the greater part of the year, chaining her to a life on the wild, barren shore and filling her with such fear and unrest during the long Winter nights that it was all she could do to restrain her impulse to flee from it all. For him and their six children the gray cottage out there was home, but it would never be hers. She was as homesick now as she had been all through the first year of her married life; she might do the work of two or three, but she never succeeded in working herself into a feeling of home.

> The sea, with its terrible, howling storms that raged all through the Winter [we read], the waves that day and night thundered and foamed upon the sand and seaweed, foamed, too, in her mind and made her sleepless, and would one day, she felt, rob her of her reason. They were long, long years. She looked forward to the day when Kristàver would sell his boats and house, move with her and the children up into the valley and take to farming. They could never be worse off than they were now.

> Every Winter he risked his life upon the Lofoten Sea, and, if one year the fishing was good, it was eaten up by the seven bad years, and they were always in poverty. But to hope to draw him from the sea to the land was like trying to change a fish into a bird, and he turned the children's minds in his direction. The eldest boy, Lars, was only 16, but he wanted to go to Lofoten next Winter; and Oluf, who was 14 in the Spring, talked of nothing else. She was like a hen with a brood of ducklings, vainly calling and enticing them away from the water.

The simile could hardly be more perfect. Johan Bojer, as Joseph Hergesheimer said of *The Great Hunger,* writes in such a way as to cause "annoyance to a world of fat comfort." And John Galsworthy adds that there is in his works a "stark realistic spirituality characteristic of a race with special depths of darkness to contend with, and its own northern sunlight and beauty." All this applies with special force to the men and women whom Bojer presents as typical of their environment and true to the life in *The Last of the Vikings*.

Kristàver Myran had become sole owner of a Lofoten boat with a reputation for capsizing so often that when it was put up for auction he was the only bidder. He had been a headman for many years, but only part owner in the boat, and what is the good of a successful fishing season once in a while when the proceeds have to be divided among six men? He owed for the boat, it is true, and would have to go still deeper into debt if he alone had to equip six men for a Winter's fishing. It was foolhardy, but he had taken the plunge, and what was done could not be undone.

There can be love in a cottage, even as humble as that of Kristàver Myran. The affection that existed between Kristàver and Màrya was not of the kind that wastes itself in words. The day was near when the Lofoten boats were making ready for their perilous voyage north. Below the boathouse at Kristàver's place lay the Seal, the craft that he and his son were about to set out in, together with their four companions:

> At Myran, where Kristàver and Màrya slept in a bed against the south wall, Kristàver woke in the middle of the night, and a little while after said softly:
>
> "Are you crying, Màrya?"
>
> "Oh, no!"
>
> "You mustn't be so unhappy about it."
>
> He was just dropping asleep again when he felt her arm about his neck.
>
> "It'll be so sad for me when you're gone!"
>
> "Oh, well, but you're so clever you will get on all right."
>
> "And you're taking them with you! Now it's Lars, and next it'll be Oluf, one after another. You're taking them away! You're taking, them away!"
>
> What could Kristàver say to this? They disagreed on this point, but in all else Màrya was the best of wives, and toiled from morning till night, only sometimes with a look of fear in her eyes. Her arms were around his neck now, and she did not quite agree with him again; but it would all come out right, for Màrya was the best of wives.

It is a moot point whether Johan Bojer is at his best when describing a homely scene like this: the gathering in the little church on the last Sunday before the sailing, when many a wife from the shore district raised her eyes from her hymn book to look across at her husband, when the hymn became a little prayer for his return from the long voyage northward, or when he deals with the sea itself and the men who are taking their lives in their hands as they set sail for Lofoten. The romantic and sentimental element in *The Last of the Vikings* is not over great. As boys will be boys and girls will be girls, Lars does leave behind him a lass, Ellen Koya, who had found a soft spot in the young fisherman's heart. But this is really subsidiary to the main theme of the book. It is fighting the battle against the angry North Sea waves that spells the great fascination of this story. If Johan Bojer is in his element on shore, even more so is the sea his element.

The Seal was one of four boats making that particular spot of the Norwegian coast their home port. There was the Storm-Bird, where Andreas Ekra was headman; the Sea-Fire, owned by Peter Suzansa, and the Sea-Flower, where lame Jacob limped about to make ready for the great adventure. Six men to each boat was the rule. The hour for departure was nigh. Màrya was standing with other wives upon the beach. Kristàver climbed back over the roof of the aft cabin to put on the steerage and then crept forward again, and dropped into the headman's place on the seat, turning his face to the land and to her, but without saying anything.

> "Let go!"
>
> There was a sound of wet rope against an iron ring as the grapnel was hauled in; a block screeched, and the broad, heavy square sail was hoisted up the mast, and, filling with the wind, was fastened obliquely across the boat; and the Seal moved and began to glide slowly into the bay.
>
> "Good-bye, Kristàver! Good-bye, Lars!" And "Good-bye!" cried many wives on the beach as they took off the kerchiefs that covered their heads and waved them in farewell.
>
> Kristàver was now a headman, who swung the tiller above his head and looked after everything on board, but he nevertheless waved his sou'wester vigorously and shouted "Good-bye!" A gust of wind flung dark streaks across the bay; the Seal heeled over, and the water foamed at her bow and in her wake, and the red pennon fluttered at the masthead. Màrya looked at it, and her face brightened. She had made it out of material that was to have been a petticoat for herself, and she had embroidered Kristàver's initials upon it with blue thread. Those who stood on the shore began to run along the beach as if trying to keep up with the boats, and the last thing that Màrya saw, as the Seal disappeared in the frosty haze, was a sou'wester waved from the stern as the topsail was hoisted.

And so they sailed away. It was Kristàver's first sailing day with the Seal, and he stood with every sense alert, trying to make acquaintance with the boat. That there was something wrong with her he saw at once. There was not the right accord between the rigging and the boat. Women and horses have their caprices, he thought to himself, and so has a boat, and he meant to tame her.

And he did. How Kristàver accomplished this task, Bojer relates in one of the most fascinating chapters of the book. It would spoil the effect of the whole not to leave it for the prospective reader.

Days and nights passed and still they kept sailing north. Lars was being initiated into the mysteries of the great deep. How wonderful it all was and yet how strenuous the life. Much of the sailing was through dangerous passages, then open water again, and on the wind-swept shore of a bay in the gray mountain-wall stood a few houses, with smoke rising from their chimneys. Lars thought that if his mother lived there she would go quite out of her mind. "Poor mother! If only Oluf will do all he can to help her this Winter!"

Lofoten is reached. Thousands of fishermen like Kristàver and his crew have assembled to make ready for the fishing. The scene is like no other in all the world. The signal flag is hoisted in the inspection office. Oars struck against one another and creaked, one boat bumped up against another and at the same time was pushed from the opposite side; swearing and threats filled the air. All wanted to be first on the fishing grounds. But the first day brought disappointment. The nets were set and hauled up without any catch worth speaking of. But hope was something that kept their spirits up. And then came the day when the sea gave up its riches in such abundance as never before in the memory of man. With what color effect Bojer sketches the life of these men, both as they are at work on the fishing banks and spending their time ashore under conditions that would be insufferable to any one but such who have known nothing different since attaining manhood.

But let us not forget the women and children left at home. A great storm was sweeping up the coast. It is unpleasant to be out on such a stormy night. It is bad enough down by the fjord, but what must it be for those who perhaps are out on the sea! Lofoten! Lofoten!

> Màrya had relighted the lamp and put the children to bed, and had returned to her weaving. The house shook with the wind, and it was a relief to her to have her fingers occupied when the gusts of the wind threatened to lift the cottage and carry it away through the night. Was she afraid? No, but she felt inclined to sing, to cry out wild, incoherent words, only to drown those shrieks of anguish out in the darkness, where the storm was like the howling of evil spirits. She worked with busy fingers. It was no ordinary piece of weaving, not homespun or linen; it was a hanging with figures woven into it, and she had learned it, and she had learned how to do it from the master forester's wife up the valley when she was a girl. This lady had lately come to her with a pattern for her to weave from. It represented the legend of Siegfried, and at present she was doing the part where Siegfried was riding his horse Crane through a great, crackling fire on the mountain in Franconia.

It is in touches like these that Johan Bojer shows his mastery in delineation:

> As she sat there with the storm about her, she seemed to be looking at her own life as she wove the great legend of long ago into her web. She was condemned to live here by the sea, which she hated. It would almost be a rest to go out of her mind some day, but she would have to take Kristàver with her. She could easily throw herself into the sea in weather like this, but she must have Kristàver with her.

They say that in Norway they read Jack London in preference to any other American writer. It is not difficult to account for this. There is a kinship between London and one who, like Johan Bojer, depicts life in all its elemental strength that must perforce appeal to a race like that which has the Vikings for its forebears.

No other European writer of the generation ever succeeded in gaining the ear of the American public more quickly than did Bojer. Before 1919 his name was virtually unknown this side the Atlantic Ocean. *The Great Hunger* was the first of his books to appear in English, *The Face of the World* likewise was published here in 1919. In 1920 appeared *Treacherous Ground* and *The Power of a Lie. Life* followed shortly afterward. In the heyday of his literary activity it is to be assumed that *The Last of the Vikings* will yet have many successors, but whether Johan Bojer can ever excel himself is doubtful.

Hans P. Lödrup   (essay date 1926)

SOURCE: "Johan Bojer," in *The American-Scandinavian Review,* Vol. XIV, No. 4, April, 1926, pp. 207-17.

[*In the following essay, Lödrup surveys critical opinion of Bojer during his lifetime and discusses several of the author's major works.*]

The Norwegian people are gifted artistically but not gifted politically. Therefore we have a disproportionately large number of great writers and distinguished artists, while we have an equally disproportionate dearth of statesmen. It is our peasantry that has been the fountainhead of artistic genius among us, and from this part of our population Bojer sprang. In being self-taught, or as Americans say self-made, he resembles many other Norwegian poets and artists, though he is probably the one who has had the most unpropitious start and the greatest difficulties to overcome. With it all, he has attained success in life.

Johan Bojer was a poor fatherless child, put out to board with a woman in Tröndelagen. No kind clergyman noticed the bright little boy and put him to school. No kind patron reached him a helping hand when he began to write. He has himself told that he was fifteen years old before he knew there was such a thing as literature in books.

Even as a child he had to work and look out for himself. The poor little boy who lived over a stable in *The Great Hunger* is Bojer himself, though, as it happened, he lived in the barracks of the non-commissioned officers' school. He entered this school because he knew no other place where a boy without money or influential friends could receive free instruction, board and lodging, clothes and even a few pennies for pocket money. After finishing the course, he turned his hand to one thing after another, sold sewing-machines, clerked in a store, and rowed in the fisheries. But no matter what he did, two passions were always with him: an insatiable desire for knowledge which made him steal time from his employer in the day and from sleep at night, and a strong urge for social advancement. When the little boy looked from the crofter's hut over to the big farm, he resolved that such a farm should be his some day; when he saw the passenger boat steaming past with the gold-banded captain on the bridge, he made up his mind that he would become such a captain, and when he was a non-commissioned officer he wanted to be a general. This tendency may be traced in his works, where it is sometimes so marked as to be not quite pleasant.

In spite of poverty, Bojer's childhood can not be said to have been unhappy. His foster-mother, Randi, was a good, kind-hearted woman who told him stories and had a genuine affection for him. In return he loved her, as he has shown by naming one of his daughters after her. He also loved the outdoors and every year makes a pilgrimage to his native parish. He once said that whenever he thought of home, it was not a house but the woods and moors where he tended cattle as a boy that he remembered. In these rather wistful words Bojer reveals something of his soul and gives us an inkling of how his early bent determined his later development.

High spirits and love of life were his from the cradle, but all through his youth he had to sacrifice pleasure to the necessity for drudging in every spare hour to acquire the education that more fortunate youths receive in the regular course of their schooling. Many men might have become bitter and old before their time, but the effect on Bojer has only been to make him more youthful and buoyant. He has simply made up for lost time. His books contain not a few instances of men who in maturer years have grasped the opportunity to enjoy the amusements from which hard work shut them out in their youth.

The fact that Bojer was, in a literary way, self-taught made him less sure in his style, when he began to write, than many men of lesser gifts. But with the appearance of his novel *A Procession of the People*—which the critic Carl Nærup called the best Norwegian novel published in the nineties—he stands forth as an author who, though he may be a little uneven (and who is not?) is nevertheless a master of his craft. This does not preclude a steady rise in his work to the high level attained in *The Power of a Lie, The Last of the Vikings,* and *Dyrendal*.

Bojer's most important books show him not only as a clever builder of plots and teller of tales but also as possessing an intellect of marked individuality. A just estimate of his works will place him in the front ranks of Norwegian literature, between Hamsun and Kinck. Hamsun is more of an artist, and Kinck is a deeper, more original thinker, but Bojer is clearer in his conception than Kinck and more intellectual than Hamsun. These qualities give the key to his popularity in the Latin and Anglo-Saxon countries. While Hamsun is loved and admired in the Slavic and Germanic world, Bojer is *le grand maître* in France. He has been awarded a prize by the Academy in Paris; his books are displayed in the shop windows there, and his stories run serially in the most exclusive literary magazines.

This is, of course, not merely accidental. It depends on kindred mentality in author and public.

Hamsun's works are the product of feeling. He is the lover and nature mystic, who intuitively knows the emotions and passions of men—their love-life and their reactions to nature—and who clothes these feelings in a style of exquisite beauty. He is the born artist, in whom the impressions of the outside world are immediately transmuted into forms of poetic art, apparently without reflection and without effort. Language with him is not merely the vehicle of his thought; it is an instrument upon which he plays and from which he evokes tones of purely musical value—all gifts that wake a response in the dreamy, poetic, musically attuned nature of the Slav and German, while they often leave the Latin and the Anglo-Saxon cold. The latter

demand, at least from the novel, something more tangible than moods and impressions: they crave facts and definite meanings that can be apprehended by the intellect and appraised in discussion.

This they find in Bojer. He is markedly intellectual. Though it was his creative imagination that drove him to write, the subjects of his books are drawn from the world of thoughts and ideas, not from that of his emotions. All generalizations of this nature are of course, halting, but with all due reservations, it may be said that in general Hamsun writes about emotions and Bojer about thoughts and ideas.

Bojer likes to take a single psychological phenomenon—the power of truth, or of a lie, or of love—and isolate it. This phenomenon he cultivates to the exclusion of everything else, invests it with a personality, and in fact almost makes it the hero of his book. His fondness for abstract ideas inclines him to the *typically* human, while Hamsun inclines to the *individually* human. Hamsun writes of men, Bojer of man. Hamsun is a romanticist, Bojer a classicist, and his classicism is in line with his orientation toward the Western nations.

In some of Bojer's books, which on the surface are ordinary realistic novels of Norwegian life, it is really not a person but an idea that is the central figure. He is so intensely absorbed in following this idea that his characters interest him only in so far as they throw light on the idea. Naturally this weakens the effect of his books as realistic pictures of life, but we must remember that his human characters are only the drapery over the real actors in this "drama of vices and virtues." It is therefore not a sign of failing power when the reader is apt to forget the persons and remember the problem; quite the contrary, for the problem *is* the person. He who would judge Bojer according to the usual standards of realistic fiction can find plenty of pegs to hang his objections upon, but this would be as unfair as to judge a man by his clothes.

Bojer began as a realist, for this is the line of least resistance. But while he wrote of people and events in his home parish, just as other peasant born writers have done, it soon became apparent that he was approaching them from an altogether different angle. He would take up a single thread in the tangled skein of human emotions and follow it in all its windings, and this task absorbed him more and more. As the philosopher after a while has to move in the domain of pure thought and tread the paths of unreality, so Bojer abstracts the single psychological phenomenon from its relation with other thoughts and ideas in the mind of the individual. He picks it up as the vivisectionist picks up with his instrument a single nerve fibre from a bundle of nerves and disentangles it from everything else. While he plays this exciting intellectual game, juggling with pure psychology, the persons naturally sink into the background. *A Procession of the People* is not so much a book about Chairman Hegge as about the ravages of politics in the mind of the politician. *The Power of a Lie* is not about Nordby but about the lie.

This power of taking general psychological observations and making them so vital that they go on living in our minds as problems is, in my opinion, Bojer's great achievement. This form of writing is far more difficult than the ordinary psychological novel. It demands brilliant presentation, great power of concentration, and tremendous energy of imagination. The idea must be traced in all its meanderings through human consciousness and must at the same time be made so vital that it grips the imagination. The author must not only have this driving force in the pursuit of his subject, but must have mastered the technique of composition and the art of telling a story entertainingly. All this is eminently true of Bojer.

The Power of a Lie (called *The Power of Faith* in the original) is without doubt the most monumental work in this part of Bojer's production. It is the story of a lie which by the power of faith becomes a truth, but outwardly it is the story of the village magnate Nordby who by a lie gets Trader Wangen imprisoned for cheating.

The lie begins its career by flying out, tiny and innocent, in the form of a slight omission—Nordby has not the courage to contradict his wife when she says, "Thank goodness you haven't signed any papers for him, so you don't lose anything."—This little omission is not with intent to deceive, but simply because he hates to risk the scene which surely would follow if he told his wife that he actually had given security for Wangen and had lost. The omission flies out into the world, lives its own life, and has consequences. It leads to other omissions, then to direct little lies, and finally to perjury in court. But on its way Nordby's lie meets the mistakes of others and encounters at last a lie on the part of Wangen. And it meets Nordby's conviction that at bottom he is not a bad fellow. In his mind his own sin becomes paler and paler with every new sin committed by Wangen. At last when his fellow citizens arrange a celebration for him, he ends by having a very good opinion of himself. The lie which sailed out into the world as light as a single feather has become a truth equal to five hens. Nordby thinks it is dreadful what lies Wangen tells, he feels quite scandalized and thanks God that he is not like Wangen. The book ends with these lines:

> When Nordby at last got into bed, he folded his hands and read a couple of verses from a hymn. He felt that God was very near him. The respect and sympathy of the parish seemed to shine into his conscience, and he had to thank God for everything.
>
> "But one thing I can't understand," he thought after a little while, "and that is how people like Wangen can stand there with a straight face and lie in court. God help people who haven't got more conscience than that."

Such is the power of faith, says Bojer. So a lie can live and wax fat until at last it becomes a truth.

This ending is too paradoxical. Bojer the wag has taken the reins from the poet and psychologist. He has not been able to resist the image of the old sinner lying there and thanking God because he is not like the publican Wangen. In spite of its paradoxical ending, however, the book is a remarkable and distinguished piece of work, one that may resist the wear and tear of centuries. There is so much virtuosity in the handling, so much keenness in the analysis, and so much originality in the conception that it has well deserved the world fame it has attained.

The Prisoner Who Sang is another of Bojer's free psychological creations in novel form. It is not so firm in composition as *The Power of a Lie* and not so monumental, but it is more elegant, more ingratiating, and perhaps even more original. It deals with the human desire to play several rôles and not always to be the same person, in other words, with that division of personality which most people have felt in themselves. Bojer once expressed it in speaking to a group of ultra-exclusive European men of letters, when he suddenly exploded, "I became a writer because I could not become a cavalry general."

Andreas Berget, the prisoner who sang, has a personality so subdivided that there is nothing left of his real self. He is a near relative of Peer Gynt, and like him a member of the onion family, all peel and no kernel. He suffers from an insatiable longing to be in the lime light, and he is absolutely unable to distinguish between good and evil—is, in fact, thoroughly amoral. Being a poor boy, the only way he can attract attention to himself is by mischievous pranks. Once at a funeral he becomes possessed with a desire to startle people and "give them new faces" as Bojer put it, and so he raps out a strong oath in a loud voice. Being totally devoid of all inhibitions, he gives way to every impulse, and inasmuch as his impulses usually take the form of wanting to make fools of people by playing a part, pretending to be what he is not, they often lead to criminal swindling. He cheats in love and in business, but is always in a radiant good humor, thoroughly enjoying the game. At last he becomes a pawnbroker and a communist agitator, a usurer and a reformer at the same time. In true Bojer style he carries the situation—the division of personality—to a point where his communist self leads a mob in attacking the business of the pawnbroker and scatters all his treasures in the street. Then the police takes a hand, and inasmuch as the pawnbroker can not be found, he is accused of having murdered him. In court he makes a clean breast of the whole story and confesses that he is the pawnbroker too. The court, of course, believes he is insane, and then he makes his great speech:

> "As a pawnbroker I often had a bad conscience, that is to say, a longing to be a better man and to see a better state of society realized. A large part of my nature gained self-expression when I fleeced the poor borrowers, and the remaining part of me obtained a place in the sun when I fought for their cause and advocated their rights in the world. Only, the demagogue might feel his gorge rising at all those oily words addressed to the crowd, and my only comfort was the thought that I myself was well anchored in reality. I was able to return to reality, however mean, before the day ended. It strengthens and refreshes a man to change his nature. As a rule the pawnbroker had only contempt for the communistic orator, and the communist hated and cursed the pawnbroker. The tension between the two kept my spirit wide-awake all times. One day the communist arranged a riot against the pawnbroker, plundered his shop and strangled him. In that way one side of our nature often takes re-

venge over the other. And might I be allowed to ask: Are there so very many in this room who are so thorough when they desire to better themselves?

"Life and theory? You demand connection between the two? If you are all honest, you will admit that nothing is more impossible. If the ideal were life, then there would be nothing for which to gaze at the sky, nothing to seek in the azure of the future. There would be no need of faith, of longing, of dreams. The moment an ideal becomes a part of life, it is changed into local administration.

"Finally I will ask every one in this room: am I not right? Most of the ladies and gentlemen present presumably call themselves Christians. Tell me in earnest: have you even for one moment out of the twenty-four hours of the day carried out the doctrines of Christianity in your lives?

"Hypocrisy? Not at all. Only when a doctrine is so lofty that it is out of reach, then only is it true and eternal. . . . As far as I am concerned I sorrowfully declare that on the day when we strangle what is evil in us we also destroy what is good, and that is why I am here now, not exactly sure of my own identity."

This is, of course, dialectics. It is paradoxical, but it is brilliant. It is an agile play with psychological facts, the like of which we have never before seen in our literature. The book is whimsical to the point of flippancy, but underneath the jest there is a deep meaning hidden and it teaches us much about ourselves that we did not know before.

A third instance of Bojer's unrealistic psychological imaginative work is the fairy tale, *The Eyes of Love,* which he has since turned into a rather uninteresting play. The idea is that love makes everything beautiful within us and around us, and like the other tales in the collection *White Birds,* it is a rapturous hymn to love. A youthful and enthusiastic poet is writing these mad fairy tales in praise of a woman. They are not all equally good; some are a little clumsy, while others are not free from foppishness; they have neither the deep wisdom of the folk tale nor Hans Christian Andersen's knowledge of human nature, but they contain beautiful thoughts; they are so young and vibrant, they warm hearts that have not yet grown so cold as to forget the bliss of loving.

Here is an example:

Such a young and lovely woman sails in among the dull week-days with music on board. Drunken beggars are silenced when she approaches. Faces marred by weeping light up when she enters. The sick forget their pain when she touches them.

The poor man becomes rich when she stands in his cottage. No food is so common that it does not turn into festive fare when she sits down to the table, and her dress may be red or white or blue, but it carries always a fragrance of white linen.

Such a young woman has an invisible fairy who does her hair, chooses her colors for her, and

dresses her. If there is a slight disarrangement in her costume, that is only an added charm. If she puts on her hat hastily, it assumes lines more graceful than any modiste could have given it. If she loses a button from her long glove, it allows her partner a rapturous glimpse of her wrist. If her shoe-string comes untied, it will afford some young man a blissful memory for life that he has been allowed to kneel down and tie it.

Or the following:

In the field as the priestess of earth, at the hearth-stone, on the virginal couch, in the temple, clad in silk or only in a fig leaf, pale or golden, always she has been the light of the world. . . . What hurts me is to think that so many millions of young women have lived and I have not seen them, not spoken one little word to them, not handed them the tiniest flower, not basked in the light of their smile.

This is Bojer the lyrist—infatuated and mad.

Yet there is still another Bojer, a solid realistic novelist who has produced a number of excellent—and some not so good—novels and stories. His best novel of this type is *Dyrendal* (published in English under the title *God and Woman*) the story of Martha, the peasant girl in the north of Norway, who gains gold and land, but is poor and barren in her soul because she is not a mother. Rarely has a man understood so well the tragedy of the childless woman. Martha is a vital figure with roots deep in the soil and a temperament colored by the landscape around her. Sometimes it is as though a sudden depth opened in her soul and allowed us to glimpse for an instant the strange mixture of tenderness and hardness, of dourness and yearning, of narrowness and boundlessness which makes up her nature. She seems to reflect the scenery, at once bleak and bountiful, with ocean depths and mountain peaks, with confining valleys and illimitable open sea.

The *Last of the Vikings* is a broadly composed and brilliantly painted picture of folk life. In addition to its literary charm, it has historical value in that it preserves a certain type of life that has lasted for centuries but is now passing with the advent of the motor boat and the reorganization of the fisheries along lines of big industry. Bojer's faculty for telling a story so that it grips the attention has never been more apparent. He knew the life through and through, the people, the places, and the customs. The book will be a classic in Norwegian literature, a modern pendant to the Nordland descriptions of Peder Dass. He plays on all strings, there are youthful idyls from the parishes, storm nights from the sea, fights about fishing-grounds, sickness, suffering, and death. Very beautiful in its mixture of homely simplicity and spiritual elevation is the chapter about Elezeus who is dying at the fishing-station and receives communion from the hands of another fisherman. It is tempting to quote this moving passage in full, but that would take too much space.

The author's last book, *Our Own People* (called *The Emigrants* in the English edition) is in a broad sense a continuation of *The Last of the Vikings*. It describes the life of the early Norwegian pioneers in America, tells how they break the virgin soil of the prairie, and how their little new community comes into being and develops. In the constant emotional swinging between their longing for home and their love of the land they have cultivated, Bojer sees the tragedy of the first generation. Wherever they are, they will long for the country where they are *not*.

This book, too, is planned on a large scale and executed with Bojer's mastery of technique. Everything falls into its place naturally, and from all that I have heard, the picture of the life of our emigrant countrymen seems well rendered and true. Nevertheless it has not quite the sense of actuality that we feel in *The Last of the Vikings;* it lacks the thousand and one tiny realistic touches that give such life to the Nordland book, and therefore it leaves us with a sense of something unlived and unfelt in spite of all technical virtuosity.

It will be apparent from this sketch that Bojer is an author with a wide sweep. His intellect is keen, his temperament vivacious; his interests are many-sided and his faculties versatile. What he lacks in his personality as a writer is a certain artistic quality. In his language there is a want of sensitiveness to the rounded and harmonious; it has rather a harshness that grates. It is possible that this is because he is a native of Tröndelagen, and if so it is temperamental. The hardness in form may be only an expression of his own primeval strength and indomitable energy. In most of his books he has broken new paths and created his own form with masterly skill. In others he has followed the broad highway of the ordinary novel and handled his subject with equal mastery. Occasionally, however, he falls into mediocrity, as in some of his less successful novels and in his dramas. But all his works have in common a bright and positive element, a belief in the powers of goodness, and a faith in the old homespun virtues, which is not usually found in his generation, but is in league with his own bright, energetic, positive nature. The vivacity of his books is not common in modern Norwegian literature, and though sometimes the sprightliness may be a little forced, it is often sparkling and characteristic.

Bojer's personality as an author is therefore complicated and it is not easy for a contemporary to say the final word regarding it—and besides Bojer is yet in the midst of his life-work. Whatever his shortcomings or his merits, it is at least certain that he is one of the most distinguished and individual of Norwegian authors and has richly deserved the world-wide fame he has won. To his friends it is moreover a pleasure to know that in his private life he is a happy man in a happy home, a man who even in the outer circumstances of his life has won in maturity the beauty and spaciousness that youth denied him.

Theodore Jorgenson   (essay date 1933)

SOURCE: "Neo-Realism," in *History of Norwegian Literature,* The Macmillan Company, 1933, pp. 443-512.

[*In the following excerpt, Jorgenson presents a thematic overview of Bojer's works.*]

A Procession is the first of a group of [Bojer's] early works, which may be given the common designation of po-

litical satires and includes broadly the productions of half a dozen years between 1896 and 1902. They are more realistic than neo-romantic. The central emphasis is on the accusation that political parties and overheated agitation tend to warp the characters of men and to draw them away from the pursuits of useful labor. Work is Bojer's gospel. The bitter campaigns which accompanied the fall of the Sverdrup ministry are in the mind of the author so many scorching desert winds leaving the country arid and desolate. He continued the satire in *The Eternal Strife (Den evige krig)* and in *Mother Lea.* Meanwhile he turned aside to another genre. After writing the rather weak play *Saint Olaf,* he published in 1897 and again in 1898 collections of short stories, symbolic fables and fairy tales. The lyric strain in him, which had made him experiment in the writing of verse during the spare hours in Borthen's office, now found expression in these imaginative lyric narratives. Throughout his life his fondness for such literature has been apparent, and novels on the order of *The Prisoner Who Sang* are hardly more than elaborate fairy tales.

Throughout the year 1897 Bojer lived in Oslo. He was ill part of the time. A chest disorder troubled him; it was necessary to rest at one of the near-by sanitariums. Nothing serious developed. Early in 1898 he was again in Paris where he renewed the acquaintance with Obstfelder and in addition met Thomas Krag and Christian Krohg. He continued to Nice, visited Corsica and Italy before he returned to Oslo in May, 1899. Late that same year he married Ellen Lange, a student at the University of Oslo and the daughter of colonel Lange of Stavanger. Almost immediately after the publication of *The Eternal Strife,* the newlyweds left for Rome where they remained during 1900 and 1901 and where the next novel, *Mother Lea,* was written. In the fall of the latter year we find the young couple back in Norway. They visited Rissa on their way to Stenkjer where the Langes then resided. Bestun became for a short time Bojer's home, and there the oldest of his three children was born in January, 1902.

The year 1902 marks the beginning of a new period in Bojer's literary production. It covers the time between the beginning of the twentieth century and the publication of *Treacherous Ground* in 1908 and includes, beside the book here mentioned, the drama *Theodora* and the novels *A Pilgrimage* and *The Power of a Lie.* These works may be called psychological morality studies. They exemplify the author's use of an idea in the service of art. In *A Pilgrimage,* for instance, the thing given at the beginning is the deterioration of a woman's character when the racial function is thwarted. Every scene in the novel is but another step in the unfolding of the one characteristic until the woman chases hither and thither in a feverish and insane desire to recover the lost child. Some of the effects used are almost mathematical in their regularity, as when in quick succession Regina Aas tells her husband, first that she has born a child out of wedlock, then that she has killed this child, and finally that since marriage she has been unfaithful—all in order to satisfy her morbid desire to rid herself of him, since he cannot help her recover the illegitimate offspring she had turned over to unknown fosterparents. Similarly in *The Power of a Lie.* The given idea is that a man may deceive his own conscience to the extent that white innocence rises out of a dark and corrupt deed. Every scene is a step in the proof. Erik Evje in *Treacherous Ground* is an example of how a certain type of idealism is essentially based on a selfish desire to have life present a fixed meaning. There must be a moral ruler of the universe or the bottom drops from under the feet of the believers and they face chaos. Here the problem is the same as that which Kinck sets forth in the characters Machiavelli and Aretino, the one strong enough to be a transvaluator, the other too weak. Bojer's method is the direct opposite of that of the old Norwegian sagas, in which certain deeds and appearances are given, certain actions are known. From these we must feel our way inward into the hearts of the characters. Consider as an instance Skarphedin in the story of Burnt Njal. The twentieth century favors the latter practice. It desires to feel the uncertainties of life, the possibility of different outcomes, and the likelihood that the future is unsettled, being made. Hence the discrediting of the rigid plot novel and the uniform praise given to psychological and social description. We may favor philosophical ideas, but we insist at any rate that the artist shall be able to sink these ideas so deeply into the stream of life that they are sensed in the manner in which the spirit of a personality is sensed from the face of the man. Bojer is not consistently able to achieve that result. His books are clear and impressive but not always richly human. . . .

Beginning with the year 1909 [Bojer] entered a third period of creative activity characterized by vibrant joy in a new fullness of life. A number of his characters experience an Indian summer during the forties of their lives, a circumstance which may no doubt be traced back into the mind of their maker. With the exception of the publication of *The Eyes of Love,* an adaptation of a story originally found in *White Birds,* and the similar dramatization of *The Power of a Lie,* the first book representing the new mood is the novel *Life* finished in 1911. There are portions of captivating beauty in the work, yet it is hard to disagree with the Oslo critics that the emphasis on the new interest in sports such as skiing, boating, and tennis does not make for depth, and the attempt to show a rhythmic recurrence of life from parents to children is not altogether convincing.

To this period of vibrant joy in a new fullness of life belong also the novels *The Prisoner Who Sang* and *The Great Hunger.* The story of Andreas Berget is the account of a man who possesses no strong inner continuity, no determining self. He is a supreme actor but the stage affords no lasting satisfaction. He must play in real life, in such a manner that people are fooled and mistake the show for reality. Happy and carefree, entirely void of the sense of moral rights, he passes through life alias this and alias that until one of his personalities is accused and brought to trial for killing another. It is a Doctor Jekyll and Mr. Hyde affair on a much larger scale but without the actual transformation of the English account. In conclusion Andreas finds that after all there is a force which integrates the various moods and personalities of man and makes of him a responsible soul. It is the love of a woman. Again we discern Ibsen's idea that the soul is not a unity as such at the beginning. It comes into being when mind-elements

are coordinated and given point under the guidance of a strong life purpose rooted in the principle of growth. The Scripture says, Where there is no law, there is no sin. Likewise we may say, Where there is no spiritual purpose based on a life function, there is no creative soul, no real continuity, only successive states. Here too we have the basis of Bojer's amoral conception of the physical world. The landslide in *Treacherous Ground* has no regard for the teleology of Erik Evje. It is only when we enter the realm of mind that moral principles have any meaning. The same idea underlies the story of Peer Holm in *The Great Hunger*. We are swept along and fascinated by the dash and the genius of the leading character only to find him in the end overtaken by the fortuitous amoral elements of existence. He stands like a badly shaken mountain pine. But as the people of this world of ours crawl back to their habitations after cities have been destroyed by earthquakes and storms, and at once begin to repair the losses, so man in his very nature is characterized by an inner persistency which drives him to continue, and by a surplus quality of soul which in the final analysis compels him to be a creator of good, one who insists that the kingdom of God shall not perish from upon the earth. . . .

Two books not hitherto discussed belong to Bojer's so-called "idea" novels. They are *The Face of the World* and *The New Temple,* the former published in 1917 and the latter, a sequel to *The Great Hunger,* in 1927. Neither is particularly satisfying. The author himself has passed unfavorable judgment upon the story of Doctor Mark by omitting it from his collected works. It is an account of a social idealist whose altruism brings ruin. *The New Temple* is an attempt to show how the religion of modern humanism may be harmonized with the worship of the existing church simply by, in a somewhat ingenious manner, filling the old bottles with a new wine. The meaning of the sacraments is to be reinterpreted and mental reservations made in cases where the intellectually inclined finds difficulties in the path of reason. The novel is pale. One must again agree with the critics that there is a heaven-wide difference between the soul agony expressed by Garborg in *Tired Men* and the rather insignificant pangs suffered by the priest of the new temple.

We have now reached the fourth and perhaps the most significant group of Bojer's works, his descriptive novels of folk life. They include *God and the Woman, The Last of the Vikings, The Emigrants,* and *The Everlasting Struggle.* In these works we find a satisfying nearness to life and a richness of artistic expression not consistently present in his other works, though who shall say that a book with the strong lift in it that *The Great Hunger* possesses will not outlive them all? In *God and the Woman* some of the "idea" novel persists. Underlying the fortunes of the master and the mistress of Dyrendal is distinctly the doctrine that woman must function racially or die. The failure of Martha Ersland to perpetuate her life in offspring and of Hans Lia to secure a natural heir to his estate are the mainsprings of their undoing. In spite of their magnificent achievement they have not found and established deep contact with the things which grow. The *Last of the Vikings* is a paean to the old Lofoten fishermen. It was customary for the small farmers in Bojer's native district

Rissa to make the northward journey every year; hence the names we meet are locally determined: Lindegaard, Myran, Skaret, Raben, and others. The splendid thing about the book is its epic grandeur. In spite of the hard circumstances under which the people labor, they are men and women of energy and action, of courage and stubborn persistence, first cousins of Rölvaag's giants. And these two authors draw nearer to each other in their emigrant sagas. Though **The Emigrants** indicates in its very title that the point of view is that of a European, while the Minnesota novelist is concerned with the making of a new nation, their two works are complementary. Not an emigrant himself, Bojer had lived, nevertheless, for years in foreign countries. He was not a stranger to the emotions of longing nor to the feelings of those who return to childhood haunts. In its central elements the book is true and genuine, a worthy companion to the story of Kristaver Myran and his Lofoten fishermen. Personally, I do not find the English title of the last book of the group suitable. Literally translated from the Norwegian it is *People by the Sea.* To be sure their life is an everlasting struggle, but the author's effort is descriptive, an attempt to create a picture of folk life without any descriptive, an attempt to create a picture of folk life without any social or moral implications. It does not appear from the work itself that the life of the poor farmers and fishermen is necessarily less happy than that of people in other circumstances. The book is a piece of descriptive narration and as such magnificent. . . .

[Bojer's] natural ability to tell a story is very great. The lucidity of his intellect is admirable. And it seems that his fine persistence, his untiring self-discipline in the artistic pursuit, has made him a creator of lasting significance.

Brian W. Downs   (essay date 1966)

SOURCE: "The New Century," in *Modern Norwegian Literature, 1860-1918,* Cambridge University Press, 1966, pp. 189-98.

[*Downs was an English author and educator who specialized in Scandinavian studies at Cambridge University. In the following excerpt, he discusses the moralist elements in Bojer's works.*]

[At 24, Bojer] published a mature, characteristic novel, *A Procession (Et Folketog,* 1896). Amid full and variegated pictures of a typical Norwegian constituency, half agricultural, half maritime, it centres on the disastrous career of the chairman of a District Council: on an admirable programme for alleviating the little man's problems and hardships, he gets elected to Parliament, to find himself not only checkmated by the party-machine, but simultaneously driven into irretrievable debt by the expenses of a politician's life. The presentation is straightforwardly realistic, unaffected by the tendencies towards the fantastic which the contemporary fiction of Thomas Krag, Hamsun and Kinck was exhibiting. It is also, discreetly and with little overt irony, shot through by a fair amount of *tendens* that has none of Kielland's openly radical satire, points indeed in a conservative direction, without, however, forfeiting

the liveliness and freshness of approach by which the new writers set such store.

Bojer was always at heart a moralist, but in his best novels he kept anything like 'special pleading' well in check. The earliest of these, *The Power of Faith (Troens Magt,* 1903) strongly resembles *A Procession* in many ways. Though Lake Mjøsa takes the place of the sea, the setting, human and topographical, is much the same; it too culminates in a public jollification; and one of the two men about whose feud the plot is constructed is brother to the hero of the older book and, like him, ends miserably. *The Power of Faith* also resembles [Peter] Egge's *Hansine Solstad,* since it too turns on an unjust accusation and its dire consequences. The essential difference between the two authors comes out very clearly from the parallels between their stories. Egge's is a tender study of his stoical heroine, the slander against whom has no loud-voiced, let alone vindictive, mouthpiece and which, though a lowering cloud over the whole of her long life, is hardly the cause of all her misfortunes. *The Power of Faith,* on the other hand, in an action confined to eighteen months or so, focuses on a hotly contested legal process with its dramatic elements of police and public trial. The chief character Norby is not the victim of the slander but the slanderer, an active, middle-aged, prosperous farmer, who wins his case through perjury and then, as far as one can tell, lives happy ever after.

Bojer has been described as a moralist, but the morality of Norby's triumph may seem in the highest degree dubious, the more so as his adversary Wanger is left penniless, broken, a convict. Bojer's intention, however, is anything but crudely ironical. He mitigates, with an insight as great as his technical skill, the shock of his tale. For all the good faith on which he prides himself, the wretched Wanger, through muddling that amounts to dishonesty, deserves to be ruined; sooner or later life would have broken him; and, innocent though he was of the forgery for which he was indicted, he had in fact, as was proved at his trial, fabricated one of the documents produced for his defence. His enemy, on the other hand, honestly believes him to be a noxious creature, whose radical activities—calamitous at that—menace the patriarchal relations between rich and poor of which he himself is an unexceptionable exponent. There is more to be admired in *The Power of Faith* than such structural dexterity. The title given to the English translation, *The Power of a Lie,* is apt enough; so would have been a more biblical one, 'The Grain of Mustard Seed', since the tragic issue has, plausibly enough, quite trivial and adventitious an origin. Bojer's own biblical title, nevertheless, has a deeper significance. What he exhibits is not a miscarriage of justice, but the progressive degeneration of mind in two self-righteous men, whose fanaticism for their shaky causes, infecting others besides themselves, finally leads them genuinely to believe as truth the falsehoods fabricated in their support.

Intrigues, involutions, the weighing of guilt by scruple and drachm have gone the way of *tendens* in *The Last Viking* (1921). It vies with Lie's *Go Ahead!* as the finest Norwegian novel of life at sea as experienced by the crofter-fishermen who set out under sail for the Lofoten banks through the winter storms. By the time that Bojer wrote, many of the details of this life had passed away, and a perspective is imposed on his picture by a foreshadowing of the all-pervading revolution wrought by the advent of steam. With the death of Kristaver Myran, master of 'Kobben', on one of his voyages, it is recognized that the last Viking Age has come to an end.

More than anything the story of Kristaver and his crew calls to mind one of the half-naïve panoramic 'murals' in which modern Norway delights. Within the panorama *The Last Viking* is a series of episodes—uproarious, heroic, touching—and each in its own way is projected with a power that makes much of Kipling's *Captains Courageous* look cheap: they range from the brooding anxiety of the women waiting at home and the administration of the last sacrament to a dying sailor in all that his mates have at hand—ship's biscuit and a dram—to the wild party for giving the youngest his footing as a *Lofotkar* ('Lofoten-chap') or the heroic battle of the sailing ships

against the trawlers when these shut them off from their accustomed fishing-grounds.

FURTHER READING

"The Power of a Lie." *The Bookman* XXXV, No. 209 (February 1909): 236.

Favorable review of *The Power of a Lie* that praises Bojer for creating a story that is "intensely suggestive and disturbing."

Randell, Wilfred L. "Three Holiday Novels." *The Bookman* LXIV, No. 384 (September 1923): 285-86.

Favorable review of *The Last of the Vikings* that discusses the novel's realistic depiction of seafaring life.

The Man Who Was Thursday

G. K. Chesterton

The following entry presents criticism of Chesterton's novel *The Man Who Was Thursday: A Nightmare* (1908). For information on Chesterton's complete career, see *TCLC*, Volumes 1 and 6.

INTRODUCTION

Often regarded as Chesterton's finest novel, *The Man Who Was Thursday* mixes elements of parable, spy fiction, and romantic fantasy as it follows the poet-detective Gabriel Syme on a mission to apprehend a mysterious anarchist known only as Sunday. Seen as humorous, bizarre, and at times diffuse by critics, the work is framed as Syme's dream-adventure and explores the existence of evil and the role of faith in the modern, materialistic world. An early work of Chesterton's, the novel invokes themes common to his writings throughout his career, including meditations on the wonder of life and the limits of human reason. In addition, *The Man Who Was Thursday* is said to be Chesterton's attack on the prevalent pessimism of his age, and an appeal for renewed optimism based on religious conviction.

Plot and Major Characters

The Man Who Was Thursday opens in the fictional London suburb of Saffron Park. Here two young poets, Lucian Gregory and Gabriel Syme, debate the relative merits of anarchy versus order. Syme, an undercover detective called upon to infiltrate the Central Anarchist Council, a secret group of seven men who plan to destroy the world, dupes Gregory into leading him deeper into the society. Managing to win the post of Thursday—one of the seven positions in the Council, each of which is named after a day of the week—Syme is brought before its remaining six members the following morning. Sunday—an imposing man of almost inhumanly large proportions—presides over the group, a motley assortment of villains: the Secretary of the Council (Monday) with his twisted smile, a hairy Pole named Gogol (Tuesday), the decadent Marquis de St Eustache (Wednesday), the almost corpse-like Professor de Worms (Friday), and a dark young physician called Dr Bull (Saturday). After some discussion of a plan to assassinate the Russian Czar and the President of the French Republic in Paris three days hence, Sunday exposes Gogol as a fraud—who, unbeknownst to Syme, was also working for Scotland Yard. Sunday, concerned that there might be a further breach of secrecy, leaves the details of the bombing to Dr Bull and the Marquis. Following the meeting Professor de Worms tracks down Syme and explains that he too is a police agent, and the two join forces only to learn that Dr Bull is likewise an undercover detective. The trio then travel to France, where Syme engages the Marquis in a duel in order to prevent him from reaching Paris and bombing the world leaders. After some swordplay the Frenchman removes his mask and introduces himself as Ratcliffe, a detective like the others. Meanwhile beset upon by Monday and a gang of masked men, a lengthy chase ensues until the Secretary catches Syme and his companions and reveals his own police credentials. Gogol soon joins the group, and all six men return to England in order to capture Sunday. The president eludes his pursuers, however, escaping by cab, elephant, and hot-air balloon. When the flight ends at Sunday's house the narrative takes on an even more fantastic tone as the six detectives are treated to the president's hospitality. After resting they are asked to clothe themselves in costumes that represent each of the six days of Biblical creation. The bewildered men are then brought before Sunday. In answer to their queries about who he really is, he replies, "I am the Sabbath . . . . I am the peace of God." Soon after, Syme awakes from this vision and finds himself again in Saffron Park. Dawn is breaking and he is still walking with Gregory, conversing as they had been before.

Major Themes

Many critics find the key to *The Man Who Was Thursday* in Syme's shifting perceptions of Sunday. The detective initially experiences a vague sense of evil in the presence of this enigmatic figure, but this foreboding is later replaced with an awed respect for the man, who is thought to represent the human failure to completely fathom the paradoxes of life and nature. Chesterton further dramatizes the limits of human understanding in the inability of Syme and the other police detectives to recognize one another for what they really are—each provides a threat that is only perceived, and is in actuality an ally in disguise. Overall, the novel is said to portray Chesterton's comic vision of the universe, one in which evil is nothing more than an illusion. Sunday, rather than being a menace to humanity, simply provides a test of Syme's faith and perseverance. In addition, the work is often seen as a social critique, in which Chesterton contrasts the noble qualities and hopeful optimism of Syme with what he saw as the prevalent attitude of pessimism and nihilism in vogue among his contemporaries.

Critical Reception

Early critical speculation about *The Man Who Was Thursday* often focused on the allegorical qualities of Sunday and a perceived lack of artistic control on Chesterton's part in the work, when not merely dismissing the novel altogether. At the time of its publication, even Chesterton saw his story as a somewhat amusing piece that was of considerably less consequence than many of his other writings. Several decades later, however, he set out to clarify some of the misconceptions that he had observed among critics. He answered them in his 1936 *Autobiography,* writing, "The point is that the whole story is a nightmare of things, not as they are, but as they seemed to the young half-pessimist of the '90s; and the ogre who appears brutal but is also cryptically benevolent is not so much God, in the sense of religion or irreligion, but rather Nature as it appears to the pantheist, whose pantheism is struggling out of pessimism." In the years since, C. S. Lewis has favorably compared the work to the dream-allegory of Franz Kafka, commenting on similarities of method and the shared theme in both writers of human bewilderment in relation to the vastness of the universe. The work has also been praised for its tongue-in-cheek humor and valued as a precursor of modern detective fiction, described by some, according to Miles Copeland, as "the best spy book ever written."

CRITICISM

William Barry   (essay date 1908)

SOURCE: "Mr. Chesterton's Allegory of Anarchism," in *The Bookman,* London, Vol. XXXIV, No. 199, April, 1908, p. 23.

[*In the following review, Barry praises* The Man Who Was Thursday *as a skillful attack against anarchistic and decadent intellectual stance.*]

There are many ways of preaching a lay sermon; and it would be strange if Mr. Chesterton did not take his own. For he combines gifts which are seldom found together. With rare insight he has detected the glory of the commonplace; he is certain that genius and the ordinary man agree in their judgment about life, death, marriage, morals, and all the things that signify. Therefore he despises in good-humoured fashion the crank, the law-breaker, the "immoralist"—senseless persons who strike an attitude because they can do nothing else. But while cleaving to the old, he arrays it in new garments of a most surprising cut and lively colours. Why should paradox be always enlisted on the wrong side? Who has a better right to laugh than the man that believes in plain and saving Realism? Laugh, accordingly, in the very thick of a struggle to defend the Highest Law, our philosopher does, yet not without grimness, for the smoke of the nether deeps circles around him. The echo of that laugh reminds us in its peculiar accent, at once grave and gay, of Robert Louis Stevenson. And, on the whole, it is Stevenson's creed that is set before us, healthy, brave, rather high-strung, tender at last with a pity that hides itself in schoolboy fun and frolic.

But all do not construe allegory when they see it; a nightmare is an uncanny sort of vision, and the crowd may not understand. *The Man Who Was Thursday* begins like any other Anarchist make-up; singularly resembling "The Angel of the Revolution," but ironical, whereas that was no more playful than a thrust with a dagger. We get the thrill and the shock and are led cleverly astray. The "special constables of order"—a conception worthy of Sir Conan Doyle—put us on the *qui vive;* but for a time bewilder us, as they ought in so good a story. Their purpose—and here Mr. Chesterton means what he says—is to keep watch and ward against the most deadly kind of Anarchism. "Yes," exclaims the "Man who was Thursday," "the modern world has retained all those parts of police-work which are really oppressive and ignominious, the harrying of the poor, the spying upon the unfortunate. It has given up the more dignified work, the punishment of powerful traitors in the State and powerful heresiarchs in the Church. The moderns say we must not punish heretics. My only doubt is whether we have a right to punish anybody else."

How few will take this as seriously intended! The blasé reader will smile and rush on, gaping to know what becomes of Syme, the gentleman-detective, who has ventured his life by joining the supreme Anarchist Council, and is bound in honour to fight without help of Scotland Yard. Such racing and chasing ensue that we are caught up in the whirlwind of it, yet always with a point of horror, strongly Stevensonian, perhaps overdone. There are crowds of dark lines in this spectrum, showing finally as burlesque, but leaving an unpleasant trail behind. No doubt, if you want to throw on canvas the "City of Dreadful Night"—which is the true name for modern unbelief and disorder—you must deepen your sable tints; only our nerves cannot well endure them. These insane eccentricities which we reject have weakened us all; a healthier generation will look back on our age of decadence with wonder and no slight contempt. But, anyhow, even by borrowing its own weapons, Mr. Chesterton strikes at the monstrous phantom which is always denying "the decencies and charities of Christendom," and he strikes hard.

In this mixture of the picturesque and the horrible there is something Japanese. We may remember among the sketches of Hokusai certain huge apparitions like the enigmatic President, "Sunday," or combats of weird beings, praeter-human and terrifying, over whom the artist flings a ray of sunshine that adds to their strangeness. At length our nightmare, which we have pursued through thick and thin, tumbles into absolute farce. The undergraduate humour of Syme breaks all bounds; and we feel hurt as we join in that mad chase after "Sunday" across London, where he plays the fool as he drives on. With sudden violence we are carried out of this harlequinade into a drop-scene, parable or what you will, and the philosophy of the book discloses itself. It is the old true Gospel of peace purchased by war, of valour standing up to be slain for its plighted word, of faith against appearances, of redemption through self-sacrifice. Was the message ever brought in a more unconventional garb? At all events, it is the genuine thing, as well as a challenge to the "science" that "announces nonentity," and the art that "admires decay." Beyond all question our intellectual anarchists proclaim a doctrine of suicide which the young, the ardent, the weaker sort, have acted upon or will act upon. To show us its meaning, with a hearty laugh at its extreme folly, may do the rest of us good. We wake from this nightmare into a world of sanity, and face the dawn with hope.

William Morton Payne (essay date 1908)

SOURCE: Review of *The Man Who Was Thursday*, in *The Dial*, Chicago, Vol. XLV, No. 520, August 16, 1908, p. 89.

[*The longtime literary editor of several Chicago publications, Payne reviewed books for twenty-three years at the* Dial, *one of America's most influential journals of literature and opinion in the early twentieth century. In the following review, he faults* The Man Who Was Thursday *for its improbable premises.*]

Among our audacious latter-day sophists, who so neatly make the worse appear the better reason, Mr. Chesterton is gaining a high place. Indeed, he may almost dispute the honors of leadership with the priest-in-chief of the cult of paradox, Mr. G. Bernard Shaw. His latest "budget of paradoxes" takes the form of a novel—or, rather, of a fantastic invention, which has to be described as fiction because it bears no conceivable relation to reality. Even the author balks at his own imaginings, and passes off the whole invention as a dream when he comes to the last chapter. It is called *The Man Who Was Thursday,* and has to do with the conflict between anarchy and order. A central council of anarchists, seven in number, bear the names of the days of the week (which accounts for our title), and, under the leadership of an awe-inspiring Sunday, develop their programme of treasons, stratagems, and spoils. The gigantic humor of the conception is that these seven men are really Scotland Yard detectives, spying upon each other; for each of them thinks that all the others are genuine anarchists. The amount of fun that Mr. Chesterton gets out of this situation may readily be imagined, as well as the opportunity it affords him for the exercise of his talent for paradox. Like most dreams, the story grows more wildly impossible as the awakening is neared. It is a highly entertaining yarn, and exhibits the author in the light in which he ought always to be viewed—the light of a man not for a moment to be taken seriously upon any subject, but simply to be admired for a combination of nimble wit with diabolical cleverness.

G. K. Chesterton (essay date 1926)

SOURCE: "*The Man Who Was Thursday*," in *G. K. C. as M. C.: Being a Collection of Thirty-Seven Poems,* edited by J. P. de Fonseka, Methuen & Co. Ltd., 1929, pp. 202-07.

[*In the following essay, which was originally published in 1926 as an introduction to Mrs. Cecil Chesterton and Ralph Neale's stage adaptation of* The Man Who Was Thursday, *Chesterton comments on the origins and themes of his novel.*]

It is the more desirable that I should write a few lines to express my thanks to those who have here paid my story [*The Man Who Was Thursday* (a play in three acts, adapted from the novel by G. K. Chesterton), by Mrs. Cecil Chesterton and Ralph Neale. Messers. Ernest Benn, Ltd., 1926.] the compliment of casting it in another and (quite probably) a better form, because long after I had given to them, and to them alone, such authorization as I am capable of giving, a rather ridiculous rivalry or invasion of their rights in the matter occurred, it would appear, in Eastern Europe. The Bolshevists have done a good many silly things; but the most strangely silly thing that ever I heard of was that they tried to turn this Anti-Anarchist romance into an Anarchist play. Heaven only knows what they really made of it; beyond apparently making it mean the opposite of everything it meant. Probably they thought that being able to see that a policeman is funny means thinking that a policeman is futile. Probably they would say that thinking Don Quixote funny means thinking chivalry futile; in other words, they are barbarians and have not learnt how to laugh. But in this case a certain consequence follows. Making fun of a policeman would always be fun enough for me. Treating this tale as a farce of balloons and escaped elephants would never trouble me; and I would never bore anybody about the meaning of the allegory. But if somebody, even in Moscow or Vienna, starts making it mean something totally different, or flatly contrary, I cannot avoid a word about its real origin or outline. I do not want to take myself seriously; it is Bolshevism, among its other crimes, that is making me a serious person for a moment.

So many people have lately been occupied in turning good novels into bad plays, that the authors of this adaption have conceived the bolder and more hopeful scheme of turning a bad novel into a good play. For though I know very little about *The Man Who Was Thursday,* only a very casual acquaintance is needed to make sure that if it is a novel it is a bad novel. To do it justice, by its own description, it is not a novel but a nightmare. And since that subtitle is perhaps the only true and reliable statement in the book, I may plead it as a sort of excuse for my share in the matter. Nightmares on the stage are not uncommon nowadays; and some of them are regarded as realistic studies, because they are examples of that very deep and bottomless sort of nightmare from which it happens to be difficult to wake up. Nevertheless, a distinction between the dreams of to-day and those of that remoter day, or rather night, is essential to understanding whatever there may be to understand. To do them justice, the new nightmares do generally belong to a night: as day-dreams belong to a day. They are aspects; they are fragmentary and, to do them justice, they are frivolous. It was not so with a certain spirit that brooded for a certain time over the literature of my youth. I can remember the time when pessimism was dogmatic, when it was even orthodox. The people who had read Schopenhauer regarded themselves as having found out everything and found that it was nothing. Their system was a system, and therefore had a character of surrounding the mind. It therefore really resembled a nightmare, in the sense of being imprisoned or even bound hand and foot; of being none the less captive because it was rather in a lunatic asylum than a reasonable hell or place of punishment. There is a great deal in the modern world that I think evil and a great deal more that I think silly; but it does seem to me to have escaped from this mere prison of pessimism. Our civilization may be breaking up; there are not wanting many exhilarating signs of it breaking down. But it is not merely closing in; and therefore it is not a nightmare, like the narrow despair of the nineties. In so far as it is breaking down, it seems to me more of a mental breakdown than a moral breakdown. In so far as it is breaking up, it may let in a certain amount of daylight as well as a great deal of wind. But it is not stifling like positive pessimism and materialism; and it was in the middle of a thick London fog of these things that I sat down and tried to write this story, nearly twenty years ago.

It is in relation to that particular heresy that much of its main suggestion must be understood. Perhaps it is not worth while to try to kill heresies which so rapidly kill themselves—and the cult of suicide committed suicide some time ago. But I should not wish it supposed, as some I think have supposed, that in resisting the heresy of pessimism I implied the equally morbid and diseased insanity of optimism. I was not then considering whether anything is really evil, but whether everything is really evil; and in relation to the latter nightmare it does still seem to me relevant to say that nightmares are not true; and that in them even the faces of friends may appear as the faces of fiends. I tried to turn this notion of resistance to a nightmare into a topsy-turvy tale about a man who fancied himself alone among enemies, and found that each of the enemies was in fact on his own side and in his own solitude. That is the only thing that can be called a meaning in the story; all the rest of it was written for fun; and though it was great fun for me, I do not forget that sobering epigram which tells us that easy writing is dashed hard reading. I think, however, the thing has possibilities as a play; because by the plan of it the changes are, as they should be in drama, only half expected but not wholly unexpected. I have been responsible for many murders in my time, generally in the milder and more vicarious forms of detective stories; and I have noticed a fashionable fallacy that is not irrelevant here. Because murdering or being murdered is generally felt by the individual involved to have something about it dramatic and striking, it is often supposed that any detective story will make a drama. The thing has been done and may be done again, but it is not easy to do. In such a story the secret is too sensational to be dramatic. The revelation comes too suddenly to be understood; and until it is understood all that ought to seem mystifying only seems meaningless. But in this foolish farce, it is at least true that the action proceeds along a certain course that can be followed, and I offer it gravely as an attempt to restore the canons of Aristotle and the classical unities of antiquity. In other words, a man may watch for the end of the play, when he would put down the book under the impression that he knew the story by having read half of it.

Evelyn Waugh   (essay date 1947)

SOURCE: *"The Man Who Was Thursday* (1947)," in *G. K. Chesterton: A Half Century of Views,* edited by D. J. Conlon, Oxford University Press, Oxford, 1987, pp. 72-4.

[*Waugh was England's leading satirical novelist of the mid-twentieth century. In such works as* Vile Bodies *(1930),* Scoop *(1938), and* The Loved One *(1948), he skewered such targets as the bored young sophisticates of the 1920s, the questionable values of the British press, and the American commercial trivialization of death. Considered a major Catholic author after his conversion in 1930, Waugh is best*

known today for his novel Brideshead Revisited *(1945), which examines the lives of members of a wealthy Catholic family. In the following essay, which was originally published in* The Commonweal *on 21 March 1947, he notes that the circumstances of the happy ending portrayed in Chesterton's novel seem improbable to readers of the post-World War II generation.*]

The need for a secret society is one that many story-tellers have felt. Most good stories are, in some fashion, the conflict between Good and Evil, and whereas it is easy enough to pile up virtues until some fairly plausible hero has been created, villains, however black the crimes attributed to them, tend to remain limp in their makers' hands. Iago is wicked, but the reasons he gives for his actions are so fatuous that few readers, offhand, can remember them. Bosola is the unwilling agent of men of diabolic character; it is impossible to take seriously their statement that they are impelled by avarice. And the Elizabethans were far nearer to the springs of Evil than Miss Agatha Christie.

The writers of detective stories, indeed, are in a peculiar difficulty. Their concern is with the mechanics of crime and the logic of its discovery, rather than with Good and Evil. But convention demands that the crime be murder. This is the accepted token-coin of extreme wickedness, yet it is one of the few sins which the civilized man can regard quite dispassionately. However misanthropic, he has never been tempted to its commission as he has been tempted, say, to adultery or suicide, and he recognizes, as perhaps he would do with other sins, could he regard them with equal coolness, that the dangers and exertions are appalling and the rewards trifling. Moreover, conscience, silenced before more alluring transgressions, is here plainly audible, interposing its voice and debunking the tempter: murder for profit—'What shall it profit a man if he gain the whole world and lose his own soul?'; murder for revenge—'Vengeance is mine, saith the Lord'; murder for love—'Love suffereth long and is kind' . . .

Only writers like Mr Graham Greene and M. Bernanos—how glibly the words come! What writers, in fact, are there like these two—who plumb the human spirit at depths where few venture, can create villains. More humble writers, who know they are qualified to deal only with rather ordinary characters, and who know that such people do not kill, are constrained, often, to exonerate their murderers either by inventing circumstances—blackmail, the threat of corruption of a loved one, etc.—in which the victim is an intolerable aggressor and his removal justifiable, in which case the forces of law are deprived of the reader's sympathy and only his intellect is engaged in the process of solution, or by borrowing from the psychologists. Schizophrenes, those rare and often harmless creatures, have become an accepted device of stage and fiction, such as identical twins were to an earlier age. The modern 'psychological-thriller' has, properly, no villain, for the crimes are not acts of free will.

But there is a third resource, the group villain—the gang, the spy-ring, the subversive organization, the secret society—which doubly commends itself to the critical reader, first by titivating the conspiracymania which is latent in most of us, and secondly by emphasizing the deep moral truth that men in association are capable of wickedness from which each individually would shrink.

The simplest case is the gang, the army of outlaws. Though there is a commercial 'racket' at the origin of it and wads of 'grands' disbursed, the essence of the gang, as it appears in fiction, is not the making of money, but an organized war against society; they take their orders, observe their own loyalties, and 'shoot it out' with the police without hope of victory. In advance of this is the organization which aims not merely at an independent existence in a law-abiding universe, but at the actual subversion of the social and moral order.

The conviction that such a conspiracy is feasible may be traced in history—for example in the Albigensian suppression and in the pogroms inflamed by the spurious 'Protocols of the Elders of Zion'. It is even more frequent in fiction. Conan Doyle, Agatha Christie, John Buchan, Francis Beeding, Edgar Wallace—almost every writer of crime stories has at one time or another made use of this expedient. The classic example, of course, is in Chesterton's *The Man Who Was Thursday,* only in that case, significantly, the whole thing turns out to be moonshine.

Significantly of Chesterton's character and age, Chesterton's cheerfulness was redeemed, but abundantly redeemed, from vulgarity only by his innocence. He was so sweet and virtuous a man that crime appeared to him as ingenious, schoolboy mischief and sin as something remote and palpably perverse, diabolic, scarcely human at all. Dr Fu Manchu was his type of villain. And he lived in an age when it was possible to retain this purity untarnished. *The Man Who Was Thursday* ends in a great chase when the Common Men rise and take arms; it is thought in cosmic anarchy; it is discovered in defence of order and truth; and the dionysiac Sunday is revealed as the beaming, tutelary, Cheeryble Brother, god of the hearth.

Could Chesterton have written like that today, if he had lived to see the Common Man in arms, drab, grey and brown, the Storm Troopers and the Partisans, standard-bearers of the great popular movements of the century; had he lived to read in the evidence of the War Trials the sickening accumulation of brutality inflicted and condoned by common men, and seen, impassive on the bench, the agents of other criminals, vile, but free and triumphant?

Chesterton was the poetic and romantic child of a smug tradition. It is typical of his age and class that the dawn of sweetness and light in which are dissipated all the night-fears of *The Man Who Was Thursday* should be the discovery that the secret society, so long hated and dreaded, proves to comprise nothing but policemen. For Chesterton the police were the angelic hosts in action; the corpulent blue figure under the Kensington lamp-post represented Justice and Order and held his commission from the innate and inalienable sanctity of popular good sense. For half the world today 'the police' are the Gestapo and the NKVD, and a very macabre parable might now be written of a poetic anarchist whose associates one by one unmask and reveal themselves as policemen, for *they* are the new secret society, so often foreseen in shadows, that conspires against the social and moral order.

Garry Wills   (essay date 1961)

SOURCE: "Paradox and Nightmare," in *Chesterton: Man and Mask,* Sheed & Ward, 1961, pp. 35-54.

[*Wills is an American editor, educator, and critic who has written on diverse topics, including Chesterton, Catholicism, and race relations. He is best known for political commentaries, especially his examination of Richard Nixon's political career,* Nixon Agonistes: The Crisis of the Self-Made Man *(1970). In the following excerpt, he places* The Man Who Was Thursday *in the context of Chesterton's developing personal philosophy.*]

The Wild Knight is typical, and a guide to Chesterton's work, precisely because it was born out of his early bafflement. It is true that Chesterton does not mention it when listing the works which sprang from this crisis, but that is almost certainly because of its attacks on priestcraft and narrow dogma. Instead, he cites *The Man Who Was Thursday* as the most complete expression of his youthful encounter with the aesthetes. Although the novel did not appear until 1908, its dedicatory poem bears out Chesterton's memory of the matter. The story of his plight is indirectly presented here (not, be it noticed, as a private fancy of his own adolescence, but as an historic mood shared by many). Solipsism and Impressionism are the foes:

> Science announced nonentity and art admired decay.

Stevenson and Whitman are the allies:

> I find again that book we found, I feel the hour that flings
> Far out of fish-shaped Paumanok some cry of cleaner things;
> And the Green Carnation withered, as in forest fires that pass
> Roared in the wind of all the world ten million leaves of grass;
> Or sane and sweet and sudden as a bird sings in the rain—
> Truth out of Tusitala spoke and pleasure out of pain.
> Yea, cool and clear and sudden as a bird sings in the grey,
> Dunedin to Samoa spoke, and darkness unto day.

The novel has those qualities Chesterton ascribed to dreams: unity of mood and wild variety of incident. Unreality overclouds Gabriel Syme, the story's hero, destroying and dissolving everything he reaches out for. This is like a story by Kafka, in which stairs melt into crumbling sand, and horses gallop but carry one nowhere. But in Kafka's tales the spell is never broken, whereas Syme takes an irrational courage into every chamber of horror and is rewarded by a final collapse in which *illusion* dissolves.

The unity of the piece is not only one of mood. There is method in Syme's madness. He climbs ordered degrees of unreason, until he reaches the top and is left alone, for a dark space, in his tower of insanity. The first fears are childish ones, mere grotesques of an imagination that has run wild. Professor de Worms is "the crooked man who went a crooked mile," the bogy man which our plastic mind can, by some mystery of idolatry, first shape and then fear.

But the next encounter, with Bull, is even more unnerving—the encounter with cold and impersonal thought. Syme is now the child who has lost his world of poetry and personality:

> Syme was increasingly conscious that his new adventure had somehow a quality of cold sanity worse than the wild adventures of the past. Last night, for instance, the tall tenements had seemed to him like a tower in a dream. As he now went up the weary and perpetual steps, he was daunted and bewildered by their almost infinite series. But it was not the hot horror of a dream or of anything that might be exaggeration or delusion. Their infinity was more like the empty infinity of arithmetic, something unthinkable, yet necessary to thought. Or it was like the stunning statements of astronomy about the distance of the fixed stars. He was ascending the house of reason, a thing more hideous than unreason itself.

The tyranny of astronomy and cold science goes with another invasion of childhood, the banishing of romance in the name of "realism":

> About the Professor's make-up and all his antics there was always something merely grotesque, like a gollywog. Syme remembered those wild woes of yesterday as one remembers being afraid of Bogy in childhood. But here was daylight; here was a healthy, square-shouldered man in tweeds, not odd save for the accident of his ugly spectacles, not glaring or grinning at all, but smiling steadily and not saying a word. The whole had a sense of unbearable reality. Under the increasing sunlight the colours of the Doctor's complexion, the pattern of his tweeds, grew and expanded outrageously, as such things grow too important in a realistic novel.

The next stage of Syme's fear is reached in his duel with the Marquis, when death hovers over him, ready to blot out all things:

> the fear of the Professor had been the fear of the tyrannic accidents of nightmare, and the fear of the Doctor had been the fear of the airless vacuum of science. The first was the old fear that any miracle might happen, the second the more hopeless fear that no miracle can ever happen. But he saw that these fears were fancies, for he found himself in the presence of the great fact of the fear of death, with its coarse and pitiless common sense. He felt like a man who had dreamed all night of falling over precipices, and had woked up on the morning when he was to be hanged.
>
> He felt a strange and vivid value in all the earth around him, in the grass under his feet; he felt the love of life in all living things. He could al-

most fancy that he heard the grass growing; he could almost fancy that even as he stood fresh flowers were springing up and breaking into blossom in the meadow—flowers blood-red and burning gold and blue, fulfilling the whole pageant of the spring. And whenever his eyes strayed for a flash from the calm, staring, hypnotic eyes of the Marquis, they saw the little tuft of almond tree against the sky-line. He had the feeling that if by some miracle he escaped he would be ready to sit forever before that almond tree, desiring nothing else in the world.

The next step into nightmare—that caused by the flight from the secretary—is more healthy but not less real. It is the fear of defeat—not mere death, but irrelevant death. The army that advances after the fugitives seems like the whole world in cry at their heels. But beyond this shared despair there is a "last and worst" fancy that comes to Syme alone. Fleeing through the mottled shadows of the forest, pursued by men in masks and supported by men who have just removed their masks, Syme begins to wonder if anything is fixed in dependable identity:

> Was not everything, after all, like this bewildering woodlands, this dance of dark and light? Everything only a glimpse, the glimpse always unforeseen, and always forgotten. For Gabriel Syme had found in the heart of that sun-splashed wood what many modern painters had found there. He had found the thing which the modern people call Impressionism, which is another name for that final scepticism which can find no floor to the universe.

Graphically the novel presents that "suicide of intellect" which Chesterton would describe in his next volume, *Orthodoxy*. The various shapes and suggestings of unreal things have led at last to Unreality itself. There is nowhere else to go. Here Chesterton must end the story, as Kafka would, in the farthest reaches of the unreal, or rescue his hero somehow.

That rescue involves the archetypal drama which hovers behind this entire pantomime of chase and nightmare. "The Council" and the "Accuser" are, in the last scene, direct references to the Book of Job. The final chase through with trumpeting and incredible beasts, is a glimpse of that animal world which Jehovah called up for Job. Syme is answered by the elephant, as Job was by Behemoth. These echoes multiply in the final chapter as the Sons of God shout for joy in the strange dance the Council witnesses. The parallels are finally established by Bull's quotation: "Now there was a day when the sons of God came to present themselves before the Lord, and Satan came also among them."

Job's challenge to a meaningless world of pain was not met by the narrow rationalizings of his friends but by the answering challenge to battle which God issued. The whirlwind offers adventure, not explanation. If Job joins the war on chaos, about which the stars shout for joy, he must live with the mysteries of free will, suffering, and evil, not resorting to his friends' refuge of optimism. Chesterton called the Book of Job the finest proof that pessimists and optimists are both wrong. And he gave his novel the same theme, making of optimism the last and most seductive temptation which Syme must meet.

The pleasant daydream of Sunday's banquet resembles the earlier stages of nightmare; joy is substituted for horror, but it is the paralyzing joy of a dream, where individuality fades into a central fire. Everything had been illusion; now everything is God. A single-textured optimism can only lead to a single-textured world—to pantheism, which all the fighters resent as a denial of their struggle. Sunday remains truly their foe insofar as he is Everything. As Chesterton said many years later [in his *Autobiography*]:

> the ogre who appears brutal but is also cryptically benevolent is not so much God, in the sense of religion or irreligion, but rather Nature as it appears to the pantheist, whose pantheism is struggling out of pessimism.

On the same page, Chesterton points to a *change* that overcomes Sunday, that figure of blind energy, of pure existential drive, when the last unveiling is reached. For Syme does rend this specious pantheism in the most violent manner. And only then does Sunday—the Lord's Day—become the Lord.

The Accuser, like Syme and the Professor, resents his scars; unlike them, however, he is seeking revenge, not explanation. He hurls at the others a taunt which Chesterton was all too familiar with, the ancient taunt of Job's diabolic afflicter—that the good have not suffered, that believers know no doubts and cannot deserve the reward of heroic rebels. Syme's answer—and Chesterton's—is brief, though it raises a thunderous echo. Syme shouts a denial out of his own experience. He has fought in the dark against all the forces in and beyond the world. He has been wrong and stupid, running down empty passages, taking journeys none of his fellows of the Council shared. He has known real isolation and a terrible solitude. The story of each man on the Council is equally heroic, sealed in his own incommunicable self. Being is an exception in each of its manifestations. It appears only in definite shapes drawn in the hardest lines against the background of nonexistence. Loneliness is the best proof of individuality.

Chesterton was just at this moment on the verge of writing *Orthodoxy,* which—growing out of his controversy with Blatchford—would be his most complete statement of the idea of *creation:* creation means a sundering, a proliferation of individuals by the rearing of boundaries. God gave man glory and adventure by giving him free will, an independent path for his mind to explore. Existence God shares with us, at each instant, a living vein and open channel into his raging nature. But essence—identity—is ours. Man's life is caught in a tense dialectic on all levels, as *Orthodoxy* would demonstrate.

With a last touch of Job's audacity, Syme flings a challenge at Sunday, who has faded and grown vague in the twilight. His amorphous energy and dissolving outline seem to lift him above the struggle the others have undergone. But when Syme asks him if he is of their fellowship of battle a new note enters the distant voice as it thunders back: "Can ye drink of the cup that I drink of?" In *Orthodoxy* Chesterton would suggest, darkly, that the Trinity

is a proof that God knows personality and dialectic in a higher form of pure action without suffering. Here he glances at the Incarnation, whereby *God*'s personality is established by His loneliness.

Chesterton saw that the simple existentialist is as unstable as the rationalist. The world of empty Forms leads to Platonic doubts and Schopenhauer's negations. But a worship of mere energy can as easily take a manic form, in Whitman's cheery effusiveness as in Nietzsche's dark worship of strength. Sunday is the god of Whitman.

Kingsley Amis   (essay date 1968)

SOURCE: Review of *The Man Who Was Thursday,* in *The New York Times Book Review,* October 13, 1968, p. 2.

[*A distinguished English novelist, poet, essayist, and editor, Amis was one of the Angry Young Men, a group of British writers of the 1950s whose writings expressed bitterness and disillusionment with society. Amis's first and most widely praised novel,* Lucky Jim *(1954), is characteristic of the movement and demonstrates his skill as a satirist. Amis later rejected alliance with any literary group, pursuing instead his own artistic aims. Throughout his career Amis sustained an interest in science fiction; he was coeditor of the* Spectrum *anthologies and was the author of one of the first major critical surveys of the genre in* New Maps of Hell *(1960). In the following essay, he offers an appreciation of Chesterton's novel.*]

Of supposedly serious contemporary writers, Gilbert Keith Chesterton was the first to make a strong and genuine impression on me. "Contemporary" is perhaps misleading: he and I only overlapped by 14 years, but I had come to value him enough to be dashed and bewildered by his death in 1936. One never quite gets over any early attachment. Even now I see something romantic, almost heroic, about Chesterton, while deploring what in those days I knew nothing of, his self-indulgent polemical writing and the whimsical playing with paradoxes so common in his later fiction. However, at least two of his novels and two or three dozen stories (mostly the justly celebrated Father Brown detective shorts) retain all their appeal.

I think it was *The Man Who Was Thursday* that started me off. I was instantly hooked by the mysterious title, the sinister subtitle—"A Nightmare"—the prefatory poem, with its again sinister hints of a vast conspiracy stealthily taking over men's minds:

> A cloud was on the mind of men
> And wailing went the weather,
> Yea, a sick cloud upon the soul
> When we were boys together.
> Science announced nonentity
> And art admired decay;
> The world was old and ended:
> But you and I were gay;
> Round us in antic order
> Crippled vices came—
> Lust that had lost its laughter,
> Fear that had lost its shame . . .
> This is a tale of those old fears,

Even of those emptied hells,
And none but you shall understand
The true thing that it tells—
Of what colossal gods of shame
Could cow men and yet crash;
Of what huge devils hid the stars,
Yet fell at a pistol-flash.

This part has an up-to-date ring, but Chesterton, who was born in 1874, was only talking about late-Victorian rationalism and the "decadent" movement of the nineties, favorite targets of his. I thought he was bringing me news of the Devil (who often turned up in the other stuff I was reading at the time), or warning me that most grown-ups were mad (an equally acceptable idea).

This was not a bad frame of mind in which to approach the novel itself. Attempts to fix a label break down: it is not quite a political bad dream, or a metaphysical adventure, or a cosmic comedy in the form of a spy story, but it has something of all these. Anyway, it is unique, and also, what is not all that much easier to bring about, magnetically readable. We open in a remote quarter of that Edwardian London which Chesterton knew so exactly and lovingly. Outside the immediate center, this cannot have been such a very different place from contemporary London: a conglomeration of linked villages, each with its own look and feel and smell, a continual variousness I have never found in any North American city.

Chesterton sets the key at once, with the special intensity he always brought to descriptions of times of day and effects of light, reminding us that he started life with ambitions to become a painter. The suburb of Saffron Park, we are told, looked more like a work of art than a real place:

"More especially this attractive unreality fell upon it about nightfall, when the extravagant roofs were dark against the afterglow and the whole insane village seemed as separate as a drifting cloud. . . . This particular evening, if it is remembered for nothing else, will be remembered in that place for its strange sunset. It looked like the end of the world. All the heaven seemed covered with a quite vivid and palpable plumage; you could only say that the sky was full of feathers, and of feathers that almost brushed the face."

Against this backdrop Gabriel Syme, poet and (as it transpires) policeman, confronts Lucian Gregory, poet and anarchist. In pursuance of a sort of bet, Gregory takes Syme to dinner in a greasy riverside pub that turns out to serve champagne and lobster mayonnaise. More surprisingly, dinner table and diners presently descend en bloc into an underground chamber—shades, or rather anticipations, of Ian Fleming's "Live and Let Die." For me, at any rate, this is much more than a coincidence. James Bond and Gabriel Syme differ in innumerable ways, but they share a quality of romance, of color and chivalry, almost of myth, that attracts me a lot more deeply than anything about the down-to-earth and up-to-the-minute heroes of writers like Len Deighton and John Le Carré. In the chamber under the pub, a secret anarchist meeting is held; not very plausibly, but after some enjoyable oratory, Syme gets himself elected in place of Gregory to the Central Anarchist Council, whose members are named after

the days of the week. So the man who has become Thursday sets out by moonlight, in a heavy cloak and carrying a sword-stick, to take the war to the enemy:

"His chivalric folly glowed in the night like a great fire. Even the common things he carried with him—the food and the brandy and the loaded pistol—took on exactly that concrete and material poetry which a child feels when he takes a gun upon a journey or a bun with him to bed." I can still feel the gentle shock of reading that sentence for the first time, that flash of realization, not that you fully understand the author, but, far rarer and more memorable, that the author knows all about you.

The Anarchist Council members turn out to be a set of frightening grotesques, not merely malignant, but with a hint of the spiritual evil that from now on begins more and more to color the tale. The eyes of Saturday are covered by black glasses, as if they were too frightful to see. Monday, the Secretary, has a smile that goes up on one side of his face and down on the other and is wrong. The face of Sunday, the huge President, is so vast that Syme is afraid that at close quarters it will be too big to be possible, and he will have to scream.

When the spectacles and the mask of anarchy are removed, however, Saturday is human enough, a policeman, in fact, from Syme's own special branch, The Last Crusade. (I would love to see that emblazoned on some door in Scotland Yard.) One by one the other Days declare themselves on the side of the law, until only the Secretary stands between police and President. But Monday is Sunday's agent, with the power of turning the world itself against the crusaders. The chase sweeps across a France of sturdy peasants and soldierly patriots and cultured men of wealth (more fun to read about, at least, than most real Frenchmen) transformed one by one, in true nightmare fashion, into fanatical friends of anarchy. Finally the champions of reason and order, and of Christendom, turn at bay. . . .

The end is fantasy in a different key, though related to what precedes, indeed giving meaning to it. At the end of a second chase, in which the pursuers are helpless in the hands of the pursued, Sunday stands revealed—as beneficent, as the deviser of The Last Crusade, as something like Pan, as God, even. Years later, in a newspaper article published the day before he died, Chesterton tried to evade this last interpretation, to my mind unconvincingly. At any rate, the book views life as one huge joke, but a kindly joke which includes and reconciles and justifies everything.

The Man Who Was Thursday is high melodrama and is written in that style. In one of his essays, with characteristically deliberate overemphasis, Chesterton claims that melodrama is much more like life than realism is. Well: I only know that, after a surfeit of supposedly realistic accounts of the workings of espionage organizations, after reading about the 20th gray man in a gray raincoat with a sawn-off Smith & Wesson Centennial Airweight at his hip, I long for The Last Crusade and Gabriel Syme with his cloak and sword-stick, and wish that there were a few more books like this.

Lawrence J. Clipper (essay date 1974)

SOURCE: "Detectives and Apocalypses," in *G. K. Chesterton*, Twayne Publishers, Inc., 1974, pp. 120-44.

[*In the following excerpt, Clipper highlights the religious themes of* The Man Who Was Thursday.]

If one wishes to date the beginning of Chesterton's commitment to religion as an answer to the problems of modern man, it is safe to point to 1908, the year of both *Orthodoxy* and *The Man Who Was Thursday*. In a later essay, he said that the novel was written "in the middle of a thick London fog of positive pessimism and materialism," and the dedication to E. C. Bentley speaks of that era when

> A cloud was on the mind of men, and wailing
> went the weather,
> Yea, a sick cloud upon the soul when we were
> boys together.

The subtitle *A Nightmare,* underscores one of its features (and also relates it to almost all his other romances). In the nightmare the hero, a young poet named Syme, hears of a Super-Council of Anarchists bent on the destruction of society, law, and religion. When Syme vows to fight this monstrous conspiracy, he joins a chapter of detectives whose sole purpose is to track down and destroy the anarchists. By accident, he is then introduced into a meeting of the Council of Seven Days, the very Anarchist Super-Council he has been seeking. The strange name is derived from the fact that its seven members carry the names of the days: the leader of the Council is a large, jovial, almost Falstaffian figure named Sunday; and he is strangely out of place, thinks Syme, at a meeting of such a sinister group. When Syme boldly asks to be made the replacement for a recently deceased member, Thursday, he is welcomed into the group.

Once inside the group, the hero has misgivings; he seems alone, cut off from all safety, surrounded by evil. In a rapid succession of shocking episodes, each of the others on the Council is revealed to be a detective enlisted in the same agency to fight the Anarchist Council; and each has been sworn in by the same large, hidden figure in a dark room. Although appearing to be Anarchists, they are really members of the police; they have been both Good and Evil, legal and illegal.

In a final fantastic sequence, the gross but harmless figure Sunday flies in a balloon to his estate, pursued all the way by his mystified lieutenants. Sunday, of course, proves to have two sides: he is Chief Anarchist and Chief of Detectives; he is the gay trickster; he is anarchic; he defies the codes of society; he is absent-minded and innocent; he is always well-meaning. (Chesterton was willing to admit that there was a touch of self-portraiture in Sunday.)

Sunday is like nature itself, or the universe; he is, indeed, Pan—the whole world, all of life. He shows that while life may appear to be dark, nasty, and brutish from one angle, from another and more informed point of view, it appears to be good. It is a matter of an individual's choosing; in having chosen to enlist in the fight against evil and nihilism, the detectives have transformed Sunday into what he really is. Their acceptance of life brings them into harmo-ny with it; they find themselves accepted and loved by Sunday, who tells them at his mansion that they can now find "pleasure in everything." Their only argument now is with one another: each is sure that Sunday's estate is modeled on the scenes of his own youth. What they have gained with their understanding of Sunday is the innocent vision of youth which Chesterton always extolled.

The Man Who Was Thursday still presents problems for the critics since it seems to be teaching the highly un-Chestertonian message that there is no evil, that evil is an illusion, that things are not what they seem. Recognizing the ambiguity, Chesterton later explained, "I was not then considering whether anything is really evil, but whether everything is really evil; and in relation to the latter nightmare it does still seem to be relevant to say that nightmares are not true." The operative word here is "everything"; the problem is not the relativity of values but the discovery that—as the Dedication emphasizes—one might take a small step in finding *some* thing good in spite of the pessimism and gloom of the Edwardian period.

Even while writing, though, Chesterton must have sensed the shaky philosophical ground upon which he stood. In the last scene, while a general Dickensian reconciliation is occurring at a magnificently described masked ball, a Satanic figure steps forward to challenge Sunday again. The relativistic conflict of most of the book makes way for pure Manicheism. "Satan" demands to know the meaning of the masquerade that Sunday has arranged. Why were the detective-anarchists forced in ignorance to play two roles at once? Why were they not granted the meaning of the game without the mummery, the deceit, the struggle, the final embarrassment?

The answer that Sunday gives is straight out of Browning's "Rabbi Ben Ezra." The detectives, Sunday informs everybody, were made to fight "evil," or think they were fighting "evil," "so that each thing that obeys law may have the glory and isolation of the anarchist. So that each man fighting for order may be as brave and good a man as the dynamiter." The struggle against evil, the very sense of an evil to be overcome—has endowed the detectives with the moral virtue spoken of by Rabbi Ben Ezra, who teaches that evil is "Machinery just meant/ To give thy soul its bent."

Chesterton, however, moves beyond Browning's concept of evil. The Tempter still confronts Sunday with piercing questions; he accuses Sunday of not having suffered the fear and doubt felt by his lieutenants during their dark agony. Sunday painfully replies, in the words of Christ, "Can ye drink of the cup that I drink of?" As the book ends, Syme's nightmare is shattered by this question, which stands as a beacon now for the hero, for Chesterton, and for the reader. *The Man Who Was Thursday* is a milestone in Chesterton's progress from the secular-Medieval fantasies of *The Napoleon of Notting Hill* to the complete acceptance of Christian mystery and duty. Serenity and hope, if it can be found at all, will come to the individual who is willing to accept the burden of the Cross.

Ian Boyd   (essay date 1975)

SOURCE: "The Pre-War Novels," in *The Novels of G. K. Chesterton: A Study in Art and Propaganda*, Barnes & Noble Books, 1975, pp. 40-76.

[In the following excerpt, Boyd centers on the various types of allegory apparent in Chesterton's novel.]

It is difficult to find any obvious common characteristic in the novels which Chesterton published between 1908 and 1914. They mark a distinctive period in his literary development and accurately reflect his political thinking in the pre-War years, but more than any other group of novels they create the impression of being heterogeneous in character. The themes found in each of them suggest his preoccupations in a particular period, but they are themes which link them not so much to each other, but to the earlier and later groups of novels. The curious double allegory of *The Man Who Was Thursday* has only a slight connection with the themes developed in the other pre-War novels, but its dramatization of a purely personal mood and its treatment of anarchy and order anticipates some of the themes dealt with in the later fiction, particularly in *The Poet and the Lunatics* and *The Paradoxes of Mr Pond. Manalive* has the same curious air of being isolated from the other novels in the pre-War group, but its treatment of the theme of wonder recalls *The Napoleon of Notting Hill* and the part played by Innocent Smith recalls the role of Father Michael in *The Ball and the Cross. The Flying Inn* is equally distinctive, although its use of type characters associates it with the early romances and its somewhat negative political satire and apocalyptic tone link it to the Distributist novels which follow it.

The peculiar allegorical quality of *The Man Who Was Thursday* presents at once its most original feature and its chief difficulty in interpretation. For there is a sense in which the one novel contains two distinctive allegories, which are indeed related, but never completely integrated into a coherent whole. The first, which might be called the personal or private allegory, presents the story of Chesterton's reaction to what he regarded as the pessimism of the nineties. The second, which might be called the public or the political allegory, is concerned with the story of an individual's conflict with an international conspiracy which in fact never exists. The relationship between the two allegories is of course obvious. The terrors of the young policeman who discovers that his enemies are secret friends are as unnecessary as the terrors of the young Chesterton who discovers that he is living in an essentially friendly universe. The private allegory is the story of a man whose enemies turn out to be friends, and the political allegory is an elaboration of his misunderstanding. The interest and the poetic power of the novel comes from the way in which the political story, which is meant to illustrate the private allegory, gradually takes on an independent life and meaning of its own. The situation which haunts the imagination long after the fears of Chesterton's alter-ego have been explained away presents a doomed hero fighting a hopeless battle against a world-wide conspiracy of wealthy and powerful men.

Chesterton's own comments on the novel illuminate only the personal allegory. On the two occasions on which he discussed the novel, he was content to emphasize the way in which it allegorized a mood he experienced in the nineties against which he finally reacted. 'It was intended', he writes, 'to describe the world of wild doubt and despair which the pessimists were generally describing at that date, with just a gleam of hope in some double meaning of the doubt, which even the pessimists felt in some fitful fashion.' On another occasion, however, he denied that the novel had anything to say about an ultimate kind of optimism: 'I was not then considering whether anything is really evil, but whether everything is really evil.' In fact Chesterton's explanation adds little to what the dedicatory poem to E. C. Bentley already made sufficiently clear. Indeed it is the poem rather than the explanation which draws attention to the way in which the novel expresses both the almost incommunicable sense of loneliness in a bewildering moral struggle and the sense that the adolescent difficulties were no less terrifying for being largely imaginary. At the same time the poem suggests the new psychological and moral poise which the novel also represents:

> This is a tale of those old fears,
>   Even of those empty hells,
> And none but you shall understand
>   The true thing that it tells—
> Of what colossal gods of shame
>   Could cow men and yet crash,
> Of what huge devils hid the stars,
>   Yet fell at a pistol flash.
> The doubts that were so plain to chase,
>   So dreadful to withstand—
> Oh, who shall understand but you;
>   Yea, who shall understand?
>
>   . . . . .
>
> Between us, by the peace of God,
>   Such truth can now be told;
> Yea, there is strength in striking root,
>   And good in growing old.
> We have found common things at last,
>   And marriage and a creed,
> And I may safely write it now,
>   And you may safely read.

Perhaps the most useful function of both Chesterton's comments and his dedicatory poem is the way in which they draw attention to the frame-story which encloses the central action of the novel. The fears of which he speaks in both instances are, as the sub-title reminds us, only a nightmare, but the nightmare takes place in the comfortable suburb which is described at the beginning and the end of the novel. The story of Gabriel Syme as a member of the Brotherhood of Anarchists must be related to the frame in which the story is placed. And the very details of the adventure in Saffron Park are important to an understanding of the dream-adventure which follows it. In the dream, the debate with Lucian Gregory is presented in another form, but it is essentially the same debate which begins in the park. A conflict in ideas is translated into the conflict of a Stevensonian romance. Even the smaller details of the frame-story throw light on the central action of the novel. The sound of a barrel-organ which Syme hears as he talks to Rosamund provides him with the courage he needs when he hears it again during his dream-meeting with the Anarchists. In the park, the music is a reminder of his love: 'His heroic words were moving to a tiny tune from under or beyond the world': In the dream, the music is a reminder of his role as a representative of the common people:

> He found himself filled with a supernatural courage that came from nowhere. The jingling music seemed full of the vivacity, the vulgarity, and the irrational valour of the poor, who in all those unclean streets were all clinging to the decencies and the charities of Christendom.

Similarly, Syme's courtship of Rosamund not only provides what may be a graceful allusion to Chesterton's own courtship of Frances in the somewhat similar artistic colony of Bedford Park, but also prepares the way for Syme's meeting with Rosamund at the end of the novel and for the part she is supposed to play in inspiring the central action of the story: '. . . in some indescribable way, she kept recurring like a motive in music through all his mad adventures afterwards, and the glory of her strange hair ran like a red thread through those dark and ill-drawn tapestries of the night.'

The meaning of the personal allegory is also suggested by the purely descriptive passages which one finds in the frame-story. This is particularly true of the description of the sunset with which the novel begins and the description of the sunrise with which it concludes. At first these passages might seem to be examples of what Ronald Knox [in his introduction to Chesterton's **Father Brown: Selected Stories,** 1966] has called Chesterton's weakness for mere scene-painting and brilliant word-pictures, but on closer examination it becomes clear that far from being irrelevant digressions, they have an obvious relation to the main action and present important emblems of what the action means. Thus the most significant and obvious thing about the Saffron Park sunset is that it is a sunset. It expresses symbolically the *fin de siècle* mood of pessimism which is the central theme of this novel. On the other hand, the quiet and remarkably effective description of the sunrise at the end of the novel expresses perfectly the way in which Syme's fears are finally transformed into a new mood of hope:

> Dawn was breaking over everything in colours at once clear and timid; as if Nature made a first attempt at yellow and a first attempt at rose. A breeze blew so clean and sweet, that one could not think that it blew from the sky; it blew rather through some hole in the sky.

The contrast suggested by the two descriptions is however more than a simple contrast between despair and hope. The particular quality of the despair is also suggested, and suggested in a way which anticipates both the dream which follows and the cautious optimism which eventually follows the dream. Thus the sunset is described in explicitly apocalyptic language: 'This particular evening, if it is remembered for nothing else, will be remembered in that place for its strange sunset. It looked like the end of the world.' The weird imagery of colours as feathers which seem to brush the earth suggests a suffocating evil and

malice, and foreshadows the story of the conspiracy: 'The whole was so close about the earth, as to express nothing but a violent secrecy. The very empyrean seemed to be a secret.' And yet, at the same time, the description also suggests an opposite mood. The 'red-hot plumes' which cover up the sun are hiding 'something too good to be seen', and the enclosed sky which seems to oppress is also emblematic of something which is called at the end of the novel 'some impossible good news, which made every other thing a triviality, but an adorable triviality'. The sky, we are told, 'expressed that splendid smallness which is the soul of local patriotism. The very sky seemed small'.

The movement from pessimism to a qualified optimism which is expressed in the frame-story's contrasting descriptions of sunset and sunrise is also represented in the dream itself. The unmasking of successive enemies who turn out to be friends has the authentic quality of the transformation of despair into something like optimism. Similarly the pursuit of Sunday by the Six Days and the investiture of the Six in their symbolic garb also suggests the discovery of an ultimate hope which lies behind the terror. In fact the entire dream can be interpreted in terms of Chesterton's sacramental view of life, according to which nature both conceals and leads to the divine. What the dream finally presents is a kind of Meredithian argument for nature's essential goodness as an ally which ultimately comes to the rescue. Thus, in one of Syme's final speeches, he interprets his adventures in language which might have been inspired by Butler's *Analogy*:

> 'Listen to me,' cried Syme with extraordinary emphasis, 'Shall I tell you the secret of the whole world? It is that we have only known the back of the world. We see everything from behind, and it looks brutal. That is not a tree, but the back of a tree. That is not a cloud, but the back of a cloud. Cannot you see that everything is stooping and hiding a face? If we could only get round in front—'

The chief imagery used in the personal allegory to present this philosophy of optimism is the imagery of masks. From one point of view, the masks represent what Chesterton regarded as the scepticism of the nineties, which had such an obsessive influence on him during his Slade school days. Thus Syme, while fleeing through the Normandy woods, sees the forest as a symbol of the scepticism represented by Impressionistic art:

> The inside of the wood was full of shattered sunlight and shaken shadows. They made a sort of shuddering veil, almost recalling the dizziness of a cinematograph. Even the solid figures walking with him Syme could hardly see for the patterns of sun and shade that danced upon them. Now a man's head was lit as with a light of Rembrandt, leaving all else obliterated; now again he had strong and staring white hands with the face of a negro. . . . Was he wearing a mask? Was anyone wearing a mask? Was anyone anything? This wood of witchery, in which men's faces turned black and white by turns, in which their figures first swelled into sunlight and then faded into formless night, this mere chaos of chiaroscuro (after the clear daylight outside) seemed

to Syme a perfect symbol of the world in which he had been moving for three days, this world where men took off their beards and their spectacles and their noses, and turned into other people. . . . Was not everything, after all, like this bewildering woodland, this dance of dark and light? Everything only a glimpse, the glimpse always unforeseen and always forgotten. For Gabriel Syme had found in the heart of that sun-splashed wood what many modern painters had found there. He had found the thing which the modern people call Impressionism, which is another name for that final scepticism which can find no floor to the universe.

But from another point of view, the masks represent not the 'mere chaos of chiaroscuro', but the sense that the frightening appearances of things hide an encouraging secret. The president of the Anarchist conspiracy who is seen only in daylight turns out to be the leader of the anti-Anarchist conspiracy who sits in the dark room and is never seen. The deadliest enemies are all of them secret friends. As C. S. Lewis remarks [in his "Notes on the Way" in *Time and Tide,* 9 November 1946], the pattern of the story suggests a comparison with Kafka:

> . . . read again **The Man Who Was Thursday**. Compare it with another good writer, Kafka. Is the difference simply that the one is 'dated' and the other contemporary? Or is it rather that while both give a powerful picture of the loneliness and bewilderment which each one of us encounters in his (apparently) single-handed struggle with the universe, Chesterton, attributing to the universe a more complicated disguise, and admitting the exhilaration as well as the terror of the struggle, has got in rather more; is more balanced: in that sense, more classical, more permanent?

The apparently unnecessary terror which the masks create is also given a meaning. For it is through this seemingly gratuitous suffering that Syme gains his new hope. He had after all joined the anti-Anarchist police force because of his exasperation with the apparent smugness of the forces of order: '. . . I could forgive you even your cruelty if it were not for your calm.' At the end of the novel, he is identified with the forces of order he had previously reviled, and it is Gregory, the one real Anarchist, who repeats his protest: 'Oh, I could forgive you everything, you that rule all mankind, if I could feel for once that you had suffered for one hour a real agony such as I—' It is precisely the suffering that Syme has undergone in the time which has intervened between the two complaints which enables him to understand the difficulty which was once his own:

> 'I see everything,' he cried, 'everything that there is. Why does each thing on the earth war against each other thing? Why does each small thing in the world have to fight against the world itself ? . . . For the same reason that I had to be alone in the dreadful Council of the Days. So that each thing that obeys law may have the glory and isolation of the anarchist. So that each man fighting for order may be as brave and good a man as the dynamiter. So that the real lie of Satan may be flung back in the face of this blas-

phemer, so that by tears and torture we may earn the right to say to this man, "You lie!" No agonies can be too great to buy the right to say to this accuser, "We also have suffered." '

And when the dream ends with Syme asking Sunday the same question and hearing the distant voice reply, 'Can ye drink of the cup that I drink of ?', the echoes from the Book of Job acquire a more particular and more religious significance. For the story of the optimism which comes through suffering is now associated with the mystery of the Incarnation and the suffering of God.

The novel does therefore work to a remarkable extent in the way in which Chesterton said it was intended to work. It can be read as a convincing allegory of the solution to a personal problem, in which fear and scepticism are transformed into a real although cautious optimism, just as the apocalyptic sunset of Saffron Park is transformed into the new dawn of romantic hope. But the personal allegory does not exhaust the novel's meaning. In dramatizing his rejection of the supposed *Zeitgeist* of the nineties, Chesterton also presents an allegory of a political problem which remains after the private problem has been solved. The nightmare has a political meaning which to a degree undercuts and reverses the personal meaning which is meant to explain the nightmare away.

The political meaning is first suggested by the nature of the philosophical police force which is supposed to combat Anarchy. This curious organization remains interesting even though the conspiracy it fights exists only in the minds of the policemen, and the conspirators and policemen alike exist only in the mind of Syme. It is interesting not only because it might provide a plot for a kind of John Buchan adventure story, but because it is very much in keeping with Chesterton's own political and social thought. What the policeman on the Thames embankment invites Symes to take part in is in fact an elaborate though secret heresy hunt. The implication, which is entirely Chestertonian in spirit, is that the educated are the real criminal class:

> 'You have evidently not heard of the latest development in our police system,' replied the other. 'I am not surprised at it. We are keeping it rather dark from the educated class, because that class contains most of our enemies. . . . The head of one of our departments, one of the most celebrated detectives in Europe, has long been of [the] opinion that a purely intellectual conspiracy would soon threaten the very existence of civilization. He is certain that the scientific and artistic worlds are silently bound in a crusade against the Family and the State.'

The nature of the supposed Anarchist movement which the policemen combat is also in line with Chesterton's misgivings about the defects of Edwardian society. His conviction that great wealth carries with it great danger both to the person who possesses it and to the society in which he lives is given vivid imaginative expression in the picture of an Anarchist movement which is controlled by an immensely wealthy group of conspirators. Sunday himself is described as a mad Edwardian financier with cosmopolitan connections and right-hand men who are South African and American millionaires. Like John Buchan's criminal millionaires, Sunday and his henchmen combine enormous wealth with nihilistic principles. And there is a similarly Buchanian flavour to the contrast between Sunday's real and apparent position. Like Lumley and Medina, he is equally capable of directing a world-wide conspiracy or taking the chair at a humanitarian meeting. It is easy to imagine Ratcliffe's description of what Sunday has done as part of the plot of Buchan's *The Powerhouse* or *The Courts of the Morning*:

> Can you think of anything more like Sunday than this, that he should put all his powerful enemies on the Supreme Council, and then take care that it was not supreme? I tell you he has bought every trust, he has captured every cable, he has control of every railway line. . . . The whole movement was controlled by him; half the world was ready to rise for him.

But there are important differences in the way in which Chesterton and Buchan treat this similar theme. Buchan's criminal millionaires are often defeated by the good millionaires who are their counterparts. There is little moral difference between the millionaire hero and the millionaire villain except that one tries to preserve the system which the other tries to destroy. And indeed, in one instance, the hero and the villain are the same person. For Castor is both the sinister cosmopolitan who creates a secret empire based on drugs and slave labour and the kindly philanthropist who destroys his own creation.

From Chesterton's point of view, Buchan's heroes and villains are interchangeable. His own thinking on this question is summed up in Colonel Ducroix's casual comment on the wealthy of a small French town: ' "Four out of the five rich men in this town", he said, "are common swindlers. I suppose the proportion is pretty equal all over the world. The fifth is a friend of mine, and a very fine fellow." ' Even the exception to this rule is a somewhat doubtful case, and Syme has no difficulty in believing that he, too, is treacherous: 'I suspected him from the first. He's rationalistic, and what's worse, he's rich. When duty and religion are really destroyed, it will be by the rich.' In Buchan's novels, the criminal behaviour of the wealthy never ceases to be a surprise: it has the special note of something monstrous, since it is the betrayal of society by those who are assumed to be its best and wisest guardians. In Chesterton's novels, the wickedness of the wealthy is more or less taken for granted: it is their occasional decency which surprises. The picture which is presented in *The Man Who Was Thursday* and which recurs throughout Chesterton's fiction is that of the wealthy as the permanent enemies of the social order and the poor as its permanent defenders:

> 'The poor have been rebels, but they have never been anarchists: they have more interest than anyone else in there being some decent government. The poor man really has a stake in the country. The rich man hasn't; he can go away to New Guinea in a yacht. The poor have sometimes objected to being governed badly; the rich have always objected to being governed at all.

> Aristocrats were always anarchists, as you can see from the barons' wars.'

Another expression of the same attitude is reflected in what is supposed to be the very organization of the Anarchist society. The inner and outer circles of the movement correspond approximately to the social division between the rich and the poor. The rank and file of the movement are for the most part simple people with genuine grievances who seek social improvement and the punishment of tyranny. Even the rhetoric which appeals to them suggests their naïvety. What they like best are the clichés of romantic revolutionaries:

> 'I do not go to the Council to rebut that slander that calls us murderers; I go to earn it.' (Loud and prolonged cheering.) 'To the priest who says these men are the enemies of religion, to the judge who says these men are the enemies of law, to the fat parliamentarian who says these men are the enemies of order and public decency, to all these I will reply, "You are false kings, but you are true prophets. I am come to destroy you, and to fulfil your prophecies." '

The serious danger is presented by the inner ring of Anarchy. This is the group which is described as a kind of church. Whereas the outer ring who repeat Anarchist jargon unthinkingly form the laity of the movement, the inner ring who are completely cynical about official Anarchist beliefs form a sort of revolutionary priesthood. The two rings represent at once the division between the rich and the poor and the moral division between what the policeman calls 'the innocent section' and 'the supremely guilty section'. The members of the inner ring do not desire social reform or improvement of any kind or even complete freedom from restraint. Indeed they possess something of Chesterton's own scepticism about the possibility of progress and something of his conviction about the reality of original sin. They are inspired by a spirit which has been described as the psychic undercurrent of revolutionary politics which, in Buddhist fashion, teaches two things only—sorrow and the ending of sorrow. Behind the slogans of this 'rich and powerful and fanatical church', one can detect a longing for death:

> They also speak to applauding crowds of the happiness of the future, and of mankind freed at last. But in their mouths . . . these happy phrases have a horrible meaning. They are under no illusions; they are too intellectual to think that man upon this earth can ever be quite free of original sin and the struggle. And they mean death. When they say that mankind shall be free at last, they mean that mankind shall commit suicide. When they talk of a paradise without right or wrong, they mean the grave. They have but two objects, to destroy first humanity and then themselves.

The complete meaning of this theory is never developed in the novel, but even in its incomplete form the description of the Anarchist conspiracy presents a suggestive critique of the revolutionary spirit. In *The Napoleon of Notting Hill* Chesterton argues the case for a balance between political idealism and irony. In *The Ball and the Cross* he suggests the need for a balance between secular and transcendental values. And in both these novels, the impossibility of social happiness resulting from mere material improvement is more or less taken for granted. But in *The Man Who Was Thursday,* he carries the argument one stage further. What he suggests is that there is an undercurrent in the desire for social reform which may eventually be turned against society itself, so that the reformers who have despaired of reform may seek a kind of Nirvana instead. In the first of the pre-War novels, Chesterton has translated his hatred of Edwardian plutocracy into a fantasy in which the revolutionary reformers and the rich coalesce for the purpose of pure nihilism, and a small band of common people make a vain attempt to rally the populace for a last desperate stand against their masters.

This is the meaning of the novel at the level of imagination. Superimposed on this political parable is the private parable about Chesterton's years of depression between 1891 and 1896. However effective and interesting the personal allegory may be, it weakens and contradicts the equally interesting and effective political allegory which is subordinated to it. The terrifying figure of Sunday becomes the somewhat unconvincing figure of the good policeman. And the story of the Anarchist Brotherhood and the ineffectual attempts to thwart it becomes first an extraordinarily detailed account of a misunderstanding and finally the inconsequential material of a nightmare. *The Man Who Was Thursday* is therefore a curiously ambivalent book. It may be read in the light of the dedicatory poem as a kind of extended commentary on the Book of Job, recounting the story of the new hope which is achieved through the anguish of doubt and isolation. At the same time it may also be read as a powerful though incomplete allegory on the social dangers of wealth and the meaning of the extreme revolutionary spirit. A personal comment on the ethos of the nineties ends as a serious political comment on a perennial political problem.

Garry Wills   (essay date 1975)

SOURCE: *"The Man Who Was Thursday* (1975)," in *A Half Century of Views,* edited by D. J. Conlon, Oxford University Press, Oxford, 1987, pp. 335-42.

[*In the following essay, which was originally published as an introduction to* The Man Who Was Thursday, *Wills discusses Chesterton's use of symbolism in the novel.*]

> Chesterton restrained himself from being Edgar Allan Poe or Franz Kafka, but something in the makeup of his personality leaned toward the nightmarish, something secret, and blind and central.
>
> Borges, *Other Inquisitions*

This 1908 novel [*The Man Who Was Thursday*] has long enjoyed a kind of underground cult among those with a special interest in fantasy. It is the story of a conspiratorial council of seven anarchists, each one named for a day of the week, with the mysterious Sunday as their president. Admirers of the tale have included J. R. R. Tolkien, C. S. Lewis, W. H. Auden, Jorge Luis Borges, and T. S. Eliot.

Kingsley Amis has frequently written about it. Yet the wider reading public remains largely unaware of it.

No wonder. It is a detective story that seems to solve itself too easily, and lose its mystery. But those who stay with it, even after they think they have seen through it, are teased back and back by its ultimately unresolved nature, all the puzzles that remain after the last pages are read. It does not give up its secrets at a glance. Even Mr Amis, despite his enthusiasm for the tale, seems to misunderstand it—as when he writes: 'What I find indigestible in the closing scenes is . . . the person of the fleeing Sunday, who at one point makes off mounted on a Zoo elephant and who bombards the pursuit with messages of elephantine facetiousness, [*Encounter,* October 1973]. He is attacking the finest clue of all. But, more than that, he lapses into the condescending attitude he came to criticize—the view that Chesterton cannot resist buffoonery, even when he is onto something bigger and more startling than a good joke (or a bad one).

But Sunday's riddles go beyond joking, good or bad; they show a cruelty in humour like the cruelty of nature itself—they are taunts thrown back at men who have been tortured. The best parts of this racy entertainment, as Borges understood, are moments of weird near-break-down:

> As he now went up the weary and perpetual steps, he was daunted and bewildered by their almost infinite series. But it was not the hot horror of a dream or of anything that might be exaggeration or delusion. Their infinity was more like the infinity of arithmetic, something unthinkable, yet necessary to thought. Or it was like the stunning statements of astronomy about the distance of the fixed stars. He was ascending the tower of reason, a thing more hideous than unreason itself.

The book is all a chase, an evasion, and a dream; a benign nightmare prolonged, page by page, beyond our waking. It has the compelling inconsequence of nightmare, its tangle of mutually chasing loves and hates, where the impossible becomes inevitable and each wish comes partnered with its own frustration. Nightmare is described in the book itself as a world of 'tyrannic accidents'. Auden and others have noticed Chesterton's power to evoke the despotic mood of dreams. Borges compared him to Poe in this aspect, and C.S. Lewis to Kafka. The reason we go on reading Chesterton's tale—after we have cracked its first secret (that all the conspirators are also, unbeknownst to each other, anti-conspirators)—is that a dream mood leads us on, linking all its incidents. It aims at an effect that intrigued Chesterton in his own disturbing dreams, one achieved in some of his favourite works of literature.

> Here is the pursuit of the man we cannot catch, the flight from the man we cannot see; here is the perpetual returning to the same place, here is the crazy alteration in the very objects of our desire, the substitution of one face for another face, the putting of the wrong souls in the wrong bodies, the fantastic disloyalties of the night . . .
>
> [Essay on 'A Midsummer Night's Dream', in W. H. Auden, *G. K. Chesterton: A Selection,* 1970]

So, even after we know that the anarchists are also cops, the dream-suspension of things in air continues—the flight from Age, through a crippling ache of snow; a slow climb up the mad tower of pure reason; the duel with a phantom who comes apart like meat being carved but will not bleed; the endless chase by anonymous somebodies who gradually become Everybody, embodying paranoia's logic. Then, after running as the quarry, the book's accumulating heroes turn and reach new stages of bewilderment as the pursuers. They knew more as the hunted than as hunters. Desperation gave them solidarity; but at a hint of victory they come apart again, each teasing at the private riddles addressed to him by Sunday. But this dominance of a nightmare mood should not blind us to the riddles addressed to us as readers. These are nicely differentiated, and cluster around two questions. Who are the conspirators? And: Who is Sunday?

THE CONSPIRATORS

> Then thou scarest me with dreams
> and terrifiest me through visions.
>
> Job 7.14

The first set of clues is almost too obvious—which makes men overlook further hints, to which the first set was only our introduction. The point is not only that everyone is in disguise, but that his disguise is revealing. Each man's secret is unwittingly worn like a shield instead of an emblem. The biggest clue can be overlooked because Chesterton has placed it so prominently in the title. A man can be Thursday only because other men are already Friday, Monday, etc. Granted, the Council of Days is a device that readers quickly penetrate; and most of them focus thenceforth on the identity of Sunday. But the riddle of Monday is not disposed of simply by knowing that he is Sunday's Secretary and also the hidden Detective's right-hand man. Chesterton tries to keep reminding us of this; but readers, so far as I can tell, still keep forgetting. When Dr Bull says, toward the end, 'We are six men going to ask one man what he means', Syme replies: 'I think it is six men going to ask one man what they mean.'

What does the Secretary, the first and most persistent of the Council, mean—with the cruel tilt of laughter as a doubt across his face? At the final banquet he will wear robes that make him more real—a pitch black garment with the struggle of first light down its expanse. He is Monday, light out of darkness, the first unstoppable questioning that is man's last boast—'And God said: Let there be light.' He comes after his fellow-conspirators in the long dream-scene of chase with a black mask on, his face a pattern of light and dark echoed in all his followers. He dwells in darkness, only to fight it, and is described from the outset as tortured with thought in its most naked form. Syme wonders why, when the Secretary gets tossed from the hood of the car, darkness comes on so soon—a minor riddle, but part of a large pattern. Monday, with his complex mind, is the simplest and truest of them all in his quest for truth. He will not stop asking impertinent questions even in the unknowable Emperor's palace.

Gogal, shaggy under his load of wild tresses, but transparent and easily found out, is as simple as the waters of the Second Day, Wednesday is the Marquis, whose absinthe philosophy brightens to the green clothing of earth. Thursday is Syme, a poet, a divider of planet from planet on a plan—as Michelangelo's sculptor-God on the ceiling shoulders moons off from the sun. Friday is the Professor, who has a nihilist's ethic of bestiality, but a deeper kinship, also, with the innocence of animals. Saturday is the last day, Man, a thing almost too open and childish to wear a disguise, an optimist of reason, the tale's French revolutionary, declaring the patent rights of man as king of the creation—each man a king.

All six of the men are puzzles, but elemental puzzles, the kind that one cannot really 'solve'. They represent man's status as a partner in his own creation—the question of man's questioning; the open energy of Gogol; the dim recesses of the Marquis; Syme's swagger; Friday's depths of despair; and Saturday's insaner hope. When Syme grieves that the conspirators have looked only on the fleeing back of the universe, we think his talk deals only with Sunday, since he is often glimpsed from behind in the story. But later, in the garden, all things—in dancing—turn a sudden face on the Council, each tree and lamppost. Everything has a story untold, an episode wandered into, a history only half-understood. And what is true of the clues is true of the detectives, who are themselves the main clues they must read. Each of them deceived the others because he was seen from behind or partially, at an odd angle. The 'back' of intellect is doubt; of subtlety, deviousness; of energy, rage. Everything in the tale, as in the world, needs deciphering, nothing more than oneself. We are all walking signs, signaling urgently to one another in a code no one has cracked. If anyone could understand himself, he would understand everything. So the last person to guess what the man called Monday means will be Monday. Sunday is not a greater mystery than the other Days, except in one respect—he is not only a clue, and a reader of clues; he also plants the clues. He may have cracked the code. That is why they go in search of him.

The tale is not an idle play with symbols. It gets its urgency and compression from the fact that it is the most successful embodiment of the seminal experience in Chesterton's life, his young mystical brush with insanity. In that sense, it is full of clues to his own mental crisis—his depression and near-suicide as an art student in the decadent 1890s. At the centre of Chesterton's best fiction there is always a moment of aporia, the dark seed of all his gaudy blossomings. In *Thursday* that moment comes when the chase is urged on by the masked Secretary:

> The sun on the grass was dry and hot. So in plunging into the wood they had a cool shock of shadow, as of divers who plunge into a dim pool. The inside of the wood was full of shattered sunlight and shaken shadows. They made a sort of shuddering veil, almost recalling the dizziness of a cinematograph. Even the solid figures walking with him Syme could hardly see for the patterns of sun and shade that danced upon them. Now a man's head was lit as with a light of Rembrandt, leaving all else obliterated; now again he had strong and staring white hands with the face of a negro. The ex-Marquis had pulled the old straw hat over his eyes, and the black shade of the brim cut his face so squarely in two that it

seemed to be wearing one of the black half-masks of their pursuers. The fancy tinted Syme's overwhelming sense of wonder. Was he wearing a mask? Was anyone wearing a mask? Was anyone anything? This wood of witchery, in which men's faces turned black and white by turns, in which their figures first swelled into sunlight and then faded into formless night, this mere chaos of chiaroscuro (after the clear daylight outside), seemed to Syme a perfect symbol of the world in which he had been moving for three days, this world where men took off their beards and their spectacles and their noses, and turned into other people. That tragic self-confidence which he had felt when he believed that the Marquis was a devil had strangely disappeared now that he knew that the Marquis was a friend. He felt almost inclined to ask after all these bewilderments what was a friend and what an enemy. Was there anything that was apart from what it seemed? The Marquis had taken off his nose and turned out to be a detective. Might he not just as well take off his head and turn out to be a hobgoblin? Was not everything, after all, like this bewildering woodland, this dance of dark and light? Everything only a glimpse, the glimpse always unforeseen, and always forgotten. For Gabriel Syme had found in the heart of that sun-splashed wood what many modern painters had found there. He had found the thing which the modern people call Impressionism, which is another name for that final scepticism which can find no floor to the universe.

The dragging in of impressionism here makes no sense except by its connection with the morbid experiences of Chesterton at the Slade School during the years 1892 through 1895, when a fashionable pessimism was cultivated by the same people who were taken with fashionable 'impressionism'.

Much of the material for **Thursday** comes directly out of the notebooks and poems of those art-school years, almost a decade and a half behind him when he wrote the novel. An early poem on suicide lies behind Chapter 10. The account of an art-school conversation is drawn on for the lantern episode in Chapter 12. The emergence from solipsism into fellowship, described in Chapter 8, lies behind much of his poetry from this period—like **'The Mirror of Madmen,'** from which I quote just the opening and closing stanzas:

> I dreamed a dream of heaven, white as frost,
> The splendid stillness of a living host;
> Vast choirs of upturned faces, line o'er line.
> Then my blood froze for every face was mine.

> Then my dream snapped and with a heart that
>   leapt
> I saw, across the tavern where I slept,
> The sight of all my life most full of grace,
> A gin-damned drunkard's wan half-witted face.

The same experience lies behind the novel's dedicatory poem, with its tribute to the two men who meant so much to him in his personal ordeal—Stevenson of Tusitala, who also rebelled against the aesthetes of *his* art school in Paris; and Whitman of Paumanok, who praised the mere existence of multiple things in a democracy of existence. In-

deed, the first sketch of what would become **Thursday** was written as an exercise in Whitman pantheism. It appears in an unpublished Chesterton notebook from the early nineties:

> The week is a gigantic symbol, the symbol of the
>   creation of the world:

> Monday is the day of Lent. (Light? Ed.)
> Tuesday the day of waters.
> Wednesday the day of the Earth.
> Thursday: the day of stars.
> Friday: the day of birds.
> Saturday: the day of beasts.
> Sunday: the day of peace: the day for saying
>   that it is good
> Perhaps the true religion is this
> that the creator is not ended yet.
> And that what we move towards
> Is blinding, colossal, calm
> The rest of God.

Chesterton opposed the chaos in himself and the life around him by considering each man's life a re-enactment, day by day, of the first verses of Genesis. One of his student letters has this passage: 'Today is Sunday, and Ida's birthday. Thus it commemorates two things, the creation of Ida and the creation of the world . . . Nineteen years ago the Cosmic Factory was at work; the vast wheel of stars revolved, the archangels had a conference, and the result was another person . . . I should imagine that sun, wind, colours, chopsticks, circulating library books, ribbons, caricatures and the grace of God were used.' Chesterton took as the ground of his hope that very sense of dissolution that threatened his sanity. By the energy of existence things keep re-emerging from dissolution. Creation uses chaos as its working material—just as the spirit, freed in dreams, uses the world as a set of signs, shifting their meaning in ways that terrify man while making him the master of 'unsignified' matter:

> If we wish to experience pure and naked feeling we can never experience it so really as in that unreal land. There the passions seem to live an outlawed and abstract existence, unconnected with any facts or persons. In dreams we have revenge without any injury, remorse without any sin, memory without any recollection, hope without any prospect. Love, indeed, almost proves itself a divine thing by the logic of dreams; for in a dream every material circumstance may alter, spectacles may grow on a baby, and moustaches on a maiden aunt, and yet the great sway of one tyrannical tenderness may never cease. Our dream may begin with the end of the world, and end with a picnic at Hampton Court, but the same rich and nameless mood will be expressed by the falling stars and by the crumbling sandwiches. In a dream daisies may glare at us like the eyes of demons. In a dream lightning and conflagration may warm and soothe us like our own fireside. In this subconscious world, in short, existence betrays itself; it shows that it is full of spiritual forces which disguise themselves as lions and lamp-posts, which can as easily disguise themselves as butterflies and Babylonian temples. . . . Life dwells alone in our very heart of hearts, life is one and virgin and unconjured,

and sometimes in the watches of the night speaks in its own terrible harmony.

['Dreams', in *The Coloured Lands*, 1901]

Chesterton was drawn back, constantly, to the Book of Genesis because of its beginning in chaos. Once one has experienced that nothingness, the emergence of any one thing into form and meaning is a triumph, the foundation for a 'mystical minimum' of aesthetic thankfulness. Then, as Blake saw, each sunrise becomes a fiery chariot's approach.

> When we say that a poet praises the whole creation, we commonly mean only that he praises the whole cosmos. But this sort of poet does really praise creation, in the sense of the act of creating. He praises the passage or transition from nonentity to entity. . . . He not only appreciates everything but the nothing of which everything was made. In a fashion he endures and answers even the earthquake irony of the Book of Job; in some sense he is there when the foundations of the world are laid, with the morning stars singing together and the sons of God shouting for joy.

[*St. Francis of Assisi* 1928]

The Council of Days not only praises this transition, but effects it—as God creates through his six days. Creation is not only *the* beginning, but is *always* beginning—with the Council of Days in on the battle against chaos from the outset. They overthrow their own darker side, their evil brother, as God had to wrestle the sea-god into bonds in the Book of Job. When the six Days gather in Sunday's garden, they have gone back beyond their childhood 'where a tree is a tree at last—to the primordial self they could only accomplish by a struggle that, illogically, *forms* that self. Their end is to arrive at their own beginning, in a puzzle Chesterton often returned to:

> It is at the *beginning* that things are good, and not (as the more pallid progressives say) only at the end. The primordial things—existence, energy, fruition—are good so far as they go. You cannot have evil life, though you can have notorious evil livers. Manhood and womanhood are good things, though men and women are often perfectly pestilent. You can use poppies to drug people, or birch trees to beat them, or stones to make an idol, or corn to make a corner, but it remains true that, in the abstract, before you have done anything, each of these four things is in strict truth a glory, a beneficent specialty and variety. We do praise the Lord that there are birch trees growing amongst the rocks and poppies amongst the corn; we do praise the Lord, even if we do not believe in Him. We do admire and applaud the *project* of a world, just as if we had been called to council in the primal darkness and seen the first starry plan of the skies. We are, as a matter of fact, far more certain that this life of ours is a magnificent and amazing enterprise than we are that it will succeed.

[*T.P.'s Weekly,* 1910]

David J. Leigh, S. J. (essay date 1981)

SOURCE: "Politics and Perspective in *The Man Who Was Thursday*," in *The Chesterton Review,* Vol. 7, No. 4, November, 1981, pp. 329-36.

[Leigh is an American educator and critic. In the following essay, he analyzes Chesterton's use of allegory in The Man Who Was Thursday.*]*

The rediscovery of Chesterton's *The Man Who Was Thursday* by the critics (and even by *Time,* April 7, 1975) has illuminated the complexity of the allegorical nightmare which even G.K.C. admitted was overloaded with meaning. Although most critics—e.g., Barker, Clipper, Wills, Youngberg—call *Thursday* Chesterton's best novel, several critics find serious flaws of incoherence. In particular, Ian Boyd finds the novel's two allegories—philosophical and political—"never completely integrated into a coherent whole" [*The Novels of G. K. Chesterton: A Study in Art and Propaganda,* 1975].

In this article, I will contend that *Thursday* can be read as a coherent pattern blending three main allegories: the approach to the Ultimate (chapters 1-12), the revelation of the nature of the Ultimate (chapters 13-15), and the social-political consequences of these two main allegories (passim). In interpreting these three allegories, the reader must adjust to the genre of eschatological allegory. In eschatological symbolism, the primary meaning dominates, in either its metaphysical implications (the Ultimate is good) or its theological implications (God has entered human history in Christ). These higher levels must retain their primacy in the sense that particular historical or political details or consequences are not to be taken too literally or to be allowed to dominate. Rather, as we shall see in Chesterton's novel, the significance of the higher level—once it is reached at the end of the tale—can enlighten the preceding political references. Like Gabriel Syme, the reader must learn to interpret in an analogical manner. And, perhaps most importantly, the reader must interpret this eschatological revelation *progressively.* At each stage of the allegory, the characters and events signify what can be grasped from a particular ongoing perspective. Read in this fashion, *Thursday* proves to be a revelation allegory in which Syme's poetic horizon is expanded step by step with each anarchist-detective he unmasks.

Most analyses of *Thursday* have noted the significance of the anarchists, from Gogol to the Secretary, as each is revealed. But no one, to my knowledge, has explicated the correlation between each anarchist and his perspective on Sunday. A close look at each anarchist shows not only such a correlation but also suggests a progression in the vision of the Ultimate in the anarchists' perspective on Sunday.

Gogol, the first to be unmasked, suggests the simple but mad idealism of a young adolescent, impulsive and eager for violent action, even if it is meaningless or ineffective. Correspondingly, his vision of Sunday is a blank, for on principle he refuses to think of the consequences or context—or the ultimate meaning—of his impulsive action. As Gogol tells Syme, "I don't think of Sunday on principle, any more than I stare at the sun at noonday." Once

Gogol is unmasked, Syme, the searcher after the ultimate horizon, is free to continue his search by asking ultimate questions. Professor de Worms, suggesting perhaps the nightmare of late adolescence with its uncontrollable fears and imagination, is revealed after a hunting chase to be an actor playing the part of a notorious German nihilist. Correlative to this "too large and too loose" youth is his picture of Sunday as an infinite Face, an unimaginable and uncontrollable Buddha. His spiritualised vision is so beyond intelligibility as to be closer to a doubt than a creed. In the Professor's words: "His face has made me, somehow, doubt whether there are any faces."

In sharp contrast, the next anarchist to be unmasked is the rationalistic Dr. Bull, who turns out to be a city clerk disguised by thick blank spectacles as a British scientist. Exposed after a confrontation in which Syme feels himself reduced to a mere object, Dr. Bull eventually sees Sunday as an infinite source of Vitality, a cosmic *elan vital* to be wondered at and analysed. Here Sunday has been transformed from the youth's unthinkable ideal (Gogol) into the late adolescent's infinite spiritual Mystery (de Worms) and now into the modern scientist's object, infinite Vitality (Dr. Bull).

The Marquis presents a more difficult case. He does not present himself as a particular philosophy, but as an embodiment of human contingency. In the duel, he appears to Syme as a personal source of imminent death, a challenge to Syme's own existence. As Syme responds during the match with the Marquis:

> All the fantastic fears that have been the subject of this story fell from him like dreams from a man waking up in bed. He remembered them clearly and in order as mere delusions of the nerves—how the fear of the Professor had been the fear of the tyrannic accidents of nightmare, and how the fear of the Doctor had been the fear of the airless vacuum of science. The first was the old fear that any miracle might happen, the second the more hopeless modern fear that no miracles can ever happen. But he saw that these fears were fancies, for he found himself in the presence of the great fact of the fear of death, with its coarse and pitiless common sense.

From this experience of human contingency, Syme learns to feel "the love of life in all living things." In combating this personal source of death, Syme senses he is confronting a diabolical threat, a Satanic force which can harm him but cannot do the one thing Syme must do—die. Correlatively, the Marquis's notion of Sunday derives from the perspective of one who has suddenly become aware of the unpredictability and incomprehensibility of death. To the deadly Marquis, Sunday is like an absent-minded tiger. The Ultimate for the Marquis—as for many who first awaken in early middle age to the reality of their own death—seems to be an arbitrary and inconsistent deadly force.

Finally, Syme reaches the most mature and yet most frightening stage in his approach to the Ultimate—that of the crooked smiling Secretary. As Garry Wills has noted, this man closest to Sunday appears in his pursuit of Syme across the French countryside as an impersonal and unin-

telligent mob. The Secretary appears even more horrible because Syme begins his flight through a forest of chiaroscuro ("Was anyone anything?"). He emerges from this chaos of scepticism into a world in which everyone he meets eventually seems to be on the side of anarchy. From the Secretary's perspective—that of the mature secular philosopher of 1900—Sunday appears to be "the final form of matter." The most frightful image of the Ultimate is that of a tragic and meaningless materialism.

Gabriel Syme, of course, is free, as a poet, from the limited horizons of each of these univocal notions of the Ultimate. He alone is able to learn from his encounters with each of these anarchists and their approaches. After listening to them, he turns from poet to prophet. As he explains:

> Each man of you finds Sunday quite different, yet each man of you can only find one thing to compare him to—the universe itself. Bull finds him like the earth in spring, Gogol like the sun at noonday. The Secretary is reminded of the shapeless protoplasm, and the Inspector of the carelessness of virgin forests. The Professor says he is like a changing landscape.

In transcending each of the others' perspective, Syme is able to see the Ultimate as revealed in reverse. The mystery of Sunday, like the mystery of the world that reflects him, is the paradoxical mystery of a person whose back is nearly always turned. In Syme's words: "But when I saw him from behind I was certain he was an animal, and when I saw him in front I knew he was a god." In the end, the confusion of the early contradictory perspectives becomes the mystery of a paradoxical revelation by "a father playing hide-and-seek with his children."

Syme's interpretation of his fellow detectives' perspectives shows not only how each fits within a progressive scheme of human knowledge of the divine, but also reveals that his own interpretation of Sunday as both "back" and "face" is incomplete. Sunday himself interrupts Syme's explanation by "coming down" in his balloon and enticing the six searchers into an eschatological paradise. If the pursuit stories reveal various philosophical approaches to the Ultimate, this final scene in Chapter 15 moves into a more explicitly Biblical revelation of the nature of God. Here the image of God is more positive and, as we shall see, more coherent with itself and with other allegorical aspects of the entire tale.

From the various parallels with the Book of Job, several critics have shown how the final episode reveals more about both the pursuers and the Pursued. Each of the detectives is here clothed in a revelatory disguise from the days of Genesis, thus suggesting each one's ultimate meaning:

> Gogol, or Tuesday, had his simplicity well symbolised by a dress designed upon the division of the waters, a dress that separated upon his forehead and fell to his feet, grey and silver, like a sheet of rain. The Professor, whose day was that on which the birds and fishes—the ruder forms of life—were created, had a dress of dim purple, over which sprawled goggle-eyed fishes and outrageous tropical birds, the union in him of un-

fathomable fancy and of doubt. Dr. Bull, the last day of creation, wore a coat covered with heraldic animals in red and gold, and on his crest a man rampant. He lay back in his chair with a broad smile, the picture of an optimist in his element.

Like Job, the searchers are not given an explanation. Sunday's self-description is a word addressed through darkness to faith. He tells them he has been a voice in the darkness commanding valour and virtue. He tells them he has been aware of them all even in their worst hour. Just at the point at which they learn the Ultimate to be personal and transcendent, Sunday tells them his real name—"I am the Sabbath. I am the peace of God."

This Jobean self-revelation in darkness immediately provokes a Jobean demand from each of the six for an answer to the problem of evil. Why—if Sunday is the peace of God—have they struggled and suffered? Once again the form of each one's objection is in accord with his earlier nature.

At this point the tale goes beyond philosophy and even the Book of Job to an explicitly Christian level. After Syme's defense of suffering as creative of valour, Syme turns to Sunday and presents the final demand: "Have you ever suffered?" Sunday's reply is more than a vague allusion to the Christian incarnation. For, in citing Jesus' response to the disciples who boasted of their right to suffer and rule, Sunday suggests the central mystery of the Redemption— "Can ye drink of the cup that I drink of ?" The image of the cup in this passage suggests not only the human suffering of God in the crucifixion, but also the preparation for it at the Last Supper and the consequences of it in both the meals of Christ's risen life and the eschatological meal in the Eucharist and in the kingdom of Heaven. The profane cup at the earlier Feast of Fear has become the cup of salvation. What had happened in the search to be an arbitrary pantheistic God behind human suffering becomes not merely the transcendent God of the Sabbath but at the same time the incarnate God of the cup of sorrows. But this draining of the chalice of suffering is only one phase in the redemptive cycle of suffering, death, and resurrection. The gospel allusion carries the weight of the central Christian paradox.

This redemptive cycle symbolised by the cup is crucial to all the previous levels of the story. For in the light of the redemptive pattern, the previous struggles are all given new meaning. This "impossible good news" that Gabriel Syme brings back from his nightmare can now make "every other thing a triviality, but an adorable triviality."

In particular, the social and political allegory is not as "vain" as Ian Boyd suggests. The "battle against a worldwide conspiracy of wealthy and powerful men" is not entirely "hopeless" for Syme in his final stage. The theological allegory can enlighten (and lighten) the political allegory. The two aspects of the theological allegory we have seen are: 1) the double face of the Ultimate, and 2) the redemptive entry of the Ultimate into the pattern of suffering and death, thus, making the pattern redemptive (the "cup"). Both of these aspects can be then applied to the political struggle. Just as the ultimate "Establishment"

proves to have two faces, so, too, the human establishment has a double potential—one for oppression and one for liberation. Certainly in 1908, Chesterton was more concerned about the oppressiveness of the larger societal forces, but his theological tale does not render all those in power "hopeless." For Sunday only *appeared* to be a magnate who had bought up industries and communications; the people (Renard, the Colonel, etc.) only *appeared* to be in arms against Syme's group. Chesterton did not work out the implications of his theological fable for the political sphere, but he was clear enough, from our reading, in asserting that evil is not ultimate—at any level. As he reflected in his *Autobiography* on this novel: "the point is that the whole story is a nightmare of things, not as they are, but as they seemed to the young half-pessimist of the '90's."

Thus, from the final perspective of the tale, we see that Sunday is revealed to be not the source of personal or political evil that he appears to be from previous viewpoints. And, most importantly, the final perspective of Sunday as redemptively involved in the process of struggle and suffering—such a perspective relativises all other viewpoints and frees the individual to enter into the personal or political struggle precisely *with hope*. The long-term political struggle with the rich and powerful is no longer a losing battle against South African and American millionaires, but a redemptive venture in which God is continually involved on the side of the suffering.

As the nightmare ends, we learn that what is needed is the eschatological vision of the poet and the religious energy of the prophet—both embodied in Gabriel Syme. For he awakes at dawn able to find the "good news" in the "adorable trivialities" of the human condition—from the political battles of "the red irregular buildings of Saffron park" to the personal meeting with the "girl with the gold-red hair, cutting lilacs before breakfast, with the great unconscious gravity of a girl."

Witold Ostrowski   (essay date 1984)

SOURCE: "*The Man Who Was Thursday*," in *Litterae et Lingua: In Honorem Premislavi Mroczkowski*, edited by Jan Nowakowski, Zaklad Narodowy im. Ossolinakich, 1984, pp. 141-52.

[*In the following essay, Ostrowski examines the relationship between the conventions of detective novels, the phenomena of nightmares, and the structure of* The Man Who Was Thursday.]

G. K. Chesterton's book *The Man Who Was Thursday* is one of the most curious and interesting literary compositions to a scholar who studies the relationship between the meaning and the structure and the typology of the novel.

Chesterton himself saw in the book "the very formless form of a piece of fiction", but a form justified by the fact that it was related to a nightmare. In fact, writing in his *Autobiography* about the disorientation of the critics which the book had provoked, he says: "But what interests me about it was this; that hardly anybody who looked at the title ever seems to have looked at the sub-title;

which was 'A Nightmare', and the answer to a good many critical questions."

NIGHTMARE AS MEANING AND FORM

Perhaps the best starting point for an analysis of this novel is to take the hint from the author and to concentrate on the word Nightmare. It implies both a certain characteristic content and a certain form in which the unpleasant content is presented.

The nightmarish character of the experience which had inspired Chesterton to write about it has been described in detail in the dedicatory poem **"To Edmund Clerihew Bentley,"** which begins with the words:

> A cloud was on the mind of men,
> And wailing went the weather,
> Yea, a sick cloud upon the soul
> When we were boys together.

The poem refers to *The Man Who Was Thursday* thus:

> This is a tale of those old fears,
> Even of those emptied hells,
> And none but you shall understand
> The true thing that it tells—

because "those old fears" were

> The doubts that drove us through the night
> As we two talked amain
> And day had broken on the streets
> E'er it broke upon the brain.

The experience of spiritual doubts and fears wafted, as it were, from the City of Dreadful Night known to J. Thomson and the 1890's had been a very personal kind of nightmare shared and therefore understood only by the two close friends. But when it found its literary expression in Chesterton's story, owing to his idiosyncrasy it became "an extraordinary book written as if the publisher had commissioned him to write something rather like *The Pilgrim's Progress* in the style of the *Pickwick Papers*" as Monsignor Knox has said [In the panegyric preached at Westminster Cathedral, 27 June 1936. Quotation after Maise Ward, *Gilbert Keith Chesterton,* 1958].

If the effect is not Kafka, it is due to the simple truth that Chesterton could not write like Kafka any more than Kafka could write like Chesterton.

But if the exuberant energy of the story seems rather to deny it the title of a nightmare, its structure perfectly confirms it. For the world presented in the story has many features of a dream. Its dreamlike quality is stressed on the very first page of the novel:

> The place was not only pleasant, but perfect, if once he could regard it not as a deception but rather as a dream.

There is a strange, unrealistic atmosphere about the setting of the book which suggests an unusual state of consciousness even before the dream begins. This is how a "strange sunset" is evoked and perceived:

> It looked like the end of the world. All the heaven seemed covered with a quite vivid and palpable plumage; you could only say that the sky was full of feathers, and of feathers that almost brushed the face. Across the great part of the dome they were grey, with the strangest tints of violet and mauve and an unnatural pink or pale green; but towards the west the whole grew past description, transparent and passionate, and the last red-hot plumes of it covered up the sun like something too good to be seen. The whole was so close about the earth as to express nothing but a violent secrecy.

The writer gives this unusual state of consciousness and its characteristic perception of the world to his main character, the poet Gabriel Syme. During his dispute with Lucian Gregory, another poet (and anarchist):

> Once he heard very faintly in some distant street a barrel-organ begin to play, and it seemed to him that his heroic words were moving to a tiny tune from under or beyond the world.

> He stared and talked at the girl's red hair and amused face for what seemed to be a few minutes; and then, feeling that the groups in such a place should mix, rose to his feet. To his astonishment, he discovered the whole garden empty. Everyone had gone long ago, and he went himself with a rather hurried apology. He left with a sense of champagne in his head, which he could not afterwards explain. In the wild events which were to follow this girl had no part at all; he never saw her again until all his tale was over. And yet, in some indescribable way, she kept returning like a motive in music through all his mad adventures like a red thread through those dark and ill-drawn tapestries of the night. For what followed was so improbable that it might well have been a dream.

The last quoted sentence is the author's sly signal that what follows is a dream. It is sly, because usually the reader does not pay proper attention to it; but formally it is as good, or almost as good, a warning of the change of the hero's mode of experience as Langland's words: "I fell asleep. And I dreamt a marvellous dream" or Bunyan's: "And as I slept, I dreamed a Dream".

The return to the day-consciousness is marked about the end of the story with a row of asterisks followed by the words:

> When men in books awake from a vision, they commonly find themselves in some place in which they might have fallen asleep; they yawn in a chair, or lift themselves with bruised limbs from a field. Syme's experience was something much more psychologically strange if there was indeed anything unreal, in the earthly sense, about the things he had gone through. For while he could always remember afterwards that he had swooned before the face of Sunday, he could not remember having ever come to at all. He could only remember that gradually and naturally he knew that he was and had been walking along a country lane with an easy and conversational companion.

The disturbances of memory, so frequently associated with remembering dreams, were accompanied by a feeling of "an unnatural buoyancy in his body and a crystal simplicity in his mind".

In stressing the similarity between older dream-visions in fiction and *The Man Who Was Thursday* we should not, however, close our eyes to the strange lack of sharpness in the transition from Syme's reality to his dream and back. The explanation why Chesterton does not follow Langland's and Bunyan's examples of sincerity and precision, but tricks the reader with: "What followed was so improbable that it might well have been a dream", is simple: he wants the reader accept, for a time, the dream for reality. This is the trick practised in modern times by many writers introducing improbable tales.

Chesterton's ambiguity in the quoted passage which describes awakening is less conventional. Let us try to understand what he means by saying: "Syme's experience was something much more psychologically strange if there was indeed anything unreal, in the earthly sense about the things he had gone through" and when he states that Syme "could not remember ever come to at all".

The answer is that the narrator of the adventures wants them to be both a nightmare in a dream and, at the same time, a real and valid human experience. In this Chesterton not only follows modern psychology, which accepts dreams as real and valid human experiences, but also follows Langland, the author of *The Pearl,* and Bunyan. All these "dreamers" spiritually grow up in the course of their dreams. The same thing happens with Syme, because Chesterton considers his message as of the utmost importance.

There is yet another feature which makes the story like a nightmare and distinguishes it as one of the most original literary creations. It is the fluidity of the presented world. Its world, instead of being merely fantastic or even mad, but one with its own stability, constantly changes into another and yet another world. It reminds one of the croquet ground in *Alice in Wonderland* in which the croquet balls were live hedgehogs, and the mallets live flamingoes and the soldiers had to double themselves up and stand on their hands and feet, to make the arches. All those elements of the game moved of their own will and playing the game was very difficult.

Something like that happens in *The Man Who Was Thursday*. Characters change not only their looks, but even identities, becoming somebody or something else. The setting changes in quick succession in the unending scenes of escape and pursuit and underneath it some disquieting cosmic dimensions are felt. And the story which began in the world of politics, changes into a street carnival rag and frolic to develop into a philosophical garden party to evaporate into total blackness. Its end seems to forget its own beginning.

SUSPICION OF CRIME AND NEED FOR DETECTION

The starting point for action is a suspicion of crime and need for detection. Syme has insinuated himself into the Anarchist Lodge's favour and has been elected Thursday, one of the seven members of the Supreme Council of Anarchy, though he is a philosophical (or ideological) policeman. Both he and his friend and ideological opponent Gregory may fear the consequences of mutual exposure and both are bound by a reciprocal pledge to be silent about each other's ideological stance.

The situation has two aspects. One is philosophical. It is revealed when Syme asks Gregory: "What is it you object to? You want to abolish Government?"

Gregory's answer shows his militant atheism, or rather anti-theism, and moral nihilism:

> To abolish God! . . . We do not only want to upset a few despotisms and police regulations: that sort of anarchism does exist, but it is mere branch of the Nonconformists. We dig deeper and we blow you higher. We wish to deny all those arbitrary distinctions of vice and virtue, honour and treachery, upon which mere rebels base themselves. The silly sentimentalists of the French Revolution talked of the Rights of Man! We hate Rights as we hate Wrongs. We have abolished Right and Wrong.

The other aspect of the situation is political and social. Its dangers are more limited, but also more immediate. Syme has developed a "hatred of modern lawlessness", because he experienced a dynamite outrage which broke windows, made him blind and deaf for a moment, and wounded some people. Anarchist terrorism has become "a huge and pitiless peril" for him. And at the same moment he joined the Anarchist Council, the Czar was to meet the President of France and a bomb attempt was being prepared to kill the two. Crime is being planned and Syme's duty as a policeman is to counteract it, especially as he had been received into the secret police to take part in what his mysterious chief in a dark room had called "the battle of Armageddon" and "the Last Crusade" even at the risk of martyrdom. So the starting point of the adventurous action is the pursuit of criminal terrorists.

But these criminals are criminals raised to at least a second power. "The common criminal is a bad man, but at least he is—says Syme—as it were, a conditional good man. He says that if only a certain obstacle be removed—say a wealthy uncle—he is then prepared to accept the universe and to praise God. He is a reformer, but not an anarchist. He wishes to cleanse the edifice, but not to destroy it. But the evil philosopher is not trying to alter things, but to annihilate them".

Syme the policeman suspects that it is the Anarchist Council of which he has become a member that forms the mind and heart of that all-destructive programme or plan which was revealed to him by Gregory as the ultimate essence of anarchism. The need for detection is created. But at the same time a new motive force interferes with the detective's intention—the impulse of escape and pursuit. Among "the six men who had sworn to destroy the world" seeds of fear and suspicion are sown by Sunday's warning of the presence of a traitor among them. Then Gogol, the pretended Pole with the decidedly Russian name, is exposed as a detective with the same kind of blue card as Syme's. And Sunday suggests that this detection of an enemy may not be the end of the purge.

This suggestion comes home and Syme becomes wary while walking London streets in a snowstorm. He soon finds that he is being pursued by a half-paralytic Professor de Worms and has no doubt left about the matter when the old man chases him like a greyhound. Their mutual confession of being both in the police is one of the turning points in the action of the story. Syme says about Sunday:

> I am afraid of him. Therefore I swear by God
> that I will seek out this man whom I fear until
> I find him, and strike him on the mouth. If heav-
> en were his throne and the earth his footstool,
> I swear that I would pull him down.

Here the idea of detection and the idea of pursuit unite. Henceforth Syme will pursue Sunday in order to detect his mystery. The action of the novel will become a chain of chases in order to detect what is endlessly escaping. Syme's declaration is the more important, because, in the perspective of the final chapters of the novel, his detective activities will continue even if Sunday should turn out to be the lord of heaven and earth.

He is not alone. The professor joins him and the following day in the early morning they surprise the sinister-looking Dr Bull who, without his dark spectacles, is revealed as a harmless young man. He is the third policeman and they plan stopping the anarchist Marquis who was to go to Paris to throw a bomb at the Czar visiting the President of France. Syme wants to stop the Marquis at Calais by engaging him in a duel and his efforts are rewarded at least with a revelation that he fights against a fellow detective.

Each of the chapters of the novel following Gogol's exposure seems to bring a new revelation of reality. In Chapter IX it is revealed that appearances deceive—nobody is what he seems to be. In Chapter X men of the same purpose fight each other and are ready to die doing so. In Chapters XI and XII entitled (from the point of appearances) "The Criminals Chase the Police" and "The Earth in Anarchy," even the friends of the law and order—the peasant, the innkeeper, the rich townsman, and the French colonel—all turn against the bewildered detectives and at last their friend Dr Renard goes so far as to shoot at them.

It seems that each new discovery brings more and more confusion and nonsense in the strife for law and order. In the end the pursued members of the Supreme Council of Anarchy realize that there was no council of this kind and that they were chased by the police and the crowd, because they were taken for anarchists. Here, by the way, Chesterton makes consciously or unconsciously, his greatest point against the lunacy of conspiracy. Conspiracy provokes counter-conspiracy and then nobody knows who is what and against whom. (The same point was made two years earlier by Joseph Conrad in *The Secret Agent*).

But this political point is implied only. The funny and absurd incidents in France are serious not so much because they belong to politics, but because they acquire, increasingly, a solemn, metaphysical or even religious dimension. The "battle" at Lancy has some relation to "the battle of Armageddon" mentioned by the invisible police chief when he had received Syme into his service. Duelling,

Syme thinks that he is fighting the Devil. Later he fights lighting his way in the falling darkness with an ancient lantern with a cross. The shout "The morning star has fallen!" is an obvious allusion to the fall of Lucifer, even though it refers to a friend's apparent betrayal. The six lines quoted from *Dunciad* expressly refer to a cosmic cataclysm in which Chaos and Anarchy begin to reign in universal darkness. They are introduced in a seemingly hopeless moment when "the Earth in Anarchy" makes "the hopeless Inspector" say: "The human being will soon be extinct. We are the last of mankind".

This is not yet the end, though. The five detectives are wiser at least by the discovery that "there never was any Supreme Anarchist Council" and that they are "all a lot of silly policemen looking at each other". The next obvious step is the pursuit of the President. This takes place in Chapters XIII and XIV mostly in London. Sunday jumps down from the hotel balcony and runs away in all possible means of transport, clowning in a wonderful circus parade round London until he soars up in a balloon stolen from the Earl's Court Exhibition.

Behind these farcical externals there is a serious purpose. The pursuit started with the need to find out what Sunday was. "What did it all mean? If they were all harmless officers, what was Sunday? If he had not seized the world, what on earth had he been up to? . . . Whatever else Sunday is, he isn't a blameless citizen". It is, again, the need for investigation, for acting on suspicion and for detection that moves all the six policemen to action.

Sunday's behaviour in their presence only deepens the riddle. He laughs at them and then declares: "I tell you this, that you will have found out the truth of the last tree and the topmost cloud before the truth about me. You will understand the sea and I shall be still a riddle" . . . "Since the beginning of the world all men have hunted me like a wolf—kings and sages, and poets and law-givers, all the churches, and all the philosophers. But I have never been caught yet . . .".

And he sharpens their curiosity by stating: "There's one thing I'll tell you, though, about who I am. I am the man in the dark room, who made you all policemen". This and his escape from the balcony are an irresistible stimulus to the natural policeman. The investigation changes into a chase.

PHILOSOPHY AND THEOLOGY FIND THE ANSWER

The careful reader of the book will observe that ever since Sunday declared himself to be a riddle to all kinds of men, a riddle like the riddle of the tree, the cloud, and the sea—he begins to change from a man into Nature. The policemen following him across the fields of Surrey become "six philosophers" who express their impressions and guesses about his nature. Each man finds Sunday quite different, but all of them compare him to the universe. His back looks brutal and beastlike; his face an archangel's. Syme says: "When I saw him from behind I was certain he was an animal, and when I saw him in front I knew he was a god". "Pan was a god and an animal"—confirms the Professor.

Here Syme identifies "the mystery of Sunday" with "the mystery of the world". At last he sums up his philosophical conclusions in this way: "Shall I tell you the secret of the whole world? It is that we have only known the back of the world. We see everything from behind, and it looks brutal . . . Cannot you see that everything is stopping and hiding a face? If we could only get round in front—".

Once this understanding of the dualism or ambivalence of Nature, and consequently of the world, and consequently of the ecology and existence of man is realized, the balloon carrying Sunday descends and the pursuers become his welcome guests.

The atmosphere changes again with the change of the setting. An old servant in the peaceful twilight of the evening, a white road, six carriages waiting for the guests, a countryhouse in a park which makes each man of them declare "that he could remember this place before he could remember his mother" suggest an unexpected ease and comfort, but also an allegory of coming home after a life full of strife and anxiety. Also in this Chapter XIV, entitled "The Six Philosopher," the Biblical allusions are continued ("Why leap ye, ye high hills?"; "It was like the face of some ancient archangel, judging justly after heroic wars".). Now it is the Bible that "provides" for every guest a role to be played at a fancy dress party that is being prepared and a costume symbolizing one of the Days of Creation according to Genesis.

Chapter XV begins with a pageantry reminiscent of medieval allegories, but instead of the Seven Deadly Sins we meet the Seven Days of Creation seating themselves on stone thrones surrounded with forest and lit by bonfires with cauldrons on them. Dancing proceeds until the fires almost die out, the merry-makers disappear into the house and stars come out. Then Sunday in his white robe sums up his own view of the events. He says:

> Let us remain together a little, we who loved each other so sadly, and have fought so long. I seem to remember only centuries of heroic war, in which you were always heroes—epic on epic, iliad on iliad, and you always brothers in arms. Whether it was but recently (for time is nothing), or at the beginning of the world, I sent you out to war. I sat in the darkness, where there is not any created thing, and to you I was only a voice commanding valour and an unnatural virtue. You heard the voice in the dark, and you never heard it again. The sun in heaven denied it, the earth and sky denied it, all human wisdom denied it. And when I met you in the daylight I denied it myself.

This is a confirmation of Sunday's ambivalence. This is also a timeless presentation of life as an endless struggle of men to keep their human dignity, for Sunday adds: "You did not forget your secret honour, though the whole cosmos turned an engine of torture to tear it out of you".

But then the final question in the investigation of Sunday's mystery is asked "in a harsh voice":

> "Who and what are you"? And the answer is: "I am Sabbath. I am the peace of God."

This answer, instead of pacifying the six, rouses their dissatisfaction in varying degrees. Only one of them says: "I understand nothing, but I am happy". The strongest objection and criticism comes from the Secretary:

> I know what you mean . . . and it is exactly that that I cannot forgive you . . . I am not reconciled. If you were the man in the dark room, why were you also Sunday, an offence to the sunlight? If you were from the first our father and our friend, why were you also our greatest enemy? We wept, we fled in terror; the iron entered our souls—and you are the peace of God! Oh, I can forgive God His anger, though it destroyed nations; but I cannot forgive Him His peace.

Here the encounter with Nature, which developed out of the encounter with Sunday the man, rises to the level of an encounter with God himself responsible for the creation of the universe and the condition of man. This is the moment for the only cosmic anarchist to appear—for Gregory. And he impersonates Satan. This is explicitly stated by Dr Bull who says: "Now there was a day when the sons of God came to present themselves before the Lord, and Satan came also among them". This is an exact quotation from *The Book of Job* in the Authorized Version. In its context the title of this last chapter of the novel—"The Accuser" and its whole content acquire a decidedly Biblical significance. *The Book of Job* is a book about the suffering of the blameless man, which had been provoked by Satan's contention that man serves God only for something that he receives. Job, the sufferer afflicted by Satan through the permission of God, comes victorious out of the trial, but his protest against the obvious injustice of his lot sounds very much like the Secretary's protest against the peace of God while people are suffering.

"Man is born unto trouble, as the sparks fly upward . . . Man, that is born of a woman is of few days, and full of trouble. He comes forth like a flower and is cut down"—these are the most familiar quotations from the Book and they are in tune with the Secretary's accusation of complacency.

But the Accuser, who says about himself "I am a destroyer" has something more to say.

The thick texture of the novel does not allow us to analyse it on one level at a time so this is the moment in which the reader ought to be reminded that all that has so far happened and all that is to come is the logical development of the question of who and what Sunday is and whether he is a blameless person. By this time he has turned into Nature and the Peace of God crowning the Creation. The investigation of his identity seems at an end, but not the judgement on him. Gregory will act as the Accuser and Syme as the Defence.

But, by an ironic twist, what in the Bible was the congregation of the Sons of God sitting in judgement over the tried man and what has already turned into a trial of God by men now is becoming trial of God and man prosecuted by Satan.

The essence of Satan's accusations seems to be an anti-

Establishment attitude which is much more popular today than it was in Chesterton's times:

> You are the people in power! You are the police—the great fat, smiling men in blue and buttons! You are the Law . . . The only crime of the Government is that it governs. The unpardonable sin of supreme power is that it is supreme. I do not curse you for being cruel. I do not curse you (though I might) for being kind. I curse you for being safe!

This supremely anarchist attitude is pervaded by hatred which may be its root ("I would destroy the world if I could").

Syme springs to the defence of man. He has received sudden illumination. What is, he asserts, has been created in justice. Each thing on the earth has to war against each other thing and against the whole universe, alone, so that each thing that obeys law may have "the glory and isolation of the anarchist". Objectively, the universe is a benevolent conspiracy, but to a subjective view it presents a frightening exterior. The individual feels isolated, he fears and suffers, because all this is essential in gaining the glory, or the dignity of man through self-reliance and courage.

This is how Syme defends man and the meaning of the world. But at the same time he realizes that Sunday, hidden behind the scenes and knowing the dual nature of existence, may not have suffered as all others had done.

He asks "in a dreadful voice", his final question in the process of detecting who and what Sunday is: "Have you ever suffered?"

Then, again, a transformation of the nightmare world takes place. Sunday's face grows "to an awful size", "filling the whole sky", and disappears in blackness. From behind Nature, which has disappeared "a distant voice saying a commonplace text" is heard: "Can ye drink of the cup that I drink of?"

The text is Christ's words from St Mark's gospel. Like its paraphrase in St Matthew, it refers to suffering and death by crucifixion, as is obvious from the scene of Jesus' agony in the garden of Gethsemane, in which the cup is mentioned again.

Thus Syme's tremendous question is not answered by Nature, but by Christ who is, according to Christian faith, both God and a Man. And being, as a man, subject to all the conditions of Nature and the miseries of human social and political history, suffered like his creation, though sinless and blameless.

That this is the correct way of interpreting the final scene in the dream, has been confirmed by Chesterton when he said [in an interview quoted by Maise Word]:

> There is a phrase used at the end, spoken by Sunday: "Can ye drink from the cup that I drink of?" which seems to mean that Sunday is God. That is the only serious note in the book, the face of Sunday changes, you tear off the mask of Nature and you find God.

What follows in the story is Syme's awakening and meeting Gregory's graceful sister cutting lilac before breakfast in her garden. This is a simple closing part of a frame-story which has no special significance, so we may leave it and return to the dream-vision.

HOW THE UNITY OF COMPOSITION WAS ACHIEVED

It is not made of such stuff as dreams are made of, but rather of many materials such as Chesterton's experience of London life in the beginning of the twentieth century and of at least one visit to France; his walking discussions with Edmund C. Bentley; their fears of political and antitheistic Anarchism; their doubts about the sense and justice of the universe; *The Book of Genesis, The Book of Job,* and the *Gospels;* and some minor literary echoes, including, which is significant, *Alice in Wonderland* and allegorical dream-visions of English religious literature.

If we ask how from this hotchpotch any literary composition could be made, the answer is to be found in Chesterton's *Autobiography:*

> I . . . was oppressed with the metaphysical nightmare of negations about mind and matter, with the morbid imagery of evil, with the burden of my own mysterious brain and body; but by this time I was in revolt against them; and trying to construct a healthier conception of cosmic life, even if it were one that should err on the side of health. I even called myself an optimist, because I was so horribly near to being a pessimist . . . All this part of the process was afterwards thrown up in the very formless form of a piece of fiction called *The Man Who Was Thursday.*

The urge to overcome late Victorian pessimism found its springboard for telling a story in the idea of investigating the mystery of existence and in Chesterton's mind this investigation meant a story of detection without crime. He has stated this in the following passage [of the interview quoted by Ward]:

> In an ordinary detective tale the investigator discovers that some amiable-looking fellow who subscribes to all the charities, and is fond of animals, has murdered his grandmother, or is a trigamist. I thought it would be fun to make the tearing away of menacing masks reveal benevolence.

Intended as a story of detection, *The Man Who Was Thursday* began, like Conrad's *The Secret Agent,* as a novel (or a burlesque of it) of political crime, in which the investigation was to be conducted by a growing number of secret policemen. This literary form it preserves until the moment when only Sunday is left as an embodied mystery of conspiracy. His escape and the chase after him as a man develop into a riotous carnival which ends with his flight in a balloon. Then, in the natural (instead of the social) setting the detectives change into philosophers, because they are members of "a special corps of . . . policemen who are also philosophers", but the detection still goes on. Sunday's behaviour also changes, but the investigation of Sunday's character and the nature of the world continues.

With the change of the men's dirty and tattered clothes for the gorgeous robes of the Seven Days or Sons of God the search for the truth behind Sunday leaves general philosophical grounds and moves towards theology or Christian philosophy, because only a philosophy based on the assumption that God has become a man can make its arguments valid. Now the predicament of man is a moral and religious problem and Gregory becomes Satan who is the Archanarchist and the Accuser of men and God. The voice of Christ solves the mystery of suffering in human existence, but only for those who accept the Christian conception of God-Man and his fellowship with men in suffering and glory. That is why Chesterton shifts from philosophy to theology.

Here the investigation ends, because the mystery has been partly detected and partly revealed.

Chesterton has called the process of detection of the nonexistent, but strongly suspected cosmic crime "the groping and guesswork philosophy of the story". And, appropriately, the story assumed the form of a nightmare with the characteristic gradual transformation of the initial presented world into a series of differing succeeding worlds. But two constant factors make it a consistent and a valid book. One of them is the process of detection as the principle organizing its plot from the beginning to the end. The other is the fact that this detective "groping and guesswork" is a "philosophy".

To put in other words, *The Man Who Was Thursday* is a novel of ideas—a clash of two opposing philosophies of life: Anarchic Nihilism, which wishes to destroy everything, and Christianity which wants to fight evil, and thus to preserve creation.

The author of the book did not start from a previously assumed philosophical position. That is why the novel is not a mere illustration of a ready-made thesis, but a real debate, just like some other novels of ideas written at the beginning of the twentieth century by H. G. Wells and A. Huxley. But at the same time it is a mystery novel with a deepening mystery and therefore one in which simple police detection must give place to other kinds of investigation. As a novel of ideas and a mystery novel it is distinctly Chestertonian. It operates with allegory and symbol and combines detection with philosophy. This combination was further developed in the detective stories of Father Brown. It is unique or rare in presenting a successful detection without crime.

Michael Coren   (essay date 1989)

SOURCE: "The Man Who Was Orthodox," in *Gilbert: The Man Who Was G. K. Chesterton*, Jonathan Cape, 1989, pp. 167-89.

[*It the following excerpt, Coren provides an overview of* The Man Who Was Thursday.]

Gilbert's second novel, a work which he was unsure of and not satisfied with, appeared in the February of 1908. Subtitled 'A Nightmare', as *The Man Who Was Thursday* it received more recognition than any of his previous writings. He dedicated it to Edmund Clerihew Bentley, with an introductory poem

> A cloud was on the mind of men,
>   And wailing went the weather,
> Yea, a sick cloud upon the soul
>   When we were boys together.
> Science announced nonentity
>   And art admired decay;
> The world was old and ended:
>   But you and I were gay;
> Round us in antic order
>   Crippled vices came—
> Lust that had lost its laughter,
>   Fear that had lost its shame.
> Like the white lock of Whistler,
>   That lit our aimless gloom,
> Men showed their own white feather
>   As proudly as a plume.
> Life was a fly that faded,
>   And death a drone that stung;
> The world was very old indeed
>   When you and I were young.
> They twisted even decent sin
>   To shapes not to be named:
> Men were ashamed of honour;
>   But we were not ashamed.
> Weak if we were and foolish
>   Not thus we failed, not thus;
> When that black Baal blocked the heavens
>   He had no hymns from us.
> Children we were—our forts of sand
>   Were even as weak as we,
> High as they went we piled them up
>   To break that bitter sea.
> Fools as we were in motley,
>   All jangling and absurd,
> When all church bells were silent
>   Our cap and bells were heard.
>
> Not all unhelped we held the fort,
>   Our tiny flags unfurled;
> Some giants laboured in that cloud
>   To lift it from the world.
> I find again the book we found,
>   I feel the hour that flings
> Far out of fish-shaped Paumanok
>   Some cry of cleaner things;
> And the Green Carnation withered,
>   As in forest fires that pass,
> Roared in the wind of all the world
>   Ten million leaves of grass;
> Or sane and sweet and sudden as
>   A bird sings in the rain—
> Truth out of Tusitala spoke
>   And pleasure out of pain.
> Yea, cool and clear and sudden as
>   A bird sings in the grey.
> Dunedin to Samoa spoke,
>   And darkness unto day.
> But we were young; we lived to see
>   God break their bitter charms
> God and the good Republic
>   Come riding back in arms;
> We have seen the City of Mansoul,
>   Even as it rocked, relieved—
> Blessed are they who did not see,
>   But being blind, believed.

This is a tale of those old fears,
  Even of those emptied hells,
And none but you shall understand
  The true thing that it tells—
Of what colossal gods of shame
  Could cow men and yet crash,
Of what huge devils hid the stars,
  Yet fell at a pistol flash.
The doubts that were so plain to chase,
  So dreadful to withstand—
Oh, who shall understand but you;
  Yea, who shall understand?
The doubts that drove us through the night
  As we two talked amain,
And day had broken on the streets
  E'er it broke upon the brain.
Between us, by the peace of God,
  Such truth can now be told;
Yea, there is strength in striking root,
  And good in growing old.
We have found common things at last,
  And marriage and a creed,
And I may safely write it now,
  And you may safely read.

The intent of the novel was set down quite clearly in the poem: an attack upon the misconceptions of fashionable decadence, a defence of the values which Gilbert, his friends and—so he thought—his God cherished so dearly. He employs the character of Gabriel Syme, a romantic young poet who is also an undercover agent working for the British police. Syme's experiences throughout the book are based in the twilight area of the nightmare, and we are never sure where reality and dream mingle or become one. Syme passes himself off as an anarchist, defeating a real anarchist poet at his own game of distorted honour and bluff. As he walks through a haunting area of London, which is Bedford Park by all appearances, he learns more of an anarchist plot and the extent of the world conspiracy. The hub of the crime is the Central Anarchist Council, consisting of seven members who are named after a day of the week. By extreme demonstrations of courage and a calm wit Syme joins their ranks. He meets all the council members, discovering that they are undercover agents working for the police, mistrusting each other until the disguises are lifted. Only one member, the President, Sunday, is loyal and true to his cause. He is more than a man, more than a monster

> The form it took was a childish and yet hateful fancy. As he walked across the inner room towards the balcony, the large face of Sunday grew larger and larger; and Syme was gripped with a fear that when he was quite close the face would be too big to be possible, and that he would scream aloud. He remembered that as a child he would not look at the mask of Memnon in the British Museum, because it was a face, and so large.

When the surreptitious detectives join together and chase President Sunday they undergo a series of outlandish adventures, eventually tracking the man who represents so much evil to his own garden. When confronted face-to-face their sworn enemy is exposed as the Chief of Police who originally gave them their orders, explaining why he was always hidden in darkness when he addressed his men. He is questioned but will only reply 'I am the Sabbath. I am the peace of God.'

Syme, the only character with any depth in the book, responds to Sunday's actions and to the appearance at the end of the novel of the real anarchist poet who he had hoodwinked earlier, with a fit of revelation; he shakes from head to foot

> 'I see everything,' he cried, 'everything that there is. Why does each thing on the earth war against each other thing? Why does each small thing in the world have to fight against the world itself? Why does a fly have to fight the whole universe? Why does a dandelion have to fight the whole universe? For the same reason that I had to be alone in the dreadful Council of the Days. So that each thing that obeys law may have the glory and isolation of the anarchist. So that each man fighting for order may be as brave and good a man as the dynamiter. So that the real lie of Satan may be flung back in the face of this blasphemer, so that by tears and torture we may earn the right to say to this man, "You lie!" No agonies can be too great to buy the right to say to this accuser, "We also have suffered."

> 'It is not true that we have never been broken. We have been broken upon the wheel. It is not true that we have never descended from these thrones. We have descended into hell. We were complaining of unforgettable miseries even at the very moment when this man entered insolently to accuse us of happiness. I repel the slander; we have not been happy. I can answer for every one of the great guards of Law whom he has accused. At least—'

> He had turned his eyes so as to see suddenly the great face of Sunday, which wore a strange smile.

> 'Have you,' he cried in a dreadful voice, 'have you ever suffered?'

> As he gazed, the great face grew to an awful size, grew larger than the colossal mask of Memnon, which had made him scream as a child. It grew larger and larger, filling the whole sky; then everything went black. Only in the blackness before it entirely destroyed his brain he seemed to hear a distant voice saying a commonplace text that he had heard somewhere, 'Can ye drink of the cup that I drink of?'

Gilbert's use of dream symbolism was a new departure for him, without doubt having its roots in the painful years of his lonely period, when his sleep as well as his waking hours were filled with nightmare visions which seemed never to leave him. He was to play down some of the theological meaning in the book, anxious that the story and the moral should stand on their own merits. He wrote that the tale was of a nightmare of things, 'not as they are, but as they seemed to the half-pessimist of the '90s . . . ' In an interview published many years later, when *The Man Who Was Thursday* was adapted for the stage, he spoke of an ordinary detective tale and the tearing away of menacing masks.

Associated with that merely fantastic notion was the one that there is actually a lot of good to be discovered in unlikely places, and that we who are fighting each other may be all fighting on the right side. I think it is quite true that it is just as well we do not, while the fight is on, know all about each other; the soul must be solitary, or there would be no place for courage.

A rather amusing thing was said by Father Knox on this point. He said that he should have regarded the book as entirely pantheist and as preaching that there was good in everything if it had not been for the introduction of the one real anarchist and pessimist. But he was prepared to wager that if the book survives for a hundred years—which it won't—they will say that the real anarchist was put in afterwards by the priests.

But, though I was more foggy about ethical and theological matters than I am now, I was quite clear on that issue; that there was a final adversary, and that you might find a man resolutely turned away from goodness.

People have asked me whom I meant by Sunday. Well, I think, on the whole, and allowing for the fact that he is a person in a tale—I think you can take him to stand for Nature as distinguished from God. Huge, boisterous, full of vitality, dancing with a hundred legs, bright with the glare of the sun, and at first sight, somewhat regardless of us and our desires . . .

FURTHER READING

Carter, Huntley. "Chesterton on the Moscow Stage." *The Outlook* LIII, No. 1362 (8 March 1924): 156-57.
   Sees in the Moscow Kamerny Theatre adaptation of *The Man Who Was Thursday* a display of the dual nature of the Chestertonian hero—as both collectivist and individualist.

Review of *The Man Who Was Thursday*. *The Dublin Review* 143, No. 286 (July 1908): 190-91.
   Calls *The Man Who Was Thursday* "a very fine parable," but faults Chesterton's lack of restraint in the work.

Youngberg, Karin. "Job and the Gargoyles: A Study of *The Man Who Was Thursday*." *The Chesterton Review* II, No. 2 (Spring-Summer 1976): 240-52.
   Analysis of *The Man Who Was Thursday* that concentrates on the work as a piece of detective fiction concerned with paradox and "the riddles of life." Summarizes by calling the novel "a fantasy-search for meaning in the modern world."

Additional coverage of Chesterton's life and career is contained in the following sources published by Gale Research: *Contemporary Authors*, Vols. 104, 132; *Concise Dictionary of British Literary Biography*, 1914-1945; *Dictionary of Literary Biography*, Vols. 10, 19, 34, 70, 98, 149; *Major Twentieth-Century Writers*; *Something about the Author*, Vol. 27; *Short Story Criticism*, Vol. 1; *Twentieth-Century Literary Criticism*, Vols. 1, 6.

Kenneth Grahame

1859-1932

Scottish novelist, short story writer, and essayist.

INTRODUCTION

Grahame established an early reputation as a writer with his short stories about children and their imaginative worlds, but he is remembered by succeeding generations primarily for the novel *The Wind in the Willows*. This animal fantasy has proven highly popular with readers of all ages since its initial publication in 1908 and has received increasing critical attention for its satire, its social commentary, and its treatment of rural and Arcadian themes.

Biographical Information

Grahame was born in Edinburgh and spent the first five years of his life with his family in Scotland. Following the death of his mother in 1864, Grahame's father sent him and his siblings to live with their maternal grandmother in Cookham Dene, Berkshire, on the Thames, and it was here that Grahame first reveled in a new-found world of English meadow and riverbank. In 1866, however, Grahame was removed from this pastoral setting when his grandmother was forced to move far from the Thames. The same year an attempt to reunite the Grahame children with their father—now suffering from the advanced stages of alcoholism—proved futile. Grahame subsequently attended St. Edward's School, Oxford, from 1868 through 1876, and although he hoped to enter the University, his uncle, upon whom he was financially dependent, forced him into a clerkship with the Bank of England. Grahame remained with the bank while pursuing writing as an avocation; a collection of essays attracted some notice, but his short stories, later collected in *The Golden Age* and *Dream Days*, brought him much greater popularity. Grahame married Elspeth Thomson in 1899, and the couple had one child, Alastair. The bedtime stories Grahame invented for his son eventually grew into his masterpiece, *The Wind in the Willows*, a novel which recreated the idyllic world the author himself had glimpsed as a child. Following the publication of *The Wind in the Willows*, Grahame traveled widely but wrote very little. He died in Pangbourne, England, in 1932.

Major Works

Grahame's first articles were published anonymously as early as 1888, but subsequent works appeared under his own name in such periodicals as the conservative *National Observer* and the decadent *Yellow Book*. The collection *Pagan Papers* drew mixed reviews, but when Grahame extracted the book's introduction and its five short stories and added a dozen more, publishing them under the title *The Golden Age*, he secured his reputation. This volume and its sequel, *Dream Days*, displayed an unsentimental view of childhood and a wry, unflattering view of adulthood; while the children in the stories thrive by indulging their imaginations, the adults—known as Olympians—are preoccupied by mundane matters. Although *The Wind in the Willows* first dismayed readers and critics who expected more stories about children, the episodic novel about a band of animals—Mole, Toad, Badger, and Rat—who live along a riverbank near the Wild Wood has eclipsed Grahame's other works in popularity.

Critical Reception

While Grahame's short story collections have receded into obscurity over the years, *The Wind in the Willows* continues to enjoy a huge following. Young readers are enticed by its sharply drawn animal characters, gentle satire, and whimsical plot. Adults, on the other hand, find a more complex work which parodies traditional literary forms, celebrates the natural world while making full use of its symbolic potential, mourns the passing of English rural life, and acknowledges a yearning for an archetypal Golden Age.

PRINCIPAL WORKS

Pagan Papers (essays) 1893
The Golden Age (short stories) 1895
Dream Days (short stories) 1898
The Headswoman (short story) 1898
The Wind in the Willows (novel) 1908
The Cambridge Book of Poetry for Children [editor] (poetry) 1916; revised edition, 1932
Fun o' the Fair (essay) 1929
The Reluctant Dragon (fairy tale) 1938
First Whisper of 'The Wind in the Willows' (short story and letters) 1944
Bertie's Escapade (short story) 1949

CRITICISM

A. A. Milne (essay date 1920)

SOURCE: "A Household Book," in *Not That It Matters*, E. P. Dutton & Co., Inc., 1920, pp. 84-8.

[*In the following essay, Milne expresses his enthusiasm for Grahame's* The Wind in the Willows.]

Once on a time I discovered Samuel Butler; not the other two, but the one who wrote *The Way of All Flesh,* the second-best novel in the English language. I say the second-best, so that, if you remind me of *Tom Jones* or *The Mayor of Casterbridge* or any other that you fancy, I can say that, of course, that one is the best. Well, I discovered him, just as Voltaire discovered Habakkuk, or your little boy discovered Shakespeare the other day, and I committed my discovery to the world in two glowing articles. Not unnaturally the world remained unmoved. It knew all about Samuel Butler.

Last week I discovered a Frenchman, Claude Tillier, who wrote in the early part of last century a book called *Mon Oncle Benjamin,* which may be freely translated *My Uncle Benjamin.* (I read it in the translation.) Eager as I am to be lyrical about it, I shall refrain. I think that I am probably safer with Tillier than with Butler, but I dare not risk it. The thought of your scorn at my previous ignorance of the world-famous Tillier, your amused contempt because I have only just succeeded in borrowing the classic upon which you were brought up, this is too much for me. Let us say no more about it. Claude Tillier—who has not heard of Claude Tillier? *Mon Oncle Benjamin*—who has not read it, in French or (as I did) in American? Let us pass on to another book.

For I am going to speak of another discovery; of a book which should be a classic, but is not; of a book of which nobody has heard unless through me. It was published some twelve years ago, the last-published book of a well-known writer. When I tell you his name you will say, "Oh yes! I *love* his books!" and you will mention *So-and-So,* and its equally famous sequel *Such-and-Such.* But when I ask you if you have read *my* book, you will profess surprise, and say that you have never heard of it. "Is it as good as *So-and-So* and *Such-and-Such?*" you will ask, hardly believing that this could be possible. "Much better," I shall reply—and there, if these things were arranged properly, would be another ten per cent. in my pocket. But, believe me, I shall be quite content with your gratitude.

Well, the writer of my book is Kenneth Grahame. You have heard of him? Good, I thought so. The books you have read are *The Golden Age* and *Dream Days.* Am I not right? Thank you. But the book you have not read—my book—is *The Wind in the Willows.* Am I not right again? Ah, I was afraid so.

The reason why I knew you had not read it is the reason why I call it "my" book. For the last ten or twelve years I have been recommending it. Usually I speak about it at my first meeting with a stranger. It is my opening remark, just as yours is something futile about the weather. If I don't get it in at the beginning, I squeeze it in at the end. The stranger has got to have it some time. Should I ever find myself in the dock, and one never knows, my answer to the question whether I had anything to say would be, "Well, my lord, if I might just recommend a book to the jury before leaving." Mr. Justice Darling would probably pretend that he had read it, but he wouldn't deceive me.

For one cannot recommend a book to all the hundreds of people whom one has met in ten years without discovering whether it is well known or not. It is the amazing truth that none of those hundreds had heard of *The Wind in the Willows* until I told them about it. Some of them had never heard of Kenneth Grahame; well, one did not have to meet them again, and it takes all sorts to make a world. But most of them were in your position—great admirers of the author and his two earlier famous books, but ignorant thereafter. I had their promise before they left me, and waited confidently for their gratitude. No doubt they also spread the good news in their turn, and it is just possible that it reached you in this way, but it was to me, none the less, that your thanks were due. For instance, you may have noticed a couple of casual references to it, as if it were a classic known to all, in a famous novel published last year. It was I who introduced that novelist to it six months before. Indeed, I feel sometimes that it was I who wrote *The Wind in the Willows,* and recommended it to Kenneth Grahame . . . but perhaps I am wrong here, for I have not the pleasure of his acquaintance. Nor, as I have already lamented, am I financially interested in its sale, an explanation which suspicious strangers require from me sometimes.

I shall not describe the book, for no description would help it. But I shall just say this: that it is what I call a Household Book. By a Household Book I mean a book which everybody in the household loves and quotes continually ever afterwards; a book which is read aloud to every new guest, and is regarded as the touchstone of his worth. But it is a book which makes you feel that, though everybody in the house loves it, it is only you who really appreciate it at its true value, and that the others are scarcely worthy of it. It is obvious, you persuade yourself, that the author was thinking of you when he wrote it. "I hope this will please Jones," were his final words, as he laid down his pen.

Well, of course, you will order the book at once. But I must give you one word of warning. When you sit down to it, don't be so ridiculous as to suppose that you are sitting in judgment on my taste, still less on the genius of Kenneth Grahame. You are merely sitting in judgment on yourself. . . . You may be worthy; I do not know. But it is you who are on trial.

Geraldine D. Poss   (essay date 1975)

SOURCE: "An Epic in Arcadia: The Pastoral World of *The Wind in the Willows,*" in *Children's Literature: Annual of the Modern Language Association Seminar on Children's Literature and The Children's Literature Association,* Vol. 4, 1975, pp. 80-90.

[*In the following essay, Poss examines pastoral themes in* The Wind in the Willows.]

Throughout Kenneth Grahame's two collections of short stories, *The Golden Age* and *Dream Days,* his narrator writes fondly of the romantic characters that he, his brothers, and his sisters read about during their childhood. The children liked to choose roles and act out the Arthurian romances, and on the particular day described below, Harold, the youngest boy, seized the occasion of his oldest brother's absence to be Sir Lancelot. Charlotte insisted on being Tristram, and the narrator, who was more inclined that day to dream than to act, accepted a subordinate role without protest:

> "I don't care," I said: "I'll be anything. I'll be Sir Kay. Come on!"
>
> Then once more in this country's story the mail-clad knights paced through the greenwood shaw, questing adventure, redressing wrong; and bandits, five to one, broke and fled discomfited to their caves. Once again were damsels rescued, dragons disembowelled, and giants, in every corner of the orchard, deprived of their already superfluous number of heads. . . . The varying fortune of the day swung doubtful—now on this side, now on that; till at last Lancelot, grim and great, thrusting through the press, unhorsed Sir Tristram (an easy task), and bestrode her, threatening doom; while the Cornish knight, forgetting hard-won fame of old, cried piteously, "You're hurting me, I tell you! and you're tearing my frock!"

[**"Alarums and Excursions"**]

The nostalgia, mock-heroism, and affection expressed in this passage are typical of Grahame's attitude toward romance. He equates the innocence of the children with its ideal world and, to the extent that both are irretrievable, the equation is valid. But he is also aware that the worlds of Homer and Malory are fallen; heroes need villains in order to demonstrate their valor. And he knows that it is only through the uncritical eyes of childhood that the heroic world can truly seem Utopian. For Grahame, the innocent, green world of Arcadia is by far the more appealing, and from time to time, quite casually, in the short stories, he allows us a glimpse of it as it was perceived by the uncomprehending child. Though the Arcadian vision remains intermittent and basically undeveloped in the stories, we can find in them the elements—both positive and negative—that would eventually lead Grahame to fashion the sweet epic in Arcadia that exists in *The Wind in the Willows*.

"The Roman Road," another story in *The Golden Age*, outlines the Arcadian alternative at its most poignant and melancholy. The narrator opens by relating how on a day "when things were very black within" he took a walk along a road which he felt might truly, as the proverb promised, lead to Rome. He meets an artist who, by some coincidence, claims to spend half his year there, and the little boy begins asking questions about the city. As the conversation develops, it becomes evident that the place they are discussing is a creation of fantasy only, and that its inhabitants are those people who have for some reason had to leave the world of poor, working mortals:

> "Well, there's Lancelot," I went on. "The book says he died, but it never seemed to read right, somehow. He just went away, like Arthur. And Crusoe, when he got tired of wearing clothes and being respectable. And all the nice men in the stories who don't marry the Princess, 'cos only one man ever gets married in a book, you know. They'll be there!"

"And the men who never come off," he said, "who try like the rest, but get knocked out, or somehow miss,—or break down or get bowled over in the *mêlée*,—and get no Princess, nor even a second-class kingdom,—some of them'll be there, I hope?"

The world which they envision is one which simply ignores death, women, and pressure to achieve. Rejecting the idea of his death, the little boy includes Lancelot, but it is clearly with the others, the gentle folk who never made it as heroes, that the adult narrator has the greatest affinity. And perhaps such types struck a respondent chord in that hero-worshipping little boy too, who so easily bypassed Arthur and Gawain to slip into the subsidiary role of Sir Kay. If we hear a wistful note here, about not getting the princess and fighting the dragons, we sense relief too, for there is something foolish and even vaguely repellent to the writer in all that activity, and he can imagine a much more satisfactory world, without the "alarums and excursions." His "reluctant dragon," a sensible spokesman for pacifism, elsewhere explains to the earnest and perplexed St. George why he will not participate in a contest:

> "Believe me, St. George," [he says]. "There's nobody in the world I'd sooner oblige than you and this young gentleman here. But the whole thing's nonsense, and conventionality, and popular thick-headedness. There's absolutely nothing to fight about from beginning to end. And anyhow I'm not going to, so that settles it!"

[*The Reluctant Dragon*]

What the dragon seeks, and what finally moves him to agree to fight and succumb on the third charge, is a chance to socialize with the villagers, narrow-minded though they may be, and to find a sympathetic audience for his poetry.

If only one man can win the princess, it seems implicit in the little boy's statement that he did not expect—nor perhaps want—to be that man. The narrator, and by inference Grahame, reveals his ambivalence about women throughout his essays, in the distaste he evinces for the typical female behavior of his older sister Selina and for the tendencies he occasionally notes in his younger sister Charlotte to follow in her footsteps—even though the little girl was still smart enough in *The Golden Age* to want to be Tristram rather than Iseult. In **"The Finding of the Princess,"** another essay in that volume, Grahame approaches the issue with his characteristic charm and indirectness, reflecting upon the subject with perhaps as much light as he was willing to give it.

By way of contrast with its title, and to establish conditions existing in his own family circle at the time of the incident, the story opens with a discussion of toothbrushes. The narrator muses on the reasons why his sisters received them before he and his brothers: "why, we boys could never rightly understand, except that it was part and parcel of a system of studied favouritism on behalf of creatures both physically inferior and (as shown by a fondness for tale-bearing) of weaker mental fibre." With this observation as a prelude, the story then moves to the child's romance. He is walking alone through a wood which leads to a garden. All his literary experience tells him that it is in such places that princesses are found, and notwithstanding his disdain for his sisters, he approaches hopefully:

> Conditions declared her presence patently as trumpets; without this centre such surrounding could not exist. . . . There, if anywhere, she should be enshrined. Instinct, and some knowledge of the habits of princesses, triumphed; for (indeed) there She was! In no tranced repose, however, but laughingly, struggling to disengage her hand from the grasp of a grown-up man who occupied the marble bench with her.

The man asks amiably where he "sprang from"; he replies that he "came up stream" in search of the princess, and then adds: " 'But she's wide awake, so I suppose somebody kissed her.' This very natural deduction moved the grown-up man to laughter; but the Princess, turning red and jumping up, declared that it was time for lunch." Indulging his own whimsy, the young man dubs him "water baby," and invites him to stay for the meal. Thus, the little boy is able to sustain his fantasy through the afternoon. When he finally leaves the couple, at their gentle suggestion, the man gives him two half-crowns, "for the other water babies," and the princess gives him a kiss. The story ends as the child drifts into a pleasant sleep, filled with dreams of this kiss. But the narrator notes that at the time he was actually more affected by the man's generosity, which he described (no pun, I think, intended) as a "crowning mark of friendship." This is understandable: a gift not for oneself but for one's friends is a gesture of regard and affection much easier to accept gracefully than an inevitably embarrassing kiss. But the judgment also suggests that the magic the child had tried so hard to attach to his real princess ultimately failed him. She was not as satisfying as the dream into which he finally incorporated her. Throughout the essay the reader can sense this contrast between the romance the little boy is trying to cast and the good-natured yet necessarily limited flesh-and-blood characters who are being called up on to fill the roles, careless of their place in history and the eyes of the chronicler upon them. From the very start the scene was wrong; the princess was awake, and maybe just a bit too awkward and embarrassed herself. How much more beautiful it would have been had she been asleep.

Heroism, heterosexual love, and death—all are approached gingerly, with occasional humor and gentle irony, in the stories of the 1890's. But a decade later, in *The Wind in the Willows,* Grahame finally develops a golden age of his own imagining rather than Malory's, and the ambivalence, is, in his own way, resolved. The ideal world that blossoms in his novel is like the world at the end of the Roman Road. It is an unpressured world of good-natured fellows who eschew nonsensical fighting. And as for the princess, no one need worry about competing for her, or living with her once she has awakened, for she is simply not there. What remains is an Arcadian world bounded by a lovely river, a Wild Wood that really threatens no evil, and a Wide World that one need never bother about at all. Through his book Grahame weaves the gentler trappings of epic, dividing it into a classical

twelve chapters, but omitting from the work all aspects of the heroic life that might cause strife and pain and eventually death.

The book opens, in the epic manner, with a statement of theme: it is to be about the "spirit of divine discontent and longing," a spirit so strong in spring that it reaches to the "dark and lowly little house" of the domestic Mole, luring him out in search of some gentle adventure. Later this same spirit draws him back home, if only for a visit, and this we recognize as the epic pattern in little: the journey out and the journey back. As in picture books, it is diminutive and relatively safe, because it is a journey within an innocent pastoral milieu. At his most heroic, the childlike Mole must make his necessary passage to the Wild Wood, and the Rat must strap on his guns to follow him, but this too quickly leads to warmth and comfort and piles of buttered toast. The Rat is there to protect the Mole, the Badger to protect them both, and the ubiquitous Friend and Helper ultimately to protect them all.

With his creation of the Friend and Helper, Grahame has neatly seized control of the gods, scaling another epic problem down to comfortable size. In "The Olympians," prefaced to *The Golden Age,* he had characterized adults by their power to affect lives with their foolishness and petulance, to blame children for the wrong offenses, and to ignore those pleasures that beckoned so obviously to the young. The Homeric gods stood in a similar relation to men, exacting vengeance, playing favorites, and generating continual concern about sacrifice, devotion, and protocol. Such Olympians, whether as adults or gods, have been eliminated from *The Wind in the Willows.* The animals in Grahame's ideal world are truly innocent, and so they are spared the anguish that questioning, knowledge, and the inevitable desire to influence their fate would produce. What they have, instead, is the benign, all but unsexed figure of Pan, who sits at the center of the book, but demands no recognition and no offerings. And unlike the Olympian gods, who were always leaving awesome and intimidating signs of their presence—whether by dazzling men with their beauty, or by metamorphosing into birds at the ends of their earthly visits—Pan bestows the gift of forgetfulness, asking no thanks for his benevolence. Dimly, in the seventh chapter, the Rat can hear this song: "*Lest the awe should dwell—And turn your frolic to fret—You shall look on my power at the helping hour—But then you shall forget*". And as he and the Mole move closer, the Rat says finally: "This time, at last, it is the real, the unmistakable thing, simple—passionate—perfect." But he cannot repeat it and shortly falls asleep, as the song fades into the gentle reed talk produced by the wind in the willows.

If gods and religion are at the center of the strife that plagues the Homeric world, women are the traditional, if unwitting, agents. Odysseus lays the blame for the Trojan War squarely on Helen's shoulders, and, contemplating the fate of Agamemnon, he declares: "Alas! . . . All-seeing Zeus has indeed proved himself a relentless foe to the House of Atreus, and from the beginning he has worked his will through women's crooked ways. It was for Helen's sake that so many of us met our deaths, and it was Clytaemnestra who hatched the plot against her absent lord." Even Penelope and a reformed and penitent Helen cannot adequately redress the balance. So Grahame, who could never find a lady to match the sleeping princess of romance, and who was evidently unhappy in his own marriage, wisely disposed of these instruments of the gods as one more safeguard against unhappiness. Occasionally, in his descriptive passages, his prose will carry him past the limits of his chaste, bachelor's paradise, and he will celebrate the sexual aspect of the natural cycles: "June at last was here. One member of the company was still awaited; the shepherd-boy for the nymphs to woo, the knight for whom the ladies waited at the window, the prince that was to kiss the sleeping summer back to life and love." But the passion he alludes to metaphorically is utterly missing (or, as for the Rat, forgotten) in his animal world.

Laurence Lerner describes the two ways in which Arcadias can traditionally accommodate sex. The first is to offer fulfillment of desire; the second to eliminate desire all together. But if, in the latter case, the characters must make a conscious effort to conquer or deny desire that they actually feel, then they are experiencing the rigors of asceticism and moving toward heroism again. The most natural path to a happy, asexual world is the path back to childhood, and Lerner translates a passage from Virgil's *Eclogues* which recalls this innocent state:

> When you were small I saw you (I was then your guide) with your mother, picking the dewy apples in our orchard. I had just entered the year after my eleventh year; already I could touch the delicate branches from the ground. I saw you and, ah, was lost: this wicked treachery of love caught me.

The world that Virgil regards with such sophisticated nostalgia is like the world of Grahame's child-men, who, despite their enjoyment of the manly and epic pleasures of hearth and home and a story well told, will never enter the year after their eleventh year. They may be threatened by the social upstarts from the Wild Wood, but they will never have their Arcadia destroyed by the passion or treachery of love.

Yet even without the help of gods and women, the comic Toad manages to create a hell for himself. The most active character in this pastoral paradise, and the only actual wanderer, Toad is also the most shallow of the lot. Perhaps this is not completely ironic, for it reflects the singleminded intensity of purpose that the hero—or at any rate the man of action—needs in order to complete his task. And if Toad's only task is to heed that spirit of divine discontent and longing presumably wherever it takes him, Grahame nevertheless indicates that it should not be taking him where it is. His pursuit of activity and novelty for its own sake is not ennobling and heroic as Toad fancies, but rather a mischanneling of a natural instinct. The other animals may travel less, but they seem to be experiencing much more. Grahame has obvious affection for Toad (Green suggests that he represents the submerged bohemian in Grahame himself), yet he is still demonstrating in Toad the problems of an unexamined life devoted to acquisition and external adventure in a world that is retreating further and further from nature.

Green writes that "most of Toad's adventures bear a certain ludicrous resemblance to Ulysses' exploits in the *Odyssey;* and the resemblance becomes detailed and explicit in the last chapter, which parodies the hero's return and the slaying of the suitors." In general, however, *The Wind in the Willows* parallels epic in a way that is more reverential than parody is. Grahame is simply being eclectic about what he can include in his own ideal world. If Toad's adventures mimic those of Odysseus, the joke is almost always on Toad. He incorporates the hero's idiosyncracies, but he is all style, without the center of strength and intelligence of Odysseus, and without the hero's true capacity for anguish.

First and most obviously, Toad shares Odysseus' delight in singing his own praises. After he seizes the same motor car for the second time, he composes a small paean of praise to his resourcefulness:

> The motor-car went Poop-poop-poop,
>   As it raced along the road.
> Who was it steered it into a pond?
>   Ingenious Mr. Toad!

Seconds later he realizes he is being pursued and shifts: "O my! . . . What an *ass* I am." While Odysseus taunts Polyphemus with the fact that it was he, "Odysseus, Sacker of Cities," who had blinded him, and never thinks to blame himself for the seven years on Calypso's island that the boast costs him, we are nevertheless aware of his compensating qualities. Without such arrogance, he would not be a sacker of cities, and had he not planned his escape from the Cyclops' cave, he and his men would have died. Had Toad, on the other hand, shown a little restraint, he might simply have spared himself and his friends a lot of trouble.

Toad's second seizure of the car followed what might have been a twenty-year jail term, rounded off by a magistrate of medieval speech patterns and Olympian irrationality from nineteen ("fifteen years for the cheek"). It would have been an epic term, had he served it, the same length of time Odysseus spent away from home before Athene secured Zeus' permission to free him from Calypso. Toad's escape is likewise arranged through the efforts of a woman, the gaoler's daughter, who, like Athene (and perhaps Nausicaa?), appeals to her father for mercy and plans on her own to let him slip out, disguising his aristocratic toad's body in the clothing of a washerwoman, as Odysseus was disguised and withered, upon his return to Ithaca, to look like an old warrior. The gaoler's daughter is goddess-like both in her control and in her affectionate tolerance of Toad's boasting. She is clearly a different order of being from Toad. The only other point at which the distinction between human and animal seems as pronounced is when the barge woman discovers Toad's identity and cries: "Well, I never! A horrid, nasty, crawly Toad! And in my nice clean barge, too!" It is a wonder that the two women have any place in *The Wind in the Willows,* but they remain part of the wide world, which is full of all sorts of perils and which is kept forever separate from the enchanted circle on the river bank.

Throughout *The Odyssey,* Odysseus longs for the pleasures of home, for his wife, and for the son he left in infancy. The longing tinges all his voyages with urgency and sadness, and the ambivalence lends depth to the character and the story. But for Toad there is never ambivalence; his exaggerated swings from joy to remorse seem due to an inability to accommodate two contrary states of feeling simultaneously. He loves his friends, but once he has left them, and until he gets into trouble, he forgets them completely. And neither is he nostalgic for his home. Instead, what seems to stir him is pride of ownership. His description to the gaoler's daughter—"Toad Hall . . . is an eligible self-contained gentleman's residence, very unique; dating in part from the fourteenth century, but replete with every modern convenience"—is, as the lady says, more in the nature of a classified advertisement than an affectionate remembrance, and she replies perceptively: "Tell me something *real* about it." Even the excitement of travel that he relates to the Mole and the Rat seems false on his lips. He speaks of "the open road, the dusty highway. . . . Here to-day, up and off to somewhere else to-morrow! Travel, change, interest, excitement! The whole world before you, and a horizon that's always changing," and the statement may faithfully record Grahame's own enthusiasm for travel. But one wonders how Toad could know, for not only does he never stay out of trouble long enough to enjoy any of his trips, but when he is momentarily free, he is preoccupied with himself exclusively. When finally plans the pre-, during-, and after-dinner speeches that his friends never let him deliver (perhaps in ironic imitation of Odysseus' long and deeply appreciated tale to the pleasure-loving Phaeacians), we anticipate nothing that will touch or excite us. It will be all ever-expanding self-congratulation.

As dramatic change does not necessarily imply growth or excitement in *The Wind in the Willows,* permanence does not imply boredom or stagnation. Enjoyment of the life on the river bank merely involves Thoreau's ability to hear a different drummer, one who is quieter, requiring greater patience and sensitivity from the listener. That pattern of pastoralism, the Mole, is not dead to the calls around him. "We others," Grahame writes,

> who have long lost the more subtle of the physical senses, have not even proper terms to express an animal's intercommunications with his surroundings, living or otherwise, and have only the word "smell," for instance, to include the whole range of delicate thrills which murmur in the nose of the animal night and day, summoning, warning, inciting, repelling. It was one of these mysterious fairy calls from out of the void that suddenly reached Mole in the darkness making him tingle through and through. . . . He stopped dead in his tracks, his nose searching hither and thither in its efforts to recapture the fine filament, the telegraphic current, that had so strongly moved him. A moment, and he had caught it again; and with it this time came recollection in fullest flood.

> Home!

Athene produced a mist which so obscured the shores of Ithaca that Odysseus did not know he had finally returned. No one could have so befuddled the faithful Mole, who was not to be diverted, and desensitized, by journeys:

"For others the asperities, the stubborn endurance, or the clash of actual conflict, that went with Nature in the rough; he must be wise, must keep to the pleasant places in which his lines were laid and which held adventure enough, in their way, to last for a lifetime."

That the Mole recognizes other modes of existence and makes this conscious decision to limit himself is in keeping with pastoral tradition. Reflecting on the genre, Patrick Cullen observes:

> Arcadian pastoral can and does satirize the artifices and corruptions of the nonpastoral world . . . but there is, implicitly or explicitly, a counterpoising awareness of the limitations of pastoral values and with that a greater sense of the multivalence of experience, a sense of the potential legitimacy of urban and heroic modes.

This "potential legitimacy" is not realized in the Toad, who is satirized for his recklessness (" 'Smashes, or machines?' asked the Rat. 'O, well, after all, it's the same thing—with Toad.' ") In the chapter entitled "Wayfarers All," however, Grahame does suggest what these other modes of existence might be. Disturbed at the autumn departure of his friends who are following the longing to go south, the Rat must face the call of adventure himself, and while the migration of the birds may be all instinct, the case of the Sea Rat cannot be so clearly explained. Grahame allows his River Rat to be enchanted by the words and the way of life of the other animal, without suggesting where instinct ends and conscious will begins. Is the River Rat tied to the river, as the birds are seasonally to the north and south? Or does the Rat's allegiance to the river spring from habit that can be changed? When the chapter is over and the Rat's seizure past, our relief for him is mingled with a sense of the validity of other styles of life, even though for the Rat and the Mole, Grahame has reaffirmed the value of pastoral, with "adventure enough, in [its] way, to last for a lifetime."

It is often stated that, with the possible exception of *The Reluctant Dragon,* the essays and short stories that Grahame wrote in the 1890's are not children's literature. Deciding on which shelf to place *The Wind in the Willows* is more difficult. There do not seem to be many children today who share Alistair Grahame's prodigious verbal faculties (he was once called "a baby who had swallowed a dictionary" [Peter Green, *Kenneth Grahame: A Study of His Life, Work and Times*]), and most of the encouragement about introducing the novel to children may be found in books that are as idealistic and nostalgic as Grahame's work itself. The reasons for the difficulties children have with the book may go beyond the occasional near-archaic words and complex metaphors. Perhaps it is the sophisticated intelligence that informs *The Wind in the Willows* that is hardest for the child to appreciate. It is the same spirit, the longing for a golden age, that infused his short stories, and although the obtrusive elegance of the narrative voice has receded, the ironies remain. Part of the pleasure of reading an Arcadia lies in the perception both of its limited but highly artful simplicity and of its ever-budding but never fully blossoming allegory. To a great extent such sophisticated perception exists for adults in all children's literature. The writer selects and guides his naive reader, manipulating facts, breaking harsh truths gently, attempting, however unconsciously, to instill an appreciation of those values that he holds most dear. But the ideal reader remains, or should remain, the child, who will take it all quite seriously, and innocently allow the writer silently to pull the strings. The ideal reader of *The Wind in the Willows,* however, knows as much as the writer. He not only understands "how jolly it was to be the only idle dog among all these busy citizens" and comprehends the metaphor of "Nature's Grand Hotel," but more important, knows, with Virgil, how it feels to be no longer too young to reach the branches, and has some sense of the "spirit of divine discontent and longing" from which the work springs.

Laura Krugman Ray (essay date 1977)

SOURCE: "Kenneth Grahame and the Literature of Childhood," in *English Literature in Transition: 1880-1920,* Vol. 20, No. 1, 1977, pp. 3-12.

[*In the following essay, Ray compares Grahame's* The Golden Age *to works about childhood by William Wordsworth and Charles Dickens.*]

Although Kenneth Grahame's current reputation rests entirely on his classic children's book, *The Wind in the Willows,* it was the appearance of *The Golden Age,* a sequence of stories about childhood, some thirteen years earlier in 1985 that made Grahame an immediate literary celebrity. Swinburne called this work "well-nigh too praiseworthy for praise," a judgment ratified by the British public in its enthusiastic response. Today *The Golden Age* and its sequel in 1898, *Dream Days* have passed out of print—and out of favor with readers and critics alike. But, in spite of such undeserved oblivion, *The Golden Age* remains a serious contribution to the body of post-enlightenment literature treating childhood as an intelligible aspect of the human experience and so retains a claim on our critical attention.

Writing in the last decade of the nineteenth century, Grahame is the natural heir of the two dominant literary figures of his age, Wordsworth and Dickens, both deeply concerned with representations of childhood in their work. The link between Grahame and Wordsworth has been briefly marked by Peter Green who, in his critical biography of Grahame, finds that *The Golden Age* sounds "the authentic Wordsworthian note." Roger Lancelyn Green points to a minor Dickensian piece, "Holiday Romance," as a major influence on Grahame: " 'Holiday Romance' seems to be the earliest literary example of that eternal theme of childhood, 'let's pretend,' which was to become the inspiration of such books as *The Golden Age* and *The Treasure Seekers.*" But neither critic has gone beyond such superficial observations to treat the presence in Grahame's stories of specific Wordsworthian motifs and of Dickensian attitudes to childhood. In effect, Grahame draws from and fuses his predecessors while systematically undercutting their most serious themes. A participant in the Neo-Pagan movement of the nineties, Grahame saw in nature not so much a source of emotional enrichment and self-awareness as an escape from the artificial structures and standards of English society. He echoes Wordsworth in depicting the child's easy exchange with nature, but he turns evasive, sentimentalizing or ironizing the consequences of this exchange. In a similar way, Grahame follows Dickens in recreating the quality of a child's vision and the texture of his world, while discarding the moral energy of his model in favor of a contemplative and remote authorial stance. The stories of *The Golden Age* combine the thematic concerns of Wordsworth's poetry and Dickens' novels while muting their powerful statements of imagination and humanity to a gentle recollection of what it once meant to be a child.

The child in Wordsworth is almost invariably a solitary, responsive to nature and more at ease in the natural world than in the world of society. The cottage girl of "We Are Seven," the child of "Anecdote for Fathers," and particularly the young Wordsworth recalled in *The Prelude* express in varied ways the harmonious relationships of the child with nature and the strain of his subjection to the demands of "civilized" adults. This attitude appears in an altered form in Grahame's stories of five orphaned children living in a household of unnumbered and frequently unnamed aunts and uncles, a household loosely based on Cookham Dene, in Berkshire, where the four motherless Grahame children were sent to be raised by their maternal grandmother while their father grieved alone at home in Scotland. To the narrator of *The Golden Age* recalling his childhood, these adults were the Olympians, remote beings who "having absolute license to indulge in the pleasures of life, . . . could get no good of it"; they are alien in their tastes, arbitrary in their judgments, comprehensible only "as in the parallel case of Caliban upon Setebos." Nature provides one method of escape from the world presided over by these Olympians, and it is here that Grahame follows Wordsworth into the English countryside.

Grahame presents us with his version of Wordsworth's moment of communion with nature in **"A Holiday,"** first of the seventeen sketches which compose *The Golden Age.* The narrator recalls a solitary ramble when "the passion and the call of the divine morning were high in my blood" and he ran "colt-like . . . in the face of Nature laughing responsive." I quote at length the following passage because it illustrates so clearly Grahame's transformation of the majesty of *The Prelude* into the intimacy of the prose sketch:

> The air was wine; the moist earth-smell, wine;
> the lark's song, the wafts from the cow-shed at
> top of the field, the pant and smoke of a distant
> train,—all were wine,—or song, was it? or
> odour, this unity they all blended into? I had no
> words then to describe it, that earth-effluence of
> which I was so conscious; nor, indeed, have I
> found words since. I ran sideways, shouting; I
> dug glad heels into the squelching soil; I
> splashed diamond showers from puddles with a
> stick; I hurled clods skywards at random, and
> presently I somehow found myself singing. The
> words were mere nonsense,—irresponsible bab-
> ble; the tune was an improvisation, a weary, un-
> rhythmic thing of rise and fall: and yet it seemed
> to me a genuine utterance, and just at that mo-
> ment the one thing fitting and right and perfect.

This child experiences the summons of nature, the blending of his senses into a single sensation, the failure of language to express his feelings. We may compare his inarticulate song to the boy of Winander blowing "mimic hootings to the silent owls, / That they might answer him" (*Prelude*). Nature does answer him, "responsive to his call," much as "Nature laughing responsive" encourages Grahame's narrator in his frolic. Both children find instinctive modes of communication with nature, untroubled by the failure of conventional language to meet their needs; and both feel an animal pleasure in their harmony with the rhythms of the natural world.

In contrast to this Wordsworthian experience, however, its framework suggests that Grahame is far more interested than the poet in the public dimensions of the world his rambler inhabits. **"A Holiday"** begins with a substantial social reality, a glorious morning, by good fortune someone's birthday and consequently a holiday from lessons and routine. There is an interval during which the narrator joins his sister Charlotte in fighting a bear, played heroically by their brother Edward, but finally he is drawn away from his usual pastimes and companions, giving himself up to the wind instead as guide and sole companion. This may remind us fleetingly of a scene in *The Prelude,* when the young Wordsworth, ice-skating with his companions, offers himself up to the wind and is rewarded by a glimpse into the workings of the universe, "even as if the earth had rolled/With visible motion her diurnal round:" Although Grahame does not allow, as Wordsworth does, that the child may instruct his elders by virtue of such unspoiled relations with nature (the Olympians are apparently beyond recall to the vision of childhood), he does follow the poet in his insistence on the effect of nature's tutelary powers on the child himself. But Grahame offers nothing comparable to Wordsworth's moment of pure vision. The wind in **"A Holiday"** proves rather to be "a whimsical comrade" with diverse motives, directing the child to one lesson after another but never leading him outside the ordinary limitations of the social and natural worlds.

The demands of the narrative form Grahame has chosen diffuse the intensity of a concentrated poetic image over an extended adventure, and Grahame's tone remains aloof and even ironic as he records the reactions of his child character to nature's instruction. The wind first leads him to a pair of lovers, a spectacle that ordinarily strikes the narrator as absurd. This time, however, the encounter seems to him appropriate and acceptable:

> and it was with a certain surprise that I found myself regarding these fatuous ones with kindliness instead of contempt, as I rambled by, unheeded of them. There was indeed some reconciling influence abroad, which could bring the like antics into harmony with bud and growth and the frolic air.

Romance is followed by morality, as the wind takes the narrator past the village church, where the local bad boy is engaged in stealing biscuits. Wordsworth's nature acts to intimidate and reprove the young thief in *Prelude,* Book I, or so he thinks, but to Grahame's hero nature seems to assert its strict neutrality in all matters of social justice:

"Nature, who had accepted me for ally, cared little who had the world's biscuits, and assuredly was not going to let any friend of hers waste his time in playing policeman for Society". And, extending this principle of amorality, Grahame next confronts the narrator with a hawk attacking a chaffinch: "Yet Nature smiled and sang on, pitiless, gay, impartial. To her, who took no sides, there was every bit as much to be said for the hawk as for the chaffinch".

The adventure reaches a climax when the wind deserts its companion at a "grim and lichened" whipping-post, inscribed with the initials of generations of past offenders. This incident may remind us of a comparable, though sterner, passage in *The Prelude,* and the differences are themselves instructive of the way in which Grahame has altered Wordsworth from the visionary mode to a whimsical narrative of boyish truancy. Wordsworth remembers a day in his childhood when, separated from his companion, he stumbled on

> a bottom, where in former times
> A murderer had been hung in iron chains.
> The gibbet-mast had mouldered down, the bones
> And iron case were gone; but on the turf,
> Hard by, soon after that fell deed was wrought,
> Some unknown hand had carved the murderer's name.
> The monumental letters were inscribed
> In times long past; but still, from year to year
> By superstition of the neighbourhood,
> The grass is cleared away, and to this hour
> The characters are fresh and visible.

The sight of the gibbet and the subsequent sight of the girl bearing a pitcher form a spot of time for Wordsworth, a sharp memory of "visionary dreariness" assuaged only when he revisits the scene years later with his beloved. The gibbet, then, with its monumental letters, comes to represent, in the design of the poem, the restorative powers of feeling where once strong emotion has occurred. If we compare the gibbet to Grahame's whipping-post, there is a striking decline from the visionary quality of Wordsworth's episode to the self-consciously literary and slightly coy finish to Grahame's adaptation:

> Had I been an infant Sterne, here was a grand chance for sentimental output! As things were, I could only hurry homewards, my moral tail well between my legs, with an uneasy feeling, as I glanced back over my shoulder, that there was more in this chance than met the eye.

Nature has offered a lesson here too, but its terms are immediate and practical: the truant returns home to find his brothers and sisters suffering the consequences of their holiday behavior. He has already absorbed the meaning of his lesson and applies it to his situation:

> The moral of the whipping-post was working itself out; and I was not in the least surprised when, on reaching home, I was seized upon and accused of doing something I had never even thought of. And my frame of mind was such, that I could only wish most heartily that I had done it.

Another way of formulating the difference between

Wordsworth and Grahame is to say that where the poet is most vitally concerned with the spiritual or philosophic implications of childhood engagement with nature, the writer of stories is interested in the child's relationship with nature as it illuminates his psychosocial existence as a brother, a nephew, a pupil. So where Wordsworth moves temporally from the distant to the more recent past, Grahame moves spatially from the natural to the social world. His narrator always leaves from and returns to a comfortable if not always congenial social framework; his sorties into nature are refreshing and expressive of his child's being, but they are finally reabsorbed into the childhood community he inhabits.

Wordsworth of *The Prelude* and Grahame have something more in common, something they share with Charles Dickens: all three authors employ an adult narrator who recollects, from the vantage of maturity, his childhood experiences and emotions. For Wordsworth the act of memory is sacramental, a way of restoring and rededicating his poetic powers, while for Grahame it is closer to nostalgia, the pleasure of recalling a happier, less complicated time of life. For Dickens, as for Wordsworth, memory is sacred and restorative; the motto of his 1848 Christmas book, *The Haunted Man,* "Lord, keep my memory green," might serve as well as the epigraph for virtually all his novels, though particularly for his novels of remembered childhood, *David Copperfield* and *Great Expectations.* But, where Wordsworth examines the way he responded to and was molded by nature in his youth, Dickens and Grahame are concerned to recreate the way their child characters observed and comprehended the social and natural worlds. Wordsworth, we might say, is interested primarily in childhood as it links the adult self to nature, Dickens and Grahame in the nature of the child himself.

The technical method that Dickens developed to transcribe the child's sense of the world is a double perspective that superimposes the voice of an adult narrator onto the perceptions of his child self. The retrospective voice can assume a great variety of tones—it may be sympathetic, ironic, amused, indignant, even uncomprehending—but at all times it provides simultaneously a wedge into the child's consciousness and an assertion of the child's essential separateness from the world familiar to his elders. The early sections of both *David Copperfield* and *Great Expectations* are wonderfully successful in evoking the private world of distortions and illuminations that the child inhabits in the midst of ordinary adult life. Here Pip recalls his early interpretation of his catechism:

> Neither were my notions of the theological positions to which my Catechism bound me, at all accurate; for I have a lively remembrance that I supposed my declaration that I was to "walk in the same all the days of my life," laid me under an obligation always to go through the village from our house in one particular direction, and never to vary it by turning down by the wheelwright's or up by the mill.

Such a passage renders with great clarity the child's characteristic methods of interpretation; on the one hand, he is painfully literal in his acceptance of language, while on the other hand his imagination is released by the effort of this literalness. Dickens, however, gains something more than faithful renderings of a child's vision from his narrative method: he can, at the same time, offer critical judgment of adult conduct and values through the child's intuitive and naive perspective. David Copperfield's description of Miss Murdstone's arrival is as complete a dissection of that harsh and unyielding woman as any adult could offer with comparable economy:

> She brought with her two uncompromising hard black boxes, with her initials on the lids in hard brass nails. When she paid the coachman she took her money out of a hard steel purse, and she kept the purse in a very jail of a bag which hung upon her arm by a heavy chain, and shut up like a bite. I had never, at that time, seen such a metallic lady altogether as Miss Murdstone was.

The details are true to the limits of David's powers of observation, yet the narrator also signals to the reader a more expansive moral statement than the frightened David could then have made.

Grahame adapts Dickens' method in chronicling the adventures of Edward, Selina, Charlotte, Harold, and the narrator in the voice of an adult appreciative of his childhood yet candid enough to wonder, as he analyzes the enormous gulf between children and Olympians, "Can it be I too have become an Olympian?" Like the adult Pip or David, this narrator remembers not simply what happened in the past, but how it all looked and felt; he evokes the texture of a child's daily life, surrounded by yet detached from adults, and the element of "let's pretend" cited by Roger Lancelyn Green is only part of a more complex treatment of childhood than "Holiday Romance" attempts.

Grahame follows Dickens in presenting childhood as a province remote from the world of adult business and routine. The children of *The Golden Age,* like virtually all of Dickens' children, are without what Grahame calls "a proper equipment of parents," but their orphanhood is not the cruel isolation of a Dickens child, in part simply because there are five of them. They act as "members of a corporation, for each of whom the mental or physical ailment of one of his fellows might have farreaching effects," squelching independent action in the service of their "Republic." And of course the Republic is united in its opposition to the Olympians, evading their demands, mocking their customs, denouncing their injustice. But if these themes sound strikingly Dickensian, it is important to note that they appear in Grahame's stories emptied of the moral attention which Dickens' novels command. Just as he dilutes the force of Wordsworthian nature by opposing it to the claims of a conventional upper-middle-class household, so Grahame defuses Dickens' anguished concern for the alienated child by making him a member of an harmonious children's society. Grahame's adults are not affectionate and nourishing, like the Dickens adults—Joe Gargery or Peggotty—who understand children, but neither are they brutal or destructive, like Dickens' sinister child-haters and exploiters. They are merely adults guilty of no more than thoughtlessness and an occasional lack of charity, a "strange anaemic order of beings," as the narrator tells us, "further removed from us, in fact, than the kindly beasts who shared our natural existence in the sun." Dickens makes use of the distance between child and adult to make strong moral judgments of individuals and of society, but Grahame is content to depict the separation of worlds without formulating any moral statements of consequence. His satire of the Olympians is mild where Dickens' is scathing, his refrain not Dickens' cry for the sustenance of childhood memories but the ceaseless lament that children must become adults at all.

With these qualifications on Grahame's use of his predecessors, we may examine one of the most successful of the *Golden Age* sketches, **"The Finding of the Princess,"** as a fusion of Wordsworthian motifs with Dickensian attitudes. Once again, as in **"A Holiday,"** it is a glorious morning, and the narrator has just been elevated to that harbinger of manhood, a toothbrush. As if counseled by "The Tables Turned," he decides to forego his customary geography lesson in favor of an unlicensed and solitary ramble on the grounds that "the practical thing was worth any quantity of bookish theoretic." Leaving familiar surroundings for an unfamiliar copse, he experiences nature in a manner that heralds a significant adventure:

> If the lane had been deserted, this was loneliness become personal. Here mystery lurked and peeped; here brambles caught and held with a purpose of their own, and saplings whipped the face with human spite. The copse, too, proved vaster in extent, more direfully drawn out, than one would ever have guessed from its frontage on the lane: and I was really glad when at last the wood opened and sloped down to a streamlet brawling forth into the sunlight.

In many ways Grahame's story may be read as an adaptation of Wordsworth's "Nutting," with its parallel journey through "tangled thickets" to a hidden bower, a banquet, and a rest amid "fairy water-breaks." But where Wordsworth's young adventurer falls victim to the temptation of the scene and violates its peace with a brutality that teaches him a lesson, Grahame's narrator leaves the natural world altogether and enters the carefully landscaped garden of a country estate. And here Wordsworth gives way to Dickens, as Grahame shifts his interest onto the hero's response to the elegant scene. With a child's insouciance, he immediately recognizes it as the Garden of Sleep and wastes no time in setting out "in search of the necessary Princess." He meets the challenge of the unfamiliar by means of an imagination stocked with the lore of fairy tales, and it is his interpretative faculty which now assumes prominence. Encountering a young couple in the garden, he ingenuously imposes his fantasy onto the scene. The young lady is of course the princess, " 'But she's wide-awake, so I suppose somebody has kissed her!' " This remark draws a blush from the lady and laughter from her companion—the observer is both naive and acute. This section of the story depends on similar jokes; the silent footman who serves a splendid lunch is "another gentleman in beautiful clothes a lord, presumably," and the child advises the couple, according to his fairy tale expertise, that they really should marry. When the narrator

wakes from a sleep in the garden, however, the natural world reasserts its primacy over the social:

> When I woke, the sun had gone in, a chill wind set all the leaves a-whispering, and the peacock on the lawn was harshly calling up the rain. A wild unreasoning panic possessed me, and I sped out of the garden like a guilty thing, wriggled through the rabbit-run, and threaded my doubtful way homewards, hounded by nameless terrors.

The panic and guilt result from no breach against nature, and his infractions of household rules are too common to disturb him in this powerful way. The moment recalls the sudden interruption of communion in **"Knotting,"** but is also Keatsian with its suggestion of panic at the loss of an imagined world and guilt at truancy from the world of men. Again, however, Grahame steps back from the implications of this episode. He sends the child home, clutching the half-crowns given him by the gentleman, recalling the lady's farewell kiss, to a token punishment. The story ends with his dream that night, a lyrical summation of the day's adventures:

> Then, nature asserting herself, I passed into the comforting kingdom of sleep, where, a golden carp of fattest build, I oared it in translucent waters with a new half-crown snug under right fin and left; and thrust up a nose through water-lily leaves to be kissed by a rose-flushed Princess.

The solitary excursion, the discovery of a hidden bower, the awakening into a terror are all Wordsworthian motifs suggesting some form of instruction or initiation. Yet the opening of the story dwells on such nursery talismans as toothbrushes and slates; the middle on the child's confounding of fantasy with society; the end on the child's imaginative response, in sleep, to his escapade—all suggestive of post-Romantic, novelistic concern with the conduct and the psyche of the child. The final dream, in fact, turns the story away from nature and toward the child's private vision, in this case shaped equally by fantasy and reality; even the word nature is used in the last sentence to refer to human nature, the physical demands of the young body. And the elegance of Grahame's style even further distances the adventure, cools down the frightened energy of the child's panic to physical exhaustion and soothing sleep. The adventure is enclosed by the aesthetic form of the adult voice which, unlike Wordsworthian and Dickensian voices, acts to reaffirm the distance between the child's vision and the adult's.

The remaining stories of *The Golden Age* show similar concern for the imaginative life of the five children. As an insulated community, they establish their own rules, customs, and conventions of behavior based in part on a sharp understanding of Olympian habits and in part on a child's delight in games of pretense. Individualism is discouraged, though it occasionally breaks through in the narrator's excursions or in Harold's solitary games of Clubman or muffinman. But the real threat to the children's society is time. We see Selina excluded from a forbidden game because she has "just reached that disagreeable age when one begins to develop a conscience"; she later shows an alarming preference for conversation with other girls of her age.

The most violent disruption comes in the final story, **"Lu-sisti Satis,"** when Edward departs for school:

> Fortunately I was not old enough to realise, further, that here on this little platform the old order lay at its last gasp, and that Edward might come back to us, but it would not be the Edward of yore, nor could things ever be the same again.

The theme, once again, is Wordsworthian in its mourning for the old childhood order; Dickens sees no comparable loss in growing up if the adult can retain the child's clarity of vision and kindliness of heart. But the expression of Grahame's regret is social, not personal. The intrusion of a world larger and more threatening than that of the Olympians is felt in Edward's pride over the badges of his new estate: the trunks bearing his name, the spending money in his pocket, his first bowler hat. And the narrator's lament that he will not return to their children's society unchanged is only a particularized and limited instance of Wordsworth's universal lament in the Intimations Ode.

The Golden Age is in many ways a classic among works about childhood, surely deserving of more attention than it has received in this century. But it is also indisputably a minor classic, because Grahame modulates aspects of his theme from the major key of Wordsworth and Dickens to his own artful yet minor key. His writing lacks the depth and range of his models; childhood for Grahame is a time of great joy and imagination, but he offers no sense of its continuity with maturity, neither Wordsworth's sense of diminishing power nor Dickens' of expanding moral perception. As an appreciation of childhood, remarkable in recreating its moods and colors, *The Golden Age* excels, but as a literary statement of the relationship of childhood to the rest of experience it falls short. The narrator of Grahame's work stands apart from his remembered youth, the ironic, urbane, and lyrical tones of his voice suggesting always detachment, never the rapprochement between past and present that for Wordsworth and Dickens meant the survival of the highest human powers.

Roger Sale (essay date 1978)

SOURCE: "Kenneth Grahame," in *Fairy Tales and After: From Snow White to E. B. White*, Cambridge, Mass: Harvard University Press, 1978, pp. 165-93.

[*In the following essay, Sale surveys* The Wind in the Willows *and considers its place within the "cult of childhood."*]

> When I took a studio at No. 4 St. George's Square, Primrose Hill, the outgoing tenant said "Let me introduce you to Dr. Furnivall. He will ask you if you can scull. If you say 'No,' he will take you up the river to teach you. If you say 'Yes,' he will take you up the river to keep you in practice. He will take you anyhow." . . .
>
> I could not help smiling as, after a little enquiry about my work, Dr. Furnivall asked, "Can you scull?" When I answered "Yes," his whole face beamed. "How jolly!" he exclaimed. "I hope you will often come up the river with us." . . . I met him shortly after nine o'clock on the appointed

morning, as he was coming from his house. Two large string bags were slung over his shoulder—one hanging in front, the other behind. These, with a third bag in his right hand, were all full of good things to eat . . . Back at Richmond the club boats went on to Hammersmith, but the Doctor would take his party to the station by way of queer narrow back streets, in one of which there was a quaint little 'tuck-shop.' Into this he would suddenly disappear, and those of the party who did not know that the floor of the shop was two steps below the level of the street, literally dived after him.

In his biography of Kenneth Grahame, Peter Green quotes this passage to illustrate the charm of F. J. Furnivall, founder of the Early English Text Society and the New Shakespeare Society, whom Grahame met shortly after he went to work for the Bank of England in the mid-1870s. Readers of Grahame will identify Furnivall immediately; bluff, cheerful, full of purpose when coming and going from excursions of great and active idleness, knowledgeable about where to go and what to take along, Furnivall is the Water Rat of *The Wind in the Willows*.

Furnivall must have been impressive, and Grahame's imagination tenacious, since it was thirty years after Grahame's first friendship with Furnivall that he published his little masterpiece, in 1908. The picture of Furnivall is useful, too, in helping us describe what seems, for our purposes at least, like a shift in Victorian consciousness. Lewis Carroll, born in 1832, grew up as the Victorian cult of childhood was first taking shape; as we have seen, the adored child for Lewis Carroll and his generation was a preadolescent girl, while the awkward, unpleasant thing to be was an active boy. Grahame, born a generation later in 1859, grew up as the cult was in full flower, and the central figure was more and more apt to be a boy. F. J. Furnivall, as Jessie Currie describes him in the passage above and as Grahame first knew him, was a grown man, but at the same time he wasn't; he is Rat, reflecting the excitement of being a fun-loving boy. Like Rat, Furnivall enjoys the perquisites of being independent, but it is his boyishness that charms our sense of him.

Grahame's first books, *Pagan Papers* (1893), *The Golden Age* (1895), and *Dream Days* (1898), were published when this new version of the ideal person had gained a firm grip on the English imagination, a hold it would not lose until World War I, when the boy, slightly older, gained his apotheosis as a young victim in Flanders. In Beatrix Potter's work we see little direct evidence of this, but it is noteworthy that all her young heroes are male, while her young females are always a little too nice to be interesting. If we look elsewhere in the period, we see signs of this cult of boyishness everywhere. Here is how Angus Wilson describes it:

> But perhaps the whole of the nineties represents the triumph of one prominent strand of romantic thought—the cult of childhood. However different their purposes, however serious their aims, there is about Rhodes and Barnato, Wilde and Beardsley, Shaw and Wells, Henley and Kipling, a boyishness at once entrancing and at times maddening. Max, the dandy born old, did

well to show the Prince of Wales standing like a schoolboy, face to the corner, before the Queen's awful displeasure; the illustrator of *1066 and All That* did right to show the naughty nineties as childish old boys. It was, not too long after, that night after night the upper and middle classes crowded out the theatre to hear Peter Pan say, "I want always to be a little boy, and to have fun."

[Angus Wilson, *The Naughty Nineties*]

The showiness or gaudiness of some of those Wilson mentions should not deter us from seeing that the shy and quiet Grahame belongs on this list and lived in this world. Henley published a great deal of Grahame's early work, and a number of issues of the notorious *Yellow Book* have Grahame stories and sketches alongside Beardsley drawings and Beerbohm cartoons.

The Golden Age and *Dream Days* were immensely popular books because they fitted so easily into this new phase of the cult of childhood. These books are almost unknown today, except perhaps for *The Reluctant Dragon,* but we will understand Grahame much better if we see why his early books were so popular, and how *The Wind in the Willows* is a transmutation of his earlier materials into ideal and enduring shape. It too is about boyishness, or, more properly, boyish manhood, about being free of adult restraint and responsibility and sex. Furnivall appears as Rat, messing about in boats and taking along good food; the rural god Pan reappears, still idolized; Oscar Wilde appears in Mr. Toad's adventures in jail. *The Wind in the Willows* goes *Peter Pan* one better; Barrie and Peter Pan acknowledge in the very act of saying what they want that it is impossible, while Grahame's ideal world on the river seems more palpable, more fully realized, more truly desirable, than *Peter Pan*. As a result, *The Wind in the Willows* lives today, perhaps more popular now than it has ever been, part of its time but blessedly not limited to it. It is loved by lovers of children's books, and also by many who care little for, or even positively dislike, most children's literature. Its pleasure is the pleasure of enclosed space, of entering a charmed circle, of living in a timeless snugness. It takes so little to turn snugness into smugness that it is no wonder that many books that seem to resemble *The Wind in the Willows* are tiresome and even objectionable. If it did not exist it might rightly be claimed that a good book with its essential emotional bearings could not be written. To try to explain this, we must look at Grahame's life, and briefly at his early work, and then slowly and carefully at *The Wind in the Willows* itself. Grahame's was not a distinctly original genius, like Lewis Carroll's or Beatrix Potter's, and it takes some stretching to call *The Wind in the Willows* a great book. But its best pages are magical, fringed with joy, and therefore irreplaceable.

Kenneth Grahame was a Scot by birth; his mother died when he was very young, and his father soon decided he wanted nothing to do with his children and sent them off to live with their maternal grandmother, who lived at Cookham Dean, Berkshire, in the Thames valley. It is easy to surmise that Grahame came to idealize childhood because his own was anything but ideal. He went to St. Ed-

ward's School in Oxford and expected to go on to the university, but the uncle who was financially supporting him thought of a university education as a needless frill, so at eighteen Grahame went to work, first in the uncle's law firm, and then in the Bank of England, where he spent the rest of his working life. He was dutiful on the job, but never known for working hard, and he was lucky enough, and good enough, to become at thirty-nine the youngest Secretary in the history of the Bank. He lived in London most of the time between 1876 and 1906; his friends were mostly bohemians, artists, and gentleman scholars, all boyishly anxious to show they weren't entirely respectable, all willing to have along someone who was eminently respectable by day but eagerly escapist by night and by weekend.

Grahame married late, after gaining financial security as Secretary to the Bank and as author of *The Golden Age* and *Dream Days*. His wife was his age, also sexually shy, used to personal independence, and emotionally retarded; their correspondence was in a kind of cockney baby talk. The marriage seems to have been unhappy and might not have lasted except for its one offspring, Alistair, born in 1900. In 1906 the Grahames moved to the Thames valley of his childhood; in 1908 he published *The Wind in the Willows* and resigned from the bank. Grahame traveled, often by himself, and moved his family into different houses in Berkshire. He wrote almost nothing. In 1920 Alistair Grahame, a student at Oxford, committed suicide, and after that his father maintained himself as a kind of living corpse. He died in 1932, and was buried on top of his son, at St. Cross Church, Oxford.

The crucial fact in Grahame's life is that he did not become the Oxford don he wanted to be and seemed suited to be. Had he done so he could have retired early into a quiet single life, and, lacking Lewis Carroll's genius and urgencies, he might never have been heard from again. Thrust into the city, he found in the Bank of England an institution in which he could believe sufficiently to make him persevere successfully in his work, but for which he was sufficiently unsuited that he had to seek escape from it constantly. The more successful he became, the more he wanted to give a form to this constant need to escape, something beyond taking walking weekends in Berkshire and long holidays in Cornwall or Italy. When he knew he would soon be appointed Secretary, he became an author; when he realized his marriage was also something from which he needed to seek refuge, he began *The Wind in the Willows*. Never having the permanent haven Oxford might have provided, he had to invent it in his books.

The first readers of *The Golden Age* and *Dream Days* tended not to recognize them as literature of fantasy and escape, because they could also be taken as witty and satiric exposés that showed children and parents as they "really" are. They are short sketches and stories about a group of five children in the same family; they idealize the children, but not into an image satisfactory to their elders, because their ideal life is gained not by doing as they are told, but by escaping from "the Olympians," their elders. By a neat ironic twist, they were therefore not thought of as children's literature at all. Their readers were adults, and people like Richard LeGalliene and Swinburne reviewed them. Those who objected did so in the name of what one reviewer called "the sacred cause of childhood," while those who loved them claimed Grahame had told the truth about children at last. Children themselves were not encouraged to read the books.

The five children in these stories are Edward, Henry, Charlotte, Selina, and a nameless lad who doubles as narrator. They are a crew, which means they may quarrel among themselves but always unite in sympathy and action whenever any one is the target of Olympian attention or abuse. They exerted a strong influence, apparently, on E. Nesbit, Arthur Ransome, Edward Eager, Mary Norton, and others, all English, all more avowedly writers of "books for children" than was Grahame, all fond of imagining the need of children to build a bastion against parents, relatives, nannies, and teachers, all frank users of the magical, the exciting adventure, or the fantastic, as Grahame himself was not, because for him freedom was all one needed to be at the heart of all fantasy and escape. I confess to finding most of these books with a young community of secular saints rather shy-making, mostly because the authors tend to work too hard to give each character some distinctive or identifying trait, which leads to mechanical writing and often to mechanical relations among the children.

That Grahame was not really seeking a realistic version of childhood in *The Golden Age* and *Dream Days* is most evident in his narrator, who experiences all the joys and dark gloom of the other children but who is frankly free to become an adult narrator whenever Grahame wishes. The result is a kind of double perspective: here is a child telling a story, building a fortress against adults; here also is an adult narrator authorizing and supporting that fortress in his nostalgia for its having never been, or its having been lost. The results tend to be unpleasant a good deal of the time. For instance, in a famous story, **"Sawdust and Sin,"** the younger sister, Charlotte, is trying to make two dolls named Jerry and Rosa sit still so she can tell them stories, while the narrator watches from a convenient hiding place:

> At this point Jerry collapsed forward, suddenly and completely, his bald pate between his knees. Charlotte was not very angry this time. The sudden development of tragedy in the story had evidently been too much for the poor fellow. She straightened him out, and wiped his nose, and, after trying him in various positions, to which he refused to adapt himself, she propped him against the shoulder of the (apparently) unconscious Rosa. Then my eyes were opened, and the full measure of Jerry's infamy became apparent. This, then, was what he had been playing up for! The rascal had designs, had he? I resolved to keep him under close observation.

On the one hand the narrator can share with Charlotte the presumption that the dolls have ears, eyes, and intentions. On the other, he can laugh at Charlotte for not understanding what Jerry's "real" intentions are. It is a convenient perch.

Charlotte goes on with a quick recounting of *Alice in Wonderland,* but ends sooner than she means to:

> "I never can make my stories last out! Never mind, I'll tell you another one."
>
> Jerry didn't seem to care, now he had gained his end, whether the stories lasted out or not. He was nestling against Rosa's plump form with a look of satisfaction that was simply idiotic; and one arm had disappeared from view—was it around her waist? Rosa's natural blush seemed deeper than usual, her head inclined shyly—it must have been round her waist.

This is smug rather than snug. Charlotte is condescended to as the little girl who plays with dolls, so absorbed in telling her stories and "getting them to listen" she doesn't know what is "really" going on. She is hardly a worthy victim of any but the briefest sally, one would have thought, but Grahame and his narrator get much mileage out of her innocence. The narrator is of course male, and superior to the girl's naïveté, and by believing in Charlotte's fantasy that the dolls are real, by poking fun at Charlotte, Grahame can simultaneously indulge his sexual fantasy and deny it is fantastic.

Thus when, a moment later, Rosa falls "flat on her back in the deadest of faints," Grahame can giggle at the doll's orgiastic swoon and poke an elbow in a reader's ribs with double entendres: " 'It's all your fault, Jerry,' said Charlotte reproachfully, when the lady had been restored to consciousness: 'Rosa's as good as gold except when you make her wicked. I'd put you in the corner, only a stump hasn't got a corner—wonder why that is.' " Ostensibly, one presumes, this is Grahame's joke on "the sacred cause of childhood," or that part of it that elevated the purity and innocence of Alice and Rosa. But in his licentiousness Grahame only reveals *his* innocence. He and Charlotte mean different things by "good" and "wicked," but he accepts the equation of goodness and sexual purity just as much as Charlotte accepts the equation between goodness and correct manners. What makes Grahame's innocence all the more culpable is that it is all done with an ostensibly adult snicker that shows he would not have dreamed of giving a copy of **"Sawdust and Sin"** either to Charlotte or to her older brother. The story fits well, thus, into *The Yellow Book,* and one can feel justified in preferring either the frank decadence of Beardsley's drawings or the totally repressed sexuality of a contemporary book like Frances Hodgson Burnett's *The Secret Garden.*

But the stories are seldom as bad as **"Sawdust and Sin,"** and Grahame can occasionally use his blend of child and adult narrator to real advantage. In **"Dies Irae,"** for instance, the boy has begun his day of wrath by gloomy brooding. He wanders outdoors oblivious of his surroundings because he is busily fantasizing revenges against aunts and others like aunts:

> A well-aimed clod of garden soil, whizzing just past my ear, starred on a tree-trunk behind, spattering me with dirt. The present came back to me in a flash, and I nimbly took cover behind the trees, realising that the enemy was up and abroad, with ambuscades, alarms, and thrilling

sallies. It was the gardener's boy, I knew well enough; a red proletarian, who hated me just because I was a gentleman. Hastily picking up a nice sticky clod in one hand, with the other I delicately projected my hat beyond the shelter of the tree-trunk. I had not fought with Red Indians all these years for nothing.

Here too a hierarchy is made, but the gardener's boy, unlike Charlotte, isn't really ridiculed, not even when he fails to distinguish a hat from a human head:

> As I had expected, another clod, of the first class for size and stickiness, took my poor hat in the centre. Then, Ajaxlike, shouting terribly, I issued from my shelter and discharged my ammunition. Woe then for the gardener's boy, who, unprepared, skipping in prematurc triumph, took the clod full in the stomach! He, the foolish one, witless on whose side the gods were fighting that day, discharged yet other missiles, wavering and wide of the mark; for his wind had been taken away with the first clod, and he shot wildly, as one already desperate and in flight.

The superiority of the gentleman to the gardener's boy is what it should be. He has read more stories, fought more Red Indians, learned about Ajax and the gods, and so knows an epic battle when he sees one and that the gods fight on different sides on different days. The style includes the gardener's boy rather than ridicules him, and so everything that shows the narrator is an adult as well as a boy shows only the boyishness of both.

In **"Sawdust and Sin"** the hierarchy makes a leer, while in **"Dies Irae"** it celebrates release, the fantastic becomes real, the gods become defenders in which anyone might wish to believe. With a writer like Lewis Carroll, leering can be a fascinating and poignant activity—as with Alice and the Duchess, or the Gnat—but with Grahame it is only a nasty trifling. He needed situations and materials in which he could be more open, where the pleasure of creating hierarchies was mostly the pleasure of being inside a charmed circle, as with the gentleman lad in **"Dies Irae,"** and thus beyond care, however momentarily, and beyond snobbery or snickering. In these early books, or so it seems to me, only in **"Dies Irae"** and **"The Roman Road,"** where a boy and a man discuss the places they'd like to go, does the open enjoyment of wanting bring pleasure free from any attendant restrictive absorption with victims, or from a nostalgia where there is no circle and the charm is all a blur.

In the decade after *The Golden Age* and *Dream Days* Grahame's life contrived to make him feel more alone and unhappy, more in need of flight and escape. After his marriage he drifted away from Furnivall and Henley and many of his bachelor friends with whom he had walked the Berkshire Ridgeway or messed about in boats on the Thames or on the Fowey in Cornwall. He also accepted a relation for which he was emotionally unfit and in which he was, apparently, sexually hopeless. After she had noted a lack of interest in him, he wrote back: "It sums it up, wot you say about 'abit o not being interested 'speshly wen its cuppled wif much natral 'gaucherie' wot as never been strove against." The two may never have spoken openly

to one another. Their child, Alistair, might serve to hold the marriage together, but only by becoming a terrible victim of his parents' separate wishes for him. Grahame's financial security was hard to enjoy since he felt hemmed in, unable to up and leave his family as his father had done, unable to stay and be the husband and father at least a part of him wished to be. It is not pleasant to think of *The Wind in the Willows* as the work of a man becoming increasingly miserable, but such seems to have been the case; he began the work as stories told in letters to Alistair to placate him and his mother for Grahame's spending so much time away from them.

Since *The Wind in the Willows* did begin in this fashion, it superficially resembles Milne's Pooh books and J. R. R. Tolkien's *The Hobbit*, all being stories fathers told their sons, written by men who never thought of themselves as authors of children's books. The resemblance, however, may be one reason people have been mistaken about *The Wind in the Willows*. Ostensibly Grahame is inventing a world to enchant his son of six or seven, but actually he is describing a world he himself had lived in so completely that it seems false to say he invented it; he had been Rat, Mole, Badger, and Toad. Somewhat nervous about its reception, Grahame himself wrote on the dust jacket that the book is "perhaps chiefly for youth," but it was really written for himself and it usually fails to please a child who has just been delighted by the Pooh books and *The Hobbit*. But thereby lies the reason for its superiority to these other books: it has none of the superior tone that mars Milne's book or the smugness that hurts Tolkien's. It is about coziness, but it never seeks an uncomfortably cozy relation with its reader or listener. Its best audience is certain children, or adolescents, or adults, people of a particular sort or in a particular mood. If there is a "good age" to give a "child" *The Wind in the Willows*, it is not the age of Alistair Grahame when he first heard it, but twelve- or thirteen-year-olds, boys especially, who need to be told or reassured that the demands of adult life—work, sex, family, aging—which loom so frighteningly for them are in fact capable of frightening everyone. If one is rather doubtful about one's suitableness as an adult, one can be enthralled by *The Wind in the Willows*, and in this as in a number of other interesting respects it resembles two books that have never been thought of as fit reading for children, John Cleland's *Fanny Hill* and Hemingway's *The Sun Also Rises*. Like the *Alice* books, it is too personal, too signed by the needs of its author, to be a children's book as the Pooh or Oz books are.

By the time Grahame wrote *The Wind in the Willows* he was almost fifty and able to see that he was, in certain important respects, never going to "grow up." He also could see the ways in which the demands of maturing could no longer levy on him as strongly as they once had. He was what he was, he loved what he loved, which is why this book is much less self-conscious and satiric than the earlier ones. "I love these little people, be kind to them," he told Ernest H. Shepard when Shepard came to see him near the end of his life to ask permission to illustrate *The Wind in the Willows*, illustrations, incidentally, so good they seem to belong to the book as much as Tenniel's of *Alice* or John R. Neill's of Oz. In one particular way, it seems a ripe book, mature: it has an unerring sense of season and of the effect certain seasons can have on us irrespective of the demands of work or school. "The River Bank" in early spring, "Wayfarers All" in October, "Dulce Domum" at Christmas, are perfect expressions of a seasonal mood. If for no other reason, *The Wind in the Willows* is part of the ongoing emotional equipment of those who love it; there are many times and situations that recall its characters and scenes with vividness and fondness. Its sense of fun carries with it a sense of belonging, of the deep rightness of this kind of pleasure.

In his biography of Grahame Peter Green plausibly reconstructs the order in which the chapters of *The Wind in the Willows* were written. First came the adventures of Mr. Toad, which were the letters sent to Alistair, chapters 2, 6, 8, 10-12, or about half the book. Next came the chapters dominated by the friendship of Rat and Mole, 1 and 3-5, which for me are the heart of the book. Last came chapters 7 and 9, "The Piper at the Gates of Dawn" and "Wayfarers All," written most frankly out of personal compulsions of Grahame's and quite unreflective of any desire to tell stories to Alistair or to write a book "perhaps chiefly for youth." But in the book as Grahame finally assembled it, the divisions I have named are not as evident as the division into something like two halves. Up to chapter 7, "The Piper," everything is of a very high order, and the early Toad episodes blend splendidly with those centered on Rat and Mole. After "The Piper," Grahame seems less certain, more forced into letting Toad dominate and into letting plot play an unwontedly large role. Ask any lover of the book to name the most memorable parts, and the answer will invariably be scenes from the first half, even though the halves were never constructed as such by Grahame.

The special and enduring pleasure of *The Wind in the Willows* is an invitation into an enclosed space, and from its first pages Rat is the essential inviter, and Mole the essential enterer:

> "Lean on that!" he said. "Now then, step lively!" and the Mole to his surprise and rapture found himself actually seated in the stern of a real boat.

> "This has been a wonderful day!" said he, as the Rat shoved off and took to the sculls again. "Do you know, I've never been in a boat before in all my life!"

The day has kept opening up wonderfully for Mole: he has reneged on his spring housecleaning and come above ground, chaffed some rabbits and discovered the river, and now he has stepped into a real boat. Something close to this could easily have happened to Grahame with F.J. Furnivall. "Lean on that!" and "Step lively!" mean Mole has become an initiate, and Mole is only delighted as Rat keeps making it clear he is only on an outer threshold " 'What?' cried the Rat, open-mouthed: 'Never been in a—you never—well, I—what have you been doing them?' " Rat's consternation is strong enough to dissolve his usual simple politeness, and Mole is so impressed by the consternation he does not notice Rat's insult of his way of life:

"Is it so nice as all that?" asked the Mole shyly, though he was quite prepared to believe it as he leant back in his seat and surveyed the cushions, the oars, the row-locks, and all the fascinating fittings, and felt the boat sway lightly under him.

"Nice? It's the only thing," said the Water Rat solemnly, as he leant forward for his stroke. "Believe me, my young friend, there is nothing—absolutely nothing—half so much worth doing as simply messing about in boats."

As an insider it is not Rat's task to persuade, advertise, or inventory activities. He gestures only, and it is Grahame's task to make the gestures seem sufficient: " 'Whether you get away or whether you don't; whether you arrive at your destination or whether you reach somewhere else, or whether you never get anywhere at all, you're always busy, and you never do anything in particular.' " This does not describe messing about in boats. It says, rather, why there is no need for such a description, because messing about in boats abolishes destination, time, and purpose, and that is the point of doing it.

Nature does not quite create such rivers, but the Thames as Grahame knew it was just such a place, a warren of streams, weirs, locks, and marshes that had been created to make purposeful navigation possible and that also made purposeless navigation delightful. Given such possibilities, "nice" is an inadequate word, and activity is just a series of doings connected with "or": on the river one does this or that or the other, and it does not matter which. There is nothing essentially boyish about Rat and his pleasures here, and certainly nothing childish or childlike. The boyishness, the childlikeness, is all in Mole:

> The Mole waggled his toes from sheer happiness, spread his chest with a sigh of full contentment, and leaned back blissfully into the soft cushions. "*What* a day I'm having!" he said. "Let us start at once!"

It is hard to praise Mole enough here. The river and Rat are so inviting that anyone might feel delight in their company, but to admit one's delight, to share it without shame—that is hard, and rare, and completing.

So Rat packs lunch:

> "What's inside it?" asked the Mole, wiggling with curiosity.

> "There's cold chicken inside it," replied Rat briefly; "coldtonguecoldhamcoldbeefpickledgherkinssaladfrenchrollscressandwidgespottedmeatgingerbeerlemonadesoda-water—"

> "O stop, stop," cried the Mole in ecstasies: "This is too much!'"

Come inside the charmed circle and there is everything, including the longest of words. Mole, an outsider but no stranger to English buffet lunches, cannot contain his delight at being continually asked to step over the line Rat keeps drawing. This is freedom, newness, springtime, friendship, and all Mole needs for his passport is his own modesty upon being asked. How wonderful, one feels, to be Mole, to be thus invited and thus accepting; the joining and sharing in things makes one feel, for once, fully alive.

What difference does it make that these characters are a rat and a mole? They speak, wear clothes, scull, pack cold lunches, and wish they could afford black velvet smoking jackets. They are much more like human beings, and individual human types, than Beatrix Potter's animals. Yet it will not do to say they are human beings, because Grahame's fantasy depends on his being able to give them so much because they are not human, because he does not have to give them an age, a biography, a past for which they might have to feel guilty, or a future they must anticipate. These are the basic freedoms which then create the possibility of those other freedoms we have just seen: messing about in boats, enjoying a full larder, making a new life, for oneself, for someone else.

So Rat and Mole are not human, for all their human apparatus. They are also, in a dimmer sense, animals, as Rat reveals when he begins to describe what lies outside the charmed circle, starting with some residents of the Wild Wood, on the opposite side of the river from Mole's house:

> "Well, of course—there—are—others," explained the Rat in a hesitating sort of way. "Weasels—and—stoats—and foxes—and so on. They're all right in a way—I'm very good friends with them—pass the time of day when we meet and all that—but they break out sometimes, there's no denying it, and then—well, you can't really trust them, and that's the fact."

Rat here resembles an Englishman describing French and Germans, but what he says is also based on the natural fact that weasels, stoats, and foxes all kill rats, so that when Rat says these others "break out sometimes," he is being English, politely understating the nasty truth, but without any taint of English insularity or prejudice. Mole then remembers "it is quite against animal etiquette to dwell on possible trouble ahead, or even to allude to it." Grahame here is touching on precisely the point Potter raises when Peter and Benjamin find the rabbit bones and skulls outside Mr. Tod's house, but his way is almost the opposite of hers. Where Potter wants to voice a horror and to find a limit to that horror, Grahame wants to have it both ways, to elevate both animal and human possibility. It is fun, but irresponsible, for human beings to ignore the future, especially the natural fact of death. Animals have, on the other hand, only the most instinctive sense of any future, nothing more than a pregnant female preparing a home, or birds migrating. Grahame's animal etiquette resembles English manners in insisting on the virtue of understatement, but it carries with it something much more important to Grahame than that: the freedom to ignore the future by not speaking of it, so that if this weekend must end, or if weasels kill rats, it is best we not even think of it. The abolition of worry about the future without abolishing the knowledge that day will break, or that summer will follow spring, encloses Grahame's animals in a secure present where all time is rhythmic time, and rhythmic time brings all the changes one needs.

Freed from the future just as Mole has been freed from his past, the two can go on so Rat can draw another boundary and secure an other enclosed space:

> "Beyond the Wild Wood comes the Wide World," said the Rat. "And that's something that doesn't matter, either to you or me. I've never been there, and I'm never going, nor you either if you've got any sense at all. Don't ever refer to it again, please. Now then! Here's our backwater at last, where we're going to have lunch."

The backwater in question has such human-made objects as a weir and a mill wheel, but they, clearly, are all right, because they are far from the Wide World, London, and the Bank of England. It is possible to stand next to the Thames, near Grahame's childhood home in Cookham Dean or his last home in Pangbourne, and feel the scale reduce itself just as Rat dictates: a weir or a canal creates a backwater, and there are woods beyond. Not far off are Maidenhead, and Windsor Castle, and the Great Western Railway, but as one stares at the quiet water, and the reeds, and the willows lining the bank, one feels the pleasure not just of quiet beauty but of being able to say: "I know you're there, nearby even, but I'm here, and staying here."

Such pleasures, lived on such a small scale, must be active to be fully felt, so that stepping inside the charmed circle and seeing the boundary drawn can feel liberating rather than confining, at which point the unwanted is excluded and the circle can be explored. In the opening chapter, one of the finest openings to any book, Grahame keeps inviting, drawing a boundary, making those pleasures into relief and release. After sculling, lunch; and after lunch, meeting the society of the river—Otter appears and disappears with graceful lack of announcement, news comes of Toad out sculling, Badger appears briefly, then departs, and Rat must explain that Badger, a denizen of the Wild Wood, "hates society." All the while we understand, as Mole does, that we are learning about the limits of enclosed space without ever arriving at a definition of what belongs inside it. But we understand more than Mole does about all this. This is the greatest day of Mole's life, and "The River Bank" is also one of the great opening chapters of any reader's reading life. But what is to follow? We know that the great failing of invented ideal worlds is not in their opening chapters but in what follows, in their tendency to become dull once we have become accustomed to their ways and means. All too often, we know, the original sensation of release—how wonderful to be free to do this, to leave all that behind—is followed by other feelings—that the space is too narrow, the blessed activity too repetitive, such that we long to return to uncertainty, hope, doubt, and despair, the future even. If Grahame's opening chapter is exhilarating, he succeeds in it in ways others have succeeded too.

Sensing his situation and its problem, Grahame introduces us to the perpetually outside insider, Mr. Toad. We know, of course, that Grahame began with Toad when writing to Alistair, but when he made a book that could embody his own deepest longings, he rightly shifted Mr. Toad from the center of attention and placed him to one side. We hear of him first from Otter's announcement that he is out on the river: "Such a good fellow, too, but no stability—especially in a boat." The phrase "good fellow" reads like a code word here, an insider's phrase, such that neither we nor Mole expect to understand it fully the first time around. We do gather, though, that "no stability" is a pun, of Grahame's and perhaps of Otter's, because not only is Mr. Toad liable to tip over in a boat, but he also is always searching for new things to do. He has sailed and houseboated in the past, and the other animals expect he will soon tire of sculling, and before he learns to manage the oars. To reinforce his point about the virtues of stability, Grahame has Mole suddenly imagine he has become a master of the oars after only one afternoon; he soon tips the boat over, and Rat has to haul him out. But Mole is a "good fellow," and learns his lessons quickly. Mastery comes through repetition, and repeated actions are the best because they teach you how to live in your landscape.

But with Toad we are not immediately clear where to stand. In the second chapter Mole says he would like to be introduced to Toad, having heard so much about him. Of course, Rat answers:

> "It's never the wrong time to call on Toad. Early or late he's always the same fellow. Always good-tempered, always glad to see you, always sorry when you go . . . He is indeed the best of animals . . . So simple, so good-natured, and so affectionate. Perhaps he's not very clever—we can't all be geniuses; and it may be he is both boastful and conceited. But he has got some great qualities, has Today."

When Rat described the stoats and weasels he drew a boundary—"They're all right in a way" but they "break out"—and we and Mole could see where and why the line is drawn so stoats and weasels will be on the other side. But it is different with Toad. "Simple" may mean "so good-natured, and so affectionate," but it is not clear how "best of animals" equals "not very clever" and "boastful and conceited." Rat is inside the circle, but we cannot see if Toad is inside or outside it. So we need to go see him, and for at least two chapters Grahame does marvelously at placing and re-placing Toad for us.

Toad is "Mr. Toad," he lives in magnificent Toad Hall, but no one ever condemns him for being rich and living ostentatiously; anyone might enjoy such splendor at least some of the time. It is the instability that is bothersome; when Rat and Mole first visit Toad Hall the boathouse has "an unused and a deserted air," because Toad has given up boats altogether. But Toad greets his visitors like "the best of animals," gives them lunch, and exultantly shows them his new toy, a gypsy caravan:

> "There's real life for you, embodied in that little cart. The open road, the dusty highway, the heath, the common, the hedgerows, the rolling downs! Camps, villages, towns, cities! Here today, up and off somewhere else tomorrow!"

The life of the open road might seem to embody instability as a principle, but clearly, also, it resembles messing about in boats; you go, and it doesn't matter where you get to because there is so much to see and do all the time. Mole, always eager to be invited, longs for the open road as he longed for the life on the river, but Rat, who knows more than Mole about this best of animals, has to be coaxed into going. For two days the open road is delightful; the animals ride, and tramp, and greet other animals, and delight in the fresh air. On the first night out, as they are going to sleep, Toad exults:

> "Well, good night, you fellows! This is the real life for a gentleman! Talk about your old river!"
>
> "I *don't* talk about my river," replied the patient Rat. "You *know* I don't, Toad. But I *think* about it," he added pathetically, in a lower tone: "I think about it—all the time!"

Toad's search, we see, is for "real life," while Rat's is not a search at all. Presumably he does not talk about the river because that would make him boastful, like Toad, a possessor of activities and places; presumably, too, he does not think about the river all the time, but it is always there, inside him, defining him.

On the third day out the animals hear a loud "Poop-poop," and the caravan is suddenly upset by a speeding automobile. Rat and Mole look at the wrecked caravan and see it is time to return home, but Toad is not the least dismayed as he sprawls on the dusty highway:

> "I've done with carts forever. I never want to see the cart, or to hear of it, again. O Ratty! You can't think how obliged I am to you for consenting to come on this trip! I wouldn't have gone without you, and then I might never have seen that—that swan, that sunbeam, that thunderbolt! I might never have heard that entrancing sound, or smelt that bewitching smell! I owe it all to you, my best of friends!"

Now "boastful and conceited," "always happy to see you," and "best of friends" all fall into place. Toad's conceit lies in his being unable to consider anyone but himself, his pleasure lies in his easy willingness to share his joy, even to give Rat credit for it. Unstable he is, so hedgerows and downs give way to swans, sunbeams, and thunderbolts, but constant he is too, in the innocent friendliness with which he conveys and shares his passions.

It is easy, we now see, to exclude the Wide World; one just messes about in boats or has lunch and all thought of it is gone. It is not difficult, apparently, to exclude weasels and stoats, because their natural instinct is to be predators, and to "break out," water rats being their prey. If all animals were simply to obey their instincts, however, then Rat and Mole would never meet, and there would be no holiday. To enjoy their lives the animals must not just professionally do as they are naturally fitted to do; they must also be amateurs, more "human," and lead life as a series of charmed possibilities. For precisely these reasons Toad cannot be easily excluded. He cares nothing for the Wide World, he is a gentleman, an amateur above all, fully enjoying what he does. He shares easily, he goes his own way, he never pries into the private concerns of others. Grahame presents him so that in a great many ways he resembles Rat. To rule him out would be most unfriendly, since it would in effect be insisting that everyone be like everyone else.

Yet Toad is dangerous. We may think at first that his defect is flightiness and faddishness as he goes from one exciting activity to the next, always scorning everything he did previously. But after Toad discovers automobiles he never develops another interest, because Grahame wants to define the problem involved here more precisely. Toad buys cars, he wrecks them, he is a menace on the highway, but he is constant to his love. His dangerousness lies in the source and the uncontrollableness of his passion. He has no natural instinct to guide him, and he has a profound and pathetic inability to resist what he mistakenly assumes are his greatest inner needs. Thus, in chapter 6, "Mr. Toad," after Badger, Rat, and Mole incarcerate him in Toad Hall, and after Toad himself seems willing to admit he has been victimized by a terrible malady, his passion leads him to escape from the others and then to become a car thief:

> Next moment, hardly knowing how it came about, he found he had hold of the handle and was turning it. As the familiar sound broke forth, the old passion seized on Toad and completely mastered him, body and soul. As if in a dream he found himself, somehow, seated in the driver's seat; as if in a dream he pulled the lever and swung the car round the yard and out through the archway; and, as if in a dream, all sense of right and wrong, all fear of obvious consequences, seemed temporarily suspended. He increased his pace, and as the car devoured the street and leapt forth on the high road through the open country, he was only conscious that he was Toad once more, Toad at his best and highest, Toad the terror, the traffic-queller, the Lord of the lone trail, before whom all must give way or be smitten into nothingness and everlasting night.

It is one of the best moments in the book, Grahame's version of hell. Like all well-conceived hells, it closely resembles heaven. Every gesture here invites, draws a boundary, and excludes the unwanted outside world, so that the grammar of hell and heaven are precisely the same. Thus Toad can never be excluded from the society of the other animals. What differentiates heaven from hell is what is excluded and included. Inside Toad's passion there is only Toad. In this passage we focus first on the car, the handle, the driver's seat, the ignition; but gradually the car disappears, having succeeded in obliterating everything else in the world: "he was Toad once more, Toad at his best and highest, Toad the terror." Perhaps the most deceiving aspect of such passions is that they convince us we are most alive, most ourselves, when we are in fact most mastered, most not ourselves. "The car responded with sonorous drone, the miles were eaten up under him as he sped he knew not whither"; that *seems* like "whether you arrive at your destination or whether you reach somewhere else . . . you're always busy and never do anything in particular," and Grahame never once implies Rat is better because he does not play with complicated twentieth-century machines. But Rat is always looking outward, keeping his windows clean and his ears waxed, delighting in whatever the river and its banks happen to show him, which is why it is possible for him to say "I think about it—all the time!" Toad is concerned with his own pulse

rate and delights only in whatever can raise it to new heights; he is bored and twitchy all the rest of the time, since now he has found his "real life." Passion, the great excluder, is thus for Grahame the great enemy, because its dangers lie within us and can never be ruled out just by drawing a boundary or evolving an etiquette that agrees not to discuss the future. To be free, to be released, to live in the present—these are crucial for both Rat and Toad. Toad's is a perversion of a way of life of which Rat is the deepest embodiment.

But here, in this passage, Grahame reaches one of his limits. It is the nature of passions that, once their temptations have been given in to, little good can result for very long, so Toad soon ends up in the dock. It is also the nature of passions to become repetitive, so that once Toad has become "Toad at his best and highest," neither Toad nor Grahame can do more than to try to climb the mountain again and again, so the adventures of Mr. Toad must become the further adventures of Mr. Toad, and these must consist mostly of the frustrations and miseries of Toad as he is kept from getting into cars. When such passions are the subject of works whose scale is larger than Grahame's they are the stuff of high tragedy; we can watch for the length of an entire work the fatal consequences of the initial passions of Faustus or Macbeth. Of course none of that is wanted here, since Toad's passion is designed to seem only the serpent in the garden of Grahame's paradise. The trouble is that after this moment of Toad's fulfillment all we can have is Toad in jail, Toad making a car out of a railroad, Toad with the barge woman, Toad regaining Toad Hall from the weasels and stoats. Perhaps he is chastened at last, but the book must end lamely since a chastened Toad is of no interest; and the unchastened Toad has had too many tales told of him already. In *The Sun Also Rises* Hemingway handles his outside insider, Robert Cohn, with greater tact and never allows Cohn to occupy the center of the stage, as Grahame does let Toad do in the later chapters. He belongs, to repeat, over to one side, and Rat and Mole belong at the center.

We have hardly done enough thus far, however, to celebrate Rat and Mole. If *The Wind in the Willows* were only the stunning opening chapter, and the two chapters with Toad before he reaches the height of his passion, the book would not be the irreplaceable work I think it is. But this is not all, and in the other non-Toad chapters Grahame tries to find ways to keep his animals inside their boundaries and, at the same time, describe their responses to impulses as powerful in their way as Toad's. Of the five chapters involved at least three seem totally successful: "The Wild Wood," "Mr. Badger," and "Dulce Domum." The other two, "The Piper at the Gates of Dawn" and "Wayfarers All," are very attractive in part, but in them Grahame is trying to do what is really beyond his capacities. Let us look at an example of each. First "Dulce Domum," the gem of the book, Grahame's wonderful story of Rat's success at the apparently impossible task of inviting Mole into his own home.

Caught in the "rapid nightfall of mid-December," far from their river home, Rat and Mole trudge through a village where a canary in a cage reminds them of how snug and warm it is to be indoors. As they go on, Rat in the lead, Mole is struck and then overwhelmed by a series of scents that come over him. He soon interprets them to mean home, his home, his old home in the ground: "Poor Mole stood alone in the road, his heart torn asunder, and a big sob gathering, gathering, somewhere low down inside him, to leap up to the surface presently, he knew, in passionate escape." This designedly resembles Toad's response when he first hears the "poop-poop" of the automobile, but it is noteworthy that Mole is not so much excited as made miserable: "But even under such a test as this his loyalty to his friend stood firm. Never for a moment did he dream of abandoning him. Meanwhile, the wafts from his old home pleaded, whispered, conjured, and finally claimed him imperiously. He dared not tarry longer within their magic circle." The word "imperiously" is an important one for Grahame. He uses it in the opening pages to describe the way Mole is commanded by the spring to leave his housecleaning and come above ground and go to the river. There, as here, the power that does the commanding is every bit as great as the passion of Toad, but it is located outside the characters, in the world, as part of the great creation of nature. The imperious command to return to one's natural habitat is made stronger here because it is December, and cold, and all living things are seeking home as their refuge.

Mole breaks away from the magic circle of the imperious smells, catches up with Rat, but then breaks down:

> "I know it's a—shabby, dingy little place," he sobbed forth at last, brokenly: "not like—your cozy quarters—or Toad's beautiful hall—or Badger's great house—but it was my own little home—and I was fond of it—and I went away and forgot all about it—and then I smelt it suddenly—on the road, when I called and you wouldn't listen, Rat—and everything came back to me with a rush—and I *wanted* it!"

This is the perfect speech to contrast with Toad's triumphant conversion to the automobile. Mole is not in heaven here, but he is a candidate for admission. What shames Mole is a power strong enough to break down his duty as Rat's friend to keep up and not to bother anyone else with his private troubles. The network of pleasures and loyalties the animals work so hard to build cannot resist such power, which is why Mole is so miserable. But Rat, best of animals, knows the crucial difference between seeking passion as a form of excitement and giving into imperial powers naturally greater than oneself. The opposite of the amateur pleasures is not anything professional, but a power essentially religious. So, insisting that Mole blow his nose to keep it keen so it can guide them, Rat takes over, himself having only to obey the need to be loyal to his friend.

When they arrive at Mole's house Mole must go on being ashamed, because all he can see is a "poor, cold little place." Rat, however, kind beyond thanks, dissolves Mole's shame, not by cheering him up but by discovering the pleasures of Mole End: "So compact! So well planned! Everything here and everything in its place!" He sets out to build a fire, gets Mole to dust the furniture, but Mole discovers a new shame: there is no food. Rat, having just

seen an opener for a sardine can, insists there must be sardines somewhere. Indeed, after "hunting through every cupboard . . . the result was not so very depressing after all, though of course it might have been better." Not "coldhamcoldtonguecoldbeefpickledgherkins," and all the rest of Rat's picnic, but sardines, a box of biscuits, and a German sausage. Rat keeps on drawing the circles, inviting Mole across his own threshold, recreating the splendors of home and thereby recreating the purpose and possibility of friendship:

> "No bread!" groaned the Mole dolorously; "no butter, no—"
>
> "No *pâté de fois gras,* no champagne!" continued the Rat, grinning. "Ah, that reminds me— what's that little door at the end of the passage? Your cellar, of course! Every luxury in this house! Just you wait a minute."

Down Rat goes, and back he comes, a bottle of beer in each hand, and one under each arm:

> "Self-indulgent beggar you seem to be, Mole," he observed. "Deny yourself nothing. This is really the jolliest place I ever was in. Now wherever did you pick up those prints. Make the place so home-like, they do. No wonder you're so fond of it, Mole. Tell us all about it, and how you came to make it what it is."

In these pages Grahame makes home both richly nostalgic and actively alive in the present. One wants to keep cheering Rat on to find more things to love, and one wants also to weep, as one's gratitude for Rat reveals the knowledge that no homecoming, no friendship, could ever quite be this good.

Then, at the end, it is the Christmas season. A group of field mice appear outside, singing carols, and Mole and Rat are delighted to see them until Mole remembers how bare his larder is and how little he can give the mice. Again Rat leaps to the occasion: " 'Here, you with the lantern! Come over this way. I want to talk to you. Now, tell me, are there any shops open at this hour of the night?' " The English are famous for shutting their shops at the slightest hint of a customary excuse or a holiday, but Grahame, self-indulgent beggar himself, concedes everything: " 'Why certainly, sir,' replied the field-mouse respectfully. 'At this time of year our shops keep open to all sorts of hours.' " No enchantment in a fairy tale, no magic picture in Oz, is more magical or enchanting than this discovery that the shops are open: "Here much muttered conversation ensued, and the Mole only heard bits of it, such as 'Fresh, mind!—no, a pound of that will do—see you get Buggins's, for I won't have any other—no, only the best— if you can't get it there, try somewhere else—yes, of course, home-made, no tinned stuff—well then, do the best you can!' " This is the triumph of snugness; the shops are all the shops in the world. They are good sturdy village shops where one can expect to find something homemade, not tinned, a meat pie perhaps. They are also market-town shops and can be expected to cater to the gentry and keep Buggins's in stock; Buggins's makes marmalade, maybe, or chutney. They are also as grand as Fortnum and Mason's and can be expected to have fresh food in the dead of winter, not just bread or apples, but tomatoes or lettuce. Only by having his scale so small can Grahame make such pleasures seem to mean everything. Only by longing for such pleasures himself could he have wanted them at all, as a last magical Christmas present, from Rat to Mole: all the dreams of home. What begins as the summons of an imperial power ends as the relaxed intense excitement of giving to a friend what he could not, were he the mightiest or most wealthy, give to himself.

But this sense of imperious powers in nature haunted Grahame, and he could not rest content with having that power be whatever drove Mole up out of his hole and then drove him back down into it. Grahame came to his world of the river and the woods with thanksgiving, he entered its courts with praise, and so he wanted to name its god. Thus, after the splendid burrowings into the houses of Mr. Badger and Mole, he makes an attempt to soar, in "The Piper at the Gates of Dawn," as high above the earth as the other chapters go beneath it. This chapter divides the book; before it we have Grahame at his very best, in all the ways we have seen thus far, and after it we have the later and less interesting Toad stories. In "The Piper" Grahame rather self-consciously tries to justify his excursions into cozy fantasy when, in fact, no such justification was needed.

It is a summer evening, and it feels, even late at night, as though the sun has never quite left this spot of earth. Rat and Mole hear that Otter's son Portly is lost, and, worried and unable to sleep, they set out to try to find him. As they row up the river, it begins to get light in the east, and Rat hears a noise, a bird maybe, the wind in the reeds: " 'Now it passes on and I begin to lose it,' he said presently. 'O Mole! the beauty of it! The merry bubble and joy, the thin, clear, happy call of the distant piping! Such music I never dreamed of, and the call in it is stronger even than the music is sweet!' " Once again, the imperious power. Mole, who only smells his powerful callers, hears only "the wind playing in the reeds and rushes and osiers," but Rat needs more, a religious summons. This is a strain in Rat that has been there all along—in his dreaming off at the very beginning while telling Mole about messing about in boats, in his writing poetry when the fit seizes him—but it seems more a part of Grahame himself than something he can make actively a part of Rat's character. We can concede Rat's "I think about it—all the time!" certainly, but this more ethereal propensity seems just not to belong. Thus, when Rat and Mole, following the piping music only Rat hears, arrive at their destination, it does not sound like Rat who is speaking: " 'This is the place of my song-dream, the place the music played to me,' whispered the Rat, as if in a trance. 'Here, in this holy place, here if anywhere, surely we shall find Him.' " We hardly seem to be in *The Wind in the Willows* at all.

It would be easy enough to explain it away. We could go back to Grahame's first book, *Pagan Papers,* and to quite a few other *fin de siècle* writers who seem to lapse into a soft religion that was not quite nature, not quite out of this world, but an aestheticism about nature; Walter Pater's hard gemlike flame is very much akin to Grahame here. Yet we should trace it a little further in "The Piper" before

making such a dismissal. As Rat and Mole come to the island to which they have been summoned, they see "the very eyes of the Friend and Helper," complete with horns and rippling muscles and shaggy limbs. Then:

> . . . last of all, nestling between his very hooves, sleeping soundly in entire peace and contentment, the little, round, podgy, childish form of the baby otter. All this he saw, for one moment breathless and intense, vivid on the morning sky; and still, as he looked, he lived; and still, as he lived, he wondered.
>
> "Rat!" he found breath to whisper, shaking. "Are you afraid?"
>
> "Afraid?" murmured the Rat, his eyes shining with unutterable love. "Afraid! Of Him? O never, never! And yet—and yet—O Mole, I am afraid!"

No one not already a worshipper of Pan would actually prefer this Rat, this Mole, this writing, to "The River Bank" or "Dulce Domum." The adjectives—"very," "entire," "unutterable"—all show a straining toward a feeling that by its thrilled vagueness makes us remember how much, elsewhere in the book, Grahame can convey with language only slightly more pinned down. Grahame may say Mole and Rat are afraid, but he himself is not; he is only thrilled at the possibility of feeling such fear.

The trouble is the context, or, in this case, the feebleness of the context. When, in the opening pages, Mole says, "So this—is—a—River!" and Rat answers, "*The* River," we have already enough of Mole's life underground, and we soon will have enough of Rat's life on the river, so that this language, which out of context is no clearer than that in the passage above, can remain gesture and still seem precise enough to describe the relation of Rat to Mole and the desirability of that relation's developing. Surprisingly little of the book, as it evolves, is actually about life on the river, but that does not matter seriously, since we have also evolving alongside the relation of Rat and Mole. But here, because the experience is religious, that relation necessarily matters less, and so we must try to look at Pan himself to see what Grahame is caring about, and of course Pan himself is, and probably must be, vague. The young otter is there, protected by Pan the Friend and Helper, but even he, the most clearly seen figure in the scene, is only putative; we know nothing of him, and Rat and Mole are looking for him mostly because it is a restless summer night, not because they know where or how to look for him. In other words, the imperious command does not arise out of anything, or, really, lead to anything beyond a rescued Porky. Pan simply is, and we must take him or leave him. Even the relation of Pan to the dawn is more suggested than carefully realized.

I don't for a minute think that in any serious way Grahame believed in Pan or in any other deity. What he knew was the intensity of his own longings to live life as an escape, as holiday, as Rat and Mole can live it and Toad cannot. He was not ashamed either of the feelings or of the intensity. Still, one of the secrets of the power of the release was some sense that grown people are not supposed to yearn that much for something that many other grown people see as the yearnings of a child. If everyone in Grahame's England had been like F. J. Furnivall, Grahame would never have been driven to become an author, or at least not the author of *The Wind in the Willows*. But everyone wasn't like Furnivall; other people took and gave orders, accepted work as a sacred duty, and expected others to agree with them. Grahame did all these things, too, and part of him believed in doing so, but the greater part of him felt himself to be an exile from a world, a childhood, a Thames life, he had never quite lived in. Lonely and unhappy, possessed by longings, he was driven to justify them. The first six chapters of *The Wind in the Willows* were the only justification he needed, but he was driven to insist on more than this. There is no radical defect involved here, only a reminder that books like this one are often written by huddled, self-protective people who can be driven toward a definition of a vaguely understood "higher experience."

How odd, thus, that someone whose writing was so personal should ever have been thought of essentially as a writer for children. If Grahame "understood children," it was not because he liked them, enjoyed their presence, or even thought about them. Rather, because he was deprived of much that goes into the usual experiences of a childhood, he remained something of a child throughout his life, perceptibly more so than the rest of us. This can be said of Lewis Carroll, too, but he was too powerful and too quirky a writer to settle for trying to create in his books a world he actually wanted to live in. Generally, it is a diminishing thing in a writer to seek to do this, because it allows the edges of the imagination to go soft and remain untested, and it is usually very difficult to tell stories that take place in ideal worlds. But Grahame did just this, and in its finest moments *The Wind in the Willows* creates and sustains a genuine ideal, one that is going to continue to appeal strongly to many people, for centuries perhaps. To be rid of the cares of personality and responsibility, to forget or never know yesterday's wrongdoings or tomorrow's needs—it is a great wish, close to universal perhaps. . . . Most writers and most people find that when they have tossed off adult tasks and human curses they have, left over, only a rather empty space. But Grahame could fill that space and invite us into the charmed circle he thereby created. He could make little sounds seem like bustle, make gestures of invitation seem like love, make food and fire feel like home.

Michael Steig   (essay date 1981)

SOURCE: "At the Back of *The Wind in the Willows*: An Experiment in Biographical and Autobiographical Interpretation," in *Victorian Studies*, Vol. 24, No. 3, Spring, 1981, pp. 303-23.

[*In the following essay, Steig examines what he perceives as a veiled eroticism in* The Wind in the Willows, *using his own childhood reading of the book as a springboard for his discussion.*]

> One does not argue about *The Wind in the Willows*. The young man gives it to the girl with whom he is in love, and if she does not like it,

asks her to return his letters. The older man tries it on his nephew, and alters his will accordingly. The book is a test of character. We can't criticize it, because it is criticizing us. As I wrote once: it is a Household Book; a book which everybody in the household loves, and quotes continually; a book which is read aloud to every new guest and is regarded as the touchstone of his worth. But I must give you one word of warning. When you sit down to it, don't be so ridiculous as to suppose that you are sitting in judgment on my taste, or on the art of Kenneth Grahame. You are merely sitting in judgment on yourself. You may be worthy: I don't know. But it is you who are on trial.

(A. A. Milne)

Among Late-Victorian and Edwardian novels of fantasy, the one which seems to have retained the greatest power to affect readers emotionally, from childhood into adulthood, is Kenneth Grahame's *The Wind in the Willows* (1908). The *Alice* books may be more challenging intellectually, but Grahame's novel has, according to my personal experience and discussions with other readers, a far more lasting effect upon the feelings and loyalties of those who first take up the book at some point in childhood or adolescence. It is indeed a "household book," and certain connotations of "household" may help to explain A. A. Milne's interdict against "sitting in judgment . . . on the art of Kenneth Grahame." Such an attitude implies that this work is inviolable, immune to analysis or criticism, because the feelings it arouses are so special and private.

From a slightly different point of view, Victorian and Edwardian novels are by and large "household books"; that is, they comprise a genre of the *Heimlich*. Charles Dickens, William Makepeace Thackeray, Charlotte and Emily Brontë, George Meredith, George Eliot, George Gissing, Anthony Trollope, Thomas Hardy, Arnold Bennett, Henry James, each in his or her own way both reveals and conceals the intimacy of emotional life within the family, between lovers, and in the individual psyche. The cliché taunt, "What's he when he's at home?" may be answered or evaded in a variety of ways. While Henry James conducts so painstaking and convoluted an analysis that it often hides more than it reveals, George Eliot merges domestic realism and moral philosophy so that the latter purports to subsume the former. Thackeray manages his evasions through the coy wiles of a characterized narrator who slips in and out of the world of his novels so that their reality remains ambiguous, while Meredith manages his fictional world through a comedy of ideas which allows for the illusion of distance from household secrets. In the Brontës and Dickens there is an overt symbolism which leads away from those secrets at the same time that it embodies them, and in the case of Emily Brontë there is in addition a cunningly elusive narrative form. Hardy's usual form of indirection is a pretension to a cosmology or, as in *The Well-Beloved,* endless talk around the main subject, while Gissing combines a supposed social realism with barely concealed sexual fantasies. And, seemingly, in Trollope and the Bennett of *Clayhanger,* there is a transparent openness, so that nothing suggests itself as hidden, and an illusion of complete revelation is created—though not to the satisfaction of some readers, who may feel, "there must be more to life."

Whereas their modernist novels may once have seemed, in contrast to those of the Victorians, to be under a new and fully conscious kind of control, with increasing biographical information we can now understand the personal ambivalences embodied in the works of Virginia Woolf and James Joyce. Yet there is a difference; for Joyce and Woolf, though Victorians by birth, knew something the Victorians did not: they knew the Victorian age with hindsight and could react against it in a way that was only just becoming possible for Hardy. Our own relationship to the Victorians is also a complex one, for we are their heirs, and though we pride ourselves on having transcended their limitations in the domestic sphere, we return eternally to them, to the household in Victorian novels, to try to understand its meaning for ourselves. As Freud found in consulting Daniel Sanders's and Jakob and Wilhelm Grimm's dictionaries, *heimlich* became long ago a virtual synonym for *unheimlich* (usually translated as "uncanny"). Thus, that which is of the household is familiar and private, even secret, and, paradoxically, strange and forbidden. What is familiar is "of the family," and therefore much of it is not to be discussed, is to be repressed, so that it becomes unfamiliar to consciousness. Superficially, the family is homey (*heimisch*); but much of what goes on in one's own or someone else's household is mysterious and, in art, likely to be expressed in indirect, evasive, or symbolic form.

The *Heimlich* has an especially important role in fantasy novels ostensibly for children, from the *Alices,* the fantasies of George MacDonald, and *The Water Babies,* to Kenneth Grahame and Edith Nesbit. While the remark that Charles Kingsley's *The Water Babies* is all about masturbation and its punishment may reflect the reductive pseudo-Freudianism of a recent critic's approach to fantasy [Maureen Duffy, *The Erotic World of Faery*], the first edition's illustrator, J. Noel Paton, came remarkably close to depicting masturbation as the central theme of the novel, as we see in his frontispiece: the naked water babies cluster around the pretty fairy, thumbs in mouths and a rapt look on their faces, a situation that for a real child of similar age usually finds the other hand on his or her genitals. Such household realities are not likely to be a part of the prior, conceptualized intentions of the author, but they may nonetheless be perceived as a part of meaning.

For the present-day critic, a central interpretive problem engendered by an attraction to the *Heimlich* in Victorian novels is that of the relation between intention, meaning, and response. Now that we are largely out of the age of anxiety about the intentional fallacy, we can once again see a work of literature as an utterance by a real person, an act of attempted expression and communication. Many now read novels as *by* Dickens, or Eliot, or James, rather than as autonomous artifacts. But it is the case with Victorian novels that while overt meanings are usually not difficult to discern, the meanings that matter, those which define the work as an aesthetic object, must be constructed by the reader in the course of his or her reading experience and will not be identical for all readers. [In a footnote, the

critic explains: "I am using 'aesthetic object' somewhat as Wolfgang Iser does, to refer to the work as constituted by the reader in the reading experience and equivalent to the 'meaning' of the work."] And if one does have the habit of reading a novel as an utterance by a historically real person, the construction of this meaning must, logically, somehow take the historical author into account.

Recent theorists of aesthetic response begin from the premise that literary meaning (as distinguished from purely lexical meaning, though even that distinction is problematic) comes into existence only when the act of reading has taken place; the text may be a potential source of meanings, but it does not contain them. For Norman N. Holland, such construction of meaning will take place inevitably in terms of the reader's individual "identity theme," an unchanging structure of ways of relating to the world and to other people. For Wolfgang Iser, the work as aesthetic object is created by the reader, who follows the instructions of the "strategies" of the text: that is, the ways the author juxtaposes norms, systems, and allusions, to create the potential for a new meaning not contained within those "background" elements themselves. Iser is less interested in the range of divergency among various readers' interpretations than he is in the ways complex narratives involve the reader as a participator in the creation of meaning; but he never completely loses sight of the inevitability of such divergency. For David Bleich, on the other hand, the reporting and self-analysis of individual response is the most important source of knowledge about literature; yet paradoxically Bleich allows for the role of biographical knowledge in the reader's construction of meaning, as such knowledge becomes a part of that reader's total perception of the text.

In my own experience as reader, teacher, and critic I have found that biographical knowledge, including knowledge of an author's other works, becomes a part of my reading-history for a given text, materially clarifying or altering meaning, and thus becoming a constitutive factor in the construction of that meaning. My tentative solution to the problem of relating response to the author's intention is to try to see the work of literature as existing simultaneously in my reading experience and in its own historical context; thus the aesthetic object becomes a constellation of meanings projected along several axes, including the author's attempt to express ideas and feelings, the values of his or her age, and my personal response as they relate to my own associations.

The experiment in interpretation I shall present here follows the actual sequence of my attempts to make sense of my experiences of reading *The Wind in the Willows*. I describe in detail my reading-history insofar as I have been able to reconstruct it, isolating and describing my responses, specifying my associations with these responses—including the circumstances in which I first read the book—and then summarizing my search in Grahame's life and other writings for explanations of the nature of the book as I perceive it, so as to construct a pathway from my subjectivity to Grahame's (or rather, my construction of it). The potential value of such an experiment goes beyond the illumination of the particular works discussed in offering an approach to the problems of relationships among text, author's milieu, reader, and reader's milieu. The relevance of such an approach to the Victorian novel in general will be suggested briefly in my conclusion.

I

The reviewer for *Victorian Studies* of Peter Green's centenary biography of Kenneth Grahame remarked only that it was "comprehensive" and "disturbing." I cannot speculate on this particular reviewer's personal reasons for feeling disturbed, but potential sources of disturbance in the biography are clear enough. Green puts forth the thesis, amply supported by the details of Grahame's life, that *The Wind in the Willows* is a transformation into symbolic form of rebellious and hedonistic impulses mildly evident in his earlier works, a process taking place under the extreme pressures of a late, unhappy, and unfulfilling marriage, being the father of a handicapped (half-blind) child, and tedious work in the Bank of England. Such an analysis might indeed be disturbing to anyone for whom reading *The Wind in the Willows* has formed a special, private set of experiences, and who does not wish those experiences to be sullied by the misery and frustration of Grahame's life.

Yet I found my adult rereading of Grahame's book more perplexing than my subsequent reading of his biography, and it is from this perplexity that the present attempt at interpretation issues. On the one hand, *The Wind in the Willows* continues to be important to many who have read it, and my own childhood reading of it was an important event for me. On the other hand, there seem to be several reasons why I, and at least some of its other adult devotees, should really dislike it. One may note that this novel's fantasy seems to be a very narrow one as an analogue of the real world. Its principal animal characters are all male, all bachelors, and all independently wealthy, conditions that obtain for few people and fewer wild animals. It is, seemingly, "clean of the clash of sex," as Grahame wrote for the publisher's blurb, as well as being a demonstrably conservative satire of aspects of upper-middle-class life, a satire whose point is now largely lost in North America and increasingly irrelevant in Britain. Furthermore, it contains a good deal of what is, on the face of it, terribly sentimental writing. We can perhaps imagine why an Edwardian reader of a certain social class might find the book delightful because of these very attributes; it is difficult to understand why it should have any appeal for modern readers who have some awareness of the exclusion of females and the class presumption of the four major characters.

The observation that there would seem to be reasons to dislike *The Wind in the Willows* applies not only to my present adult perspective but to my first reading of the book in 1946, when I was ten-and-a-half. When I first proposed to teach Grahame's book in a course on children's literature which I shared with a colleague, his first reaction was, "I hate that book, with all that awful religious stuff," and I found myself nonplused because I could recall nothing religious about *The Wind in the Willows* and would have expected that I, as an avowed atheist from early childhood, would have found almost any book with overt religious content offensive by the time I was ten. Similarly, at ten I was on the brink of early adolescence and extremely interested in girls; why a book about bachelors, devoid of female characters (except for two who appear briefly), should have appealed to me at that stage seemed another mystery.

The context of my first reading turns out to be significant in reconstructing that first response. I was in a camp in the Adirondacks, my first full summer away from home, and in the infirmary with a cold. The inevitable feelings of separation and loss were complicated by the fact that my parents were counsellors at the camp, which meant that while I was away from home I was only ambiguously away from them. Upon rereading the book as an adult my general impression was that three of Mole's experiences had been the most important parts of it for me in childhood. The first occurs in the first chapter when Mole comes out of the ground in springtime and sniffs the air:

> It all seemed to be too good to be true. Hither and thither through the meadows he rambled busily, along the hedgerows, across the copses, finding everywhere birds building, flowers budding, leaves thrusting. . . .

> He thought his happiness was complete when, as he meandered aimlessly along, suddenly he stood by the edge of a full-fed river. Never in his life had he seen a river before—this sleek, sinuous, full-bodied animal, chasing and chuckling, gripping things with a gurgle and leaving them with a laugh, to fling itself on fresh playmates that shook themselves free and were caught and held again.

As I can reconstruct my response it was one of delight, of identification with Mole, and a great feeling of comfort. For the first eight years of my life summers had been spent at my family's place in Connecticut, away from the deadness and heat of a New York summer; this place had been sold in 1945, and we summered that year in Long Island. Only now, in my first summer in camp, did it come home to me forcefully that Connecticut was gone forever; Mole's rediscovery of spring and discovery of the river are associated permanently for me with each summer's return to the green woods, and the wide brook that ran through our property. Thus in the circumstances surrounding my first reading of *The Wind in the Willows,* several kinds of felt loss and regained delight are layered upon one another.

These layers of feeling are increased and deepened in my recalled response to Mole's return to his home in the ground in the fifth chapter, "Dulce Domum." Having entered the upper world and then the dangerous Wild Wood, where he and friend Rat have been given shelter by the avuncular Badger, Mole is struck with nostalgic longing—which he experiences as smell, a point I will take up below—for his home; but because Rat won't listen to him and keeps on walking, Mole is finally overcome: "The Mole subsided forlornly on a tree-stump and tried to control himself, for he felt it surely coming. The sob he had fought with so long refused to be beaten. Up and up, it forced its way to the air, and then another, and another, and others thick and fast; till poor Mole at last gave up the struggle, and cried freely and helplessly and openly, now that he knew it was all over and he had lost what he could hardly be said to have found." Mole then explains to Rat, amidst further sobs, what his trouble is: ". . . it was my own little home—and I was fond of it—and I went away and forgot all about it—and then I smelt it suddenly—on the road, when I called and you wouldn't listen, Rat—and everything came back to me with a rush—and I *wanted* it!—O dear, O dear!—and when you wouldn't turn back, Ratty—and I had to leave it, though I was smelling it all the time—I thought my heart would break.—We might have just gone and had one look at it, Ratty—only one look—it was close by—but you wouldn't turn back Ratty, you wouldn't turn back!"

This is followed by the now fatherly Rat's insistence that they go immediately to Mole End and by the rhapsodic passages of Mole's rediscovery of his home, beginning with an "electric thrill . . . passing down" his body which, though described as "faint," is strong enough to be felt by Rat through physical contact with Mole. Smell leads Mole to his home, but once Mole End is attained smell drops out of the narrative and is replaced by Mole's bourgeois delight in seeing his possessions again, as well as the oral delight in the "provender so magically provided" by working-class field mice children who have come singing Christmas carols.

My associations with this episode are no less specific or vivid. In addition to feelings of loss and return, an incident from age four has the most direct association with my response to "Dulce Domum." Mole's speech ending, "Ratty, you wouldn't turn back!" recalls the time when, on a snowy day my father picked me up at nursery school, assuming that my mother wouldn't be able to make it in time from her job because of the snow. Just as the bus arrived I spotted my mother waving to us from the other side of Central Park West. My father didn't see her and started loading me into the bus despite my protests that I wanted to go to my mother. I don't remember whether I actually wept, but the frustration, the helplessness of the small child to communicate something of great emotional importance comes back to me even today with great force when I read those passages in *The Wind in the Willows*.

The difficulty of relating childhood memory to adult response and interpretation may be suggested, however, by what I am able to make of the predominance and subsequent elimination of *smell* in "Dulce Domum." Intuitively, I feel that smell is an important component of the secret, the *Heimlich,* the forbidden. As Ernest Schachtel points out, smell is the sense in children most subject to conditioning and suppression by adults. It is closest to an animal sense, at least initially lacking in conceptual discrimination, but in a child's development it is most closely allied with feelings of shame, guilt, and disgust. It is perhaps for these reasons that I have no precise memories associated with Mole's smelling of his home, but retain a strong feeling that this is related to some of my most basic childhood experiences. And thus for me the replacement of smell by sight as the dominant feeling in Mole's return to his home is akin to a shift from early childhood to more adult, conceptual ways of thinking and feeling. But how

much of my response here is based on traces of childhood memory and how much is a construct based on my reading of Freud and Schachtel is difficult to say. One must recognize that all memories—like all interpretations—are constructs whose ultimate truth can never be established.

Grahame himself stresses that Mole's return is a kind of temporary regression: Mole sees "clearly how plain and simple—how narrow, even—it all was; but clearly too how much it all meant to him, and the special value of some such anchorage in one's existence. He did not at all want to abandon the new life and its splendid spaces, to turn his back on sun and air and all they offered him and creep home and stay there; the upperworld was all too strong, it called to him still, even down there, and he knew he must return to the larger stage." The very image of an underground home suggests a return to some womblike comfort or, more resignedly, to the grave. My own particular association with this aspect of Mole's return, however, is the comfort of being ill in bed, waited on by adults, and in the context of my first reading more specifically the infirmary at camp, which removed me temporarily from the challenges of a group situation and allowed me to be waited on by a young and interesting nurse. Whether *The Wind in the Willows* is, as Grahame wrote at least twice, free of problems and free of sex, remains to be determined—and thus, whether my association of the book with a budding interest in girls is purely contingent on the circumstances of my first reading.

The seventh chapter, "The Piper at the Gates of Dawn," contains expressive imagery which in some ways recalls "Dolce Domum." Again, loss is an initial theme: little Portly, the baby otter, is missing, and his father expresses his sense of desolation to Mole and Rat. But the father's sense of loss becomes the occasion for a new set of emotions to be experienced by Mole and Rat as they search for Portly. These feelings begin for Rat with what is apparently the piping of a bird, which is for him "so beautiful and strange and new! Since it was to end so soon I almost wish I had never heard it. For it had roused a longing in me that is pain, and nothing seems worth while but just to hear that sound once more and go on listening to it for ever." Mole hears nothing "but the wind playing in the reeds and rushes and osiers," but Rat hears the sound again, and, "rapt, transported, trembling, he was possessed in all his senses by this new divine thing that caught up his helpless soul and swung and dandled it, a powerless but happy infant in a strong sustaining grasp."

Finally, as they row closer, Mole hears as well, and is likewise "caught . . . up, and possessed . . . utterly." Reaching the island the two are struck with an ever-deeper awe; Rat trembles "violently," and Mole's emotions are described at length:

> Perhaps he would never have dared to raise his eyes, but that, though the piping was now hushed, the call and the summons seemed still dominant and imperious. He might not refuse, were Death himself waiting to strike him instantly, once he had looked with mortal eye on things rightly kept hidden. Trembling he obeyed, and raised his humble head; and then, in the utter clearness of the imminent dawn,

while Nature, flushed with fulness of incredible colour, seemed to hold her breath for the event, he looked in the very eyes of the Friend and Helper; saw the backward sweep of the curved horns, gleaming in the growing daylight; saw the stern, hooked nose between the kindly eyes that were looking down on them humourously, while the bearded mouth broke into a half-smile at the corners; saw the rippling muscles on the arm that lay across the broad chest, the long supple hand still holding the pan-pipes only just fallen away from the parted lips; saw the splendid curves of the shaggy limbs disposed in majestic ease on the sward; saw last of all, nestling between his very hooves, sleeping soundly in utter peace and contentment, the little, round, podgy, childish form of the baby otter, . . .

"Rat!" he found breath to whisper, shaking. "Are you afraid?"

"Afraid?" murmured the Rat, his eyes shining with unutterable love. "Afraid! Of *Him?* O, never, never! And yet—and yet—O, Mole, I am afraid!"

Then the two animals, crouching to the earth, bowed their heads and did worship.

When little Portly awakens he searches for the "demi-god" like "a child that has fallen happily asleep in its nurse's arms, and wakes to find itself alone and laid in a strange place . . . till at last the black moment came for giving it up, and sitting down and crying bitterly." But Rat and Mole do not weep because they have been granted the "gift of forgetfulness." They feel "strangely tired," with a lingering sense of contentment, and by the end of the chapter Rat is asleep in the boat, "with a smile of much happiness on his face." My adult response to this chapter is a mixture of revulsion and identification. No doubt this chapter is what my colleague referred to as "that awful religious stuff," with its obvious paralleling of Pan and Christ. The swooning worship is a bit heavy for me now, but I have the sense that my childhood response was positive, if not to Pan himself, then to the gamut of emotions experienced by Rat and Mole. I am fairly sure that as a child I skimmed the overtly religious passages and responded to the complex of emotions: that sense of suddenly seeing things clearly, the awe before nature (once again, for me inextricably tied up with my own lost childhood Arcadia), but also the feeling of being completely taken care of by an adult, expressed in quite different ways in the description of Portly between the hooves of Pan and the other animals' worshipful submission to his power.

Pan is here, one might think, the same fantasized demigod about whom Grahame wrote seventeen years earlier in **"The Rural Pan."** But whereas in the latter essay Pan has the ephemeral quality of immanence in nature, in the seventh chapter of *The Wind in the Willows* he is incarnated, with different results. For me, two main things emerge from the passage describing Pan: the lingeringly stressed details, with an emphasis on his power and muscular beauty, and the way in which the otter's child is cradled between his hooves, sleeping with the contentment of a young child in its mother's arms. This strikes me as the embodiment of father and mother in one figure, and the animals' response combines a worship of the nurturing mother (nature, referred to metaphorically as "she" early in the paragraph) with a submission to the all-powerful but benign father. Perhaps in part through an unconscious sense of this I felt (and still feel) that Mole's and Rat's experiences in the seventh chapter are intensely erotic, from the initial intoxications of melody, to the violent trembling at the sight of "things rightly kept hidden," the peak of intense experience in the combination of love, fear, and worship, followed by the gradually falling intensity of emotion (as the animals move into forgetfulness), to the physical exhaustion which leaves Mole "half-dozing in the hot sun," and "the weary Rat . . . fast asleep."

Roger Sale has recently written that if you "ask any lover of the book to name the most memorable parts . . . the answer will invariably be scenes from the first half [that is, up to chapter seven]," and though this is unverifiable and probably untrue—since many readers consider Toad the center of the book—it happens to fit with my own reading-history. Toad, delightful though he is, just did not exercise the same magic upon me, nor does he today. Intellectually, one may see the toad as the id, the representative of chaotic and dangerous desires. Of the four animal friends, he is the one who violates codes of good behavior and even becomes an actual criminal in his theft of automobiles. But at age ten, such acting-out was not recognizable as part of myself; it was low comedy, amusing but viewed from a distance.

Insofar as I can analyze my childhood reading of the book, then, the dominant meaning has to do with loss, which begins with the sense of separation from one's mother in infancy, repeated in various ways—literal and symbolic—as one develops; and in the more particular sense, for me, of loss of a place that was home in a more tangible way than a series of apartments over the years—a home that had been periodically regained and temporarily lost with the expectation of recovery each summer. These feelings carry over into the newly threatening loss involved in summer camp, in growing into adolescence, in having to make my own way with an unfamiliar group of my peers, and in the mysteries of adult sexuality as well as the delights and anxieties of a potentially new relationship to girls. In the latter regard, the "Piper at the Gates of Dawn" chapter is important not because it addresses the problem of sexuality directly, but because its rise and fall of emotion, with the revelation of the mystery at the peak, approximate the feelings I was tentatively beginning to connect with becoming an adolescent. In this respect it is an excellent example of what I see as the indirection with which the *Heimlich* is presented in Victorian novels, though in a book intended for children the indirection is perhaps especially oblique.

It is not difficult to see where a plausible interpretation of the personal meaning of *The Wind in the Willows* for its author intersects with my own set of meanings, constructed from adult and memory of childhood response. Loss, deprivation of place, and the desire to escape from the city seem to dominate Grahame's life. Having lost his mother when he was not quite five and, effectually, his father as well (since James Cunningham Grahame soon gave up care of his young family to their maternal grandmother), he spent the remainder of his childhood in Cookham Dene, Berkshire, Cranbourne near Windsor, and St. Edward's School, Oxford, coming to love the Berkshire and Surrey downlands and the Thames valley, as well as the still very medieval city of Oxford. There seems little doubt that his uncle's refusal to permit him to enter Oxford University was experienced as another loss, of a place he had come to consider his own, and that London and a clerkship in the Bank of England (of which he eventually became secretary) were antipathetic to his natural feelings.

Peter Green sees the appearance of Pan in the seventh chapter as one manifestation of a rebellious element in Grahame's character, expressed mildly elsewhere in such essays as **"The Rural Pan,"** but Green takes Toad as a much more direct expression of Grahame's ambivalence, since the open rebel is associated with the motorcar—which Grahame abhorred—and is ultimately punished. The Pan of chapter seven Green deprecates as "desexualized, paternalized," and "a projection of Edwardian ruralism, post-Beardsley social opposition, wistful yearning for conformity, an urge towards some replacement for Arnold's God as a comforting Father Figure". Yet, as my summary should have suggested, the feelings expressed in the chapter are more complex than this, in its vision of a motherly father, as well as a distinctly sensual, masculine one, perhaps implying symbolically a boy's erotic feelings for his mother, sublimated into a homoerotic image whose quality Grahame could never acknowledge directly.

Considering how concrete the details of physical description are in the text, it seems strange that a psychoanalytic writer such as Lili Peller could describe the form of the "Faun" as one which, "barely perceived, dissolves and melts into the foliage"; but Peller is classifying *The Wind in the Willows* as an "Early Tale," which appeals to young, preoedipal children, and in which sex is reassuringly denied through the mask of sexually unspecific animals. The fact that this particular children's book seems to be read and treasured by many adults, however, and is often first read in preadolescence, makes a difference. What might be comforting denial to a young child may be, for one on the brink of adolescence, an equally comforting, and equally disguised, affirmation of sexual feelings. This latter remark speaks to my own adult and reconstructed childhood responses, but Grahame is at once more elaborately evasive and revelatory than I have yet suggested. The statement that the animals are seeing "things rightly kept hidden" sounds very close to the concept of the *Heimlich,* just because things at home, things private and secret (and repressed) have a disturbing (*unheimlich*) effect when revealed in distorted or symbolic form. And the duplicity goes even further, for Grahame takes the trouble to tell us that Mole feels "no panic terror": yet etymologically and conventionally in English "panic terror" is precisely what one is supposed to feel at the sight of Pan. If the intense emotions felt by the animals contain no element of "panic terror," are we to believe that they are entirely serene? This is borne out neither by the "objective" content of the text nor by my own response to it. As we shall see, Gra-

hame's conceptual understanding of what is "in" his text is open to question in a number of ways.

II

After my adult rereading I wanted to see whether Grahame's other works contained any elements comparable to the veiled eroticism I thought I detected in the seventh chapter of *The Wind in the Willows.* Peter Green suggests that one can find in the earlier works more explicit and thus less powerful expressions of Grahame's impulses and conflicts which are converted into symbolic form in the later book. The rejection of adults as lofty, uncaring, unreasonable "Olympians" in *The Golden Age* and *Dream Days* becomes in *The Wind in the Willows* a symbolic rejection of ever growing up, though with the compromise with conformity expressed in Mole, Rat, and Badger's treatment of the troublesome Toad. As Green speculates about the success of the two books of sketches about children, the fin-de-siècle temperament was ready for a revelation of the gulf between the adult's world and the child's; and to some extent we are still part of that modern temperament which had its roots in late-Victorian days. But there are other patterns and emphases in those sketches which can be related directly to the notion of "things rightly kept hidden," although they are in fact expressed quite overtly.

Half of the eighteen sketches in *The Golden Age* and of the eight in *Dream Days* deal with one or more of four related themes: children's curiosity about adult love life, boys' curiosity about girls, children's voyeurism, and heterosexual feelings or fantasies in young boys. In **"A Holiday"** [*The Golden Age*] the narrator tells of leaving his brothers and sister to follow the summons of nature, taking the "hearty wind" for his guide:

> A whimsical comrade I found him ere he had done with me. Was it in jest or with some serious purpose of his own, that he brought me plump upon a pair of lovers, silent, face to face o'er a discreet unwinking stile? As a rule this sort of thing struck me as the most pitiful tomfoolery. Two calves rubbing noses through a gate were natural and right and within the order of things; but that human beings, with salient interests and active pursuits beckoning them on from every side, could thus—! Well, it was a thing to hurry past, shamed of face, and think on no more.

But the "magical touch in the air" causes him to regard "these fatuous ones with kindliness instead of contempt, as I rambled by, unheeded of them"—a fairly clear statement of the child's somewhat unwilling acknowledgment that sex between humans is natural.

The same narrator, describing himself at an earlier age in **"The Finding of the Princess,"** presents an adventure in which he first fantasizes finding "the necessary Princess," and then suddenly believes he has found her in the person of a young woman "laughingly struggling to disengage her hand from the grasp of a grown-up man". He is naively open with the couple about his belief that she is a princess, and they take him into the house and give him a sumptuous meal. There is a dual perspective, and we understand that the young woman and man regard the boy with a patronizing and careless amusement. When leaving, the child sees the couple walking with arms around each others' waists down the path, and on turning for home he is "possessed" by "a wild unreasoning panic, and . . . sped out of the garden like a guilty thing . . . hounded by nameless terrors". That night he dreams of himself as a fish, thrusting "up a nose through water-lily leaves to be kissed by a rose-flushed princess". The connections among the child's feelings are left unstated, but one may feel that the sudden access of guilt and panic has to do with his afternoon's episode of voyeurism, while the concluding dream with its imagery of swimming, thrusting, and the "rose flush" hints at something more than a merely abstract desire for a "princess."

In contrast, **"The Burglars"** is a straightforward, amusing account of the children's taking the spooning curate and their Aunt Maria as burglars and causing them much embarrassment. The sketch opens with some speculation by the children as to what "spooning" is, and Edward (the eldest) can only conclude lamely that "it's just a thing they [adults] do, you know". Sexual curiosity is the dramatic motive of this sketch, though the dénouement is mild farce, revealing the "spooners" as ridiculous. The *Heimlich,* the private, secret aspects of the family, is here as a part of the story's propositional content, but as in most of the other sketches it is not presented with much force and is overlaid with a tone of knowing adult irony. The strongest instances of presented emotion are **"The Magic Ring,"** one of a group of sketches in *Dream Days* dealing with boys' budding interest in girls, and **"Its Walls Were as of Jasper,"** the emotional power of which comes from its total lack of explanation.

The first of these sketches is probably the most overtly erotic. It tells of the boys' visit to a circus, during which the narrator falls in love, first with Coralie, the "Woman of the Ring,—flawless, complete, untrammelled in each subtly curving limb", and then more profoundly with Zephyrine, the Bride of the Desert, a "magnificent, full-figured Cleopatra." As in **"The Finding of the Princess,"** this sketch ends with the narrator dreaming, this time of Zephyrine, with the eyes of the white-limbed Coralie glimmering at them in reproach. Here we are clearly on the verge of masturbation fantasies. But **"Its Walls Were as of Jasper"** is much more ambiguous. The narrator is taken by his aunt (there are no parents in these books, likely a reflection of Grahame's own childhood) to a large country house where he is promptly ignored by the adults. Wandering from room to room he takes down a picture book and, after an initial disappointment that it is in a foreign language, discovers in it pictures that image some of his own fantasies. There is nothing specifically sexual, though one page on which he focuses depicts a wedding. But when discovered by his hostess, he is spanked soundly and made to suffer with the *Sabbath Improver*. It is never made clear what his particular crime has been, beyond the fact that he is being denied indulgence in fantasy and made to feel guilty about it. (The spanking itself is sexually ambiguous: in the text the boy's fantasies are interrupted with his own *"Ow! Ow! Ow!"* and the book is "ravished" from the boy's grasp by his "dressy" hostess.)

I find it most significant that Grahame took such pains to

deny that *The Wind in the Willows* contains either problems or sex, considering that his two previous books are full of both. And there is one surprising passage in the novel which may illustrate the degree of self-deception of which he was capable. At the beginning of the second chapter, following Mole's ecstatic discovery of the river at the end of the first chapter, we are told that Rat has been swimming in the river with his friends the ducks and annoying them by diving down to tickle their chins. He has composed a five-stanza song which he calls "Ducks' Ditty." I shall quote stanzas one, four, and five:

> All along the backwater,
> Through the rushes tall,
> Ducks are a-dabbling,
> Up tails all!
>
> . . . . .
>
> Everyone for what he likes!
> We like to be
> Heads down, tails up,
> Dabbling free!
>
> High in the blue above
> Swifts whirl and call—
> We are down a-dabbling
> Up tails all!

Assuming that Grahame had no conscious intention of slipping in an allusion which would appeal to adults' salaciousness while bypassing innocent children, this poem strikes me as a remarkable example of Victorian doublethink, the ability to know something and deny it to one's consciousness simultaneously. For "uptails all" has a long history as a slang expression referring to sexual intercourse. The *OED* gives as its first meaning, "the name of an old song and its tune," and one has to seek pretty assiduously in that chaste dictionary to piece together the meaning that is historically primary. Even if Grahame did not know the old vulgar song, it is unlikely that he did not know Robert Herrick's poem, "Up tailes all," included in *Hesperides*, and in which the meaning is perfectly clear. Herrick was one of Grahame's favorite poets, and one of the four, after Shakespeare, who led the list for numbers of poems included in Grahame's idiosyncratic anthology of poems for children.

In context, the double entendre seems at first to make little sense, but referring again to my own responses and associations, and to the end of the first chapter, in which Mole is described as "emancipated" because he has "learnt to swim and to row, and entered into the joy of running water," I find a generalized sensuality in swimming, which amounts to being touched all over one's body, and in boating, in the alternation of struggling against the water's resistance and submitting to its force in drifting. Note also that Rat's tickling the ducks' necks is a kind of aggressive teasing of their bodies, done while he is swimming, which Rat (unlike a real water rat) does for sheer enjoyment. Not that this is much to build a full-scale interpretation on, for the sexual implications are not carried through in this chapter, as Toad soon turns up and attention is focused on him. But the very presence of the salacious allusion amounts to a kind of denial of its meaning, in the context of a book whose author guaranteed it to be "clean of the clash of sex." Putting this together with the erotic aura of chapter seven, I have to conclude that Grahame's insistence on the absence of sex is a clue to his conscious awareness of it in many of the earlier sketches about children, and at least a repressed awareness of its presence in *The Wind in the Willows*.

That presence is discernible through reader-response and its analysis, taken in combination with the evidence of Grahame's other works and the details of his life. One may wonder what Grahame thought of Aubrey Beardsley's title page design for *Pagan Papers*, showing two strange faun creatures, one, seemingly male and in human dress, looking wistfully at the other, who is naked and perfectly ambiguous sexually. Certainly there is little in *Pagan Papers*, apart from three of the six pieces later moved to *The Golden Age*, that even hints at the erotic. Beardsley may have been indulging his own preoccupations rather than actively interpreting the content of a somewhat misleadingly titled book. But sexual ambiguity is one of the feelings I find evoked by the "panic" scene of the seventh chapter of *The Wind in the Willows*. One way of explaining Grahame's making all of the principal characters male, animal, and without the usual animal characteristics of predatoriness or sexual need, is that he was engaging in a kind of denial which subsequently manifested itself in those two strong statements about the absence of problems and sex. It seems less useful to label the animals "phallic," as Maureen Duffy does, than to try to capture, subjectively, the dramatic and narrative feeling and tone, and to place these in relation to Grahame's life and other writings.

III

In the context of late-nineteenth and early twentieth-century literature, Kenneth Grahame may look like something of an anomaly: a man who in the 1890s published one mild book of essays and two bestselling volumes of sketches about childhood, and who then wrote only one more book, which in the year of its appearance evoked a good deal of confusion in his former admirers because it was so different from his previous work, but which has remained the book by which he is remembered—a book not clearly either for children or adults, and which overtly resembles no other volume that we normally think of as a Victorian or Edwardian novel. Yet that book is, as Peter Green has shown, in its own way as much a transformed autobiography as *David Copperfield, Wuthering Heights,* or *The Mill on the Floss*. Each of these novels and many others of the period resemble Grahame's fantasy-novel in that each has an overt content of propositional meaning which overlies a strong, though disguised, emotional content of the forbidden. If the programmatic meaning of *The Wind in the Willows* is the misbehavior and reform of Mr. Toad, that of *David Copperfield* is that David's heart must mature from its infatuation with Dora to the true love of Anges; but Murdstone and Heep have already been shown, quite overtly, to be his doubles, and there is no evidence but narrative assertion that David has really escaped the shadows of his childhood by the conclusion of the novel.

Emily Brontë is more elusive in her elaborate narrative layering, and yet the *heimlich* concerns of brother-sister love are to be found at the base of the overt tale of Romantic love fulfilled only in death. In a quite different way Eliot in *The Mill on the Floss* places the most private, familial matters at the emotional center, and yet structures the novel in terms of a moral and philosophical program which is then subverted or at least distorted by the wish fulfillment fantasy of the book's ending. With Henry James the typically Victorian programmatic content seems to disappear, and yet fantasies of the private and forbidden are admitted through other kinds of indirection: the "uncanny" mystery of *The Turn of the Screw,* the innocent viewpoint of the child in *What Maisie Knew,* or the endless talk around the subject by an elderly man "innocently" in love with the heroine in *The Awkward Age*.

It is not my intent to suggest that *The Wind in the Willows* is a universally serviceable paradigm for Victorian and Edwardian novels. For one thing, these simplified generalizations must stem in part from my own preoccupations as a critic and a person: primarily, the search for hidden meanings. But I contend that the exploration of meaning along subjective and biographical axes provides a dialectical basis for intersubjective syntheses, initially between critic and author, and potentially, if the critic's experiences bear any resemblance to others', between critic and other readers. In the area of Victorian literary domesticity, where the *Heimlich* so often masquerades as a synonym of the *Heimisch* instead of the *Unheimlich* (rather as Mrs. Rochester's sex-mad screams are for such a long time attributed to the placid Grace Poole), the approach may prove to be one of the most fruitful methods for recovering meanings that really matter to us.

John Anderson   (essay date 1982)

SOURCE: "Kenneth Grahame (1920)" in *Art & Reality,* Janet Anderson, Graham Cullum, Kimon Lycos, eds., Hale & Iremonger, 1982, pp. 157-61.

[*In the following essay, Anderson discusses the characteristics of Grahame's prose style.*]

Kenneth Grahame's writing belongs to what might be called the literature of the countryside. Not only does it deal with the significance of common things, of growth, of open-air delights; it draws attention to the way in which the countryside is significant in history. These qualities are to be found also in Chesterton and Belloc, the latter of whom has enshrined them in the poem at the end of *The Four Men*:

> He does not die that can bequeath
> Some influence to the land he knows,
> Or dares, persistent, interwreath
> Love permanent with the wild hedgerows;
>> He does not die, but still remains
>> Substantiate with his darling plains.

George Bourne, in his *Memoirs of a Surrey Labourer,* makes it quite clear that such historical significance resides in persons. There is nothing 'literary' about his attitude; he describes country life as it is lived and his description is direct and free from literary allusions. With Chesterton, Belloc and Kenneth Grahame there is at least a hint of the pathetic fallacy, and little description of country life as it is actually lived by those whose lot it is to till the fields and tend the crops and animals thereon.

Perhaps Kenneth Grahame comes nearer than either of them to the 'John Barleycorn' attitude, even though the very titles of the first two **Pagan Papers**—'Romance of the Road' and 'Romance of the Rail'—indicate the romanticism which is expressed in Kenneth Grahames's case by his somewhat learned and literary views, and there is a strong suggestion that the countryside is being described from the point of view not merely of the 'educated' but of the comfortable class. In this respect Chesterton, and to a great extent, Belloc, achieve a more objective attitude, though their Romanist views do not permit of a quite non-sentimental outlook (cf. Chesterton's interpretation of history in the matter of the Crusades). In none of them, of course, do we get simple nature-worship; all recognise the importance (or the necessity) of work and toil, yet sometimes, in **Pagan Papers,** there is a suggestion of literature and life (especially that of the countryside) as amusement, as reflection for the jaded—not as something that is actually lived. And connected therewith, there is a certain 'insincerity'—a search for the *mot juste,* for *neat* ways of saying things, for the sake of neatness and not for the things. This characteristic also appears in the literary style of the 'I' of **The Golden Age** and illustrates how 'fancy' can lead to *inconsequence,* to having things praised for their associations and not for themselves. At other times, again, there is a suggestion that men seek, and have sought, the idyllic: that there is a real and possible life of this kind, with its own economies and its own enjoyments: that, at least, it is a kind of life into which one can sink for awhile, and in which, if one could stay, it would be well. Then, again, there is the notion that all we have are glimpses of something that is now unattainable.

For Kenneth Grahame the golden age was in the past, both as regards the race and as regards individuals. In **"The Lost Centaur,"** he asks if the lamentable cleavage between men and animals that has taken place somewhere along the line of development might not have been avoided, thus leaving the world with beings of a 'dual nature', comprising 'the nobilities of both and the baseness of neither'. And of ourselves, he says: 'As we grow from our animal infancy and the threads snap one by one at each gallant wing-stroke of a soul poised for flight into Empyrean, we are yet conscious of a loss for every gain, we have some forlorn sense of a vanished heritage.' What most endears these pagan worlds to him is the absence of didacticism, and though the rhythm of his prose gives an effect of rhetoric, there is thus often the saving grace of a certain ironical criticism of business and of systems of ends (i.e., of definite objects or goals), ranging from that of the strenuous holidaymakers in 'Loafing', 'their voices clamant of feats to be accomplished', to the more whimsical paper, called 'Deus Terminus', with its final request for a 'fat and succulent stationmaster' to be offered up on 'the altar of expiation'. There is, too, evidence of a certain *satyric* mentality (cf. his fondness for the musical god, Pan) which has none of the sadness of Belloc or the buffoonery of Chesterton; but there is, unfortunately, not enough of either quality to

save the work from being judged both 'literary' and cathartic—something to amuse, to distract and 'interest'.

It is in **The Golden Age** itself that we find this ironical criticism of convention as the world is seen through the eyes of a child. *He,* for example, is not allowed to do as he likes, but *they* (the Olympians) are, only they have forgotten how to like (cf. the wish that fails because it never acts).

> These elders, our betters by a trick of chance, commanded no respect, but only a certain blend of envy (for their good luck) and pity (for their inability to make good use of it). . . . Having absolute licence to indulge in the pleasures of life, they could get no good of it. They might dabble in the pond all day . . . they were free to fire cannons and explode mines in the lawn; yet they never did any of these things. No irresistible Energy haled them to church o' Sundays: yet they went there regularly of their own accord, though they betrayed no greater delight in the experience than ourselves.

Even in **The Golden Age,** 'fancy' intrudes to some extent. Instead of the recognition of play as useless work for its own sake, we have the children's activities glamourised. The impracticability of the 'practical' is not to be shown by means of 'fancy' or romance, but by means of things themselves as contrasted with ends or purposes. The earth and the children's kinship with it are not presented directly, but are treated with an insistence on the joys of retrospection, which comes perilously near the 'Cult of Immaturity'; but if it is a cult of anything, it is the cult of romance, which is not a childish thing at all. There is a certain amount of romance in Cook's 'Littlemen' in *The Playway,* but through it all, these 'Littlemen' are eminently practical. One might rather say that Grahame puts a romantic flavour over things that would later in life seem romantic, but were not so at the time. It is true that tales of knights and chivalry were far less interesting than paddling and other childhood activities, but Grahame sheds on these the light of romance that comes with memories in after years.

This is a good book, a better than **Pagan Papers** and superior, too, to **Dream Days**. It is nearer to things themselves and has fewer allusions, though it is still burdened by romance. Its excellence lies in the fact that it shows the working of simple motives, the going direct to some object, the cultivation of things in themselves—things not tied up with other people's expectations. In a word, it deals with the age of innocence, a theme which is strongly grasped; and for that reason alone, it is not a children's book, but quite simply a work of art, with certain incongruities like the foisting of literary enthusiasms on 'I', etc., but good in spite of that.

In **Dream Days** we find a greater tendency to epigram, much longer stories (suggesting a spinning out, or the intrusion of alien material) and more 'grown-up' stories. The title, too, is bad, standing as it does for the development of one of the defects in the previous book. There is also some affectation, a certain striving after 'fine writing' and, as a result, the poses are no longer boys' poses—they are too thoughtful. This preciosity leads to making fun by mixing up childishness and grown-upness—by a notion of the incongruity of a child's imaginings. But this position is not really sound for the child does not mix toys with his 'grown-up' adventures.

Perhaps the suggestion in the title is that we have here a halfway stage between the Age of Innocence and the Age of Convention—a conventionalised innocence, as it were—a compromise. But (except for the absence of 'Edward'), the background seems much the same, and the ages of the children very little different; the age is not yet the age of puberty. At any rate, the stories are told from a more external point of view—that of making fun of the child instead of entering into his diversions. They are *pictorial* rather than dramatic, and the atmosphere partakes too much of the 'jolly-good-fellow' spirit, of Bohemianism as well as of reflectiveness. The last story in the book is much the best; it captures some of the spirit of *The Golden Age* and avoids the smartness that has crept into much of *Dream Days*.

In *Books and Persons,* Arnold Bennett describes *The Wind in the Willows* as 'an urbane exercise in irony'. What we have in Kenneth Grahame generally, and *The Wind in the Willows* in particular, is a criticism of *habits* as contrasted with spontaneous activity; *or* of straight lines as contrasted with cycles—a criticism, in a word, of rigidity (i.e., of 'morals'). This is presumably the function of all comedy, whether in the form of irony or not, and just as it stands for criticism against 'morals', so it stands, in general, for art and literature, for things themselves against pretences (for the removal of hypotheses), for variety against uniformity—in a word, for beauty.

At the same time, there are in the book (cf. the chapter headed 'Wildwood'), objections to 'adventure without responsibility', such as those indulged in by Toad, as much as to 'responsibility without adventure'. These attitudes on the part of the author are both inartistic, for art is not *random* (as moralists assume); it is not a mere outbreak; it has rules. The important point is to follow the rules of things them selves, not to set up rules over and above them, i.e., not to set up standards from without. Things *have* measures. In addition to this defect, there is, as in the other books, a certain amount of 'fine writing' and some incongruity as in Otter's description of the snow.

But in the wonderful Pan episode ('The Piper at the Gates') we have the sense of great moments; of the lifting of veils; of inspirations that cannot be recaptured, but that somehow lead us on thereafter. There is also a sense of security, of a watcher and helper, of 'nature' that carries us though in *spite* of our efforts; not end, nor yet origin, but being (cf. 'the god who made things as they are'). We have, too, a notion of harmony behind strife; of value behind valuation. This is all romanticism (yet of a realistic sort), and may be compared with *furgen,* which is much more romantic and gives far less sense of actuality.

Kenneth Grahame achieves this sense of actuality in many ways. For instance, among his animals we find the notion of servants, of foreigners, of tradesmen and all sorts of specialists just as we find them in real life. Yet over the whole work he casts a poetic spell, perhaps because he gives such lively expression to our own longings for 'adventure'. It is interesting to see how he treats adventure itself in the four main characters of the book. Mole embarks upon it from ignorance and interest; Rat from poetry (romance) and because he enjoys it; Toad from vanity and Badger from necessity—he is quite willing to undertake adventures when they have to be undertaken, but he is fundamentally fond of peace and security. As Arnold Bennett says, 'they are human beings, and they are meant to be nothing but human beings. . . . The superficial scheme of the story is so childishly naive, or so daringly naive, that only a genius could have preserved it from the ridiculous'; and it is 'no more to be comprehended by youth than *The Golden Age* was to be comprehended by youth'. It is, in fact, an unusual and wonderful work, and both in it and in *The Golden Age,* Kenneth Grahame, although his output his output is so small, shows himself an artist of very great ability.

Carlee Lippman   (essay date 1983)

SOURCE: "All the Comforts of Home," in *The Antioch Review,* Vol. 41, No. 4, Fall, 1983, pp. 409-20.

[*In the following essay, Lippman considers the notion of "comfort" as it applies to* The Wind in the Willows.]

There are times in life when innocence seems very far away, like something once dreamed and long forgotten. Almost forgotten. That residue in us that reminds us of another time, another state, never really vanishes, but lives to prick and disturb. The disturbance takes the form of a yearning for the simpler, the gentler, the aimless day, the cricket-loud back porch, the meadow more green and more yellow than nature herself planned. Idealized memories long since rigidified as picture postcards.

And there is nothing strange about this. Hazy reveries, half-remembered visions, do not a civilization make. We are better equipped for a life of toil without such encumbrances. If we are intelligent and opt for contentment, we do our best to brush off the small gnawings of these impossible pleasures. If, however, we are unable to relinquish them, the suffering can be exquisite.

The cure? Insanity, permanent infantilism, living through one's children, through other people's children, writing for one's children. Aha! Writing for one's children! You mean, of course, writing for oneself? You wince. I've hit a nerve. You blush, and it's all there in your face. Don't shut the notebook, hiding it under the *Times Literary Supplement.* You're not alone. The world is full of aging children in business suits, models of seriousness, studies crammed with adult toys.

"Not all people who think they are writing for children are really doing so," says Jean Karl in *From Childhood to Childhood.* Whatever his intentions, Kenneth Grahame wrote *The Wind in the Willows* for his son. That we know. And we feel certain his son enjoyed it, as multitudes after him have done. But we feel certain, too, that Kenneth Grahame enjoyed the writing of it more than anyone else did the reading of it. Why? Because *The Wind in the Willows* is one of the most perfect wish-fulfillment books of all times. An extravagant claim? Perhaps. But an extravagant book. A book, curiously, about animals. And very curious animals. Curiously like people. Kenneth Grahame writes about animals because it is more gratifying to write about animals. They don't have to go to work and stay out of reform school. Their lives are rich and wonderfully private.

But a glimpse wouldn't be out of order. One of the joys of an animal life is described very satisfactorily by the Water Rat, known to his friends as "Rat." Rat is speaking to Mole about his life on the boats (this perfectly in keeping with the aquatic animal Rat is), and certain obvious inferences may be drawn from his words:

> In or out of 'em [boats], it doesn't matter. Nothing seems really to matter, that's the charm of it. Whether you get away, or whether you don't; whether you arrive at your destination or whether you reach somewhere else, or whether you never get anywhere at all, you're always busy, and you never do anything in particular; and when you've done it there's always something else to do, and you can do it if you like, but you'd much better not.

Such are the words of wisdom Rat offers us, words that thud rather dully on the dulled eardrums of the *homme d' affaires.* Words that speak rather directly to aimless, time-rich childhood. But of course Rat is only talking about *boats.*

And then there's Mr. Toad, who doesn't appear until the narrative is fairly well advanced. When he does appear, it is with great éclat and tumult, and with total disregard for conventions. He is, in fact, the most egregious of the characters, committing larger-than-normal crimes, not stooping to half-measures. He does, for example, steal a motor car under the eyes of its owner:

> As if in a dream he found himself, somehow, seated in the driver's seat; as if in a dream, he pulled the lever and swung the car round the yard and out through the archway; and, as if in a dream, all sense of right and wrong, all fear of obvious consequences, seemed temporarily suspended.

"Temporarily suspended," or never apprehended? The distinction, at this point, is hardly material; Toad has lost his mind, and acts with a sense of tragicomic vainglory:

> . . . as the car devoured the street and leapt forth on the high road through the open country, he was only conscious that he was Toad once more, Toad at his best and highest, Toad the terror, the traffic-queller, the Lord of the lone trail, before whom all must give way or be smitten into nothingness and everlasting night.

The sense of a self-mythologizing figure is very strong here, a pathetic being whose self-appraisal is based on the uncertain marriage of epic and cheap adventure story. One can hardly help but feel something parallel in many of today's drivers, whose vehicles lift them out of the tiny sphere of their actual power and exalt them to some demiurgical area of consequence.

Kenneth Grahame certainly feels free to use the children's

story form for his own purposes. Mr. Toad is of course apprehended (how could it be otherwise, considering the flagrancy of his crime?) and condemned to prison. We are not spared the details of his internment, the description of which ends: "The rusty key creaked in the lock, the great door clanged behind them; and Toad was a helpless prisoner in the remotest dungeon of the best-guarded keep of the stoutest castle in all the length and breadth of Merry England." Even the casual reader will be struck by the chantlike quality of this description. The gradual and explicit encasement of Mr. Toad in various layers of impenetrability makes for a vivid image of isolation and misery. The final, Dickensian irony of "Merry England" augments the sense of despair and at the same time points to the actual presence of a world outside, a world apart, from which Toad has just been separated.

What about the Toad-in-prison chant here? What does it mean; what purpose does it serve? It has some of the purposes we mentioned above, emphasizing Toad's isolation and the impregnability of his cell. But the chant has at the same time an effect nearly opposite to that of emphasis. The chant makes more acceptable the reality, which it encases in rhythmic formula. Our faculties for warding off painful information are lulled as we watch the chant unwind itself to its sinister conclusion. As Toad is a literal prisoner of the British penal system, so we have become helpless prisoners of our mimetic abilities. We can't let the chant go, and similarly, it won't let us go. However much we sympathize with Toad, however much we can't bear to think of his coming to grief, we must follow the inexorable chant, which leads us out and away from Toad, into the free world that is Merry England.

Such is the power of chants, a power strong enough that it should not be entrusted to children. Yet that is precisely at whom most chants are directed, at hapless children whose critical abilities have not developed to the point where they know they are being manipulated. Reciting a chant, one pays the dues of slavery.

The Wind in the Willows is not, however, a sinister book. Written for children in an age when it was still considered possible to "mold" them, it carries with it a feeling of moral responsibility, of not wanting children to suffer on its account. For this reason, its chants, though horrible, are not *that* horrible; they do not push much past the bounds of other children's literature, in which beloved characters are regularly threatened and always rescued. The chant, therefore, is in itself a parody of other situations, in which the hero is wrongfully imprisoned under dire circumstances, in the rustiest and dustiest of dungeons. The more secure the dungeon, after all, the more credit for escaping from it. Childhood fantasy does not warm as readily to characters' walking out the unlocked doors of minimum-security prisons.

This chant differs from others in that the prisoner in question is a toad, one who speaks, wears clothes, drives motor cars. But a toad nonetheless. That fact is what makes the parody so exquisitely amusing. All the old machinery is being trundled out, the whole literary arsenal reinvoked, all for the sake of a toad, self-important though he may be. That sort of illogical juxtaposition, while not too outré for childhood fantasy work, is also a source of pleasure for adults, and certainly for Kenneth Grahame. There is something supremely irreverent about taking the classic forms and inserting into them an unclassic form—that of a toad. Such variation on a theme, ready-made for children's literature, becomes in this way a mechanism of freedom—the subversion of forms through their deliberate and sedulous use.

Leaving Toad to sweat it out in his language-bound cell, we return to the cozier homes of the animals without criminal records. But alas, even the most comfortable of nests—animal or human—begins to feel a little too snug on occasion. "The larger stressful world of outside Nature" does after all furnish us with a good deal of interest and information. In some way the book (and life itself) is a struggle between precisely these two poles—cloistered comfort, and the hunger for the new, the strange, the adventurous. "How do we know when we are having an adventure?" asks Sartre. A surprisingly difficult question to answer. How much easier to know when we are *not* having an adventure, when we are curled up in the same old corner, nose on our paws, thoughts on nothingness. For the animals in the book, this level of consciousness is pleasant enough, and is, in fact, their usual state. But at moments the innocent paradise is invaded by alien desires, which often carry with them tragic consequences, as in the case of Toad. Rat, being more sensible, suffers less from the problem. But even he is not immune:

> Restlessly the Rat wandered off once more, climbed the slope that rose gently from the north bank of the river, and lay looking out towards the great ring of Downs that barred his vision further southwards—his simple horizon hitherto, his Mountains of the Moon, his limit behind which lay nothing he had cared to see or to know. Today, to him gazing south with newborn need stirring in his heart, the clear sky over their long low outline seemed to pulsate with promise; to-day, the unseen was everything, the unknown the only real fact of life. On this side of the hills was now the real blank, on the other lay the crowded and coloured panorama that his inner eye was seeing so clearly.

This then, is the other movement in the book, the swing back, the reaction. The seemingly hermetic sphere of home and comfort contains within it, as part of its basic equipment, the seeds of restlessness and discontent. Such discordances are what give comfort whatever meaning it may have, formless and ill-defined concept that it is. One might be tempted to view the book in terms of an alternation between comfort and the discontent that leads to adventure.

In this passage the question of whether or not to accept the world as given is put to us in a series of balanced, antithetical statements. Again, Grahame is using the concrete expository style of the children's story to reflect on more abstract issues. What Rat sees when he looks around is a "great ring of Downs" that blocks his vision and defines his horizon, "his Mountains of the Moon, his limit behind which lay nothing he had cared to see or to know." It is this very tangible limitation of vision that is responsible

for the upwelling of dissatisfied consciousness—consciousness of being in a world that has literally shrunk before one's eyes—those same eyes that now see it very differently. It is not that Rat hadn't known about the world beyond; rather, until today he hadn't cared. The world for Rat was more than literally bounded by that "great ring of Downs"; the psychological void beyond it was unimaginable because undesired, unsummoned.

The Day of the Birth of Desire is heralded by a magic dissolution of boundaries. A world hitherto crowded with sensuous information has turned into a "real blank," a devastated, shell-shocked area from which the mind has been withdrawn, from which one turns in weariness and loathing as the last object disappears from mental sight. At this nadir, a movement toward conservation is generally initiated, an impulse toward holding onto what we have, an expression of the paralyzing fear of the void. We resist death because it will take from us what we have, with hardly a promise of replacement. As an alternative, the "great ring of Downs," the "simple horizon," the "Mountains of the Moon," or even the jail cell, seem greatly preferable.

Rat has taken a step (mental, for the moment) that tends toward the breaking up of his world, the destruction of the little realm of comfort and acceptance that was heretofore all he could have imagined. Actually, imagination had not played any real part among the forces and energies that had maintained the world in place up to now. Instead, a dull sort of nonexamination of the given had kept everything going, had left Rat in the center of a universe that did not feel unduly small (or perhaps Rat did not feel unduly large).

The birth of imagination is not without pain. One looks at the present furnishings of the world and sees only how different they could be. "On this side of the hills was now the real blank, on the other lay the crowded and coloured panorama that his inner eye was seeing so clearly." As our perspicacious narrator reminds us, imagination can take a spatial form. It is the thing that is there, not here, that is on the other side of the hills, just out of sight. Imagination functions as the making present of an absence. Were the desired or imagined object in fact present, imagination would at that instant cease to serve a purpose. It is shed, in fact, as readily as innocence.

But the two are not synonymous, far from it. Clearest for our present purposes is to view imagination as one of the qualities opposite to innocence. Imagination is the ability to visualize and perhaps desire what is not present to the senses. It is a source of discontent. By its very nature, it shows us possibilities without putting them into our hands; we look at those hands, empty as they are, and wish to fill them with the dazzling colors and seductive shapes that are just out of reach. We now know those hands to have a purpose, long unsuspected, a purpose for the present denied them. Desire grows with the realization of futility; the glimpse of another world blinds us to any source of satisfaction in this one. Is not imagination therefore at cross-purposes with innocence? Does it not obliterate the happy state of occupying a whole world uncritically and fully?

The alternative—in Grahame's book—to restless imagination is a much-emphasized comfort and delight in one's surroundings. Such comfort can overtake us at any moment, and often in the most unlikely places. Witness what happened to Toad, for example, in his jail cell:

> When the girl returned, some hours later, she carried a tray, with a cup of fragrant tea steaming on it; and a plate piled up with very hot buttered toast, cut thick, very brown on both sides, with the butter running through the holes in it in great golden drops, like honey from the honeycomb. The smell of that buttered toast simply talked to Toad, and with no uncertain voice; talked of warm kitchens, of breakfasts on bright frosty mornings, of cosy parlour firesides on winter evenings, when one's ramble was over and slippered feet were propped on the fender; of the purring of contented cats, and the twitter of sleepy canaries.

The sensuous nature of this passage is irresistible. The narrator permits himself a lavish expenditure of adjectives to describe two rather simple items—hot tea and hot toast. These are basic constituents of an ordinary British diet, but rarely before have they seemed such an exquisite luxury. It is not simply hot tea, or steaming tea, but "fragrant tea *steaming* on it." The verb lends a certain unexpected but nonetheless welcome emphasis. Tea that is actively steaming is in little danger of cooling, at least in the space of a few paragraphs. But there is little time to worry about the temperature of the tea; hot toast immediately rears its lovely head, and is, without doubt, the *pièce de résistance*. All the possible virtues of toast are presented to us in loving detail. Unlike the one or two cold, begrudged slices one is usually offered for breakfast. Toad's plate is "piled up with very hot buttered toast, cut thick." A lot of it, and thick. Largesse, nothing less. And to moisten the bargain, butter. But not just butter. Butter that is aggressively butter, "running through the holes in it in great golden drops, like honey from the honeycomb." Butter flowing effortlessly, liquid ore, butter sweet as honey.

As important as the immediate appeal to the senses is the process of association the toast triggers in Toad's mind. As he sniffs the repast, he thinks of an array of situations in which comfort and contentment are featured. "Warm kitchens," "cozy firesides on winter evenings," "slippered feet propped on the fender," "purring cats," all epitomize in varying ways a high level of British *Gemütlichkeit*. This comfort is imbibed through the dual pleasures of food and warmth—every grown embryo's dream.

Somewhat more eclectic, and less an appeal to basic human comfort, is the passage describing the picnic lunch the Water Rat gave the Sea Rat (more about him later). The following is decidedly not for the faint-hearted:

> There he [Water Rat] got out the luncheon-basket and packed a simple meal, in which, remembering the stranger's origin and preferences, he took care to include a yard of long French bread, a sausage out of which the garlic sang, some cheese which lay down and cried, and a long-necked straw-covered flask contain-

ing bottled sunshine shed and garnered on far Southern slopes.

The details of this passage are exquisite, perhaps even more so than those of the preceding one. There, we had a high degree of descriptive and connotative excellence; here, we have something close to poetry. "A sausage out of which the garlic sang" surely surpasses our narrative expectations for a novel, let alone a children's story. So too does the wine's introduction, pure metaphor, pointing as it does to distant lands of unstinted warmth and sunlight. The "simple meal" that the Water Rat packs is not in the least carelessly assembled. His concern to provide something in accord with "the stranger's origin and preferences," is more than echoed in the control exercised by the narrator as he prepares an expository plate for us. The unexamined life is not worth living and the unexamined meal equally unpalatable. At least as far as a self-indulgent narrator is concerned. One who eats his words. And with great pleasure.

We are now almost at the heart of the comfort question in this book. Earlier we advanced the theory that comfort is somehow to be equated with innocence. Comfort was satisfaction with "things as they are," leading to the lack of desire to look further, a kind of blissful unexamination. To this we had opposed imagination, with all its perils of restlessness and unquelled desire. But we knew there was something facile about this dichotomy. Rigorous examination would find flaws in it. And indeed, less than rigorous examination has to lead to the conclusion that there is more than one side to comfort. Perhaps what finally grinds us down is the total impression purveyed by an accretion of passages such as the two cited above. A toad tempted by salaciously dripping toast is in itself just a freak, a momentary lapse in propriety. And the "simple picnic" that turns rapidly into an elaborate feast of language is also a forgivable small aberration. But the two of them, taken together and in combination with numerous other examples of frank hedonism, are much too rich a diet. They lead rather directly to linguistic gout, unless carefully monitored. They also lead to a reexamination of the comfort question. If comfort is simple innocence, then what about this glut of sensuously comfortable situations? Is it comfort or self-indulgence to dream of (and write about) foods that do more than satisfy hunger? Isn't there a big difference between contentment with one's cell and crust of bread, and the other sort of comfort that comes from oversatisfaction and hyperstimulation of the senses? Where is the virtue of contentment with one's lot, if there is no possibility of discontent?

So we can evaluate the comfort question in the following terms: It is indeed a luxury, and a self-indulgence, to write a children's book and cram it full of such wish-fulfillment items as sumptuous foods and cozy kitchen fires. But this sort of pleasure, vicarious in the highest degree, it among the most harmless in the world, not excepting the Peeping Toms and the Sneaking Sues. As we read *The Wind in the Willows*, a particular mind's thought process is revealed to us with unaccustomed frankness. With each new passage on the related subjects of food, comfort, and home we find an additional piece for study. The aggregate reveals a personality that we might call obsessive, but that has found a way to deal with its obsessions—by flaunting them in the pages of a children's book. The fact of having animals eating and dreaming about food is a slight decoy; we cannot help but be struck by the absurdity of a water rat envisioning garlic sausage, or a toad sating its hunger with buttered toast and tea (and make it hot). But such is the thin stratagem (or obvious projection) used here. There is no real hope or attempt to deceive, but an almost pure expression of innocent pleasure.

Earlier, we spoke of comfort as the antithesis of imagination. In proceeding, we seem to have changed the status of comfort, demolished it as a real object, and instead subsumed it in the concept of imagination. The comfort conveyed by imagining buttered toast is a purely imaginary comfort, highly satisfying though it may be.

There is an imagination that leads inward, another that points outward. Both kinds are the work of the same faculty, but the products of each, the objects envisioned, are quite different. Both kinds of imagination are represented in Grahame's book, and the counterbalance is quite delicate. As one might assume, home and its benefits require one type of imagination. One thinks back to what one knows, what one has experienced. In the process, horizons shrink somewhat, as the focus of desire is increasingly narrowed until it includes a finite number of objects or situations. The magnification of these few objects, their overcareful description, is the sort of imaginative work that is carried on in the book. Objects and situations are actually recreated in this fashion, given a new emphasis, as is the case in a still life, for example. And that is, in a sense, what Grahame's descriptions are—virtual still lifes. Buttered toast frozen forever with the butter dripping lustily from it, with an eternally available store of associations that go with it, such marvels are the work of imagination, defier of time and space. This sort of imagination abolishes the barriers between memory and future time, between the already-perceived and the yet-to-be-apprehended. It keeps intact the family mansion that has long ago crumbled.

The other kind of imagination, the outward-pushing, is also present in this remarkable children's story. One might say it needn't be, that there is enough internal texture to keep animals, children, and adults enthralled for millenia. But Kenneth Grahame heroically battles against the pleasantly otiose, the overstuffed chair and the warm hearth, in order to poke a cold but questing nose outside the window. In this posture, our second kind of imagination comes into play, bringing with it the dreams of a place that is not home. Such a specific role is left to a rather specific character—the Sea Rat. What better sort of character than a sailor—animal or human—to do the work of emissary from another world? A sailor on a ship who knows no real home, only ports, homes for the night, easily abandoned in the next day's sailing. Such a character introduces himself to our Rat, Water Rat, whose home is the river, but one very specific spot on that river.

The two meet, as we said, and dine together on the finest continental cuisine, replete with garlic and sparkling wine. Then, as a sort of *quid pro quo*, the Sea Rat speaks a little about his life on the water, speaks to a spell-bound Water

Rat who has never known about another, the other, existence, but who is gratifyingly open and accepting:

> The quiet world outside . . . receded far away and ceased to be. And the talk, the wonderful talk flowed on—or was it speech entirely, or did it pass at times into song—chanty of the sailors weighing the dripping anchor, sonorous hum of the shrouds in a tearing North-Easter, ballad of the fisherman hauling his nets at sundown against an apricot sky, chords of guitar and mandoline from gondola or caique? . . . Back into speech again it passed, and with beating heart he was following the adventures of a dozen seaports, the fights, the escapes, the rallies, the comradeships, the gallant undertakings; or he searched islands for treasure, fished in still lagoons and dozed day-long on warm white sand. . . .

Calling this passage an encapsulated sea epic would not be overstating the impression it makes on the reader, through the Water Rat, who has surrendered himself body and soul to this teller of tales. For the child reader, this fact is enough to fascinate; for the literary critic (or other cynic), this is a "story-within-a-story," testimony to unsuspected levels of complexity.

Above all else, this passage is an exercise in imagination. Sea Rat tells, but Water Rat "sees." Word pictures are painted and are envisioned, admired, re-created. Sea Rat and Water Rat are alike effaced in the telling, and wholly unconscious of self. Only the verbal pictures remain, floating in the air, dominating with suggestive power. For Water Rat, all these images are very new and very strange. Obvious though it may be, there is a good deal of difference between traveling and remaining at home. Home connotes, among thousands of other things, a stable collection of objects with which to fill and define a life. And we've certainly had enough glimpses of animal home life—British style. Here, though, we have a different arena for thought, an arena virtually without limits because it has no fixed points. A ship docking at different ports—classic symbol of restlessness and, to a certain extent, irresponsibility—is the life the Sea Rat offers the Water Rat. It is a life without any guarantees of a table with buttered toast or a hearth fire sempiternally burning. It is, in short, a life of risks and, possibly, of rewards. It is also the sort of life an Englishman sitting in front of a comfortably modulated fire, munching buttered toast, would like to contemplate. In this setting, our Englishman would be using the outward-pointing imagination we mentioned above, the one that thinks toward objects and contexts never before seen, decidedly "not Home," alien.

It is this imagination we worry about in terms of innocence. Rat hears the Sea Rat's stories and immediately vows to go off to sea, all his former friends and associations forgotten. The sort of contentment on which innocence is built and that is necessary for its complete flowering is impossible in a mind in which restlessness and curiosity have been awakened. Imagining oneself in another state, one inevitably knows the limitations of this one and of oneself. From placid unconsciousness of self, one reaches the stage of self-contemplation and self-criticism. And once infected, it is no easy achievement to travel the road back to the uncritical being who fills his skin with no wrinkles, born to the role.

But Grahame's is a book whose very excesses lead back to the placid fount of consciousness. A few brave gestures, a few baby steps in some new direction, and then a somewhat hurried, if dignified, retreat. Here with the Sea Rat, where imagination is perhaps at its most rampant, even here we can't avoid the homeward motion. His subversive account ends, ". . . the merry home-coming, the headland rounded, the harbour lights opened out; the groups seen dimly on the quay, the cheery hail, the splash of the hawser; the trudge up the steep little street towards the comforting glow of red-curtained windows." Home again, home again, home again. The "weary traveler" is welcomed with open arms, back to the womb that he never really left. His voyages around the world were just a displacement, a temporary break in the living continuum. Imagination, rebellious for a time, could not help but come back to itself, back to the home, origin of contentment and peace, nest of innocence.

And as we come home to *The Wind in the Willows,* we see that it never pretends to be more than a children's story. Yet its underpinnings have all the subtlety of a well-made novel. Little flashes of excitement, large doses of innocent comfort—the mixture gives us a first-rate mental beverage, beneficial to both heart and brain. Were the concoction prepared by the Devil himself, it could hardly be more seductive.

Neil Philip   (essay date 1985)

SOURCE: "Kenneth Grahame's *The Wind in the Willows*: A Companionable Vitality," in *Touchstones: Reflections on the Best in Children's Literature,* Vol. 1, Children's Literature Association, 1985, pp. 96-105.

[*In the following essay, Philip provides reasons why* The Wind in the Willows *remains a favorite book of both children and adults.*]

"Vitality—that is the test," wrote Kenneth Grahame, in his introduction to *Aesop: A Hundred Fables* (1899). It is a test *The Wind in the Willows* passes, for Grahame's best-known book possesses in abundance that quality by which Ezra Pound defined the true classic: "a certain eternal and irrepressible freshness." A. A. Milne called it a "Household Book": one to be kept constantly at hand, referred to, quoted, read aloud.

But it is also, it must be admitted, a very strange book. Early reviewers were entirely flummoxed by it, expecting another wickedly exact portrait of childhood in the mode of Grahame's highly successful collections of stories *The Golden Age* (1895) and *Dream Days* (1898). Instead they were offered a tale of humanized animals—or animalized humans—in which the characters are at one moment life-size water rats, moles and toads, and are at another hitching life-size horses to gypsy caravans and taking to the road, where they mix on equal terms with humans; a tale with two distinct narrative threads, one of gentle celebration of simple, riverside pleasures, the other of hectic farce—and with two interpolated mystical chapters that seemed to have nothing to do with the rest.

To make matters worse, Grahame was, at the time of publication in 1908, Secretary of the Bank of England.

The book was soon assimilated, however, soon taken to its readers' hearts, and it now forms Grahame's chief claim to fame. His meagre other writings are now read for their relationship to *The Wind in the Willows,* if at all. It is one of the handful of books that every English child is bound to meet; and every English-speaking child should. Yet it is also a book intriguingly poised between literature for children and for adults, while its story is propelled by the logic of make-believe, it is shaped by an adult perception of make-believe's limitations, and expressed in a prose elaborately simple.

Grahame's first published writings were essays for literary journals of the eighteen-nineties, including *The Yellow Book* and W. E. Henley's *National Observer.* Many of these were collected in ***Pagan Papers*** (1893), which also contained the earliest stories of *The Golden Age.* Other gifted writers—Arthur Ransome, J. M. Barrie—produced similarly vapid verbal confections during this time: all, like Grahame, looked to R. L. Stevenson as their model. Grahame's early essays are imitations of Stevenson's; his stories of child life are a series of narrative glosses on a specific essay, "Child's Play" in *Virginibus Puerisque* (1881).

Stevenson's essay on play provided Grahame with a key to his feelings of dispossession: children "dwell in a mythological epoch, and are not the contemporaries of their parents." Of the attitude of children to adults, Stevenson says that "we should be tempted to fancy they despised us outright"; Grahame's frequent word for the children's feelings for "the Olympians" is "contempt". But while Grahame took to heart many of Stevenson's wise and perceptive comments on children's make-believe, he disregarded Stevenson's opening statement, that "the regret we have for our childhood is not wholly justifiable". Grahame's adults—save a few fantasy benefactors—*are* contemptible, "without vital interests and intelligent pursuits"; Grahame takes as much pleasure as Saki in constructing imaginary retrospective revenges on them.

For Grahame, then, children's ability and willingness to cheat themselves with invention is an unmitigated good. But though the stories in *The Golden Age* and *Dream Days* describe the world of make-believe with vivid accuracy, they do not enter it. The narrator is at a distance, can afford, indeed, to be amused as well as envious. This is not so in *The Wind in the Willows*.

My point can perhaps best be appreciated by considering a passage in the story **"A Saga of the Seas"** in *Dream Days,* in which the narrator recollects a particularly involved and involving daydream piratic escapade. The boy's method of narrative construction is to follow the desired storyline, providing and discarding incidental characters and props in an arbitrary and ad hoc manner, according to necessity rather than likelihood. "As for the pirate brigantine and the man-of-war, I don't really know what became of them. They had played their part very well, for the time, but I wasn't going to bother to account for them, so I just let them evaporate quietly." This is precisely Grahame's own narrative technique in *The Wind in the Willows*. He wrote in 1919 to Professor G. T. Hill, who had queried Mole's domestic arrangements, "I would ask you to observe that our author practises a sort of 'character economy' which has the appearance of being deliberate. The presence of certain characters may be indicated in or required by the story, but if the author has no immediate use for them, he simply ignores their existence."

The book's famous incongruities stem from Grahame's deliberate adoption of a narrative voice rooted in the tradition of make-believe rather than fiction. In the make-believe world it does not matter if a toad brushes his hair (a source of distress to Beatrix Potter), or if a rat says to a mole, "I like your clothes awfully, old chap . . . I'm going to get a black velvet smoking suit myself some day." Grahame is wonderfully deft at handling the transitions of size that are such a trouble to his illustrators and stage adaptors. With one adjective, for instance, he reduces Toad from washerwoman-size to toad-size: "One big mottled arm shot out and caught Toad by a fore-leg, while the other gripped him fast by a hind-leg." The barge-woman's "big" arm expels Toad from the human world. In *The Wind in the Willows,* Grahame incorporates for the first time into his narrative stance the truth observed by Stevenson, that "nothing can stagger a child's faith; he accepts the clumsiest substitutes and can swallow the most staring incongruities."

Toad, Rat and Mole are not only characters in a narrative arranged according to the principles of make-believe; they also order their own lives in the same fashion. Here Toad—in part an affectionate mockery of aspects of the character of Grahame's son, in part perhaps a caricature of Oscar Wilde—is of chief interest. To observe Toad, deprived of real transport, resort to an arrangement of chairs on which he crouches, "bent forward and staring fixedly ahead, making uncouth and ghastly noises," is to recall Stevenson's observation that though adults can daydream while sitting quietly, a child needs "stage properties": "When he comes to ride with the king's pardon, he must bestride a chair". When Toad translates his make-believe into action, the Olympians, again in Stevenson's words, "reach down out of their altitude and terribly vindicate the prerogatives of age": "Mr. Clerk, will you tell us, please, what is the very stiffest penalty we can impose . . . ?" Toad's downfall is presented as farce, not tragedy; but it is a rueful farce, shot through with Grahame's painful consciousness of the distance between his own imaginings and reality.

Like many children's books, *The Wind in the Willows* originated as bedtime stories told to the author's son. Grahame improvised the tale for his son Alastair, and when separated from him continued it in letters, which survive and have been published as *First Whisper of 'The Wind in the Willows'* (1944). He then wrote the whole story out as a novel, and added the two mystical chapters, "A Piper at the Gates of Dawn" and "Wayfarers All". "A Piper" stands directly between the portion of the story that was told and the portion that was sent in letters.

We cannot, of course, know what relation the spoken story had to the early chapters of the book. It seems likely that the reflective, lazy, elegiac quality of these chapters, with their rounded, serene prose and their uneventful evocation of simple affections and simple pleasures, reflect Grahame's taste more than Alastair's. Though these are the passages that linger in the mind, they are not the ones of most immediate interest and appeal to small children, to whom Mr. Toad is the novel's chief character.

Whatever the need to provide entertainment for his son, there is no doubt that *The Wind in the Willows* shapes and expresses Grahame's own deepest longings. The boy in the story "Mutabile Semper" in *Dream Days* describes the means of access to his land of Cockayne: "you're going up a broad, clear river in a sort of a boat". Nature for Grahame is not red in tooth and claw, but a nurturing, idyllic, cozy world in which one can escape the pressure of adult responsibilities and the confines of adult behaviour. In "The Magic Ring," also in *Dream Days,* he writes, "To nature, as usual, I drifted by instinct," to console a disappointment. For all its rural setting, *The Wind in the Willows* is not a countryman's book, but a townsman's potent blend of recollection and fantasy: wish-fulfilment, not observation.

Mole, who escapes from underground to the fascinations of the riverbank, is a fantasy image of Grahame himself, recalling, on the very first page, the central figure of the childhood stories. The resemblance between the opening of *The Wind in the Willows* and the opening of the first story in *The Golden Age*, "A Holiday", is very striking. In "A Holiday", Grahame writes,

> the soft air thrilled with the germinating touch that seems to kindle something in my own small person as well as in the rash primrose already lurking in sheltered haunts. Out into the brimming sun-bathed world I sped, free of lessons, free of discipline and correction, for one day at least. My legs ran of themselves, and though I heard my name called faint and shrill behind, there was no stopping for me.

Here is the corresponding passage in the first paragraph of *The Wind in the Willows:*

> Spring was moving in the air above and in the earth below and around him, penetrating even his dark and lowly little house with its spirit of divine discontent and longing. It was small wonder, then, that he suddenly flung down his brush on the floor, said 'Bother!' and 'O blow!' and also 'Hang spring-cleaning!' and bolted out of the house without even waiting to put on his coat. Something up above was calling him imperiously.

For the first five chapters, before Toad begins his independent adventures, the narrative focus barely leaves Mole for an instant; there is a case for seeing in Grahame's sudden diversion of attention away from Mole and onto Toad, whose adventures were already set down in the letters to Alastair, a serious flaw in the book's construction, caused by the difficulty of marrying the fantasy which was a solace for Grahame with the fantasy which was an entertainment for Alastair. The existence of the exuberant farce of Toad in written form compelled Grahame to change direction, and to remove Mole from his central position. That for Grahame, Mole, not Toad, was the book's protagonist is proved by one of his suggested titles, fortunately unused: *Mr. Mole and his Mates.*

But, willy-nilly, Toad does take over the book, the moment he takes to the road. A comparison of the letters in which his story is first charted and the chapters in which it took final shape is highly instructive. The difference between the two texts is not so much that between something dashed off and something crafted, but between a story genuinely for children—or rather a child—and one with more ambiguous purposes. It is clear that Grahame kept the letters in front of him as he wrote, simply expanding and refining the existing text: but the final result is very different in flavour. To some eyes, the letters may appear a sort of plot summary without the subtle resonance of the book's full cadences; to others, the simple directness of the letters, and their robust good humour, will mark them as Grahame's only true children's story. Compare:

> He stepped out into the road to hail the car, when suddenly his face turned very pale, his knees trembled & shook, & he had a bad pain in his tummy.
>
> *(Letters)*

> He stepped confidently out into the road to hail the motor-car, which came along at an easy pace, slowing down as it neared the lane; when suddenly he became very pale, his heart turned to water, his knees shook and yielded under him, and he doubled up and collapsed with a sickening pain in his interior.
>
> *(Final text)*

The intimacy of the letters has given way to a more formal relationship between writer and audience. This happened inevitably as Grahame sought to attach the succinctly related story of Toad's adventures to the book's early chapters written with his natural expansiveness, and without the restriction of an immediate child audience.

This task of marrying up two different stories written in two different moods caused endless problems, and they can be traced in the book's textual inconsistencies. Take Badger's speech, for instance. In the letters, he says of the cold tongue, "It's real good." In the book, he says, "It's first-rate." That shows the difference between the texts in a nutshell: but Grahame—recognizing, perhaps, that Badger is most convincing when he says real good rather than first-rate—did not completely expunge the no-nonsense speech of the letters. In the book as in the letters, Badger defends Toad's ungrammatical "learn 'em" against Rat's strictures: "What's the matter with his English? It's the same what I use myself." Yet this is the same Badger who earlier in the book, in a passage written exclusively for publication, speaks like this:

> "This very morning," continued the Badger, taking an armchair, "as I learnt last night from a trustworthy source, another new and exceptionally powerful motor-car will arrive at Toad Hall on approval or return. At this very moment, perhaps, Toad is busy arraying himself in

those singularly hideous habiliments so dear to him, which transform him from a (comparatively) good-looking Toad into an Object which throws any decent-minded animal that comes across it into a violent fit. We must be up and doing, ere it is too late."

But to say that *The Wind in the Willows* is structurally shaky is not to condemn it. It is this very "flaw", the book's openness to being read as chiefly the story of Mole or chiefly the story of Toad, which allows such a range of response, and appeals to such a range of temperaments. And there is also, of course, a third strand to the narrative, the mild nature mysticism and wanderlust expressed in the two interpolated chapters, "The Piper at the Gates of Dawn" and "Wayfarers All". The poetic prose of these chapters, and their pallid Edwardian paganism, are the only elements of the book with which I am myself entirely out of sympathy; but these chapters were important to Grahame, and have been to many of his readers. Grahame was by no means alone in his attraction to Pan—as Somerset Maugham put it in *Cakes and Ale* (1930), "Poets saw him lurking in the twilight on London commons, and literary ladies in Surrey and New England, nymphs of an industrial age, mysteriously surrendered their virginity to his rough embrace"—but it was his unique achievement to reduce the savage god to a sort of woodland nanny. Again, a strand of Grahame's neo-paganism derives from Stevenson, but how bitterly resonant is Stevenson's sentence in "Pan's Pipes" *(Virginibus Puerisque),* in the light of Grahame's life and work: "Shrilly sound Pan's pipes; and behold the banker instantly concealed in the bank parlour!"

Some of Grahame's nature mysticism, and some too of his descriptive style, derives from the work of Richard Jefferies, whose *Wood Magic* (1880) is an important precursor of *The Wind in the Willows*. But Grahame has not Jefferies' astringent eye, and where he is most like Jefferies, he is least impressive. Here is Jefferies, from "The Pageant of Summer" *(The Life of the Fields,* 1884):

> It was between the may and the June roses. The may-bloom had fallen, and among the hawthorn boughs were the little green bunches that would feed the redwings in autumn. High up the briars had climbed, straight and towering while there was a thorn, or an ash sapling, or a yellow-green willow to uphold them, and then curving over towards the meadow. The buds were on them, but not yet open; it was between the may and the rose.

> As the wind, wandering over the sea, takes from each wave an invisible portion, and brings to those on shore the ethereal essence of ocean, so the air lingering among the woods and hedges— green waves and billows—became full of fine atoms of summer. Swept from notched hawthorn leaves, broad-topped oak-leaves, narrow ash sprays and oval willows; from vast elm cliffs and sharp-taloned brambles under; brushed from the waving grasses and stiffening corn, the dust of the sunshine was borne along and breathed.

And here is Grahame, from chapter three of *The Wind in the Willows:*

> The pageant of the river bank had marched steadily along, unfolding itself in scene-pictures that succeeded each other in stately procession. Purple loosestrife arrived early, shaking luxuriant tangled locks along the edge of the mirror whence its own face laughed back at it. Willow-herb, tender and wistful, like a pink sunset-cloud, was not slow to follow. Comfrey, the purple hand-in-hand with the white, crept forth to take its place in the line; and at last one morning the diffident and delaying dog-rose stepped delicately on the stage, and one knew, as if string-music had announced it in stately chords that strayed into a gavotte, and June at last was here.

Jefferies is by no means the only influence traceable in *The Wind in the Willows.* Perhaps the most interesting, bearing in mind Grahame's association with *The Yellow Book* and his horror of the Wilde trial (which his biographer Peter Green suggests contributed to the characterization and the fate of Toad,) is Oscar Wilde. Wilde's story "The Devoted Friend" (*The Happy Prince and other tales,* 1888), opens with the words, "One morning the old Water-rat put his head out of his hole." Wilde's Water-rat puts into words the burden of *The Wind in the Willows:* "Love is all very well in its way, but friendship is much higher."

Grahame himself had no real friends. His first biographer Patrick Chalmers wrote that he "never made intimate friendships with his fellows"; whatever his relationship with Frederick Furnivall, who taught him to row, Grahame neither contributed nor subscribed to the volume of memoirs of Furnivall edited by John Munro in 1911, though his cousin Anthony Hope did both. In an essay **"The Fellow That Goes Alone"** (*St. Edward's School Chronicle* 1913, reprinted in full in Green's *Kenneth Grahame*), Grahame dwells on the story of St. Edmund being greeted by a child who says "Hayle, felowe that goest alone" (a quotation from Caxton that we know was twice transcribed in the now-lost ledger book that contained Grahame's earliest work). Grahame writes, "Specially we should envy him his white vision in the meadow; for which he should be regarded as the patron saint of all those who of set purpose choose to walk alone, who know the special grace attaching to it, and ever feel that somewhere just ahead, round the next bend perhaps, the White Child may be waiting for them."

The redemptive child waiting round the corner in this cherished notion of Grahame's is not Christ, but his own lost childhood self. He told Constance Smedley (in a conversation recorded in her *Crusaders,* 1929, and quoted by Green), "I feel I should never be surprised to meet myself as I was when a little chap of five, suddenly coming round a corner . . . The queer thing is, I can remember everything I felt then, the part of my brain used from four till about seven can never have altered. . . . After that time I don't remember anything particularly." As Barrie put it: "Nothing that happens after we are twelve matters very much."

Despite making a virtue of "going alone", Grahame did,

at least in his younger days, appreciate a particular sort of easy male companionship, a society of free cheerful talk, no petticoats, no irksome responsibilities. The folklorist Edward Clodd, Secretary of the London Joint Stock Bank while Grahame filled the same post at the Bank of England, and consequently an acquaintance, held gatherings at Aldeburgh each Whitsun which encapsulated what Peter Green has called the "weekend myth". George Gissing records in his diary for 6 June, 1895: "These men's parties at Whitsuntide have been an institution with Clodd for many years; he has had numbers of well-known men down at his home. Everything simple, but great geniality and heartiness." This is the atmosphere recalled to Patrick Chalmers by one of Grahame's bank colleagues, Sidney Ward, who went on rural weekends with him: they took long walks, followed by chops cooked over an open fire, and "great chunks of cheese, new bread, great swills of beer, pipes, bed, and heavenly sleep".

The lure of the country for clerks and city men was not exclusive to Grahame. It was expressed in essays of rural escape by writers such as Edward Thomas and Arthur Ransome, and in a splendid poem, "Week-End", by Harold Monro (*The Silent Pool and Other Poems,* 1942). The countryside was not for working in: it was a place for rest and recreation. Furnivall catches the mood in a passage quoted in Bernard O'Donoghue's *Selected Poems of Thomas Hoccleve,* confiding that when editing Hoccleve he took his papers to his holiday farm but, "never untied the string. Bother Hoccleve! where would he come in, with the sunshine, flowers, apple-orchards and harvest about?"

This romantic idea of the country relates both to the club-bable, roomy atmosphere of the all-male riverbank world, and to Grahame's oddly wrong-headed notions about his own book. In July 1908, he wrote a blurb for the fly-leaf, claiming that *The Wind in the Willows* was

> A book of Youth—and so perhaps chiefly for Youth, and those who still keep the spirit of youth alive in them: of life, sunshine, running water, woodlands, dusty roads, winter firesides; free of problems, clean of the clash of sex; of life as it might fairly be supposed to be regarded by some of the wise small things *"That glide in grasses and rubble of woody wreck".*

He expanded on this in a letter of 10 October 1908 to Theodore Roosevelt: "Its qualities, if any, are mostly negative—i.e.—no problems, no sex, no second meaning—it is only an expression of the very simplest joys of life as lived by the simplest beings of a class that you are especially familiar with and will not misunderstand." *The Wind in the Willows* is a densely layered text fairly cluttered with second meanings (though not, as Grahame's phrase may imply, *double entendre*): but Grahame could not for his own peace of mind afford to admit it.

One of these second meanings, and one for which the book has come under considerable attack in recent years, is the book's political ethos. In chapter eleven, while Rat, Mole, Badger and Toad prepare to storm Toad Hall, "the bell rang for luncheon." Grahame's "character economy" enables him to evade the question: "Who rings the bell?" For his animal heroes form a leisured class which implies for its continuation a servant class, whom we never see. Instead the rough, uncouth "Wild Wooders" are built up into a class enemy, uncomfortably like the Victorian working class. We find in *The Wind in the Willows* echoes of the middle class hysteria consequent on the West End riots of February 1886, in which the mob were, as *The Times* put it, "loafers and loungers of a pronounced type."

Yet though on one level the book encodes genteel Victorian paranoia about the mob, the anarchy Arnold and Ruskin felt heaving below the surface restraints of civilized society, to interpret the book in these simple political terms would be to read it perversely. For though the stoats and the weasels may be seen as the beastly working class, they are also, more truly, the forces which for Grahame threaten and destroy the ideal life: the destructive part of human nature, and the inconvenient demands of human society. To consider the riverbank world as a working economy is to misread Grahame's escape fantasy, and mistake its implications. For in its paean to the simple uncluttered pleasures of friendship, it works to warm, not chill, the reader; while class prejudice may impinge on the book, human feeling drives it. And as George Sturt wrote in *A Small Boy in the Sixties* (1927), "One's mind easily forgets rubbishy opinions, while one's tissues take permanent growth from feelings."

"I love these little people," said Grahame to the illustrator E. H. Shepard. "Be kind to them." That love communicates; in *The Wind in the Willows* Grahame created, out of a thwarted and lonely imagination, one of the most companionable of all English classics: a book which enters and nourishes the mind, and whose plangent rhythms establish a resonance that enriches and enlivens one's sense of language, of landscape, of life.

Humphrey Carpenter   (excerpt date 1985)

[*In the following excerpt, Carpenter addresses Grahame's interest in a pastoral paradise and his vision of it in* The Wind in the Willows.]

SOURCE: "Kenneth Grahame and the Search for Arcadia" and "*The Wind in the Willows,*" in *Secret Gardens: A Study of the Golden Age of Children's Literature,* Houghton Mifflin Company, 1985, pp. 115-25, 151-69.

Anyone studying Grahame's life and work will quickly find himself indebted to Peter Green's immensely skilful biography of him (1959), arguably the best book ever written about an English children's author. Nevertheless, Green may be wrong in one of his major conclusions. Chiefly on the evidence of Grahame's two books about childhood, *The Golden Age* (1895) and *Dream Days* (1898), he concludes that Grahame had a largely unhappy childhood, marked by emotional deprivation, and suggests that it was this which largely influenced him to write these two books—and so, indirectly, to become the author, a decade later, of *The Wind in the Willows.* Yet *The Golden Age* and *Dream Days* seem to suggest precisely the opposite—that Grahame's childhood (or at least the part of it that these two books deal with) was unusually happy.

Grahame was born in 1859, the son of an Edinburgh law-

yer who shortly after the boy's birth became a legal official in Argyllshire, and moved his wife and family there. Kenneth was the third child; when he was five, his mother gave birth to another, and shortly afterwards she died of scarlet fever. The father decided that he could not cope with the children after his wife's death, and sent them south to live with her mother, a Mrs Ingles, who resided in the Thames-side village of Cookham Dene in Berkshire. There Kenneth, his two brothers, and his sister, spent about three years, after which their grandmother decided that the house was not suitable for her any longer, and took them with her to a cottage at Cranbourne in the same country. Next, Mr Grahame decided that after all he would like to have his children back, and they were duly sent up to Scotland; but the experiment was not a success, and back they came. The father, always a *bon viveur,* now devoted most of his energies to the bottle, and soon vanished to France, where he seems to have scraped some sort of a living by teaching English. Kenneth never saw him again alive, but many years later was suddenly summoned across the Channel to sort things out after the father had died penniless in a Le Havre boarding house.

Peter Green makes out (as do the biographers of Lewis Carroll) that it was the death of the mother which profoundly affected his subject, and caused a trauma which was closely related to his becoming a writer. The father, he says, meant by comparison nothing at all to Kenneth, who presumably resented the casting-out of himself and his siblings after their mother's death. That experience cannot exactly have endeared his father to Kenneth; and yet one wonders whether Mr Grahame senior should be dismissed quite so briskly from the son's life. There are two important facts about him: that he took to drink, and that he ran away to France. Both were forms of escape from the intolerable pressures of life, and it is exactly this kind of escape—this ducking responsibility—which forms a major theme in Grahame's writing. His first published book, *Pagan Papers* (1893), which came out in the year after his father's death, is brimful of fanciful accounts of men who do just the sort of thing his father had done:

> This is how Fothergill changed his life and died to Bloomsbury. One morning he made his way to the Whitechapel Road, and there he bought a barrow . . . He passed out of our lives by way of the Bayswater road . . .

> That stockbroker . . . who was missed from his wonted place one settling-day! . . . They found him in a wild nook of Hampshire. Ragged, sun-burnt, . . . he was tickling trout with godless native urchins . . .

> 'Mr ——— did not attend at his office today, having been hanged at eight o'clock in the morning for horse-stealing.' . . .

> There was once an old cashier in some ancient City establishment, whose practice was to spend his yearly holiday in relieving some turnpikeman at his post . . .

And so on and so on. Respectable City men run away, become lock keepers on the Thames, turn into vagabonds wandering the remote country villages, 'die to Bloomsbury.' And all this is described with the deepest envy and admiration, and not a hint of censure. Is not Grahame, in these musings (which contain a germ of the characters of Toad, Rat, and Mole), looking wistfully over his shoulder at his father's all-too-successful escape? Certainly Grahame's passion for things continental, the constant longing to follow the sun southwards which possessed him from his early adult years, and which he was only able to gratify by occasional and rather sober trips through Europe, seems to have been motivated by a desire to follow in his father's steps. All these feelings united to create one pole of his personality, which we might call the Wanderer.

At the other pole was Kenneth Grahame the Home-lover. All those moves from one house to another in childhood must have played a part in his obsession with creating a snug, neat little home for himself, which runs through *The Wind in the Willows* (Mole End, Rat's bachelor home, Badger's splendid underground quarters) and may also be discerned in his early essays and letters. To a friend, he confessed that he had a recurrent dream of

> a gradual awakening to consciousness in a certain little room, very dear and familiar . . . always the same feeling of a home-coming, of the world shut out, of the ideal encasement. On the shelves were a few books—a very few—but just the editions I had sighed for, the editions which refuse to turn up, or which poverty glowers at on alien shelves. On the walls were a print or two, a woodcut, an etching-not many. . . . All was modest—Oh, so very modest! But all was my very own, and, what was more, everything in the room was exactly right.

> [Quoted in Peter Green, *Kenneth Grahame*]

All Grahame's writing was produced by tension between those two poles, the Wanderer and the Home-lover. *The Wind in the Willows* was the outstanding result of it, but one may also observe it in *The Golden Age* and *Dream Days,* which are explorations of the security and homelovingness of childhood, and also a search for some more distant goal, which can only be achieved by the child wandering away from home, either in imagination or in actual fact.

Neither book conveys any sense of deep unhappiness, of regret for parents dead and lost, of a lack of love. The two books describe a family of parentless children living in the house of some maiden aunts, under the supervision of these ladies, a governess, and the occasional visiting uncle; and after the narrator's initial observation that he and his brothers and sisters lacked 'a proper equipment of parents' there is not even a hint of regret for what might have been. Certainly Aunt Eliza (who is the nearest we get to a portrait of Grahame's grandmother) is a rather unlikeable, unsympathetic Victorian who lacks even the slightest understanding or tolerance of what children like doing and thinking; and she and the others of her kind are characterised by the narrator as 'the Olympians', both stupid and indifferent to children's needs. But the Olympians play only a small part in the story. Sometimes, quite unpredictably, they intervene in the doings of Edward, Harold, Selina, Charlotte, and the nameless boy-narrator, as when

a circus visit is promised by them, and is then suddenly withdrawn to be replaced by a threatened garden party. They may be relied upon, too, to punish apparent wrongdoing without any questioning of its real nature or cause. But for most of the time the Olympians are simply not in evidence; the children are left free to do what they want, to an extent that would astonish their modern successors, and such rules as do exist—for instance, attendance at schoolroom lessons—are broken again and again without dire consequences:

> Harold would slip off directly after dinner, going alone, so as not to arouse suspicion, as we were not allowed to go into the town by ourselves. It was nearly two miles to our small metropolis, but there would be plenty of time for him to go and return . . . Besides, he might meet the butcher, who was his friend and would give him a lift . . .

> . . . I vowed, as I straddled and spat about the stable-yard in feeble imitation of the coachman, that lessons might go to the Inventor of them. It was only geography that morning, any way: and the practical thing was worth any quantity of bookish theory. As for me, I was going on my travels . . .

> Harold tumbled out of the trough in the excess of his emotion. "But we aren't allowed to go on the water by ourselves," he cried.

> "No," said Edward, with fine scorn: "we aren't allowed; and Jason wasn't allowed either, I daresay. But he *went!*" . . .

> We made our way down to the stream, and captured the farmer's boat without let or hindrance . . .

And though the circus visit has been called off, the children nevertheless manage to get there, accepting a random offer of a lift from a neighbour, the Funny Man. The Olympians have about as little actual influence on their lives as did the original Olympians on the daily lives of the Greeks; Grahame, who knew his classical literature pretty well, chose their name carefully.

These books, then, are not the product of an unhappy childhood. On the contrary, they are a record of a time so free from worry, so peculiarly happy, that later life could never quite measure up to it. Grahame once remarked to a friend that

> I feel I should never be surprised to meet myself as I was when a little chap of five, suddenly coming round a corner . . . I can remember everything I felt then; the part of my brain I used from four till about seven can never have altered.

> [Green, *Kenneth Grahame*]

That his character at that age—the time he was living at Cookham Dene—should seem to him detached from the rest of his life indicates that his experiences in those years must have seemed utterly different from anything that happened before or after; one is reminded of C. S. Lewis's remark that his time in the trenches during the First World War, and the memory of all the horrors there, 'is too cut off from the rest of my experience and often seems to have happened to someone else.' Great unhappiness would presumably produce this effect; but in Grahame's case we can scarcely doubt, from the evidence of *The Golden Age* and *Dream Days,* that it was exactly the reverse which inspired this sense of detachment—his childhood self had experienced a life of freedom, contentment, and excitement which other experiences could never match.

His achievement in these books was, of course, the recovery of this childhood self, the ability to bring it alive again on the page. Not that the books are autobiography: it is impossible to relate much in them with any certainty to Grahame's actual experiences (for example, there are five children in them, as opposed to the four Grahames), and Peter Green points out that at least some details in them were taken from other families and children of his acquaintance. None the less a process of recall has taken place. Grahame does not assume the *persona* of his child-self, and narrate the books in that voice; perhaps he had felt that Jefferies' *Bevis* (which he would have known well, being an admirer of Jefferies' ruralist writings) lacked a certain vitality because its author had chosen to see everything in it through the boy's eyes. Instead, Grahame retains all his adult sophistication, and uses it to describe the child's feelings. The result seems arch at first, and certainly the prose is sometimes irritatingly ornate; but the reader who is prepared to accept this device uncomplainingly soon finds that it creates a 'Chinese box' effect, and the presence of Grahame-the-child becomes oddly more real because Grahame-the-adult seems to be stressing his separateness from him:

> Why does a coming bereavement project no thin faint voice, no shadow of its woe, to warn its happy, heedless victims? Why cannot Olympians ever think it worth while to give some hint of the thunder-bolts they are silently forging? And why, oh, why did it never enter any of our thick heads that the day would come when even Charlotte would be considered too matronly for toys?

This comes in a story—the final one in the collections—which tells how the toys are packed up, without the children's consent, to be sent off to a London hospital; but, late at night, the children raid the parcel, extract a few of their favourites, and bury them in the garden—not so that they can play with them again, but because 'The connexion was not entirely broken now—one link remained between us and them.' The meaning of the metaphor is obvious: for Grahame, and so for his readers, childhood itself lies buried at the foot of that tree in the paddock; a few turns of the spade, and it will be out in the light again. *The Golden Age* and *Dream Days* are themselves an act of exhumation.

A lesser writer than Grahame might have performed that act with no deeper purpose than mere nostalgia; the result would then have been trite. But Grahame has no particular interest in childhood for its own sake; he is not setting out, as Jefferies was, to understand the emotions and the imagination of boyhood just for itself; nor is he trying to show his readers how sweet or charming children really are—such as the creators of the Beautiful Child had done,

with horrid results. Indeed, Grahame's children are not especially likeable. They have no special depths of character—Edward, the eldest, is rather shallow, and neither of the girls has anything in particular to commend her; only Harold, the younger boy, is at all a memorable figure in himself, possessed of a quirky imagination. They are all far less entertaining to read about, in themselves, than E. Nesbit's Bastable children. The point is that to write about them, and what they thought and felt, was only the half-way house in Grahame's self-imposed mission. He wished to revisit childhood because of the possibilities it offered of Escape.

If the notion of Escape was planted in him by his father's behaviour during his early years, the later part of his childhood and his early adult life seem to have encouraged him to contemplate a kind of spiritual running-away because of the constraints they imposed on him. He was sent to St Edward's School, Oxford, where he had to endure the usual kind of public school toughness, and then was denied his very strong desire to become an Oxford undergraduate. His family believed that a University education would be both unnecessary and expensive, and instead they secured him a clerkship in the Bank of England. Not surprisingly, many commentators, following Peter Green, have regarded Grahame's apparent desire to escape, in his writings, from the world of conventional late Victorian society as a natural result of his having been pressed, in this fashion, into an alien mould.

Yet the facts do not quite accord with this interpretation. However shy and reserved Grahame may have been (and, according to many accounts, he was very retiring in manner), he does not seem to have hated public school at all; indeed he was one of the heroes of St Edward's in his days there, gaining his First XV Rugby colours and becoming the head boy of the school—the behaviour of Mr Toad rather than Mole. And as for the Bank of England, far from being a repressive, authoritarian institution likely to frown upon any individuality of spirit in its employees, it was in Grahame's day notable, even notorious, for its tolerance and even encouragement of eccentricity. It was a quaint repository of tradition whose staff worked short hours, and where pandemonium often reigned while business was supposedly being conducted—the staff ate and drank heavily on the premises, kept pet animals, and amused themselves at all hours oblivious of decorum. Any distaste Grahame may have felt for the Bank in his early years there is more likely to have been on account of its licentious character than any repression it exercised over him. And the evidence is that, far from hating his work there, he found it extremely congenial; for he rose extremely quickly through its ranks, and in 1898 actually became Secretary, one of its highest offices—at thirty-nine he was one of the youngest people to have done so. No doubt the Bank did inspire conflicting feelings in him—there is some evidence that he found the responsibility of his job there a burden—but it would be wrong to paint it as the monster from which he wished to escape. That monster, if it existed, seems to have been of a more subtle nature; one might suspect it to have been London itself.

By Grahame's day, hatred of urban life, and of the harm

that the industrial revolution had steadily done to English society during the previous hundred years, had become a major theme in English writing. After Dickens and Mayhew (and the evangelical writers) had had their say at describing the miseries of the urban poor, there had come those Pre-Raphaelites who believed that a return to sanity lay through medievalism and the old craft methods. A wide range of writers from Ruskin to Kingsley had tried to find other answers to the dilemmas of industrialisation, but no magic solution appeared, and the problem merely got worse and worse. In view of this it is scarcely surprising that more and more writers were seeking landscapes that were far from what Ruskin called 'that great foul city—rattling, growling, smoking, stinking—a ghastly heap of fermenting brickwork, pouring out poison at every pore'.

It was in this climate that the nature writings of Richard Jefferies found an enthusiastic audience, and Grahame was among those who lapped them up. He devoured George Borrow too—he often refers in his writings to *Lavengro,* Borrow's prose Scholar Gipsy tale which offers even wider landscapes into which to escape. Meanwhile, in Grahame's actual daily life, more practical possibilities of flight were offered by his friend F. J. Furnivall, a Muscular Christian (he was a disciple of Maurice) who had founded the Early English Text Society—thereby reviving many pre-industrial English romantic narratives—and who ran a working men's rowing club on the Thames. Furnivall took Grahame sculling on the river, and seems to have contributed to the character of the Water Rat, with his passion for messing about in boats. Even more important, he was the first person steadily to encourage Grahame with his writing, and it was largely thanks to him that in the late 1880s Grahame began to have essays and prose sketches accepted by London magazines.

Grahame's early writings are very much in the manner of Robert Louis Stevenson—the first Grahame book to be published, *Pagan Papers,* closely resembles the style and subject matter of Stevenson's essay collection *Virginibus Puerisque,* which had appeared about a dozen years earlier; there is even an essay in the Stevenson book called 'Child's Play' which may have helped to suggest *The Golden Age,* with its discussion of children's imaginations. *Pagan Papers* also owes a little to the Decadents, with whom Grahame was marginally associated (he published several pieces in the *Yellow Book*), in its praise of the rural god Pan, whom Grahame claims to detect lurking in all the most secluded rural spots. but the 'paganism' of the book is not really of a kind that the Beardsley-Wilde circle would have understood: Grahame's pagan desires are not remotely priapic, but simply epicurean in the old classical way, and in essay after essay he extols the pleasures of the hearty country walk, the pints of beer and the tobacco pipe in the rural inn—much as his unconscious disciple C. S. Lewis did half a century later. And even these are only halfway houses in the great game of Escape: the Ridgeway along the Berkshire downs is chiefly loved not for the pleasures it itself can offer, but because it leads to a gleam of the English Channel, and so over to Europe and the Mediterranean climate where living can really begin. And what is Grahame escaping from? From the machine age, not because of the harm it had done to its workers or its city dwellers (Grahame took no interest himself in such social problems), but because it denied the possibility of dreaming dreams and seeing visions. Grahame did not actually dislike machines for themselves—he speaks of having 'a sentimental weakness for the night-piercing whistle', and even of 'the enchanted pages of the railway A.B.C.' The trouble is that they were not enchanted enough: 'The crowning wrong that is wrought us of furnace and piston-rod', he writes, 'lies in their annihilation of the steadfast mystery of the horizon, so that the imagination no longer begins to work at the point where vision ceases.' He pleads for a return to the story-book world, in which 'there was always a chance of touching the Happy Isles'.

The first part of *Pagan Papers* is all in this mode, with its whimsical accounts of vanishing stockbrokers and City men who become tramps. The second part consists of the realisation of the dream of Escape in much richer terms—for in *Pagan Papers* were first printed many of the sketches that later went to make up *The Golden Age.* In this context, more than when they later appeared in a separate book, their function in Grahame's psyche becomes clear. By returning to childhood in these prose sketches, he is able to indulge the Escape dream to its fullest. For the five children who dwell under the shadow of the Olympians are constantly escaping, in fact and in imagination, from their mundane lives into worlds of quite extraordinary fancy.

The dominating notion in these *Golden Age* sketches is that of the Good Place, the Golden City, an Arcadia which can always be reached in imagination, and whose shores one may occasionally touch in fact. In one of the stories (in *Dream Days*) the narrator confides to a girl-neighbour his familiarity with just such a place:

> Of course it's just a place I imagine . . . but it's an awfully nice place—the nicest place you ever saw . . . Generally it begins by—well, you're going up a broad, clear river in a sort of boat. You're not rowing or anything—you're just moving along. And there's beautiful grass meadows on both sides, and the river's very full, quite up to the level of the grass. And you glide along by the edge. And the people are haymaking there, and playing games, and walking about; and they shout to you, and you shout back to them and they bring you things to eat out of their baskets, and let you drink out of their bottles; and some of 'em are the nice people you read about in books. And so at last you come to the Palace steps . . .

In this instance the Palace itself proves something of a disappointment to the adult reader—its contents are chiefly chocolates, sweets, and fizzy drinks. The dream, in fact, is more enticingly suggested when the goal of the Golden City is not quite reached, as in the story **'Its Walls Were as of Jasper'**, in which the children visit, in their imagination, the Arcadian landscape in one of the pictures which hangs in the Olympians' house, but can never quite see what lies behind the corner. Sometimes they make actual journeys and discover real approximations to the Good Place. In one story the narrator crawls through a fence and finds himself in a garden fit for a fairy tale, with what seems to be a real Princess being courted by a Prince. The grown-ups do not disillusion him, for the very good reason that his child's perception of them actually enriches their own lives. In another, similar story the children go boating up the river (how often water occurs in this context with Grahame) and find a remote house and garden where a girl they meet there seems to them a true fairy tale creature. And indeed she really has been imprisoned by an aunt, after an unhappy love affair. Best of all, in the story **'The Roman Road'**, the narrator encounters an Artist (clearly the adult Grahame himself) who, to his astonishment, shares his own dream of Arcadia, and would dearly love to get there—despite the fact that he has been to, and actually lives in, what the boy imagines to be a real Arcadia, the city of Rome:

> 'You haven't been to Rome, have you?' I inquired.
>
> 'Rather,' he replied briefly: 'I live there. . . . I'm a sort of Ulysses—seen men and cities, you know. In fact, about the only place I never got to was the Fortunate Island . . .'
>
> 'Wouldn't you like,' I inquired, 'to find a city without any people in it at all?'

The boy goes on to describe his Good Place in childish terms: 'You go into the shops, and take anything you want—chocolates and magic-lanterns and injirubber balls—and there's nothing to pay . . .' And to his surprise, the Artist understands him:

> 'Do you know,' he said presently, 'I've met one or two fellows from time to time, who have been to a city like yours—perhaps it was the same one. They won't talk much about it—only broken hints, now and then; but they've been there sure enough. They don't seem to care about anything in particular—and everything's the same to them, rough or smooth; and sooner or later they slip off and disappear; and you never see them again. Gone back, I suppose.'
>
> 'Of course,' said I. 'Don't see what they ever came away for; *I* wouldn't . . .'

And so the adult Grahame and the boy Grahame part company, vowing to meet again one day in that city, and the boy

> went down-heartedly from the man who understood me, back to the house where I never could do anything right. How was it that everything seemed natural and sensible to him, which these uncles, vicars, and other grown-up men took for the merest tomfoolery? Well, he would explain this, and many another thing, when we met again . . . Perhaps he would be in armour next time—why not? He would look well in armour, I thought. And I would take care to get there first, and see the sunlight flash and play on his helmet and shield, as he rode up the High Street of the Golden City.
>
> Meantime, there only remained the finding it. An easy matter.

The Golden Age became a bestseller when it was published in 1895, but its popularity was not on account of its delicate, subtle accounts of the search for Arcadia. It was loved by the majority of its readers simply because here at last was an unsentimental, funny, but still true-to-life way of portraying children. A few reviewers—true Olympians—were simply unable to believe that children can be as contemptuous towards adults as those in Grahame's book are to the aunts and uncles; one Professor Sully, author of a book called *Children's Ways,* spoke sternly about 'a dishonour done to the sacred cause of childhood . . . a tone of cynical superiority which runs through the volume'. Those who had worshipped the Beautiful Child for several decades were, not surprisingly, disconcerted to have their idol dethroned in favour of a more realistic image. But most reviewers recognised a masterpiece, and agreed with Swinburne, who spoke of *The Golden Age* as 'well-nigh too praiseworthy for praise'. Grahame's reputation was made at one stroke; he became a literary lion, and when *Dream Days* appeared three years later it was lapped up just as greedily by the public. And in that same year, 1898, E. Nesbit began to write her Bastable stories, which showed very clearly the influence of Grahame in the way she portrayed children.

Grahame himself meanwhile fell virtually silent as a writer for many years after *Dream Days* was published. Did he feel he had betrayed a very personal secret in talking so publicly of his search for Arcadia, for the Golden City? At all events he seemed not to know where to look next in his quest for it.

. . . . .

Though the notion of Escape dominates *The Golden Age* and *Dream Days* as strongly as it does the stories of Beatrix Potter, Kenneth Grahame was incapable of finding any real-life escape route from the pressures of his existence. In the years that followed the publication of *Dream Days* (in 1898) he became even more deeply trapped in a life which was far from what he desired. The consequence was that, for a whole decade after *Dream Days* had appeared, he maintained a virtual literary silence.

One can deduce from *The Golden Age* and its sequel that Grahame was not short on the romantic instinct; if those stories are to be trusted, he had, at least in childhood, a habit of falling in love with unattainable idealised females (a baker's wife, a girl in spangled tights at the circus, and other dream-princesses). It appears that their very unattainability was part of the attraction; certainly Grahame reached his late thirties without coming anywhere within hailing distance of marriage, and the only relationship which might have led that way seems to have ended because the lady (apparently a cousin) was too 'forward', and actually made advances to him. But then, quite suddenly, he was hooked and landed by one Elspeth Thomson.

She was the daughter of a Scottish inventor whose mother had remarried after the father's death, and had brought Elspeth to London. The girl—if she could still be called that, for she was only two years younger than Grahame—was a kind of ferociously flirtatious blue-stocking. As a child she had specialised in whimsically precocious friendships with Tennyson and other great literary men, and she had kept up the habit of pursuing successful writers. Grahame was at first merely one such prey. Unfortunately the fact that he wrote stories about children made her all the more fascinated by him. By the late 1890s the fashion for sentimentality towards children and childhood was at its height. Grahame's own writings had helped to nurture it, though of course they were not intended to be taken sentimentally. Elspeth Thomson was among those who adored *The Golden Age* simply because it was about children, without realising that it was implicitly opposed to softhearted attitudes towards the young. In fact she was a worshipper at that by now much-visited temple, the shrine of the Beautiful Child. And she even enrolled Grahame himself temporarily into her religion.

Wensdy arnoon

My Dearie

Fanx fr mornin letter wich I redd *insted* o gettin up & ketchin a bote wot wos goin to Exmouf it wasn't tickler erly but Id ad a rarver wakefle nite so ventchly I sor the bote steem orf . . . My room as a balkiny & a stript ornin & looks over the arber so I sees the botes I orter ketch goin orf wich is next bes ter ketchin of em . . .

Goodbye darlin pet & I wish you were here . . .

Your lovin

Dino

This—though one finds it hard to believe it at first—is Kenneth Grahame writing to Elspeth Thomson in the early months of their courtship. Mock baby-talk was the *lingua franca* between the two of them, though one can hardly imagine it was a language Grahame would ever have wished to speak, left to his own devices. But Elspeth conducted things very cunningly, taking advantage of an illness of his to pay unchaperoned visits, thereby compromising him (it seems) to a point where marriage was almost obligatory. They were married in the summer of 1899. There is a tradition that Grahame's sister Helen, astonished by the newspaper announcement of the impending wedding and herself detesting Elspeth, asked Kenneth if the marriage was really going ahead, and he answered in a tone of the deepest gloom, 'I suppose so; I suppose so.'

It was a disaster from the beginning. Elspeth immediately conceived a child, but it would appear that Kenneth thereafter shied away from sex. Elspeth poured out, in the bad poems she wrote in large quantities, her resentment at his coldness and neglect of her, and when the child, Alastair, was born she made him the focus of all her hopes and affections. Unfortunately Alastair was blind in one eye from birth and generally sickly, but Elspeth treated him as an incipient genius, so that he developed a precocious, cheeky manner which nauseated Grahame's friends.

Grahame himself made a few feeble efforts to extricate himself from the situation. He spent as much time as possible in the company of male friends who understood and shared his nature and his tastes, notably Arthur Quiller-Couch, at whose home at Fowey in Cornwall he was a frequent visitor. The Fowey river and estuary contributed more than is generally realised to the setting of *The Wind in the Willows,* while another Fowey resident, a mildly eccentric boating bachelor called Edward Atkinson, seems to have been among those whose personality went to make up the Water Rat. Another form of Escape tried by Grahame in the early days of his marriage was moving his family back to the setting of the happiest part of his childhood; for in 1907 he took a house at Cookham Dene by the Thames. But nothing could really ease things. During 1904 both parties made more serious moves to extricate themselves: Elspeth spent much of the year away from home, taking the cure at a Lincolnshire spa, and while she was still away Kenneth set off alone for Spain on one of his southward migrations that were as near as he dared go to real escaping. But then Alastair contracted peritonitis, and both parents had to return home. No further attempts at a separation were made, possibly because by this time Kenneth had begun to rediscover his old escape route, writing.

> Presently the tactful Mole slipped away and returned with a pencil and a few half-sheets of paper, which he placed on the table at his friend's elbow . . . When he peeped in again some time later, the Rat was absorbed and deaf to the world; alternately scribbling and sucking the top of his pencil. It is true that he sucked a good deal more than he scribbled; but it was joy to the Mole to know that the cure had at least begun.

The Wind in the Willows began as bedtime stories for Alastair in May 1904, just as the child had reached his fourth birthday. Or rather, that part of the book which concerns the adventures of Toad originated in this fashion. But those adventures form only one of several layers in the book; the others are very different in character, and one cannot imagine that their creation had much to do with Grahame's son.

Alastair was nevertheless the catalyst for the simplest elements in the story. The original night-time tales told to him sound much as if they were in imitation of Beatrix Potter, whose books were just then beginning to appear, with great success; they were certainly known to Grahame, for the rabbits in his short story 'Bertie's Escapade', written at the same time as *The Wind in the Willows,* are called Peter and Benjie. The first stories told to Alastair are reported to have been about 'moles, giraffes & water-rats', a fairly random selection of the sort of creatures Beatrix Potter might have written about, though the giraffe seems incongruous and soon dropped out. The Toad appears to have arrived fairly early on. Probably the saga continued in a random way over the next three years; certainly in May 1907 when Alastair was on holiday with his governess, his father was writing him story-letters in which Toad's adventures were well under way. The first of these letters refers to Toad supposedly being 'taken prisoner by brigands' and a ransom being demanded, but this proves to have been one of Toad's tricks; the truth (the letter says) is that he climbed out of the window early one morning, went to a hotel, stole a motor car, and has vanished. 'I fear he is a low bad animal,' says Alastair's father.

In subsequent letters, written over the next four months, Toad's exploits are described much as in the published book, at first in terse synopsis form, but gradually in full-length narrative.

The book could have been published in this form, simply as a farcical account of the career of the irrepressible Toad. Grahame, however, seems to have shown no desire to do this, and quite rightly. Toad's encounters with the English judicial system—police, magistrate, prison warders—and his flight from prison via engine cab, canal boat, and stolen horse have a certain energy, resembling eighteenth-century picaresque, and Toad is an amiable trickster of the standard folk-tale type. But this idiom was not Graham's *forte,* and he does not seem very comfortable in it. There is a certain amount of parody—of Harrison Ainsworth's historical novels in the scene where Toad arrives at the prison (" 'Oddsbodikins!' said the sergeant of police . . . "Rouse thee, old loon, and take over from us this vile Toad, a criminal of deepest guilt' "), and of George Borrow's *Lavengro,* in the scene where Toad sells the horse to the gypsy (" 'He's a blood horse, he is, partly; not the part you see, of course—another part' "). But this all suggests uneasiness of authorial control; the parodies would mean nothing to children, so who is Grahame writing for? As W. W. Robson has observed, in the prison sequence 'the authorial or editorial voice itself seems to have gone slightly crazy'. Perhaps Grahame felt he should be writing a different kind of book. At all events he was soon doing so.

He continued to work at Toad's adventures after the story-telling to Alastair had ceased, at the encouragement of Constance Smedley, an American lady who represented the magazine *Everybody's* in England. She lived near Grahame in Berkshire and was sent by her editor to persuade him to write another book. It seems that she discovered that he was telling the story of Toad to Alastair, and encouraged him to put it on paper; under protest he responded, and this later stage of work on *The Wind in the Willows* brought it gradually to the form we know. It was published in 1908.

There is nothing remarkable about the fact that the original bedtime stories for Grahame's son concerned animals. Largely thanks to Beatrix Potter, many Edwardian children (or at least those with inventive parents or nursemaids) must have been listening to the same sort of thing. Alastair himself was nicknamed Mouse. But at some point Grahame must have realised, if only subconsciously, that an animal story also provided the perfect vehicle for the kind of thing he most wanted to write.

His disastrous marriage had made him turn with deeper passion than ever to the things that had concerned him in *Pagan Papers* and the *Golden Age* stories: complete emotional freedom from the control of 'grown ups'; a boyish delight in outdoor pursuits sought not for muscular exercise but spiritual refreshment; and always a longing glance towards the far horizon which offers the possibility of complete and utter Escape—flight to an Arcadia even more perfect than that offered by these daydreams. Suddenly, in the chapters of *The Wind in the Willows* that he wrote after the Toad adventures were complete, all these things burst out.

And bursting out is just what happens at the beginning of the book. As anyone who studies it alongside Grahame's biography must realise, Mole's burrowing up to the surface at the start of Chapter One is the author himself letting his deepest preoccupations break out from their prison in his mind and come into the daylight. Pretence does not have to be kept up any more. 'This is fine!' Mole says to himself. 'This is better than whitewashing!'

The greatness of *The Wind in the Willows* lies largely in what comes next. Of all the Victorians and Edwardians who tried to create Arcadia in print, only Grahame really managed it. His opening chapter gives a full, rich portrait of the earthly paradise, expressed in a symbol that is likely to strike a chord with all readers and was particularly meaningful to his own generation: the River.

The immediate source of the landscape and characters of *The Wind in the Willows*—apart from the slight influence of Beatrix Potter on the Toad chapters—is Richard Jefferies. In *Bevis* you may find the same languorous description of water's edge and woodland, while *Wood Magic* supplies the notion of tribal and social upheavals among the animals, and even has passages where words are whispered by the reeds, the river, and the wind. But there is little suggestion of Grahame's River—with a capital R—in Jefferies' book. Rivers are, of course, timeless symbols in literature, but the late Victorians found a special meaning in them. By the middle of the nineteenth century, Britain's rivers in general and the Thames in particular had been tamed by a system of locks and weirs, and the decline of the old commercial barge traffic (taken away first by canals and then by railways) left them open, as they had never been before, as a pleasure ground for anyone who cared to pick up a pair of oars. In consequence, thousands of those who lived in the sprawling towns and whose lives were dominated by urban industrial society—Londoners very much among them—were taking to the water. Grahame had observed this during his early days at the Bank of England, when he helped with F. J. Furnivall's working-men's rowing club. Indeed, he seems to have known about the River as an escape route since his schooldays at St Edward's in Oxford, where there was not only the Thames but its tributary the Cherwell to explore in skiff or punt. Many times in *The Golden Age* the experience of Escape is bound up with a journey by water, usually along a willow-fringed river; and so it must have been for many young men in Grahame's time. One literary result of this was Jerome K. Jerome's *Three Men in a Boat* (1889), to which *The Wind in the Willows* has more than a slight resemblance. Jerome's book, though outwardly far more comic than Grahame's, slips again and again into ponderous musings which, poor stuff though they are, show their author's awareness of the River as a numinous subject.

Grahame, then, was choosing a very popular symbol when he expressed the Arcadian life in terms of the River Bank. In many ways he was writing specifically about the *bachelor* Arcadia, unencumbered by women. Mole's first meeting with the Water Rat, their picnic together with its catalogue of good food, and their homeward row during which Mole makes a fool of himself by grabbing the oars and upsetting the boat, is a perfect expression of the delights of the all-male life as enjoyed by Grahame in the company of such friends as Furnivall, Quiller-Couch, and his Fowey boating acquaintance Edward Atkinson—a life without many responsibilities, but certainly not without etiquette. The shy, slightly effeminate, and privately rebellious Mole, bursting out from his private confines, is both coming to terms with his own nature as he 'entered into the joy of running water' (a phrase strikingly reminiscent of *The Water-Babies*) and is being initiated into the outdoor, gently muscular world that Kingsley, Furnivall, and the other Christian Socialists knew so well, a world which offered them a form of Escape which was quite adequate for high days and holidays.

It is in one sense a very restrained world. No questions must be asked about people's private activities, and Badger and Otter appear and vanish without apology ('Animal etiquette forbade any sort of comment on the sudden disappearance of one's friends at any moment, for any reason or no reason whatever'). But there is deeply warm friendship for anyone who wants it and is acceptable to this all-male group:

> 'Look here! I really think you had better come and stop with me for a little time . . . And I'll teach you to row, and to swim, and you'll soon be as handy on the water as any of us.' The Mole was so touched by his kind manner of speaking that he could find no voice to answer him; and he had to brush away a tear or two with the back of his paw.

Only three things mar the perfection of the landscape. One is the Wild Wood. In recent years it has become customary to regard *The Wind in the Willows* largely as a social allegory, with the Wild Wood and its inhabitants standing for the rebellious proletariat. This layer of meaning undoubtedly exists within the book, as we shall see; but in the opening chapter it is not touched upon. Here, with the River Bank standing so clearly for all that is good, comradely, and humane in (male) human nature, the Wild Wood intrudes itself darkly into a corner of the picture as a symbol of the unpleasant possibilities of one's personal psychology, the unhealthy imaginings (presumably chiefly sexual) which are apt to cause disturbances when vigilance is relaxed:

> 'Well, of course—there—are others,' explained the Rat in a hesitating sort of way. 'Weasels— and stoats—and foxes—and so on. They're all right in a way—I'm very good friends with them—pass the time of day when we meet, and all that—but they break out sometimes, there's no denying it, and then—well, you can't really trust them, and that's the fact.'

The second threat is one we have met already in Grahame's writings. The River is not in itself the extent of the visible landscape; it forms a boundary or frontier, and there are other possibilities beyond it, chief among them the allure of the far horizon, the Wide World, 'Where it's all blue and dim, and one sees what may be hills or perhaps they mayn't, and something like the smoke of towns,

or is it only cloud-drift?' This is Escape taken to its furthest possibilities, real flight from all responsibility, just as Grahame's father had flown from his family and vanished across the Channel. In *The Golden Age,* full-blown Escape of this sort was treated as a positive, morally acceptable goal—the Roman Road to the perfect city. In *The Wind in the Willows,* a more mature work which shows the imprint of Grahame's increased knowledge of the world, it is recognised for what it really is, a dangerous siren-call that the person of sense cannot dare to listen to:

> 'Beyond the Wild Wood comes the Wide World,' said the Rat. 'And that's something that doesn't matter, either to you or me. I've never been there, and I'm never going, nor you either, if you've got any sense at all. Don't ever refer to it again, please.'

But Grahame also knows that the call cannot be silenced, and later in the book it is the disciplined Rat, rather than the inquisitive, jejune Mole, who responds to it and nearly succumbs.

The third and final threat to the River Bank, and to the stability of the dream, is that which in the event nearly triumphs: Toad Hall. It was a work of some ingenuity for Grahame to link his comic narrative about Toad to his Arcadian vision of the River Bank. Later in the book, Toad's uncertain social position, his *nouveau riche* ambitions, are the principal source of the comedy. But at the beginning, before *The Wind in the Willows* has become a social parable, Toad is not a *parvenu* so much as a psychological misfit. In the structure of the book's first chapter he represents the threat to the individual from the excesses of his own nature. He constantly 'goes over the top'. While Rat and Mole indulge soberly in the gentle pleasure of 'messing about in boats', Toad goes 'a-pleasuring' to excess, and gorges himself on what should be simple delights:

> 'Once, it was nothing but sailing,' said the Rat. 'Then he tired of that and took to punting. Nothing would please him but to punt all day and every day, and a nice mess he made of it. Last year it was house-boating . . . He was going to spend the rest of his life in a house-boat. It's all the same, whatever he takes up; he gets tired of it, and starts on something fresh.'

> 'Such a good fellow, too,' remarked the Otter reflectively. 'But no stability—especially in a boat!'

'Stability' is precisely the quality that Toad lacks. He is certainly 'a good fellow': even at the height of his misdemeanours he retains the fundamental sympathy of his fellow-creatures. But he cannot refrain from over indulgence, and he entirely lacks that *gravitas* or sobriety which is abundantly possessed by Mole, Rat, and Badger, and which is essential to the proper enjoyment of the Arcadian life of the River Bank. Many real-life models for Toad have been suggested: Grahame may have had in mind the tantrums and outrageous behaviour which his own son Alastair is reported to have often indulged in; he may very likely have been thinking of Oscar Wilde, whose scandalous excesses had recently (he was imprisoned in 1895) implicated much of English male society, particularly the Yellow Book circle in which Grahame himself had briefly moved. What seems certain is that, within the structure of the early chapters of *The Wind in the Willows,* Toad is meant to represent Everyman as much as are Mole and Rat, but in his case Everyman run riot. He is not, in this early part of the book, a Till Eulenspiegel or a jester so much as a warning.

The second chapter, 'The Open Road', expounds this further. Toad's *hubris* has now led him to dismiss the River as a 'silly boyish amusement', and he sets off for 'the Life Adventurous'. But his attempt to reach the Wide World—the ultimate Escape—by such crude means is doomed to failure. Toad is restlessly dissatisfied with the new horizons; the journey ends in the ditch (with the ruin of the horse-drawn caravan), and Toad's sights become set on yet another form of excess (the fast motor car). His companions Rat and Mole pine for the River Bank.

By now, we may suspect that the River is not just a symbol for the perfect bachelor life, but for something greater, perhaps Imagination itself. Is not Mole the apprentice artist discovering the possibilities of the imaginative life, and being initiated into it by Rat, already practised in it? We are constantly being told that Rat is a poet; Mole is at first contemptuous of his poetry-writing:

> 'I don't know that I think so *very* much of that little song, Rat,' observed the Mole, cautiously. He was no poet himself and didn't care who knew it; and he had a candid nature.

But his increasing experience of the River Bank changes his attitude. When he and Rat encounter the great god Pan on the enchanted island, Mole cannot at first hear the music of the Pan-pipes which bewitches Rat, but then he does:

> Breathless and transfixed the Mole stopped rowing as the liquid run of that glad piping broke on him like a wave, caught him up, and possessed him utterly.

And finally, when Rat is undergoing a spiritual-psychological crisis, and is fighting the siren-call of the south in 'Wayfarers All', it is Mole who perceives that the cure for his friend's condition is poetry—and who himself turns poet in his attempt to win his friend back to the River Bank:

> Casually, then, and with seeming indifference, the Mole turned his talk to the harvest that was being gathered in, the towering wagons and their straining teams, the growing ricks, and the large moon rising over bare acres dotted with sheaves. He talked of the reddening apples around, of the browning nuts, of jams and preserves and the distilling of cordials; till by easy stages such as these he reached midwinter, its hearty joys and its snug home life, and then he became simply lyrical.

By the conclusion of the book, then, Mole is fully initiated into the life of the Imagination, the life of the artist. He who at the start 'was no poet' is now 'simply lyrical'.

Toad is a poet too, but his odes are hymns of self-love; not without merit, perhaps, and a little resembling the boasts of great heroes in ancient literature, but ultimately the poetry of excess and self-indulgence:

> He got so puffed up with conceit that he made up a song as he walked in praise of himself . . . It was perhaps the most conceited song that any animal ever composed.

> 'The world has held great Heroes,
>   As history-books have showed;
> But never a name to go down to fame
>   Compared with that of Toad!'

Yet Toad, too, grows in wisdom, and by the end of the book has learnt to keep his boastful poems to himself. He recites 'Toad's Last Little Song' in the privacy of his bedroom, and then, descending to the banquet celebrating his return to Toad Hall, maintains a discreet silence. Poetry has been restored to its rightful place in the order of things.

If the Wild Wood—the subject of the book's third chapter—symbolises the darker side of human psychology, it also has a place in that layer of *The Wind in the Willows* which examines the proper and improper role of Imagination in the individual's life. Here, it seems to stand for the tangle of rich and dangerous symbolism which threatens the mental life of even the most sober of artists. The image is not unusual; for example, Charles Williams, friend of C. S. Lewis, used the wood Broceliande to carry just this meaning in his Arthurian cycle of poems, *Taliessin through Logres.* Williams described this wood as 'a place of making', from which either good or evil imaginings may come, and so it is with Grahame's Wild Wood.

The most striking fact about the Wild Wood is that, despite its threatening nature, Badger dwells at the heart of it; and Badger is the most wise and perfectly balanced character in the book, with his gruff common sense, his dislike of triviality (he chooses to come into Society only when it suits him), and his strength of character which can—at least temporarily—master even the excesses of Toad. Badger is, of course, a portrait of a certain kind of English landed gentleman, but he is far more. He is the still centre around which the book's various storms may rage, but who is scarcely touched by them. He is, one may surmise, the deepest level of the imaginative mind, not easily accessible; perhaps he stands for inspiration, only visiting the artist when it chooses, and then behaving just as it wishes. 'You must not only take him *as* you find him, but *when* you find him,' Rat says of Badger. Above all he is not to be sought out deliberately: 'It's quite out of the question, because he lives in the very middle of the Wild Wood.' The deepest level of the imagination dwells (as surely it must) right in the middle of spiritual or psychological danger.

Mole, the artist who has not yet learnt the wisdom of his craft, ignores all warnings and determines to plunge into this danger zone in the hope of getting some sort of imaginative reward. He 'formed the resolution to go out by himself and explore the Wild Wood, and perhaps strike up an acquaintance with Mr Badger'. The result is predictable: at close quarters the wood terrifies him, with its nightmare visions of sinister faces, its whistlings, and its patterings.

Again, the wood's threat may be sexual—the artist's mental equilibrium is perhaps being threatened particularly by sensual imaginings. Rat's remedy for it is male companionship: 'If we have to come, we come in couples, at least; then we're generally all right.' Yet when Mole collapses in terror at the very centre of the wood, it offers, surprisingly, a womb-like security:

> At last he took refuge in the deep dark hollow of an old beech tree, which offered shelter, concealment—perhaps even safety, but who could tell?

So Anodos takes refuge in the arms of the maternal beech tree in George MacDonald's *Phantastes:* ' "Why, you baby!" said she, and kissed me with the sweetest kiss of wind and odours.'

But the Wild Wood offers, at the heart of its sexual tangle, an even more womb-like refuge than the hollow of the beech: Badger's own home, entered by 'A long, gloomy, and, to tell the truth, decidedly shabby passage'. The words 'womb-like' are, indeed, quite inadequate to describe the sense of security and return to childhood conveyed by Grahame's description of Badger's home. And with this description, we come to the heart of Grahame's Arcadian dream.

The description is worth quoting at length. Badger flings open a stout oak door, and Rat and Mole find themselves in his kitchen:

> The floor was well-worn red brick, and on the wide hearth burnt a fire of logs, between two attractive chimney-corners tucked away in the wall, well out of any suspicion of draught. A couple of high-backed settles, facing each other on either side of the fire, gave further sitting accommodation for the sociably disposed. In the middle of the room stood a long table of plain boards placed on trestles, with benches down each side. At one end of it, where an arm-chair stood pushed back, were spread the remains of the Badger's plain but ample supper. Rows of spotless plates winked from the shelves of the dresser at the far end of the room, and from the rafters overhead hung hams, bundles of dried herbs, nets of onions and baskets of eggs. It seemed a place where heroes could fitly feast after victory, where weary harvesters could line up in scores along the table and keep their Harvest Home with mirth and song, or where two or three friends of simple tastes could sit about as they pleased and eat and smoke and talk in comfort and contentment. The ruddy brick floor smiled up at the smoky ceiling; the oaken settles, shiny with long wear, exchanged cheerful glances with each other; plates on the dresser grinned at pots on the shelf, and the merry firelight flickered and played over everything without distinction.

The Kitchen, described in these terms, is as universal a symbol as the River. Whereas the River is the expression of the adult Arcadia, with its challenges and its rules and its excitements, the Kitchen suggests another kind of Golden Age.

Its appeal is multiple. It hints at the mead-halls of such poems as *Beowulf;* Grahame says that 'heroes could fitly feast' in it, a phrase whose alliteration faintly recalls Anglo-Saxon verse. To Grahame's generation it must also have had William Morris-like hints of an earlier, pre-industrial, and therefore ideal society where distinctions of class seemed unimportant when food was being dealt out, and men of all ranks sat together in the lord's hall or by the yeoman farmer's hearthside. And, more sharply for Edwardian readers than for those of the present day, there is a suggestion too of a return to childhood. Many of Grahame's generation spent much of their early life being cared for by domestic servants, and so as small children lingered often in the kitchen, watching the pots and the joints of meat cooking on the great ranges or spits. Walter de la Mare, born fourteen years after Grahame, was still in time to have this experience, shared with his brothers and sisters. As his biographer Theresa Whistler writes:

> They had their breakfast in the kitchen with Pattie [the servant], while [their mother] was served her toast alone . . in the drawing room . . The children's lives revolved in great part around Pattie's spry, neat figure in the kitchen . . . Pattie's old range had a roasting jack with a winding clock, and dripping-pan underneath. When the children came home ravenous from school, if a joint was roasting, Pattie would open the little door below and supply them with hot bread and dripping . . . In [de la Mare's] fairy tales for children, magic and remoteness are often given for backcloth an old-fashioned kitchen, minutely described and as warmly relished.

There is a suggestion of the Kitchen in many of the outstanding children's books which preceded *The Wind in the Willows*. In *The Water-Babies*, Tom comes, at the end of his exhausting climb down Lewthwaite Crag, to the cottage of the old school-dame, where he peeps through the door:

> And there sat by the empty fireplace, which was filled with a pot of sweet herbs, the nicest old woman that ever was seen . . . At her feet sat the grandfather of all the cats . . . Such a pleasant cottage it was, with a shiny clean stone floor, and curious old prints on the walls, and an old black oak sideboard full of bright pewter and brass dishes . . .

George MacDonald's preferred symbol of deep security is the Library in the Castle, yet even he touches upon the Kitchen at moments. It is from a cottage kitchen that Tangle and Mossy set out on their quest in 'The Golden Key', while in *The Princess and Curdie* the moral decay of the king's household is largely expressed in terms of the disgusting state of the castle kitchen:

> Everywhere was filth and disorder. Mangy turnspit dogs were lying about, and grey rats were gnawing at refuse in the sinks. . . . [Curdie] longed for one glimpse of his mother's poor little kitchen, so clean and bright and airy.

Lewis Carroll, of course, was not concerned with the establishment of a positive Arcadia, but his anti-Arcadia has, as one of its most memorable features, a kitchen where everything has gone deliberately wrong:

> The door led right into a large kitchen, which was full of smoke from one end to the other . . . The cook took the cauldron of soup off the fire, and at once set to work throwing everything within her reach at the Duchess and the baby— the fire-irons came first: then followed a shower of saucepans, plates, and dishes.

Beatrix Potter's Mrs Tiggy-Winkle and Tailor of Gloucester, both true Arcadians, live in kitchens, but it was left to Grahame to give full expression to this symbol of deep, childlike security. As Rat and Mole sit down to supper by Badger's great hearth, they find themselves truly 'in safe anchorage', and know 'that the cold and trackless Wild Wood just left outside was miles and miles away, and all that they had suffered in it a half-forgotten dream'.

It is now—and only now—that *The Wind in the Willows* begins to become a social drama, a narrative about the English middle class and the threat to its stability. The meditations on the subject of the artistic imagination, on Escape, and on the deep need the individual has for the womb-like security of home, do not disappear from the book. They return in force in the chapters 'Dulce Domum' and 'Wayfarers All', while the Pan chapter 'The Piper at the Gates of Dawn' is an attempt to go beyond the plain, homely Arcadia of Badger's kitchen and describe a more spiritualised utopia. But, in general, after Badger's home has been reached the book turns into something more like a socio-political allegory.

Something of class distinction has been suggested from the beginning. The Mole, scrabbling up to the surface and running across the meadows in his delight at freedom, brushes officious toll-gate-keeping rabbits aside in a manner resembling that of a member of the upper middle class dealing with tiresome government clerks. On the other hand, when he first meets the Rat there is a suggestion that here is someone subtly his social superior, who leads a leisured gentlemanly existence while Mole is a creature of routine, who inhabits a more lowly home. Badger, of course, is a member of the old aristocracy, living unmolested in the very heart of the Wild Wood by virtue of the authority that birth and breeding have conferred upon him, not to mention his vast tunnelled dwelling which gives him access to any part of the landscape—the great country house and its estate dominating the villagers. The young hedgehogs sheltering from the snow and breakfasting in his kitchen refer to him as 'the Master', and address Rat and Mole as 'sir' and 'you gentlemen'. When Badger shows Mole the extent of his underground domain, and explains that it owes its grandeur to the fact that it is the ruins of an ancient city, Grahame is surely suggesting that society at its best and most stable is built on the foundations of past cultures.

Toad represents the opposite of this stability. His exact social position is never made clear; he is described as behaving like 'a blend of the Squire and the College Don', and it is clear that Toad Hall has been in his family for more than one generation; yet the narrative constantly gives the impression that he is a *parvenu* whose family has bought its way into the squirearchy rather than inherited its position. Badger censures Toad for 'squandering the money your father left you', and there seems to be a hint that Mr Toad senior made that money in the cotton trade or something less decorous. What is absolutely certain is that Toad's behaviour is letting the side down, is threatening the position of the entire *bourgeoisie* and upper class. Badger says to him severely:

> 'You knew it must come to this, sooner or later . . . You're getting us animals a bad name in the district by your furious driving and your smashes and your rows with the police. Independence is all very well, but we animals never allow our friends to make fools of themselves beyond a certain limit; and that limit you've reached.'

This passage is to some extent misleading, in that it suggests that Toad's sin is to damage the reputation of the animal inhabitants of the River Bank with 'the police', that is, the humans. Grahame is not, however, talking about this. (He is never certain about the animals' relation to the human world around them—this is perhaps the one major flaw in the concept of the book—and at times, as here, the uncertainty obtrudes.) What he is really saying is that Toad is letting down his class and exposing it to danger, as subsequent events make clear. Toad's absence in prison leaves Toad Hall vacant for the Wild Wooders to occupy and claim as their own. Irresponsible behaviour among the *bourgeoisie,* the *rentier* class, has weakened the defences of that part of society, and made it vulnerable to riot and revolution.

One can have little doubt that this layer of meaning exists within the book. It appeared in print, in 1908, at a time when England, like much of western society, had experienced many decades of social unrest, and when anarchy or revolution was an all too familiar terror. Peter Green, in his biography of Grahame, speaks of the Wild Wooders as 'like the urban mob-anarchists of every Edwardian upper-middle-class nightmare'. He argues persuasively that the story has 'an unmistakable social symbolism'. Yet it is hard to persuade oneself that Grahame was so very much aware of this symbolism, or took much conscious interest in contemporary social unrest. Certainly, shortly before he began to invent the Toad element in the book's plot, in November 1903, he himself was threatened at gunpoint in the Bank of England by a lunatic of socialist tendencies, and this episode is perhaps echoed at the moment when a ferret sentry fires at Toad. But apart from this, there is little evidence that Grahame took the kind of interest in current social events that may be found, for example, in Beatrix Potter's journal. One is inclined to judge that the 'social symbolism' of *The Wind in the Willows* is in the nature of almost accidental colouring, acquired because of the time in which it was written, rather than present strongly in its author's mind.

The parallels between the Wild Wooders and the socialist-anarchist mob threat are not in any case very many. Mole, walking through the Wild Wood and seeing 'evil wedge-shaped faces', may be experiencing something of the emotions of an Edwardian gentleman inadvertently finding himself in the London slums, but the episode has more about it of nightmare than rational social fear. Moreover, the Wild Wooders, inasmuch as they are described at all (and remarkably little is actually said about them), do not behave like a working-class mob. When they get possession of Toad Hall they act just like dissipated gentry—like Toad himself, in fact, 'lying in bed half the day, and breakfast at all hours . . . Eating your grub, and drinking your drink, and making bad jokes about you'. The speech given by the Chief Weasel is not rabble-rousing by a mob leader but a typical piece of after-dinner oratory at a banquet:

> 'Well, I do not propose to detain you much longer'—(great applause)—'but before I resume my seat' (renewed cheering)—'I should like to say one word about our kind host, Mr Toad. We all know Toad!'—(great laughter) . . .

This is the atmosphere of an undergraduate dining club, or a cheerful gathering of City clerks, not a piece of revolutionary fervour. *The Wind in the Willows* does not anticipate *Animal Farm*.

If, despite this, the Wild Wooders are *en masse* the social inferiors of the River Bankers—and there is no clear evidence to support this—then possibly they represent the rural rather than the urban working classes, for there is a passage near the end of the book where a mother weasel speaks to her child much as a cottager might have addressed her offspring when the local gentry of Grahame's era came in sight:

> 'Look, baby! There goes the great Mr Toad! And that's the gallant Water Rat, a terrible fighter, walking along o' him! And yonder comes the famous Mr Mole, of whom you so often have heard your father tell!'

In fact, one suspects that Grahame himself saw the behaviour of the Wild Wooders not in terms of contemporary English society, but as something like the suitors of Penelope in the *Odyssey,* who have to be cast out by Ulysses before he can regain his home. The final chapter of *The Wind in the Willows* is entitled 'The Return of Ulysses', and Peter Green has pointed out that there are other Homeric references within the book, most notably the description of the arming of Badger, Rat, Mole, and Toad before their attack on Toad Hall.

If one accepts that *The Wind in the Willows* is not primarily a social parable, one is likely to judge that the dominating element of the book is that which celebrates the pleasures of existence among the River Bankers. Within this part of the story, on the simpler level, Grahame is talking about the cheerful bachelor-like existence of himself and his friends, as they lead the kind of life sought by men of their class since the days of Kingsley and Tom Hughes. More subtly, he is concerned with the artistic imagination and its delights and dangers. And this higher level is the only one which easily assimilates everything in the book, and makes a coherent whole of it.

On this level, Rat and Mole are not simply the apprentice and the experienced artists, but different facets of the same artistic mind. Mole is by turns timorous and rash, while Rat alternates between dreamer and practical man-of-the-world. One begins gradually to feel that Mole is the artist's personality as a human being (he closely resembles many aspects of Kenneth Grahame himself), while Rat is an expression of the two sides of an artist's actual work: inspiration (Rat's dreaminess) and craftsmanship (his practical knowledge of boats). The meeting ground of the two is the River, Imagination itself, with its 'babbling procession of the best stories in the world, sent from the heart of the earth to be told at last to the insatiable sea'.

Both Rat and Mole are vulnerable to certain urges which threaten to upset the stability of the relationship. Mole is markedly home-loving, and would half like to desert the River Bank (imagination and artistic creation) for the very mundane pleasures of his own home. In 'Dulce Domum', the brilliant chapter describing his rediscovery of that home one winter's evening, Grahame subtly suggests that Mole has no real artistic taste: the courtyard of his house is decorated with 'brackets carrying plaster statuary—Garibaldi, and the infant Samuel, and Queen Victoria, and other heroes of modern Italy'; and in the centre of a goldfish pond is 'a fanciful erection clothed in . . . cockleshells and topped by a large silvered glass ball that reflected everything all wrong and had a very pleasing effect'. The hint of vulgarity, of mass-produced works of art purchased from chain stores, contributes to a picture of the reluctant artist fleeing for his real pleasures to very off-duty surroundings. Rat wisely allows Mole a night in this setting before luring him back to the River Bank and his true vocation. Rat himself has an equally strong temptation in the opposite direction, to abandon the life of the imagination for a life of purely sensual pleasure. The Sea Rat—an exact mirror-image of himself in all but experience—tries to lure him away from his own habitat and occupations into a world that is not merely Grahame's adored Mediterranean landscape but also a life of lotus-eating, a lazy tasting of pleasure that spells death to artistic creation. (The Sea Rat, it should be noted, is not himself a sailor; he takes no part in the work of the crew, but lazes in the captain's cabin while they are labouring.) Was Grahame thinking particularly of the excesses of some of his fellow-writers of the 'nineties?

Within this scheme of the book, with Badger (as we have said) personifying pure inspiration, and Toad's adventures symbolising the threat to the artist from the unstable nature of his own personality, one turns to the chapter 'The Piper at the Gates of Dawn', which stands at the centre of the book, in the expectation that here Grahame will make some positive statement about the artistic imagination which will bind the rest of the book together. But any such expectation is disappointed. Grahame has chosen, at this crucial place, to introduce yet another major character or symbol, the great god Pan himself, whose pipes are heard and who is then glimpsed himself by Rat and Mole. The episode makes plenty of sense within the book's examination of the theme of the artistic mind: it is Rat (as we have noted) who hears the Pan-pipes first, and Mole only comes to be aware of the presence of the god thanks to the persuasion and influence of Rat ('Now you must surely hear it! Ah—at last—I see you do!') But Pan does not seem to be the right figure to stand for the pure artistic inspiration, the experience of real poetry, which is what the chapter is intended to convey.

Grahame, it should be noted at this point, rejected conventional religion. *The Golden Age* mocks the Olympians for going to church on Sundays 'though they betrayed no greater delight in the experience than ourselves'. Peter Green records that the Calvinism of his parental upbringing followed by the 'social Anglicanism' of his grandmother's home 'had damned Grahame's natural spring of faith at the source'. He was drawn aesthetically to the ritual of the Roman Catholic church, which lured him as did all things Mediterranean, but his rational mind could not apparently accept Christian doctrine. In this, of course, he resembled other outstanding practitioners of children's literature, and like them he wrote for children partly because it seemed to offer a way to the discovery of an alternative religion. But though his River Bank and Wild Wood stir, at the moment when he is writing most subtly, something like religious awe in the reader, he is quite unable to evoke specifically religious feelings just at the moment when he wants to. 'The Piper at the Gates of Dawn' is embarrassing because it summons up the very 'nineties figure of Pan, who reappears again and again in mediocre 'pagan' writings of the period by Grahame and his contemporaries. Grahame's description of him is a ghastly error in taste:

> . . . the rippling muscles on the arm that lay across the broad chest, the long supple hand still holding the pan-pipes only just fallen away from the parted lips; . . . the splendid curves of the shaggy limbs disposed in majestic ease on the sward . . .

Just when we should be encountering pure poetry we have a piece of bad late Victorian art, with the sexual potency of the Pan of classical literature replaced by something resembling 'The Light of the World'. W. W. Robson has suggested that people who dislike 'The Piper at the Gates of Dawn' do so because they are hostile to religion. But this is to suppose that the chapter conveys any real sense of the religious or numinous.

However, it not only misses true religious art but is redundant within the scheme of the book. Badger and the Wild Wood are surely more than adequate symbols for the deepest level of the artistic imagination, and Mole's encounter with them both is the book's central crisis. The River Bank stands perfectly for the day-to-day life of the artist. The exploration of these themes in the supposedly more heightened terms of 'The Piper at the Gates of Dawn' is just not necessary; the thing has already been done as well as it possibly could be.

The Wind in the Willows has nothing to do with childhood or children, except in that it can be enjoyed by the young, who thereby experience (though they do not rationally understand) what its author has to say, and are able to sense some of its resonances. C. S. Lewis observed that it is a perfect example of the kind of story which can express things without explaining them. Taking as an example the character of Badger, whom he described as an 'amalgam of high rank, coarse manners, gruffness, shyness and goodness', Lewis argued that 'The child who has once met Mr Badger has got ever afterwards, in its bones, a knowledge of humanity and English social history which it certainly couldn't get from any abstraction.' In this sense *The Wind in the Willows* has a claim to be regarded as the finest achievement of children's literature up to the date at which it was written, and perhaps afterwards. It is crammed full of experience of human character, almost unfailingly wise and mature in its judgements, and yet largely accessible to children. It does not frighten in the way that *Alice* often does; it is never condescending, nor does it present an oversimplified view of the world. It has nearly as much irony and comedy as Beatrix Potter's stories while being far more ambitious. Yet it is also faulty. 'The Piper at the Gates of Dawn' is an error or judgement on a grand scale, and there are smaller lapses again and again in the book—the awkward question of the human-animal relationship, the self-conscious self-parodying authorial manner during the account of Toad's brush with the law, and overindulgent scenic descriptions, reminiscent of Richard Jefferies or Edward Thomas at their most run-of-the-mill. Though it is fine enough in structure, one feels that it is often shakily executed, and that the exercise could scarcely be repeated successfully, so near does it come at times to collapse.

Certainly Grahame himself never repeated it. *The Wind in the Willows* was his last book, and after it he gave up the struggle to rescue himself from his marriage and the general impossibility of his life. He resigned early from the Bank of England and led an empty retirement. His son Alastair, to whom the book had first been told, was found dead on a railway line while an undergraduate at Oxford in 1920, and though the inquest verdict was accidental death the evidence points to suicide. This event provides an ironic link with another Edwardian who wrote a great work of literature for children; for the child who, more than any other, was the 'real' Peter Pan met his death a year later, in not dissimilar circumstances and only a few miles away from that of the boy who had provided the impetus for *The Wind in the Willows*.

Lesley Willis   (essay date 1988)

SOURCE: " 'A Sadder and a Wiser Rat/He Rose the Morrow Morn': Echoes of the Romantics in Kenneth Grahame's *The Wind in the Willows,*" in *Children's Literature Association Quarterly*, Vol. 13, No. 3, Fall, 1988, pp. 108-11.

[*In the following essay, Willis traces the influence of English Romantic literature on* The Wind in the Willows.]

> The Seafarer, refreshed and strengthened, his voice more vibrant, his eye lit with a brightness that seemed caught from some far-away sea-beacon, filled his glass with the red and glowing vintage of the South, and, leaning towards the Water Rat, compelled his gaze and held him, body and soul, while he talked. Those eyes were of the changing foam-streaked grey-green of leaping Northern seas; in the glass shone a hot ruby that seemed the very heart of the South, beating for him who had courage to respond to its pulsation. The twin lights, the shifting grey and the steadfast red, mastered the Water Rat and held him bound, fascinated, powerless. The quiet world outside their rays receded far away and ceased to be.
>
> [Kenneth Grahame, *The Wind in the Willows*]

Through this blend of Coleridge's "The Ancient Mariner" and Keats's "Ode to a Nightingale," Kenneth Grahame expresses the central tension of *The Wind in the Willows*. On the surface, nothing could be clearer than the paramount value of home and community and the merit of accepting (with decent allowance for personal growth) one's own limitations; the movement of the whole book is towards the integration of isolated or unregenerate animals into a well-ordered community bounded by the borders of what was formerly the Wild Wood. Even Toad, who exhibits, to borrow Jane Austen's words, "vanity, extravagance, love of change, [and] restlessness of temper," (*Emma*) is finally induced to play the role his community requires of him.

Yet beneath the apparently steady development of domestic and social tranquillity—Toad's aberrations are amusing rather than threatening—a conflict exists between the desire for security and the desire for adventure and change which results, not in a decisive victory for the former, but in a contained tension in which the pull for security provides the outer framework. At the root of this conflict is the fear, on the one hand, of the danger inherent in trying to fulfil one's longings, on the other, of the stultifying effect of too much security. The danger inherent in safety itself appears through the pervasive prison motif; the fascination of adventure is reinforced by allusions to Romantic poetry and references to that most changeable aspect of nature, the sea. In the image of the Ancient Mariner, the two last are united.

The arch-adventurer in *The Wind in the Willows* is Toad, who sums up his philosophy in his encomium on life in the canary-coloured cart:

> "Here today, up and off to somewhere else tomorrow! Travel, change, interest, excitement! The whole world before you, and a horizon that's always changing!"

This certainly has a flavour of Baudelaire's "les vrais voyageurs sont ceux . . . qui partent/Pour partir," but there is precious little of the Ancient Mariner in Toad, in spite of his travels, his anti-social behavior, his punishment and his occasional ventures into poetry. The one possible allusion to Coleridge's Mariner is found when Toad steals the motor-car parked outside the Red Lion; the lines "But swift as dreams, myself I found/Within the pilot's boat" echo in the description of Toad's state of mind, a passage the even, anaphoric structure of which suggests poetic metre:

> As if in a dream he found himself, somehow, seated in the driver's seat; as if in a dream he pulled the lever and swung the car round the yard and out through the archway; and, as if in a dream, all sense of right and wrong, all fear of obvious consequences, seemed temporarily suspended.

But Toad sees land and water only as thoroughfares. He lacks the respect and love for them which the others feel, and he certainly has none of the passionate awareness of nature which the Ancient Mariner develops in the course of his wanderings. And Peter Green persuasively argues in his book, *Kenneth Grahame*, that Oscar Wilde is the person to whom the character of Toad owes most.

The Ancient Mariner presents himself in the second of two quasi-mystical chapters—"The Piper at the Gates of Dawn" and "Wayfarers All"—which were apparently the last to be incorporated into the text (Green). He appears as the Sea Rat, a figure whose exotic appeal is undiminished by any of Toad's absurdity. The Sea Rat, or Adventurer, is "lean" to the Ancient Mariner's "lank" and, while he does not have the Mariner's "skinny hand," "his paws were thin and long"—which, again, suggests Coleridge's "thou art long, and lank, and brown." The Ancient Mariner's "glittering eye" becomes an eye "lit with a brightness that seemed caught from some far-away sea-beacon," and Ratty finds at the end of the tale that the Adventurer is "still holding him fast with his sea-grey eyes."

There is never any suggestion that the Sea Rat has committed a crime against nature; Grahame, like Jane Austen in *Mansfield Park*, is content to "let other pens dwell on guilt and misery." The fascination of the Sea Rat, is, however, inseparable from the dangerous instability revealed by his reason for setting out on his previous voyage: "Family troubles, as usual, began it. The domestic storm-cone was hoisted." And he admits, perhaps with more politeness than sincerity, that the life of a "freshwater mariner" is "a goodly life . . . no doubt the best in the world, if only you are strong enough to lead it." But Ratty is incapable of heeding such hints. His own discontent has predisposed him to listen to the Sea Rat, and he gradually sinks into a hypnotic trance in which he loses control of the situation; he is "held . . . body and soul," he is "mastered" and "held . . . bound, fascinated, powerless." Ratty plays a far from reluctant Wedding Guest to the Sea Rat's Ancient Mariner in a passage which shows at once the seductiveness and the danger of the "Life Adventurous"; and the extent of the danger is brought home when we find that "his eyes . . . were glazed and set and turned a streaked and shifting grey—not [Ratty's] eyes, but the eyes of some other animal."

Allusions to Keats's "Ode to a Nightingale" reinforce the sense of Rat's loss of control and the risk he runs of loss of self. The glass, shining with "a hot ruby that seemed the very heart of the South," suggests Keats's "beaker full of the warm south," while Keats's hope that he may "drink, and leave the world unseen,/And with thee fade away into the forest dim" is realized in Ratty's case by the "twin lights" that mesmerise him—a well-known brainwashing technique—so that "the quiet world outside their rays receded far away and ceased to be." The analogy, however, is not complete, for in Grahame's passage the person, not the world, begins to "fade far away" and "dissolve"; and, while Keats, like the Sea Rat, wants to escape conflict and responsibility, the Water Rat is closer to the "thou among the leaves" who has never known disease, decline or the waning of love.

The paradox of the Sea Rat is that he is both Mariner and Anti-Mariner, for Grahame wants to show not only that adventure is dangerous but that, in the long run, it is disappointing. Though the Seafarer, like the Ancient Mariner, is gifted with "strange power of speech," his tale has oddly prosaic touches which his listener is too entranced to notice. When Ratty supposes that the Adventurer must be "months and months out of sight of land, and provisions running short, and allowanced as to water, and your mind communing with the mighty ocean, and all that sort of thing," the Sea Rat replies that he is "in the coasting trade, and rarely out of sight of land." And, while his account of Venice makes the Water Rat "[float] on dream canals and [hear] a phantom song pealing high between vaporous grey wave-lapped walls," the Seafarer seems quite as concerned with the joys of eating in Venice as with its beauty—indeed, the food motif recurs so frequently in his discourse that Ratty finally takes the hint and fetches a well-packed picnic basket.

The greatest paradox of all is that the Sea Rat's call to adventure involves the acceptance of death, not as the ultimate means of escape which Keats envisions, but as the ultimate reality. "Take the Adventure, heed the call, now ere the irrevocable moment passes! 'Tis but a banging of the door behind you," says the Seafarer. But animals such as Ratty and Mole are afraid of "the banging of the door," for it means abandoning the illusion of an eternal present and moving into the relentless sequence of time in which, one day, a point will be reached when "the cup has been drained and the play has been played." Coleridge's Ancient Mariner has passed beyond the reach of time, but the Sea Rat is very conscious that "the days pass, and never return"—and he alone, among all Grahame's characters, can say "I am ageing."

Under the circumstances, we can understand why Ratty behaves "like one that hath been stunned,/And is of sense forlorn"; the crucial question is whether one can also say that, like the wedding guest, "A sadder and a wiser rat,/He rose the morrow morn." Sadness there certainly is after Ratty's encounter with the Seafarer—the sense of a once-in-a-lifetime opportunity missed—but such wisdom as accrues to Ratty derives not from the Seafarer but from Mole, who long before learned, by experiencing the fear of death, that "he must be wise, must keep to the pleasant places in which his lines were laid and which held adventure enough, in their way, to last for a lifetime."

Writing about "Wayfarers All," Peter Green comments that "Mole here is the respectable, conformist side of Grahame: conscientious, practical and loyal, he stands for all the domestic and public virtues." But Mole also has Romantic associations, although, his earlier adventures notwithstanding, they have nothing to do with the Romantic journey. The associations of Mole are with scenes of domestic nature of the type that appeal to Wordsworth, and this emerges clearly in the chapter entitled "The Piper at the Gates of Dawn," in which Mole and Ratty meet the Pan-like "Friend and Helper" on a willow-fringed island in the river. Although Ratty, as a poet, hears more of the song in the reeds than does his friend, we see the vision through Mole's eyes. And Mole, as a child of the earth, bears some resemblance to the lowlier figures in Blake's "Book of Thel"—which begins with the lines "Does the Eagle know what is in the pit?/Or wilt thou go ask the Mole?" (Thel's Motto). While the allusions to Blake's

poem are less direct than the allusions to Coleridge and Keats in the passage already discussed, it does not seem unduly fanciful to think that Mole in this chapter owes something to the Lilly, who "bow'd her modest head," and to the Clod of Clay, who "rais'd her pitying head" and then "fix'd her humble eyes" on the Queen of the vales. The very rhythm of the sentence "Trembling he obeyed, and raised his humble head" could place it in "The Book of Thel"—and certainly the whole scene is reminiscent of the vale in which Thel wanders by the River of Adona.

Mole is well qualified to reanimate Ratty's interest in "the things that went to make up his daily life," and the exigency of the moment when Ratty is transported by the Sea Rat's vision raises him to unaccustomed eloquence:

> Casually . . . and with seeming indifference, the Mole turned his talk to the harvest that was being gathered in, the towering wagons and their straining teams, the growing ricks, and the large moon rising over bare acres dotted with sheaves. He talked of the reddening apples around, of the browning nuts, of jams and preserves and the distilling of cordials; till by easy stages such as these he reached mid-winter, its hearty joys and its snug home life, and then he became simply lyrical.

This is Mole's only venture into the role of muse, and it differs widely from Toad's earlier "[playing] upon the inexperienced Mole as on a harp" while he describes the "Life Adventurous." Mole wants Ratty to observe, not to speculate, and he is finally gratified by seeing his friend give a proper direction to his imaginative powers through writing poetry.

In Mole and Ratty, the domestic side of Romanticism—rural life—is balanced against its more dangerous exotic appeal, and comes out victorious. But this triumph is tinged with sadness and even with fear of the potentially dulling effect of opting for security. The clear allusions to Coleridge, Keats and Blake find an unequal but perceptible counterpart in the more diffuse motif of the caged bird—an incongruous presentation of a potent Romantic symbol of freedom. Even the canary-coloured cart, that paradoxical compound of home and journey, has its caged inhabitant—a bird within a bird. And the gaoler's daughter keeps not only a canary, "whose cage hung on a nail in the massive wall of the keep by day . . . and was shrouded in an antimacassar on the parlour table at night," but also "several piebald mice and a restless revolving squirrel." Interestingly, the several varieties of prisoner—Toad is one—are detailed in the chapter which separates "The Piper at the Gates of Dawn" from "Wayfarers All."

The fullest treatment of the ambivalent image of the caged bird occurs when Ratty and Mole walk through a human village as they return from (another paradox) a hunting and exploring trip with Otter:

> It was from one little window, with its blind drawn down, a mere blank transparency on the night, that the sense of home and the little curtained world within walls—the larger stressful world of outside. Nature shut out and forgot-

ten—most pulsated. Close against the white blind hung a bird-cage, clearly silhouetted, every wire, perch, and appurtenance distinct and recognizable, even to yesterday's dull-edged lump of sugar. On the middle perch the fluffy occupant, head tucked well into feathers, seemed so near to them as to be easily stroked, had they tried; even the delicate tips of his plumped-out plumage pencilled plainly on the illuminated screen. As they looked, the sleepy little fellow stirred uneasily, woke, shook himself, and raised his head. They could see the gape of his tiny beak as he yawned in a bored sort of way, looked round, and then settled his head into his back again, while the ruffled feathers gradually subsided into perfect stillness.

Even the favourable contrast with the situation of Ratty and Mole—"a gust of bitter wind took them in the back of the neck, a small sting of frozen sleet on the skin woke them as from a dream, and they knew their toes to be cold and their legs tired, and their own home distant a weary way"—cannot disguise the fact that the bird is a prisoner.

"A Robin Red breast in a Cage/Puts all Heaven in a Rage," says Blake ("Auguries of Innocence"); and although canaries are bred to captivity, there is something inherently unfitting about the idea of a caged bird. The universal association of birds with freedom is reflected in the fact that Ratty's restless longing to leave home is at least in part a response to their fall migration: "Even as he lay in bed at night he thought he could make out, passing in the darkness overhead, the beat and quiver of impatient pinions, obedient to the peremptory call." The two poems to which Grahame alludes in describing the Adventurer's call—"The Rime of the Ancient Mariner" and the "Ode to a Nightingale"—are renowned for their powerful bird images, and though Grahame mentions neither the albatross nor the nightingale their connotations of freedom are implicit in the passage.

But animals in *The Wind in the Willows* must learn that they cannot hope for the freedom of birds, and the whole idea is amusingly deflated when Toad—known for his unrealistic attitude to life—is thrown from a motor-car:

> Toad found himself flying through the air with the strong upward rush and delicate curve of a swallow. He liked the motion, and was just beginning to wonder whether it would go on until he developed wings and turned into a Toad-bird when he landed on his back with a thump . . .

And Toad is not the only one who "land[s] on his back with a thump." Ratty, like Mole before him, "must keep to the pleasant places in which his lines were laid," and Mole is rewarded for his enterprise and heroism before and during the retaking of Toad Hall (not for nothing is there a statue of Garibaldi in his garden) by supervising clean-up operations and filling out a large pile of invitation cards.

Throughout *The Wind in the Willows* the call to a new experience or an unknown place is seen as appealing. Mole hears it at the very beginning of the book; like the infant Samuel whose statue adorns his garden, he feels that "something up above was calling him imperiously." But

never does the call seem more attractive than in "Wayfarers All." The Seafarer's voice is "vibrant," his eyes are "of the changing foam-streaked grey-green of leaping Northern seas" and he "compelled [Ratty's] gaze and held him, body and soul, while he talked." Ratty, for his part, is merely "bound, fascinated, powerless." But the many words connoting agency or motion which Grahame uses in connection with the Seafarer do more than make this animal appear vital and fascinating. They underline the fact that the call is away—away from the safe, the predictable, the familiar, and (in the tradition of the Romantic hero) towards the uncertain, the new, the extraordinary.

The passage quoted at the beginning of this paper brings out the contrast between resignation and desire, for it is full of contrasts—North and South, grey and red, speech and silence, stasis and motion—and they are interrelated in such a manner as to convey that sense of not-quite-resolved tension, of reasonably happy compromise, that underlies the surface calm and playfulness of the novel. For the call—a poignant and disturbing element in an otherwise tranquil life—must sometimes be resisted, but it will always be heard.

Mary DeForest   (essay date 1989)

SOURCE: "*The Wind in the Willows*: A Tale for Two Readers," in *Classical and Modern Literature*, Vol. 10, Fall, 1989, pp. 81-7.

[*In the following essay, DeForest explains the similarities between Toad in* The Wind in the Willows *and Homer's* Ulysses.]

First published in 1908, Kenneth Grahame's masterpiece, *The Wind in the Willows,* has appealed to readers of all ages. The child who hears the story enters its cozy river world with its pleasant inhabitants, Mole, Ratty, and Badger. In counterpoint to the peaceful charm of this world are set the lunatic adventures of Toad, who has successfully shaken off the trammels of responsible behavior. The adult who reads to the child gets a more subtle enjoyment because the pattern of the story follows that of one of the most venerable pieces of literature, the *Odyssey*. Under the mottled skin of the Toad can be discerned the features of Ulysses.

One of the most versatile characters in literature is Ulysses. Even his name is mutable. Homer knew him as Odysseus, but as heirs to the Romans we call him Ulysses. A master of disguise, he plays many roles, king, beggar, and husband. So versatile is he that he has even freed himself from his epic tradition. The sailors of children's fiction have him in the background. The name of Captain Nemo surely comes from the pseudonym, Nobody, which Ulysses gave to the Cyclops. In the *Just So Stories,* the whale was taught moderation by Kipling's sailor of "infinite-resource-and-sagacity." But Grahame was the first, it seems—ten years before Joyce's *Ulysses*—to take Ulysses out of a nautical context and to present him in an entirely different shape, that of a wealthy Toad.

Ulysses was never imagined as being at rest. In the *Odyssey,* we see him eagerly pressing his way home. Once there, however, he was prevented by later writers from remaining at ease with prosperity and a wife. Instead, Dante has him leave Ithaca to find the world's edge, summoning his aged comrades with these stirring words:

> fatti non foste a viver come bruti,
> ma per seguir virtute e canoscenza.
>
> [*Inferno*]

Tennyson's Ulysses also summons his comrades with an appeal to their valor:

> You and I are old;
> Old age hath yet his honor and his toil.
> Death closes all; but something ere the end,
> Some work of noble note, may yet be done,
> Not unbecoming men that strove with Gods.
>
> (Tennyson, "Ulysses")

Grahame's Toad is modeled on the Ulysses of Tennyson and Dante. The adult reader's attention is drawn to Toad's contrast with Homer's hero. In the *Odyssey*, we meet Ulysses sitting on the beach of Calypso's island, in the middle of nowhere, with tears in his eyes. In utter contrast, when we first meet Toad, he is sitting on a wicker lawn-chair, with a map on his knees and a discontented expression on his face. The man sits on an empty beach, the Toad in a civilized lawn. Toad has the world identified and delineated on a map, while Ulysses is surrounded by the trackless, nameless wastes of sky and sea. Like the Ulysses of Dante and Tennyson, Toad calls on his friends to join his wanders, to experience life to the full by travelling around the country in a canary colored cart:

> You surely don't mean to stick to your dull fusty old river all your life, and just live in a hole in the bank, and boat? I want to show you the world! I'm going to make an animal of you, my boy.

The ironies in Toad's determination to make animals out of a Water Rat and a Mole make the parody of Dante and Tennyson all the more delightful.

All children have the fantasy of driving their parents' car and Toad's fatal involvement with the motor-car involves him in wonderful adventures. For the adult reader, however, the "poop-poop" of the motor-car parodies the song of the sirens, which enchanted Ulysses. The Homeric hero took the precaution of plugging his crew's ears with wax, so that he could listen to the song without being harmed. Thus, while he, pierced by the beauty of the song, struggled to break free of the bonds, his sailors acted on his instructions and bound him more securely. Ulysses wanted to hear the song without crashing his boat. Toad, however, seems as enamored of the crash as he is of the ride. Consequently, just as the sirens' island was festooned with the bones of mariners, so Toad's carriage-house accumulates a mountain of motor-car fragments. After seven crashes, perhaps more, Toad's friends imitate Ulysses' crew by physically restraining him. Locked in his room, the ridiculous animal sulks, beguiling his solitude with dramatizations of his earlier car crashes:

> He would arrange bedroom chairs in rude resemblance of a motor-car and would crouch on the foremost of them, bent forward and staring fixedly ahead, making uncouth and ghastly noises, till the climax was reached, when, turning a complete somersault, he would lie prostrate amidst the ruins of the chairs, apparently completely satisfied for the moment.

Eventually, Toad manages to trick Ratty into leaving the house unattended. He pretends to be dying and while his friend goes for the doctor, he sneaks out of the window. Barely hours after he escapes, Toad manages to steal a motor-car, crash it, get arrested, and be sentenced to twenty years in prison. While he languishes in a dungeon, so deeply immured that the jailors speak medieval English, let us review the pattern of the story so far.

The disparity between Toad and Toad's conceited vision of himself is quite delightful. His friend the Water Rat knows him best:

> He is indeed the best of animals. . . . So simple, so good-natured, and so affectionate. Perhaps he is not very clever—we can't all be geniuses; and it may be that he is both boastful and conceited. But he has got some great qualities, has Toady.

Whatever these great qualities may be, they are not those of Ulysses, famed for his intelligence and endurance. We first hear of Toad from Otter, who says that he is unstable, always changing from one obsession to the next. Moreover, unlike Ulysses who defies danger, persists, and prevails, Toad is timid, as Ratty points out, and in adversity he gives way to despair.

But in his own mind, Toad is a hero. Boasting about his deception of Ratty, he reveals how absurd is his opinion about himself:

> Smart piece of work that! . . . Brain against brute force—and brain came out on top—as it's bound to do.

While the child is amused and delighted by the two Toads, the adult reader can savor the contrast of each with the figure of Ulysses. Toad fancies himself as a Ulysses, a creature of infinite resource and sagacity. When he boasts about his deception of the Water Rat we can see that he imagines himself another Ulysses, prevailing over brute force by his intelligence. The Trojans, the Cyclops, and the suitors could attest to Ulysses' automatic competence. Toad, however, prevails against his friends, not through intelligence but by a cheap trick. The story confirms Ratty's estimation: Toad is boastful and rather stupid. In contrast, the wily Ulysses learned modesty after he was persecuted by Poseidon for boastfully giving his name to the blinded Cyclops. The heroic figure of Ulysses looms over the absurd Toad. Just as the story makes playful allusion to Ulysses' adventures, and as Toad envisions himself another Ulysses, so the real character of Toad emerges as an anti-Ulysses.

Toad's incarceration reveals the same three levels of narrative. In the *Odyssey,* Ulysses was saved by a princess who happened to be washing clothes near where he was cast ashore. Naked as he was, he prevailed on her to give him clothes from the ones that she and her maids were washing. The product of a civilized society, Nausicaa gave him clothes because she was a pious, well-brought up, young lady. She also, Homer implies, fell in love with him, and the world-weary man was given the chance to start life anew with a young bride in a rich land.

Grahame splits the figure of Nausicaa into two separate characters: the maiden and the washer-woman. Nausicaa was the daughter of the island's king, who would send Odysseus home to Ithaca; the daughter of Toad's jailor helps him to escape from prison, when, like a true anti-hero, he has given up. Nausicaa gave Odysseus clothes because she was noble and just; the washer-woman is of an inferior class and is being bribed to defy justice. The jailor's daughter has romantic possibilities, since she resembles not only Nausicaa but also Phoebe in the *Yeoman of the Guard*. The story pattern implies that a romance will take place, and Toad actually fancies that she really is in love with him. Fleetingly (and hilariously), he regrets the gulf in their social class that would prevent their being married. In reality, however, the girl is not in love with Toad at all. Her original motive in meeting him was to get him to do tricks like sitting up or eating from her hand. Here, too, the pattern of the story and Toad's conceitedness make Toad into a Ulysses, while reality shows us an entirely different Toad.

In prison, through the help of the girl, Toad comes to terms with his feelings for home. Toad Hall stands in ironic contrast to Ulysses' palace on Ithaca. "Finest house on the river," Toad puffs, when he first meets the Mole. Then he blushes when he catches the amusement shared by the Rat and the Mole. But even when he boasts, he has no real appreciation of his house. Asked by the girl to describe Toad Hall, he answers her:

> "Toad Hall," said the Toad proudly, "is an eligible self-contained gentleman's residence, very unique; dating in part from the fourteenth century, but replete with every modern convenience. Up-to-date sanitation. Five minutes from church, post-office, and golf-links. Suitable for—."

Subtly, Grahame conveys that Toad has never come to terms with his own feelings about his house. He can talk about it in vague grandiosity—"finest place in the county," but pressed for detail, he can only repeat what sounds like an advertisement. Since he has never given his house a serious thought, he cannot say anything about it in his own words. This the little girl teaches him to do. As he tells her about his ancestral home, he becomes worthy of it.

No parody of the *Odyssey* would be complete without mention of the gods. In a world where Toad is hero, the humans are gods. Indeed, the motor-car which comes from the world of humans does resemble the fateful gifts of the gods which have such dire consequences for mortals: Pandora, the necklace of Harmonia, the arms of Achilles, and, more recently, the coke bottle in *The Gods Must Be Crazy*. Toad, of course, gets this backwards. As he dresses up for a drive, he sees himself as the "heaven-born driver," the deus ex machina.

Purveyors of so dangerous a gift, humans are promoted to the level of Olympian deities. At least it may seem like a promotion, but the Olympians had a personal meaning for Grahame, the grown-up world which he pillories in his book, *The Golden Age*. Unreasonable, unfair, and insensitive, Grahame's Olympians are entirely concerned with surface: clothing and profession. In *The Wind in the Willows,* the surfaces have hardened into uniforms. Most of the adults are officials of justice: bewigged judges, vizored prison guards, fat, red-faced policemen. These are the just gods of Homer translated onto a human plane. The Homeric gods rewarded Ulysses' piety and furthered his just cause; Grahame's human Olympians try to punish Toad for hubris. Thus, he is sentenced to four years for his crimes and fifteen years for his cheek to the rural police.

But the minions of the law are thwarted by the scheme of the little girl, who realizes, as children always realize, that grown-ups never look below the surface, that they see only the costume, not the person in the costume, the handwriting and not the words. How silly—a toad disguised as a washer-woman, but in this disguise Toad finds his way home by train, by barge, and by horse. Even the barge-woman who figures out that Toad is no laundress fails to penetrate his disguise, to see that he is not human. Like the Olympians in Grahame's *Golden Age,* the adult world may be superior to Toad, but it is blind all the same.

If the Toad repents, and this is doubtful, his change takes place without adult intervention. As soon as he sees the Water Rat, Toad bursts into an eager account of his deeds:

"Oh, Ratty!" he cried. "I've been through such times since I saw you last, you can't think! Such trials, such sufferings, and all so nobly borne! Then such escapes, such disguises, such subterfuges, and all so cleverly planned and carried out! Been in prison—got out of it, of course! Been thrown into a canal—swam ashore! Stole a horse—sold him for a large sum of money! Humbugged everybody—made 'em all do exactly what I wanted! Oh, I *am* a smart Toad, and no mistake! What do you think my last exploit was? Just hold on till I tell you—."

Ratty, who is a considerate person, settles him in comfortably and then hits him with a few home-truths.

> Now, Toady, I don't want to give you pain, after all you've been through already; but seriously, don't you see what an awful ass you've been making of yourself? On your own admission you have been handcuffed, imprisoned, starved, chased, terrified out of your life, insulted, jeered at, and ignominiously flung into the water—by a woman, too! Where's the amusement in that? Where does the fun come in? And all because you must needs go and steal a motor-car.

The last chapter, entitled "The Return of Ulysses," overtly evokes the scene where Odysseus takes possession of his ancestral home. The banquet, the secret of the house, even the punishment of the intruders (here cast as stoats and weasels) all bring the heroic paradigm to mind. Once again, far from filling Ulysses' shoes, Toad is barely tolerated by his comrades and gets in their way. The parody spares us the slaughter of the wicked intruders and treacherous maids. Their only punishment is to clean up the mess they have made and to reform.

Thus, we see that while the imaginations of Toad and the narrator can recreate Ulysses-in-Toad, his actions reveal he is an anti-Ulysses, lacking courage, resolve, resource, and intelligence. His only great qualities are his warm-heartedness and the affection he inspires in his friends. In fact, if you reread the book, you will find that my analysis has distorted its emphasis. The story is not with Toad, whose adventures streak through like a crazy comet, glorious and irrelevant, but rather with his friends and the day-to-day adventures by the River. With delightful irony, Grahame has fashioned them on the minor characters of the *Odyssey:* like the crew, they restrain Toad, and like his loyal servants, they help restore him to Toad Hall. But in fact they have the qualities that marked Ulysses in Homer. Ratty is like Ulysses, quick-witted and poetic. Badgers have Ulysses' endurance, as Mole is told in one of the great speeches of the book:

> Well, very long ago, on the spot where the Wild Wood waves now, before ever it had planted itself and grown up to what it now is, there was a city—a city of people, you know. Here, where we are standing, they lived, and walked, and talked, and slept, and carried on their business. Here they stabled their horses and feasted, from here they rode out to fight or drove out to trade. They were a powerful people, and rich, and great builders. They built to last, for they thought their city would last for ever. . . . People come—they stay for a while, they flourish, they build—and they go. It is their way. But we remain. There were badgers here, I've been told, long before that same city ever came to be. And now there are badgers here again. We are an enduring lot, and we may move out for a time, but we wait, and are patient, and back we come. And so it will ever be.

At the celebratory party, the Toad presents a decorous appearance, as he murmurs:

> Badger's was the mastermind; the Mole and the Water Rat bore the brunt of the fighting; I merely served in the ranks and did little or nothing.

This sounds like modesty, but is the simple truth. Gone is his earlier flamboyance: in our last view of Toad, he has his hair combed down on either side; he looks down his nose and murmurs polite nothings.

But alone in his room, the unregenerate Toad peeks at his reflection in the mirror. Whatever appearance he may hold up to the outside world, in the privacy of his own room, he is free, and his song of praise for his own exploits is a kind of mini-Odyssey.

> The Toad—came—home!
> There was panic in the parlour and howling in the hall,
> There was crying in the cow-shed and shrieking in the stall,
> When the Toad—came—home!

Thus, *The Wind in the Willows* offers the child an opportunity to explore the extremes, wanderlust and domesticity, doughty isolation and companionship, civilization and nature, responsibility and rebellion. But such a book sustains the child beyond childhood, and when it is our turn to read to children, when we see the literary jokes that mark the book as a classic, we perhaps convey to the child that sense of another world, as yet unattainable but one that can be attained through age, and through participating in great literature. This sense of ever-expanding horizons can only stimulate the child's imagination, and confer the healthy sense that the world is richer than can immediately be understood.

John David Moore   (essay date 1990)

SOURCE: "Pottering About in the Garden: Kenneth Grahame's Version of Pastoral in *The Wind in the Willows,*" in *The Journal of the Midwest Modern Language Association,* Vol. 23, No. 1, Spring, 1990, pp. 45-60.

[*In the following essay, Moore argues that the Arcadian world portrayed in* The Wind in the Willows *is actually an "uneasy Eden."*]

In his introduction to what has become accepted as Kenneth Grahame's classic of children's literature, A. A. Milne writes:

> One does not argue about *The Wind in the Willows*. The young man gives it to the girl with whom he is in love, and if she does not like it, asks her to return his letters. The older man tries it on his nephew, and alters his will accordingly. The book is a test of character. We can't criticize it, because it is criticizing us. As I wrote once: It is a Household Book; a book which everybody in the household loves, and quotes continually; a book which is read aloud to every new guest and is regarded as the touchstone of his worth.

Even if we allow for the hyperbole common in such encomiastic introductions, Milne's pronouncement suggests an attitude that should not be dismissed lightly. Milne at first, it seems, is trying to establish Grahame's book as an inviolable aesthetic artifact. We are reminded of Oscar Wilde's celebrated comment: "I find it harder and harder every day to live up to my blue china." Milne treats the book as a beautiful household implement, which is by no means inappropriate considering that Grahame's work has its roots in *fin-de-siècle* aestheticism. More is involved here, however, than the recognition of an artistic icon. Dumbness in the face of the aesthetic object betrays acknowledgement of values that must be taken on faith, felt but not expressed. Moreover, the dumb appreciation of Grahame's book grants admission to a "household" of the worthy. Roger Sale speaks of reading Grahame's book as "entering a charmed circle, of living in a timeless snugness." For Milne, being worthy of this book allows one to enter inner sanctums that suggest comfy domesticity—a marriage, a comfortable inheritance, a household.

The book itself abounds in scenes of domestic coziness, charmed circles in their own right wherein we meet a mole, a water rat, a badger, each dwelling in comfortable womb-like burrows that exude that particularly British domestic security for which Grahame's book is often most remembered. Domesticity is a central value among Grahame's animals. At the close of the book's only epic moment, the liberation of Toad Hall from a band of unsavory stoats and weasels, the chief concern is with clean linen and plates of cold tongue. Much of the book, like Milne's introduction, is concerned with inviting the right people in and keeping the wrong people (weasels, stoats, rabbits) out. Charmed domestic interiors also seem to have preoccupied Grahame's life. In a letter to a friend, Grahame records a recurrent dream of "a certain little room, very dear and familiar" where he has "always the same feeling of a home-coming, of the world shut out, of the ideal encasement," and where "all was my very own, and, what was more, everything in the room was exactly right."

In *The Wind in the Willows,* the circle of charmed enclosure, "ideal encasement," expands to include a landscape as memorable in its comforts as the homey and sometimes sentimental interiors. It is important that this is a book with a map, an enclosed space whose boundaries are significant. Within its borders we find an inner sanctum, a piece of countryside that for the most part is as domesticated as the homes of Rat, Mole, or Badger. This map, like Milne's introduction, defines inside and outside, insiders and outsiders. Rat verbally draws this map for us within the book's first chapter. Mole here asks Rat what lies in the distance:

> 'Where it's all blue and dim, and one sees what may be hills or perhaps they mayn't, and something like the smoke of towns, or is it only cloud-drift?'
>
> 'Beyond the Wild Wood comes the Wide World,' said the Rat. 'And that's something that doesn't matter, either to you or me. I've never been there, and I'm never going, nor you either, if you've got any sense at all. Don't ever refer to it again, please. Now then! Here's our backwater at last, where we're going to lunch'.

The eye is drawn back from expanding distance and the smoke of towns to the immediacy of slow backwaters and thoughts of lunch, domesticity enclosed in a wicker picnic basket. Rat's verbal mapping and the map itself, drawn for Grahame by E. H. Shepard, draw attention to what is excluded as well as what is included. To the north of Toad Hall, yet in no distinct direction (as if we should never need or want to find the way), are printed the words, "to the town." And all around the map's borders lies simply the Wide World, of which we should think nothing though its very presence defines the space for the charmed existence Grahame portrays.

As we gaze into this carefully mapped world, it becomes clear that the passports Milne sees the book granting or denying are passports for the land of pastoral. Within this map whose boundaries are supported by allusion to yet exclusion of the town, the smoke of cities, we find a soft landscape of cottages and cattle, sheep pens and weirs, rivers and canals, woods and fields, and finally the prominently situated palatial country house of Toad Hall. In pastoral the comforts of domesticated interiors are extended and included in a landscape.

The Wind in the Willows has long been recognized as a Georgian pastoral, and such terms as "Arcadian" and "idyllic" figure loosely into most discussions of the book. To consider Grahame's book as a pastoral is by no means to ignore its status as children's literature. It is rather to accept William Empson's extension of pastoral to include such productions of nineteenth-century child cult as *Alice in Wonderland,* in which the old pastoral opposition of country and court, of shepherd and courtier, is transformed into an opposition of child and adult. Indeed, children and childhood have been endemic to pastoral from the beginning; children's literature merely aligns itself with elements that had been there from the start. The fourth of Virgil's *Eclogues* announces the arrival of an Arcadian age, its commencement marked by the birth of a child. Arcadia or the Golden Age is the mytho-historical childhood of the race. Projected into the future it becomes Utopia, or the New Jerusalem, the kingdom for which we must become as little children to enter. Following the invention of children's literature, the Golden Age becomes a personal childhood as well. *The Golden Age* is also one of Grahame's early books in which he looks "Back to those days of old, ere the gate shut to behind me," and reflects upon adult stupidity "and its tremendous influence in the world." In Grahame's fictional treatment of his own childhood, the adults are "Olympians." Like Hesiod's Golden Age, which is ended through the whim of the Olympian Zeus, the Golden Age of Grahame's childhood seems to crumble under the ignorant hands of adults.

Yet these Golden Ages, these Arcadias and their mytho-historical destruction or projected reinstitution, are all finally adult concerns. In the earlier conventions of pastoral it is often the sophisticated courtier who writes of the virtues of the country and mimics the naive, childlike shepherds at masque or ball. In children's literature it is the adult who gives us the children's Arcadia, writing a way into the garden of childhood, mapping its borders in adulthood's "light of common day." The irony of the matter is commonplace—childhood, like Arcadia, must be left to be truly appreciated. The child, the shepherd, the peasant, all finally live in ignorance of their Arcadian bliss. They are total insiders, and it is only the outsider who can see, often with a disturbing, covert superiority and resentment, the perfection such a state affords. The country becomes pastoral only when entered from the city, and childhood becomes Arcadian only when recaptured in adulthood.

Though *The Wind in the Willows* is thought of as a children's book, there are, strictly speaking, no children in it. In *The Golden Age* and *Dream Days* Grahame reenters his rural childhood home of Cookham Dene as a child, though a child with a very adult voice. In *The Wind in the Willows* a pastoral childhood world is again recreated, but this time it is entered through animals who are an attempted syntheses of adults and children. Like adults, they look after themselves; like children, they don't hold jobs, and they take the world's comforts for granted. More accurately, Grahame's animals are old boys enjoying the childhood Eden that is ideally available only in geriatric retirement. The recent euphemism, "Golden Agers," certainly applies here most evocatively.

Grahame's animals are adults freed from the restraints of adulthood, free to engage in childlike pottering. The Water Rat potters with nature poetry and "messes about in boats." Mole shirks the responsibility of spring cleaning, pops out of his hole in joyous and rebellious rebirth, and joins Rat for a life of gentlemanly repose on the river. At home, "Mole End," we see that Mole potters about with beer and skittles, and collects cheap plaster statuary—"Garibaldi and the infant Samuel, and Queen Victoria, and other heros of modern Italy". The reclusive Badger potters about digging and fitting out additions to his den, expanding the regions of domesticity beneath the Wild Wood. Finally, Toad potters about with boats and gypsy carts, though his pottering turns to maniacal frenzy when he discovers that threat to all England's rural bliss, the motor car. For Rat, Mole, and Badger this is a life of changeless natural rhythms and invisible incomes. It is the world of unsupervised childhood enhanced by the supposedly adult awareness that childhood is the best of times.

We are aware here of an ambivalence towards child and adult. The invention of animal old boys attempts an eradication of distance between adult and child, but finally plunges us into an ambivalence that is endemic to pastoral itself. Questions arise. Which is better—to be an ignorant innocent in Eden or a wise and retrospective adult sneaking back into the garden in a bid for second childhood? Is it better to be an inarticulate rustic, or a sophisticated courtier or landed gentleman who can see the dryad in the shepherdess and neo-classical landscapes amid rural squalor?

As Raymond Williams has pointed out, the values of pastoral are most often ambivalent, contradictory, ironic, and certainly distorting in more than strictly literary ways. The oppositions between city and country, courtier and clown, are never as neatly drawn as the pastoral voices throughout the tradition would have us believe. In Williams's treatment of pastoral we become aware of the importance of positioning, of viewpoint, attitude, and most crucially, class. Pastoral is undeniably ideological, and thus impels us to locate the power controlling the instrument of pastoral vision.

Insofar as children's literature often shares central elements with pastoral tradition, the attention both Williams and Empson bring to the ideological ironies, ambiguities and distortions of pastoral reveals ways in which children's literature too can be examined for its ideological underpinnings and in the process be aligned more strongly with a cultural tradition whose literature is not so dependent on a specialized sense of audience for its definition. To look at children's literature as Williams and Empson look at pastoral is to see much of the literature that surrounds childhood, especially that which assigns childhood ideal value, as expressions of ideological power. Childhood, like idealized rural life, becomes shaped from outside, enclosed within an ideal space in an ironic parallel to the enclosure of rural lands that so changed the look of rustic England in the eighteenth and nineteenth centuries.

This sense of enclosure in both children's literature and pastoral in general involves an exclusionism that on the level of social class is especially pronounced in the production of pastoral. William Empson defines pastoral as literature about but not by or for the people, and questions how often it is even about them. To the extent that pasto-ral is utopian (one thinks of William Morris's *News from Nowhere*) it can suggest a proletarian power. But in general pastoral rarely frees itself from a conservative position. It not only can evoke possibilities, but also can legitimatize an existing order, or what appears to be one. It can also attempt both, as Grahame's book appears to do both in terms of generating a childlike vision and in mapping an ideal rural space that may look like a timeless Arcadian past but involves values that suggest a status quo.

I observed earlier that Milne's introduction attempts to mystify the book, to remove it from any possibility of critical discussion and leave us only with an inarticulate aesthetic response. This is often a position taken when deeply felt values are at stake. And indeed Milne's caveat to the reader links aesthetic response to values, to social judgments. The appropriate aesthetic reaction will admit one to a special order of things, a community described as a household. The aesthetic response is no longer purely aesthetic, but also social and possibly political in its implications.

Pastoral and its commentators often attempt the separation of the political and the aesthetic, the Utopian and the Arcadian. W. H. Auden's "Vespers" provides a useful example of the problems involved in such distinctions. Here the Arcadian and the Utopian are presented as antitypes—Auden, with some self-irony, taking the position of the Arcadian. The two meet and:

> Neither speaks. What experience could we possibly share?
>
> Glancing at a lampshade in a store window, I observe it is too hideous for anyone in their senses to buy: He observes it is too expensive for a peasant to buy.
>
> Passing a slum child with rickets, I look the other way: He looks the other way if he passes a chubby one.

Auden's Arcadian assumes it is clear that "between my Eden and his New Jerusalem, no treaty is negotiable." Each, it seems, necessarily excludes the other. Yet both share the principle of exclusion:

> In my Eden a person who dislikes Bellini has the good manners not to get born: In his New Jerusalem a person who dislikes work will be very sorry he was born.

And once we enter either paradise, we find that distinctions are not all that clear. We only have to look at William Morris's craftman's Utopia in *News from Nowhere* to see that art, though perhaps not that of Bellini, fits in quite comfortably and even necessarily. And we need not look far into the seemingly most unpolitical literature of Arcadia to find what might be called an aesthetic worship of noble rural labor. Nor does Arcadian labor exclude the machine. It is no surprise to find that "even the chefs will be cucumber-cool machine minders" in the New Jerusalem of Auden's Utopian. But the machine, insofar as it is a nostalgic, aesthetic artifact, also has a place in the garden of Auden's Arcadian:

> In my Eden we have a few beam-engines, saddle-

tank locomotives, overshot waterwheels and other beautiful pieces of obsolete machinery to play with

Auden, as Arcadian, finally begins to suspect that political and aesthetic versions of pastoral are caught up in one another. Crucial questions arise, suggesting on the one hand shared illusions and on the other a sort of necessary symbiosis:

Was it (as it must look to any god of cross-roads) simply a fortuitous intersection of life-paths, loyal to different fibs?

Or also a rendezvous between two accomplices who, in spite of themselves, cannot resist meeting

to remind the other (do both, at bottom, desire truth?) of that half of their secret which he would most like to forget,

forcing us both, for a fraction of a second, to remember our victim (but for him I could forget the blood, but for me he could forget the innocence)

Auden still prefers the Arcadian vision, since no blood, it seems, is shed to purchase it. Yet both visions have their victims, and because of this the poem finally attempts a position distanced from the business of ideals altogether.

The symbiotic relationship between the aesthetic and the political that Auden's poem begins to suggest and accept is also implied in Milne's introductory remarks. Like our attitudes towards Bellini or work, our responses to Grahame's book will determine whether or not we are the right sort to share in the secret harmonies of an idyllic order. The principles of inclusion and exclusion at work in Grahame's pastoral fantasy aim at establishing the idyllic harmony. Yet the ambivalent relation of pastoral to both aesthetic and political positions creates an inevitable dissonance. We should be prepared to find problems, contradictions beneath the placidity of Grahame's rural world.

The ostensible harmony of this world is that of landscape, the natural environment that to some degree in all pastoral defines the life of the Arcadian inhabitants. Pastoral is about fitting into a landscape, about what can and cannot be included in what is always felt to be a balanced natural order.

What we notice most in Grahame's landscape is a river, a river to which the action and also, as we shall see, the inaction of the book returns again and again. It is where Ratty, the poet of the river, makes his home. It is on an island in this river where we meet a rather domesticated variety of the Great God Pan, the guardian deity of this Arcadia, and the inspiration of much of the armchair sensualism of Grahame's Georgian contemporaries. It is to the river that the errant Mr. Toad unexpectedly returns with a plunge at the close of his anti-pastoral adventures with motor cars and prison cells. The river defines the life of this pastoral community. When Rat answers Mole's query, "And you really live by the river?," it is clear that he lives by it as by a principle:

'By it and with it and on it and in it,' said the Rat. 'It's brother and sister to me, and aunts and company, and food and drink, and (naturally) washing. It's my world, and I don't want any other. What it hasn't got is not worth having, and what it doesn't know is not worth knowing.'

The principle of the river becomes clearest in the Rat's description of that particular form of pottering called "messing about in boats":

'—about in boats—or *with* boats,' the Rat went on composedly, picking himself up with a pleasant laugh. 'In or out of 'em, it doesn't matter. Nothing seems really to matter, that's the charm of it. Whether you get away, or whether you don't; whether you arrive at your destination or whether you reach somewhere else, or whether you never get anywhere at all, you're always busy, and you never do anything in particular; and when you've done it there's always something else to do, and you can do it if you like, but you'd much better not.'

To live by the river is to live the comfortable paradox of Pastoral—to be active yet inactive, changing yet changeless, aimless yet purposeful. It is the innocent irresponsibility associated with childhood recaptured. The river defines the central rhythm of pastoral life—the natural rhythm of the seasons, change contained by repetition.

The river defines a life of pottering, the dawdling existence that fits the characters into the landscape. And of course it also helps to be an animal. To the idealizing mind the animal appears to be always at one with its surroundings. It is always in its proper place and realizes the perfection of its being at every moment. In a comment remembered by his wife, Grahame observes that:

Every animal, by instinct, lives according to his nature. . . . No animal is ever tempted to belie his nature. No animal in other words, knows how to tell a lie. Every animal is honest. Every animal is straightforward. Every animal is true—and is, therefore, according to his nature, both beautiful and good.

Like the river, Grahame's animals, unlike men or even idealized children, supply an image of being that is variable but at root changeless.

Mr. Badger discourses upon the animal and the human while giving the Mole a tour through his extensive underground dwelling. We here discover that beneath the Wild Wood lie the ruins (possibly Roman) of a city, parts of which Badger has incorporated into his own residence. In his brief discourse upon these ruins, Badger speaks as part of the changeless rural landscape, as an animal. He tells us that the human builders of this city were a glorious race:

'They were a powerful people, and rich, and great builders. They built to last, for they thought their city would last for ever.'

'But what has become of them all?' asked the Mole.

'Who can tell?' said the Badger. 'People come—

they stay for a while, they flourish, they build—
and they go. It is their way. But we remain.
There were badgers here, I've been told, long before that same city ever came to be. And now
there are badgers here again. We are an enduring
lot, and we may move out for a time, but we
wait, and are patient, and back we come, and so
it will ever be.'

We are here viewing a sort of subterranean version of a
picturesque landscape by Piranesi, whose message in part
is typical—*sic transit gloria mundi*. But the focus is less on
the ruins than on the enduring figures of Mole and Badger.
To a degree they appear here as genteel tourists. But because Badger is also speaking as an animal, he and Mole
resemble the rustics in typical picturesque landscape who
continue about their business with little regard to the images of transcience that surround them. The image of the
rustic merged with the countryside is only slightly removed from the image of the animal adapted to its environment. The price paid for seeing the rustic as a part of
his landscape is dehumanization. The rustic becomes an
unconscious creature dead to the harmony in which he
lives with his surroundings. We must remember that the
phrase "Et in Arcadia ego" was an epitaph. The most
complete harmony with a landscape is attained only in
death.

Grahame tries to avoid this problematic dehumanization
by beginning with the animal and dressing him up—not
as the rustic but as the gentleman. Superficially, Grahame's animals appear as "Ourselves in Fur," suggesting
the instructive animals of beast fable. Yet with the possible
exception of Mr. Toad, who has no fur at all, these animals
are not didactic in any obvious sense. Nor are Grahame's
animals accurately general humanity in fur. Over the fur
Grahame's characters are decked out with a significant
wardrobe of plus fours, tweed jackets, white flannels, and
lounging slippers, sartorially denoting a social class and
its sensibility.

The tastes and values of Rat, Mole and Badger suggest
middle-class status, though it is difficult to determine the
exact position of these animals within the bourgeoisie.
Mole's taste for beer and skittles and plaster statuary, the
preponderance of sardines and sausages in his larder, and
his conversations with Rat about the bargains and expenses involved in furnishing his home all suggest the
"shabby genteel." On the other hand the sense of comforts
taken for granted and the reticence about sources of income suggest a higher class standing, though certainly not
as high as that of the landed Mr. Toad.

It is perhaps easier to be accurate when considering the
values, the sensibilities expressed by Grahame's characters. Grahame's ideal bourgeois animal is the urban bachelor, the man of leisure, the old boy, the tourist in the country who has decided to stay, bringing the misogynous values of the men's club into the rural cottage. This is indeed
a society of retired boyish chums where there are no girls
allowed. There are women in Grahame's book. The Otter,
we presume, has a wife—at least he has a child. Toad
meets a vulgar barge-woman and a manipulative jailer's
daughter, but they inhabit a world outside the cozy pastoral borders, the world of Toad's anti-pastoral adventures.

Within Grahame's idyllic community, the "chequered
shade" of pastoral landscape acts as a purdah, keeping
women out of view. Nor was Grahame unaware of this exclusion. He once observed with a note of satisfaction that
he had used his animal characters "to get away . . . from
weary sex problems" and that his book was "clean of the
clash of sex." [Peter Green, *Kenneth Grahame*]

The urbanity of Grahame's gentlemen animals dictates
that some topics, women among them, should not be mentioned. With these zoomorphic gentlemen, urbanity is a
matter of instinct. Manners, customs portrayed as animal
nature—"animal-etiquette" as Grahame calls it—bring
the drawing room (or more accurately the gentleman's
den) to the country, where the ideal natural man can be
enclosed in domestic comfort. Instinctual etiquette is a
matter of polite exclusion. Both animal and human necessities are either mentioned with polite periphrasis or not
mentioned at all. Badger's necessary hibernation is referred to as being "busy." The animal reality of predaci-
ty—Otter's diving in mid conversation after a fish, the
danger posed to moles and rats by weasels and stoats—is
also excluded from polite discussion. Except where the
rich Mr. Toad is concerned, the human matter of money
is usually ignored with typical gentlemanly discretion.

Instinct is the ideal, natural version of social values in this
Arcadia. It is the principle of inclusion and exclusion that
maps the borders of Grahame's domesticated countryside
and defines the value of being at home, of fitting into the
landscape. In the chapter, "Dulce Domum," Mole is
drawn home, back to his tunnels, to his plaster sculpture
and beer and skittles, as any animal would be drawn to its
den or lair—by smell, an animal instinct that here, however, only thinly disguises a human sense of nostalgia.

Instinct keeps Grahame's characters in touch with the
pastoral order, drawing them home when they drift away
from their assigned places and activities. Some hibernate,
some migrate, some wander freely beyond the pastoral
borders because it is their nature—like the Sea Rat, whose
stories of exotic travel nearly lure the River Rat away
from his home in the river bank. Home, the sense of one's
proper place in a seemingly natural arrangement, consistently asserts its power. Rat, with the help of the domestic
blandishments of the Mole, quells his wanderlust and reconciles himself to sedate homelife and pottering with poetry. The anti-pastoral adventures of Toad end with a return
to Toad Hall's grandiose domesticity. Each of Grahame's
animals gravitates to his proper place.

The fantasy of the animal in its environment is finally a
fantasy of class stability envisioned as natural order. One's
home is one's social position. This is most evident when
we consider Toad Hall, the typical country house whose
palatial form dominates the map of Grahame's countryside just as it dominates the landscapes of much British
pastoral vision.

It is from the windows of the great country houses that
much that has passed for pastoral landscape has been arranged. Raymond Williams has noted the centrality of the
great rural seat in the creation of an ideological vision of
"natural" order, an order of social values that disguises

the real presence of work, exploitation, and consumption. The view from the country house, as Williams observes, presents "a rural landscape emptied of rural labour and of labourers." This view can be recognized in such seventeenth-century place poems as Jonson's "To Penshurst" and Carew's "To Saxham," and in such eighteenth-century improved landscapes as those at Stourhead or Chatsworth. In "To Penshurst" fruit and game, the produce of the countryside, offer themselves willingly to the table, and the rustic appears only as a thankful consumer of lordly charity. In the designed landscapes of Repton and Capability Brown, we see an ordered Arcadia where everything that can be aesthetically (and ideologically) included fits in its proper place. In accordance with the paintings of Claude Lorrain, even the cattle have assigned places, kept at an aesthetic distance through the ingenious invention of the ha-ha, a fence kept tactfully from view at the bottom of a ditch. In such engineered Arcadias the more genuine and often disturbing elements of rural life—in one case an entire village—have been removed from a scene that now becomes scenery.

The countryside surrounding Toad Hall is not exactly a Repton design, but it does suggest aesthetic arrangement—a small village out of view from the Hall, tree lines, lawns. Even beyond the grounds, where Mole, Badger, and Rat dwell, the landscape is shaped into the picturesque interplay of woods and fields. The labor which shapes this agricultural landscape at the idyllic core of *The Wind in the Willows* is visible only when it is picturesque. The most we really see of rural labor is an idyllic glimpse of Grahame's animal peasants gathering in their winter stores. The scenery for Grahame's chronicle of leisure—tilled fields, hedge rows, a canal with barges, a new iron bridge—is shaped by invisible labor. Visible labor is removed to the cities and towns where we meet some of it during Toad's adventures. In Grahame's idyllic countryside we see mainly the products of labor. The pastoral halls of Penshurst, the tables at Toad Hall and even the larders of the middle-class bungalows of Rat, Badger, and Mole are supplied with food as if by magic.

Viewed from the position of Toad's country house, Grahame's landscape is a social design, a map of class hierarchy where every animal has its place. The Toad, with his ancestral wealth is at the top and center, though he mingles freely with the bourgeois gentlemen of wood, field, and river. Below these characters are the rabbits, hedgehogs, stoats, and weasels. The hedgehogs, the young ones any rate, are respectful and subservient to the point of demeaning docility. Rabbits, though Rat calls them "a mixed lot," are generally mindless and treated with contempt. They suggest a deprecating image of the rustic laboring class as dense, apathetic, healthy, and of course prolific. When Otter solicits a rabbit for information about the Mole, who has become lost in the low rent districts of the Wild Wood, he has "to cuff his head once or twice to get any sense out of it at all." Otter then proceeds to ask why the rabbits did nothing to aid the Mole, who was being pursued by stoats and weasels:

> 'You mayn't be blest with brains, but there are hundreds and hundreds of you, big stout fellows, as fat as butter, and your burrows running in all directions, and you could have taken him in and made him safe and comfortable, or tried to, at all events.' "What us?" he merely said: "Do something? us rabbits?" So I cuffed him again and left him. There was nothing else to be done.'

Rabbits present a demeaning image of the lower orders as fat, stupid, and apathetic, but weasels and stoats present the lower classes as dangerously vicious and predatory. The Rat, however, tries to be fair to them:

> 'They're all right in a way . . . I'm good friends with them—pass the time of day when we meet, and all that—but they break out sometimes, there's no denying it, and then—well you can't really trust them, and that's the fact.'

We have heard this sort of thing all too often, these hesitant, qualifying, speciously reasonable and polite deprecations of classes and races. Grahame's Arcadia is here beginning to look more like a country club and his pastoral river bank more like the suburbs. "The bank is so crowded nowadays," complains the Rat, "that many people are moving away altogether. O no, it isn't what it used to be, at all". Behind the apparently idyllic stability of this pastoral setting lies a sense of threatening flux—not the predictable, comfortable flux of river and season contained by stable natural process, but the disturbing movements of social instability. Rat's complaints voice the anxiety of suburbians escaping the crowding of the cities only to find they have brought the congestion with them. The creation of pastoral community becomes a matter of zoning. One must constantly worry about the wrong elements moving in next door.

This element of threatened stability, however, is what makes *The Wind in the Willows* a story and not a mere still life in words. Moreover, the static coziness of the book is made all the more cozy when we are conscious of what it excludes. Badger's house is all the more comfortable because we know that outside weasels and stoats roam through the snow. The core of the book remains a static idyll, but what there is of cohesive plot involves a threat to the idyllic order.

Much of the book seems to reject adventure as a threat to stability. The Rat's wanderlust induced by the Sea Rat's tales is finally treated as an aberration, a sickness to be cured by long hours of convalescence in domestic peace. Yet adventure is no stranger to pastoral. In Longus's *Daphnis and Chloe* the static bliss of the unspoiled hero and heroine is interrupted and tested by adventurous intrusions from the outer world, the disturbing influences of pirates and thoughtlessly worldly gallants. The stability of the pastoral order is strengthened by confrontation with what opposes it. We feel less like we are constructing Utopia and more like we are returning to a status quo.

The threat to Grahame's pastoral order is class instability, people not knowing their places. Most evidently the threat comes from below—weasels and stoats who "break out" and take over Toad Hall, enacting the nightmare of any Tory remembering Bloody Sunday in 1887 or the Pall Mall riots of 1886. Yet from the standpoint of Grahame's animal bourgeoisie, it is not this simple. It is Toad and his adventures that are at root responsible for opening the respectable banquet rooms of Toad Hall to the vulgar feasting of the rabble. Toad's irresponsibility betrays weakness that is open to attack. He presents a flabby and decadent appearance to the lower orders. Toad, the landed rentier, will not keep his proper place but instead roams the countryside in motor cars, an image of senseless, destructive change, bringing the speed and stench of the city into the countryside. Toad loses the sense of home that is so important to the stability of the other animals. Moreover, Toad violates the traditional and idealized role of the landed aristocrat. In one of his many short-lived moments of repentance, Toad defines what he should be—a stable, respectable figure at the center of an aesthetically designed landscape of the good old days, merrie England:

> 'I've had enough of adventures. I shall lead a quiet, steady, respectable life, pottering about my property, and improving it, and doing a little landscape gardening at times. There will always be a bit of dinner for my friends when they come to see me; and I shall keep a pony-chaise to jog about the country in, just as I used to in the good old days, before I got restless, and wanted to do things.'

It is not so much just doing things that is Toad's problem. Toad too "messes about in boats" for a time. And his aimless journey in a gypsy cart with Rat and Mole fits well with the pastoral ethic of pottering, the winding road being at first only another version of the river. Toad violates the code of pottering, however, when he turns to the motor car and becomes obsessed. The car becomes an *idée fixe*, and pottering turns into disruptive passion.

Toad's violation of pastoral principles provides us with the other half of *The Wind in the Willows*. Though interspersed with sections of Grahame's idyllic still life, Toad's adventures seem to form a distinctly independent story—comic, picaresque, satirical. It is a story of the things that must be excluded in the mapping of Grahame's Arcadia—machines, cities, bureaucracies, women. Toad's spendthrift, riotous obsession takes him into a world of motor cars and railroads, prisons and courtrooms, and finally, officious nurses, patronizing jailer's daughters, and "common, low, *fat*" barge women.

Though this world is clearly opposed to the nostalgic and misogynous "old boy" values of pottering in the countryside, once Grahame plunges into its comic roguery there is no overt opposition to it. The conventions of a comic braggadocio's adventures are comfortably accepted. We are in another order of things and the rules are different. Toad on the road is a sort of comic, nursery version of the debauched squire, squire Thornhill made humorous and, for the most part, harmless.

Taken by themselves, Toad's adventures seem to harmlessly exercise an anarchical energy. It is how the book gets adventure out of its system. Grahame allows us to enjoy this energy while it lasts, but finally we see its dangers. These adventures are like the trickster tales of the Till Eulenspiegel variety in which we revel in the feats of the prankster but also accept the sober necessity of his ending up on the gallows. For Toad, however, there remains a place within the pastoral community. And Gra-

hame never lets us forget the governing idyllic context in which Toad's adventures occur. The Toad chapters are interspersed with chapters of pastoral stasis reminding us of the world Toad has left behind in his obsessive rambles. Moreover, Toad's adventures are framed by incidents in which Toad is joined by his stable bourgeois chums.

At the end of Toad's escapades, in the chapter, "The Return of Ulysses," Mole, Rat, and Badger help to retake Toad Hall in a sort of mock heroic assault in which Toad is cast as a not so wily but much self-inflated Ulysses. The mock heroic element is, however, largely superficial, for at root the final chapters involve the serious business of restoring order to the Arcadian community. The rabble must be put in its place. Weasels and stoats, once subdued, are put to work tidying up around Toad Hall, restoring the virtues of ordered domesticity. And they learn to doff their hats and say "Sir" like the hedgehog children. Toad too must be put in his place; he must live up to the middle-class notion of an aristocrat. We note that it is Toad's class inferiors who bring him into line. Ironically, it is the continually rising middle-classes who seek to preserve at least the facade of an old aristocratic order. Toad's wealth is never condemned; nor is his ostentation, for it is manifested in larges. His braggadocio is an eccentricity to be tolerated and his faddishness is in some ways only a more expensive sort of pottering. All this makes up the charm of the landed aristocrat, the old boy par excellence. What is threatening to the arrangement of Grahame's map of Arcadia are Toad's instability and obsessive passions.

The rule in this Arcadia is that nothing is ever of all consuming importance. This is why Rat's wanderlust is finally rejected; like Toad's motor cars, it blocks out everything else. The world of *The Wind in the Willows* is a world of moderation, of middle grounds. The social center of the charmed pastoral circle is the middle-class, and toads, like weasels and stoats must be placed securely in relation to this gravitational center. The dominant action in Grahame's book involves putting things into alignment, balance. Arcadia becomes a juncture of city and country, a suburbia where the class values of the city obtain in the form of an instinctual urbanity. Ironically, this urbanity involves exclusion not so much in fact as in polite form. The distant smoke of towns, the fear of the predatory lower orders are not expunged; it is just bad manners for cultivated bourgeois animals to mention them.

The comfortable arrangement of Grahame's pastoral world, as with all pastoral designs perhaps, hides ironies and contradictions amid its cozy green hills and vales. A number of these are embodied in the demi-god, Pan, who is the genius of Grahame's Arcadia. Grahame's therianthropic god suits an Arcadia whose citizens portray the cultivated natural man as an animal in tasteful leisure dress. Pan, though half beast, is hardly half gentleman. Yet it is Pan that we meet in one of Grahame's idyllic chapters where the simpler prose of rural description gives way to the purple prose of aesthetic parlor paganism. Grahame's suggestive, pseudo-mystical prose tries to convince us that we are here up against something truly awesome and sublime. Yet we cannot escape the irony. What is Pan doing at the center of a book proudly "free from the clash of sex?" What is a god, whose name gives us the word "panic," doing in an Arcadia founded on moderation? This Pan, mentioned only as *"Him"* by Rat and Mole, is meant to be awe inspiring—Rat registers the appropriate response by saying he is not afraid, yet afraid. Yet Pan's immediate function in the plot of this chapter is somewhat sentimental. Pan, called "the Friend and Helper," finds the lost Otter child. This Pan seems to merge with a cheap Victorian print of the Good Shepherd. He seems really to belong with Mole's collection of plaster garden statuary. This is a Pan made safe for a middle-class Arcadia, where instinct is equivalent to decorum and custom. As the genius of Grahame's suburban, sexless garden, Pan appears as a castrated Priapus. He is the god of nature certainly, but not nature red in tooth and claw. He is the Pan of *fin-de-siècle* aesthetic paganism, though much tamer than anything in Beardsley or even Swinburne. As an aesthetic version of the goat god, this Pan finally does fit into the middle-class menagerie of well-dressed animals; the ideal Arcadian aesthete is not merely half man, half animal, but half animal, half aging dandy.

The final purpose of Pan in Grahame's garden is apparently to offer a principle of forgetfulness, primarily the forgetting of intense, sublime experience. Pan bestows forgetfulness "Lest the awful rememberance should remain and grow, and overshadow mirth and pleasure, and the great haunting memory should spoil all the after-lives of little animals helped out of difficulties, in order that they should be happy and light-hearted as before." Here again Grahame includes something in the act of rejecting it. Such intense experience is the problem. It is Toad's problem—trying to live the passionate, intense moment again and again. Grahame's Arcadia tries to cultivate a quiet celebration of equivalent moments, a domestic aestheticism of the everyday, a living up to mundane things. It is the aesthetic ethics of Wilde's blue china again. Grahame tries through his characters to approximate the ideally perceived ability of the animal to live completely in each moment, in an eternal status quo free from the disturbing memories that make history. As badger tries to demonstrate, men and their cities have history, animals and their environments do not. In *The Wind in the Willows* what memory there is becomes disguised often thinly, as instinct—remembering one's place, remembering the natural cycle in its changelessness. But this cycle is finally only a version of history appropriate to the charmed circularity of a conservative Arcadian status quo.

And it is not finally forgetfulness itself that is so important, but forgetting the right things—ignoring the slum child with rickets if you are an Arcadian, ignoring the chubby child if you are an Utopian. The problem of pastoral is the problem of what to ignore. The construction of Grahame's Arcadia depends on ignoring sex, women, machines, labor, the friction of class. The intrusion of the city into the country must be ignored above all for herein lies the greatest irony. As Raymond Williams has pointed out, the creation of much pastoral vision depends on that intrusion. In *The Wind in the Willows,* we cannot for very long escape Grahame's identity as a city man, the secretary of the Bank of England, a man who was part of the urban institutions that have made Toad Halls possible,

now make comfortable suburban life and gentlemanly rural escape possible, and finally make possible the homogeneity of country and city. Grahame's animals, like himself, are finally not natives to a rural order, nor is this rural order really native to the countryside. At the top of the rural order we find Mr. Toad, but we doubt that he is any more a native than his urbane middle-class neighbors. We suspect, as with most proprietors of great country estates, that Toad's position originates in the financial power of the city. If there are any true natives in Grahame's countryside, they are the rabbits, weasels, and stoats, and we have seen what sort of treatment they come in for.

If we do not look beyond the pastoral conventions of Grahame's world, we see a community of insiders, each in his cozy, appropriate place. But conventions have ideological roots, and when we glimpse the larger context of Grahame's countryside, what lies hidden in and around its borders and beneath the surface of its woods and fields, we see that Grahame's country gentlemen are outsiders, builders of a suburban Eden that may eventually reproduce that city whose ruins lie beneath Grahame's Wild Wood. It is an uneasy Eden. As we enter it through Milne's introduction, we see there is a problem with letting the wrong sort in. The supposedly timeless order of this suburban garden is threatened by what is brought from outside—more and more river bankers—and what is already there—stoats and weasels who don't know their place.

Pottering about is offered as a solution, an escape. One can be a childlike old boy animal lost in a series of equally valuable moments—writing mediocre verse, messing about in boats, strolling the country lanes. But such moments exclude more and more of their context. Finally the borders of Grahame's map enclose less and less. The circle shrinks until we are back inside the book's central domestic space, "ideal encasement" in the subterranean homes of Mole, Rat, and especially the reclusive Badger. The Arcadian principle becomes agoraphobia and the Arcadian landscape becomes a series of cozy rooms, rooms ironically intertwined with the ruins of a city.

FURTHER READING

Biography

Chalmers, Patrick R. *Kenneth Grahame: Life, Letters and Unpublished Work.* London: Methuen & Co., 1933, 321 p.
　　The first biography of Grahame, relying unduly upon the saccharine and sometimes unreliable reminiscences of Grahame's widow, Elspeth.

Graham, Eleanor. *Kenneth Grahame.* London: Bodley Head, 1963, 72 p.
　　A brief biographical and critical study from a noted children's writer.

Green, Peter. *Beyond the Wild Wood: The World of Kenneth Grahame, Author of* The Wind in the Willows. New York: Facts on File, 1983, 224 p.

An abridgement, in larger format and with new illustrations, of Green's full-scale 1959 biography.

Green, Peter. *Kenneth Grahame, 1859-1932: A Study of His Life, Work and Times*. London: John Murray, 1959, 400 p.

Argues that Grahame was far more complex than critics and readers had realized, and identifies a number of late nineteenth-century issues and concerns in his work. Green finds Grahame a more troubled figure than does Chalmers.

Prince, Alison. *Kenneth Grahame: An Innocent in the Wild Wood*. London: Allison & Busby, 1994, 384 p.

The most substantial biography to date. Prince identifies Elspeth Grahame's embroideries and exaggerations in both Chalmers and Green.

Criticism

Gilead, Sarah. "Grahame's *The Wind in the Willows*." *Explicator* 46, No. 1 (Fall 1987): 33-6.

Discusses the significance of the River in Grahame's novel.

Gillin, Richard. "Romantic Echoes in the Willows." *Children's Literature* 16 (1988): 169-74.

Illustrates Grahame's use of themes from Keats, Coleridge, and Wordsworth.

Hunt, Peter. "Dialogue and Dialectic: Language and Class in *The Wind in the Willows*." *Children's Literature* 16 (1988): 159-68.

Investigates Grahame's avoidance of "class dialect" in situations that otherwise suggest class differences.

Kuznets, Lois R. *Kenneth Grahame*. Boston: Twayne, 1987, 156 p.

A critical and biographical study from an authority on Grahame and children's literature in general. Includes an annotated bibliography of selected secondary sources.

———. "Kenneth Grahame." *Writers for Children: Critical Studies of Major Authors Since the Seventeenth Century*, edited by Jane M. Bingham, pp. 247-54. New York: Charles Scribner's Sons, 1988.

A brief critical survey of Grahame's work.

———. "Kenneth Grahame and Father Nature, or Whither Blows *The Wind in the Willows*?" *Children's Literature* 16 (1988): 175-81.

Examines the "idyllic male-only animal world" of Grahame's novel.

Milne, A. A. Introduction to *The Wind in the Willows*, by Kenneth Grahame, pp. vii-x. New York: The Heritage Press, 1940.

A graceful appreciation from a fellow-writer who dramatized the novel.

Parker, W. M. "The Children's Advocate: Kenneth Grahame." In *Modern Scottish Writers*. Edinburgh: W. Hodge & Co., 1917, pp. 125-38.

An appreciation stressing and elucidating Grahame's particular "charm" as a children's writer.

Robson, W. W. "On *The Wind in the Willows*." In *The Definition of Literature and Other Essays*, pp. 119-44. Cambridge: Cambridge University Press, 1982.

Considers the novel in a wider literary context and identifies its "artful artlessness" as a vehicle "for more serious purposes."

Smith, Janet Adam. Preface to *The Golden Age*, by Kenneth Grahame, pp. v-vii. New York: Garland, 1976.

A brief exposition of the reasons some children have appreciated a collection not specifically intended for them.

Swinnerton, Frank. "A Bedside Book." In *Tokefield Papers, Old and New*, pp. 175-81. London: Hamish Hamilton, 1949.

Swinnerton praises *The Wind in the Willows* for crossing "the boundary between the world we know and the world of dreams."

Thum, Maureen. "Exploring 'The Country of the Mind': Mental Dimensions of Landscape in Kenneth Grahame's *The Wind in the Willows*." *Children's Literature Association Quarterly* 17, No. 3 (Fall 1992): 27-32.

Argues that the novel consists of a series of journeys, all of them entailing explorations of and changes in consciousness.

Watkins, Tony. " 'Making a Break for the Real England': The River-Bankers Revisited." *Children's Literature Association Quarterly* 17, No. 3 (Fall 1992): 34-5.

Suggests that the continued popularity of *The Wind in the Willows* may derive from readers' fantasy of the "real England."

Additional coverage of Grahame's life and career is contained in the following sources published by Gale Research: *Children's Literature Review*, Vol. 5; *Contemporary Authors*, Vol. 136; *Dictionary of Literary Biography*, Vols. 34, 141.

Robert (Smythe) Hichens

1864-1950

English novelist, short story and nonfiction writer, dramatist, poet, screenwriter, and autobiographer.

INTRODUCTION

Primarily known for his novels, Hichens is frequently described as a writer who failed to fulfill his early promise. He devoted himself to his craft for over sixty years, composing more than forty novels, numerous short stories, and several plays, but his greatest triumphs appeared during the first decade of his career. He initially achieved fame with *The Green Carnation,* a satire on the Aesthetic Movement that caused a sensation in England. Ten years later he published his most critically acclaimed and popular work, *The Garden of Allah,* a romance set in Northern Africa that sold nearly a million copies and was adapted for both stage and screen. During the remainder of Hichens's career, he continued to experiment with subject matter, producing social satires, romance novels, supernatural and occult fiction, and detective stories. While a few of these works were quite popular, for the most part they enjoyed only modest success.

Biographical Information

Born in Speldhurst, Kent, Hichens decided at an early age that he wanted to be a musical composer. Although his father, a rector at a parish in Canterbury, hoped he would attend Oxford, Hichens instead entered Clifton College in Bristol, where he studied piano and organ, and he later enrolled at the Royal College of Music in London. Despite some success as a lyricist, Hichens became convinced that he did not have enough talent to become a distinguished musician. Still in his early twenties, he then decided to pursue his other great interest, writing. Hichens had been writing since he was in his teens, mostly short stories and poetry, but he had also composed three novels, one of which, *The Coastguard's Secret,* was accepted for publication on the condition that Hichens pay half the cost of producing it. After studying for a year at the London School of Journalism—his experiences there provided some of the material for the semiautobiographical novel *Felix*—Hichens began writing articles for newspapers and contributing stories to periodicals, including the *Pall Mall Magazine.* He originally sent *The Green Carnation* to the *Pall Mall Magazine* for serialization, but the editor recommended it to a book publisher. A witty *roman à clef* that satirized fashionable London society and the figures associated with the Aesthetic Movement, notably Oscar Wilde, *The Green Carnation* was an immediate success that made Hichens a celebrity when it was learned he was the anonymous author. Shortly after the appearance of *The Green Carnation,* Hichens succeeded Bernard Shaw as music critic for the *London World.* He resigned from this position three years later and devoted the rest of his life to travel and writing. Hichens traveled extensively throughout Northern Africa, Egypt, Italy, Sicily, and the Orient, locales that figure prominently in his books. He also spent a great deal of time in Switzerland, where he was living at the time of his death in 1950.

Major Works

During the early part of his career, Hichens wrote three types of fiction: social satires on current fads in fashion and the arts; romance novels, many of which are studies of amoral or deviant behavior; and stories about supernatural and occult phenomena. Critics agree that his best works, with the exception of *The Green Carnation,* belong to the second category. The most memorable of these is *The Garden of Allah,* which describes the love affair between a lonely British spinster, Domini Enfilden, and a renegade Trappist monk, Boris Androvsky, who meet in a tourist town in Algeria and ultimately spend a passionate honeymoon in the North African desert. Hichens's portrayal of Androvsky's moral dilemma and his evocation of the desert landscape and its captivating effect on the two main characters proved enormously appealing to both readers and reviewers. Upon publication, *The Garden of Allah* went through five editions in just three months. It retained its popularity for some years afterward, as well; it was produced as a play in both New York (1911) and London (1920), and it was filmed three times. Hichens's other important works in this category, *The Call of the Blood* and its sequel, *A Spirit in Prison,* also treat the theme of forbidden love. In *The Call of the Blood,* which takes place in Sicily, a newly married Englishman, Maurice Delarey, has an affair with a peasant girl named Maddalena after his bride, Hermione, interrupts their honeymoon to visit a friend in England who is dying. Maurice is killed by Maddalena's father, but Hermione is led to believe that he drowned. *A Spirit in Prison,* set on an island in the Bay of Naples, concerns the friendship that develops between the daughter of Maurice and Hermione, Vere, and Maddalena's illegitimate son by Maurice, Ruffino. Criticism of *The Call of the Blood* and *A Spirit in Prison* echoed commentary on *The Garden of Allah.* Both novels were praised for their psychological insight, but critics were even more impressed by Hichens's depiction of local color, many of them finding his vivid pictorial descriptions more interesting than his narratives. Among the most noteworthy of Hichens's works dealing with occult and supernatural phenomena are the novels *Flames* and *The Dweller on the Threshold,* which explore such ideas as psychic influence, personality transference, and reincarnation, and the short stories "The Return of the Soul" (from *The Folly of Eustace, and Other Stories*), "How Love Came to Professor Guildea" (from *Tongues of Conscience*), and "The Black Spaniel," all of which concern reincarnation and the transmigration of souls between humans and animals. After the publication of *A Spirit in Prison*, Hichens divided his time between fiction and drama, but from the 1920s through the 1940s, he devoted most of his energy to the writing of novels, hoping to capitalize on the vogue for detective fiction. The best-selling *The Paradine Case*, which was made into a movie, is representative of Hichens's crime stories in its exploration of human psychology.

Critical Reception

Commentary on Hichens's works is scarce after the 1920s. Earlier critics, recognizing the talent displayed in *The Green Carnation* and *The Garden of Allah*, were puzzled by the mediocrity of most of his subsequent publications. By way of explanation, they cited his flagging sense of humor, growing obsession with detail, and increasing tendency to overanalyze. Although popular interest in Hichens's works was renewed when he began publishing detective novels, none of his crime stories rivaled the success of *The Green Carnation* or *The Garden of Allah*.

PRINCIPAL WORKS

The Coastguard's Secret (novel) 1886
The Green Carnation (novel) 1894
An Imaginative Man (novel) 1895
The Folly of Eustace, and Other Stories (short stories) 1896
Flames: A London Phantasy (novel) 1897
The Londoners: An Absurdity (novel) 1898
The Slave (novel) 1899
Tongues of Conscience (short stories) 1900
Felix: Three Years of a Life (novel) 1902
The Garden of Allah (novel) 1904
The Woman with the Fan (novel) 1904
The Black Spaniel, and Other Stories (short stories) 1905
The Call of the Blood (novel) 1906
A Spirit in Prison (novel) 1908
Bella Donna (novel) 1909
The Dweller on the Threshold (novel) 1911
The Fruitful Vine (novel) 1911
Mrs. Marden (novel) 1919
Snake-Bite, and Other Stories (short stories) 1919
After the Verdict (novel) 1924
Dr. Artz (novel) 1929
The Paradine Case (novel) 1933
The Gardenia, and Other Stories (short stories) 1934
The Power to Kill (novel) 1934
The Afterglow, and Other Stories (short stories) 1935
The Sixth of October (novel) 1936
Daniel Airlie (novel) 1937
The Journey Up (novel) 1938
Secret Information (novel) 1938
That Which Is Hidden (novel) 1939
The Million: An Entertainment (novel) 1940
Married or Unmarried (novel) 1941

A New Way of Life (novel) 1942
Too Much Love of Living (novel) 1947
Yesterday: The Autobiography of Robert Hichens (autobiography) 1947
Nightbound (novel) 1951

CRITICISM

Frederic Taber Cooper (essay date 1912)

SOURCE: "Robert Hichens," in *Some English Story Tellers: A Book of the Younger Novelists*, Henry Holt and Company, 1912, pp. 342-75.

[*An American educator, biographer, and editor, Cooper served for many years as literary critic at the* Bookman, *a popular early twentieth-century literary magazine. In the following essay, he surveys Hichens's early works, from* The Green Carnation *to* The Fruitful Vine, *commenting on his themes, style, and development as a writer.*]

It is almost a score of years since Mr. Robert Hichens first sprang into local notoriety through *The Green Carnation,* which set all London buzzing hotly anent the identity of its bold literary and social lampoons. It was just ten years later that he obtained at last an international recognition, with *The Garden of Allah,* in which for the first time, and perhaps for the last, the inherent bigness of his theme and the titanic majesty of his setting shook him out of his studied pose of aloofness and sardonic cynicism, and raised him to unexpected heights. And almost at the close of a second decade, Mr. Hichens visited America, to find himself, for the passing hour, one of the most widely discussed of modern novelists, with his latest novel giving promise of becoming a "best seller," his earlier triumph, *The Garden of Allah,* demanding a second recognition in dramatic form, and he himself receiving the doubtful tribute of full-page interviews in the Sunday supplements. Accordingly, Mr. Hichens seems to be one of the contemporary British story tellers about whom it is distinctly worth while to ask: How much of this popular acclaim is merited on sound literary grounds, and how much of it is not?

Before attempting to answer specifically this natural and legitimate question, it seems profitable to call attention to the treatment which Mr. Hichens has received at the hands of his critics during the past eighteen years as an illuminating example of the average professional reviewer's shortness of memory and lack of prophetic intuition. A glance over the files of the leading English literary reviews leaves the reader amazed at the suavity with which the critics of Mr. Hichens's more recent popular triumphs ignore the many harsh aspersions they cast upon his earlier volumes, and the completeness with which most of them seem to have forgotten their one-time aversion to certain salient features of his style, his technique and his attitude towards life, all of which are just as marked and most of them just as offensive to-day as in the days when he was trying to startle a stated public into attention, by eccentricities like *Flames, The Londoners* and *The Slave.*

For, if we examine Mr. Hichens with dispassionate frankness, refusing to be dazzled by those physical and moral mirages of the desert, of which he possesses the incomparable and magic trick, we must realize that, although he has gained immensely in sheer craftsmanship, and although his instinct for the unerring right word has become surer with practice, his verbal color more brilliantly lavish, his style more fluent and less epigrammatically crystalline, his development has nevertheless been peculiarly homogeneous and consistent. That he has grown, it would be idle to deny; but the growth has been logical, and on certain definite and predestined lines. His gifts, and some of his faults as well, have attained ampler dimensions with the passage of years; but gifts and faults alike, there is scarcely one of them, the seeds of which might not have been found already germinating and taking vigorous root in the now almost forgotten *Green Carnation*. It is worth while, as a bit of pertinent literary history, to call to mind the terms in which Mr. Arthur Waugh first brought this volume to the attention of American readers, in his monthly London letter to the New York *Critic:*

> At last London has a sensation. The quiet of the early autumn is broken by the explosion of a genuine bombshell, and every one is rushing to read *The Green Carnation*. . . . It is a satire, brilliant and scintillating, upon the literary and social affectations of the hour; and a more daring, impertinent and altogether clever piece of work has not been produced for many years. . . . The writer remains anonymous and his preference for secrecy is not surprising, for if it is possible for good-humored satire to make enemies, he would scarcely find a friend left. Nobody is spared. Mr. Oscar Wilde is, as the title implies, the principal butt of the brochure, but almost every conspicuous writer and personage is touched to the quick.

From the very nature of its naked and unashamed personalities, this first volume was handled rather gingerly by the reviewers, most of whom were fain to dismiss it, after the euphemistic manner of the *Academy,* as a mere "caricature of an affectation in life and literature, an abnormality, a worship of abstract and scarlet sin, which must by its very nature pass away with the personality that first flaunted it before a wondering, half-attracted, half-revolted world." To-day the unwholesome interest of its theme has passed away like a whiff of foul gas; and in its place remains the interest of the human document, for it shows that the author was even then, just as he is to-day, concerned primarily with the abnormalities of life, seeking by preference the tainted mind, the stunted soul, the pathological body. In spite of a life-long straining after startling effects, Mr. Hichens has no great and original fertility of plot. Many another novelist before him has built stories upon the themes of metempsychosis; of a woman's slavery to the glitter of jewels or to the fool's paradise of opium; of hereditary fires of passion, that betray a bridegroom on his honeymoon into forgetting the marriage service, or a renegade monk into breaking his vows. Mr. Hichens's distinction lies rather in his special gift for taking world-old problems and modernizing them, warming them over to suit a jaded palate, with a dash of the deca-

dent spirit and a garniture of *Fleurs de Mal*. Any one who has read Henry James's *Ambassadors* must remember the sensations of the mild and scholarly Mr. Strethers during his first afternoon in Chad Newsome's Paris apartment, while he listens to the conversation going on blithely and carelessly around him, and wonders helplessly whether all those well-dressed, well-mannered guests really mean all the unspeakable things that they seem to be uttering, or whether his own mind has suddenly become strangely perverted and is playing him tricks. The episode inevitably comes to mind in connection with Mr. Hichens's novels, for it precisely portrays the impression that, with malice aforethought, he contrives to leave upon the mind of his readers. He seems to delight in bringing them to a sudden full stop, with a gasping protest, "Surely, he never could mean that!"—and then, at the turn of the page, leaving them with a bewildered and shamefaced wonderment how they could have entertained, even for a moment, such outrageously indecent thoughts!

That this is no arbitrary and one-sided view of Robert Hichens, any one may readily convince himself by merely taking the trouble to glance over the contemporary reviews of his several books. These reviews, with few exceptions, and quite regardless of their favorable or unfavorable tone, form a rich thesaurus of the various English synonyms,—and sometimes the French synonyms as well, when Anglo-Saxon resources run low,—of such words as morbid, neurotic, pathological, decadent, salacious and unclean. It is true that since the appearance of *The Garden of Allah,* less emphasis has been laid upon the unwholesomeness of Mr. Hichens's themes, and more upon the vivid color and scintillating brilliance of his style. It may even be conceded that there is justice in this change, and that, on the whole, his later books are more normal, more human, than his earlier. Nevertheless, the taint persists. There is no escaping the obvious fact that his interest is always in the exceptional, rather than in the average, type. Strange people, bizarre customs, alien skies, men and women vainly struggling against some overmastering obsession, physical disability or mental lesion, a long nightmare procession of the socially and morally unfit,—such as they mentally file before us, is the impression left by the leading characters of Mr. Hichens's novels.

Now the fault with Mr. Hichens is not too great a frankness about life. It is not that he looks upon the world without illusions, recognizing the plague-spots of human nature and ruthlessly stripping them bare. A bold, uncompromising handling of hypocrisy and avarice, frailty and vice is one of the canons of the realistic creed. There is more disease and degradation in Zola's *Lourdes* than in all the pages ever penned by the author of *The Black Spaniel*. And the reason why *The Black Spaniel* is an unwholesome book, while *Lourdes* is not, is simply this: That when he has occasion to expose the ugliness of life, Mr. Hichens, unlike Zola, either cannot or will not emulate the purely scientific zeal of the surgeon, dissecting away a diseased tissue. Underneath the surface impersonality of the realist, one discerns a spirit of prying and unwholesome curiosity, gloating over the forbidden and the unclean. "When I am what is called wicked, it is my mood to be evil," are the words that Mr. Hichens puts into the mouth of Reggie

Hastings, in *The Green Carnation*. "I must drink absinthe, and hang the night hours with scarlet embroideries; I must have music and the sins that march to music." And, if we are content not to stretch the comparison unduly, these phrases are not a bad characterization of the salient qualities of much of Mr. Hichens's fiction. He, too, is fond of hanging the night hours with scarlet embroideries, of showing us sins that keep pace to sensuous rhythms. Like the French artist, Fromentin, one of Mr. Hichens's forerunners in discovering and interpreting Algeria, he has suffered from an innate tendency to see what is picturesque, spectacular, even pretty, rather than what is truly great; and, as with Fromentin, Algeria taught him how to do the bigger thing. It was not until he replaced his "scarlet embroideries" with the vast monochrome of the African sky, the tinkle of drawing-room music with the sublimity of desert silence and solitude, that he attained, for once at least, an epic amplitude of canvas and of theme.

As a bold and effective colorist, Mr. Hichens deserves cordial commendation. His skill in vivid pictorial description is beyond dispute. Whether it be a glimpse of a crowded London street, the turquoise blue of Italian sea and sky, or the burning reach of sun-ravished desert, his printed words seem to open up a vista of light and warmth, a moving picture wrought of dissolving and opalescent hues. His colors lack the riotous romanticism of a Théophile Gautier, the wistful melancholy of a Pierre Loti, the frankly pagan sensuousness of a d'Annunzio,—yet he owes something of its varied richness to each of these. It is obvious that he loves color for its own sake,—much as his heroine in *The Slave* loves the gleam of jewels,—and flings it on lavishly, just as he flings on other forms of ornamentation, purely decorative in purpose, with the result that his backgrounds are often crowded with superfluous and confusing detail. This tendency has grown upon him year by year; it is only in his shorter stories that he has learned the value of restraint. *The Garden of Allah, Bella Donna, The Fruitful Vine,* one and all would have gained much by a well-advised and ruthless pruning.

There is a popular impression that Mr. Hichens is a writer of uncommon versatility; and when we consider that his themes range from the morphine habit to the transmigration of souls, and his stage settings from a London drawing-room to the Sahara desert, and from the Nile to the Italian lakes, this impression seems at least superficially justified. But when we begin carefully to sift them over and mentally slip each plot into its respective pigeon-hole, we find that, underneath all his shifting scenes and varied topics, Mr. Hichens's interest in life narrows down to just one form of obsession, namely, the study of human imperfection, the analysis of those various lesions in body, mind or soul which, like a flaw in the heart of a gem, brand certain men and women as unfit,—at best, to be classed as eccentrics, and at worst as monstrosities. Viewed from this point, his themes fall naturally under three heads: first, his social satires, or studies of the passing fads, foibles, petty vices and hypocrisies on which the world of fashion smiles indulgently; secondly, certain mental delusions, occult phenomena, psychopathic hallucinations, such as form the underlying idea of stories of *The Black Spaniel* type,— in which each reader must decide for himself whether he is reading an allegory, a diagnosis of a curious form of insanity, or a report to the Society for Psychical Research; and, thirdly,—and to this class belong practically all of Mr. Hichens's later serious novels,—studies in moral depravity, chronic and often incurable maladies of the human soul.

Because of this threefold classification of his stories, it is impracticable to survey Mr. Hichens's writings in anything approaching chronological order. His sardonic enjoyment of the social extravagance of the passing hour is more or less apparent in every book that he writes, and lends sharp characterization to many an unforgettable minor character. Yet the only volume since *The Green Carnation* in which it would be fair to say that social satire is, first, last and all the time, the main issue, is *The Londoners,* in which the pretensions of smart society, the pomps and vanities of Mayfair, are, as Mr. Hichens's own sub-title implies, reduced to an absurdity. Of the second class of plots, or those dealing with occultism and pseudo-psychic phenomena of the Jekyll-Hyde order, we have, besides *The Black Spaniel,* a number of weird and fantastic short tales and two novels, *Flames: A London Phantasy,* one of his earliest efforts, and *The Dweller on the Threshold,* which is one of his most recent. This group of stories represent various degrees of cleverness; but they one and all leave the impression that the author has not put the best of himself into them. They simply are the embodiment of certain fantastic ideas which in hours of perversity happened to riot through his brain, and which later he could not bring himself wholly to reject. There is a loathsome and uncanny horror about a theme like that of *The Black Spaniel,* that obviously fastened leech-like upon the abnormal side of Mr. Hichens's nature and refused to let go its hold. Yet, even in this instance, the strongest of all his occult horror tales, the thing is not quite achieved. By over-insistence upon obvious details, by underestimating the intelligence of his readers and explaining his meaning in words of one syllable, as though to an audience of little children, he defeats his purpose, and destroys the last vestige of plausibility. Mr. Hichens is too much of the earth, earthy; he is far too interested in the frailties and perversions of the flesh, to gain credence when writing of the transmigration of souls or the vagaries of disembodied spirits. Consequently, it is with his third class of stories, serious studies of human delinquency, that we must mainly concern ourselves, in order to take a fair measure of Mr. Hichens, as artist and as student of human nature.

Neither is it worth while to linger over his shorter stories, in any of the three subdivisions. What has so often been said in regard to the collection of Egyptian and Algerian tales that swell the volume containing *The Black Spaniel* to its required three hundred and odd pages, namely, that they were fugitive pages from his note-book for *The Garden of Allah,* applies in the main to most of his shorter efforts. He is essentially a writer of the sustained effort type; and it is consequently only fair to judge him by his full-length volumes. If evidence were needed to support the contention that, other things being equal, he ministers by preference to a mind diseased, then such a collection of tales as *Tongues of Conscience* would furnish fertile illustrations. There is, for instance, the story of the famous painter whose peace of mind is destroyed because he holds himself responsible for having inspired a street urchin with a passion for the sea, and the boy subsequently was drowned; or again, in **"The Cry of the Child,"** we have a young doctor, in whose ears there rings ceaselessly the dying cry of his own child, whom he had cruelly neglected in its last hours; and still again, in **"How Love Came to Professor Guidea,"** we are told how a materialistic man of science becomes subject to the obsession of a degraded spirit,—a hideous bit of morbidity, which might pass for a study in insanity, if the author had not precluded that explanation by showing us the Professor's parrot offering its crest to the caresses of unseen fingers, and mimicking the endearments of the invisible and loathsome visitant.

But, as it happens, the longer stories are even more to our purpose than the short tales. Already in 1895, his second published volume, *An Imaginative Man,* clearly reveals the author's natural bent. Briefly, it is the story of an intellectual and highly cultivated man who is destitute of natural affections:

> He (Denison) had never loved his kind, and never even followed the humane fashion of pretending to love them. . . . It amused him to observe them under circumstances of excitement, terror or pain, in a climax of passion or despair. . . . He liked people when they lost their heads, when they became abnormal. Anything bizarre attracted him abnormally.

This curiously unnatural personage marries a charming and devoted wife, because he chooses to suspect something enigmatic about her. Later, when he is forced to recognize that she is normal and simple and true-hearted, his interest turns to a dislike akin to hatred. Accordingly, he leaves her, and, after amusing himself for a time in Egypt, watching the impotent rebellion of a boy in the last stages of consumption, he ends his useless career by dashing out his brains against the Sphinx, with which he has perversely become enamored. Among the press-clippings of that period there is one opinion upon which it would be presumptuous to try to improve:

> It is a story to remain a splendid monument to unwholesome fancy, a thesaurus of morbid suggestion, which exalts mere vulgar suicide into an intellectual resource of the weary-minded, and degrades the humanity of virtue into mere animal instinct.

As a companion picture to this unnatural man, Mr. Hichens shortly afterwards gave us an equally unnatural woman, in the person of Lady Caryll Allabruth, the heroine of *The Slave*. Lady Caryll is obsessed by one consuming passion, jewels,—by which, of course, Mr. Hichens wishes to symbolize all the futile luxuries for which women, from time immemorial, have sold themselves. She is fortunate in meeting, while still quite young, an Anglicized Oriental of great wealth, who can lavish upon her diamonds, pearls and rubies, who understands her through and through, without one remnant of flattering illusion, and who actually wins her by the dazzling splendor of one huge and matchless emerald. It is her own husband who, in the course of the story, sums her up as follows:

> She was born to live in a harem, petted, as an animal is petted, adorned with jewels as a sultan's favorite is adorned. Such a life would have satisfied her nature. Her soul shines like a jewel and is as hard. . . . A certain class of women has breathed through so long a chain of years a fetid atmosphere, of intellectual selfishness, has sold itself, body, mind and soul, so repeatedly for hard things that glitter, for gold, for diamonds, for the petted slave-girl's joys, that humanity has absolutely dwindled in the race, just as size might dwindle in a race breeding in and in with dwarfs. In Caryll, that dwindling light of humanity has gone out. My wife is not human.

Now, it is extremely convenient for a woman who happens not to be human to have a husband who, although aware of the fact, does not seem to mind; so it was rather unfortunate for Caryll Allabruth that her husband died, ruined by her monomania for jewels. In her poverty, however, Lady Caryll managed to retain the one matchless emerald with which he had won her. This emerald is subsequently stolen; and, since it is the one thing left in life for which she cares, and all other means of recovering it fail, Lady Caryll consents to become the burglar's bride, in order that the emerald's green fires may once more burn upon her breast. All of which, in spite of its melodramatic extravagance, rests upon a foundation of perverse and sardonic logic that is eminently characteristic.

The next two volumes, in point of time, while unmistakably expressing the same outlook upon life, show a distinct gain in the direction of sobriety and self-restraint. *Felix* and *The Woman with the Fan,* although neither of them a book of real importance in itself, at least revealed Mr. Hichens as a novelist worth watching for better reasons than merely because he could attract attention with a flow of epigram, as insistent as the cracking of a whip. Moreover, although he had not learned to draw sympathetic characters,—and it is seriously to be questioned whether he ever will learn,—he at least began to get rather nearer the average human level of understanding than in the case of Denison or Lady Caryll. The heroine of *Felix* is not naturally inhuman; she is simply a victim of the drug habit, an unfortunately common and pitiable human weakness, although repulsive and rather nauseating when forced in intimate detail upon our notice. If Mr. Hichens's purpose was to do for the opium habit what Zola did for alcohol in *L'Assommoir,* it is a pity that his misunderstanding of the realistic method has resulted in defeating his object. Zola got his effects by tireless and uncompromising accumulation of facts, flung at us almost defiantly, with no attempt to palliate or to obscure. What his characters made of these facts, whether they understood them, believed them, acted upon them or not, was all of secondary importance; facts, as nearly as he could get them, were the be-all and the end-all of his novels, their excuse and apology for existence. Mr. Hichens, on the contrary, cannot be frank, even if he wants to be; he always proceeds by indirection. It is so much easier to suggest than to tell plainly an unsavory fact, and then trust the reader's mind to go to greater lengths than the printed page would dare to go! In *Felix* we have probably the best and most extreme case of this method to be found in the whole range of its author's writings. Felix himself is in no wise abnormal; on the contrary, he is just the plain, ordinary variety of young fool, the Kipling type of fool, whose rag and bone happens, to his more complete undoing, to be further complicated with a hypodermic needle. Felix pays a brief visit to Paris, where fate wills it that he shall meet a certain little tailor who in youth had the honor to make Balzac a "pair of trousers without feet," and who initiates Felix into the endless delights of the *Comédie Humaine.* This whole episode of the little tailor stands out luminously against a background of human slime. It is the sort of thing that Mr. W. J. Locke can do so supremely well, a page that might have fluttered loose from *The Belovèd Vagabond.* When the final reckoning of Mr. Hichens's achievements is to be cast up, this little masterpiece of Balzac's tailor ought to count heavily on the credit side.

As for the story of Felix as a whole, it is undeniably strong,—as strong as escaping sewer gas. Having read the *Comédie Humaine,* Felix flatters himself that human nature holds no secrets from him; he plunges, hot-headed, into the turbulence of London's fast set, men drugged with ambition, women drugged with vanity, with avarice, with opium. There is an all-pervading sense of something unexplained and inexplicable. Felix's inexperience hangs like a heavy veil before our eyes, and we are forced to grope with him, to piece fragments of evidence together, just as he does, and, like him, often to piece them wrong. Especially, out of the other loathsome and unclean horrors, there looms up, as nauseously offensive as some putrescent fungoid growth, a certain corpulent, bloated, blear-eyed little dog, symbolic of human bestiality. The present writer can recall no episode in modern fiction, not even in the audacities of Catulle Mendès, which, after a lapse of some years, still brings back the same sickening qualm of physical illness.

The Woman with the Fan, although not by any means lacking in audacities, came as a welcome contrast to its predecessor. In addition to its odd title, it had a somewhat startling cover design, the nude figure of a woman apparently going through some sort of a drill with an open fan. This figure, which proves to be a marble statuette known as *Une Danseuse de Tunisie,* plays a rather important part in the development of the story. It is the fan which makes the statuette wicked, one of the characters repeatedly insists; and the thought which is symbolized by the statue is that of the Eternal Feminine degraded by the artificial and the tarnish of mundane life. In applying the symbolism of this statuette to his heroine, Lady Holme, Mr. Hichens seems to have taken a perverse pleasure in confusing right and wrong, idealism and sensuality. Lady Holme's friends constantly identify her with the statuette, and beg her to "throw away her fan," meaning that there is a taint of wickedness about her, and that she is capable of higher things. The facts in the case, however, hardly fit in with this theory. Stripped of its symbolism, the book is a study of the two elements which go to make up human love, the physical attraction and the psychological. Viola Holme is a woman in whom the finer elements of character lie dormant. She is married to a man of the big, athletic, primitive sort, "a slave to every impulse born of passing physical sensations." She knows that of poetry, music, and

all the finer things of life he has not, and never will have, the slightest comprehension. She knows, too, that he loves her only for the surface beauty of her hair, her eyes, her symmetry of face and form, and that if she lost that beauty on the morrow, his love would go with it. And yet she loves him, in spite of his crudeness and his many infidelities, because he satisfies the demands of that side of her nature which is the strongest,—the side which "holds the fan." Other men, the men who urge her to "throw the fan away," offer her a different kind of love, because there are times when they see in her eyes and hear in her voice, when she sings morbid little verses from d'Annunzio, the promise of deeper emotions than her husband ever dreamed her capable of. Now, a woman of Viola Holme's temperament would never voluntarily "throw aside her fan," and Mr. Hichens is a sufficiently keen judge of women to be aware of it. Nothing short of an accident in which the statuette is broken will accomplish this miracle. So fate is invoked, in the shape of an overturned automobile, and Lady Holme struggles back to consciousness, to find her famous beauty gone forever. In its place is a mere caricature of a human face, a spectacle so repellent that, of all the men who formerly professed to worship the "inner beauty of her soul," only one has the courage to renew his vows, and he a poor, broken-down inebriate, as sad a wreck as herself. Such, in bare outline, is the story of [*The Woman with the Fan*] and each reader may apply the symbolism to suit himself. A hasty, snap-shot interpretation would be that Lady Holme would have become a better woman, mentally and morally, if she had discarded her coarse-minded husband and replaced him with a lover of more artistic temperament. But such an interpretation would do scant justice to Mr. Hichens's subtlety. The physical and spiritual elements of love, he seems to say, are too curiously intermeshed to be readily separated; there is no love so earthly that it does not get a glimmer of higher things, no love so pure and idyllic that it does not crave some slight concession to the flesh. If she would hold love, the modern woman must be content to remain a little lower than the angels, she must hold to her fan.

In spite of the implied confession of weakness in solving a rather big problem with the unsatisfactory makeshift of an accident, [*The Woman with the Fan*] is obviously, even now as we look at it in the light of his later achievements, so much bigger and stronger and more vital than all that went before it, that *The Garden of Allah,* when it followed shortly afterwards, ought not to have been the surprise that it actually was. Of this book, the one really big and enduring contribution that Mr. Hichens has made to modern fiction, there is really absurdly little to say. It is so simple, so elemental, so inevitable in all its parts. It may be epitomized with more brevity than many a short story. There is a certain Trappist monk, Androvsky, who, after twenty years of silent obedience to his order, breaks his vows, escapes from bondage, and, meeting Domini Enfilden, an independent English girl with a lawless strain of gipsy blood in her veins, woos her with a gauche and timid ardor, and carries her off for a mad, fantastic honeymoon into the heart of the African desert. The desert, so says a Moorish proverb, is the Garden of Allah; and here the renegade monk, fleeing from his conscience, with confession ever hovering on his lips, and doubly punished through dread of the anguish awaiting his innocent bride when enlightenment comes to her, finds the solitude too vast, the isolation too terrifying, the imminence of divine wrath too overwhelming to be borne. It drives him back to the haunts of men, even in the face of a premonition that amounts to certainty, that his secret must be laid bare and his short-lived and forbidden joy be ended. Now the theme of a man breaking the holiest vows for the unlawful love of a woman is one of the commonplaces in the history of fiction. It is the majestic simplicity of his materials, the isolation of his man and his woman, the sublimity of his remote, unfathomable background, that combine to raise this exceptional book almost to the epic dignity of the First Fall of Man. As has already been insisted, in connection with each succeeding book, Mr. Hichens does not possess the faculty of frankness. That Boris Androvsky is a sinner, bearing the burden of an unpardonable and nameless misdeed, is a fact that we grasp almost at the outset; but Mr. Hichens would have been false to his own nature, if he had not, before revealing the secret, forced us to suspect his hero of every known crime against man, nature and God. But suddenly his theme seems to have taken possession of him, to have raised him against his will, perhaps without his knowledge, out of the pettiness and subterfuge that have dwarfed so much of his work, into the full light of truth and sympathy and understanding. In a certain sense, the book seems to have written itself; it is a fantastic piece of word-painting, done with a tropical luxuriance of color, a carnival of Algerian pageantry and African sunshine; and everywhere and all the time, is an all-pervading sense of the mystery, the languor, the thousand blending sights and sounds and scents of the Orient. Long after the final page is turned, you cannot shut out from your eyes the memory of the desert, "with its pale sands and desolate cities, its ethereal mysteries of mirage, its tragic splendors of color, of tempest and of heat"; you cannot forget the throbbing pulsations of burning air, the vast endless monochrome of earth and sky, the primeval tragedy of an erring man and woman, helpless motes in the glare of universal sunshine, impotently fleeing from an avenging God. It is this one book which entitles Mr. Hichens to a serious consideration among the novelists of today. Without it, he could have safely been passed over in silence.

It follows that, in various degrees, all the books that Mr. Hichens has given us since *The Garden of Allah* are in the nature of an anti-climax; and for that reason they may be somewhat briefly and summarily dismissed. One recalls with a certain amount of cordial appreciation another and briefer story of Algeria called *Barbary Sheep,*—a book that owes its charm chiefly to its delicate and almost flawless artistry, and its lack of any pretension to be more than it actually is. Just a bit of idle playing with fire, a young English couple gaining their first glimpse of African life and African temperament; and while the husband spends his days, and sometimes the nights, tirelessly hunting Barbary Sheep, the young wife, restless, unsatisfied, craving excitement, is drifting rashly into an extremely dangerous intimacy with a cultured and suave young Arab, an officer in one of the native regiments. What might so easily have become a tragedy is brought to a safe and final solution by the removal of the Arab from further participation,

through his death at the hands of a fanatical dervish. And to the end we have the delicious irony of the utter unconsciousness of the phlegmatic English husband, so intent on Barbary Sheep that he passes his wife, where she crouches among the rocks, in the desert moonlight, equally unsuspecting, as he passes, the menace of her Arab lover, and the death-blow that an instant later removes that menace.

Then we have the much overpraised Sicilian story, *The Call of the Blood,* and its stronger and more sanely appraised sequel, *A Spirit in Prison.* Aside from an almost pagan frankness in their unashamed recognition of physical passion, these are conspicuously clean volumes, with little if anything of the author's earlier perversity. The chief weakness in *The Call of the Blood* lies in the unconvincing character of the leading episode, the one upon which the whole structure of the story hinges: namely, the fact that Hermione, the young English wife of Maurice Delarey, feels herself compelled to leave him before their honeymoon in Sicily is half over, in order to hasten to the bedside of Emile Artois, the Frenchman who has long been in love with her, and who is said to be dying. During the brief weeks of her absence, her husband, who has inherited through his grandmother a strain of Sicilian blood, yields to the call of this remote strain and falls under the spell of a young peasant girl's transient beauty, promptly paying the penalty of death at the hands of the peasant girl's kinsmen. Of the true facts of this tragedy Hermoine is never told; she knows only that her husband was drowned, and that she lost some precious weeks of happiness by her absence at the bedside of the Frenchman whom she did not love and who has lived, while the Englishman whom she did love has died. So, believing him to be the perfect type of honor and fidelity, she consecrates herself to lifelong widowhood.

It is at this point that *The Call of the Blood* breaks off, with a young and still beautiful woman wasting her best years in mourning for an unworthy man, while the right man, who knows the truth and might easily win her if he chose to speak, feels that his lips are sealed by his unwillingness to destroy her ideal. *A Spirit in Prison* takes up the story some seventeen years later. The scene is no longer Sicily, but a tiny island in the Bay of Naples, to which the widowed bride retired at the time of her bereavement, to await the birth of her child, and in which she and Vere, the daughter, now a girl of sixteen, still have their home. The Sicilian peasant girl, for whom Hermione's husband proved false to her, also had a child, who is now a sturdy young fisher lad, with eyes that are strangely reminiscent of some one whom Hermione has known, some one in the distant past whom she either cannot or will not name even to herself. Her attention is first called to the fisher lad by the interest that he awakens in her daughter, Vere; for the girl, by some curious instinct, has recognized the ties of kinship and has made the boy her protégé and comrade. It takes very little time for Artois, who still loves Hermione with patient hopelessness, and for Gaspare, her faithful old servant, to learn the truth about the boy's parentage; and these two men instinctively conspire to keep Hermione in ignorance. But by doing so they unconsciously prolong her suffering; because her spirit is struggling in the prison of delusion, and can win freedom, and with it love and happiness, only through full knowledge of the truth. Altogether, these two volumes make up a strong, clean, tender human story, admirably handled to bring out all the values that the plot contains. It revealed Mr. Hichens as an interpreter of Italian life somewhere midway between Richard Bagot and Marion Crawford, less pedantic than the former, yet lacking the geniality of the creator of *Saracinesca*.

Mr. Hichens might, had he chosen, have gone on indefinitely from this point, doing the fairly innocuous, fairly entertaining sort of story, and letting us little by little forget the days when a new volume from his pen meant an alternate gasp and shudder at the turn of each page. But it is not in his nature to be content with doing the innocuous thing. He insists upon being conspicuous; and if the only way of being conspicuous is to shock a startled world into attention, he stands ready to do so. Just two more novels demand a passing word: **Bella Donna** and **The Fruitful Vine**. Of these two, the former is of no special importance, either in theme or in detail,—although in its heroine he has created one more unwholesome and abnormal type that lingers in the memory. At the opening of the story, Mrs. Chepstow is summed up as "a great beauty in decline":

> Her day of glory had been fairly long, but now it seemed to be over. She was past forty. She said she was thirty-eight, but she was over forty. Goodness, some say, keeps women fresh. Mrs. Chepstow had tried a great many means of keeping fresh, but she had omitted that.

The facts about Mrs. Chepstow, which Mr. Hichens regards as of moment, are that in the zenith of her youth and beauty she was divorced by her husband; that, having made a failure of one life, she resolved that she would make a success of another; that for a long time she kept men at her feet, ministering to her desires,—and then suddenly, as she approached forty, "the roseate hue faded from her life, and a grayness began to fall over it." In other words, to catalogue the book roughly, it is one more of the many studies devoted to *L'Automne d'une Femme*. And so, at the opening of the volume, we meet Mrs. Chepstow, in the consulting-room of a famous specialist, Dr. Meyer Isaacson, confiding to him certain facts about herself, physical, mental and moral facts, which the reader is not allowed to overhear, which the woman herself never alludes to again, but which Mr. Hichens has no intention of allowing the reader to cease for one moment to ponder over, with a more or less prurient curiosity. Incidentally,—and to this extent alone is her confession justified structurally,—it is the memory of what she confided to him that at a crucial hour hurries Dr. Isaacson on a desperate, headlong Odyssey to the Nile, in order to save a friend and keep Mrs. Chepstow from the sin of murder. But all of this is, frankly, rather cheap stuff, and quite unworthy of the author of **The Garden of Allah**. It makes a normal-minded reader somewhat exasperated to see a rather rare talent deliberately misused.

Only one other volume, **The Fruitful Vine,** remains for discussion. The setting is modern Rome, the leading characters two married couple, both English, Sir Theodore

Cannynge and his wife, Dolores, Sir Theodore's closest friend, Francis Denzil and his wife Edna—and just one Italian, Cesare Carelli. Cannynge, having lost his first love in a painful tragedy years before, remained unmarried almost until middle age. At the opening of the story Dolores has for ten years been his wife, but no children have come to them. Whatever regrets he may have felt have remained unspoken; until within a year his whole interest seemed to center in his diplomatic career, first in one European capital, then in another. But when the inheritance of an independent fortune came almost simultaneously with the loss of his great ambition, the Austrian Embassy, in a moment of pique he resigned, and from that time on had more time for thought than was good for him. Finally comes the day when, fresh from a visit to Denzil's home, full of the merriment of children's voices, he catches up his wife's Chinese poodle by the throat and, while the miserable little beast writhes and coughs and blinks, tells her violently: "Look at it! This is all we've got, you and I, to make a home—after ten years!" Dolores is not surprised; she has felt instinctively that sooner or later this outbreak was bound to come. None the less it hurts her—just as every one of his almost daily visits to Denzil's home, blessed with a fruitful vine in place of a barren one, has hurt her. She is not jealous of Edna, Denzil's wife, although she knows that the idle gossip of Rome has settled their relations for them. The Roman world would be incapable of understanding that the attraction might be the children and not the woman. Dolores's troubles, however, are only just beginning. Francis Denzil, husband of "the happiest woman in Rome," is suddenly stricken down with cancer of the larynx, is operated upon and never rallies. His last request is that Sir Theodore will be a second father to his little son—and Sir Theodore promises. From this time onward, Dolores sees less and less of her husband; a vicarious fatherhood has taken possession of him, absorbed him, made him a new man. When the summer comes, he disappoints her regarding her long-cherished plan to visit London, and insists upon taking a villa at Frascati, so as to be near the Denzil children. Then comes a day when Dolores rebels, packs her belongings and goes by herself to Lake Como, to escape the torture of neglect. Meanwhile Roman gossip has been busy in coupling her name with that of another man, that of Cesare Carelli. Since he was a mere boy, Carelli has been faithful to just one woman, the Mancini. But suddenly and quite recently it has become common knowledge that he has definitely broken with her. Why? asks Rome insistently; Romans do not do such things; a man may be untrue to his wife, but a lover remains faithful. There must be some other woman—and Rome is quick to find her in Dolores. As the Countess Boccara tells Dolores to her face, with a malicious little stress on the pronoun: "The rupture happened in the summer, very soon after you left Rome, *cara*." Now it is while Dolores is in hiding at Como, and just at the crucial moment when the insistent thought has first taken possession of her, "If I could only give Theodore a child!" that Carelli tracks her down—and this is the beginning of the tragedy that the reader at once foresees is inevitable. What actually follows may be put into a dozen words. Dolores does give a child to Sir Theodore—a child of alien parentage—but she never reaps the harvest that she has hoped for, the harvest of reawakened love; because the child costs the mother her life, or rather, not the child, but her own loosened hold upon life itself, due to a loathing of her own deed. As for Carelli, he is truly Italian in his inability to conceive of Dolores's real motive. For love, yes, that he could understand; but for motherhood, never! And when the woman is dead, and the stricken husband is just awakening to his loss, the Italian thinks to square accounts by claiming his child. But his revenge misses fire. His revelation simply results in quickening Sir Theodore's own self-knowledge, and he says at last in all humility: "She was better than I, better than I!"

Such is the story of **The Fruitful Vine,** analyzed as generously and as sympathetically as possible. It is written with extraordinary power, and it is thrown into strong relief against a background of rare richness, the vari-colored background of the Roman world. Of the inherent bigness of his theme, the pathos of barrenness, the tragedy of a woman who sees her husband's love alienated because she fails to give him sons and daughters, there can be no question:—just as there can be no question that Mr. Hichens has, perhaps unwittingly, done his utmost to debase it. He has given his theme certain perverse twists that put it on a level even lower than that of Elinor Glyn's much-discussed *Three Weeks*. It was cheap workmanship, and not an unworthy plot, that made *Three Weeks* the ephemeral, negligible book that it was. But in **The Fruitful Vine** we are asked to believe that a delicately nurtured, refined and cultivated Englishwoman, who worships her husband, is willing to do him the ultimate, crowning wrong that any wife can do, and foist upon him, as his son and heir, an interloper that has not even the redeeming grace of being a child of love, but one more basely begotten, more purely meretricious than half the nameless waifs that crowd the asylums! And in asking this, he simply insults our intelligence. All his finished craftsmanship cannot make the volume otherwise than futile.

To sum him up in a few words, we have in Mr. Hichens a story teller of much brilliance who has deliberately chosen to prostitute his gifts to the gratification of unhealthy tastes. He has preferred the sensational notoriety of the passing hour to the less flamboyant successes of enduring worth. He has given us a few books that are fairly innocuous and just one book that deserves to live. And the danger of according the full measure of praise to **The Garden of Allah** lies in this: that by granting its greatness, we may seem by implication to put the stamp of approval on the author's other works, so many of which, unfortunately, are mentally and morally unclean.

Harold Williams   (essay date 1918)

SOURCE: "The Contemporary Novel," in *Modern English Writers: Being a Study of Imaginative Literature, 1890-1914,* Sidgwick & Jackson, Limited, 1919, pp. 355-416.

[*In the following excerpt, which was originally published in 1918, Williams provides an overview of Hichens's novels in which he judges their relative strengths and weaknesses.*]

There are aspects in which the novels of Mr. Robert Hichens are not unlike those of Mr. Conrad. He combines elements of romance, of realism, and the study of motives, causes and mental phenomena. When a young man he came to London to become a student of the Royal College of Music; but by a happy inspiration he chose the moment when the æsthetic movement was at its height to publish a witty and spirited satire upon its extravagances. **The Green Carnation** (1894) was the book of the moment and a popular success. It deserved its success, for it was the most pointed satire of any length directed against the æsthetic movement. The epigrams and paradoxes of Esmé Amarinth are those of Wilde hardly veiled. "Everything that is true is inappropriate" has all the ring of Wilde's manner; and the length and breadth of the æsthetic moral philosophy is well summed-up in the remark of Lady Locke—"We are to aim at inducing a violent rash that all the world may stare at."

Thenceforward Mr. Hichens was committed to the path of literature, and, diverging from his first direction, the writing of satiric extravaganza, he turned to more thoughtful and serious work, till with the most subtle and psychologically intricate of his books, *A Spirit in Prison* (1908), he exhausted his powers, and his later volumes, despite the best efforts of the author, break down under the strain of trying to catch the former vigour and closeness of analysis. In **Bella Donna** (1909) the fantastic element of Mr. Hichens' imaginative faculty overpowers his sense of reality and proportion, and the narrative collapses in a painfully melodramatic effort to represent the glamour of the Orient. But this is to anticipate, and to pass over a number of exceptionally strong and thoughtful novels.

The Green Carnation was followed by **An Imaginative Man** (1895), a study in morbid pathology and a satire upon the shams of modern life, and **The Folly of Eustace** (1896). But the curious and original **Flames** (1897), a story of spiritualistic phenomena and psychic influences, was the most remarkable of his earlier tales. **Felix** (1902) illustrates the *illusions perdues* of a young Englishman, who is fired with literary ambitions, after meeting with the tailor who once made trousers for Balzac. The book is partly a tale of the lost ideals of rose-white youth, and partly an indictment of literary and social life in London. This and **The Woman with the Fan** (1904), a well-constructed book, are, compared with the occultism of **Flames,** realistic novels of the common world. But it was between the years 1904 and 1908 that Mr. Hichens reached his best in craftsmanship, insight and concentration with the three long novels, **The Garden of Allah** (1904), **The Call of the Blood** (1906) and its sequel, **A Spirit in Prison**. In these novels, conscious that he was beginning to exhaust his store of observation of English social life, and anxious to study the psychology of simple, passionate and unsophisticated men and women, he carried his scene afield to Northern Africa and Sicily. **The Garden of Allah** has a double thread running through its pages—the fascination of the vast silences of the sandy desert and the spell of the Roman Catholic faith. Mr. Hichens shows himself an excellent topographical writer in these tales.

> They were near Beni-Mora now. Its palms appeared far off, and in the midst of them a snow-white tower. The Sahara lay beyond and around

it, rolling away from the foot of low, brown hills, that looked as if they had been covered with a soft powder of bronze. . . . In this pageant of the East she saw arise the naked soul of Africa; no faded, gentle thing, fearful of being seen, fearful of being known and understood; but a phenomenon vital, bold and gorgeous, like the sound of a trumpet pealing a great *réveillé.* As she looked on this flaming land laid fearlessly bare before her, disdaining the clothing of grass, plant and flower, of stream and tree, displaying itself with an almost brazen insouciance, confident in its spacious power, and in its golden pride, her heart leaped up as if in answer to a deliberate appeal.

The desert in its influence upon the heroine of Mr. Hichens' story plays a part comparable to Egdon Heath in Mr. Hardy's *Return of the Native.* It governs the narrative and moulds the characters of those men and women who come in contact with it. Against the sombre colours of the desert is set the somewhat melodramatic love-story of an English girl and a renegade Russian monk. As Boris, the monk, hears the call of love and the world, so in *The Call of the Blood* Maurice Delarey, half English, half Sicilian, is hurried by his passionate southern blood into faithlessness to his wife and a tragic end. But it is in the sequel, *A Spirit in Prison,* that Mr. Hichens gives us his finest and closest work as a student of the mind. A long novel, it is perfectly co-ordinated, and the development of the theme—the bondage of the spirit shielded by a lie—is used with extraordinary skill and power. *A Spirit in Prison* is a fine piece of writing, and immeasurably Mr. Hichens' most substantial work. *Bella Donna* represented a great falling off, and only too evidently betrayed weariness and laboured effort. In his attempt to reproduce the atmosphere of *The Garden of Allah*—the spell of the Orient—Mr. Hichens became so unbalanced as to suggest comparison with Ouida. *The Dweller on the Threshold* (1911) restored the scene to England, and reverted to the subject of psychic influence; but, compared with *Flames,* it was a brief and slight piece of writing. *The Fruitful Vine* (1911) is weaker than his best writing, but it is the one book of the last few years which does Mr. Hichens the least discredit. In *The Way of Ambition* (1913) he tells cleverly the story of a musical composer forced against his will into writing for success, and his consequent downfall. He has a thorough knowledge of his situations and the many types of people whom he introduces, but the characters are wire-drawn and wanting in true life-likeness.

Mr. Hichens' chief failing in his more ambitious novels is an absence of that humour which he possessed in abundance when he wrote *The Green Carnation.* In later years he takes himself too seriously and coldly. In analysis of human character and motive an intellectual egotism and aloofness renders his characters chilling and unsympathetic. He cannot sink himself in the people of his imagination. Even in *A Spirit in Prison* his manner tends to be intellectually objective. On the other hand Mr. Hichens succeeds in uniting his narrative to the broader and more important issues of life and the moral workings of the universe. *Flames* exhibits the power of mind upon mind for evil; *The Call of the Blood* illustrates the forces of heredity

and unconscious memory; *A Spirit in Prison* and *The Fruitful Vine* point the moral of the revenge exacted by circumstance for falsehood even in a good cause. These are motives patient of great dramatic treatment, and Mr. Hichens has the instincts of the dramatist. But his work is inexplicably unequal in its quality. *Felix* is slight in invention, thought and treatment compared with work that went before; *The Dweller on the Threshold* makes a surprisingly lame use of a subject—psychic influences—which the author had used already with far greater power in *Flames;* and *Bella Donna* drops to the grotesque when contrasted with *The Garden of Allah.* If Mr. Hichens had not reasserted himself with *The Fruitful Vine* it would be natural to say that he had completely written himself out in 1908, the year of his greatest, his most complex and his most convincing novel in the exposition of character—*A Spirit in Prison.* Among English novels written within this century this book, in its close analysis of character and motive, in the poetry of its background, and in the breadth with which Mr. Hichens outlines his moral drama, stands out as a noble and distinctive achievement.

Abel Chevalley (essay date 1921)

SOURCE: "Development of the English Novel during the Past Thirty Years," in *The Modern English Novel,* translated by Ben Ray Redman, Alfred A. Knopf, 1925, pp. 117-34.

[*In the following excerpt, which was originally published in French in 1921, Chevalley contends that Hichens's later works did not fulfill the promise of his earlier writings.*]

Why has [Robert Hichens] not given us all that he promised? It seems that he has lost himself in an excess of analysis, in a vain effort to attain the inaccessible, which may perhaps be explained by his musical education and his essays in occultism.

In 1894 he published *The Green Carnation,* a cutting satire on the æsthetic and symbolist movement, which made him famous. *An Imaginative Man* (1895) contains a curious pathological study, and lays bare the lies of an artificial civilization. *Felix* (1902) depicts a young Englishman, enamoured of literature, who discovers Balzac's tailor, becomes famous, loses his illusions, and serves as pretext for a mordant picture of literary life in London. Who could divine in these ironic productions the future author of *A Spirit in Prison*? *Flames,* in 1897, had revealed the secret tendency of his mind. It is a story of occultism, curious, original and morbid. But there was nothing to make one foresee the sudden blooming of his talent about 1904, after a period of meditation and work. For him, as for many other contemporary novelists, those years between 1903 and 1904 are a date of capital importance.

In 1904 he published *The Garden of Allah,* in 1906 *The Call of the Blood,* in 1908 *A Spirit in Prison.* These three books contain the best of his work.

After this, Robert Hichens quits England and goes to Africa and Sicily in search of an atmosphere that is simpler, closer to nature, in which passion stalks nakedly. *The Garden of Allah* is the desert in the vicinity of Biskra; the love of a young Englishwoman for a Russian ex-monk; the mysterious attraction that Catholicism exercises upon weary souls. *The Call of the Blood* portrays a half-Sicilian Englishman, Delarey, who is led by the hereditary awakening of passions to betray his wife and to perish in a violent death.

The Sahara and Sicily are not merely the principal themes, they are almost the heroes of these two powerful books, which made a sensation in their day. *A Spirit in Prison* follows *The Call of the Blood* and contains an inexorable but interminable analysis of the effects produced by a moral lie, even though told in the best of causes, on him who utters it and on him who profits by it.

Since then, Mr. Hichens has written nothing that is reminiscent of these three books.

Lacon (essay date 1925)

SOURCE: "Mr. Robert Smythe Hichens," in *Lectures to Living Authors,* Houghton Mifflin Company, 1925, pp. 93-9.

[*In the following essay, Lacon writes in the form of a lecture to Hichens on the overall course of his career.*]

There was once a singular institution called, somewhat grandiloquently, the London School of Journalism. I gather from the public press that schools purporting to teach the art of writing, journalistic or other, flourish even in the present day: there may even, by now, be another bearing the same title. They arise, and fade, and rise again. And there is, I suppose, a certain part of the journalistic trade that can actually be taught—given a teacher who knows his business. At the worst the anxious beginner can be cautioned against certain offences—against the unblushing use of outworn clichés, or of the split infinitive. But why you should have frequented the school in question I cannot say. Possibly you thought, in those early days, that there really was a Mystery of Journalism to which the initiated might provide a key. Possibly it was already clear to you that the school itself might be productive, in the future, of good copy. Or it may be that parental foresight insisted upon this ante-chamber to Bohemia, to make sure that your character should not be ruined by a too early and facile success. In any case you became a pupil, together with at least one other writer of reputation, Mr. Francis Gribble. Genius, we know, will out: it is as difficult to conceal as murder: as hard to eradicate as hereditary gout. Probably the easy methods of the ingenious gentleman who ran the establishment did little either to improve or impair the style of these eminent authors.

The curious may find this same School of Journalism portrayed, with little more than a touch of caricature, in the pages of *Felix,* a novel in which there is more autobiography than we are accustomed to find in your works. Perhaps for this reason, I have always regarded it as one of your best books. It came at a fortunate period, when you had already written enough to gain command of your material, and before you had acquired the verbosity that distinguished some of your later novels.

You are one of the few literary men who know something about music. Many authors have dabbled in painting: not many have been attracted by the mysteries of harmony and counterpoint. Samuel Butler, it is true, advanced some way up both avenues; but at the moment I can recall no other name to brigade with yours. For it was your earliest ambition to become a musical composer, and you actually went through a course of study for that purpose at Bristol and in London. If, at the ripe age of thirty, you had not made a hit with *The Green Carnation,* it is possible that you might have achieved fame by another route. But *The Green Carnation* set people talking. It was a clever book, of a kind that often attains success through curiosity. Several well-known persons, Oscar Wilde among the number, were understood to be discoverable in its pages, under a thin disguise. The *roman à clef* has often proved the propriety of its name by unlocking the gates of Fame's forecourt.

Perhaps it dates you a little to say that the book was published in 1894. We were both young then, and the literary world had its fashions no less than it has now. Men, and women, now dead or forgotten, were in the forefront of the new movement: magazines and reviews sprang up like mushrooms in the night: little poets produced slim books of verse, even as they do now; and brilliant young writers coruscated in somewhat artificial prose under the fostering wing of the late W. E. Henley, then editor of the *National Observer.* There followed, during the next three years, *An Imaginative Man, The Folly of Eustace, Flames,* and *The Londoners.* I have often wondered, especially now that you have attained to a certain success in the theatrical world, why this last book has never been adapted for the stage. The earlier part of it is admirable farce, carried on with immense spirit. Towards the end, it is true, it degenerates into a sort of knockabout humour. But it possesses a charming young American lady masquerading in man's clothes who should make the fortune of any play.

With added years came a sort of seriousness. Did you despise the precious gift of humour; or did it merely fade away, as such gifts will? The faculty for writing farce seemed to have been lost when, in 1901, you published that melancholy attempt at boisterous fun, *The Prophet of Berkeley Square.* It seems almost incredible that this book could have been written by the same hand that produced *The Londoners.* Some of the critics began to express doubts as to your future. Would you prove yet one more of that band of young writers who were destined not to redeem their early promise? However, you pulled yourself together and gave them *Felix,* which was much better stuff. I do not say that it is a great novel, but it will bear reading more than once—which is more than can be said of most novels in these degenerate days. It has characterization: there is pathos to be found in it as well as humour. The critics revised their opinion, and agreed that you might still go far.

In a sense, I suppose, you have, though it must be confessed that your more recent books have not shown an improvement commensurate with your increased years. You have "arrived," it is true. Just twenty years ago you brought out *The Garden of Allah,* and your name was made. Incidentally you discovered a formula—always a dangerous discovery for an artist to make. Put in a few words, that formula may be stated as The Importance of the Elderly Woman. Before your happy arrival she had been neglected by the novelist: her fading charms were treated with levity or, even worse, with an exaggerated sympathy. And yet the lady of forty to fifty years felt within herself that she still had the capacity for adventure: she saw no reason why she should retire so early into the background and be content to watch her younger rivals taking all the prominent parts. Women were beginning to emancipate themselves: year by year they were growing determinedly younger, especially if they chanced to be unmarried. Yet it was undeniable that the dreaded borderland of Middle Age was near at hand: they snatched, with a courage born of despair, at the chance of one real adventure before quitting the arena. It was Hichens who had the wit to perceive this cardinal fact, and to turn it to his own advantage. While your comrades blindly concentrated their energies on the young and unformed heroine you struck out boldly into the Saharan desert and showed how Algeria still held possibilities for the courageous woman who had lost her first youth, but retained the primitive instincts of her sex. It was said—I know not with how much truth—that *The Garden of Allah* and *Barbary Sheep* were responsible for a vast number of adventurous tourists (a large proportion of them ladies of a certain age) taking tickets to Biskra and the borders of the Sahara.

From the selling point of view, I take it that you found your formula useful enough. It must be remembered that women have always been the great novel-reading section of the community, and, which is even more important, the great distributors of fame. Rumour, with her thousand tongues, was justly painted as of the female sex. And the woman of forty-odd has ever been wont to find solace for her fading charms in the imaginary love-affairs of others. She, above all others, is the great dispenser of fortune to the struggling novelist; and the man who can touch her heart most nearly, who can persuade her that the dangerous fascination of some women really increases rather than deteriorates with advancing years, is assured of success. The only trouble attendant on his good fortune lies in the fact that publishers have an unpleasant knack of demanding that a good formula, once found, shall be worked for something more than it is worth. It is difficult to persuade these unimaginative gentlemen that an artist cannot walk contentedly for ever round the same circular track. To put Pegasus in harness is bad enough, but it is too much to try and turn him into a mill-horse.

The heroine of *The Call of the Blood* was also a lady whose adventures began (somewhat to her discomfiture) rather late in life. I suppose this book and its sequel, *A Spirit in Prison,* may be said to have secured your position as a serious novelist—one of those who can be trusted to deal with a psychological problem with that detail and exhaustiveness that the British public demand from a clever writer before they consent to prepare his pedestal. It was in these two books that I first noticed a tendency on your part towards a distressing verbosity. *The Call of the Blood* was kept alive by the strength of the plot, the Sicilian setting, and the admirable character sketch of Gaspare: in the sequel there was less material but even more fluency.

Some of us began to fear that you had fallen in love with mere length for its own sake, and that your future novels might outrival in size some of the mammoths of antiquity.

In common with Mr. Eden Philpotts, a novelist of about your own standing, both as regards age and general reputation, you have been apt to take your relaxation, after writing one of your more important books, in the composition of something trifling on a smaller scale. Thus, after *The Garden of Allah* you published *The Black Spaniel,* which is more like an anti-vivisection tract than a novel: after *A Spirit in Prison* came a book on Egypt and its monuments and *Barbary Sheep*: between *Bella Donna* and *The Fruitful Vine* you brought out a book on the Holy Land and a psychological story called *The Dweller on the Threshold*. These intercalary works may not have always displayed you at your best, but they possess at least the negative merit of conciseness. We had begun to predict for you a distinct future in the literary world. You could write: you had abundance of ingenuity, and an eye for a dramatic situation. Indeed, that eye may have been too good. *Bella Donna* was dramatized—with a success that may prove to have been her author's ruin.

I have been re-reading during the last few days some of your earlier works, for I always like to refresh my memory on these points before I definitely commit my opinion of any author to the printed page. I read *Felix* once again, and my good opinion of the book was confirmed: I read also *The Londoners* and wondered what subtle quality in it that made me laugh so consumedly in 1897 had evaporated after seven-and-twenty years. I remember distinctly the first time I read that story, for it was in a club library, and on the mantelpiece of the palatial room was displayed a placard with the word SILENCE inscribed thereon in big letters. Perhaps it was just that placard that made me choke and gurgle with dissimulated laughter, as one laughs hysterically at church or during a funeral. But no! it certainly was funny: it was screamingly funny in parts. And yet now I can read it soberly enough, without more than an occasional quiet chuckle. The fact is, that farce has to be very good indeed if it is to live. There was a time when Jerome's *Idle Thoughts* laid the foundation stone of a new school of British humour: you are more likely to yawn over it now than to laugh. And yet *Pickwick* survives. To preserve it from decay farcical writing needs an especially large infusion of humanity.

St. John Adcock   (essay date 1928)

SOURCE: "Robert Hichens," in *The Glory That Was Grub Street: Impressions of Contemporary Authors,* The Musson Book Company Limited, n.d., pp. 105-14.

[*An English author whose works often concern the city of London, Adcock served as editor of the London* Bookman *from 1923 until his death in 1930. In the following essay, he focuses on Hichens's literary beginnings and his novel* The Garden of Allah.]

There is a tradition that every novelist began as a writer of verse, and if Robert Hichens did not exactly conform to it, he did not altogether break with it, for in his youth he wrote both verse and prose, but without regarding either as the business of his life. His first absorbing ambition was to become a musician; he sacrificed a career at Oxford to this end, and, leaving Clifton College, studied music for some years at Bristol and at the Royal College, in London. His instruments were the piano and the organ, and he acquired a considerable mastery of them. He never made his début professionally, but played several times in public at charity concerts with success that was satisfying enough; but he was not one of those who mistake the desire to achieve for the power to achieve; he always had a healthy instinct for looking facts in the face, a long-sighted faculty of self-criticism; and he was not slow to realise that however hard he might practise he would never be able to make a great musician of himself; and as soon as he felt sure of this he abandoned the attempt to do so.

Through all that experimental period he had been writing tales, essays, recitations, and scores of lyrics for music; his lyrics alone in one year brought him in over a hundred pounds. One of the first lyrics he sold, **"If at Your Window"**, was set to music by Ethel Harraden, sister of Beatrice Harraden, the novelist; another, **"A Kiss and Good-Bye"**, was set by Tito Mattei and sung by Madame Patti at the Albert Hall.

"In the natural pride of my heart," Robert Hichens confessed to me when we were talking of this some while ago, "I took a seat in the stalls and waited in a fever of anxiety to hear how it would come off. It was received with such enthusiastic applause that I was lifted into a heaven of delight, but as Madame Patti returned, in response to insistent cries of 'Encore!' I was tumbled headlong down out of my heaven by hearing two voices from the seats just behind me: 'What a lovely song that was!' one exclaimed rapturously. 'Yes,' the other grudgingly agreed, 'but what awful rot the words of these songs always are!' "

Born in 1864, Robert Hichens was the eldest son of Canon Hichens, Rector of St. Stephen's, near Canterbury. He was about twenty-four when he decided that there was no future for him as a musician and began to feel his way toward a different goal. So far, he had been writing stories mainly for his own amusement; he had also written two long novels which he had never dreamt of publishing; but a third, written when he was seventeen, *The Coastguard's Secret,* he offered to a publisher, and was so impressed when that publisher said he was willing to risk half the cost of publishing it that he risked the other half himself and his book appeared, and was not unkindly received by the reviewers.

But it languished, and died, and has long been out of print. I could not lead Hichens to tell me more of it than that it was a kind of ghost story—a very bad one—merely the crude sort of thing you would expect from a youngster still in his 'teens. When, after the brilliant success of *The Green Carnation,* the publisher of *The Coastguard's Secret* urged that the time was ripe to put out a new edition of it, its author was filled with direst alarm and by prayer and protest dissuaded him from his purpose.

Seeking the best way to his new goal, while that now unobtainable novel was still the only one to his name, Hichens became a pupil at the late David Anderson's School of Journalism; shortly before he joined, Francis Gribble had left it, and among his fellow-pupils were Bernard Hamilton, Guy Berringer and Cranstoun Metcalfe.

I gathered from Robert Hichens that he had endowed Felix, in his novel of that name, with certain of his own characteristics and some of his own autobiography. And if you turn to *Felix* you will find there delightfully amusing descriptions of Sam Carringbridge and his School of Journalism in the Strand which tally closely enough with what Hichens told me of his experiences with David Anderson. At a loose end in London, Felix, then only one-and-twenty, meets Hugo Arliss, learns that Arliss is "a sucking Kipling" studying at Sam's School, and eagerly accepts the offer of an introduction to that institution. He calls, and being summoned into Mr. Carringbridge's presence, finds him a large, handsome, urbane personage, beautifully dressed and smoking a cigar:

> "Mr. Hugo Arliss told me about your school," Felix began, in an unusually low voice and feeling soothed almost as if by a narcotic.
>
> "Mr. Arliss, a charming, intelligent, gentlemanly fellow. I am very much attached to him," said Mr. Carringbridge. . . .
>
> "I met him in France," said Felix. . . . "Arliss advised me to see if I could enter at your school for a year. I am very keen on trying to write."
>
> "It is a great profession. The journalist is a power. . . . You know my terms?"
>
> Felix jumped—the last sentence came with such a mellifluous abruptness from Mr. Carringbridge's bright red lips.
>
> "No. Arliss didn't———"
>
> "Dear careless fellow. One hundred guineas payable to me on the day I sign the agreement. You merely hand me your cheque and I bind myself forthwith to give you the advantage—if it be one, possible not!—of my personal teaching and experience for one whole year, and to allow you the free and unfettered use of the writing-hall you have just passed through. I also give you ink———"
>
> A generous smile illumined his face.
>
> "It's awfully good of you," Felix had murmured, before he knew that he was going to murmur anything.
>
> "But not pens and paper. I find young men prefer to consult their personal taste in those matters, and therefore I give them free scope. About ink there is less divergence of opinion, and mine, I believe, gives general satisfaction. I am glad if it is so. I never drive the young."
>
> "No?" said Felix.
>
> "Never. I lead them, perhaps. I show them what a man can do, has done. You see the volumes on that table? . . . Those contain the leading articles written by me for the *Daily Recorder* during twenty-five years of active journalistic life. My pupils can read them at any time."

"You must have worked tremendously hard," said Felix, counting the volumes.

There were eight of them, and they were tremendously fat. He felt almost awe-stricken. Mr. Carringbridge indulged himself and Felix in a lotus-eating smile.

"I have been through the mill," he replied lazily. . . . "If my pupils like to take me as an example they would do well to follow," he continued, "they can. I come up from Brighton every day by the nine o'clock train. But I never drive them. I trust them. I rely on them. I give them complete liberty. When do you propose to come?"

At the end of his term, Felix was assured by Carringbridge that he would certainly get on; not perhaps as a journalist, but he had detected greater than journalistic gifts in him and urged him to develop these. It is more than likely that, at the end of his term at David Anderson's School, Anderson gave Hichens similar advice. Anyhow, at Anderson's Hichens worked hard, writing all manner of descriptive and leading articles and submitting them to him, and at the same time he was sending manuscripts to the magazines and newspapers, having many rejected and a steadily increasing proportion accepted. About this date and in the few succeeding years, he contributed articles to the *European Mail* and the *Evening Standard* and, like so many authors who have since become famous, supplied his quota of "turnovers" to the late lamented *Globe*. But he was not destined to be a journalist, even though for a time he did musical and dramatic notes for *Hearth and Home,* the *Gentle-woman* and various other papers, and succeeded Bernard Shaw as musical critic of the *World.*

Returning in those early years from a holiday in Egypt, Hichens wrote a story, **"The Collaborators"**, and sent it to the *Pall Mall Magazine.* The editor, Sir Douglas Straight, promptly accepted it, and asked for more, and more were sent and taken. When, in 1894, Hichens offered him *The Green Carnation,* Sir Douglas saw it was quite unsuitable for a magazine serial but, recognising its brilliance, forwarded it with a strong recommendation to Heinemann, the publisher. The success of *The Green Carnation*—which, apart from the boyish *Coastguard's Secret,* was Hichens's first book, was immediate and immense. As everyone knows, it satirised Oscar Wilde and the esthetic movement, then in full blast. It was written without the least touch of malice, and merely because the subject was ready to hand. Hichens only knew Wilde casually; had met him no more than four times before he wrote the book, and never met him after; and so far as he heard Wilde took it all in good part and with characteristic imperturbability.

Curiously enough, though it came out while *The Green Carnation* was still the sensation of the day, *An Imaginative Man* met with but moderate success, and a year later *The Folly of Eustace* was scarcely more fortunate. *Flames* (1897), that finely imaginative, haunting, spiritualistic romance, had a more stirring reception, and after discussing it at large in the *Review of Reviews,* W. T. Stead gave us a tabloid edition of it for a penny; nevertheless, it fell short of the triumph of *The Green Carnation.* Hichens's seven books of the next seven years were acclaimed by the critics but their sales were not extraordinary, yet they included *The Londoners, Felix,* and so poignant and masterly a story as *The Woman with the Fan.* In the year after *The Woman with the Fan,* however (1905), appeared *The Garden of Allah,* and then the reading world hesitated no longer. Within three months that greatest of Hichens's novels had run through five editions, and how many it has gone through since I would not say at a venture. Of his fourteen more recent novels—*Barbary Sheep, The Call of the Blood, Bella Donna,* down to *The God Within Him* (1926)—able and popular as they are, none has reached the high literary and imaginative qualities or the popularity of *The Garden of Allah.*

He has felt the lure of the stage, and among plays of his that have been produced are *Daughters of Babylon,* in collaboration with Wilson Barrett; *The Medicine Man,* with H. D. Traill, in which Irving played the principal part; *Becky Sharp, The Real Woman, The Voice from the Minaret,* but the dramatic power and long success of *The Garden of Allah,* which he dramatised in 1920, has eclipsed them all.

For long past Hichens has had no settled home in this country. He came to London in 1884, when he was twenty, and lived here for fifteen years. Then a troublesome illness affected his nerves, and finding the endless noise and hurry and excitement of the town unendurable, he went abroad to look for the seclusion and quiet that were necessary to him. He became very much of a dweller in hotels, with a pleasant place where he could work at peace in Sicily. He laughs at the notion of a novelist roaming the earth in search of human material or local colour. Living in Sicily, he came to know its atmosphere, its spirit, its people, and was moved to write about them as spontaneously as he was moved to write of London while he lived here. *Felix* and *The Londoners* are not more essentially born of London than *The Call of the Blood* is of Sicily, or *The Garden of Allah* more essentially inspired by the magic and glamour and mystery of the desert. His stories grow in his mind out of whatever life happens to be round about him. He had no thought of writing anything about the Sahara until he had been there many times, but by degrees the strange spell of it laid hold upon him, and it was not until after a seventh sojourn in the desert that he was moved to begin writing *The Garden of Allah.*

On one of those seven occasions, he visited a Trappist monastery and, drawn by its air of perfect restfulness, said he wished he could stay there for a while. "We take guests," remarked the lay brother who was showing him round. "We should be glad to have you if you do not mind living very simply". For three weeks Hichens lived there frugally, sleeping in one of the small, bare cells. From there he went into the desert with the Arab poet whom in the novel he has named Batouch, for his guide, and as they stood one evening gazing across the waste of sand toward the sunset, a chance phrase of Batouch's woke in him a first vague thought of *The Garden of Allah.* Talking in his usual dreamy monotone, Batouch said, "This is the garden of oblivion. In the desert one forgets everything, even the desire of one's soul". This saying somehow called a vision of the secluded, prison-like monastery back into its hearer's mind, and with it came a fancy of bringing one of the monastery's silent tenants out here into the desert and letting him forget, in this garden of oblivion, his vows, his hopes, his God, and be willing to lose even his soul for the love of a woman.

But another five years passed before the story shaped itself and he could see his way through it, and then he spent the better part of two years translating it into words, slowly and with infinite pains which were amply justified by the result. For whatever else may be lost in the desert, it was there that, as a novelist, Hichens found himself.

FURTHER READING

Criticism

Payne, William Morton. Review of *The Green Carnation,* by Robert Hichens. *The Dial* XVII, No. 201 (1 November 1894): 266-67.
> Maintains that the popularity of *The Green Carnation* will be short-lived.

Priestley, J. B. Review of *After the Verdict,* by Robert Hichens. *The London Mercury* X, No. 59 (September 1924): 541.
> Judges *After the Verdict* to be unrealistic.

Review of *The Garden of Allah,* by Robert Hichens. *Punch* (26 October 1904): 306.
> Maintains that the appeal of *The Garden of Allah* lies in its character development rather than in its descriptive detail.

Review of *A Spirit in Prison,* by Robert Hichens. *The New York Times Book Review* (19 September 1908): 506.
> Considers *A Spirit in Prison* representative of the new method Hichens adopted in *The Garden of Allah,* in which scenic description takes precedence over dialogue and character development.

Additional coverage of Hichens's life and career is contained in the following source published by Gale Research: *Dictionary of Literary Biography*, **Vol. 153.**

Daisy Miller

Henry James

The following entry presents criticism of James's novella *Daisy Miller* (1879). For information on James's complete career, see *TCLC*, Volumes 2, 11, and 47; for discussion of his novella *The Turn of the Screw* (1898), see *TCLC*, Volume 24; for discussion of his novel *The Portrait of a Lady* (1881), see *TCLC*, Volume 40.

INTRODUCTION

Considered among his finest works of fiction, *Daisy Miller* was James's earliest "international novel" to achieve popular and critical success. Lacking much of the narrative complexity for which James would later become known, the story recounts the exploits of a young American girl in Europe and dramatizes the theme of innocence beset upon by modern society. Likewise, the novella traces many significant themes that James explored in his other early works, including the contrast between American and European culture and the constraints that society places on individual freedom.

Plot and Major Characters

The plot of *Daisy Miller* centers on two individuals, Daisy Miller, a pretty and headstrong young woman from Schenectady, New York, and Frederick Winterbourne, a young American expatriate residing in Europe. Winterbourne first encounters Daisy in the Swiss resort town of Vevey, where she is vacationing with her ineffectual mother and sickly nine-year-old brother Randolph. Charmed by Daisy, Winterbourne—who is prone to circumspection rather than action— categorizes her as a "pretty American flirt," and when he returns to Geneva looks to his aunt, Mrs. Costello, for advice in dealing with the situation. After a brief excursion with Daisy to the Castle of Chillon back in Vevey, Winterbourne again returns to Geneva, and while there receives some letters from his aunt, now in Rome where she has recently made the acquaintance of Daisy. In her letters, Mrs. Costello hints at some impropriety on Daisy's part, claiming that she has become "very intimate with some third-rate Italians." In reality Daisy's Italian acquaintance is Eugenio Giovanelli, who suffers more from poor judgement than low character. Winterbourne, nonetheless, travels to Rome to meet his aunt and to visit Daisy, who has been seen more and more with Giovanelli. About her behavior Daisy is confronted by Mrs. Walker, another American socialite residing in Europe like Winterbourne's aunt. Daisy refuses to listen to the older woman and agrees to go with Giovanelli to the Colosseum at night—an unseemly act in the eyes of Walker, Costello, and Winterbourne. In addition, all fear that Daisy might contract malaria from being out in the city at night. When Winterbourne goes to retrieve Daisy, he finds her and Giovanelli at the Colosseum, where Daisy—angered by the assumptions made about her character and by Winterbourne's easy acceptance of the gossip—defiantly claims that she does not care if she falls ill. Shortly afterward Daisy shows signs of exposure to the disease and soon dies. Later Winterbourne goes to Daisy's grave in the Protestant cemetery in Rome where he meets Giovanelli, who proclaims Daisy's innocence.

Major Themes

According to most critics *Daisy Miller* is a work primarily concerned with the nuances of character and the effects that social values and manners have on individual actions. James himself declared the novella to be about innocence, specifically Daisy's innocence in conflict with the sophistication of the modern world. Yet critics have observed that he portrays her character with a tone of irony that highlights her willful and reckless behavior. These ambiguities of character were also commented on by James, who claimed to have produced a poetic, rather than a strictly critical, portrait of Daisy. General consensus has since aligned Daisy with the natural world, and made her a personification of spontaneity and freedom. Contrasted with this is the character of Winterbourne. Overly deliberate and superficial, he has come to represent the stultifying and deceptive qualities of Victorian society. And, while Winterbourne appears to be forthright and honorable, James reveals that he is having an affair with "a very clever foreign lady"—a gender-related hypocrisy that forms another theme in *Daisy Miller*. Commentators also have speculated as to who is the real protagonist of the novella. Many have argued that Daisy is merely the object of other people's perceptions and that the work is really about Winterbourne. As a result, much of the recent criticism on *Daisy Miller* has focused on Winterbourne's self-deceptive enslavement to Puritanical standards of behavior, his misogyny, and his complicity in destroying Daisy.

Critical Reception

While James initially had great difficulty finding a publisher for *Daisy Miller*, when the novella made its appearance in *The Cornhill Magazine* in 1879, it created a huge uproar among the American reading public. William Dean Howells observed that the country was split between "Daisy Millerites and anti-Daisy Millerites." The latter were scandalized by Daisy's behavior, which was thought to flout Victorian standards of womanly conduct. Nevertheless, the ensuing publicity brought James to the forefront of the American literary scene. And, while contemporary critical appraisals of the work were generally positive, twentieth-century critics have since elevated it to the status of a minor masterpiece. Such praise has focused on James's incisive portrayal of character and his compelling investigation of the cultural differences between the Old and New Worlds, a theme that he was to more fully dramatize later in *The Portrait of A Lady*.

CRITICISM

Henry James   (essay date 1909)

SOURCE: A preface to *Daisy Miller, Pandora, The Patagonia and Other Tales*, Charles Scribner's Sons, 1909, pp. v-viii.

[*In the following excerpt, James discusses the inspiration for his novella* Daisy Miller, *and the difference between his original, real-life observations of character and the final product of his art.*]

It was in Rome during the autumn of 1877; a friend then living there but settled now in a South less weighted with appeals and memories happened to mention—which she might perfectly not have done—some simple and uninformed American lady of the previous winter, whose young daughter, a child of nature and of freedom, accompanying her from hotel to hotel, had "picked up" by the wayside, with the best conscience in the world, a good-looking Roman, of vague identity, astonished at his luck, yet (so far as might be, by the pair) all innocently, all serenely exhibited and introduced: this at least till the occurrence of some small social check, some interrupting incident, of no great gravity or dignity, and which I forget. I had never heard, save on this showing, of the amiable but not otherwise eminent ladies, who weren't in fact named, I think, and whose case had merely served to point a familiar moral; and it must have been just their want of salience that left a margin for the small pencil-mark inveterately signifying, in such connexions, "Dramatise, dramatise!" The result of my recognising a few months later the sense of my pencil-mark was the short chronicle of *Daisy Miller,* which I indited in London the following spring and then addressed, with no conditions attached, as I remember, to the editor of a magazine that had its seat of publication at Philadelphia and had lately appeared to appreciate my contributions. That gentleman however (an historian of some repute) promptly returned me my missive, and with an absence of comment that struck me at the time as rather grim—as, given the circumstances, requiring indeed some explanation: till a friend to whom I appealed for light, giving him the thing to read, declared it could only have passed with the Philadelphian critic for "an outrage on American girlhood." This was verily a light, and of bewildering intensity; though I was presently to read into the matter a further helpful inference. To the fault of being outrageous this little composition added that of being essentially and pre-eminently a *nouvelle*; a signal example in fact of that type, foredoomed at the best, in more cases than not, to editorial disfavour. If accordingly I was afterwards to be cradled, almost blissfully, in the conception that *Daisy* at least, among my productions, might approach "success," such success for example, on her eventual appearance, as the state of being promptly pirated in

Boston—a sweet tribute I hadn't yet received and was never again to know—the irony of things yet claimed its rights, I couldn't but long continue to feel, in the circumstance that quite a special reprobation had waited on the first appearance in the world of the ultimately most prosperous child of my invention. So doubly discredited, at all events, this bantling met indulgence, with no great delay, in the eyes of my admirable friend the late Leslie Stephen and was published in two numbers of *The Cornhill Magazine* (1878).

It qualified itself in that publication and afterwards as "a Study"; for reasons which I confess I fail to recapture unless they may have taken account simply of a certain flatness in my poor little heroine's literal denomination. Flatness indeed, one must have felt, was the very sum of her story; so that perhaps after all the attached epithet was meant but as a deprecation, addressed to the reader, of any great critical hope of stirring scenes. It provided for mere concentration, and on an object scant and superficially vulgar—from which, however, a sufficiently brooding tenderness might eventually extract a shy incongruous charm. I suppress at all events here the appended qualification—in view of the simple truth, which ought from the first to have been apparent to me, that my little exhibition is made to no degree whatever in critical but, quite inordinately and extravagantly, in poetical terms. It comes back to me that I was at a certain hour long afterwards to have reflected, in this connexion, on the characteristic free play of the whirligig of time. It was in Italy again—in Venice and in the prized society of an interesting friend, now dead, with whom I happened to wait, on the Grand Canal, at the animated water-steps of one of the hotels. The considerable little terrace there was so disposed as to make a salient stage for certain demonstrations on the part of two young girls, children *they,* if ever, of nature and of freedom, whose use of those resources, in the general public eye, and under our own as we sat in the gondola, drew from the lips of a second companion, sociably afloat with us, the remark that there before us, with no sign absent, were a couple of attesting Daisy Millers. Then it was that, in my charming hostess's prompt protest, the whirligig, as I have called it, at once betrayed itself. "How can you liken *those* creatures to a figure of which the only fault is touchingly to have transmuted so sorry a type and to have, by a poetic artifice, not only led our judgement of it astray, but made *any* judgement quite impossible?" With which this gentle lady and admirable critic turned on the author himself. "You *know* you quite falsified, by the turn you gave it, the thing you had begun with having in mind, the thing you had had, to satiety, the chance of 'observing': your pretty perversion of it, or your unprincipled mystification of our sense of it, does it really too much honour—in spite of which, none the less, as anything charming or touching always to that extent justifies itself, we after a fashion forgive and understand you. But why *waste* your romance? There are cases, too many, in which you've done it again; in which, provoked by a spirit of observation at first no doubt sufficiently sincere, and with the measured and felt truth fairly twitching your sleeve, you have yielded to your incurable prejudice in favour of grace—to whatever it is in you that makes so inordinately for form and prettiness and pathos; not to say sometimes for misplaced drolling. Is it that you've after all too much imagination? Those awful young women capering at the hotel-door, *they* are the real little Daisy Millers that were; whereas yours in the tale is such a one, more's the pity, as—for pitch of the ingenuous, for quality of the artless—couldn't possibly have been at all." My answer to all which bristled of course with more professions than I can or need report here; the chief of them inevitably to the effect that my supposedly typical little figure was of course pure poetry, and had never been anything else; since this is what helpful imagination, in however slight a dose, ever directly makes for. As for the original grossness of readers, I dare say I added, that was another matter—but one which at any rate had then quite ceased to signify.

B. R. McElderry, Jr.   (essay date 1955)

SOURCE: "The 'Shy Incongruous Charm' of 'Daisy Miller'," in *Nineteenth-Century Fiction*, Vol. 10, No. 2, September, 1955, pp. 162-65.

[*McElderry was an American educator and critic whose studies focus predominantly on the works of such American realists as Mark Twain, Henry James, and Thomas Wolfe. In the following essay, McElderry reveals James' intention of portraying Daisy as innocent by quoting a letter he wrote on the subject soon after the publication of his novella.*]

The best-known comment by Henry James on his story *Daisy Miller* is found in two long paragraphs at the beginning of his "Preface" to volume XVIII of the New York Edition. Written nearly thirty years after the original publication, the account is not very illuminating. James tells the anecdote on which he based him story, and explains that it was published in *Cornhill* after being rejected by a Philadelphia magazine. "Flatness indeed," he continues, "one must have felt, was the very sum of her story. . . ." Yet from it, "a sufficiently brooding tenderness might eventually extract a shy incongruous charm." Years later a lady reproached him for wasting his talents in falsifying the heroine. To this he replied that "my supposedly typical little figure was of course pure poetry, and had never been anything else. . . ."

There is, however, a little-known letter written not long after *Daisy Miller* was published, which is much more specific in accounting for the story. It is preserved in a memoir of Mrs. Lynn Linton, together with Mrs. Linton's inquiry, which prompted James's letter. Mrs. Lynn Linton (1822-1898) was a well-known English novelist and journalist. In her earlier years she was a vigorous partisan for women's rights, but in 1868 (ten years before *Daisy*) she wrote a series of anonymous articles attacking "The Girl of the Period" for unfeminine traits. Mrs. Linton's concern for feminine manners continued for the rest of her life, and as she makes clear in her letter to James, involved her in an acrimonious dispute over *Daisy Miller*.

My Dear Mr. James,

As a very warm dispute about your intention in *Daisy Miller* was one among other causes why I have lost the most valuable intellectual friend I ever had, I do not think you will grudge me

half a dozen words to tell me what you did really wish your readers to understand, so that I may set myself right or give my opponent reason. I will not tell you which side I took, as I want to be completely fair to him. Did you mean us to understand that Daisy went on in her mad way with Giovanelli just in defiance of public opinion, urged thereto by the opposition made and the talk she excited? or because she was simply too innocent, too heedless, and too little conscious of appearance to understand what people made such a fuss about; or indeed the whole bearing of the fuss altogether? Was she obstinate and defying, or superficial and careless?

In this difference of view lies the cause of a quarrel so serious, that, after dinner, an American, who sided with my opponent and against me, came to me in the drawing room and said how sorry he was that any gentleman should have spoken to any lady with the "unbridled insolence" with which this gentleman had spoken to me. So I leave you to judge of the bitterness of the dispute, when an almost perfect stranger, who had taken a view opposite to my own, could say this to me! . . .

Mrs. Linton's agitation had its effect. James replied with his customary grace, and with unusual definiteness.

My Dear Mrs. Linton,

I will answer you as concisely as possible—and with great pleasure—premising that I feel very guilty at having excited such ire in celestial minds, and painfully responsible at the present moment.

Poor little Daisy Miller was, as I understand her, above all things *innocent*. It was not to make a scandal, or because she took the pleasure in a scandal, that she "went on" with Giovanelli. She never took the measure really of the scandal she produced, and had no means of doing so: she was too ignorant, too irreflective, too little versed in the proportions of things. She intended infinitely less with G. than she appeared to intend—and he himself was quite at sea as to how far she was going. She was a flirt, a perfectly superficial and unmalicious one, and she was very fond, as she announced at the outset, of "gentlemen's society." In Giovanelli she got a gentleman—who, to her uncultivated perception, was a very brilliant one—all to herself, and she enjoyed his society in the largest possible measure. When she found that this measure was thought too large by other people—especially Winterbourne—she was wounded; she became conscious that she was accused of something of which her very comprehension was vague. This consciousness she endeavoured to throw off; she tried not to think of what people meant, and easily succeeded in doing so; but to my perception she never really tried to take her revenge upon public opinion—to outrage it and irritate it. In this sense I fear I must declare that she was not *defiant*, in the sense you mean. If I recollect rightly, the word "defiant" is used in the tale—but it is not intended in that large sense; it is descriptive of the state of her poor little heart, which felt that a fuss was being made about her and didn't wish to hear anything more about it. She only wished to be left alone—being herself quite unaggressive. The keynote of her *character* is her innocence—that of her *conduct* is, of course, that she has a little sentiment about Winterbourne, that she believes to be quite unreciprocated—conscious as she was only of his protesting attitude. But, even here, I did not mean to suggest that she was playing off Giovanelli against Winterbourne—for she was too innocent even for that. She didn't try to provoke and stimulate W. by flirting overtly with G.—she never believed that Winterbourne was provokable. She would have liked him to think well of her—but had an idea from the first that he cared only for higher game, so she smothered this feeling to the best of her ability (though at the end a glimpse of it is given), and tried to help herself to do so by a good deal of lively movement with Giovanelli. The whole idea of the story is the little tragedy of a light, thin, natural, unsuspecting creature being sacrificed as it were to a social rumpus that went on quite over her head and to which she stood in no measurable relation. To deepen the effect, I have made it go over her mother's head as well. She never had a thought of scandalising anybody—the most she ever had was a regret for Winterbourne.

This is the only witchcraft I have used—and I must leave you to extract what satisfaction you can from it. Again I must say I feel "real badly," as D. M. would have said, at having supplied the occasion for a breach of cordiality. May the breach be healed herewith! . . . Believe in the very good will of yours faithfully,

H. James

And that—"as concisely as possible"—was James's intention in ***Daisy Miller***. This was the method of the "brooding tenderness" which "eventually extract[ed] a shy incongruous charm" for James's most popular story.

Edmond L. Volpe (essay date 1958)

SOURCE: "The Reception of *Daisy Miller*," in *The Boston Public Library Quarterly*, Vol. X, January, 1958, pp. 55-9.

[*Volpe is an American author and educator. In the following essay, he refutes the tradition that* Daisy Miller *was poorly received by critics, citing instead the social uproar it created and its effect of perturbing readers, rather than critics, nationwide.*]

At the time of its publication Henry James's ***Daisy Miller,*** according to literary tradition, was not well received by the American critics. The author is supposed to have been reviled by his countrymen for his unflattering portrait of the American girl. Modern scholars have wondered why there should have been such a reaction to what is really a sympathetic portrayal of Daisy, but no one, in print at least, has questioned the validity of the tradition. Richard Foley, in his study of the reception given to James's works in American periodicals, noted that though "the maga-

zines reported . . . ***Daisy Miller*** had been objected to on the grounds that it maligned the American young lady, it was well received by those [magazines] examined." The discrepancy between the reports by the magazine writers and their own favorable comments has been generally ignored, probably because several months after the appearance of ***Daisy Miller*** a brief discussion of its reception (attributed to William Dean Howells) in the "Contributors Club" of the *Atlantic Monthly* included quotations from "some critical experts" who regarded the tale as "servilely snobbish" and "brutally unpatriotic."

Who these "critical experts" were and in what publications they made such statements is a mystery. A search through the literary periodicals of the period has revealed no statement about the novel that even approximates the tone of these quotations. On the contrary, the tale was very well received. No critic questioned James's patriotism or accused him of snobbishness. Only one reviewer wondered if Daisy had been intended to represent the typical American girl:

If the anomalous mother and daughter who are the chief figures in Mr. James's ***Daisy Miller*** were seriously presented by him as typical representatives of our country-women—while admitting that such a mother and daughter are as much within the range of possibility as the Siamese twins and has as equitable a title to be set up as types—we should affirm that they have not enough of general or special resemblance to any really existent class to lend probability to caricature. It is obvious, however, that Mr. James had no such purpose in this brilliant and graceful trifle.

No writer in an American periodical provided the "Contributor Club" commentator with his quotations, nor did the reviewers in the New York or Boston newspapers. The only New York journal that printed a full-length review of the novel was the New York *Times,* and that was laudatory. In Boston, where the novel was first published, it produced almost no reaction in the daily or weekly newspapers. The Boston *Evening Transcript* usually devoted a full column or two to book reviews; on the day James's tale was listed under "Books Received" there were reviews of several other works mentioned, including a Grocer's manual, a Latin grammar and a book on ornithology. The Boston *Post* on November 11, 1879 offered the most elaborate review:

Daisy Miller is a bright little story, an *affaire du coeur*. The scene of the story is laid in Switzerland—in Vevey, in fact, one of the most charming retreats that skirt the shore of Loch Leman. It is an entertaining little tale of what befell two hearts in that far-off country, and one may while away a half hour with pleasure and no harm done.

It is possible that in the "Contributor's Club" passage Howells was quoting oral criticism; the following month, however, the same column made specific reference to published criticism:

To read the silly criticisms which have been printed, and the far sillier ones which are every day uttered . . . would almost convince us that we are as provincial as ever in our sensitiveness to foreign opinion. It is actually regarded as a species of unpardonable incivism for Mr. James, because he lives in London, to describe an underbred American family . . .

There is no ambiguity in these lines: James has been attacked by American critics; but by whom and in what publication, Howells did not say. None of the other magazine writers who corroborate the statement is specific either. In the "Our Monthly Gossip" column of *Lippincott's Magazine* (October, 1879), the writer maintains that two novels "*The Story of Avis* and *Daisy Miller* are in much greater demand [by magazine editors] in consequence of the severity of a few reviewers in dealing with them." The *Nation*'s critic, reviewing the book a month after publication, wrote: "Certainly no American book of its size has been so much read and so much discussed, as far as our memory runs back." And the critic in the *Century* declared that the novel was

> . . . much criticised in the United States for the uncomplimentary character of its heroine . . . The character is denounced as exaggerated in the extreme, and only applicable to Americans in Europe who are the scandal and terror of their fellow-travelers.

Yet neither the *Nation* nor the *Century* critic mentions printed criticism. Howells, in a letter to James Russell Lowell on June 22, 1879, describes the reaction to the novel as a "vast discussion in which nobody felt very deeply, and everybody talked very loudly. The thing went so far that society almost divided itself in Daisy Millerites and anti-Daisy Millerites." It is a social rather than a critical controversy that Howells presents in this letter. Had there been so vigorous a literary attack upon James as the "Contributor's Club" passages indicate, surely there would have been some mention of it in the literary gossip sections of the periodicals. But neither the *Literary World* with its "Literary Table Talk" nor the *Outlook* with its "Literary Notes" referred to any controversy over *Daisy Miller*.

The New York and Boston newspapers, too, failed to make any reference to an attack upon James or his novel. The New York papers reflected instead a developing popular interest in the novelist. He was spoken of frequently in the "personal" and "literature" columns during the first few months of 1879, and on June 4 of that year the New York *Times* carried on its editorial page a discussion of the international social problem which mentioned the resentment aroused by *Daisy Miller:* "There are many ladies in and around New York to-day who feel very indignant with Mr. James for his portrait of Daisy Miller, and declare that it is shameful to give foreigners so untrue a portrait of an American girl."

The evidence, therefore, is that *Daisy Miller* perturbed many readers, particularly women, but not the critics. In comparison to the manner in which James's biography of Hawthorne was received, the reception of the story was excellent. In 1880, sparked by George Lathrop's denunciation, a number of American authors accused James of being unpatriotic; and many editorial writers pounced upon him for his "unAmerican" attitude. It is possible that the receptions given these two works have, over the years become confused.

In his letter to Lowell, Howells declared that he was pleased with the furor *Daisy Miller* had created, because in "making James so thoroughly known, it would call attention in a wide degree to the beautiful work he has been doing so long for very few readers and still fewer lovers." He may have been primed for trouble long before the tale's publication in book form. In his preface to the novel in the New York edition, James stated that he had originally submitted the story to a Philadelphia magazine (*Lippincott's*) the editor of which (John Foster Kirk) had promptly returned it without comment. Puzzled, he appealed to a friend "for light, giving him the thing to read." The friend "declared that it could only have passed with the Philadelphia critic for 'an outrage on American girlhood.' " There is nothing to prove that Howells was that friend, but if he was, or even if he had been informed by James of the incident, he would have been ready to defend the novel against expected attacks.

There is another possible solution to the mystery: that a midwestern or western newspaper has provided Howells with the quotations he used. But even if such a review were discovered, the tradition that *Daisy Miller* received a poor critical reception in the United States is obviously untrue.

James W. Gargano   (essay date 1960)

SOURCE: "Daisy Miller: An Abortive Quest for Innocence," in *South Atlantic Quarterly*, Vol. 59, Winter, 1960, pp. 114-20.

[*In the following essay, Gargano contends that* Daisy Miller, *considered as Winterbourne's and not Daisy's story, is "essentially the study of a young man's quest for innocence, a virtue for which his society has alienated itself."*]

When John Foster Kirk rejected *Daisy Miller* as "an outrage on American girlhood," he unhappily misled critics of Henry James's novel into an obsessive preoccupation with its heroine. In his preface to the New York edition, James himself, perhaps still smarting from his rebuff, waives consideration of other aspects of the novel in his excessive concern with justifying his portrait of the maligned Daisy. Howells, too, because of the nature of his subject in *Heroines of Fiction,* focuses discussion of the novel on the appealing heroine.

Critical preoccupation with Daisy has fostered the view that the theme of the novel is the peril of a good but naïve American girl in a stiffly conventional society. This simplification ignores the fact that Frederick Winterbourne, as the central intelligence, represents the consciousness upon which the events and characters of the novel have the greatest impact. Since he is always on the scene, observing, discriminating, and seeking to unravel the mystery of the enigmatic Daisy, the drama must, if James's art can be said to have any intention, structurally center in him. He, I believe, is the subject of the novel and not merely the lens through which Daisy's career is seen. His story has a richness that makes *Daisy Miller* more than a thin commentary on the lawless innocence of the American girl.

Winterbourne's visit to Vevey begins an experience which can be described, in one of James' favorite words, as an "initiation." In other words, Winterbourne leaves a world of fixed values, and adventures into a foreign one where only innate sensibility and large sympathy can guide him and where commitment to a restrictive code will surely hurt him. His attraction to Daisy, by wrenching him out of his moral and social insularity, offers him an opportunity to enlarge his consciousness and gain the psychic fulfilment that James's characters constantly seek and very rarely find in love. Thus, for all her independent charm, Daisy exists to test Winterbourne's ability to grow beyond his hitherto narrow and one sided state into a fully realized human being.

Considered as Winterbourne's story, *Daisy Miller* is essentially the study of a young man's quest for innocence, a virtue from which his society has alienated itself. It is by no means accidental that Winterbourne meets Daisy in a garden—commonly associated with innocence—or that the severe Mrs. Costello describes the girl as romping "on from day to day, from hour to hour, as they did in the Golden Age." Indeed, the *mis-en scène* of the first section of the novel cleverly foreshadows the later conflict between innocence (here related to freedom) and the dark assumptions with which Winterbourne faces life. Winterbourne is visiting Vevey, which, because it resembles "an American watering-place," exhibits a more relaxed social life than is to be found elsewhere in Europe. Vevey is further identified with freedom by its proximity to the Castle of Chillon, unmistakably associated with Bonivard, a famous foe of tyranny. With typical finesse, James immediately emphasizes the spiritual distance between Vevey and Winterbourne, who "had an old attachment for the little capital of Calvinism." Certainly Geneva, later referred to "as the dark old city at the other end of the lake," symbolizes a rigidly conventional way of life whose forms mask a Puritan distrust of spontaneous and natural behavior. Winterbourne, who significantly attended school in Geneva and has many friends there, constantly assesses his new experiences by the standards of his spiritual home.

Vevey is the appropriate scene for Winterbourne's rencounter with a bewildering girl who "looked extremely innocent." But since innocence is the very thing in which Geneva has lost faith, Winterbourne consistently misreads Daisy's character and seeks to ferret out the *arrière pensée*, the dubious motive behind her artless conversation. Still, his admiration of her constitutes a self-betrayal, a persistent belief in innocence perhaps rooted in his American origin and fortified by the romantic idealism of youth. Lacking as yet a fatal rigidity, he is offered an opportunity to discover innocence and escape the propriety that menaces the full flowering of his nature.

Winterbourne's initiation begins in a comic manner calculated to show his inability to appreciate instinctively the innocence of Daisy's character. When, contrary to the code of Geneva, he speaks to the unmarried Daisy, he wonders whether "he has gone too far." He risks "an observation on the beauty of the scene" and wrongly assumes that an excursion to Chillon with the girl must perforce include her mother as chaperone. When he attempts to classify her, she undermines all of his stuffy and inapplicable generalizations. He decides that she may be "cold," "austere," and "prim" only to find her spontaneous and as "decently limpid as the very cleanest water."

Winterbourne's perplexity in the presence of innocence indicates the extent to which he is "morally muddled." Unable to believe in natural goodness, which usurps freedoms of speech and action, he must analyze it with the suspicious rationalism of Geneva and thus miss its essential luster. Distrusting the authority of his feeling for Daisy's "natural elegance," he complacently pronounces her a flirt:

> Winterbourne was almost grateful for having found the formula that applied to Miss Daisy Miller. He leaned back in his seat; . . . he wondered what were the regular conditions and limitations of one's intercourse with a pretty American flirt.

Winterbourne's comic ineptness demonstrates how poorly Geneva's formulas have prepared him to understand innocence.

His self-assurance is so halfhearted, however, that he takes his problem to his aunt, Mrs. Costello, the most reliable social authority he knows. Going to her with "a desire for trustworthy information," he suddenly betrays an inchoate perception of Daisy's nature. Though he uncritically allows Mrs. Costello's reference to the girl's "intimacy" with Eugenio to "make up his mind about Miss Daisy," he generously declares, "Ah you're cruel! . . . She's a very innocent girl!" In spite of his aunt's innuendoes, he holds to his purpose of taking Daisy to Chillon. Indeed, his momentary defection from Geneva appears so extreme that Mrs. Costello is confirmed in her refusal to be presented to his new acquaintance.

Winterbourne's recognition of Daisy's innocence may represent impatience with the stringent code of Geneva, but it can by no means be interpreted as thoroughgoing disillusionment. He sees only enough to be less blind than Mrs. Costello; if he departs from the dictates of propriety, he does so with customary prudence. Lacking the ardor and recklessness of a rebel, he is temperamentally doomed to swing in permanent vacillation between opposing claims. He has sensibility enough to be "touched, mortified, shocked" when he perceives Daisy's hurt at Mrs. Costello's refusal to see her; yet he is too tepid to do anything more than think of sacrificing "his aunt—conversationally." Even his trip to Chillon—perhaps his most daring action—is followed by his symbolical return to the bleak city of conformity. In his paralyzing introspection and most of his behavior, he is a morbid, though superficially cultivated, latter-day Puritan.

Nevertheless, before his visit to Rome, Winterbourne has found Daisy's innocence appealing enough to defend. On the free soil of Vevey, he has even dared to take an unchaperoned young lady on an excursion. He may cut a comic figure in his attempts to reduce Daisy's ingenuous license to formula, but his mind is open to impressions that the bigoted Mrs. Costello refuses to receive. Since Rome, however, is the city where one behaves as the Romans do, Winterbourne's capacity for freedom and conversely the extent of his commitment to Geneva are tested there.

The Roman phase of the novel ironically dramatizes the disintegration of Winterbourne's somewhat nebulous faith in innocence. In the presence of Daisy's critics, he defends her in a manner which reveals a desire to strengthen his own faltering belief in her. To Mrs. Costello's indictment of the Millers, he timidly responds: "They are very ignorant—very innocent only, and utterly uncivilized." When Mrs. Walker's carriage appears in the Pincian Gardens to rescue Daisy from her "tryst" with Giovanelli, Winterbourne again insists upon the girl's innocence, but as he does so he "reasoned in his own troubled interest." Indeed, before Mrs. Walker's intrusion, he had himself explored all manner of doubts about the "fineness" of Daisy's character. Obviously, then, in his debates with the girl's critics he is confronting, and only temporarily triumphing over, his own sinister suspicions. Basically, he never triumphs at all, for after his colloquy with Mrs. Costello he "checked his impulse to go straightway" to visit Daisy and after his bout with Mrs. Walker he confesses, "I suspect, Mrs. Walker, that you and I have lived too long at Geneva." His evaluation of himself is so accurate that when Mrs. Walker affords him a chance to return to Daisy, and thus to conquer his doubts, he permits mere appearance, "the couple united beneath the parasol," to undermine his insecure faith in innocence.

Winterbourne's desertion of Daisy in the Pincian Gardens (again the garden suggests innocence) characterizes him as incapable of embracing values larger than those of his parochial society. His acuteness in recognizing the cruelties of Mrs. Costello and Mrs. Walker is not vision, and his persistent defense of Daisy is hardly courage. With a finicky, formal taste, he wants his innocence wellbred and prudent, not realizing that innocence is by nature averse to calculation. When Daisy asks him if he thinks she should desert Giovanelli and enter Mrs. Walker's carriage, he advises her to "listen to the voice of civilized society." Sententiously, stiffly—Daisy describes him as having no more "give than a ramrod,"—he lectures her about the "custom of the country" and the "ineptitude of innocence."

His final incapacity to champion innocence is shown when, Mrs. Walker having turned her back on Daisy, he is "greatly touched" by the girl's "blighted grace" but characteristically does nothing more than accuse Mrs. Walker of cruelty. It is no wonder that he soon feels "that holding fast to a belief in [Daisy's] 'innocence' was more and more but a matter of gallantry too fine-spun for use." He admits that "he had helplessly missed her, and now it was too late." Yet, he cannot completely abandon his belief in an innocence that once charmed as well as bewildered him until he discovers Daisy and Giovanelli together in the Colosseum at night. Then, with "final horror" as well as "final relief," he capitulates to Geneva:

> It was as if a sudden clearance had taken place in the ambiguity of the poor girl's appearances and the whole riddle of her contradictions had grown easy to read. She was a young lady about the shades of whose perversity a foolish puzzled gentleman need no longer trouble his head or his heart. That once questionable quantity *had* no shades—it was a mere black little blot.

Winterbourne's quest has thus ended in a typically Puritan repudiation of innocence. Now, giving greater faith to his new discovery of Daisy's "evil nature" than he had ever given to his timid belief in her goodness, he spurns her with a severity as inhumane as Mrs. Costello's and Mrs. Walkers. His last conversation with the girl is a caustic revelation that his nature has shriveled rather than expanded. He counters her assurance that she is not engaged to Giovanelli with a confession of indifference made "with infinite point." "It was a wonder," says James, "how she didn't wince for it." Essentially the slave of a society that worships form and ignores humane considerations, he lifts his hat and leaves her while Daisy cries out, "I don't care . . . whether I have the Roman fever or not!" Even Daisy's death-bed message, reminding him of their trip to Chillon (freedom) and disavowing the rumors concerning Giovanelli and herself, leaves him intransigent and unaffected.

Winterbourne's harsh certainty about Daisy's character convicts him of a fatal coldness of heart fostered by the sin-obsessed society of Geneva. Having failed to respond to Daisy's need for affection, he can gain enlightenment only from without, never from within. Ultimately, he must be convinced of Daisy's purity by the impressionable fortune hunter, Giovanelli. Their short conversation after Daisy's burial brings home to Winterbourne how irremediably the dark old city has played him false. He has seen innocence—the only kind of innocence this complex world affords—and has conspired with Mrs. Costello and Mrs. Walker to kill it. Listening to Giovanelli's elegy to Daisy, he is made to face his own incredible error:

> "She was the most beautiful young lady I ever saw, and the most amiable." To which he added in a moment: "Also—naturally!—the most innocent."
>
> Winterbourne sounded him with hard dry eyes, but presently repeated his words, "The most innocent?"
>
> It came somehow so much too late that our friend could only glare at its having come at all.

Months later Winterbourne reveals to Mrs. Costello that he has brooded over and measured the depth of his mistake. Nevertheless, though he locates the cause of his failure in his "foreign" education, his wisdom culminates in a retreat to Geneva. The quest for innocence has thus merely brought him experience of his own lugubrious inadequacy to transcend—even with the advantage of knowledge—the sham and cruel proprieties of the dark old city.

Carol Ohmann   (essay date 1964)

SOURCE: "*Daisy Miller*: A Study of Changing Intentions," in *American Literature*, Vol. XXXVI, No. 1, March, 1964, pp. 1-11.

[*Ohmann was an American author and educator. In the following essay, she argues that James' attitude toward Daisy shifts over the course of the novella, beginning as a comedy of manners critical of Daisy and ending as a poetical treatment of her innocence.*]

Henry James's most popular nouvelle seems to have owed its initial prominence as much to the controversy it provoked as to the artistry it displayed. **Daisy Miller** caused a bitter dispute in the customarily urbane dining room of Mrs. Lynn Linton; it gave American writers of etiquette a satisfying opportunity to chastise native mothers and daughters (Daisy should have had a chaperone; dear reader, take heed); it brought Henry James himself, while he sat in the confines of a Venetian gondola, a round scolding from a highly articulate woman of the cosmopolitan world. The causes of argument, of course, were the character of James's heroine and the judgment her creator made of her. In late Victorian eyes, Daisy was likely to be either wholly innocent or guilty; James, either all for her or against her.

Today, Daisy's notoriety attends her only in her fictional world. We take her now as one of our familiars; we invoke her, in the assurance that she will come and be recognized, as an American figure both vital and prototypical. Thus Ihab Hassan, for example, joins her in his *Radical Innocence* with Twain's Huck Finn and Crane's Henry Fleming, and notes that all three are young protagonists faced with "the first existential ordeal, crisis, or encounter with experience." Taking Daisy with appreciation and without alarm, we also re-read her character and re-evaluate her moral status. We seem to meet James's sophistication with our own, by agreeing on a mixed interpretation of Daisy: she is literally innocent, but she is also ignorant and incautious. Or, as F. W. Dupee writes [in *Henry James: His Life and Writings*, 1956], and his view meets with considerable agreement elsewhere in our criticism, "[Daisy] does what she likes because she hardly knows what else to do. Her will is at once strong and weak by reason of the very indistinctness of her general aims."

Our near consensus of opinion on **Daisy Miller** seems to me largely correct. I certainly do not want to dismiss it, although I do wish to elaborate upon it and ground it in Jamesian text and method. At the same time, however, I wish to suggest that our very judiciousness is supported by only part of James's nouvelle and that other parts, certain scenes in Rome, really call for franker and more intense alignments of both sympathy and judgment. In a sense, the early and extreme reactions to Daisy were adequate responses to James's creation. Whether black or white, these responses did at least perceive that the final issue of the nouvelle was a matter of total commitment. In short, I think James began writing with one attitude toward his heroine and concluded with a second and different attitude toward her.

I

James begins his nouvelle by building a dramatic, and largely comic, contrast between two ways of responding to experience—a contrast at once suggested by the first-person narrator in the opening paragraph:

in the month of June, American travellers are extremely numerous; it may be said, indeed, that Vevey assumes at this period some of the characteristics of an American watering-place. There are sights and sounds which evoke a vision, an echo, of Newport and Saratoga. There is a flitting hither and thither of "stylish" young girls, a rustling of muslin flounces, a rattle of dance-music in the morning hours, a sound of high-pitched voices at all times. You receive an impression of these things at the excellent inn of the "Trois Couronnes," and are transported in fancy to the Ocean House or to Congress Hall. But at the "Trois Couronnes," it must be added, there are other features that are much at variance with these suggestions: neat German waiters, who look like secretaries of legation; Russian princesses sitting in the garden; little Polish boys walking about, held by the hand, with their governors. . . .

The carefree exuberance, the noisy frivolity, of the American visitors is set against the quiet formality and restraint of the Europeans, who hold even their little boys in check.

James repeats his opening contrast in virtually every piece of dialogue that follows. While the hero Frederick Winterbourne is an American by birth, he has lived "a long time" in Geneva, the "little metropolis of Calvinism," the "dark old city at the other end of the lake." And Winterbourne's mode of speech suggests the extent to which he has become Europeanized. In Vevey, he finds himself "at liberty," on a little holiday from Geneva. He takes a daring plunge into experience; with no more than a very casual introduction from her little brother Randolph, he speaks to Daisy Miller. "This little boy and I have made acquaintance," he says. Daisy glances at him and turns away. In a moment, Winterbourne tries again. "Are you going to Italy?" he asks. Daisy says, "Yes, sir," and no more. "Are you—a—going over the Simplon?" Winterbourne continues. Shortly afterwards, as Daisy continues to ignore him, Winterbourne "risk[s] an observation upon the beauty of the view." Winterbourne's feelings of "liberty" and of "risk" and, later, of "audacity" become ironic in conjunction with his speech. For all his holiday spirit, his language is studiously formal, his opening conversational bits, unimaginative and conventional.

In opposition to Winterbourne, Daisy often speaks in the language of extravagant, if unoriginal, enthusiasm. In her opinion, Europe is "perfectly sweet. . . . She had ever so many intimate friends that had been there ever so many times. . . . she had had ever so many dresses and things from Paris." She wants to go to the Castle of Chillon "dreadfully." Or, unlike Winterbourne again, Daisy speaks in an idiom that is homely and matter-of-fact. When Winterbourne asks, "Your brother is not interested in ancient monuments?" she rejects his formal phrasing and says simply, "[Randolph] says he don't care much about old castles."

For all their differences, Winterbourne and Daisy may still be capable of *rapprochement*. Toward the end of Part I, Daisy teases Winterbourne out of his formality and makes him, for a moment, speak her language—makes him, for a moment, express himself enthusiastically. "Do, then, let me give you a row," Winterbourne says. Daisy replies, "It's quite lovely, the way you say that!" And Winterbourne answers, "It will be still more lovely to do it." Winterbourne is, and Daisy notices this, a "mixture." He is not quite, or at least not yet, thoroughly Europeanized.

Winterbourne may be influenced by Daisy, but he is also subject to the sway of his aunt. Mrs. Costello is a woman of few words. When Winterbourne asks her, in Vevey, if she has observed Mrs. Miller, Daisy, and Randolph, she raps out the reply: "Oh, yes, I have observed them. Seen them—heard them—and kept out of their way." Epigram is Mrs. Costello's favorite way of speaking and perfectly expresses the inflexibility of her approach to experience. Her principles of value have long been set—she need only apply them. Whatever is vulgar, whatever is improper, she condemns out of hand, and shuns. Sage and spokesman of the American set abroad, she guards a *style* of life and reveals its furthest limit of permissible emotion by exclaiming, "I am an old woman, but I am not too old—thank Heaven—to be shocked!"

The opening, then, and indeed the chief focus of *Daisy Miller* is a comic portrayal of different ways of living, different manners. In the social settings with which they are identified, in the ways they speak, as well as in what they say, the various characters range themselves along an axis that runs from the natural to the cultivated, from the exuberant to the restrained.

In the conflict between Geneva and Schenectady, there is, I think, little doubt of the direction James gives our sympathies. Presented with the collision between the artificial and the natural, the restrained and the free, we side emotionally with Daisy. We sympathize with Winterbourne, too, to the extent that he seems capable of coming "alive" and to the extent that he speaks up in favor of Daisy to Mrs. Costello in Vevey and, later, in Rome, to Mrs. Costello and also to Mrs. Walker, another American who has lived in Geneva. For the rest, however, our emotional alliance with Winterbourne is disturbed or interrupted by his Genevan penchant for criticism. At his first meeting with Daisy in Vevey, Winterbourne mentally accuses her—"very forgivingly—of a want of finish." But when Daisy blithely announces that she has always had "a great deal of gentlemen's society," Winterbourne is more alarmed. He wonders if he must accuse her of "actual or potential *inconduite,* as they said at Geneva."

In Rome, although Winterbourne defends Daisy to the American colony publicly, he is privately, increasingly shocked by her friendship with the "third-rate" Italian Giovanelli. Her walks with Giovanelli, her rides with Giovanelli, her tête-à-têtes in her own drawing room with Giovanelli—all worry Winterbourne. He imitates Mrs. Walker in scolding Daisy. And so he removes himself farther and farther from her. When he finally comes upon her with Giovanelli in the Colosseum at night, he thinks that she has certainly compromised herself. And he is relieved. For his personal feelings for Daisy have gradually been overwhelmed by his intellectual involvement in the problem of Daisy. He is relieved and "exhilarated" that the "riddle" has suddenly become "easy to read." He promptly judges Daisy by her manners—as Mrs. Costello and Mrs. Walker have already done—and condemns her. "What a clever little reprobate she was," he thinks, "and how smartly she played at injured innocence!"

He learns otherwise too late. He knows, for a moment at the end of the nouvelle, that he has made a mistake; he knows he has wronged Daisy because he has stayed too long abroad, has become too rigid in his values. Yet his knowledge does not change him. The authorial voice concludes the tale by mocking Winterbourne's return to the narrow social code of restraint and prejudice:

> Nevertheless, he went back to live at Geneva, whence there continue to come the most contradictory accounts of his motives of sojourn: a report that he is "studying" hard—an intimation that he is much interested in a very clever foreign lady.

Like so many Jamesian heroes, Winterbourne has lost the capacity for love, and he has lost the opportunity to come to life.

As Winterbourne judges Daisy, judges her unfairly, and completes her expulsion from the American set in Rome, our sympathy for her naturally increases. But I think James does not—save through a certain pattern of symbolic imagery to which I wish to return in a moment—guide us to any such simple intellectual alignment with his American heroine.

Daisy's sensibility has very obvious limitations, limitations we hear very clearly in the statement that Europe is "perfectly sweet." Daisy is more intensely alive than anyone else we meet in Vevey or Rome. But James hints from time to time at a possible richness of aesthetic experience that is beyond Daisy's capabilities—a richness that would include an appreciation of the artificial, or the cultivated, not as it is represented by the mores of Geneva but by the "splendid chants and organ-tones" of St. Peter's and by the "superb portrait of Innocent X. by Velasquez."

And Daisy has other limitations. The members of the American community abroad are very much aware of one another's existence. True, they use their mutual awareness to no good purpose—they are watchbirds watching one another for vulgarity, for any possible lapse from propriety. But Daisy's social awareness is so primitive as scarcely to exist. At Rome, in the Colosseum, Winterbourne's imagination cannot stretch to include the notion of unsophisticated innocence. But neither can Daisy's imagination stretch to include the idea that manners really matter to those who practice them. She never realizes the consternation she causes in Rome. "I don't believe it," she says to Winterbourne. "They are only pretending to be shocked." Her blindness to the nature of the American colony is equalled by her blindness to Winterbourne and Giovanelli as individuals. While Winterbourne fails to "read" her "riddle" rightly, she fails to "read" his. She feels his disapproval in Rome, but she is not aware of his affection for her. Neither does she reveal any adequate perception of her impact on Giovanelli. To Daisy, going about with Mr. Giovanelli is very good fun. Giovanelli's feelings, we learn at the end, have been much more seriously involved.

James therefore hands a really favorable intellectual judgment to neither Geneva nor Schenectady. He gives his full approval neither to the manners of restraint nor to those of freedom. His irony touches Daisy as well as the Europeanized Americans. And the accumulation of his specific ironies hints at an ideal of freedom and of vitality and also of aesthetic and social awareness that is nowhere fully exemplified in the nouvelle. To be from Schenectady, to be from the new world, is to be free from the restrictions of Geneva. But merely to be free is not enough.

II

Such, then, in some detail are the Jamesian dynamics of social contrast that give us our prudent estimate of Daisy—a heroine innocent and exuberant and free, but also unreflective and insensible of the world around her. But, as I have already suggested, this estimate does not receive support from the whole of the story. To begin with, prudence leads straight to the conclusion that Daisy dies as a result of social indiscretion. What began as a comedy of manners, ends in the pathos, if not the tragedy, of a lonely Roman deathbed and burial. And there is, it seems to me, in this progress from the Trois Couronnes to the Protestant cemetery a change in tone so pronounced, a breach in cause and appropriate effect so wide, as to amount to a puzzling disruption of James's artistry.

To be sure, James tries to make Daisy's death inevitable, and to make it so within, as it were, the boundaries of his comedy of manners. Early in Part II, at Mrs. Walker's late one afternoon, Daisy remarks that she is going to take a walk on the Pincian Hill with Giovanelli. Mrs. Walker tries to dissuade her from the impropriety—a walk at such a time in such a place with such a dubious companion. It isn't "safe," Mrs. Walker says, while Mrs. Miller adds, "You'll get the fever as sure as you live." And Daisy herself, as she walks towards the Pincian Hill with Winterbourne, alludes to the fever: "We are going to stay [in Rome] all winter—if we don't die of the fever; and I guess we'll stay then."

With these remarks, James foreshadows Daisy's death, and links her fate with her carelessness of the manners of restraint. But these preparations do not successfully solve his difficulties either of tone or of cause and effect. They croak disaster far too loudly, far too obviously, and, still, the punishment no more fits the crime than it does in a typical cautionary tale.

In Part I, James has already used the words "natural," "uncultivated," and "fresh" to describe his heroine. And in the choice of the name, Daisy, he may have suggested her simplicity and her spontaneous beauty. In Part II, just after the opening scene at Mrs. Walker's, James follows up the implications of these epithets—"natural," "uncultivated," "fresh"—and of the name Daisy and gives them a somewhat different significance.

In Rome, after Winterbourne has been taken up in Mrs. Walker's carriage and set down again, he sees Daisy with Giovanelli in a natural setting—a setting that James describes in brilliant and expansive terms. Daisy and Giovanelli are in the Pincian Garden overlooking the Villa Borghese:

> They evidently saw no one; they were too deeply occupied with each other. When they reached the low garden-wall they stood a moment looking off at the great flat-topped pine-clusters of the Villa Borghese; then Giovanelli seated himself, familiarly, upon the broad ledge of the wall. The western sun in the opposite sky sent out a brilliant shaft through a couple of cloudbars, whereupon Daisy's companion took her parasol out of her hands and opened it. She came a little nearer and he held the parasol over her; then, still holding it, he let it rest upon her shoulder, so that both of their heads were hidden from Winterbourne. This young man lingered a moment, then he began to walk. But he walked—not towards the couple with the parasol; towards the residence of his aunt, Mrs. Costello.

This scene links Daisy with the natural world, and links her with that world more closely than any other scene James has so far given us. And it suggests that the distance between Winterbourne and Daisy is greater even than the distance that separates artificial from natural manners, greater than the distance that separates restraint from free self-expression.

That suggestion becomes a certainty on the Palatine Hill:

> A few days after his brief interview with her mother, [Winterbourne] encountered her in that beautiful abode of flowering desolation known as the Palace of the Cæsars. The early Roman spring had filled the air with bloom and perfume, and the rugged surface of the Palatine was muffled with tender verdure. Daisy was strolling along the top of one of those great mounds of ruin that are embanked with mossy marble and paved with monumental inscriptions. It seemed to him that Rome had never been so lovely as just then. He stood looking off at the enchanting harmony of line and colour that remotely encircles the city, inhaling the softly humid odours and feeling the freshness of the year and the antiquity of the place reaffirm themselves in mysterious interfusion. It seemed to him also that Daisy had never looked so pretty; but this had been an observation of his whenever he met her. Giovanelli was at her side, and Giovanelli, too, wore an aspect of even unwonted brilliancy.

Here Daisy is not identified with a particular society, as she was with the gay American visitors by the lakeside and in the garden of Vevey, but simply and wholly with the natural world, which has its own eternal and beautiful rhythms. Birth is followed by death, and death is followed again by birth. And the beauty of the natural world—the world to which Daisy belongs—is supreme. Rome has never been so lovely as when its relics are "muffled with tender verdure." The monuments of men, the achievements of civilization, are most beautiful when they are swept again into the round of natural process. At the moment, Daisy seems to share the natural world, as she did in the Pincian Garden, with Giovanelli. But at the end of the nouvelle that "subtle Roman" is quite aware of Daisy's distance even from himself. He knew, beforehand, that the Colosseum would not be for him, as it was for Daisy, a "fatal place." "For myself," he says to Winterbourne, "I had no fear."

Once Daisy is identified with the world of nature, we see that she is subject to its laws of process. Her very beauty becomes a reminder of her mortality. So the scene on the Palatine (unlike the scenes at Mrs. Walker's and on the way to the Pincian Hill) does prepare us effectively for Daisy's burial in the Protestant cemetery; it does convince us that her death is inevitable.

III

Yet James's use of his symbolic natural imagery is at once a gain and a loss. If it solves, almost at the eleventh hour, certain difficulties of tone and of cause and effect regarding Daisy's death, it also leaves us with some permanent breaks in the nouvelle's unity of structure. If Daisy is translated or transfigured in the end into a purely natural ideal of beauty and vitality and innocence, then what relevance has that ideal to Schenectady, or to Geneva? If Daisy's death is "fated," does it matter at all what Winterbourne does? And what sort of agent is Giovanelli? Or can we even call him an agent? Hasn't James made inconsequent by the end of his tale, the dramatic conflict—the conflict between two kinds of manners—that he set up in the beginning? The contrast in manners seems to suggest, to hold up as an ideal, a certain way of responding to life. This ideal would combine freedom and vitality with a sophisticated awareness of culture and society. Yet the symbolic imagery of the Palatine Hill seems to elevate natural freedom and vitality and innocence into an ideal so moving, so compelling, that all other considerations pale beside it. Or, if I rephrase my questions about Schenectady and Geneva, Winterbourne and Giovanelli, and answer them in terms of James's creative experience, they come to this: James began writing *Daisy Miller* as a comedy of manners and finished it as a symbolic presentation of a metaphysical ideal. He began by criticizing Daisy in certain ways and ended simply by praising her.

James's friend in the Venetian gondola was, at least in a general way, aware of his transfiguration of Daisy. And James records her opinion—in effect her scolding—in his preface to the New York edition of his nouvelle:

> "[Daisy's] only fault is touchingly to have transmuted so sorry a type [as the uncultivated American girl] and to have, by a poetic artifice, not only led our judgement of it astray, but made *any* judgement quite impossible. . . . You *know* you quite falsified, by the turn you gave it, the thing you had begun with having in mind, the thing you had had, to satiety, the chance of 'observing': your pretty perversion of it, or your unprincipled mystification of our sense of it, does it really too much honour. . . ."

James virtually accepts his friend's criticism. Elsewhere in the preface, speaking in his own voice, he says that, when his nouvelle was first published, the full title ran: *Daisy Miller: A Study*. Now, for the New York edition, he subtracts the apposition "in view of the simple truth, which ought from the first to have been apparent to me, that my little exhibition is made to no degree whatever in critical but, quite inordinately and extravagantly, in poetical

terms." It appears, then, that James's natural symbolic imagery and his translation of his heroine into a metaphysical figure were unconscious developments. Only after he wrote his nouvelle did James himself discover and acknowledge his own "poetical terms."

Once he had discovered those "terms," he chose to emphasize them, not only in his preface, but also in his text for the New York edition. Viola R. Dunbar has already noted that in a number of places in the final version of *Daisy Miller* James eases his criticism of Daisy and bears down more heavily on the Europeanized Americans. Briefly, he places more stress on Daisy's beauty and innocence, and he associates her more frequently with nature, and more pointedly. At the same time, he gives more asperity to the judgments of Winterbourne and Mrs. Costello and Mrs. Walker. And it is interesting to note as well that James inserts very early in Part I at least two suggestions of Daisy's final transfiguration. She looks at Winterbourne "with lovely remoteness"; she strikes him as a "charming apparition."

These revisions, though, are occasional and do not essentially change *Daisy Miller*. In the New York edition, as well as in the original version, it remains a narrative of imperfect unity, a work that shows unmistakable signs of shifting authorial intention and attitude. And yet, as I have already suggested, James's idealization of his heroine is a matter of gain as well as loss. It resolves certain problems about Daisy's death. More importantly, it adds to the emotional appeal of the second part of the nouvelle. In other words, even if James may have lost something in intellectual consistency by introducing the poetry of Daisy, even if he does to some extent throw away his original comedy of manners, his symbolic natural imagery nonetheless intensifies our response to his story. Again, I return to the articulate lady in the gondola: "As anything charming or touching always to that extent justifies itself, we after a fashion forgive and understand you."

The ideal of a purely natural vitality and freedom and innocence is a strongly, and persistently, attractive ideal. It is attractive, especially, to American writers, and in one variation or another we have, of course, met it before—in Melville, for example, in Hawthorne, in Fitzgerald, in Faulkner. We take James's Daisy Miller, rightly, as prototypical. My purpose here has been to suggest that her relationship to certain major areas of our American experience is even more various than we may previously have thought.

John H. Randall III   (essay date 1965)

SOURCE: "The Genteel Reader and *Daisy Miller*," in *American Quarterly*, Vol. XVII, No. 3, Fall, 1965, pp. 568-81.

[*In the following essay, Randall maintains that* Daisy Miller *satirizes the mores and manners of late nineteenth-century American society.*]

In an age in which one president is criticized for having a Boston-Harvard accent and another has it held against him that his speech is that of the Pedernales Valley, the concern with manners is far from dead. Manners may be an expression of nationality, or section, as well as morals; and many are content to judge the person by them alone. In a stable society such as once might have been presumed to exist, this may have been possible. But society has not been stable in America or Europe for quite some time. Whenever two people meet, there is apt to be a comedy of misunderstanding, and when people from different cultures meet, the chances are considerably multiplied. Below manners lies personality, which must be reached somehow; we ignore it at peril to our civilization. But the chances for misinterpretation are great, and the result is not always comic. So it might be instructive to look at a classic literary example of misjudging character through manners: the blunders of the ill-starred Winterbourne in trying to understand the elusive Daisy Miller.

In all fairness to Frederick Winterbourne, we must admit that the difficulty in judging character through manners is one of which he is not exactly unaware. When the American colony at Rome ostracizes Daisy and he is struggling to divine her attitude toward their treatment of her, he can come to no certain conclusion: ". . . he was vexed at his want of instinctive certitude as to how far her eccentricities were generic, national, and how far they were personal." This vexation was unfortunately not shared by contemporary reviewers of *Daisy Miller,* who wrote as if they knew exactly what they thought of her. Although emphatic, their opinions did not always coincide; they include the assertion that Daisy was bad-mannered and had more money than moderation (New York *Times*), that Daisy and her mother were "impossible" eccentrics (*Harper's*), that American young ladies abroad are usually dreadful (*The Nation*), and, from the other side of the Atlantic, that Daisy was a delightful exotic, while Americans abroad in general are censorious and dreary snobs (*Blackwood's*). True, on our own shores Daisy had a few defenders, notably William Dean Howells, but in general Yankees—or at least reviewing Yankees—were furious with her. This may be a sign of continuing American sensitivity about the behavior of other Americans abroad, but the whole problem of the difficulty in judging character through manners was left untouched. Subsequent critics have recognized the difficulty other characters in the tale have in judging Daisy, but more often than not have gone on to give their own opinions of her, which vary from praise to blame in a manner not unlike that of the early reviewers, although they are not so vehement about it.

The cause lies in James' method of presentation. Throughout the story Daisy is seen from the outside, we perceive her words and actions through the eyes of Winterbourne, who is not a very effectual observer. His effectuality is hampered by his being a servitor of Mrs. Grundy—or of Mrs. Costello, as she is called in the story. It is noteworthy that Mrs. Grundy, or Mrs. Costello, is an American, not a European; that Winterbourne, although protesting faintly, is subservient to her; and that his final betrayal of Daisy, when he lets her know in the Colosseum scene that he thinks her a bad girl, occurs when he gives in to Mrs. Grundy. He is entirely too much in awe of public opinion and hesitates to judge or act for himself. Daisy, on the

other hand, is all too independent in judgment and action. Both come to a bad end, one in the Colosseum, the other in James' sarcastic little final paragraph. What are we to think of this? Does public opinion always get in the way of evaluating others? Is true judgment through manners possible?

It may be helpful to formulate certain attitudes and pose certain questions about them, the answers to which will depend on our own view of life:

1) Daisy is so unaware of or defiant toward form that she goes her own way, not caring what Rome thinks of her or what the Americans think of her. The question is, should she care?

2) She is interested in Winterbourne and can't find any way to reach him: he's too chilly. The question: does she try hard enough?

3) Much of the story concerns itself with attitudes toward gossip and rumor and the tremendous pressure exerted by a not-too-well-informed public opinion. Should one give it too much weight?

4) Below all this lies the problem of whether or not we can judge people. Can we even understand them, especially when they come from or interact with people of different cultures; or are they finally inscrutable? We know what Joseph Conrad thinks; can we tell what Henry James thinks in this story?

I submit that the answers each of us gives to these questions will depend on our attitudes toward spontaneity and formality, feminine and masculine courtship roles, individualism and group-centeredness, and finally the mystery of human communion and love. Since Henry James has presented Daisy purely from the outside, leaving us to draw what conclusions our temperaments and training incline us to, it strikes me that he has given us a double-jointed story which admits of more than one interpretation of the characters, depending, as I have said, on our own view of life.

This may account for the variety of responses to the story on the part of contemporary reviewers, but where does James stand? Can we tell? I think we can. I think he has written a very ironic tale in which social class and the snobbishness that goes with it brings out the worst in everybody, except Mr. Giovanelli. The preoccupation with manners is so great that the characters have forgotten the original purpose of manners: to make social intercourse easier and more pleasant. Everyone except Mr. Giovanelli is afraid to be simple and direct; their sophistication undercuts their humanity, and even Mr. Giovanelli's entanglement with the class system and incomprehension of American manners interferes with his judgment when he lets Daisy persuade him to take her to the Colosseum by moonlight, which he clearly should not have done.

Here a distinction may be in order. The eyes of all the characters may be fixed upon Daisy, but the focus of the story is not on Daisy's fate, which is somewhat underplayed, but on the fate of those who observe and respond to her. Of these, Mrs. Costello and, to a lesser degree, Mrs. Walker, may be taken as exemplifying in a transplanted setting all that has been said by De Tocqueville and John Stuart Mill about the tyranny of public opinion in a democracy. They are sorry snobs, and that is all there is to it. The cases of Mr. Giovanelli and Winterbourne are more instructive, since, as we shall see, the Roman moves toward comprehension of Daisy's character, the American away from it. It is the American—who is traditionally supposed to judge people as individuals, free from class bias—who makes a dreadful blunder, and the European—who is traditionally supposed to see everything in terms of manners and social class—who comes to a true understanding of Daisy's worth.

During most of the story the question of Daisy's character is up in the air, and the other characters are as much at sea concerning her as the reader is. (No doubt this is the result of a deliberate effort on James' part.) We are not shown the workings of Mr. Giovanelli's mind, but we are shown Winterbourne's:

> Was she simply a pretty girl from New York State—were they all like that, the pretty girls who had a good deal of gentlemen's society? Or was she also a designing, an audacious, an unscrupulous young person? Winterbourne had lost his instinct in this matter, and his reason could not help him.
>
> . . . . .
>
> And then he came back to the question whether this was, in fact, a nice girl. Would a nice girl—even allowing for her being a little American flirt—make a rendezvous with a presumably low-lived foreigner? . . . It was impossible to regard her as a perfectly well-conducted young lady; she was wanting in a certain indispensable delicacy. . . . But Daisy, on this occasion, continued to present herself as an inscrutable combination of audacity and innocence.

Since none of the characters knows what Daisy is like until after she is dead, it might be interesting to speculate about her character in accordance with what little James has told us about her. In fact, we might draw up two contrasting interpretations of her, labeled "Daisy *pro*" and "Daisy *con*," depending on our attitude toward that series of paired opposites I mentioned a few paragraphs back. If we do so, the result might be something like this:

1) Daisy *pro*: Assuming that Daisy was serious in the message she left for Winterbourne on her death bed and that, in his words, "she would have appreciated one's esteem," she has had a hard time with a man of Winterbourne's frostiness; he is hardly a knight on a white charger. Not only does he let gossip rule him, he uses it as an excuse to mask his own hesitancies and nonassertiveness. On this level, Daisy and Winterbourne are prototypes of a long series of noncouples in American fiction and prefigure the theme of the headstrong girl and the ineffectual man. (They certainly prefigure Lily Bart and Lawrence Selden in Edith Wharton's *House of Mirth*.) But the headstrong girl is not at all happy that the man is ineffectual. She keeps waiting for him to show some interest in her; he does nothing. He not only believes but is glad to believe the gossip about her, jumps to a quick conclusion about her in the Colosseum, thinks she is a bad girl and decides he's been

wasting his time. She's friendly, she's playful, she tries to let him know she's interested in him, but all to no avail; he's just dead. He's Winter-born, and Winter, as Northrop Frye tells us, is the time for irony and satire.

If this interpretation is correct, Daisy, piqued by Winterbourne's unwillingness to commit himself, is stung into spending most of her time with Mr. Giovanelli. Winterbourne has refused to stand up for her when she is criticized by the American colony, he has declined to commit himself when she twits him by pretending to be engaged to Mr. Giovanelli; Daisy might well echo the wail of Liza Doolittle in *My Fair Lady*: "Words, words, words!" And so she visits the Colosseum by moonlight with Mr. Giovanelli. Why does she risk the *perniciosa* by going to the Colosseum at night? I suppose because she is young, because she doesn't believe anything seriously bad will ever happen to her ("I never was sick, and I don't mean to be! . . . I don't look like much, but I'm healthy!") William Hazlitt began a famous essay by declaring that "No young man believes that he shall ever die." The same holds true for Daisy Miller, and it might be said that, insofar as she is a type, no young American girl believes she will ever be compromised.

2) Daisy *con*: According to this interpretation, Daisy is a "pretty American flirt" who is not really interested in Winterbourne at all, but merely in demonstrating her own power over men. She comes to dominate, and ends up by becoming a victim. She is self-centered, headstrong, petulant and not really interested in anyone but herself. She wants everyone to dance attendance on her, she wants always to remain uninvolved and dominant; with her, it is all taking and no giving. Her refusal to accept criticism and her attitude that "nobody tells *me* what to do" render her insufferable. Although she left a last message for Winterbourne, if she had recovered from her fever, she would have changed her mind about him. She has been spoiled by an ineffectual mother and an absentee father who is busy piling up dollars in Schenectady ("My father's rich, you bet!"); his deputy is her little brother Randolph, who represents in miniature the unpleasant bragging American tourist who goes through Europe, cigar in hand ("I can't get any candy here—any American candy. American candy is the best candy"). Daisy refuses to take advice from anybody, man or woman; and when Winterbourne tries to keep her from meeting with Mr. Giovanelli and insists he will stay with her when she persists, she thinks he is trying to manipulate her, when he is only trying to help her ("I have never allowed a gentleman to dictate to me, or interfere with anything I do"). But she herself is not above manipulating men by means of her sex appeal; she is not so much innocent as selfish. Daisy uses sex appeal to attack the class system, which is hurting her; she sets up an oscillation which makes women strike at her through the class system; then she hits back at them through her power over men. Although she may not have social standing, Daisy is a plutocrat as well as a beauty, and she well knows the power of these two things. It is even possible to give an economic interpretation of Daisy Miller, especially after reading Thorstein Veblen on women as status symbols. It would run somewhat like this: the reason Daisy blushes and is offended when Win-

terbourne suggests she may be in love with Giovanelli is that a young American woman is encouraged to regard her marriageability as her market value and use it as a bargaining counter. This involves not admitting that she cares for a man until he has spoken for her and has been accepted, i.e., until her market value has been wisely invested in a blue-chip engagement and she herself is safe. In suggesting that Daisy may be in love with Giovanelli, Winterbourne is driving her market value down and putting her in the position of appearing to allow herself to be hypothecated by Giovanelli. This view shows Daisy as a business woman and sees her motives as a mixture of commercial bargain-hunting and sexual prudery. Fantastic as it sounds, this view may have something to recommend it; it's clearly not the whole story, but it may be there.

It now appears that we have been reading two different stories, one entitled "Poor Daisy Miller, or, A Good Man Is Hard to Find" (Henry James himself inclined to this view, both in his letter to Mrs. Linton and in his preface to the New York edition of the tale), and the other, "Cold-Hearted Daisy, or, The Selfish Young American Flirt." The latter will appeal to any man in a misogynistic mood; I myself think the story is double-jointed and there is truth in both titles. But perhaps there is a third story we haven't read yet; Henry James may be counting on the genteel reader's stock responses. It was common for European authors addressing a European audience to begin a story with a stereotype of an unattractive American, and then gradually present the character in a more and more favorable light. An example contemporary with James was "Ouida" (Miss de la Ramée), of whom Elizabeth Hoxie writes:

> In *Moths* (1880), . . . it was easy to take offense at Miss de la Ramée's picture of Fuschia Leach, the "wild little republican" with the "high, thin voice," who said "cunning" for "nice" and rested "her feet on an ottoman, her hands behind her head, a rosebud in her mouth, and a male group around her." Nevertheless, Fuschia proved popular because of her high spirits ("everybody delights her and everything is fun to her").

In such stories the author plays a trick on his audience by eliciting a stock response from it. The reader, presented with a character at whom people jeer, thinks he understands the story; he feels sophisticated but is only responding to a stereotype. Then as the character is more fully presented in more human terms, he does an about-face as he gradually perceives he has been taken in. James does the same thing in **Daisy Miller,** only in this case the trick is perpetrated on an American audience responding to the story of an American abroad. The reader first sees Daisy through the eyes of Randolph, her awful little brother, who thinks all things American are best except his sister. Then Daisy meets Winterbourne, without a formal introduction, through the same brother; she "picks him up" and wangles an invitation from him to visit the castle of Chillon. The reader, if he is sufficiently genteel and places a high enough value on formal manners, winces at this image of his countrywoman abroad; snobbery and prudery combine to make him agree with Winterbourne that

Daisy must be either a sexual adventuress or else a dreadfully vulgar parvenu. Then he encounters Mrs. Costello and has all his convictions as to Daisy's vulgarity thrown back in his face, and this from a woman who is as narrow, rigid and heartless a snob as one is likely to meet among Americans in Europe. The reader becomes uneasy; this is not quite the company he wanted to keep. Then he begins to criticize Winterbourne for keeping and listening to such company. He finds that the Americans in Rome, who are the first group he is likely to identify with, are actually the last people whose judgment is to be trusted; it is the poor despised Mr. Giovanelli, upon whom they all look down, who has the final and kindest word on the case. The genteel reader's own snobbery is exposed to him and revealed as the ridiculous and destructive thing it is.

From this point of view the story is about the shameful waste which can result, not only from snobbery, but from sheer ineffectuality and blindness, as James ticks off first the snobs, Mrs. Costello and Mrs. Walker, then Mr. Giovanelli, who is kind but ineffectual, then Winterbourne, who is neither effectual nor kind. So the true title of the story we have been reading may turn out to be "Only a Woman, or Daisy Revealed: Stereotypes Are We All Until We Get to Know Each Other if It's Not Too Late." For if the genteel reader has been responding to stereotypes, so have the characters in the novella. Mrs. Costello and Mrs. Walker obviously are; more interesting are the responses of Mr. Giovanelli and Winterbourne. We are not told much about Mr. Giovanelli; he may indeed have started out as a fortune hunter (James tells us "Winterbourne afterwards learned that he had practiced the idiom [English] on a great many American heiresses"), but then again he may merely be a young man out to have a good time in life, in short, a male Roman counterpart of Daisy Miller. Like her, he is good looking and attractive; like her he is looked down upon by those who are confident they can judge people through manners; as in her case, when the problem of sincerity *versus* opportunism comes up, the question is decided against him. His one real blunder, which has deadly consequences for Daisy, is allowing her to persuade him to take her to the Colosseum by moonlight; and this couldn't possibly be attributed to self-seeking. Apparently this arises from an incomprehension of alien manners (he thinks American girls must be allowed to make all their own decisions) and an excess of gallantry to someone above him on the social scale (he acquiesces in everything the lady wishes to do, even when for health's sake he should have taken a firm hand). For this he pays heavily. There is every reason to believe that he means it when he tells Winterbourne after the burial, "She was the most beautiful young lady I ever saw, and the most amiable. . . . And she was the most innocent." Being in awe of her, he had thought she knew what she could and could not do (including on the level of physical survival); when she falls ill and dies, he realizes that she was just as fallible as poor ordinary European mortals after all.

Mr. Giovanelli may begin in incomprehension of Daisy, but he ends as the only character who realizes she is to be treated with consideration and kindness; and this may be as close to the "truth" about a human being as we are likely to get. With Winterbourne the case is otherwise. He, like the other Americans in the tale, sees life through the spectacles of the picturesque. What he responds to is a guidebook view of life, not life itself. Since this is the way in which genteel American readers of the 1870s may be presumed to have responded to stories about Europe, it should have been instructive to them to observe Winterbourne's fate. For most of the nineteenth century, the ability to respond aesthetically to the beauties of nature and of European antiquities was supposed to be a class trait. If one were a member of the upper classes, one might have it; if not, one did not. We see this in the stories and sketches of Washington Irving; we see it in the genteel heroes and heroines of Fenimore Cooper. It is still present in Henry James, especially the early James of the 1870s, although by that time he was already beginning to see his way around it and satirize it. What had begun as a fresh and original way of perceiving the irregular beauties of nature, untrammeled by neoclassical symmetry, had rigidified by James' time into a stock response and a badge of class status; part of the snobbery of the American characters in the story is their stereotyped response to the picturesque. That this stock response can put blinders on one person and give him a distorted guidebook view of life is dramatized in the Colosseum scene, where Winterbourne, by seeing everything through the spectacles of the picturesque, actually prevents himself from seeing what is really going on.

The scene begins with Winterbourne's taking an evening walk to the Colosseum, where he starts to quote Byron's famous lines from "Manfred" just before he sees Mr. Giovanelli and Daisy, who see him first. The moonlit scene before him and the lines from Byron induce a romantic revery which puts him in the worst possible frame of mind to cope with the action-demanding realities which suddenly thrust themselves on him. Here the picturesque is one of the elements which help produce the catastrophe, since it leads him to a mood of unearned exultation followed by a precipitous drop from the sublime to the bathetic. As Daisy calls out to him, he is once again involved with his old fear of women and his inability to assert or commit himself, which he evades by hiding behind the skirts of Mrs. Grundy. James writes:

> When, on his return from the villa . . . Winterbourne approached the dusky circle of the Colosseum, it occurred to him, as a lover of the picturesque, that the interior, in the pale moonshine, would be well worth a glance. . . . Then he passed in, among the cavernous shadows of the great structure, and emerged upon the clear and silent arena. The place had never seemed to him more impressive. One-half of the gigantic circus was in deep shade; the other was sleeping in the luminous dusk.

This is just what every genteel traveler in Europe was supposed to feel. The reader is lulled into thinking he is listening to someone who is *au courant* and knowledgeable. But Winterbourne has seen nothing new or fresh or revealing in the scene; it is a stock response. As he stands there he begins to murmur Byron's famous lines from "Manfred" (III, iv, 1-45) which begin:

> The stars are forth, the moon above the tops
> Of the snow-shining mountains.—Beautiful!
> I linger yet with Nature, for the Night
> Hath been to me a more familiar face
> Than that of man . . .

Winterbourne clearly feels more at home with the moonlit scene than with the man and woman he is so unexpectedly to meet. The lines continue:

> I do remember me, that in my youth,
> When I was wandering—upon such a night
> I stood within the Coliseum's wall. . . .

and go on in a vein of sentimental musing on the ruins of time which induces in Manfred a pleasant melancholy. He continues:

> And thou didst shine, thou rolling moon, upon
> All this, and cast a wide and tender light . . .
> Leaving that beautiful which still was so,
> And making that which was not, *till the place*
> *Became religion,* and the heart ran o'er
> With silent worship of the great of old,—
> *The dead but sceptred sovereigns, who still rule*
> *Our spirits from their urns.*
>
>   [Italics mine]

We do not know how far Winterbourne has a chance to proceed in the soliloquy before seeing Daisy, but the mention of "Byron's famous lines" should have been enough to call up the whole quotation for the nineteenth-century reader. It is plain that the dead still rule the spirit of Winterbourne; the entire passage as used in this context is an implicit criticism and indictment of this snobbish and ineffectual young man. For, as he walks to the middle of the arena, he sees on the steps which form the base of the great cross in the center a man and a woman, whom from their conversation he recognizes to be Mr. Giovanelli and Daisy. Then at last he is able to make up his mind about her: "She was a young lady whom a gentleman need no longer be at pains to respect." Not only does he come to an erroneous and damning conclusion about her; he is glad to do so, feeling that he has at last been taken off the hook and is no longer under the necessity of committing himself. The reason he does not immediately advance toward her is not the fear that his judgment may be wrong but "the sense of the danger of appearing unbecomingly exhilarated by this sudden revulsion from cautious criticism." When Daisy calls out to him that he is snubbing her, he does try to save her from malaria, but he hurts her by laughing at her and informing her of his brutal judgment that he thinks her a bad girl:

> Then, noticing Winterbourne's silence, she asked him why he didn't speak. He made no answer; he only began to laugh . . . "*Did* you believe I was engaged the other day?" she asked.
>
> "It doesn't matter what I believed the other day," said Winterbourne, still laughing.
>
> "Well, what do you believe now?"
>
> "I believe that it makes very little difference whether you are engaged or not!"
>
> He felt the young girl's pretty eyes fixed upon him through the thick gloom of the archway; she

was apparently going to answer. But Giovanelli hurried her forward. "Quick! quick!" he said; "if we get in by midnight we are quite safe."

". . . Don't forget Eugenio's pills!" said Winterbourne, as he lifted his hat.

"I don't care," said Daisy, in a little strange tone, "whether I have Roman fever or not!"

She is bewildered; she is hurt. This knowledgeable-sounding young American actually knows nothing and has acted with complete inhumanity toward her. What she says about not caring if she falls ill is more than mere petulance; she is saying that now she doesn't care what happens to her; then she falls ill and dies. In a very real sense, Winterbourne, for whom she cared, has contributed to her death.

All of Winterbourne's vices contribute to undo him with Daisy in the Colosseum scene, but it is his over-indulgence in the picturesque which gives him a distorted view of reality and helps prevent him from acting like a man. The picturesque is the killer here; like any form of sentimentality, when overdone it can mislead people into being extremely cruel. It is significant that the concluding lines from the Manfred quotation run:

> 'Twas such a night!
> *But I have found our thoughts take wildest flight*
> *Even at the moment when they should array*
> *Themselves in pensive order.*
> [Italics mine]

It is a pity that Winterbourne couldn't continue to the end of the quotation; if he had, he might have learned something helpful to know.

Soon after his soliloquy, Manfred dies of guilt and remorse for unknown but terrible crimes not specified by his creator. His final speech to the spirit that is summoning him to hell contains the lines

> I have not been thy dupe, nor am thy prey—
> But was my own destroyer, and will be
> My own hereafter. . . .

Winterbourne too has committed terrible "crimes" which are indirectly but clearly specified by Henry James: they resemble those of John Marcher in *The Beast in the Jungle*. He lives on, but he is as good as dead; and he has helped kill the youth of Mr. Giovanelli and the life of Daisy Miller. The two male characters are contrasted with each other, for although the young Roman and the young American are both interested in Daisy and both contribute to her death, their response to the experience is totally different: the Italian shows a vast moral superiority to the traveler from the New World. As Daisy turns from an unknown quantity to a human being for Mr. Giovanelli, she turns from an unknown quantity to a stereotype for Winterbourne. Or, rather, not an unknown quantity but a puzzle. For Daisy is a puzzle to Winterbourne, a pretty little puzzle. When he thinks he has the puzzle figured out, he solves it with a stereotype, and a derogatory one at that. This explains the use of the picturesque in the Colosseum scene; Winterbourne responds only to stereotypes, whether in nature, in architecture or among mankind.

Now we see why the story focuses on those around Daisy rather than on Daisy herself. The question of Daisy's worth, or even of what she really is, is irrelevant to the moral imperative that she is entitled to consideration and respect as a human being; and, in the story, Mr. Giovanelli alone gives that to her. We don't find out much about Daisy, but we do find out what Winterbourne is like. Winterbourne doesn't care at all about the truth of the matter; he is afraid to face it, for the truth may involve him with other people and frighten him by bringing him face to face with himself. So he prefers the appearance of respectability rather than life; appearances are safer, he thinks; all the best people believe in them. But the man who finds the appearance of respectability more important than truth misses out on the best things in life and never understands anyone at all. Henry James, although something of a snob, was also and more importantly an artist; and he was not so big a snob as he has sometimes been pictured or as some of his readers were and are.

But what of the genteel reader all this time? If he were perceptive enough, he would have had his little universe shattered; he would see that the implicit criticism and condemnation of Winterbourne is a condemnation of his own habits and tastes. But, judging from contemporary reviews, this is exactly what did not happen. The reviewers remained genteel; they reacted not perceptively but angrily. In a perverse way, this proved James' point; the carapace of gentility was so thick as to be impervious to ridicule, which only aroused a defensive and self-righteous anger. So I will have to confine my comments to how the readers might have reacted, had they read the story with attention rather than indignation.

In presenting the Colosseum scene to us, James is dramatizing and satirizing the American nineteenth century's most cherished concepts of "culture" and "civilization": "Europe," the picturesque, the daylight-moonlight metaphor of the romantic movement, the genteel, the cult of sexual purity and respectability in young American womanhood. Perhaps the preoccupation with respectability can best sum it up. And overconcern with respectability kills Daisy Miller; "the letter killeth." When Winterbourne approaches Daisy and Mr. Giovanelli in the Colosseum, they, intensely conscious of their surroundings, imagine he looks like an old-time lion or tiger eyeing the Christian martyrs. This is neither as playful nor as far-fetched as it sounds. For fantastic as it at first seems, Winterbourne actually *is* a lion ready to devour poor Daisy. As a representative of the American colony at Rome, he is quite exhilarated to see her sacrificed to that crowd; in the words of another line from Byron, she is "butchered to make a Roman holiday." In every sense including the physical one, Daisy Miller is a martyr to the genteel tradition on the very spot where the Christian martyrs died centuries before. The barbarousness of degenerate Rome gives way to the barbarousness of the invading Americans; like the Romans, they too think of themselves as highly civilized. And the reader? One by one he sees his genteel idols smashed before his eyes: Europeans are frankly spontaneous; Americans are rigid formalists; the ruins of antiquity are deadly, not life-giving; "respectability," far from civilizing people, dehumanizes them; the cult of sexual purity kills life itself. One could go on: the "untrustworthy" "lower-class" European becomes the noblest Roman of them all; the genteel American abroad becomes an agent of death and destruction comparable to the ancient persecutors of the martyrs; the American colony at Rome becomes the howling mob that once filled the Colosseum with their bloodlust, interested only in the brutal gladiatorial games of the *haut monde* in which to turn thumbs down on a person means instant death for him. The genteel audience should have squirmed under self-scrutiny when it saw that the un-Manfred-like "crimes" of Winterbourne are exactly the crimes of negation, exclusion from human sympathy and snobbish cruelty that were most likely to be committed by the genteel nineteenth-century American Puritan reader. This story is about the disintegration of value (as are Edith Wharton's *House of Mirth* and Scott Fitzgerald's *Great Gatsby,* both of which were influenced by it), and it contains a revealing glimpse of cultural history. It shows a falling-off in value from the plain living and high thinking of pre-Civil War Boston (for in the story America *is* Boston); the land of the free has become the home of the genteel. The Americans in this tale have taken the ideals of an earlier America and stood them on their heads—something they would never have done with their persons. By their whole way of living, they have taken the pre-Civil War statement of Emerson's, that transcendentalism was a Saturnalia of faith, and inverted it. Instead, they enact a Saturnalia of snobbery and unbelief, and this not in the New England where their far-off ancestors had once proposed to found a city on a hill, but in eternal Rome, where indeed the entire world can see.

Motley F. Deakin   (essay date 1969)

SOURCE: "Daisy Miller, Tradition, and the European Heroine," in *Comparative Literature Studies*, Vol. VI, No. 1, March, 1969, pp. 45-59.

[*Deakin is an American author and educator. In the following essay, he places Daisy Miller within the tradition of European literary heroines found in the works of Turgenev, Cherbuliez, George Sand, and Mme de Staël, and argues that, in these contexts, Daisy is symbolic of the ideal of freedom.*]

When William Dean Howells selected Daisy Miller as the one Jamesian character to emphasize in his *Heroines of Fiction,* he did her two great services. First, he, as the dean of American critics, certified her important position in both the Jamesian canon and in the literary world at large. Second, he affirmed by both precept and example that she would be understood best not as an isolated phenomenon but as a part of a literary tradition. The reasons for Daisy's significance have been examined often enough; one need only add that since Howells stated his preference, other Jamesian heroines—Isabel Archer most forcefully, and, not far behind her, Milly Theale and Maggie Verver—have challenged his prescriptive choice. In contrast, Daisy's relevance as a phenomenon within some particular literary tradition does need to be studied. We do not know enough about what influences conditioned her conception.

If we follow Howells' precedent, then we find that this tradition is purely English and American, the heroines of which "are of easily distinguishable types, and their evolution in their native Anglo-Saxon environment has been, in no very great lapse of time, singularly uninfluenced from without." Which all sounds most promising until we begin examining the American part of this tradition and Daisy Miller in particular, for then the usefulness of Howells' assertion becomes questionable. The tradition that Howells presents in his two-volume study is overwhelmingly English; what is American is but a fraction, or, as Howells describes it, "wilding off-shoots," whose main representatives—whose very substance really—constrict to only Hawthorne's heroines and Daisy Miller herself. We wonder about the importance and memorableness of Howells' other examples in that American tradition: Marjorie Daw, Miggles, Nellie Armitage, Aurora Nuncanou, Jane Marshall, Jane Field. We are even puzzled at how we can place them in this tradition Howells is postulating when, without his aid, we would first have to guess at the identity of many of them. Nor, when we try to place Daisy Miller in Howells' English tradition, can we find much resemblance between her and Emma Woodhouse or Jeanie Deans, Amelia Sedley or Dorothea Brooke, who seem representative in one way or another of the host he lists. Only occasionally, in, say, Elizabeth Bennet or Catherine Earnshaw or Clara Middleton, does one find qualities in these English heroines that seem comparable to Daisy's; and we might further note that though Howells presents the two earlier heroines, curiously he did not like Meredith's novels and had not read *The Egoist.* So, though we can accept Howells' premises, his guidelines are not too helpful.

Looking to James for aid, we find his position not so explicit as we would wish. Certainly he was conscious of the need for tradition, especially for the literary artist: his admiration for Balzac and his study of Hawthorne are evidence enough. But to him Daisy was as ostensibly American as empirical evidence could make her; she was representative of an evanescent phenomenon that suddenly appeared on the European scene during the decade 1860-70 and then as quickly vanished. These facts taken at face value make Daisy an objective rendering of an existing reality without any marked relation to a literary tradition, American or otherwise.

But though one may wish to read *Daisy Miller* in this way, he must recognize too that the creative mind seldom works so simply, and certainly not James's. We should remember that several of James's early efforts in fiction, including that so obviously American novel, *Washington Square,* are adaptations of literary works by foreign authors. We should recall too that James's personal experience as a boy and a young man had, in large part, nullified for him any chauvinistic notion of what constitutes an individual's identity. His impulse was always to break beyond the national boundary, and when he could not do so physically, he found his escape through books. So what James brought to the creation of Daisy was a sense of life that, for his generation, was singularly emancipated and broadly informed. And though James may have styled himself a realist, the world of his mind, as evidenced in his fiction, is one replete with ambiguities and complexities, images and figures, that had been actuated, not by knowing the security and stability of living in one place, but rather by experiencing the tension and excitement of moving through the flux of new and continually changing environments. The one constant that remains is human nature, which in an important, ultimate sense is unweighted by larger, social or nationalistic identifications. All of this means that insofar as Daisy is concerned, James most probably would not have seen her simply as the product of Schenectady but, rather, would have taken what he needed in her creation from whatever sources were available—sources which for him were various. In *Daisy Miller* the result should be something less clear and simple than would at first appear, and the character of Daisy should exemplify some attributes that would transcend the limiting identifications of upstate New York or even of America.

The clue to this literary tradition we are seeking lies, I think, in James's placing Daisy in a scene neither English nor American, and in the insistence of both James and Howells that this character in this scene postulates the International Situation. For proof we note that James has set Daisy in an atmosphere reverberating with other names and other histories which impinge upon and color our response to Daisy—names and histories which do not belong just to the other characters in the story but rather are evoked by the setting or other referents. Thus we should recognize that Daisy is moving in and being influenced by a new and different world, not necessarily the same as the world of the transplanted American dowagers who surround her.

This is a world long since familiar to James both as fact and fiction. As a tourist he had attentively watched and noted what he needed for the realistic accouterment of a Daisy Miller. But just as important, as a "devourer of libraries" he had already observed many other fictive heroines move through this same setting—heroines who, because of similar forces and tensions conditioning them, may be found to resemble Daisy both in their attributes and their fates. It *is* significant that Daisy is American, but it is *equally* significant that the great crisis of her life is experienced in Europe. Expressed in terms of literary influence, one could say that James's affinities with the continental authors were, in his early maturity, stronger than what he felt for the English, and though the American Hawthorne certainly exerted his influence, he was but one against a whole array of other, equally significant but non-American writers. Thus one would expect that if a literary tradition helpful in enlarging our understanding of Daisy Miller is to be found, it would more probably appear in the novels of these European authors James admired than in the Anglo-Saxon tradition Howells postulated.

In his critical essays James has left an abundant record of his reading. Looking through them we are struck by the frequency with which he notes and delineates the fictive heroines he encountered. With persistence he expresses admiration for them while at the same time ignoring the masculine element he may have met. But even among the heroines he discriminates, selecting for special commendation those young maidens who demonstrate a flair of inde-

pendent individuality that reminds one of Daisy. If we try to place these heroines in some kind of order, we soon become aware that it is not so profitable to try to determine when the young James read what novel. However, it is important to realize that James's interests tend to attenuate as the authors he read are removed from him chronologically; his favorites seem to be of his generation or, more often, that of his father, but certainly not much more removed than that of his grandfather. But even within this relatively short period of time, if we place in chronological order those fictive heroines who both fascinated James and have qualities comparable to Daisy's, we still can construct a tradition significant in both its fictive and its historic connotations.

The development of this tradition, and particularly of Daisy's place in it, is best seen if we approach it at that point in time most contiguous to Daisy. So we must start with Turgenev, whom James both admired and knew personally. His heroines appeared to James to be "one of the most striking groups the modern novel has given us." James's admiration even carried him to the point of asserting a similarity between the American and Russian characters: "Russian young girls . . . have to our sense a touch of the faintly acrid perfume of the New England temperament—a hint of Puritan angularity." In these heroines James found a strong will, an ability to resist, to wait, a sense of honor more exigent than that of the men they love. Their strength of character is so powerful that it exceeds their formal significance in their respective novels; though they are not the centers of the novels in which they appear, they often dominate them.

The best examples are Marianna (*Virgin Soil*) and Elena (*On the Eve*). As future brides of revolutionaries, their assurance and sense of purpose commend them as embodiments of a Daisy-like independence of spirit. Dedicated to freedom, both personal and public, they resent oppression and inequality. "Justice satisfies but does not gladden them; while injustice, to which they are frightfully sensitive, stirs them up to the very bottom of the soul." But, despite their unselfish devotion to commendable ideals, they irritate a public that thinks they set a bad example for other girls. They are iconoclasts. Unlike Daisy, who is usually accepted as at least representative of part of that American society from which she comes, Turgenev's heroines personify a disturbing new force in Russian society. Marianna is proud and surly: "from her whole being there emanated a strong and daring, impetuous and passionate element." She longs for freedom "with all the force of [her] unyielding soul," a freedom to be realized only in a complete, selfless dedication to a noble cause. Elena, James's expressed favorite, has this same impetuous and passionate element. Like Marianna, she thirsts for the opportunity to do good, to help the poor, the hungry, and the sick. Leading an intense but lonely life, she ignores parental authority, asserting her independence at the age of sixteen. She dawdles in boredom until, through love and a new-found sense of purpose it embodies, she discovers a direction for her life. Finally, she realizes personal freedom through her dedication to the cause of political freedom which her husband symbolizes. The response of these two heroines to life is not formed so much by a groping ignorance as by an intuitive understanding of the forces that impel them to action. Their activities are not marked by the gaucheries and surges of pudency that usually characterize young innocence. Instead, they move with assurance to their fates. As literary cousins of Daisy Miller, they offer a sense of liberating humanity, a strength and moral beauty that to some extent informs James's own creation. But there is a difference: Daisy knows only a present, whereas Turgenev's heroines anticipate a future, even though over that future hangs the pall of death.

Moving back in time to Victor Cherbuliez, a French author whose heroine is actually cited in **Daisy Miller** and thus is the most obvious link with this tradition we are tracing, we find on examining his novel *Paule Méré* that the stories of James and Cherbuliez have much in common. They both explore the theme of social disorientation, examining the effects of rigid conventions on a young girl not sympathetic to them. Like **Daisy Miller,** *Paule Méré* relies for its clash of personal and social attitudes in part on regional and national distinctions, though it also derives some of its effect from the more romantic concept of the superior, liberated role of the artist in society. The male protagonists in both novels cannot resist the pressures of convention, thus exposing the unprotected heroines to the crushing power of these pressures. Both novels present a protest against these inhuman social forces, but both also contain the bitter recognition that they are invincible, destroying as they do the young innocents.

Paule Méré is the child of a Venetian dancer and a Genevan father of strict Calvinistic background, a background that informs, to an extent, Winterbourne's character in **Daisy Miller**. Since the paternal side of the family thought it best that the child be removed from the environment of the theater, she is given into the care of her father's parents on the condition that her mother not see her. The child is raised in this somber Geneva household, always cautioned against her tainted maternal ancestry, but always secretly drawn to the brilliant image of her mother. From her mother she has inherited a talent for and delight in aesthetic pleasures, but she is compelled to look upon them as sinful. Finding it impossible to suppress her artistic impulses, she seeks refuge with friends. Misunderstood by society and finally by the man whom she loves, she "dies of a broken heart because her spontaneity passes for impropriety." This innocent and ardent spirit must exist in a society whose password is *Qu'en dira-t-on?* She is imprudent, perhaps, but this is "la dernière vertu qu'apprennent les âmes généreuses." For herself and those whom she loves, she insists on a faith in the integrity of one's spirit that would transcend conventions and appearances. But in the opinion of this society's religious leader, M. Gérard, Paule suffers from two incurable maladies, "le mépris des convenances et le goût du fruit défendu." Judging her most generously, this society can only say:

> Voulez-vous savoir son plus grand défaut? Cette chere enfant a mauvaise tête. On a toujours les défauts de ses qualités. Sa droiture est cause qu'elle manque de souplesse; elle ne sait pas se plier aux circonstances ni patienter avec la vie, et quand la vie lui manque de parole, la chaleur

de ses ressentiments trouble la justesse naturelle de son jugement.

In this society a young girl who respects herself can take seriously only "le tricotage, la couture et le catéchisme." It regards "l'enthousiasme, l'imagination, toute supériorité de l'esprit comme autant de dangers et de piéges tendus à la vertu." The weight of its disapprobation finally destroys Paule Méré.

But though James does give special prominence to Paule Méré, he could have found just as adequate an analogue for Daisy from the long list of feminine protagonists created by that earlier and greater artist, George Sand. He knew her novels and in his early criticism wrote admiringly of them. These heroines are often creatures of instinct and impressions, natural and simple in their responses. Rarely well-educated, they exemplify a self-learned, self-imposed creed that distinguishes them from other characters in these novels. Even Indiana, the simplest and weakest of them, has a will of iron, an incalculable force of resistance against any oppression, even to the point of death, the fate of many of these heroines. Forced back upon themselves by their unwillingness to accede to the demands of society, they have developed habits of introspection and self-examination. They are superior women in their dedication, their moral virtue, or their genius. Though rarely exhibiting great physical courage, "elles ont souvent le courage moral qui s'exalte avec le péril ou la souffrance." They are a compound of sentiment and intelligence. When they surrender to sentiment they suffer; when they are guided by intelligence they survive, but only at the risk of renouncing something cherished. To Consuelo, who embodies so much of the best in George Sand, this desire for renunciation is instinctive but is supported and made rational by her dedication to her art, an attitude congenial to James as person and as author. The situations of these heroines are often morally ambiguous. Unattached, at variance with society, they often suffer from the acts of men weaker or more conscious of convention than they. Surrounded by selfishness and intrigue, they are victimized by appearances and their own generous natures. Sometimes they succeed in retaining their social integrity, sometimes they fail, but, as their author intended, they always capture the sympathies of the reader. Unlike Cherbuliez, Sand does not make use of the International Situation, seeking no further than personal or family attachment for relevant social compulsion. Indiana is Creole, but socially this does little more than make her a provincial. Of greater significance is Consuelo's early attachment to Venice, for this city meant for both Sand and Cherbuliez an ambiance conducive to the development of the artist. It meant the same to James, though, oddly enough, it, like the rest of Italy, represents for these earlier authors a freer, more relaxed social order, whereas James finds there a sordid, cynical appearance of conformity as well.

Thus George Sand helps fill out the tradition we are tracing. But if we are to find its origins we must move beyond Sand to that other great literary feminist, Mme de Staël, who seems more clearly a seminal force, a shaper of literary trends and traditions. With her we are coming to the limits of James's interests. He mentions her less often and wrote no critical study of her; still he does make enough scattered allusions to her to indicate that he was familiar with her and her work.

Her novels *Corinne* and *Delphine* are theses on the problems of the socially disoriented woman. Both novels could serve as examples of the ironic epigraph found on the title page of *Delphine:* "Un homme doit braver l'opinion; une femme doit s'y soumettre." But if she must submit, still first she will always resist. This resistance is necessary, for, like George Sand, Mme de Staël intended her works as defenses of herself, as vindications of her own unorthodox opinions and actions. Consequently, in all circumstances these heroines are commendable. Even in adversity they can only be pitied, not condemned. To them, as to both George Sand and Mme de Staël, the villain must always be society.

Corinne is the literary antecedent most clearly useful to James. It is Mme de Staël's defense of the artist, stating as it does the romantic concept of the artist's inherent superiority, his strength of perception, his greater moral virtue and passionate attachment. Like Paule Méré, Corinne is of mixed nationality, thus affecting, as Cherbuliez and James do, a tension between two cultures. Her father is a British aristocrat, her mother is Italian. Though she combines qualities of both countries, she responds most evidently to Italy and its attributes of beauty, spontaneity, pleasure, and freedom. Here she can gratify her aesthetic interests and delight in knowledge. To her, Britain, in contrast, represents conventions, duty, and joyless obligation conceived of as morality. In that country a woman was thought to be of questionable virtue if she tried to assert herself, and for her efforts she could gain nothing. The opposite was true in Italy, for there Corinne was admired as an improviser in poetry and music, a talent that exemplified the imaginative élan governing her life. Accompanying this Orphic gift she had, like Faust, a desire for vast, profound learning which she could also gratify in Italy, but not in Britain. Every object that arouses Corinne's affection she can love with the same impetuous ardor, whether it be art and learning, or country, or the man she hopes to marry. With this affection she combines a constancy, an impulsive generosity that is too often misunderstood and exposes her to the disapprobation of a society which finally destroys her. This conclusion is possible because, as is characteristic of this whole literary tradition, Corinne, despite her allure and strength, cannot control the action of the novel, an action which turns not on her love for the hero, Oswald, but on the conflict he feels between his love for Corinne and his desire to obey the last wishes of his dead father. Caught between the liberating force of love and the constraint of filial obedience, he sacrifices Corinne to a conscience burdened with guilt and remorse. On her side, by surrendering to her love for Oswald, a love conceived romantically as overpowering and total, Corinne cannot forestall or turn away the fatal consequences of her devotion. Unlike Daisy, who dies a maligned innocent little aware of a threat to her freedom, Corinne is alert and committed but is also powerless in the grasp of her passion. As a victim of love, Corinne exudes an erotic sentiment characteristic of the Romantic Movement and reminiscent of a host of earlier heroines—a sen-

timent that, though later diminished and viewed negatively as scandalous impropriety, still informs *Daisy Miller*.

As support to this pervasive sentiment, a similar romanticism colors the setting of *Corinne,* to which James—who, like Winterbourne, could quote Byron, that symbol of social misanthropy, in the Colosseum—responded sympathetically. The Italian scene, in particular, is presented with an enthusiasm, a comprehension and sympathy, that James would have appreciated, for a relevant correspondence exists here between *Corinne* and *Daisy Miller* in both the choice of subject and its picturesque presentation. The most striking parallel is the emphasis placed on that magnet to the romantic spirit: the Colosseum. Corinne does not seek her fatal rendezvous there, as Daisy does, but she is attracted to it nonetheless, because it excites in her a confusing multiplicity of responses, all delightful to the romantic spirit. Corinne comes to it as to a church, kneeling before its huge black cross set in soil once accursed but now sanctified to the memory of the martyrs sacrificed there. There too she senses reverberations of old Rome and, among these crumbling ruins, even an escape into Nature. But no one effect dominates, for each melts into the other, especially when seen, as it is by both Corinne and Daisy, at night, the time favored by romantic devotees of this scene. At this place and time she can feel her soul "frissonne et s'attendrit tout á la fois en se trouvant seule avec la nature," and she can cry out in longing and ecstasy. The romantic sentiment felt for the Colosseum is still strong enough to draw Daisy to it, but the attenuation of its attraction becomes evident in Daisy's incapacity to see this somber scene as anything more than "pretty."

But the Colosseum is dangerous too, because here lurks malaria, a malignancy mysterious and inseparable from the beauty and charm of its environment. The fascination Corinne feels for the Colosseum is symptomatic of an impulse towards death to be found in the whole tradition from *Corinne* to *Daisy Miller*. This imminence of death foreshadowing the fates of so many of these heroines may be seen as perhaps the most dramatic evidence allying the tradition of the socially emancipated woman to the larger literary fascination with the gothic, erotically motivated theme of the persecuted woman. In the social evaluation with which we are concerned here, the urge towards death appears motivated by the exigencies of the victim's relation to society: society requires the sacrifice of its opponents. The larger tradition depends, rather, on a privately motivated cruelty: the villain must persecute and destroy his victim. Within the more limited tradition considered here, the tradition of the socially disoriented woman, the compulsion toward death seems to indicate a morbid scepticism about the efficacy of the individual's revolt.

As an influence on *Daisy Miller,* Mme de Staël's other novel, *Delphine,* does not seem so immediately significant as *Corinne.* It does, however, develop a concentration of interest upon the superior woman and her relations to society that establishes with clarity the tradition in which Mme de Staël's successors could work. Abandoning the romantic scene and the emancipated genius, the author concentrates here on Delphine as an example of natural goodness caught in the power of a society hostile to her.

Delphine, an orphan and a widow, unfamiliar with a sophisticated society, schooled by her former husband to love philosophical inquiry and the natural impulses of the heart, is forced, as Mme de Staël felt she herself was, into an intimate relationship with a society she can not respect but is forced to fear. Singularly independent in her judgments, she finds it difficult to submit her sense of rightness to the laws, let alone to the opinions, of society. If the true desire of her soul is not in accord with the proprieties of society, then those proprieties must be ignored. If she were to succeed socially she would be forced to lead a life "politiquement ordonnée," a life of calculated dissimulation. To live even comfortably in society Delphine must suppress everything that could distinguish her among women: her "pensées naturelles, mouvements passionnés, élans genereux de l'enthousiasme." The opinions of society are the consensus of the bourgeoisie—of mediocrity which "ne suppose rien au delá de sa propre intelligence, et regarde comme folie tout ce qui le dépasse." The author argues that in America, where Delphine's husband, M. d'Albemar, had served in the Revolutionary War, this constraint is mitigated and the laws and the customs are more humane. In part it is this spirit of revolutionary America, as conveyed through M. d'Albemar to his wife, that motivates Delphine's opposition to the society she finds in Paris. Natural, generous, impulsive, she responds as well to the liberating urge of the French Revolution. A society so freed, she feels at first, will acquiesce in her actions, motivated as those actions are by empathy and a desire to alleviate unhappiness and suffering. But she is disappointed. She is born too late. The Revolution manifested politically the personal ideals impelling Delphine into opposition to a society no longer stirred by the clarion of that Revolution. So she must die: society must claim its victim.

Here, caught up in the surge and violence of the liberating impulse rocking France, Mme de Staël projects into her autobiographical novels her sense of its significance as it affected her personally. In her, later in George Sand, transmuted in Cherbuliez, and transferred to a new scene and a new revolution in Turgenev; the impulse to freedom, the desire for individual emancipation, is continuous. What is conscious revolt in Mme de Staël becomes finally an accepted, natural, quiescently felt attitude in Daisy Miller. A revolutionary ideal has become a convention, but in the process it has changed, losing its enthusiasm and some of its power to stir men's hearts. By the time it reaches Daisy, this ideal is flattened and attenuated; it is diminished to deportment and manners. As a result, Daisy comprehends only dimly the ideal of freedom which she symbolizes.

This European aspect of Daisy's antecedents is a curious irony, considering the apparent cohesiveness of Daisy's American identification. But that cohesiveness is not the only reality of the story. What we have taken as Daisy's American indifference to propriety can also be seen as an acquisition, an adaptation of an older and larger foreign tradition. The independence she exemplifies, in part coddled in the social vacuum of the American Frontier, had also roiled up in defiance to the repressive stagnation of the more ancient, denser European social scene. If it was a response to an American ethos, it was also a revulsion from a European miasma; it was in either form an expression of a will to be free.

Thus, when a naïve, ill-prepared Daisy returns to the battleground which first gave meaning and purpose to her innocent free will, it is proper that she too resist as best she can. But it is also inevitable that, like so many heroines before her, she should be defeated by the same force that gave her, as an exemplification of this tradition, a reason for being. If she will not conform, society must punish her; it must, one could even say if he sees her death as something more than accident, claim her as a victim. For somehow we must find a justification for the enormous irony of her death. It seems something less than satisfactory to explain that death away by attributing it to chance, or to Daisy's perverse willfulness, or to Winterbourne's need to be taught a lesson. Is it not more satisfactory to accept the postulate of the tradition we have examined here and say that her death becomes a social and symbolic necessity? Writing in the American tradition that James knew, Howells had refused to recognize this necessity. In his novels he allowed those of his heroines for whom James expressed admiration a happier future with marriage and children at the end of it, and his precedent, not James's, was followed by later writers. By letting Daisy die, James allied himself to an essentially traditional, European resolution to a theme that by this time offered him the opportunity to break with it. But he chose not to and consequently succeeded in making *Daisy Miller,* at first so stark and slight a record of actuality, into a story of resonating cultural significance.

R. P. Draper　(essay date 1969)

SOURCE: "Death of a Hero? Winterbourne & Daisy Miller," in *Studies in Short Fiction*, Vol. 6, Fall, 1969, pp. 601-8.

[*Draper is an English author and educator. In the following essay, he studies the character of Winterbourne, and demonstrates the ways in which he is the central figure in* Daisy Miller.]

"She goes on from day to day, from hour to hour," says Mrs. Costello of the heroine of *Daisy Miller,* "as they did in the Golden Age. I can imagine nothing more vulgar." This unconscious echo (unconscious, that is, as far as Mrs. Costello is concerned) of *As You Like It* lends a comic absurdity to her notion of vulgarity. It is perhaps true that to lead the free, untrammelled life of the Forest of Arden in the formally moral, but, in reality, cynical atmosphere of Rome is a kind of sentimental indulgence possible only to the unsophisticated, "vulgar" mind. In such a context, however, the word has a boomerang effect. It damns the sophistication of those who gloss over the nastiness of their "fallen" world with the manners and taste of cultured society, making the ignorance and simplicity of the "vulgar" almost a positive value. This is a pastoral effect that makes the association with *As You Like It* an appropriate one, and it would be possible to argue that "a pastoral" would be a better qualification of the title than "a study." It would certainly have the merit of directing the reader's attention away from Daisy's significance as a character-study, which has only limited value, and towards her much more important role as a focus for other people's opinions—above all as a focus for the uncertainty and moral confusion of the character who is the real centre of the tale, Winterbourne.

Early readers of *Daisy Miller* found Daisy an offensive representation of American womanhood abroad. Manners have so changed that the point of the story, though not lost, is much more likely to seem to the modern reader to lie in the offensiveness of expatriate Americans like Mrs. Costello and Mrs. Walker. Neither attitude is correct. Daisy is culpable in her self-will. She bridles at any hint of interference. "I have never allowed a gentleman to dictate to me," she says to Winterbourne, "or to interfere with anything I do." A little earlier we learn that Winterbourne remembered a compatriot's saying that American women "were at once the most exacting in the world and the least endowed with a sense of indebtedness." Daisy has her share in this fault, too. Indeed, what is called her flirtatiousness seems to be more of this nature than anything suggesting the provocativeness of a coquette. She is the very embodiment of the spirit of youth with its paradoxical combination of selfishness and ingenuousness, which yet, through warmth and spontaneity, makes an almost irresistibly strong appeal.

For the purposes of the story (and who could one expect to be more aware of the story *as* story, with its own artistic purposes, than Henry James?) this appeal is directed at Winterbourne. It is he who gives form and meaning to the story, and it is primarily through his consciousness, or "point of view," that the events are narrated. As Maxwell Geismar says [in *Henry James and His Cult,* 1964], ". . . it is Winterbourne's own conflict, his repressed love for Daisy, the attraction beneath his disapprobation, which carry the story along." After all, we know very little about Daisy at first-hand. If we were meant to think primarily of her, we should want to know a great deal more about what is going on in her mind. Certainly, we are not completely ignorant of this. We can guess, for example, that she tells Winterbourne that she is engaged to Giovanelli in order to challenge him to come out of his shell, and that she promptly denies it afterwards because she wants to make sure that he has not misunderstood her. It is instinctive with her to challenge response from Winterbourne—not, that is, to provoke him "sexually" (as that word is commonly used, though I think it *is* in a deeper, and quite underogatory sense, sexual provocation), but to try to compel him to overcome his "stiffness" and to defy convention for the sake of real feeling. This is evident in her reply to Winterbourne's warning that if she continues her present behaviour towards Giovanelli, people will give her the cold shoulder.

> Daisy was looking at him intently; she began to colour. 'Do you mean as Mrs. Walker did the other night?'
>
> 'Exactly!' said Winterbourne.
>
> She looked away at Giovanelli, who was decorating himself with his almond blossom. Then looking back at Winterbourne—'I shouldn't

think you would let people be so unkind!' she said.

> 'How can I help it?' he asked.
>
> 'I should think you would say something.'
>
> 'I do say something'; and he paused a moment. 'I say that your mother tells me that she believes you are engaged.'
>
> 'Well, she does,' said Daisy very simply.

If it is strange that Daisy leaves her mother in doubt about so important a matter, it is that much more significant that she clears up Winterbourne's doubt. But the major point of the dialogue is the challenge issued by Daisy, and unhappily missed by Winterbourne, that he should stand up for her. I have called it a challenge to defy convention, and so it is, as convention seems to operate among these Europeanised Americans; but it might equally well be called a challenge to live up to the standard of gentlemanliness that he and they jointly profess. A "gentleman" would protect her, whereas all that Winterbourne's good intentions amount to is an attempt to persuade her to conform to the usual appearances, to do in Rome as the Romans do. Either way, the discussion brings us back to Winterbourne rather than to Daisy herself. It is what she represents for him, rather than what she is in herself, that ultimately counts.

It matters a great deal, of course, that Daisy dies of Roman fever—at once a natural and a symbolic death; a death that she brings on herself by her folly, and a death in which Giovanelli, Winterbourne, and expatriate American society all have a share. James's artistic tact allows the climax of the story to have all these implications. And yet it is much more of a significant climax for Winterbourne than for anyone else. With regard to Daisy herself it is pathetic; with regard to him it is as nearly tragic as his Prufrockian nature will allow. To appreciate why this is so it is necessary to consider Winterbourne's "case."

The story begins and ends with him. He is a vaguely drifting idler, "an extremely amiable fellow", rumored to be "extremely devoted" to a Genevan lady older than himself—James's colloquial *extremely* has its own ironic effect, since caution rather than extravagance seems to be his key-note. According to sound dramatic practice, James introduces him to Daisy via her younger brother. Quite apart from sounding the note of America, as the Old Pretender would say, in strident fashion, this enables a comment to be made on Winterbourne's Europeanised notions of how women are to be approached: "It seemed to Winterbourne that he had been in a manner presented. . . . In Geneva, as he had been perfectly aware, a young man was not at liberty to speak to a young unmarried lady except under certain rarely occurring conditions. . . ." The fact that he dares to make such an advance to Daisy is in his favour, but it is not unambiguously so, for there is a faint suspicion that he feels able to treat her with freedom because he is free not to respect her. Daisy's honesty and freshness attract him, but he is at the same time confused—"amused, perplexed and decidedly charmed." Should he condemn her for "laxity of deportment"? He is troubled by the very fact of having lost his instinct for knowing such things. "He felt that he had lived at Geneva so long that he had lost a good deal; he had become dishabituated to the American tone." James follows his soliloquising with absorbed interest. This is the thing: how the betwixt-an-between Winterbourne, out of instinctive touch, gropes to find a category that will fit Daisy Miller, and at last hits upon the useful formula "pretty American flirt."

In the second section of the tale, Winterbourne applies to his aunt whom he hopes to make the guarantor of his good behaviour in Daisy's eyes—though, once again, this tells us more about himself than it does about Daisy. He is the one who thinks it necessary, and it is his own uncertainty that is further revealed. James, with cool irony, informs us that Winterbourne listens with interest to Mrs. Costello's slightly malicious gossip that "helped him to make up his mind about Miss Daisy," and he presses the conversation further, "with a desire for trustworthy information," to find an echo of his previous thought in Mrs. Costello's assertion: "You have lived too long out of the country. You will be sure to make some great mistake. You are too innocent." The tone here is comic:

> 'My dear aunt, I am not so innocent,' said Winterbourne, smiling and curling his moustache.

> 'You are too guilty, then!' Winterbourne continued to curl his moustache, meditatively.

One laughs both with and at Winterbourne and his aunt. But the serious words *innocent* and *guilty* also make their effect. James has placed his character beautifully between them. It is his dilemma that he is both innocent and guilty, and does not know which part of himself to prefer. He shelters behind the curling of his moustache, which can be taken as either a consciously Byronic self-parody, or as complacent enjoyment of the right to repudiate mere innocence (on the basis of his experience with the lady of Geneva, perhaps?). Such ambiguity surrounds all Winterbourne's actions. Daisy by comparison is single-minded and spontaneous. When she makes the expedition to Chillon, she has no "guilty" sense that she is eating forbidden fruit. It is Winterbourne who thinks in these terms: "To the young man himself their little excursion was so much of an escapade—an adventure—that, even allowing for her habitual sense of freedom, he had some expectation of seeing her regard it in the same way. But it must be confessed that, in this particular, he was disappointed."

Section three transfers the action to Rome. Some of the most delightful paragraphs in the story are indebted to James's journalistic experience in evoking the spirit of place, and can be read for just that. But place is also tinged with implications for manners and morals. I have already referred to Daisy's death from "Roman fever," and likewise to the presence of a mysterious lady in Geneva. The historical associations of the Castle of Chillon in the second section provide a contrasting backdrop to the freedom and chatter of Daisy herself. Once again, the piquancy of this contrast depends on the double perception of Winterbourne, who, in this respect, is an indispensable reflector of the author's awareness. (Winterbourne's informed appreciation of European culture provides an obvious comic contrast to Randolph's belief that the best place he has

seen is the *City of Richmond,* but it is not—any more than Philip Herriton's comparable appreciation of Italy in Forster's *Where Angels Fear to Tread*—an unqualified asset.) He expects some credit for having missed out on Bologna and Florence on his way down to Rome, only to find that Daisy reproaches him for not having come more quickly; and, in fact, the reference to what he has missed, even though it forms no more than a comment on what is passing through his mind, has the almost unreasonable effect of making him appear to value too much the very cultural opportunities that he foregoes. The weight of European things combines with the restraint of European manners to impede the natural warmth of response that Daisy might otherwise call forth in him. Accordingly, it is above all in Rome, where both these influences are at their strongest, that the challenge of Daisy Miller comes to its crisis. The off-stage opposition of Mrs. Costello is replaced by the on-stage friendship (which turns to ostracism) of Mrs. Walker; and this has its grand, dramatic expression (inflated language for a trivial episode, perhaps, but James's art is to make convincing mountains out of apparent molehills) in the scene of the carriage on the Pincio.

The confrontation of Daisy and Mrs. Walker provides a black-and-white contrast. The intermediate shades in which James is chiefly interested belong once more to Winterbourne. Daisy's association with Giovanelli makes his own moral disorientation yet more acute. While being vexed with himself for what he begins to recognize as a strong "inclination" towards her, he would welcome evidence that she is indulging in an amour with Giovanelli, for then "to be able to think more lightly of her would make her much less perplexing"—that is, he would have an avenue of escape from his own perplexity. But Daisy continues to present "an inscrutable combination of audacity and innocence." He, therefore, has to face her first explicit challenge—though the fact of its being so explicit is a measure of the extent to which he has failed in response to the instinctive challenge that Daisy constitutes in her self—when she demands of him: "Does Mr. Winterbourne think . . . that—to save my reputation—I ought to get into the carriage?" The advice he gives is prudent: to get into the carriage. But James makes it more interesting to the reader by attributing it to "gallantry" rather than prudence, with the gloss that "the finest gallantry, here, was simply to tell her the truth; and the truth, for Winterbourne, as the few indications I have been able to give have made him known to the reader, was that Daisy Miller should take Mrs. Walker's advice." James's first-person intrusion in this sentence is not a clumsy lapse from his point-of-view technique, but a timely reminder that it is such a technique that he is employing. The truth here is only the truth "for Winterbourne." What the truth for Daisy is, or what *the* truth is, it is not among the purposes of the story to unfold. And the truth "for Winterbourne" is inseparable from his image of himself as a person of gallantry—which I take to be a facet of his image of himself as a gentleman. Although it is to his credit in this instance that he does not indulge in the kind of gallantry that is mere compliment, but feels bound to speak as he thinks, his answer disturbingly reveals that he cannot make a like discrimination between appearance and reality where the question of a young woman's "reputation" is concerned. His answer implies what Daisy's question had challenged him to deny, that reputation *is* a matter of appearances. The conclusion of the episode, which James so places that it is also the conclusion of the third section, confirms this. Winterbourne shows a touch of fire in his defence of Daisy before Mrs. Walker. He speaks "angrily," and his earlier, private misgivings about having been too long in Europe flash out in the sharp comment, "I suspect, Mrs. Walker, that you and I have lived too long at Geneva!" Yet his intention to rejoin Daisy—which might have been his commitment to a growing self-criticism—is deflected by no more than the action of her parasol in screening her head and Giovanelli's from view. It is what this appears to signify that makes the young man direct his steps, not towards the couple, but towards Mrs. Costello; and the structure of the story tells us that this is a serious relapse, for Mrs. Costello, who has never even condescended to know Daisy, ought to have been relegated to an earlier stage of Winterbourne's development.

The last section is the one in which Daisy's conduct has something of the air of wilfulness, but she also has justice on her side, notably in her criticism of the false Roman propriety that considers flirtation more appropriate in married than in unmarried women. Mrs. Walker's cutting her lends force to this criticism. Vulgarity is seen to lie on the side of "culture" rather than Daisy's "audacity and innocence." Winterbourne, not yet free from his vacillation, despite the significant move made at the end of the third section, can be ironic to his aunt about the quality of that culture that she upholds; but when he muses to himself upon the meaning of Daisy's determination to accept Giovanelli's company, he finds that "holding oneself to a belief in Daisy's 'innocence' " is "more and more a matter of fine-spun gallantry." In reality the "gallantry" has worn thin. He concludes that "She was 'carried away' by Mr. Giovanelli." The scene in the Colosseum, where he, too, cuts Daisy, is a consequence of this. Although he again vacillates to the extent of trying to cover his intention from Daisy, the outcome is a final move in the Mrs. Costello direction, made "with a sort of relief " that he is at last released from ambiguity: "She was a young lady whom a gentleman need no longer be at pains to respect."

As in *The Wings of the Dove*—for which *Daisy Miller* is in so many ways a preliminary sketch, in spite of the great difference between the characters of Daisy and Milly—the story ends not with Daisy's death, but with the realization by her diffident lover of what he had lost both in her and in himself. The shreds of evidence contributed by Mrs. Miller (Daisy's insistence that she never was engaged) and Giovanelli (he knew that she would never marry him) provide a sufficient force in this delicately counter-weighted story to swing Winterbourne right through the arc of his apparently resolved ambiguity to the opposite recognition that he had done Daisy an injustice. If it had been D. H. Lawrence writing the story (which, admittedly, is to suppose that its whole tone and tempo would have been different, but not, I believe, fundamentally its theme) Winterbourne's failure would have appeared more explicitly as a missed opportunity with "one of the lords of life." James, limited to impressions upon Winterbourne's consciousness, and given more to the irony of understatement,

nevertheless hints at a similar conclusion. The final variation on the recurrent motif of Winterbourne's having lived too long in Europe is James's way of saying this. "You were right," says Winterbourne to Mrs. Costello, "in that remark that you made last summer. I was booked to make a mistake. I have lived too long in foreign parts." To say in such a way to Mrs. Costello that she was right is to indicate firmly that she was, and is, wrong, in her sense of the phrase, but also conveys to the reader Winterbourne's final understanding that a certain quality of life has atrophied in himself.

The ironic and ambiguous expression of Winterbourne's failure is of a piece with his character and with James's method of telling his story. A great change has taken place, but the surface remains intact. We assume that Winterbourne's attendance on his aunt continues as before, and the last paragraph tells us that he has returned to Geneva, and probably to the mysterious lady there. Unlike Romeo, he passes not from a Rosalind to an ultimate commitment to his Juliet, but from Rosalind to a half-hearted relationship with Juliet, and back to his Rosalind again. That is the sort of tragic hero he is—not one that opens the Shakespearean stops, or excites the Lawrentian indignation, but a tragic figure for all that in a muted fashion. He has failed to answer Daisy's challenge; and her death, touching as it is, is less the point of the story than the stifling of instinct in himself that his act of "injustice" to her represents. James, as the ending of *The Turn of the Screw* illustrates, is quite capable of making a death scene the highly dramatic conclusion to one of his stories; but it would have been quite inappropriate to end *Daisy Miller* with the heroine's death, for this would have meant contradicting the whole emphasis of this particular story. It is the hero's slow, lingering, and almost comically *un*-dramatic death that is the main theme, and his ironically distanced, but unavailing struggle for life that provides the material of the slender plot.

John Holloway (essay date 1969)

SOURCE: An introduction to *Daisy Miller: A Study*, The Heritage Press, 1969, pp. v-xvi.

[*Holloway is an English author and educator. In the following essay, he discusses the evolution of theme in* Daisy Miller, *claiming that the novella dramatizes "the fate of innocence in a devious and sophisticated world," but agrees with James in the assessment that the story is more a poetic than a critical study of Daisy's character.*]

It is nearly a century since *Daisy Miller* was published by Leslie Stephen in *The Cornhill Magazine* of 1878, and today it is strange to seek out, on the reserve shelves of some big library, the dusty *Cornhill* volumes for those years, and to find, on their yellowing pages and among their heavy black Victorian illustrations, James's spirited and incisive *allegro*. But his *nouvelle* caught the spirit of that time: its preoccupations were not James's alone. If *Daisy Miller* depicts a contrast between American and European manners, the *Cornhill*, not long before, had run an article precisely about the greater freedoms of youth in the New World. Its account of the 'bright, cheery, hearty, simple ways of the young people . . . straying on the sands of Newport' makes one think of James's '**An International Episode,**' almost a companion piece to *Daisy Miller*; and the titles of other contemporary *Cornhill* pieces—*The Tyranny of Fashion*; *The Decay of Fine Manners*; *Mara, or the Girl Without References* ('it is a curious symptom . . . that alacrity with which moral people jump at the idea of an improper connection')—all these details recall James's story, and help to show its typicality in a certain sense.

James himself, in writing of his story a generation later, adverted to his own 'incurable prejudice in favour of grace.' In this early period his style was at its most lucid, and nothing he ever wrote displays that prejudice in favour of grace with more luminous delicacy. The very name of its heroine points to this: 'Daisy' is a pet-name, supplanting his heroine's prosaic, baptismal 'Annie P.' with enchanting appositeness—her delicately trim spontaneity is indeed daisy-like.

James had incomparable resources for giving his story its crisp, summery charm (one quite forgets that the Roman part is as a matter of sober fact set in the winter season). He had a rich response to the landscape of Europe, especially its cultivated landscape; and at this time at least he still had a wonderfully alive, direct, yet decorous sense of young femininity, and almost a woman's awareness of the brilliant subtleties of *haute couture*. Paintings by Manet like 'Olympia,' or Renoir's 'The Box,' with their scintillating responsiveness to texture (whether of cloth or skin), and to fashionable dress, were painted only a few years before *Daisy Miller* was written.

At this period also, James still displays the same order of sensibility to every *nuance* of conversation, and plays colloquialism and formality exquisitely against each other. His meticulous, slightly old-fashioned use of French ('*tout bonnement*'; 'a young lady *qui se passe ses fantaisies*') adds another touch of refined cosmopolitan charm. Even the note of colloquialism is unobtrusively modulated from character to character:

> '. . . You won't *back out?*' she said.
> 'I shall *not be happy* till we go!' he protested.

With Daisy it is the product of quick but guileless wits; with Winterbourne, her would-be lover, it is scrupulous, well chosen, flat ('I think you had better get into the carriage'), a product of his self-confessed 'stiffness'; in Mrs. Costello, his aunt, plainness of speech goes with a narrow if often good-humoured self-assurance; and in the 'earnest' Mrs. Walker it expresses a rather more kind-hearted conventionality. James's spare and lucid dialogue does not prevent *Daisy Miller* from being a masterpiece of character portrayal.

Yet, while James has beautifully discriminated the outward style of his characters in this *nouvelle,* their inward natures remain more opaque. How, to begin with, ought we to see the shaping idea of the story? James says in his *Notebooks* that it is 'of the international family,' like '**The Siege of London**' or '**Lady Barberina**'. One of the very greatest Jamesians, Leon Edel, has interpreted it as centred upon a contrast between a 'child of nature and of freedom' who 'refuses to yield her innocence,' and the 'super-subtle alien codes' of 'the Europeans, . . . the Europeanized Americans.' Certainly in a novel like *The Europeans,* which is of the same year as *Daisy Miller,* or in the savage little *Four Meetings* of the year before, James saw a contrast between the Old World and the New, of a kind almost wholly favourable to the latter. But his sense of this whole rich field, and its interaction with other permanent interests of his, seem to me to vary from work to work.

It would not be right to think that James always saw Europe as super-subtlety and America as innocence, or that he thought of Europe as the only place with a rigidified 'high society.' In writing in his *Notebooks* some years later, he glosses 'an international tale, a tale of the *Daisy Miller* order,' with the phrase, 'the eternal question of American *snobbishness abroad*.' In '**An International Episode,**' there is an American high-society just as there is an English one: more 'bright, cheery, hearty,' much more conscious of intellectual culture; but its members feel insulted by the suggestion that they are not of the 'aristocracy.' As for subtlety, the conversation between the English and the American aristocratic ladies at the end of the story is a miraculously elegant display of barbed, pregnant high-society amiabilities on both sides. In '**The Siege of London,**' New York society is too rigid to admit the enchanting but much-married Westerner Mrs. Beck, while London society does so simply because she is 'amusing.'

In '**Pandora**' (1884) the American lady Mrs. Dangerfield is convinced that American society is full of 'distinctions, of delicate shades, which foreigners are too stupid to perceive'; and later in the story, another American lady says to a visitor from Europe, 'How we do puzzle you!' and he replies, ' . . . But of course, we are very simple.'

Coming back to *Daisy Miller* with these works in mind, one cannot but be struck by the idea that James is not constructing a general contrast between American and European *mores* at all. The two ladies who so much condemn his heroine are themselves both American. They have both resided in Europe, but this is not why Mrs. Grundy has won them to her side. Mrs. Costello makes it clear that her values are those of American 'society':

> 'But don't they all do these things—the young girls in America?' Winterbourne inquired.
>
> Mrs. Costello stared a moment. 'I should like to see my granddaughters do them!' she declared grimly.

—'American snobbishness abroad,' in other words. Critics have stressed how the line, 'You have lived too long out of the country,' which Mrs. Costello addresses to Winterbourne, points implicitly, and from James's own position, to the fact that he has lost his awareness of youthful American innocence. But Mrs. Costello herself meant simply that prolonged absence has made him unaware of social vulgarity by home standards. Daisy herself—innocent as she is of anything that could be called Europeanization— is perfectly well acquainted with the idea of respectability, mentions propriety twice, speaks of her 'reputation,' and blushes or goes pale several times over, rather as any young lady might. The point about Daisy is not that she is encountering a 'rigid and complex' society for the first time, but that she has as good as no idea of what, by American standards or any other, 'propriety' consists in, and also that she has what can at most be described as a very intermittent interest in the whole subject.

Finally, one must register the position of Giovanelli, the not altogether engagingly personable Italian with whom she compromises herself. This young Italian (again, the name tells one something) had the truest and also the most humane and life-affirming insight into Daisy's character. This least American of the characters—this negation of everything American as the story sees it—not only recognizes Daisy's true nature but very much cares about it, and that disinterestedly. He wanted a rich American wife ('. . . Mr. Giovanelli, who spoke English very cleverly—Winterbourne afterwards learned that he had practised the idiom upon a great many American heiresses'), and was setting aside his own ambition, simply to enjoy the company of 'the most beautiful young lady I ever saw, and the most amiable.' He was a humane enough man to find it worth his while to waste his time.

Thus, anything by way of a contrast between European and American life was not James's concern in this particular tale. Rather, he used an international setting for a quite general theme: the fate, irrespective of nationality, that so easily befalls innocence and directness in a devious and sophisticated world. *Daisy Miller* is thus close to *Washington Square,* published only three years later. True enough, Catherine Sloper's innocence and directness in that novel are not quite those of Daisy. The later heroine has less brilliance, and more of something that perhaps makes up for that. But *Washington Square* recounts Catherine's destruction through the dried-up sophistication and calculatingness of others: 'She was sickened at the thought that Mrs. Penniman had been let loose, as it were, on her happiness,' while Winterbourne and his two dowagers were 'let loose' on Daisy's youthful happiness; and sophisticated, calculating and dried-up they all were in their various ways. If that is not quite the whole truth, it is for a most interesting reason, and an unexpected one: Daisy herself was also let loose on that precious article.

James's intention was unquestionably to portray his heroine as an instance of endearing innocence: there happens to be a contemporary letter, written by himself, which decisively confirms this. Mrs. Lynn Lynton, an Englishwoman of literary pretensions, wrote to James shortly after the tale was published, saying that she had quarrelled with a friend over its meaning, and asking him to adjudicate. In his reply, James was explicit. Daisy 'went on' with Giovanelli, he said, because she was 'above all things innocent.' She had 'a little sentiment about Winterbourne, that she believes to be quite unreciprocated'; but she was 'too innocent' to be 'playing off Giovanelli against Winterbourne.' What the story recounted was the 'little tragedy of a light, thin, natural, unsuspecting creature being sacrificed to a social rumpus that went on quite over her head.'

Thirty years later, James revised *Daisy Miller* for the 'New York' collected edition of his works. He gave much added stress to the innocence and naturalness of the heroine, and sharpened the contrast between her and the other characters. 'That pretty American girl' is expanded into 'that little American who's so much more a work of nature than of art.' But Mrs. Costello's tongue becomes sharper than ever. 'Skinny little' gets inserted into the mild words of 1878, 'Oh, the [. . .] mother is just as bad.' Winterbourne now refers to Giovanelli as a 'thing,' rather than a 'man'; and James himself now degrades Giovanelli all the way down from 'brilliant' to 'glossy.'

Professor Carol C. Ohmann, in an interesting essay on the tale, has argued that Daisy is 'identified . . . simply and wholly with the natural world which has its own beautiful and eternal rhythms' and that, taken all together, James's revisions make this clearer than ever. Certainly, they emphasize Daisy's naturalness; but hardly in this Wordsworthian sense in which even her death could seem part of the transience-in-renewal of nature. Rather, it is a question of an older sense of the word, where the focus is on human not scenic nature. Changes in the other characters by no means go to make them more social and artificial in contrast to a more 'natural' Daisy—but merely a little nastier.

Viola R. Dunbar has put forward the view that James was free to give added emphasis to Daisy's charm and naturalness, because he abandoned the idea that she was typical of American girlhood. But the key words in his Preface to the New York edition mean something more than this. Here they are (my italics):

> . . . the simple truth, which ought from the first to have been apparent to me, that my little exhibition is made to no degree whatever in *critical* but, *quite inordinately and extravagantly,* in *poetical* terms.

This does not mean that James had written a Wordsworthian story while only half realizing it, nor that the contrast between 'critical' and 'poetical' is one simply between the representative and the idiosyncratic. I think it means that James saw how *Daisy Miller,* judged as a whole, exposed itself to a serious and limiting criticism; and he met this not by attempting a direct victory over what exposed it to criticism, but by making his story in effect less ambitious than it had been at first.

James's position over sophisticated society and the sincere individual was something of a self-contradiction. He always had an enchanting vision of innocence and sincerity, and he saw how the predatory conventions of society did those things violence. But at the same time he could not have accepted the only terms on which what he hated in high society might have been done away with. Society, with its elegance and its finesse, enchanted him also, and made up his life. He understood inward spontaneity and vitality less as Hardy or Lawrence or Yeats did—from within and first hand—and more with the external awareness of a delighted and perceptive social being. To portray someone who threw off society by virtue of an altogether superior inward power, and so could rebel and succeed with rebellion, was outside his range. His 'outsiders' are like Mrs. Headway in **'The Siege of London'** and Pandora Day in **'Pandora,'** whose primal, self-made virtue establishes them as insiders after all.

Daisy Miller illustrates these facts. It is something rather less rigorous than really to have been 'A Study' (James dropped the sub-title when he revised the text), and it is 'poetic' rather than 'critical,' partly because the author's judgement of his heroine is extraordinarily lenient. This is not because propriety matters in itself but because, in Daisy Miller's own particular circumstances, it mattered so little that to go mixed up with it *either way* was to betray a terrible triviality of mind. Daisy was in love, and the man she loved returned that love—or nearly—but needed some help before he could say so. Here are indeed circumstances in which independence of 'super-subtle' alien codes could stand one in good stead. But what does Daisy do with her 'nature' and 'freedom'? It is her doing as much as his that neither lover glimpses the full truth until too late. True, he has a difficulty that she does not feel: but could that be a matter of indifference to a woman who loved him?

Meanwhile, Daisy fills in with the company of Giovanelli. Giovanelli may indeed have had an acute and humane appreciation of the 'amiable' and 'innocent'; but he also displays a truly savage egocentricity. Even if we suppose that he is meant to have no inkling of the feelings of Daisy or of Winterbourne each for the other, he certainly knows that he is abetting Daisy's social ostracism, and over Daisy's death James is most careful to make plain his murderous selfishness: 'For myself I had no fear . . . [it is the second time he is made to proffer this gigantic self-inculpation]. *If she had lived, I should have got nothing.*' This second observation follows at once after the first. His modest words are the words of an unconscious brute. Perhaps James was catching something of what used to be thought a 'southern,' a 'Mediterranean' type.

In this story, then, the author was really much more on the side of "polite" society than transpires at first, or than he seems himself to have realized at the time. He enchants us with Daisy's innocence, exquisite face, bright wit, and lovely clothes, but his 'child of nature and freedom' is no real indictment of the world she has to live in: if anything, her blindness and destructiveness exceed its own. For total consistency in his 'study,' James would have had either to create another child of nature and freedom, one who could bring larger and more valid energies to her independence—or to treat Daisy's tragedy not as the 'little' tragedy of one who was merely a child 'over' whose 'head' it was that things 'went on,' but as the more substantial tragedy of one who, without realizing it, was a destructive caricature and trivialization of the great inward dimension of life.

The result was that when he revised his story he simply made it less 'social' altogether. Daisy is now a little less to be seen as standing in any exact context, and so inviting us to exact 'study,' of tensions between society and the individual. More, she is (to use words from his later text) a 'charming apparition,' a figure of 'lovely remoteness.'

James understood his own difficulties, and met them with his own masterly sophistications; but the enigmatic charm and grace of his heroine remain in one's mind, long after the problems raised by her story have receded.

Donald E. Houghton   (essay date 1969)

SOURCE: "Attitude and Illness in James' 'Daisy Miller'," in *Literature and Psychology*, Vol. XIX, No. 1, 1969, pp. 51-60.

[*In the following essay, Houghton examines the theme of illness as a manifestation of cultural difference in* Daisy Miller.]

Oscar Cargill's definition of James' "international novel" [in his introduction to James' *Washington Square* and *Daisy Miller,* 1965] indicates how close James came in so many of his novels to presenting the psycho-physical experience we now refer to as culture shock. "If Turgenev had originated 'the international novel,' James was to perfect and more sharply define it. An 'international novel' is not simply a story of people living abroad, as in Hemingway's *The Sun Also Rises,* but it is a story of persons taken out of the familiar contexts of their own *mores* where their action is habitual and placed in an element, as in a biological experiment, where everything is unfamiliar, so that their *individual* responses can be examined." Cargill, of course, is using the term "biological experiment" metaphorically, but in fact the experience of encountering a foreign culture where "everything is unfamiliar" often does have "biological" implications which go far beyond the physiological consequences of a mere change of climate, food, and drinking water. In James' *Daisy Miller* the experience of Europe affects adversely the health of a number of Americans visiting Europe, and it would appear that the Americans become ill not so much because of any objective circumstances in the new environment but as a result of attitudes the Americans take toward that environment.

The relation of illnesses to mental states in James' novels has been suggested by Napier Wilt and John Lucas [in *Americans and Europe: Selected Tales of Henry James,* 1965]: "Europe has the power to inflict pain, visit ill, work disaster only upon those Americans who arrived or remained in the wrong spirit." The "wrong spirit" is the belief that America is superior to Europe in about every way and that the American does well to resist, ignore, or retreat from any aspect of European life he does not immediately like. Several characters in *Daisy Miller* have the "wrong spirit," and as a result Europe visits ills upon them ranging from minor discomforts to a fatal disease. Those Americans like Winterbourne and Mrs. Walker, who accept Europe on its own terms, thrive while there. On the other hand, Americans like Mrs. Costello, Randolph, and Mrs. Miller take a negative attitude toward Europe. They survive their tour, although uncomfortably, by developing neurotic symptoms which keep to a minimum unpleasant or dangerous encounters with the unfamiliar European culture. Finally there is Daisy, whose sudden switch from a highly positive to a highly negative attitude toward Europe leads to her death.

Mrs. Walker and Winterbourne have the "right" attitude and remain healthy throughout the novel. Both are long-time residents of Europe. Whatever pain Europe may have inflicted upon them upon their arrival is now in the past. Mrs. Walker's health, happiness, and social success result in part from the fact that she came to terms with European culture. "Mrs. Walker was one of those American ladies who, while residing abroad, make a point, in their own phrase, of studying European society. . . ." As a result of her study, Mrs. Walker has come to know the rules, she abides by them, and she cuts from her social circle anyone who endangers her own position by not following what she calls the "custom here." Like Mrs. Walker, Winterbourne is quite comfortable in Europe because while in Rome he does as the Romans do. His advice to others is to "go by the custom of the place." Winterbourne's adjustment is so complete that he apparently comes to prefer Europeans to Americans. We hear at the end of the novel that he probably will make a permanent alliance with "a very clever foreign lady."

Winterbourne's aunt, on the other hand, has not succeeded in adjusting to Europe or making Europe adjust to her, with the result that Europe is to her still a painful experience. Mrs. Costello suffers from sick headaches. A social climber who gave Winterbourne to understand that she exerted a considerable influence in social circles back home in New York, she evidently has not been socially successful in Europe. Too proud to associate with Americans touring the continent and yet not having been accepted by European society or the society of Europeanized Americans, she has developed sick headaches and withdrawn from society altogether. Upon his arrival at Vevay, Winterbourne goes at once to call upon Mrs. Costello, but "his aunt had a headache—his aunt had almost always a headache—and now she was shut up in her room, smelling camphor. . . ."

Mrs. Costello "admitted that she was very exclusive. . . ." This is her way of explaining her unconscious withdrawal to protect herself from further unsuccessful and painful social encounters in Europe. In her anxiety over her social position she has repressed her desire to enter European society. The headaches are a symptom of this repression.

Once present, the headaches become useful to Mrs. Costello. They serve as an acceptable, face-saving excuse for not succeeding in European society and for not risking further humiliations. She "frequently intimated that, if she were not so dreadfully liable to sick-headaches, she would probably have left a deeper impress upon her time." The headaches also serve to protect her from the unpleasantness of having to meet people like the Millers, whom she considers below her. Both Winterbourne and Daisy understand that Mrs. Costello uses her headaches to her advantage. When Daisy suggests a meeting between her and his aunt, Winterbourne is embarrassed:

> "She would be most happy," he said; "but I am afraid those headaches will interfere."
>
> The young girl looked at him through the dusk.
>
> "But I suppose she doesn't have a headache every day," she said, sympathetically.
>
> Winterbourne was silent a moment. "She tells me she does," he answered. . . .
>
> "She doesn't want to know me!" she said suddenly.

Winterbourne's reply to Daisy at this point summarizes the relation between Miss Costello's headaches and what Mrs. Costello has come to call her "exclusiveness": "My dear young lady," he protested, "she knows no one. It's her wretched health."

The three members of the Miller family in Europe suffer in varying degrees from ill health, and the illness of each appears to be related to the attitude each takes toward Europe. To Randolph the only good thing about the trip to Europe was the ship, but "it was going the wrong way." Daisy tells Winterbourne, "He doesn't like Europe. . . . He wants to go back . . . he wants to go right home." Randolph tells Winterbourne, "My father ain't in Europe; my father's in a better place than Europe." Later Randolph tells Winterbourne that he hates Rome "worse and worse every day!" Randolph's teeth are coming out, no doubt from natural causes, although Randolph blames Europe even for this: "I haven't got any teeth to hurt. They have all come out. . . . I can't help it. It's this old Europe. It's the climate that makes them come out. In America they didn't come out."

Randolph's strong disapproval of Europe, however intense, is not accompanied by deep anxieties and neurotic symptoms that occur in the travelling adults. He is too young to have arrived in Europe with any special hopes or expectations and so he is not shocked or bitterly disappointed by the fact that Europe has nothing to offer him. He is also too young for Europe to expect much from him and so he is not faced with the kind of decisions which might set up conflict within him. Still, since Randolph does want to return home, the longer he stays in Europe the more likely he too will be subject to frustrations and the development of neurotic symptoms. There is some evidence that this may be happening already. Randolph does not sleep well. Daisy tells Winterbourne that Randolph "doesn't like to go to bed" and that she believes Randolph doesn't "go to bed before eleven." Later when Daisy and Winterbourne join Mrs. Miller, the three discuss Randolph's sleeping habits:

> "Anyhow, it ain't so bad as it was at Dover," said Daisy Miller.
>
> "And what occurred at Dover?" Winterbourne asked.
>
> "He wouldn't go to bed at all. I guess he sat up all night in the public parlour. He wasn't in bed at twelve o'clock: I know that."
>
> "It was half-past twelve," declared Mrs. Miller, with mild emphasis.
>
> "Does he sleep much during the day?" Winterbourne demanded.
>
> "I guess he doesn't sleep much," Daisy rejoined.
>
> "I wish he would!" said her mother. "It seems as if he couldn't."

Like Mrs. Costello, Randolph instinctively protects himself from Europe by keeping to a minimum his exposure to the place:

"Your brother is not interested in ancient monuments?" Winterbourne inquired, smiling.

"He says he don't care much about old castles. . . . He wants to stay at the hotel."

Mrs. Miller does not like Europe any more than Randolph, but as an adult she can not indulge in the outspoken criticism of Europe which provides some therapeutic release for Randolph. Mrs. Miller is not well, and her "illness" appears to be an adaptive symptom to keep to a minimum further encounters with foreign ways. Like her son, Mrs. Miller does not sleep well. When Winterbourne asks Daisy at one point if her mother had gone to bed, Daisy says, "No, she doesn't like to go to bed. . . . She doesn't sleep—not three hours. She says she doesn't know how she lives. She's dreadfully nervous." Later in Rome, Winterbourne says to Mrs. Miller, "I hope you have been well since we parted at Vevay," and she replies, "Not very well, sir." Randolph volunteers the information to Winterbourne that Mrs. Miller has the dyspepsia and that the whole family has it, him most of all. Mrs. Miller then blames her illness on Europe: "I suffer from the liver. . . . I think it's this climate; it's less bracing than Schenectady. . . ."

It is, of course, not the climate but the total impact of Europe upon her which causes Mrs. Miller's suffering. Her blaming the European climate reveals only her general attitude toward her total experience of the continent. That her illness is psychosomatic, caused by her negative stance toward Europe, is underscored by James in this same scene after Winterbourne has had "a good deal of pathological gossip" with Mrs. Miller and attempts to change the subject by asking her how she liked Rome. "Well, I must say I am disappointed," she answered. "We had heard so much about it; I suppose we had heard too much."

Mrs. Miller's illness stems from the anxieties attendant upon her having to face daily, even hourly, the strange and unfamiliar. She labels her illness "dyspepsia" and then uses her discomfort to ward off further pain. She withdraws from Europe as much as possible. Early in the novel, Daisy informs Winterbourne that they were all going to the Chateau de Chillon "but my mother gave out. She suffers dreadfully from dyspepsia. She said she couldn't go." Later Daisy tells Winterbourne that her mother doesn't like "to ride around in the afternoon" and on still another occasion she tells him that her mother "gets tired walking around." When Daisy and others are talking with Mrs. Walker about a forthcoming party and also about Daisy's new Italian boy friend of uncertain character, Mrs. Miller senses she is about to encounter another array of new experiences and problems she has never had to face back home. Her instinctive response, like that of Mrs. Costello and Randolph, is to retreat from danger: "I guess we'll go back to the hotel." She and Randolph do so, leaving Daisy to face alone a decision which turns out to be a life and death matter.

The picture James gives of Daisy's psycho-physical state in Europe is quite different from that of the others. The novelties of Europe charm rather than threaten her. Consequently, she has no occasion to be anxious and she does not develop the neurotic symptoms which insulate Mrs. Costello, Randolph, and Mrs. Miller from Europe. Daisy, on the contrary, is "carried away" with enthusiasm for Europe and wants to widen rather than narrow her experience of the place. Until very near the end of the story she enjoys good health. When she does finally become ill, her illness is not a protective psychosomatic symptom which comes from within, but a disease contracted from without. Her fatal illness, however, does resemble the illnesses of the others in one important way: it is causally related to a negative attitude she finally takes toward Europe.

Mrs. Costello, Randolph, and Mrs. Miller develop neurotic symptoms which prevent their experiencing Europe in any significant way. While they will return to America as innocent and ignorant of Europe as they were when they arrived, at the same time they *do* survive to return. Daisy's lack of apprehension over *surface* differences, on the other hand, allows her to enjoy Europe and good health for a long time, but her health and happiness last only until she discovers, with startling suddenness, a *fundamental* difference between American and European values which she can not accept. Unlike the others whose ailments help to spare them from any direct confrontation with Europe, Daisy, with a father in America and a mother back at the hotel with dyspepsia and with no knowledge of the realities of European traditions and taboos, unknowingly drifts into a crisis situation unprecedented in her experience.

The crisis comes in the scene in which Daisy is about to take a walk on the streets of Rome in the company of the questionable Mr. Giovanelli. Winterbourne and Mrs. Walker know that what Daisy is about to do is dangerous from many points of view, but their warning to her is put so delicately that Daisy does not get their meaning. She understands that considerable pressure is being put upon her not to walk with Giovanelli, but she does not understand why. She thinks they may be concerned over her health. Before Mrs. Miller left for the hotel, she had warned Daisy, "You'll get the fever as sure as you live. Remember what Dr. Davis told you!" When the more sophisticated Mrs. Walker tells Daisy that walking at this "unhealthy hour" under these circumstances is "unsafe," Daisy still thinks she is talking about catching Roman fever. Daisy does not realize that Mrs. Walker is speaking metaphorically and is warning her against doing something which would not only be potentially dangerous to her health but which also would be damaging to her reputation. Mrs. Walker then makes her meaning explicit: "You are old enough, dear Miss Miller, to be talked about."

In one terrible moment Daisy understands what all the fuss has been about. She understands for the first time the full sexual and moral implications for Europeans and Europeanized Americans of what she is about to do. It is a traumatic and psychologically violent moment for Daisy. She is at once confronted with the facts of European life and the facts of life in general, facts which she had previously been ignorant of or had unconsciously avoided. A gradual *unconscious* withdrawal from her dangerous and painful predicament is not an alternative open to Daisy. It is an either-or matter: she must either walk with Giovanelli or not walk with him, and the decision must be made here and now on the streets of Rome with Winterbourne and Mrs. Walker on one hand and Giovanelli on the other awaiting her decision.

Shocked, outraged, and hurt by her discovery, Daisy is in no state of mind to weigh the matter carefully and deliberately. As Frederick Hoffman points out [in *Freudianism and the Literary Mind,* 1957], decisions made under such circumstances are likely to be impulsive and irrational, even self-destructive:

> An uninhibited drive toward satisfaction of unconscious wishes (or expenditure of libidinal energy) would lead to death. The wish needs instruction in the shock of reality; if the character of the inhibition is moderate, the shock will lead to readjustment; if the reality is too suddenly and too brutally enforced, the effect will be a traumatic shock, leading to one of several forms of compulsive behavior.

Daisy chooses complete freedom rather than cultural and moral relativism and walks with Giovanelli. It is the dangerous rather than the protective choice and her walk leads to illness and death.

Daisy's resolve to make a moral principle out of not conforming to European customs finally leads her to the scene of her most daring indiscretion, the Roman Colosseum. It is there she receives through Winterbourne the final condemnation by society of her character and it is there she contracts the malaria which leads to her death. The causal relationship between her death and her attitude toward Europe is clear, since Daisy would not be in the Colosseum with Giovanelli at this unhealthy hour if she were not intent on flouting European standards of conduct.

In this climactic scene, the contrast between sickness and health is used ambiguously by Daisy and Winterbourne to refer both to Daisy's physical state and to her moral condition. When Winterbourne first sees Daisy there, his first thought is of "the craziness, from a sanitary point of view, of a delicate young girl lounging away the evening in this nest of malaria" and he warns her of the great danger she is exposed to. But since Winterbourne is also much concerned with and aware of Daisy's moral state, he is also telling her that he thinks she is being corrupted by this Roman and that she will suffer from this. He tells Daisy that "you will not think Roman fever very pretty. This is the way people catch it." Since Daisy's discovery of the realities of European culture came through her ultimately understanding metaphorical meanings, particularly those related to health and sickness, she is now alert to the double meaning in Winterbourne's warning and answers him in kind: "I don't care . . . whether I have Roman fever or not!" But Daisy is very fond of Winterbourne and still cares about his opinion of her. She wants him to know that he has been mistaken to judge her morals by her manners, her character by appearances only. Extending the metaphor further, she conveys this final message to him: "I never was sick, and I don't mean to be!. . . . I don't look like much but I'm healthy!"

What Daisy says is true only in the sense she is still innocent sexually, but she has by now contracted malaria and

so is fatally ill. James' novel also suggests that anyone who ignores or defies society to the extreme that Daisy did is "sick" also in the psychological sense, sick even unto death.

Ann Wood   (essay date 1972)

SOURCE: "Reconsideration," in *The New Republic*, Vol. 167, No. 24 & 25, December 23 & 30, 1972, pp. 31-3.

[*In the following essay, Wood records her impressions of* Daisy Miller, *noting that Daisy, as an example of the typical American girl, is ultimately "public property"—little more than an object to be acted upon.*]

And there she was, Daisy Miller, the American Girl, pretty, vulgar, vulnerable, formally presented to the public in 1878 by the young Henry James. She charmed, angered, and amused Anglo-American readers in her own day, provided her author with his only commercial success, and lingers potently today with still provocative claims on the American imagination. I know that her story has long held a tenacious and personal if somewhat elusive fascination for me. I read it over a decade ago on my first trip to Europe, in the midst of my own complicated discovery that I too was the American Girl; I passed it on later as prescribed reading to a young man I knew—a not very subtle reminder of the privileges and perils of involvement with such a creature; I have taught it half a dozen times with undiminished interest. Yet I was never much like Daisy Miller. I wouldn't have liked to think of myself as being "pretty"; I have never dressed fashionably or even well; and I have always fancied myself as some sort of an intellectual. Why do I care about flat little Daisy in her fine clothes? I think it is because she reveals what I and others, whether rightly or wrongly, welcomed and dreaded daily in our youth and retained a sense of later: the fact that the American Girl is absolutely and quintessentially public property.

James creates Daisy's reality for his readers not by illuminating her interior life, but by throwing a flood of light on her exterior existence. This is not just James' technique, but Daisy's substance as James understood it. Chronic over-exposure is somehow part of her nature. We learn a great deal about the American Girl from the fact that *Daisy Miller* is not really about Daisy Miller, but rather about other people's opinions of Daisy Miller. This is not to say that anyone in the book, with the possible exception of Winterbourne, gives her close scrutiny and careful analysis, or tries to understand her. No, the issue at hand is simply whether those observing her will accept or reject her. Daisy does not at first realize that she can only be chosen or discarded, but James does. She is somehow a product and the only question can be whether or not one wants to buy. *Daisy Miller* taps the paralyzed anxiety of American girlhood in a way that shuttles me back to adolescent nightmares of the terrors of wallflowerdom. Accepted or rejected, loved or hated, living or dead? Which?

Daisy, so pretty, so processed, so dependent, comes from a country which has Hollywood in its future. Absurd as it may sound, she anticipates to me the tragedy of Marilyn Monroe. Daisy Miller exists only as she pricks the imagination of her public. Her obliviousness to this fact is but a sign of unconscious proficiency; an acquired trait has *per force* become instinctual. She is a professional attention-getter. But the attention which creates her also transfixes and traps her. And like Monroe, what beauty she possesses is in her slightness, her final powerlessness to save herself, her inevitable fragility. Monroe died, I sometimes think, of her inability to stop pleasing; Daisy, her faint fictional prototype, from a rather desperate decision to displease. But she has for me some of the same pathos. An ever-present audience which has ceased to comprehend, if it ever did, can sometimes leave the performer with no recourse but suicide.

Perhaps I could say that *Daisy Miller* is finally not about Daisy, but about her audience which is hostile as well as uncomprehending. One of the many ironies of Daisy's fate is that her author is less interested in her plight than he is in her enemy's problems and methods, for these are much closer to his own difficulties of self-definition than Daisy's unverbalized struggle. Her audience of opponents is essentially parasitic, and its chosen weapon is naturally that of the parasite: gossip, that "confidential" talk by which we form and flay those who in some way perform for us. The process of gossip already engages James' attention: it was in certain ways to be the model for his novelistic craft. He shows its function here to be not as a protection for traditional conventions and ideals in a stable society, but rather as a substitute for them in a transplanted and unstable community of emigrés and tourists forced to make critical pretension take the place of inherited values. In the world of *Daisy Miller,* gossip is not the traditional home-grown, over-the-back-fence garrulous and wayward chatter of washing day, but a kind of art, the perfected form of curiosity and malice by which alienated men and women create and discard each other's personalities and their own. Gossip is the culture of the dispossessed, and as such, provides the art of innuendo, the technique of suggestiveness by which the articulate exert their power in James' fiction. The expatriate society of Daisy's Rome relies on scandal and the snide as a means both of self-expression and of social manipulation.

Yet, although their talk sets the terms of Daisy's destruction, it in no way brings the event about. That task James assigns to Frederick Winterbourne, a young American long domiciled in Geneva who turns out to be Daisy's major enemy and James' chief concern. He is the most important member of Daisy's audience for he alone is potentially a critic in the real sense of the word. He himself causes little comment, generating only rather vague, uninformed rumors about a possible mistress. The scent he leaves is apparently faint, veiled, undecided; he is essentially privatized and inaccessible. But he is drawn to Daisy, and while his "set" is that of the emigrés who denounce her, he long resists the gossip which passes as judgment. If he is a bit disdainful, at least he is disdainful of everyone. He wants, and tries, to judge for himself.

Daisy knows perfectly well that only Winterbourne of those around her can possibly spring her from her trap or permanently condemn her to it. James shows her accepting, even willing her death as soon as she realizes that he has emotionally dismissed her. Yet in the face of her utter need of him, why does she treat him as she does? It is clear from the start that Daisy likes Winterbourne; it is equally clear that, once arrived in Rome, she does everything she can to make herself unappealing to him. Yet given her dilemma as James has displayed it, she has no other course of action open to her. Her struggle for survival must involve putting her head on the block and calling for execution.

To cease being a product and to become a person, Daisy must annihilate her market value as irrelevant. To be sure that Winterbourne cares for her self, she must demand that this most ceremonious and "stiff" of young men accept her when she is absolutely unacceptable. And perhaps at the bottom of her lawless little heart lies a belief that if she all but destroys herself, he will have to intervene, and massively. This is a perverse way of looking for love, the tactic of one who does not know what love is, the strategy of "an American girl," whose father is absorbed in business, whose mother is absorbed in stolid domesticity, whose brother is absorbed in himself. Daisy's world, as James reveals it to us, is a singularly loveless one. Her distinction is that, no matter how confusedly, antagonistically or backhandedly, she is looking for something her experience could hardly have told her existed, and for which, if found, she might well have had no adequate response.

Winterbourne's failure to cipher her inverted code is hardly surprising, but it spells tragedy not just for Daisy, but for him. One might well ask why, since James makes it crystal-clear that there is nothing in Daisy herself which would attract a man of taste like Winterbourne. She is pretty, but she is deficient. She comes from a society where there are no long-standing cultural traditions, and she is plainly an advertisement of their absence. Small wonder, James seems to be hinting, that she has a "monotonous" voice, that her language is impoverished past the power of any degree of prettiness to camouflage ("well," a kind of non-word, is, too tellingly, her favorite word). Predictably, Europe is a closed book to her.

Yet James knows that Winterbourne needs Daisy not perhaps for what she is—for James is as uninterested in that problem as are her fellow characters—but for the experience she offers to one in Winterbourne's position. Winterbourne is of course an expatriate, who pursues "studies" in Geneva, and enjoys quoting Byron at night in the Colosseum. He has adopted the role of sentimental traveler, a well-worn one in the brief annals of American fiction, and one whose viability Henry James in 1878 had every reason for wishing to test and understand.

Just three years before writing *Daisy Miller,* after nearly a decade of vacillation, James had left America for good. He had heralded his decision in 1875 by an allegorical story called **"Benvolio,"** whose hero, in choosing New England over Europe, sacrifices his creativity to his morality. James knew that he could not meet the cost such a sacrifice would impose on him. Yet he never lost his belief in the possibilities for important literature in America. When he wrote Howells in 1880 that he (Howells) was "magnificently and heroically right" in deciding to work from within American culture, I see no reason for doubting his sincerity. He knew, however, that Howells lacked what an American writer to be great must have, "A *grasping* imagination," the ability for "sniffing . . . the very earth of our foundations" and there to find the "very heart" of human nature. Melville had it, although James seems not to have known it, but James, as he surely at bottom felt, did not. James needed, as F. W. Dupee and Leon Edel have shown, to be an outsider, even a voyeur, in order to create, to be, as he put it, "an observer in a place where there is most in the world to observe."

Furthermore James wanted to establish the value of American literature by making it *art,* even at the sacrifice of mass appeal. James Russell Lowell could still proclaim "Let no man write a line that he would not have his daughter read," and the daughters of the land read him with pleasure. But Howells tells us that New Englanders, "especially the women," disliked James' work. James desired, as he later frankly put it, to reclaim the novel from "the ladies and children—by whom I mean . . . the reader irreflective and uncritical." In other words, he wished to write in some sense an intellectual fiction, one which could not be written for a nonintellectual audience. His final if limited success was to be as a writer in a recreated patronage system of authorship—working long and arduously to please the discriminating few—not under the pressures of a commercial system—working systematically and perhaps superficially to capture the uncritical many.

James' decision to expatriate was probably the right one, and his intelligence in finding a crucial distinction between Scylla and Charybdis fine. That same intelligence, however, never let him forget that he had taken the least debilitating of two potentially debilitating options. Winterbourne is the expression of this awareness. If the American Girl *Daisy Miller* displays for James the dangers of over-advertisement attendant upon the essentially commercialized life-style which he had rejected, the expatriate male in that story exhibits the perils of over-privatization attendant upon the esthetic one which he had chosen. The mutual need of these two figures is inevitable and transparent.

As Winterbourne listens to Mrs. Miller discussing her liver ailments, or young Randolph boasting about America and his own perversity, he has the air of a man politely and resolutely swallowing the unswallowable at an unsuccessful dinner party. In actuality, he is being fed the coarse bread of life. Indeed, in the Millers' unconscious candor lies Winterbourne's only chance of replenishment. Daisy and her relatives are invaluable to him as they are to James, because they spread before him the vast vistas of the "vulgar," the flat terrain of American mass culture that his residence in Europe has safely yet dangerously distanced to a subculture for him.

And Winterbourne finds not just comedy but magic and excitement both in the new and in the casual freedom with which it is offered. He marvels at the easy aplomb Daisy shows chatting about her personal life or riding in public on a boat unescorted except by a gentleman friend. Who can tell what other astonishing transformations of experi-

ence she can accomplish? It is Winterbourne's pretentious aunt who, in discussing Daisy's unabashed display of familiarity with her Italian friend, identifies her appeal: " 'she thinks of nothing. She goes on from day to day, from hour to hour, as they did in the Golden Age.' " It is precisely Daisy's extraordinary public quality which is her "innocence" and her attraction. It is her denial, perhaps her ignorance, of dark corners which draws Winterbourne—and James—to her in mingled envy, hope and disdain. Unawares, Daisy suggests the tantalizing half-promise of a golden vulgarity, the release from the strain of cultural and sexual privatization—the essential resource of liberation. Winterbourne, perhaps like James, distrusts this promise but his torment is that he does not disbelieve it. He destroys, but he regrets.

This is where the book ends, not with Daisy's death but, characteristically, with the *effect* of her death on Winterbourne, and with James' penetrating and subtle analysis of his predicament. Geneva, the "little metropolis of Calvinism" to which Winterbourne returns and whose Puritan aspects James carefully stresses, represents all too clearly the literal historical origin of New England. Geneva, whose young ladies never do as Daisy did, symbolizes here, as New England was in part to do in James' book on Hawthorne, a spirit of hostility to the free play of the imagination. Ironically, Winterbourne, in following the "gossip" of his countrywomen, has simply chosen as guide the New England conscience debased and operating in alien territory. He has traveled only to stay at home, and worse, in doing so, he has nourished not his creativity but his guilt. This was the fate that James himself was to try to avoid, although not perhaps with complete success.

Here the book closes, yet I cannot close, as James intended I should, on Winterbourne's loss, because that is not the real force of the story for me. There is a certain self-pity lurking amidst James' ironies here, and perhaps I want some of my own. Yes, poor Winterbourne, James seems to be telling us, and I sympathize even while I note Daisy's displacement. Like all those other introspective, somewhat ineffectual and self-condemning observer-figures who decide and re-decide through the pages of James, Hawthorne and Howells, Winterbourne, James implies, must finally bear the burden of life. By a curious logic, it is apparently only the good-looking, nonconforming woman or girl who has the privilege of dying and leaving that rather unemployed man who failed to understand her a permanent sinecure of self-indulgent grave-tending. Of course it is not so simple, but still I am drawn to Daisy not just because Winterbourne deserts her, but because in a sense James does too. It is of her essence that she does not quite "belong," even in her own book. She *is* so vulnerable, this Daisy Miller, an American Girl whose superficiality is her complexity. She never knows she is pathetic, decked out in Daddy's trophies but without Daddy, emblem and victim of mass culture, addicted to attention and ignorant of love, perishing of that inability to articulate peculiar to a cult figure obscurely dissatisfied with its cult, losing her audience but not her image: the eternal object. Who looks at her, who owns her, who kills her, who buries her, who misses her, who writes about her, and why—

that's what matters, there's her story. Dear Daisy, when they've all gone home, do you exist? I need to know.

Ian Kennedy (essay date 1973)

SOURCE: "Frederick Winterbourne: The Good Bad Boy in *Daisy Miller*," in *Arizona Quarterly*, Vol. 29, No. 2, Summer, 1973, pp. 139-50.

[*In the following essay, Kennedy characterizes Winterbourne as a "Puritan romantic" whose repression and hypocrisy lead to sexual predation.*]

As James Gargano pointed out in his excellent article, "*Daisy Miller*: An Abortive Quest for Innocence," critical attention has concentrated obsessively on the heroine of James's most popular nouvelle and has consequently ignored the fact that its central character is, in fact, Frederick Winterbourne. From the time of John Foster Kirk's denunciation of *Daisy Miller* as "an outrage on American girlhood" the debate over the character of Daisy has rolled on inconclusively, but as soon as one recognizes that the only character in the story whom we see from the inside is Winterbourne, and that it is through him that we receive most of the evidence upon which any judgment of Daisy must be based, it becomes obvious that what one thinks of Daisy is to a large extent dependent on and in any case secondary to what one thinks of Winterbourne.

Gargano regards Daisy as a *ficelle* who "exists to test Winterbourne's ability to grow beyond his hitherto narrow and one-sided state into a fully realized human being," and the story as the drama of his attempt and ultimate failure to overcome the conditioning of Calvinistic Geneva such that he can acquire the ability to recognize, believe in, and appreciate that state of natural innocence, the existence of which is denied by the Puritan ethical code of the Europeanized Americans in Geneva and Rome. In "The Genteel Reader and *Daisy Miller*,"—the best essay yet written on the work—John H. Randall III argues persuasively that Winterbourne is James's vehicle for a scathing satirical attack on the inhumane and sentimental mores of "the genteel nineteenth-century American Puritan reader," that all Daisy wants is to be treated with the consideration and respect due to any human being, and that instead of this she elicits from Winterbourne snobbish cruelty and a heartless exclusion from human sympathy. Randall sees these reactions of Winterbourne to Daisy as the result of an "overindulgence in the picturesque which gives him a distorted view of reality and helps prevent him from acting like a man," and from the failure of Winterbourne to treat Daisy as a human being he extrapolates his theory that James is attempting to reveal the extent to which the values of his genteel readers are savagely inhumane rather than, as they imagine, cultured and civilized.

Both Gargano and Randall regard Winterbourne, therefore, as a representative figure. Gargano sees him as sufficiently less rigid than his aunt and Mrs. Walker to be capable of redemption from their stultifying code of respectability, and for Randall he is the embodiment of the distorted values not only of the Europeanized Americans, but of *Daisy Miller*'s original American readers in general. Yet James expends considerable energy in the first half of the nouvelle depicting the individual characteristics of his protagonist, and although Winterbourne does perform a representative function to some extent, most of the interest and significance of his relationship with Daisy derives from those very aspects of his character and attitudes which deviate from the norms embodied in Mrs. Costello and Mrs. Walker. Any attempt to categorize Winterbourne as a representative type must, therefore, both logically and in justice to the care with which he is characterized, begin with his individual attitudes, personality, and behavior. Indeed, it is in his individualistic interpretation of the code of behavior which Daisy ignores, rather than in any strict conformity to it, that he reveals himself to be in some ways both a more vicious and, as far as Daisy is concerned, a more dangerous character than anyone else in the story.

From the start there is an ambivalence about Winterbourne which arouses uncomplimentary suspicions about him. He lives in Geneva and has "an old attachment for the little metropolis of Calvinism" where he has made and kept "a great many youthful friendships," so one assumes that he does not find the Puritan mores of the city and its inhabitants in any way oppressive. Yet we learn simultaneously that he is "extremely devoted" to an older, foreign lady who lives in Geneva, and "about whom there were some singular stories." It appears, therefore, that Winterbourne, although attached to the center of Calvinism, is having an affair there, an affair, moreover, which he and the lady concerned are at pains to hide from any degree of public exposure since "Very few Americans—truly I think none—had ever seen this lady." And so, beneath an outward appearance of conformity to the social conventions of the Puritan ethic, Winterbourne hypocritically pursues his individual sociomoral freedom.

This inconsistency in his character is evident again immediately after the narrator has given us the background information about him. Daisy's brother, Randolph, approaches Winterbourne and asks for a lump of sugar: "Yes, you may take one," he answered; "but I don't think too much sugar is good for little boys," a comment which reflects in miniature Winterbourne's own situation in Geneva, and simultaneously shows us for the first time the stiff pomposity of his speech. It is revealing to compare the ensuing conversation with Randolph, who, as his mother later says, is not much like an infant, to the dialogues between Pemberton and Morgan in "The Pupil"; Winterbourne suffers by the comparison, for, unlike Pemberton, he consistently talks down to the boy and treats him as an object of amusement rather than as a person. This is apparent again a few pages later when, during his first conversation with Daisy, Winterbourne uses Randolph to elicit information about his sister. The description of this—Winterbourne learned more about her "by catching hold of her small slippery brother and making him stand a few minutes by his side"—does not in itself reflect too badly on Winterbourne, but in retrospect it can be seen as the first of a series of occasions on which he uses people, without regard for their own wishes, to attempt to insinuate himself into Daisy's favor.

He uses his aunt's name and the promise of an introduction to her to persuade Daisy that he is respectable and a gentleman; then, when Mrs. Costello refuses to associate with the Millers, we are told that:

> for a moment [he] almost wished her sense of injury might be such as to make it becoming in him to reassure and comfort her. He had a pleasant sense that she would be all accessible to a respectful tenderness at that moment.

In other words, he sees the possibility of using the rejection for the same purpose as he had intended to use the promised introduction, and the passage continues: "He felt quite ready to sacrifice his aunt—conversationally"; "conversationally," but no more, for to sacrifice her further than in conversation behind her back would be to preclude the possibility of being able to use her again, in some way or another, in the future—capital should be invested, not squandered. It may seem at first appearances rather extreme to view Winterbourne's feelings for his aunt in this harsh light, but we are never given any reason to suppose that he has any affection for her, rather the opposite since he is prepared "to admit" to Daisy that "she was a proud rude woman," and the only reason given for his attendance on her is that "He had imbibed at Geneva the idea that one must always be irreproachable in all such forms," especially, one suspects, if that aunt is "a widow of fortune." When he first meets Mrs. Miller Winterbourne's first recorded observation of her, an assumption that "she opposed such a course" as the projected excursion to Chillon, is immediately followed by: "but he said to himself that she was a simple easily-managed person and that a few deferential protestations would modify her attitude." Again, the wishes, desires, approval or disapproval of the other person have no influence on Winterbourne, whose only interest in them is to discover the easiest way to prevent them from obstructing his pursuit of his own pleasure, and it is noticeable that he intends to use his manners and cultivated speech, "a few deferential protestations," to overcome Mrs. Miller's supposed disapproval. Finally, at the Castle of Chillon, Winterbourne tips the custodian generously with the desired result that he "ended by leaving them quite to themselves"; an arrangement of no great significance in itself, but noticeable as yet another example of Winterbourne's habit of using people in a manner that is superficially harmless, but basically unscrupulous. It is clear, moreover, that both his moral hypocrisy and his repeated exploitation of others are used by Winterbourne primarily to establish and maintain himself in such a position in his relations with women that he can enjoy a far freer degree of intercourse with them than either society, or he himself, in public, would possibly condone.

Although illegitimate children and clandestine love affairs are a constant feature of James's novels, he is delicate, often to an exasperating extent, in his treatment of sexual matters. It would take a psychologist to explicate properly Winterbourne's sexual character and its probable behavioral manifestations in any given context, but there is sufficient evidence for even the nonspecialist to see that, in keeping with the contrast between his appearance of social conformity and his hidden deviance from Puritan norms of behavior, the respectable surface of Winterbourne's attitudes and behavior towards Daisy covers a licentious nature which he reveals several times despite his efforts to suppress it. John Randall has shown how Winterbourne's inhumane social behavior is a result of his viewing reality with the warped vision of a Puritan romantic, and this same characteristic makes him, in sexual terms, superficially and in his own view of himself, a gentlemanly romantic lover, a gallant knight clad in the armor of righteousness, but in reality a potential sexual monster who regards Daisy "as one of the old lions or tigers may have looked at the Christian martyrs," as she herself puts it, or, in other words, as an object to be sexually devoured.

In the original edition of *Daisy Miller* it is said early on of Winterbourne that "He had a great relish for feminine beauty; he was addicted to observing and analyzing it." In the New York edition, however, this sentence has been amended to read: "He took a great interest generally in that range of effects [Daisy's complexion, nose, ears, and teeth] and was addicted to noting and, as it were, recording them." The substitution of "great interest" for "great relish" weakens the sentence in a manner which James cannot have recognized, for the irony of the statement is subtly suggested in the original contrast between the lip-smacking, fleshy word "relish" and the subsequent claim that this interest in women is limited to the esthetic and intellectual activities of observation and analysis—which itself seems unlikely in a twenty-seven-year-old male. The real key, however, is that we already know that Winterbourne's attentions to women are not limited in this way, for he is having an affair with an older woman; and although it is the narrator who asserts that his interest is in observation and analysis it seems reasonable to take this as Winterbourne's own view of the matter, for it is characteristic of his practice of self-deception.

Perhaps what is most revelatory of Winterbourne's social and sexual attitudes towards people is his reductionism. Just as he speaks to the precocious Randolph as "little boy" in the abstract, as it were, and instantly classifies Mrs. Miller as a "simple, easily-managed person," so his most constant occupation throughout the nouvelle is his attempt to find the appropriate formula for Daisy Miller. When he acknowledges at the end that he has made a mistake with regard to her, he means simply that his final classification of her as a young lady "about the *shades* of whose perversity a foolish puzzled gentleman need no longer trouble his head or his heart. . . . That once questionable quantity . . . was a mere black little blot" was a mistake, and that she was in fact a "nice girl" after all. But this mistake is of little importance, for the real error of judgment is the assumption that one can reduce people to the level of objects with appropriate species labels, and Winterbourne is puzzled by Daisy simply because the individuality which she shares with all other human beings is given, in her case, such strong outward expression that we can see that his reasoning about her is inevitably wrong because it is based on a false premise. Winterbourne himself never perceives this fact, and so he returns, symbolically, to Geneva at the end of the story.

But why is Winterbourne so obsessively determined to categorize Daisy in the first place when his interest clearly extends beyond what would be aroused by an anomaly in his mental filing cabinet? It seems clear that he is from the first strongly attracted to her sexually. He is very struck by her physical charms; he jumps at the chance to take her to Chillon and is insistent to the point of indiscretion, in view of the presence of Mrs. Miller, that she carry through the proposal of a row on the starlit lake. But Daisy confuses and perplexes him because he conceives of women as belonging to three types; they are "low," in which case they may command one's sexual attention in private, but not one's public recognition or respect; or they are ladies, or "nice girls," who command one's respect but with whom sexual relations are impossible; or, thirdly, they are "persons older than Miss Daisy Miller and provided, for respectability's sake, with husbands—who were great coquettes; dangerous, terrible women with whom one's light commerce might indeed take a serious turn." This third type again reveals the hypocritical double standard which Winterbourne observes; the husbands provide outward respectability while the wives engage in amours, and the tone and phrasing of the last clause suggest that Winterbourne regards a man's liability to become involved with such women in a rather fatalistic way; there is no suggestion that one should take physical or mental steps to avoid such entanglements and, indeed, one assumes that Winterbourne's own "foreign lady" in Geneva is in this class.

In the middle of his first conversation with her Winterbourne "was inclined to think" that Daisy is "a pretty American flirt"; and as she accepts his proposal to go with him to Chillon and in turn proposes that he take her for a row, his estimate of her character becomes increasingly light. As his aunt says when he refers to Daisy as "a very innocent girl," he does not himself sound convinced of this. "She is a young lady," says Mrs. Costello, "who has an intimacy with her mamma's courier," and Winterbourne pounces on the last phrase and repeats it as a question in a way which suggests that his interpretation of the word "intimacy" is as extreme as possible, which is a reflection of his idea of Daisy's character. And again and again in the first half of the story it is made clear that Winterbourne already regards Daisy as a young lady whom a gentleman need no longer respect, but whom he has no intention of avoiding, rather the opposite. He reveals this when he asks his aunt to confirm his notion of Daisy as "the sort of young lady who expects a man sooner or later to—well, we'll call it carry her off." Mentally comparing Daisy with his "pretty cousins in New York" whom he has heard described as "tremendous flirts," but whom Mrs. Costello would never dream of allowing to go on a sight-seeing expedition with a young man without the company of a chaperone, he decides that "she did go even by the American allowance rather far"—the reader is left to make his own estimate of how much Winterbourne thinks, and clearly hopes, "rather far" might be. When Daisy and her mother retire for the night Winterbourne is left feeling very puzzled, "but the only very definite conclusion he came to was that he should enjoy deucedly 'going off' with her somewhere." The next morning, we are told, Daisy has appointed to meet him in the hotel lobby, which is not "the place he would have chosen." We learn further that "he could have believed he was *really* going 'off' with her," that he would have preferred the greater intimacy of a private carriage to the public steamer by which she chooses to travel, and that he is worried lest she embarrass him socially by talking loudly, laughing too much, and wanting to move around the boat.

Three conclusions emerge from this evidence. Firstly, Winterbourne decides, despite his protestations to Mrs. Costello, that Daisy is not a nice girl and consequently he proceeds to try to treat her as one treats such women; that is, he wants to meet her and travel with her privately rather than publicly, since in public she might embarrass him, all the world can see that they are together, and there is less possibility for intimacy. Secondly, having reduced Daisy to a representative of a familiar type, having, by observation, satisfactorily analyzed her, his interest in her should, theoretically, cease to exist, since his interest in women is supposed to be esthetic and intellectual, but instead, on the contrary, he now starts treating her as an object for the gratification of his own sensations—the freight for his skiff and a female whom he feels no compunction about lying to about the existence of his lady friend in Geneva. Thirdly, he has wish-fulfillment mental images of Daisy as the object of an abduction and of himself as the abductor, and far from appearing cheerful and jolly on the trip to Chillon he is so preoccupied with this autoerotic image of himself that Daisy comments on his appearance of gravity and says: "You look as if you were taking me to a prayer-meeting or funeral."

Leslie Fiedler has argued that Daisy is an example of the archetypal character, "the Good Bad Girl," who is always, whatever she does, essentially "virginal though indiscreet." Examined from the same angle Winterbourne may be classified, by analogy, as the Bad Good Boy, whose external behavior is so proper that the rigidly strict Mrs. Costello is "greatly pleased with him," but whose repressed libidinal instincts and romantic self-deceptive, squinted vision of reality makes him potentially a very dangerous character with whom no careful mother would be wise to trust her daughter.

Only two characters in the story, however, ever give any sign of recognizing Winterbourne for what he is, Mrs. Costello, and, interestingly enough, Daisy—but then Daisy, innocent or not, is in the best position to judge since she is the object of Winterbourne's sexual attention. In the course of his first conversation with his aunt, Mrs. Costello warns Winterbourne:

> I really consider you had better not meddle with little American girls who are uneducated, as you mildly put it. You've lived too long out of the country. You'll be sure to make some great mistake. You're too innocent.

To which Winterbourne "protested with a laugh and a curl of his moustache, 'My dear aunt, not so much as that comes to!'" Whereupon she quickly and acutely retorts: "You're too guilty, then!" And Winterbourne does not reply. Later that evening Daisy proposes the row by starlight which Winterbourne so pressingly insists on accomplishing, and when she gives up the project and retires instead to bed her parting words to him are: "I hope you're disappointed or disgusted or something!" which is exactly how one would expect Winterbourne to react; disappointment in the loss of the sensation of guiding "through the summer starlight a skiff freighted with a fresh and beautiful young girl," disgusted at being disappointed, and also, superficially and in accordance with his professed respectability, disgusted at the whole idea in the first place. Again, in Rome, when Winterbourne accuses Daisy of being a flirt and then expresses the wish that she would "flirt with me, and me only," she replies perceptively "you're the last man I should think of flirting with. . . . you're too stiff," for a man like Winterbourne cannot flirt, he cannot enter into a relationship with any woman in a light-hearted way because, as a Puritan romantic, his consciousness of sex is too intrusively obsessive. Finally, Daisy's apparently casual characterization of Winterbourne in the Colosseum as "one of the old lions or tigers" who ate the Christian martyrs again reveals her recognition, which may be subconscious, of his potential sexual ferocity.

This study has concentrated on the first half of *Daisy Miller* because it is at Vevey that the character of Winterbourne is revealed. What happens in Rome follows up the character delineation by showing how such a person behaves in a given set of circumstances. James Gargano has written: "In the presence of Daisy's critics, he [Winterbourne] defends her in a manner which reveals a desire to strengthen his own faltering belief in her." It is clear that Winterbourne's defense of Daisy is ambiguous and unconvincing, but it seems that this is because although he himself unconsciously disbelieves himself, his conscious mind has to produce some justification of his continuing interest in her as a substitute for the sexual truth which the Puritan consciousness refuses to recognize. Similarly, he justifies to himself an intense dislike of Giovanelli, which is in reality simple sexual jealousy, by immediately classifying him, although unjustly as it turns out, as "a music-master or a penny-a-liner or a third-rate artist," and the jealousy which is the hidden motive for this vituperation of the *cavaliere avvocato* (gentleman lawyer) is revealed in Winterbourne's next words "damn his fine eyes!" His attempts to defend Daisy before her critics may also be seen, therefore, as a subconscious refusal to give up his own sexual hopes of Daisy, for as long as her relations with Giovanelli can be seen as innocent there is still a chance for Winterbourne, but this is complicated by the fact that he cannot believe Giovanelli to be innocent also, and he attributes to him his own licentiousness; hence the unconvincing nature of his defense of Daisy's conduct. When he finds them together in the Colosseum at midnight these attempts to convince himself collapse and, in keeping with his character, his sexual jealousy breaks out in scornful contempt of the object of his frustrated attention, not because he now regards Daisy as a low woman, for he has done this all along, but because he is convinced that Giovanelli's relationship with her is sexual, and that his own sexual ambitions have consequently been frustrated irrevocably.

Finally, the discovery of Daisy's innocence causes Winterbourne to feel ashamed of himself. He expresses this as a failure to recognize that "she would have appreciated one's esteem," in other words he recognizes that she was, after all, a lady, or "nice girl," and therefore to be respected, or esteemed. He still fails to realize, however, that his

guilt feelings, which he broods over intermittently all winter, derive from his having pursued as a sexual object one who turned out to be a lady, or one of the sexually untouchables; "She would have appreciated one's esteem" is, therefore, once again his conscious reason for a feeling the real roots of which are more complex.

It seems unlikely that James realized what sort of person he was creating in the character of Winterbourne, and it is probable that he set up the ambivalence in his personality in order to use him as a vehicle for an essentially social theme, as Gargano and Randall suggest. But man is a sexual as well as a social animal and it is natural that Winterbourne's sexual as well as his social nature should be revealed in a study of his relationship with a pretty young girl. Sociomorally he is a hypocrite whose conformity to the Puritan ethic and social code of "respectability" is a public display of virtue beneath which he practices his private vices. It is consistent with this character, therefore, that he should display the same pattern in his sexual nature. Outwardly he is a gentleman, romantic but asexual, with whom any virgin should be safe on a desert island, but the mask of the Puritan romantic hides the fires of a repressed libido which seeks to devour the objects of its sexual attention as the lions and tigers of old did the Christian martyrs. In contrast to Daisy, the Bad Good Girl, he is the archetypal, dangerous Good Bad Boy.

Louise K. Barnett (essay date 1979)

SOURCE: "Jamesian Feminism: Women in 'Daisy Miller'," in *Studies in Short Fiction*, Vol. 16, No. 4, Fall, 1979, pp. 281-87.

[*In the following essay, Barnett compares the limitations society places on women with Winterbourne's self-imposed social and personal restrictions.*]

Although Henry James satirizes the idea of a women's movement in *The Bostonians,* his constant exploration of the tension between individual self-realization and social restriction often focuses upon the way in which society particularly shapes the behavior of women. A number of James's heroines must give up some degree of personal fulfilment and freedom because of social realities. The fine spirit of Isabel Archer is "ground in the very mill of the conventional," just as Marie de Vionnet, another valued heroine, must be sacrificed to Chad Newsome's social obligations of marriage and career. Kate Croy and Charlotte Stant struggle against the limitations placed upon them by their social position as women without means. Resignedly or ruefully, all of these women accept the terms of society, try to achieve self-realization within its confines, and remain within the system after their defeat. Only in Daisy Miller does James portray a woman whose innocent devotion to her own natural behavior causes her to flout society wilfully and persistently. The contrast between what Daisy wants and what other women in the novella have, and between the amount of freedom allowed by society to Daisy and to Winterbourne, constitutes James's clearest indictment of the restrictions society imposes specifically on women.

Through a number of emblematic settings ranging from

the castle of Chillon to the Protestant cemetery, and through a spectrum of characters, *Daisy Miller* explores the options available to women. The odyssey of experience which Daisy, "the child of nature and of freedom," undergoes reveals society's desire to confine women within a narrow and rigidly defined sphere. While those women who accept their circumscribed existence pay varying prices of neurotic illness, ineffectuality, and hypocrisy, the woman who ignores social prescription is punished by ostracism and death. Although the women characters uphold the system which restricts them, the chief arbiter of society for Daisy is a man, the aptly-named Winterbourne. As a definer and enforcer of the bourne or boundary of social propriety, whose verdict has the life-denying implications of winter, Winterbourne represents the masculine world which has ultimate control over the lives of women.

Significantly, Winterbourne is strongly attached to Geneva, a city identified with Calvinism and its social reflection, a decorum which is both narrowly conventional and hypocritically relaxed. The innocent and natural association of young people is strictly controlled and even discouraged: "In Geneva, as he had been perfectly aware, a young man was not at liberty to speak to a young unmarried lady except under certain rarely occurring conditions." Such a view is sustained in Rome by Mrs. Walker, a lady who "had spent several winters at Geneva" and is thus linked to Winterbourne's position both seasonally and geographically. In spite of the severity with which Geneva controls the behavior of young unmarried girls, married women of a certain age enjoy a clandestine sort of freedom, vaguely conveyed by James's statement that some "singular stories" existed about Winterbourne's mysterious foreign lady. Geneva also prescribes a standard of conduct towards relatives, which Winterbourne dutifully conforms to: "He had imbibed at Geneva the idea that one must always be attentive to one's aunt."

Although Winterbourne from time to time expresses an awareness that Geneva has narrowed his perspective, he is unwilling to repudiate its values. When Daisy upbraids him for seeking out Mrs. Walker's company in Rome rather than her own, she remarks: " 'You knew her at Geneva. . . . Well, you knew me at Vevey. That's just as good.' " Daisy has no way of knowing that Geneva prescribed the familial obligation that brought Winterbourne to Vevey; his real world is "the dark old city at the other end of the lake." Daisy's unsuccessful attempt to be a natural and free person within a rigid and hypocritical society is framed by Winterbourne's coming from and returning to Geneva, its Calvinistic code of social behavior *and* its allowable liaisons with older women.

1

With Winterbourne as observer and mediator, *Daisy Miller* develops as a series of confrontations between Daisy and those women who live under the sign of Geneva. In the resort world of Vevey, where Winterbourne and Daisy first meet, social decorum is embodied in Winterbourne's aunt. Denied a more constructive career, Mrs. Costello has channeled her energies into the negative occupation of social exclusiveness. Always on the verge of realization about the life-inhibiting aspects of conventionality, Win-

terbourne finds Mrs. Costello's picture of the "minutely hierarchical constitution" of the society she presides over "almost oppressively striking." Herself victimized by the demands of propriety, Mrs. Costello has internalized the rules of society and devoted herself to oppressing others in its name. In the service of these standards her will has become so inflexible that she tells her nephew, apropos of acknowledging the social existence of the Millers: " 'I would if I could, but I can't.' " Nevertheless, more than a touch of picque may be felt in her comment to Winterbourne: " 'Of course a man may know every one. Men are welcome to the privilege!' "

That Mrs. Costello might have been more at home in this larger masculine world seems likely: her lack of rapport with her children indicates that she was ill-suited to the maternal role. She is described as "a person of much distinction, who frequently intimated that, if she were not so dreadfully liable to sick-headaches, she would probably have left a deeper impress upon her time." Believing that there is a disparity between potential and achievement in her life, Mrs. Costello has sick headaches both as a rationalization for and a psychogenic response to her frustrations.

Mrs. Costello's exclusiveness prevents her from censuring Daisy's behavior in person, a task undertaken in Rome by Mrs. Walker, "the lady from Geneva." While Mrs. Walker strenuously opposes Daisy's walking about without a proper escort, her name suggests that by virtue of conforming to the conventions—being a mature married woman—she is allowed to walk with more freedom than society allows Daisy. Because she prefers a carriage, however, Mrs. Walker's name may be an ironic reflection of the confinement of her own spirit within socially prescribed boundaries. Her "little crimson drawing-room . . . filled with southern sunshine" indicates a passionate nature, but Daisy's remark that Mrs. Walker's small rooms are suited to conversation rather than dancing shows that this nature is not given physical expression.

Ineffectual and ignorant, Daisy's mother is a still lesser version of the absolute represented by Mrs. Costello. As she says to Winterbourne about Giovanelli: " 'I suppose he knows I'm a lady.' " Bewildered by an unfamiliar milieu, which makes her social lapses more plausible, Mrs. Miller nevertheless advances hesitant prescriptions which show a rudimentary sense of the proprieties in force at Geneva. When Daisy complains about her brother, Mrs. Miller rebukes this violation of family loyalty. She also expresses a feeling of vague impropriety when Randolph is boastful and when Daisy refuses to say whether or not she is engaged. Mostly, Mrs. Miller fails to see social infractions because she has a decidedly practical bent. When Mrs. Walker warns Daisy that her contemplated walk on the Pincio is not safe, Mrs. Miller immediately thinks of the danger to her daughter's health rather than to her reputation. Her explanation of Daisy's delayed arrival at Mrs. Walker's party is similarly unsophisticated: the impracticality of Daisy's dressing so early obscures for Mrs. Miller the impropriety of her remaining alone with her Italian suitor.

Like Mrs. Costello's headaches, Mrs. Miller's dyspepsia is both a response to the paucity of meaningful activity in her life and a substitute for it. She becomes animated only when discussing her illness, an affliction which at least makes her important to one person—her doctor:

" 'He has so much to do, and yet there was nothing he wouldn't do for me. He said he never saw anything like my dyspepsia, but he was bound to cure it. I'm sure there was nothing he wouldn't try. He was just going to try something new when we came off. Mr. Miller wanted Daisy to see Europe for herself. But I wrote to Mr. Miller that it seems as if I couldn't get on without Dr. Davis.' " The European trip which deprives Mrs. Miller of this one entirely satisfactory human relationship was commanded by her husband. Given a luxurious leisure which she can make little use of, and unable to play significant maternal role for her headstrong children, Mrs. Miller has a chance to exhibit competence only during Daisy's fatal illness. With a limited and specific task, that of nursing her daughter, she is able to be efficient and, for once, "perfectly composed."

2

Of the two vistas to be seen from Vevey—"the sunny crest of the Dent du Midi and the picturesque towers of the Castle of Chillon"—one images the world of nature and, metaphorically, Daisy's character; the other is a symbol of the societal repression whose less obvious forms constrain the other women in James's novella. To the Daisy Winterbourne meets at Vevey society means people, particularly gentlemen admirers. Successful in the more fluid ambience of New York, where even Winterbourne's proper cousins are "tremendous flirts," Daisy neither feels the weight of nor comprehends the prohibitions of society expressed in Mrs. Costello's snub. Her reaction is merely unoffended wonder: " 'Gracious! she *is* exclusive!' " Another embodiment of society's power, the castle of Chillon, is equally uninstructive to Daisy. It is fitting that Winterbourne should guide Daisy on the excursion to Chillon—the first of a series of juxtapositions of Daisy to a symbol of group tyranny over the individual—for after his first impulse to take Daisy's part against his aunt, Winterbourne consistently tries to persuade Daisy to abide by the social proprieties. Daisy's response to the paraphernalia of punishment is instinctive antipathy: "She flirted back with a pretty little cry and a shudder from the edge of the *oubliettes*." Chillon is an emblem of society's severest forms of repression, but Daisy has not yet perceived its relevance to herself.

Winterbourne follows up his introduction to Daisy with a continuing effort to place her in the proper social category, but the stereotypes he tries to apply—"pretty American flirt," "nice girl," "young lady whom a gentleman need no longer be at pains to respect"—always turn out to be inadequate. Because the forms of social behavior obviate the need of individual decision—prescribing the correct treatment of aunts, unmarried girls, and married women—finding the right label for Daisy, reifying her with the application of some pat formula, would reassure Winterbourne. Uncertain how to categorize Daisy, he is correspondingly uncertain how to act towards her and is

reduced to taking his cues from her. Daisy resists his classification and thus eludes his comprehension.

After Vevey, where Mrs. Costello and Chillon suggest the ostracism and confinement society accords its rebels, Daisy is made aware of society's disapprobation by Mrs. Walker's attempt to enclose her both within her carriage and within her social code. Taking a position she never retreats from, Daisy expresses a desire to alter society rather than her own behavior. She concludes, meaningfully: " 'If I didn't walk I should expire.' " Walking is the simple physical activity performed by an autonomous individual and also the motion of life itself, in contrast to the rigidity of social prescription and the stasis of death. For Daisy, life without the freedom to move under her own power and by her own direction is unthinkable.

When Daisy turns from Mrs. Walker's importunings to Winterbourne, she exhibits a realization that men are the final arbiters and wielders of power. Her appeal is not for the social truth Winterbourne gives her, but for support. Instead of joining Winterbourne in the repressive world of social propriety which his stiffness reflects, Daisy wishes to entice him into her pastoral world of innocence and spontaneity. Winterbourne is tempted, as he was at Vevey, but social decorum impels him to acquiesce to a lady's command, i.e., to join Mrs. Walker in her carriage. His reluctance to accompany his friend and his pondered comment—" 'I suspect . . . that you and I have lived too long at Geneva!' "—reveal Winterbourne's irritation at this point with the restrictions imposed by propriety. When pressed by Mrs. Walker to give up Daisy, he vacillates characteristically. In asserting that there will be "nothing scandalous" in his attentions to Daisy, Winterbourne still imagines that he can have both Daisy and society, but in walking towards his aunt's residence and away from Daisy, he shows his most deeply felt commitment. And, of course, he casually exercises a prerogative denied to Daisy—that of freely walking about alone.

The climax of the novella makes Winterbourne's position clear to Daisy; in his rejection she sees the impossibility of having both freedom and social approval, individuality and community. Significantly, the Roman fever which later kills Daisy is first mentioned in conjunction with her intention of behaving improperly by walking to the Pincio alone. Her death establishes a link between social disapproval and fever: had Daisy not violated a social taboo by going to the Colosseum at night with Giovanelli, she would not have been exposed to the fever. Daisy's own remarks give a further twist to the theme of society's responsibility. Before Winterbourne explicitly rejects her, Daisy affirms her good health: " 'I never was sick, and I don't mean to be!' " After he pronounces his judgment, made in the name of that Geneva doctrine which keeps young women under strict surveillance, Daisy no longer cares whether or not she gets malaria.

Both Winterbourne's and Giovanelli's lack of susceptibility to the fever reiterates again the theme of society's imprisonment of women. Men already have the prerogatives which Daisy lays claim to: it should be just as imprudent for Giovanelli or Winterbourne to go to the Colosseum, but the first shrugs off the danger while the second thinks of it only after satisfying his desire to imbibe the romantic atmosphere for a bit. James's description draws our attention to the enchantment of the setting:

> The evening was charming, and he promised himself the satisfaction of walking home beneath the Arch of Constantine and past the vaguely lighted monuments of the Forum. There was a waning moon in the sky, and her radiance was not brilliant, but she was veiled in a thin cloud curtain which seemed to diffuse and equalize it. When, on his return from the villa (it was eleven o'clock), Winterbourne approached the dusky circle of the Colosseum, it occurred to him, as a lover of the picturesque, that the interior, in the pale moonshine, would be well worth a glance. He turned aside and walked to one of the empty arches, near which, as he observed, an open carriage—one of the little Roman street-cabs—was stationed. Then he passed in, among the cavernous shadows of the great structure, and emerged upon the clear and silent arena. The place had never seemed to him more impressive. One-half of the gigantic circus was in deep shade, the other was sleeping in the luminous dusk.

The division of the ruin into light and dark areas, and the recitation of Byron broken off in mid-quote, illustrate Winterbourne's conflict: his oscillation between Daisy and the customs of "the dark old city," between the risk-taking of individual assertion and the safety of social prudence. James's vivid rendering of the scene, which impresses us with its charm and powers of attraction, indirectly points up another contrast. Winterbourne's innocent desire to see the Colosseum by moonlight is socially acceptable, albeit medically unwise. The same innocent desire in Daisy is a scandalous violation of propriety.

In death Daisy returns to nature, but she is also locked away in a place suggestive of Geneva, the Protestant cemetery. Hypocritically, the society which ostracized her turns out for her burial in a "number larger than the scandal excited by the young lady's career would have led you to expect," perhaps in vindication of the collective mores no longer threatened by Daisy. Winterbourne returns almost immediately to his life in Geneva, "stiff" because of its repression of natural feelings and its rigidly conventional behavior, but safe because it lacks the puzzling and unpredictable qualities of natural self-expression.

3

Daisy remains the most uncompromising and uninhibited of James's many freedom-seeking heroines, a resister of patriarchal authority who "has never allowed a gentleman to dictate to [her] or to interfere with anything [she does]." She breaks rather than bending to social demands. Mrs. Costello's mocking gossip, Mrs. Walker's overt rudeness, and Winterbourne's final cruel rejection of Daisy all reveal the entity opposing her to be mean-spirited and reductive, able to respond only in a negative fashion to natural vitality and innocence. In creating a spectrum of socially approved but sterile feminine existences, James contrasts Daisy's desire for freedom with the confinement of other women in artificial and trivial spheres. Ironically, much

of the freedom society prohibits to Daisy is allowable to Winterbourne, but he has confined himself within a sterile and restricted mode of existence, the victim of his own temperament and choice rather than of society's coercion.

Richard A. Hocks   (essay date 1980)

SOURCE: "*Daisy Miller*, Backward into the Past," in *Henry James Review*, Vol. 1, No. 2, Winter, 1980, pp. 164-78.

[*Hocks is an American author and educator who has written extensively on Henry James. In the following essay, he examines* Daisy Miller *from the perspective of one hundred years of criticism. Highlighting developments in critical perspective and revisions in James's thoughts on the novel, he explores the characters of Daisy and Winterbourne and the thematic issues that they raise.*]

> Here you have the work of a great psychologist, who has the imagination of a poet, the wit of a keen humorist, the conscience of an impeccable moralist, the temperament of a philosopher, and the wisdom of a rarely experienced witness of the world.

> —W. D. Howells on Henry James

1. THE PRESENT

Although there is a lingering untrue truism that, with the publication in 1878 of *Daisy Miller,* James "invented the international novel," what is both enduring and true is that, with the character of Daisy Miller herself, James auspiciously identified as his special imaginative territory the plight of the international American girl. Well after he had transmuted her into Isabel Archer of *The Portrait of a Lady* and, much later, into Milly Theale of *The Wings of the Dove*—by which time he was willing to consent to the view that "my supposedly typical little figure [Daisy] was of course pure poetry, and had never been anything else"—even then James was likely to be identified as the author of *Daisy Miller*. A tale that was pirated immediately in this country, that sold twenty thousand copies in pamphlet form in weeks, that was oft reprinted, translated, and given a different form as a play and even as a hat, and that generated some heated discussion when it first appeared, *Daisy Miller* was as close as Henry James ever came to becoming a popular novelist in his own lifetime. To committed Jamesians, especially in the American academy, *Daisy Miller* has frequently seemed like a mixed blessing within the novelist's momentous and immense body of work, for it occupies, along with *The Turn of the Screw*, perhaps, a somewhat disproportionate importance in that canon.

Yet that importance still persists and will, I should think, continue to do so. For one thing, those who teach Henry James often discover each year that, as with *The American,* so much a piece of the same vintage, university students respond exceedingly well to *Daisy Miller*, respond to it despite—I shall shortly argue even because of—the outmoded manners that constitute the narrative conflict. For another thing, the tale itself remains accessible to students and teachers alike because of its beautifully swift focus on the antagonism between Daisy and the Europeanized "gang" abroad, because of the vividly convincing "moral muddlement" rendered by James of his register Frederick Winterbourne, and because of the yet uncomplicated syntax of James's prose idiom—another element in common with the much-taught book *The American*. For still another thing, Daisy's plight, her character, and her willingness to take risks against the conventional mores all appeal immediately to the deep feminism of these times; the specific issues may seem tame, even quaint, but a great many young women college students, upon reading *Daisy Miller* for the first time, are convinced at once that she is their "sister." They see in her not only a victim of Victorian views about the conduct of women, but more generally a sacrificial victim of some amorphous "societal" set of "female expectations," of traditional "role models," the challenging of which is for them the first, or close to the first, priority of our own times. (It is always tempting at that juncture for a teacher to inform his students that *Daisy Miller*, after being rejected unceremoniously by an American publication, was first accepted and printed in the *Cornhill* by none other than Virginia Woolf's father!) That Daisy's principal antagonists are themselves women, older women with a sort of moralist-custodian station, is a feature of this tale that particularly appeals to these young readers; they "empathize" with her in that conflict, one in which men like Winterbourne are permitted to have their Geneva lady friends without any criticism from the Mrs. Costellos and Mrs. Walkers of the world, but in which Daisy herself is abominated, as it were, by these same vindictive ladies. A double standard derived from men but enforced by women! Finally, even the fantasies of such young college women, I recently discovered to my great surprise, may manage to connect up with the story of Daisy Miller: a particularly vivacious student informed the present writer and her own classmates that, upon reading this tale, she immediately "understood" Daisy because she herself had always wished to appear at her mother's bridge party, or else cocktail party, in a bathing suit! Both the fuss and the challenge to respectability were very important.

Those students who are sympathetic to the woman's movement and who are otherwise students of literature go on, of course, to read *The Portrait of a Lady* rather soon after their baptism into Daisy's cause. But after *The Portrait* they are not so sure what to think. If they have by then become appreciative readers of James, they will obviously read other tales and some of the other novels, perhaps, but they will no longer "relate" to James, or to his young American heroines, in quite the same way. One might even, at that stage, inform the few students who remain after the natural attrition process of the existence of *The Bostonians,* though hastening to add that James himself thought so poorly of it that he chose to omit it from the New York Edition! For those exceedingly few students who eventually become Jamesians themselves, it is henceforth perhaps Kate Chopin or Edith Wharton, not the author of *Daisy Miller,* who will better represent for them the late nineteenth and early twentieth-century American contribution to "women's literature." And yet, like all readers who come to admire Henry James, these last will

permanently wish they could puzzle out the "bottom line" on this issue in the fiction of James.

But of course the great majority of responsive young readers of *Daisy Miller* are precisely *not* the small sifted group above; they are those who feel an instinctive affinity with Daisy, yet one that hardly compels them to undertake the later prose style or sensibility of Henry James. In short, *Daisy* perhaps continues, in a real sense, to be as close as James can come to popularity, and this despite the vast and distinguished academic criticism and scholarship given to him. As for the young "feminist" response to the tale? It is anything but easy to know how much to challenge that response; how much, really, to complicate it— though complicate it, I am convinced, one should. But how much? The issue is a surprisingly intricate one, for not only is the tale itself far more intentionally ambivalent than a pro-sister-Daisy reading might wish it, but the cultural ambience out of which that reading comes manages to recomplicate things. For instance: it is not so hard to perceive, with Leslie Fiedler, that Daisy is, from a certain angle, the "Good Bad Girl" recast, the "virtuous whore," the "*mythically* innocent" figure, and the "prototype of all those young American female tourists who continue to baffle their continental lovers with an innocence not at all impeached, though they have now taken to sleeping with their Giovanellis as well as standing with them in the moonlight." Yet this kind of insight gives us but the lightest of Daisy's threads of continuity with our own day. Likewise, the instinctive response by young college students, especially young women, to Daisy's cause and "feelings" will remind us that these students too are after all themselves "intelligent but presumptuous" American people prepared to "affront their destiny," and thus that James always knew generically of what he wrote. But neither revelation is quite the "complicating cultural ambience" to which I referred before. Even less, nay least, penetrating is the sort of cultural interpretation that says the young sisters of Daisy Miller are today similarly poetic, endlessly baffling and appealing, and wonderfully "audacious and innocent" while pursuing merely a different, or heightened, set of goals, such as "self-fulfillment," a "nonsexist," "non-judgmental" social order, a "healthy sexual identity," or even a full "economic equality." That kind of analysis does not really complicate anything very much, although, like Fiedler's approach, it does exhibit a thread of continuity between Daisy's drama and our own day. But what I meant earlier by a complicating cultural ambience is, rather, something very different. It is my sense that, when studying *Daisy Miller,* the most enthusiastic young students, especially the pro-sister-Daisy interpreters and, if I may so metonymize it, the "bathing suit" response, depend in no small measure on the "quaintness" of the mores in conflict, depend on the formality, even, of the acts of conduct in question. In other words, I sense that the innocently anachronistic forms themselves, not to mention Daisy's own sexual innocence, are central to a contemporary response by the young reader to Daisy's predicament. I do not say that this young college reader has the more refined and ambiguous understanding of the story that the Jamesian has. Indeed, that reader does not, for, whereas the adult Jamesian will wish to emphasize the novelist's realism and, especially, his vigorous departure from siding with any Victorian value system, the young student may, without quite realizing it, be responding to a certain inchoate attractiveness in Victorian formalities, imperatives, and even conceptions of respectability. To put this another way, I sense that the young American reader may be attracted to the "outmoded manners" in conflict within the story in a way not unlike the way Daisy herself responds so excitedly on those few occasions that Winterbourne speaks hyperpoetically, formally, and anachronistically to her—" 'Dearest young lady,' " he cries, " 'have I come all the way to Rome only to be riddled by your silver shafts?' "; and Daisy typically explodes, " 'Just hear him say that!' " It is surprising just how often that sort of exchange occurs in the tale. In teaching *Daisy Miller* we are, properly enough, attuned to James's critical position. But I think our students who, after all, no longer need convincing that they are free and entitled to abide by the manners of nineteenth-century Schenectady (which is, after all, what Daisy "perpetrated," and nothing more)—such students find instead intrinsically fascinating the sort of formal code with which Daisy has to contend.

This is one reason, then, why *Daisy Miller* will most likely keep that "disproportionate importance" in James's canon. It will continue to attract young Americans, and now especially young women, to Daisy's cause; yet that very enthusiasm will, I believe, continue to be fed by a subterranean romance for the past, a kind of dimly understood nostalgia for a social context in which the high drama of such outmoded manners is still possible. If this assessment is correct, there is much irony in the fact that the student so taken with Daisy and her predicament can consciously only transfer her terms of allegiance with Daisy to her own contemporary cultural or sexual goals, ones which, enunciated now primarily by the language and thought of behavioral psychology and counselling—e.g., "feeling good about oneself," "personal growth," "sexually active," "non-judgmental," "reproductive freedom," "getting in touch with my feelings," "letting me be me," "a good self-image," "pro-activist input"—can hardly fail to reinforce the sort of jadedness which gave rise to the attraction of Daisy's charmingly "other" version of the moral drama in the first place.

These few reflections on *Daisy Miller* and the modern student are occasioned in part by the frame of a "centennial" consciousness, to be sure; but they arise pertinently too as a meditation on a very recent study of American social fiction by C. Hugh Holman, whose title *Windows on the World* not only recalls a famous passage in James's Preface to *The Portrait of a Lady* but whose argument contends, against the current academic fashion, for the significance of Realism as a fundamental American literary mode. Holman reminds us of what Realism and its ramifications were for the novel of society, but also points out the appropriateness of the Realistic Movement to the cultural and intellectual milieu out of which it came. He summarizes that overall view with words that evoke immediately the essential spirit of James and his contemporaries and that speak directly to the meaning, then and now, of a touchstone-document of imagination like *Daisy Miller*.

The surface details, the common actions, and the minor catastrophes of a middle-class society constituted the chief subject matter of the movement. Most of the realists avoided situations with tragic or cataclysmic implications. Their tone was comic, frequently satiric, seldom grim or somber, even when situations have—as they often do in Henry James's novels—tragic overtones.

I believe that realism as it was self-consciously practiced by the American novelist in the last half of the nineteenth century was the literary mode that most adequately embodied the assumptions of the thoughtful American of *that* time, as existential romanticism seems to embody the assumptions of ours. The major tenets of realism were called forth by the postulates of the American dream; at its apex realism proved to be a reasonably accurate expression of that dream; and the decline of realism into doctrinaire naturalism, symbolism, and expressionism in our century has been the result in part of a decline in an active faith in that dream. This position is, I believe, in accord with the facts of literary history.

Indeed, Holman's formulation not only "accords with the facts of literary history," it simply evokes at once, as was said before, the very world of James's social and moral vision. When we teach *Daisy Miller* now to our responsive students we are deeply obligated by the "facts of literary history" no less than by the complexity of James's imagination to present the nouvelle as the true, critical dialectical inquiry it is. But we must also recognize, by virtue of the same facts of literary history since 1900 with the diminished importance of realism, that the nostalgic reach backward to the "quaintness" of the moral issue on the part of present-day readers, ourselves as well as our students, is as intrinsic to our collective character and circumstance as Daisy's instinctive response to the flowery language of courtly romance. It is that sense of a "backward imagination" that I have found lacking in the cultural approach epitomized, on the one hand, say, in Leslie Fiedler's view, or in the less formal "literary" application, primarily through feminism, of the language and thinking of counselors and therapists; in a strange quirk of recent history, requiring only a centenary, the obsessions of Victorian sentimentality—the family, motherhood, the respectability of the "Young Girl" (as Howells denominated her in his *Criticism and Fiction*)—are about to be replaced by the sentimentality of our own era, that of sexuality and feeling good about ourselves. We are becoming perhaps the new Mrs. Walkers and Costellos with, from their point of view, such unlikely doctrines! No wonder, then, that our enthusiastic students think uncritically that they "understand" at once what it is Daisy "feels," despite the fact that the tale never enters within her point of view. But no wonder, also, that the same students cannot help but be charmed deep within their being by the presence of a moral and social code like that which Daisy dared to flout.

II. THE MIDDLE PAST

To present *Daisy Miller* as the "true dialectical inquiry it is," and thus to present it also as a vintage expression of the literary milieu described by C. Hugh Holman, it may be helpful to take brief stock of certain configurations found in the critical literature of the work. Perhaps it should first be said that virtually all of its legendary "rumpus," and particularly its alleged "outrage on American girlhood," has been greatly overstated. Indeed, this notion, one that has accompanied the academic history of this story for years, is simply not to be found in the *written* contemporary reviews and response to *Daisy Miller,* with the exception on occasion of remarks by Howells, who of course attributes the sense of outrage elsewhere. Doubtless there was some talk along these lines, but the written record will not justify the legend. On the other hand, what cannot be overstressed is the extent to which *Daisy Miller* did immediately "click" in the reading public, did create overnight its vogue; in no time at all everyone did seem to know what "a Daisy Miller" was, in much the same way that today we all know immediately what "an Archie Bunker" is. In that respect, Howells' casual reference in *The Rise of Silas Lapham* to Daisy Millerism, or even his well-known comment about society's dividing itself into "Daisy Millerites and anti-Daisy Millerites," is well justified, for it is after all possible to disagree about her in literary conversation while all participants agree that James's portrayal was appropriate and, to a greater or lesser extent, on target. If that sounds more like an academic discussion of the story than its supposed contemporary disrepute and scandal, that is nevertheless closer to what appears to have been the case. Everyone seems to have recognized Daisy as a "real" phenomenon, and the number of contemporary allusions to her, both individually and generically, is even astonishing. Yet what is finally compelling is the extent to which James's story had the effect of "teaching" the real Daisy Millers to behave differently, and even the extent to which he himself, along with others, believed that Daisy was almost an extinct species by, say, 1905.

There is some reason to believe, however, that James later thought Daisy extinct for reasons quite different from those marked by natural changes or increasing tolerance in social manners within international society. That James thought differently about the whole issue is almost surely the case. James may have felt by the first decade of this century that his Daisy Miller figure was inevitably more jaded than he had portrayed her earlier and was perhaps even sinister. Indeed, his reaction in this regard is almost a synecdoche for the reaction C. Hugh Holman points to in the demise of literary realism when it begins to lose faith in, and feel the decay of, the American dream. In other words, James's reconsideration of Daisy, a grimmer, more "realistic" reconsideration, we might say, is meanwhile symptomatic of the decline of Realism as the dominant literary movement!

This crux and paradox is, I believe, central to an understanding of James and of the *Daisy Miller* text that eventually came out of James's revision for his New York Edition. The viewpoint that Daisy had lost her innocence for James, a view corroborated by his portrayal of Julia Bride and by his discussion of those contemporary young Daisies in his later "Preface," is one that must register on the literary historian following the lead of C. Hugh Holman.

It is one side of the equation. But what is likewise part of that same moment, both for James and for literary history, is the other side of the equation. The American Daisy-figure underwent an idealized transformation, while the cultural ambience associated with her became, for James's sensibility, part of a poetic past subject to the ravages of the present. In other words, "the decline of active faith in that [American] dream" at the turn of the century, of which Holman speaks, took the form in James of subjecting the international American girl to the corruption of the modern world. In the case of Maggie Verver it meant fighting like nature herself red in tooth and claw against a hideous modern evil "seated all at its ease where she had only dreamed of good. . . . like some bad-faced stranger surprised in one of the thick-carpeted corridors of a house of quiet on a Sunday afternoon." Like Isabel Archer, another of Daisy's sisters, Maggie Verver had to fight for her life in a domestic framework of deception and brutal manipulation. It might even be said that, unlike Isabel, Maggie had no choice but to become deeply tainted morally, suffer the "miasma" of the corruption of modern life in order to survive.

In the case of Milly Theale, James even went so far as to identify her with the very poetry of Venice, a poetry, that is, which James interpreted as tied intimately to the beautiful city's own slow, inevitable decay from within, an intricate conception and interpretation that anticipates by about ten years a comparable one by Thomas Mann. James's haunting explication of Venice as "the poetry of misfortune" provides for us a deep analogue by which Daisy Miller, no less than her own prototype in his cousin Minnie Temple, had now been transformed into the Milly Theale phenomenon. "Is it the style," he asks, while pondering Venice's immemorial beauty,

> that has brought about the decrepitude, or the decrepitude that has, as it were, intensified and consecrated the style? There is an ambiguity about it all that constantly haunts and beguiles. Dear old Venice has lost her complexion, her figure, her reputation, her self-respect; and yet, with it all, has so puzzlingly not lost a shred of her distinction. Perhaps indeed the case is simpler than it seems, for the poetry of misfortune is familiar to us all, whereas, in spite of a stroke here and there of some happy justice that charms, we scarce find ourselves anywhere arrested by the poetry of a run of luck. The misfortune of Venice being, accordingly, at every point, what we most touch, feel and see, we end by assuming it to be of the essence of her dignity. . . . What was most beautiful is gone; what was next most beautiful is, thank goodness, going—that, I think, is the monstrous description of the better part of your thought. Is it really your fault if the place makes you want so desperately to read history into everything?

By the time the metamorphosis of the Daisy figure into Milly Theale and the poetry of her misfortune had taken place, James had likewise begun to turn, at least partially, again toward Hawthornean romance as the vehicle for this tenor. In this respect James is, once more, a legitimate barometer of the change Hugh Holman points to in the beginning of the decline of Realism's dominance at the turn of the century. We have already noted, of course, that the elder James of the New York Edition was apt to refer to Daisy as having been "pure poetry." James's comments are confirmed by the findings of those scholars who have studied at close hand his textual revisions for the New York Edition. The consensus is that James's revisions serve to coat his earlier comedy of manners with a symbolic and poetic overlay, one that emphasizes not only Daisy's charm and the general disagreeableness of her critics in the story, but especially that stresses her symbolic ties to nature, ties which, inevitably, betoken also her subjugation to its laws and processes. It is thus at once an idealization of his heroine which, at the same time, makes symbolic connections with her fragile mortality. While it is most understandable that interpreters of James's nouvelle will wish to see this textual evidence as confirmation that Daisy was innocent, blameless, and beautiful of spirit, a true and modern victim whose Colosseum death is as unprovoked as those of the Christian martyrs preceding her, my own viewpoint is that James's revisions, together with his statements in the New York "Preface," have more to do with his own reinterpretation of the cultural past epitomized in the American girl abroad, a reinterpretation as "the poetry of misfortune," a perspective in which the elements of romance are part of the real, the "poetry" even part of the "monstrous" realization of a decay in the dream. Above all, perhaps, it was clear that in the New York Edition James would no longer prefer to emphasize his comedic objectivity and distance from the heroine in a comedy of manners by titling his nouvelle "A Study": the affinities with Milly Theale and the cultural reconceptions she symbolized made that impossible. Thus, despite the fine academic criticism James has received, no one, I think, has perceived this deep connection between Daisy and Milly any better than did Howells. He writes [in *North American Review* 176 (1903)]:

> Milly Theale is as entirely American in the qualities which you can and cannot touch as Daisy Miller herself; and (I find myself urged to the risk of noting it) she is largely American in the same things. There is the same self-regardlessness, the same beauteous insubordination, the same mortal solution of the problem. Of course, it is all in another region, and the social levels are immensely parted. Yet Milly Theale is the superior of Daisy Miller less in her nature than in her conditions.

. . . . .

If one had to pick a single feature, or perhaps two, which have become crucial in interpreting the text of *Daisy Miller* by academic critics, those would be, first, the emphasis on James's "middle point of view" in the conflict he portrays, and, second, the importance to the story of Winterbourne, who is, after all, our narrative register rather than Daisy (who remains instead the "phenomenon" she is and could no longer quite be were we permitted within her consciousness). For obvious reasons these two approaches tend to overlap, because James's balanced objectivity relies in part on his, and our, keeping in mind that Daisy is perceived and evaluated from without, which in turn

means from a point of view largely, but not entirely, that of Winterbourne. In the 1950's, for example, F. W. Dupee and Christof Wegelin represent two versions, if you will, of a balancing interpretation of the tale. Dupee emphasized that Daisy was indeed no martyr, but that James was addressing critically the *sentiment* of the American girl and the "legend of American innocence," not merely participating romantically in it himself (as James in retrospect, we recall, thought he had done erroneously in the case of Newman in *The American*). "Daisy's death" in the Colosseum, observed Dupee [in *Henry James,* 1951], "if it proves anything, proves that not every superstition is a fraud." For Wegelin, on the other hand, James's critical distance was keynoted by the fact that all of Daisy's own critics and censors in the story are Americans in Europe, a colony which bends over backwards to ape European practices and judgments. In this framework it is, of course, appropriately ironic that Mr. Giovanelli, the one actual European in the tale, pronounces accurately the "innocence" to Daisy's character denied by her own Europeanized compatriots! In still another vein, Leon Edel perceived James's social criticism to lie in no small measure in the "unerring vision which James had of the total abdication, by the mass of American parents, of all authority over their children."

But I think it fair to say that the most elucidative energy expended on *Daisy Miller,* at least in its comparatively recent critical history, has been a refocusing on Frederick Winterbourne as the Jamesian "center" of the story. Perhaps one measure of this refocus is a most recent comment *au contraire* by Edward Wagenknecht, in his book *Eve and Henry James,* that in the "one hundred years that the story has now been in existence, has a single human being ever read it not because he was interested in Daisy but because he was interested in Winterbourne?" Perhaps not, yet one can hardly blame a number of Jamesians for gravitating in the direction they have. Daisy is, after all, seen from without, is indeed misinterpreted from without; so it is natural to follow, as it were, the story's own narrative lead. This seems especially appropriate since all know that James himself became preeminently concerned with, and masterful at, developing the viewpoint character. Finally, a Winterbourne-focus in *this* tale does not divert us from the social conflict or "international theme" which comprises James's real subject, since Winterbourne is himself a solid representative, albeit in a softer key, of the Europeanized American colony comprising the story's collective antagonist.

In any case, there is no gainsaying the tendency toward a kind of emphasis in the past twenty years to the effect that Winterbourne is really the pivotal character. This view was taken in Wayne C. Booth's influential study *The Rhetoric of Fiction,* but his emphasis remains there primarily technical; others, however, have sought to construct social, cultural, psychoanalytic, or moral interpretations of *Daisy Miller* extracted from a reading of, or by way of, the character of Winterbourne. With occasional exception, these readings concur that Winterbourne is morally culpable, as his name insinuates; indeed that he freezes to death this American Daisy as effectively, let us say, as Emily Dickinson's frost in her poem "Apparently with no Surprise." Perhaps this is only a newfangled way of continuing to read the story with a strong sympathy for Daisy's beauty, freedom, innocence, and vulnerability. But on closer inspection one discovers also that the real villain, for these commentators, is Puritanism, whether American- or Geneva-style; or, worst of all, the two symbolically combined in the chilly Winterbourne. What is foremost to that position, then, is that James's famous tale is a harsh indictment of Puritanism, either in cultural or in sexual terms, or in both. Yet a new and interesting variation on this tendency in recent years to center on Winterbourne is provided by Holman in *Windows on the World*. He argues that *Daisy Miller* takes its place in a long line of distinctively American narratives which are adaptations of the nineteenth and twentieth-century Bildungsroman. In a group extending from Hawthorne's "My Kinsman, Major Molineux" to *All the King's Men,* Holman notes the persistence of the witness or spectator-characters, individuals who undergo a development toward wisdom and maturity by watching what happens to others, and who most often are instructed "in a dark dimension of life which that witness might otherwise never have seen." This version of the rite of passage associated with the *Bildungsroman*

> comes not actually from his own experience or his own response to trials or actions or even from what is directly done to him, but from what he witnesses being done by and to others. The initiation through which he passes results from witnessing action not from taking it. That structure, in which a witness or a narrator watches actions by others and learns from them, has reappeared in so many American novels dealing with the maturing, development, or education of characters that it may be considered truly a peculiarly American form of the *Bildungsroman*.

Holman's argument is valuable primarily for his isolating a native sub-genre of the *Bildungsroman* rather than for his breaking much new ground on our analysis as such of *Daisy Miller*. And yet, what his remarks do perform for the nouvelle is an extremely helpful move away from using Winterbourne as the principal target for alleged anti-Puritan, anti-sexual-repression statements by James. Modern criticism has, I think, been wise to concentrate on the figure of Winterbourne, for one's reading of Daisy's character and her larger symbolic meaning is not impaired by that focusing; it is in fact enhanced. But psycho-sexual criticism, with its inevitable pillorying of "Puritanism," misses the whole point of James's moral world, at least in his international fiction. The drama of inner conflict, whether social or sexual, is the exciting stuff of James's viewpoint characters, especially when they are Americans. These critics sometimes seem to forget that James has created his own share of characters with emancipated views and practices in the domain of sexuality, and they are not the more compelling for it. Winterbourne's tale, if it is his tale, is essentially about the making of a Europeanized American. That sad and deleterious process has only completed itself by the very end, when his alternative possibility, in the person of Daisy, has been closed, and he returns to Geneva and to a "clever foreign lady." But we seem to forget that the issue was still in doubt only

as long as he inclined toward Daisy's innocent and affecting ways and also kept vacillating from one moment to the next: thus, for example, when his aunt tells him Daisy "has an intimacy with her mamma's courier," Winterbourne, who had just before concluded that Daisy was an innocent American flirt, is caught off guard—" 'An "intimacy" with him?' Ah there it was!" There, of course, it was not; not even for Winterbourne, who changes his mind numerous times again before the story's climactic scene in the Colosseum. To put what is often said of him in a sort of obverse way, as long as Winterbourne remained truly puzzled by the question of Daisy's sexual innocence he was potentially worthy of her and worthy of our sympathetic engagement with him as narrative "center." Winterbourne's alliance with Geneva in the story does, I concede, suggest symbolically his association with the sources of Calvinism. But it primarily stands, I believe, for his amphibious attachments—national, cultural, and social—to the old and now worlds. It was really, without his knowing it, the new world element within his "queer mixture" that responded to the free spirit from Schenectady.

III. THE PAST

In 1870 James lost his beloved cousin Minnie Temple. Eight years later his conception of Daisy owed something central to his memory of her. Most important was a quality they both had of moral spontaneity, of questioning given institutions, and of a general natural free-spiritedness. Most different between them were Minnie's intellectual interests and her capacity for personal introspection—in that respect James's cousin resembles more the character of Isabel Archer. Still another element in common between Minnie and Daisy is, of course, their premature deaths. This parallel may be of particular importance, inasmuch as James seems always to have believed that Minnie's death, terrible as it was, at least precluded her discovery of the full extent of the world's evil. James always felt that she had died, not only betimes, but before the inevitable disillusionment with her reading of life had set in. Yet James simultaneously believed that he himself, and also his brother William, had been thrust rudely out of their own innocence and youth by her death. It is only extending slightly James's own lifelong analysis of the meaning of Minnie's death to suggest, then, that her liberation, even by death, from the darker interpretations of life became the occasion and even the requirement that James accept and convey them, as it were, for her. Daisy's abrupt death functions in a similar way in *Daisy Miller*. She remains, we are told, first by Giovanelli and then twice in echoing repetition by Winterbourne, " 'the most innocent!' " And Winterbourne, who is the exact same age as was James when Minnie died in 1870, is left with the burden of consciousness, the loss of his own spiritual innocence. The manner of Daisy's death, too, suggests not so much a martyrdom perpetrated by the bad accusatory Americans—even though Winterbourne's reaction once she is *at* the Colosseum is, as she says, " 'he cuts me dead!' "—rather it suggests that the "Roman fever" she catches is worldly evil, which is pervasive, whether she knows it or not. Whatever one might say of Winterbourne, his aunt, or Mrs. Walker, it might be suggested that

Giovanelli's friendship, which Daisy prized, was somewhat less than elevated from his side by his willingness to take her to the "fatal spot." His explanation that he had no fear for himself and that Daisy " 'did what she liked' " is accompanied by his raising "his neat shoulders and eyebrows to within suspicion of a shrug." From a certain angle, Giovanelli's actions and explanations are closer to the unprotected condition of life, the cruel Roman fever of experience, than is the misjudgment or even the rejection, on passionate ground, by Winterbourne. What is clearest at the end is that, apart from her own family, Winterbourne is the only one who continues to reflect on Daisy's fate and its implications for himself.

As is not the case with the later James, however, character analysis as such, whether of Winterbourne or of Daisy, will take us only so far. To appropriate Winterbourne's own language, the two principals in this story are "booked to make a mistake" with one another because the reactions by each to the other are culturally and socially predetermined and are psychological only in a subsidiary way. Given our general recognition that Henry James developed an extraordinary capacity in his mature fiction to translate cultural issues into the dominion of individual psychology, the emphasis in *Daisy Miller* remains at the level of social determinism; it is fundamentally what the nouvelle immediately following it was called, "an international episode." And it is not even necessarily a better intrinsic piece of work than the latter (which has also its Daisy Miller/Isabel Archer American girl in the person of Bessie Alden). What it does have, however, is the special conflict and mutual misunderstanding that arises between the "natural" American free spirit and the complicated response to that spirit by the Europeanized American who is at once attracted and repelled by it. Yet it is still, at least at this stage in James's career, a case of a quasi-tragedy through cultural implantation; or we might want to call it a social comedy of errors with a darkening and lyric edge.

For this reason, Daisy's name functions emblematically in the tale in a way that would almost be worthy of James's predecessor Hawthorne. She is, of course, the North American "daisy," thus by association a "natural" and "common" flower from the region of her native land: indeed, Winterbourne's initial response to what he thinks of as her "natural elegance" is much in keeping with this typology. Etymologically, as several critics have mentioned in passing, she is the "day's eye"; I think it is interesting that not only does she, like certain species of the daisy, "close up again" at night when she visits the Colosseum with Giovanelli, she also puts off her earlier nighttime sojourn with Winterbourne to the castle of Chillon at Vevey until another time when it becomes instead a daylight excursion. And even though Mrs. Costello, so to speak, "cuts her dead" verbally when hearing about the Chillon outing—"And that . . . is the little abomination you wanted me to know!"—nevertheless Daisy herself is anything but "closed up" by that earlier expedition with Winterbourne. Thus, while the two trips to Chillon and the Colosseum are clearly structural opposites in the story, and are largely ironic in the fact of the two companions and the different social conventions governing Vevey and

Rome (so that Winterbourne is, in a sense, the prototype of Giovanelli while at Vevey), the same structural opposition is enhanced with additional meaning when looked at through the iconography of Daisy's name.

But Daisy's name also carries emblematic associations with the other principal species of the flower, the European plant, sometimes called the "English daisy." Here I suspect we have not so much a type to which Daisy herself refers, as with the North American species, but more the expectations made *of* her by critics and verbal adversaries throughout the tale. For this latter European species of daisy is commonly referred to as "bachelor's button," suggesting, as boutonniere, a number of images antithetical to Daisy's free-spiritedness and natural state, indeed suggesting elements of conformity, of unlimbered rigidity, of exactness and precision, all by dint of being severed from the natural soil. (Daisy, we recall, continually calls Winterbourne "stiff"; Winterbourne, in lamenting often that Daisy fails to "compose," is surely not thinking of the "bachelor's button," but I am not sure James himself does not have that, along with much else, in mind.)

Still another meaning connected with Daisy's name is the colloquial, or slang, expression of "daisy" meaning something which is fine, first-class, first-rate. A beautifully memorable use of the word that way, an ironic use, is by Mark Twain when characterizing Natty Bumppo's following the canonball track in "Fenimore Cooper's Literary Offenses." This slang meaning parallels, perhaps, something of the ambiguous resonance we are left with in our reflection upon Daisy after taking stock of many factors, both those denoting her natural elegance and victimization as well as those denoting her foolishness, stubbornness, and, more than once, a sort of tactless crudity. More immediately, the "daisy" of the slang meaning conveys, I think, the sort of dramatized ambivalence concerning her which is found in Winterbourne's puzzled consciousness.

Let me say that, having taught James and written about him for many years, I have found "allegorical" approaches to his fiction halting, to say the least. My analysis here, however, by way of Daisy's name, is meant to elaborate two points. First, I have meant to suggest that these emblematic features tie into and support the very same kind of social drama we would ordinarily explicate without such typology. Second, I wish to suggest again by this approach the extent that Daisy Miller is primarily governed by cultural determinism, and is not primarily an example of James's depth and complexity at rendering individual psychology. Though other Jamesians may doubtless disagree, it is my own view that, in the novelist's later, more complex idiom, the typology of his fictional names is in itself less enhancing, but instead functions as a kind of first-level framework of meaning and interpretation, the point of which is usually to be complicated and qualified through further analysis—as with "Marcher" and "May," for instance, in *The Beast in the Jungle*.

In a somewhat different vein, yet pointing to the same overall meaning, James's craftsmanship in *Daisy Miller* is particularly evident in his masterful use of verbal foreshadowing, one of the strongest features of his mature fiction as well. Thus, in addition to the kind of ironic adumbration found in Winterbourne's early excursion to Chillon with Daisy at Vevey, we find that the early designation by Mrs. Costello of Daisy as "a horror" actually anticipates the very term for the emotion Winterbourne feels when he finally makes up his mind against her in the Colosseum: "Winterbourne felt himself pulled up with final horror now—." Such verbal echoing has the force of aligning Winterbourne with his aunt, thus telling rhetorically against him despite the fact that the moment comes to us from within his own consciousness. Still another, powerfully subtle case of such verbal foreshadowing in ***Daisy Miller*** occurs in connection with the phraseology of going "too far." When Winterbourne first meets the young lady, he "wondered whether he had gone too far, but decided that he must gallantly advance rather than retreat." After a number of references throughout to Daisy's having gone too far by exceeding the limits of propriety, we find, once again in the climactic Colosseum scene, that Winterbourne's original motive for visiting is said to be the following: "The air of other ages surrounded one; but the air of other ages, coldly analysed, was no better than a villainous miasma. Winterbourne sought, however, toward the middle of the arena, a further reach of vision, intending the next moment a hasty retreat." The configuration here of a "further reach of vision" followed by a "hasty retreat" is an extraordinary case of the sort of "reflexive" language James mastered in his fiction throughout his career. The literal reasons—to gain a more general look and then leave before the bad air harms him—give way quickly to the key idea that Winterbourne has, with Daisy, been struggling to extend his vision, to discover her special goodness and beauty (and his own shortcomings in the light of that discovery) but is now about to "retreat" hastily again into the prejudices and judgments of others against Daisy when, in the next moment, he sees her there with Giovanelli. The same phrasing of his now "retreating" also, of course, reverses the earlier articulation at Vevey when he was cast in a different role, as we have seen. James's conscious, intentional use of such phrasing is unquestionable. In this case, for instance, he altered the Scribner's text from the earlier version so that the idiom would carry the full reflexive force just described.

Winterbourne's moral failure in James's tale, as many readers agree, occurs the next moment he recognizes Daisy's presence in the Colosseum with Giovanelli and determines for himself that she is base. He feels himself, as we have seen, "pull up with final horror now—"

> and, it must be added, with final relief. It was as if a sudden clearance had taken place in the ambiguity of the poor girl's appearances and the whole riddle of her contradictions had grown easy to read. She was a young lady about the *shades* of whose perversity a foolish puzzled gentleman need no longer trouble his head or his heart. That once questionable quantity *had* no shades—it was a mere black little blot. He stood there looking at her, looking at her companion too, and not reflecting that though he saw them vaguely he himself must have been more brightly presented.

James's moral "ricochet," as before, is the great achievement here. Who else could inform us that Winterbourne's false conclusions about Daisy, conclusions in the very act of forming in his reflective consciousness, are themselves only too clear to the reader, so that, whatever shade of truth may attach from them to Daisy and to her companion, Winterbourne himself is, without of course his perceiving it, all the "more brightly presented" in his transgression against Daisy's character? Who but James could do that—make the very articulation immediately subject to the light of moral reflex, while on its surface level the passage only says that Winterbourne was more visible by moonlight than the two he just now condemned? So tight in this respect is James's moral landscape that should we, say, want to embroider the surface meaning, as by calling Winterbourne "caught in a shaft of light," or some such parallel, we could hardly avoid expounding figuratively the inner meaning along with it. All of this is, certainly, a function of the creative principle James was later to call "operative irony"; generically it is the same kind of irony that elsewhere occurs when, for instance, Mrs. Costello and Winterbourne both claim at different times that Winterbourne has "lived too long out of the country"—each attaching opposite implications to that shared proposition.

But in the passage above the operative irony is particularly dense, because there it converges with several other verbal and thematic elements, and does so at this appropriate moment of crisis. Thus, the "sudden clearance" connects beautifully and ironically with the "further reach of vision" from the earlier passage. Likewise, the "final relief" he feels has the effect of his letting go of the uncertainty which has been the hallmark of his "Puritan" vacillations concerning Daisy, the presence of which uncertainty, I would argue against some commentators, has merited on his behalf our sympathetic engagement. Especially important to the passage, however, is the language and meaning attached to the issue of "shades," language, I should add, entirely introduced by James into the later Scribner's text. Whether we think of it as shades of interpretation of Daisy's character (her "riddle" as Winterbourne also calls it) or perhaps as shades of moral and ethical responsibility, in which case it might well apply to both main characters, the whole conception at this moment of "shading" is imaginatively deep and powerful. Daisy herself, of course, has been from the start transparent in her absence of coquetry, of discrimination, or of subtlety of any kind (except perhaps her deeper attraction to formal and courtly expressions on the part of her admirers). Winterbourne, by contrast, has, by virtue of his own "queer mixture" of European and American allegiances (symbolized by his "Geneva-ness") translated that shadowy ambiguity into his vacillation regarding Daisy. This moment of ironic epiphany, then, manages to reverse and fuse both sides of the moral equation. Winterbourne finally discards "shades," thereby being himself exposed to our moral censure; Daisy simultaneously takes on the shades Winterbourne discards, for not only does she literally sit there in vague silhouette obscured from the moonlight, she moves swiftly out of the tale, as well as the Colosseum; this disappearance effectively leaves us to ponder, not so much about her essential character as about her judgment, especially with respect to this last, and final, episode in her short history. James's transpositions here of Winterbourne's shades and shadings into Daisy and of Daisy's transparency into Winterbourne (don't *we* judge and condemn him right at this moment with a decisiveness comparable to that of Daisy's censors in the tale generally?)— these constitute a feature which is found in his finest work. For those who have studied it, his extraordinary inversions of lightness and darkness in *The Portrait of a Lady* will be seen at once to function in the same way.

Jamesians should know, of course, that shades and nuances constitute in the last analysis virtually a microcosm of James's own epistemology and aesthetic practice. Winterbourne's relinquishing of "shades" at the crucial moment in effect pits him against everything James stands for as a writer. But whereas Daisy eventually "retreats" from us into the obscurity just mentioned, her character and her judgments while "planted straight in front" of us throughout the tale do anything but vindicate her, at least from this perspective of "shades." It is not Daisy's directness or obvious lack of ulterior design in her negotiations with people, any more than, say, Billy Budd's, which tells against her in this respect. It is, rather, her absence of real consciousness itself. In this sense it is almost a moot point whether we hold that her inward life is withheld from us because of James's choice of point of view, or that he made that choice because he wished to qualify Daisy's various positive qualities—naturalness, absence of guile, fresh beauty, true innocence—in this one important direction. Again, the comparison with Billy Budd is possibly instructive, for Melville apparently found, at one stage of composition, that he could not tell the story adequately without a Captain Vere, without, that is, a character who possesses a reflecting consciousness. The point is all the more acute when we recollect that James's principal quantum leap forward with the American girl after Daisy is his conception of Isabel, one which, as he insisted so strongly in the later Preface, constituted a singular decision to make this "frail vessel" type his reflecting consciousness as well. That decision transformed, among other things, "A Study" into "The Portrait," a figure into a character properly speaking. Yet it is remarkable to recall how much Isabel too is direct, is natural, is devoid of guile, possesses a fresh American beauty and a moral spontaneity. And it is just as remarkable to recollect that, on one level, Daisy fulfills James's famous Isabel-formula of the engaging, presumptuous "young woman affronting her destiny." But the difference, that Isabel's story is told from within, marked a momentous change in the whole trajectory of James's career, at least with respect to his international fiction and his conception of the American girl. Daisy's lack of maturity and judgment, as opposed to her beauty, innocence, and "poetry," is signified in her absence of reflection and consciousness. In that sense she resembles more the character in *The Portrait* of Henrietta Stackpole, although Henrietta has many more ideas, however blunt and unsifted by any real thoughtfulness, than does Daisy. In her own story Daisy reveals a capriciousness, usually based on the enjoyment of a "fuss," which effectively precludes any inward life whatever. She "chatters" in a way that, semantically as well as socially, sometimes resembles more the sound of a scattergun than the verbalization of real thought. That she is only one step removed from her mother is at times painfully obvious. And the fact that the

two of them share in central and southern Europe only the topics of brother Randolph and Schenectady's Dr. Davis is wincing.

Even so, Winterbourne's oft-repeated sense that Daisy's various parts fail to make an "ensemble," or that she somehow doesn't quite "compose," has occasionally suggested to this writer a qualification James made in his otherwise strong approbation of the fiction of his colleague Howells. My point is not, obviously, one of comparing the minds of Daisy and Howells, but of recalling that, for James, composition had its analogues outside the aesthetic sphere. Perhaps Howells, whose imagination and dominion was, from James's viewpoint, particularly American, and whose work and method is dominated sometimes by long and uninterrupted conversations, could be said to exhibit a kind of spiritual kinship with Daisy. Perhaps it might be added that Howells represented in his fiction something like the highest terms of a tutored vision of the sensibility which in its primitive state resides in Daisy. And this is only to say, too, that perhaps Winterbourne is, in his primitive state, something like the answering sensibility in James himself.

Although the emphasis is on the appeal, Winterbourne's formulation of Daisy's "queer little native grace" hints at her limitations as well. James's own Winterbourne-like formulations from his later "Preface," that with a "sufficiently brooding tenderness" he could "eventually extract" from Daisy as his subject "a shy incongruous charm," hints at the same appeal and limitation. The word "incongruous" especially echoes her "want of finish," her absence of "form" which Winterbourne frequently remarks to himself. Daisy is, then, as much a "queer mixture" as is Winterbourne himself. Even the young man's potential for romantic love for her is a mixed issue. While it is certainly the case that he "liked her awfully" and that, as much as anything else, Winterbourne's conflicts with her in Rome arose from a combination of jealousy and disappointment that she had not been pining away for his arrival, it is equally true that: "It pleased him to believe that even were twenty other things different and Daisy should love him and he should know it and like it, he would still never be afraid of Daisy. It must be added that this conviction was not altogether flattering to her: It represented that she was nothing every way if not light." This judgment by Winterbourne is sufficiently of a piece with the James of the later "Preface." Indeed, here the later Scribner's text makes the assessment more generalized, more "reliable," less Winterbourne's own opinion subject to a distorting lens. And since it is already the consensus of those who have studied the matter that James chose to render Daisy herself more poetic and idealized in the revised text, it suggests that at no time, early or late, did James fail to perceive his heroine's limitations. A "lightweight," in Jamesian terms, most often means someone without sufficient consciousness.

Daisy and Winterbourne were not really star-crossed lovers, because they never did have a sufficient meeting of minds to become lovers in anything but a preliminary sense. At best they were perhaps complementary figures. Daisy's enthusiasm and spontaneity needed to be tempered by a capacity for analysis, reticence, discrimination, if you will the critical faculty, whereas Winterbourne, as she kept insisting to him, was not spontaneous enough, hadn't enough "give." One of the most humorous aspects to the story, yet finally a sad one, is that unconsciously Daisy is reaching out for Winterbourne's funny-bone; when she teases him time and again she is truly searching for his American "funny" side, which is still latent within him, but which is already obstructed, as her opposing latent possibilities are obstructed, by presuppositions culturally planted and entrenched within their beings. Out of the Daisy/Winterbourne opposition were to emerge the great sets of American and European opposing correlatives in the international fiction of James. Nature required art; activity and energy required meaning and consciousness; innocence required experience; freedom demanded an awareness of life's limitations; the ethical temperament required its aesthetic understanding; spontaneity must always inhabit the conditions of history and custom. Daisy's will was at once strong and weak by virtue of the indistinctness of her aims and, of course, the absence of any critical reflection on them. Her family situation betrayed the same problem, for it is clear from the vivid presence of Randolph, of her mother, and the situation of her absent "downtown" father, that they all inhabited a vacuum, all were deprived (as our early novelists themselves lamented) of a cultural "content." Winterbourne, like many another James character to come, was flawed spiritually by his preconceptions, by his either-or thinking, by the very "relief" he experiences, both early and late, when he thinks he has discovered "the formula." And so the story does remain a true dialectical inquiry, as well as an unforgettable early success of James and of American Realism. With the great international novels ahead of him, and certain very special lessons learned from this piece of work as well as from its predecessor, *The American,* it was to be James himself, rather than Winterbourne, who had discovered the formula.

Carey H. Kirk   (essay date 1980)

SOURCE: " 'Daisy Miller': A Reader's Choice," in *Studies in Short Fiction*, Vol. 17, No. 3, Summer, 1980, pp. 275-83.

[*In the following essay, Kirk argues that James's narrative strategy in* Daisy Miller *is designed to promote alternate and even contradictory interpretations of characters and themes in the novel.*]

Any overview of the past century's critical responses to *Daisy Miller* reveals a radical shift in readers' sympathies with its characters. The genteel American audience of James's day was outraged and insulted by Daisy's liberated behavior, but modern sensibilities identify Winterbourne as the principal offender against human decency. They accuse him of being everything from an emotional cripple to an unfeeling criminal, and now count Daisy as his almost innocent victim.

This change of allegiance can be explained, of course, by a shift in cultural attitudes towards women and manners in general, and by the increased perceptiveness of modern interpreters. But the present critical consensus should by no means be considered the final assessment of the characters' relative worth. In *Daisy Miller* James has designed a story that will continue to challenge readers' interpretive skills and cause their attitudes toward Daisy and Winterbourne to vacillate for a considerable time to come.

The author has constructed this study to promote his audience's confidence that they can choose the right side in the contest between the central characters. James flatters their discernment by providing a variety of literary allusions that are distinctly uncomplimentary to Winterbourne. Mrs. Costello's request that her nephew bring her that "pretty novel of Cherbuliez's—'Paule Mëré'—" is a delicate revelation that Winterbourne's aunt, and by extension Winterbourne, read books with the same insensitivity that they read people.

For the reader upon whom nothing is lost, James begins and ends his story with certain Byronic allusions which reflect negatively on Winterbourne for his attitude and conduct toward Daisy. Their tour of the castle of Chillon reminds one not only of Bonnivard, the Genevan freedom fighter, but also of "The Prisoner of Chillon." Byron's Bonnivard, freed from six years' confinement, ends the poem expressing these sentiments about his release:

> At last men came to set me free;
>   I ask'd not why, and reck'd not where;
> It was at length the same to me
> Fetter'd or fetterless to be,
>   I learn'd to love despair.
> And thus when they appear'd at last,
> And all my bonds aside were cast,
> These heavy walls to me had grown
> A hermitage—and all my own!
> And half I felt as they were come
> To tear me from a second home:
> With spiders I had friendship made,
> And watch'd them in their sullen trade,
> Had seen the mice by moonlight play,
> And why should I feel less than they?
> We were all inmates of one place,
> And I, the monarch of each race,
> Had power to kill—yet, strange to tell!
> In quiet we had learn'd to dwell;
> My very chains and I grew friends,
> So much a long communion tends
> To make us what we are:—even I
> Regain'd my freedom with a sigh.

James surely intends one to identify Bonnivard's ambivalent attitude toward his imprisonment and emancipation with Winterbourne's own preference for a repressed emotional life. The American expatriate's brief escapade with Daisy at Chillon is the only real departure from his wonted life style, and ironically, he must free himself from Daisy before being reshaped in his accustomed mold. If Winterbourne has learned to love the spiders and mice of his Havisham world, how will he ultimately view the healthy Daisy except as an intruder on his privacy? Or going one step further, if, like Byron's Bonnivard, he has begun to coexist peacefully with the creeping things of darkness, Winterbourne may have actually become inimical to creatures of light and life.

James rounds off *Daisy Miller* by associating Winterbourne with Manfred's reminiscence of the Coliseum by moonlight. The evocation of another Byronic hero this time serves by contrast to highlight Winterbourne's timidity. His fear of contagion from the Coliseum and his general unwillingness to hazard faith in Daisy clash nicely with Manfred's daredevil posture. But Manfred also resembles Winterbourne to the extent that Byron's protagonist has in some mysterious way killed a woman he loved, "Not with my hand, but heart, which broke her heart; / It gazed on mine, and wither'd" (II,ii). James goes to some pains to show the murderous effect of Winterbourne's callous remark to Daisy that "it makes very little difference" what he formerly thought about her or her supposed engagement to Giovanelli. Daisy's reply that she no longer cares whether she has Roman fever or not indicates at least a broken will, if not a broken heart.

Although it takes a careful and experienced reader to catch these clues which James plants as evidence against Winterbourne, once observed, the author's literary intelligence appears to have indicated his protagonist on a charge of criminal homicide. But Winterbourne's harsh treatment from recent critics and from James as well still does not convict him or close his case. Murder is a serious accusation, and the too reticent Winterbourne deserves to have his side fairly heard.

In fact, James also provides some basis for his defense. At the very least, a good lawyer might plead Winterbourne's crime as involuntary manslaughter rather than premeditated murder, and at the very most, an exceptional advocate could move for dismissal of the charges against Winterbourne on the grounds of self-defense, indeed, justifiable homicide.

To prove Daisy a dangerous and predatory American female is difficult because all the evidence for or against her, of course, comes to the reader at second hand, some of it hearsay. In addition, those characters who speak or act against Daisy, like Mrs. Costello or Mrs. Walker, are portrayed as distinctly unpleasant snobs. Still, James does make it possible to view Daisy as a girl on the make who selfishly attempts to use Winterbourne to satisfy her social and psychological needs.

When we first encounter Daisy at Vevey, we learn that before her encounter with Winterbourne, she has had little contact with European society; she has been unable to attract the attention of gentlemen. But by his response to her aggressive and unpredictable behavior, particularly over the proposed moonlight row to Chillon, Winterbourne accidentally reveals to Daisy the way to achieve what she wants. In a sense, this puzzled and fascinated young man is her first successful experiment on the continent, and since her provocative behavior works on him, she presses her strategy as far as possible, both in Vevey and later in Rome.

This is a natural role for Daisy because she is a spoiled child, used to having her own way, and much like a grown-up version of Hawthorne's Pearl, she cannot be made "amenable to rules" either. She does not seem capable of an outright quarrel with social strictures and can only be genuinely shocked by Mrs. Walker's cold shoul-

der. She has not realized how unacceptable her behavior has become. But she does know how she got her first gentleman and obstinately presses her initially rewarding strategy too far. Daisy loses the attention and "esteem" of Winterbourne, whose admiration and solicitude she perhaps needed the most. In a social sense, he could, by his association, provide her with the respectability that she had sacrificed for the sake of her strategy.

Daisy also tries to use Winterbourne to compensate for certain emotional and intellectual deprivations that she has suffered. First, Daisy has been indulged completely in a material sense, but is obviously very much ignored by both her absent father and her mother, who has been "invisible" until forced to give her daughter "the advantage of her society" as Daisy is dying. Obviously, the center of attention is her untamed brother, Randolph, whom she finds "real tiresome" because he limits the family's activities in Europe. Randolph is "very smart" and intended for college. Whatever Daisy's intellectual limitations, she has not been sufficiently educated to give Randolph instruction even though he is only nine. Daisy requires Winterbourne's guiding devotion and well-educated authority to make up for what she has been denied by her parents. "Daisy went on to say that she wished Winterbourne would travel with them and 'go round' with them; they might know something, in that case." As the sophisticated interpreter of the European scene, he can be her sympathetic mentor.

But Daisy is the classic case of a personality who, having been denied so much, demands too much by way of compensation. She not only tantalizes Winterbourne to gain his attention, but she also tries to remake him in her own image. Whatever good Daisy might do Winterbourne by relaxing his stiffness and lowering his public inhibitions is merely incidental to Daisy's need to reduce a detached authority figure to an undisciplined passion. In addition to using her relationship with Giovanelli to make Winterbourne jealous, on one occasion after another Daisy gibes Winterbourne about his stiffness and formality. When he finally bridles a bit, Daisy replies that if she had "the sweet hope of making [him] angry," she would taunt him further. Since Daisy's own absence of restraint can be attributed to her parents' lack of guidance, what better revenge than to inflict her own weakness on an agent of power and control? Winterbourne, then, is potentially useful to Daisy not only as a source of needed affection and attention but also as a surrogate target for her aggression against uncaring authority.

When Daisy finds that she cannot manipulate Winterbourne completely and he rejects her as immoral, she behaves exactly like the spoiled child, who, unable to have its own way with its parents, threatens them by endangering itself—by holding its breath or hitting its head, for example. Going to the Coliseum in the first place and then not caring whether she has Roman fever or not are just such self-destructive tactics, but in this case, the child hits its head too hard and dies.

Daisy, however, nearly manages to control Winterbourne from her grave in the Protestant Cemetery. The occasion of her death and funeral allows Giovanelli to reveal her innocence and Winterbourne's mistake. But Winterbourne's real error is not recognizing that Daisy is too infantile to meet the requirements of adult sexual behavior; he does not see that her needs are more and less than sexual. But Winterbourne at least reasserts his own maturity when he returns to Geneva and "a very clever foreign lady," who suffers neither from the emotional or intellectual stuntedness of Daisy Miller.

Winterbourne's only other error in regard to this typical American girl is having no fear of her and thinking her a "very light young person." "I may affirm that with regard to the women who had hitherto interested him, it very often seemed to Winterbourne among the possibilities that, given certain contingencies, he should be afraid—literally afraid—of these ladies; he had a pleasant sense that he should never be afraid of Daisy Miller." But the very affection that Daisy inspires in him simply makes Winterbourne more vulnerable to her vengeance against the authority that he represents to her. The observation of Winterbourne's "cynical compatriot" that pretty American women "were at once the most exacting in the world and the least endowed with a sense of indebtedness" perfectly describes Daisy's dangerous ambivalence to her suitor. Her needs for emotional and intellectual stimulation from sources of power appear to be insatiable and are incompatible with her simultaneous desire to take revenge on authorities who neglect her.

Viewed from this psychological vantage point, Daisy could well be an unpredictable and dangerous little beast with an appetite for expatriate American males. James at least has not allowed her to remain the completely innocent Christian martyr eyed by the Winterbourne lion in her own flattering simile. "Well, he looks at us as one of the old lions or tigers may have looked at the Christian martyrs!' " Daisy herself appears to be more tiger than lady.

I have played the devil's advocate here not to exonerate Winterbourne, nor to strike an even balance in the evidence of the case, nor even to adjust a certain bias in recent criticism of the tale, but to indicate that James has given his reader another side to be on. However, the variety or validity of readers' efforts to form alliances with the characters of *Daisy Miller* is not nearly so important as the method which the writer uses to provoke his audience to make such choices. Involving readers in fiction is for James more than simply appealing to individual temperaments. Inquiring into possible responses to *Adam Bede,* he writes:

> In every novel the work is divided between the writer and the reader; but the writer makes the reader very much as he makes his characters. When he makes him ill, that is, makes him indifferent, he does no work; the writer does all. When he makes him well, that is, makes him interested, then the reader does quite the labour. In making such a deduction as I have just indicated, the reader would be doing but his share of the task; the grand point is to get him to make it. I hold that there is a way. It is perhaps a secret; but until it is found out, I think that the art

of story-telling cannot be said to have approached perfection.

James does make the reader of *Daisy Miller* labor, and his method of doing so may illustrate a nearly perfect story-telling technique.

The novelist's strategy consists first of interlacing *Daisy Miller* with strong suggestions of order and explanation which tempt the audience to make deductions and arrive at solutions regarding the events and characters of the tale. Its characters are radically opposed, its plot is straightforward, and its settings are clearly delineated. James's readership is immediately confronted by the story's two-part structural clarity. Geneva's association with a constricting Puritanism set against the expansive and sensuous richness of Rome presents the audience with a choice of contrasted settings. Perhaps Vevey, as a kind of middle ground, suggests compromise or resolution of opposites.

In addition, *Daisy Miller* exhibits three thematic layers; a reader can quickly discern its social, moral and psychological levels. In even succession, questions arise over Daisy's etiquette, her reputation, and finally her motives. And as previously pointed out, Jame's well placed literary allusions appear to stress the moral corruption of certain characters in contrast to the natural virtues of another—a favoring of American over European values reinforced by the author's use of some obvious symbolism present even in the names of characters, "Daisy" and "Winterbourne." *Daisy Miller* invites its audience to focus selectively on or among two or three well-defined alternatives.

Clearly, an initial contact with the story can inspire a reader with the confidence to attempt an interpretation; however, James also puts up strategic barriers against comprehension. He includes disorienting and disorganizing ingredients that prevent a sense of final resolve or satisfaction in the audience. The author obfuscates matters by making everything in the tale happen in the distance of Winterbourne's perspective. And Winterbourne is not reliable—he is confused about Daisy; Daisy is confused about Europe; and Giovanelli, Mrs. Costello and Mrs. Walker all misjudge Daisy. The difficulties which the characters have correctly perceiving the actors and events in their story both create and mirror the reader's own stumbling blocks to understanding *Daisy Miller*.

Nor is the *nouvelle*'s setting as substantially constructed as it might first appear. James's introduction of the "Trois Couronnes" at Vevey is excessively roundabout. Initially, this unnamed hotel is only one of "an unbroken array of establishments . . . of every category, from the 'grand hotel' of the newest fashion, with a chalk-white front, a hundred balconies, and a dozen flags flying from its roof, to the Swiss *pension* of an elder day, with its name inscribed in German-looking lettering upon a pink or yellow wall, and an awkward summer-house in the angle of the garden." Then, from this jumble, James singles the establishment out as being more luxurious and mature than its neighbors. It is like an "American watering place," but then it is not. Indeed, when it is finally labeled the "Trois Couronnes" with all that title's association with orthodox numeration and hierarchy, the narrator introduces a nameless "young American" and does not know whether his protagonist is more concerned with the analogies between the "Trois Couronnes" and American hotels or the differences between them. Clarification alternates with muddle, and certainty with ignorance so that even in the outward exactness of the story's opening description, James has managed to blur the identification of part of the setting as well as Winterbourne's sense of national affinities.

But if Winterbourne is confused about American characteristics and personalities, we might assume that his extensive European experience has enabled him to understand and deal accurately with a variety of international environments. Instead, Rome seems to bring out the very worst in Americans, like Winterbourne or Mrs. Walker, conditioned in any way by Geneva's precepts. The "bloom and perfume" of a Roman spring gives a Calvinistic predisposition to see the worst in human nature all the excuse it needs to do so, and thus, Winterbourne misconstrues a fallen Daisy. The neat arrangement of James's setting in fact provokes disordered impressions for both the author's characters and his readers.

Distinct thematic elements also merge with disturbing results for the reader who tries to maintain a grip on them. " 'They are hopelessly vulgar,' said Mrs. Costello. 'Whether or no being hopelessly vulgar is being "bad" is a question for the metaphysicians. They are bad enough to dislike, at any rate; and for this short life that is quite enough.' " And if Mrs. Costello mixes the story's social dimension with the moral, Winterbourne's lame efforts to understand the real Daisy after she is ostracized by her compatriots ends in a jumble as well. "He was angry at finding himself reduced to chopping logic about this young lady; he was vexed at his want of instinctive certitude as to how far her eccentricities were generic, national, and how far they were personal. From either view of them he had somehow missed her." Winterbourne's question could well prompt the reader to inquire whether *Daisy Miller* is public comedy or private tragedy. But as her erstwhile suitor is deaf to the true Daisy, even the most refined critical ear misses a dominant tone for her multifaceted history.

In light of these many discordant elements, it should be obvious by now that any interpretive stance for or against either Daisy or Winterbourne, no matter how temporarily satisfying, cannot stand up to thorough scrutiny for long. The best that can be said for my elaborate case against Daisy, for example, is that James includes just enough suspicious evidence to warrant a psychological investigation, but the substantiation of specific charges against her must depend on my own imaginative justification. Likewise, of course, efforts to make a solid case against Winterbourne must follow the same uncertain procedure as my speculative use of Byronic allusion.

James's strategic presentation of the characters, settings, and themes of *Daisy Miller* gives the reader just enough suggestion of possible interpretive solutions to pull him into a trial analysis of the tale. But almost simultaneously, the author disconcerts that same reader and playfully pushes him away from any fulfilled sense of having completely understood his thematic intentions for the story. Then, out of what must be a sense of increasing frustration, the reader may, without any actual justification, supply his explanation of the tale's significance. Thus, by initial fascination or final frustration, James manages to "interest" or engage the reader of *Daisy Miller* with what is, secret or not, highly effective story-telling.

Although this literary strategy could not serve for a figure in the Jamesian carpet (his later style added another dimension to his art and could repel or attract readers almost entirely by itself), the author's stratagem in *Daisy Miller* is like an interworked pattern in some mosaic which must be observed from a certain angle to be visible. James's successful *trompe d'oeil* can only be understood as a process which the reader experiences through a progressive interaction with the tale. If one were to stand away from the story and view it critically after the fact of close reading, the figure would disappear. One would be left merely with a static perception of competing values; one would tend to downplay the forces of disorientation in the work or write them off as enriching ambiguities or ironies. And one might inevitably be lured into an ethical judgment of *Daisy Miller*'s characters and certain convictions about James's attitude towards them.

But perhaps we have all along had more respect for James's reputation for authorial detachment and impersonality than many critics of *Daisy Miller*. Or perhaps we have already been convinced of the limitations that must be placed on testing fictional characters by standards applicable to fully responsible human beings. What we do not sufficiently understand, I think, are the tactical maneuvers which novelists, even very detached ones, employ to tempt readers to treat fictional constructs as real people, literary meanings as actuality. I have attempted to reveal one such strategy employed in *Daisy Miller,* but this strategy is so successful at creating a sense of "felt life" in the story that readers will be drawn back again and again to adjudicate the claims for and against Daisy and Winterbourne, for and against naive extroversion or sophisticated introversion. Suggestions of symmetry and order will urge them on, just as the ever-present agents of disorder will make their certainties and conclusions but temporary conjectures. James has arranged that the critical reader of *Daisy Miller,* just as much as Winterbourne, is "booked to make a mistake," and this reader, also like Winterbourne, could easily remain unaware of the real sources of his error.

Frankie Wilson and Max Westbrook (essay date 1980)

SOURCE: "Daisy Miller and the Metaphysician," in *American Literary Realism 1870-1910*, Vol. XIII, No. 2, Autumn, 1980, pp. 270-79.

[*In the following essay, Wilson and Westbrook investigate the metaphysical aspects of* Daisy Miller, *as well as its resemblance to certain mythological stories.*]

According to Henry James, "Experience is never limited, and it is never complete; it is an immense sensibility, a kind of huge spider-web of the finest silken threads suspended in the chamber of consciousness, and catching every air-borne particle in its tissue." James's fiction, consistently faithful to this thesis, seems to contain always one more nuance, one more complexity.

Critics writing on *Daisy Miller,* however, accept the judgments of characters who, by the Jamesian definition of experience, are not qualified to judge. Mrs. Costello has no desire to explore complications but the critical consensus accepts her simplistic analysis of Winterbourne: his problem is that he has been living "too long out of the country." Winterbourne seeks a formula to live by, but the consensus accepts his belated discovery of Daisy's innocence as if it were a tardy but meaningful revelation. Actually, Winterbourne has allowed himself only two possible views of Daisy, *good* or *bad,* which does not suggest that he has learned to make discriminations in the "immense sensibility" of human experience.

What happens in *Daisy Miller* cannot be evaluated by the snobbish disinterest of Mrs. Costello or by the absolutes of her Calvinistic nephew. Daisy is innocent, yes, but Henry James was not content with one-dimensional character portraits. The habit of his mind was to explore. With *Daisy Miller*—subtitled *A Study*—his probings led him through the context of social innocence and into the troublesome land of primal innocence, something closer to the Undine myth than to the "victimized innocence" of Catherine Sloper in *Washington Square.* Daisy is undone because she is a creature of inclinations, a willful child of nature whose vulnerability is more psychological than social. She is undone, also, by Winterbourne's failure to love her, but the reasons for Winterbourne's failure go beyond society's corruption of good manners from grace to tyranny and include a Calvinistic betrayal of his own primal self.

When Winterbourne protests that the Millers are " 'innocent only' " and " 'not bad,' " the distinction does not interest Mrs. Costello. The Millers, she argues, are " 'hopelessly vulgar,' " bad enough so that one knows not to associate with them, which is sufficient information for this life. She says, " 'Whether or no being hopelessly vulgar is being "bad" is a question for the metaphysicians.' " Clearly, it is not a question for Mrs. Costello. It is equally clear, however, that the question is of intense interest to the author of *Daisy Miller.* The "metaphysician," it follows, is Henry James.

Winterbourne, for his part, is interested and even bedeviled by the question of Daisy; but he seeks a "formula," an answer that will save him the pain of confrontation with himself. At the beginning of the story, he is said to be "studying." Rumors mention a mysterious "foreign lady—a person older than himself." At the end of the story, he is again said to be "studying" and to have, perhaps, a "very clever foreign lady." In brief, he is back where he started, the implication being that he has learned nothing, or that anything he may have learned has not come with fire sufficient to change his life of Calvinistic retreat.

Beyond manners, and invisible to the snobbish eyes of Mrs. Costello and the categorical eyes of Winterbourne, is another dimension. After establishing his hero and the

setting, James introduces the Miller family—all a bit strange—through a puzzling character, the oft-noted but never-analyzed Randolph. A nine-year-old little brother with only seven teeth and a face that is "aged," who carries a sinister alpenstock "the sharp point of which he thrust into everything that he approached . . .", a child who talks and intimidates as Randolph does is not the ordinary little brother.

Wearing red hose and a red cravatte, Randolph is introduced as he pauses in front of Winterbourne: " 'Will you give me a lump of sugar?' he asked, in a sharp, hard little voice—a voice immature, and yet, somehow, not young." James and many others were concerned about a current issue, the damage done to spoiled rich children being dragged around Europe, but that does not account for Randolph, who looks like a homunculus and is sometimes a classically impossible child. At Mrs. Walker's, Randolph declares, " 'We've got a bigger place than this. . . . It's all gold on the walls.' " And when his mother replies that she told him he would " 'say something' " improper, he snaps back, " 'I told you,' " and gives "Winterbourne a thump on the knee." Randolph is not a Tom Sawyer grown rich.

Like his parents, he has dyspepsia. Like his strangely passive mother, he suffers from insomnia. Randolph—in face, voice, and manner—is an amorphous combination of the child and the old man. Henry James as metaphysician is weaving his "spider-web."

Randolph is unshaped, an energy of inclinations, a striking example of what C. G. Jung calls the "irrational third," the child at a preconscious stage of development and with an uncertain potential. Far from being odd merely, or a sociological example merely, Randolph is very much his sister's little brother. Both are in a primal state of development. Both follow their inclinations. For his role as the one who introduces Daisy to Winterbourne, Randolph is specifically appropriate.

Daisy's manner, like her prepared-for entrance, is carefully managed. She poses before Winterbourne, before *his* bench, with the garden and light just right. James is creating a portrait, a technique he often used to interweave the inner and outer worlds. In *The Ambassadors,* for example, Strether sees the canoe come drifting in, just right, to complete the picture, as if by surprise and yet as if from the personal unconscious.

In keeping with the autonomy associated with the unconscious, Daisy is very much in command. She is not silent, at first, from being shy, and then suddenly talkative, from shyness released. Daisy is "not in the least embarrassed." She is "neither offended nor fluttered" by Winterbourne's forwardness. She has posed for him, in front of his bench. He responds. She looks at him briefly, then looks away, and waits. Daisy is a cool and even aggressive innocent, and there is—in the presentation and withholding of her self, in her elfin emissary, in her affinity for garden, water, and the dark—a suggestion of the natural in the archetypal sense of that word.

Beyond the social themes, the realistic basis of *Daisy Miller,* there are parallels with Nathaniel Hawthorne's Beatrice, Freud's concept of the *unheimlich,* Rudolph Otto on the nouminous, Jung on the unconscious, and with the myths of Lamia and Undine. These parallels, we think, argue for a corrective in our standard reading of Daisy. By definition, a social innocent is *too* self-conscious and gives excessive weight to the rules and powers of propriety and the dating game. A primal innocent is just the opposite: there is no blushing or flirtatious self-consciousness, and social rules are not felt to be real. That which brings pleasure—sugar, dinner parties, or whatever—is desired, but what is real to the primal innocent is inclination; and the development of the self is in jeopardy. Daisy's manners are American, but her psyche is unformed by any standards—European or American—and the person invited to love her will contribute to the decisions of her developing soul by his capacity to love or to betray. And that is why she responds to Winterbourne as if they were old friends, then turns away, blank. Daisy breaks rules by inclination, not from ignorance; her being is at stake, potential.

Dangers awaiting the primal innocent, furthermore, are substantive and personal as well as social. Thus the frightening delicacy of Henry James makes it seem, at times, that the innocent Miss Daisy may be evil after all. One can even begin to imagine that something is going on between Eugenio and Daisy. In the scene in which Daisy teases Winterbourne about the 11:00 p.m. boatride, for example, Eugenio's role is suggestive of the sinister; and yet Daisy teases him, even flirts with him, as her helpless mother watches. Then suddenly, with the information that Randolph is finally asleep, the whole scene is dropped. The passive mother makes a rare decision, assuming Daisy's assent, which comes automatically as the mother knows it will: with Randolph in bed, they will now retire. Supporting evidence comes from Daisy's love of the dark, the hint that she can see in the dark (as her mother approaches from a distance), her many and often mysterious gentlemen friends, and her disturbing affinity for the miasma of the Colosseum, where she settles down peacefully in the moonlight, as if at home in a place of evil and death.

But before the Colosseum scene—at the party, when Mrs. Walker snubs Daisy—all hints of evil are undercut. Suddenly, a marked change occurs in the story. Daisy, who seems to know exactly what she is doing, who has been told the rules repeatedly by her mother and by Winterbourne and his friends, is genuinely surprised and hurt. How can that be? After all her social experience in America and Europe, after all the explanations by so many people, after acknowledging the finality of her decision not to get into Mrs. Walker's carriage ("' . . . you must give me up' "), how can she be shocked? It is not possible to believe that Daisy is naive to the point of idiocy. Her shock cannot be accounted for in terms of social innocence; but it can be accounted for, we believe, in terms of primal innocence. Daisy is energized by a spontaneity long since buried in the Calvinistic soul of her friend Winterbourne, and the harsh forces of propriety are not yet real to her nature. Daisy, in fact, resists the loss of her preconscious state of being: "'I don't think I want to know what you mean. . . . I don't think I should like it.' " Since it is difficult to mature without betraying the spontaneous preconscious, Daisy accepts those social rules which are games merely, but rejects the threat of a developing consciousness.

When the harsh forces of society do finally penetrate her spontaneous nature, she changes. Society for Daisy is pleasure, not ultimate reality as it is for Mrs. Costello, and its loss is merely the loss of one possible source of pleasure. But Winterbourne's refusal to return her love—a refusal sponsored and supported by social forces—is a rejection of her being. Daisy is jolted rather than guided toward consciousness. Her independence does not mature from the spirit toward the world, as it might were she moved lovingly into it by Winterbourne. She becomes defiant. With her natural joy short-circuited, she moves toward despair. The manner of telling the story changes also, with the narrator using ironic language to describe Daisy's detractors: "these shrewd people had quite made up their minds"; her fellow countrymen "desired to express to observant Europeans the great truth that . . . Miss Daisy Miller . . . was not representative—was regarded by her compatriots as abnormal."

"Innocent" and "bad" are abstract categories used by Calvinists, gossips, snobs and other narrow-minded people who are impatient with distinctions. James the metaphysician is concerned not only with types and combinations of innocence and evil but with the drama of meta-physics, a changing land in between. And the concern is pervasive. Even the apparently innocent Mr. Giovanelli has his dark moments. He must have known, without needing any information from Mrs. Walker, that Daisy's reputation would be injured if she strolled with him on the Pincio. Did Giovanelli mean to appease Daisy at any cost, or feel that he had a better chance of marrying her if she had no American friends? The rhetorical sequence of the conversation in the cemetery is worth considering. Winterbourne asks Giovanelli " '[w]hy the devil' " he took her to that " 'fatal place.' " Giovanelli says " 'she wanted to go.' " Winterbourne rightly says this is " 'no reason.' " Under pressure to explain why he took Daisy to a place he knew to be lethal, Giovanelli says, " 'If she had lived, I should have got nothing. She would never have married me, I am sure.' " In what way is that an answer to the question asked? It strains critical good manners to think that Giovanelli, finding that he could not have Daisy, consciously tried to kill her, or let her commit suicide; but ominous possibilities have been suggested in this scene and *passim* and are substantive to the story.

The special tension of James, that air of things beings up for grabs, unknown, not yet through happening, is due in part to his fascination with human intercourse as a drama in which the end—*contra* the predestination of Calvinism—is *not* determined. Daisy is warned, and Winterbourne was "booked" to make a mistake; but the motivations and decisions of both involve character, an identity which describes but does not prescribe. Daisy, like Alice Staverton and May Bartram, is potential, alive, asking to be loved; and Winterbourne, like Spencer Brydon and John Marcher, is also in dramatic suspension, his soul too at jeopardy.

A critical language for this dimension of *Daisy Miller*—no claims of influence intended—is available in the Undine myth. In *The Uncreating Word: Romanticism And The Object,* Irving Massey provides an excellent and useful analysis.

> The real problem is that consciousness itself, without the intervention of other people [Winterbourne is excessively self-conscious, and he lives, essentially, without other people], produces a division between the inner and outer dimensions of the self [Winterbourne vacillates between his attraction for Daisy and his Calvinistic suspicions].

For *self* read "Winterbourne," for innocence read "Daisy," as Massey continues:

> A self which has become an object is a contradiction in terms. The attempt of the self to escape the status of an object is the pursuit of innocence, the attempt to recapture the primal, preconscious harmony. But it is an attempt which is doomed, for the self that wishes to recall its object-self is already compromised. It has been guilty of the original act of objectification; it is contaminated with self-consciousness. And consciousness is incompatible with innocence; inevitably, it leads toward experience, a sinister state which in these terms turns out to be strangely similar to abstraction or theory.

The Undine myth itself, as told by Massey, bears a striking relevance to **Daisy Miller:** "The story begins with the arrival of a young knight at the shore of the lake." Then a young girl arrives, a "quicksilvery, willful, temperamental girl, totally spoiled and uncontrollable. . . . On being crossed in a whim, she stamps out into the night." Later, she is discovered "on an island in the midst of a torrent . . . lying in the moonlight, apparently completely unafraid." After persuasion by the knight, Undine "finally agrees to return." But she does not return "because of any sense of impropriety in her behaviour or of duty or guilt towards her foster-parents. She is innocent. . . . She does not know the meaning of repression or voluntary self-frustration."

Winterbourne is unable to persuade his primal innocent to return; but the end, for Daisy and Undine, is the same, and the parallels are clear. Daisy's strong desire to enter society is coupled with an even stronger determination that her gentlemen friends must not tell her what to do. Daisy's cheerful American manners are coupled with a strange affinity for water and darkness. She wears Paris gowns in exquisite good taste but is nicknamed "Daisy."

The Undine parallel, furthermore, helps explain why Daisy must die. She is not an American flirt who is disappointed in romance and therefore courts death, a reading which reduces Daisy to contradictory stereotypes. The actual case on which the story is based does invite sentimentality, and James may well have felt the tug; but **Daisy Miller** is not the story of a romantic pining-away. On the level of character motivation, Daisy is hurt by Winterbourne's perfidy and does something she is not supposed to do, something like climbing too high or too far out because someone one loves does not love in return. On the psychological level, not to be loved in youth is not to develop to the next stage. Growth stops. Undine, as Massey

explains, "has no soul; totally moved by the elements and the natural forces of the world, she will, at the end, dissolve and return to them." Daisy, a lovely and natural American girl, is innocent, in part, because she is motivated more by the vitality of what she feels and sees and wants than she is by the importance of society's strictures. This is her charm, her present personality, but it is also dangerous. If the primal innocent does not grow and mature beyond her natural vitality, then she must return to nature, back to the sea, or, in Daisy's case, "beneath the cypresses and the thick spring-flowers."

Again, we do not intend to argue that Daisy *is* Undine or that Henry James (who *was* interested in psychological and occult materials) made conscious use of the Undine myth. The intent of the comparison is to suggest a critical language to account for specifics in the story which cannot be accounted for by the simplistic terms of social innocence and social knowledge.

This argument holds not only for Daisy herself, but for Winterbourne. If the standard reading is correct, Winterbourne is a good and sensitive man who—too late—understands Daisy. But this approach does not account adequately for Winterbourne's actions or attitudes, especially as regards Daisy, nor does it explain the emphasis on Calvinism. What is the purpose of the narrator's odd and seemingly pointless conjectures about Winterbourne's reasons for staying so long at Geneva? The first explanation is assigned to friends: Winterbourne "was at Geneva 'studying.' " The second explanation, offered by "certain persons," somehow different from friends, is that Winterbourne "was extremely devoted to a lady who lived there—a foreign lady—a person older than himself." Then a third explanation is offered, one which comes directly from the narrator:

> Very few Americans—indeed I think none—had ever seen this lady, about whom there were some singular stories. But Winterbourne had an old attachment for the little metropolis of Calvinism; he had been put to school there as a boy, and he had afterwards gone to college there—circumstances which had led to his forming a great many youthful friendships. Many of these he had kept, and they were a source of great satisfaction to him.

Winterbourne, as we see later, has probably never had a proper romance. And yet the mysterious foreign lady *does* exist. When Daisy assumes a "mysterious charmer in Geneva," Winterbourne is amazed: "How did Miss Daisy Miller know that there was a charmer in Geneva?" The narrator then tells us that Winterbourne, "who denied the existence of such a person," is "divided between amazement at the rapidity of her induction and amusement at the frankness of her *persiflage.*" Daisy is just now, he feels, "an extraordinary mixture of innocence and crudity."

It seems that an affair, for this Calvinist, is dirty, something to be denied, a secret to be kept by American colleagues, who are presumably too refined to mention such matters (his friends say he is "studying"). It is only those who are really enemies (and Winterbourne is too nice and neutral to earn an enemy) who would mention the foreign lady or who (being Europeans) would ever be allowed to see the proof of her existence. For Daisy to sense the possibility of an affair is for her to be guilty of "crudity," even though her manner of chattering on in romantic anger is a sign of her "innocence." Winterbourne, in short, has already denied his foreign lady as, later on, he will deny Daisy. He has associated sex with the unmentionable, something gentlemen do not discuss. And a lady, of course, must not even realize the existence of such things.

What, then, are Winterbourne's motives? Repeatedly, he is struck by how pretty Daisy is. He likes her personality. He finds that her unaffected response to life tugs at his inner being. Outwardly, he defends Daisy as being, after all, innocent. In the privacy of his consciousness, he associates Daisy's charm with wickedness. The contradiction becomes clear when he listens to his aunt's report on the Millers:

> "I shouldn't wonder if he [Eugenio] dines with them. Very likely they have never seen a man with such good manners. . . . He probably corresponds to the young lady's idea of a Count. He sits with them in the garden. . . . I think he smokes."

Clearly this is gossip: "I shouldn't wonder," "Very likely," "He probably," "I think." And yet Winterbourne accepts these conjectures as the truth. These "disclosures" help "him to make up his mind about Miss Daisy. Evidently she was rather wild." But when Mrs. Costello challenges the "respectability" of the Millers, Winterbourne pretends to be hurt: " 'Ah, you are cruel!' said the young man. 'She's a very nice girl.' "

The "division between the inner and outer dimensions" of Winterbourne's "self " coincides in detail with the fragmentation described by Massey. Winterbourne thinks of Daisy as a type, he searches for a "formula" by which to accommodate his mixed feelings, he vacillates between thinking of her as good or bad, he contradicts himself by saying one thing and feeling the opposite, and he is intrigued as much by the hope that Daisy will prove to be virtuous as by the oblique titillation of the opposite possibility:

> If, therefore, Miss Daisy Miller exceeded the liberal license allowed to these young ladies [Mrs. Costello's granddaughters], it was probable that anything might be expected of her. Winterbourne was impatient to see her again, and he was vexed with himself that, by instinct, he should not appreciate her justly.

The paratactical implications are that Winterbourne is "impatient to see her again" *because* "anything might be expected of her"; and the words "instinct" and "justly" are left to carry a deceptive, disturbing, and very Jamesian ambiguity.

So the critics are right to quote Mrs. Costello: Winterbourne has "lived too long out of the country." But this is merely the first strand in the metaphysician's web. Winterbourne has become, also, a foreigner to his own inner feelings. He cannot read his unconscious or natural self any better than he can read Miss Daisy. And the critics

are right to say that Daisy is an American innocent, but her innocence is also a profoundly human determination to assert the original self, to resist the desire of consciousness to capture and enslave the unconscious. Youth wants to be what it wants to be.

Thus it is appropriate for the climax to come on a special territory. The moonlit night in the Colosseum—suggesting the unconscious—is for Winterbourne unbearable. Confronted with this ancient presence, unable to rationalize further with gentlemen-at-the-pub thoughts of Daisy as a woman capable of "anything," Winterbourne refuses to love his Lamia, Beatrice, or Undine. This is his personal tragedy; for, as we see in **"Pandora,"** Henry James believed it was possible for a Daisy Miller type to be rescued by love.

Pandora Day has a vague father and mother, comparable to the vague Mrs. Miller and absent Mr. Miller (the preconscious is in need of a guide). Pandora's little-brother-Randolph has become a disturbingly independent youth of poise and strength. He is detached but contented, and older people recognize and respect his confident personality. Pandora herself is Undine matured, the amalgamation of consciousness and unconsciousness which Daisy Miller, with better luck, might have achieved. Count Otto Vogelstein, a "stiff" Germanic version of Winterbourne, is reading a story entitled *Daisy Miller* and doubting his ability to analyze Americans scientifically (Winterbourne's "formula"). The Count takes Pandora to be a flirt. She seems innocent yet forward, completely unaware of social restrictions. But this "Daisy" is married and mature. She is able to maintain her spontaneous charm and to function successfully at the presidential level of American diplomatic circles on behalf of her husband.

The implication of **"Pandora,"** confirmed by *Daisy Miller* itself, is that Winterbourne's statement to Daisy at the Colosseum is terribly wrong: " 'I believe that it makes very little difference whether you are engaged or not!' " And his conclusion after Daisy's death is, however formal, unmistakably right: "It was on his conscience that he had done her injustice." But Winterbourne, to the very end, sees with the intellect. He is fragmented, a man with a good but timid will, living in fear of confrontation. Below the level of propriety and consciousness there exists another part of the self, a reality signalled by language and story: " 'Quick! Quick!' " pleads Giovanelli at the Colosseum, " 'if we get in by midnight we are quite safe.' "

Robert Weisbuch   (essay date 1993)

SOURCE: "Winterbourne and the Doom of Manhood in *Daisy Miller*," in *New Essays on Daisy Miller and the Turn of the Screw*, edited by Vivian R. Pollak, Cambridge University Press, 1993, pp. 65-90.

[*In the following essay, Weisbuch examines Winterbourne as a literary type—the bachelor—whose misogyny, obsessiveness, and self-absorption are his defining characteristics.*]

1

Henry James is like the modern jazz masters in this: He

begins with the simplest romantic themes, then builds intricacies upon them until the once-clichés speak to all the subtle richness of social existence. With Daisy Miller and her reluctant suitor Frederick Winterbourne, the theme is no more than "opposites attract," and the trick is that one pole of that opposition is so constructed as to make the attraction deadly. "Stiff" Winterbourne brings doom to Daisy and a different doom to himself; through him, James tallies the evils of a misconstructed masculinity.

It's a multifaceted opposition between the failed lovers, but at base simple as motion through the world. Daisy Miller moves. She "goes on," "goes round," "goes too far," well over a hundred times in the text. "She goes on," a particular persecutor remarks, "from day to day, from hour to hour, as they did in the Golden Age." No enthusiast of the dynamic, Mrs. Costello "can imagine nothing more vulgar." Too blithely regardless, alive, American, and unknowing amidst the miasma of history, "strolling along the top of one of those great mounds of ruin that are embanked with mossy marble and paved with monumental inscriptions," Daisy comprehends her life principle lightly and perfectly: "If I didn't walk I should expire," she tells an inaptly named Mrs. Walker. Mrs. Walker, representative of a society of parlors, never does walk, but chases Daisy in her carriage to persuade her against walking. "If I didn't walk I should expire," says the girl of gardens and the vibrant moment, surprised into opposition; and when she cannot walk any longer, she dies, a latest Roman sacrifice to a world of rooms and rules.

These too are simple, her perfect understanding and her nasty doom. Daisy begins simply, fills out only to defend that simplicity, and expires into mythy apotheosis: the "most innocent" of all young ladies by the account of the cured opportunist Giovanelli, whose judgment is unimpeachable in an assessment that holds no stakes for him. James, amazed that readers followed Winterbourne in making Daisy's innocence a point of dispute, ever after seconded the Italian's judgment.

Daisy's continuing and finally ennobled simplicity is not what we usually expect from fiction, where characters generally complicate themselves in the course of their experiences. But James means for us to see Daisy's complexity as not inherent. The terrible ambiguity, the vexing mystery of her status as innocent or vixen, have nothing to do with her inherent quality, simple as a Daisy can be; they are all evoked by Winterbourne's misshapen assessment. It is not really her story but Winterbourne's, and there the complications are killing.

Frederick Winterbourne does not go on or go too far, as he too accuses Daisy of doing. After his first words with Daisy, "He wondered whether he had gone too far; but he decided that he must advance farther, rather than retreat." But his advances *are* half-retreats, and he vacillates throughout: hesitating to visit Daisy on his arrival at Rome once he hears of her as "surrounded by half-a-dozen wonderful moustaches" or running comic opera between Mrs. Walker's carriage of imperial respectability and the scandalously free-walking Daisy. Progressively in the second, Roman half of the tale, Giovanelli succeeds Winterbourne as active suitor, and Winterbourne, retreat-

ing or receding, supplants the protective courtier Eugenio as eugenic guardian. Finally, spying Daisy with Giovanelli at night in the Colosseum, "as he was going to advance again, he checked himself; not from the fear that he was doing her injustice, but from a sense of the danger of appearing unbecomingly exhilarated by this sudden revulsion from cautious criticism. He turned away," seeking secrecy for his hideous emotion, relief that now he can find surcease from his vacillating movements in the sure (but wrong) knowledge that Daisy is corrupt. Her goading causes him to turn again and advance, but only to scold Giovanelli, for Roman fever is potential in the dank night air of the ruins. This prudential warning is not so gallant, given that he had meant to retreat a last time before issuing any such warning, leaving Daisy to possible death—which he then goes on to cause, killing her spirit by his dismissal.

After Giovanelli's disclosure, Winterbourne confesses, "I have lived too long in foreign parts," the last and most shocking of many sexual puns in the tale. But then he goes round. "He went back to live at Geneva," where the contradictory rumors by which James's narrator introduces him are renewed, "a report that he is 'studying' hard—an intimation that he is much interested in a foreign lady."

With Daisy, Winterbourne advances and retreats, recedes, and finally reverts. But without her he is motionless, he sits, he idles. That is how we find him in the garden of the hotel at Vevey, until Daisy's brother and then Daisy interrupt his stasis. In his very first description as "a young American," Winterbourne seems something other, a European idler; like one of Conrad's tropical emigrés, little is known about him. It is startling what we do not know about Winterbourne. Who are his parents? Has he siblings? We are told that he has many friends in Geneva, but only one male friend appears on the scene and that briefly, with information of Daisy at the Doria. Daisy is from Schenectady, her limitation but not her fault, but where is Winterbourne's hometown? Why, really, is he in Geneva, or in Europe at all? Where does he get the money to do nothing? What does he wish to do? He has been in bed with a woman, perhaps many, but has he ever loved? And what is he "studying" other than sex in Geneva and Daisy in this narrative?

I think there are answers to some of these questions and answers to why we do not know the answers to others, awful disclosures about this "young American" who to Daisy "seemed more like a German." The answers have to do with such matters as cash and class, labor and idling, sexuality and something that is its reduction and defeat. I am sorry the answers have to do with these subjects, so predictably present are such matters in the interpretation of books at our own cultural moment. But James knew his cultural moment, knew himself in it, too, and *Daisy Miller* is one of his many attempts to state the moment and to free himself from it.

I do not mean to deny the international theme that readers find in the tale but to sharpen it. James is certainly telling a story about cultural bigotry in which an American man who has neglected his origin has an opportunity to educate an American girl all too provincially limited, and by this interchange has an opportunity to go not "on" or "round" or "too far" but home. The necessary aging of young America is at issue. Daisy's death dramatizes a worry that the new nation cannot grow up into a world of vicissitude; and as all of Daisy's accusers are expatriate Americans, not one of them the real thing, James is warning, much as Mark Twain would do in limning the pretensions of the Mississippi River culture in *Huckleberry Finn,* of an American attempt to become culturally mature the wrong way, by grotesquely aping the nightmare aspects of European sophistication. When Mrs. Costello speaks of "the minutely hierarchical constitution" of New York society, America appears feudal. In all this there is the sense of missed opportunity, not only for Daisy and Winterbourne, but for America and Europe to form that Jamesian compact in which American vitality and European knowledge and manners would combine to save the West. Yet there is something beyond the international theme, something that makes even Winterbourne's self-blame, put in the "lived too long in foreign parts" lexicon of that theme, half a misnomer and a rationalization, and I want to get at what it is.

2

Our questions about Winterbourne may resolve into a single, gigantic problem: What is it to be a man? In the American decades before the Civil War, a new definition of manhood was getting fashioned, and with a rapidity possible only in a new nation formed at a late stage of Western civilization. Industry, and the changes it effects in social organization and individual personalities, came pell-mell upon an America just learning to know itself. "Here, as in a theater," wrote James Russell Lowell, "the great problems of anthropology . . . are compressed, as it were, into the entertainment of a few hours." An extremely insecure aristocracy, for instance, is barely established before it finds itself rudely jostled. "The older ideologies of genteel patriarchy and artisan independence were being challenged by a new middle-class ideology of competitive individualism," writes David Leverenz, adding, perhaps a bit too simply, "The new middle-class won, and its ideology of manhood as competitive individualism still pervades American life." The significantly absent Mr. Miller is one such winner, remaining behind in what Winterbourne imagines his Italian rival would consider "that mysterious land of dollars." But Winterbourne's confusion over Daisy suggests that commercially energetic America is a mystery to him as well, for Winterbourne is one of the losers in this redefinition of manhood. We know that he had been "put to school" in Geneva by his parents at about the age of Daisy's brother Randolph. Familial wealth is the implication, supported as well by the circumstances and snobbery of Winterbourne's aunt. That is, Winterbourne comes from a shaky displaced aristocracy that has found a shaky home in Europe. In England, Leverenz notes, "a similar class conflict . . . had ended with the gentry reestablishing control by 1870," and although we might wish to complicate this assertion—labor certainly has some claims on an approved manhood in Victorian fiction—the defeat of the many socialist revolutions across Europe by forces of royalty in the 1840s did make the continent a more comfortable site for monied lassitude. America,

Fenimore Cooper had written decades earlier, "possesses neither the population nor the endowments to maintain a large class of learned idlers," idlers such as Frederick Winterbourne, lifelong "student."

Thus Winterbourne's permanent vacation in Geneva is a choice; he has chosen not to enter into his own time and into the fray of "competitive individualism." This gives particular point to Daisy's characterization of Winterbourne's speeches as "formal" and "quaint." Winterbourne's lectures to Daisy on the nature of who is and is not a gentleman add to the anachronistic lexicon by which he seeks to assert his class superiority.

Winterbourne is willing to compete only by standards that rely on a code of behavior closely allied with inherited caste. He refuses free market competition and this refusal has everything to do with his romantic behavior. When Winterbourne abandons Mrs. Walker's carriage, apparently enlisting in Daisy's cause, he spies her with Giovanelli behind the same parasol prominent in his own first flirtation with her at Vevey, and the narrator's phrasing implies a major moment in Winterbourne's advance-retreat scenario: "This young man" (and the epithet focuses the issue of manhood) "lingered a moment, then he began to walk. He walked—not towards the couple with the parasol; towards the residence of his aunt, Mrs. Costello"—where he can take his revenge in the sure condemnation of Daisy she will provide. He had done just the same on his arrival in Rome when he heard of Daisy surrounded by the moustaches; he will do the same differently when he hears of Daisy and Giovanelli in company again, retreating more aggressively to tell momma, informing Mrs. Miller that her daughter is "going too far." When he does confront Daisy directly, it is as a parent, not a lover, lecturing her on propriety to the point that Daisy for once evinces resentment. She notes that Winterbourne has failed to offer her tea as a gentleman suitor should; and to his "I have offered you advice," Daisy rejoins, "I prefer weak tea!", suggesting the degree to which Winterbourne dilutes his romantic presence by his learned condescension. In the Colosseum, when Winterbourne indicates to Daisy his condemnation, he does so by opting out of competition, telling her that "it makes very little difference whether you are engaged or not." Daisy, echoing the phrase, soon says "I don't care . . . whether I have Roman fever or not." In the tale's sentimental causality, Winterbourne's renunciation of interest in Daisy causes Daisy's renunciation of life. As he enters the Colosseum Winterbourne recalls Byron's description of it in *Manfred,* but he might better have recalled Manfred's confession that he killed his beloved, "Not with my hand but heart, which broke her heart, / It gazed on mine and wither'd" (II. ii. 118-19). Winterbourne would rather kill than compete, and his response to challenge, tallying with the response of his class in arenas other than the romantic, is refusal and disdain.

"You needn't be afraid. I'm not afraid," Daisy tells him when he is forced to admit that Mrs. Costello will not meet her, and we sense that Winterbourne fears more generally. Yet it is unanswerable whether he takes his aristocratic stance because he is afraid—of a world of change, of impulses in himself that would force him to choose against his lifelong choice of class—or whether he is afraid because he has chosen an aristocratic stance that demands the loss of what he calls "instinct."

This is not to argue that James is, by contrast, glorifying the ascendancy of the mercantile class in America. As many readers have noted, the disorder of the Miller family, and forms of naiveté that approach the callow in Daisy herself, serve James as a harsh critique upon this class. Mr. Miller's absence from the family journey suggests a gendered distinction good for no one, as the man remains home making more money while the wife and children "get culture" (though never getting it at all). The son, Randolph, is "hard" as the lumps of sugar he criticizes, charmless, uncontrollable, and oddly "aged" with a voice "not young." Europe to Daisy is "perfectly sweet," the Colosseum "so pretty," all with a reductive condescension that is the sweet echo of Randolph's jingoist convictions that American candy and American men are "the best." Their mother suffers from a bad liver that is the equivalent of Mrs. Costello's headaches, these figures of opposing classes both substituting a narcissism of the body as pain for healthful purpose. The Millers too display a familial entropy that is a low result of the democracy that has advanced them. Mrs. Miller "is always wearing my things," Daisy laughs as her mother appears wrapped in Daisy's shawl, but it's a significantly unfunny inversion of roles. Daisy is as much an unofficial orphan as Winterbourne, and the absence of appreciation and authority in her own family may well draw her to the paternalistic, culturally authoritative, and quaint Winterbourne.

Winterbourne cannot meet the challenge, however, for he and his female advisors are part of a fragile, essentially nouveau, American aristocracy that is not real aristocracy at all any more than these expatriates are real Europeans. The problem is less class division and prejudice than it is class confusion and anxiety. Winterbourne and his ilk make hyperbolic any true European conventions in order to stake a nervous claim to beyond-Miller status. "Real" Europe is problematic in itself as, in a commercial age, filthy lucre makes embarrassing appearances amidst the leisure of the European upper class. As early as the second sentence of the tale, the narrator notes of Vevey that "the entertainment of tourists is the business of the place." The highest status hotel in Vevey, where the Millers reside, was built on the site of an old castle, both a reason for its status and a sign of the capitalist transformation of society. An actual establishment, its name, the "Trois Couronnes," implies both nobility and coins. The mishmash of the commercial and the aristocratic in Europe is one reason why its poetry-inspiring history is portrayed in the tale as dead-in-life, miasmic, not so much informing the present as sickening it.

Winterbourne too is financial, however much he wishes to disdain the world of economic struggle. As Ian Kennedy points out [in *Arizona Quarterly* 29, No. 2 (1973),] when the narrator tells us that Winterbourne "had imbibed at Geneva the idea that one must always be attentive to one's aunt" just after he has described Mrs. Costello as "a widow with a fortune," James uncovers the savage, selfish

underpinning of the Genevan ideal of duty and of Winterbourne's fidelity to it and to his aunt. In a sense, attendance upon his wealthy aunt is Winterbourne's job.

He has yet another, and Daisy points to it when, at Chillon, she senses that Winterbourne is returning to Geneva because of a liaison. Bravely turning her hurt to a sally, she taunts, " 'Does she never allow you more than three days at a time? . . . Doesn't she give you a vacation in summer? There's no one so hard worked but they can get leave to go off somewhere at this season, I suppose.' " No champion of freedom like Byron's Bonnivard, this prisoner of Chillon yet shares that hero's terrible adjustment to the loss of liberty.

Even this momentary intimation of Winterbourne as prostituted makes his contempt for Giovanelli broadly hypocritical. On meeting the Italian, Winterbourne decides that "he is only a clever imitation" of a gentleman and he makes this claim in terms of labor: "He is a music-master, or a penny-a-liner, or a third-rate artist." Winterbourne himself is, by occupation, no more and something less; and if Giovanelli indeed has "practiced the idiom" of speaking in English "upon a great many American heiresses," one expects that Winterbourne has had to adapt to a few adopted idioms himself: "He had known, here in Europe, two or three women—persons older than Miss Daisy Miller, and provided, for respectability's sake, with husbands—who were great coquettes—dangerous, terrible women, with whom one's relations were liable to take a serious turn." Who is the imitation of a gentleman? Giovanelli, by the unemployed Winterbourne's account, turns out to be a "perfectly respectable little man" who is in fact a *cavaliere avvocatto,* and this gentleman lawyer ends by entering a plea for a true perception of Daisy's innocence. Just as the Italian takes Winterbourne's resigned place as amoroso in the narrative, though never in Daisy's affections, so too he takes Winterbourne's place finally in the reader's regard. Giovanelli is not Winterbourne's gigolo opposite so much as his double, and finally his better.

This then is the economic Winterbourne: an emigrant out of fear of practicing the American ideal of equal competition, an unemployed idler whose sense of aristocratic breeding is prostituted by fortune hunting. We must recall that Winterbourne is no confirmed villain, at least not until the final words of the tale when he refuses the true illumination, the grace of understanding his own character that Daisy's death has afforded him. His very attraction to Daisy is proof of a residue of possibility in him and of a desire for a non-Genevan self-reformation. But the forms this attraction takes have everything to do with the class alliances Winterbourne had made; and when we ask, given such choices, what kind of manhood emerges, the answers constitute an encyclopedia of misogyny.

3

One of Henry James's great surprises is his occasional penchant for broad effects. I began by insisting that his basic plots are often melodramatic, and his naming of such characters as Daisy and Winterbourne is obviously allegorical. Noting such effects often makes James's reader queasy, and this is most true as regards the sexual puns.

Can the Master, the writer's writer who provides the "sense of the sense," actually be thought to indulge in such adolescent double entendre? The answer is affirmative, for James will exploit the whole register of meaning making. The character always intends the more or differently figurative meaning of such words, the socially sophisticated meaning; but James intends all meanings, including those that betray the character's unsublimated self.

The words that attach to yet another of Winterbourne's alter egos, Daisy's brother Randolph, offer such a case. Unsettlingly older than his age, Randolph's voice is "sharp, hard," his eyes "penetrating." He carries a long alpenstock, "the sharp point of which he thrust into everything that he approached—." He "poked his alpenstock, lance-fashion, into Winterbourne's bench," calls the sugar Winterbourne has afforded him "har-r-d," and then "got astride of" the alpenstock. He speaks again in "his little hard voice," and converts his alpenstock finally "into a vaulting pole."

Daisy's "small, slippery brother" at times seems something of a walking penis; his aggressive energy—remeeting him in Rome, Winterbourne compares him to "the infant Hannibal"—represents everything in American competitive manhood that Winterbourne had fled. Yet Winterbourne is not so apart from these tendencies and this phallicism as we first think.

Shortly after Winterbourne "wondered if he himself had been like this in his infancy, for he had been brought to Europe at about this age," Daisy appears, and Winterbourne is described as "straightening himself in his seat, as if he were preparing to rise." Much later, in Rome, Daisy on four occasions criticizes Winterbourne as "stiff." The social meaning of the adjective seems to oppose the romantic, as when Winterbourne tells Daisy he does not dance and Daisy replies, "Of course you don't dance; you're too stiff." But I want to argue that the phallic condition of "stiff" opposes romance as well. The dance of respectful courtship demands flexibility and motion; the sexual love of women and men requires an appreciation of the entire person, not a stiff, phallic reduction of the Other. Daisy is right beyond her knowing when she refuses Winterbourne's request to "flirt only with me" because, in her words, "You're too stiff." Just as Winterbourne attempts to live apart from his commercial age and thus becomes almost a fortune hunter, so in fleeing American competitive manhood and his own American "instinct" as he calls it, Winterbourne reduces his sexuality to the state of Randolph's, preadolescent and yet ever so hard.

James labors to establish Winterbourne's trouble at the outset, in Winterbourne's first meeting with Daisy, as he dramatizes Winterbourne's leaking libido in terms of an extended act of perception. This is how Winterbourne views the girl:

> They were wonderfully pretty eyes; and, indeed, Winterbourne had not seen for a long time anything prettier than his fair country-woman's various features—her complexion, her nose, her ears, her teeth. He had a great relish for feminine beauty; he was addicted to observing and analys-

ing it; and as regards this young lady's face he made several observations.

> It was not at all insipid, but it was not exactly expressive; and though it was eminently delicate Winterbourne mentally accused it—very forgivingly—of a want of finish.

In three sentences, James packs seven overlapping kinds of inhumanity, seven deadening sins. The first I would term *exploitative or acquisitive perception*. Winterbourne itemizes Daisy's features in such a way—her eyes, her teeth—as to make her an object or himself a horse trader. His "relish for feminine beauty" is resentable too. It suggests a practice of *connoisseurship*, an emotional distancing both affectedly aristocratic and somehow prurient, pornographic.

Seeing through the eyes of others is yet a third form of Winterbourne's blindness. Does the face lack a finish?, Winterbourne worries, and we worry that someone else is setting the standards. Note as we approach the passage that Daisy's glance is "perfectly direct and unshrinking" yet not "what would have been called an immodest glance." Discrimination is a Jamesian essential, and naming is as natural as Adam, but this is the world's postlapsarian naming—"what would have been called"—not Adam's.

Winterbourne's *obsessive categorizing*, his classificatory zeal, is another function of his hand-me-down mentality. Earlier, when Daisy first appears, "she" is immediately made a "they" by Winterbourne: "How pretty they are"; and later, he questions, "were they all like that, the pretty girls who had a good deal of gentlemen's society? Or was she also a designing, an unscrupulous young person?" Winterbourne will not allow women to be, will not grant them an integrating wholeness, will instead dissect and categorize. And when they don't fit, when humanity refuses such reduction—agreeing to Winterbourne's accusation, Daisy responds, "I'm a fearful, frightful flirt! Did you ever hear of a nice girl that was not?"—he will dismiss them brutally, as he does at the Colosseum. Under an ominously "waning moon," Daisy is revealed to him, all falsely, as unscrupulous indeed and he experiences his unbecoming exhilaration "by a sudden revulsion from cautious criticism." The cautious criticism is dehumanizing in itself, the bipolarities deadening. James has his final joke on Winterbourne when, after implying the gross inadequacies of the either-ors, he allows Daisy an innocence even in Winterbourne's dichotomizing terms. Winterbourne's "cautious criticism" of categories and types is his attempt to halt experience in aristocratic, hierachical stillness; his final revulsion from it, itself fearful in a refusal to live with mystery, is less a refutation than an extension of it.

This categorizing has yet another aspect that constitutes his fifth sin of perception, one that we might call *testing*. In the early description of Daisy, Winterbourne tests her against various ideals of socially respectable appearances; and soon, in a moonlit scene that anticipates the finale in the Colosseum, Winterbourne suggests a boat ride to Chillon, primarily to see how far Daisy will go. Acceptance of the invitation would doom Daisy in Winterbourne's opinion and rid him of the bothersome ambiguities of his own creation, but for this pathetic relief he must wait upon Rome.

A sixth form of inadequacy in the early passage coexists with all the others, together constituting *the sins of the spectatorial*. As John H. Randall III writes [in *American Quarterly* 17 (1965)], Winterbourne "sees life through the spectacles of the picturesque. What he responds to is a guidebook view of life, not life itself." This marks him a cultural parvenu in his comments on the sights of Europe. When, for instance, he quotes Byron on entering the Colosseum, he reminds us of all those nineteenth-century American anglophiles who are described nicely by Benjamin Goluboff as "the alluder on the landscape," insecure travelers from the raw New World taking "a sort of examination in cultural literacy." Winterbourne flunks the more crucial exam of understanding, for he is about to exemplify the final lines of Byron's Colisseum description, "The dead but sceptered sovereigns who will rule / Our spirits from their urns" (III. iv. 40-41). Just so, when Mrs. Costello requests that her nephew bring her *Paule Méré*, she seems unaware that the Cherbuliez novel, published in Geneva, concerns the victimization of a brave woman, an older Daisy, by a weak husband reminiscent of Winterbourne and by a society much like Mrs. Costello's own.

When Winterbourne directs this same effete, meaning-emptying appreciation toward Daisy, it bespeaks that removal from life that is also a removal from self. This self-removal provides another reason for Winterbourne's wish to visit Chillon with Daisy: "[H]e had never yet enjoyed the sensation of guiding through the summer starlight a skiff freighted with a fresh and beautiful girl." The sophisticated but crude "freighted" underlines once more the dehumanizing of Daisy, the "fresh and beautiful girl" the categorizing tendency of this collector of experiences. But there is also here a sense of Winterbourne, if you will allow me an anachronism, watching a motion picture of his own life. He can produce such a movie even when he is not present in a particular scene, as when he arrives in Rome and is discountenanced by the news that Daisy is surrounded by moustaches, "a state of affairs so little in harmony with an image that had lately flitted in and out of his own meditations; the image of a very pretty girl looking out of an old Roman window and asking herself urgently when Mr. Winterbourne would arrive." This is uproariously self-flattering—Winterbourne Studios is consistently partial to its owner-star—but it is also self-negating, for one cannot live a life while obsessively observing it. Such self-consciousness even harms those attempts at manipulation that always undercut Winterbourne's moments of empathy. When he senses that Daisy is hurt by his aunt's refusal to meet her, Winterbourne decides it might be "becoming in him to attempt to reassure her. He had a pleasant sense that she would be very approachable for consolation." Winterbourne imagines unstiffening—though only in a most becoming way and only to get what his stiff self desires—but by the time Winterbourne Studios has produced the scene in his head, Daisy's mother appears and his bad chance is lost. Life *is* for Daisy; it is always about to be for the screening room hero, though perhaps this is fortunate given his designs on it.

But Winterbourne is not a public actor, and if he creates his own scenes, he does not wish upon himself the eyes of others. He is secretive, and *guilty privacy* is his seventh sin. In the passage in which he itemizes Daisy's features, he is looking but his thoughts are not seen. This privacy is apt in a man who lives his only vital life behind closed doors and at absolute odds with the social manners he espouses so recklessly. James takes an early revenge on this hypocrite gossip by having his narrator speak of him in the falsely respectful, secretly savage voice of the society to which Winterbourne belongs:

> [W]hen his friends spoke of him, they usually said that he was at Geneva, "studying." When his enemies spoke of him they said—but, after all, he had no enemies; he was an extremely amiable fellow, and universally liked. What I should say is, simply, that when certain persons spoke of him they affirmed that the reason of his spending so much time at Geneva was that he was extremely devoted to a lady who lived there—a foreign lady—a person older than himself. Very few Americans—indeed I think none—had ever seen this lady, about whom there were some singular stories. But Winterbourne had an old attachment for the little metropolis of Calvinism; he had been put to school there as a boy.

Each of the narrator's false hesitations to disclose something unpleasant constitutes a cut. The unseen lady—foreign, then older, finally singular in the stories told of her—is also Winterbourne's unseen life and suggests a reason for Winterbourne's interest in "coming off" with Daisy to Chillon secretly. He can thus deny her freshness and the jolt it might give to his pornographic, musty self. Winterbourne associates the libido with the hidden—that is why he despises meeting Daisy in the hotel hall (not simply because it is vaguely vulgar) and it is why, once they arrive at Chillon, he bribes the custodian to leave them alone, yet another act that characterizes his economic cheating. It is also why he cannot believe in Daisy's appearance of innocence, because his own appearance is so unnaturally fashioned to disguise what resides in Geneva and in himself. What Winterbourne half wishes is to make Daisy taboo, for then she can enter his dirty little world and he will not have to leave it. That he also half wishes to leave it is what saves him a measure of sympathy. That he decides against this second chance is what ends all sympathy and dooms his manhood, as I will suggest a bit later, to a fate literally worse than Daisy's death because it constitutes damnation.

4

There is one element of Winterbourne's first long description of Daisy's appearance and of his entire encounter with her that is so obvious as to be hidden. It is best expressed in a law Leverenz constructs for Hawthorne's short story, "The Minister's Black Veil": "My wish to invade his privacy is an evasion of my own." Winterbourne's invasion of Daisy's privacy, his dressed-up, vulgar desire to know, as Cathy Davidson puts it, " 'Does she or doesn't she?'," is a way to evade questions about his own capacity for love. Troubled, frightened, Winterbourne runs from the world of male competition and surrounds himself with two kinds of women: the adultresses in Geneva and the prudish widows in Vevey and Rome. These two kinds are really one kind, halves of a determined double standard whereby, in Mrs. Costello's words, "a man may know everyone."

Our major reaction is to exclaim against the women's society that castigates Daisy for wholly inoffensive and open actions while allowing for Winterbourne's hidden profligacies, "not morality but conformity," as William E. Grant writes [in *Studies in Short Fiction* 11 (1974)]. And certainly we feel the force of female self-punishment: "[W]omen characters uphold the system which restricts them," Louise K. Barnett notes [in *Studies in Short Fiction* 16 (1979)]; and Davidson rightly calls these women "misogynous" [in *Arizona Quarterly* 32, No. 4 (1976)], adding that women like Mrs. Costello and Mrs. Walker "will seek to be men" and take on their authority. But my main interest is in the degree to which Winterbourne submits to them. He "acquiesces in their power," writes Susan Koprince. He is, in Motley Deakin's summation, "the captive of women."

He is the captive of both kinds of women. That he experiences the adultresses in Geneva as "dangerous, terrible" suggests a fearful subordination, suggested as well by Daisy's taunt that his present lover in Geneva will not even give him, her employee or servant, more than a few days off. Winterbourne thus does not appear sexually potent even in the gossip of his liaison with this woman about whom singular stories have been told. However wild the unnamed woman may be, he is emasculated by the relationship. Just so, when Winterbourne runs to Mrs. Costello or Mrs. Walker to discuss Daisy, curl his moustache as he may, he seems a woman himself. With Daisy alone, he becomes traditional male lawgiver; but Daisy, the one relief in this chaotic environment of misgendering, refuses him this authority: "I have never allowed a gentleman to dictate to me, or to interfere with anything I do."

Winterbourne is castrated once more, but by Daisy less than by himself. He has taken this parental stance toward her, as I argued earlier, to avoid real competition. Indeed, Daisy's whole attempt with Winterbourne is to help him locate his manhood. This is the motive for all her teasing and taunting, to persuade him to behave as a man toward her but via love rather than authority. Thus when she is buried doubly inaptly—a Daisy dying in the spring, buried in cultural loneliness in the small Protestant cemetery in the world capital of Catholicism—James has his narrator describe her grave as a "raw protuberance among the April daisies." Davidson sees here an Easter resurrection, with Daisy becoming "the patron saint of a repressed sexuality." But Daisy's fate is Christlike only twistedly. When James earlier recalls the Resurrection by employing the phrase "On the evening of the third day," he is referring to Mrs. Walker's party, where Mrs. Walker's snub makes Daisy look "with a pale, grave face at the circle near the door." And the "raw protuberance" of Daisy's grave suggests a swelling in two ways ironic. As a female swelling, it is an image of death in the place of pregnancy, new birth, all that Daisy's youth and vitality promised. As

a phallic protuberance, it suggests death's cause and Winterbourne's stiff loss.

Indeed, Winterbourne has entered forever the deadening, emasculating creed of what we might call the women's religion in *Daisy Miller*. I mean religion almost and terribly literally, for the expatriates' hellish code has usurped the place of the church. There is in fact a scene in St. Peter's where

> A dozen of the American colonists in Rome came to talk with Mrs. Costello, who sat on a little portable stool at the base of one of the great pilasters. The vesper-service was going forward in splendid chants and organ-tones in the adjacent choir, and meanwhile, between Mrs. Costello and her friends, there was a great deal said about poor little Miss Miller's going really "too far."

In this ugly scene, the women have taken to themselves the heavenly judgment that is St. Peter's office. And in the same paragraph Winterbourne hears from his friend of Daisy and Giovanelli viewing the portrait of Pope Innocent, a portrait the misnamed Pope himself called *troppo vero*, as the renowned Velazquez painting reveals a cynic of worldly intrigue. The Pope's name underscores Daisy's own innocence while his face in the portrait, as Adeline Tintner writes [in *Essays in Literature* 6 (1979)], makes for "a vivid contrast" between the worldly head of state and "the secular, free-wheeling, free-thinking American Protestant girl who doesn't hesitate to turn her back on his Holiness and his so-called 'shrine.'"

James gives us something of an encapsulated history of Western religion in this slight tale of Geneva, "the little metropolis of Calvinism," and "the cynical streets of Rome." With its accusatory conviction of innate depravity and its ability to live down to it, Geneva begins a process of destroying Daisy that Rome, city of ordained convention and the pernicious leavings of pagan and Christian history, completes. The attitudes of the expatriates who paganize the Church are yet the direct result of a long misprizing of the religious spirit by religion itself.

Entering the Colosseum, Winterbourne spies Daisy seated in the shadow of "the great cross in the centre" and, in Daisy's light words, he "looks at us as one of the old lions or tigers may have looked at the Christian martyrs." But this is only the culmination of a process in which the expatriates translate religious and moral idealism into Victorian aggression devoid of real principle. Winterbourne finally adopts his aunt's view that "one does one's duty by not—not accepting" such Americans as the Millers. For Mrs. Costello, deep ethics is pretension: "Whether or no being hopelessly vulgar is being 'bad' is a question I leave to the metaphysicians." Mrs. Walker, who wishes to conventionalize Daisy rather than exclude her, does make metaphysical the socially conventional: She theologizes "Thank heaven I have found you," and, with "her hands devoutly clasped," attempts to persuade Daisy against walking in the company of men. "Extremely devoted" by the account of "certain persons" to the lady in Geneva, "awfully devoted" to Daisy in Daisy's joking phrase, Winterbourne finally takes his vows in the priesthood of the expatriates. Again, it is worth emphasizing that this is a choice, for Daisy, no metaphysician herself, has come to represent an alternative. Refusing Mrs. Walker's invitation to join her in her victoria for some moral instruction, Daisy says, "I don't think I want to know what you mean. . . . I don't think I should like it"; and the simple relativism of her "People have different ideas!" gains a resonance against this creed of absolutism born of ennui and worse, a creed well defined by the narrator when he characterizes Winterbourne's thought of consoling Daisy as "a perilous mixture of gallantry and impiety." But this emptying of the spirit succeeds in the world, leaving Daisy's memory and Henry James alone in opposition.

5

That is where Winterbourne ends, and in a moment we will name the place, but where does he originate? We do know Winterbourne's place in a literary sense, for this man of categories himself belongs to a category of male characters who populate nineteenth-century literature in America and England. He is the bachelor figure, bespeaking in the nineteenth century an anxiety of cultural exhaustion, the worry of a discontented civilization whose complaint is voiced by Winterbourne when he cannot type Daisy because "he had lost his instinct in this matter, and his reason could not help him." The loss is not simply of the American instinct but of instinct itself—spontaneity, real awe rather than artificial appreciation, vitality, everything Daisy has and he lacks. Emily Brontë's Lockwood, George Eliot's Casaubon, Melville's gourmands in his "Paradise of Bachelors" who substitute the gustatory for the romantic and heroic, any number of Hawthorne's males who victimize women to their own destruction—all are Winterbourne's literary kin. The bachelor, as I have written elsewhere,

> is a grotesque with an oversized intellect, a shrunken body, and a shrivelled heart. He refuses the human community; he will not risk relatedness, preferring to experiment on others or to observe them from a voyeuristic distance. Crippled by self-consciousness, if he loves he often runs away to maintain an equilibrium that is passion's defeat. Impotent and vengeful, highly intellectual but unwise, he sells his soul for a sullen invulnerability that is itself fraudulent, for his great need is to impress others.

This is Winterbourne's literary lineage.

The bachelor is a function not only of over-civilization but of a tradition in male authorship in the Romantic period by which the femme fatale is cleared of charges. Such writers as Keats and Hawthorne engage misogynist legends that blame evil on women and rewrite them to redefine the evil as inherent in the manner that men view women; and this has everything to do with Daisy Miller and with James and *Daisy Miller*.

James's explicit allusions in the tale are to Cherbuliez and Byron, and the latter particularly has to do with that cultural fatigue we are describing. If Byron's heroes suffer an exhaustion of spirit from idealistic questing, Winterbourne, fleeing such quest while alluding to Byron, suffers *weltschmerz* squared and without glory, as a "Manfred

Manqué," in Susan Koprince's phrase. But the most powerful influences on *Daisy Miller* are not explicit. Central here is Hawthorne, about whom James was to write a full book in the next year. Richard Brodhead argues persuasively [in *The School of Hawthorne*, 1986] that "influence" is too mild a term to apply to the relation between Hawthorne and James, that James "perfectly internalized" Hawthorne from his earliest writing, giving fiction the dignity of internal literary history.

Daisy Miller is such a thoroughly meditated variation on Hawthorne's tale "Rappaccini's Daughter" that it seems folly to enumerate the parallels—Winterbourne's resemblance to Hawthorne's Giovanni in their voyeurism, secrecy, failure of faith, and destructive conformity to an ethic of cynical skepticism parading as respectability, Daisy's resemblance to Hawthorne's Beatrice in their joint status as femmes fatales who are far more sinned against than sinning. It is more to the point to quote a single passage from Hawthorne: "Blessed are all simple emotions, be they dark or bright!" exclaims the narrator. "It is the lurid intermixture of the two that produces the illuminating blaze of the infernal regions." In Winterbourne's case, while the "lurid intermixture" of his feelings prepares Daisy's doom, his demand for resolution seals it. In the "luminous dusk" of the Colosseum, with his "sudden illumination," Winterbourne unknowingly perceives via the darkness visible of his own sick spirit. Hawthorne's tale also connects James to Keats, for Hawthorne's Beatrice, poisonous yet pure, is herself a reminiscence of Lamia, the snake-turned-woman who captures a lover but sweetly, and who is destroyed by the lover's demand to show off his prize in a public wedding. She is ruined by his egotism and by his faith in a sophist teacher, Apollonius, the equivalent of Hawthorne's Baglioni and James's Mrs. Costello. Winterbourne stands with Giovanni (whose name, played upon, becomes Giovanelli and a better spirit in James's redaction) and Keats's callow, publicity-seeking Lycius as apparently pleasant if shallow youths who are yet male murderers.

But Hawthorne's tale goes back further, to an Italy older than Daisy's or Beatrice's. Beatrice was Dante's beloved, and the history of the poet's sublimation of his lust for her, to the point where he can experience God through her, is the ideal development that Hawthorne's Giovanni and James's Winterbourne fail miserably to achieve. Through Hawthorne, James reaches back to Dante's Rome—and to Dante's Satan, for Winterbourne's name is redolent of the Devil of the *Inferno*. Dante portrays a wintry Satan, devoid of all light and warmth, icily fixed in that loneliness that is the appropriate form of his utter self-love. The only motion available to Dante's Devil is the futile beating of his wings. Like Dante's lesser damned ones, like Winterbourne in the devastating final sentence of James's tale, Satan is condemned to endless repetition. The beating of his wings only fixes him more firmly in that ice which is the image of his hatred of others. This failed motion, repetitive yet worsening, also characterizes Winterbourne, incapable of "going on" or "going too far," capable only of "going round" and getting nowhere, beating his wings. By this network of allusions, James is saying nothing so crude as that Satan is Winterbourne's real identity. He is saying something worse, that this is the rough context for understanding what Winterbourne by his choices has made himself become.

But what has James become in the act of writing *Daisy Miller*? It is certainly possible that James was working through the premature death of his beloved iconoclastic cousin Minnie Temple, that Daisy is a less intellectual surrogate for this real woman who died at an early age. For a more meaningful answer, we can refer to the relation between Hawthorne and another of his bachelors, Coverdale in *The Blithedale Romance*. As character-narrator, Coverdale bears a structural resemblance to Winterbourne, though James as narrator occasionally opens just enough narrative distance from his hero to satirize him, as in the early passage on what Winterbourne's theoretical enemies might say. Coverdale too is an idler, a more-and-more minor poet, a voyeur, an analyzer, a skeptic conformist, full of jealousy and lust and punished by the narrative into learning less and less of the truth of the individuals with whom he is obsessed. He misses all the major scenes, just as Winterbourne is progressively shut out of Daisy's life, staring at an occluding parasol. Yet in many ways Coverdale seems Hawthorne's avatar, for his refusal to share the utopian hopes of the Blithedalers mirrors Hawthorne's reaction to his summer at Brook Farm. So too, James, reaching a point in his expatriation where he might have feared "living too long in foreign parts," and, more important, opting out of that revolution in American manhood whereby the new middle class had established competitive individualism, a rivalry for dominance, as its leading principle, much resembles Winterbourne. What Irving Howe writes of Hawthorne and Coverdale [in *Politics and the Novel*, 1957] may serve exactly for James and his Winterbourne. Howe notes the conflict in Hawthorne between a social self which "could summon no large enthusiasm" and "a powerful impulse within him" that "worked to assault and deride that scepticism." Thus Coverdale "is a self-portrait of Hawthorne, but a highly distorted and mocking self-portrait, as if Hawthorne were trying to isolate and thereby exorcise everything within him that impedes full participation in life." This seems to me exactly true of James in relation to the materials we have discussed.

With one exception. I think James has achieved something better here and throughout his career than merely an exorcism. Leverenz notes that the writers of Hawthorne's generation sought a manhood that would refuse the old aristocratic requisites but also would avoid the new demands upon manhood of rivalrous individualism. Instead, he writes, they sought, by the creation of heuristic, unsettling narratives, to unseat themselves and their readers, to "fashion styles of self-dispossession." Just so, James refuses the aristocracy of Winterbourne and the competing party of Randolph and Mr. Miller. That other alternative of self-dispossession, the one that feels what cannot be reasoned and questions all without the need for finality, is the manhood Winterbourne fails to locate and James practices. It is the site where manhood becomes ungendered and begins to become sexed humanity.

FURTHER READING

Bibliography

Ricks, Beatrice. *Henry James: A Bibliography of Secondary Works*. Metuchen, N.J.: The Scarecrow Press, Inc., 461 p.
> Contains a bibliography of criticism and early reviews of *Daisy Miller*.

Criticism

Cargill, Oscar. An Introduction to *Washington Square and Daisy Miller*, by Henry James, pp. vii-xxv. New York: Harper & Brothers Publishers, 1956.
> Outlines sources for *Daisy Miller* and compares the work to James's novel *Washington Square*.

Coffin, Tristram P. "Notes and Queries." *Western Folklore* XVII, No. 4 (October 1958): 273-75.
> Claims that in her "independence of thought and action," "laudable innocence," and "straightforward distrust of subtlety" Daisy Miller is similar to the heroes of western cowboy novels.

"Daisy Miller; and The Laughing Mill." *The Saturday Review* (London) 47, No. 1,227 (3 May 1879): 561-62.
> Generally positive review of *Daisy Miller* that nevertheless finds the story's conclusion dissatisfying.

Dunbar, Viola R. "The Revision of *Daisy Miller*." *Modern Language Notes* LXV, No. 5 (May 1950): 311-17.
> Surveys revisions James made for the 1909 New York Edition of *Daisy Miller*.

Dupee, F. W. "The Tree of Knowledge." In *Henry James*, pp. 74-112. Garden City, N.Y.: Doubleday & Company, Inc., 1956.
> Includes a discussion of *Daisy Miller* as an ironic tribute to the American girl.

Fiedler, Leslie A. "The Revenge on Woman: From Lucy to Lolita." In *Love and Death in the American Novel*, pp. 291-336. New York: Anchor Books, 1992.
> Briefly comments on Daisy Miller as being "finally and unequivocally innocent" despite the uproar of indignation her character created among American readers.

Geist, Stanley. "Portraits From a Family Album." *The Hudson Review* V, No. 2 (Summer 1952): 203-6.
> Study of Daisy's character that emphasizes her "absolute metaphysical freedom" in conflict with the realities of modern society.

Goodspeed, Edgar J. "A Footnote to *Daisy Miller*," *The Atlantic Monthly* 153, No. 2 (February 1934): 252-53.
> Suggests a possible real-life source for the character of Daisy Miller.

Hoffman, Michael J. "Realism as Vision and Style." In *The Subversive Vision: American Romanticism in Literature*, pp. 101-28. Port Washington, N.Y.: Kennikat Press, 1972.
> Explores *Daisy Miller*'s theme of an innocent individual in a repressive society.

Newberry, Frederick. "A Note on the Horror in James's Revision of *Daisy Miller*." *Henry James Review* III, No. 3 (Spring 1982): 229-32.
> Observes James's multiple inclusions of the word "hor-

ror" in the 1909 revision of *Daisy Miller,* noting a verbal play on its similarity to the word "whore" and its consequent bearing on interpretations of Daisy's character.

"Recent Novels." *The Nation* (New York) XXVII, No. 703 (19 December 1878): 386-89.
> Includes a review of *Daisy Miller* that calls the work a "true" and "clever" study of character.

Review of *Daisy Miller. Harper's New Monthly Magazine* LVIII, No. CCCXLIV (January 1879): 310.
> Short commentary on the unrealistic qualities of Daisy and her mother.

White, Richard Grant. "Recent Fiction." *North American Review* CXXVIII, No. 266 (January 1879): 91-110.
> Contains a brief review of *Daisy Miller* that comments on the nature of the title character as a faithful portrait of "a certain sort of American young woman."

Additional coverage of James's life and career is contained in the following sources published by Gale Research: *Concise Dictionary of American Literary Biography,* 1865-1917; *Contemporary Authors,* Vols. 104, 132; *DISCovering Authors; DISCovering Authors: British; Dictionary of Literary Biography,* Vols. 12, 71, 74; *Major Twentieth-Century Writers; Short Story Criticism,* Vol. 8; *Twentieth-Century Literary Criticism,* Vols. 2, 11, 24, 40, 47; *World Literature Criticism.*

John Maynard Keynes

1883-1946

English economist.

INTRODUCTION

Keynes is considered one of the foremost economists of all time. His *The General Theory of Employment, Interest and Money* transformed the course of economic thought with its controversial interpretation of the causes of unemployment and prescriptions for its remedy. The impact of this book on twentieth-century economic history—known as the Keynesian Revolution—has been profound, encompassing economic method, theory, and policy.

Biographical Information

Born and raised in Cambridge, England, Keynes grew up in an atmosphere that fostered intellectual achievement. His father, John Neville Keynes, was a noted logician, economist, and a registrar at Cambridge University, while his mother, Florence Ada Keynes, was a writer and social welfare advocate as well as the first woman mayor of Cambridge. Keynes attended Eton from 1897 until 1902 and then entered King's College, Cambridge, on a scholarship in mathematics and the classics. During his freshman year at Cambridge, Keynes was invited to join an intellectual group called "The Apostles" that met periodically to discuss literary, philosophical, political, and aesthetic questions. Among the members of the Apostles were Leonard and Virginia Woolf, Lytton Strachey, E. M. Forster, and Bertrand Russell, all of whom would later become leaders of the exclusive circle of intellectuals and artists known as the Bloomsbury Group. Through his association with the Apostles, Keynes became introduced to the philosophy of G. E. Moore; critics note the pervasive influence of Moore's *Principia Ethica* on Keynes's *A Treatise on Probability*, his only philosophical work, as well as on his economic methodology. After graduating from Cambridge with a master's degree in mathematics, Keynes studied economics for a year in preparation for a civil service examination. In 1906 he was assigned by the British government to the India Office; the knowledge he gained there formed the basis of his first book, *Indian Currency and Finance*. Keynes resigned from the India Office in 1908 to join the economics faculty at Cambridge. He taught at Cambridge until 1915, when he returned to government service as a Treasury official. By the end of World War I, Keynes had risen to a prominent position in the Treasury and was responsible for managing foreign-exchange arrangements. Although he seemed destined for great success as a public official, Keynes's trip to the Paris Peace Conference as economic adviser to Prime Minister Lloyd George caused his career to change directions once again. Appalled by the political maneuverings of the conference and convinced that the reparations policies imposed upon

Germany were excessive, Keynes resigned from his Treasury post. Shortly after, he published a stinging indictment of the Versailles Treaty, *The Economic Consequences of the Peace*, which provoked international controversy and made Keynes famous. During the 1920s, Keynes resumed his teaching duties at Cambridge, pursued an active business life in London as a financial consultant and insurance company executive, and was named bursar at King's College. Around the middle of the decade, Keynes became convinced that he needed to develop a strong theoretical foundation to support his belief that public expenditures would be useful in lowering unemployment. This conclusion became the impetus for *A Treatise on Money* and the *General Theory*. By the time the *General Theory* appeared, politicians and economists all over the world were searching for a way to reverse one of the longest depressions in economic history; orthodox, or classical, economic policy, which held that prosperity would return if prices and wages were lowered, was not promoting recovery anywhere. Keynes's *General Theory* was quickly accepted by many economists as an answer to the world's economic tragedies, and when Keynesian fiscal measures began to produce the desired results, he became widely viewed as the savior of capitalism. The *General Theory* also influenced economic thinking on how World War II should be financed. When the war commenced, Keynes returned to the British Treasury and was consulted on all important questions regarding the economic management of the conflict. He was a principal negotiator at the Bretton Woods Conference in 1944, where he played a significant role in the inauguration of the International Monetary Fund and the World Bank. His last major public service was his negotiation in 1945 of a multi-billion-dollar U.S. loan to England. He died of a heart attack on April 21, 1946, shortly after returning from an economic conference in Savannah, Georgia.

Major Works

The revolutionary content of Keynes's economic theory, the bulk of which is contained in *A Treatise on Money*, the *General Theory*, and, to a lesser extent, *A Tract on Monetary Reform*, developed out of his active involvement in England's economic problems during the 1920s and 1930s. During the 1920s, he advocated economic policies, either in an official capacity or as an independent expert, that he arrived at largely by intuition. In *The End of Laissez-Faire* and *Can Lloyd George Do It?*, he recommended a government-sponsored program of public works to get the unemployed off welfare, but these works lacked a theoretical foundation, and *A Tract on Monetary Reform*, which also suggested that government intervention could curb unemployment, was unsuccessful at refuting the classical argument, or so-called "Treasury view," that government spending financed by loans would cause inflation or crowd out private investment. In *A Treatise on Money* and the *General Theory*, Keynes sought to establish a firm theoretical basis that would explain the reasoning behind his policy proposals. In *A Treatise on Money*, he attempted to replace the classical explanation of money and its function in the economy, known as the quantity theory of money, with a more dynamic model that related booms and slumps to oscillations in the credit cycle and that described the causal processes by which the price level is determined. It was not until he began composing the *General Theory*, however, that Keynes was able to completely break away from the quantity theory of money. When the *General Theory* was published, it was viewed as a powerful challenge to orthodox economic theory, which held that a decrease in the wage level would stimulate employment because firms would take on more labor at a lower price, and that the interest rate would always adjust in such a manner as to prevent variations in savings and investment from causing any change in spending. Keynes declared this theory nonsense, tracing the origins of unemployment not to excessively high wages but to the total purchasing power in the economy, or aggregate demand. While classical economists focused on the individual firm or household, Keynes looked at output and employment as a whole. He maintained that a decrease in wages would not stimulate employment because it would lower the overall demand for goods and services, thereby causing prices to drop. He also contended that the classical economists erred in thinking that savings would always be equal to investment, arguing that there are times when savers wish to save more than investors are willing to invest, causing part of output to go unsold and leading producers to cut back on employees. Keynes placed great emphasis on the idea that private investment was a function not only of interest rates but also of expectations about costs and demand for products in the future. He was skeptical that monetary policy in the form of lower interest rates would provide a sufficient stimulus to business investment in times of severe economic depression to bring the economy back up to a level of full employment. He therefore proposed that fiscal measures such as public works or subsidies to afflicted groups were the only possible correctives to prolonged unemployment.

Critical Reception

On January 1, 1935, during the course of writing the *General Theory*, Keynes wrote to George Bernard Shaw: "I believe myself to be writing a book on economic theory which will largely revolutionise—not I suppose at once but in the course of the next ten years—the way the world thinks about economic problems." Keynes's prophecy proved accurate. Quickly after the publication of the *General Theory*, governments everywhere began adopting policies advocated by Keynes or associated with his name, a trend that continued for over thirty years. By the late 1940s, his theories had been incorporated into textbooks in the United States and England, and millions of students were introduced to the idea of national income accounting. Keynes was not without his critics, however. While many scholars attributed the economic prosperity experienced after World War II to the adoption of Keynesian policies, some insisted that it was the result of other factors, such as rearmament in Europe and the United States after the outbreak of the Korean War, improved international economic relations, and new technology that stimulated large amounts of private investment. Keynes was also attacked by hard-line communists, who argued that the *General Theory* was an attempt to save capitalism with remedies he knew to be ineffective. In the 1970s, with the onset of rising inflation and unemployment, the popularity of Keynes's ideas plummeted. Many economists traced the weakening of private investment to growing budget deficits and maintained that inflation was the result of the Keynesian policy of high employment, which had caused too great an increase in wages. Today, Keynes's policies remain in a state of official disfavor, but there are large numbers of economists who contend that the world's current economic problems are the result of the pursuit of anti-Keynesian ideas. The dispute over the validity of Keynes's ideas has taken shape in a vast amount of literature written by professional and academic economists. Immediately after the publication of the *General Theory*, classical economists sought to dispel the notion that Keynes was proposing a drastic change in economic thought by arguing that Keynes's ideas were a special case of orthodox equilibrium theory. In the ensuing years, additional attempts have been made to reconcile classical economic theory with the existence of involuntary employment, further undermining the revolutionary content of the *General Theory*. Other economists, and a large number of socialists, have read the *General Theory* as a radical threat to the capitalist system. These conflicting interpretations have resulted in large part from the vagueness and incomprehensibility of certain parts of the *General Theory*, which has allowed scholars to conjecture what Keynes meant to be saying. Among the most common types of studies on Keynes are expositions of specific aspects of his theory, such as investment, savings, consumption, and interest; analyses of the development of his economic thought, primarily as revealed in *A Tract on Monetary Reform*, *A Treatise on Money*, and the *General Theory*; examinations of the relationship between his theories and his policy proposals; and studies attempting to establish the difference between Keynes's own ideas and the various schools of Keynesian thought his works have inspired. The publication of Keynes's collected works by the Royal Economic Society and the centenary of his birth in 1983 prompted countless reassessments that further added to the growing literature on Keynes. In recent years, scholars have placed greater emphasis on Keynes's philosophical beliefs as expressed in *A Treatise on Probability*, studying the moral underpinnings of his economic method and tracing his theory of investment expectations to his ideas on probability and induction. As many of Keynes's critics point out, the passionate controversy he has inspired is evidence of the depth and range of his ideas. In the minds of most scholars, this fertility of thought, combined with his enormous influence on economic theory and policy, justifies his reputation as the twentieth-century's most important economist.

PRINCIPAL WORKS

Indian Currency and Finance (nonfiction) 1913

The Economic Consequences of the Peace (nonfiction) 1919

A Treatise on Probability (philosophy) 1921

A Revision of the Treaty: Being a Sequel to "The Economic Consequences of the Peace" (nonfiction) 1922

A Tract on Monetary Reform (nonfiction) 1923

The Economic Consequences of Mr. Churchill (nonfiction) 1925

A Short View of Russia (nonfiction) 1925

The End of Laissez-Faire (lecture) 1926

Can Lloyd George Do It? An Examination of the Liberal Pledge [with H. D. Henderson] (pamphlet) 1929

A Treatise on Money (nonfiction) 1930

Essays in Persuasion (essays) 1931

Essays in Biography (essays) 1933

The Means to Prosperity (nonfiction) 1933

The General Theory of Employment, Interest and Money (nonfiction) 1936

How to Pay for the War: A Radical Plan for the Chancellor of the Exchequer (nonfiction) 1940

Two Memoirs: Dr. Melchior, a Defeated Enemy, and My Early Beliefs (memoirs) 1949

The Collected Writings of John Maynard Keynes. 30 vols. (nonfiction, essays, philosophy, memoirs, letters, lectures, notebooks, and pamphlet) 1971-89

CRITICISM

Allan G. Gruchy   (essay date 1949)

SOURCE: "J. M. Keynes' Concept of Economic Science," in *The Southern Economic Journal*, Vol. XV, No. 3, January, 1949, pp. 249-66.

[*In the following excerpt, Gruchy examines Keynes's economic thought at its various levels of analysis—from his theory of output and employment, to his theory of the capitalist order, to his set of proposals for remedying the capitalist system as it was then operating in England—illustrating how his views on the nature of economic science adhered to and diverged from the orthodox position of the Cambridge school.*]

I

Recent attempts to reduce Keynes' economics to the general textbook level raise the very interesting question as to what after all are his views concerning the nature of economic science. If one were to accept the view of economics found in Paul A. Samuelson's *Economics, An Introductory Analysis* (1948) as representative of Keynes' position, then the latter's economics would turn out to be a highly formalized body of thought. As is well known, however, "Keynesian economics" and "the economics of Keynes" are not always one and the same thing. When Samuelson defines economics as a science which "can concern itself only with the best means of attaining given ends," he is of course, restating the Robbinsian definition that "Economics . . . is concerned with that aspect of behavior which arises from the scarcity of means to achieve given ends." [L. Robbins, *An Essay on the Nature and Significance of Economics Science.*] While such a highly formalistic view of economics may satisfy both Robbins and Samuelson, it is considerably removed from the view of economics which underlies Keynes' work. His economics is what he describes as a "moral science," that is to say, a science which never fails to emphasize the fact that economics, like other social sciences, is in the final analysis concerned with an explanation of actual human problems. When Keynes defines economics as an "interpretation of current economic life," or as a study of "the economic society in which we live," he gives preference to a view of economic science which, though less broad than that of the historical and institutional schools, is nevertheless not nearly as narrow as the view of economics held by those who find the essence of their science in mathematico-logical analysis.

When Keynes entered Cambridge in 1902, ideas about the nature of economic science were well summarized in John Neville Keynes' *Scope and Method of Political Economy* (1890) and Alfred Marshall's *Principles of Economics* (1890). These views stressed economics both as a study of pure theory and as a body of concrete generalizations which had a great deal to contribute to social betterment. Cambridge economics was at this time a unique combination of the abstract and the humanistic. Sidgwick, the elder Keynes, Marshall, and others could move with ease from the consideration of a highly abstract question of pure theory to some very concrete issue of the day. If Cambridge economics appeared at times to be lost in the rarified atmosphere of high abstraction, it was equally evident that at other times it could come down to earth to deal with the less precise matters of daily living. To be sure, the Cambridge economics to which the younger Keynes was introduced in the early years of this century was far from being as realistic as some of the opponents of economic orthodoxy would have liked it to be. But, in spite of its limitations, the economics of Sidgwick, Edgeworth, and Marshall commanded the respect of a large circle, and was in a flourishing state when the younger Keynes turned from his mathematical studies to the less precise science of economics.

It is quite clear from a consideration of Keynes' basic views relating to the nature of economics that he works within the Cambridge tradition. There is in his work the same emphasis upon a hard core of pure theory which dominates the whole of the upper reaches of economic inquiry. Keynes, like Marshall, is known to many readers as a specialist in the field of pure or abstract economics. His ***General Theory*** overshadows everything else that he wrote. Furthermore, like his predecessors in the Cambridge school, Keynes reveals a strong preference for a deductive approach to economic analysis. Although it may be said that he is more aware than some of his orthodox predecessors of the historical trends in economic life, nevertheless Keynes, true to the Cambridge tradition in economics, is not very strongly attracted by historical, cultural, or sociological analysis. As with Marshall, he might deplore the excesses of the mathematical economists, but he could never bring himself to adopt the more sociological or culturalistic approach of a Hobson, a Veblen, or a Marx.

Along with the other members of the Cambridge school Keynes realizes that there is much more to economics than just the field covered by pure theory. Surrounding the core of pure theory is a rather indefinite realm of analysis which Neville Keynes described in his study on the scope and method of political economy as the field of "concrete economics." Concrete economics, not being satisfied with merely deductive analysis, supplements pure theory by providing economic generalizations which relate primarily to a given period or a given state of society. Marshall drew attention to the same matter by making a distinction between the "foundations" of economics and its "superstructure" [*Principles of Economics*]. The superstructure of economics is erected on a foundation of general or universal principles, but it does not itself possess any universality since it purports to explain only the operations of a particular economic society. Following in the footsteps of his father and of Marshall, Keynes writes about levels of analysis which extend from the bare bones of pure theory to the more complicated but much less precise interpretations of the real economic world. Like his Cambridge predecessors, he seeks to erect on the essentials of pure theory an inductive superstructure which will bridge the gap between pure and applied economics. For Keynes as for Marshall economic theory of the pure variety is only preliminary or introductory to those more inductive economic studies which are the ultimate goal of the economist's analysis.

If Keynes' over-all views relating to the nature of economic science are basically similar to those of other members of the Cambridge school, the question then arises, Wherein does he differ from Sidgwick, Edgeworth, Marshall and other exponents of neoclassicism? If Keynes clings to his father's distinction between "abstract" and "concrete" economics, how does he improve upon the latter's generation? It is now a widely held view that the younger Keynes' work amounts to something of a revolution in economic thinking. Economists today speak and write about the Keynesian Revolution or the New Economics of Keynes. They do not mean to imply, however, that Keynes has some radically new ideas relating to the general nature of economics as a science, or that he has deserted the Cambridge school for, say, the institutional or historical school. What these economists are saying is that the bottle may be old but the wine is definitely quite new. Keynes has poured a new content into the inherited molds of pure and concrete economics. He has taken Marshall's "economic foundations" apart, rebuilt the substructure of economic science, and then erected a superstructure of economic interpretation which was only hinted at in various places in Marshall's works. It is now clear that Keynes has done much more than merely reshuffle the Cantabrigian cards. He has also developed novel ideas like those of Hobson, Gesell, and other exponents of economic heterodoxy. Although the final result is to many economists a strange mixture of Cambridge economics and some theories similar to those found in the "underworlds of Karl Marx, Silvio Gesell or of Major Douglas" [*The General Theory*], Keynes himself saw nothing incongruous about his combination of orthodox and heterodox ideas. On the contrary, he appears to have regarded himself as representative of the most recent step in the further development of Cambridge economics.

II

Since Keynes' early views about the nature of economics were greatly influenced by Alfred Marshall, the latter's views will serve as a useful point of departure for a study of Keynes' opinions on the same matter. Marshall defined economics as "a study of mankind in the ordinary business of life" [*Principles of Economics*]. This definition is so general that it may be made to include a study of economic life anywhere and at any time. Marshall, however, had no special interest in any country but England in the last quarter of the nineteenth and the first quarter of the twentieth century. His economics turns out to be a study of mankind in the business of making a living in a capitalistic economy such as was found in England from 1875 to 1914. What Marshall actually does is to restrict his definition of economics until it becomes a study of the competitive capitalism which reached the pinnacle of its development in England about the time that he published his *Economics of Industry* (1879). His method of expanding the definition of economics is to work out first the "foundations" of his science and then to move on to its "superstructure." He explains that his first volume on the principles of economics is only a general introduction to the study of economics, whereas the second volume, which never appeared, was to have dealt with the superstructure of his science. Marshall intended to develop various levels of economic analysis which would extend from the precise analysis of pure theory on the one hand to the complex analysis of the concrete economic system on the other hand.

Marshall very significantly points out that the economist's shifting from the foundations of economics to its superstructure is not just a matter of introducing reservations to pure theory. He is aware that much more than a simple transfer is involved. Somewhere along the line, as the economist moves upward in his analysis toward the real economic world, he has to make a fundamental intellectual adjustment. This change in analytical approach involves substituting a new framework of analysis for that which was found useful in the lower levels of pure theory. Pure theory, Marshall points out, is only an introduction to economic studies. He goes on to say that "it is especially needful to remember that economic problems are imperfectly presented when they are treated as problems of statical equilibrium, and not of organic growth. For though the statical treatment alone can give us definiteness and precision of thought, and is therefore a necessary introduction to a more philosophic treatment of society as an organism; it is yet only an introduction." What Marshall had in mind is quite clear. As the economist ascends the ladder of scientific analysis, moving towards an interpretation of the complex flow of real economic events, he finds it necessary to substitute a new view of the economy as a "social organism" for the preliminary view of it as a "statical equilibrium." In other words, on higher levels of analysis he has to use a new framework of interpretation which makes room for many of the data of concrete economic life not considered by pure theory.

At this point in his thinking Marshall was on the verge of constructing a theory of the capitalist economic order which would have been applicable to English conditions in the half-century running from 1865 to 1914. He was about to provide an explanation of the era of economic development which coincided with his own life-experience, and in an interpretation of which his principles or "economic foundations" would have been very useful. Unfortunately, Marshall found himself unequal to the task. All that we now have to go upon are a few scattered references to what the superstructure of his science would have been made to include had he been able to develop it. He did explain that, whereas his first volume on principles dealt with "the theory of stable equilibrium of normal demand and supply," in his projected second volume normal action was to have been replaced by the concrete action of the real economic world. "Normal action falls into the background," Marshall wrote, "when Trusts are striving for the mastery of a large market; when communities of interest are being made and unmade; and, above all, when the policy of any particular establishment is likely to be governed . . . in subordination . . . to some campaign for the control of markets. Such matters cannot be fitly discussed in a volume on Foundations: they belong to a volume dealing with some part of the Superstructure." Here Marshall dropped the matter. In doing so he failed to develop a theory of the capitalist economic order within the new organismal framework of analysis to which he made reference in the preface of his *Principles*.

Marshall's thinking about the two fields of economic analysis, the one relating to the foundations of the science and the other to its superstructure, always remained in a somewhat unsettled state. At first, as Keynes tells us in his biographical sketch on Marshall, the latter had planned to write a number of monographs on special economic problems and then to compress these studies into a general economic treatise. It turned out, however, that Marshall reversed this procedure and never succeeded in raising his exposition of the superstructure of economics to the level of his work in the field of pure theory. In spite of all his efforts he did not get much beyond thinking of the superstructure of economic science as something of a catchall into which various specialized studies could be placed. As a consequence of his failure to work out the implications of his view of the economic system as a "social organism," Marshall was unable to provide that much needed unity for his concrete economic studies which would have given them something of the scientific status possessed by his work in the field of pure theory. But where Marshall failed Keynes enjoyed more success. It is to Keynes' credit that he sharpened the whole analysis relating to the superstructure of economics by providing the necessary unity for empirical studies of the economic system. In Keynes' work this unity takes the form of a theory of the capitalist order in the light of which concrete economic studies are given their full meaning.

III

Keynes, like Marshall, starts off with a very general definition of economics. He takes economics to be an "interpretation of current economic life" [*Essays in Biography*]. This broad definition is soon narrowed, however, so that economics becomes a study of "the economic society in which we live" [*The General Theory*]. Since the society in which Keynes lived was basically capitalistic, it is not surprising that his economics turns out to be an interpretation of "an economy of individualistic capitalism" [*The General Theory*]. He was more specific than was Marshall, who started with a very general definition of economics but never reached the point of actually declaring his science to be a study of the way in which economic life is organized under the system of individualistic or laissez-faire capitalism. In taking economics to be "the interpretation of current economic life" or a study of "the economic society in which we live," Keynes occupies a position midway between the formalism of Lionel Robbins and the institutionalism of the heterodox economists. Robbins emphasizes the formalistic aspects of his science when he states that economics is a study of "that aspects of behavior which arises from the scarcity of means to achieve given ends." Keynes, the man of action, could find little intellectual satisfaction in Robbins' formalistic approach, although there is much in the latter's work with which he could agree. Nor did Keynes find himself attracted by the broad cultural approach of a Sombart or a Veblen. Like other economists in the English classical tradition, he did not go so far as to make his science a study of the economic aspect of human culture, as do the institutionalists and their followers. In this connection Keynes was much closer to Marshall than to Hobson or the Webbs. This close adherence to the Marshallian position undoubtedly accounts for some of Keynes' antipathy to the work of Marx, who was a forerunner of both the historical and the institutional schools.

In developing his views on the nature of economics Keynes follows Marshall by making use of the idea of various levels of economic analysis which vary from the most formal at the one extreme to the most realistic at the other extreme. Keynes explains that at the bottom of the scale are found the bare bones of pure economics. This type of economics is concerned with what he describes as "comparatively simple facts which are known with a high degree of precision." At this low level of analysis the primary aim of the economist is to "imagine and pursue to their furthest points the implications and prior conditions of comparatively simple facts" [*Essays in Biography*]. The economist endeavors to reduce his analysis to constructions of pure form. As he rises above the level of pure economics, the facts of economic life become increasingly less simple and less precisely known. Economic interpretation grows more realistic but also more difficult to handle. The logical schematism of pure theory is now clothed with generalizations which owe much to the economist's "practical wisdom" and his wide acquaintance with the facts of the real economic world. Finally, at the top level is found "economic interpretation in its highest form," which constitutes the economist's ultimate goal. Keynes explains that this high-level analysis provides an economic interpretation of the complex and incompletely known facts of experience. It presents an interpretation of that "current economic life" which Keynes regards as the final goal of economic studies. This high-level economic analysis, based as it is on Keynes' "amalgam" of logic, intuition, and wide acquaintance with the facts, not only moves far beyond the realm of pure theory but also leads one a long distance toward the establishment of "useful results."

Keynes did important work at various levels of economic analysis. At the lowest level he provided his pure theory of output and employment as a whole, while at the top level he worked out his empirical interpretation of the current phase in the development of the capitalist system. His theory of most recent era in the evolution of the capitalist system is much less developed than his pure theory of employment. This is not surprising when one considers Keynes' intellectual background and his training as an economist. Cambridge economics has always been much stronger in the realm of pure theory than in that of more concrete economic interpretation. Alfred Marshall and others gave Keynes a thorough training in the foundations or general principles of economics, but they did not prepare him equally well for a study of the superstructure of the science. Marshall had little to say about the economic system as an emerging process or historical continuum. He was therefore ill-equipped to introduce Keynes to the kind of economic thinking which is necessary for the development of a theory of the capitalist order. Keynes might have been better prepared for the higher levels of economic analysis had he made a thorough study of the work of Marx, Veblen, Hobson, and other exponents of economic heterodoxy. In spite of the limitations imposed by a traditional, neoclassical training and later, by a busy life, Keynes made considerable progress in developing these higher levels of economic analysis where pure theory merges into a more empirical interpretation of the actual economic system.

Keynes' work at the lower levels of economic analysis was not intended as a substitute for the pure theory which had been developed by earlier economists. He is quite explicit in stating that much of the pure theory of his orthodox predecessors has an enduring value, and that "it is impossible to think clearly on the subject without this theory as a part of one's apparatus of thought." [*The General Theory*]. What Keynes accepts from earlier economists is their theory of the individual firm, which assumes a given volume of employed resources and then explains the distribution of these resources between different uses under equilibrium conditions. Orthodox theory did not raise the question as to what it is that determines the actual level of employment of resources. It was merely assumed by the orthodox economists that all available resources would be employed. Keynes abandons this assumption and makes a problem out of what was taken for granted by his orthodox predecessors. He wants to know what it is that determines the actual level of employment of available resources, since in the modern world this level fluctuates widely. It is for this reason that he describes his goal at the lower levels of economic analysis as "the pure theory of what determines the *actual employment* of the available resources." [*The General Theory*].

What Keynes does, in effect, is to graft on to the inherited pure theory of the individual firm or industry a theory of output and employment as a whole. He finds it necessary to enlarge the received field of pure theory, because it proves to be an unsatisfactory stepping stone to higher levels of economic analysis. Keynes points out that, since Marshall's pure theory relates to a commodity economy or an economy of refined barter, it necessarily ignores the "peculiar properties of money as a link between the present and the future" [*The General Theory*]. The result is that the doors to a broader interpretation of the concrete economic order are for the most part closed to the orthodox economist. In developing his pure theory of employment Keynes makes certain that he avoids the pitfalls to which his orthodox predecessors fell victims. His theory of employment is constructed within the framework of a monetary economy which takes account of money as "a subtle device for linking the present to the future." The central doctrine in Keynes' explanation of a monetary economy is his theory of expectations. The basic assumptions of this theory are that the future is not "fixed and reliable in all respects," and that business expectations, since they are liable to disappointment, are capable of influencing the present. Keynes' theory of expectations leads to a consideration of highly sensitive liquidity preferences, instabilities in the flow of real investment, and wide fluctuations in output and employment as a whole. On the basis of these and related ideas he constructs his well-known general theory of employment which "can be summed up by saying that, given the psychology of the public, the level of output and employment as a whole depends on the amount of investment" ["**The General Theory of Employment,**" *Quarterly Journal of Economics,* Feb., 1937].

What is especially significant about Keynes' theory of employment, as compared with Marshall's theory of the individual firm, is that it opens rather than closes the way to analysis on higher and more concrete levels. As E. A. G. Robinson has pointed out in his review of Keynes' life and work, the latter developed his theory of employment as a tool to aid him in explaining the functioning of the mature capitalistic economy. [E. A. G. Robinson, "John Maynard Keynes, 1883-1946," *Economic Journal,* March, 1947]. The major problem of the capitalistic system, according to Keynes, is the lack of sufficient investment outlets to absorb the planned savings of the upper income groups. What Keynes needed was a corpus of pure theory which would throw some light on the role of investment in economic life. His theory of employment, with its attention centered on investment as the most significant single factor influencing the level of output and employment, meets this important theoretical need. Furthermore, Keynes' interest in the role of investment in economic affairs provides the bridge between his pure theory and his more inductive interpretation of the actual capitalistic system. As we shall see, it is Keynes' treatment of the investment problem which unites the various levels of economic analysis running from his pure theory of employment to his concrete theory of the capitalistic order. Our analysis will reveal that there was in Keynes' mind a much greater unity or coherence than is evident in his many scattered writings. He had visions of a unified thought system which, unfortunately, he put on paper only in a very fragmentary form.

IV

So much for Keynes' work in the field of pure theory. What remains to be investigated is his work on those higher levels of economic analysis toward which his pure theory points. It is on these higher levels that Keynes develops his theory of the capitalist order which not only makes use of his general theory of output and employment but which also goes far beyond it. At this point in his theorizing Keynes is concerned with an explanation of the concrete economic system. He finds that the isolation of a few factors and the study of their interrelations is not enough for the purpose at hand. The economist, says Keynes, must go beyond the logical analysis of pure theory to combine logic with intuition and a wide acquaintance with the facts. He has to turn to "practical wisdom" or intuition for guidance as to what is most significant in the "extreme complexity of the actual course of events" [**The General Theory**]. The logic of pure theory is useful in unravelling the complexities of economic life once these complexities have been placed in some kind of an analytical framework, but logic comes into service primarily after the major outlines of the problem have been intuitively grasped. In other words, logic is analytical but never selective, as is Keynes' "practical intuition." Of course, intuitive insight must be grounded in what Keynes refers to as a wide acquaintance with the facts, for there is always the danger that intuition may draw more heavily upon fancy than upon fact.

As Keynes moves above the level of pure theory he introduces his concept of the economic process or the historical continuum which supplies him with a new framework of interpretation. For short-run purposes he uses an equilibrium framework of analysis by the aid of which he analyzes those short-run changes in economic activities which result in pushing the rate of new investment to the point where the marginal efficiency of capital in general approximates equality to the rate of interest. This equilibrium approach, however, is found by Keynes to be unsatisfactory for the type of economic analysis which seeks to include more than the limited number of isolated factors considered by his general theory of employment. When he wishes to cover a wider range of factors, Keynes thinks of the economic system in terms of an economic process. He then moves from the equilibrium of pure theory to a consideration of the "psychological equilibrium" of a particular phase in the evolution of the capitalistic system [**A Tract on Monetary Reform**]. It is this psychological equilibrium or balance between various economic classes which is the center of interest in his theory of mature capitalism, just as "the position of equilibrium" between the marginal efficiency of capital and the rate of interest is the focal point in his general theory of employment.

Marshall likened the concrete economic system to a social organism, but the term "organism" is much too biological for Keynes. He follows Alfred N. Whitehead in preferring the term "process," which he uses to describe the actual economic system [**Essays in Biography**]. This system, as Keynes sees it, is an economic process which is passing through a number of developmental stages. Currently we are in an "era of transition from economic anarchy to a regime which deliberately aims at controlling and directing economic forces in the interests of social justice and social stability" [**Essays in Persuasion**]. It is this current "phase of capitalism" which is Keynes' special concern on the higher, more concrete levels of economic analysis. He provides his interpretation of "the kind of system in which we actually live" against the background of an era of transition from one stage of capitalistic development to the next stage. Since this era is like Whitehead's "event" which incorporates within itself the past, the present, and the future, it is not surprising to find Keynes writing that the economist should "study the present in the light of the past for the purposes of the future" [**Essays in Biography**] This is precisely what he attempts to do when he is developing his theory of capitalism on the higher levels of economic analysis.

Interpretations of the capitalist process revolve around considerations of such matters as the theory of capitalist development, the class organization of a capitalist society, the breakdown of capitalism, and the role of government in a capitalist economy. We can briefly analyze Keynes' theory of capitalism in the light of these four basic questions. Although he is well aware of the phases or eras through which capitalism has passed, Keynes offers no theory of capitalist development. There is nothing in his explanation of capitalism which is comparable to Marx's or Veblen's technological interpretation of the course of capitalist development. Keynes very largely ignores this question, and concentrates instead upon an interpretation of the "present stage of human affairs." He has much to say about class organization in contemporary economic society. According to his interpretation, the many different classes in a modern capitalist society are divided into the two major categories of the productive (or active) and the unproductive (or inactive) classes [**A Tract on Monetary Reform**]. The productive classes are mainly concerned with "enterprise," while the unproductive classes, the rentier, have "accumulation" as their main interest. As long as there was a proper balance between enterprise and accumulation, the economy could function satisfactorily; but, unfortunately, in the current phase of mature capitalism accumulation tends to gain the upper hand as against enterprise. The rentier are successful in preserving their share of the national income by maintaining high interest rates. These high interest rates discourage enterprise, and result in low rates of investment accompanied by low levels of output and employment.

The breakdown of capitalism occurs when the heavy hand of the inactive classes interferes with the full functioning of the economy. To make matters worse, the governing classes, by failing to understand the nature of the problem, persist in policies which only serve to support the rentier classes and to perpetuate the chronic stagnation of business. An understanding leadership, Keynes feels, would strive to correct the unbalance between enterprise and accumulation, but such leadership is difficult to discover. This is why he describes the breakdown of capitalism as "nothing but a frightful muddle, a transitory and an *unnecessary* muddle" [**Essays in Persuasion,**]. The breakdown is not made inevitable by the push of technological developments, as Marx and Veblen would have it. Instead, it is the result of misunderstanding on the part of short-sighted politicians and ultra-conservative civil servants who continue to preach the gospel of laissez-faire in an age which calls for greater "collective action" [*Essays in Persuasion*].

Keynes' theory of the role of the state is also quite different from that of Marx and other exponents of economic heterodoxy. The state's role, in Keynes' opinion, is that of a "balancing factor" which seeks to preserve the proper "psychological equilibrium" between the various economic classes [*The General Theory, A Tract on Monetary Reform*]. Whenever there is the danger that the inactive classes are about to take for themselves too large a share of the national income, the government steps in to correct this situation. It levies high income and inheritance taxes to weaken the operation of the hereditary principle in the transmission of wealth and the control of business. Or the government benefits new wealth at the expense of old, and arms enterprise against accumulation, by depreciating money and keeping interest rates down. This latter procedure was followed in the nineteenth century, but where there is a scarcity of new investment outlets, as is the case today, the depreciation of money is not enough to restore the balance between the productive and the unproductive classes. The government then seeks to restore the balance by lowering interest rates and creating new investment outlets. Eventually, however, if the pure interest rate were to become zero, the problem of balancing enterprise against accumulation would disappear along with the rentier as well. At such a time the state would still be concerned with many other problems of economic balance. There would be the problem of equating the risks and the returns on new private investments having doubtful prospective yields, and also the problem of balancing the wants of the current generation against the needs of future generations.

Keynes' theory of the capitalist order plays a very important role in his thought system. It provides the nexus between his work in the field of pure theory and his proposals with respect to actual economic problems. It is a mistake to assume that the economist moves directly from pure theory to the field of applied economics, where general principles are modified to meet the requirements of the actual data of real life. Between pure and applied economics lies the economist's theory of the economic order, into which are fitted his generalizations from the field of pure theory. This theory of the economic order provides a unity or frame of reference for the field of applied economics without which the applications of pure theory tend to degenerate into an indiscriminate handling of a wide variety of unrelated problems. Unfortunately, many economists fail to elaborate the theory of the economic order which canalizes their thinking as they go about making use of the generalizations of pure theory. In some instances the presence of such a theory is not even admitted; in others only a few fragments of any such theory are made available to the reader. Even Keynes is not very explicit about the theory of capitalism which runs like a single colligating principle throughout his life's work. He does, however, provide enough so that his theory of the economic order may be brought together without too much difficulty on the part of his readers.

Keynes has not drawn attention to some of the problems to which his thinking leads when he makes use of his concept of the scientist's intuition. Although economists can agree on the results of their logical analysis, they do not readily reach agreement about the results of their intuitive understanding of the facts. If one accepts Keynes' definitions and also the logic with which he strings these definitions together, then he can also accept Keynes' conclusions in the field of pure theory. It is easy to see why there is considerable agreement with Keynes in respect to his "general theory" but much less agreement with his interpretation of the evolving capitalistic system or with his proposals for handling concrete economic issues. If one does not accept Keynes' intuitive understanding of the course of economic events, then he will very likely reject Keynes' theory of capitalism and also his suggestions for the handling of actual economic problems.

All economists employ both logic and intuition to some extent in developing the theory of the economic order which unites their work in the fields of pure and applied economics. But they are not always willing to admit that their work shows the influence of both intuitive and logical analysis. This is true of some of Keynes' followers, who have much to say about his pure theory of employment but little to say about his theory of capitalism. These economists appear to believe that the only problem is one of securing a clear understanding of Keynes' pure theory. When this goal is achieved, the investigator is supposed to be prepared to step directly into the field of applied economics. Other economists go beyond Keynes' pure economics to make use of a theory of capitalism, but they do not focus attention on this theory. It is clear that, although such a theory underlies their work, it rarely comes to the surface where it can be examined and criticized by the reader. In general Keynes' followers fall considerably behind their master, who pushed boldly beyond the realm of pure theory to construct a theory of the capitalist order.

v

It is quite clear from the preceding analysis that Keynes' thinking about the nature of economic science falls into a clear-cut pattern. Although he never wrote extensively on the question of the nature and scope of economics, Keynes always had in mind a very comprehensive view of his science. . . .

Keynes divides the science of economics into two major fields of interest, the first one being concerned with pure economics and the second dealing with the concrete or empirical aspects of the science. He further subdivides the field of pure theory into the theory of the individual firm or industry on the one hand and the theory of output and employment as a whole on the other hand. The first subdivision of pure theory is concerned with the operations of the individual firm and the distribution of the product resulting from the use of a given supply of resources. This first type of pure theory is primarily concerned with the allocation of a given supply of resources under the equilibrium conditions of full employment. The second subdivision of pure theory deals with fluctuations in output and in the amount of employed resources. It endeavors to explain what it is that brings about fluctuations in the levels of output and employment which vary from full employment to much less than full employment. Keynes is careful to point out that there are no contradictions between these two subdivisions of the field of pure economics. On the contrary, they complement each other. He explains that when the level of full employment of resources is reached "the classical theory of the individual firm comes into its own again from this point onwards" [*The General Theory*]. His criticism of the first subdivision of pure theory is not that it contains any logical flaws, but that it cannot solve many of the problems of the actual world because its premises are not sufficiently grounded in reality. Working with a different set of assumptions, Keynes expands the inherited field of pure theory so as to make it include new general principles which are found useful in dealing with the economic problems of the twentieth century.

The field of concrete economics is divided by Keynes into two parts, the first dealing with the theory of the economic order and the second with the application of economic principles to concrete problems of the economy. His theory of the economic order presents a much broader interpretation of the functioning of the capitalist economy than does his theory of output and employment as a whole. It covers a wider expanse of economic experience, and attempts to deal with facts which are not known with a high degree of precision. In spite of its limitations Keynes' theory of the capitalist order plays a very important role in his thinking. It carries his analysis much closer to "the actual world" than does his pure theory. This is true because his generalizations of pure theory are of a more "logical" than "experiential" nature. They do not make sufficient room for the facts of experience which do not follow of "logical necessity." Keynes' theory of the capitalist order fills a need not met by his work in the field of pure theory. It provides a framework for the analysis of "the actual phenomena of the economic system . . . which are not logically necessary" [*The General Theory*]. Keynes points out that there is no logical reason why the economic system should not be violently unstable. But the historical or empirical facts are that the capitalist system remains for long periods in a "chronic condition of subnormal activity." He explains these empirical facts by turning to the environmental and psychological conditions found in a modern capitalist economy. At this point in his work Keynes goes beyond his pure theory; and, generalizing from experience, he lays the foundation for his theory of capitalism.

After Keynes has developed his general principles of pure theory and his concrete theory of capitalism, he is prepared to apply his theory to practice. He then moves to the field of applied economics where solutions of economic problems are worked out with the aid of whatever generalizations his science provides. In this field of economics Keynes is far removed from the simple facts of pure theory. The material upon which he works is intractable; the data are incompletely known; and logical analysis, proving to be inadequate, has to be supplemented by the economist's practical intuition and wide acquaintance with the facts. Keynes points out that there are no conclusive tests, either formal or experimental, in economics and other social sciences. It is not surprising, in this situation, that agreements between economists on proposals for the solution of economic problems are difficult to secure. Nor is it surprising that it is Keynes' applied economics which is the most controversial portion of his work. His proposals for economic reform have not always been well defined. They range from very specific suggestions for monetary control by the central authority to the rather vague recommendation of a "somewhat comprehensive socialisation of investment" as the only means of securing an approximation to full employment. Writing as he frequently did *sub specie temporis,* Keynes did not always clearly distinguish between the short-term and long-term aspects of his thinking; nor did he always clearly relate his economic proposals to these various aspects of his work. This failure to integrate sufficiently well his analyses and his proposals has resulted in varying interpretations of Keynes' economics. Some economists describe his work as a type of "depression economics," while others assert that its generality makes it independent of any particular phase of the cycle. Whatever one may think of the general import of Keynes' economic thinking, it is quite apparent that he left his work open to widely varying interpretations.

This analysis of Keynes' views on the nature of economics reveals that in the general outlines of his thinking on this particular problem he has not radically departed from the position of the Cambridge school. What he has done has been to give new content to old categories. The world passed through many changes in the years between the first publication of Marshall's *Principles* (1890) and the appearance of Keynes' *General Theory* (1936). Economic doctrines which had been considered adequate in 1890 were found in need of much revision 40 years later. This was a need that Keynes endeavored to meet without departing too far from the general scheme of things created by earlier members of the Cambridge school. He complemented Marshall's theory of the individual firm with his own theory of aggregate output and employment. More than this, Keynes went beyond Marshall's undeveloped theory of the economy as a social organism to work out a theory of the mature capitalist order. He succeeded in developing the superstructure of the science of economics in a manner which would certainly have commanded the admiration, if not the assent, of his illustrious teacher. It is Keynes' position that Alfred Marshall was unable to make much progress in interpreting the economic system as a "social organism" because his pure economics was in itself deficient. He explains that Marshall, in the realm of pure theory, had done little more than graft the marginal principle and the principle of substitution on to the Ricardian long-period equilibrium analysis. Marshall's pure economics, with its emphasis on the allocation of a given supply of resources, proved to be an inadequate introduction to the development of a theory of the competitive capitalism of his time. It could not have been surprising to Keynes that Marshall's second volume on the superstructure of economics never made its appearance, since the first volume on general principles closed so many doors to a study of the concrete economy as a part of the great historical process.

Keynes' contributions to the development of economics when considered from the broadest viewpoint may be summarized as a successful, though incomplete, integration of the various levels of economic analysis running from pure to concrete economics. Marshall and his generation had failed to integrate satisfactorily these various types of economic analysis. Their failure to do so prepared the way for a growing separation between the pure and concrete divisions of their science. In the last quarter of the nineteenth century pure and concrete economics tended to move in opposite directions. The pure economist tended to ignore the problems which were of interest to more empirical investigators; while the applied economist was prone to carry on his studies without much attention being paid to the contributions of pure economics. In spite of the warnings of Marshall, Robbins, and others, concrete economics continued to be little more than an amorphous omnium-gatherum to which was consigned a vast and growing flood of monographic literature. It has been Keynes' contribution to remedy this deficiency in the work of earlier economists of the orthodox school. He directed his pure theory toward the concrete problems of his times. More than this, Keynes created a bridge between pure and applied economics in the form of a theory of the capitalist order. The final product of his efforts is an integration of pure and concrete economics which, although it is far from being complete, nevertheless marks an important step forward in the progress of the science of economics.

The deficiencies which are found in Keynes' views on the nature of economics are those that are usually associated with the Cambridge school. He reproduces the somewhat formalistic, anticulturalistic bias of Sidgwick, Edgeworth, and Marshall. The strongest part of Keynes' work is that which deals with the more formal aspects of economic theory. Although he goes far beyond the earlier members of the Cambridge school in developing a theory of the capitalist order, Keynes' empirical economics is by no means as well developed as his pure economics. It has already been pointed out that Keynes offers no theory of development as a substitute for the technological interpretation provided by the heterodox economists. His theory of capitalism does not come to grips with some of the most important facts of twentieth-century economic life. Furthermore, it remains in a very fragmentary form. Like some other members of the Cambridge school, Keynes had an aversion to broad economic treatises. He much preferred to emulate the pamphleteering of Ricardo, Malthus, and Jevons. "Economics," Keynes wrote, "must leave to Adam Smith alone the glory of the Quarto, must pluck the day, fling pamphlets into the wind, write always *sub specie temporis,* and achieve immortality by accident, if at all" [*Essays in Biography*]. Having a strong preference for the monograph over the general treatise, Keynes could not be expected to get very far with the broad outlines of a theory of the economic order.

There is in Keynes' work a strong humanistic bias which leads him to a decidedly functional view of his science. Marshall had come to economics from prior studies in metaphysics and ethics. His interest in ethical matters continued long after he had taken up economics as his major study. This is evident from the way in which the first chapter of Marshall's *Principles* introduces the subject of poverty. He pointed out in his introductory chapter that it is the hope of reducing poverty "which gives to economic studies their chief and their highest interest." He viewed economics as a science which would become increasingly useful as a weapon in the fight against human misery. This functional view of economic science is reproduced in the work of Keynes, who was much more concerned with "social" than with "private" advantage. But there is a fundamental difference in the functional view of economics held by Marshall and Keynes. Marshall hoped that economics would prove to be a useful tool for the betterment of the laissez-faire economy of his time; but Keynes held no such view, for he was essentially anti-laissez-faire in his general outlook. He regarded economics as an aid in the establishment of a partially-controlled economy in which the government would assume responsibility for the good working of the investment process. It was to defend the view that "a large extension of the traditional functions of government" is required by the economic circumstances of the twentieth century that Keynes found it necessary to change radically the contents of the pure and concrete economics handed down by Sidgwick, Edgeworth, Marshall, and other members of the Cambridge school. In this doctrinal reconstruction Keynes moved far beyond the orthodox position to which he was introduced when he first entered Cambridge. As a consequence, although the shell of his economics may still be described as orthodox, its contents are largely a contribution of novel twentieth-century thinking.

Arthur Smithies   (essay date 1951)

SOURCE: "Reflections on the Work and Influence of John Maynard Keynes," in *The Quarterly Journal of Economics*, Vol. LXV, No. 4, November, 1951, pp. 578-601.

[*In the following excerpt, Smithies surveys Keynes's career, commenting on the relationship between his economic theories and his philosophical beliefs, his views on domestic and international economic policy, his method of argument, the success of his policy proposals, and the political consequences of his theories.*]

I

The publication of Mr. Harrod's biography of Keynes will enable many of us who were not his intimates to reflect on his personality and achievement in a way that was not possible before. It will enable those who knew but one aspect of his many-sided life to form some idea of his extraordinary versatility.

Mr. Harrod deserves our gratitude for his painstaking investigations and our congratulations for not being overpowered by his eminent subject. However, I am not entirely happy about Mr. Harrod's biographical method, which bears distinct marks of indebtedness to Lytton Strachey. We can be reasonably sure that Strachey was not lurking in a corner of Queen Elizabeth's boudoir, and we therefore know where we stand. With Mr. Harrod, it is difficult to disentangle the parts of his work that are based on direct personal experience, of himself or others, from his vivid interpretations. Consequently many readers will find the extracts from Keynes's correspondence and the plain statements of fact the most useful parts of the book. However, the more I have worked with the book, the more I have liked it.

As Mr. Harrod says in his preface: "Keynes' contributions to the theory of economics were closely related to [and usually followed] his practical proposals and these in turn were closely related to his general philosophy. An understanding of the background of his thought is indispensable for a correct interpretation of his conclusions"—and for an explanation of his eminence and of the seeming paradoxes in his career. What were the motives of the man who inspired more enthusiasm and more consternation than any economist since Marx? What was the extent of his influence on the course of events in his own country and in the world? Did he help to undermine capitalism or to sustain it? Did his influence help to produce the results he intended or did he reap the whirlwind? What light does his career shed on his own famous thesis on the potency of ideas?

Keynes, like most if not all of the great figures in economics, has striven to influence events as well as to explain them; and the effects of economic theories on human action cannot safely be relegated by economists to other branches of social science.

In this article I shall discuss some of the perplexing questions about Keynes's intent and influence on the basis of the evidence presented by Mr. Harrod, Professor E. A. G. Robinson, and others and by Keynes's own published work.

II

From Mr. Harrod's account of Keynes's childhood and his time at Eton, one does not get any hint of the unique, controversial, and rebellious figure of the future, although one may catch a glimpse of the brilliant emissary of his country and the distinguished member of the House of Lords. Brilliance, distinction, and intolerance of stupidity were all evident. But he was intolerant of bad sermons, not of sermons as such. He was preoccupied with winning prizes and he liked to row boats. He disliked the idea of getting up early in the morning for military training, but he celebrated the Boer War victory with the largest flag in Eton—and forty years later was to call for three cheers for Colonel Blimp and the Old School Tie. He was and remained thoroughly content with England and English institutions, particularly those exemplified by Cambridge and Eton. The only possible breach with conformity at Eton came from his Congregationalist and liberal family background. In fact he was everything one would expect the gifted son of a happy intellectual family to be.

His tutors and friends confidently expected eminence, but I think it was eminence along well-accepted lines. It was easy to imagine that he might end up as Lord Chancellor in an Asquith government, which is what Trevelyan may have had in mind.

While home and Eton confirmed Keynes's belief in the traditions in which he had grown up, Cambridge, and later Bloomsbury, planted the seeds of rebellion, although they were to lie dormant for a decade and then to sprout, one feels, by the accident of circumstance. Keynes's rebelliousness was of no ordinary kind. It was rebellion against "madmen in authority," lunatics (a favorite word)—bankers and politicians—men who acted according to the dictates of their prejudices and automatic rules rather than according to the light of reason in fields where Keynes felt reason should prevail. It was a rebellion against the bank chairmen who deprecated "the expenditure of mental agility" and desired "straightly to face the facts rather than find a clever way around them" [***Essays in Persuasion***].

One detects little sympathy for popular causes as such. Although Keynes was president of the Liberal Club at Cambridge and took part in election campaigns, I do not get the impression that he felt he was fighting for great causes. As far as the record goes, the social revolution that was accomplished in England between 1906 and 1910 neither excited his sympathy nor stirred his imagination.

Mr. Harrod is quite right, I believe, to stress Keynes's friendship with Strachey. Strachey's attitude towards Queen Elizabeth and Queen Victoria is very much like Keynes's reaction to traditional economic beliefs. Strachey felt obliged to show that Victoria was a dumpy little woman and that Elizabeth owed her success to inability to make up her mind, not because he was a republican but because he had an intellectual and aesthetic distaste for traditional English historians. Keynes must have derived the same kind of satisfaction from his opposition to bankers and politicians and, later on, to stuffy nineteenth century economists.

But comparison with Strachey is as interesting for the differences as for the similarities it reveals. Keynes did not espouse causes merely because he was against stupidity and error, but because he was in favor of measures for the general betterment. Curiously enough Mr. Harrod attaches little, if any, importance to the ideological influences to which Keynes was exposed as an economist. In fact he rather goes out of his way to deprecate Marshall's influence on Keynes, who is quoted as saying, "He [Marshall] was an utterly absurd person, you know." It seems to me that, as an economist, Keynes was the product of English Utilitarianism. (In fact, what English economist is not?) When confronted with the same issues, I can easily imagine that Keynes and John Stuart Mill would be in agreement on the necessity, the feasibility, and the nature of the action by the state required to promote the common good.

In view of his own protestations to the contrary, to call Keynes a Utilitarian may appear a solecism. But he tended to associate Utilitarianism with Bentham and laissez-faire, rather than with J. S. Mill, and he must have had a curious idea of Bentham; otherwise how could he refer, as he does in **"Early Beliefs,"** to "the final reductio ad absurdum of Benthamism known as Marxism"? And he was also more concerned with denying hedonism as an ethical doctrine than with disputing the validity of the body of economics derived from it. In his essay on Edgeworth he writes "The later Marshall and the later Edgeworth and many of the younger generation have not fully believed [in the utilitarian psychology]; but we still trust the superstructure without exploring too thoroughly the soundness of the original foundations" [*Essays in Biography*].

Keynes's policy recommendations, like John Stuart Mill's, were made to advance the general welfare and not primarily to advance the relative position of any economic or social class, and his attitude to social questions was intellectual and moral rather than emotional. He refused to join the Labor Party because it was a class party and proclaimed that, if he was forced to decide, the social revolution would find him on the side of the class to which he belonged—the educated bourgeoisie. Nevertheless his faith in the power of the human intellect to solve social problems kept him out of the Conservative Party. The Liberal Party was where he belonged. Keynes liked and admired Lord Oxford because of his intellect, disliked and distrusted Lloyd George because of his emotions, and never had any close ties with any labor statesman. And I wonder whether he ever quite forgave Mr. Churchill for the return to gold.

Keynes had no desire to create a world that was unfit for the bourgeois intellectual to live in; the measures he proposed were designed to eradicate misery and suffering and to eliminate injustice. But he showed a marked preference for monetary and fiscal measures that were elegant in operation and anonymous in their direct effects. And, so far as I can see, he was never particularly concerned with the campaign for social security, which was quite in line with his general economic ideas.

He advocated income redistribution because it would increase the propensity to consume, not because of a desire for equality. He looked forward to "euthanasia of the rentier" because rentiers neither toiled nor spun nor served any decorative purpose. There is a profound difference between Keynes's approach and Beveridge's program for full employment through a campaign against Want, Disease, Ignorance and Squalor.

However, to understand Keynes's performance as an economist and a publicist, we must turn from his adherence to Utilitarianism to his reaction from it as an ethical principle. As he proclaims in **"Early Beliefs"**, his religion, and that of Strachey and his friends, was G. E. Moore and his *Principia Ethica*. He says: "We were among the last of the Utopians, or meliorists as they are sometimes called, who believe in a continuing march of progress by virtue of which the human race already consists of reliable, rational, decent people, influenced by truth and objective standards, who can be safely released from the outward restraints of convention and traditional standards and inflexible rules of conduct, and left from now onwards to their own sensible devices, pure motives and reliable intuitions of the good," and "we had no respect for traditional wisdom or the restraints of custom. We lacked reverence . . . for everything and everyone. It did not occur to us to respect the extraordinary accomplishment of our predecessors in the ordering of life . . . or the elaborate framework which they had devised to protect this order."

The ritual of the religion was introspection and conversa-

tion. While the good was indefinable, good states of mind could be ascertained by asking the right questions. "The appropriate objects of passionate contemplation and communion were a beloved person, beauty and truth, and one's prime objects in life were love, the creation and enjoyment of aesthetic experience and the pursuit of knowledge."

This memoir was Keynes's bequest to the world, and he presumably felt it fitting to withhold this revealing clue to his personality until after his death. It is a curious mixture of retention and recantation. He says: "It seems to me looking back . . . it was a purer, sweeter air by far than Freud cum Marx." On the other hand, by the time he wrote (1938) he had come to realize that D. H. Lawrence could with some justice object to a religion that tended to regard the finer human emotions merely as subjects for "brittle" discussion. And one does not have to be endowed with Lawrence's passionate nature to feel somewhat dismayed to find these first-class intellects preoccupied with questions such as: "If A was in love with B because A's spectacles were not strong enough to see B's complexion, did this altogether, or partly, destroy the value of A's state of mind?" [*Two Memoirs*].

A religion that centers its attention on the individual and on the relations between individuals may keep its adherents pure and unspotted by the world, but it does not necessarily enable them to understand the world. For instance, one cannot fail to be struck by Keynes's failure to attach sufficient importance to Marx or to realize that the world was condemned to be a different and more disagreeable place because of the "Marxian and Freudian religions." He acquired and retained a sublime faith in the power of the intellect over the forces of history. In *The End of Laissez Faire* he stated that "A study of the history of opinion is a necessary preliminary to the emancipation of the mind." His thesis was that if we could be brought to realize how slender were the philosophical supports for laissez-faire, it would lose its potency. And he seems to have felt that Marx could have been dealt with in the same way. For Keynes that fact that ideas, whether well- or ill-founded in the first instance, had been absorbed into the culture of a country over a period of more than a century seemed to make little difference.

The main direct effect of Keynes's "religion" on his economic opinions was that it led him to deplore preoccupation with the money motive. This led him to see a gleam of hope for Russia, and to have little sympathy with the United States until the closing years of his life. It probably accounted in part for his dislike for businessmen and bankers. He could never have regarded the entrepreneur as the romantic figure that Schumpeter did. And with his own extreme rationality, he showed his contempt for money by making a fortune before he got up in the morning.

The indirect effects were far more important. Moore and his circle may have equipped Keynes for the "long struggle of escape" that might otherwise have been impossible. Other economists—Pigou and Robertson—whose purely intellectual endowments were not inferior to his did not attempt it. And his faith in his intellectual powers enabled him to put forward his opinions with the dazzling assurance in which he was unique.

But all that would have meant little, as it did for his friends, in the world of public affairs were it not for the heritage of economics, the purposefulness acquired in his early years, and what Mr. Harrod calls the presuppositions of Harvey Road: the belief that "the government of Britain was and would continue to be in the hands of an intellectual aristocracy using the methods of persuasion." In fact an England that continued to exist on those lines seemed the only place where the good life according to Moore would be possible.

III

Keynes, the economic reformer, was one of the consequences of the peace. It is clear that he felt that nothing more than the meliorative program of the Liberal Party was needed in the pre-1914 world. He might never have realized what powers of persuasion he possessed had not the white heat of indignation compelled him to protest against the Versailles settlement. In a less turbulent world, Keynes's contributions to economics might have been confined to such technical questions as whether India should adopt a gold exchange standard in place of the gold standard.

The story of the *Economic Consequences* is too well known to require descriptive comment here. It seems clear from the structure of the book that what stirred Keynes most was the fact that the negotiations were dominated by political passions, which excluded both magnanimity and rationality; and his dislike for Lloyd George was all the greater because Lloyd George was an Englishman, who should have known better. That, it seems to me, outweighed in his mind the importance of the economic argument that the reparations proposals were bound to break down. There was nothing in the peace settlement or its negotiation that resembled *Principia Ethica*.

The moral fervor of the *Economic Consequences* added great emphasis to Keynes's argument about the transfer question. Of course the existence of a transfer problem in addition to the problem of raising the resources internally is implicit in much of the classical theory of international trade, but it was assumed that countries would submit to the adjustments required to attain international equilibrium. Keynes's new emphasis was that the whole impact of reparations on the standard of living of the paying country—resulting both from increased taxation and from the possible worsening of its terms of trade—should be considered in determining the feasibility and desirability of a reparations plan. Of course the pressure of events might itself have propelled that issue into the limelight with or without Keynes. In any event, what was novel then has become a commonplace today. International adjustments are rarely considered without full regard to their internal impact. In fact, one frequently has the impression that nothing but internal impact receives serious attention.

Apart from the reparations question, Keynes's main preoccupation during the twenties and thirties was to secure freedom for his own country to achieve "stability of prices, credit and employment" [*Tract on Monetary Reform*].

First it was necessary to secure freedom from the international gold standard, which made independent national action impossible, and, second, it was necessary to win freedom from the Treasury point of view at home.

In the chaotic world of today, the international proposals of the *Tract on Monetary Reform* (1923), which were then thought sensational, seem no more than moderate. Essentially Keynes proposed that the United Kingdom should continue the system of managed exchange rates that had emerged during the war. Every Thursday the Bank of England should announce the price of gold with the same lack of fanfare as it announced the discount rate. It should allow fluctuations in its gold reserves to offset seasonal and other short-run shifts in the demand and supply of foreign exchange, but beyond that should direct its exchange rate policy and its discount policy toward the attainment of internal price stability. There was to be no question of exchange control or import control. In fact the United Kingdom had maintained specie payments throughout World War I largely on Keynes's advice.

The doctrine of the *Tract* is briefly: "Thus inflation is unjust and deflation is inexpedient. Of the two perhaps Deflation is . . . the worse; because it is worse, in an impoverished world, to provoke unemployment than to disappoint the *rentier*. It is easier to agree that both are evils to be shunned. The individualistic capitalism of today, precisely because it entrusts saving to the individual investor and production to the individual employer, presumes a stable measuring rod of value, and cannot be efficient— perhaps cannot survive—without one." It is interesting to observe this early recognition—one of the main theses of the *General Theory*—that deflation of the price level cannot be accomplished without unemployment. But, if so, how can stability of employment and stability of the price level be preserved when the latter requires the correction of inflationary tendencies? The *General Theory* resolved the dilemma in favor of stability of employment—at a time when the danger of inflation seemed slight. What would Keynes have written today, when individualistic capitalism may be imperilled by instability of the standard of value?

Unfortunately, neither then nor subsequently did Keynes attach enough importance to the possibility of conflict between the twin objectives of stability of employment and stability of the price level.

Keynes's advice was not followed. The government decided to return to gold at the prewar parity and committed the country, probably unwittingly, to the consequent deflation and unemployment. When it abandoned gold in 1931, it did so because it could do nothing else. The highly successful system of exchange management that prevailed during the thirties corresponded closely to the ideas of the *Tract*.

It seems clear that national and international monetary management was always Keynes's first love as a control device. It was an elegant instrument that could, in his view, be administered by the kind of men who ought to control the Bank of England. It required a minimum of administration and permitted a maximum of individual freedom from control.

The decision to return to gold and the consequent deflation and unemployment in England and the world-wide depression of the thirties naturally led Keynes to think more in terms of a direct attack on unemployment, and also to remold his theories to support the new burdens they had to carry; the Quantity Theory of Money provided a doctrinal base that was adequate for the prescriptions of the *Tract*.

In 1924, Keynes supported Lloyd George's plan for extensive public works to combat unemployment, but he went further and advocated that savings be diverted from foreign to home investment. He argued that there was an immediate connection between long-term foreign investment and exports. Even if the United Kingdom made funds available to foreigners, British exporters would still have to compete with the exporters of other countries to satisfy the increased demand; and there were bound to be leakages in the course of internal adjustment that would prevent the British export trade from obtaining the full benefits of increased foreign investment in the shape of increased demand for their products. And, secondly, he argued that there were institutional and legal reasons why investors preferred foreign to home investment. Consequently, he urged government programs to undertake home investment and measures to make home investment more attractive for private investors. It is important to note, however, that Keynes did not, at that time, advocate any measures to restrict the flow of foreign investment.

In 1926, Keynes took part in an abortive effort to organize an export cartel in the cotton trade, and in 1930 made his most serious break with tradition in international policy. He joined the protectionist camp and advocated a revenue tariff as a temporary measure to relieve unemployment. This move probably disappointed his friends more and outraged his opponents less than anything else in his rebellious career. His friends saw almost a wanton disregard for principle. But were they not too harsh? He had fought the battle for flexible exchange rates and devaluation and had lost. Judged by today's standards of economic conduct, an economist would not be criticized severely if he advocated a tariff where devaluation was the right remedy, but seemed politically out of the question. Nevertheless, Keynes continued to urge protection till within a few months of England's departure from the gold standard. After England did devalue, Keynes urged postponement of the tariff question, but it was too late. As Mr. Harrod says: "In the event Britain went off the Gold Standard, which removed the need for protection, and had protection also, and then failed to give any lead for international reconstruction."

When the United States torpedoed the World Economic Conference in 1933, Keynes commented with an article, **"President Roosevelt is Magnificently Right,"** and a month or two later stated in an article [in *New Statesman and Nation*], "I sympathize, therefore, with those who would minimize, rather than with those who would maximize, economic entanglement between nations. Ideas,

knowledge, art, hospitality, travel—these are things which should of their nature be international."

If economic rivalry could be eliminated by policies of national self-sufficiency, the cost in terms of restrictions on the international division of labor could be considered slight. But have not attempts at self-sufficiency in fact exacerbated rather than reduced international rivalry? And with modern restrictive policies, the very types of international intercourse that Keynes valued have been the first to suffer.

This seems to have been the high-water mark of Keynes's economic isolationism. I use that term rather than economic nationalism or autarchy since at no stage of his thinking did he urge beggar-my-neighbor policies for their own sake. The discriminatory policies of Dr. Schacht were utterly alien to his temperament and inclination. The *General Theory* envisaged a world where trading countries attained internal stability and were thereby enabled to enjoy the fruits of the international division of labor. *The Treatise on Money* proposed an international monetary authority on the lines of what Bretton Woods might have been. And when Keynes negotiated the British Loan, he based his case on Britain's total balance of payments rather than its prospective dollar deficit. His sole objective so far as I can see was to secure for individual countries, and his own country in particular, freedom of internal action, and, thereby, to meet the conditions necessary for international stability.

IV

So much, for the moment, for Keynes's views on international economic policy; let us return to his opinions on domestic policies. Throughout the twenties and thirties he consistently advocated public works expenditures financed by borrowing as a major remedy for unemployment. And his intellectual efforts—*The Treatise on Money, The Means to Prosperity,* and the *General Theory*—were stimulated largely by the need to build a theoretical structure to support the point of view that he knew intuitively to be right. The theoretical structure of the *Tract* was thoroughly inadequate for the purpose and, if anything, supported the Treasury point of view that there was a single lump of real savings available for all investment purposes. Public works expenditure would then either cause some inflation or divert real investment from private channels.

Mr. Harrod properly reminds us that the *Treatise on Money* (1930) was a great work for its time and that, for some of his basic ideas, Keynes was greatly indebted to Professor D. H. Robertson, whose merits have received less than their just due in the Keynesian Wonderland. Nevertheless, with its analytic preoccupation with the price level and its policy concern with unemployment, it is rather an awkward halfway house between the *Tract* and the *General Theory;* it is like an agreeable prewar building with large picture windows cut into it. The *Means to Prosperity* (1934) completed the foundation of the new orthodoxy by incorporating the Kahn multiplier.

In 1936, the *General Theory* appeared. This is not the place to discuss details of its analytical structure or to debate the validity of its reasoning. I want rather to summarize the main conclusion with respect to the operation of the economy and the policy that Keynes invited economists to accept on the basis of his analysis. In my opinion these are:

(1) The mainspring of economic activity is effective demand which can expand or contract in relation to supply as a result of spontaneous decisions by consumers, investors, or government. In contrast to the Treasury view, an expansion of demand in one sector normally results in an expansion of the total, and not in a corresponding decrease elsewhere, which would be the case if the rate of interest performed the role assigned to it in traditional theory.

(2) Changes in effective demand produce changes in output and employment in the same direction. Wages and prices also change in the same direction, but in normal times quantity effects outweigh price effects in importance. The initial effects of changed demand are magnified by multiplier effects. It is interesting to note that through his insight into the investment process or through his lack of it, Keynes did not close his system with a formal "accelerator" relationship.

(3) With given productivity of labor, the price level depends on the wage level. Wage rates are rigid at least in the downward direction, and can only be reduced through the pressure of unemployment. Hence there may be direct conflict between employment stability and price stability or adherence to the gold standard at a fixed parity. The process of deflation is so wasteful and unjust that policy objectives that require deflation to achieve them should be abandoned.

(4) Changes in the money supply affect the economy through the rate of interest. While contraction can produce deflation, an expansion of the money supply is likely to have little effect if interest rates are already near their lower limit. And since Keynes held that the quantity of money does not affect consumption, increases in the money supply are not viewed with alarm.

(5) The only automatic mechanism through which the economy can adjust itself to a deficiency of effective demand is the long process by which unemployment reduces wage rates and consequently the demand for money and interest rates. Since an increase in the quantity of money will produce the same results more quickly and painlessly, there is no reason why deflation should ever be relied on as a remedy for unemployment.

(6) Modern industrial economies are likely to suffer from an excess of thrift rather than a deficiency of it. Consequently, one of the main reasons that have been advanced in the past for the inequality of incomes and against a progressive income taxation has disappeared. On the contrary, such measures are desirable because of their effects on the propensity to consume.

(7) If effective demand is maintained in the short run, long-run growth will look after itself. Although this proposition is not explicitly stated, surely it is implicit in the *General Theory;* and Keynes does state that economic

growth would have been more rapid under Malthus than it was under Ricardo.

The inference is that stability of employment can be achieved through a combination of fiscal and monetary policy plus some direct planning of investment. Stability of the price level requires a wage policy that limits general wage increases to productivity increases. The possibility of conflict between social reform and economic progress disappears, since reform, within reasonable limits, has beneficial effects on the propensity to consume and redistribution can be carried a long way without impairment of incentives to enterprise.

No wonder that the future seemed bright and that many of us felt that at last we had been given a creed of which, as economists, we could be proud. Even before publication of the *General Theory,* Keynes himself was supremely confident that he would revolutionize economic thought. He said so in a letter to Bernard Shaw in 1935, and added: "When my new theory has been duly assimilated and mixed with politics and feelings and passions, I can't predict what the final upshot will be in its effect on action and affairs. But there will be a great change, and, in particular, the Ricardian foundations of Marxism will be knocked away." What did happen may have been further beyond his powers of prediction than he thought. Perhaps he cannot be expected to have foreseen the war and its aftermath. But did not his rare gifts of persuasion carry with them special responsibilities to foresee the consequences of what he said?

V

With the onset of the war, Keynes set about putting the *General Theory* into reverse in order to provide a remedy for inflation. By a combination of higher taxes and compulsory saving, the disadvantages of open or suppressed inflation were to be avoided. The analysis of the *General Theory* also greatly influenced economic thinking on war finance through the whole English-speaking world, and calculation of the inflationary gap became one of the favorite occupations of economists. Looking back on these exercises, in which I took part with as much enthusiasm as anyone, they now seem rather futile. No government was prepared to close the gap by taxation, and when the time to which the calculations related came around it had necessarily been closed by something—savings in some form or price increases. Consequently, it was very difficult, if not impossible, to see whether the original estimate was right. Anyway, everyone was too busy to try.

Every government found it necessary to rely far more heavily on direct controls than almost any economist recommended; and one is led to wonder whether there was something wrong with the economists' diagnosis. I think the inequities that would result from reliance on a purely fiscal attack on inflation were overlooked. Unless a tax system were progressive enough to equalize incomes, short supply commodities would go to the higher income groups; rationing is required to attain commonly accepted standards of equity. And the Keynesian preoccupation with income as the main determinant of consumption leaves out of account the possibilities of consumption out of capital. Nothing short of expenditure control in some form or other can adequately control consumption.

The subordinate role accorded to the stock of money in the *General Theory* led Keynes to persuade his government to follow a cheap money policy throughout the war, and the British example probably encouraged the United States to follow the same course. Undoubtedly this policy was effective in its avowed purpose of holding down the burdensomeness of national debts—even more effective than its advocates expected. For the postwar inflations that were in part stimulated by wartime cheap-money policies have meant in fact that the war was financed at negative real rates of interest.

Keynes's efforts on the international field during the last years of his life paralleled efforts in the same direction on this side of the Atlantic to lay the foundations for a workable international economic system in the postwar period. But whereas the American approach from the outset involved action in the fields of both finance and commercial policy, Keynes, until a late stage, centered his hopes on financial arrangements.

In some respect Keynes's efforts to secure workable postwar settlements resembled his protest in the *Economic Consequences*. This time it was his function to claim the same magnanimity towards impoverished allies as he had previously claimed for a defeated enemy. I cannot agree with those of his critics who allege that he acted from an exclusively English point of view. The Clearing Union proposal was designed to provide dollar aid to all the European allies without favor to anyone. It was only after the amounts provided through the Fund appeared inadequate that Keynes was forced to urge the claims of his own country. Throughout he was supported by a strong conviction of the moral rightness of his case.

In his view, the economic requirements of a workable international system rested on four main premises:

(a) In addition to cancellation of Lend-Lease obligations, the United States should extend economic aid to its allies: the $20 billion drawing rights contemplated in the Clearing Union at the time seemed impossibly large. Actually the United States has provided about that amount—through the Marshall Plan, the British Loan, actual drawings on the Fund, and UNRRA. Whether the unconditional provision of this sum at the outset would have produced equally satisfactory results is an interesting question to discuss but an impossible one to answer.

(b) The main responsibility for international adjustments lay on creditor countries. They could either extend credit or accept more imports. Such steps could be taken by creditors without hardship to themselves, while adjustments required of a debtor would necessarily be painful. This one-sidedness in the Keynesian view was its greatest weakness. He failed to realize what subsequent experience has proved to be true—that the provision of aid encourages debtors to continue in their debtor position.

(c) Exchange rate adjustments are the proper corrective for fundamental disequilibria, but credit and reserves should be used to preserve exchange stability in the face of temporary disturbances of international balance. At the time of Bretton Woods, Keynes seemed to attach a good deal more importance to exchange stability than he did in the *Tract* twenty years earlier. I have never understood why the Americans and the British came to legislate so much exchange rigidity into the Bretton Woods Agreement or what experience made them decide that competitive exchange depreciation was a major evil to guard against. It seems to me to be a much more fundamental matter to invoke the "scare currency clause" than to require debtors or creditors to alter their exchange rates. Yet a system of flexible exchange rates could make the scarce currency clause unnecessary.

(d) Adequate financial arrangements are necessary for the creation of conditions where an expanding and multilateral world economy are possible. However, until relatively late in the practical negotiations Keynes seemed to feel that financial arrangements were all that should be undertaken and he entertained no hope for removal of restrictions on trade. But by the time of his death he had become an ardent and eloquent advocate of the ITO Charter. And he consistently regarded sterling convertibility as an important policy objective. He ended his life in the confident hope that the basis for a new world order had been achieved.

VI

Many of the Keynesian "heresies" of the twenties and thirties have become commonplace today. The Versailles settlement was discredited; the international gold standard has been abandoned and countries have thus won the freedom to pursue their internal policies unhampered by external restraint; governments have become aware that fiscal policy can exercise a potent influence on production, employment, and the price level; the interest rate has become a subject of national policies; progressive taxation has been used to accomplish a great redistribution of income in most countries. Yet, five years after his death, the world, with its new-found freedom to act in the economic sphere, is not the world that Keynes would have liked to see. The economic terms imposed on Germany made even less sense this time than last time; the international economy is hampered by exchange control and discrimination; it requires a major financial crisis to induce a country to alter its exchange rate; governments are reluctant to use fiscal and monetary controls to prevent inflation and prefer direct controls of prices and rationing; in his own country egalitarian policies have gone a long way towards the euthanasia not only of the rentier but of the educated bourgeoisie as well.

Had Keynes's advice been followed in its entirety during the twenties and thirties, the world would have been a more prosperous and agreeable place today. A world war and a world depression might have been avoided. The most rabid opponents of his policies would be better satisfied than they now are. But that is hardly an accolade. Many economists have given advice which, if followed, would have avoided disaster. Keynes, however, provided a program for a sinful world as he saw it; others felt it must be purified before a cure was possible. But this has furnished a basis for criticism as well as commendation.

Keynes's hostile critics complain that his condonation made the world more sinful, while friendly critics can charge, with some justice, that he did not seem to realize how sinful the world really was.

Keynes hoped for a world where monetary and fiscal policies, carried out by wise men in authority, could ensure conditions of prosperity, equity, freedom, and possibly peace. His view thus stood out in marked contrast to those who believed that profound structural changes in the economy were necessary to cure admitted economic ills— including socialists, who believed that the means of production should be nationalized, and so-called liberals, who felt that national economies should be atomized. There is no doubt in my mind that Keynes was more nearly right than his adversaries, but it is painfully clear that in the conduct of both national and international affairs his hopes have by no means been fully realized. In part, governments have not been prepared to accept his advice to the full, especially when action to curb inflation was needed; in part, the liberation from ancient prejudice that he achieved has produced consequences that he neither liked nor foresaw.

Throughout his career Keynes's successes seem to have been consistently marred by the same kind of miscalculations that were as deeply rooted in his personality as his successes and that may have been inherent in his kind of success:

(a) He attempted to tear down ideas, institutions, and reputations to a greater extent than was necessary to make room for his arguments. Furthermore, he overestimated his own power to eradicate old ideas, including some of his own, and put new ones in their place.

(b) He failed to recognize that some of his remedies might worsen the diseases they were designed to cure and might deprive the economy of its immunity to others.

(c) He clung to the "presuppositions of Harvey Road" and ignored important facts of modern political life. He thus hoped that his economic ideas could be put into practice outside the arena of partisan politics, but failed to realize that his own efforts tended to make that impossible.

I shall now try to illustrate these points by specific references to Keynes's writings.

(a) After rereading the *Economic Consequences of the Peace,* I have come to feel that the attack on the protagonists, especially Wilson, was a mistake. Of course, it strengthened Keynes's case against the Treaty to show that it was not only economically unworkable but also immoral and that it represented a betrayal of the high principles with which the Conference began. But, to use a Keynesian expression, was it not "sheer lunacy" to deliver a devastating attack on Wilson when everything hung in the balance on this side of the Atlantic? Or did Keynes really want the Senate to reject the Treaty? Had that been his intention, would he have amended a single phrase of the text? It is, of course, impossible to assess what effect this aspect of the book had on American opinion—Mr. Harrod makes a valiant attempt to show that it had none—but the risks were so great that it would have been

safer to base the attack on economic principles rather than to reach for ethical arguments. But Keynes always seemed impelled to appeal to the most comprehensive principles he could; and when one recalls his early training one can easily understand why.

My second illustration relates to Keynes's attack on the gold standard. In 1924 and 1925, the great issue was not whether England should or should not return to gold, but what the exchange rate with the dollar should be—the traditional $4.86 or the existing $4.40. It was the decision to return to $4.86 that required deflation in Britain and added to the forces that made it necessary to abandon gold in 1931. Keynes lost his fight in the twenties; he might have been more successful had he limited his objective and urged a return to gold at a workable parity with the dollar rather than a rejection of the entire mythology of gold. Such a course might not only have been good tactics at the time but might have had a useful effect on attitudes in the future. At present we seem to have the worst of both worlds. The idea of fixed formal parities is by no means dead, while the general disrepute of the gold standard, which Keynes helped to produce, has been reflected in a general reluctance, despite high-sounding protestations to the contrary, to regard convertibility of currencies as a serious policy objective. We are a long way from the system of flexible exchange rates that Keynes envisaged in the *Tract on Monetary Reform*.

Of course, Keynes urged abandonment of the gold standard in principle largely to secure for governments freedom of internal action. But is that not a will-o'-the-wisp anyway? The gold standard implies willingness to inflate or deflate on appropriate occasions; flexible exchange rates imply willingness to allow the cost-of-living to change in relation to money wages; and even a system of direct control of foreign trade, if it is to work, must be supported by an internal policy that avoids a state of general excess demand.

In his later years Keynes said his purpose was to achieve for gold the position of a constitutional, instead of an absolute, monarch. But the British constitutional monarchy has emerged from an adaptation of the ideas and institutions of the past to the needs of the present. It is a pity that, in his early years, Keynes did not pay more attention to his metaphor.

A third, and perhaps the most obvious, example of Keynes's attempts to destroy too much is his treatment of saving in the *General Theory*. As far as I can see, a general attack on the ideology of private saving, which is what the *General Theory* amounts to, was quite unnecessary for Keynes's purposes. His aim was to demonstrate the possibility of lack of balance between saving and investment and to point to the need for compensatory or sustaining action by governments. Keynes like almost everyone else was afflicted with myopia by the Great Depression and evidently felt that no reduction in private saving that a change in attitudes might produce could be excessive, but the war and postwar years have proved him to be wrong.

The attack on saving accounts for much of the distrust or hostility that the *General Theory* provoked. While I cannot agree with Schumpeter that Keynes himself had an anti-capitalist bias, he provided grist for the mills of those who did. Surely his interest and intention was to provide a policy for those who wanted to make capitalism succeed. He could hardly hope to de-socialize socialists and, far less, to de-communize communists. The **General Theory** could have been a finer piece of analysis and could have won more of the kind of support that it needed, had its author felt less impelled to make sweeping changes in ethics as well as economics. While the Keynesian Revolution was a glorious one, it was and still is incomplete. Its economic consequences are thus somewhat analogous to the political consequences of the French Revolution. Despite high-sounding statements of principle, the old ideas have shown an obstinate refusal to die.

Professional economists date the Keynesian Revolution from the publication of the **General Theory** in 1936. But, as we have seen, Keynes's own ideas on policy had matured years before his theoretical structure; and they were not particularly original with him. Pressure of events had driven England to a system of managed exchange rates during the first war; Lloyd George had proposed public works in 1924; cheap money ideas, to which Keynes did not at first subscribe, had a long history. In this country, the fiscal policy of the thirties was dictated largely by the political and humanitarian necessity to provide relief for labor and agriculture; the internal monetary policy was in line with Federal Reserve tradition; and the decision to devalue in 1933 certainly owed nothing to Keynes. It is possible that had the **General Theory** never been written we would by now have reached a pragmatic Keynesianism that tended to unite rather than to divide American opinion.

Keynes himself did not always seem to realize how far the system he wanted to create depended on the retention of traditional ideas. In the **End of Laissez Faire** (1926), he sought to weaken the entire foundations of the individualistic creed. He stated in effect that the arguments for laissez-faire are undermined "by the complications which arise—(1) when efficient units of production are large . . . (2) when overhead or joint costs are present, (3) when internal economics tend to the aggregation of production, (4) when the time required for adjustments is long, (5) where ignorance prevails over knowledge, and (6) where monopolies and competition interfere with equality of bargaining. . . ." In the **General Theory** all these points were overlooked, and Keynes built his analytical model on the assumption of perfect competition. This assumption goes to the heart of the matter: unless the doctrines of laissez-faire can be broadly held to apply in the field of individual behavior, fiscal monetary policies, while necessary to any solution of the problem of economic stability, cannot be held to provide a complete solution.

(b) The extent to which the competitive assumption is not valid provides the basis for the frequent criticism that Keynesian fiscal and monetary remedies are not only a palliative rather than a cure but in fact worsen the diseases they are supposed to cure. I believe it to be true that Keynesian involuntary unemployment arises from price rigidities of various kinds in the economy—the ultimate

rigidity may be the inability of the interest rate to become negative. By the doctrine of the **General Theory** itself, if there were no rigidities, the economy would rapidly deflate under the impact of deficient demand; the real money supply would increase; interest rates would fall and investment and employment would rise. The criticism is that, if it is generally known that the government can and will sustain effective demand, rigidities will persist or increase. To be convinced that the criticism has validity, one has only to reflect that cutting money wages, either in single industries or across the board, has practically dropped out of professional and popular discussion of remedies for unemployment. Were the Keynesian escape not available, wage cutting could not have become a closed issue.

All this does not mean that Keynesian remedies should be rejected. The only practicable course of action may be to face the prospect of increasing rigidity in the economy and to learn how to live with it. I believe such an attitude is more nearly right than the opposite extreme that requires competitive conditions to be achieved before fiscal and monetary remedies are applied. But a middle course seems better than either extreme. Keynes, himself, seems to have reached this point of view when he belatedly gave his support to the ITO Charter, and when he made his famous posthumous plea that the classical medicine should have a chance to do its work.

(c) Had Keynes's political presuppositions been fulfilled, had it been possible to vest economic power in a body like the Court of the Bank of England that had become converted to the Keynesian Enlightenment, everything might have turned out according to his plan. Exchange rates, interest rates, government expenditures, and taxation all could have been adjusted from time to time according to a rational design to promote economic well-being. That is the kind of hope that we, as economists, habitually entertain and which we cannot abandon entirely so long as we have faith in general economic principles. Nevertheless, Keynes's own career demonstrates that the proclamation of general principles and the promotion of economic enlightenment does not always produce the desired results.

Is it not fair to say that Keynes's attack on the gold standard and the classical theory of interest helped to make exchange rates and interest rates hot political issues and materially reduced the chances that in the future they could be determined in courts of economic wisdom? At any rate, that is what has happened. Britain could hardly have returned to gold in 1925 had there been wide political understanding of what was being undertaken; in 1949, devaluation was obstructed by the fact that the mysteries of economics had been revealed to the politician and he was able to discourse freely on the terms of trade and the relation of the exchange rate to the cost of living. Again it has clearly become impossible, as a political matter, for the Federal Reserve system to resort to the hard money policy of the late twenties. The cheap money policy, which was introduced largely on the basis of economic argument in the thirties, has accumulated political support the longer it has been continued. As a result of the popular spread of economic understanding, we have lost a large part of the freedom that was once enjoyed, and frequently abused, to put monetary policy into reverse. Had he lived to see the present inflationary period, Keynes might have had second thoughts about the stupid banker who felt that the interest rate was not a proper subject for free thought.

In more general terms, Keynesian economics has demonstrated to the most potent political groups—in business, labor, and agriculture—that they have a short-run interest in inflation. On the other side, it is generally realized that short-run interests in deflation are confined to those who can keep both their incomes and their jobs. The knowledge that deflation means lower profits and usually means unemployment has practically ruled it out as an economic remedy.

It is not my purpose here to bemoan the present or yearn for the past; it is merely to point out that the world of today differs from what Keynes hoped for in part because of the political consequences of the economic ideas that he did so much to promote. He looked forward to a situation where stability of employment, stability of the price level, and freedom from direct controls of prices and wages could all co-exist. It now appears possible that this combined objective is unattainable; and that the political demand for high employment and the general refusal to tolerate even short-run unemployment may mean increasing resort to direct controls.

One of our few glimpses of Keynes's view of the postwar world is contained in his letter to Hayek in June, 1944, in which he writes of the *Road to Serfdom:* ". . . morally and philosophically I find myself in agreement with virtually the whole of it; and not only in agreement with it, but in a deeply moved agreement." But he goes on to say that what we want is more planning rather than less. "But the planning should take place in a community in which as many people as possible, both leaders and followers, wholly share your own moral position. Moderate planning will be safe if those carrying it out are rightly oriented in their own minds and hearts to the moral issue. This is in fact already true of some of them. But the curse is that there is an important section who . . . wish to serve not God but the devil." In short, the *planners* should all have gone to Cambridge fifty years ago. And, in the meantime, Keynes himself had helped to discredit some of the beliefs that he now felt they should entertain. However, all who feel that we can and should look forward to the future with hope rather than with despair will prefer Keynes's answer to Hayek's, and so far no better answer than his to one of the most serious dilemmas of our time has been given.

In 1919, Keynes failed to impress high authority with his political acumen. Sir Eyre Crowe of the Foreign Office wrote of him: ". . . in politics his illustrations are seldom related to logic. That is because he has as little aptitude or taste for politics as you or I have for the refinements of economic speculation." And in *The World Crisis* (1929), Mr. Churchill pronounced his verdict: "His qualifications to speak on the economic aspects [of the Peace Treaty] were indisputable; but on the other, and vastly more important, side of the problem he could judge no better than many others."

In the final, bitter, episode of Keynes's career the question of management of the Fund and Bank came to a head. At Bretton Woods, the management issues had been the province of secondary committees; the protagonists of the Conference devoted their attention to matters of "substance." At Savannah, Keynes realized that management was of critical importance: were the Fund and Bank to be allowed to operate with the quiet discretion of traditional, but enlightened, central banks; or were their operations to be conducted in the glare of politics? That was the issue epitomized in the debate over the nature of the management and the location of the institutions. I think this debate was more than a clash of personalities. The debates over the institutions in forty legislatures may have prescribed for them a political future. It is also possible that the non-political status that Keynes urged for them was their only hope of real success.

In 1919, Keynes's indignation was aroused and his respect for Wilson diminished as he saw the Fourteen Points twisted and distorted by political demands for punishment and security. He was to live to see his own high hopes distorted in a similar way. He was not a Presbyterian, but his strength and his weaknesses depended heavily on his own religion.

VII

Of course, it is easy, and even fashionable at the present time, to dwell on Keynes's limitations and miscalculations. We do not know what the world would have been like without his influence. It is quite possible that his doctrines have, on balance, provided a unifying influence and that without them there could be no semblance of agreement on national or international economic policies.

All I have tried to do in this essay is to show that his proposals, in many instances, failed to produce the results that he himself intended. In short, his career illuminates the weakness of the predictive power of economics. It suggests, moreover, that the way to improvement does not lie in limitation of its subject matter, which is too frequently involved in efforts to make economics "scientific." The answers to many of the vital questions in economics lie outside its traditional boundaries and depend on a deeper understanding of political and social forces than we have usually thought necessary for our purposes.

Whatever the verdict of history on Keynes may be, it is unlikely that anyone who ever saw him will dispute this personal impression by Professor Robbins: ". . . I often find myself thinking that Keynes must be one of the most remarkable men that have ever lived—the quick logic, the birdlike swoop of intuition, the vivid fancy, the wide vision, above all the incomparable sense of the fitness of words, all combine to make something several degrees beyond the limit of ordinary human achievement. . . . He uses the classical style of our life and language, it is true, but it is shot through with something which is not traditional, a unique unearthly quality of which one can only say that it is pure genius."

Paul Lambert (essay date 1963)

SOURCE: "The Social Philosophy of John Maynard Keynes," in *Annals of Collective Economy*, Vol. XXXIV, No. 4, October-December, 1963, pp. 1-33.

[*In the following excerpt, which is a translation of chapter five from his study* L'oeuvre de John Maynard Keynes, *Lambert provides a chronological study of Keynes's writings, portraying the economist as the founder of a "new liberalism" that sought to reconcile the individualistic spirit of capitalism with the need for government intervention to ensure full employment.*]

I. THE SOCIAL PHILOSOPHY OF KEYNES: AN ASPECT OF THE NEO-LIBERAL MOVEMENT

As my book [*L'oeuvre de John Maynard Keynes*] is intended to serve a scientific purpose, I shall not attempt to make any critical comparison between Keynes's social philosophy and my own; instead I shall describe and refute the interpretations I consider to be mistaken. I shall refrain from expressing my personal opinions, except where I consider this absolutely necessary.

In the outline biography of Keynes which I gave in the first chapter I described how, when he was a student at Cambridge, he was the president of the Liberal Club, and how he subsequently maintained his contacts with the British Liberal Party. I also described the part he played in the direction of various liberal reviews and the influence he exercised in the publication by the Party of *Britain's Industrial Future* in 1928; just before the 1929 elections he took up his pen in defence of the book [in *Can Lloyd George Do It?*].

Keynes was thus a liberal, but not in the conventional sense of the term.

The pure liberals of the 19th century believed in the automatic interplay of a number of different factors. They believed that the common welfare was automatically brought about by the inevitable convergence of private and public interests. They believed that social justice was automatically achieved because every factor of production received the equivalent of its marginal product. They believed that economic progress was automatically achieved; the law of markets assured them that the act of production inevitably created, in sufficient volume, the market required to absorb the goods produced, while competition forced entrepreneurs to reduce production costs and to make innovations. At the international level the equilibrium of balances of accounts and the distribution of precious metals was automatically maintained.

In addition, the two motivating factors controlling all these automatic processes—personal interest and competition—were natural factors which made their influence felt wherever the State did not prevent them from doing so. This it was which inspired Bastiat to write: "The wisdom of God is revealed and His glory demonstrated not only by the pattern of the heavens but also by the pattern of society" [*Harmonies economiques*].

Keynes did not deny the existence of all these factors; but he did deny the existence of some which were of vital importance in the old liberal doctrine. Moreover, he was of the opinion that none of them had sufficient virtue to provide a full justification for it.

Of all the principal social philosophies prevalent today—neo-liberalism, the social teachings of the church, communism, socialism—only one—neo-liberalism—offers houseroom for Keynes's beliefs.

Although no two neo-liberals are alike—as I shall show later—one can offer a definition of neo-liberalism which will embrace them all. I propose the following definition: first of all, the neo-liberal believes that the system of private ownership of capital is, in practice at least, superior to any other economic system; secondly, he condemns the principle of *laissez-faire* and is in favour of State action calculated either to lay down the boundaries of private enterprise in such a way as to enable competition to operate effectively or to supplement the activities of private enterprise in sectors where, owing to special circumstances, competition cannot make itself felt; alternatively, intervention by the public authorities may be designed to remedy the failures or mistakes of private enterprise in matters relating to the preservation of natural wealth, distribution, employment and production.

By their rejection of the doctrine of *laissez-faire* the neo-liberals broke down the barriers which during the 19th century clearly separated the champions of liberalism from those of State intervention; on the other hand, whenever they attempted to state exactly what the State should do, they split into a multitude of conflicting factions.

The old liberal system did at least offer two great advantages from which it drew strength, namely a doctrine which, from the logical standpoint, offered no flaws and a remarkable unity of views within the school of its supporters. Admittedly, the latter might be moderates or extremists; but their discussions on the sphere of activity of the State almost invariably related to questions which were not strictly economic in character—whether, for instance, the State should subsidise artists, provide education for the poor, or maintain standards in the medical profession. The only major controversy on which the school was ever divided was that of the privilege of issuing banknotes; and even that was soon forgotten.

In inducing the State to intervene in the economy the neo-liberals introduced into Bastiat's harmonious economic system an irreconcilable element of discord, the degree of influence of which it was possible to foresee in advance. For this reason—and it is important to remember it—there could not be any fundamental agreement within the new school.

If one reads the records of the meetings of the symposium organized by Walter Lippmann on 26-30 August 1938, at which it is often said that the neo-liberal movement was founded, and if one reads the work of Hayek, Rougier or Röpke, one finds them to be permeated throughout with controversy either on the interpretation of the main phenomena encountered within our economy or on the framing of a plan of action. Mises was of the opinion that the State is responsible for the existence of cartels; his theory was refuted by Detoeuf and Mantoux. When Rueff brought up once again his old theory that unemployment benefit is the cause of long-term unemployment he was vigorously attacked by Condliffe. Lippmann considered the joint-stock company a pernicious institution; Mises and Marlio were in favour of it. Röpke and Lippmann held completely irreconcilable views on the subject of social security. Röpke considered that full employment was "a mirage"; but at the same time the Liberal Party and the liberal trade unions in Belgium were demanding that a clause guaranteeing the right to work should be included in the national constitution.

In the circumstances it would be completely arbitrary to refuse to consider Keynes a neo-liberal on the grounds that his particular brand of interventionism was rejected by some other neo-liberal.

Some time ago I had a brief clash with Röpke on this question [P. Lambert, "Keynes et le néo-libéralisme. A propos d'une note du professeur Wilhelm Röpke", and W. Ropke, "Réponse au Professeur Lambert", in *Industrie*, August, 1953]. I proffered the same definition of neoliberalism as that given above and stated: "If one accepts this definition, then Keynes must clearly be classified as a neo-liberal. But this definition may be untenable. Before we can decide whether it is or not, we must see what alternative definition is offered." In his reply Röpke fails to deal with this specific point. He does not deny that Keynes shows liberal tendencies; but immediately he has made this concession he qualifies it by stressing the changeability of Keynes's views. The field of social philosophy is, however, the field in which Keynes remained consistent throughout his career; the whole of the present chapter brings this out. In addition, Röpke speculates on whether "as a result of this praiseworthy determination on Keynes's part it has proved impossible to use his doctrines and those of the post-Keynesian period as powerful weapons of collectivism"; he answers this question in the negative. First of all, Röpke's views on the subject are entirely personal and fail to carry conviction. Other writers disagree with him entirely; one example is L. R. Klein, who wrote: "The Keynesian policy is, indeed, a conservative one because it aims at conserving free-enterprise capitalism" [*The Keynesian Revolution*]. A more important factor is that, in the interests of objectivity, one must classify an author according to his own intentions rather than on the basis of the consequences to which his teachings have given rise against his will.

Keynes is not merely a member of the neo-liberal school; he is in fact its founding father.

This last aspect of Keynes's work is often not understood. We find, for instance, such a scholarly writer as Maurice Ansiaux stating in January 1940 that neo-liberalism was first evolved in the United States and consequently giving exaggerated importance to Walter Lippmann's book *The Good Society,* published in 1938. Keynes laid down the main lines of neo-liberal thinking long before Lippmann. Not unnaturally, some of his ideas were formulated by earlier writers, such as Dupont-White and Léon Walras; but Keynes was the first person to set forth coherently and clearly the main theses of the new school.

In two short articles entitled respectively **"Am I a Liberal?"** and *The End of Laissez-faire,* Keynes offered first of all, the name for the new school of thought (neoliberalism), secondly, a refutation of the *laissez-faire* doctrine; thirdly, a definition, in terms of Bentam's formula, of what a government should and should not do (the Lippmann symposium was later to consider this problem in exactly similar terms); and fourthly a theory reconciling the existence of an extremely large sector of private ownership and initiative with the taking of regulatory action by the State. These points will be dealt with in detail in this chapter.

The same fundamental beliefs were visible in Keynes's writings even before 1925.

II. FROM 1913 ONWARDS:
SCEPTICAL ATTITUDE TOWARDS THE "AUTOMATIC REGULATORS"

In his first book, written in 1913 and entitled *Indian Currency and Finance,* Keynes stated that the gold standard was not an automatic regulator. He argued that equilibrium in balances of payments was maintained, not only by bank rate policies, but by deliberate measures taken by the central banks to invest abroad when conditions were favourable and to recall those investments when the national balance of accounts was showing a deficit.

The United Kingdom was the only country to confine itself to adjusting bank rate. Keynes explains this by reference on the one hand to the fact that Great Britain was in the main the creditor of the international short-term loan market and, on the other hand, to the organisation of the English money market. He showed how what was believed to be irrevocable and lasting was in fact contingent and precarious. He explained the phenomena which the old Liberal school attributed to the unchanging and universal character of natural law in terms of positive and therefore changeable laws and of the particular conditions obtaining at a given time and a given place.

"To illustrate how rare a thing in Europe a permanent and automatic gold standard is", he wrote, "let us take the most recent occasion of stringency—November 1912." This was the time of the Balkan war, and during that month gold was selling at a premium varying between 0.75% and 1% in France, Germany, Russia, Austria-Hungary and Belgium. In addition, several countries, by policies which Ansiaux described as "policies of petty expedients", placed restrictions on exchanges of banknotes for gold in order to check gold outflows.

Many theorists have ignored these facts or treated them as minor incidents of a fortuitous character. Keynes, on the other hand, concentrated all his attention on them; for him they were a sign of the fragility of the gold standard system. Let us consider this for a moment. The only reason why the 1912 crisis was not a serious one was the speed with which the attendant political and military events took place. It was sufficient to show that the existence of the gold standard presupposed at the very least a general atmosphere of confidence. If the latter were to disappear, the gold standard system would break down.

In the same book Keynes gave vent to his dissatisfaction with the Gold Standard system in the following terms:

> The time may not be far distant when Europe, having perfected her mechanism of exchange on the basis of a gold standard, will find it possible to regulate her standard of value on a more rational and stable basis. It is not likely that we shall leave permanently the most intimate adjustments of our economic organism at the mercy of a lucky prospector, a new chemical process, or a change of ideas in Asia.

He also expressed in this book his deep-rooted aversion to saving in the form of cash accumulation. . . .

III. 1919 TO 1923:
AN APPEAL FOR CONTROL OF THE MONETARY SYSTEM TO SAFEGUARD INDIVIDUALIST SOCIETY

In *The Economic Consequences of the Peace,* written just after the First World War, Keynes explained the instability of the economic equilibrium of the years prior to 1914.

He attributed the equilibrium which existed before the 1914-1918 war to factors which no longer existed. The first of these factors was the thoughtlessness of the working classes as well as of the capitalist class; the latter saved and saved to accumulate capital and went on saving and accumulating endlessly . . . "Saving was for old age or for your children; but this was only in theory—the virtue of the cake was that it was never to be consumed, neither by you nor by your children after you . . ." and the working classes, "from ignorance or powerlessness, tolerated the inequalities of distribution which made saving of this kind possible".

The second factor was the one-way flow of capital from the older capitalist countries to the younger countries. Even the interest earned on the capital so invested was ploughed back in the same way.

This point deserves some comment. Keynes underlines here the principal reason for the success of the gold standard system during the 19th century and gives added coherence to the ideas he first put forward in *Indian Currency and Finance*. As Rosenstein-Rodan emphasised later, the new countries repaid their debts simply by contracting new loans. If they had had to clear off their indebtedness they would soon have paid out the whole of their gold reserves and gone off the gold standard. It is true to say that after 1919 the prevailing and persistent insecurity prevented international capital movements from serving once again as a regulator.

The third fortuitous cause of the previous equilibrium invoked by Keynes was this: the countries of Europe had concentrated all their efforts on industrial development and had in consequence become dependent on the New World for their food supplies. For many years there had been no latent danger in this situation, as there were abundant supplies of wheat available to meet demand. But as the population—in America as well as in Europe—rose, the terms of trade became less and less favourable to the industrialised countries; the Europeans had to work more and more to obtain the same amount of corn.

Keynes was mistaken here. Between 1875 and 1940 the terms of trade moved irregularly but consistently against the countries offering raw materials and foodstuffs for sale. In other words, the strength of the position of the industrialised countries was to increase still further after the First World War.

Keynes also emphasised, in *The Economic Consequences of the Peace,* the destructive effect of inflation on the capitalist system: "Lenin was certainly right. There is no subtler, no surer, means of overturning the existing basis of society than to debauch the currency. . . ."

In 1923, in *Monetary Reform,* Keynes took up this subject again and examined it in more detail.

Here we come face to face with one of the main pillars of the structure of Keynes's social philosophy.

Keynes believed that, if private enterprise and individualism generally were to continue to exist, capital—or at least a large proportion of it—should be privately owned. In this he was genuinely liberal. But he could see that the society to which he belonged with his whole being was threatened by excessive fluctuations in price and employment levels, and in order to save society he sought an instrument which would prevent or at least check these fluctuations. It was thus Keynes's liberal convictions which made him a supporter of government intervention.

In what way did sudden changes in general price levels endanger private capitalism? Keynes explained it in a striking manner, not by reference to the steadily germinating seeds of revolt which inflation sowed among the working classes, but by showing how inflation gradually broke up the capitalist class itself.

In times of inflation savers, whose activities had made possible so much investment (and the equilibrium of the gold standard) throughout the 19th century, are discouraged from further saving; some are ruined and others are hesitant to throw good money after bad. At the same time business men are prospering; but their prosperity is unhealthy. The profits they receive are the result of chance and of events beyond their control; they can no longer feel that their profits are the reward of their labours. Thus they lose confidence in themselves and feel discredited. In contrast, during a period of deflation when falls in prices are to be expected, business men will attempt to limit their losses; if they "expect a fall, it may pay them, as a group, to damp production down, although such enforced idleness impoverishes society as a whole". This attitude constitutes a challenge to the principle that levels of production are governed by the profit motive.

Private capitalism requires a stable instrument for the measurement of values for its survival because under it the two tasks of saving and production are allocated to two separate social groups—the rentier and the entrepreneur. It is essential that the cash flow between the two should remain stable.

Thus "it is one of the objects of this book" to induce the authorities responsible for national currencies to prevent or lessen cyclical price movements. The task of counterbalancing individual forecasts of changes in general price levels "by setting in motion some factor of a contrary tendency" is a staggering one. Keynes considers a policy involving such measures as "an improvement on the policy of sitting quietly by". Inflation may be an evil, but deflation is an even greater evil "because it is worse, in an impoverished world, to provoke unemployment than to disappoint the rentier".

The entire development of Keynes's social philosophy is signposted in these passages. We must not forget that *A Tract on Monetary Reform* was written six years before the beginning of the great depression. Once Keynes had become convinced that monetary measures by themselves were insufficient to break the cycle, he was logically led to seek other means of doing so and to recommend more radical steps.

Let us consider some of the other main ideas put forward in this book.

Returning to a theme he originally touched on in *The Economic Consequences of the Peace,* he lashes with his irony the belief, held by so many 19th-century liberals, that love of accumulated wealth and moral virtue went hand in hand.

> The savings were seldom drawn on, and, accumulating at compound interest, made possible the material triumphs which we now all take for granted. The morals, the politics, the literature, and the religion of the age joined in a grand conspiracy for the promotion of saving. God and Mammon were reconciled. Peace on earth to men of good means. A rich man could, after all, enter into the Kingdom of Heaven—if only he saved. A new harmony sounded from the celestial spheres. 'It is curious to observe how, through the wise and beneficent arrangement of Providence, men thus do the greatest service to the public, when they are thinking of nothing but their own gain'; so sang the angels.

The book contains another doctrinal judgment: inflation, with all its inherent injustices and dangers, does at least have the merit of reducing the share of the national income which goes to lending capitalists and rentiers. If inflation were to disappear it would have to be replaced by "the scientific expedient, the capital levy". He answers conservative protests as follows:

> Nothing can preserve the integrity of contract between individuals, except a discretionary authority in the State to revise what has become intolerable. The powers of uninterrupted usury are too great. If the accretions of vested interest were to grow without mitigation for many generations, half the population would be no better than slaves to the other half. . . .
>
> Changes in Death Duties, Income Tax . . . have received the same denunciations from the absolutists of contract,—who are the real parents of Revolution.

In other respects, . . . Keynes was still in 1923 very much a pure liberal. This is clear from the views he expresses when touching on subjects such as exchange control, speculation, subsidies, price-fixing, rent restriction, campaigns against profiteering, and excess profits taxes. As time went by he inclined more and more towards support of State intervention in these different fields. To sum up, it may be said that, although Keynes started out as a neo-liberal, his social philosophy went through several stages of development which gradually estranged him from the neo-liberal beliefs closest to the doctrines of 19th-century liberalism.

IV. 1925-26:
KEYNES LAYS DOWN THE MAIN LINES OF NEO-LIBERALISM

In 1925 and 1926 Keynes wrote four short works: *A Short View of Russia* (1925), **"Am I a Liberal?"** (1925), *The End of Laissez-faire* (1926) and **"Liberalism and Labour"** (1926).

He defines Leninism as a mixture of a new type of economic activity with a new type of religion. After stressing all which separates a liberal of his type from Bolshevism, he expresses considerable interest in an experiment in which the desire of the individual to accumulate personal wealth is debarred as a motivating factor in economic activity. His conclusion is: "I should like to give Russia her chance; to help and not to hinder."

But is he a genuine liberal? It all depends on the meaning one attaches to the term. He believes in a "new liberalism", the mission of which he describes as follows:

> The transition from economic anarchy to a régime which deliberately aims at controlling and directing economic forces in the interests of social justice and social stability will present enormous difficulties both technical and political. I suggest, nevertheless, that the true destiny of new liberalism is to seek their solution.

Keynes described the tasks of the new liberalism in greater detail in a pamphlet with the striking title *The End of Laissez-faire*.

He begins by challenging a number of the concepts of 19th-century liberalism. He refuses to accept that natural law confers inalienable rights on those who possess or acquire wealth; that private and general interests are necessarily convergent; or that individuals gathered together in a social unit and taking decisions collectively are always less far-sighted than they would be acting as individuals.

What programme does he offer?

First of all, he considers it essential to develop new structures—semi-autonomous bodies "subject in the last resort to the sovereignty of the democracy expressed through Parliament" of which the Port of London Authority is an example. It would obviously be undesirable to nationalise some limited companies which had already to a considerable extent "socialised themselves" in that the management was no longer under the control of the shareholders and was more concerned with maintaining the firm's reputation and stability than with seeking the maximum profit. But a number of large undertaking, and in particular public utility services—"water, gas, electricity and other business requiring a large fixed capital, still need to be semisocialized".

To improve the functioning of the economy "a deliberate control of the currency and of credit by a central institution" would be required. Other essentials would be an information agency collecting and publishing factual information on the business world in order to combat uncertainty and ignorance, and a population policy aiming at the determination and achievement of an optimum population level and structure.

One may think that this is not very much; on the other hand, one may think that for its time it is a great deal. But in any case these are only examples. The main aim is one of achieving rationalisation and coordination without restricting private enterprise and the spirit behind it.

Keynes's conclusion was as follows: "For my part, I think capitalism, wisely managed, can probably be made more efficient for obtaining economic independence than any alternative system yet in sight, but that in itself it is in many ways extremely objectionable."

In **"Liberalism and Labour"** he sums up the problem facing humanity in the following striking sentence: "The political problem of mankind is to combine three things: economic efficiency, social justice, and individual liberty."

In offering this definition of the problem he adopts a position very close to that of democratic socialism, and he is aware of the fact: "I am sure that I am less conservative in my inclinations than the average labour voter." But he opposed many demands of the trade union movement, and State socialism, the slogans inherited from Marx and the concept of the class struggle were anathema to him. He could never have become a member of the Labour party. On the other hand, if he had had to choose between voting Conservative and voting Labour he would have voted Labour, and even went so far as to say that anyone who disagreed with him and was ready "to die in the last ditch for capitalism" should leave the Liberal party.

He expresses his desire to see the Liberal and Labour parties join forces in the following terms: "Great changes will not be carried out except with the active aid of Labour. But they will not be sound or enduring unless they have first satisfied the criticism and precaution of liberals."

V. THE DOCTRINES OUTLINED IN A TREATISE ON MONEY (1930)

Keynes's fear that the system of private capitalism might break down under the pressure of the two forces of price instability and employment instability came to the surface again in 1930, when, at the end of *A Treatise on Money,* he was reflecting on the world economic depression which had recently set in. He wrote:

> It has been my role for the past 11 years to play the part of Cassandra, first on the economic consequences of the peace and next on those of the return to gold. I hope that it may not be so on this occasion.

> If this (income deflation) occurs, our present régime of capitalistic individualism will assuredly be replaced by a far-reaching socialism.

It may be said that the doctrine of full employment was

outlined in the *Treatise*. In his concern with the problem of securing the desired stability of prices and employment, Keynes concentrated his attention primarily on prices up to 1926; from then onwards, he became more and more concerned with employment. He denies that the "stimulus of distress" is the only means of bringing about savings and technical improvements; there are certain types of improvements which can only be achieved "in an atmosphere of optimism and abundance". He goes on to make a critical analysis of Robertson's thesis that the trade cycle plays a progressive part and that it would be dangerous to allow it to disappear entirely. He lays great stress on "the loss of output due to involuntary unemployment (which is a greater evil than the overtime worked during a boom is a benefit)".

In one passage in which Keynes states his preference for a gradual rise in incomes and the prices of consumer goods we recognize a throwback to an earlier and more long-standing concern, namely the search for methods of reducing the share of the national income taken by rentiers, of loosening "the grip of the dead hand". This concern permeates the whole of Keynes's writings.

On the other hand, in the *Treatise* we find the first significant signs of a change in Keynes's attitude on the problem of free trade and protection. . . . [In] 1923 Keynes described himself as a 100 per cent. free trader. In *A Treatise on Money* he recognised, firstly, that the imposition of a customs duty may improve terms of trade at the expense of foreign countries, and secondly that in certain circumstances the establishment of customs barriers may lead to an increase in overall investment and employment and thus to a "net gain" for the country as a whole.

Lastly, Keynes's valued judgments on the problem of distribution deserve closer consideration, as they throw a good deal of light on his fundamental beliefs.

Given that the main motive for economic activity in a capitalist system is the profit motive, Keynes concluded logically that to counter a depression one must increase profit margins. He expressed the idea even more clearly in 1930, when addressing the Macmillan Committee in the following terms: "You have first of all to do something to restore profits and then rely on private enterprise to carry the thing along" [quoted in R.F. Harrod, *The Life of John Maynard Keynes*]. To conclude from this that Keynes had no objections or scruples concerning the earning of profits or misgivings regarding their rightness is a short step which many commentators have blithely taken without further thought.

[In *A Treatise on Money* he] began by recalling that, during the first phase of a boom, prices increase faster than incomes (not including profits). "The difference is arbitrarily distributed among the members of the entrepreneur class as a permanent addition to the latter's wealth; or they can usually secure more of the gains of the inflation than they suffer of the losses of the deflation." The reason why he accepts this state of affairs is that "the advantages to economic progress and the accumulation of wealth will outweigh the element of social injustice, especially if the latter can be taken into account and partially remedied by the general system of taxation—and even without this remedy, if the community starts from a low level of wealth and is greatly in need of a rapid accumulation of capital".

Admittedly, "a socialist system which was directed with perfect knowledge and wisdom" could, by legislative action and without social injustice, fix the rate of accumulation and bring about transfers of productive resources from one kind of production to another. But—"an individualist system" requires the stimulus of profit. The problem was, in fact, one of choosing the drawbacks one was prepared to accept.

Keynes did not exhaust this subject in *A Treatise on Money;* he took it up again in the *General Theory*.

In this book Keynes does not lose sight of the fact that the choice between the present and the future also raises a problem of social justice. He admits that the unrestricted placing of money abroad on loan may increase the rate of growth of the leader nation's wealth, but points out that this is achieved "by putting off the day at which the workers in the country can enjoy, in the shape of higher wages, the advantages of this accumulation of capital". From there, he goes on to make an extremely important point which is of particular significance to the countries with authoritarian State planning today, for it raises the whole question of economic democracy. He writes:

> Nineteenth-century philosophy was wont to assume that the future is always to be preferred to the present. But modern communities are more inclined to claim the right to decide for themselves in what measure they shall subscribe to this austere doctrine.

VI. THE DOCTRINE OF FULL EMPLOYMENT AS DESCRIBED IN THE GENERAL THEORY OF EMPLOYMENT, INTEREST AND MONEY (1936)

The *General Theory* is the keystone of Keynes's social philosophy. His writings after 1936, such as *How to Pay for the War* (1940) and the speeches on the Keynes Plan or at Bretton Woods (1943-44) merely deal with the application of the doctrine to a specific problem. I shall therefore concentrate now on the *General Theory* except where it proves necessary to refer to an earlier or a later text to complete the picture.

1. *Rejection of the Law of Markets.*

To his previous challenges to various tenets of old-style liberalism Keynes now added a new and extremely important challenge. He questioned the argument that the very fact of production creates a market sufficient to absorb the goods produced.

. . . [The] law of markets had for many years been under attack from "pessimists" or "heretics", some of whom had actually demonstrated its invalidity. But their demonstrations were either misunderstood or ignored, and failed to make any impression on the overwhelming majority of economists. Keynes's talent and prestige, applied to contemporary events, were sufficient to enable him to refute Say's law convincingly enough to carry with him the majority of the economics teachers of his time and, through them, the succeeding generations. The final rejection of

the law of markets may thus be said to date from the appearance of the *General Theory*.

The spectacle presented by the capitalist system during the time of the depression had already drawn from Keynes the disillusioned comment that "capitalism . . . is not intelligent, it is not beautiful, it is not just, it is not virtuous—and it doesn't deliver the goods". As there no longer remained even any theoretical guarantee of the marketability of the goods produced, he was led to the doctrinal conclusion that "it is certain that the world will not much longer tolerate the unemployment which, apart from brief intervals of excitement, is associated—and, in my opinion, inevitably associated—with presentday capitalistic individualism" ["**National Self-Sufficiency**", in *Yale Review*, 1933, and *General Theory*].

It should not be thought that this conclusion led Keynes into the socialist camp. What he wanted to do was to replace the existing system by a system which, while remaining individualistic in essence, could secure full employment and other types of social progress.

2. *Was Keynes Opposed to Saving?*

In any given set of circumstances there is an optimum level of saving. If the volume of saving exceeds that level it is excessive; if it falls short of that level it is inadequate. This was the thesis put forward by Malthus; it was put forward by Keynes as well. One would therefore be wrong in describing Keynes as opposed to saving.

It is true that he opposed the tendency to save during the Great Depression; during that period it was far more important to consume more in order to stimulate production. But in at least three different places in the *General Theory* he very clearly stated that in a different situation, if full employment was achieved, the only way to finance investment without inflation was through saving. When in 1948, after several years of full employment in Great Britain, Joan Robinson wrote "Saving once more becomes a virtue" she was merely repeating what Keynes had already said.

In 1940, Keynes himself explained that compulsory or voluntary saving was essential to the war effort. He said: "We have become so accustomed to the problem of unemployment and of excess resources that it requires some elasticity of mind to adapt our behaviour to the problem of full employment and of resources which are no longer adequate to supply our needs. . . . Voluntary savings would serve this purpose if they were sufficient. In any case, voluntary savings are wholly to the good and limit to that extent the dimensions of our problem" [*How to Pay for the War*].

3. *Extension of the Sphere of Activity of the State: Planning.*

According to Keynes, all the evidence available suggested that a reduction in interest rates would not by itself suffice to bring the level of economic activity up to the feasible maximum. "A somewhat comprehensive socialisation of investment will prove the only means of securing an approximation to full employment." In addition, responsibility for the implementation of this new policy was to lie with the organs of central government; this would imply "a large extension of the traditional functions of government" [**General Theory**].

If the State is to play a much more important part in economic life, as Keynes envisaged, it will inevitably have to study, foresee and co-ordinate—in other words, *plan*—the measures it takes in the economic field. This corollary is not dealt with in the **General Theory**; but Keynes set down his views on the subject in 1944 in a letter to Professor Hayek. The latter had just published his book *The Road to Serfdom*. The fundamental argument of this book is that there is a close relationship between the fundamental freedoms of the citizen and private ownership of capital, between the freedom of the entrepreneur and the freedom of every individual; and that if the State attempts to plan economic activity, even to an extremely limited extent in the early stages, it will inevitably be forced to take more and more measures of a increasingly authoritarian character until a completely totalitarian régime exists.

Keynes begins his letter by confirming his attachment to the principles of individualism. "Morally and philosophically I find myself in agreement with virtually the whole of it (the book); and not only in agreement with it, but in a deeply moved agreement." He goes on to express the opinion that, from the economic standpoint, Hayek has made a mistake in basing his reasoning on the "very doubtful" hypothesis that planning will not be effective. Indeed, the opposite is "quite likely". He agrees, however, that an increase in the efficacity of a given plan cannot be accepted as a valid reason for sacrificing precious liberties.

Keynes then turns to his "only serious criticism." He points out that Hayek himself admits the impossibility of achieving either total abstention by the State from all interference in economic activity or absolutely universal planning in practice. He therefore considers it illogical to argue that the slightest step towards planning will inevitably lead to catastrophe. "According to my ideas, you greatly under-estimate the practicality of the middle course. . . . I should conclude your theme very differently. I should say that what we want is not no planning, indeed I should say that we almost certainly want more. But the planning should take place in a community in which as many people as possible, both leaders and followers, wholly share your own moral position."

4. *Scope of Private Initiative.*

Private initiative and enterprise were to be left plenty of scope. Keynes felt that there was no reason to socialise all economic activity. He wanted to be sure that the consumer's freedom of choice would be maintained and considered that, if production was raised to the highest possible level, the actual use to be made of the goods produced should be determined by the price mechanism.

The objection to this argument usually put forward is that consumers are given satisfaction in proportion to the size of their incomes and that the price mechanism is only acceptable if one presupposes a fair system of distribution. Keynes does not reply directly to this argument; he does, however, implicitly answer it by his proposals concerning means of drastically reducing social inequalities. . . .

5. *Increased Consumption and a Drastic Reduction of Social Inequalities.*

Obviously, the achievement of full employment will not by itself solve the whole of the social problem. It will, however, make an overall solution much easier to reach. First of all, if full employment is to be achieved and maintained, it is essential that consumption or investment—or, better still, both—should increase.

The proof of the assertion that Keynes is the most frequently quoted and the least frequently read of all economists is to be found in the fact that some of his commentators actually believe that he recommended the building of pyramids as the most desirable form of investment. How is it possible not to sense the bitter irony of the passage contained in the following sentence: "It would, indeed, be more sensible to build houses and the like; but if there are political and practical difficulties in the way of this, the above would be better than nothing."

The **General Theory** also refuted the principal argument in favour of inequality of distribution, namely that such inequality was essential if the substantial volume of saving necessary for investments was to be maintained. In practice, however, in all periods of under-employment—and under-employment has prevailed most of the time—saving has done more harm than good. In addition, the techniques of collective saving have evolved considerably since the 19th century. Lastly, an increase in the volume of investment will increase incomes and give rise to an equivalent volume of saving, even if income is distributed in a more equitable fashion.

Keynes goes even further. His desire was "to increase the stock of capital up to a point where its marginal efficiency had fallen to a very low figure". When this had been achieved, profit would be no more than "an allowance for risk and the costs of skill and supervision". To those who fear that such a reduction in profits will act as a brake on economic activity in the private sector, Keynes replies with an amusing metaphor taken from gambling. He argues that gambling is just as fascinating whether the stakes are high or low: "much lower stakes will serve the purpose equally well, as soon as the players are accustomed to them".

Lastly, if a policy of full employment is to be applied effectively, interest rates must be kept at extremely low levels. This would involve "the euthanasia of the rentier". Keynes has no sympathy whatever for the rentier class; rather the opposite is the case. "Interest today rewards no genuine sacrifice, any more than does the rent of land."

It must be admitted that these last two theses—those concerning the future of profits and interest—are of doubtful validity; in the **General Theory** their significance is not spelt out with sufficient clarity.

On the subject of the reduction of interest rates, Keynes expresses a number of reservations, the exact significance of which it is difficult to assess. For instance, if the propensity to consume throughout the community (including the State) rose to such a level as to give rise to the danger that net saving would cease entirely, it might be necessary to reintroduce "a reward in the shape of interest". However, Keynes went on to say: "But even so, it will still be possible for communal saving through the agency of the State to be maintained at a level which will allow the growth of capital up to a point where it ceases to be scarce."

These remarks immediately call forth the following comments:

1. *Danger of inflation.* If during a period of full employment the checks of discount and interest rates are not to be applied and inflation is nevertheless to be avoided, State-controlled machinery for the rationing and distribution of credits will have to be set up.

2. *The euthanasia of the rentier and problems of financing.* If interest rates are kept down at such low levels that nobody derives any benefit from lending out the money he has saved, new institutions with the ability to finance undertakings and public institutions will have to be established. Keynes's reference to collective saving centralised by the State gives only an extremely vague idea of the changes which would be necessary. The State would have to obtain the money needed to provide the credits by taxing the incomes of undertakings. In view of Keynes's general outlook it is doubtful whether he would have pushed the logic of his thinking to such an extreme.

3. *Persistent shortages of capital.* Keynes was of the opinion that the shortage of real capital might come to an end "within one or two generations". For some reason Keynes did not look further afield than the older and more advanced countries, which he considered as forming a single, homogeneous and exclusive unit. The economies of these countries are obviously affected by events taking place throughout the world. One has only to think of the economically under-developed countries, which contain the majority of the world's population, to realise that there is a very considerable world-wide shortage of capital.

4. *Monopolies and elements of monopolies.* Even in the more advanced countries considered individually, the hope that large scale investment could by itself bring about a substantial reduction in profit levels suggests that the influence of monopolistic factors in competition has been under-estimated.

For all these reasons I am of the opinion that the Keynesian concept of a gradual disappearance of unearned incomes, of interest as such and of pure profit as an automatic consequence of the application over a considerable period of a full employment policy smacks of utopianism.

6. *International Problems: War and Peace, Free Trade and Protection, World Currency.*

A policy of full employment would turn the attention of governments to the development of home markets and thereby make for peace throughout the world. In this connection the passage in the exposition of this thesis in which Keynes refers to the theory of imperialism deserves recall. He writes: "War has several causes. Dictators and others such, to whom war offers, in expectation at least, a pleasurable excitement, find it easy to work on the natural bellicosity of their peoples. But, over and above this, facilitating their task of fanning the popular flame, are the economic causes of war, namely the pressure of population and the competitive struggle for markets. It is the second factor, which probably played a predominant part in the 19th century, and might again, that is germane to this discussion."

Let us examine the commercial policy Keynes proposes.

He admits that a certain amount of customs protection will sometimes be necessary, either to stimulate a greater variety of activities in a country in which productive resources are concentrated in too few branches or to enable an individual State to isolate itself from the contagion of an international depression. Generally speaking, however, countries should strive to approximate as nearly as possible conditions of free trade by adhering to an international policy of full employment. No country should ever take steps to increase employment in its own territory which would have prejudicial effects in other countries.

An international currency should facilitate transactions. There can be no question of returning to the gold standard, which requires for its operation substantial changes in discount and interest rates and allows crises to spread rapidly. The international currency would be controlled by a supranational authority. The balances held by creditor nations could be lent to debtor nations, in the same way that in individual countries those who require money can, through the banking system make use of the resources of those who have money. The international currency could be bought with gold but would not be convertible into gold; it might even become possible eventually for the international authority to fix the price of gold at such a low level that it would lose its monetary value completely; this would make human and capital resources available for more useful work. Lastly, a number of countries would exercise control over international capital movements; for in such a system it would be essential to prevent the flight of capital from a particular country for political reasons and—even more important—to prevent investment abroad rising to such an excessive degree that interest rates at home would rise and the policy of full employment would thereby be jeopardised.

7. *A General View of Keynes's "New Jerusalem".*

If we now consider Keynes's **General Theory** together with his earlier teachings, we are in a position to trace the main outlines of his vision of "The New Jerusalem".

1. Certain joint-stock undertakings with large amounts of invested capital were to be reorganised as "semi-autonomous bodies", i.e. public corporations which in the last resort would be under parliamentary control.

2. The sphere of action of government would be broadened to enable it to pursue a population policy and a full employment policy.

3. The State would act in accordance with planning techniques which would safeguard the fundamental freedoms of the individual; economic activity would be carried on within the political framework of democracy.

4. Private ownership would continue to prevail in a very

wide field; production would continue to be regulated and orientated by the wishes and choices of consumers.

5. The full and permanent employment of productive forces would lead to an increase in consumption and in the volume of socially useful investment.

6. Considerable progress would be made in reducing inequalities in the distribution of wealth. In addition, Keynes was of the opinion that a policy of full employment would eventually lead to the disappearance of unearned profits and of the rentier class.

VII. REACTIONS OF OTHER SCHOOLS OF THOUGHT TO KEYNES'S SOCIAL PHILOSOPHY

1. *The Attitude of the Old-Style Liberals and the Neo-Liberals.*

As we saw earlier, in 1925 and 1926, Keynes laid down the fundamental principles of the whole of the neo-liberal school, namely rejection of the doctrine of *laissez-faire* and of any limitative delineation of the boundaries of State activity and the maintenance of a substantial sector of private ownership.

This does not, however, mean that all the neo-liberals accepted the Keynesian doctrine; in fact, only a few of them ever did so entirely.

The very general principles I have recalled in this chapter can serve as a basis for a number of systems which may differ considerably according to whether one adopts an extensive or restrictive approach in defining the sphere of activity of the State. I have already said that neo-liberalism is not a doctrine; it is a whole gamut of doctrines ranging from a liberalism bordering on *laissez-faire* liberalism to a doctrine bordering on socialism.

Keynes, like his disciple Beveridge, adopted a position at the leftward end of the scale—the end bordering on socialism.

As a result, Keynes's doctrines were attacked—sometimes with extreme ferocity—by the liberals who had remained faithful to the teachings of Bastiat (for example Ludwig von Mises) and the majority of the neo-liberal economists. Jacques Rueff loudly drew attention to "the fallacies of Lord Keynes's *General Theory*" ["Les erreurs de la théorie générale de Lord Keynes", in *Revue d'économie politique*, January-February, 1947]; Röpke, as we have seen already, considered Keynesianism as a stepping-stone to collectivism; Hazlitt was infuriated by the prospect of the "euthanasia of the rentier" [H. Hazlitt, *The Failure of the "New Economics"*]. All of them were convinced that, whatever Keynes might say, State intervention of the Keynesian type would smother all individual enterprise and that full employment would lead to ill-chosen investments, a general falling off in productivity and dangers to freedom. . . .

It is impossible to evaluate scientifically the validity of the opinion of the liberal economists that the Keynesian system is fundamentally unstable and must inevitably form a stage on the road to some form of socialism; all these opinions are typical value judgments. The same is true, incidentally, of any reply to the question which one continu-

ally has to ask oneself when reading these writers' works, namely: what would be the chances of survival of a capitalist system left to its own devices?

Some of them, however, distorted Keynes's thought to the point of caricaturing it. Here are some examples:

1. Hazlitt described Keynes's policy as a "policy of perpetual inflation".

2. Cortney wrote that for Keynes "there is not only too much saving, but this latter is practically a sin" [P. Cortney in *The Critics of Keynesian Economics,* edited by H. Hazlitt].

3. In the opinion of von Mises, Keynes shared "the pseudo-philosophy of those who can think of nothing else than to dissipate the capital accumulated by previous generations" ["Stones into Bread, the Keynesian Miracle" and "Lord Keynes and Say's Law", two articles written in 1948 and 1950 and published in *The Critics of Keynesian Economics,* edited by H. Hazlitt].

4. According to Stagg Lawrence Keynes's views on investment were in essence as follows: "Digging holes and filling them again can be more useful socially than the private accumulation of wealth. . . . Building useless pyramids can be more desirable socially than building a railroad. . . . The government should control and direct all investment." [*The Critics of Keynesian Economics,* edited by H. Hazlitt].

2. *The Communist Attitude.*

From the communist review *La Nouvelle critique* one learnt for the first time in 1949 of the pernicious influence which Keynes's ideas were having on certain militants on both sides of the Iron Curtain.

> No other bourgeois social philosophy . . . has ever infiltrated the ranks of the workers' organisations so dangerously. . . . Even the communist party in the U.S.A. was tempted by the blandishments of Keynesianism, and its former Secretary-General, Earl Browder, nearly led his party into a deviation. . . . In the Soviet Union a debate on the work of the economist Varga showed how deeply the insidious influence of Keynes's mistaken views on the role and the nature of the capitalist State had penetrated. . . . A general critical analysis of a number of books and articles by Soviet economists . . . shows that Varga's erroneous views are shared by an entire group of students of economics. [*La nouvelle critique,* February and July-August, 1949]

It was therefore essential that the official views of the party on the Keynesian theory—that is to say, an absolute and categorical condemnation of them—be issued as soon as possible. Writers like J. Domarchi and P. Sweezy, who compared Keynes with Marx and even suggested that the work of Keynes had thrown new light on certain passages of *Capital,* were viewed with grave suspicion by their Marxist colleagues. Varga finished by writing his own self-criticism; in it he abased himself so much that one is tempted to wonder whether he was not being a little malicious.

All this took place under Stalin's rule. Since then the official views of the Communist party on Keynesism have not changed; this is clear from a number of books published since 1949 and from articles recently published in Soviet economic reviews.

A communist is of course perfectly entitled to draw attention to this evidence; Keynes was never either a communist or a marxist. Unfortunately these writers—as is so frequent among writers of their tendency—are all too easily led to substitute insult for argument. They claim that Keynes filled in "exactly" with the group of economists whose task it was to "propose remedies known in advance to be ineffective" in order to be able to comply with "the orders" of the capitalist system. He has been accused of being "the personal and indefatigable champion of British imperialism", and a number of his followers have been described as "the most effective instigators of the Third World War".

Some of the communist attacks deserve further study, as they throw a great deal of light on the communist social philosophy itself.

The first line of attack is the accusation that all Keynes was trying to do was to save capitalism. It is true that Keynes wished to save private enterprise and a large sector of private ownership; but at the same time he was proposing major changes in a system which in his opinion inevitably gave rise to economic depressions and accepted intolerable injustices within itself. If the system condemned by Keynes and the system he proposed are both to be tarred with the same capitalist brush, then the wielder of the brush must in fairness explain that the new system is not capitalistic in the same way as the old one. What the communists are doing, in fact, is using the same word to cover two substantially different things. Here again, a communist or a socialist may quite legitimately refuse to accept the mixed-economy system of the type envisaged by Keynes as a goal to work towards. But to over-simplify the problem in this way implies failure to understand what the adversary is driving at and consequently to fail to come to grips with him.

The second line of attack is the affirmation that full employment is impossible except under communism. The report submitted by Mr. Khrushchev to the 22nd Congress of the Communist Party of the USSR contains the statement that "the bourgeois myth of full employment is nothing but a sinister farce". In earlier years this attitude had been justified by reference to Stalin's dictum that "You will never be able to force a capitalist to act in a manner prejudicial to his own interests and accept a lower rate of profit to satisfy the needs of the people" [*La nouvelle critique,* February, 1949]. Let us take one example of what actually happens: In 1944 in Great Britain taxpayers with incomes of less than £250 per year only paid 2 1/2 per cent. of their incomes in tax, while persons earning more than £10,000 per year paid over 80 per cent. of their incomes in tax. What capitalists are willing to accept is irrelevant; what matters is what the State, under the pressure of complex capitalist, non-capitalist and anti-capitalist forces, will compel them to accept. One often hears communists putting forward arguments of the following kind:

"The resumption of the armaments race, first in Germany and later in the United States, is the only way of reabsorbing unemployment." If an armaments policy has an effect of this kind, then one can no longer say that full employment is impossible. And what is to prevent the State from obtaining the same end by expenditure of a different kind—namely social investments?

We now come to the last major communist objection to Keynesianism, namely that Keynes would not in any way reduce the domination of the capitalist class by broadening the influence of the public sector, because the State is merely a reflection of the will of that class (or part of that class; the terms "capitalism", "financial capital" and "monopoly capital" are used as if they were synonymous).

This is in essence a restatement of a thesis originally advanced by Marx and amplified by Jules Guesde and Lenin. When Marx originally advanced this hypothesis he was, admittedly, making an over-hasty generalisation. But this generalisation was based on the actual situation in his time; a State which forbade occupational associations and strikes and permitted child labour could deservedly be called a lackey of capitalism. Today, however, this hypothesis clearly does not correspond to the facts. When Varga, in his condemned book, wrote that the State, "in its desire to make the most rational use possible of all the resources of the country in the prosecution of the war, continually clashed with private interests of different capitalist undertakings which wished to earn the maximum profit", he was recording a fact. But in this case the facts are misleading.

Evidence of the difficulty of closing one's eyes to the facts all the time can be found in the refutation of the Keynesian philosophy by W. Foster, the Chairman of the Communist Party of the USA. In the middle of this refutation, Foster was incautious enough to state that Roosevelt had encouraged the organisation of a powerful trade union movement and in so doing earned the undying hate of the big capitalists. Foster had thus fallen into exactly the same error as Varga. How could Roosevelt, as the head of a State which was merely the reflection of the will of the capitalist class, have done anything displeasing to his masters?

Those responsible for framing communist ideologies continue determinedly to close their eyes to the facts. As long as the Communist Party continues to uphold Lenin's views on the nature of the State, it will be unable to understand recent developments in non-communist countries.

3. *The Attitude of the Socialists.*

The publication of the **General Theory** was welcomed with enthusiasm by a large number of socialist theorists. G. D. H. Cole considered that it was the most important piece of economic writing since Marx's *Das Kapital*. During recent years a number of socialist parties have adopted resolutions in support of proposals expounded in their original forms by Keynes. André Philip wrote in 1952, albeit with some misgiving, that Keynes had supplanted Marx as the guide of socialist thought.

Obviously, this remark is not be taken literally. Although Keynes was an extremely left-wing neo-liberal with beliefs approximating to those of socialism, he never actually stepped into the socialist camp. A socialist who was prepared to accept the social philosophy of Keynes as it stands would in so doing abandon his allegiance to socialism.

The fact that capital is the source of economic power never disturbed Keynes. Apart from the suggestion that the choice between catering for the present and catering for the future should be taken in agreement with the people as a whole (which we referred to in discussing *A Treatise on Money*), Keynes never expressed any desire for economic democracy. In this connection his lack of interest in the position of the co-operative movement throughout the world is characteristic. No socialist could be satisfied with a situation in which undertakings with large amounts of invested capital would be "semi-socialised" merely because in such a situation they would take public opinion into account and work to secure stability rather than the maximum short-term profit. Nor could a socialist consider as definitive a system in which most of the decisions would be taken by capitalist undertakings, even within the framework of a general State plan. Lastly, no socialist could rely entirely on the maintenance of full employment to abolish unearned incomes, unearned interest and unearned profit and relinquish all desire to introduce structural reforms to hasten the achievement of this end, for he cannot accept the belief that (apart from questions of the total volume of production) the market machinery secures the best possible use of the factors available.

Some socialists are in fact open opponents of Keynesism. Professor Mossé, for example, wrote a violently anti-Keynesian article for *La revue socialiste*. But this article is based on an extremely personal interpretation of both the socialist and the Keynesian doctrines.

Mossé seems quite content with a stagnant kind of socialism; he writes: "Once production has risen to a sufficiently high level the primary task is the distribution of wealth and leisure." In other words, in his brand of socialism full employment is considered as a "ridiculous" aim. [Robert Mossé *Le Keynésisme devant le socialisme,* offprint from *La revue socialiste,* 1949 and 1950].

Mossé goes on to offer the following interpretation of the *General Theory:* "Whatever one may say, he (Keynes) has remained faithful to the law of markets. . . . (a study of the distribution of incomes) would show that there are certain persons with high incomes who, owing to social inequalities, are unable to spend their entire incomes. Keynes does not explore this field at all. . . . In Keynes's view the construction of pyramids would be just as profitable to society as the manufacture of mining equipment. . . . He entirely ignores the problems of distribution of incomes."

In these circumstances, how is it that a number of socialists have accepted Keynes's teachings?

The *General Theory* gives short shrift to the beliefs on which liberal social philosophy had been based for a century—the law of markets and the invariably desirable results obtained by giving free rein to the profit motive. In the circumstances it is understandable that the book could be interpreted by socialists as the triumph of some of their own ideas. On the positive side of the balance sheet they found the thesis that a depression can be checked, not by decreasing wages, but by increasing demand and that a more equitable distribution of incomes would have a stabilising effect on the economy; the objective of full employment aroused echoes of their own long and unremitting struggles to secure recognition of the right to work; and his strictures on interest and unearned income reminded them of Saint-Simon's outbursts against "incomes obtained without labour". They could quite legitimately think that, although the *General Theory* was not socialist in character, it nevertheless represented considerable progress towards socialism. Keynes's book offered neo-liberals and socialists a possibility of reaching an understanding—even if it were only a temporary one—within which they could frame a new economic policy.

In conclusion, it should be mentioned that Keynes won the sympathy of the socialist movement early in his career by his criticism of the Treaty of Versailles and by his defence of the miners during the 1926 strike.

VIII. KEYNES WAS NOT THE FOUNDER OF A NEW FAITH

Keynes won over thousands of people to specific aspects of his theories or his social philosophy; but only very few people conceive the New Jerusalem in exactly the same way as he does. He has many disciples but no followers.

This cannot be attributed to his consistent and all-pervading rationalist outlook; Ricardo, Bastiat and Marx all appealed solely to the reason of their readers but nevertheless had faithful followers.

If a social philosophy is to inspire faith it must be expressible in a few simple, coherent affirmations. Keynes's social philosophy is too complex and attempts to reconcile too heterogeneous a set of elements.

He demonstrates the instability and precariousness of so many different kinds of equilibrium and then proposes a new equilibrium which many people consider equally unstable and precarious. He suggests that, if private ownership and private enterprise are to continue to reign in a broad sphere, the scope of collective action must be greatly extended and the individual entrepreneur must be content with a relatively modest remuneration. . . .

Nothing could be more illustrative of the difficulty of creating an entirely Keynesian faith than consideration of the careers of Roy Harrod and Joan Robinson, Keynes's two favourite pupils, who are mentioned in the preface to the *General Theory.* Harrod was impressed above all by the liberal content of the books, bitterly criticized the Labour experiment during the years immediately following the Second World War and moved towards a Conservative point of view, while Joan Robinson took the step which Keynes himself had consistently refused to take and became a socialist.

Thus Keynes stands in a peculiar position among those thinkers who have influenced the course of history. He did not proclaim his own social philosophy as an immutable creed and rally a new army in its support; instead he delicately influenced existing social philosophies and persuaded the leaders of already existing groups to take up his goals as their own.

Izumi Hishiyama   (essay date 1969)

SOURCE: "The Logic of Uncertainty According to J. M. Keynes," in *The Kyoto University Economic Review*, Vol. XXXIX, No. 1, April, 1969, pp. 22-44.

[*In the following excerpt, Hishiyama maintains that* A Treatise on Probability *had a direct bearing on the* General Theory, *particularly with regard to the two essential components of Keynes's principle of aggregate demand, investment and consumption, both of which, according to Keynes, contain an element of uncertainty that is not mathematically calculable.*]

I

I think that one chapter has been left untouched in the studies about J. M. Keynes which have been made so far. It is none other than the relationships between *A Treatise on Probability* and *The General Theory*. Because *A Treatise on Probability* was Keynes' first painstaking work, I believe in a certain sense that the study of these relationships will serve to clarify the changes of his thought from his early days up to the latter.

Though it is to be expected that some would say that setting up a proposition like that would be quite meaningless in the case of Keynes, I think that even if a doubt of that kind might be aroused, it would be natural in the case of Keynes. It seems to me that among all the prominent scholars in the past and present there are few scholars like him who have been unsophisticated out of a bad habit of insisting on the conventional way of thinking. Of course he has never insisted on his own assertions. It is likely that some may dare criticise him, saying that he is eccentric. As is well known, in his *Treatise on Money,* 1930, he criticised the formula (the cash balance equation) asserted in his *Monetary Reform,* 1923, and also in his *General Theory of Employment, Interest and Money,* 1936, he abandoned the essential part (fundamental equations) of his *Treatise on Money.* He further proceeded to make a severe, if not fatal, criticism of the classical economists, among whom he himself belonged for a long time and he attempted to extricate himself from their field. Viewed from this angle, I would rather think that a deeper development of one's thought would, above all other things, have meant to Keynes to criticise the very concept in one's own mind, to make a conquest of it and to attempt to extricate oneself from it.

On the other hand, it is also commonly known that he had something of the personality of a current critic having an acute realistic sense. Thus no point of the vicissitudes of current problems ever escaped being timely grasped by Keynes' sharp sensibility. The innumerable variety of economic problems which had given rise with bewildering rapidity during the period from the end of the World War I to the great depression, such as the problems concerned with post-war disposal and rehabilitation measures, the system of currency and price stabilisation, chronic unemployment and depression and what not, together with their resulting economic diseases, came into existence, carrying particular phases and colours in each case. As it acted in concert with each case, Keynes' diagnosis and his prescription slips showed some changes one after the other. In this way he never stayed at the same place; just as if he were running water. Whatever specific time he may be taken up at, we always find him in the posture of a man of thought who is attempting to face the future by doing away with the past. In a word, he is, as it were, always "a man on his way." If one turns his mind toward the past from the viewpoint of such man of thought, the past must have reflected on his mind not as what should be taken over but as what should be abandoned. The past must be something incomplete or immature, if not something erroneous. The harder the effort is made to trace the changed course of his original thought, the oftener the chances to think in that way increase. If viewed from this aspect, it may appear to be meaningless to make a quest for the relationships between his *General Theory,* which was intimately conceived by Keynes, and his *Treatise on Probability,* which was the crystallisation of his primitive thought. In this way this very point in question has been almost left (duly?) untouched by those who have been regarded as specialised Keynes scholars. Neither L. R. Klein, S. E. Harris, A. H. Hansen nor D. Dillard, etc. has made mention of even a few words with respect to the *Treatise on Probability,* not to speak of the above mentioned point in question. Even J. A. Schumpeter, who has been so well-known for his profound knowledge, did not grasp the meaning of the *Treatise on Probability* as having been anything more than "an outlet for the energies of a mind" [*Ten Great Economists: From Marx to Keynes*]. Because many other scholars one after another have done nothing but contribute to the spread of such views, the specific problems concerned with a *Treatise on Probability* have been left untouched, being buried in oblivion for the period of thirty years since the publication of *The General Theory,* and there has been at least no room left in any economist's concern to be taken up by these problems.

It may be said that the reason why a *Treatise on Probability* has been disregarded by those who have made a study of Keynes is, not because it was immature or that it has been replaced by his own thought in later days, but because it was an achievement in a field having nothing to do with economics, or because it had no concern whatsoever with the formation of his economic thought. Maybe it was assumed that the line of thought in terms of a *Treatise on Probability* and that which has penetrated through *The General Theory* by integrating the thoughts in the field of his economics were, so to speak, two parallel lines, neither of which would ever cross the other. Or rather, the truth might lie in the fact that a *Treatise on Probability* has never been read, and that those specialists interested in this field who perused the theory so happened to show no interest in Keynes' economics. Let it be what it may, it is anyway an indisputable fact that the re-examination of the part that the *Treatise on Probability* played in forming Keynes' thought, specifically in systematising his economic thought has never been attempted before, being completely neglected by those who have made a study of Keynes' works. And if it can be assumed that such a point in question does have some weight which cannot be disregarded, then it follows that the various studies conducted about Keynes so far are characterised by a blind point of a serious nature. As for me, I am of the opinion that this point in question should by no means be neglected, and therefore my judgement leads to the conclusion that the studies about Keynes in the past are not free from such a blind point.

The *Treatise on Probability* is not a book that deals with the technique and mathematical application of probability as the title may suggest. It is a product of a far more extensive and ambitious way of grasping the nature and role of probability. Speaking briefly, its aim is to compose a new logical foundation rather than the creation of a new logic on the basis of empirical science. Such a way of taking up the problem is very clearly expressed in his quoted line of Leipzig's words, which may be cited here as follows: "J'ai dit plus d'une fois qu'il faudrait une nouvelle espèce de logique, qui traiterait des degrés de Probabilité." Since the main subject of a *Treatise on Probability* lies in the clarification of 'a new type of logic' (une nouvelle espèce de logique) to provide a logical basis of empirical science, it would not be entirely wrong to say that this book treats the methodology of empirical science, if expressed in recent words. Therefore, the relationship between a *Treatise on Probability* and *The General Theory* can be, in a sense, comparable to that between J. S. Mill's *System of Logic* and his *Principles of Political Economy,* or that between Jevons' *Principles of Science* and his *Principles of Political Economy.*

For the purpose of making a thorough study of the meanings of J. S. Mill's thought on economics it would probably be essential to make a close examination of his system of logic. The same should be held true with regard to the case of Keynes. That is, for the purpose of clarifying the theoretical meaning of his thought on economics developed in his *General Theory* it would be necessary to examine his system of logic. In the meanwhile, speaking of the system of logic of Keynes, there is no such book except his *Treatise on Probability,* and it can be seen that Keynes sacrificed his whole youthful life, when his intellectual energies were brought into full play, only to complete this book in which he wanted to accomplish the task of creating a new type of logic which could well be set up against Mill's system of logic. This book is not anything like a layman's piece-work, but is literally one of his life works, as commented on by R. F. Harrod. It appears to me, as far as my view is concerned, that Keynes' philosophical thought, being different from the case of economic thought, grew to maturity in his youthful days and that his systematical thought of logic which bloomed in his youth never came to be revised in all his life. In the case of Keynes, if described in a more or less exaggerated manner, his philosophical vision with respect to the methodological foundation of his theoretical framework came to be established during the period of his earliest intellectual formation, and the development of his thought filled with seeming diversities and changes that took place afterwards, up to such time when his *General Theory* was published, was something like sparks flying apart just before a gigantic lense set in the frame of such a vision was about to be focussed

on a certain point. It appears to me that those who made a study of Keynes in the past have all been dazzled too much by such brilliant sparks and that they have failed to recognise the other side of Keynes' thought—that element which kept wandering in hope of finding a place to settle down, taking root deep in the basic layer of his superficially ever-changing thoughts, i.e. that ever-lasting philosophical element.

Be the matter as it may, how suggestive it is that the very first field of study from which Keynes set forth to begin his scholastic itinerary was principally concerned with the theory of probability and the theory of money. To recompose the theory of probability as a fundamental logic common to the empirical sciences by straightforwardly accepting the uncertainty which spreads its wings in the field of experience as a natural and normal element on the one hand, and to make complete research of a theory and practice of all monetary phenomena in which uncertainty makes its most prominent appearance in the economic field on the other—all these were none other than the subjects of his study to be pursued by himself when Keynes launched himself in to the study of a science. As already mentioned, it seems that the study of the systematisation of empirical and inductive logic based on the concept of probability was completely finished in his early days, being maintained as such without any modification throughout all his life. Contrariwisely, however, the systematisation in the field of his economic thought, which was started from his study of money and which was integrated in a voluminous *General Theory,* through a series of various works on money and banking, was characterised by repeated destruction and creation, criticism and reconstruction, being forced to pass through a long painful gestation period. Disregarding the danger of too much simplification, if the formation of Keynes' thought is to be briefly and symbolically summarised, it can be reduced to the following two fields of systematisation: (1) *logic* based on *probability* and (2) *economics* based on *money.* Now then, our present problem is to examine whether or not an everlasting straight line originating from *probability,* and a diversified, and so to speak, spiral line originating from *money* respectively, determine each independent field of its own which will never cross the other. Needless to say, I think that these two fields are connected by close relationships with each other, and that in the intersection of these two lines should lie the *raison d'être* of a new microcosm, in opposition to the old classical microcosm which is composed of Mill's inductive logic and deterministic economics mainly concerned with *real* matters taken over by A. C. Pigou through the ideas held by J. S. Mill and A. Marshall.

Viewed from this angle, it follows that the system of *A Treaties on Probability* should be regarded as an essential component element of the thought of Keynes, being coupled with the system involved in *The General Theory.* Therefore, it can fairly be said that almost all of the scholastic studies and literature in the past which did not take this point up deviated from the fundamentally important point in question, if viewed both from the standpoint of a far-sighted grasping of the systematical thought of Keynes and from the standpoint of the clarification of the theoretical meaning of his economic thought. Consequently, the subject matter of my present study about Keynes, in brief, can be focussed on clarifying that the two abovementioned different categories of thought, or fields, are connected together in meaningful relationships, that the two lines originating from *probability* and *money* respectively should intersect, and still further that his systematised economic thought should be rebuilt on Keynes' logic of uncertainty.

II

It seems that among Keynes' systematised economic thought concentrated in the ***General Theory,*** one of the groups of problems which has some relationship with the thoughts concerned with the theory of probability is *the theory of inducement to invest or the theory of investment decisions,* and another one of them is *the theory of propensity to consume or the theory of the consumption function.* Now, as is generally known, since these two problems are no more than the essential elements of the so-called principle of effective demand, if it could be made clear that these theories are based on a consistent ground in terms of the theory of probability, then our assumption that the Keynesian theory of probability has some meaningful relationships with his systematised economic thought could be corroborated. However, even if it is made clear that the theory of probability is related to the theory of investment inducements and the theory of the consumption function, it does not follow that the way in which the relation comes to arise and its nature are exactly identical in both cases. In my opinion the theory of probability and the theory of investment inducement are directly related, and such a combination is very natural. The reason is because the problem of investment is concerned with the way of selecting a probable course of action under uncertain anticipation. Putting it another way, because the problem resolves itself into a problem of selection or decision under uncertain conditions, the concept of probability comes to be naturally formed in consciousness. Taking the way of thinking advanced in the ***General Theory*** for example, if a little more concrete explanation is to be given, it runs as follows. Generally speaking, the decision to produce new capital goods, such as machines or buildings, will be governed by the production cost and the expected market price. Now then, when the price of capital goods is expected to exceed production cost, the production of capital goods, i.e. investment will be stimulated. In other words, the scale of investment will be determined at the level where the price and production cost come to be equal. Nevertheless, the price of capital goods depends upon two factors: one is the rate of interest and the other is the expectation of the future profit from capital goods. When the rate of interest goes down, other conditions being equal, the price of capital goods will go up, and similarly when the expectation of the future profit turns out favourably, its price will also go up. The way in which the price of these capital goods fluctuates is a plain fact to be easily understood by analogical inference if our eyes are turned to the daily price fluctuations of valuable securities, although these are not real assets like machines and buildings, which can be looked upon as representative of real capital assets. Now, if roughly expressed, the rate of interest ac-

cording to Keynes, once the quantity of money is fixed, is determined by the propensity of the public to hold money. However, various motives of the public for holding money in possession for future use are governed by the anticipation or judgement with respect to the future. On the one hand it is needless to say that the anticipation of future profit from capital goods is also to be governed by judgement having an uncertain element. Therefore, it necessarily leads to the conclusion from all that has been stated that, if the production cost of capital goods is given, then investment after all is to be based on two different judgements with respect to the future—the preference of the public to hold money in possession and their opinion of the future profit from capital goods. Because these judgements are of an extremely uncertain nature, they are not based on safe and definite grounds. Putting it another way, in the case of the selection of a course of action, the result of which will become known not instantaneously on the spot but more or less in the distant future, however complex and confusing its phenomenal form may appear to be, it appears to me that the structure of inference based on the theory of probability has its roots deep in the background of such judgements. Therefore, it can fairly be assumed that the way of thinking in terms of the theory of probability is not inessential in Keynes' theory of investment inducement or the theory of investment decisions, and that there does exist a very close relationship at the very bottom of the foundation.

As to the so-called theory of the consumption function, viewed from the chronological sequence of Keynes' thought, it must have been formed in his mind as a flashing light in relatively later days, possibly immediately after the publication of the ***Treatise on Money*** in 1930. It can be assumed that the concept of a fairly stable consumption function must have come to his mind through the formulation of an investment-multiplier prepared by his student R. F. Kahn, as its inevitable assumption, rather than as a result of its by-product. If it is permissible to view it in this way, then it may be considered that the theory of the consumption function, at least as far as its *genetic* ground is concerned, has nothing to do with the theory of probability. If so, where should the relationships between the theory of the consumption function and the theory of probability be sought? As to this question, the following two points seem to be worthy of note: one is the problem of statistical generalisation and statistical stability, the other being the problem concerned with Keynes' way of interpreting the so-called aggregation.

Now, if seen from the standpoint of empiricism, it would be permissible to think that the theory of the consumption function is concerned with a kind of statistical generalisation. If consumption and income are grasped as an aggregated quantity of an economy as a whole, then the theory of the consumption function would indicate the plain fact that the move of aggregate consumption is governed *principally* by the move of aggregate income. Of course, the propensity of the public to consume may be affected by a number of factors, such as conditions of income distribution, their attitudes toward the future, etc., and also by the rate of interest to a certain extent. However, if income increases, consumption increases, too, but the rate of the increase of the latter is smaller than that of the former. In brief, the increment of consumption C is always smaller than the increment of income Y. Moreover the ratio of C to Y (this is called the marginal propensity to consume) is positive and less than 1. Keynes asserts that this characteristic prescribes the "normal shape of the function of consumption" of a society and it forms the "fundamental psychological law" of an economic society [*General Theory*]. Now then, if the law pertaining to the function of consumption, to which the characteristic (it may now be expressed by ϕ) that is mentioned in the above can be ascribed as an inevitable conclusion, is grasped as a kind of statistical generalisation, it is clear enough that it will be formed on the basis of the theory of probability.

A statistical law does not so strictly require universal soundness that even one exception will lead to its abandonment. For instance, although the drawing of a conclusion that *all* swans are white, based on data which show that this or that or those swans are white, may be regarded as inductive reasoning in conformity with the classification of Keynes' *Treatise on Probability,* it should rather be looked upon not as statistical induction but as universal induction. In a case of statistical induction the proposition to be clarified would show that *most* swans are white, or that the probability that a swan is black is such and such, based on data that this or those swans are white and the other one is black. If the same reasoning is applied to the law presupposed in the function of consumption, the characteristic ϕ, which prescribes that the marginal propensity to consume is positive and less than 1, is not necessarily found to be true, depending on each individual case. It may so happen that all of the increased portion of income may be consumed in one case, or that more than the increased portion may be spent in another case. In other words it seems that each individual case is governed by a variety of arbitrary factors which may transgress the regularity of a law. Nevertheless, when it comes to the aggregate of many individual cases, i.e. a large majority phenomenon, the existence of the law comes to be clearly accepted, and this can be boiled down to the proposition that *most* of so many cases have the characteristic ϕ. Or similarly statistical generalisation will always arrive at the form showing that "the probability, that an instance taken at random from series S will have the characteristic ϕ, is p" [*A Treatise on Probability*]. Viewed from this standpoint, I should think that there is room to contemplate the problem of the *stability of the propensity to consume,* on which the stability of the economic system was regarded to depend by Keynes, in close relationship with the statistical stability in *A Treatise on Probability*.

Now, if the concept of the consumption function, thinking that aggregate consumption has a stable relationship with aggregate income, is concerned with the existence of a law to be drawn *empirically* from the aggregates, the problem of examining a rational ground for such an empirical generalisation is still left to be clarified. That it is possible to confirm the stability of the propensity to consume through a statistical procedure is not the answer to the problem; it simply gives its first step. It is because the attempt to clarify in a reasonable and *a priori* way the reason why it becomes so is still left untouched. If stated in a slightly more concrete manner, it is because whether the relationships of regularity drawn from the aggregated group which is indicated in the function of consumption can be consistently connected with the traditional theory of the reasonable preference of consumers or not, in other words whether it is possible to draw the macroscopic theory of the consumption function in a theoretically consistent form from the microscopic theory of consumers' preference or not—such problems, i.e. the so-called aggregation problem in contemporary economics—are still left untouched. In his *General Theory,* Keynes did not refer specifically to this problem, and he did not solve it, either, though it is natural that he could not. However, what is meant by the problem of aggregation, if viewed from a slightly wider angle, is none other than the problem of clarifying the logical ground for the empirical generalisation observable among aggregates. If further put in other words, the problem may also be generally concerned with the logical ground for inductive inference. If it is permissible to view it in this way, for the reason that in the first place the problem of clarifying the logical ground for the inductive inference in general, including the statistical inference, was one of the main issues in Keynes' *Treatise on Probability,* it would be possible as well to think that the methodological foundation provided by Keynes himself with respect to the aggregation problem in contemporary economics had already been perfunctorily given in one sense.

In the meanwhile, needless to say, the problem of aggregation has the nature of being applied not only to the consumption function but also to the so-called aggregate supply function, to the investment demand function also, and even further to the money demand function or liquidity preference function. Now, as the field of view is widened from the market of consumer goods to that of capital goods and further to that of securities, it can be seen that uncertainty comes to intervene in the behaviour of microscopic economic constituents as an overwhelming element which can not be disregarded. Under such circumstances how much appropriateness can the traditional microscopic theory, which generally disregards uncertainty, or which is based on a plain or tacit presupposition that it is possible to predict uncertainty in a numerically measurable form, have as a well-founded basis of the inductive law of regularity confirmed empirically from the majority phenomena that have taken place in the market? In this connection, G. Ackley states that, because the *a priori* analysis in support of Keynes' consumption function (i.e. the theory of the consumers' preference) is no more than "an abstract timeless analysis of rational behavior using a minimum of psychological assumptions," it would be impossible to infer a "generalisation that can be used to predict or describe behavior which is observed over time in a changing world" [*Macroeconomic Theory*]. Thus, it is interesting that he has expressed his frank doubt as to the *a priori* argument in support of the consumption function. Such doubts, I am sure, will grow stronger and stronger as his eyes are turned from the market of consumer goods which he had in his mind exclusively to the market of capital goods or securities. Although I can not agree with Ackley's assertion, drawn from his unsophisticated empiricism, which maintains that "the stability . . . the consumption function can only be established empirically," as to the very way the aggregation problem is taken up from the aspect of modern economics, I can not help raising a doubt of the same kind as that of Ackley. It seems to me that the only reasonable way of solving the so-called aggregation problem would be to provide the inductive generalisation or inductive inference relating to the behaviour of an aggregate with a justifiable ground *in terms of the theory of probability* by straightforwardly and clearly contemplating the uncertainty in the decision or activity of each individual random member who is a component part of such an aggregate. Be the matter as it may, it appears that the problem of the confrontation of the microscopic system and the macroscopic system is still covered by a thick mist. Viewed from such a way of thinking, since it appears that the systematic thought of Keynes' theory of probability has some meaningful relationship with the above mentioned problem, it would be necessary to make an examination of this point in question by going back to *A Treatise on Probability*.

III

To begin with I have to give my answer to one question. That is, even if it were a fact that Keynes attached much importance to the concept of probability when he was composing his empirical argument, such a matter is not one that occurred only in the case of Keynes, and we have still the question, 'Was not the element of uncertainty and the concept of probability similarly considered in fact even in the so-called classical theories?' Is the relationship between Keynes' theory and the theory of probability something fundamentally different in nature, as a matter of fact, in comparison with the relationship between the classical theory and the theory of probability? I shall give my opinion about this question in general here.

I have a firm belief that classical theories had a full acknowledgment of the point that the element of uncertainty did have a more prominent effect on the producers' preference than on the consumers' or more so in the market of capital goods than in the market of consumer goods, and still more so in the field of investment than in other fields. However, it seems to me that classical economics ordinarily completely did away with such uncertainty, and by presupposing the socalled stationary state, or even if they had it in their mind, by presupposing that it was possible to grasp it through either the concept of the numerically measurable probability distributions or probability, they thought that the existence of uncertainty did not call for the necessity of making a fundamental modification of the intrinsic nature of their basic model characterised by its deterministic nature.

In the meantime, because it is too commonly known that many classical economists used to presuppose the stationary state in their arguments, such a point will not be taken up here, but there is, I think, the necessity of making explanation with illustrations about the particular point, in a sense to prevent some misunderstanding too, that they in fact took the above-mentioned uncertainty into account. For example, A. C. Pigou, who succeeded and developed the theories of Marshall, the great master of classical theories, advocated in his *Economics of Welfare* that the uncertainty-bearing on the part of producers should be regarded as one kind of independent factor of production, maintaining that what investment meant in the actual world, where some future event could not be perfectly predicted, was in a sense to expose resources under uncertainty. Now, the uncertainty that supervenes with a certain type of investment, according to Pigou's view, is to be manifested in its full play in a certain probability distribution of the expected gain of the investment. He calls it "a scheme of prospective returns." Thus, investment can not be anything more than getting possession of a certain probability distribution which is to be manifested in a scheme of prospective returns, by laying out a certain amount of money in a manner similar to the case of betting. Now, it was considered that the degrees of probability of each prospective return, making up the component element of such probability distributions, could be clearly made known. Consequently it follows that the 'mathematical expectation' of the probability distributions in question could be interpreted as being something numerically measurable, the mean value of which could be obtainable if the product of each prospective return with the probability of attaining it was added together. However, the prospective return which ought to be a real measure of the uncertainty-bearing should be not the average or actually expected rate of return but that amount by which the latter exceeds the return of a perfectly safe investment (e.g. consols). In short, it should not be something vague and non-measurable but a definite and calculable value.

Thus, the uncertainty element in the field of investment, as far as Pigou's view is concerned, is something probable, but because it can after all be grasped in a certain and clear probability distribution, he asserts that its mathematical expectation is calculable. And so it may be a fair guess to say, assuming from his idea of identifying "the most probable return" with "the most frequent return," that his thinking is grounded on the theory of statistical frequency which was integrated by J. Venn. However, even if it was assumed that he took the uncertainty element into account in the field of production or investment, the frame of his deterministic way of thinking with respect to production still remains to be as such without being affected at all. The reason is because, according to Pigou's way of thinking, this particular element of the uncertainty-bearing in the case of investment, is firmly seated in the same analytical structure of marginal productivity in the same capacity and in an exactly similar manner as in the case of three other factors of production, such as nature, labour and capital (i.e. waiting). Therefore, if the above-mentioned view of uncertainty is taken, even if the uncertainty arising out of investment for resources is taken into consideration, it does not necessarily follow, speaking of the problems of the so-called optimum allocation of productive resources, that the nature of the primary model which was composed on the condition of certainty should be fundamentally modified. Needless to say, if Pigou's point of view is taken, the consideration of uncertainty did not come to give any impetus to reorganise the deterministic way of thinking into the way of thinking in line with the theory of probability.

But Keynes is different. The reason is because the foundation-stone on which his theory was composed is different, however similar the nature of Keynes' way of thinking may superficially appear to be to that of the scholars of the classical school. Though paradoxically it may sound, even if it were proved how far Keynes' way of thinking is different from that of the classical economists, unless such analysis takes up the difference in the foundation on which respective ways of thinking were grounded, it can not be sufficiently complete. Anyway, Keynes never overlooked the specific points that classical theories represented by Pigou, Edgeworth, etc. did take up; not merely the stationary state, which was supposed to be governed by certainty, but the world in which the parts to be played by *change* and *expectation* was sufficiently taken into consideration, i. e. the system in which uncertainty was taken into consideration. However, according to him, in the classical economists' way of thinking, "at any given time facts and expectations were assumed to be given in a definite and calculable form" [**"The General Theory of Employment,"** *Quarterly Journal of Economics,* 1937], and he further maintained that, even if the uncertainty and risks were recognised, "they were supposed to be capable of an exact actuarial computation." In other words they thought that by means of "the calculus of probability" uncertainty could be reduced to "the same calculable status as that of certainty itself." In connection with this Keynes drew a conclusion to the effect that such a way of thinking was of the same type as the methodology which was adopted in the Benthamite philosophy to calculate pleasure and pain, or gain and loss in ethical behaviour.

As far as Keynes' view is concerned, it will lead to the following conclusions that, even if it is supposed that the uncertainty element was taken into consideration in the way of thinking of the classical economists, it was presupposed to have been something definitely calculable through the concept of numerically measurable probability, that the presupposition of mathematical expectation of probability distributions with respect to the so-called reasonable economic decision was no more than the technique of converting uncertainty into certainty, and that through such instrumentality the classical system could not be anything else than a system of certainty in which facts and expectations were grasped in a calculable and definite form at any given time. Thus, all that has been said will lead to the conclusion that the nature of their system after all has nothing fundamentally different from that type of "system in which the amount of the factors employed was given and the other relevant facts were known more or less for certain" [**"The General Theory of Employment"**], i.e. the nature of the model in a stationary state where no uncertainty element is involved at all.

According to Keynes, uncertainty prominent in the field of economics, especially in the field of investment, is a peculiar characteristic inherent not merely in economic phenomena but also in the structure of inference underlying empirical science, which is universally unavoidable in such human behaviour that is being obliged to make alternative judgements of which the results will more or less show up in the future. Especially in the field of economics this characteristic must be substantial as well as decisive. The reason is because among all human behaviour which

is influenced by the *preoccupation* with the prospective result, one of the most important ones is something of an economic nature, i.e. "Wealth" or "the accumulation of Wealth." "The whole object of the accumulation of Wealth is to produce results, or potential results at a comparatively distant, and sometimes at an *indefinitely* distant, date. Thus the fact that our knowledge of the future is fluctuating, vague and uncertain, renders Wealth a peculiarly unsuitable subject for the method of classical economic theory" [**"The General Theory of Employment"**].

It appears that Keynes made use, in a very strict sense, of the term 'uncertainty' which arises in the economic field, particularly in the field of accumulation. It is not something which can be grasped by means of measurable probability as in the case of the classical theory. Since the ratio to win at roulette or in a raffle is calculable probability, as is widely known, uncertainty in this sense is different from that which is meant by Keynes. Viewed from this angle, it is needless to say that the uncertainty which is to be indicated in Pigou's "scheme of prospective returns" does not belong to genuine uncertainty (in the sense meant by Keynes), because in the case of Pigou mathematical expectation is calculable. Uncertainty in the real sense of the word is something neither predictable nor calculable, something to which no measurable probability or even the concept of probability distribution is applicable. Unfortunately, the uncertainty arising in the accumulation of wealth is none other than this kind of uncertainty. Thus, viewed from this angle, it follows that the classical theory is "one of these pretty, polite techniques which tries to deal with the present by abstracting from the fact that we know very little about the future" [**"The General Theory of Employment"**]. In this connection, because I think it very useful to remember a comment made by D. H. Robertson, successor of A. C. Pigou, in which Robertson frankly expressed his doubts about his master's analysis, it may be cited here as follows: "The ultimate uncertainties of the business life are precisely those which cannot be insured against or pooled in this way. Indeed it is arguable that Pigou's 'scheme of uncertainty' paints too narrow a picture of the whole problem, since often the businessman not only does not know what point on a 'scheme of uncertainty' he will hit, but has only the vaguest idea what the scheme of uncertainty is" [*Lectures on Economic Principles*].

What is most important for the problem now under discussion is not a theoretically consistent system but how the core of uncertainty in the economic field should be prescribed. To the eyes of Keynes it may have appeared that those classical economic systems which completely disregarded such uncertainty that was beyond the probability-calculation, must have been no more than "market-place idols," in the sense that they did not penetrate to the core of substantial uncertainty inherent in economic phenomena, however theoretically consistent they might have been in themselves. However, it must be admitted that if our eyes are cast upon aggregated economic activities, something of regularity can be empirically confirmed from a macroscopic point of view, through the mechanism of the market. However, if our eyes are once turned from the microscopic view to the foundation of the preferences of individuals, we are confronted with an entity of uncertainty as if it were a mollusc which we cannot take hold of. Thus, we are again confronted with the conception of uncertainty which has its root deep in the background of the problem arising out of the opposition between the microscopic and macroscopic ways of thinking.

Now, it seems to me that the difference in the ways of thinking with respect to the concept of uncertainty and probability held by Keynes and the classical economists can be concretely and straightforwardly seen in the theory of money and the rate of interest. In other words it is said that this very difference is in itself an outstanding characteristic of the Keynesian theory of inducement to invest or the theory of investment decisions, in which the above-mentioned theory is included as one train of thought. But, before taking up such a proposition now, I shall turn to the way of thinking in *A Treatise on Probability* and see how Keynes generally grasped the concept of uncertainty and probability.

IV

As far as I can see, it appears that the concept of uncertainty or probability of Keynes' own creation is expressed in a very vivid manner in his criticism of "the theory of statistical frequency" which was advanced in his *Treatise on Probability*. Taking this as a clue, I shall now make my approach to this problem. Before going into any further discussion, let us not forget that whenever the classical economists took uncertainty into account, they grounded their reasoning on the concept of objective probability on the presupposition of the theory of statistical frequency and the resulting concept of uncertainty which was prescribed by it.

Now, the essence of the theory of statistical frequency can be briefly put as follows: Taking the uncertainty-bearing of Pigou already referred to as an example, the proposition that the probability of producing a prospective return of 10 by spending 100 for a certain investment is f/n, means that this particular investment is one of a group of a great number of investments of the same type as the one mentioned—the f/n ratio of which produces the return of 10. And it follows that the very existence of a series of investments having the frequency of f/n to produce a prospective return of 10 is purely an empirical phenomenon, and they should be determined exactly in the same way as in the case of any other matter of fact. Viewed from this angle, probability is something ultimately concerned with a series of certain events in the form of frequency in respect of a certain characteristic. Then, the problems relating to probability come to be something to indicate intensively the results of experience (for instance what has been experienced about the aggregate of a certain type of investment).

If based on such theory, probability must be understood to be characterised by an objective frequency which is inherent in the aggregate of all the cases experienced, and it follows that it should have some definitely known numerical values in all cases rather than that it might have. Now, when it is said in our daily argument that there is no knowing about probability or that probability is vague,

it can fairly be said that it is all because of our poor or incomplete knowledge of probability and not because of objective probability itself. For example, the reason why the probability of a certain type of investment to produce certain prospective returns is not clear is not to be ascribed to the characteristics of probability distribution itself of the said investment-returns, but is to be ascribed to the incompleteness of our knowledge or information with respect to the matter. The reason is, if based on the frequency theory, because "the probabilities are relative, not to our knowledge, but to some objective class, possessing a perfectly definite truth-frequency" [*A Treatise on Probability*]. In other words probability is something provided objectively to the events which have been experienced. In a word it means *objective* probability.

What is meant by probability by Keynes differs substantially from this. Probability, according to him, is the probability of an inference or an argument. It is the probability not of events but of propositions. As in the case of the frequency theory, probability is not something objectively innate to the aggregate of events. It is "in an important sense *relative to given premisses*" as the probability of the conclusion of a certain inference. Putting it another way, it is concerned with actual or hypothetical information or knowledge which forms the presupposition of inference. Now, in just as much proportion to the difference among informations or knowledges on which the presupposition of inference is to be formed, the extent of the probability of that proposition may vary. In short, Keynes' probability is a subjective probability. In this sense it is also something concerned with "the degree of rational belief" in a proposition. But, it is not something based on inference in order to draw a conclusion with "demonstrative certainty" as in the case of the geometry of ideal space or a syllogism, though it can be called rational belief. It is something based on the "arguments from premisses leading to conclusions which are reasonable but not certain," i.e. a probable and reasonable inference. Keynes further states that almost all of the empirical sciences and our daily behaviour depend on such a probable inference. In this way it is seen that Keynes' theory of probability is not something concerned with the nature inherent in the objective *events* in themselves, as in the case of the frequency theory, but with the nature of subjective *inference* with respect to the events. In other words it treats the varied degrees of confidence aroused from the inference of drawing an uncertain, though reasonable, conclusion.

Viewed from such a standpoint, what defects could there be in the theory of statistical frequency? The concept of probability held in the frequency theory is clearly understandable by anybody because of its objective and measurable nature, but it cannot throw light on the process of forming our reasonable belief itself. In other words, it can not be really useful in making our decision. Now, in the ordinary activities of daily life and also in almost all of the empirical sciences, however differently they may be characterised in their abstractness, universality or consistency, the process of inference based on experience lies deeply rooted at the bottom. In short, our activities or sciences are closely connected with the process of empirical inference. Moreover, the meaning of such inference can not be after all anything else other than the preference for a certain conclusion to be drawn through a reasonable procedure from a given presupposition. Thus, fundamentally speaking, reasonable *inference* means reasonable *preference,* which can be seen in the statement made by Keynes to the effect that "probability is the study of the grounds which lead us to entertain a *rational* preference for one belief over another." It is needless to say that many of the reasonable inferences used in our daily life or empirical sciences aim at no demonstrative certainty, but do have a more or less probable nature, because there can not be any room to make a preference to 'alternatives' in the process of drawing a definite conclusion by demonstration, as in the case of geometry.

In the meanwhile, if the basic nature of probable inference lies in determining "which alternatives it is *reasonable to prefer,*" then probability comes to be something concerned with the "logical grounds of decision" and it leads us to the conclusion that, if such a reasonable decision were concealed in the core of our life, then probability would be something that comes in contact with the very roots of both ordinary life and scientific life. If viewed from such an angle, statistical probability cannot be useful either as "the guide of life" or as "the guide of decision." Moreover, "in following it we are not acting according to reason." In short, it comes down to the fact that statistical probability cannot be a sufficient condition for *reasonable preference.* This can well be guessed to be the meaning of Keynes' statement to the effect that "We may call a statistical frequency a probability, if we choose; but the fundamental problem of determining which of several alternatives is logically preferable still awaits solution."

Nevertheless, what is the reason for saying that statistical probability is not sufficient to be made the logical ground of our preference? I shall give a further explanation about this point by taking the analysis made by Pigou as an example again. Illustrations with respect to *a certain type* of investment which takes *a certain type* of probability distribution of prospective returns are given in Pigou's analysis. However, there is a risk in such a simplification of missing the very core of the decision for investment, because what is important for anybody who makes the decision to invest is the selection among several types of investment. Now then, let's suppose that there are so many types of investment and each of them has a probability distributions of its own type respectively. Thus, what is important for the decision of investors is a selection among so many mathematical expectations which are substantiated by their own inherent statistical frequency. Then, it follows that each objective probability distribution (of prospective returns) in correspondence to the difference due to the type of investment is taken for granted in this case. In other words, it is not put in question how the statistical frequency (objective probability), on which our preference or decision is presupposed, comes to be formed. But, when the process through which the above-mentioned probability distribution is formed is further analysed, it can easily be understood that a number of factors affect the foundation of the 'real value' of each statistical probability, which may govern our decision in some measure. Therefore, if viewed from subjective probability, the probability of statistical

frequency peculiar to each type of investment should be put in question. In other words the *probability* (in the sense held by Keynes) of the proposition, saying that the probability of producing a given prospective return through a given type of investment is p, should be put in question. Be the matter as it may, it is sure enough that the order of the mathematical expectation peculiar to each type of investment does not precisely reflect that of the preference for the decision to make an investment. It seems to me, as referred to before, that Keynes cherished the opinion that the classical economists' thoughts were based on Benthamite logic. What is meant by such a comment is that even in Benthamism it was presupposed that the order of preference for an ethical decision was supposed to correspond precisely to that of the mathematical expectations (of the expected virtue or pleasure), and that the behaviour-pattern of this type was completely taken over as the foundation of an economic decision by the classical economists. Consequently it might be said that if this viewpoint is taken, the behaviour-pattern presupposed by Pigou in the background of the investment decision is substantially grounded on Benthamite logic.

Be the matter as it may, because the mathematical expectations substantiated by statistical probability can not be a sufficient condition for forming a logical foundation for our decision, there arises a necessity of building up a new systematised way of thinking of probability, in which all the factors that have been given away for the reason of being subjective or non-measurable from the aspect of the theory of statistical frequency should be comprehended. The reason is because such a system of thought can only be really useful as a 'logical ground of decision' or as a 'guide of life.' Keynes' statement to the effect that "My *Treatise* is concerned with the *general* theory of arguments from premises leading to conclusions which are reasonable but not certain" can be interpreted in such a way (italics mine).

In the meantime, probability in the theory of statistical frequency is characterised by its clearness and measurableness. Perhaps it is because of such characteristics that this theory has come to be generally accepted. But what really matters lies neither in a clear definition of probability nor in the logical consistency of a way of thinking, but *in finding a logical ground for our decision or preference* having its root deep in the bottom of our inference. If viewed from such a standpoint, even such a problem as to whether the probability of a conclusion of our inference is measurable or not is not a substantial matter. However, in many instances probability which is concerned with the degree of our rational belief is not measurable. Frequently it is something which can not even be compared. In a case like this "Nor have we any *prima facie* indications of the existence of a common unit to which the magnitudes of all probabilities are naturally referable. A degree of probability is not composed of some homogeneous material, and is not apparently divisible into parts of like character with one another."

It is, needless to say, with his criticism against the fundamental conception of the classical economists, on the one hand, that Keynes limited the meaning of probability very strictly, finding it impossible to grasp the real uncertainty in the economic field through the concept of a measurable and objective probability, but we should not overlook on the other hand that such an idea sprang from a motif in *A Treatise on Probability,* which maintained that the concepts of uncertainty and probability which lie deep in the logical ground for decision or preference were neither measurable nor comparable. Leaving the matter as it is, it appears to me that Keynes had an idea that the concepts of uncertainty or probability in the economic field make numerical comparison impossible in the substantial meaning of the word. If viewed in this way, Keynes' sharp criticism in his *Treatise on Probability* of the theory of statistical frequency, the motive of which was to discover the 'logical ground for decision,' was the first criticism ever made of classical economic thought which took up the problem of uncertainty and probability in this theory, and at the same time it was consistent in its groundwork with his later criticism of classical thought.

Another criticism raised by Keynes against the theory of statistical probability is his opinion that the concept of objective probability cannot be a reasonable ground for empirical inductive inference. As already mentioned before, to seek 'the logical justification' of inductive inference in general, including the statistical inference in the concept of probability, i. e. to attempt to reinterpret the 'inductive law' in terms of the theory of probability, was part of his main subject matter. What is regarded as important for this subject matter lies not in whether the way of thinking in the theory of statistical frequency has logical conformity or not, but whether "the body of probable argument, upon which the greater part of our generally accepted knowledge seems to rest can be explained in terms of it (the frequency theory)." Can it be possible, as a matter of fact, that such an inference can be drawn from the assumption of statistical frequency? Keynes gave a negative answer with respect to this question after making an examination, for example, of various presuppositions on which the conclusion of Darwin's *The Origin of Species* was based, which may be quoted as follows: "Not only in the main argument (in 'The Origin of Species'), but in many of the subsidiary discussions, an elaborate combination of induction and analogy is superimposed upon a narrow and limited knowledge of statistical frequency. And this is equally the case in almost all everyday arguments of any degree of complexity. The class of judgements, which a theory of statistical frequency can comprehend, is too narrow to justify its claim to present a complete theory of probability."

Thus, it leads us to the conclusion that the problem of rebuilding the logical ground for inductive inference through a new concept of subjective probability, instead of statistical objective probability, was still left to be solved by Keynes. What forms the main subject of Part III of *A Treatise on Probability* is none other than this problem. Through all that has been discussed I have shown the general nature of the concept of uncertainty and probability held by Keynes, in comparison with that of objective probability, which had its root deep in the foundation of classical thought. Then, it is self-explanatory from the composition of the problem briefly stated at the beginning of Section II that how the theory of inducement to invest, or the theory of investment decisions, maintained by Keynes should be recomposed based on the above mentioned new concept of subjective probability is our next problem to be solved.

John Kenneth Galbraith   (essay date 1971)

SOURCE: "How Keynes Came to America," in *Essays on John Maynard Keynes,* edited by Milo Keynes, Cambridge University Press, 1975, pp. 132-41.

[*In the following essay, which was first published in 1971, Galbraith explains how the ideas contained in the* General Theory *were disseminated and eventually adopted in the United States.*]

> 'I believe myself to be writing a book on economic theory which will largely revolutionize—not, I suppose, at once but in the course of the next ten years—the way the world thinks about economic problems.'
>
> —Letter from J. M. Keynes to George Bernard Shaw, New Year's Day 1935.

The most influential book on economic and social policy so far in this century, *The General Theory of Employment, Interest and Money,* by John Maynard Keynes, was published in 1936 in Britain and a few weeks later in the United States. A paperback edition is available in the United States, and quite a few people who take advantage of this bargain will be puzzled at the reason for the book's influence. Though comfortably aware of their own intelligence, they will be unable to read it. They will wonder, accordingly, how it persuaded so many other people—not all of whom, certainly, were more penetrating or diligent. This was only one of the remarkable things about this book and the revolution it precipitated.

By common, if not yet quite universal agreement, the Keynesian Revolution was one of the great modern accomplishments in social design. It brought Marxism in the advanced countries to a total halt. It led to a level of economic performance that now inspires bitter-end conservatives to panegyrics of unexampled banality. Yet those responsible have had no honours and some opprobrium. For a long while, to be known as an active Keynesian was to invite the wrath of those who equate social advance with subversion. Those concerned developed a habit of reticence. As a further consequence, the history of the revolution is, perhaps, the worst told story of our era.

It is time that we knew better this part of our history and those who made it, and this is a little of the story. Much of it turns on the almost unique unreadability of *The General Theory* and hence the need for people to translate and propagate its ideas to government officials, students and the public at large. As Messiahs go, Keynes was deeply dependent on his prophets.

The General Theory appeared in the sixth year of the Great Depression and the fifty-third of Keynes's life. At the time Keynes, like his great contemporary Churchill, was regarded as too clear-headed and candid to be trusted.

Public officials do not always admire men who say what the right policy should be. Their frequent need, especially in matters of foreign policy, is for men who will find persuasive reasons for the wrong policy. Keynes had foreseen grave difficulty from the reparations clauses of the Versailles Treaty and had voiced them in *The Economic Consequences of the Peace,* a brilliantly polemical volume, which may well have overstated his case and which certainly was unjust to Woodrow Wilson.

Later in the twenties, in another book, he was equally untactful toward those who invited massive unemployment in Britain in order to return sterling to the gold standard at its pre-war parity with the dollar. The man immediately responsible for this effort, a highly orthodox voice in economic matters at the time, was the then Chancellor of the Exchequer, Winston Churchill, and that book was called *The Economic Consequences of Mr Churchill.*

From 1920 to 1940 Keynes was sought out by students and intellectuals in Cambridge and London; was well known in London theatre and artistic circles; directed an insurance company; made, and on one occasion lost, quite a bit of money; and was an influential journalist. But he wasn't really trusted on public questions. The great public trade union which identifies trustworthiness with conformity kept him outside. Then came the Depression. There was much unemployment, much suffering. Even respectable men went broke. It was necessary, however unpleasant, to listen to the candid men who had something to say. This is the terrible punishment the gods reserve for fair weather statesmen.

It is a measure of how far the Keynesian Revolution has proceeded that the central thesis of *The General Theory* now sounds rather commonplace. Until it appeared, economists, in the classical (or non-socialist) tradition, had assumed that the economy, if left to itself, would find its equilibrium at full employment. Increases or decreases in wages and in interest rates would occur as necessary to bring about this pleasant result. If men were unemployed, their wages would fall in relation to prices. With lower wages and wider margins, it would be profitable to employ those from whose toil an adequate return could not previously have been made. It followed that steps to keep wages at artificially high levels, such as might result from the ill-considered efforts by unions, would cause unemployment. Such efforts were deemed to be the principal cause of unemployment.

Movements in interest rates played a complementary role by insuring that all income would ultimately be spent. Thus, were people to decide for some reason to increase their savings, the interest rates on the now more abundant supply of loanable funds would fall. This, in turn, would lead to increased investment. The added outlays for investment goods would offset the diminished outlays by the more frugal consumers. In this fashion, changes in consumer spending or in investment decisions were kept from causing any change in total spending that would lead to unemployment.

Keynes argued that neither wage movements nor changes in the rate of interest had, necessarily, any such agreeable

effect. He focused attention on the total of purchasing power in the economy—what freshmen are now taught to call aggregate demand. Wage reductions might not increase employment; in conjunction with other changes, they might merely reduce this aggregate demand. And he held that interest was not the price that was paid to people to save but the price they got for exchanging holdings of cash, or its equivalent, their normal preference in assets, for less liquid forms of investment. And it was difficult to reduce interest beyond a certain level. Accordingly, if people sought to save more, this wouldn't necessarily mean lower interest rates and a resulting increase in investment. Instead, the total demand for goods might fall, along with employment and also investment, until savings were brought back into line with investment by the pressure of hardship which had reduced saving in favour of consumption. The economy would find its equilibrium not at full employment but with an unspecified amount of unemployment.

Out of this diagnosis came the remedy. It was to bring aggregate demand back up to the level where all willing workers were employed, and this could be accomplished by supplementing private expenditure with public expenditure. This should be the policy wherever intentions to save exceeded intentions to invest. Since public spending would not perform this offsetting role if there were compensating taxation (which is a form of saving), the public spending should be financed by borrowing—by incurring a deficit. So far as Keynes can be condensed into a few paragraphs, this is it. *The General Theory* is more difficult. There are nearly 400 pages, some of them of fascinating obscurity.

Before the publication of *The General Theory,* Keynes had urged his ideas directly on President Roosevelt, most notably in a famous letter to the *New York Times* on 31 December 1933: 'I lay overwhelming emphasis on the increase of national purchasing power resulting from government expenditure which is financed by loans.' And he visited F.D.R. in the summer of 1934 to press his case, although the session was no great success; each, during the meeting, seems to have developed some doubts about the general good sense of the other.

In the meantime, two key Washington officials, Marriner Eccles, the exceptionally able Utah banker who was to become head of the Federal Reserve Board, and Lauchlin Currie, a former Harvard instructor who was director of research and later an economic aide to Roosevelt (and later still a prominent victim of McCarthyite persecution), had on their own account reached conclusions similar to those of Keynes as to the proper course of fiscal policy. When *The General Theory* arrived, they took it as confirmation of the course they had previously been urging. Currie, a highly qualified economist and teacher, was also a skilled and influential interpreter of the ideas in the Washington community. Not often have important new ideas on economics entered a government by way of its central bank. Nor should conservatives worry. There is not the slightest indication that it will ever happen again.

Paralleling the work of Keynes in the thirties and rivalling it in importance, though not in fame, was that of Simon

Kuznets and a group of young economists and statisticians at the University of Pennsylvania, the National Bureau of Economic Research and the United States Department of Commerce. They developed the now familiar concepts of National Income and Gross National Product and their components of National Income and Gross National Product was the saving, investment, aggregate of disposable income and the other magnitudes of which Keynes was talking. As a result, those who were translating his ideas into action knew not only what needed to be done but how much. And many who would never have been persuaded by the Keynesian abstractions were compelled to belief by the concrete figures from Kuznets and his inventive colleagues.

However, the trumpet—if the metaphor is permissible for this particular book—that was sounded in Cambridge, England, was heard most clearly in Cambridge, Massachusetts. Harvard was the principal avenue by which Keynes's ideas passed to the United States. Conservatives worry about universities being centres of disquieting innovation. Their worries are surely exaggerated—but it has occurred.

In the late thirties, Harvard had a large community of young economists, most of them held there by the shortage of jobs that Keynes sought to cure. They had the normal confidence of their years in their ability to remake the world and, unlike less fortunate generations, the opportunity. They also had occupational indication of the need. Massive unemployment persisted year after year. It was degrading to have to continue telling the young that this was merely a temporary departure from the full employment norm, and that one need only obtain the needed wage reductions.

Paul Samuelson of M.I.T., who almost from the outset was the acknowledged leader of the younger Keynesian community, has compared the excitement of the young economists on the arrival of Keynes's book to that of Keats on first looking into Chapman's Homer. Some will wonder if economists are capable of such refined emotion, but the effect was certainly great. Here was a remedy for the despair that could be seen just beyond the Yard. It did not overthrow the system but saved it. To the non-revolutionary, it seemed too good to be true. To the occasional revolutionary, it was. The old economics was still taught by day. But in the evening, and almost every evening from 1936 on, almost everyone discussed Keynes.

This might, conceivably, have remained a rather academic discussion. As with the Bible and Marx, obscurity stimulated abstract debate. But in 1938, the practical instincts that economists sometimes suppress with success were catalysed by the arrival at Harvard from Minnesota of Alvin H. Hansen. He was then about fifty, an effective teacher and a popular colleague. But most of all he was a man for whom economic ideas had no standing apart from their use.

The economists of established reputation had not taken to Keynes. Faced with the choice between changing one's mind and proving that there is no need to do so, almost everyone opts for the latter. So it was then. Hansen had an established reputation, and he did change his mind. Though he had been an effective critic of some central propositions in Keynes's *Treatise on Money,* an immediately preceding work, and was initially rather cool to *The General Theory,* he soon became strongly persuaded of its importance.

He proceeded to expound the ideas in books, articles and lectures and to apply them to the American scene. He persuaded his students and younger colleagues that they should not only understand the ideas but win understanding in others and then go on to get action. Without ever seeking to do so or being quite aware of the fact, he became the leader of a crusade. In the late thirties Hansen's seminar in the new Graduate School of Public Administration was regularly visited by the Washington policy-makers. Often the students overflowed into the hall. One felt that it was the most important thing currently happening in the country, and this could have been the case.

The officials took Hansen's ideas, and perhaps even more his sense of conviction, back to Washington. In time there was also a strong migration of his younger colleagues and students to the capital, and Keynes himself once wrote admiringly of this group of young disciples. The discussions that had begun in Cambridge continued through the war years in Washington. One of the leaders, a close friend of Hansen's but not otherwise connected with the Harvard group, was Gerhard Colm of the Bureau of the Budget. Colm, a German refugee who made the transition from a position of influence in Germany to one of influence in the United States in a matter of some five years, played a major role in reducing the Keynesian proposals to workable estimates of costs and quantities. Keynesian policies became central to what was called post-war planning and designs for preventing the re-emergence of massive unemployment.

Meanwhile, others were concerning themselves with a wider audience. Seymour Harris, another of Hansen's colleagues and an early convert to Keynes, became the most prolific exponent of the ideas in the course of becoming one of the most prolific scholars of modern times. He published half a dozen books on Keynes and outlined the ideas in hundreds of letters, speeches, memoranda, Congressional appearances and articles. Professor Samuelson, mentioned above, put the Keynesian ideas into what became (and remains) the most influential textbook on economics since the last great exposition of the classical system by Alfred Marshall. Lloyd Metzler, now of the University of Chicago, applied the Keynesian system to international trade. Lloyd G. Reynolds, at a later stage, gathered a talented group of younger economists at Yale and made that university a major centre of discussion of the new trends.

Nor was the Harvard influence confined to the United States. At almost the same time that *The General Theory* arrived in Cambridge, Massachusetts, a young Canadian graduate student named Robert Bryce arrived from Cambridge, England. He had been in Keynes's seminar and had, as a result, a special licence to explain what Keynes meant in his more obscure passages. With two or three other Canadian graduate students, Bryce went on to Ottawa and to a succession of senior posts culminating in Deputy Minister of Finance. Canada was perhaps the first country to commit itself to a firmly Keynesian economic policy.

Meanwhile, with the help of the academic Keynesians, a few businessmen were becoming interested. Two New England industrialists, Henry S. Dennison of the Dennison Manufacturing Company in Framingham and Ralph Flanders of the Jones and Lamson Company of Springfield, Vermont (and later United States Senator from Vermont) hired members of the Harvard group to tutor them in the ideas. Before the war they had endorsed them in a book, in which Lincoln Filene of Boston and Morris E. Leeds of Philadelphia had joined, called *Toward Full Employment*. It was only slightly more readable than Keynes. In the later war years, the Committee for Economic Development, led in these matters by Flanders and the late Beardsley Ruml, and again with the help of the academic Keynesians, began explaining the ideas to businessmen.

In Washington during the war years the National Planning Association had been a centre for academic discussion of the Keynesian ideas. At the end of the war Hans Christian Sonne, the imaginative and liberal New York banker, began underwriting both N.P.A., and Keynesian ideas. With the C.E.D., in which Sonne was also influential, N.P.A. became another important instrument for explaining the policy to the larger public. (In the autumn of 1949, in an exercise of unparalleled diplomacy, Sonne gathered a dozen economists of strongly varying views at Princeton and persuaded them to sign a specific endorsement of Keynesian fiscal policies.)

In 1946, ten years after the publication of **The General Theory,** the Employment Act of that year gave the Keynesian system the qualified but still quite explicit support of law. It recognised, as Keynes had urged, that unemployment and insufficient output would respond to positive policies. Not much was said about the specific policies but the responsibility of the federal government to act in some fashion was clearly affirmed. The Council of Economic Advisers became, in turn, a platform for expounding the Keynesian view of the economy and it was brought promptly into use. Leon Keyserling, as an original member and later chairman, was a tireless exponent of the ideas. And he saw at an early stage the importance of enlarging them to embrace not only the prevention of depression but the maintenance of an adequate rate of economic expansion. Thus in a decade had the revolution spread.

Those who nurture thoughts of conspiracy and clandestine plots will be saddened to know that this was a revolution without organisation. All who participated felt a deep sense of personal responsibility for the ideas; there was a varying but deep urge to persuade. But no one ever responded to plans, orders, instructions, or any force apart from his own convictions. That perhaps was the most interesting single feature of the Keynesian Revolution.

Something more was, however, suspected. And there was some effort at counter-revolution. Nobody could say that he preferred massive unemployment to Keynes. And even men of conservative mood, when they understood what

was involved, opted for the policy—some asking only that it be called by some other name. The Committee for Economic Development, coached by Ruml on semantics, never advocated deficits. Rather it spoke well of a budget that was balanced only under conditions of high employment. Those who objected to Keynes were also invariably handicapped by the fact that they hadn't (and couldn't) read the book. It was like attacking the original Kama Sutra for obscenity without being able to read Sanskrit. Still, where social change is involved, there are men who can surmount any handicap.

Appropriately Harvard, not Washington, was the principal object of attention. In the fifties, a group of graduates of mature years banded together in an organisation called the Veritas Foundation and produced a volume called *Keynes at Harvard*. It found that 'Harvard was the launching pad for the Keynesian rocket in America'. But then it damaged this not implausible proposition by identifying Keynesianism with socialism, Fabian socialism, Marxism, Communism, Fascism and also literary incest, meaning that one Keynesian always reviewed the works of another Keynesian. More encouragingly, the authors also reported that 'Galbraith is being groomed as the new crown prince of Keynesism (sic)'. Like so many others in similar situations, the authors sacrificed their chance for credibility by writing not for the public but for those who were paying the bill. The university was unperturbed, the larger public sadly indifferent. The book evidently continues to have some circulation on the more thoughtful fringes of the John Birch Society.

As a somewhat less trivial matter, another and more influential group of graduates pressed for an investigation of the Department of Economics, employing as their instrument the visiting committee that annually reviews the work of the department on behalf of the governing boards. The Keynesian Revolution belongs to our history; so accordingly does this investigation.

It was conducted by Clarence Randall, then the exceptionally articulate head of the Inland Steel Company, with the support of Sinclair Weeks, a manufacturer, former Senator and tetrarch of the right wing of the Republican Party in Massachusetts. In due course, the committee found that Keynes was, indeed, exerting a baneful influence on the Harvard economic mind and that the department was unbalanced in his favour. As always, there was a handicap that the investigators, with one or two possible exceptions, had not read the book and were otherwise uncertain as to what they attacked. The department, including the members most sceptical of Keynes's analysis—no one accepted all of it and some very little—unanimously rejected the committee's finding. So, as one of his last official acts before becoming High Commissioner to Germany, did President James Bryant Conant. There was much bad blood.

In ensuing years there was further discussion of the role of Keynes at Harvard and of related issues. But it became increasingly amicable, for the original investigators had been caught up in one of those fascinating and paradoxical developments with which the history of the Keynesian (and doubtless all other) revolutions is replete. Shortly after the committee reached its disturbing conclusion the Eisenhower administration came to power.

Mr Randall became a Presidential assistant and adviser. Mr Weeks became Secretary of Commerce and almost immediately was preoccupied with the firing of the head of the Bureau of Standards over the question of the efficacy of Glauber's salts as a battery additive. Having staked his public reputation against the nation's scientists and engineers on the issue (as the late Bernard De Voto put it) that a battery could be improved by giving it a laxative, Mr Weeks could hardly be expected to keep open another front against the economists. But much worse, both he and Mr Randall were acquiring a heavy contingent liability for the policies of the Eisenhower administration. And these, it soon developed, had almost as strong a Keynesian coloration as the department at Harvard.

President Eisenhower's first Chairman of the Council of Economic Advisers was Arthur F. Burns of Columbia University and the National Bureau of Economic Research. Mr Burns had credentials as a critic of Keynes. In his introduction to the 1946 annual report of the National Bureau, called 'Economic Research and the Keynesian Thinking of Our Times', he had criticised a version of the Keynesian underemployment equilibrium and concluded a little heavily that 'the imposing schemes for governmental action that are being bottomed on Keynes's equilibrium theory must be viewed with scepticism'. Alvin Hansen had replied rather sharply.

But Burns was an able economist. If he regarded Keynes with scepticism, he viewed recessions (including ones for which he might be held responsible) with positive antipathy. In his 1955 Economic Report, he said, 'Budget policies can help promote the objective of maximum production by wisely allocating resources *first between private and public uses;* second, among various governmental programmes.' (Italics added.) Keynes, reading these words carefully, would have strongly applauded. And, indeed, a spokesman for the N.A.M. told the Joint Economic Committee that they pointed 'directly toward the planned and eventually the socialized economy'.

After the departure of Burns, the Eisenhower administration incurred a deficit of no less than $9.4 thousand millions in the national income accounts in the course of overcoming the recession of 1958. This was by far the largest deficit ever incurred by an American government in peacetime; it exceeded the *total* peacetime expenditure by F.D.R. in any year up to 1940. No administration before or since has given the economy such a massive dose of Keynesian medicine. With a Republican administration, guided by men like Mr Randall and Mr Weeks, following such policies, the academic Keynesians were no longer vulnerable. Keynes ceased to be a wholly tactful topic of conversation with such critics.

Presidents Kennedy and Johnson continued what is now commonplace policy. Advised by Walter Heller, a remarkably skilful exponent of Keynes's ideas, they added the new device of the deliberate tax reduction to sustain aggregate demand. And they abandoned, at long last, the doubletalk by which advocates of Keynesian policies combined advocacy of measures to promote full employment and economic growth with promises of a promptly balanced budget. 'We have recognised as self-defeating the effort to balance our budget too quickly in an economy operating well below its potential', President Johnson said in his 1965 report.

Now, as noted, Keynesian policies are the new orthodoxy. Economists are everywhere to be seen enjoying their new and pleasantly uncontroversial role. Like their predecessors who averted their eyes from unemployment, many are now able to ignore—often with some slight note of scholarly righteousness—the new problem, which is an atrocious allocation of resources between private wants and public needs, especially those of our cities. (In a sense, the Keynesian success has brought back an older problem of economics, that of resource allocation, in a new form.)

We have yet to pay proper respect to those who pioneered the Keynesian Revolution. Everyone now takes pride in the resulting performance of the economy. We should take a little pride in the men who brought it about. It is hardly fitting that they should have been celebrated only by the reactionaries. The debt to the courage and intelligence of Alvin Hansen is especially great. Next only to Keynes, his is the credit for saving what even conservatives still call capitalism.

Harry G. Johnson   (essay date 1972)

SOURCE: "The Early Economics of Keynes," in *The American Economic Review*, Vol. LXII, No. 2, May, 1972, pp. 416-21.

[*In the following essay, Johnson examines the relationship between Keynes's plans for the International Monetary Fund system, established after World War II, and his early economic work, specifically, his thoughts on the Indian currency problem and his views on international monetary relationships directly after World War I.*]

The Royal Economic Society has this year published the first eight of a projected twenty-four-volume series of *The Collected Writings of John Maynard Keynes*. Six of them are already in print or in library; the other two, edited by Elizabeth Johnson, contain a great deal of hitherto unpublished material on Keynes's activities from his graduation from Cambridge until his resignation from the Treasury in 1919. These two volumes throw a great deal of light both on the character, personality, and intellectual development of Keynes, and on the nature of economics as conceived and utilized, in both the academic world and in government, in the period up to and including the First World War. But I have no time to discuss these interesting matters.

It is tempting, in a very brief review of Keynes's early economics such as this, to attempt to discover in that early work the seeds of *The General Theory*. In the context of 1971, however, it seems to me far more interesting to look into his earlier work for signs of the evolution of thought that led up to Bretton Woods, the Keynes plan, and the establishment of the International Monetary Fund. These signs are to be found in the two major incidents with which these books are concerned: his work on Indian currency and finance, culminating in his brilliant feat of persuading the Royal Commission to change its conclusions on a crucial issue in international monetary management; and the views on international financial relationships in the broad sense that led him to write *The Economic Consequences of the Peace*.

The Indian currency problem, as Keynes first encountered it, was very briefly as follows. In 1892, the government had decided in favor of a gold rather than a silver or bimetallic standard, and had accordingly closed the mints to the minting of silver rupees and rupee notes as a token currency. The minting of silver rupees involved a substantial seigniorage profit for the government but required the maintenance of a reserve of silver and gold coins for exchange against inflows of domestic notes or of money from abroad. But gold was the standard, and maintaining the standard required two things: maintenance of a gold reserve in India and maintenance of a reserve of liquid sterling assets in London. The central problem for policy was that those who had favored, and still supported, the adoption of a gold rather than a silver standard believed that a gold standard required the actual circulation of gold coins and wanted reforms designed to promote the use and circulation of gold coins in India.

Keynes's main contributions to the debate at this stage were to advocate a gold exchange standard with a token silver coin circulation and to assert both that the existing Indian currency system was a gold exchange standard and that, in line with the evolution of the gold standard elsewhere, it should become more so, rather than being forced to move toward a full-bodied gold standard. Notable among his arguments in this connection were that gold coins in actual circulation are the part of the total currency least available to the monetary authorities in times of difficulty, so that centralization of the gold reserves in the hands of the authorities is the optimal policy; that gold in circulation loses the monetary authority the seigniorage on the fiduciary issue it replaces; that the revenue obtainable by investing international reserves in liquid sterling assets rather than barren gold was a significant consideration for India; and that it was inefficient to handle payments imbalances by actual physical movement of gold to and from India rather than by transfers of funds in London. In all these respects, Keynes's arguments foreshadow the structure of the post-Bretton Woods international monetary system, in which gold remains the reserve anchor of the system but the cost of holding it is reduced so far as possible by the substitution for it of interest-bearing credit instruments.

A financial scandal and a series of articles in *The Times* led to the establishment of the Royal Commission on Indian Finance and Currency, of which Keynes was nominated a member. Though he was the youngest member of the commission, it is quite clear from both his questioning and the acceptance of most of his arguments that, apart from Lionel Abrahams of the India Office, he was the only person involved on either side of the hearings who understood the monetary issues involved in the Indian currency system.

One of his most important contributions was a lengthy memorandum on an Indian State Bank [*The Collected Writings of John Maynard Keynes,* Vol. 15, *Activities: India and Cambridge, 1906-14,* pp. 148-211], eventually published as a separate section of the commission's *Report,* remarkable, in view of the short space of time which Keynes had to prepare it, for its exhaustive treatment of constitutional and operational issues and its command of relevant experience in other countries. His main concern was with establishing an economical currency system that would not tie up an excessive amount of resources in barren reserves. Yet it is interesting, in view of the emphasis in recent years on the need for developing countries to economize on international reserves and use expansion of the domestic money supply to finance economic development, on the basis of essentially Keynesian theory, to observe that Keynes the academic was roundly criticized by Abrahams the bureaucrat for his excessively conservative unwillingness to allow the resources accruing from seigniorage on the coinage and the expansion of the fiduciary issue to finance Indian industrialization (Vol. 15, pp. 214-15).

Later in the proceedings of the commission, Keynes was able to throw his weight successfully against those who wanted to expand the circulation of gold coin in India and to write into the *Report* many of the arguments contained in his book on *Indian Currency and Finance*. His major contribution to the *Report,* however, was made in the penultimate stages of drafting it, when he was laid low in Mentone with diphtheria, and his colleagues through half-understanding of his views arrived at a draft that would have made it impossible to provide an elastic currency and have accentuated the commitment of the resources backing the Indian money supply to sterile investments in reserves. The story is a complex one, both economically and diplomatically, and can only be understood by a careful reading of the editor's connecting text (Vol. 15, pp. 237-65); and Keynes won his point largely because it could be met by two very simple changes of wording, the import of which his fellow commissioners were presumably incapable of understanding.

The key issue, in very simple terms, was whether the fiduciary circulation of twenty crores of rupees to be permitted against the paper currency circulation should be a maximum, or whether the normal reserve of forty crores of rupees should be considered a minimum; and in the latter case, whether the minimum reserve ratio of one-third should apply to the note circulation gross or net of the government's own holdings of currency. By inducing the commission to settle for a minimum normal absolute cash reserve rather than a maximum fiduciary issue, and application of the reserve ratio to the net circulation of notes, Keynes freed the hands of the Indian monetary managers to provide an elastic supply of credit through the lending out of seasonally surplus cash and to invest money holdings above the normal at their discretion in domestic or foreign earning assets. The final *Report* thus came out against a rigid gold-circulation or proportional-gold-reserve standard, and in favor of a much more economical and flexible minimum-absolute-reserve standard, or more briefly an intelligent gold-exchange standard. (Unfortunately, the outbreak of the First World War led to the shelving of the *Report,* and India did not get a central bank until 1935.)

Keynes's activities in the period of approaching and initiated war, August-December 1914 [*The Collected Writings of John Maynard Keynes,* Vol. 16, *Activities: The Treasury and Versailles, 1914-19,* pp. 3-72], present him in a not altogether attractive light as a young man anxious to obtain an important job in wartime economic management and not too scrupulous about taking sides with the Treasury and the Bank of England against the commercial banks and the City of London to further his ambitions. He surged forward with a memorandum and subsequent articles and correspondence against the proposal of the joint stock banks to suspend gold convertibility of sterling, arguing correctly (and consistently with his earlier ideas on Indian finance) that the purpose of reserve holding is external and for use in emergencies and that the proper policy was to replace the internal gold circulation by notes; and he was cock-a-hoop about Lloyd George's taking his point that suspension of the Bank Act with respect to the maximum on the fiduciary issue was not equivalent to suspension of gold convertibility but instead a means of strengthening the ability to maintain convertibility.

Subsequently, he busied himself in preparation for the hoped-for Treasury appointment in studies of the initial wartime financial arrangements of Germany, France, Russia, and other allied countries. A major theme of these studies, which recurs persistently in his later work for the Treasury on problems of interallied finance, is the irrationality of the approach of other countries to the domestic position and international use of gold. Gold was the focal point of all the problems of interallied finance with which Keynes was concerned during this period, through the American entry into the war and the peace treaty negotiations; and there are some interesting though not very direct parallels between Keynes's efforts to induce the Americans to understand the reserve currency position of sterling in that period and recent American efforts to induce the Europeans to understand the reserve currency position of the dollar. There can be no doubt that Keynes's prolonged grappling with the role of gold in the context of interallied finance in the First World War stripped his mind of any lingering remnants of the prewar mystique of gold, drove home to him the importance of proper management of international credits, and laid the foundations for his bold and brilliant proposal of the "bancor" system as the basis for post-World War II international monetary reconstruction. At the same time, he remained thoroughly persuaded of the necessity of maintaining the convertibility of sterling into gold at a fixed parity—some of his arguments for specie now appear rather specious (Vol. 16, pp. 9-10)—and the ideas he formed in relation to Britain's special position among the allies as the only reserve currency country undoubtedly influenced the details of his "bancor" plan—though by that time his experience of the adverse effects on British employment of an overvalued currency in the 1920's had converted him to the concept of the "adjustable peg."

Keynes's early work at the Treasury was hectic, heady,

and highly varied, involving not only his main concern of interallied finance but also other issues such as inflation—contemporary Keynesian antimonetarists would be well advised to read his memorandum on **"The Relation of Currency Inflation to Prices"** (Vol. 16, pp. 76-78)—and an artful deal, rather tactfully glossed over by the editor, to relieve the Government of India, to the benefit of the British consumer, of the surplus of Indian wheat created by that Government's desire to prevent inflation of Indian food prices by embargoing the export of wheat at a world price far above the domestic Indian price.

In 1915-16, Keynes became involved in the general issue of wartime economic management, which happened to focus on the issue of conscription—an issue on which his personal concern about his conscientious objector friends of Bloomsbury joined hands rather uncomfortably with his views on the economics of the situation. Briefly, his position was that, unless Britain could drastically cut home consumption by increased taxation of the middle and lower classes, it had to choose between continuing to support its allies with munitions and material, and fielding a larger army of its own (Vol. 16, pp. 110-25 and 157-61); and he argued, rather emotionally but correctly in the light of subsequent history, that the former course represented the best course for beating Germany. (It would also have eased the problems of the peace treaty negotiations, which were intimately associated with the fact that Britain in effect supplied her allies with American goods financed by British debts to the United States.)

This piercing through of the veil of money and finance to the underlying real economics of the allocation of output and specifically of labor resources has generally been held to be the great contribution of "Keynesian economics" to financial management in the Second World War; hence it is important to note both that Keynes had arrived at this approach already in the early stages of the First World War, and that its application requires none of the novelties of *The General Theory*—Keynes was able to handle the monetary aspects of the approach quite satisfactorily with elementary quantity theory, including the concept of "hoarding." (The concept of the inflation tax appears in Vol. 16, p. 127.)

In February 1917, Keynes was made head of a new division of the Treasury, charged with responsibility for all questions of external finance, which in practice meant financial relations with the Americans. The details, which are hauntingly reminiscent of the same relations after the United States entered the Second World War, deserve only a brief comment here. Keynes encountered the same three major problems as recurred on the later occasion—difficulty in effecting firm bargains with administration officials who had ultimately to wangle their bargains through a suspicious Congress, difficulty in winning U.S. understanding of the allied-war-finance implications of Britain's reserve-currency role, which centered on getting U.S. acceptance of the use of American loans to other allies to repay their loans from Britain, and the refusal of American opinion to allow American aid to be spent on goods from non-U.S. sources—and his haughtiness and impatience toward the Americans, which sometimes had to be restrained by his official and political seniors, gave him a reputation for rudeness that made him less effective than he might have been.

After the Armistice, Keynes became concerned with the question of reparations, and subsequently with the negotiation of the Peace Treaty. The **"Memorandum By The Treasury on The Indemnity Payable by The Enemy Powers for Reparation and Other Claims"** (Vol. 16, pp. 344-83), which he prepared, is a masterpiece of applied economic analysis, assessing both the claims that the allies might make for specific war damage and Germany's capacity to pay, finding the latter less than the former but in a comparable range of magnitude, and recommending quick rather than protracted payment, in the awareness that in the latter case Germany would have to build up her exports at the expense of Britain's traditional industries. A more important consideration, which dominated Keynes's reaction to the Peace Conference, was that no sovereign country had ever been or could be forced into a position of abject economic servitude for a substantial period of years.

Keynes attended the Peace Conference in Paris as the senior Treasury member of the British delegation and the official representative of the British Empire on the Supreme Economic Council, and eventually resigned in disgust at the terms of the resulting treaty. Much of his writing at that time is cannibalized in his *The Economic Consequences of the Peace,* and needs no summary here. What stands out from the record (Vol. 16, Ch. 5) is his desperate humane effort to get Europe and especially the defeated enemies started on the path to reconstruction in the face of the wildly unrealistic demands of the European allies for massive reparations and the growing incomprehension of and hostility toward these allies of the United States, which then as in the Second World War, in accordance with the anti-European and sport-oriented psychology of America, showed more love for the defeated opponent than for its own seconds in the ring. Keynes tried increasingly frantically to clear the financial problems of war debts and reparations out of the way of the relief of German and Austrian misery, first by a proposal to cancel out war debts (which for a time was an official British proposal) and then by a proposal for a joint guarantee of reparation bonds to be issued by Germany, only to be met by a U.S. refusal to recognize the problem or consider the proposed solution. The mood in which he resigned is illustrated by two letters both of which begin with the statement "on Saturday I am slipping away from this scene of nightmare. I can do no more good here" (Vol. 16, pp. 469 and 471).

What does all this tell us, in the way of suggestion about the formative experiences that helped to lead Keynes up to his major role in the establishment of the International Monetary Fund system? Very little of specific substance, it must be confessed, apart from the fundamental idea that monetary and financial institutions and arrangements should be designed to promote the prosperity and progress of the people, and the belief that it is worth the while of an intelligent and knowledgeable man who has the opportunity to influence decisions to hand on and to keep proposing potentially negotiable plans so long as there is any hope of circumventing the blind unreasoning stupidity of the politicians. One might go further, stretching a point, and see in Keynes's concern for the milk-starved children of Austria the seeds of his later concern for establishing an international monetary system that would preserve and guarantee the priority of domestic full employment over the potentially hideous discipline of external balance, which was the original intention of his "bancor" proposal, however far the International Monetary Fund system in practice has drifted from that intention. But Keynes's concern in this period was with the problem of an impossible war-created structure of international debts and claims within a fixed-exchange-rate system rather than with the international monetary system itself. Later in 1919, he participated in a conference of bankers and others in Amsterdam, which among other things discussed the possibility of a new international currency; but that story is reserved for a subsequent volume in the *Collected Writings*.

Elizabeth Johnson   (essay date 1972)

SOURCE: "John Maynard Keynes: Scientist or Politician?" in *Journal of Political Economy*, Vol. 82, No. 1, January-February, 1974, pp. 99-111.

[*In the following excerpt, Johnson discusses the nature of Keynes's involvement in British political life and economic policy. Johnson's essay was originally read as a paper on September 5, 1972, at the annual meetings of the British Association for the Advancement of Science.*]

John Maynard Keynes—scientist or politician? The reader of the popular press of a generation ago would have had no doubt of the answer. Keynes, a swinging weather vane of a man, was the most unscientific of individuals—a cartoonist's dream. He was Keynes the india-rubber man: the *Daily News and Chronicle* of March 16, 1931, carried an article headed "Economic Acrobatics of Mr. Keynes" and illustrated it by a sketch of "A Remarkable Performance. Mr. John Maynard Keynes as the 'boneless man' turns his back on himself and swallows a draught"—the draught, a glass marked "15 per cent Protection." After years of preaching the virtues of free trade, he had first announced the end of laissez faire and now urged a revenue tariff on the country. As an exasperated political opponent remarked on another occasion—complaining of the man who in 1925 said wage costs were too high and in 1929 wanted higher prices: "It is difficult to reconcile Mr. Keynes the politician with Professor Keynes the economist. He seems to be both right and wrong! [Sir Laming Worthington-Evans, Conservative secretary of state for war, in a letter to the *Evening Standard,* May 6, 1929].

Keynes himself had no such difficulty. In his own opinion, he was always right. He had a clear idea of his own role in the world; he was the economist—at first Cassandra, croaking prophecies of doom about the economic consequences of reparations and the gold standard, prophecies which came all too true—and then as he gathered stature, the chief economic adviser to the world, to the chancellor of the exchequer of the day, to the French minister of finance whoever he was, to the president of the United

States. To elaborate, Keynes the economist initially thought of himself as the educator, the persuader, the man who would assemble all the relevant information and thereby start the reverberation of public opinion that would echo back to the politicians who, he said, "have ears but no eyes" ["**Reconstruction in Europe. An Introduction,**" *Manchester Guardian Commercial,* May 18, 1922]. . . . Then as he became established as an expert, he came to think of himself more as the economic scientist, the technician, the mechanic who is called in to fix the machine when the self-starter is broken. He looked forward to the time when economists would be consulted like dentists and hailed President Roosevelt as the first head of state to take theoretical advice as the basis for large-scale action.

"For the next 25 years, in my belief," he wrote in 1932, "economists, at present the most incompetent, will be nevertheless the most important, group of scientists in the world. And it is to be hoped—if they are successful—that after that they will never be important again" ["**The Dilemma of Modern Socialism,**" *Political Quarterly* 3 (April-June 1932)].

Keynes had a generally low opinion of politicians as charlatans who manipulated the public with their propaganda and obstinately clung to the accepted shibboleths until the winds of change forced them to tack. He knew himself to be an intellectual and a scientist, but he was a very *political* economist, addressing himself to the big problems of his time. As the high tide of the nineteenth century ebbed away and the waves of the twentieth came rolling in, as the world struggled out from the aftermath of the 1914-18 war with its old antagonisms and old sovereignties, the new hopes of peace and progress were bogged down by old debts and old habits. Poverty stood in the midst of what should have been plenty, and in Britain, less hard hit than Germany or the United States, one quarter of the working population was unemployed. How was the world to get out of this mess? In Britain, what could be left to the individual and what must be done by the state? No longer would "private ambition and compound interest . . . between them carry us to paradise" ["**Liberalism and Industry,**" in *Liberal Points of View* (1927), edited by H. L Nathan and H. Heathcote Williams]; the system could no longer be trusted to correct itself. The problems were political problems and for Keynes they were intellectual ones.

For all that, he was a natural politician. He inherited the Liberal politics of his parents and at Cambridge was a Liberal president of the union. During the early part of his life, he often appeared on the platform to speak for Liberal candidates. He was asked to stand for election himself many times—by all three parties—but he preferred the more powerful background role of expert counselor and adviser. Yet he had, in fact, so many of the traits of the politician and they seemed to come so naturally and were so much a part of his personality that it is hard to think that they could not have influenced his advice.

He was an opportunist who reacted to events immediately and directly, and his reaction was to produce an answer, to write a memorandum, and to publish at once. He was

into everything, be it the German mark or the French franc, birth control, the Lancashire cotton trade, buying British, economic sanctions, compulsory savings for a joyful hereafter. In the World War II treasury, he nearly drove some of his colleagues crazy with his propensity to keep a finger in every pie. "Don't just stand there, do something," would have been his present-day motto. Discussing unemployment in 1930, he said: "If we just sit tight there will be still more than a million men unemployed six months or a year hence. That is why I feel that a radical policy of some kind is worth trying, even if there are risks about it" ["**Unemployment**" (broadcast discussion with Sir Josiah Stamp), *Listener,* February 26, 1930]. Both Conservative and Labour governments—in the "fatalistic belief that there never can be more employment than there is," as Keynes said ["**Mr. J. M. Keynes Examines Mr. Lloyd George's Pledge,**" *Evening Standard,* March 19, 1929]—sat tight over the twenties and thirties, instructed by the civil servants of the treasury school whom he once characterized as "trained by tradition and experience and native skill to every form of intelligent obstruction" ["**Democracy and Efficiency**" (interview with Kingsley Martin), *New Statesman and Nation,* January 28, 1939].

Keynes instead was ready with ideas—ideas of his own, and the current ideas of others that he made his own—and ready with recipes for trying them. They were practical, inventive solutions—such as his proposal to use legislation, originally framed to permit the government to stockpile war materials, for the additional purpose of minimizing price fluctuations. Characteristically, the proposal might be presented as a three-, four-, five-, or more point agenda. He explored alternatives, giving what he considered the preferred order of adoption. Often he tied up a package deal; he was always happy if he could pick off two birds with one stone and get in a little social benefit while solving an economic problem. He was always ready to commit himself to definite figures—unkind persons said that he made them up. Other people say that he was very good at making them up, and that he had a sense, a feel, for what the right figure ought to be. In any case, he cannot be blamed entirely for making up figures, for well into the 1920s there was a great scarcity of economically relevant statistics; it was Keynes who laid the foundations for providing this branch of economic information in Britain.

In doling out his economic prescriptions Keynes's style was to make a direct appeal to action—to governments, to heads of state (as in his "**Agenda for President Roosevelt**") or to individual citizens. Often it was an appeal for internationally concerted action. At the planning stage of the World Economic Conference of 1933, he urged all governments *simultaneously* to adopt programs of public spending, supported by gold certificates issued by the Bank for International Settlements, to restore world prosperity. "What is the charm to awaken the Sleeping Beauty, to scale the mountain of glass without slipping? If every Treasury were to discover in its vaults a large *cache* of gold . . . would that not work the charm? Why should not that *cache* be devised? We have long printed gold nationally. Why should we not print it internationally? No reason in the world, unless our hands are palsied and our wits dull" ["**The World Economic Conference, 1933**," *New Statesman and Nation*, December 24, 1932].

This call to action is typically phrased. As Keynes himself said: "Words ought to be a little wild—for they are the assault of thoughts upon the unthinking" ["**National Self-Sufficiency**," *New Statesman and Nation*, July 15, 1933]. Talking on the radio about unemployment in 1931, he hazarded the guess that whenever you saved five shillings you put a man out of work for a day; on the other hand, whenever you bought goods you increased employment. "Therefore, Oh patriotic housewives," he paeoned, "sally out tomorrow early into the streets and go to the wonderful sales which are everywhere advertised. You will do yourselves good—for never were things so cheap, cheap beyond your dreams. Lay in a stock of household linen, of sheets and blankets to satisfy your needs. And have the added joy that you are increasing employment, adding to the wealth of the country because you are setting on foot useful activities, bringing a chance and a hope to Lancashire, Yorkshire, and Belfast" ["**The Problem of Unemployment**" (broadcast talk), *Listener*, January 14, 1931].

I have not consulted the contemporary newspapers to learn whether this appeal showed up in the department stores' takings in the January sales, but one result is recorded—the cartoonists had a field day depicting the middle-class "little woman" sallying forth on a spending spree, loading up hubby with parcels and saddling it all on Mr. Keynes. Were these words a little too wild? In a radio discussion two years later, Keynes was careful to explain the difference between hoarding and *useful* saving ["**Saving and Spending**" (broadcast discussion with Sir Josiah Stamp), *Listener*, January 11, 1933].

But I should give you the rest of the quotation about words. Keynes finished it by adding, "When the seats of power and authority have been attained, there should be no more poetic license."

He liked to call for timely action—*now is the time* to buy sheets, to appoint a board, to settle the world's currency system—and he had his favorite words. He was fond of using the phrases "the prospects for" and "the progress of " and the word "consequences" in his titles. He was always ready to present his "drastic remedy" or his "radical plan" or to approve a "bold measure"—he fancied himself as the *enfant terrible*. He was optimistic—where others saw the beginning of a long industrial decline, he felt the country was "in the middle of a painful adjustment" ["**Investments Abroad**" (letter), *Times*, (London), March 13, 1930]. Addressing international delegates to a meeting of the National Council of Women (his mother was president) in June 1930, he explained that England was suffering "from a sort of *malaise* of wealth"—saving money faster than she was spending it, economizing on the use of labor faster than finding outlets for it, raising the standard of living a little too fast—and he described these phenomena as "the growing pains of progress, not the rheumatism of old age" ["**The Prosperity of England. Mr. Keynes's Reassuring Picture**," *Manchester Guardian*, June 18, 1930].

On this occasion, he talked of England's social achievements, in which he took pride. He had a strong vein of patriotism, in spite of his internationalism during the twenties. He was perpetually fussing about the possibility that British lending abroad was diverting funds from investment in home industry. (Was he, subconsciously, like the colonel in "Dr. Strangelove," worrying about the sapping of "precious bodily fluids"?) He did not want to see his country become a rentier nation and miss out on the action, he had his own ideas about how Britain should honor her debts before devaluation, and he looked to her to take the initiative and leadership in all his international proposals.

He enthusiastically supported any leader whom he thought could make the running. After the terrible things he had said about Lloyd George, that goat-footed Welsh Witch, in connection with the Treaty of Versailles, he supported him vigorously in the election of 1929 and wrote the pamphlet that became the textbook of the Liberal campaign. When taxed with what he had said about Lloyd George's conduct of the coupon election, he replied: "I oppose Mr. Lloyd George when he is wrong; I support him when he is right." It was the same with Winston Churchill. And in December 1930 Keynes commended the enterprising spirit of Sir Oswald Mosley in putting forward a national economic plan ["**Sir Oswald Mosley's Manifesto**," *Nation and Athenaeum*, December 13, 1930], but he did not write about Mosley after that.

He was flexible. Having, after much thought, deserted free trade to recommend a revenue tariff with all his might, the moment that England left the gold standard and made such a tariff economically unnecessary, he dashed off a letter to the London *Times* calling attention to the now primary importance of devising a sound international currency system; the discussion of domestic protection should wait until later, he said ["**After the Suspension of Gold**," *Times* (London), September 29, 1931]. And, as the rest of the country breathed a half-sigh of relief after painfully climbing out of the slump, he looked ahead in two *Times* articles to ask how to avoid a future occurrence of such a situation ["**How to Avoid a Slump**," *Times* (London), January 12 and 13, 1937].

Flexibility—or inconsistency? "Inconsistency" was the word that he was branded with. When he was attacked for coming over from free trade to a revenue tariff, he lampooned his critics:

> I seem to see the elder parrots sitting round and saying: "You can *rely* upon us." Every day for 30 years, regardless of the weather, we have said, "What a lovely morning!" But this is a bad bird. He says one thing one day and something else the next ["**Economic Notes on Free Trade II. A Revenue Tariff and the Cost of Living**," *New Statesman and Nation*, April 4, 1931].

Even Keynes's critics had to admit that he never tried to pretend when he changed his mind. And he usually explained just why he had done so. But he was not always so flexible. When he was still in his thirties, he was youthfully uncompromising, insisting that the Treaty of Versailles must be revised, unwilling to live with it and accept it as a political necessity. As time went on, he became more amenable to compromise: "My own view is that I want as much as I can get," he wrote of a League of Nations proposal in 1930; "but I do not want to wreck the whole project by asking for more than I can get" ["**The Draft Convention for Financial Assistance by the League of Nations**" (letter), *Nation and Athenaeum,* December 13, 1930]. In the course of time, he even came to tone down—publicly, that is—some of his caustic language. Writing to the literary editor of the *Daily Mail* about some small alterations that he wished to make in an article on England's war debts to America, "chiefly with the object of avoiding strong language," he replaced the phrase, "when one reads the rubbish reported from Congressmen, much of it altogether beneath the intelligence and dignity of human nature," by the much milder observation, "when one reads what Congressmen say to reporters" [unpublished letter to R. J. Frew, Keynes Papers, Marshall Library, Cambridge University, December 10, 1932].

Between the two wars he was very visible, energetic, and vigorous on the surface of English political life. Articles, pamphlets, and books appeared perfectly timed for the opening of a conference, the preparation of the Budget— or perhaps the preparation of the public for the inevitable economic consequences of some past decision or event. The political pamphlets were priced at 6d. and 1/-; *The General Theory* sold for 5/-. Margot Asquith objected to the publication of the article on the American debts in the *Daily Mail:* "You sd. have sent it to the *Times,* as those who read the *Daily Mail* are mostly in the Servants Hall (I never take it in)" [unpublished letter, Keynes Papers, Harshall Library, Cambridge University, January 2, 1933]. He was careful to send his articles, punctiliously presented, to the London *Times,* the *Manchester Guardian,* the *Nation,* and the *New Statesman;* at the same time, he never missed an opportunity to publish the same material in more swashbuckling form in the *Daily Mail,* the *Daily Express,* and the *Evening Standard.*

But as with every real politician, nine-tenths of the iceberg was invisible. Only the small group of those in the know could have been aware of his leadership in 1920 in organizing an appeal to the League of Nations for an international loan and also the first international conference of economic experts in Brussels—civil servants, not politicians; his part in the thinking and research which went into the Yellow Book that reviewed and restated the objects and aspirations of the ailing Liberal party; the questioning that led to his adoption of the revenue tariff policy in the behind-doors Economic Advisory Committee, months before he expressed this change of heart in public; his crucial dominance of the Macmillan Committee of Inquiry into Finance and Industry. And just like every practicing politician, he maintained contact with an extensive network of influential friends and acquaintances to whom he could go for help if necessary, because they would do the same with him. His correspondence files are almost a *Who's Who* for an era—not only in the fields of economics and politics, but also in society, literature, and art. The day that he surfaced and was observed lunching alone with Ramsay MacDonald, the stock market rose.

All these characteristics show Keynes as a natural born

and highly efficient, ever alert politician. With his Eton Pop, Cambridge Union background, he was born to the purple, if this was what he wanted. Yet he insisted that politics was not his role, that he was more valuable in his chosen capacity as adviser. It was a case of emotion versus intellect; some of his contemporaries thought of him as an emotionless, coldly logical machine. Writing of Lloyd George's political craft with introspection into his own personality clearly in mind, he remarked: "A preference for truth or for sincerity *as a method* may be a prejudice based on some aesthetic or personal standard, inconsistent, in politics, with practical good" [*A Revision of the Treaty;* also in *Essays in Persuasion*]. In middle age, he was able to write, "I still suffer incurably from attributing an unreal rationality to other people's feelings and behaviour (and doubtless to my own, too)" ["**My Early Beliefs,**" in *Two Memoirs*]. His radical approach—"The Republic of my imagination lies on the extreme left of celestial space" ["**Liberalism and Labour,**" in *Essays in Persuasion*]—seemed to destine him for the Labour rather than the Liberal camp, but he shied away from Labour dogmatism and anti-intellectualism. To proclaim any dogma as infallible and applicable in all cases, he said, debating the merits of the two parties, was "voluntarily to shut oneself out from any scientific approach to economic problems by means of experiment and investigation" [Report of Liberal Summer School Debate with Tom Johnston, M.P., *Manchester Guardian,* August 4, 1928]. Also, the Labour party was a class party, Keynes said, "and the class is not my class. . . . the *class* war will find me on the side of the educated *bourgeoisie*" ["**Am I a Liberal?**" in *Essays in Persuasion*].

In considering Keynes, one can never forget his social background. The son of cultivated, thrifty, donnish parents—nonconformist in outlook though apparently not overtly religious—brought up at the close of the nineteenth century in comfortable middle-class Cambridge, polished and finished at Eton and King's, and sophisticated by Bloomsbury and the high-ranking civil service, making and losing a fortune and reestablishing himself again before he was 40—these were personal experiences that made him what he was. The man had a confidence, springing partly from his parents' established place in Cambridge society but more powerfully from the consciousness of his own intellect which won him an even more exalted place in the outside world before he was 35.

As the son of his philosopher father and socially conscious mother, he sought in politics a party that in the changing conditions of the time would create a society both economically just and economically efficient, while still preserving individual liberty. He stayed with the Liberals, the party of his parents, by standing intellectually outside of it, despite his campaigning and committee work and participation in summer schools. From his parents he inherited the late Victorian nonconformist belief in the necessity and possibility of the improvement of society by the application of reason and the sense of obligation to one's social inferiors that went with it. (The same attitudes appear in the Fabianism of the Webbs, but Keynes seems to have regarded the Webbs as a little naïve.)

Large-scale unemployment was the basic problem that Keynes came to focus on. His received view of the world was of a society in which each man had his appointed place, and it was an injustice for him not to be allowed to feed his family and retain his self-respect in fulfilling the task ordained for him. Economic theory then taught the belief that if there were not enough jobs, the laboring force would divide up the supply of work, driving down wages in the process—a hardship to the worker and no challenge to the employer to make himself more efficient, Keynes said. His solution, when he wrote **"The Question of High Wages"** in 1930 [*Political Quarterly* 1 (January 1930)], was to increase the workers' real wages by providing social services. He told a story about the little girl who, asked if the poor should be made like the rich, replied, "No, it would spoil their characters" [**"Mr. Keynes's Lecture"** (letter), *Manchester Guardian,* November 19, 1929]. The story was offered tongue-in-cheek, but does one detect the social worker's instincts of his mother?

An achievement that gave Keynes great satisfaction was his wartime scheme for compulsory savings or, as he later chose to call it, "deferred pay." He considered that he had made it "outrageously attractive" to the working class [Report of Talk to the Fabian Society, Keynes Papers, Marshall Library, Cambridge University, February 21, 1940], although the working class seems to have been singularly unenthusiastic about it. He regarded it, characteristically, not just as an expedient for financing the war, but as an opportunity to demonstrate the difference between the totalitarian and the free economy. "For if the community's aggregate rate of spending can be regulated, the way in which personal incomes are spent and the means by which demand is satisfied can be safely left free and individual . . . the only way to avoid the destruction of choice and initiative, whether by consumers or by producers, through the complex tyranny of all-round rationing. . . . This is the one kind of compulsion of which the effect is to enlarge liberty. Those who, entangled in the old unserviceable maxims, fail to see this further-reaching objective have not grasped, to speak American, the big idea" [**"Mr. Keynes's Plan, Control of Boom and Slump"** (letter), *Times* (London), April 10, 1940].

Toward the end of *How to Pay for the War,* he sums up the scheme as "the perfect opportunity for social action where everyone can be protected by making a certain rule of behavior universal." It is economically just, it is economically efficient—and the smell is undeniably paternalistic. Keynes grappled with the problems of the twentieth century, but he was born in a big house in Harvey Road, Cambridge, in 1883, and he never really extricated himself from the view of society, and his own position therein, in which his parents had reared him.

Unemployment was a problem that according to orthodox theory should not exist, but it was the problem that would not go away. He grappled with it with a moral indignation and persistency that conjures up the spirit of another great grappler, John Bunyan, the subject of a biography by Keynes's maternal grandfather, the nonconformist minister, John Brown. "Is not the mere existence of general unemployment for any length of time an absurdity, a confes-

sion of failure, and a hopeless and inexcusable breakdown of the economic machine?" Keynes demanded in a radio dialogue with Sir Josiah Stamp. Stamp, so addressed, observed: "Your language is rather violent. You would not expect to put an earthquake tidy in a few minutes, would you?" [**"Unemployment,"** *Listener,* February 26, 1930].

It took the years from 1923 to 1936 for Keynes to tidy up the theory of the earthquake. In an address on the occasion of the centenary of the death of Malthus, Keynes quoted Malthus himself on the relation of experience to theory, distinguishing between that partial or confined experience that a man gains "from the management of his own little farm, or the details of the workhouse in his neighbourhood"—which is "no foundation whatever for a just theory"—and "that general experience, on which alone a just theory can be founded." Keynes claimed for Malthus "an unusual combination of keeping an open mind to the shifting picture of experience and of constantly applying to its interpretation the principles of formal thought" [**"Robert Malthus: Centenary Allocation,"** in *Essays in Biography*]. Here, in his emphasis on constant referral back to the facts, he stated his own ideal of how a social scientist ought to work.

As I have documented earlier in this paper, Keynes behaved from day to day in public like a working politician. In private, he was deeply and seriously concerned with the science of economics. He kept coming back to the central problem that the existing theory would not explain. At first, he was content to dazzle by demonstrating that a fuller knowledge of economic theory and statistics than his professional colleagues possessed would support different conclusions than their understanding of the economic orthodoxy had led them to. But eventually, his intellectual honesty and his concern for economic science brought him to believe that it was not the incompetence of the orthodox economists that was at fault, but the received theory itself. Modifications within the framework of orthodox economics were not enough; a frontal attack on the framework itself was required.

So Keynes produced the *General Theory* as a proof—by the standards of the prevailing economic orthodoxy itself—that, contrary to orthodoxy, the normal state of economic society was not full employment, but general unemployment. As a corollary, government policies to raise the level of employment were not mistaken and arbitrary interferences with a well-functioning and efficient economic machine; instead, government interference was absolutely necessary in order for the machine to work at all. Thus, Keynes behaved as a scientist in the crucial sense: having found the existing body of scientific knowledge in economics increasingly unsatisfactory as a tool for solving the problems that he considered important, he produced a new and rival theory that would explain the discrepancies between the orthodoxy and the facts of observation—discrepancies which formerly had to be explained as special cases.

Recalling Malthus on partial and general experience, how much did Keynes's enthusiasms, his inventiveness, blind his science? One of his early reactions to unemployment was to put it down to overpopulation, a critic accused him of letting his advocacy of birth control affect his conclusions (*New Statesman* 1923). If he was less of a patriot would he perhaps have been so troubled by the idea of foreign lending? If his upbringing had not inclined him to think of foreign food as less wholesome than home grown, or if he had not bought a Sussex farm for himself and invested a lot of his college's money in a large farm estate in Lincolnshire, would he, after he reverted from his 1931 recommendation of a revenue tariff to his lifelong belief in free trade, have made an exception for tariff protection to agriculture? If his father had been a docker, and not a well-to-do academic philosopher, how would he have dealt with unemployment?

Keynes's origins and place in society strongly influenced and limited his scientific thought. There is a passage in *The Economic Consequences of the Peace* where he describes the expectations of a man of his station in pre-1914 society: while he worked on his papers, sipping his morning tea in bed, other people cooked and washed and cleaned, providing all his wants—even if he needed money to travel, he could send his servant to the bank. Keynes assumed, extrapolating from his own experience, that "any man of capacity or character exceeding the average" could attain this position.

In the world as it was then, security and independence were the lot of a few; the housewives whom Keynes urged to go out and buy sheets were middle-class housewives with money in the bank to provide for the future. Yet, in his ideal society, he desired security and independence for everybody. However, he could conceive of it only in terms of his own experience: social happiness was employment for every one, each in his appointed place, his own niche.

Keynes, armed with all the advantages of his upbringing, believed unquestioningly that anyone in England with enough ambition could rise to his proper position in society. Nor did he have any question as to whether it was just for a man who had risen as rapidly as he had to be able to rely so implicitly on the full-time dutiful service of others who did not have those advantages. (What were the thoughts of the servant, who earned perhaps £1 a week, when he was sent to the bank to fetch £10 or £50? Keynes was fortunate if the servant, like himself, did not bother his head about it.) Social injustice existed only in there not being enough jobs to go around. If there were servants with talents or character above their appointed stations, they deserved help, financial or advisory, from their betters; it was the obligation of the employer and ultimately the state to make it up to them in welfare benefits and other social transfers.

So that, although Keynes thought of himself as a radical, one can see that he took a conservative, even an archaic view of society. His "radical" solution of government maternalism has now become the received orthodoxy. Even so, his social philosophy made a great leap forward: he said that it is wrong for a government to expect people to study, work hard, be honest and responsible, in order to fit themselves for a place in a society presumed to be anxious to employ and make good use of them, when in fact the economic policy of that government precludes a large number of its citizens from having an opportunity

for employment and a decent career; government has a responsibility to society to follow an economic policy that will satisfy these expectations.

We are left with two problems that did not trouble Keynes. We still have not solved the problem of equal opportunity, which Keynes took as a matter of course. We do not yet know how to reconcile the boring nature of many jobs with freedom for the human spirit; Keynes, who thought about it in terms that reflected his own social background, looked forward to more automation, less work, and the enrichment of leisure time by cultural activities provided by the state.

In summary, in my judgment, Keynes was a politician, but a politician whose constituency was not electoral but intellectual—he had to be a scientist to be a politician. And he was a good enough scientist, with a strong enough sense of scientific integrity, and a strong enough aesthetic preference for truth, to recognize eventually that the social science he knew was not good enough to solve the problems he recognized as politically important and that he had to reform the science to make it politically relevant and useful. He was a scientific political economist. One can emphasize either the "scientific" or the "political"—and which adjective one emphasizes depends on whether one is writing a political biography of the man himself or a history of economic thought—but both adjectives are appropriate and both are necessary to characterize what the man was and what he contributed to British society and British social history.

D. E. Moggridge (essay date 1976)

SOURCE: "The Economist," in *John Maynard Keynes*, Penguin Books, 1976, pp. 20-41.

[*In the following excerpt, Moggridge describes the general character of Keynes's thought, his method of approaching economic problems, and his views on the making of public policy.*]

Before examining the development of Keynes's economic ideas . . . , one should try to get inside the man and the mind behind the ideas in question—one must become aware of his habits of thought, his methods of working, his views as to the nature of economic inquiry, and the like. Fortunately, although Keynes did not leave behind an autobiography or a treatise on the nature of economic inquiry, his drafts, correspondence, comments on the work of others, and asides provide one with enough clues to begin to catch the flavor of the economist.

Perhaps the best starting point is to look . . . at the intellectual environment from which Keynes emerged—at Cambridge. There was a distinctive characteristic in the work of the founding generation of modern Cambridge economics which many of its successors share. Alfred Marshall, A. C. Pigou, Henry Sidgwick, and Neville Keynes in their work as a whole regarded economics as a moral science. Although they accepted a theoretical distinction between positive and normative arguments, they saw that the two were closely intermingled in practice. Thus Pigou characterized Marshall's development:

"Starting out then with the view that economic science is chiefly valuable, neither as an intellectual gymnastic nor even as a means of winning truths for its own sake, but as a handmaid of ethics and a servant of practice, Marshall resolutely set himself to mould his work along lines conforming to his ideal" [A. C. Pigou, ed., *Memorials of Alfred Marshall*]. Or, as Keynes put it to Harrod in 1938, during the discussion of the latter's presidential address to the Royal Economic Society, "Scope and Method of Economics"—and of Jan Tinbergen's *Statistical Testing of Business Cycle Theories:*

> It seems to me that economics is a branch of logic, a way of thinking; and that you do not repel sufficiently firmly attempts . . . to turn it into a pseudo-natural science. . . .
>
> Economics is a science of thinking in terms of models joined to the art of choosing models which are relevant to the contemporary world. It is compelled to be this, because, unlike the typical natural science, the material to which it is applied is, in too many respects, not homogeneous through time. The object of a model is to segregate the semi-permanent or relatively constant factors from those which are transitory or fluctuating so as to develop a logical way of thinking about the latter. . . .
>
> Good economists are scarce because the gift for using "vigilant observation" to choose good models, although it does not require a highly specialised intellectual technique, appears to be a very rare one.
>
> In the second place, as against Robbins, economics is essentially a moral science and not a natural science. That is to say, it employs introspection and judgements of value. . . .
>
> I also want to emphasise strongly the point about economics being a moral science. I mentioned before that it deals with introspection and with values. I might have added that it deals with motives, expectations, psychological uncertainties. One has to be constantly on one's guard against treating the material as constant and homogeneous. It is as though the fall of the apple to the ground depended on the apple's motives, on whether it is worthwhile falling to the ground, and whether the ground wants the apple to fall, and on mistaken calculations on the part of the apple as to how far it was from the centre of the earth. [**The Collected Writings of John Maynard Keynes** (hereafter cited as *JMK*), XIV, 296-97, 300].

One aspect of the ethical nature of Cambridge economics, both in Marshall's day and later, was a strong commitment to certain practical social ends. Keynes noted it clearly of Marshall in his charming obituary notice (*JMK,* X, 161-231). Pigou observed the same tendencies in Keynes, in terms surprisingly similar to his comment on Marshall twenty-four years earlier.

> Both [Keynes and Marshall] were alike in their single-minded search for truth and also in their desire that the study of Economics should serve, not as a mere intellectual gymnastic, but direct-

ly, or at least indirectly, for the forwarding of human welfare. . . . In his **General Theory** there are some, as I think, unwarranted strictures on parts of Marshall's *Principles*. But that in no wise meant that he had ceased to be a firm disciple of the "Master."

[A. C. Pigou, "The Economist," in *John Maynard Keynes, 1883-1946*]

Other contemporaries of Keynes also remarked repeatedly on Keynes's extremely practical bent as an economist: his dislike of theory for theory's sake, his almost complete absorption in questions of policy. It was this characteristic that lay behind his choice of emphasis in handling theoretical problems in the **General Theory**. As he told J. R. Hicks in June 1935: "I deliberately refrain in my forthcoming book from pursuing anything very far, my object being to press home as forcibly as possible certain fundamental opinions—and no more." In fact, Keynes's ideal economist was in many respects a practical, if right thinking, technician—a dentist, to borrow one of his phrases. In his own work as an economist, Keynes might almost find himself classified as an extraordinary civil servant, using traditional modes of analysis until they broke down and then proceeding to fashion new tools to fill in the gaps—little more. Keynes saw the economist as providing an essential element in the possibility of civilization—a role that echoed Marshall's hopes in his inaugural lecture:

> It will be my most cherished ambition . . . to increase the numbers of those, whom Cambridge, the great mother of strong men, sends out into the world with cool heads but warm hearts, willing to give some at least of their best powers to grappling with the social suffering around them; resolved not to rest content till they have done what in them lies to discover how far it is possible to open up all the material means of a refined and noble life.

[Pigou, ed., *Memorials of Alfred Marshall*]

This practicality colored all of Keynes's working life as an economist. It came out clearly in his comments on the work of others—as a reader of manuscripts for publishers, editor of the *Economic Journal,* unofficial civil servant, or general reader. A typical reply to a possible *Journal* contributor, dated April 1944, runs: "I do not doubt that a serious problem will arise when we have a combination of collective bargaining and full employment. But I am not sure how much light the analytical [economic] method you apply can throw on this essentially political problem." Again, in October 1944, when asked to comment on the idea of "functional finance"—a theoretical attempt to devise a general rule for countercyclical budgetary policy to maintain full employment—he remarked that "functional finance is an idea and not a policy; part of one's apparatus of thought but not, except highly diluted under a considerable clothing of qualification, an apparatus of action. Economists have to be very careful, I think, to distinguish the two." Useful words to consider again after a period when economists have provided us with ideas masquerading as policy in such forms as the Phillips Curve "explaining" the relation between money wage claims and unemployment.

This leads us on to another characteristic of Keynes, one not unexpected in the author of *A Treatise on Probability*. For Keynes, more than most, approached all problems with a mind that attempted to get to the fundamental basis of an argument or a system of ideas. As one Treasury economist-colleague of the World War II period put it in a letter:

> I would say that what dominated his approach to any matter was a philosophy—a habit of mind. He was always ready and eager to make the best possible synthesis of the available data, thence to carry this reasoning where it might lead him and to *offer* (repeat offer) conclusions. But unlike many, he never forgot the fundamental importance of premises and the invalidity of good reasoning on incomplete premises (Propn. 2.21 of [Russell's and Whitehead's *Principia Mathematica*] refers). So while it was usually impossible to attack his reasoning, he was always ready and willing to revise his conclusions if his premises were attacked and could be shown to be wrong or imperfect. He could be pretty difficult in resisting attack, but if it succeeded— never mind whether from the office boy, or the office cat for that matter—he had the tremendous capacity of always being willing to start afresh and re-synthesise. . . . So the continuing value, as it seemed to me, of so much of his work in that time was in provoking critical examination and analysis of the facts of the situation— the premises.

It was Keynes's seriousness concerning assumptions and premises that underlay much of the purpose of the *General Theory*. There, Keynes attacked his "classical" contemporaries, not because they disagreed with him on policy proposals in connection with the slump—in fact, many of them wrote joint letters to *The Times* with him and sat on committees exhibiting a fair degree of unanimity in their reports—but because he believed that their policy recommendations were inconsistent with the premises of the theory they used to explain the situation. One must remember that he singled out Professor L. C. Robbins, the economist with whom he disagreed perhaps most on policy throughout the 1930s, as almost alone among his contemporaries as one whose "practical recommendations belong . . . to the same system as his theory" (*JMK*, VII, 20n). Thus in 1937, after the publication of Pigou's *Socialism versus Capitalism*, Keynes could write to Richard Kahn: "Many thanks for sending me a copy of the Prof's new book. As in the case of Dennis [Robertson], when it comes to practice, there is really extremely little between us. Why do they insist on maintaining theories from which their own practical conclusions cannot possibly follow? It is a sort of Society for the Preservation of Ancient Monuments" (*JMK*, XIV, 259). In the 1930s Keynes believed that this inconsistency between premises and conclusions was a source of weakness in the economists' attempts to influence policy. For, on occasion, it led to unnecessary and unhelpful public controversy that obscured the issues at stake. Thus he attempted to get his professional colleagues to reconsider their premises. . . .

With a knowledge of this aspect of his approach to problems one can understand more fully Keynes's many con-

tributions to public and professional discussion. In *The Economic Consequences of the Peace* (1919) he was questioning the assumptions concerning the nature of the European economic system implicit in the peace treaties following World War I. Similarly, in *The Economic Consequences of Mr. Churchill* (1925) he questioned the authorities' assumptions concerning the international economic position of Britain in 1925 and the mechanism of adjustment to a higher exchange rate following their decision to return to the gold standard at what he believed was an overvalued rate. Again, in his discussion of the early econometric work of economists such as Tinbergen, Keynes, who was not unsympathetic to such work and was at the time founding the Cambridge Department of Applied Economics, turned—as was natural for both Keynes the economist and Keynes the author of *A Treatise on Probability*—to the assumptions and premises of the methodology involved. In fact, perhaps Keynes's great influence as a molder of professional economic and public opinion came from his efforts to set out clearly the implicit assumptions of others for scrutiny rather than to quibble over details.

Despite Keynes's emphasis on the premises of arguments and his care in the development of many of his own ideas—exemplified by the definitional chapters of his *General Theory* which took an immense (indeed, inordinate) amount of his time during 1934-35—it would be very misleading to leave the reader with the picture of a remorseless logician. For Keynes was the most intuitive of men. Moreover, in a series of what must certainly be introspective passages, he recognized the role of intuition in the work of others in the course of his biographical essays on Newton, Malthus, and Marshall (*JMK*, X). The Marshall passage, written in 1924 while he was wrestling with the early drafts of what became *A Treatise on Money* (1930), is perhaps the most useful in this connection:

> But it was an essential truth to which he held firmly that those individuals who are endowed with a special genius for the subject of economics and have a powerful economic intuition will often be more right in their conclusions and implicit presumptions than in their explanations and explicit statements. That is to say, their intuitions will be in advance of their analysis and their terminology. Great respect, therefore, is due to their general scheme of thought, and it is a poor thing to pester their memories with criticism which is purely verbal.

> (*JMK*, X, 211n)

The intuitive nature of Keynes's thought processes comes out clearly at many points in Keynes's work as an economist. Occasionally, in his discussions with possible contributors to the *Economic Journal*, he might make the nature of his thought process explicit and write, "You have not expressed it in a way in which I am able to bring my intuition to bear clearly." Similarly, in the development of his *General Theory* one can see from students' lecture notes, correspondence, and drafts that Keynes had intuitively grasped most of the essentials of his system as early as 1932. However, if there was no doubt about the truth, there was considerable trouble over the proof, and it took another three years of redrafting and discussion to clothe that intuition in what he regarded as a technically adequate form for the purposes at hand. With Keynes intuition represented an early, but essential, stage in the act of creation. Very hard, systematic work then went into developing the scheme of thought for the consumption and persuasion of the world at large.

Believing that intuition normally ran a little way ahead of formal analysis, Keynes naturally expected a considerable amount from his readers. He made his position most clear in a 1934 draft preface for the *General Theory:*

> When we write economic theory, we write in a quasiformal style; and there can be no doubt, in spite of the disadvantages, that this is our best available means of conveying our thoughts to one another. But when an economist writes in a quasi-formal style . . . he never states all his premises and his definitions are not perfectly clear-cut. He never mentions all the qualifications necessary to his conclusions. He has no means of stating, once and for all, the precise level of abstraction on which he is moving, and he does not move on the same level all the time. It is, I think, of the nature of economic exposition that it gives, not a complete statement . . . but a sample statement . . . intended to suggest to the reader the whole bundle of associated ideas, so that, if he catches the bundle, he will not be the least confused or impeded by the technical incompleteness of the mere words. . . .
>
> This means, on the one hand, that an economic writer requires from his reader much goodwill and intelligence and a large measure of co-operation; and, on the other hand, that there are a thousand futile, yet verbally legitimate, objections which an objector can raise. In economics you cannot *convict* your opponent of error—you can only *convince* him of it. And, even if you are right, you cannot convince him, if there is a defect in your own powers of persuasion and exposition or if his head is already so filled with contrary notions that he cannot catch the clues to your thought which you are trying to throw to him.

(JMK, XIII, 469-70)

It was this point of view, a result of Keynes's own habits of thought and work, that explains his unusually fierce reactions to criticism, as on the occasion of Professor F. A. Hayek's review of his *Treatise on Money*. In replying to it, Keynes turned on Hayek's most recent book as follows:

> The reader will perceive that I have been drifting into a review of Dr. Hayek's *Prices and Production*. And this being so, I should like, if the editor will allow me, to consider this book a little further. The book, as it stands, seems to me to be one of the most frightful muddles that I have ever read, with scarcely a sound proposition in it beginning with page 45, and yet it remains a book of some interest, which is likely to leave its mark on the mind of the reader. It is an extraordinary example of how, starting with a mistake, a remorseless logician can end up in Bedlam. Yet Dr. Hayek has seen a vision, and though when

he woke up he has made a nonsense of his story by giving the wrong names to the objects which occur in it, his Khubla [*sic*] Khan is not without inspiration and must set the reader thinking with the germs of an idea in his head.

(JMK, XIII, 252)

When one looks at Keynes's copy of Hayek's review, the most heavily annotated article in the surviving copies of his journals, one finds he wrote at the end: "Hayek has not read my book with that measure of 'goodwill' which an author is entitled to expect of a reader. Until he does so, he will not know what I mean or whether I am right." Perhaps a similar reaction to what he believed to be unsympathetic criticism helped to mar (from Keynes's side) the once pleasant and fruitful relationship between Keynes and D. H. Robertson in the course of the 1930s.

One final consequence of Keynes's habits of thought and working is his use of "the Cambridge didactic style" in presenting his arguments. This was another way in which his writings often followed those of Marshall. When either Keynes or Marshall faced a subtle, but complex problem in pursuing an argument, he would use all the resources at his command to solve it. However, having solved it, rather than taking the reader through the analytical process he had completed, he would provide him with a strategic short cut which would save the reader from considering the problem, yet leave the author's flank protected against possible professional criticism. As Keynes described Marshall's use of the method:

> The lack of emphasis and of strong light and shade, the sedulous rubbing away of rough edges and salients and projections, until what is most novel can appear as trite, allows the reader to pass too easily through. . . . The difficulties are concealed; the most ticklish problems are solved in footnotes; a pregnant and original judgment is dressed up as a platitude. . . . It needs much study and independent thought on the reader's own part before he can know the half of what is contained in the concealed crevices of that rounded globe of knowledge which is Marshall's *Principles of Economics.*

(JMK, X, 212)

Keynes himself, being more willing to "fling pamphlets to the wind" and "trust in the efficacy of the co-operation of many minds," was, perhaps, less of a master of the "style" than Marshall, but it is always there to trap the unwary in his more formal writings.

So far, I have concentrated on Keynes's mental processes—his habits of thought and his characteristic methods of attacking problems. However, one cannot understand Keynes's work completely without some reference to his views on how government policies were made in Britain and on the appropriate types of policy. With his emphasis on the practical, his almost desperate desire to influence policy, and his numerous attempts to persuade policymakers (both privately and publicly), they are vital for an appreciation of his work as an economist.

As a day-to-day working economist, looking out on the

world of his age, Keynes was very much the rationalist—perhaps too much so. His career represented a constant campaign bristling with moral indignation at the harm perpetrated by "madmen in authority," "lunatics" (a very common word in his vocabulary), and others who acted according to prejudice and rules of thumb rather than according to reason carefully applied to an evolving situation—whether in making peace treaties, exchange rate decisions, unemployment policy, or mundane administrative decisions. His assessment of Beaumont Pease, chairman of Lloyds Bank, in 1924 is characteristic:

> Mr. Pease . . . deprecates thinking, or—as he prefers to call it—"the expenditure of mental agility." He desires "straightly to face the facts instead of to find a clever way round them," and holds that, in matters arising out of the quantity theory of money, as between brains and character, "certainly the latter does not come second in order of merit." In short, the gold standard falls within the sphere of morals or of religion, where free thought is out of place.
>
> (*JMK*, IX, 188-89).

Similarly he wrote to the Chancellor of the Exchequer in February 1944 concerning the Bank of England's opposition to the proposals for what would become the International Monetary Fund:

> The Bank is not facing any of the realities. They do not allow for the fact that our post-war domestic policies are impossible without further American assistance. They do not allow for the fact that the Americans are strong enough to offer inducements to many or most of our friends to walk out on us, if we ostentatiously set out to start up an independent shop. They do not allow for the fact that vast debts and exiguous reserves are not, by themselves, the best qualifications for renewing old-time international banking.
>
> Great misfortunes are not always avoided, even when there is no difficulty in foreseeing them, as we have learnt through bitter experience. I feel great anxiety that, unless a decisive decision is taken to the contrary and we move with no uncertain steps along the other path, the Bank will contrive to lead us, in new disguises, along much the same path as that which ended in 1931. That is to say, reckless gambling in the shape of assuming banking undertakings beyond what we have any means to support as soon as anything goes wrong, coupled with a policy, conceived in the interests of the old financial traditions, which pays no regard to the inescapable requirements of domestic policies. Ministers should realise that these things . . . are what the trouble is all about.

Keynes always believed that "a little clear thinking" or "more lucidity" could solve almost any problem. Throughout his career, he used every available means to achieve it, and his methods reflected his conception of the policy process and of the forces shaping public opinion. In addition, he always carried with him what Harrod calls "the presuppositions of Harvey Road" [R. Harrod, *The Life of John Maynard Keynes*]—those of his youth—including the following: reform was achieved by the discussion of intelligent people; public opinion must be wisely guided; the government of Britain would be in the hands of an intellectual aristocracy using the method of persuasion.

In Keynes's view, the political elite of civil servants, politicians, important journalists, and the like was open to two influences—rational persuasion and public opinion. As Keynes saw it, the elite played a dual role: not only was it privy to its own "inner opinion" but it also formed part of the "outside opinion" expressed in public speeches, newspapers, and other forms of public comment. Through its links with "outside opinion," the elite could, and in Keynes's view should, influence the public in general and prevent too large a gap emerging between the inner and outer opinions on any event. Keynes also saw the force of changing economic events as perhaps the most important other long-run determinant of opinion among the public at large. In his view, persuasion could lead to an articulation of this outside opinion, as well as alter inner opinion. Thus Keynes, in his impatience to short cut normal long-run tendencies and influence events in the direction he desired, saw his exercises in persuasion as performing a dual role. For they would remove and undermine old prejudices, highlight likely trends, and generally prepare the ground among the public at large, so that the elite, once persuaded, could lead rather than follow, guide rather than obfuscate. If the elite did not do so, Keynes could be rather bitter. In 1940, during his campaign for stronger wartime anti-inflationary measures, he remarked to Reginald McKenna, an old fellow campaigner:

> In truth the trouble is not with public opinion at all. The public are ready for anything and as good as gold. It is the bloody politicians whose bloody minds have not been sufficiently prepared for anything unfamiliar to their ancestors. If the thing were to be sponsored and put across with responsible leadership, there would be practically no opposition at all.
>
> Since my *Times* articles [the early version of **How to Pay for the War**] I have appreciably revised my proposals, and indeed made them a good deal more palatable to Labour. Last week I had discussions both with the Labour Front Bench and with the T.U.C. [Trades Union Congress], and enjoyed the latter particularly. What, if anything, will come of it all I do not know. Nothing, I should rather expect, until after a lag. But the public mind, judging from my fairly voluminous correspondence and discussions I have had in various groups, has made quite gigantic progress in the last two months, and in two or three months more, or at the worst six months, the fruit may be ripe on the bough.

In Keynes's view of the policy process, private meetings with ministers, M.P.s and officials, broadcasts, and articles in *The Daily Mirror* all had their part to play.

In his efforts at persuasion, particularly in the case of the inner opinion, Keynes had great faith in rationality. He believed that individuals could rationally appreciate the appropriateness of a line of policy. Proper persuasion could wear down prejudices and inhibitions and open previously unexploited areas for choice. After all, wasn't that Keynes's experience with the 1919 peace treaties and later with the gold standard? Thus Keynes could write to T. S. Eliot in 1945 on the possibilities of a successful policy of full employment: "It may turn out I suppose, that vested interests and personal selfishness may stand in the way. But the main task is producing first the intellectual conviction and then intellectually to devise the means. Insufficiency of cleverness, not of goodness, is the main trouble. And even resistance to change as such may have many motives besides selfishness." This credo, plus his own faith in his personal powers of persuasion, provides an essential clue to many aspects of Keynes's behavior as an economist. For example, it certainly gave rise to his faith in the possibilities of active economic management, and from the 1920s often made him its most optimistic advocate. It also lay behind his approach to the 1945 American Loan negotiations—his belief that the Americans, on the basis of his masterly exposition of the case, would see (as had the British Treasury and cabinet) the sense of justice, as he called it, and offer Britain a large gift to ease the transition to peacetime conditions in the interests of the postwar world. (Characteristically, when he found his premises concerning American opinion to be untrue, he changed his ground quickly and experienced much subsequent difficulty in persuading the Treasury and the cabinet to adapt to his new appreciation of the situation.) Possibly, it also lurked behind his frequently expressed, if rather naïve, view that a rational appreciation of the situation would very often lead to a single policy proving acceptable to opinion generally. Overtones of this point of view abound in his papers and published work, other than his *Tract on Monetary Reform* (1923), where he was prepared to be more catholic in his allowance for divergences in opinion. However, toward the end of his life, Keynes at times accepted that his presumption of rationality, with its consequential effects on his approach to the policy process, was another reflection of his early beliefs as an Apostle and member of Bloomsbury. As he told the memoir club in 1938:

> As cause and consequence of our general state of mind—when young we completely misunderstood human nature, including our own. The rationality which we attributed to it led to a superficiality, not only of judgment, but also of feeling. . . . I still suffer incurably from attributing an unreal rationality to other people's feeling and behaviour (and doubtless to my own, too). There is one small but extraordinarily silly manifestation of this absurd idea of what is "normal," namely the impulse to *protest*—to write a letter to *The Times,* call a meeting in the Guildhall, subscribe to some fund when my presuppositions as to what is "normal" are not fulfilled. I behave as if there really existed some authority or standard to which I can successfully appeal if I shout loud enough—perhaps it is some hereditary vestige of a belief in the efficacy of prayer.

> (*JMK,* X, 448)

But Keynes did not espouse causes merely because he was opposed to stupidity and error and wanted to increase the scope for rationality in public affairs. He clearly had a con-

ception of a desirable society. Unlike some of his predecessors, such as W.S. Jevons or Marshall who made some attempt to study and understand the lives of ordinary people and had decided to pursue political economy as a result of what they had learned, Keynes's conception of the desirable society was based much less on widespread observation and experience. In fact, there is no record in Keynes's case of any such observation or attempt to understand the lives of ordinary men and women beyond his strong interest in the agricultural workers on his college's estates after 1928. Although he certainly wished to improve the lives of ordinary people, Keynes's approach to the problem of doing so had its roots in the attitudes and experiences of his childhood and of Bloomsbury—in a strong but more abstractly based moral commitment to remove stupidity, waste, and absurdities. This may partially explain his greater interest in what one might call the problems of macro reform rather than those of micro reform. There is no indication that as an undergraduate or in the years immediately afterward he took any great interest in the questions of social reform that were then the subject of extensive public debate. Moreover, in the 1920s, in his attempt to change Liberal party policies, his reference to social questions centered on what he referred to as "sex questions"—"birth control and the use of contraceptives, marriage laws, the treatment of sexual offences and abnormalities, the economic position of women, the economic position of the family" (*JMK,* IX, 302-303). These perhaps had rather more to do with Bloomsbury than anything else. Finally, during World War II, his involvement with the Beveridge proposals for social insurance and allied services which set the pattern for the postwar welfare state in Britain was primarily limited to that of a good Treasury man concerned with the financial implications of the scheme and attempting to trim it down where politically easiest. Nonetheless, despite its basis, Keynes's view of the good society has proved remarkably influential.

Keynes was, for want of a better word, a "neoliberal," perhaps one of the earliest. By his own admission, Keynes lay at the "liberal socialist" end of the broad spectrum of political and social thought that runs to Ludwig von Mises and Hayek and successors such as Milton Friedman at the other. From the beginning, Keynes had rejected *laissez faire* in its dogmatic form, probably more completely than had Marshall and Pigou before him. From the beginning, he emphasized the essential fragility of the economic order which others took to be natural and automatic and emphasized the need for conscious management. Thus in *Indian Currency and Finance* (1913) he noted: "The time may not be far distant when Europe, having perfected her mechanism of exchange on the basis of the gold standard, will find it possible to regulate her standard of value on a more rational and stable basis. It is not likely that we shall leave permanently the most intimate adjustments of our economic organism at the mercy of a lucky prospector, a new chemical process, or a change of ideas in Asia."

From the mid-1920s, Keynes went further and actively developed a clear "social and political philosophy." Then, in a series of essays and speeches, largely designed to shift the Liberal party from the issues that had concerned it before

1914 to ones more suited to the postwar world, he provided a statement of his political and social creed, which, with minor amendments, was to last him for the rest of his life. Along with other essays, they clearly demonstrate that he was an extremely bad "party man," who used political parties as vehicles for his ideas and detached himself from them when they proved unhelpful. These essays also demonstrate that he regarded contemporary capitalism as a necessary, but not permanent, evil—a system which, although ugly, delivered the goods (except for a period in the 1930s) reasonably efficiently, safely channeled potentially disruptive energies into less harmful channels, and, owing to the role of convention in human affairs, capable of considerable reform without affecting its longer-term performance in accumulating the capital necessary to "solve" the economic problem. At all times, capitalism was a means, albeit a morally distasteful one, to an end, and Keynes did not believe that "there is an economic improvement for which revolution is a necessary instrument" (*JMK,* IX, 267). In the organization and management or contemporary capitalism, he saw the areas for state intervention or action, the agenda of government, as pragmatically chosen. For Keynes, the optimistic rationalist with "the presuppositions of Harvey Road," had no fear of bureaucrats and officials, provided they all held the appropriate moral outlook. As he wrote to Hayek in June 1944 on reading the latter's *Road to Serfdom:*

> I should say that what we want is not no planning, or even less planning, indeed I should say that we almost certainly want more. But the planning should take place in a community in which as many people as possible, both leaders and followers, wholly share your own liberal moral position. Moderate planning will be safe if those carrying it out are rightly orientated in their own minds and hearts to the moral issue. . . .
>
> What we need, therefore, in my opinion, is not a change in our economic programmes, which would only lead in practice to disillusion with the results of your philosophy; but perhaps even the contrary, namely, an enlargement of them. . . . I accuse you of perhaps confusing a little bit the moral and the material issues. Dangerous acts can be done safely in a community which thinks and feels rightly, which would be the way to hell if they were executed by those who think and feel wrongly.

Keynes briefly summed up his political creed for *The New Statesman* in 1939:

> The question is whether we are prepared to move out of the nineteenth century *laissez faire* state into an era of liberal socialism, by which I mean a system where we can act as an organised community for common purposes and to promote social and economic justice, whilst respecting and protecting the individual—his freedom of choice, his faith, his mind and its expression, his enterprise and his property.

It was from this position that Keynes was prepared to experiment with his, perhaps, over-optimistic view of the powers of persuasion, to release men from the yoke of drudgery and privation, to allow and encourage them to enjoy the finer things of life, both material and spiritual, and to prepare the world for "the economic possibilities for our grandchildren" when "we shall once more value ends above means and prefer the good to the useful." Thus it is not surprising that he should use a radio talk **"Art and the State"** to propose a massive program of public works to make the south bank of the Thames, from County Hall to Greenwich, "the equal of St. James's Park and its surroundings" or that he should take the Arts Council so seriously. Keynes always wanted to put and keep the economic problem in perspective, behind other matters of greater and more permanent significance.

Richard Kahn   (essay date 1978)

SOURCE: "Some Aspects of the Development Keynes's Thought," in *The Journal of Economic Literature*, Vol. XVI, No. 2, June, 1978, pp. 545-59.

[*In the following excerpt, Kahn examines Keynes's changing attitudes towards the quantity theory of money, as revealed in* A Tract on Monetary Reform, A Treatise on Money, *and the* General Theory. *The critic also discusses Keynes's views on the behavior of money wages and the causes of inflation.*]

In this brief essay I have picked out certain particular strands of thought, on the basis partly of theoretical significance and partly of relationship to economic policy.

Monetary economics is in a state of shameful confusion. One example is the common failure to distinguish between "crowding out" in a physical sense and in a financial sense. At a time when labor bottlenecks and scarcity of productive equipment are wide-spread, the doctrine is a matter of common sense. In the financial sense it takes us back to the notorious "Treasury view" of 1929—that if more saving is devoted to one purpose, less is available for other purposes, so that it is impossible to reduce unemployment by trying to increase investment. What is completely overlooked is Keynes's discovery that—when, as at the present time, there is plenty of surplus labor and equipment—an increase of investment results in an equal increase in saving.

Then there is the severe controversy between monetarists and Keynesians; likewise there is the controversy whether a reduction in real wages is required to reduce unemployment.

The word "Keynes" has become a term of abuse. It seems worthwhile to go back and enquire what Keynes actually thought and wrote, at the expense of adding yet one more (necessarily brief) to the many published surveys, of which Professor Don Patinkin's is a good example.

Keynes was born on 5 June 1883. He published **The Tract on Monetary Reform** in 1923 at the age of 40; the **Treatise on Money** in 1930 at the age of 47; and the **General Theory of Employment, Interest and Money** at the age of 50. It had been a long and painful process of escape from traditional economics.

In his popular writings Keynes was well ahead of his serious books. ***Can Lloyd George Do It?*** by Keynes and Hubert Henderson, published in 1929, is based, in essence, on Keynes's ideas about the main cause of unemployment and the character of the remedy. But it lacked a complete theoretical foundation. For example, he noted that one of the resources that can enable new investment to provide a net addition to the amount of employment "comes from the savings which now run to waste through lack of adequate credit." Some years were to elapse before Keynes realized that in this sense savings do not "run to waste," but are not made.

The gradual change in Keynes's attitude towards the Quantity Theory of Money illustrates the development of his thought. Irving Fisher is regarded as the great codifier of the Theory, in his *Purchasing Power of Money.* He did not however, do more than express the truism in its well-known algebraic form. The character of any causation is not apparent. Keynes, in his *Tract,* states that "his exposition follows the general lines of Professor Pigou and Dr. Marshall rather than the perhaps more familiar analysis of Professor Irving Fisher." There is more in this than the formal difference between expressing the theory in terms of the velocity of circulation of money and the value of the transactions that take place in the course, say, of a year, and in terms of the stock of money and the stock of money expressed in real value.

> Marshall had pointed out that: changes in the rapidity of circulation of money are themselves incidental to changes in the amount of ready purchasing power which the people of a country find it advantageous to keep in their own holding. This amount is governed by causes, the chief of which can be seen with but little trouble.

But

> This "Quantity doctrine" is helpful as far as it goes: but it does not indicate what are the "other things" which must be assumed to be equal in order to justify the proposition: and it does not explain the causes which govern "rapidity of circulation." It is almost a truism.

Pigou codified Marshall in the form of his "Cambridge equation," which expresses the relation between the stock of money and the stock of money expressed in real terms. He emphasized at the outset that there was no "fundamental disagreement [between him and Irving Fisher] about the real causes at work" ["The Value of Money," *Quarterly Journal of Economics,* Vol. 32, November, 1917]. Later in the article, however, he wrote of his presentation:

> It focusses attention on the proportion of their resources that people choose to keep in the form of titles to legal tender instead of focussing in on "velocity of circulation." This fact gives it, as I think, a real advantage, because it brings us at once into relation with volition—an ultimate cause of demand—instead of with something that seems at first sight accidental and arbitrary.

According to this view, the causative process takes the form of decisions as to the amount of wealth that individuals, as a whole, wish to hold in the form of money. Given the quantity of money, the price-level has to accommodate these decisions.

In the *Tract,* Keynes is at one point as orthodox on the subject of the Quantity Theory as an earlier economist, and more orthodox than many. He had been encouraged to become an economist by Alfred Marshall, whom he knew well, as a result of Marshall's friendship with his father, the Cambridge logician and economist who wrote the *Scope and Method of Political Economy.* But Keynes was far more strictly monetarist than Marshall and Pigou.

The Quantity Theory he said was "fundamental. Its correspondence with fact is not open to question." He quoted a saying of Goschen's, of sixty years earlier—it could with much more justification be repeated today—that "there are many persons who cannot bear the relation of the level of prices to the volume of currency affirmed without a feeling akin to irritation." Keynes in 1923 shared Goschen's contempt for such Philistines.

And yet a few pages further on Keynes denied the validity of the Quantity Theory, in the form in which it is normally presented, except "in *the long run,* in which we are all dead." A change in the quantity of money, in a period shorter than that long run, is itself the cause of a change in the ratio of the quantity of money to the price-level.

Six months after the *Tract* was published, Keynes started work in July 1924 on a new book, which six years later was to be published in two volumes under the title of ***A Treatise on Money.*** The Quantity Theory of Money continued for a time to dominate his thinking, although the part played by investment in working capital began to assume an important role.

It was at this stage that Dennis Robertson was working on his *Banking Policy and the Price Level.* Already in November 1915, in his preface to his book on *Industrial Fluctuations,* Robertson wrote that the war had "compelled clear thinking on the real nature of saving and investment in the most unlikely quarters."

In a letter addressed to Robertson after the publication of his ***General Theory,*** Keynes wrote: "I certainly date all my emancipation from the discussions between us which preceded your *Banking Policy and the Price Level.*" As Professor Sir Austin Robinson put it in his obituary of Keynes, *Banking Policy and the Price Level* was the first book "to bring home to us in Cambridge . . . the essential distinction between the act of saving and the act of investment" ["John Maynard Keynes, 1883-1946," *Economic Journal,* Vol. 57, March, 1947]. In his introduction Robertson wrote of his discussions with Keynes: "Neither of us now know how much of the ideas contained [in chapters V and VI] is his and how much is mine." Keynes, in his preface to his ***Treatise,*** refers to the "penetrating light cast by Mr. D. H. Robertson on certain fundamental matters."

In 1926 Keynes was hoping that his new book would be published in 1927. It was not published until 1930.

Keynes's long struggle over a period of six years to produce a version of the ***Treatise*** worthy of publication was directed partly to an escape from the stranglehold of the

Quantity Theory of Money in its crude form. In the end Keynes was able to write that "the forms of the quantity theory . . . on which we have all been brought up . . . are but ill adapted" for the purpose of exhibiting "the causal process by which the price level is determined. . . . They do not, any of them, have the advantage of separating out those factors through which . . . the causal process actually operates during a period of change."

Five pages further on, Keynes wrote that the conclusions that he drew from his Fundamental Equations

> are, of course, obvious and may serve to remind us that all these equations are purely formal; they are mere identities; truisms which tell us nothing in themselves. In this respect they resemble *all other versions of the quantity theory of money*. Their only point is to analyse and arrange our material in what will turn out to be a useful way for tracing cause and effect, when we have vitalised them by the introduction of extraneous facts from the actual world. [italics added]

Keynes seems to have been so much under the spell of the Quantity Theory that he could write about his Fundamental Equations as though they were "versions" of the Quantity Theory; although, up to this point in his book, the quantity of money does not figure in them in any sense.

Seven pages further on, Keynes attempted a reconciliation with the Quantity Theory. It was not successful. But in it can be seen the seed of what in the *General Theory* was to flourish under the name of the Liquidity Preference Theory. This Theory explained how the quantity of money exercises a causative influence by helping to determine the rate of interest—or more generally, as we would put it now, the state of credit and the price levels of securities, both fixed-interest and equities.

And yet, another three pages on Keynes insisted on a symbolic presentation, which must to most readers of the time have appeared to have been a reaffirmation of the Quantity Theory in its simple form.

Later on in the book, Keynes was more explicit. He wrote that under equilibrium conditions "the quantity of money available for the Industrial Circulation *does* (if habits and methods are unchanged) rule the situation. Equilibrium conditions prevail *'when the price-level is in equilibrium with the cost of production.'* " In the section of the book from which I am now quoting, the *modus operandi* of price determination ceases to be the conventional determination by the quantity of money only when equilibrium is disturbed as a result of the rate of physical investment failing to match thriftiness. And yet much earlier in the book, the Fundamental Equations indicated that the price level under conditions of equilibrium is determined by money costs of production per unit of output. There is a serious internal inconsistency in the *Treatise*.

The baby had been born but the umbilical cord had not yet been cut.

Keynes's insight grew immediately after he had completed the *Treatise* in September 1930. A year later, in the course of a special preface to the German edition, he criticized the well-known concept of forced saving. It was often supposed to be the result of, and equal to, an expansion of bank credit. This "forced" saving was regarded as supplementing "voluntary" saving—the value of an economy's physical investment being equal to the sum of the two. This doctrine, together with the concept itself of "forced" saving, Keynes completely rejected. Investment creates the necessary "voluntary" saving, quite irrespective of the extent to which it is financed by the banks.

Later in 1931 and early in 1932, Keynes was making rapid progress towards a completely new formulation. The *General Theory* was finished at the end of 1935 and published early in 1936, five years after the *Treatise*.

Towards the end of his *General Theory*, Keynes did provide a symbolic expression, involving four elasticities of response, which he wrote "can be regarded as a generalised statement of the Quantity Theory of Money." He added: "I do not myself attach much value to manipulations of this kind . . . . I doubt if they carry us any further than ordinary discourse can." He referred to a warning he had given a few pages back:

> It is a great fault of symbolic pseudo-mathematical methods of formalising a system of economic analysis . . . that they expressly assume strict independence between the factors involved . . . ; whereas, in ordinary discourse, . . . we can keep "at the back of our heads" the necessary reserves and qualifications. . . . Too large a proportion of recent "mathematical" economics are merely concoctions, as imprecise as the initial assumptions they rest on, which allow the author to lose sight of the complexities and interdependencies of the real world in a maze of pretentious and unhelpful symbols.

The equation that presents the so-called Quantity Theory is, of course, correct. But it is not an equation. It is an identity, like so many so-called equations in economics. An identity may be a useful means of avoiding error, but it cannot, taken by itself, prove anything about causation.

A large volume of literature now exists comparing the *Treatise* with the *General Theory,* commenting on the transition. To discuss the subject—still more the commentators—would require several articles. I confine myself to some personal comments.

Looking back, I find astonishing the confusion of thought of those of us, who, directly or indirectly, were in close touch with Keynes in Cambridge. Donald Moggridge describes it in Volumes XIII and XIV of the Royal Economic Society edition of *The Collected Writings of John Maynard Keynes*.

In the *Treatise* Keynes concentrated on the determination of the prices of consumption-goods and capital-goods rather than on their outputs. This seemed to us to be made by an entirely different Keynes from the co-author of *Can Lloyd George Do It?*, published in 1929, a year earlier than the *Treatise*. Actually, Keynes devoted a considerable part of the practical second volume of the *Treatise* to fluctuations and unemployment.

When I re-read my own letters to Keynes, I found them

so confused that I had difficulty in believing that they were written by the author of my article, written nine months earlier ["The Relation of Home Investment to Unemployment," *Economic Journal,* Vol. 41, June, 1931]. In our discussions of the price level of capital goods, we seem to have failed to appreciate how Keynes brought in expectations. In developing his Fundamental Equation, Keynes took the price level of new investment goods simply as given, reserving its examination to a later part of the chapter.

When he got on to the subject, he began with the prices of securities, explaining their determination by expectations of the returns likely to be received on securities in the future and by the quantity of savings deposits (and the rate of interest paid on them). He wrote in terms of "bullishness" and "bearishness" of the public, and of "two opinions." The actual price level of investments he regarded as the resultant of the sentiment of the public and the behavior of the banking system. But he then allowed himself to become completely confused by the two quite different meanings of the word "investment"—in securities and in new capital goods. (This is one of the rare occasions on which the French vocabulary is richer than the English. Joan Robinson, taking a hint from John Hicks, has established the word *placement* for investment in securities.)

Keynes wrote:

> The price level of investments as a whole, and hence of new investments, is that price level at which the desire of the public to hold savings deposits is equal to the amount of savings deposits which the banking system is willing and able to create.

He got himself involved in confusion between securities and capital goods. The prices of capital goods, of course, depend on expectations about their future earnings, not on the future earnings of the equities which they underlie. There is some relation between the two. There is also, quite obviously, a relation between the prices of equities and the prices of the capital goods that underlie them. But the former are subject to fluctuations larger, and different in character, from the latter.

Here, despite its faults, are to be found the germs of the Liquidity Preference Theory of the *General Theory*. The Liquidity Preference Theory of the *General Theory* also involves a serious fault. The expectations relate to fixed-interest securities—to "the complex of rates of interest for varying maturities which will rule at future dates." In Chapter 13 there is no place for equities as part of a man's wealth. Keynes's failure to present his theory of determination of the rate of interest in terms of "portfolio analysis" can be explained by his ardent desire to make his presentation as simple as possible, in the hope of carrying conviction to those unwilling to be convinced. But he should have explained—both in this and in other contexts—the character of his simplifying assumptions.

The following passage is significant:

> Whilst liquidity-preference due to the speculative-motive corresponds to what in my *Treatise on Money* I called "the state of bearishness," it

is by no means the same thing. For "bearishness" is there defined as the functional relationship, not between the rate of interest (or price of debts) and the quantity of money, but between the price of assets and debts, taken together, and the quantity of money. This treatment, however, involved a confusion between results due to a change in the rate of interest and those due to a change in the schedule of the marginal efficiency of capital, which I hope I have here avoided.

Keynes's chapter on the marginal efficiency of capital is based on the prospective future yield of a capital asset which, together with the rate of interest, determines the price of the asset.

Keynes was not a man who easily got worried or lacked confidence in himself. But without allowing his spirits, which were normally buoyant, to be affected, he was at no stage satisfied with his accomplishment. On the evening on which he finished the *Treatise,* he wrote to his mother: "Artistically it is a failure—I have changed my mind too much . . . for it to be a proper unity."

Five months before he completely finished the *General Theory,* Keynes wrote to me: "I am in the stage of not liking my book very much." Joan Robinson recalls that in reply to a note from her: "I hope you are not suffering from author's melancholy," Keynes replied: "Author's melancholy did set in at the end. I feel I have not been worthy of my task."

Eight months after he had finished the *General Theory,* Keynes wrote to Sir Ralph Hawtrey:

> I may mention that I am thinking of producing in the course of the next year or so what might be called *footnotes* to my previous book. . . . Of course, in fact, the whole book needs rewriting and re-casting.

It would have given Keynes intense pleasure had he lived to hear Pigou, in November 1949, partially renounce his review of the *General Theory* ["Mr. J. M. Keynes' *General Theory of Employment, Interest and Money,*" *Economica,* Vol. 3, May, 1936]. It was a moving occasion. It took the form of two lectures delivered to a large audience of Cambridge dons and undergraduates. Referring to "the kernel of Keynes' contribution," as set out on page 246 of the *General Theory,* Pigou said:

> Whatever imperfection there may be in his working out of the fundamental conception embodied there, the conception itself is an extremely fruitful germinal idea. In my original review article on the *General Theory* I failed to grasp its significance and did not assign to Keynes the credit due for it. Nobody before him, so far as I know, had brought all the relevant factors, real and monetary at once, together in a single formal scheme, through which their interplay could be coherently investigated.

I turn now to Keynes's treatment of the behavior of money wages. It will serve to illustrate the attitude towards the Quantity Theory of Money of the Keynes of the *General Theory* if I begin by outlining the attitude of many Keynesians to the extremely serious problem presented today by inflation. According to the monetarist school of thought, the remedy is to prevent the supply of money from increasing faster than the rate of increase of the national product added to such modest rate of rise of the price level as appears acceptable. We are assured that, after a period of some years, the economy will settle down in a happy state of tranquil growth, with the price level rising at a modest rate.

Part of the Keynesian comment about such a policy is that a decline in the ratio of the supply of money to the value of output would mean rising rates of interest, and a progressive failure of the supply of credit to meet the needs of industry, falling prices on the Stock Exchange, and bankruptcies at an increasing rate. Unemployment would grow progressively and would reach a level which was politically unacceptable, before it had an appreciable influence, if any at all, on the outcome of wage bargaining.

Already in his *Treatise on Money,* Keynes had drawn the fundamental distinction between cost inflation and the kind of inflation that shows itself in profits being abnormally high. The distinction is brought out sharply in his Fundamental Equations. Underlying a rising price level are two elements. The first is a rising rate of efficiency-earnings—the rate of money earnings per unit of output. This Keynes called *income inflation*. The second element Keynes called *profit inflation*. It is the result of the level of demand being such as to push prices above earnings per unit of output, resulting in profits being abnormal.

In so far as the abnormal profits are earned in the production of consumption goods, they are earned at the expense of real wages. Incidentally, here we can trace the seed of what was, over 20 years later, to become the post-Keynesian theory of the distribution of income. In so far as the abnormal profits are earned in the production of capital goods, real wages are not directly affected. But such profits encourage an increase in the rate of investment—the output of capital goods—and this results in abnormal profits being earned in the production of consumption goods as well.

As I have already indicated, Keynes had not, when he completed the *Treatise,* broken entirely loose from the trammels of the Quantity Theory of Money. But here we have a theory of determination of the price level in which the Quantity Theory plays no explicit part. Implicitly it appears through monetary influences on the output of capital goods. In this particular part of the *Treatise,* monetary influences appear in the form of the market rate of interest. Following Wicksell, the great Swedish economist, Keynes described as the natural rate of interest that rate of interest which would result in such an output of capital goods—such a rate of investment—as would entail no profit inflation. But inflation could still take the form of income inflation, as a result of money wages rising faster than productivity.

By introducing income inflation as a possibility consistent with the absence of profit inflation, Keynes improved on Wicksell. Keynes has been accused of either failing adequately to acknowledge his debt to Swedish economists or of failing to profit from their pioneer work. Professor

Gunnar Myrdal, in his rightly famous book on *Monetary Equilibrium,* published in German in 1933, wrote:

> The English school of theorists has only slowly arrived at Wicksell's statement of the problem. . . . J. M. Keynes' new, brilliant, though not always clear, work, *A Treatise on Money,* is completely permeated by Wicksell's influence. Nevertheless Keynes' work, too, suffers somewhat from the attractive Anglo-Saxon kind of unnecessary originality, which has its roots in certain systematic gaps in the knowledge of the German language on the part of the majority of English economists.

Keynes did, in fact, admit in the *Treatise*—referring to books by Ludwig von Mises, Professor Hans Neisser, and Professor Friedrich Hayek—that he would have made more references to them if his knowledge of German had not been so poor. "In German I can only clearly understand what I know already."

Wicksell was available to Keynes only in German. Keynes certainly derived the phrase "natural rate of interest" from Wicksell. And he regarded Wicksell's book as sufficiently important for me to translate. Sir Roy Harrod's view is that "the process of thought by which Keynes reached his conclusions was independent, and not derived from the study of Wicksell" [*The Life of John Maynard Keynes*].

The truth seems to lie closer to the implications of Professor Gunnar Myrdal's phrase "systematic gaps in the knowledge of the German language" than to that of his phrase "completely permeated."

On this issue we have Keynes's own testimony, in an article published in 1937, replying to an article by Professor Bertil Ohlin. Keynes wrote that Sir Ralph Hawtrey and Dennis Robertson had "strayed from the fold" of classical economics sooner than he had. He regarded Sir Ralph Hawtrey "as [his] grandparent and Mr. Robertson as [his] parent in the paths of errancy," and he had "been greatly influenced by them." Keynes might have adopted "Wicksell as [his] great-grandparent, if [he] had known his works in more detail at an earlier stage in [his] own thought and also if [he] did not have the feeling that Wicksell was *trying* to be 'classical' " [included in volume fourteen of *The Collected Writings of John Maynard Keynes,* p. 202, fn. 2].

Professor Myrdal, in his recent book of essays, called *Against the Stream,* does actually praise Wicksell because he "was always eager to root his new ideas in thoughts which, after laborious study, he had found expressed somewhere in the great literature, in part from the beginning of the nineteenth century." This view, taken by Professor Myrdal, confirms Keynes's complaint that Wicksell was *trying* to be classical.

In fact, Professor Myrdal's own book, *Monetary Equilibrium,* is strongly based on classical thought as the following quotation indicates: "The 'natural' or, as Wicksell sometimes says, the 'real,' rate of interest is defined as the marginal increment in 'physical productivity' of the services of land and labour when they are saved."

That is by the way. I was saying that Keynes improved on Wicksell by demonstrating the compatibility of income inflation, due to money wages rising faster than productivity, with the market rate of interest being equal to the natural rate; and so he demonstrated the compatibility of income inflation with profit inflation: whereas Wicksell defined the natural rate as the rate of interest that would result in stability of the price level.

The fact that later on, in his *General Theory,* Keynes abandoned the use of Wicksell's term "natural rate of interest" is irrelevant to the issue of the degree of Wicksell's influence on Keynes.

It is unfortunate that Keynes failed in his *General Theory* to refer to Professor Myrdal's book. But although it was published in German in 1933, the English translation was not published until 1939.

Keynes's concept of income inflation, published 44 years ago, fits in with much modern thinking about the causes of inflation. Although Keynes abandoned the actual phrase in his *General Theory,* he strengthened the logical basis of the concept. One of the important contributions of the *General Theory* is what Sir John Hicks, in his recent book on *The Crisis in Keynesian Economics,* calls the *"wage theorem."* Keynes had already in his *Treatise* enunciated the doctrine, which emerged logically from his discovery of income inflation. The money wage is the fulcrum on which rests the whole structure of everything expressed in terms of money—all prices, incomes of every kind, and all money values. A higher level of money wages means that everything expressed in terms of money is higher in the same proportion. The one important exception is the quantity of money. If it is held constant, a higher money wage means that in real value—in terms of its purchasing power over labor and goods—the quantity of money is reduced. The only important influence on the real state of the economy of a higher money wage takes the form of the higher rates of interest, and the general tightening of credit, which result from a reduction in the real value of the quantity of money.

In addition, all incomes and debts fixed contractually in terms of money are smaller in real value as a result of the moneywage being higher. I am, of course, abstracting from effects on exports and imports.

The basis of the fundamental role of the money wage in determining all prices, money incomes, and money values is that money wages not only form part of costs of production but, because they are to a large extent spent, they form part of total purchasing power expressed in terms of money. The higher costs resulting from a higher level of money wages are met by the resultant addition to demand in terms of money; while in real terms demand is unaltered.

Keynes's analysis of the behavior of money wages is unsystematic and unsatisfactory. His failure to consider adequately how wages would, or might, behave under conditions of fairly full employment is attributable to the high level of unemployment with which he was faced and to his belief that, apart from war, unemployment would never fall to a really low level. His main concern was not with rising wages but with certain aspects of falling wages. First of all, he stressed the extreme reluctance of money wages to fall even under the pressure of severe unemployment. Sir John Hicks points out that in 1933 in this country, "the wage-index had fallen no more than 5 per cent below its level in the mid-twenties." In the early 1930's the number of unemployed rose above 2 million—above a percentage of 20—and in 1932 was about 2,800,000—a percentage of 28. During the last stages of Keynes's completion of his *General Theory,* in 1934 and 1935, unemployment was falling, but it remained over 1,200,000.

The difficulty of securing a fall of wages had been the basis of the argument used by Keynes in *The Economic Consequences of Mr. Winston Churchill.* Even if severe unemployment in the unsheltered industries did result in some fall of wages, "wages will not fall in the sheltered industries, merely because there is unemployment in the unsheltered industries. Therefore, you will have to see to it that there is unemployment in the sheltered industries also."

Keynes had to contest the very widely held view that, quite apart from favorable effects on exports, if only wages fell more heavily, unemployment would be reduced. He argued emphatically that lower wages simply meant lower purchasing power and that far from unemployment being reduced, it would be increased if a fall of wages resulted in an expectation of further falls of wages and prices.

Furthermore, a really heavy cut in wages, resulting in a heavy fall of prices, would seriously endanger the financial position of companies that were partly financed by loans and debentures. As a result, the financial position of banks would be threatened. Although their assets would rise in real value to the same extent as the deposits held with them, some of their borrowers would become bankrupt. The solidarity of the whole financial system would be threatened.

Keynes was mainly concerned, in the *General Theory,* with the failure of economists and others to appreciate the reluctance of money wages to fall and to realize that even if they did fall, unemployment would not be diminished, except in industries subject to competition with overseas suppliers.

However, he did write something about the relationship between the behavior of money wages, and the level of demand as reflected in the level of employment. He expressed such a relationship in what would today be regarded as the wrong form. He referred to a rise of the level of money wages in response to a rise of demand and employment, whereas today we would refer to the relationship between the rate of increase of money wages and the level of employment. This is just one aspect of the fact that Keynes's concepts were designed for an economy in a state of depression. Similarly, he would discuss the influence of a change in the actual quantity of money as opposed to a change in its rate of growth.

Among the forces responsible for the behavior of money wages, Keynes mentioned "the power of trade unions" [*A Treatise on Money*], the greater readiness of entrepreneurs to give way to pressure "when they are doing better business," and "the psychology of the workers and the policies of employers and trade unions" [*General Theory*]. However, there is no analysis of the problem. The only reasoned statement that I have been able to find either in the *Treatise* or in the *General Theory* is the following in the *General Theory*.

> . . [this] accords with our experience of human nature. For although the struggle for money-wages is . . . essentially a struggle to maintain a high *relative* wage, this struggle is likely, as employment increases, to be intensified in each individual case both because the bargaining position of the worker is improved.

So we find that, as long ago as 1936, Keynes regarded what is now called the "leap-frogging effect"—or the wage-wage spiral as opposed to the wage-price spiral—as the main cause of rising wages. This is the view many of us have held for some years.

Keynes added that "these motives will operate within limits," and that the level of money wages in practice fluctuated very little. His belief was dominated not only by contemporary experience, with heavy unemployment, but also by the "fair measure of stability of prices" between 1820 and 1914, which he attributed to "a balance of forces in an age when individual groups of employers were strong."

As to full employment, Keynes wrote that "when a further increase in the quantity of effective demand produces no further increase in output . . . we have reached a condition which might be appropriately designated as one of true inflation." But he had written earlier, "full, or even approximately full, employment is of rare and short-lived occurrence."

There are passages in the *General Theory* that seem to suggest that there is one quite definite level of demand, resulting in a level of employment which can be described as a "state of full employment." As Sir John Hicks, in his recent book, remarks.

> when the Keynes theory is set out in this textbook manner . . . it is bound to give the impression that there are just two 'states' of the economy: a 'state of unemployment' in which money wages are constant, and a 'state of full employment' in which pressure of demand causes wages to rise.

Some of the gross over-simplifications of Keynes's analysis of which the textbooks are shamefully guilty are attributable to Keynes's burning desire to be understood. To clarify his presentation, he was apt to give a misleading impression of believing in a number of simple relationships. Many of his readers have failed to realize that the simplifying assumptions made for the sake of clarity are not to be taken literally.

But actually, in the relationship between the behavior of money wages and the level of employment, no such excuse is admissible. Keynes stated clearly in a number of passages that, to quote one of them, "the wage-unit may tend to rise before full employment has been reached." On the previous page he had recognized that, in general, the demand for some services and commodities will reach a level

beyond which their supply is, for the time being, perfectly inelastic, while in other directions there is still substantial surplus of resources without employment.

It seems odd that, in the passages I have quoted, Keynes seemed to regard the behavior of the level of money- wages as though it was open to a choice of policy. That was not his view at all. Already in the *Treatise* he had written:

> It is more important to have a system which avoids, so far as possible, the necessity for *induced* changes [in the behavior of moneywages], than it is to attempt to stabilise the price level according to any precise principle, *provided always that the rate of change in the price level is kept within narrow limits.* [italics added]

Of course, it always was Keynes's view that, to quote from *The Economic Consequences of Mr. Winston Churchill,* a policy of trying to reduce wages and prices "by intensifying unemployment without limit . . . is a policy . . . from which any humane or judicious person must shrink."

In the middle of the Second World War, an article in the *Economic Journal* by Professor Hayek, on "A Commodity Reserve Currency" [Vol. 53, June-September, 1943], gave Keynes an opportunity, at a time when in the Treasury he was deeply involved in postwar problems, to air his views in public in the today more relevant context of coping with an upward surge of money wages as opposed to reluctance of money wages to fall. In a *Rejoinder* to Professor Hayek's article [**"The Objective of International Price Stability [Rejoinder to Hayek],"** *Economic Journal,* Vol. 53, June-September, 1943], Keynes mentioned "attempts to confine the natural tendency of wages to rise beyond the limits set by the volume of money," which rely on "the weapon of deliberately creating unemployment. This weapon the world, after a good try, has decided to discard."

> Keynes referred to the view that in a capitalist country this policy is doomed to failure because it will be found impossible in conditions of full employment to prevent a progressive increase of wages. According to this view severe slumps and recurrent periods of unemployment have been hitherto the only effective means of holding efficiency wages within a reasonably stable range. Whether this is so remains to be seen. The more conscious we are of this problem, the likelier shall we be to surmount it.

So Keynes foresaw that there would be a problem. He did not foresee that nothing would be done about the problem until it had gotten out of hand. He did not foresee the order of magnitude of the problem. The terrifying size of the problem is today attributable in the United Kingdom partly to the failure of all governments before July 1961 to be fully conscious of the existence of the problem, still more of its potential order of magnitude.

A note by Frank Graham, the Princeton Professor, on the Keynes versus Hayek controversy, refers to correspondence that had passed a year earlier between himself and Keynes ["Keynes vs. Hayek on a Commodity Reserve Currency," *Economic Journal,* Vol. 54, December, 1944]. In a letter to Graham, Keynes had asked:

How much otherwise avoidable unemployment do you propose to bring about in order to keep the Trade Unions in order? Do you think it will be politically possible when they understand what you are up to? My own preliminary view is that other, more reasonable, less punitive means must be found.

Keynes was also corresponding in 1943 on the same subject with Benjamin Graham, the famous advocate of an international composite buffer stock. Keynes explained his view that:

If money-wages rise faster than efficiency, this aggravates the difficulty of maintaining full employment . . . and is one of the main obstacles which a full employment policy has to overcome.

. . . The more aware we were of the risk, the more likely we should be to find a way round other than totalitarianism. But I recognized the reality of the risk.

Keynes failed to foresee that, 29 years after the end of the war, the percentage rate of increase of money costs of production in a number of industrial countries would have reached double figures.

Keynes was essentially a man of moderation. He would have had difficulty in accepting as a possibility the degree of stupidity in advanced countries indicated in such figures.

Keynes's unawareness of the magnitude of the problem with which industrial countries generally, and ours in particular, were to be faced is echoed in various documents written towards the end of the war. Keynes, preoccupied with various talks with the Americans, could devote little time to the drafting of the Coalition Government's White Paper on *Employment Policy*. But there is no evidence that he wanted more emphasis to be given to the problem of curbing the upward tendency of wages, to which one perfunctory page is devoted.

Beveridge [*Full Employment in a Free Society*] quotes from an article published anonymously in *The Times,* a warning by Professor Joan Robinson. "In peacetime the vicious spiral of wages and prices might become chronic." He took the problem somewhat more seriously than the Government and devoted two and a half pages to it, in the course of which he wrote:

The primary responsibility of preventing a full employment policy from coming to grief in a vicious spiral of wages and prices will rest on those who conduct the bargaining on behalf of labour. The more explicitly that responsibility is stated, the greater can be the confidence that it will be accepted. . . . Wages ought to be determined by reason, not by the methods of strike and lockout. Ordeal by battle has for centuries been rejected as a means of settling legal disputes between citizens.

Keynes had, in *The Economic Consequences of the Peace,* expressed his horror of inflation. There we find the famous statement that "Lenin is said to have declared that the best way to destroy the capitalist system was to debauch the currency." Keynes added that "Lenin was certainly right." In the first chapter of his *Tract on Monetary Reform,* published in 1923, he analyzed the great injuries inflicted both by heavy inflation and by heavy deflation, and expressed himself on balance in favor of stability of the price level. "Inflation is unjust and deflation is inexpedient," he wrote. "Of the two perhaps deflation is, if we rule out exaggerated inflations such as that of Germany, the worse."

Keynes obviously regarded the upward and downward movements of the price level both between 1914 and 1922 and during and after the Napoleonic Wars as altogether exceptional. He believed himself to be living in a country in which, as in other advanced industrial countries, the price level was quite remarkably stable. In the *Treatise,* Keynes referred to "the sensational rise of prices" in Britain between 1550 and 1650. The price level rose by 200 percent between 1500 and 1650. The average annual rate at which it rose was 0.75 percent. That is the degree of inflation which Keynes regarded as abnormal. Even more exceptional was the fall of prices in 1930 to which Keynes referred as he was completing the *Treatise*.

During the Second World War, the official cost-of-living index rose at an average annual rate of about 6 percent—a remarkable achievement, part of the credit for which is due, not only to Keynes, but also to those civil servants, many of them economists, who gladly followed his lead. It was quite largely due to cooperation between the Government and the Trade Union Council (TUC).

There is nothing in the *General Theory*—rather the contrary—that anticipates Keynes's growing awareness that if unemployment ceased to be a serious problem, it would be replaced by the problem of pressure to raise money wages faster than productivity. But while the *General Theory* was going through the press, it continued to be discussed with Keynes by his disciples, particularly by Professor Joan Robinson, who included an essay on the subject in a book published in 1937 [*Essays in the Theory of Employment*], which Keynes read in draft and approved in its final form.

In a comment on the *Australian Full Employment White Paper,* Keynes wrote in June 1945: "One is also, simply because one knows no solution, inclined to turn a blind eye to the wages problem in a full employment economy" (quoted in Moggridge and Howson ["Keynes on Monetary Policy, 1910-1946," *Oxford Economic Papers,* Vol. 26, no. 2, July, 1974]).

At this point I shall go back for a moment to Keynes's letter to Benjamin Graham of December 1943. Keynes wrote:

The task of keeping efficiency-wages reasonably stable (I am sure they will creep up steadily in spite of our best efforts) is a *political* rather than an economic problem. [Quoted in Moggridge and Howson, italics added]

In the course of his "Inaugural Keynes Lecture" delivered . . . [on April 22, 1971 (included in *Proceeding of the British Academy,* Vol. LVII)], Austin Robinson quoted the following passage from a letter written by

Keynes in 1944, as editor of the *Economic Journal,* to an author who had submitted an over-formalistic analysis of the problem of inflation:

> I do not doubt that a serious problem will arise as to how wages are to be restrained when we have a combination of collective bargaining and full employment. But I am not sure how much light the kind of analytical method you apply can throw on this essentially *political problem.* [italics added]

It is clear to me that these references to the problem of rapidly rising wages as being political point to incomes policy. But Keynes had absolutely no idea of the terrifying orders of magnitude which recent years have displayed.

Josef Steindl   (essay date 1983)

SOURCE: "J. M. Keynes: Society and the Economist," in *Keynes's Relevance Today,* edited by Fausto Vicarelli, The Macmillan Press Ltd, 1985, pp. 99-125.

[*In the following excerpt, Steindl judges the contemporary relevance of Keynes's ideas. Basing his arguments on a discussion of several key topics in the criticism on Keynes, he outlines the main points of Keynes's economic theory, illustrates how the unorthodox content of the* General Theory *developed out of Keynes's active involvement in the formulation of economic policy during the 1920s and 1930s, identifies the focal points in the critical attacks on the* General Theory, *discusses the way in which the revolutionary arguments of the* General Theory *were undermined, and comments on the consequences of the defeat of many of Keynes's international finance proposals following World War II. Steindl's essay was drawn from the English-language translation of* Attualità di Keynes, *which was first published in Rome in 1983.*]

I THE PARADIGM

What was it that Keynes stood on its head in economics? Perhaps an idea of it can be conveyed in simple words. The analogy between the individual household and society as a whole which many economists as well as laymen use in their reasoning is misleading. Conclusions drawn from this analogy, Keynes showed, are false. Thus for the individual household saving (spending less than one's income) leads to an accumulation of assets. For society as a whole when people spend less they reduce each other's income and the wealth of society is reduced. That for the economy as a whole the relations are different, that spending determines income and not the other way round, is not immediately accessible to common sense which bases itself on the day by day experience of the household. The truth of the matter is revealed only by studying the circular relations in a society (spending-income-spending). This shows that there are feedbacks which for the individual household or firm are unimportant because of its small scope but which for a large unit, such as for example the public sector, will be very important. In economics as in other fields the scope of reasoning is enlarged beyond the field of everyday experience and intuition and produces results in flat contradiction with it.

The instrument for analysing the circular relations in an economy are the national accounts. They are a double entry book-keeping for the society, whole groups like households, business or government being represented by separate accounts, as are also activities like investment, consumption and so on. The systematic development of national accounting received its great impetus from Keynes and his theory. The style of theorising which made use of the concepts of national accounting became widespread only through Keynes although it was known to Quesnay and Marx. Known as macroeconomics it became crucial for the discussion of economic policy problems. It offers a convenient way between the sterility of the Walrasian general equilibrium and the limited scope of the partial analysis of Marshall, because it is couched in terms of variables which are statistically measurable and at the same time relevant for national economic policy.

A special case of circular interrelations in the economy concerns wages. Here it is the analogy between the firm and the economy as a whole which gives rise to the usual faulty reasoning: for a single firm, if it could pay a lower wage rate, the advantage were obvious and would probably lead to an expansion of output. But how different are the relations in the economy as a whole! The general level of prices is strongly influenced by costs and in a closed economy with no foreign trade costs consists mainly of wages. A general increase or decrease in wages will therefore, on simple assumptions, be passed on to prices. Thus, Keynes concludes, workers and trade unions in a closed system will not be in a position to determine the general level of real wages. This shows the lack of realism of the neoclassical view that workers could always bring about full employment if they are prepared to reduce the level of real wages sufficiently.

For Keynes the volume of employment is determined not by real wages but by demand for goods. The variability of production in the cycle is evident and the bottleneck which limits production is most of the time demand.

Let us turn to another characteristic of Keynes's thinking. For him the only real economic constraints which limit our policy options are scarcities of real resources—of labour, skills, machines, factories, land, raw materials, exhaustible resources. If we cannot make use of them this must be due to institutions, superstition or to our own stupidity. We should be wary therefore of the argument 'There is no money for it' and always ask whether there is any real scarcity involved or not. This naturally leads to a critical attitude towards institutions, especially financial ones. Institutions, this is definitely Keynes's view, have to be such as to make possible the full use of the available real resources. They will not do so automatically or on the basis of very simple precepts such as proposed by Hayek (neutral money) or the monetarists. Keynes therefore had no respect for the tenets of financial orthodoxy— the gold standard, balanced budgets, sound finance—in so far as they merely hindered a rational use of available material resources.

Reference has been made above to the circulation of flows in the economy (transformation of cost into income, income into spending, spending into cost again). This stream is not kept moving by itself, it is always in danger of draining away into leakages constituted by savings. The driving force which replenishes the stream and keeps it moving is investment in plant, equipment etc. The central role of investment as the prime force of accumulation is one of the most distinctive characteristics of the Keynesian view of the economy. The strategic position of investment is due to the length of life of equipment and structures and to the uncertainty of the return. Investment thus depends on expectations which in the last resort can not be fully justified by calculation because of basic uncertainties, so that ultimately investment is based on a kind of optimism ('animal spirits'). Investment, unstable by itself, is rendered even more unstable by the apparatus of finance which is interposed between the saver and the investor. The speculative element in investment is reinforced by the speculative character of the markets for financial instruments, claims of all kinds based on debt. Instability is therefore a basic feature of the system.

Every theory rests on simplification. A characteristic simplification of Keynes is the closed system. It is easy to see why: the circularity of the relations is evident only in the closed system, while in the open system it is interrupted.

But there is also a moral behind it. In a closed system the conflicts of interest between different countries are eliminated, one nation cannot gain at the expense of another. One is therefore thrown back on devices other than sponging, robbing and stealing. The closed system represented the world as a whole.

There is no denying that Keynesian policies meet their greatest difficulty at the point where the system is open, in the balance of payments. There are two ways of confronting these difficulties: the one is to close the country more or less by suitable protectionist measures. The other is to unite all countries in a common international order which will safeguard their interests by the establishment of suitable rules.

II AMNESIA

Conventional wisdom tells us that short of a real cataclysm the technical achievements of a society cannot be lost again. Yet most economists seem to have completely forgotten what Keynes as well as the experience of several decades taught them about full employment. They talk in terms of the treasury view of 1930 ('crowding out'), of budget deficits creating high interest rates, of increasing employment by lowering wages internationally. It is a collective cultural amnesia. Only the system of national accounts remains standing as a lasting monument of the era, difficult to destroy because it was so elaborately built over the whole world.

III THE IMPACT ON HISTORY

A technique that has been forgotten? But was it ever tried? It may be—and it has been—argued not quite unconvincingly that the high employment experienced in the decades after the war has materialised largely without the active help of government policies consciously based on Keynesian economics; and that on the first occasion these

policies were really badly needed worldwide—in 1974-75—they were not applied.

It is true that the high level of post-war employment was partly due to fortuitous circumstances which might perhaps have produced it even had Keynes never existed, namely

(a) The re-armament in the US and Europe following the outbreak of the Korean war in 1950.

(b) The spin-off from war time and post-war military developments leading to or facilitating the introduction of new products which required large investments.

(c) The massive transfer to Europe of old technology from the US to which the Continent had practically had no access in the interwar period and during the war: this was facilitated by the Marshall plan and it led to considerable investment activity.

(d) The international economic cooperation which was the corollary of the military alliance of the West and which removed the balance of payment constraints standing in the way of expansion.

The same kind of skeptical view is also suggested by the fact that Schacht and the economic administration of Nazi Germany quite successfully applied full employment policies when the *General Theory* had not yet been published. Yet all this will not suffice to settle the issue.

IV KNOWLEDGE AND HISTORY

The question is whether employment techniques and theories are similar to technological knowledge. That this played a role in history can hardly be in doubt although it is a tricky task to describe it.

When we consider the relation of knowledge and material development of history we must free ourselves of primitive ideas of unilateral causation. We may get some help from the concept of feed-back and perhaps also from the view that an idea plays a role in history only when 'the time is ripe for it'. What would this mean? Presumably it means that the idea or knowledge must combine with other events or developments in order to become relevant ('it must fall on fertile ground'). We must also remind ourselves that the idea itself arises from a certain historical background which is fairly obvious in the case of the Keynesian ideas. Thus the idea (consciousness) exists between a flow of history which produces it and another flow of history which receives it as seed.

The economics of Keynes whether he wanted it or not in the course of time has become successively associated with one or another of the great streams of events and policies of our time.

In the first place it became associated with the finance of the war in Britain. It was in this context that the system of national accounts was developed by E. Rothbarth, J. E. Meade and R. N. Stone. Keynes and his friends intended to use this in order to overcome the inhibitions of the orthodox bankers and treasury officials against war finance by borrowing: The accounts would show them how the deficits were duly covered by a corresponding amount of saving.

The association of Keynesianism and war finance did not stop there. It was relevant to the post-war rearmament in so far as it removed the scruples of orthodox finance and instead pointed to the benefits obtained in increased employment, prosperity and industrial profits. It may be controversial how far these considerations contributed to armament, but it seems plausible that the military-industrial complex in the United States was somehow wedded to a Keynesian ideology.

A different and hardly controversial association is the welfare state. This ideology arose as a reaction against the horrors of the war and a sign of newly awakened social consciousness in the élite of a society which had been rather impervious to the suffering of the victims of the pre-war depression and which felt darkly how much this had contributed to the war. It represented also a re-assertion of the newly gained political consciousness of the workers.

In Britain it found its first expression in Sir William Beveridge's work on social security and his 'Full Employment in a Free Society' as well as a series of government papers.

The welfare state in the course of time was realised in all industrial countries. It involves a large increase in the public sector and a good deal of built-in stabilisation: This means that a large part of any additional spending comes back in increased revenue and that tends to stabilise the economy.

Another ideological stream which recruited Keynes as an ally or used him as an instrument was of wider political significance. It arose from the need of western capitalism, tainted by the pre-war experience, to change its image so as to be able to face up to the competition of communist propaganda in the cold war. In fact, Keynesian economics was ideally suited for that purpose: it promised an effective reform of capitalism which freed it from some of its most ugly features. The idea that capitalism could be salvaged by Keynesian thought was eagerly embraced by social democrats and somewhat less vociferously by the conservative business community. The best witness to this was the enthusiasm for consumption which dominated the post-war business world. The bitter denunciation of Keynes by established Marxism only reflected these attitudes.

The business community accepted the Keynesian paradigm in spite of their innate dislike of some of its features (role of the state, association with welfare policies).

On the basis of these considerations we can understand the spirit of the Keynesian era: the prevailing ideology of growth and of consumption, and a tremendous optimism which becomes evident and striking once we compare it with the pessimism which took hold of the same strata of society in the 1970s. It was as if by a kind of Aladdin's lamp Keynes had posthumously called up the 'animal spirits' which in his view were the prime movers of the investment process.

It appears then that the earlier quoted arguments about the irrelevance of Keynesian innovations to the post-war development are not the full story. On a balanced view they had a profound influence though this rarely took the form of government deficit spending.

V NOT A RETIRING SCHOLAR

The novel and unorthodox ideas of Keynes were laid down systematically in his *General Theory of Employment, Interest and Money* (1936) which together with two earlier books, *A Tract on Monetary Reform* (1923) and *A Treatise on Money* (1930) formed the bulk of his theoretical output. Preceding this, however, over a long time beginning in 1919, there was a vast amount of work of a more practical nature dealing with problems of economic policy which arose from the events of the time. It has to be realised that a large part of Keynes's working time and interest was taken up not by the university in Cambridge but by an active engagement in the formulation of economic policy, either in an official capacity, mainly during and after the two world wars, or as an independent writer, lecturer and expert, mainly between the two wars. There was no lack of challenging problems: The condition of Europe after the war, the special problems of post-war Britain—the high burden of war time debts and the need for structural adjustments, mass unemployment which never ceased to be a problem until the second world war, the return to the gold standard at an over-valued rate for the pound sterling (1925), which could be maintained only at a heavy cost in high interest rates and unemployment and was finally given up in 1931 in favour of a floating pound, and in the further course the shift of British policy from free trade to protectionism.

It is surprising that the work of Keynes on these policy questions, apparently guided by a very strong intuition and acute observation, anticipated to a very large extent the results he reached much later and by tortuous routes in his academic work on a theoretical plane.

In fact he advocated public works as a remedy for unemployment consistently and strongly from 1924 onwards. To finance the public works he proposed that the money should be taken out of the sinking fund. There he immediately came into conflict with Treasury views. In view of the crushing burden of the public debt the Treasury was trying to accumulate a surplus year by year in order to repay some of the debt. They were not willing to let Keynes raid their fund.

The works Keynes had in mind concerned transport, communications, electricity transmission, docks and ports and housing. He wanted to include in these schemes also private investment financed by treasury loans or guarantees and subject to technical advice and guidance by a semi-public authority.

Keynes also considered as a source of finance the rechannelling of the considerable funds which year by year were flowing into foreign investment. Of the funds raised on the capital market five times as much was going into foreign investment than into home investment. He argued that the effect of these foreign investments on export and thus on employment in Britain was small whereas an investment of the same sums in Britain would to a very large part increase output and employment there. Keynes was not very explicit about the methods to be employed; he did not clearly advocate a control of capital movements. Needless to say he was touching one of the most neuralgic points of the City. His arguments suggest that he hoped to make the home investments so much more profitable that the foreign investment would be 'crowded out'.

In carrying on his campaign for an active employment policy Keynes felt again and again the need to defend himself on a very general philosophical ground against the accusation of heresy: 'I bring in the State; I abandon *laissez-faire*,—not enthusiastically, not from contempt of that good old doctrine, but because, whether we like it or not, the conditions for its success have disappeared' [quoted in R. F. Harrod, *Life of John Maynard Keynes*]. He pleaded that private initiative was lacking in the execution of the big projects he had in mind and which would yield from 5 to 9 per cent (he was obviously thinking of the risks involved).

In his lecture **The End of Laissez-Faire** he pointed to saving and investment as activities which could not be left to the free play of the market but which necessitated the intervention of the State.

Another recurring theme is the contrast between enterprise and thrift: 'It should be obvious that mere abstinence is not enough by itself to build cities or drain fens. . . . It is enterprise which builds and improves the worlds' possessions' [*Treatise on Money*]. In social terms the contrasting pair may be translated into: Industry *versus* the rentier. It is obvious where Keynes's sympathies lay and how acutely he felt the oppressive consequence of a crushing and prolonged debt on an economy and a country. One of the main elements in his proposed post-war settlement was the cancellation of all war debts. Later in a discussion of the financial situation of France, a country which carried the heavy burden of an excessively large rentier class, he recommended price inflation as a way out of the impasse.

And, of course, cheap money policy was a natural concomitant of Keynesian concern for investment and government borrowing. This leads to one of the greatest issues in the inter-war economic policy debates: The return to the gold standard. Keynes, almost alone, passionately opposed it. It corresponded to the interest and the opinion of the City of London that the return should take place at the pre-war rate to the dollar, an issue in which the prestige of the City was at stake. Keynes argued that at this rate the pound would be overvalued by about 10 per cent; a deflation of the wage and price level would be necessary to maintain an equilibrium of payments at this level, with unpleasant economic and social consequences: the existing unemployment would be increased. In fact, on a plain reading of the subsequent events the fears were fully justified. Britain had to keep the rate of interest high in order to prevent an ever pressing outflow of money to New York and this as well as the heavy damage to exports, especially in the critical case of coal, led to great unemployment and to the general strike in 1926. Keynes's opposition against the gold standard was, however, not confined to the particular rate: He had from the beginning developed a policy preference for devaluation as against deflation. He wanted

priority to be given to internal policy concerns and not to the establishment of fixed currency relations. The gold standard, he said, bound the City to Wall Street both with respect to interest rates and to price developments.

Faintly visible behind this debate is a fundamental issue which divided and distinguished Keynes from his compatriots and contemporaries. It is the theme of a lesson which he tried to teach them untiringly, beginning with the famous chapters on Europe in the **Economic Consequences of the Peace**. He said that the world was not the same after this war and that it would never again be the same. He did not share the nostalgic sentimentality of the British middle class who imagined that it was possible to return to the pre-war Britain where they had been so happy. A special part of this illusion was that the City of London would reconquer and maintain its former place in the world. Keynes destroyed this illusion in a cutting passage of merciless logic.

In the last resort when Churchill called in outside experts to state their case, Keynes remained completely isolated.

The most mature statement of employment policies from that time is contained in the pamphlet **Can Lloyd George Do It?** written jointly with Hubert Henderson. The Treasury view that public works would merely crowd out private investment is countered by a *reductio in absurdo*: since large private investment projects are not different from public investment why should they not also crowd out other investment? The Treasury view thus seemed to imply that employment could never be increased at all. In reality there were three sources of finance for the public investment: the saving in payments to the former unemployed; the reduction in foreign lending (this argument apparently here applied to the export surplus); and 'the savings which now run to waste through lack of adequate credit' [*Can Lloyd George Do It?*]. This tormented expression of the fact that there are potential savings which are not tapped for lack of investment illustrates the terrific struggle for adequate expression of an insight grasped intuitively. In the same pamphlet there are also vague statements of the multiplier effect. There is also reference to the structural maladjustment which was then complicating the problem of unemployment. The change in structure required a shift of manpower from declining to growing industries. But the necessary condition for such a shift from the declining industries, argued the authors of the pamphlet, is that 'jobs have first been created elsewhere, and employers are crying out for men'. In another paper ['The Great Slump of 1930', included in the *Treatise on Money*] there is a foretaste of the Keynesian theory of a general shift in wages: '. . . if wages are cut all round, the purchasing power of the community as a whole is reduced by the same amount as the reduction of costs'; a change in wage cost extending to all industries and all countries leaves everybody where he was before.

When the recession came Keynes abandoned his free trade principles in favour of protectionism. To most people this seemed a *volte face;* but it might be said that he was only developing a principle which he had asserted before when he expressed his preference for devaluation against deflation: the priority of the internal equilibrium and employment of a country in its relation to the outside world. We shall meet this theme again in the discussions on the international currency order.

The preceding selection of points and arguments from the writings on economic policy may serve as an introduction to a more general observation.

The genesis of the *General Theory* offers a good illustration for the view that important innovations in economic theory are distilled from intuitive solutions of the economic policy problems of the day. The revolutionary content of the *General Theory* was pre-established in the economic policy writings which arose from the deep and passionate engagement of Keynes in the issues of his day.

Moreover the writings on economic policy show a very continuous and consistent line of development up to 1936 with an impressive constancy of certain themes and principles. By contrast, the development on the theoretical plane was erratic, with wild jumps and turn rounds by 180 degrees. Keynes had very little respect let alone awe in front of the great bankers, the City men, the civil servants and politicians or the paraphernalia of their trade. He felt a master in this milieu. But when he entered the maze of academic thinking he was burdened by traditions from which he gained his freedom only after a long struggle. He wrestled with the quantity theory through two books and did not completely extirpate it even in the third. He based his *Treatise on Money* on the assumption of constant total output, an assumption which was underlying most of the faulty reasoning of the 'classical' theory and which blocked the way to the *General Theory*.

The contrast between the two worlds is shown also in the style. The style of Keynes is at its best not in his theoretical work but when he writes on economic policy. His power to reduce an analysis to its essentials, to give concrete shape to abstract considerations so that you feel you can touch and hold them is superb. He gives his best when he tries to speak to the general public.

VI THEN AND NOW: ANALOGIES AND PARALLELS

Can the economic issues which were the subject of heated debates in the 1920s be of any interest to us today? The distance which separates us from this time is thrown into light if we consider that radio broadcasting was introduced in 1921, that the first flight over the Atlantic by Lindbergh took place in 1927; television, computers and robots were subjects of science fiction and atomic power the term in an equation in a new fangled physic's theory which nobody could understand. But the issues which Keynes and his opponents debated have a surprising and terrifying resemblance to similar issues today.

We have again to do with mass unemployment today, although the victims are now better cared for than they formerly were. And it is again the dominant wisdom that it is due to excessive wages that they cannot be employed.

Then and now the arguments against effective action include 'crowding out' and the burden of the public debt. This burden, interestingly enough, is today much lower than at the time of Keynes: in the UK the interest pay-

ments were 24 per cent of central government expenditure in 1920 and rose to 40 per cent in the late 1920s.

After the Second World War, up to a few years ago, they were less than 14 per cent. The change was in the same direction in other countries.

It is quite true that this burden is bound to increase. The reason is not so much increased borrowing of governments as high interest rates. And here there is a very strong parallel between Britain in the twenties and Britain, as well as Europe, today. Lord Kaldor considers the two periods as the first and second reign of the monetarist dogma (using the term in a rather wide sense). In both cases vital interests were sacrificed on the alter of an exotic deity: the interest rate was kept high in order to prevent the outflow of funds. In the first period, though, the policy was decided inside the country, while the second case it was imposed on Europe from outside, and very difficult to avoid in the circumstances.

Another parallel strikes the eye if we think of Keynes's attitude to capital exports. He had complained that the financial apparatus was predominantly geared to the needs of other countries and not of home investment. Today the foreign investment of Britain is by far less important than it was; the great foreign lending of the British banks is offset by borrowing abroad. But the complaint remains that the banks are neglecting the interests of home industry. In addition its international involvement makes the system extremely unstable. Incidentally, it would be highly amusing if we had a comment from Keynes on the functioning of the joint stock system today, with the take-over movement as its central feature.

Notwithstanding all the analogies, there is one difference which distinguishes our time: inflation. While for that reason one argument against expansion—that it would lead to rising prices and wages—is more credible now that it was in the deflationary inter-war years (it was used nonetheless even then) we must not blind ourselves against the immense harm that deflation did in those years. By reducing the value of real estate and other tangible assets as well as cash flows, it increased the number of foreclosures and insolvencies.

Today, it is true, the high interest policy together with decreasing inflation rates tends to produce a similarly depressing effect on the value of real assets.

Turning now to the wider aspect of social attitudes: Can we not find analogies today to the nostalgia which Keynes found in the British middle class who were longing to go back to pre-war times? In a nostalgia, that is, for the pre-welfare state? It would seem to be equally utopian, but it can explain the strength of neo-conservativism in US and Britain. Perhaps there is at least a small bit of topicality in the remarks which Keynes made about the capitalists of the time after the First World War: 'They allow themselves to be ruined and altogether undone by their own instruments, governments of their own making, and a Press of which they are the proprietors' [*The Economic Consequences of the Peace*].

And the inability of politicians, conservative as well as social democratic, to grasp the least bit of Keynes's ideas or to share his distaste for the stupid waste of humanity and ruin of his country? Alas, the analogies abound.

VII THE OPEN ENDS OF THE GENERAL THEORY

The *General Theory* is not always a paragon of clarity, unequivocal and unambiguous, nor does it represent a very complete and consistent system. As Keynes said '. . . the whole book needs re-writing and re-casting'. The gaps in the argument of the *General Theory* stand out in relief very distinctly when we compare it with the work of M. Kalecki [*Theory of Economic Dynamics* (1954)] which otherwise offers a close parallel to it.

The book does not contain any distribution theory and distribution is rarely mentioned in it. In consequence the propensity to save is defined so as to refer to the income of the nation as a whole, in other words to a kind of average behaviour. The importance which the distribution of income has for the propensity to save is completely left in the dark although it is perfectly sure that Keynes was only too well aware of it. Aggregation is definitely carried too far here. The distinction between retained profits of business and saving of rentiers and other people outside enterprises is obscured although it is relevant for Keynesian arguments.

The importance which this omission has for the later exegesis of the *General Theory* will soon become obvious. In this connection it is also noteworthy that monopoly in all its forms is largely absent from the scene except for the trade unions. In the discussion of money and real wages perfect competition is explicitly assumed. As an implication of this Keynes was still carrying with him a part of the ballast of the 'classical' tradition the bulk of which he had successfully discarded: he believed that an increase in demand must necessarily lead to increased prices of manufacturing goods with the implication of inevitable fall in real wages in the upswing of the cycle. It was later shown by J. G. Dunlop and L. Tarshis that a negative correlation between real wages and the cycle did not exist.

A second and perhaps the most important point concerns the method and the meaning of the *General Theory*. Is it a general equilibrium theory which describes the relations within a system which would keep it at rest provided it were not disturbed from outside, or is it a process analysis which shows step by step how a system starting from given initial conditions develops from one day to the next? The general equilibrium is a state to which the system ineluctably strives wherever it may start from and which it will reach provided there is no outside interference. Where does this concept come from?

In problems of mathematical physics we often have to do with a transitory solution to a differential equation which, starting from given initial conditions, vanishes after a certain span of time and leaves only the permanent solution which is independent of the initial conditions and determined only by the parameters of the equation. This permanent solution seems to correspond to the equilibrium which economists have in mind when they speak rather vaguely of 'dominant and permanent forces'. But in physics the whole process lasts only a small fraction of a sec-

ond. In economics long term equilibrium requires years or rather decades to work itself out.

In the intervening time the conditions of the system change repeatedly so that equilibrium has no chance of ever being reached. In view of that there is hardly any empirical basis for the statements about long-term equilibrium. The basis is largely *a priori* and, one suspects, often ideological. The situation may be rather better for short period partial equilibrium.

Now in its essence the Keynesian thinking was not concerned with general equilibrium. For one thing his practical mind militated against it. How indeed should one use such a theory in dealing with problems of practical economic policy? His famous dictum 'In the long run we are all dead' [*A Tract on Monetary Reform*] shows what he thought of long term equilibrium. When he explained the volume of investment by the state of expectations and discussed their instability he was evidently thinking in terms of process analysis. Yet he has not been sufficiently consistent and clear in pursuing this line. We miss in his work the systematic use of lags which we find in Kalecki and which must necessarily be an essential feature of a process analysis in economics. Thus the lag between investment decisions and investment is for Kalecki a reason why investment determines saving and not the other way round. Again one has to think of the decisive role of lags in the cobweb or in any other cycle.

At the same time we find Keynes talking in terms of equilibrium concepts such as in chapter 18 ('The General Theory of Employment Re-stated') and also in connection with the aggregate supply and demand functions. By this lack of complete clarity he opened the door through which the Trojan horse of the neoclassical synthesis could enter.

A further problem concerns the failure to distinguish between short and long term rates of interest which is puzzling to the reader. By rate of interest he meant the long term rate, and his alternative to investment in bonds (consols) was only money. The short term assets had then to be considered as money unless he disregarded their existence in the context altogether. The last interpretation is the more plausible one; since Keynes introduced the money supply as an exogenous variable he could not plausibly include short term assets in it.

Kaldor has drawn attention to the fact that the quantity of money is always exogenous in Keynes's exposition of the theory of interest and he sees in this a survival of the quantity theory of money. In so far as the quantity of money (ultimately also of base money), and not only its velocity, responds to the amount of transactions, increasing in boom and declining in recession, it is endogenous in character. This side of the picture is never seen in Keynes, because he implicitly always deals with open market operations in his exposition of interest theory.

Conspicuous by its absence from the *General Theory* is a theory of the trade cycle. Bits and pieces relevant to the subject are strewn all over the place but they do not amount to a theory. It would be unfair to blame Keynes for this omission; but one cannot help contemplating how much more committed to dynamics the book would have looked had he gone further in this direction. There are two further subjects which are under-represented in the book although Keynes had plenty to say about them in his practical policy writings: the open economy and long-term development. Both are so extensive and so complicated that Keynes had every justification to leave them out. They are mentioned here only because it has become fashionable to dwell on them, especially on the failure of Keynes to extend his theory to the long run. The tacit implication of this criticism is that he ought to have gone into general equilibrium theory. It was to his credit that he did not.

VIII THE COUNTER-ATTACK

The dismantling of the *General Theory* started as soon as it was published if not before, and with the prominent participation of some of Keynes's friends and colleagues. The method was to prove that the new theory did not differ as much as Keynes claimed from the conventional ('classical') equilibrium theory, that it was only a special case of it, or applicable only under narrowly restricted circumstances.

The attackers naturally profited from the weaknesses pointed out above. Thus Harrod ['Mr. Keynes and Traditional Theory', *Econometrica*, Vol. 5, January, 1937] blatantly asserted that the marginal efficiency of capital was nothing else but the marginal productivity known to neoclassical theory, and in this way assimilated the *General Theory* to the neoclassical distribution theory. He could do this only because Keynes had been so vague and uncommitted with regard to distribution theory. The identification was a travesty. Marginal productivity relates specifically to factor substitution. Marginal efficiency, by contrast, relates primarily to an expansion of output capacity; it depends on the state of demand and on the exploitation of new technical know how. The broader meaning of Keynes's concept results from the fact that it refers to an economy in which there is no full use of resources and in which the dynamic possibilities of new technical methods come into play. These influences are embodied in the concept of expectations.

The review of Harrod as well as that of Hicks ["Mr. Keynes and the Classics: A Suggested Interpretation", *Econometrica*, Vol. 5, April, 1939] which was destined to become very influential, uses, however, a more fundamental way of attack by addressing itself to the very meaning of the *General Theory*.

The method is to misunderstand and misinterpret the *General Theory* as an equilibrium theory, a procedure which as we have seen has been facilitated by Keynes himself. By this trick all the distinctive and revolutionary features of Keynesian theory vanish and dissolve into thin air. What sense is there in a system of mutually dependent variables to argue that investment determines saving and not the other way round? The concept of effective demand as an active agent looses its meaning for the same reason. It is true that Keynes did talk of a long-term equilibrium with a "relative stability" [*Collected Writings of John Maynard Keynes,* Vol. VII, pp. 249-54].

What he described there—and it is worth re-reading—is a tendency to long-term unemployment characteristic of our system, and he added that it must not be taken as a necessity but should be changed.

The specific line taken by Hicks in his interpretation is directed towards money and interest. His main concern is to insist that an increased inducement to invest or an increase in the propensity to consume would raise the rate of interest *via* an increased demand for money on account of the transactions motive. How could Keynes, he asks, maintain that the rate of interest would not rise in these circumstances (when more money would be needed for the increased volume of business transactions)? The answer is probably that Keynes assumed the long term rate of interest to respond only very slowly to a change in the conditions of the money market (which corresponds to experience). But however that may be, the conclusions drawn by Hicks are quite amazing. He does not deny the essential Keynesian position that the rate of interest is a monetary phenomenon depending on institutions only and determined by banking policy. Yet he maintains that by demonstrating that the rate of interest must rise in the circumstances described above he has approximated the Keynesian system to that of the "classics". But for the "classics" the rate of interest is determined by material scarcity, of capital or of saving, not by institutions or policy. Yet for Hicks the Keynesian system is now, after his "corrections" concerning the rate of interest, different from the traditional classical system only under special circumstances: It is a "slump economics" or also: "the general theory of employment is the economics of depression".

It is a puzzle why Keynes did not defend himself against the interpreters who no sooner than his theory was born endeavoured to replace it by a changeling of the most doubtful character. In fact, he thanked Harrod for his review. But those who at that time underwent the conversion from "classics" to Keynes can still remember what a strenuous intellectual adventure it was. It must be realised that Keynes was surrounded by complete incomprehension of a public stunned by the novelty of his ideas. It may be that Harrod wanted to be helpful by dressing up the bogey man in impeccable academic clothes, and that Keynes took it in this way. What neither of them realised at that time was that the distortions of the first hour would grow into a ruling system called neoclassical synthesis. This theory dominated the universities in the decades in which full employment ruled in the outside world. It said that in the long run a *laissez-faire* system would re-establish and maintain full employment and that the deviations from it were temporary and unimportant.

Members of this school tended to be split personalities, putting on in turn the Keynesian hat when they advised the Administration on economic policy of the day, and the neoclassical hat when they wrote on highbrow economic theory.

A particular subspecies of the neoclassical synthesists was wont to argue that since full employment was safeguarded in any case by the Keynesian demand management, it was fully legitimate to apply neoclassical reasoning to the present world.

In this way the thought of Keynes was gradually undermined so that the take-over of the university departments by a combination of pure neoclassicists and monetarists could proceed fairly quickly. The appropriate moment for this was dictated by events outside the universities: The calling off of Keynesian policies by the leading powers.

IX HAVE KEYNESIAN POLICIES FAILED?

Before the 1970s what impressed the observer of the post-war scene was how much fuller employment was maintained than Keynes had ever expected.

When Sir William Beveridge had put the full employment target at 3 per cent Keynes wrote to him: "No harm in aiming at 3 per cent unemployment but I shall be surprised if we succeed."

The post-war unemployment rate in Britain, and in most European countries as well, was of the order of 2 per cent or less until the 1970s. In the US the figure was rather larger. The high levels of employment were realised with—what seems to us now—relatively moderate rates of inflation (of the order of 3 per cent in the 1950s and 4 per cent in the late 1960s). It has to be borne in mind, though, that this favourable result was facilitated by an improvement of the industrial countries' terms of trade in relation to the third world.

For quite a long time, therefore, the maintenance of high levels of employment succeeded much better than Keynes himself had expected.

To understand the crisis of the 1970s fully we have to realise, that even before the overt difficulties of that time certain unfavourable factors were active behind the façade of prosperity.

One of them was the fact that in some countries Keynesian policies had never been wholeheartedly adopted. The US had only a fleeting relation to full employment. Congress could be reconciled to it only when it was bound up with the military-industrial complex. The adherence to full employment policy therefore weakened in 1969.

Germany had been forced into full employment in the early fifties from outside, by an export boom. In the later sixties she pursued a restrictive monetary policy which contributed decisively to the weakening of private business investment since that time.

Great Britain departed from the cheap money policy of the early post-war years in 1951; monetary controls played a larger role since then. Full employment policy in Britain was qualified by the recurrence of balance of payments crisis (sometimes provoked by the refusal to devalue when it was necessary—in 1964) which were partly due to a structural weakness of the foreign balance and partly due to a tendency of wage levels to run ahead of those of her competitors. While in the earlier period (up to the middle sixties) the economy was overstrained owing to large defence spending, it later lost its impetus because private investment flagged.

But the weakening of investment may not have been exclusively a result of the policies pursued, it may also have come from certain structural changes in the capitalist system. The concentration of business proceeded and this tended to increase the fear of excess capacity and a cautious attitude to investment. A symptom of the weakening interest in real investment was the take-over movement, a growing interest in financial manipulation as opposed to production. The weakening of private investment was the direct cause of the growing budget deficits, a development which reached its climax after the recession of 1974-75.

If Keynesian policies are said to have failed in the 1970s this can only mean that continuing full employment has proved impossible because it has led to insuperable difficulties. Most prominent among these difficulties is the tendency for "efficiency wages" (as Keynes termed wages per unit of output) to drift upwards and thus to cause inflation. This has always been stressed by the close followers of Keynes, Joan Robinson, Lord Kahn and Lord Kaldor. Keynes himself foresaw the difficulty, and stated that this was a political question.

This is indeed confirmed by the observation that restraint on wage levels operates in a climate of social consensus (Sweden, Austria, Germany, Switzerland) whereas wage inflation is uncontrollable in a climate of social confrontation (Italy, Great Britain, France before De Gaulle and after 1968). It appears that inflation is the expression of a latent conflict about income distribution which is carried on continuously, with everybody passing on the bill which nobody wants to pay. It may also be more than a coincidence that wage inflation characteristically dominates in countries with unstable government: Great Britain has only once in the post-war period had a government (Macmillan) which lasted longer than five years. The "see-saw" is bound to act as a de-stabiliser on economic calculations. Italy with a permanently unstable government is another example.

The wider socio-political aspects of full employment policy no doubt would deserve close study. The long period of full employment and prosperity has wrought considerable social changes; sometimes these changes have come, in typical Marxian fashion, in conflict with existing rigid structures, and social and political tensions have resulted. An outbreak of such tensions occurred in 1968 with the student movement and militant workers' unrest, simultaneous in a number of countries, in France verging for a moment on social revolution. The wage explosion 1968-70 followed in the wake of these signs of social impatience. By way of a feedback process (wage-price-wage spiral) a wage explosion confined to one year increased also the inflation rates of the following years. The effects of the wage explosion might still have been managed if it had not been for subsequent events: the transition to fluctuating exchanges removed an important restraint on wages, and the divergence of inflation rates in different countries was thereby increased. To this was further added the *hausse* in commodity prices in 1973 and the oil shock at the end of that year.

After the recession in 1974-75 had started it soon became obvious that the US and Germany had given up full employment policies. This was a political choice. These countries had not done all they could to explore alternative ways, such as an incomes policy based on social consensus instead of confrontation. Moreover, by letting the dollar drift downwards, US inflation was powerfully stimulated. Nor is it clear that inflation would have been worse than it actually was if the US had pursued a policy of expansion to absorb the excess of labour supply. This would have avoided the loss in productivity growth which drove up the wage cost per unit of output, and which resulted from stunted growth of GDP and low capacity utilisation.

But while the preoccupation with inflation was understandable in the US where owing to less social security private saving is more widely important than in Europe, giving up full employment in Europe represented a more surprising change of policy. Some countries such as France were holding out for an expansionist policy in 1975, and they were ultimately forced to give it up only because of Germany's restrictive policies. Thus the ultimate victory of the restrictionist policy almost everywhere resulted not from independent decisions of the different countries, but was to a large extent brought about by the pressure which the creditor countries with their low inflation rates brought to bear on the rest of the industrial world.

This leads to a subject which has to be treated separately in detail. It concerns the worsening in international economic relations which started in the late 1960s. That the foreign balance was the neuralgic point in his policies Keynes knew only too well and in his later years he was entirely occupied with this complex of questions.

X THE DEFEAT

The war changed the position of Keynes: from an outside critic he became a member of the establishment, holding a highly responsible office in the Treasury. He was concerned with war finance on which he had written an analysis which became the basis for a new understanding of this subject [*How to Pay for the War*]. In particular he introduced the concept of the inflationary gap, the difference between the amount of effective demand and the available supply, as a measure of the degree of inflation.

The policy of cheap money pursued during this war was due to his influence and in consequence it became known as a 3 per cent war as opposed to the 5 per cent war 25 years earlier. The easy money policy and the large treasury borrowing was made possible by the strict controls of the British was economy which created a dam for the large excess of incomes over available civilian supplies, channelling it off into saving: beside exchange control there were the physical controls at home—raw material controls and extensive rationing of consumer goods. Curiously enough, rationing did not meet with the approval of Keynes. It competed with his own "deferred payment" scheme of taxes to be repaid after the war. This scheme was applied in practice only to a very limited extent, and rationing which corresponded more nearly to the strategy proposed by Kalecki, became the effective instrument for dealing with the inflationary gap. In this question Keynes was less advanced than the war time civil service which, driven by necessity, came to understand very well the administrative and socio-politic advantages of the strategy of rationing ("fair shares").

The main concern of Keynes was, however, external finance. This involved, in particular, the negotiations with the United States which, from the Mutual Aid Agreement over Bretton Woods to the Financial Agreement were carried out by him.

In the Keynesian work of these war years two different but interwoven themes were present: One was ensuring the survival of Britain by procuring finance for its pressing needs day by day. The other was to lay the plans for a new international order of currencies, applying Keynesian thinking on a world scale. The two were, unfortunately, not unrelated. Britain, completely drained of reserves by 1940 and having sacrificed two-thirds of her exports, was dependent on supplies offered by the United States as "Lend and Lease" which was granted on the understanding that Britain would "pursue a policy, in cooperation with the United States, for world recovery and prosperity" [Harrod, *Life of John Maynard Keynes*].

American ideas on what this policy was to be were coloured by the free trade ideology of the State Department and its leader Cordell Hull. This corresponded to the interests of a creditor country of great industrial efficiency. A special bugbear was discrimination, one of its forms being non-convertibility of currencies. A ban on discrimination was the chief content of the "consideration" demanded of Britain. After being first mentioned in the Atlantic Charter it became Article VII of the Mutual Aid Agreement. This was directed against Britain's Imperial Preference and it also would have rendered impossible any bilateral practices. Convertibility was insisted on in the Bretton Woods Agreement with a period of grace of 5 years which was reduced to two years in the Financial Agreement of 1945 (the conditions for the post-war loan).

Now to the Keynesian vision of an international order. It started from a specific problem, the prospective difficulties of post-war Britain, but it had a much more general significance.

Keynes had already in 1933 thought of an international currency order which would secure abundant liquidity and therefore obviate the aggressive scramble for gold or equivalent reserves which destabilised and depressed the level of world trade and which forced weaker countries into a deflationary policy of unemployment. In the early stage of the war Keynes considered two alternative ways of avoiding a recurrence of the conditions of the interwar period: Britain, with American assistance, could employ Keynesian remedies for unemployment and trade depression on a world scale. This involved also measures for stabilising commodity prices by means of Buffer Stocks, proposed in a Memorandum for the War Cabinet on the International Regulation of Primary Products. Proposals for the finance of the Buffer Stocks were also contained in the plan for the Clearing Union. (These plans were gradually lost sight of in view of the pressure of currency problems and also owing to Keynes's illness). Or else, Britain, thrown back on her own devices, would have to make use of the bilateral techniques developed in Germany by Schacht. Pursuing the first alternative Keynes set to work from 1941 on to develop his famous plan for an International Clearing Union. Its idea was to base the international monetary order not on gold but on a central fund into which each country (in accordance with a quota settled for each country) would pay in its own currency and from which it would obtain the right to draw within certain limits whatever currencies it needed to balance its foreign accounts. In this way the fund would act as a clearing house for the countries of the world, it would settle surpluses and deficits in their balance of payments by a general reckoning up.

The most important aims pursued by the plan for a Clearing Union were the following:

(a) Adequate reserves were to be created and an equitable and reasonable distribution of these reserves was to be guaranteed.

(b) Arrangements were to be made to counteract the existing bias against the debtor countries and in favour of the creditor countries, which favoured depression. Not only persistent debtor countries but equally also persistent creditor countries were to be forced to contribute their part to the adjustment whenever a disequilibrium arose. In this way the bias in favour of depression characteristic of the present system was to be avoided.

(c) It was to be recognised that adjustment of exchange rates were necessary and reasonable in certain circumstances. Therefore rigidity of exchange rates was not proposed, but the opposite extreme, fluctuating exchanges, was also excluded.

The aim was not only to start the countries off on expanding trade, but also to prevent disequilibria from arising, or to correct them if they arose, and to maintain a continuing expansionist climate. The plan was criticised for not going far enough by Kalecki and Schumacher. But no doubt the plan offered a chance for the revival of world trade after the war.

At this point, however, the harsh realities of the other preoccupation of Keynes came into play. The United States had drawn up a rival plan, the White-Plan, which was strongly based on gold, did not provide adequate reserves and did not correct the bias in favour of the creditor.

After negotiations in September-October 1943 a Joint Statement of the United States and Britain was published in April 1944 which leaned essentially on the US proposals. It constituted the defeat of Keynes's aims. In Britain it was passionately opposed by Hubert Henderson, Joan Robinson and Thomas Balogh. The Joint Statement was the basis for the Bretton Woods conference in July 1944 and the Savannah conference 1945 from which the International Monetary Fund and the World Bank emerged.

Bretton Woods involved nothing essentially new. The ruling system became a gold-dollar exchange instead of a gold-sterling exchange. As predicted by Henderson, Balogh and Joan Robinson the system was not in a position to stand up to the post-war strain which resulted from the contrast between the demand of an impoverished Europe and the output capacity of the US and led to a large excess demand for dollars. This danger had been soft-pedalled by Keynes who had made himself the defender of his own undoing. When Britain, in an attempt to carry out the obligation contracted against the loan of 1945, introduced convertibility in 1947, the Bretton Woods system effectively broke down, because this move failed instantaneously. In the further course of events, the international payments system was kept going only owing to massive American loans and investments and chiefly to Marshall aid which constituted in a way a realisation or substitute for Keynesian plans for the recovery of the world.

It seems that Keynes was beaten by historical necessity, in so far as he happened to represent a waning power (although this was not essential for the principles he stood for). This interpretation is not generally shared. Lord Kahn thinks that the British position was stronger than it seemed and that a great part of the concessions might have been avoided. Keynes had been a very sick man which affected his stamina and his whole outlook. (He died four weeks after return from the Savannah conference).

The defeat of Keynes is still felt today. From Bretton Woods and Savannah a wide arch is spanned to our own time. The countries of Europe, trusting in the existence of a working international order, have been induced to open themselves up with regard to trade and payments. But, it is obvious by now, a workable international order does not exist. Countries find themselves helplessly thrown about by arbitrary movements of capital and exchange rates. They are, as Keynes had warned on the eve of the return to gold, bound to Wall Street in their interest rate policy. A house of cards—the Euromarket—has been built up, which is exempt from any kind of national or international control. It is the ultimate triumph of *laissez-faire* in the matter of finance. Where is the lender of the last resort to which, on an international level, banks will be able to turn if this structure starts crumbling?

The decisive defeat of Keynesian policies did not come in the domestic sphere of wage policy, it occurred in the international field. Indeed, the two digit inflation in industrial countries which is widely regarded as the rock on which Keynesian policy had been ultimately stranded was itself merely the consequence of uncontrolled *laissez-faire* in the international commodity markets. This regime was pleasant enough for the industrial countries in so far as it turned the terms of trade in their favour in the 1950s and 1960s. But the low commodity prices led to neglect of investment in the plantations and mines, so that the output could not cope with the sudden increase in demand in the world boom of the early seventies.

The point of Keynes's Buffer Stock Scheme had been precisely to avoid this: by maintaining adequate and stable prices it was to secure a steady development of supplies.

In a different way also the case of oil demonstrates the consequence of *laissez-faire:* the excessively low prices of the pre-OPEC times made the industrial world wasteful of oil and drove it into an extreme dependence on oil producers who then took revenge on their former exploiters. Here too, international agreements between producers and consumers might have avoided the extreme changes of the terms of trade. Moreover, the Clearing Union would from the start have prevented frustration of development countries by giving them adequate credits for investment. This should have reduced the latent tension between

North and South and therefore the likelihood of "ganging up" on either side.

The "invisible hand" has certainly not left traces of any kind of rational ordering; instead the visible heavy hand of creditor countries has imposed their policies on others.

If Keynes was defeated, it was not on the plane of logic: It was on the plane of power. Was he then, was the Clearing Union and the Buffer Stock Scheme, utopian? Yes, and it looks even more so today. Yet it is said that utopians are the greater realists. We are today faced with the same questions which confronted Keynes in the years 1939-41 in his thinking on international relations. We have practically not got any further in the meantime. If we want to start anew, we have to start where Keynes left off.

Bill Gerrard   (essay date 1988)

SOURCE: "Keynesian Economics: The Road to Nowhere?" in *J. M. Keynes in Retrospect: The Legacy of the Keynesian Revolution*, edited by John Hillard, Edward Elgar, 1988, pp. 125-52.

[*In the following essay, Gerrard charts the development of what he terms "mainstream Keynesianism"—the various attempts made by economists since the publication of the* General Theory *to reconcile classical economic theory with the existence of involuntary employment—and assesses the value of these developments with respect to economic theory, method, and policy.*]

INTRODUCTION

Economics in the last fifty years has been mainly Keynesian economics, inspired by Keynes' ***General Theory***. Keynes challenged classical theory, the then prevailing orthodoxy in economics. Classical theory concluded that the economy tends automatically to a position of full employment if the price mechanism is free to operate in all markets. Keynes claimed to have broken away from this orthodoxy by showing that it is possible for involuntary unemployment to occur without any automatic tendency to recovery.

Keynesian economics has been an attempt to understand and elaborate on Keynes' claim, coupled with the development of appropriate policies to overcome involuntary unemployment. But within Keynesian economics, there have been and still are many deep divisions over just exactly what causes involuntary unemployment. Many Keynesians have tried to understand Keynes from the standpoint of classical theory. This is what I would call *mainstream Keynesianism*—Keynesianism that remains firmly wedded to the *market-theoretic approach* of classical theory but arrives at Keynesian conclusions. Mainstream Keynesianism is the search for the 'missing link' that reconciles the existence of involuntary unemployment with the market-theoretic approach.

Over the years there have been many attempts to provide the Keynesian missing link—the IS-LM model, the neoclassical synthesis, the disequilibrium and neo-Walrasian analyses, and the recent work on imperfect competition and imperfect information. Yet all these varied contribu-

tions can, I believe, be interpreted as a coherent research programme in which each new phase of development flowed from the perceived deficiencies of the previous phase. The object of this paper is to elaborate on this interpretation of mainstream Keynesianism and to offer an evaluation of the contribution of mainstream Keynesianism to the development of economic thought.

KEYNESIANISM PHASE I

The IS-LM model

The IS-LM model is the starting-point for mainstream Keynesianism. The IS-LM model was developed by Hicks (1937) as an attempt to clarify the General Theory. It captured the essential change in the 'style' of economic theory that Keynes had instigated. Classical theory takes a 'bottom-up' approach, concentrating on the determination of prices and physical quantities within individual markets. The focus is on the micro-level, on the behaviour of rational economic agents. The macro-results of classical theory, such as full-employment equilibrium and the neutrality of money, are clearly derived from its microfoundations. Keynesian economics, on the other hand, focuses directly on the macro-level, dealing with the determination of aggregate monetary flows.

The IS-LM model analyses the demand-side of the economy in terms of three aggregate behavioural relationships:

1 the consumption (or savings) function;

2 the investment function; and

3 the demand for money function.

Given these three functions, the level of money income and the rate of interest are determined such that the goods and money markets are in equilibrium simultaneously.

On its own, however, the IS-LM model is inadequate for an analysis of unemployment. The reason lies in the change to the macro-style of theory. The IS-LM model derives the equilibrium level of aggregate *money* income. But the level of employment (and unemployment) depends on the level of physical output, i.e. *real* income. To move from monetary flows to employment levels it is necessary to determine the composition of money income in terms of physical output and nominal value. Without a solution to this 'transformation problem' the IS-LM model cannot analyse unemployment. Hicks bridged the theoretical gap between the aggregate monetary flow and the level of employment (what could be called the 'Keynesian dichotomy') by the assumption of a fixed money wage. Given this assumption, it follows that the level of money income and the level of employment are positively related. Hence a position of full employment is associated with a particular level of money income. This creates the possibility of an unemployment equilibrium in which the demand-side of the economy is in equilibrium at a level of money income below that necessary for full employment.

The Hicksian IS-LM model views the General Theory as an inversion of the classical vision of the economy in which the supply-side drives the whole system. In the IS-LM model, the supply-side exerts no causal influence in the determination of the level of employment. Instead, the level of employment is entirely consequent on the demand-side. This implies two fundamental breaks with the method of classical theory. First, the economy is no longer seen in purely market-theoretic terms since there is no labour market. The money wage is assumed to be exogenously given rather than being determined by the forces of demand and supply. Secondly, there is now an element of *sequentialism* introduced into the theoretical structure. The classical theory of general equilibrium is concerned with the *simultaneous* determination of all prices and quantities. In the IS-LM model this simultaneity is retained only with respect to the demand-side. The supply-side outcomes (i.e. output and employment levels) are now entirely consequent on the demand-side rather than being co-determinate.

The methodological innovations of the IS-LM model were never made explicit. Instead the 'Keynes v. the Classics' debate centred on the theoretical implications of Keynes. The obvious 'innovation' of Keynes is the multiplier, the notion that investment and saving would be brought into equilibrium by changes in the level of money income. In classical theory any change in aggregate demand would be completely offset by the automatic movement of the appropriate price, namely, the rate of interest. In Keynesian theory, however, any change in aggregate demand would create a reinforcing multiplier effect through the consumption function.

But, according to Hicks's analysis, the consumption function is not incompatible with classical theory. Indeed, it follows directly from the micro-analysis of consumer behaviour under budget constraints. The consumption function falls into the background in classical theory because the level of money income is fixed by the money supply via the quantity theory of money. The existence of a multiplier effect requires the possibility that any given money supply can be associated with various equilibrium levels of money income. It is precisely just this possibility that is denied by the quantity theory of money, but is created by liquidity preference, the notion that the demand for money depends partly on the rate of interest.

Liquidity preference prevents the rate of interest from automatically adjusting to the natural rate, thus ensuring the sufficiency of aggregate demand. Liquidity preference introduces monetary factors into the determination of the rate of interest. This destroys the classical dichotomy and creates the possibility that the equilibrium rate of interest may not be the natural rate of interest (now defined as that rate of interest which generates a level of investment equal to the level of savings that is associated with the full employment level of money income).

For Hicks then, the crucial innovation in the ***General Theory*** is liquidity preference. But, as Hicks points out, liquidity preference is not really an innovation of Keynes. It can be seen as an extension of the Cambridge demand for money function which had already been proposed most notably by Lavington. Whereas the original Cambridge demand for money function considered money only in its role as a means of exchange, liquidity preference introduces money's other role as a store of wealth. On this view, the importance of Keynes lies in his being the first to appreciate the significance of this development. A similar conclusion is drawn on the multiplier effect which, although highlighted by Keynes, had been proposed originally by Kahn.

The view of Keynes that emerges from Hicks is very much that of an economist making a 'great leap forward' in the development of classical theory. In theoretical terms, the 'leap forward' consisted of the development of liquidity preference and its consequences, coupled with the macro style of presentation. That Hicks saw Keynes as wholly within the orthodox tradition is evident from his argument that Keynes' theory is just a special case of what Hicks called the 'Generalised General Theory', of which classical theory and so-called Treasury view are other special cases. In effect, all that Keynes is seen to have done is to give a sophisticated elaboration of the problems of demand-side maladjustment, particularly those created by the influence of monetary factors on the rate of interest. The extreme case of this occurs when the demand for money becomes infinitely elastic with respect to the rate of interest when the economy is in a liquidity trap. This possibility is what Hicks terms 'Mr Keynes' Special Theory'. Later, Keynesians also considered demand-side maladjustment caused by investment being interest-inelastic.

The difference between the form of the classical and Keynesian analyses of demand-side maladjustment due to the Keynesian introduction of liquidity preference leads to a crucial difference in consequences. Whereas in classical theory there exists an automatic tendency for the rate of interest to adjust to ensure a return to a full employment equilibrium (in the absence of any supply-side problem), there is no such tendency in the Keynesian theory. Following on from this, the importance of Keynes' theoretical contribution lies in its provision of a justification for the need for systematic government intervention to ensure sufficient aggregate demand to maintain full employment. This policy implication became the very essence of Keynesianism. Furthermore, this *necessity* for demand management became associated with the *need* to use fiscal policy especially if the economy is caught in a liquidity trap and/or investment is interest-inelastic. In both these circumstances monetary policy is rendered completely ineffective and there is no crowding-out effect to reduce the effectiveness of a fiscal expansion.

The neo-classical synthesis

The IS-LM model focuses on the demand-side of the economy with the employment implications of any demand-side equilibrium being derived by using a fixed money-wage assumption to bridge the 'Keynesian dichotomy'. From the orthodox point of view, this assumption is the crucial weakness of the IS-LM model since, in effect, it removes the entire supply-side of the economy from the analysis. Thus the orthodox theorists viewed the IS-LM model as only a partial equilibrium analysis which had to be extended into a general equilibrium analysis by introducing the labour market. This is exactly what Modigliani (1944) did in his paper 'Liquidity Preference and the Theory of Interest and Money'. The consequences were inevitable:

It is usually considered as one of the most important achievements of the Keynesian theory that it explains the consistency of economic equilibrium with the presence of involuntary unemployment. It is, however, not sufficiently recognised that, except in a limiting case . . . , this result is due entirely to the assumption of 'rigid wages' and not to the Keynesian liquidity preference.

Bringing the labour market back into the model returns the analysis to its classical market-theoretic form. If the labour market is competitive there is a tendency for the real wage to adjust to ensure full employment. The substantive Keynesian innovation is the introduction of liquidity preference which alters the process whereby sufficient aggregate demand is generated. Given that the rate of interest is now influenced by both real and monetary factors it is possible that, at the existing aggregate price level, the equilibrium rate of interest may not be the natural rate. To compensate for this, it now falls on the aggregate price level to adjust to ensure the sufficiency of aggregate demand. If there is a lack of aggregate demand the price level tends to fall which increases the real value of the money supply and in turn produces an expansion-inducing fall in the rate of interest—the so-called *Keynes effect*. Thus in the *neo*-classical model, real wage adjustments ensure a full-employment level of aggregate supply while a combination of interest rate and price adjustments ensure sufficient aggregate demand. Again the money wage plays a crucial role. There is a unique money wage that renders consistent the supply-determined real wage and the demand-determined price level.

Having reintroduced the labour market, Modigliani found, not surprisingly, that, except for a limiting case, involuntary unemployment (i.e. a level of unemployment above the natural rate) is caused by 'rigid [money] wages'—the traditional classical argument of supply-side imperfection leading to real wage maladjustment. The limiting case to which Modigliani referred is the situation in which the natural rate of interest is too low to be attainable. This can happen either because of the existence of a liquidity trap or because investment is so interest-inelastic that the natural rate of interest is negative. Hence the limiting case is that of interest rate maladjustment leading to a below full employment level of aggregate demand. The causes of involuntary unemployment are essentially the same as those provided by the classical theorists prior to Keynes. The only Keynesian innovation is to alter the analysis of interest rate maladjustment on the demand-side through the introduction of liquidity preference.

Modigliani laid the foundations for the emergence of the *neo-classical synthesis* in which orthodox theorists believed that they had integrated Keynes within the classical tradition. The neo-classical synthesis combines the market-theoretic theory with the Keynesian macro 'style' of analysis. The basic vision is that the economy is a generalized market system in which demand-and-supply analysis is the starting-point for understanding the operation of individual markets. The macro-style of analysis comes into its own when the focus of attention moves from partial equilibrium to general equilibrium. Macro-economics provides a means of 'getting a handle on' the important interrelationships between markets, the multiplier effect being the most prominent. The Keynesian Revolution became regarded as a revolution only in style in which the basic vision of the economic system remained unaltered.

If a market-theoretic approach is adopted, it follows that, in general, the perfect flexibility of all prices (including wages and interest rates) ensures a continual tendency towards a position of generalized market-clearing and, in particular, a full employment equilibrium. This is a basic truth accepted by all who work within the neo-classical synthesis. This implies that if there is a prolonged period of involuntary unemployment, it must be caused by the existence of imperfections that are blocking the free operation of competitive forces on the supply-side and/or the demand-side. The market-theoretic approach necessarily leads to *imperfectionist* theories of involuntary unemployment. The crucial issue becomes the evaluation of the degree of imperfection present in the market economy.

The Keynesian-neo-classical debate

The Keynesian-neo-classical debate was a debate *within* the neo-classical synthesis. Both schools accepted the market-theoretic approach and adopted imperfectionist theories of unemployment. They agreed over the fundamentals but differed over the extent and persistence of imperfections in the market economy and whether or not other automatic mechanisms existed which could overcome the effects of these imperfections. The Keynesians were characterized by their belief in the significance of imperfections and in the lack of automatic adjustment mechanisms that would be effective within a short-run time-scale. The neo-classicals, on the other hand, argued for the efficacy of the price mechanism. The Keynesian-neo-classical debate focused on four specific issues.

The form of the aggregate behavioural functions

The consumption function In the Keynesian consumption function, it is the level of current income which determines the level of current consumption. This is the most crucial relationship in Keynesian theory since it is responsible for generating the multiplier process. An increase in the current flow of income leads to an increase in the flow of consumption which, in turn, leads to a further increase in income and so on. Neo-classical theorists, on the other hand, have tended to play down the role of current income, stressing instead the importance of wealth (both current and expected) as well as the rate of interest, as the determinants of consumption. Friedman's permanent income hypothesis and Ando and Modigliani's life-cycle hypothesis are examples of the neo-classical consumption function in which current consumption is partly stock-determined as well as flow-determined (Friedman, 1957; Ando and Modigliani, 1963). The less flow-determined is consumption, the more stable is the economic system, since, in the event of a fall in current income, agents can liquidate some of their stocks of wealth in order to maintain a constant level of consumption.

The investment function Neo-classical theorists see the rate of interest as the most significant determinant of the level of investment, Jorgenson's 'cost of-capital' theory being a more sophisticated development of this traditional supply-side theory of investment (Jorgenson, 1967). Keynesians, on the other hand, have stressed demand-side factors, usually presented in terms of an *accelerator* mechanism in which the level of investment is determined by changes in the income flow. The accelerator mechanism reinforces the instability effect of the multiplier process.

The demand-for-money function Neo classical theorists remained firmly wedded to the quantity theory tradition with a relatively interest-inelastic demand-for-money function, the rate of interest being considered essentially a non-monetary phenomenon. Keynesians took a diametrically opposed view, seeing the rate of interest as a significant factor in the money market rather than the goods market. The Keynesians have argued for an interest-elastic demand-for-money function, the liquidity trap being an extreme case. One important development from the Keynesian viewpoint was Baumol's demonstration that the transactions demand would also be sensitive to the rate of interest (Baumol, 1952).

Overall, in the debate over the aggregate behavioural functions, the neo-classicals have argued for the level of aggregate demand to be the outcome of a stock allocation process in which the rate of interest plays a key equilibrating role. This implies that the economic system is reasonably stable around a full employment equilibrium. Keynesians, however, have tended to highlight the potential instability of the system. This instability is created by the level of aggregate demand being primarily determined by the income flow, stock adjustments and the rate of interest having only a minimal impact in the goods market.

Growth

The Keynesian-neo-classical debate over the *short-run* stability of a market economy had its *long-run* counterpart in the debates between the Keynesian Harrod-Domar growth model and Solow's neoclassical growth model (Harrod, 1939; Solow, 1956). The Harrod-Domar model merged the multiplier and accelerator mechanisms to model the long-run growth path of an economy. The result was the famous knife-edge solution in which it is shown that there is no automatic mechanism to ensure that an economy grows at a rate sufficient to ensure full employment over time. The neo-classical response was to argue that factor-price adjustments provided just such a mechanism. The emergence of long-run involuntary unemployment would tend to lower labour costs relative to capital costs, thereby inducing a transfer towards more labour-intensive production techniques. Thus even in the long run the price mechanism is sufficiently effective to ensure a Golden Age growth path in which full employment is maintained over time as the labour force grows.

The wealth effect

The wealth effect is the overall impact on the level of aggregate demand caused by a change in the real value of the stock of wealth following a change in the aggregate price level. Keynesians argued that the wealth effect operated *indirectly* via the Keynes effect. A price deflation could increase aggregate demand by inducing an investment-stimulating fall in the rate of interest as agents engage in a portfolio readjustment process to remove their excess

real cash balances by buying bonds. Keynesians believed that the expansionary effect of a price deflation would be small, there being no effect at all if the economy is in a liquidity trap or if investment is interest-inelastic. Both these situations would render the Keynes effect inoperative.

Neo-classicals countered by arguing that the Keynesians had a very restricted view of the wealth effect. Not only did the wealth effect operate indirectly via the rate of interest, it also had a *direct* impact on the level of aggregate demand via the 'Pigou effect'. This direct wealth effect follows necessarily from the various neo-classical consumption functions which all include some form of asset variable as a primary determinant of current consumption. The existence of a direct wealth effect ensures that the price mechanism will overcome automatically any involuntary unemployment caused by demand-side maladjustment. Through the Pigou effect, a fall in the aggregate price level will compensate for any inadequacy in the interest rate adjustment mechanism (i.e. the Keynes effect) caused by the existence of a liquidity trap or by investment being interest-inelastic. Thus the Pigou effect overcomes Modigliani's limiting case of demand-side maladjustment, implying that an involuntary unemployment equilibrium occurs if and only if there is supply-side maladjustment. In other words, in the neo-classical view of the world, the ultimate cause of an involuntary unemployment equilibrium is the presence of wage rigidity in the labour market.

Policy implications

Since they believed that involuntary unemployment is due to a lack of aggregate demand, Keynesians advocated government intervention to increase aggregate demand. Furthermore, Keynesians tended to adopt a *fiscalist* stance—a belief that fiscal policy is more effective than monetary policy. Fiscalism is a necessary consequence of the Keynesian belief that the Keynes effect is of relatively minor importance. In such circumstances, fiscal policy becomes all-powerful since there is no crowding-out effect to reduce its impact. On the other hand, monetary policy becomes completely ineffective since the causal chain linking the money and goods markets is broken if there is a liquidity trap or if investment is interest-inelastic.

Neo-classicals argued against an expansionary fiscal policy on two grounds: (1) the crowding-out effect of any fiscal expansion would be very significant: and (2) anyway the problem lay on the supply-side not the demand-side since the price mechanism would be sufficient to overcome any demand-side maladjustment.

KEYNESIANISM PHASE II

Patinkin's disequilibrium analysis

The link between phases I and II in the development of Keynesian economics is provided by Patinkin in his book *Money, Interest and Prices* (1956). Once the direct component of the wealth effect is considered, movements in the aggregate price level overcome any interest rate maladjustment on the demand side of the economy. Hence, if the economy is in equilibrium at below full employment there must be supply-side maladjustment—i.e. wage rigidity.

Patinkin expressed this conclusion in terms of what he called his 'coexistence theorem': the coexistence of money wage flexibility and equilibrium precludes involuntary unemployment. Keynesian economics becomes just the macro-analysis of the effects of wage rigidity—a classical diagnosis of the causes of unemployment.

Patinkin concluded that if Keynes was saying something new, the **General Theory** had to involve a change in the *method* of analysis. Keynesianism Phase I had reached classical conclusions because it retained the classical method that treated involuntary unemployment as a *static equilibrium* phenomenon. Wage rigidity necessarily follows as the cause of this unemployment with the implication that a return to full employment requires a reduction in the real wage rate. An alternative that, according to Patinkin, was adopted at least implicitly by keynes, is to see involuntary unemployment as a *dynamic disequilibrium* phenomenon. It is this change in approach that marks the beginning of Keynesianism Phase II.

The change in method from a static equilibrium analysis to a dynamic disequilibrium analysis meant that involuntary unemployment was no longer seen in terms of rigidities that prevented any adjustment, but rather in terms of slow *speeds of adjustment*. Involuntary unemployment is caused by the inevitable time-lags involved in the dynamic process of adjustment towards equilibrium. On this view the Keynesian-neo-classical debate is not about the degree of flexibility of prices (including wages and interest rates). Rather it concerns the speed of adjustment of the market mechanism, the neo-classicals believing the market mechanism to be relatively quick whereas the Keynesians believe it to be relatively slow, thereby leading to significant levels of involuntary unemployment during any period of disequilibrium.

Patinkin explained the difference between neo-classical and Keynesian analyses by comparing their respective analyses of the effects of a fall in aggregate demand. In the neo-classical analysis, the fall in aggregate demand automatically triggers market forces which tend to offset it quickly. In particular, the fall in the aggregate price level generates a rise in aggregate demand via the wealth effect. Given the temporary nature of the fall in aggregate demand, firms do not reduce their output and employment levels. Thus no involuntary unemployment occurs under the neo-classical analysis.

In the Keynesian analysis, aggregate demand recovers relatively slowly so that the adjustment process becomes prolonged. Firms eventually have to reduce their output and employment levels to bring them into line with current sales, thus creating involuntary unemployment. In effect, the demand constraint faced by firms in the goods market forces them to move to positions *off* their output supply and labour demand curves. Given the existing set of market prices and wages, firms would like to sell more output and employ more labour but are prevented from realizing these wishes by the lack of aggregate demand. The involuntary unemployment that occurs in the Keynesian analysis is a disequilibrium phenomenon since there are forces at work, albeit slow-working, which will move the economy away from this position. The excess supply of labour will tend to push down the money wage rate while the non-realization of desired output supply will tend to lead firms to reduce their price levels. The combination of price and wage deflation will eventually ensure that there is sufficient aggregate demand for a return to full employment.

Thus, under Patinkin's analysis, involuntary unemployment can exist in a system in which all markets are perfectly competitive and prices and wages are flexible. Money wage rigidity is no longer a necessary condition for the existence of involuntary unemployment. Rather, involuntary unemployment arises from the slowness of adjustment following an exogenous disturbance that reduces aggregate demand. The persistence of insufficient demand eventually forces firms to reduce their output and employment levels. The involuntary unemployment that results is a disequilibrium phenomenon since a slow-working adjustment process exists which will eventually return the economy to a full-employment equilibrium. Hence involuntary unemployment is necessarily dynamic in nature, involving movements off the demand and supply schedules of agents.

This disequilibrium analysis has two important policy implications. First, it justifies government intervention to stimulate aggregate demand in the event of involuntary unemployment emerging when the speed of the self-adjusting mechanisms within the economy is too slow to ensure a return to full employment within an 'acceptable' time-period. The justification for government intervention is not based on *a priori* principles but is a matter of empirical investigation on the speed of adjustment and political judgement over what constitutes an acceptable period of disequilibrium. Secondly, the view of involuntary unemployment as a dynamic disequilibrium phenomenon implies that a fall in real wages is neither a necessary nor a sufficient condition for the rapid re-establishment of a full-employment equilibrium. If an economy is at full employment and a exogenous shock reduces the level of demand, involuntary unemployment occurs even though the real wage is at the market-clearing level. The return to full employment does not, therefore require a fall in the real wage. The notion that a real wage is necessary for a return to full employment arises from the use of static equilibrium analysis in which involuntary unemployment is ultimately seen to be due to wage rigidities.

Clower and the dual decision hypothesis

In his 1965 paper 'The Keynesian Counter-Revolution: A Theoretical Appraisal', Clower (1979) produced a disequilibrium analysis that complemented Patinkin's contribution. Whereas Patinkin had been concerned with the effects on the labour market of excess supply in the goods market, Clower was concerned with the effects on the goods market of excess supply in the labour market. Clower dealt with the 'other side of the coin' as regards the implications of the price mechanism having a slow speed of adjustment.

Clower proposed the *dual decision hypothesis*. Given the existing price vector, households plan their notional consumption demand on the basis of some notional level of income to be obtained from the sale of their labour services. If the household sells its notional supply it will have sufficient income with which to achieve its notional level of consumption. However, if the household fails to sell its notional labour supply, actual income is less than notional income. The failure to realize notional income necessitates a second round of decisions by the household in which actual consumption demand is reduced. This actual consumption demand based on realized income is what Clower called *effective* demand—demand that can be effected in the market.

Notional consumption demand equates to effective consumption demand at the aggregate level if and only if full employment pertains since, by definition, this is the only circumstance in which all workers realize their notional labour supply. Thus, if involuntary unemployment emerges in the labour market, via the dual decision hypothesis, this will have a spillover effect on the goods market—excess supply in the labour market will generate excess supply in the goods market.

Generalized disequilibrium analysis and the neo-Walrasian interpretation of Keynes

The analyses provided by Patinkin and Clower are complementary. Patinkin showed the process whereby the emergence of excess supply in the goods market would generate excess supply in the labour market while Clower showed the process whereby excess supply in the labour market would generate excess supply in the goods market. These two processes obviously interact in a mutually reinforcing manner. From Patinkin's analysis a fall in aggregate demand leads to involuntary unemployment which, in turn, from Clower's analysis, leads to a further fall in aggregate demand, and so on. There is, in other words, a *multiplier effect* by which an initial disturbance is transmitted through the economy and thereby perpetuated. The integration of the separate analyses of Patinkin and Clower was achieved by Barro and Grossman in their 1971 paper 'A General Disequilibrium Model of Income and Employment'.

Barro and Grossman show that, in the absence of price adjustments, the emergence of excess supply in the goods market sets in motion a multiplier process which continues until the economy reaches the quasi-equilibrium in which firms have adjusted their output and employment levels in line with the level of effective demand in the goods market. At this quasi-equilibrium, all agents are optimizing, given the constraints placed on their decisions by the persistence of generalized excess notional supply. The consistency of these constrained behaviour patterns means that the economy may suffer a period of prolonged involuntary unemployment. But such a position is still a disequilibrium one since eventually the pressure of excess notional supply in the goods and labour markets will bring about a fall in prices and money wages. The fall in the price level will induce a positive wealth effect which will stimulate aggregate demand and thereby begin a multiplier process in an expansionary direction, resulting in a return to a full-employment general equilibrium.

Generalized excess supply is the disequilibrium position generated by an adverse movement on the demand-side.

Barro and Grossman recognized that this is only one type of disequilibrium. They also considered the case of generalized excess demand caused by an increase in aggregate demand in the goods market which firms are unable to match by increased output and employment levels. Equilibrium is eventually restored when the aggregate price level rises, inducing a fall in demand by lowering the real value of wealthholdings.

Generalized excess supply and generalized excess demand are not the only types of disequilibrium. In his 1976 Yrjö Jahnsson lectures Malinvaud extended generalized disequilibrium analysis to cover three cases:

Case I: *Keynesian unemployment*—excess supply in both the goods and the labour markets.

Case II: *Repressed inflation*—excess demand in both the goods and the labour markets.

These are the two cases analysed by Barro and Grossman, both cases being generated by demand-side movements and, therefore, amenable to correction by Keynesian demand-management policies.

Case III: *Classical unemployment*—excess supply in the labour market combined with excess demand in the goods market.

Malinvaud's case of classical unemployment is a supply-side-generated position of disequilibrium. A rise in the real wage leads firms to reduce their output and employment levels, thus creating unemployment in the labour market even though there is no lack of aggregate demand in the goods market. Clearly, Keynesian demand-management policies are ineffective in dealing with classical unemployment since such unemployment is due solely to the real wage being too high. Malinvaud's dichotomy between Keynesian unemployment caused by lack of demand and classical unemployment caused by too high real wages is a significant advance on Phase I Keynesianism where ultimately lack of demand was seen to be caused by too high real wages.

The disequilibrium approach was set within the Walrasian framework by Clower (1979) and Leijonhufvud (1968; 1971; 1979). Walras had suggested that a market economy would tend towards a position of general equilibrium as if there is an *auctioneer* determining prices in all markets simultaneously on the basis of the quantities demanded and supplied by individual agents. Walras postulated a process of *tatonnement* in which the auctioneer would continue to adjust prices in response to excess demands and supplies until all markets cleared, a position of Walrasian equilibrium. Then and only then would trading take place between individual agents. In other words, in the Walrasian model there is no *false trading*, i.e. trading at non-market-clearing prices. It follows that, in a Walrasian equilibrium, all agents are able to effect their notional demands and supplies.

The neo-Walrasian interpretation of Keynes developed by Clower and Leijonhufvud sees the General Theory as the first attempt to deal with the removal of the auctioneer and the *tatonnement* adjustment process from the Walrasian model. The neo-Walrasians make the fundamental assumption that price adjustment is sluggish relative to quantity adjustment. Hence without an auctioneer prices may get stuck at a level that does not imply generalized market-clearing, creating the possibility of false trading in which agents are unable fully to realize their notional demands and supplies. The disequilibrium theories deal with the implications of false trading, showing how, in the absence of efficient price adjustment, agents will adjust the quantities they actually buy and sell. The self-reinforcing nature of the quantity adjustment process creates a multiplier effect which carries the economy towards a quasi-equilibrium in which agents are optimizing given the quantity constraints generated by the departure from Walrasian equilibrium.

Neo-Walrasian analysis has followed two main lines of development:

The non-tatonnement approach This approach, adopted by the French school, has been concerned with the implications of replacing the *tatonnement* process by different quantity adjustment processes in which prices remain fixed. Attention has focused on how the agents form their demands in the face of constraints and on the effects of different rationing schemes. Various rationing schemes have been used: deterministic and stochastic, manipulable and nonmanipulable (i.e. whether or not the ration depends on the effective demand expressed by the agent . . .).

The imperfect information approach The Walrasian assumption of an auctioneer-plus-*tatonnement* is an 'as if' representation of an economy in which agents have sufficient information to ensure that general equilibrium is achieved. Neo-Walrasian analysis, by dropping *tatonnement,* is trying to deal with a world in which agents possess only imperfect information and foresight. It is informational imperfections which create the possibility that the economy may not reach a full employment equilibrium quickly. This approach forms the essence of Leijonhufvud's interpretation of Keynes, the **General Theory** being seen as an attempt to generalize orthodox theory beyond its self-imposed straitjacket of perfect knowledge and perfect foresight.

To summarize: phase II Keynesianism sees involuntary unemployment as a dynamic disequilibrium phenomenon created by the relative slowness of price adjustment. In the absence of an efficient price mechanism, quantity adjustments initially predominate so that in the short-run a fall in aggregate demand generates a downward adjustment of output and employment on the supply-side. The short-run inefficiency of the price mechanism is caused by informational imperfections. However, although phase II Keynesianism provides a sophisticated analysis of the *implications* of quantity adjustment processes when prices fail to respond, there is no explanation of why prices fail to respond. The slowness of price adjustment is assumed as the starting-point and, although there is an attempt to justify this assumption on the grounds of imperfect information, there is no explanation as to why agents with imperfect information do not lower price in the face of demand deficiencies.

KEYNESIANISM PHASE III

Both phase I and phase II Keynesianism derived the existence of involuntary unemployment on the assumption of exogenously-determined price and wage rigidities. However they did differ in the nature of justifications given for the rigidity assumption. Whereas phase I Keynesianism ultimately came to focus on *imperfect competition* in the labour market, phase II Keynesianism focused on the problems of *imperfect information*. Phase III Keynesianism, which covers the most recent Keynesian writing dating from the mid-1970s, can be seen as an attempt fully to incorporate competitive and informational imperfections (albeit in separate models) within choice-theoretic models, with the aim of deriving the existence of an unemployment equilibrium on the basis of optimizing behaviour by agents without any imposed restriction on the flexibility of wages and prices. Phase III Keynesianism, therefore, offers an end to the search for the microfoundations of Keynesian macroeconomics.

Imperfect competition

This approach starts from the premise that if an economy is *structurally perfect*—that is, all markets are perfectly competitive—it will tend towards full-employment equilibrium. It follows, therefore, that the emergence of an unemployment equilibrium must be due to the existence of structural imperfection. If there is monopoly power on the supply-side of a market, optimizing behaviour on the part of the monopolist results in supply being lower and price higher than the perfectly competitive outcome. The quantity-restricting effect of monopoly power makes the theories of imperfect competition, particularly Chamberlin's monopolistic competition, an obvious source for the provision of the microfoundations of involuntary unemployment.

The imperfect competition approach has been adopted by several Keynesian theorists in recent years such as Grandmont and Laroque (1976), Benassy (1976), Hart (1982) and Snower (1983). Hart, for example, considers the case where groups of workers have monopoly power in only one particular labour market, and firms have monopoly power in only one particular product market, there being no bilateral monopolies. All optimize knowing the *objective* (i. e. actual) demand curves that they face, the position of the demand curves depending on per capita income which is determined endogenously. Hart finds that the resulting imperfectly competitive equilibrium (ICE) will generally be at below full employment, provided that the labour markets are not all perfectly competitive:

> . . . the crucial assumption has been the existence of imperfect competition in labour market—it is this that is responsible for the existence of under-employment in our basic model.

The existence of monopoly power in the labour market is a necessary and sufficient condition for an underemployment ICE in Hart's model. An under-employment ICE does not require firms to possess monopoly power in the product market.

The imperfect competition approach to involuntary unemployment has been taken a step further by Weitzman (1982) who argues that imperfect competition is itself a symptom of an even more fundamental problem, that of increasing returns to scale. In a world of constant returns to scale there can be no monopoly power in the product market since there are no barriers to entry. Furthermore, there can be no involuntary unemployment since the existence of constant returns to scale implies that the involuntary unemployed are able to become self-employed, producing to fulfil their own demands. Constant returns to scale would mean an economy in which agents are self-sufficient. There is no necessity for units of organized production (i.e. firms) since costs are independent of the scale of production:

> Once granted the powerful assumptions of strict constant returns to scale and perfect competition, the essential logic of an adjustment mechanism seems inescapable. Unemployment equilibrium is impossible in a constant returns world. To have a genuine theory of involuntary unemployment requires a genuine theory of the firm,—i.e. an explanation of the organisation or process from which the unemployed are excluded.

It is this idealistic world of self-sufficiency which Weitzman argues that the classical theorists believed to be a valid 'as if' parable about the behavior of actual economies. This classical belief was enshrined, according to Weitzman, in 'Say's Law of Markets':

> 'Say's Law of Market's, the doctrine that supply creates its own demand, is . . . a label for the kind of story being told about a quantity adjustment mechanism which increases output when there is slack capacity. The parable describes how an economy can automatically produce itself out of unemployment by a balanced kind of bootstraps operation . . . Say's Law means that an exact scale replication, by the unemployed, of the production pattern of the employed economy will take place in a linearly homogeneous production system and that it is self-supporting because it generates an equiproportionate increase in demand . . .
>
> The role of Say's Law as an adjustment parable is crucial to the classical belief that underlying forces to restore the economy away from 'temporary derangements' back toward full employment equilibrium.

It follows that in order to create the possibility of an unemployment equilibrium it is necessary to introduce increasing returns to scale. Such technological conditions provide the *raison d'être* for the existence of firms and explain why the involuntarily unemployed cannot haul themselves out of unemployment by their own bootstraps by becoming self-employed. They cannot do so because increasing returns to scale necessarily creates barriers to entry since new small-scale entry will face substantial cost disadvantages. Thus increasing returns to scale leads to an imperfectly competitive structure at the micro level and the possibility of involuntary unemployment at the macro level. Imperfect competition is, according to Weitzman, 'the natural habitat of effective demand macroeconomics':

> . . . If you want to build from first principles

a broad based microeconomic foundation to a general equilibrium theory that will explain involuntary unemployment, you must start from increasing returns and go the route of imperfect competition. Otherwise, you will forever be struggling one way or another to evade the basic truth of Say's Law under strict constant returns to scale. Modelling the failure of coordination implicit in an 'inability to communicate effective demand' requires increasing returns and product diversity.

Imperfect information

Whereas the imperfect competition approach deals with the implications of structural imperfection on the assumption that agents have perfect information about the demand curves they face, the imperfect information approach deals with the implications of relaxing the perfect information assumption but in circumstances of structural perfection (i.e. universal perfect competition).

The problem of imperfect information is being approached in at least two distinct ways. First, there is the *conjectural equilibrium* approach in which agents, without perfect knowledge of the demand conditions they face, make their supply decisions on the basis of the conjectures they hold about the demand conditions. An alternative is the *transactions cost* approach in which agents find it costly to identify, contact and negotiate with a suitable trading partner. These two approaches can be seen as complementary, the existence of transactions costs being the *cause* of the informational imperfections and the use of conjectures the necessary *consequence*.

The conjectural equilibrium approach The starting-point for the conjectural equilibrium approach is Arrow's discussion of disequilibrium in a perfectly competitive market (1959). Arrow pointed out that the assumption that a perfectly competitive firm is a price-taker is valid only at the market-clearing price. If a perfectly competitive market does not clear, all firms are not able to sell their desired level of output at the market price. In these conditions, firms will no longer continue to be automatic price-takers. Instead, they will become price-makers with the possibility of increasing their sales by lowering price.

Negishi (1979) and Hahn (1978) have used Arrow's insight as the basis of an explanation for why prices may be rigid at non-market-clearing levels. If a perfectly competitive product market does not clear, firms become quantity-constrained, forcing each to make a conjecture about the demand curve it faces. At the existing market price, each firm can sell any level of output up to its quantity constraint. In order to sell any more output the firm will have to lower its price. Thus beyond the quantity constraint the firm faces a downward-sloping demand curve whereas up to the quantity constraint its demand curve is horizontal. This creates a kinked conjectured demand curve with an associated discontinuous marginal revenue curve. The situation is very similar to Sweezy's kinked demand curve analysis of oligopoly, the kink in that case being created by the conjectured asymmetry in rival firms' reactions to the direction of the price adjustment of an individual firm.

The kinked conjectured demand curve gives two very important results:

1 Given the firm's conjectures, price rigidity emerges as the profit-maximizing response to a situation of non-market-clearing.

2 It may be profit-maximizing to maintain price in the face of moderate reductions in cost.

Thus the conjectural equilibrium approach can explain why profit-maximizing firms with the power to adjust price may choose to keep prices constant in the face of excess supply in the product market. Price rigidity becomes an endogenously-generated outcome of optimizing behaviour by agents who have imperfect information about their demand curves. Optimizing behaviour in such circumstances may not be able to overcome quantity constraints created by a lack of aggregate demand. This opens up the possibility that Keynesian demand-management policies may have a role to play. Furthermore, the conjectural equilibrium approach throws doubts on the ability of wage cuts to provide a supply-side stimulus since it is likely that prices in the product market would not respond.

Negishi has extended the conjectural equilibrium approach to the labour market to show how wage rigidity can emerge even if the labour market is perfectly competitive. Suppose that the money wage is above the level necessary for full employment. In a world of imperfect information individual workers conjecture that they can increase their probability of gaining employment by lowering their wage aspirations. However the higher probability of employment is gained at the cost of a lower wage and, therefore, a lower derived utility from employment. Wage aspirations will be reduced until the marginal benefits (via a higher probability of employment) from a lower wage equal the marginal costs (via a lower derived utility from employment). At this point, the money wage becomes rigid and this may occur at a wage above the market-clearing level.

In the conjectural equilibrium approach, therefore, wage and price rigidities can appear at non-market-clearing levels as the result of optimising behaviour with imperfect information. Wage and price rigidities are no longer an exogenously imposed assumption. It should be noted that the conjectural equilibrium approach admits of a Walrasian full-employment equilibrium as a possible outcome unlike the imperfect competition approach which denies the possibility of a Walrasian equilibrium if there is sufficient structural imperfection. This implies that, if the ultimate cause of involuntary unemployment is the existence of monopoly power, a return to full employment requires structural change.

The transactions cost approach Whereas the conjectural equilibrium approach deals with the implications of using conjectures in the absence of perfect information, the transactions cost approach focuses directly on the cause of imperfect information, namely, the existence of costs of information acquisition. This approach has been developed by Howitt (1985) who starts from the assumption that transactions costs are higher the thinner the market

so that as the level of activity increases in a market the average cost of transacting per unit sold falls. Howitt finds that an economy can get stuck at an unemployment equilibrium with a low level of activity where transactions costs are so high as to outweigh the gains from any attempt by firms to sell more output and by workers to sell more labour. Once an economy falls into a low-activity trap in which the low level of trade and the high level of transactions costs are mutually reinforcing, only an exogenous stimulus to the level of activity from, for example, a fiscal or monetary expansion can set in train a multiplier-type process in which the increase in activity lowers transactions costs, thereby giving a further boost to the level of activity, and so on.

Howitt identifies the problem of the collective good nature of transactions costs. If individual agents each expand their level of activity, they each generate a positive externality in the form of lower transactions costs which collectively may be sufficient to support profitably the expanded level of activity. But in the absence of some agency to coordinate an overall expansion of activity, no individual agent will find it profitable to set the ball rolling by expanding its own activities. Hence, rational economic agents, acting from their individual point of view, perpetuate unavoidably a sub-optimal outcome. It is a Prisoner's Dilemma-type situation in which no individual has sufficient information to provide any basis for believing that everyone will act in the common good. Without such information, the resulting unemployment equilibrium is inevitable and creates a clear case for some form of collective intervention.

MAINSTREAM KEYNESIANISM: AN EVALUATION

This survey of developments in mainstream Keynesianism has sought to portray the enterprise as a coherent research programme initiated by Keynes' ***General Theory,*** with each new phase flowing from the perceived deficiencies of the previous phase. But what has this research programme achieved? The following assessment considers three dimensions of mainstream Keynesianism: its theoretical contribution, its method and its policy prescriptions.

Keynesian theory

Classical theory adopted the market-theoretic approach to understanding the economic system. Its fundamental premise is that if the economy has a universal perfectly competitive market structure in which all agents optimize, the price mechanism ensures that there is sufficient aggregate demand to promote a full-employment equilibrium. This is the essential truth of Say's Law as applied to a generalized market economy. Perfect structure plus perfect behaviour leads to perfect outcome. The macro-outcome of full employment necessarily follows from the twin micro-foundations of a universal perfectly competitive market structure and the rationality of economic agents who possess perfect information, this informational requirement being enshrined in the Walrasian notion of a fictional auctioneer.

The market-theoretic approach implies an imperfectionist theory of unemployment. If the economy settles at an unemployment equilibrium, the ultimate cause must either be structural imperfections such as monopolistic competition in the product markets and trade unions in the labour markets, or informational imperfections that prevent the price mechanism from fully operating.

The principle claim advanced by Keynes in the *General Theory* is the possibility that, due to a lack of demand, an economy could be at a macro-equilibrium with involuntary unemployment. Mainstream Keynesianism has been a continued attempt to substantiate Keynes' claim. The IS-LM model was the first step since it provided a clear presentation of Keynes' macro-analysis, showing how the key aggregate demand-side behavioural patterns in the *General Theory*—i.e. the consumption, investment and demand-for-money functions—interacted to produce an unemployment equilibrium. But, because mainstream Keynesianism remained firmly wedded to the orthodox market-theoretic approach, the question naturally arose as to how Keynes' macro-analysis could be reconciled with market-theoretic micro-foundations. The search was on for the micro-foundations of Keynesian macroeconomics. From the market-theoretic perspective, a lack of aggregate demand necessarily implies that the price mechanism is not fully operating. Ultimately, this must be caused by the existence of imperfections, either structural or informational, which prevent market forces from ensuring the achievement of general equilibrium. The principal contribution of Keynesian theory has been to elaborate on, in ever greater detail, the various imperfectionist theories of unemployment.

Phase I Keynesianism highlighted two sources of imperfection that could render the price mechanism ineffective: money wage rigidity on the supply-side and degenerate behavioural patterns on the demand-side, such as a liquidity trap or interest-inelastic investment. These demand-side imperfections are all extreme cases and, anyway, are open to the non-classical counter that the law of supply and demand would only exert itself at the macro-level by another route (e.g. the Pigou effect). Thus, in the absence of such extreme cases, phase I Keynesianism ultimately reduced to a money wage rigidity explanation of unemployment, rationalized in terms of the structural imperfection of the labour market.

Phase II Keynesianism provided a sophisticated analysis of how sluggish price adjustment could result in involuntary unemployment. The neo-Walrasians justified the assumption of short-run price rigidity in terms of informational imperfections, symbolized by the removal of the auctioneer and the no false trading restriction from the Walrasian system. But this neo-Walrasian analysis failed to give any clear explanation as to why imperfect information would lead optimizing agents to prefer quantity adjustment to price adjustment in the short run.

Phase III Keynesianism has sought to 'tie up the loose ends' by clarifying how the two types of imperfection, structural and informational, can lead to involuntary unemployment. The imperfect competition approach has dealt with the effects of structural imperfection, especially in the labour market, while the implications of imperfect information have been pursued by the conjectural equilibrium and transactions cost approaches. The conjectural

equilibrium approach has been particularly important since it has provided an explanation of why imperfect information can lead to price rigidity at non-market-clearing levels. Phase III Keynesianism is the culmination of the earlier phases, a final explicit formulation of the inevitable imperfectionist causes of unemployment that follow from the market-theoretic approach.

Overall Keynesian theory must be regarded as having provided a valuable extension of classical theory by developing a greater understanding of the effects of imperfections in the system. There is no fundamental conflict between the mainstream Keynesians and the Classicists since they share a common perspective, that of rational economic agents operating in a generalised market context. The debate has been essentially an empirical one over the degree of imperfection present in actual economies, a debate within a single paradigm rather than between two fundamentally separate paradigms.

Keynesian method

Garegnani (1976) has distinguished two fundamental dimensions of economic analysis, the dimension of *method* and the dimension of *theory*. By method is meant the underlying vision, the abstract conception of the world which provides the criteria for selecting what it is intended to explain. The actual attempts at explanation form the theory, the hypotheses about the causal relationships between the selected variables. Applying this distinction to mainstream Keynesianism, one must conclude that since Keynesian theory has developed within the market-theoretic approach, it has necessarily interpreted Keynes as having remained firmly wedded to the orthodox method of economic analysis. Keynesian theory has sought to explain, in terms of optimizing behaviour by individual agents, how an unemployment equilibrium could occur within a generalized market economy, the inevitable conclusion being that structural and/or informational imperfections are responsible. It is natural to ask whether or not in reaching this conclusion Keynesian economics has finally uncovered the ultimate meaning of Keynes' *General Theory*. As Grossman (1972) so aptly put it, was Keynes a 'Keynesian'?

Grossman's question can never be answered definitively since the ultimate meaning of Keynes is but a mythical Holy Grail, much sought after but never quite found. The reason for this lies in the nature of method itself. Method constitutes what Polanyi termed the tacit dimension of knowledge, the formless bounds within which the process of theoretical formulation takes place. 'We always know more than we can tell.' Keynes' own method of analysis in the *General Theory* is tacit and therefore unknowable in any definite objective manner. What the various interpretations of the *General Theory* represent are attempts to render the *General Theory* consistent from the perspective of some *imposed* frame of reference. These interpretations are not the result of investigation, but are preconceived ideas of order into which the *General Theory* is perceived to fit. Likewise this survey of mainstream Keynesianism is an attempt to impose a particular frame of reference that shows the consistency between many diverse theoretical contributions.

From this view, mainstream Keynesianism must be seen as the attempt to interpret the *General Theory* in terms of the orthodox market-theoretic method. This has been by far the most common approach but it is not the only possible approach. Indeed there is much in Keynes' writings which could be interpreted as a rejection of the orthodox method:

> For a hundred years or longer English Political Economy has been dominated by an orthodoxy. That is not to say that an unchanging doctrine has prevailed. On the contrary. There has been a progressive evolution of the doctrine. But its presuppositions, its atmosphere, its method have remained surprisingly the same, and a remarkable continuity has been observable through all the changes. In that orthodoxy, in that continuous transition, I was brought up . . . But I myself in writing [the *General Theory*], and in other recent work which has led up to it, have felt myself to be breaking away from this orthodoxy, to be in strong reaction against it, to be escaping from something, to be gaining an emancipation. [*The Collected Writings of John Maynard Keynes,* Vol. VII, p.xxxi]

To interpret Keynes in terms of the orthodox market-theoretic approach is necessarily to deny that Keynes broke away from the method of classical theory. This leads to bounded vision of the highest order, preventing the development of alternative interpretations that give more credence to Keynes' own stated views on the contribution of the *General Theory*. It is for this reason that the interpretations of Keynes proposed, most prominently, by Shackle (1967) and Joan Robinson (1964), which Coddington (1976) has termed *Fundamentalist,* have always remained on the margins of the debate over what Keynes really meant.

Keynes claimed to have developed a more general theory of unemployment that went beyond classical theory which dealt exclusively with frictional and voluntary forms of unemployment, the only possible forms of unemployment that could be conceived of within classical theory. Involuntary unemployment could not exist in the market-theoretic view of the world. A theory of involuntary unemployment necessarily required a change in method. By remaining within the bounds of orthodox method, mainstream Keynesian theory has been unable to view involuntary unemployment as anything other than unemployment caused by structural and/or informational imperfections, precisely those types of unemployment that Keynes defined as voluntary and frictional, respectively. Thus one, as yet not fully developed, answer to Grossman's question, would be that Keynes was much more than just a 'Keynesian'. In what respects Keynes moved beyond the traditional market-theoretic approach is as much in need of debate today as it was when the *General Theory* was first published some fifty years ago.

Keynesian policy

The early phase I Keynesian focus on the demand-side at the macro-level gave a clear justification for Keynesian demand-management policies in stark contrast to the primarily *laissez-faire* stance implied by classical theory. In-voluntary unemployment was due to a deficiency of aggregate demand, a deficiency which could be overcome by direct government intervention in the goods market through a fiscal expansion. This, however, has proved to be the high point in Keynesian policy prescription. Ever since there has been a progressive lessening of the theoretical justification for Keynesian demand-management policies as a cure for unemployment.

The main 'nail in the coffin' for Keynesian policies from the theoretical perspective was the switch in theoretical emphasis from macro-demand-side analysis to micro-supply-side analysis. This began with Modigliani and the ensuing neo-classical synthesis which viewed money wage rigidity as the ultimate cause of involuntary unemployment. From this perspective Keynesian policies are dealing with the symptoms, namely demand deficiency, rather than with the fundamental problem of too high a level of real wages due to the structural imperfection in the labour market. Keynesian policies would only work if they created sufficient price inflation to lower the real wage to its market-clearing level. The necessary condition for this to happen is that labour does not use its monopoly power to pursue a real wage resistance objective. This requires either labour to suffer from money illusion or some form of agreed incomes policy in which labour accepts cuts in its living standards in return for higher levels of employment. Otherwise a fiscal expansion would result only in wage-price spiral with little or no effect on output and employment levels.

If the fundamental problem is structural imperfection in the labour market there is no reason to suppose that increasing demand in the goods market will provide a means of returning to full employment that avoids the necessity of structural change in the labour market. This point has been reiterated recently by the imperfect competition approach in phase III Keynesianism, in which structural imperfection in the labour market precludes the attainment of a Walrasian (full-employment) equilibrium.

The other strand of development in Keynesian theory that is concerned with the problems of informational imperfection has also become less clear in its policy implications. Initially, the assumption that imperfect information would result in quantity constraints, did provide a rationale for Keynesian demand-management policies to overcome the quantity constraints. However, once attention moves away from quantity constraints as the supposed symptoms of imperfect information and turns instead to the specific form of the imperfections in the information sets of individual agents, it is no longer clear that traditional Keynesian policies have any role. Although the conjectural equilibrium and transactions cost approaches have both resulted in models in which demand-management can be effective, it is possible that alternative forms of informational imperfection may render such policies ineffective. Thus the efficacy of government macro-intervention remains an open question, depending on the precise nature of the informational problems. These concerns have led Barro and Grossman, individually, to have 'second thoughts' on the policy implications derived from their earlier work on non-market-clearing disequilibria. Barro, for example, in 1979 wrote:

> . . . by mechanically leaving opportunities for mutually desirable trades, the non-market-clearing approach makes government policy activism much too easy to justify. When the arbitrariness of supply unequal to demand is replaced by a serious explanation, such as imperfect information about exchange opportunities, for the failure of private markets to achieve some standard of efficiency, the case for government intervention becomes much less obvious.

Overall the message is clear. In turning more and more towards the analysis of structural and informational imperfections in the micro-environment as the ultimate cause of macro-coordination failures, Keynesian theory has, inevitably, become much more ambiguous in its policy prescriptions since it just does not follow that an economy plagued by imperfections in its micro-foundations will necessary respond to intervention at the macro-level.

KEYNESIAN ECONOMICS: THE ROAD TO NOWHERE?

Keynesian economics began with Keynes' claim to have produced a theory that explained involuntary unemployment. For Keynes, involuntary unemployment resulted from a lack of aggregate demand caused ultimately by too low a level of investment. The solution according to Keynes was the 'socialization of investment' which, in practice, came to mean government demand-management, primarily by the use of fiscal policy instruments.

However, since those seemingly revolutionary early days of Keynesianism, mainstream developments have really been a retreat back inside the orthodox citadel, the citadel which Keynes claimed to have left behind. On the theoretical side, Keynesian economics has sought to rationalize demand deficiency within the orthodox market-theoretic approach, the inevitable conclusions being that demand deficiency at the macrolevel is a symptom of either structural or informational imperfections at the micro-level, the traditional explanations of unemployment. Mainstream Keynesian theory has elaborated on the effects of introducing imperfections into classical theory. In so doing, many theoretical innovations have been made within classical theory in the name of Keynes. This in itself is an important contribution to the development of economic theory not to be dismissed lightly. But the Keynesian adherence to the orthodox method leaves Keynesian theory open to the criticism that it does not warrant the name 'Keynesian', denying as it does Keynes' claim to have escaped from the old ideas. Furthermore, on the policy side, the corollary of the theoretical developments has been the removal of any clear justification of Keynesian demand-management policies. Keynesian economics in its mainstream form has been a road to nowhere new.

Mark Blaug   (essay date 1990)

SOURCE: "The Keynesian Revolution," in *John Maynard Keynes: Life, Ideas, Legacy*, The Macmillan Press Ltd, 1990, pp. 25-37.

[*In the following excerpt, Blaug attempts to explain the phenomenal success of the* General Theory *and the unprecedented rapidity with which Keynes's theories were adopted by professional economists.*]

The impact Keynes had on economics with his book *The General Theory* is what is known as the Keynesian Revolution in economic thought. This Keynesian Revolution is one of the most remarkable episodes in the entire history of economic thought; never before had the economics profession been won over so rapidly and so massively to a new economic theory, and nor has it since. Within the space of about a decade, 1936-46, the vast majority of economists throughout the Western world were converted to the Keynesian way of thinking. Many of those early converts felt themselves impelled to repudiate virtually the entire corpus of received economic doctrine, taking up the Keynesian system with an ardour that is more commonly associated with religious conversions. Moreover, it was the younger generation who proved most susceptible to the Keynesian infection; criticism of Keynes came almost solely from the older members of the profession. In short, the Keynesian Revolution comes close to conforming to a 'scientific revolution' as defined by Thomas Kuhn, involving a sense of theoretical 'crisis', the emergence of a radical new 'paradigm', and a pronounced generation gap in the response of scientists to the clash of the old and new paradigms.

Can we explain this phenomenon? That is the question we shall be asking in the pages that follow. The most popular explanation of Keynes's success was that he provided a more ingenious explanation of mass unemployment than did his orthodox contemporaries. I choose my words carefully. It is frequently said that pre-Keynesian or so-called 'classical economics' could not explain the unemployment of the 1930s. But this is careless language, because there was never any problem about 'explaining' unemployment with the aid of pre-Keynesian theory, drawing on the general notion of market imperfections. In particular, unemployment could be and was explained in orthodox terms by real wages being held above market-clearing levels, by protective tariffs, by an overvalued currency (at least in the case of British unemployment before 1931), by rigid prices due to monopolies and cartels, by misguided monetary policies, etc., etc.

It is true that both money and real wages had fallen sharply in the United States from 1929 down to the trough of the Depression in 1933, while all the time American unemployment had worsened rather than improved. The British case was more ambiguous—relative constancy of money wages and gently rising real wages—but nevertheless it was the world-wide persistence of unemployment in the 1930s that gradually sapped confidence in the orthodox explanations. Thus, it is possible to argue that Keynesian economics gave a more convincing explanation of *protracted* mass unemployment than did orthodox theory, and that is why it won over a large part of the professional academic community.

Nevertheless, this still fails to account convincingly for the unprecedented speed with which Keynes conquered economic opinion. The staggering fact remains that Keynesian economics took only twelve years (and by some criteria, only five or six years) to win the approval of the vast majority of professional economists. It is always arbitrary to date the completion of an intellectual revolution, but one obvious and simple measure is the number of years it takes for the new approach to be incorporated into elementary textbooks. The first textbook of elementary economics to expound the Keynesian system was *The Elements of Economics* (1947) by Lorie Tarshis. It failed to catch on, possibly because it stuck too closely to Keynes's own exposition in **The General Theory**. The same year saw the publication of *The Keynesian Revolution* by Lawrence Klein and *The New Economics: Keynes' Influence on Theory and Policy,* an influential collection of papers about Keynesian economics edited by Seymour Harris. But it was the appearance of Paul Samuelson's *Economics: An Introductory Analysis* (1948), twelve years after the publication of **The General Theory,** that marked the final triumph of Keynesianism. The book opened with a section on the determination of national income along entirely Keynesian lines, using the 45-degree line diagram that Samuelson had himself invented in 1939. Samuelson's book soon proved to be the most successful economics textbook of all time, and its popularity brought Keynes to literally millions of students in the USA and elsewhere. It took many more years for Keynes to conquer professional opinion in Germany, Italy and France, but in the USA and Britain the battle was, for all practical purposes, won by 1948.

It could be argued that the apotheosis of Keynes came even earlier in 1944, when the UK White Paper on *Employment Policy,* William Beveridge's *Full Employment in a Free Society,* and *The Economics of Full Employment: Six Studies in Applied Economics* by the Oxford Institute of Statistics, followed one another within the space of nine months. One could even claim that the battle was won still earlier in 1941 or 1942. A British Budget of 1941 was couched in the spirit and even the letter of Keynes, and we now know that Roosevelt's economic advisors in the White House were committed to the Keynesian framework by 1942. At any rate, what opposition there was to Keynes among academic economists, civil servants and government advisors virtually disappeared during the Second World War, which proved indeed to be something like a laboratory experiment in the effectiveness of Keynesian ideas of demand management. It is the amazing rapidity of the Keynesian ascendancy that poses the problem for any convincing account of the Keynesian Revolution.

At one time, in the early bloom of the Keynesian Revolution, it was common to attribute Keynes's triumph simply to his superior policy proposals. Orthodox economists offered no remedies for the depression except a balanced budget and an all-round deflation to force down real wages; only Keynes advocated a deliberately unbalanced budget and compensatory spending on public works. More recent historical research has thoroughly undermined this mythical picture of Keynes as a 'voice crying in the wilderness'. Much of the mythology that still surrounds popular accounts of the Keynesian Revolution relies on disguising the radical difference in the state of pre-Keynesian economics in the USA and Britain. There were some outstanding economists in the USA who favoured monetary over fiscal measures in dealing with the Depression, but the majority of US economists strongly supported a public works programme financed by borrowing, and went out of their way to attack the concept of an annually balanced government budget as an old-fashioned dogma. Indeed, the erosion of the shibboleth of balanced budgets and the adoption of the doctrine of 'spending America out of depression' had been virtually completed in Washington circles by 1936 without the benefit of Keynes's **General Theory**. Moreover, the US experience with wage deflation discouraged any belief in the efficacy of wage-cutting as a cure for unemployment, even among the conservative critics of the New Deal. In short, US economists inside and outside the universities generally favoured policies before as well as after 1936 which we now think of as Keynesian—and the same is true of Germany and the Scandinavian countries.

Almost as much might be said of Britain, except that the depressed conditions of the 1920s, in contrast to the great American boom of that decade, and the return to the gold standard at the pre-war parity between 1925 and 1931, produced somewhat greater diversity of policy recommendations among British than among US economists. Besides, the case for wage-cutting as a cure for unemployment was always better for Britain than for the United States, first because real wages had declined much less in the 1930s in Britain than in the USA, and second because Britain was more of an open economy than the USA. In addition, the gap between official thinking in Whitehall and the academic community of economists was much greater in Britain than in America. The 'Treasury View' that public spending must crowd out private investment, and thus leave aggregate demand no greater than before, had no standing among British academic economists but was held by Treasury officials throughout the 1930s. In consequence, Britain alone among the major Western industrial nations eschewed any hint of public works and deficit finance to promote domestic recovery in the 1930s, and instead relied on cheap money, high tariffs, devaluation and a number of supply-side policies. There has long been wide support among British economists for loan-financed public works, but the overvalued pound in the late 1920s produced a small school of "structuralists', such as Arthur Pigou, Edwin Cannan and Henry Clay, who attributed unemployment to real wages being too high, especially in the declining staple industries. These structuralist arguments largely faded away after Britain left the gold standard in 1931, only to be replaced by the US monetary over-investment theories of the business cycle advocated by Friedrich Hayek, the leader of the Austrian School of Economics, and Lionel Robbins.

According to the Austrian theory of the business cycle, slumps are the necessary consequence of the 'forced saving' associated with undue credit expansion in the previous boom; they should be allowed to run their course like a fever, so as to give way to the healthy boom that will inevitably follow. The protracted nature of the inter-war slump in Britain was explained by the collapse of the gold standard and the proliferation of wage- and price-fixing arrangements that had undermined the natural recuperative powers of the economy. This view, perfectly represented by Lionel Robbins' *The Great Depression* (1934), concluded that wage-cutting, however desirable, was inexpedient, and besides it was the inflexibility of all prices and not just wages that exacerbated the Depression. Little followed from all this in the way of practical action, but the conditions for recovery, Robbins seemed to suggest, were a return to free trade, a stable currency based on the gold standard, and institutional reform attacking the myriad ways in which governments promoted monopolies and cartels. The Hayek-Robbins viewpoint fell on deaf ears and attracted so little attention that Keynes did not even bother in *The General Theory* to mention either Hayek's *Prices and Production* (1931) or Robbins's *Great Depression* (although there was a footnote referring to Robbins), choosing instead to direct all his ammunition against Pigou's highly abstract and profoundly obscure *Theory of Unemployment* (1933). Of course, there was no single canonical text that characterised the whole of British economic thinking on anti-Depression policies, and hence Keynes was virtually driven to invent a straw man of what he called 'classical economics' to dramatise his battle with orthodoxy. Summing up, it is fair to say that there was a pre-Keynesian orthodoxy on policy matters in Britain—free trade, the gold standard, balanced budgets, debt redemption, and structural reforms—but it was a creed of bankers, businessmen, civil servants and politicians, not of academic economists. The economists were largely in agreement on everything except free trade, and in any case were at pains to sink their differences in favour of proposals like easy money and loan-financed public works.

The very first sentence of the preface to *The General Theory* announces that it is a book addressed to Keynes's fellow economists, and therefore that 'its main purpose is to deal with difficult questions of theory and only in the second place with the applications of this theory to practice'. Thus, Keynes attacked 'classical' economists not because they disagreed with him about action to remedy the slump but because he thought that they were wedded to ideas that were inconsistent with the policies they were advocating. Hence the footnote reference to Robbins in *The General Theory*: 'It is the distinction of Professor Robbins that he, almost alone, continues to maintain a distinct scheme of thought, his practical recommendation belonging to the same system as his theory.' What Keynes sought was capitulation on the theoretical front and, as he said in a letter to George Bernard Shaw on January 1, 1935: 'I believe myself to be writing a book on economic theory which will largely revolutionse—not I suppose at once but in the course of the next ten years—the way the world thinks about economic problems', a prediction that proved to be perfectly accurate. Let us remind ourselves once again of the principal theoretical features of Keynesian economics:

1. A shift in method from micro- to macroeconomics, from the long period to the short period, from real to monetary analysis, and from the variation of prices to the variation of quantities as central objects of analysis.

2. Both aggregate consumption and aggregate savings are taken to be stable functions of income, but investment is treated at least partly as autonomous, inherently volatile, and subject to pervasive uncertainty.

3. Saving and investment are said to be carried out by different people for different reasons and are only brought into equilibrium by changes of income itself.

4. The rate of interest is explained in monetary terms as a function of the stock demand for money interacting with an exogenously determined supply of money.

5. Real wages are treated as determined by the volume of employment rather than the other way around.

At the bottom of the entire schema is the Great Heresy that an equilibrium level of income and output need not correspond to a situation of full employment, and indeed that the economy is very likely to get stuck in a low-level unemployment equilibrium trap, there being no spontaneous, self-adjusting mechanism that will necessarily drive the economy to employ the entire labour force and to utilise the capital stock to full capacity. There is no doubt that it was this heresy combined with Keynes's demonstration of the 'paradox of thrift'—in an economy with unemployment more saving means more, not less, unemployment—that gave Keynesian economics its subversive, left-wing coloration and which earned it so much enmity from conservatives, particularly in the United States. In places in *The General Theory,* Keynes went so far as to suggest that the poor have higher marginal propensities to consume than the rich, implying that output and hence employment could be raised by redistribution of income from the rich to the poor. In addition, he suggested that capitalism, when left to its own devices, was doomed to 'secular stagnation', not just in the distant but possibly in the near future. No wonder, then, that *The General Theory* proved irresistible to young economists, radicalised by years of depression. And yet all this does not exhaust the list of appealing features in *The General Theory*.

One of Keynes's critical analytical decisions in moving away from his *Treatise on Money* towards *The General Theory* was to abandon the type of sequence of 'period analysis' that characterised monetary economics and the business cycle literature of the 1920s and instead to adopt the now familiar static equilibrium mode of analysis in which all the relevant variables of the model refer to a single period of time. It was this decision to handle essentially dynamic problems with a static apparatus that led him to define income, saving and investment in such a way as to make realised saving identically equal to realised investment, which related consumption and income via the consumption function, and which in turn defined the instantaneous multiplier as the reciprocal of the marginal propensity to save. The use of this equilibrium method confused many of Keynes's earlier readers, who were accustomed to price theory employing comparative statics and monetary theory employing period analysis, but it was precisely this heterodox use of statis equilibrium analysis applied to a monetary economy that was out of equilibrium that gave Keynes's theory its allegoric rigour and analytical simplicity.

In addition, Keynes worked hard to define all his variables in operational terms, relating them whenever possible to actual or potentially available data. In so doing he rode on the back of the statistical revolution that was already well on the way when *The General Theory* was published. Colin Clarke's *The National Income 1924-1931* (1932) and Simon Kuznets's *National Income 1929-1932* (1934) testify to a tradition of national income accounting that predates the publication of *The General Theory*. Nevertheless, Keynes's treatment of income as the chief determinant of consumption and the importance assigned in his theory to final outlays of consumption and investment, not to mention the one-period definitions of saving and investment, gave an enormous stimulus to the statistical measurement of income and outlays. Official estimates of national income appeared first in the United States in 1935, the year before *The General Theory*. By 1939, official and unofficial estimates were available for thirty-three countries, and it is no accident that the first official estimates in the United Kingdom were prepared in 1940 by James Meade and Richard Stone, two of Keynes's disciples, stimulated by Keynes's own use of national income estimates to analyse the prospective inflationary gap in *How to Pay for the War* (1940). By the end of the Second World War, official national income accounts appeared in almost all industrialised countries and were invariably presented in the $Y = C + I + G$ format of Keynesian economics.

There was a pre-Keynesian macroeconomics, but it was contentious, complex and cast almost entirely in non-operational terms, such as the degree of 'roundaboutness' of the economy, the level of hoarding and dishoarding, forced saving, overindebtedness, underconsumption and the like. Keynes achieved a drastic simplification of macroeconomics or, more cynically expressed, he achieved the optimum level of difficulty for intellectual success—not so simple as to be immediately accessible without some effort and yet not so complex as virtually to defy comprehension. An essential additional ingredient in the success of *The General Theory* was its open-endedness and sheer fecundity. Keynes was fond of the method of overkill or arriving at the same conclusion from several different angles. Thus, Chapter 17 of *The General Theory* on 'The Essential Properties of Interest and Money' seeks to produce the central Keynesian conclusion that 'unemployment equilibrium' is possible and even likely without the aid of the building blocks developed in the previous sixteen chapters. Likewise, . . . Chapter 19 on the 'Changes in Money Wages' resorts to as many as half a dozen different arguments intended to demonstrate the impracticability and undesirability of cutting money wages as a cure for unemployment. *The General Theory* is littered with digressions, puzzles requiring solution, and a wealth of theoretical hints awaiting further development. This efflorescence of ideas, a sense of the cup running over, was one of the elements of its appeal. It is a poorly constructed book that frequently reads more like a set of random notes than a systematic treatise, but even this quality of undue haste only enhanced its intellectual effectiveness.

Have we now finally accounted for the Keynesian Revolution? Not in my opinion. Economists do not adopt new theories just because they are simple, elegant, rigorous,

ideologically convenient and politically appealing. They demand that their implications should be confirmed by the available data. In the final analysis, what they really find persuasive is that the theory should predict some novel, hitherto unsuspected facts, which now suddenly make sense by being 'fitted into' a more general framework, Keynesian economics in fact came equipped with a number of new predictions.

The principal novel prediction of Keynesian economics is that the value of the instantaneous multiplier is greater than unity, and that the more than proportional impact of an increase in investment on income applies just as much to public as to private investment, and indeed just as much to consumption as to investment spending. In other words, fiscal policy is capable, at least in principle, of raising real income up to the full employment ceiling within a single time period.

The notion that a government can spend its way out of depression predated Keynes's *General Theory* and derived from the quantity of theory of money, at least in its short version. David Hume, one of the founders of the quantity theory of money, had argued as early as the eighteenth century in favour of creeping inflation: a steady continual increase in the supply of money is partly transmitted to real output and is therefore not simply inflationary. The monetary writing of a number of early twentieth-century economists, including the young Keynes himself, had long familiarised economists with the short-run, disequilibrium interpretation of the quantity theory of money; in fact, this was the standard pre-Keynesian framework for demonstrating the efficacy of a loan-financed public works programme. The trouble was that the argument was loose and imprecise and hence was vulnerable to objections based either on the 'Treasury View' or on the sheer administrative costs of mounting such schemes at short notice.

Keynes learned from Richard Kahn, his young pupil, how to calculate, however crudely, a precise value for the income multiplier, and in so doing he placed the case for demand management on an entirely new footing by making it seem incontrovertible. The case relied on the notion of consumption as a stable function of income and *The General Theory*'s definition of saving and investment as two sides of the same coin, and it followed as a matter of logic that any increase in real income and employment could be achieved by a sufficiently large autonomous increase in consumption, or investment or government expenditure. This was a novel prediction, not only in the sense that it was unknown before Keynes's *General Theory,* but also because it was an unsuspected implication of the concept of the consumption function combined with the peculiar Keynesian definitions of savings and investment; it was not just any consumption function but one in which the marginal propensity to consume lies between zero and one, is smaller than the average propensity to consume (the ratio of consumption to income), and declines as income rises. These three characteristics of the Keynesian consumption function were simply asserted by Keynes in *The General Theory,* but all three mini-predictions were in fact confirmed in 1942 by the first set of comprehensive national income data for the United States.

The same thing is *not* true of the greater-than-unity value of the expenditure multiplier, Keynes's principal prediction. Keynes himself estimated the British multiplier to be 1.5, but some of his disciples produced estimates in 1938, 1939 and 1941 of between 2.0 and 3.0, and in one case of even more than 3.0. Because of various 'leakages' into taxes, imports and savings, as well as the slow rate at which the secondary and tertiary effects show up, the true figure in most countries, we now think, is perhaps only just in excess of 1.0. In consequence, some revisionist economic historians have recently expressed doubts about Keynes's remedies in the circumstances of the 1930s, arguing that the fiscal stimulus designed to produce full employment in the severely depressed pre-war British economy would have had to have been so large as to entail physical planning on a war-time scale.

It is worth noting that Keynes himself would *not* have been as startled by the recent revisionist interpretations of the inter-war British economy as we are. He was perfectly aware that government budgets in the 1930s were so small that any budgetary deficit could only have had a miniscule effect on national income. For example, the fall in income experienced by the United States and the United Kingdom between 1929 and 1933 was so great that public expenditure would have had to have increased by 50-70 per cent to have filled in the gap. However, that is only to say that Keynes, at least in *The General Theory,* did not actually advocate budgetary deficits as a tool of stabilisation policy, but rather monetary policy in conjunction with the stabilisation of investment by means of a permanent rise in the proportion of income spent by governments—that is what was meant by his famous recommendation of 'the socialisation of investment' in the closing pages of his book.

Let us sum up. It may be convincingly argued that the Keynesian system was never put to the test before the war, that budgetary deficits in the 1930s were never large enough to produce the Keynesian results—in short, that Hitler's rearmament programme was the only New Deal that actually succeeded in eliminating unemployment, but that in no way affects the point I have been trying to make: *The General Theory* gained adherents because Keynes made a novel prediction that seemed highly likely to be true. The virtual disappearance of unemployment during the Second World War was perceived to be, rightly or wrongly, a dramatic corroboration of the central Keynesian prediction. In the same way, the full employment and overall employment conditions of the 1950s and 1960s were everywhere attributed to the deliberate pursuit by governments of Keynesian policies, although it was in fact private investment that filled the post-war gap in effective demand. In other words, the evidence for Keynes's central prediction is not compelling even now, but that is simply to say that what seems compelling at one time in history is not necessarily seen to be persuasive with the benefit of hindsight forty or fifty years later.

The principal new prediction of the Keynesian system was that fiscal policy by itself is capable of generating a full-employment level of income. But there were many other novel facts predicted by *The General Theory,* some of which were influential in attracting additional adherents to Keynesianism: for example, that there are significant differences in the marginal propensities to consume of households at different income levels; that the interest-elasticity of investment is very low; that, on the contrary, the interest-elasticity of the demand for money is very high; and, finally, that the average propensity to consume of the community tends to decline as national income rises, indicating that the threat of secular stagnation in mature economies will get worse as they grow richer. It turned out eventually that aggregate consumption and saving is relatively insensitive to change in the distribution of income, but in the 1930s young American Keynesians placed as much emphasis on income redistribution as on deficit spending as a way out of the Depression. Similarly, Keynes himself never ceased to believe that investment was sufficiently responsive to reductions in the rate of interest to make monetary policy a potent instrument for raising employment additional to fiscal policy. But a number of empirical studies by young British Keynesians soon showed that the interest-elasticity of investment was not much greater than zero, and this encouraged the belief that Keynesianism was tantamount to the thesis that private investment is bound to fall short of full employment. Lastly, imminent stagnation was a constant theme in the Keynesian literature, and, in the influential writings of Alvin Hansen, Keynes's leading American disciple, was converted into the very essence of the Keynesian message. To show how widely stagnationism was held, it is only necessary to mention that it was primarily responsible for the almost universal belief among economists in 1945 that the post-war era would commence with a sharp slump. The doctrine that industrialised countries in the twentieth century faced a chronic deficiency of effective demand because private investment was bound to fall behind full-employment savings was one of Keynes's novel predictions; it was a false prediction and it was not essential to Keynesian economics, but it was nevertheless a prediction that gained him followers in the early days of the Keynesian Revolution.

Another one of Keynes's erroneous predictions was the proposition that the average propensity to save is a declining function of income, a prediction that was at first confirmed by cross-section budget studies of family expenditure patterns, which literally exploded in the late 1930s and early 1940s. In 1946, Kuznets's *National Product Since 1869* brought home the distinction between cross-section data that confirmed, and time-series data that refuted the prediction of a negative association between the saving-income ratio and the level of national income. In other words, when we compare rich and poor households at one moment in time, it is true that richer households save a larger fraction of their income than do poorer households; but when we compare households over time it is not true that they save a large fraction of their income as they become richer. The attempt to reconcile this contradiction resulted in the Duesenberry Relative Income Hypothesis, the Modigliani Life Cycle Hypothesis and the Friedman Permanent Income Hypothesis. These hypotheses spanned more than a decade of theoretical and empirical work on the savings function inspired by Keynes's *General Theory,* but nevertheless travelled light-years away from the rather simplistic consumption and savings function originally stipulated by Keynes.

Keynes had deliberately assumed a closed economy in *The General Theory,* but the spending multiplier applies just as much to the spending of foreigners on exports as it does to domestic spending. That the foreign trade multiplier is typically greater than unity and that income effects are quantitatively more important than price effects in bringing the balance of payments into equilibrium are other new predictions of the Keynesian system, and followers of Keynes soon explored them, even if Keynes himself ignored them. The invention of the Phillips Curve in 1958 and the manner in which it was grafted on to Keynesian economics is yet another example of the amazing fertility of the Keynesian system. Of course, we have now moved well beyond the year 1948 which, we earlier argued, marked the completion of the Keynesian Revolution as a process of gaining the endorsement of the economics profession. But it is worth remembering that there is a sense in which the Keynesian Revolution is still going on. After degenerating in the 1960s and being virtually supplanted by 'monetarism' and 'rational expectations', Keynesian economics has made something of a comeback in recent years. Macroeconomics is once again trying to explain the failure of labour markets to clear in the face of unemployment—that is, to give new theoretical answers to the old Keynesian question. The spectre of Keynes continues to haunt macroeconomics, as is shown by the endless books and articles on 'What Keynes really meant', 'should have meant', and 'must have meant'.

What, in conclusion, accounts for the Keynesian Revolution? What makes economists adopt a new theory? Economics is not like physics; nor it is just a body of substantive findings about the judgements and political preconceptions of economists. Nevertheless, new economic doctrines do not find a ready audience among economists unless they can promise to produce new findings about the economy that are eventually confirmed by historical and statistical analysis. Thus, it was not just ideology, an animus against capitalism, a desire to cock a snook at the older generation, or simply a preference for something new, that drove economists into the Keynesian camp. Keynes had caught a measure of substantive truth about the working of an economic system that had not been vouchsafed to his predecessors, and that is fundamentally why economists in the 1930s adopted Keynesian economics.

J. B. Davis   (essay date 1991)

SOURCE: "Keynes's View of Economics as a Moral Science," in *Keynes and Philosophy: Essays on the Origin of Keynes's Thought,* edited by Bradley W. Bateman and John B. Davis, Edward Elgar, 1991, pp. 89-103.

[*In the following excerpt, Davis discusses Keynes's understanding of economic method in terms of his philosophical beliefs, focusing on his conception of economics as a moral science and his emphasis on the role of individual value judgments in the construction of economic models.*]

J. M. Keynes's theoretical understanding of economic method is one of the less well understood dimensions of his thought, both because Keynes's thinking, unlike that of most economists, was motivated by serious reflection on philosophical questions, and because Keynes's particular philosophical heritage—rooted as it was in early reflections on the philosopher G.E. Moore's *Principia Ethica*—was quite different from that of other Cambridge economists. Accordingly, although Keynes repeated the Cambridge view that economics is 'essentially a moral science and not a natural science' [*The Collected Writings of John Maynard Keynes,* (hereafter referred to as *CW*), 7, Vol. XIV, p. 297], that his own understanding of this notion and the method of economics had its origins in Keynes's own distinctive philosophical development perhaps suggests that Keynes transformed the Cambridge understanding of economic method, much as he transformed its conception of the economy.

Indeed, the methodological thinking of the Cambridge school did undergo considerable change in the space of three generations. At the end of the nineteenth century, Henry Sidgwick, Alfred Marshall, and John Neville Keynes, while hesitant to say economics sought universal laws on the model of natural science, nonetheless agreed that the empirical generalization of well established facts was a meaningful enterprise. Moreover, while each was aware of the role of value judgments in economics, there were few doubts concerning the validity of the normative-positive distinction, since Nassau Senior had come to underlie the idea of economics as an objective intellectual enterprise. By contrast, by the mid-twentieth century, it could well be said that many at Cambridge, in the words of Joan Robinson, believed that 'the positive and normative [could not] be sharply divided', and that empirical work in economics was fraught with such difficulty that it could hardly be granted the role hoped for it at the beginning of the century. John Maynard Keynes, then, in virtue of his ties to both the earlier and later Cambridge economists, might naturally be thought the pivotal figure in this development.

Yet that Keynes's early philosophical thinking was largely formed under the impact of a reading of Moore's *Principia,* rather than in a conscientious study of the methodological convictions of the first generation of Cambridge economists, also suggests that Keynes's impact on the development of Cambridge methodological thinking may well have been relatively slight, given the fact that most economists at Cambridge after Keynes were either unacquainted with Moore's thought or simply uninterested in it. From this perspective, it might well be surmised that Keynes's considerable prestige, combined with his often severe criticism of his predecessors, discouraged interest in earlier methodological views, while, because Keynes's own early intellectual development was highly specific to a relatively private early philosophical experience, those attracted to Keynes's economic theories found it difficult to understand, or indeed feel much sympathy toward, those philosophical notions that ultimately came to underlie his view of economics as a moral science. In effect, later Cambridge economists had to innovate methodologically on a rather narrow doctrinal base, portions of which were likely to be altogether unappealing; and this, it could be concluded, makes a case for methodological discontinuity rather than development in the thinking about economics in the Cambridge school.

Moore, it is interesting to note, was a student of Sidgwick's in ethics at the turn of the century, and thus might have reinforced the Sidgwick-Marshall-Neville Keynes tradition in methodological thinking for J.M. Keynes. However, Sidgwick, whose seven-edition *The Methods of Ethics* was meant to synthesize the competing nineteenth-century moral philosophy traditions of J.S. Mill's utilitarianism and William Whewell's intuitionism (much as Marshall's authoritative *Principles* was meant to do for economics), never persuaded Moore that utilitarianism was coherent. As a result, Moore was to go on to revive the longstanding Cambridge Platonist tradition in his intuitionist *Principia,* and this set of ideas accordingly became the basis for Keynes's own early philosophical views. Indeed, Keynes's first major work, his *Treatise on Probability,* acknowledged and drew heavily on these Moorean beginnings. In effect, then, Keynes's early philosophical thinking reached back in time over the first generation of Cambridge economists to a prior intellectual tradition at Cambridge. While this is arguably the reason Keynes's thinking about economic method has rarely been well explained, at the same time such beginnings provide new opportunities and resources for explaining Keynes's methodological thinking. What, then, were Keynes's early philosophical positions as they might relate to Keynes's later understanding of economic method?

KEYNES AND INDIVIDUAL JUDGMENT

Keynes's 1938 characterization of economics as a moral science depends centrally upon conceiving economics as an art. In believing economics as art, however, one gives up the customary, natural science view of scientific method whereby one assumes individual instances are assimilated under general principles in relatively unproblematic fashion, and in its place rests greater emphasis upon the economist's capacity to exercise individual judgement regarding the novelty of the particular instance and the significance of data generally. Keynes suggests this in his 1938 statement in asserting that economics is 'a branch of logic, a way of thinking' (*CW,* XIV, p. 297), and by emphasizing his conception of what was involved in working with models of economic relationships. On this view, 'it is the essence of a model that one does *not* fill in real values for the variable functions' since to do this was to deprive a model of 'its generality and its value as a mode of thought' (Ibid.). Thus, an economic model for Keynes possesses an important element of indeterminacy which demands a capacity for individual judgement.

These convictions recall Keynes's earlier interest in individual judgement in his first reflections upon Moore's *Principia.* In his unpublished 1904 **'Ethics in Relation to Conduct'** paper, Keynes noted that Moore's recommendation to follow general commonsense rules of conduct when estimating the probable remote future effects of one's actions was often of little value when past experience bore little relation to the future. Indeed, Keynes went on to argue, probability statements ought not to be understood as simply registering what has occurred in some given proportion of past cases—in effect, the frequency theory of probability—but rather should be thought to represent one's estimate of the justification needed to make some statement, given the evidence at one's disposal. This implies that, even when one possesses some record of past experience regarding the likelihood of a future event, that evidence must nonetheless still be evaluated for its bearing on the conclusion at hand. Individual judgement accordingly took on particular significance for Keynes from the outset of his intellectual career, so that, unlike others in the early Cambridge methodological tradition, Keynes always evidenced a considerable scepticism toward the use of *a posteriori* general principles in economics.

Keynes, however, was by no means of the opinion that legitimate general principles were non-existent. When, after some delay, he finally published his first and only philosophical study, the **Treatise on Probability,** Keynes asserted that probability relationships concerned '*a logical relation between two sets of propositions*', and that 'logic investigates the general principles of valid thought'. What Keynes principally inherited from Moore, in fact, was the view that one could intuit, or grasp, in an act of individual judgement, general *a priori* relationships. This had been the central doctrine of *Principia Ethica,* where Moore had advanced the view that the good was *sui generis* and could only be grasped in and of itself. It was also the key position in Keynes's [**Treatise on Probability**], where Keynes asserted that it was not possible to define probability, and that our knowledge of probability relationships depends upon our 'direct acquaintance' with logical relations between propositions.

At the same time, in Keynes's mind this 'direct acquaintance' with the logical relationships between propositions retained an important connection with individual judgement. In arguing that probability relationships were objective and logical, Keynes had asserted that propositions were not probable in and of themselves, but rather only probable in relation to a particular body of knowledge embodied in other propositions. This implied, he noted, that probability theory possesses both subjective and objective dimensions, since

> . . . [W]hat particular propositions we select as the premises of *our* argument naturally depends on subjective factors peculiar to ourselves, [while] the relations, in which other propositions stand to these, and which entitle us to probable beliefs, are objective and logical.

One's 'direct acquaintance' with the logical relations between propositions, then, depends importantly upon one's judgement concerning the evidence relevant to the desired probability judgement, since were our 'premises' to change, we would generally discover ourselves directly acquainted with altogether different probability relationships. Keynes, in fact, took this to be a particular strength of his account.

> Reflection will show that this account harmonises with familiar experience. There is nothing novel in the supposition that the probability of a theory turns upon the evidence by which it is supported; and it is common to assert that an

opinion was probable on the evidence first at hand, but on further information was untenable. As our knowledge or our hypothesis changes, our conclusions have new probabilities, not in themselves, but relatively to these new premises.

Thus, although the knowledge of probability relationships is a knowledge of general *a priori* logical principles, for Keynes this knowledge depends significantly upon the exercise of individual judgement.

All of this, Keynes went on to allow, imposes a certain relativity on probable knowledge that many might well surmise undermines the objective character of that knowledge.

> Some part of knowledge—knowledge of our own existence or of our own sensations—is clearly relative to individual experience. We cannot speak of knowledge absolutely—only of the knowledge of a particular person. Other parts of knowledge—knowledge of the axioms of logic, for example—may seem more objective. But we must admit, I think, that this too is relative to the constitution of the human mind, and that the constitution of the human mind may vary in some degree from man to man. What is self-evident to me and what I really know, may be only a probable belief to you, or may form no part of your rational beliefs at all. And this may be true not only of such things as *my* existence, but of some logical axioms also. Some men— indeed it is obviously the case—may have a greater power of logical intuition than others.

Keynes himself, of course, had little doubt that probability relationships were indeed objective. Yet whether this is the case, or whether Keynes was justified in thinking probability relationships objective, is not at issue here. Rather what is important to establish in the present context is whether there is a connection between this early emphasis Keynes places on individual judgement and what Keynes later understands about the need for individual judgement in economic models.

Certainly there is some question regarding whether or not Keynes's early philosophical thinking in this regard underlies his later thinking about economic method. In a later memoir, **'My Early Beliefs'**, Keynes repudiated some of his earliest philosophical thinking, especially in regard to his early expressions of confidence concerning the unimportance of relying on rules in judging what was right or wrong to do. Yet, although this might well seem to imply that less emphasis should be placed on the role of individual judgement in Keynes's later methodological thinking, or that individual judgement has an altogether different meaning for Keynes in his later work, the fact that in the same year (1938) as his **'My Early Beliefs'** memoir Keynes also emphasized the importance of economists' capacity for individual judgement in his moral science characterization of economics suggests that his **'My Early Beliefs'** critique was only concerned with the need to reassess the role of individual judgement in ethics proper. What is there then in what Keynes believes, distinctive of economics as a moral science that might be explained by Keynes's earlier philosophical ideas?

KEYNES ON INTROSPECTION AND JUDGEMENTS OF VALUE

In his 1938 characterization of economics as a moral science Keynes had also noted that economists make important use of introspection and judgements of value in their elaboration of economic models.

> I also want to emphasise strongly the point about economics being a moral science. I mentioned before that it deals with introspection and with values. I might have added that it deals with motives, expectations, psychological uncertainties. One has to be constantly on guard against treating the material as constant and homogeneous

(*CW*, XIV, p. 300).

Economics is a moral science, then, because it is principally concerned with individuals' 'motives, expectations, [and] psychological uncertainties'. This explains why its subject matter is neither 'constant' nor 'homogeneous' and why the methods of natural science are inappropriate in economics. In effect, individuals' observed behaviour correlates in varying degree with their inner thoughts and intentions, so that economists must make significant use of introspection and judgements of value to be able to model individuals' behaviour. Introspection would enable the economist to ascribe motives to individuals, given their observed behaviour; and judgements of value would enable the economist to weigh the strength of individuals' commitments to various courses of action they have undertaken. Indeed, by consulting one's own case the economist could be expected to be able to 'segregate the semi-permanent or relatively constant factors from those which are transitory or fluctuating' (*CW*, XIV, pp. 296-7), since one would presumably have a clearer sense of an individual's motives by examining one's own likely motives in similar circumstances than by examining that individual's observed behaviour.

This perspective on economic method, as is well known, was not original to Keynes. The earlier Cambridge tradition of Sidgwick, Marshall and Neville Keynes had also emphasized introspection and judgements of value in economic method, although not much attention was devoted to examining the assumptions inherent in so doing. Maynard Keynes, however, had good reason to think more carefully about the presuppositions of employing these methods, since introspection and judgements of value necessarily involve the exercise of individual judgement. That is, were one to assess another's motives by comparison with one's own case, this would clearly involve consulting one's own particular reaction to the particular circumstances encountered by another. Although reasoning by analogy in this manner certainly presupposes some knowledge of general relationships between individuals and their circumstances, the idea of case-by-case comparisons is nonetheless one that fundamentally concerns individual judgement.

Of course, there is much that is obscure in the idea of describing another's thoughts and intentions on the basis of one's own, and consequently whether it makes sense to say one can consult one's own case in order to evaluate that of others is not easily answered. On the one hand, if we are entirely unique and distinct individuals, then our individual circumstances will not be comparable. On the other hand, if we do not differ significantly in our personal motives and valuations, then our behaviour should be sufficiently similar and transparent that it could well be treated as 'constant and homogeneous'. Keynes, of course, rejected this latter alternative. Indeed, his resistance to a natural science conception of economics stemmed precisely from his conviction that individuals were insufficiently similar in experience and circumstance for their thoughts and intentions to be predicted solely on the basis of their observable behaviour. How, then, was he able to argue that individuals were unique and distinct, and that at the same time introspective individual judgement was meaningful? Here, attention to Keynes's early philosophical thinking is again valuable.

Shortly after his first critique of Moore's *Principia Ethica* in his 1904 **'Ethics in Relation to Conduct'**, Keynes completed two additional papers on the *Principia* for presentation to the Apostles, **'Miscellanea Ethica',** dated July-September 1905 and **'A Theory of Beauty',** dated September-October 1905. Although the papers investigate a number of difficulties in Moore's reasoning, for our purposes here, Keynes's conclusions regarding the proper application of Moore's principle of organic unities is of particular interest. Moore's principle of organic unities concerned the philosophical relationship between the value of a whole and the value of its parts, and stated that the value of 'a whole bears no regular proportion to the sum of the values of its parts'. On the basis of this, Moore had gone on to argue that the universe as a whole constitutes an organic unity, and that it was accordingly one's moral duty to promote the good of the universe itself. Keynes found this conclusion unrealistic on the grounds that it made nonsense of the idea of moral duty. He then reasoned that the universe is not the organic whole whose value is at issue in ethics, and that this indicated that, where value is concerned, the principle of organic unities is only properly applied to the individual mind.

> In ethical calculation each individual's momentary state of mind is our sole unit. In so far as a state of mind has parts, to this extent I admit the principle of organic unities: it is the excellence of the state as a whole with which we are concerned. But beyond each individual the organic principle cannot reach.
>
> ['Miscellanea Ethica']

That is, the individual mind alone can be said to constitute an organic unity and, accordingly, moral duty only concerned promoting good states of mind in individuals.

The implications of Keynes's position, however, go beyond questions of ethics. That the individual mind is an organic unity implies both that its activity can only be explained in terms of principles appropriate to it as a whole and that the mind's parts—an individual's thoughts and feelings—are themselves principally to be explained in terms of the activity of the individual mind as a whole.

Moreover, that for Keynes every individual mind constitutes an organic unity in and of itself, and that organic connection does not apply across individual minds implies that the principles that govern relationships between individual minds are different in nature from those appropriate to the individual mind. In effect, then, Keynes's redirection and reapplication of Moore's principles of organic unities effectively establishes a principle of autonomy for the individual as well as the foundations for an account of the nature of relationships between individuals. Individuals are distinct by virtue of the personal integrity of their mental experience, although, in a manner still to be explained, they share this autonomy with one another.

More formally, Keynes's redirection of Moore's organic unities principle provided Keynes with rudimentary criteria for individuating the individual economic agent via the determination of the conditions for individual identity through change. Generally speaking, one can claim one has successfully distinguished an individual of any sort when one can trace a set of characteristics that identify that individual through a period of change in other characteristics of that individual. Keynes's ascription of an organic unity to the mental contents of an individual accomplishes this since, though an individual's particular thoughts and feelings certainly change, for Keynes, because the individual mind always constitutes an organic unity and an individual's thoughts identify that individual, this implies that an individual's new thoughts and feelings remain the thoughts and feelings of that same individual.

This is of no little import. Although individuals are conventionally taken to be different and distinct from one another (often by virtue of their physical distinctiveness), whether one can in fact justify this distinctiveness is crucial to any methodological strategy that depends upon assessing the thinking and motives of others. Indeed, possessing criteria for individual identity is indispensable to any coherent explanation of introspection and judgements of value, since these methods presuppose some degree of intellectual autonomy on the part of the individual having recourse to them, in order to justify the claim that individuals can treat their own cases as a source of independent information regarding the motives and intentions underlying the observed behaviour of others. Put simply, the elaboration of individual identity criteria is a necessary, though not sufficient, condition for employing the methods of introspection and judgements of value. Such criteria are not sufficient in themselves, however, because establishing the distinctiveness of an individual's thought process does not also establish the representativeness of that thought process. That is, introspection and judgements of value can only be said to be authoritative if the thinking of the individual making such judgements can be said to be both distinct from and representative of the thinking of those individuals in economic life whose behaviour is to be explained. Does Keynes, then, also have a conception of the representative individual that would permit the economist taking his or her imagined responses to a set of circumstances confronted by others as typical of those individuals' likely responses to those circumstances?

KEYNES AND 'THE APPROXIMATE UNIFORMITY OF HUMAN ORGANS'

From quite early in his intellectual career Keynes did indeed struggle to define a sense in which an individual's thinking could be said to be typical of the thinking of individuals generally. Although, arguably, Keynes felt some difficulty in establishing this latter dimension of human thought, nonetheless he clearly believed that an individual's thinking could be explained both in terms of a capacity for individual judgement reflecting upon that individual's own particular experience and a capacity to reason in a manner that might be said objective in an intersubjective sense. This is apparent in Keynes's 1905 **'Miscellanea Ethica'** paper, where Keynes draws a distinction between what an individual can think and feel and what an individual ought to think and feel.

> [I]t is plain that the idea and the emotion appropriate to any given sensation are partly dependent on the nature and past history of the individual who feels. This is obvious enough; we ought not all to have precisely similar states in similar physical circumstances; common sense and the commandments are agreed on that. But we can in many cases abstract that element which ought to vary from man to man. Assuming the approximate uniformity of human organs, we can often—say what, apart from peculiar circumstances, a man *ought* to think and feel:—not indeed what he *can* think and feel—that will *always* depend upon his nature and his past.

Thus Keynes allows a role for individual judgement, but also supposes that one can often say what another individual would likely think and feel, on the grounds that there exists an 'approximate uniformity of human organs'. Since individuals possess essentially the same constitution, it is not unreasonable to say that we often anticipate what another will think and do under normal circumstances, although this does not of course preclude unexpected behaviour on the part of individuals, since an individual's behaviour is also to be explained by his or her 'nature and past history'. But economics surely is concerned with explaining average behaviour and thus, on Keynes's view, the economist would not be unjustified in supposing introspection and judgements of value produce defensible opinions about agents' motives and intentions.

This notion of a common intellectual and motivational constitution, it should be noted, has already been seen to underlie Keynes's thinking in his *Treatise on Probability*. There Keynes asserts that 'logic investigates the general principles of valid thought' which form the basis for rational belief. While probability judgements do possess a subjective dimension in the individual's selection of premises, this should not obscure the objective character of probability in Keynes's view.

> But in the sense important to logic, probability is not subjective. It is not, that is to say, subject to human caprice. A proposition is not probable because we think it so. When once the facts are given which determine our knowledge, what is probable or improbable in the circumstances has been fixed objectively, and is independent of our opinion. The theory of probability is logical, therefore, because it is concerned with the degree of belief which it is *rational* to entertain in given conditions, and not merely with the actual beliefs of particular individuals, which may or may not be rational.

Keynes's position in this regard, it is true, is not invulnerable to the considerable emphasis Keynes also placed on individual judgement in the [*Treatise on Probability*], especially in his above noted discussion of 'the relativity of knowledge to the individual'. Yet at the same time, Keynes obviously saw two dimensions to an individual's thinking—subjective and objective sides—and this conviction is what is at issue in an analysis of his claims for economics as a moral science.

Indeed, when Keynes came to confront F. P. Ramsey' criticism of the *Treatise on Probability* as indefensibly objectivist, Keynes allowed that there was something to Ramsey's complaint, while still insisting that Ramsey's account of probabilities as subjective was nonetheless lacking in an important regard.

> Ramsey argues, as against the view which I put forward, that probability is concerned not with objective relations between propositions but (in some sense) with degrees of belief, and he succeeds in showing that the calculus of probabilities simply amounts to a set of rules for ensuring that the system of degrees of belief which we hold shall be a consistent system. Thus the calculus of probabilities belongs to formal logic. But the basis of our degrees of belief—or the *a priori* probabilities, as they used to be called—is part of our human outfit, perhaps given to us merely by natural selection, analogous to our perceptions and our memories rather than to formal logic

> (*CW*, X, pp. 338-9).

Thus, although it may not be possible to speak of objective probability relations between propositions in the manner desired in the [*Treatise on Probability*], for Keynes even Ramsey's view should not be regarded as a fully subjective one, since it still presupposes 'our human outfit' is somehow responsible for the rules that define the calculus of probabilities. How 'our human outfit' might function to produce a coherent, intersubjective calculus of probabilities, admittedly, is not explained by Keynes. It is clear, nonetheless, that despite the considerable weight Keynes placed on individual judgement in his philosophical thinking, this somehow always operated against a backdrop of intersubjective intellectual capacity among individuals.

This emphasis should be placed in proper perspective. When Keynes argued in 1938 that economics is a moral science, he specifically contrasted his view to that of Lionel Robbins, who Keynes characterized as supporting the view that economics is a natural science (*CW*, XIV, p. 297). Robbins, of course, is especially well known for his *An Essay on the Nature and Significance of Economic Science* argument that interpersonal comparisons of utility are inappropriate in economics if economics is to be regarded as a science. For Robbins, interpersonal utility comparisons essentially depend upon value judgements, and value judgements, in contrast to judgements of a factual nature, are not verifiable and thus not scientific. Robbins's critique had a dramatic impact on economists when it appeared, since it created significant doubts among economists concerning the legitimacy of redistributive social welfare policies, which had been standard in economics since Marshall. Indeed, Robbins's argument was an important stimulus to Roy Harrod's Presidential Address to Section F of the British Association, 'Scope and Method of Economics', which was published in the September 1938 *Economic Journal.* Keynes's own remarks about Robbins and economics came in correspondence with Harrod prior to the latter's August presentation of the Address. Robbins also responded to Harrod in a December 1938 *Economic Journal* comment.

Accordingly, that Keynes argued that economics is a moral science, and that it justifiably employs introspection and judgements of value (or value judgements), should be taken to stand in direct opposition to Robbins's position. In claiming one can consult one's own imagined reaction to given circumstances, and then analogically assess the motives and intentions of economic agents whose behaviour is to be explained, Keynes confronts essentially the same issues that Robbins addressed in arguing against interpersonal utility comparisons. Moreover, it might well be said that the focus of the issue for Keynes—as clearly it is for Robbins—is whether it is methodologically reasonable to make value judgements in economics, since Keynes allows that introspection also involves judgements of value, when one assesses the strength or force of a presumed motive ascribed to a given economic agent analogically from one's own case. How, then, might Keynes have justified his proposed reliance on judgements of value (or value judgements) in light of Robbins's assertion that such judgements cannot be scientific?

First, Keynes, from the time of his 1904 **'Ethics in Relation to Conduct'** critique of Moore's reliance on the frequency theory of probability, clearly believed that the evidence potentially favourable to a given proposition always requires interpretation. This implies that individual judgement is indispensable to empirical argument, and also that judgements of value are involved in an investigator's assessment of the quality and significance of evidence at hand. On this view, Robbins's model of an *a posteriori* verification of empirical propositions—where the facts effectively speak for themselves—misrepresents scientific practice, since empirical verification lacks the exceptional standing claimed for it and does not offer a clear methodological alternative to using judgements of value. Second, however, Keynes unlike Robbins, believed that judgements of value could be reasonably objective, and that this provided positive justification for their (selective) use in economics. Keynes early on argued, in his **'Miscellanea Ethica'** paper, that a reapplication of Moore's organic unities principle made it possible to ground moral judgements more securely than Moore had done in his *Principia Ethica,* and thus that moral judgements could generally be thought objective. This conclusion was supported by Keynes's distinction between what one actually thinks and feels and what one ought to think and feel. Although certainly it is not always straightforward how these are distinguished, nonetheless in Keynes's view there is a difference between them. In contrast, it is fair to say that from

Robbins's point of view, judgements of value are invariably associated with what individuals happen to think and feel, since there is no agreed-upon manner—no method of verification—in which one can say how one ought to think and feel.

Indeed, it is the willingness or unwillingness to claim that a genuine difference exists between what one actually thinks and feels and what one ought to think and feel that separates the respective positions of Robbins and Keynes on the use of introspection as a methodological strategy in economics. Robbins, in his critique of interpersonal utility comparisons, argued that there was no means of testing the magnitude of one individual's satisfaction derived from a given income as compared with that of another, and that the effort to do this inevitably necessitated value judgements.

> Introspection does not enable A to measure what is going on in B's mind, nor B to measure what is going on in A's. There is no way of comparing the satisfaction of different people.

Keynes, however, did not associate scientificity exclusively with verification through measurement, and thus did not regard the lack of measurability and the attendant recourse to value judgement in introspection as an indication of non-objective judgement. In part, he believed this because he believed value judgements could be objective in the sense of it being possible to say what an individual ought to think and feel in given circumstances, so that it was not necessary for example, as Robbins thought, to say that one could never compare two individuals' satisfaction with a given income.

As a methodological approach, accordingly, introspection depends upon defending the possibility of there being certain kinds of value judgements—namely, those that are objective in the sense of being intersubjectively defensible. To be able to consult one's own imagined reaction to circumstances experienced by others, and treat this projected response as informative about others' motives and intentions, one must be able to say with confidence that, since individuals ought generally to be expected to respond to such circumstances in certain ways, one's own projected response in a situation can be thought representative of those of others. This is, as noted above in connection with Keynes's discussion of 'the approximate uniformity of human organs', a matter of having some methodological foundation for explaining the intersubjective side of human judgement to accompany his attention to individual judgement. Both, it was argued, are necessary to an account of the representative individual employed in introspective analogical reasoning, since the individual consulting his or her own case must be both distinct and typical of those whose behaviour is observed. Robbins, unlike Keynes, was reluctant to attribute 'an approximate uniformity of human organs' to individuals, and thus a capacity in judgement to individuals whereby economists' introspective judgements of others' thoughts and feelings could be thought legitimate. In effect, Robbins, saw but one dimension to human nature—namely, that especially subjective side that Keynes associated with the capacity for a distinctively individual judgement, and which is today associated with the complete exogeneity of taste.

CONCLUSION

Keynes's moral science view of economics has received little attention, no doubt due in part to the inaccessibility of its philosophical foundations, but also undeniably to the modern trend in methodological thinking that treats economics as what Keynes termed for Robbins a natural science. Keynes's understanding, however, is provocative, in that it links this methodological conception to fundamental questions concerning the theory of the individual in economics. That is, since Keynes's implicit defence of introspection and judgements of value is rooted in a dual nature theory of the individual, the question naturally arises whether a justifiable commitment to this methodological approach entails a revision of economists' theory of the individual economic agent. In the discussion here, it should be emphasized, the plausibility of the more controversial component of Keynes's view—'the approximate uniformity of human organs'—has not been assessed. Nor, moreover, has the relationship between individual judgement and an intersubjectively objective human judgement been explored in a manner that provides much more than an introduction to the idea of the representative individual. These further investigations, nonetheless, are arguably central to an understanding of not just Keynes's methodological views, but, more importantly, to an understanding of his theoretical strategies concerning the independent variables, 'in the first instance', of *The General Theory*—the propensity to consume, the marginal efficiency of capital schedule and the rate of interest. Accordingly, further investigation of these questions must necessarily take as its reference point the logic of the theory of the individual.

Robert Skidelsky   (essay date 1992)

SOURCE: An introduction to *John Maynard Keynes*, Vol. 2, Allen Lane The Penguin Press, 1994, pp. xv-xxix.

[*In the following excerpt, Skidelsky discusses Keynes's efforts to reconcile his private values with his public duties, focusing on the moral underpinnings of his economic theories. The first volume of Skidelsky's biography was published in 1983 and the second volume originally came out in 1992.*]

'My purpose is to tell of bodies which have been transformed into shapes of a different kind.' This second volume of biography tells the story of Keynes's metamorphosis from aesthete, philosopher and administrator into world saviour. It is a reshaping of life-purpose which gives his middle and later years a melancholy afterglow, despite their extraordinary achievement.

After the First World War, Keynes set out to save a capitalist system he did not admire. He found himself in a world emptied by war of its old faiths and certainties; one in which monsters prowled, ready to devour what remained of Europe's civilisation. The collapse of the American economy in 1929 closed, so it seemed, the circle of despair. In 1939, the European war, suspended in 1918, broke out again. 'We can regard what is now happening,' Keynes wrote in June 1940, 'as the final destruction of the optimistic liberalism which Locke inaugurated. . . . For the first time for more than two centuries Hobbes has more message for us than Locke. . . .'

The contrast with the cloistered, but hopeful, world of prewar Cambridge in which he grew up could not have been starker. He was the child of a late-flowering Edwardian Enlightenment which believed—against much evidence, to be sure—that a new age of reason had dawned. The brutality of the closure applied in 1914 helps explain Keynes's reading of the interwar years, and the nature of his mature efforts. This book is about his attempt to restore the expectation of stability and progress in a world cut adrift from its nineteenth-century moorings. He brought in the State to redress the failings of society, not because he loved it, but because he saw it as the last resource. His genius was to have developed an analysis of economic disorder which justified forms of state intervention compatible with traditional liberal values. He was the last of the great English Liberals.

It is worth recalling the main features of his early story. Professor John Vincent, in reviewing the first volume of my biography in the *Sunday Times* of 6 November 1983, wrote, 'Had Keynes died in 1925, he would be remembered as a minor don, an economic technician of obsolete views, a powerful wartime civil servant, a fringe figure in Bloomsbury, and a good College bursar; in other words, not remembered at all.' This is wrong: he would have been remembered for *The Economic Consequences of the Peace,* his outburst against the Treaty of Versailles. But, apart from this, Vincent is right. In 1920, Keynes was thirty-seven, and had given no hint of greatness in the sphere in which he would excel—economics. But for the war, it is not clear that he would have stuck to economics, or the life of a Cambridge don.

Keynes was born and bred for success. He was the product of two Nonconformist stocks, distinguished by brains, religious and didactic vocation and practical ability. A strong sense that one's duty to oneself entailed duty to others ran through both sides of the family, though with Maynard Keynes's father, Neville Keynes, this was a cheerless credo, his passions being much more clearly of a private nature. Those who see the imaginative flair coming from the Brown-Ford side of the family, and the administrative ability as the Keynes legacy, ignore the large role which aesthetic enjoyments—particularly those of the theatre and music—played in Neville Keynes's life. Maynard Keynes was very much his father's son, minus the anxiety which made intellectual work a misery to Neville Keynes. His tendency to preach to mankind, and legislate for its welfare, he got from his mother.

Keynes's was a precocious, pampered, but above all *successful* childhood. There was no 'unhappy' upbringing to overcome. This was partly due to the supportive nature of his home background and the enlightened regime of College at Eton. But Keynes also realised from an early age that his cleverness gave him a pathway to success in dealing with adults. Cleverness was the alternative to submission or rebellion: or, to put it another way, through cleverness one can manipulate any situation to one's advantage. But to what end? At school, Keynes excelled in both classics and mathematics; a notable gift for friendship coexisted with a facility for administration. He was cut off from normal 'boyhood' by his exceptional intelligence and lack of physical grace; at the same time he quickly learnt how to manipulate that 'normal' world, and at Eton was both an intellectual leader and a social success. His cleverness, his breadth of interests and the contrast between his private allegiances and the public nature of his abilities already mark him out as exceptionally interesting.

As a Cambridge undergraduate and postgraduate, a clerk in the India Office and Fellow of King's College, Cambridge, Keynes, before the war, played out the dichotomies of his childhood on a larger stage. The main contrast in this period is between the esoteric nature of his ideals and friendships, centred on the philosophy of G. E. Moore, the Apostles, Bloomsbury and the cult of homosexuality, and the growing range of his public activities as a civil servant, College administrator, economist, occasional politician and member of a Royal Commission. Between 1906 and 1914 nothing seemed so important to Keynes as the pursuit of knowledge and love. His *Treatise on Probability* was finished in 1914; the passionate phase of his love affair with the painter Duncan Grant came to an end in March 1909, when Duncan Grant told him that he was no longer in love with him, while retaining an affection that was 'exceedingly strong'.

> His feelings towards people [Duncan Grant wrote to James Strachey on 22 April 1909], their strength and fullness, their purity of substance, even his lack of moods make him to me a most lovable character. But I cannot any longer believe myself to be *in* love with a person who sometimes bores me, sometimes irritates me, & from whom I can live apart without being unhappy, however much I like to be with him.

Although Keynes was to have other boyfriends, the period 1908-11 is the high point of his absorption in the abstract passions of the mind, and the secret affairs of the heart, though the pattern of mental work in the context of a loving relationship was to be reproduced when he married the ballerina Lydia Lopokova in 1925.

In the First World War, Keynes's 'divided nature' came out in his simultaneous opposition to the official war aim of a fight to the finish with Germany and his work, at the Treasury, for 'a government I despise for ends I think criminal'. As he put it to Duncan Grant in 1917, 'I pray for the most absolute financial crash (and yet I strive to prevent it—so all I do is a contradiction to all I feel).' The tug within him between the rational, pacifist values of Bloomsbury—'I had become I suppose in a sense unpatriotic, as I suppose most artists must do,' Duncan Grant wrote to his father—and the calculations of Whitehall is seen at its sharpest in this period. It was not in Keynes's nature to give up *either*—an attitude he tried to rationalise by using his official position to protect his friends from conscription, and deploying financial arguments to minimise Britain's involvement in military fighting on the Western Front. This was Keynes's version of the Faustian bargain: intelligence could play a part in mitigating barba-

rism. The alternative interpretation of his conduct was put by his friend David Garnett: 'Who are you? Only an intelligence they need in their extremity. . . . A genie taken incautiously out of King's . . . by savages to serve them faithfully for their savage ends, and then—back you go in to the bottle.' The tension of this double loyalty drove Keynes to breaking point. In 1916 he declared himself a conscientious objector to conscription, although he had already been exempted by the Treasury; and he did finally break down at the Paris Peace Conference in 1919, returning, shattered, to England, to denounce Lloyd George's peace policy with a vehemence made more savage by pent-up hostility to his war policy. *The Economic Consequences of the Peace* (1919) made Keynes a world figure. Thus one could say that, in the end, he got the better of the bargain, since his Treasury experience, and the uses to which he put it in his book, gave him the position of intellectual leadership which he needed to remould economic theory and policy in the inter-war years.

It is hard even now to get Keynes's personality and achievement into focus. My own treatment has been greatly influenced by Alasdair Macintyre's fine book, *After Virtue,* published in 1981: a discussion of what happens to a culture when the attempt to justify ethics by religion or tradition comes to be seen as offensive to 'reason'. In such a culture, Macintyre suggests, moral discussion becomes interminable, since unaided reason provides no basis for agreement. Values are privatised or personalised, habitual virtues undermined; public discourse shifts to means, to technique—the one area in which rational agreement might still be sought and achieved. Such a culture produces two kinds of representative character: the Aesthete and the Manager. The aesthete pursues sensual enjoyment without limit; the manager manipulates social relations in the interests of stability. The twentieth-century 'characters' thus embody the impasse which moral discourse has reached. They are the inheritors of the collapsed Christian world-view. On occasion, Macintyre writes, the two characters may be found 'in one and the same person who partitions his life between them.'

Keynes is a leading, possibly the leading, twentieth-century example of this type of 'partitioned' character, the finest flower of an autumnal civilisation. The main cleavage running through his life is precisely that between the worlds of Bloomsbury and Whitehall. Someone who avowed his lifelong commitment to G. E. Moore's ideal of friendship and beauty was also the conscious stabiliser of social systems. But what is the connection here between private and public duty, one's duty to oneself and one's duty to the world?

Moore evaded the dilemma. He held ethical ends—conceived as states of mind—to be self-evidently good or bad. Apart from this, there was an inherited world of rules and duties. Moore argued that it was only for the sake of good states of mind—'in order that as much of them as possible may at some time exist . . . that any one can be justified in performing any public or private duty'. But there was no obvious connection between the ethical programme he advanced and the inherited morality to which he subscribed. Keynes tried to improve on Moore by detaching the question of what we ought to do from conventional morality, and linking it instead to individual judgement of probabilities attaching to different courses of action. Thus he tried to close the circle of reason. The theme of his *Treatise on Probability,* at which he worked for eight years prior to 1914, is that probability can be, and should be, the 'guide of life'. But Keynes's judgements of probability, no less than Moore's ethical judgements, rest on intuition. This attempt to ground moral reasoning in the judgements of rational individuals breaks down when it becomes apparent that people's intuitions of goodness and right conduct differ, and there is no appeal outside individual intuition by reference to which those differences might be resolved. The result is moral disorder.

Looking back, it seems clear that the Moore-Keynes programme of secularising moral philosophy rested, as Keynes later admitted in **'My Early Beliefs'**, on the tacit assumption that human beings in England, or more narrowly Cambridge, in 1900 or thereabouts were already so constituted by their history as to be 'reliable, rational, decent people, influenced by truth and objective standards, who can be safely released from the outward restrains of convention and traditional standards and inflexible rules of conduct, and left, from now onwards, to their own sensible devices, pure motives and reliable intuitions of the good'. It presupposed, that is, that, left free to choose, individuals would choose what was good and right; and that these choices would add up to what was good and right for the whole community. Eventually Keynes came to understand that the search for truth could take place fruitfully only within a shared cultural framework. In economics one could not have good conversations unless there had been a prior meeting of minds on the intuitive level. But as a young man his faith in the ability of unanchored rational argument to discover the truth was complete.

Everyone agrees that Keynes was the most intuitive of men. But if we abandon his own early view of intuition as a culture-free insight into logical relations or, more generally, the nature of 'truth', there are interesting questions to be asked about the sources of his own intuitions. He used to say that his best ideas came to him from 'messing about with figures and *seeing* what they must mean' (italics added). From his earliest years Keynes was fascinated by numbers, which were perhaps more 'real' to him than people or situations. Yet he was famously sceptical about econometrics—the application of mathematical and statistical methods to the analysis of economic data, chiefly for the purpose of explanation and forecasting. The truth seems to be that numbers were for him simply clues, triggers of the imagination, rather like anecdotes are for the non-mathematically minded. People often talked about the 'magical' quality of his mind. His imagination was filled with the legends, fairy tales, myths, secular and Christian, of his childhood, which he freely drew on, much like Freud, to make patterns of the behaviour of his own times. The legend of King Midas, for example, is a recurring motif in his work, the clue to the riddle of economic stagnation. What made Keynes more (and in the opinion of some less) than an economist was that his understanding of what was happening was influenced much more by the drama and poetry of the West, which re-

mained lifelong companions, than by the theorems of classical economics, many of which never got 'under his skin'. Economics was a game he could play, a language he could use, a powerful tool of thought; but the sources of his understanding of economic life lay outside, or beneath, its own characteristic ways of reasoning.

Keynes became more thoughtful as he grew older, without losing the sharp edge of his mind. For the young Keynes and his friends, casting off Christian 'hocus pocus' was pure gain. It liberated morality from its dependence on superstition. Keynes habitually referred to Victorian moral discourse as 'medieval' or 'barbarous', echoing the eighteenth century's contempt for the Christian world-view of the Middle Ages revived in Victorian England. The result of shedding superstition was confidently expected to be an improvement in morals, but even more importantly an improvement in the language of moral justification. The age of reason had dawned for a second time after the Victorian night. Later in life, Keynes was not so sure. 'Our generation—yours & mine . . . owed a great deal to our fathers' religion,' he told Virginia Woolf in 1934. 'And the young . . . who are brought up without it, will never get so much out of life. They're trivial: like dogs in their lusts. We had the best of both worlds. We destroyed it yet had its benefits.' In practice, Keynes's own life was shaped by the Cambridge tradition in which he grew up. This embedded the quest for individual excellence in a setting of public duty. For it was to their ancient universities that Victorian England looked for its 'clerisy'—its spiritual and intellectual leaders. But this tradition, too, had become a fragment of a vanishing whole, and was kept going by habit rather than by reflection. Indeed, when Keynes actually reflected on the problem of reconciling one's 'duty to oneself' with one's 'duty to the world'—notably in his essay on **'Egoism'** in 1906, but intermittently throughout his life—he reached the familiar modern conclusion that these duties were in fact irreconcilable. Thus the lack of any close connection between private and public virtue, or rather the lack of a language in which such a connection could be conclusively demonstrated, first emerges as a problem in Keynes's moral philosophy, though he continued to live his own life as though such a connection existed.

The difficulty of getting Keynes's 'character' right arises to an unusual extent from the weakening of the Nonconformist culture which had previously 'formed' character and held unruly propensities in check. The strong, well-defined 'characters' of Victorian biographies were not just the fictions of conventional biographical language; rather the kind of language being used about them had itself helped form their characters. The biographer of a 'modern' subject like Keynes has a more difficult task. The notion of character has been replaced by the concept of 'personality' or 'nature'. Implicit in such formulations is an absence of coherence: one's 'nature' is a bundle of possibilities, a myriad of sensations, spilling out in different directions, more like a stream than a compact building. Heredity, family, school, class all play their part in Keynes's formation. But the way he developed also reflected the dissolution of the Puritan character-type. What Daniel Bell, in his book *The Cultural Contradictions of Capitalism,* calls the 'disjuncture' between the moral and material orders finds in Keynes its representative expression. Keynes's 'character' was a set of stratagems, a matter of checks and balances which allowed his life's work to unfold. His sense of duty triumphed in the end because the world needed to be saved from its folly.

Such a nature is difficult to grasp for the uncomplicated, and it eluded his contemporaries. Discerning associates were well aware that Keynes was 'not of a piece', and were puzzled to know what, if anything, the pieces added up to. Oswald Falk, who perhaps knew him best of all in the years covered by this book [1920 to 1937], saw him as a succession of 'masks', and wondered whether he could have 'any identity in solitude'. The masks were physical as well as mental. The playful eyes and sensual mouth were covered up by the conventional disguises—the military moustache, the dark suits and homburgs which he wore even on picnics—of the man of affairs.

Kingsley Martin did a profile of him for the *New Statesman* of 28 October 1933 (to go with Low's famous cartoon . . .), which emphasised his liquidity of mind and temperament, so 'terrifying and bewildering to the cautious and the solidly rooted'. But the point is that the solidly rooted found the world crumbling beneath them and needed to be rescued by a liquid mind able 'to run round and over an obstacle rather than to dispose of it'.

> Since he is troubled with sympathies and prejudices rather than with principles [the *New Statesman* assessment continues], the best policy is to find him a new premise; in a few minutes he may be successfully discovering for you all the arguments in support of your own conclusion.

This comment is representative of many. Keynes used to say, 'Every morning I wake up like a new born babe.' Quentin Bell recalls his immense persuasiveness in arguing any theory which at the time he believed, or perhaps just interested him, or amused him. Partly this was a sheer delight in showing off his cleverness. But people wondered: where was the core of him? His intellectual playfulness led Beatrice Webb into a spectacular but understandable misjudgement: 'Keynes is not serious about economic problems; he plays chess with them. The only serious cult with him is aesthetics: the Chinese conception of the art of a pleasurable or happy man with a secured and sufficient livelihood. . . . ' This was written in her diary on 19 June 1936, four months after the publication of the *General Theory*! Dennis Robertson likened his mind to a powerful searchlight, moving from object to object, ignoring the interconnections of the whole. But suppose there were no interconnections left, only fragments? The rapidity with which he took up and discarded plans was equally startling. He was the first to realise when a cause was lost, and adapt himself to the new situation with equal elan, while the more solid were still trying to catch with his project of the day before yesterday. Yet looking at his ideas and plans over his lifetime there is a remarkable consistency in his *understanding* of his age.

> Keynes is so affectionate, loyal and warm blooded [the *New Statesman* goes on] that until one

meets him in opposition one may not understand where he gets his reputation for arrogance. He has an unavoidable consciousness that he is intellectually superior to the great ruck of mortals. He does not suffer fools. He minds about culture and personal freedom, but not at all about equality; he hates waste more than he hates suffering, and he is quite capable of being ruthless when he wants his own way. He is the most benevolent, impish, dangerous and persuasive promoter of ideas, and his eyes, arresting, commanding and challenging at times, are at others as soft and lively as bees' bottoms in blue flowers.

We must turn to Oswald Falk for the most penetrating analysis of Keynes's 'mental fabric':

> . . . I wonder [he wrote to Keynes on 2 February 1936] . . . whether analysis is your fundamental mental process, whether it doesn't follow, with a somewhat grudging struggle at rational justification, rather than precede synthetic ideas, which are your real delight, and with which from time to time you startle and shock the majority. Didn't Newton once say that his ideas reached him by some mysterious route which he could not explain? And isn't there something in the view that a new idea . . . may . . . be the product of the . . . moral feeling of an age, floating around us, and ready for apprehension by the most *sensitive* minds by other than reasoning processes? And isn't it the artist rather than the scientist who apprehends these ideas? Is your mind really so typically western as superficially it appears to be? I believe not. Brilliant as your analysis may be, I believe it is a veneer rather than the substance of your mental fabric. And that explains perhaps in part the hostility which you arouse amongst the more truly western minds of some of your fellow economists, scientists in the narrower sense, bogged in the muddles of their analysis . . . and either unwilling to admit or unable to realise that an idea, which is attainable, is something very different from a truth, which is not, and that the attainable idea is essential for the conduct of our lives.

Keynes's economics, at their most general, can be seen as the reflection of the 'moral feeling' of the age, intuited by an extraordinarily *sensitive* mind; but a mind also habituated to responsibility and duty. The decay of Victorian values freed Keynes to experiment with new ways of living and also alerted him to the need for new forms of social control. We have here a clue to the paradox of how the speculator in morals, ideas and money could win over the solid men in City suits to revolutionary concepts of economic management. He was not, after all, improbably cast as the 'saviour of capitalism'. Social systems are never saved by true believers, the virtues appropriate to going down with the ship rarely being suitable for the arts of navigation. The manipulation of economies by governments was but an extension of the management of external relations which Keynes had long practised to protect his private life. The projects conjured up by his nimble mind fitted a world no longer solidly rooted in Victorian certainties.

For Keynes's teacher Alfred Marshall, the connections between economics and culture, wealth and welfare, were still relatively unproblematic. Material prosperity, Marshall believed, was the necessary condition of moral growth: a 'gentleman' needed £500 a year. And business life was, for Marshall, itself a form of moral and moralising activity: sacrificing present enjoyment to make things which people needed to make them good. By the twentieth century this reciprocal connection between commerce, culture and morals, too readily assumed by the Victorians, could not be taken for granted, decreasingly so as the century unfolded. Today the main object of business activity is to make a quick profit, the quicker the better. The main object of contemporary statecraft is to make societies ever richer. To what end, and with what effect on individual and social virtue, we no longer ask, and scarcely dare think about. Keynes was the last great economist to hold economics in some sort of relation with the 'good life'. But already the language available to him to talk about the relationship sounded threadbare. What, in fact, was the connection between being rich and being good? Keynes was troubled by such questions but could make little progress in answering them. It became sufficient to keep the existing system of wealth-creation going, because its collapse would be more horrible than its success.

Keynes started devising his projects of economic management at a moment when the Victorian certainties had broken down—irretrievably shattered by the First World War—and Victorian motives to virtuous behaviour and self-improvement had weakened. The breakdown of the self-regulating market was the most spectacular example of the weakening of the civil society inherited from the Victorians. The chief symptom of this breakdown was persisting mass unemployment, though it was some time before Keynes identified it as the problem which it was to be his life's work to solve. He was a monetary economist and he always approached economic disorder from the side of money. The disturbing influence of money on the real economy—on the production of goods and services—is a constant factor in his thinking from his earliest pre-war economic writings to his *General Theory*. But the role of money in his theory of economic disorder shifted over time, though how much this was due to a change of terminology rather than a change in his understanding of the world is unclear.

He starts with the theme that the specific virtues associated with economic self-regulation—he singles out self-restraint and long-run thinking—presuppose, or depend on, stability of the price level. The earliest symptom of post-war economic disorder was the collapse of the stable measuring rod—money—in terms of which economic activities were valued and proportioned to each other. However, it was not the fact of inflation or deflation which caused economic activity to oscillate, but the uncertainty about the future course of prices on the minds of economic decision-makers. The effect of uncertainty on economic behaviour—on decisions to save, invest and provide employment—emerges as a major theme of Keynes's earliest theoretical book, *A Tract on Monetary Reform* (1923). In these circumstances, the duty of the monetary authority is to secure a supply of money consistent with establishing a firm expectation of zero inflation. It is deeply ironic that a theory which started off by proclaiming the necessity of stable prices for stable production should have degenerated into the dogma that 'inflation doesn't matter'.

Two paths led on from this early statement to Keynes's mature theory. First, he came to see money not so much as a cause of uncertainty as a way of dealing with uncertainty. The function of money as generalised purchasing power offered the possibility of withholding it from production and consumption, and Keynes almost implies it was invented for this purpose. Depressions arise, Keynes wrote in his *Treatise on Money* (1931), when money is shifted from the 'industrial circulation' into the 'financial circulation'. The emphasis Keynes placed on the function of money as a store of wealth, as an escape from commitment, as a measure, not of purchasing power, but of mistrust of the future, was one of his original contributions to economics. That wealth-holders should want to keep their assets liquid in an unsettled world was not perhaps a surprising revelation to this most liquid of men.

Keynes's second contribution, in the *General Theory of Employment, Interest, and Money* (1936), was to show that an economy had no natural tendency to full employment; that it could be naturally adjusted to a low level of inactivity, like an invalid to ill-health; and that, in these circumstances, an external intervention was required to restore it to vigour. This challenged head-on the inherited economic doctrine that no equilibrium position short of full employment was possible. Thus the withdrawal from investment, which the existence of money made possible, could set up a train of repercussions which left the economy in stable equilibrium short of full employment.

These are simple expressions of technical ideas in economics. But in his more philosophical writings Keynes links the power of money to disturb economic self-regulation to the tendency for money itself to become an object of desire, rather than a means to satisfy desires. His most profound and poetical pages on economics have to do with the encroachment of money values on use values, the triumph of making money over making things. For Keynes, as for the classical economists, Depressions are the wages of sin, only the sin is not spending too much, but spending too little on the things which make for a 'good life'. From this standpoint the Keynesian Revolution may be seen as an attempt to remoralise the capitalist economy—in Ruskin's words, to produce 'wealth' rather than 'illth'. This was undoubtedly part of its attraction to many on the left. These are the moral resonances in Keynes's technical arguments which can be heard by those willing to listen. They are not part of the logic of the arguments themselves. Economics was already too far removed from being a moral science for it to carry moral arguments. It was another fragment of a vanishing whole, soon to disappear into the black hole of mathematics.

Keynes did the best he could with the intellectual and cultural means at his disposal. It is impossible to think of anyone who could have done better. It is unfair to accuse him of trying to treat a moral crisis with a technical fix. The most palpable failure of individualism at the time was economic. He saw the state as a yet unexploited resource, our 'iron rations'. Moderate collectivism, applied in time, could avert the more extreme varieties then on offer. The risk seemed small compared to the risk of doing nothing. Who is to say that he was wrong? We have since learnt something about the pathology of governments, and of the economic and welfare systems managed and regulated by governments. The chief question for our own time is whether measures to stabilise economies can be combined with effective checks on governments, bureaucracies and producer groups. It is not a question we can put to Keynes. . . .

The simple message of Keynes's economics seems to be that, when a society's self-governing mechanisms break down, it needs more governing from the centre. This is the 'managerial' response to the breakdown of values. The aesthetic response is to substitute personal for public ends. Keynes combined the two by saying that good states of mind could not be enjoyed in collapsing societies. Moreover, his economic theory, which justified putting idle resources to work by means of public expenditure, could be invoked in support of his aesthetic ideals. 'If I had the power today,' he wrote in 1933, 'I would surely set out to endow our capital cities with all the appurtenances of art and civilisation on the highest standards . . . convinced that what I could create I could afford—and believing that money thus spent would not only be better than any dole, but would make unnecessary any dole. For with what we have spent on the dole in England since the war we could have made our cities the greatest works of man in the world.'

Keynes was as good as his word. Even as he was putting the finishing touches to his *magnum opus* in 1935, he was financing and supervising the building of the Cambridge Arts theatre—his personal contribution to the ideal of the civilised society.

David Felix   (essay date 1995)

SOURCE: "Theorizing of the Middle Period: A Treatise on Money," in *Biography of an Idea: John Maynard Keynes and the "General Theory of Employment, Interest and Money,"* Transaction Publishers, 1995, pp. 67-83.

[*In the following excerpt on* A Treatise on Money, *Felix discusses the genesis of the work, the weaknesses in its argument, and its contemporary critical reception.*]

In Keynes's lifetime of inexorable success, his *Treatise on Money,* his only work to go beyond one volume, was the grand exception. In it all of his strengths and weaknesses were given space in which to play themselves out to the greatest extent: his gift for exquisitely refined syllogizing and fluent management of contradictions, practical intimacy with business and finance, mathematical and verbal artistry, a generalist's taste for history and other disciplines, skill in shaping of the material to fit the theory, and his faith in his intuition. A genius had released his creativity too freely. Yet the failure left behind a wealth of materials that would be reworked into *The General Theory,* his greatest achievement, with scintillating fragments left over for his distinguished service to nation and community of nations.

Keynes was building upon the work of Knut Wicksell, the great Swedish economist and contemporary of Marshall. Seeing stable prices as basic to economic stability, Wicksell concentrated on the investment-saving relation, subject of his brief book, *Interest and Prices.* This relation was affected for good and ill by another relation, that between the two Wicksellian interest rates. One, which Wicksell called "the natural rate of interest on capital," was actually the rate of the return on capital, or profits in brief, the other being "the rate of the interest on loans" or the "market rate." If the natural rate (profits) was higher than the market rate (the cost of funds), entrepreneurs would be encouraged to borrow more to expand production, resulting in price increases and boom conditions. If, on the other hand, the market rate was greater than the natural rate, Wicksell concluded ominously, entrepreneurs would reduce investment and "prices will fall continuously and without limit." Hence, price and general economic stability, the great objective of Keynes's *Tract on Monetary Reform,* was best achieved when the market rate was most nearly equal to (but still lower than) the natural rate. Wicksell's doubled relation, investment-saving/natural interest rate-market interest rate was the armature around which the theorist Keynes wound the elaborations of his *Treatise on Money.* Keynes the policymaker, meanwhile, was placing more and more emphasis on low interest rates to encourage business investment and so increase production and employment.

Encouraged by Keynes's ambiguities on the Wicksell-Keynes relation, Harrod and Moggridge have loyally attributed independent creation to him. Thus, while Wicksell flourished a long generation before him, the *Treatise* discussed the great Swede as if he and Keynes were contemporaries, with Wicksell perhaps a half-step behind. It began with a suggestion of equality of effort and effect: "In substance and intention Wicksell's theory is closely akin . . . to the theory of this treatise . . ." But then Keynes continued the sentence with a comment that would reduce the value of Wicksell's contribution and so put his own above it: ". . . although he was not successful . . . in linking up his theory of the bank rate to the quantity equation." At another point Keynes wrote, "I feel that what I am trying to say is the same at root as what Wicksell is trying to say." Here the late Professor Wicksell (1851-1926) seems to be still trying to keep up with Keynes. Inspection shows the absolute dependence of Keynes's *Treatise on Money* on Wicksell's *Interest and Prices.*

It was actually in pursuit of Dennis Robertson's thinking, a fact that he more easily admitted, that Keynes conceived of his treatise. Robertson was evidently better acquainted than Keynes with the Continental economists, Wicksell notably. Robertson's prewar dissertation, he had pursued the quite Wicksellian concern with industrial fluctuations. Returned from the war, he had first written the graceful and illuminating *Money* (1922), which became a leading textbook on the subject, for Keynes (general editor of the Cambridge Economic Handbooks in one of his proliferating capacities). Returned to his older preoccupation, Robertson then undertook his 103-page, richly suggestive *Banking Policy and the Price Level: An Essay in the Theory* of the Trade Cycle, which would be published in January 1926, a profoundly Wicksellian—and somewhat Keynesian—exercise. Indeed its title more accurately describes Keynes's book than the one Keynes eventually chose. Keynes, meanwhile, was thinking out his basic idea and in July 1924, in a pattern he would repeat in the case of *The General Theory,* wrote the first of a series of tables of contents that served as outlines of the work-in-progress. He achieved a second table of contents on 9 October; on 30 November, he completed the third one, *and,* as the informed Lydia, "I have begun the new book!—today, and have written one page." A few weeks earlier, on 12 October, he had written her, "I met Dennis and took him back to my room. I told him the contents of my egg and he told me the contents of his."

Maynard and Dennis collaborated on both books, although the collaboration of Dennis most affected the origins and foundations of Maynard's book, while Maynard most affected the two major, penultimate chapters of Dennis's book, which comprised nearly half of the latter and much of its sense. In his introduction Dennis wrote that chapters 5 and 6 had been "rewritten . . . so drastically at [Keynes's] suggestion that I think neither of us now knows how much of the ideas therein contained is his and how much is mine." In 1928, approaching completion of the *Treatise,* Maynard wrote Lydia, "Dennis came in last night and we had a long talk about the new theory. I think it will do . . . but it owes a great deal to him." And to Wicksell, one might add.

Personally tender, professionally demanding, and profoundly different, Maynard and Dennis inflicted deep and complex agony upon each other. Maynard, objecting confidently to a thesis of Dennis, wrote Lydia, "I'm *sure* it's wrong; so afterwards I went round to bully him again and almost to say he ought to tear it up and withdraw it from publication." This led to the collaborative chapters. For his part, Dennis, who had been moderately severe about Maynard's work, sent him a revised draft of his book, signaling, "I am so unconfident that I should always like to put at the top of everything I write, 'Nobody must believe a word of what follows.'" These contrasting personal characteristics would lead to equally different theoretical and policy conclusions.

Richard Kahn, who would succeed Robertson as Keynes's junior collaborator-in-chief, commented dryly, "It is difficult . . . to pretend that Robertson's tortured writing and Keynes's tortured collaboration . . . were conducive to clarity of thought" [*The Making of Keynes' "General Theory"*]. But the process *was* conducive to a creativity of thought, however obscure, out of which came brilliant work, however contradictory, by both collaborators. Robertson, realistically self-abnegating about his own professional specialty, took the position on page 1 that "far more weight must be attached than is now fashionable . . . to certain *real,* as opposed to monetary and psychological causes of fluctuation." On policy he argued that fluctuations could be "relatively desirable" and that the "*immediate* interest of the manual worker" could not be used as a standard against which to judge economic policy: "[I]t may well be that the ultimate interest even of

the wage-earning class . . . is best served by a measure of industrial instability." In pure theory Keynes might agree, but, as Robertson well knew, Keynes the policymaker balanced off Keynes the theorist. For the moment Keynes's policy toward his protégé's book was to ignore the conclusions already expressed or reserved for the final chapter and concentrate on the joint analysis of the classically Wicksellian investment-saving relation in chapters 5 and 6, which led well beyond Wicksell. In this way Keynes helped shape the analysis in a form that could lead, if he knew where he meant eventually to arrive, to *his* conclusions.

In those two chapters Robertson plunged into a new vocabulary articulating new conceptions, or, at least, variations of older ideas so original that they suggested new ways of thinking. Quirky, insecure emotionally beneath the intellectual insecurity, he was demanding too much of himself by his own standards and trying to achieve exquisite precision beyond the capacity of the economist's professional language. For saving he employed the word "lacking" to express its essential character as liquid wealth reserved for business investment. Among other examples "dislacking" meant consuming more than earned; "abortive lacking," hoarding; "automatic splashing," consuming more than intended; and "imaginary capital," national security or prestige as "immaterial wealth." In attributing reality to what was lacking and its variants Robertson was according just importance to the *non*existence of various economic components. He was also noting the importance of intentions as well as faits accomplis. All this profoundly affected the contemporaneous construction of Keynes's *Treatise on Money* and, perhaps with a stronger effect in the long run, the foundations of *The General Theory,* loosening the cause-and-effect relationships of neoclassical economics for the first and helping effectively to deny them for the second. But then, as Robertson made clear, Keynes was an important originating force in the thinking behind the two chapters.

In the second of the jointly created chapters, however, Keynes permitted Robertson sufficient independence to move toward non-Keynesian conclusions. Robertson had already mentioned the positive values of fluctuations and instability. At a certain point in the trade cycle characterized by excessive prices, he went on in his expressive language, a responsible banking system had to restrain the boom "by churlishness" in meeting increased demand for circulating capital. (Keynes's prewar paper had advocated a similar caution.) But "a secondary fall" occurs, which further lowers prices and "begets a further 'unjustifiable' decline on the side of industrial output." Now, having changed his thinking, Keynes would demand easier rather than restrictive credit even before he had conceived of a complete theoretical rationale, and the discouragement of Robertson's last chapter further widened the difference between the two. Robertson emphasized the dangers of hampering recovery and doubted the value of "heroic capital development" and "the once heretical, but now perhaps over-respectable policy of 'public works.'" If Keynes accepted most of the analysis, he rejected the hopelessness of his friend's policy advice. In the *Treatise on Money* and in his actions to influence policy he moved on toward *his* conclusions.

Keynes began writing the treatise with a bold statement of the conception he intended to develop, entitling it "A Summary of the Author's Theory." This appeared in a draft of the proposed first chapter, written, as noted above, in November 1924. He explained that for numerous reasons the amount of money available for production was imperfectly coordinated with the need for it. One result was the credit cycle (also called, as Robertson preferred, the *trade* cycle), with the "supposed remedies . . . capable . . . of aggravating the disease [while the] credit cycle itself, by causing . . . further fluctuations . . . tended to bring about its own repetition." Confidently, he continued, "If this analysis of the credit cycle is correct, it makes the nature of the cure fairly obvious." He had to grant, "Before, however, we can reach this goal, we must concentrate on a somewhat troublesome analysis." Hence, he intended to comprehend the essential nature of the credit cycle and show how to correct its destructive fluctuations. In the end, if the cure was obvious, the way to achieve it, beginning with the analysis, was indeed troublesome. The process took six years and incorporated itself in at least seventeen successive draft tables of contents projecting Keynes's theorizing forward, and an ultimate physical expression in 2 volumes, 7 "books," 38 chapters, and 689 pages.

At one point Keynes specified, "Booms and slumps are simply the expression of the results of an oscillation of the terms of credit about their equilibrium position." But at another he mentioned Ralph G. Hawtrey, director of financial enquiries at the Treasury and a prolific writer on monetary economics, as having "gone a good deal further than I . . . in arguing that the credit cycle is a 'purely monetary phenomenon.' " In fact, scattering shreds of the problem throughout the treatise, Keynes argued alternately as if his credit cycle was a purely monetary phenomenon and as if every conceivable real factor, economic or otherwise, affected it.

To penetrate to the essence of his credit cycle Keynes felt obliged to develop a new instrument. Before the replacement is studied one should examine what it is that he proposed to replace. The accepted explanation for beginning to understand money and its function in the economy was the quantity theory and its mathematical instrument, the quantity equation. The equation can demonstrate many important aspects of the behavior of money by setting up an equality, hence its character as *equation,* between two pairs of variables. (The nonmathematical reader should be reassured that this explanation will not enter into mathematics any deeper than to mention the formula to be translated into plain English.) One such quantity is $MV = pY$, where M is the quantity of money in a given economy; V, the velocity of turnover of money in the purchase of newly produced goods (or services); p, the price index; and Y, the level of real income. Thus, at any moment, the amount of money multiplied by its turnover rate must equal the price expressed as an index times the amount of real income. This can be made more meaningful if we put it to work in situations known to the reader. What would happen if the amount of money doubled in a short time, as occurred in Germany or Russia in the early 1920s or, to pick a period nearer to us, the Russia of the early 1990s? If the V for velocity and the Y for real income did not change, a doubling of M, the money quantity, would require a doubling of p to maintain the equality. Thus, the price index or price paid for the average good or service would double. With this one has an elementary sense of inflation, an important phenomenon in the life of money.

One more step will add useful meaning. Suppose that M-money was doubled but the statisticians reported that prices had tripled. The equation would continue to be an equation and produce equality if V for velocity, for example, were increased as M increased. That makes sense. If a swift inflation is in progress, people would tend to turn their income into purchases faster because they realize that it was losing value as long as it was expressed in money. The German hyperinflation of 1923 was the classic example of accelerating money-quantity *and* money-velocity increases, with workers paid daily or more often so that they could hurry to make their purchases before prices increased again. Thus the quantity equation inexorably at work.

Wicksell had been unhappy with the quantity theory and devoted a chapter of *Interest and Prices* to attacking it as a "mere truism." But he pulled himself up short: "It is far easier to criticize the quantity theory than to repeal it by a better or more correct one." He devoted the rest of the chapter to showing the failures of the theory's opponents and concluded: "So it is no good; the quantity theory cannot be thrown overboard. . . . The quantity theory is the most competent of all the methods of interpretation that have so far been advanced of the oscillations of the general price level. . . . It must be put up with." To Keynes, Wicksell was another of his teachers he was obliged to correct.

Keynes did so by saying: "The fundamental problem of monetary theory is not merely to establish identities or statical equations relating (e.g.) the turnover of monetary instruments to the turnover of things traded for money." Remaining in its character as a truism, as Wicksell himself had conceded, the quantity theory had failed to go beyond postulating identities. Hence, it had failed to "analyz[e] the different elements involved in such a manner as to exhibit the causal process by which the price level is determined." The old theory had also failed to develop a dynamic character and so pursue monetary phenomena in their movement through the economy. It will be simpler to begin with the first objection and leave the problem of dynamics for later.

In order "to exhibit the causal process" Keynes broke down the components of the economy into many more elements than the quantity theory felt competent to manage. Thus, his more complex analysis distinguished between "windfall profits" and those defined as the "normal remuneration of entrepreneurs," the earned equivalent of workers' wages as opposed to unearned good fortune. While Keynes explained the principle behind the distinction, he did not show how the earned and unearned parts of income could be identified in the real economy. Thus, as he remarked, "the income of holders of ordinary shares will usually include elements of each of these items." One asks how the tax authorities could implement a law that set different tax rates on the shareholders' part of a given firm's earned and unearned income. The distinction, causing more problems wherever it appeared, ran all through the economy. Yet it was only one of the many that Keynes saw in money itself.

Money was subject to a continuing process of division. Initially Keynes categorized it into income and business and savings deposits. In another movement, however, he divided savings deposits into demand and time deposits. Returning to them a dozen chapters later, he found that he had to "cut . . . across our division of the total quantity of money . . . into *industrial* . . . and *financial circulation*," the first comprehending all income deposits and part of business deposits, and the second taking the rest of the business deposits plus all of the savings deposits. He did not explain how one could calculate with these multiple, shifting categories.

Under the rubric of money, inflation itself became a cluster of four categories. There were income inflation (wages, salaries, and normal profits), profit inflation ("windfall" profits), and commodity and capital inflation. Keynes was characterizing these inflations by their origins, the given variant of inflation expressing itself in disproportionate increases in given economic sectors, thus in earnings or windfall profits, or the prices of consumer or capital goods. The logic of the *Treatise* could do nothing with such categories since, as Keynes had to concede, one form of inflation often led to others: "The occurrence of either a commodity inflation or of a capital inflation will tend to cause a profit inflation; and a profit inflation will bring about an income inflation." One generally supportive interpreter wrote that Keynes had simply confused production increases with price increases. Moreover, while Keynes had verbally and mathematically defined his four inflations, he refused to define the fundamental term "inflation" itself, as he had withheld the definition of "probability," crucial aspects of the *Treatise*'s money vanishing into the indefinable. With money lost in these confusions, Keynes was unable to develop his promised method of price-level determination. He was no more successful when he used his own apparatus to provide a dynamic theory.

In the *Tract on Monetary Reform* . . . Keynes had satirized comparative statics, the method employed by the quantity theory, which permitted believing economists "only [to] tell us that when the storm is long past the ocean is flat again." The best the theorists of the old theory could do was to describe economic phenomena at given stages, without filling in the interstices between the stages. But neither he nor any other economist to date has produced a genuinely dynamic economics. One reason, among many, is the intrusion of noneconomic factors into the "tempestuous seasons" he wanted to study, for example, the political factors he noted in his two books on "economic consequences." Another reason is "chaotic behavior," which resists analysis. "[O]ff-equilibrium behavior

remains to this day a rather fuzzy area of economic investigation," one dictionary of economics put it.

The dynamics of the *Treatise* is barely more than promise. Keynes touched directly upon the transition process in four passages totaling a half-dozen pages in the whole book. Only in the last is a suggestion of movement to be found. There Keynes conceived of a notation for monetary velocity that signified greater than normal or "unity" velocity when investment was "in excess," unity when investment and savings were equal, and less than unity when investment was deficient. This is possibly a pregnant conception, but it led to no actual examination of patterns of monetary fluctuations. Book 4, another heuristic effort, is promisingly entitled "The Dynamics of the Price Level" and seems to aim at its essence in the section, "The Problems of the Transition." But Keynes fell upon an "essential awkwardness" due to the fact that a change in the "quantity of bank money is algebraically consistent for a time with more than one set of consequences." Hurled back by too many such ambiguities, he was reduced to an essentially anecdotal narrative of insecurely specified causes and effects in various sectors of the financial economy. At one point in the final chapter, on international disequilibrium, Keynes dispensed with his dynamics to scramble to the security of "the new position of equilibrium as compared with the old," thus the theoretically spurned comparative statics. (Remaining with this latter method, he made no effort to apply dynamics in *The General Theory*.) So much for the dynamics of the *Treatise*.

Keynes's replacement for the quantity equation, asserting their superiority in their name, was, collectively, his ten fundamental equations. They appeared, assigned to chapter 4 of Book 1, in the fifth known table of contents, dated 6 April 1925, some nine months after the first one. From that point to the last draft table of contents the fundamental equations grew in importance from one chapter to eight chapters, making up all of Book 3. They increased beyond that. Keynes had then decided on a two-volume work, the first volume dealing with the pure theory of money, and the second, the applied theory. He shifted five of the eight fundamental-equation chapters from the first volume to the second volume as the ensemble of Book 5, and wrote three new chapters around the equations to replace them in volume 1. In sum the completed *Treatise* devoted 11 chapters and 181 pages to the fundamental equations. They were its engine and drive train as well.

What do the fundamental equations tell us? The final equation, when translated into words, arrives at this ultimate statement: "Price level of output as a whole equals production cost plus (unearned profit divided by total output)," or price equals cost plus profit. Accusing the quantity equation of too simple a formulation, Keynes had produced an even simpler one, useless in theoretical exposition and empty of meaning. In its denial of supply-demand price determination, resting on the classical labor theory of value, it is also reactionary. The distinguished American-Israeli monetary economist Don Patinkin, the supportive interpreter mentioned above, concluded, "[H]e all too frequently shifted unawares across the slippery line that lies between tracing 'cause and effect' (as Keynes put it) and simply repeating tautologies inherent in those equations." With its failed fundamental equations the *Treatise on Money* remains immobile at its starting point.

If the fundamental equations must be left behind, as economic science has confirmed, Keynes himself had reactionary second thoughts about the inadequacy of the quantity equation. At least twice he restored it in the *Treatise* to accomplish what his own equations failed to do for him. In volume 1 he tried to explain "The Relation of the Price Level to the Quantity of Money," as the section title put it, and had to call in the enemy for help. Introducing a new equation, he admitted that it "bears a family relationship to Professor Irving Fisher's familiar equation," which was a variant of the quantity equation. Once again, at the beginning of volume 2, Keynes remarked disarmingly, "I may appear to the reader to be reverting to the old-fashioned 'quantity of money' approach." On the next page he granted it baldly, "Let us write our quantity equation as follows."

Keynes the historian tried to strengthen his pure theory with the fifty-four-page chapter 30, "Historical Illustrations," which found inflation more beneficial then deflation in line with his recent thoughts on policy. In the case of Spain, France, and England he could see "an extraordinary correspondence between periods of profit inflation and of profit deflation, respectively, with that of national rise and decline." But then he had to grant that "the decline and fall of Rome was contemporaneous with the most prolonged and drastic inflation yet reported." Other historical illustrations cooperated no better with the *Treatise*'s theory.

Like Keynes's equally unsuccessful theory of speculative "credit-cycling," the *Treatise* was a vain effort to anticipate the movement of the credit cycle. In his theorizing, the monetary authority operating through a central bank, unlike the private speculator, could go beyond anticipation and control or, at least, powerfully influence that movement in terms of its responsibility for the general welfare. This was the central message of the *Treatise on Money*—to grant extraordinary power and responsibility of the managers of money. Following Wicksell, Keynes saw the credit cycle being generated by price changes as related to costs, thus creating either profits or losses and leading to increases or decreases, respectively, in production and employment. The proper monetary leadership would try to reduce the oscillation with the help of stable prices and so maintain the economy in a continuing state of profitability by way of the appropriate levels of production and employment. It was for this reason that Keynes campaigned incessantly, after the postwar boom had broken, for lower interest rates, thus lower investment costs. Easy credit, however, remained a simplistic solution to a perverse problem. Indeed the prewar Keynes, one may recall, specifically counseled against it as productive of a boom surely enough, but a boom inevitably pursued by crisis and slump. The *Treatise* of the postwar Keynes only obscured the problem under a heap of irrelevant theoretical refinements.

Having failed to achieve an effective theory for a national economy like Great Britain's, Keynes shifted onto inter-

national terrain, where a sensible order of things might assist domestic reform. A powerful "supernational bank" would manage the value of gold according to a commodity index; it would also set the international bank rate and engage in open-market operations. Looking back to Keynes's conception of a central bank for India, it looked forward to the International Monetary Fund and the World Bank, which Keynes would help conceive and bring into existence. But such a bank was much more powerful than the latter two *plus* the Federal Reserve Board, the Bank of England, and the Banque de France. While it was visionary to constructive effect, the idea that nations would give up command of their own economies to such a bank was, to use a favorite adjective of Keynes's, crazy.

When the *Treatise* was published, the contemporary reality joined perversely with a paralyzing theoretical error to make the book's acceptance even more difficult. Its model of the economy assumed constant output based on full employment, Keynes having innocently accepted that neoclassical assumption while attacking its theory. Great Britain's 10-percent unemployment for the period 1922-30 made the assumption look odd, and it appeared odder when the figure rose to almost 15 percent in 1930 itself before increasing to 22.5 percent in 1932. The *Treatise* did allow for unemployment, but it was usually placed just over the horizon, following a fall in prices, and not seen as a central concern. With the fundamental equations expressing the full-employment conception rigidly, Keynes was led to provide a reductio ad absurdum of his own logic. This became known as the "widow's cruse fallacy" from his reference to the Bible story about the miraculously refilled oil cruse of the widow who helped the prophet Elijah (1 Kings 17:9-16). Thus, he concluded that profits spent by entrepreneurs on "riotous living" had no other place to go except back to the entrepreneurial pockets as still more profits accrued, the pattern repeating itself indefinitely. On the other hand, if they had losses, saving to pay the losses generated an equal amount of additional losses, again in a repetitive series, this time ending in bankruptcy. This is one of a number of examples, others to follow, in which Keynes became his own severest critic.

Keynes dealt with the apparent contradiction between book and reality in two ways, both constituting exceptions. In the year of the *Treatise*'s publication he inserted a ten-page section in volume 2 on "The Slump of 1930," in which he speculated on the possibility of a continuing decline, with increasing unemployment and a "far-reaching socialism" replacing "capitalist individualism." If this matched up with what was threatening to happen in the real economy it denied the book's neoclassical theory. The other exception was his parable of a community producing and consuming one product, bananas. A thrift campaign then plunged it into a deep depression that might end with a production halt, total unemployment, and starvation for all. Once again, if this had its realistic suggestiveness, it was achieved by ignoring the *Treatise*'s theory.

The banana parable is worth pursuing for another reason, its seductive absurdity. One can speculate that its relation to the real circumstances justified its use precisely because it did not obey the *Treatise*'s economic laws. Indeed, the parable has received perhaps more attention than the rest of the book. But it is a false analogy, failing to relate to economic science as well as to the economics of the book. A one-product community cannot represent an economy. In that society there is nothing for which the one product can be exchanged, hence no exchange, no buyers and sellers acting independently—none of the economy's essential characteristics. The banana community is a production unit or aggregation of such units functioning under administrative and not economic laws. Yet the parable, seized upon out of desperation, has been taken seriously as an instructive analogy.

In another effort to break out past the theoretical limits of the *Treatise,* also veering into the pragmatic dimension, Keynes speculated on enlisting the monetary cranks as auxiliaries. At the very least they could serve to balance off those nay-sayers to reform, the bankers. The *Tract on Monetary Reform*'s doubts about the virtue of gold had called up a grateful correspondence from the heretics, who sensed in Keynes a fellow believer. Their 200 years of flourishing existence, he agreed, argued powerfully "that the orthodox arguments cannot be entirely satisfactory." While questioning the cranks' lack of a theory of money and interest, he was now more tolerant of their errors than he had formerly been in the case of John Hobson. Keynes agreed with them that the bankers were not trying to maintain the optimum level of employment. His reasoning, advancing beyond the *Treatise,* was already en route to *The General Theory,* where his objections to the heretics' approach would be forgotten.

Keynes ended the book with an abrupt, three-page "Conclusion" attached to the final chapter. He had to grant that the book had not achieved what he had set out to do: "Is monetary theory more ready to take the critical leap forward which will bring it into contact with the real world?" His answer was a promise: "I believe that the atmosphere . . . is favorable to such a result." He was admitting that the result was still in the future. Referring to his ambition to create a dynamic theory, he similarly claimed for his treatise no greater role than that of "a contribution to this new phase of economic science." And so he made his escape from the book—from the theory he could not think out.

Keynes should not have been so surprised and hurt by the negative comments among the many favorable and even awed reviews. He had been his own first critic, beginning to separate himself from the *Treatise* in the preface itself: "The ideas with which I have finished are widely different from those with which I began. . . . There are many skins which I have sloughed still littering these pages." It was an extraordinary service that he demanded of his readers: identify those discarded parts and move sympathetically with the theorist to the indistinctly identified newer ideas. Whatever admissions he had made in the book, he still had faith in its fundamental statement, however ineffable, and defended it dexterously against reviews lacking sufficient sympathy to grasp it. But even the best reviews presented difficulties. The friendly fellow economist (and railway chairman) Josiah Stamp saluted it as "the most penetrat-

ing and epoch-making since Ricardo," but had to admit he did not understand all of it [*Economic Journal* 41 (June 1931)]. Similarly, the Harvard economist John H. Williams mentioned its "rare combination of penetration in theoretical analysis, grasp of mathematical statistical method, and felicity of expression." But he found important parts confusing and complained of a "sense of my shortcomings" in understanding the whole ["The Monetary Doctrines of J. M. Keynes," *Quarterly Journal of Economics* 45 (August 1931)]. Two reviews were particularly painful.

In a long review article Dennis Robertson crystallized out his resistance to Keynes's newer ideas, ["Mr. Keynes's Theory of Money," *Economic Journal* 41 (September 1931)]. In a covering note he had to write Maynard that he could not "subscribe to the fundamental analysis of your *Treatise*." His comments, noting Keynes's prefatory doubts, agreed with him that the book failed to achieve the "harmonious synthesis" that his ideas needed, thus the contradictory introduction of the fundamental equations as both truisms and operative causes in the economy. If Dennis was a friend, Friedrich von Hayek, the young but already formidable Austrian, then at the London School of Economics, was a friendly acquaintance. His two-part review ["Reflections on the Pure Theory of money of Mr. J.M. Keynes," *Economica* 11 (August 1931)] began by agreeing with Robertson's that the *Treatise* was "the expression of a transitory phase in a process of rapid intellectual development." Protesting the "almost unbelievable" and "inconsistent use" of terms in such distinctions as the division of profits into earned and unearned, Hayek found the book's essential argument lacking a clear conception of capital and saving. More specifically, he found its author ignorant of the Austrian theory of capital, the source of the Wicksellian ideas upon which Keynes himself had built. Keynes reacted personally as well as professionally to both reviews.

Keynes's basic public position was that neither critic had understood the book. "Mr. Robertson's difficulties" were due "to our minds not having met on certain large issues" [**"A Rejoinder,"** *Economic Journal* (September 1931)]. Privately he had written comments on the galley proofs and passed them on to Richard Kahn, whom he was finding useful as a personal editor and similarly collaborative replacement for Dennis. Kahn bravely defended Robertson on one point. At another criticism Keynes burst out, "Mr. Robertson's last paragraph . . . yes!—a mere relic of Sadistic—well, not so much barbarism as puritanism. But at this point psycho-analysis must take charge." Kahn advised, "I hope that you will decide to *omit*." Keynes omitted. In the case of Hayek, Keynes began by finding his thought so rooted in a different theory that he could not comprehend new ideas. But then Keynes began "drifting into a review," in his words, of Hayek's *Prices and Production,* which he found "one of the most frightful muddles I have ever read." Hayek was a misdirected "remorseless logician . . . end[ing] up in Bedlam" [**"The Pure Theory of Money: A Reply to Dr. Hayek,"** *Economica* (November 1931)]. (In his response Hayek suggested that Keynes might be "trying to distract the attention of the reader . . . by abusing his opponent" ["A Rejoinder to

Mr. Keynes," *Economica* 11 (November 1931)]. This writer easily agrees with the justice of either's critique of the other's work.) Keynes's copy of the Hayek review had thirty-four penciled marks or comments, one of them regressing to adolescence: "He evidently has a passion which leads him to pick on me." If Keynes's more professional expressions defended the book with his usual skill, he himself was not convinced.

On 5 January 1931, two months after the *Treatise* was published, Keynes wrote to an economist-correspondent [Bertil Ohlin], "My own feeling is that now at last I have things clearer in my own head, and I am itching to do it all over again." From that January until May, Richard Kahn, Joan and E. A. G. (Austin) Robinson, and others among Keynes's younger professional associates gathered together in the "Circus," as it became known, "to digest it, to understand its implicit assumptions, and, inevitably, to criticize it" [D. E. Moggridge, *Maynard Keynes*]. With their help Keynes's thoughts on the *Treatise* were moving insensibly into the thoughts constructing *The General Theory*.

FURTHER READING

Biography

Harrod, R. F. *The Life of John Maynard Keynes.* New York: Harcourt, Brace and Co., 1951, 674 p.
> The official biography.

Hession, Charles H. *John Maynard Keynes: A Personal Biography of the Man Who Revolutionized Capitalism and the Way We Live.* New York: Macmillan Publishing Co., 1984, 400 p.
> A reevaluation of Keynes's life that explores aspects of his personality, especially his bisexuality, first brought to light in Michael Holroyd's biography of Lytton Strachey (1967) and the collection of essays on Keynes edited by his nephew Milo Keynes (1975). Hession emphasizes the integral relationship between Keynes's early, private life and his later achievements and quotes freely from Keynes's writings in order to display his habits of thought and literary style.

Moggridge, D. E. *Maynard Keynes: An Economist's Biography.* London: Routledge, 1992, 941 p.
> A biography largely based on Keynes's own papers. Moggridge was one of the editors of *The Collected Writings of John Maynard Keynes.*

Skidelsky, Robert. *John Maynard Keynes.* Vol. 1, *Hopes Betrayed, 1883-1920*; Vol. 2, *The Economist as Saviour, 1920-1937.* New York: Penguin Books, 1994, 447 p., 731 p.
> A biography focusing on the conflict between Keynes's public and private lives, between the government policies it was his duty to enact and the values and ideals associated with his Cambridge upbringing and the Bloomsbury Group. Skidelsky studies Keynes's work as an economist within the context of the decay of Victorian morals, viewing his economic theories as an "attempt to restore the expectation of stability and progress in a world cut adrift from its nineteenth-century moorings."

Criticism

Bateman, Bradley W., and Davis, John B., eds. *Keynes and Philosophy: Essays on the Origin of Keynes's Thought.* Aldershot, Hants, England: Edward Elgar, 1991, 146 p.
> Seven essays on the philosophical foundations of Keynes's economic thought.

Bleaney, Michael. *The Rise and Fall of Keynesian Economics: An Investigation of Its Contribution to Capitalist Development.* London: Macmillan, 1985, 218 p.
> Assesses the impact of Keynesian economic strategies on the advanced capitalist world and charts the rise and fall of Keynes's popularity among Western economists from the 1930s to the 1980s.

Butkiewicz, James L., Koford, Kenneth J., and Miller, Jeffrey B., eds. *Keynes' Economic Legacy: Contemporary Economic Theories.* New York: Praeger Publishers, 1986, 229 p.
> Proceedings of a conference held in honor of the centenary of Keynes's birth at the University of Delaware, January 11-13, 1984. Participants at the conference discussed new research in the Keynesian tradition, focusing on such topics as rational expectations, the reduction of the natural rate of unemployment, and wage rigidity.

Chick, Victoria. *Macroeconomics after Keynes: A Reconsideration of the "General Theory."* Cambridge, Mass.: MIT Press, 1983, 374 p.
> Assesses Keynes's modern relevance, finding that, although the *General Theory* is in need of revision, it "gives a far richer understanding of the structure of macroeconomic interactions and methods of analysing them than much of what has been written since."

————. *On Money, Method and Keynes: Selected Essays,* edited by Philip Arestis and Sheila C. Dow. New York: St. Martin's Press, 1992, 227 p.
> Twelve essays by Chick written over a period of twenty years. Most of the essays are critiques of different aspects of the neoclassical understanding and application of Keynes's ideas.

Coddington, Alan. *Keynesian Economics: The Search for First Principles.* London: George Allen & Unwin, 1983, 129 p.
> Identifies and explores three schools of thought to which the term "Keynesianism" applies. Coddington's main focus is on how Keynes's ideas have been developed and adapted by later economists in an attempt to counteract potential malfunctions in the economy.

Davis, John B. *Keynes's Philosophical Development.* Cambridge: Cambridge University Press, 1994, 196 p.
> Examines the development of Keynes's philosophical views in relation to his economic theory. Davis finds that Keynes's philosophical thought changed radically over the course of his career and that his later philosophy forms the basis of his arguments in the *General Theory.*

Eatwell, John, and Milgate, Murray, eds. *Keynes's Economics and the Theory of Value and Distribution.* New York: Oxford University Press, 1983, 294 p.
> Essays on the relationship between theories of value and distribution and theories of output and employment. The collection is a contribution to a developing line of inquiry into Keynesian economics initiated by the work of Pierangelo Garegnani.

Gerrard, Bill, and Hillard, John, eds. *The Philosophy and Economics of J. M. Keynes.* Aldershot, Hants, England: Edward Elgar, 1992, 253 p.

Collection of essays designed "to stress the contemporary relevance of Keynes and to promote an interdisciplinary approach which transcends the limitations of orthodox economic perception." The volume is divided into three parts. The essays in part one emphasize the organic interdependence of Keynes's ideas on method, theory, and practice; those in part two explore Keynes's views on competition; and those in part three approach Keynes from four different perspectives—Keynesian, post-Keynesian, psychoanalytic, and Marxist.

Gilbert, J. C. *Keynes's Impact on Monetary Economics.* London: Butterworth Scientific, 1982, 280 p.

Monograph that includes an introduction to Keynesian economics and separate sections devoted to the theories of Keynes's disciples, the practical implications of Keynesianism, and the commentary of some of Keynes's most important critics, including A. C. Pigou, D. H. Robertson, F. A. von Hayek, and Milton Friedman.

Hillard, John, ed. *J. M. Keynes in Retrospect: The Legacy of the Keynesian Revolution.* Aldershot, Hants, England: Edward Elgar, 1988, 229 p.

Collection of essays that evolved out of a series of lectures, seminars, and workshops held at the University of Leeds in 1986 to commemorate the fortieth anniversary of Keynes's death and the fiftieth year since the publication of the *General Theory.* The contributors reevaluate Keynes's legacy from various perspectives and seek to determine whether his theories offer solutions to current economic problems.

Johnson, Elizabeth S., and Johnson, Harry G. *The Shadow of Keynes: Understanding Keynes, Cambridge and Keynesian Economics.* Oxford, England: Basil Blackwell, 1978, 253 p.

Volume of essays intended to further the reader's understanding of Keynes as both an economist and a historical personality. The collection is divided into five parts, which are respectively devoted to Keynes the man, the Cambridge atmosphere before and after World War I, Keynes's early work on Indian currency and finance, the Cambridge environment of his followers in the 1950s, and Keynesian economics in his own day and as it has evolved.

Kahn, Richard F. *The Making of Keynes' "General Theory."* Cambridge: Cambridge University Press, 1984, 305 p.

Studies the development of Keynes's thought up to the publication of the *General Theory,* with particular attention devoted to the activities of Cambridge economists during the 1930s.

Keynes, Milo, ed. *Essays on John Maynard Keynes.* Cambridge: Cambridge University Press, 1975, 306 p.

Collection of essays treating the many facets of Keynes's personal life and career. Included are essays on Keynes's economic theory as well as essays that are largely biographical, dealing with such subjects as Keynes's association with the Bloomsbury Group, his relationship with Lydia Lopokova, and his interest in the arts.

Klein, Lawrence R. *The Keynesian Revolution.* 2d ed. New York: Macmillan Co., 1966, 288 p.

A study of the development and application of Keynes's economic theories. Klein deals with a number of leading

issues in Keynes criticism, including the relationship between Keynes's ideas and classical economics, the relationship between the *General Theory* and Keynes's earlier writings, and the relationship between Keynes's theories and the economic policies that have been based on them.

Lawson, Tony, and Pesaran, Hashem eds. *Keynes' Economics: Methodological Issues.* London: Croom Helm, 1985, 265 p.

Twelve essays on the methodological issues associated with Keynes's theories, covering such topics as rationality, expectations, and econometrics.

Milgate, Murray. *Capital and Employment: A Study of Keynes's Economics.* Studies in Political Economy, Vol. 1, edited by John Eatwell. London: Academic Press, 1982, 217 p.

Reassesses the nature of Keynes's contribution to economic thought in light of the dominant contemporary interpretations of his work. Milgate rejects orthodox marginalist economic theory in favor of a redevelopment of the classical theory, identifying links between Keynes's theory of output and employment and the surplus approach to value and distribution of the classical tradition.

Minsky, Hyman P. *John Maynard Keynes.* New York: Columbia University Press, 1975, 181 p.

Examines aspects of the *General Theory* that, according to Minsky, have usually been ignored in standard interpretations of the work. Minsky groups these "neglected" facets of the *General Theory* under three subject headings—"decision-making under uncertainty, the cyclical character of the capitalist process, and financial relations of an advanced capitalist economy"—and argues that they contain the true revolutionary thrust of the work.

Moggridge, D. E., ed. *Keynes: Aspects of the Man and His Work.—The First Keynes Seminar Held at the University of Kent at Canterbury, 1972.* London: Macmillan, 1974, 107 p.

Proceedings of the first seminar held in honor of Keynes at Keynes College, University of Kent, which was founded in 1968. The chief speakers at the seminar were the noted Keynes scholars Roy Harrod, Eric White, Donald Moggridge, and Roger Opie.

O'Donnell, R. M. *Keynes: Philosophy, Economics and Politics. The Philosophical Foundations of Keynes's Thought and Their Influence on His Economics and Politics.* Houndmills, England: Macmillan, 1989, 417 p.

Argues that "a substantial, wide-ranging and highly illuminating set of connections exists between Keynes's philosophy and his economics and politics." O'Donnell's study is divided into two parts. In the first section, he explores the fundamentals of Keynes's philosophy, focusing on *A Treatise on Probability*; in the second section, he relates Keynes's philosophy, especially his theory of rationality under uncertainty, to his economic and political thought.

Patinkin, Don. *Keynes's Monetary Thought: A Study of Its Development.* Durham, N. C.: Duke University Press, 1976, 163 p.

Examines the relationship between *A Tract on Monetary Reform, A Treatise on Money,* and the *General Theory,* emphasizing that discussion of the *Tract* and the *Treatise* by Keynes's colleagues greatly influenced the development of the *General Theory.*

―――. *Anticipations of the "General Theory" and Other Essays on Keynes.* Chicago: University of Chicago Press, 1982, 283 p.

Four-part collection of essays in which Patinkin discusses what he views as the "central message" of the *General Theory*, the theory of effective demand (Parts I and II); elaborates on Keynes's concept of the multiplier and his policy views (Part III); and studies the interactions between the macroeconomic and econometric revolutions between the two world wars (Part IV).

Thirlwall, A. P., ed. *Keynes and International Monetary Relations: The Second Keynes Seminar Held at the University of Kent at Canterbury, 1974.* London: Macmillan, 1976, 126 p.

Proceedings of the second seminar held in honor of Keynes at Keynes College, University of Kent. The success of the first Keynes seminar—held in 1972 and attended by several well-known Keynes scholars and a number of Keynes's relatives and colleagues—prompted its organizers to plan the conferences on a biannual basis.

Vicarelli, Fausto. *Keynes: The Instability of Capitalism.* Post Keynesian Economics, edited by Sidney Weintraub. Philadelphia: University of Pennsylvania Press, 1984, 194 p.

Examines how Keynes's vision of capitalism was shaped by the economic problems of his day and assesses the logic and validity of the *General Theory*.

―――, ed. *Keynes's Relevance Today.* London: Macmillan, 1985, 206 p.

A volume of essays in which the various contributors seek to determine whether Keynesian policies offer a solution to the economic problems of the 1980s.

Wood, John Cunningham, ed. *John Maynard Keynes: Critical Assessments.* 4 vols. London: Croom Helm, 1983.

Contains 150 previously published essays on Keynes dating from 1936 to 1981, all of which first appeared in English-language professional journals. The editor claims that the collection includes all the essays on Keynes considered seminal by professional economists; articles that, taken together, provide a thorough account of Keynes's life and thought; and the articles on Keynes that are most useful to historians of thought, contemporary economists, and policy makers.

Worswick, David, and Trevithick, James, eds. *Keynes and the Modern World: Proceedings of the Keynes Centenary Conference, King's College, Cambridge.* Cambridge: Cambridge University Press, 1984, 269 p.

Proceedings of an international conference held July 15-16, 1983, in celebration of the centenary of Keynes's birth. The theme of the conference—Keynes's continuing relevance—is debated by thirty professional economists.

Additional coverage of Keynes's life and career is contained in the following sources published by Gale Research: *Contemporary Authors*, Vol. 114; *Dictionary of Literary Biography Documentary Series*, Vol. 10.

Georg Simmel

1858-1918

German sociologist and philosopher.

INTRODUCTION

Simmel is credited as the founder of sociology as a distinct field of scientific study. While focusing on the study of society and social relationships, Simmel's works reflect his interest in a variety of disciplines, including psychology, philosophy, religion, and art. Although he is often faulted for the lack of systemization in his sociological thought, Simmel was an influence on the works of such later writers as Georg Lukács and Max Weber.

Biographical Information

The youngest of seven children, Simmel was born in Berlin. His father, a successful Jewish businessman who converted to Catholicism, died when Simmel was quite young. His mother's family background was also Jewish, but she was a practicing Lutheran and had her son baptized in that religion. Although he later left the Lutheran church, Simmel concerned himself with the philosophical questions of religion over the course of his life. An inheritance allowed him to study history and philosophy at the University of Berlin. He received a doctorate in 1881 and was a lecturer at the university from 1885 to 1900. He then served as professor extraordinary, an unpaid office, until 1914, when he accepted a position at the University of Strasbourg. He retired from teaching in 1918 and died that same year.

Major Works

A key aspect of Simmel's work was the "tragedy of culture," which refers to his view that the very structures that facilitate social interaction significantly conflict with the interests of the individual. For Simmel, this struggle was most clearly exemplified by the relationship of people to money. In his *Philosophie des Geldes (The Philosophy of Money),* Simmel asserted that the exchanges made possible by the use of money served to alienate individual's from their interior, personal lives. He believed that this state of affairs held true for all societies, whatever the nature of their economic system. Simmel expressed many of his ideas in essays on a wide range of subjects, including art and literary criticism, women's rights, and city life.

Critical Reception

Simmel's broad scope of interests and lack of systematic methodology has posed the greatest challenge to both his critics and his admirers. Simmel's severest detractors have viewed his work as the superficial reflection of middle-class German society at the turn of the century. The wide-ranging subjects of his essays have led some critics to regard Simmel as lacking focus. In Europe and the United States, however, his ideas have continued to influence social theorists. Simmel was a member of a discussion group that included Georg Lukács and Max Weber, both of whom reveal their serious consideration of Simmel's ideas in their own works. Weber expanded on Simmel's observations on the conflict between form and content in modern life. Although critical of what he termed Simmel's irrationalism, Lukác's used Simmel's analysis of money in his interpretation of alienation in the writings of Karl Marx.

PRINCIPAL WORKS

Das Wesen der Materie nach Kants physischer Monadologie (philosophy) 1881

Über sociale Differenzierung: Soziologische und pyschologische Untersuchungen (sociology) 1890

Die Probleme der Geschichtsphilosophie: Eine erkenntnistheoretische Studie (philosophy) 1892; revised edition, 1905 [*The Problems of the Philosophy of History,* 1977]

Einleitung in die Moralwissenschaft: Eine Kritik der ethischen Grundbegriffe. 2 vols. (philosophy) 1892-93

Philosophie des Geldes (sociology) 1900 [*The Philosophy of Money,* 1978]

Kant: Sechzehn Vorlesungen gehalten an der Berliner Universität (philosophy) 1904; revised edition, 1913

Philosophie der Mode (sociology) 1905

Kant und Goethe (philosophy) 1906; revised edition, 1916

Schopenhauer und Nietzsche: Ein Vortragszyklus (philosophy) 1907 [*Schopenhauer and Nietzsche,* 1986]

Soziologie: Untersuchenungen Über die Formen der Vergesellschaftung (sociology) 1908; [*The Sociology of Georg Simmel* (partial translation) 1950; *Conflict and the Web of Group-Affiliations* (partial translation) 1955]

Hauptprobleme der Philosophie (philosophy) 1910

Philosophische Kultur: Gesammelte Essays (philosophy and sociology) 1911; revised edition, 1919

Die Religion (sociology) 1912 [*Sociology of Religion,* 1979]

Goethe (criticism) 1913

Deutschlands innere Wandlung (lecture) 1914

Das Problem der historischen Zeit (philosophy) 1916

Rembrandt: Ein Kunstphilosophischer Versuch (criticism) 1916

Grundfragen der Soziologie (Individuum und Gesellschaft) (sociology) 1917 [*The Sociology of George Simmel* (partial translation) 1950]

Der Krieg und die geistigen Entscheidungen: Reden und Aufsätze (sociology) 1917

Der Konflikt der modernen Kultur: Ein Vortrag (sociology) 1918

Lebensanschauung: Vier metaphysische Kapitel (philosophy) 1918

Vom Wesen des historischen Verstehens (sociology) 1918

Schulpädagogik (lectures) 1922

Zur Philosophie der Kunst: Philosophische und kunstphilosophische Aufsätze (philosophy) 1922

Fragmente und Aufsätze aus dem Nachlass und Veröffentlichungen der letzten Jahre (essays) 1923

Rembrandtstudien (criticism) 1953

Brucke und Tür: Essays des Philosophen zur Geschichte, Religion, Kunst, und Gesellechaft (philosophy) 1957

Georg Simmel, 1858-1918: A Collection of Essays (essays) 1959

On Individuality and Social Forms: Selected Writings (sociology) 1971

Georg Simmel: Sociologist and European (essays) 1976

On Women, Sexuality, and Love (essays) 1984

CRITICISM

Leopold von Wiese (essay date 1910)

SOURCE: "Simmel's Formal Method," in *Georg Simmel*, edited by Lewis A. Coser, Prentice-Hall, Inc., 1965, pp. 53-7.

[*In the following essay, which originally appeared in* Archiv für Sozialwissenschaft und Sozialpolitik *in 1910, von Wiese offers a consideration of Simmel's method for analyzing social relationships.*]

Georg Simmel's **Sociology** is today understandably viewed with the greatest interest by all those who believe in the future of sociology as a science. Although these **Investigations into the Forms of Association** are broad in scope, the work is fragmentary and incomplete, as its author intended it to be. He would not—could not—present a complete, closed system; the only aim of the book is to clarify his fundamental conception of the problem of sociology by means of a series of applications. The author states:

> As a consequence [of the basic conception], it is out of the question to attempt anything more than to begin and to point out the direction of an infinitely long path; and any systematically final completeness would be, at the least, self-deception. An individual can attain completeness here only in the subjective sense, by reporting everything he has succeeded in observing.

This is a very important advance over the older sociologists, who foundered on their mania for systems (I need mention only Ratzenhofer). To this rejection of completeness, Simmel adds the narrow delimitation of sociology as a science. It is to his credit that he has clarified the difference between the general modern tendency to view the objects of various sciences sociologically (but without detracting from their independence and autonomy), and the creation of sociology as a new science. Because of the intellectual demands of the present age, it is more and more frequently recognized today that the objects of the traditional humanities (cultural and moral sciences [*Geisteswissenschaften*]) find realization only within the framework of society. This sociological *method* in the moral sciences is the legacy of the nineteenth century. The establishment of sociology is an altogether different thing. Although the latter cannot bring new facts, new material, to light, it draws "a new line through otherwise well-known facts." It establishes new points of view, new abstractions. The various older social sciences have as their objects the contents of social processes, corresponding to the particular real areas of social life (such as economics, jurisprudence, and so on); sociology, however, examines the *forms* of association. That is to say, it examines the phenomena of human cooperation, altruistic and antagonistic interaction, the modes of reciprocal influence and mutual interpenetration in all their numberless purposes and diverse contents. The manifold forms in which association is realized are to be conceptually released from these diverse contents and analyzed as psychic phenomena of a special kind. But despite this [socio]psychological basis, sociology is in no sense a branch of psychology. Although sociology deals predominantly with psychic facts, it does not do so in order to discover the laws of psychic processes; the aim of sociology is, rather, to grasp the "objectivity of association" (which, however, as was said, is "carried by psychic processes"). In the same way that, on the one hand, psychology and sociology are not identical, so, on the other hand (and as in all special sciences), social science proper is distinct from its epistemology and its metaphysics. According to Simmel, the question of the position of society in the cosmos belongs to the metaphysics of sociology, while sociological epistemology includes the questions "Is society possible?" and "Does society exist outside of us or only in our consciousness?" and the like; so that these problems are relegated, like their metaphysical counterparts in philosophy, to defined subdisciplines.

Here Simmel has eliminated all of sociology's claims to encyclopedic-universal significance, all pretension that it ought to be the all-inclusive integration of the particular social sciences. Nor is he the least interested in extending the perspective of the natural sciences to the facts of human society. But, as indicated, Simmel limits the task of sociology even further: the content-material of social relations is to play as small a role as possible in this social science; he is interested only in the formal aspects of association. A question arises: Is such a limitation to the forms of association possible? The chapters of his work are well worth reading (their specific content cannot be examined here); but does the way in which Simmel carries out his program demonstrate the possibility and the fruitfulness of his method?

To begin with, one must beware of considering form as incidental or subordinate to content. The essence of a thing is often more clearly revealed in its form than in its content. And so it is in this case: by ignoring the content of social interrelations as much as possible, one may achieve a liberation from coincidental, temporary, unessential elements—and this alone makes possible a more profound insight into human nature as such. Hitherto-veiled secrets of the human mind, potential for human development, human motives and aspirations only now become clear. The essence of culture is not revealed by searching for it in too much concreteness—in compact, hard particularities and their summations. This external narrowing of the field of sociology signifies a valuable deepening, an internal expansion of its power of insight.

In posing the problem of sociology, I can never let the one goal out of sight: the image of man and of society must be purified of prejudice; it must emerge from our scrutiny more clearly and more genuinely than has hitherto been possible, without sociology, through metaphysical ethics and traditional political and cultural philosophy. In my opinion, Simmel's method brings us nearer to this goal (no matter to what extent Simmel may be motivated by purely abstract, scientific aims; no matter how much he may perhaps consider his social forms as ends in themselves). To that extent I am ready to consider his way as correct, and to see in his sociology a significant advance over all past attempts. But it seems to me that this science of the forms of association is in need of certain guiding ideas—of a unified goal—if it is to proceed from repeated analyses to the attainment of a concluding synthesis. This is especially true of Simmel's work: as far as I can tell, his investigations run the danger of ending in scattered fragments. Surely they contain not only a great many fine observations, but also peaks of the most valuable insight; but they lose themselves in playing with the fullness of forms with the subtlest and nicest of nuances. At times the interweaving of his thoughts resembles a spider's web studded with glittering drops of dew; but a substantial breeze can destroy it. The danger of his thread of thought becoming unravelled would have been avoided had Simmel established solid fundamental conceptions to carry the system. Above, I made no objection to Simmel's fragmentalism; in **Sociology** this is understandable and proper. But it is another question whether or not Simmel is at all capable of overcoming this tendency. I entertain doubts as to whether his analytic method can ever reach synthesis. This does not diminish his scientific importance. But when one is forced to pass judgment on the direction in which he wants to lead sociology, then one must indeed ask whether this fragmentary and incomplete character is not a disadvantage intimately linked with the essence of his thought. Unless I am greatly mistaken, Simmel has already published on various other occasions, as independent essays, many of the individual chapters dealing with the problem he poses. I must say that they impressed me as more effective when they were thus separated. Here, where they are side by side as parts of a whole, the lack of transition from one to another is striking. Out of the numerous notions about the manifold forms of association there does not emerge a central doctrine of the forms of association. The distinction between the form of association and its content is much more comprehensible in any single essay than it is here, where the formal analyses are compiled in a great heap, without any systematic sustain-

ing connection. In any case, this accumulation of thought-fragments is readable as a sequence only because of the fact that, with all his tendency toward abstraction, Simmel is by no means clumsy in dealing with concepts (*kein "Begriffskrüppel"*); that is, his presentation has great aesthetic attractiveness. From a certain aspect I would even call his sociology the sociology of an aesthete, a sociology for the literary salon. Simmel is a cultural psychologist with a cosmopolitan cast of mind. In his work we never encounter mere book-wisdom or dry, pedantic erudition; rather, one feels the rich internal agitation of the explorer: his examples are vivid, interesting, psychologically well-selected, and presented with individual originality. In short, inner experience means more to him than dry scholarship. But in its mosaic form and its aestheticism, this sociology has a distinctly personal, Simmelean character. The same method in the hands of Mr.——— (no, I had better name no names!) would be unbearable. And so I would reach the following summary:

The limitation of sociology to the doctrine of the forms of association seems to me an important advance capable of introducing clarity into a great deal of confusion. But even more important than this establishment of an independent discipline is the transition to the sociological *method* in the existing particular branches of cultural science. To elaborate the sociological aspects of economics, jurisprudence, ethics, religion, philology, geography, and so on—*that* is of primary importance.

Célestin Bougle   (essay date 1912)

SOURCE: "The Sociology of Georg Simmel," in *Georg Simmel,* edited by Lewis A. Coser, Prentice-Hall, Inc., 1965, pp. 58-63.

[*In the following excerpt originally published in a 1912 book-length study of German philosophy in the nineteenth century, Bougle views Simmel as essentially a psychological thinker.*]

In the large volume which he entitles **Sociology: Investigations into the Forms of Association,** Simmel claims that he is not offering a system but rather a great number of examples designed to show the kinds of generalizations one can make in sociology; and he does this if only that he might be able to use what Descartes described as the appropriate "bias."

Why is it that history neither is nor can be a science? Perhaps it is because, in the last analysis, the subject matter of history is a fluid complexity which must be grasped in its totality. And so it is not surprising either that the study of history should reveal more variations than consistencies, or that historians should find it difficult to establish causality between the myriad of occurrences. However, if one agreed to limit himself to a particular perspective and to abstract from the variations in content so as to focus only on the constant forms, then he would, perhaps, arrive at a series of observations the significance of which would extend beyond the range of the particular fact. It was by abstraction—i.e., by concerning itself only with spatial forms—that geometry established itself; and it was by abstraction that linguistics established itself as the science concerned with linguistic forms. Similarly, one could establish sociology as the discipline concerned only with social forms.

Of course, in one sense everything is social—just as, in one sense, everything is psychological; but we have been able to progress in our understanding of the functions of the mind without taking into account the various subject matters with which these functions are concerned. In the same way it is possible to study the modes and effects of sociation without being concerned with the various ends which sociation serves. In a word, it is possible to study what happens *in* society by looking at what happens *because of* society. The proof of this lies in the fact that the forms of sociation vary independently of social ends and social ends vary independently of the forms of sociation. Undoubtedly content influences form, but it does not determine it. Whatever the *ends* of an association—whether political, religious, or economic—it is legitimate to examine it to see how parties are organized, how work is divided, and how competition is organized among its members. It is Simmel's concern to emphasize those phenomena which are common to the workings of diverse associations. Whatever the substantive nature of the societies he might examine, he will subject them to an abstract analysis aimed at discovering how, for example, the relations among individuals vary according to whether superiority is vested in one individual, conceded to a group, or incarnated in some principle above and beyond the group as well as to the individual. Again, when he talks of competition, it is not in order to study a specific example of competition—whether economic, religious, or aesthetic—but to study the functions of conflict in general, so as to see what kinds of alliances it involves, by what means the social order defends itself against the divisive consequences to which conflict might give rise; and so on. The same approach determines his interest in secret societies, whether these are groups of conspirators or of thieves, of visionaries or of debauchees. His approach would lead him to try to discover the typical interrelations which secret societies, precisely because they are secret, tend to institute among their members.

From all this we can see that when Simmel talks of social forms, he doesn't simply mean the external forms of society. *L'Année Sociologique* groups under the title *social morphology* everything that concerns land and population—i.e., the geographical and demographical bases of the existence of collectivities. As far as Simmel is concerned, the study of these two topics constitutes but a small part of social morphology. Although he certainly pays attention to a completely "external" fact (such as the social significance of numbers and their variations), he also utilizes information about an institution (such as an aristocratic regime), about a process (such as competition), and about a quality (such as the secret character of a group).

It is difficult to summarize the intricacies of Simmel's extremely ingenious and subtle insights, and perhaps it would be best to indicate the results he gets from his approach by offering a few illustrative examples.

When discussing superiority, we said that it can be exercised by an individual, by a group, or by a collective principle which stands over and above individuals. We must trace the consequences of these various hypotheses.

A group of individuals may be subordinated to an individual who either represents or opposes them, but usually in either case the subordination has the effect of unifying the group. This fact explains the principal advantage of monarchies: they establish unity among the population. It might well be that the Greek city-states decayed because they lacked a superior authority which, by dominating the several parties, could have unified them. Furthermore, this unity can take one of two forms: it can be either leveling or hierarchical. Sometimes the dominating person endeavors to impose universal degradation on all his subjects; from this is derived the well-known relationship between despotism and egalitarianism. At other times the dominating person may cede some fraction of power to—or find himself deprived of some fraction of power by—one or more of the diverse and numerically unequal strata of society. Thus the latter, in turn, come to possess varying degrees of influence over the uses of power. In both cases, the supremacy of the ruler is explained by the fact that, although the subjects subordinate but a segment of their personalities, the ruler dominates them by mobilizing the full force of his personality. Supremacy and personality are intimately linked.

The character of the relationship between superior and subordinate is noticeably different when domination is exercised by a group of persons rather than by a single individual. The subjects may find themselves either more harshly or more justly treated. Domination by a group is impersonal and, because of this, it is less arbitrary; but it also means that less consideration is given to the personalities of the subordinates. Domination may be exercised through the intermediation of agents (though this is a very specific sociological phenomenon, occurring only in societies which are already developed). When it is, it assumes a quite special quality. When exercised administratively, domination may be more severe in one case and less severe in another.

Superordination may at times belong, not to one group, but to two; in this case the subordinates find it easier to reduce the extent of their dependency. Yet, again, if they are totally without initiative they tend to suffer more because of the plurality of their rulers: "It is not good to have two masters." If they [the subordinates] retain even a minimum of liberty, they would do well to exploit the divisions among their superiors: *duobus litigentibus tertius gaudet.* During the *ancien régime* the Third Estate was *tertius gaudens* between the monarchy and the feudal nobility. Moreover, groups which are superior to another group are seldom completely equal among themselves; there are degrees of supersubordination among them, and this results in that essentially sociological phenomenon: hierarchy. As hierarchical gradations become rationalized, they lessen the intensity of the subordination, because the subordinate is now provided with a means of recourse against his immediate superior.

The supremacy of a principle, of an impersonal idea elevated over and above individuals, also serves to render subordination less onerous to the subordinated. It has the effect of bringing even the superiors into the ranks of the subordinates: they become obliged to render allegiance to the very order which they themselves first promulgated and prestige, in some way, gets detached from them and becomes attached to the principle they represent or to the function they fulfill. Under the sway of a principle, superiority is legitimized by its coincidence with the common interest; thus, the inferior has the feeling of working alongside his superior. The relationship of subordination undergoes a change, subjectively speaking, and becomes one of cooperation.

There are two main ways in which society might develop so that individuals could regard themselves as equals. It might develop in such a way that the various positions of power could be, and in fact are, filled by different people; or it might develop into a series of social circles which would enable the same individual to envisage himself as superior in one aspect and inferior in another.

This does not mean that the relationship of subordination would—or even could—disappear: it is essential to the continuance of society. Yet, when superiority becomes detached from the personality of the individual to whom it was originally linked, then one can hope that the state of subordination will continue to lose more and more of the humiliating connotations it has for the subordinates.

One can expect that suggestive insights might be forthcoming from an application of this method to the study of secret societies. Simmel shows that, whether the group is of conspirators or of thieves, of visionaries or of debauchees, the secret [society] has the function of protection. If such societies are to fulfill their functions, it is necessary for the members to have full confidence in one another. It is thus important that they should learn to keep silent (and "the apprenticeship of silence" well may have been the best training for moral intensity). It is also important that one word of command should be able to get them to obey without question and even without understanding. Because of this, formulas and ritual practices are designed which are aimed at minimizing the independence of the individual wills and maximizing their integration. And because of this comes the establishment of a strict hierarchy in which the separate functions correspond to the various stages of initiation. And so, precisely because they are secret, these voluntary and highly self-conscious associations establish a rather mechanical organization.

These summaries are too brief, and they lose the wealth of detail which is so charming a facet of Simmel's analyses. Yet, they at least enable us to catch a glimpse of the richness of the psychological deductions with which his work abounds. Can this kind of sociology be anything other than psychology? If one *were* to draw this conclusion, Simmel would not object. He confesses—or, rather, he insists—that the interactions which seem to him to be the constituent elements of social life are, in fact, psychological phenomena. And for him, as for Tarde, the analysis of mental interaction is the essence of sociology. (We show elsewhere how extensive are the similarities between Simmel's methods and those of Tarde.) Instead of studying the large-scale institutions (churches, political organizations, commercial enterprises) which dominate individu-

als and which, it seems, come to possess a life of their own, Simmel prefers to examine topics which to him are more fruitful; and so he studies sociation "at the moment of birth," or the relations and mutual influences among individuals. These serve to explain the lives of social entities just as intercellular physiochemical relations explain the life of the organism.

After all is said and done, social wholes have for Simmel but a provisional reality, and this must give way as we come to a better understanding of the interactions from which they are derived. For his part, he readily admits that a perfect science would ascribe reality only to individuals and their interactions; and he is satisfied only when he has directed our attention to a form of explanation based on elements, molecules, or the "social atoms."

Whichever way you look at it, Simmel's thought moves away from that of Durkheim and approaches that of Tarde.

It is all too easy to tell where these methods lead and to what conceptions they commit us. For Simmel, sociological explanations are descriptions of inner experiences—i.e., they are explanations which recount what happens in those small spheres called *souls* when these are brought into contact with one another. By their very nature, such explanations offer much in the way of speculation and little in the way of proof. Because of this, one often feels that Simmel's analyses, although extremely subtle, belong mostly to the realm of probability. His method has drawn severe criticism from those—both in the social sciences and in the other sciences—who are concerned with accumulating the greatest possible number of objective and methodically established truths. Sometimes his critics have shown themselves to be hostile toward a sociology of this type, which seems to stand midway between art and science. One can legitimately reply to this by stating that there is also room for this type of sociology. Even though Simmel's formulations may not go beyond the realm of probability, they are profound and intricate, and they should definitely be codified, classified, and offered for examination. And it is beyond doubt that, had Simmel chosen to be a more objective sociologist, he would have found it much more difficult to be so suggestive a "moralist."

Alfred Mamelet (essay date 1914)

SOURCE: "Sociological Relativism," in *Georg Simmel,* edited by Lewis A. Coser, Prentice-Hall, Inc., 1965, pp. 64-73.

[*In the following excerpt from his 1914 study* Le relativisme philosophique chez Georg Simmel, *Mamelet finds that Simmel's work is distinguished from that of his contemporaries by its philosophical qualities.*]

Simmel's conception of sociology is, from the outset, clearly opposed to contemporary French sociology. The latter is predicated upon regarding social facts as something possessing two characteristics: exteriority and constraint. French sociology has its origin in traditionalism and positivism. It is anti-individualist; and political and historical contingency has effected a link between this anti-individualism and the notion of the existence of a social order. Preoccupied above all with putting restrictions on individual initiative in areas of social and political organization, the traditionalists and Auguste Comte endeavored to show that the social order, like the physical order, has its own laws which are superior to individual wills, and that individuals cannot transgress these laws without precipitating grave calamity. Their concern for social organization and stability (a concern which would legitimize the state of French society as it was at the beginning and middle of the nineteenth century), and their concern to contain the revolutionary spirit supplies the explanation of the opposition which Comte and the traditionalists established between the individual and society. By working with this opposition as a base—i.e., by defining the social fact in terms of exteriority and constraint, and as standing over and against individual will—contemporary French sociology has persisted in excluding individual actions and interactions from the realm of sociological research. In fact, it has even tended to disregard them; and, consequently, it has neglected to study those forms of sociation which emphasize not the constraint of an institution, but the interaction of free individuals—i.e., all the forms of modern society. The Simmelian conception of sociology has the advantage over the Durkheimian conception in that it is much wider in scope and is thus applicable to liberal and democratic societies (in which the individual is a free agent, a voter or legislator, and as such an active force for progress) as well as to authoritarian societies (in which the mass and tradition are everything and the individual nothing). This does not mean that this emphasis leads Simmel to adopt the thesis held in France by Tarde. According to this thesis sociological facts are essentially psychological facts. Simmel is as concerned as Durkheim to establish sociology as an independent science, distinct both from psychology and history. But he tries to gain this status for sociology by utilizing concepts which are less abstract, less all encompassing, and closer to concrete and living reality than the concepts of exteriority and constraint. These concepts—all of which can be grouped under a category which carries the full import of relativism, i.e., *reciprocity in interaction*—are, as we have seen, those of domination and subordination, of competition, of imitation, of opposition, of the division of labor, and so on. These are concepts which, while procuring the establishment of a specifically *sociological* (as opposed to a psychological or historical) form of explanation, can still leave room for all the varieties of individual action, from the most dependent to the most free. The relativist point of view has been able to provide a single answer to the problem which, in France, has resulted in the two separate answers of Durkheim and Tarde: namely, the problem of freeing sociology, as a science, from the tutelage of psychology while at the same time keeping it as close as possible to concrete reality.

This fundamental difference between Durkheim's conception of sociology and the Simmelian conception immediately gives rise to another important difference. According to Simmel, sociology should not limit itself, as does Durkheim's sociology, to the study of social macrocosms which are objectified, large-scale, synthetic, secondary, and detached from the human interactions from which they derive; it should show us the microcosmic structures of society and help us to grasp the detail of the processes of which large-scale institutions—such as states, churches, corporations, the family and so on—are the result. A comparison between the living organism and society might elucidate what is omitted by studying only macrocosms. The large-scale institutions are to society what organs are to the organism. Yet we understand the organs of the living body only when we know how they are formed, and their formation is the result of an infinity of intra[cellular] and intercellular processes. Consequently, we must analyze these processes. The same is true for society. The large-scale institutions which constitute the organs of the social body cannot be properly understood unless one analyzes the elementary processes from which they derive and which govern the formation of the social tie. At the same time, it is necessary to beware of drawing any false conclusions from this analogy between the organism and society, for to Simmel it has a purely methodological significance:

> There is definitely no question here of any analogy, sociological or metaphysical, between social reality and organic reality. It is solely a question of an analogy in the *method* of studying those two orders of reality. It is a question of discovering the threads which have been spun, and the delicate relationships which have been established between men. The continual weaving of these relationships constitutes the basis of all those large-scale structures which attain objectification and acquire a life of their own. These altogether *primary* processes (which turn individual reality into social reality) are as deserving of formal analysis as are the events in, and formation of superior and complex structures [*sind also . . . der formalen Betrachtung zu unterziehen*]; and the reciprocities of particular actions which occur at this level and which hitherto have been unsubjected to theoretical examination must be envisaged as playing a part in the general process of sociation.

Although these processes are, in point of fact, psychological processes, sociology can claim the right to analyze them because, as is shown in **Probleme der Geschichtsphilosophie,** a distinction can be made between—on the one hand—phenomena in the processes which clearly obey the laws of psychology, and—on the other hand—the function of these processes, which is amenable to analysis by the forms of sciences other than psychology, in particular by the forms of sociology: "The scientific study of psychic reality is not necessarily psychology." This reality can be approached from different standpoints and can be grasped by different sciences.

> It is of course a fact that when, for example, men influence each other, or when one man submits to something done by another, that this is a psychic phenomenon. Each particular instance of such a phenomenon can be comprehended only by the use of psychological methodology—i.e., by the use of hypotheses based on psychological constructs and by an interpretation of data which is rendered objective through the use of psychological categories. Yet the adoption of an-

other scientific perspective enables one to by-pass the psychological analysis as such, and to go on to analyze, to examine, and to rearrange the content in such a way that it can be comprehended as coming under the concept of sociation.

From this perspective—which is that of sociology as Simmel understands it—it is the forms of interpersonal relationships which restructure the subject matter: and these forms are precisely those which have already been listed—viz., domination, subordination, competition, imitation, opposition, and so on. . . .

Simmel feels that sociology gains the status of an independent science when and if it concerns itself with the study of these diverse forms of sociation. In *Soziologie* the study of these forms has already been carried out to a large extent and, although it is not necessary to go into the book in detail, it is necessary to trace its main outlines and to point out the major areas of interest. It is by utilizing the concept of *form* that, for example, Simmel tries to demonstrate the influence exercised on the internal structure of social groups by the size of the group. Then again, he seeks to determine the forms and the psychological conditions and the social consequences of domination, subordination, competition, and the struggle for life; or to unravel the effect of the necessity for secrecy on the structure of secret societies; or to examine the main forms and consequences of the encounter and intermeshing of social circles such as families, professions, nations, and so on. He tries to analyze the influence of poverty and wealth on social organization and on interpersonal relations. He tries to establish the conditions necessary for the conservation and perpetuation of groups (conditions which he finds in the incessant interaction between group members), and to determine the influence of space on social organization. Finally he seeks to understand the principal factors leading to the growth of societies and to the appearance of free and differentiated individuals. Although the book ends only after numerous digressions (one of the most intriguing being the analysis of the sociological significance of the senses, in particular [that] of smell), it is throughout motivated by one concern: namely, to show how, and under what influences psychological subject matter can assume a variety of social forms which are themselves reducible to that archtypical relativist category—viz., that of *reciprocity* in the interaction between individuals.

A sociology conceived of in this way shares with all other exact sciences—moral, political-economic, historical—the fact of having two boundaries with philosophy: viz., a frontier where it begins and a frontier where it leaves off. Of these two philosophical domains which border sociology as an exact science,

> . . . one concerns the conditions, the basic concepts, and the hypotheses of a particular piece of research. These cannot be said to be contained only in that research for they are the necessary conditions for it. Philosophy is utilized in a second way when the particular piece of research is raised to a level of generalization and synthesis which puts it in contact with concepts and problems which have no place either in experience or

in completely objective knowledge. The first domain is that of the epistemology, and the second that of the metaphysics of sociology. The latter presents two problems (which are usually, and with reason, confused in everyday thought). The unsatisfactory fragmentary nature of piecemeal knowledge, combined with the poverty of the generalizations and truths which can be derived from it, tend to lead to a reliance on speculation as the means of giving them greater significance: and along with this tendency goes the inclination to formulate a unifying system in order to make up for the contradictions in, and lack of cohesion among, the fragments of piecemeal knowledge. Side by side with this metaphysical inclination (the direction of which is determined by the state of knowledge) comes another (which is directed by another dimension of reality) in which is invested the metaphysical significance of the subject matter. It is this to which we refer when we talk about the *direction* or the *end,* or about the *absolute* substance underlying all relative phenomena, or about *value* or *religious significance.* In relation to society this problem gives rise to such questions as: Is society the goal of human existence or is it a means for the individual? Does it help him? Or, conversely, does it hinder him? Is society acting optimally when it simply maintains itself? Or when it facilitates the realization of some objective good? Or when it inculcates moral qualities in the individual? Can one draw an analogy between the stages of societal development and the cosmic processes, in the sense that the social relations of man must be seen as premised on a general rhythm or form which, while in itself alien to particular phenomena, is the basis of these, and is equally impartial in its control over the essential forces of material reality? In sum, can society be said to possess a metaphysical or religious meaning, or is such a thing reserved for individual souls only?

These are essentially philosophical questions which relate to social philosophy rather than to sociology.

In truth *Soziologie* does not answer these questions. All Simmel gives, at the very most, are some fragmentary outlines in various journals. In these he defines his conception of the unity of life. . . . However, in recompense, Simmel does offer, in *Soziologie,* some very important statements on the theory of sociological knowledge. These statements, which are concerned with the philosophical domain of sociology rather than with sociology as an "exact" science, provide a definition of Simmelian sociology and serve to distinguish it from the French school. It is important to offer a succinct analysis of these formulations.

The theoretical problem posed by sociological knowledge is: How, in general, is society possible? It is true that one might be tempted to turn to history for an answer to this problem, but history can in no way account for the origin of the societal tie. Simmel uses an idea with which Auguste Comte was very taken, and shows, quite easily, that society could not have originated in an initial conviction as to its utility because such a conviction is of necessity the product of a long social evolution: i.e., the idea that social action is more effective than individual action could only have been arrived at a posteriori. This means that, if, in fact there are any necessary preconditions for the existence of society, then they must be discovered through a priori reasoning, and this involves, not the historian, but the philosopher as theoretician of knowledge. All the same, in spite of formal similarities, it is not possible to equate the question "How is society possible?" with the seemingly analogous problem posed by Kant: i.e., "How is nature possible?" Kant's solution cannot be applied to the sociological problem—and, for a variety of reasons, it would not be enough to rely on the synthetic function of the categories of knowledge.

The unity of society is not of the same order as the unity of nature. The unity of nature is the result of the activity of the observer who effects unity by means of separate and various categories of apperception—i.e., with the aid of a perceptual schema. The unity of society is independent of the synthesizing activity of the observer. It is effected directly and spontaneously by the action of the social elements themselves entering into a reciprocity of interaction. Furthermore, the quality of the relations which are established among, and which unify, the members of the social body are distinguished from those which unify the physical world in that while the latter is the world of juxtaposition, the former is the world of living complementarity. Finally, if one puts oneself in the position of the observer, it is clear that the unity which our perceptions can effect in the physical world is much narrower than that which we can effect in the social world. This is a result of the comparative simplicity of physical reality, which is composed of a relatively small number of homogeneous and impersonal elements which obey general laws, while society, on the other hand, is composed of a multitude of individual elements which are heterogeneous and irreducible. In effect, natural objects differ from the elements of the social body in that they exist only through our representation of them, while the latter—i.e., individuals—seem to us to have an existence independent of our representations. And this existence is as absolute and unconditional as is our own. If society *is* our representation, it is not so in the same way as is nature. The problem then becomes one of finding out, first, how we can treat other individuals as objects of analysis without ceasing to recognize that they have an existence independent of us and that in some ways they exist as objects in and of themselves, and, second, how we can envisage them as members, as such, of the society of which we are also part. This transformation of others from being objects in themselves to being objects of our representation and members of society is clearly dependent upon the use of categories, which are purely a priori conditions of social knowledge.

Simmel sees three principal categories.

The first has already been defined in *Probleme der Geschichtsphilosophie* as one of the a priori's which determine the nature of historical research. It is the impossibility of ever possessing totally adequate knowledge of other individuals—i.e., of understanding them in those aspects which make them different from us. Thus, since we are forced to content ourselves with a fragmentary representation, we are led to generalize the traits which we have es-

tablished empirically by putting them into a priori categories—*class, profession, party,* and so on. We come to know the individual through these general concepts—i.e., as a member of a class, or of a profession, or of a party, and we postulate this identity as his essential nature. By abstraction we limit, and by generalization we extend, the representation which we have of his individuality. The result of this is the denial of the individual because our methodology is such as to be unable to represent what is essentially irreducible in the individual. Simmel's formulation seems to be the opposite of Schopenhauer's. To Schopenhauer the individual is not real but is, rather, a construct of our representations, which therefore falsify reality. According to Simmel (and here he expands on one of the themes on which he was most insistent in the *Probleme der Geschichtsphilosophie*), the individual is of the essence of reality, and social thought—being suprapersonal, abstract, and general—is valid only because our representations are so inadequate and because of their pragmatic utility. This is the only justification for the use of concepts. This position of Simmel's emphasizes once again the clash between his sociological thought and that of Durkheim's school. The difference is both between nominalism and realism and between criticism and dogmatism.

The second category of sociological knowledge is based on the notion that social life does not incorporate the individual in his entirety, but that each individual preserves a section of his personality which is his own alone. This constitutes, so to speak, his private property. It remains quite irreducible; it is extrasocial and persists side by side with those segments of his personality which engage him in society as a member of such and such a social group. This concept is clearly the theoretical complement of the first. It limits itself to postulating the existence of a *foro interno,* of something in and of itself, and thus provides a notion which the first category could not contain. At the same time, it preserves the franchise of psychology and history side by side with that of sociology. Moreover, in practice the subject matters of the two categories are in incessant interaction. The extrasocial self maintains a reciprocity of interaction with the social self (the extrasocial self constituting the result of social influences; the social self devoting itself to directing the reaction of the individual to those influences). The very real and profound unity of the individual conforms to the basic Simmelian principle of relativity when it is seen as being founded on this reciprocity of ongoing action.

Finally, the third category—which is a synthesis of the first two—concerns the inequality of social elements (unequal that is, not in their worth but in their content and in their destiny). Because of this inequality it would seem that each social element—i.e., each individual—participates in society by playing a particular role to which he is destined. Individual life (as defined by the second category) enters into contact with social life (as defined in the first category). Society is fully developed and socialization is complete only when the extrasocial life of the individual is fully integrated with the social body of which he is part. This integration would result in a perfect society (all moral or eudemonistic senses of the word *perfect* being excised), but it seems that it would be possible only in the event that the individual comes to accept the necessity of putting himself in the role for which he was made. From this it follows that socialization cannot be held to be a simple matter of the net effect of a multiplicity of efficient causes, but as rather a goal of the conscious individual—the causal sequence which eventuated in the establishment of society transforms itself into a teleological sequence. From now on, society appears as an environment in which each individual finds an already prepared place which determines the role he is to play. The interactions whose play constitutes the web of social life are realized inside this teleological sequence—i.e., in that complementarity of individual rights and social duties which is the ultimate reciprocity guaranteeing both individual autonomy and the conservation and progress of society. This complementarity and reciprocity constitute the fundamental law of civilized, democratic societies. When compared to the sociology of the Durkheimian school—which, it can be claimed with some truth, ascribes social reality only to undifferentiated and passive masses, or to prehistoric hordes, to primitive epochs, or to atrophied and decadent societies—it seems that Simmelian sociology has the great merit of being applicable to modern societies in which the individual is both legislator and citizen.

This is, in outline, Simmel's conception of sociology. Its essential distinguishing mark lies in its philosophical nature. Although it is—or, rather, because it is—the subject matter of an exact and positive science, social reality, like all other dimensions of reality, is embedded in philosophy. It is involved in philosophy in two different ways. First, because theoretical elaboration is necessary for the representation of social life; and, second, because—over and above positive knowledge—there is room for speculation relinking the social with the unity of life. And over and above all is a fact that, in the innermost part of the scientific study of society, one discovers the dominance of philosophical concepts whose application extends well beyond society. The sociology of Simmel is very clearly governed and directed by his relativist point of view, in particular by the notion of the complementarity and reciprocity of action—a notion which has already been applied in all other scientific disciplines. To Simmel the establishment of sociology as an independent, positive science in no way means the end of philosophy—on the contrary, for the theory of knowledge and of metaphysics retains all their prerogatives by virtue of their connection with this new science. It is this fact which is the source of the difference between the Simmelian and the contemporary positivist conceptions of sociology. It would appear that contemporary positivist sociology is too apt to deny the claim of philosophy to have a function and too eager to subsume it under scientific technique.

Emile Durkheim   (essay date 1918)

SOURCE: "Sociology and Its Scientific Field," in *Georg Simmel*, edited by Lewis A. Coser, Prentice-Hall, Inc., 1965, pp. 43-9.

[*In the following essay, which first appeared in French in 1918, Durkheim characterizes Simmel's works as "intriguing" but concludes that they fall short of the objectives and scientific standards of sociology.*]

A science which has barely begun to exist has, and initially is bound to have, only an uncertain and vague sense of the area of reality that it is about to approach, and the extent and the limits of that area. It can gain a clearer picture only to the degree that it proceeds with its studies. And the heightened awareness of its subject matter that it acquires in this way is of the greatest importance; for the path of the scientist is the more secure the more orderly it becomes; and the more methodical it is, the more exact is the account that he can render of the territory he is invading.

Sociology has reached the point at which it is opportune to make every effort to bring about such progress. If some reactionary critics, unwittingly under the influence of the prejudice which always militates against the formation of new sciences, reproach sociology for not knowing the precise subject matter with which it intends to deal, they can be told that such ignorance is inevitable in the first stages of study and that our science came into being only yesterday. It must not be forgotten, especially in view of the favorable reception that sociology is given now, that, properly speaking, Europe did not have as many as ten sociologists fifteen years ago. To this must be added that it is asking too much of a science that it define its subject matter with excessive precision, for the part of reality that it intends to study is never neatly separated from other parts. In fact, in nature everything is so connected that there can be neither a complete break in continuity nor any tooexact boundaries between the various sciences. Nevertheless, it is urgent that we obtain, if we can, a clear idea of what constitutes the domain of sociology, where this domain is found, and what signs serve us in recognizing the complex of the phenomena with which we must deal—even if we neglect to fix boundaries, which are necessarily indeterminate anyway. This problem is all the more urgent for our science, because if we do not attend to it, its province may be extended to infinity: there is no phenomenon—from physiochemical ones to properly social facts—which does not take place in society. Hence we must accurately isolate social facts and must show what it is that forms their unity in order to avoid reducing sociology to nothing but a conventional label applied to an incoherent agglomeration of disparate disciplines.

Georg Simmel has made a notable, an almost violent, effort to trace the limits of the subject matter of sociology. The basis of his argument is the idea that, if sociology is to be, it must constitute a particular system of investigations that are perfectly distinct from those of the sciences which have long existed under the names of *political economy, history of civilization, statistics, demography,* and so on. The difference lies in the fact that these other sciences study what occurs in society, not society itself. The religious, moral, and legal phenomena which they treat occur within particular groups; but these groups must themselves be the object of a different inquiry, one which is independent of these others; and it is precisely this independent study that constitutes sociology. With the help of the very society which they form, men living in society achieve many kinds of different ends—some religious, others economic, still others aesthetic, and so on; the special sciences have as their subject matter the particular processes by which these ends are attained. But these processes are not in themselves social—at least, they have a social character only indirectly and only insofar as they develop in a collective environment. These sciences, therefore, are not properly sociological. In the complex usually called *society,* there exist two kinds of elements which must be clearly distinguished: there is the content, the diverse phenomena that occur among the associated individuals; and there is the container, the association itself, within which such phenomena may be observed. Association is the only truly sociological thing, and sociology is the science of association in the abstract.

> Sociology must not seek its problems in the material of social life, but in its form. . . . It is on this abstract consideration of the social forms that the entire right of sociology to exist is founded, just as geometry owes its existence to the possibility of abstracting pure forms from material things.

But by what means is this abstraction given concrete form? If every human association develops with particular ends in view, how can one isolate association in general from the varied ends which it serves, and ascertain its laws?

> By putting together associations devoted to the most diverse purposes and eliminating what they have in common . . . the differences, presented by the particular ends around which societies form, mutually cancel each other out, and the social form alone appears. A phenomenon—the formation of parties, for instance—may be observed in the world of art as well as in those of politics, industry, or religion; if we trace what occurs in all these milieus, irrespective of the diversity of ends and interests, it will be possible to determine the laws of this particular manner of grouping. The same method will allow us to study domination and subordination, the formation of hierarchies, the division of labor, competition, and so forth.

It seems that in this fashion sociology is furnished with a clearly defined subject matter. We think, however, that in reality such a conception serves merely to keep it tied to metaphysical ideology when it actually shows an irresistible need to emancipate itself from this sphere. We do not contest the right of sociology to constitute itself by means of abstractions because there is no science that could be established otherwise. The abstractions must be methodically disciplined, however, and must separate the facts according to their natural distinctions; otherwise, they are bound to degenerate into fantastic constructions and vain mythology. The old political economy also claimed the right to make abstractions, and, in principle, it cannot be denied this right; but the use it made of it was vitiated because the basis of every one of its deductions was an abstraction that it had no right to make; that is, the notion of a man who, in his action, was moved exclusively by his personal interest. This hypothesis cannot be determined at first sight from the beginning of the investigations; we are

able to evaluate the impulsive force which personal interest can exercise on us only after repeated observations and methodical comparisons. Without them, there is no way of ascertaining whether there is in us something definite enough that it can be isolated from the other factors of our conduct and be considered apart from them. Who can say that between egoism and altruism there is the decisive separation which common sense unreflectively erects between them?

To justify the method advanced by Simmel, more is needed than to refer to the sciences that proceed by abstraction—namely, proof that the abstraction espoused is undertaken according to the principles with which every scientific abstraction must conform. By what right are the container and the content of society separated, and separated so radically? Only the container is claimed to be of a social nature; the content is not, or only indirectly so. Yet there is not a single proof to confirm such an assertion which, though far from being accepted as a self-evident axiom, may yet overwhelm a student.

To be sure, not all that happens in society is social; but this cannot be said of all that occurs *in* and *through* society. Consequently, in order to eliminate from sociology the various phenomena which constitute the web of social life, one has to demonstrate that they are not the work of the collectivity, but come from wholly different origins to place themselves within the general framework constituted by society. We do not know whether this demonstration has been attempted or whether the research that such a demonstration presupposes has been initiated. Yet it is immediately clear that the collective traditions and practices of religion, law, morality, and political economy cannot be facts less social than are the external forms of the collectivity; and if one deepens the study of these facts, one's first impression is confirmed: everywhere we find society at work elaborating them, and their effect on social organization is evident. They are society itself, living and working. What a strange idea it would be to imagine the group as a sort of empty form of trivial cast that can indifferently receive any kind of material whatever! The claim is that there are arrangements which are encountered everywhere, whatever the nature of the ends attained. But clearly, all these ends, despite their divergences, have characteristics in common. Why should only these common characteristics; and not the specific ones, have social value?

Such abstraction is not only unsystematic in that its effect is to separate things that are of the same nature, but the result of it, which is intended to be the subject matter of sociology, lacks all specificity whatever. Indeed, what are the meanings of the expression *social forms* and *forms of association in general*? If one wanted to speak only of the manner in which individuals are placed in contact with one another in association, of the dimensions of association, of its density—in a word, of its external and morphological aspect—the notion would be definite; but it would be too restricted to constitute, by itself alone, the subject matter of a science. For it would be equivalent to reducing sociology to the exclusive investigation of the substratum on which social life rests. As a matter of fact, however, our author attributes to the term *social forms* a much more extended significance. By it he understands not only the modes of grouping, the static condition of association, but also the most general forms of social relations. The term refers to the largest forms of relations of every kind that mesh in society and to the nature of the phenomena with which we are presented as being directly pertinent to sociology—the division of labor, competition, imitation, or the state of the individual's liberty or dependence vis-à-vis the group. Between these relations and the other, more special ones, however, there is only a difference of degree. How can a simple difference of this sort justify so definite a separation between two orders of phenomena? If the former constitute the subject matter of sociology, why must the latter, which are of the same kind, be excluded from it? The basis which the proposed abstraction seems to constitute when the two are opposed as container and content disappears once the significance of those words is more exactly specified, and it becomes clear that they are no more than metaphors, inexactly applied.

The most general aspect of social life is not, for that matter, either content or form, any more than it is any one of the special aspects which social life shows us. There are not two kinds of reality which, though intimately connected, are distinct and separable; what we have instead are facts of the same nature, examined at different levels of generality. And what, incidentally, is the degree of generality that such facts need in order to be classified among sociological phenomena? We are not told; and the question is one to which there is no answer. This suggests how arbitrary such a criterion is and how it gives us free rein for extending the boundaries of the science. While pretending that it defines research, it actually leaves it to the fancy of the individual. There is no rule for deciding in an impersonal manner where the circle of sociological facts begins and where it ends; not only are the boundaries mobile, which is quite legitimate, but it is not clear why they should be located at this point rather than at another. It must be added that, in order to study the most general types of social actions and their laws, one has to know the laws of more special types, since the former cannot be investigated and explained without systematic comparison with the latter. In this respect, every sociological problem presupposes a profound knowledge of all those special sciences that should be placed outside sociology but which sociology cannot do without. And since such universal competence is impossible, one has to be satisfied with summary knowledge, which is rapidly gathered and cannot be subjected to any control.

These are the characteristics of Simmel's investigations. We appreciate their subtlety and ingenuity, but we think it impossible to trace the main divisions of our science as he understands it in an objective manner. No connection can be discovered among the questions to which he draws the attention of sociologists; they are topics of meditation that have no relation to an integral scientific system. In addition, Simmel's proofs generally consist only of explanations by example; some facts, borrowed from the most disparate fields, are cited but they are not preceded by critical analysis, and they often offer us no idea of how to assess their value. For sociology to merit the name of a science,

it must be something quite different from philosophical variations on certain aspects of social life, chosen more or less at random according to the leanings of a single individual. What is needed is the formulation of the problem in a way that permits us to draw a logical solution. . . .

Ferdinand Tönnies   (essay date 1918)

SOURCE: "Simmel as Sociologist," in *Georg Simmel,* edited by Lewis A. Coser, Prentice-Hall, Inc., 1965, pp. 50-2.

[*In the following essay, which was originally published in* Frankfurter Zeitung *in 1918, Tönnies argues that Simmel is better described as a social psychologist than as a sociologist.*]

After Schäffle's precedent, and apart from books of momentary importance, Simmel was the first to give the title *Soziologie* (*Sociology*) to a major work in the German language. The objection has been raised that the title does not correspond to the content, which offers nothing of a systematic nature. But Simmel appears to defend himself against this criticism in advance, by prefacing the work only with the demand that the reader keep firmly in mind throughout the book the question raised about the problem of sociology in the first chapter, "since otherwise these pages might appear as a collection of unrelated facts and reflections." Thus to characterize this insightful work would, however, be an injustice, for the subtitle, "Investigations into the Forms of Association" ("Vergesellschaftung"), sufficiently indicates that Simmel was concerned only with theory. . . .

On Social Differentiation: Sociological and Psychological Investigations (1890), the work which first established Simmel's name, contains his fundamental methodological ideas, so that its fifth chapter, **"On the Intersection of Social Circles,"** is partly taken over into the larger work. At the time, I said in a discussion of the little volume that there remained in it something at times unsure and perhaps even unfinished. I would not dare to make this criticism of the later sociological works; rather, it seems as if this unfinished quality had here become a special art, characterized by suggestion, shading, halftones, and seemingly magical light effects. It is more than a coincidence that Simmel, who in his last years wanted to be entirely a philosopher and had a special love for aesthetics, selected Rembrandt as his hero.

The title of that earliest work is significant in another way: differentiation is the very mark of Simmel's thought. It contains much of the wisdom of that old style of thinking which has been described as a mental facility for inventing unexpected similarities. His mind, it has been said, is totally set upon analysis; and this, of course, is correct. Social objects are for him always given conditions (*Gegebenheiten*) whose essence he seeks to discover by approaching them, so to speak, with the psychological knife, differentiating them and illuminating them by revealing their elements. It has been said that, in this process, he sometimes grinds them to a fine dust so that, in the end, nothing remains but a homeopathic dilution to which only faith can give an immanent essentiality. In reality, however, Simmel did not lack synthetic capability (although he rarely used it) so much as he lacked that vision and intuitive power which can grasp the uniqueness (*das Eigentümliche*) of elemental forces and motives and show the meaning of that uniqueness within the larger context of all life.

His investigations, therefore, rarely concern themselves with large-scale historic phenomena of social life. No matter how many remarkable examples his profound erudition marshals in support of his fine differentiations, he prefers to seize upon completely timeless, general problems, such as super[ordination] and subordination, conflict, secret societies, self-preservation of the social group, the spatial ordering of society, the expansion of the group, and the development of individuality. These are all significant objects, and he treats them with a multiplicity of charming observations, brilliant insights, and blinding dialectics; but he never fully attains the recognition that the most proper objects of sociological inquiry are the social structures (*Gebilde*) which arise out of the thoughts of men themselves, out of their subjects. To distinguish sharply all mental objects (*Gedankendinge*), such as alliances and leagues, clubs and cooperative societies, parishes and states, churches and orders, from the "groups" and "circles" which are externally recognizable—that, in my opinion, is the precondition for the solution of the specifically sociological problem. It must be said that Simmel stubbornly avoided seeing this fact. His real achievements must therefore be relegated more to social psychology—a field which, admittedly, was little enough cultivated—rather than to sociology proper. But in that field lay his real excellence. One can best grasp the magical versatility of his highly skillful thought by looking through the index of the volume which he entitles *Soziologie*. But the most important thing, from the scientific point of view, will be found wherever he most closely approaches the proper object of sociology, as for example in the fifth chapter, on secrecy and secret societies, and in the eighth, on the self-preservation of the group. And in a different direction we find the same thing in the *Philosophy of Money* which has justly received so much attention. Here he is dealing with an objective structure (*Gebilde*) which confronts the subjective mind "as norm." Simmel well knows that this has a far wider relevance, but he does not develop its importance further.

Thus even the most recent little book, *Fundamental Questions of Sociology,* clings to the notion that the most general form of "association" is reciprocity (*Wechselwirkung*), and charmingly elaborates that the latter's "play-form" is conviviality (*Geselligkeit*), which, he says, is related to its concrete form as the work of art is to reality! One remembers that on the night before the opening of the first Congress of Sociologists in Frankfurt (1910) Simmel presented his delicate meditations about the sense of liberation and relief which precisely the more profound men find in conviviality. If these observations approach coquetry, if elsewhere—in a "sociology of the senses"—Simmel makes perfume accomplish "a unique synthesis of individual-egotist and social teleology in the olfactory sense," nevertheless all such spiritual amusements were meant in earnest and in the most profound sense. Yet they were not suited for advancing recognition of the enormous complexities of social life and, to some extent, even provoked a ridicule they did not deserve.

The meritorious achievement of Simmel is not confined to sociology alone. But here also this insightful man will leave profound traces. German scholarship has lost in him one of its brightest lights. He, too, fell in the turmoil of World War [I], as Lamprecht, Lexis, Schmoller, and Wagner had before him. None of them saw its outcome, and all were spared the anxiety which we must bear about the future of the German spirit and the future of European humanity.

Donald N. Levine   (essay date 1957)

SOURCE: "Some Key Problems in Simmel's Work," in *Georg Simmel*, edited by Lewis A. Coser, Prentice-Hall, Inc., 1965, pp. 97-115.

[*In the following excerpt from his 1957 doctoral dissertation, Levine delineates major themes in Simmel's work.*]

The Simmelian corps may be conveniently divided according to the three viewpoints Simmel mentioned for analyzing things human: the individual, the social, and the objective. Under objective culture are to be found his various contributions to ethics, epistemology, aesthetics, and metaphysics, comment on which lies beyond the scope of this study. Under the viewpoint of individual personality are to be found his studies of a few historic personalities—Michelangelo, Goethe, Rembrandt are the main ones—and occasional statements which reveal a rough working theory of personality. His aim in the study of the great personalities is always to disclose the inner unity, the form or essence, the "formula of the destiny of his soul" which underlies the diverse contents and expressions of the subject's life.

Simmel's theory of personality, like most prepsychoanalytic conceptions, is restricted to the psychology of the ego. It is dominated by two images. One image represents the self as a unity born of the interaction of psychic elements, just as the forms which sociology studies are unities born of the interaction among social elements. The other image, more specific and more often employed, presents the personality as divided into a central core and a periphery:

> In the inevitably symbolic language of all psychology: our soul seems to live in two layers, one of which is deeper, hard or impossible to move, carrying the real sense or substance of our life, while the other is composed of momentary impulses and isolated irritabilities.

> We can designate certain relations of the ego to its contents only by the graphic symbol of a definite or a changing distance between them. . . . We divide our inner existence into a central ego and contents distributed around it.

The more heterogeneous the peripheral contents, the more vividly does the form of the inner unity appear:

> Conflicting tendencies can arise just because the individual has a core of inner unity. The ego can become more clearly conscious of this unity the

more he is confronted with the task of reconciling within himself a diversity of group interests.

Only the frequent alternation of [peripheral] contents reveals the ego to consciousness as the abiding center amidst the stream of psychic phenomena.

Some of the other questions concerning the personality which Simmel discusses include: whether the individual is attracted more by others who are like him or unlike him, whether the ego is strong or weak, [and] whether [it is] more homogeneous or more differentiated.

The forms of social interaction, comprising the third area of Simmel's contribution, may be arranged under these headings: *social processes, social types,* and *developmental* patterns. The following lists of these forms give but a crude picture of Simmel's sociological problems. Many of the terms involved have meanings that become clear only in context, and the mere titles of the problems convey little idea of what particular questions are being discussed. . . .

Social processes refers to relatively simple, relatively stable, configurations of social interaction. The main social processes treated by Simmel are:

From *Über soziale Differenzierung:*

Attribution of guilt to a collectivity;
Group cohesion and solidarity (as a function of size and relations with outsiders);
Elementary collective behavior (the "social level");
Formation of parties, partisanship;
The division of labor.

From *Philosophie des Geldes:*

The forms of change of possessions (robbery, giving presents, reciprocal giving, tradition-sanctioned "gifts" and exchanges, haggling, exchange at fixed prices);
Money;
Representation;
The form of the double relationship whereby two phenomena which spring from the same *Grundmotiv* tend on the one hand toward reciprocal increase and, on the other, toward repression of one by the other;
The concentration of energy;
The forms of a fully rationalized order;
Personal independence in interpersonal relations;
Participation in associations that does not involve the whole personality;
The mutual reduction of both parties in a relation to the status of pure means;
Intensity of opposition between parties when they have a common origin.

From *Soziologie:*

Formal characteristics of the small group;
Forms of small groups (socialistic communities, religious sects, aristocracies);
The mass;
Relations of the individual to the norms of a group (custom, law, honor, individual morality);
Number as a basis for group organization;

The social party;
Isolation;
Freedom, in the form of liberation from ties, power over others;
The dyad;
Monogamous marriage;
Associations of three or more members;
Reconciliation through a mediator;
Divide et impera;
Subordination under a single leader;
Opposition to the ruler;
Appeal to a higher tribunal;
Unification through common subordination (leveling, gradation);
Upward gradation;
Simultaneous super[ordination] and subordination;
Subordination of group to a member versus to an outsider;
Subordination under a plurality, where the plurality is [*a*] unified, [*b*] disunited, [*c*] stratified;
Subordination under ideal norms;
Forms of individual subordination to a group (social pressures, internalized social norms, objective morality);
The ruler's subjection of self to law he has himself made;
The contract;
Freedom of a small group within a large group;
Assimilation of the upward mobile section of an opposed group to the ranks of the superordinate group;
Conflict;
Unification;
Hatred of the "enemy of the group";
Jealousy;
Envy;
Begrudging;
Competition;
Rivalry;
Unification through conflict;
Forms of termination of conflict (disappearance of the object of conflict, victory, compromise, conciliation);
Irreconcilability;
Confidence;
Acquaintance;
Discretion;
The secret;
Adornment;
The secret society;
The letter;
The confederation of associations;
Co-optation;
The hereditary office;
The facilitation or obstruction of entry or exit of members in a group;
Honor;
The group organ;
General forms of group persistence (rigidity and conservatism, flexibility and liberality);
Faithfulness;
Gratitude;
The boundary;
The fixed location as a center of activity;
The rendezvous;
The minority group;
Wandering;
Correlative formal categories applicable to any

processes (the primary individual element, the narrow circle, and the wide circle).

From *Philosophische Kultur:*

Fashion;
Coquetry;
Love;
Play forms of association;
Sociability;
Social games;
Conversation.

If, instead of regarding association from the point of view of the total interactive process, one focuses on the typical characteristics of a person when engaging in the various sorts of interaction, one obtains a picture of particular social types. Besides discussing competition, for example, one may speak of *the competitor;* one may discuss *the coquette* as well as *coquetry.* [One] perspective discloses the invariant structures of social experience; the [other] reveals the variety of forms assumed by human nature qua social.

Simmel moves readily from the one sort of discussion to the other. In many instances he finds it more useful to describe forms of interaction from the vantage point of social type. Indeed, in some cases this is necessary, for sometimes "characteristics of an element which could originate only in the relation between this and another element . . . come to be essential qualities of that element, independent of all interaction."

The main social types Simmel discusses are:

From *Philosophie des Geldes:*

The less involved party in a relation;
Forms determined by the individual's relation to money (the coveter of money, the miser, the dissipator, the ascetic poor, the modern cynic, the blasé type).

From *Soziologie:*

The mediator;
The nonpartisan;
The arbitrator;
The *tertius gaudens* (passive—enjoying advantages accidentally bestowed by one of the conflicting parties; active—exploiting extant paralysis of forces, or throwing his strength to one side);
The superordinate;
The subordinate;
The renegade;
The middleman;
The priest;
The merchant;
The woman;
The poor;
The bourgeois;
The stranger;
The aristocrat.

From *Philosophische Kultur:*

The adventurer;
The hero of fashion;
The feminine;

The masculine;
The forms of youth and age;
The genius;
The coquette;
The professionals with little specialization but relatively high status (the lawyer, the salesman, the housewife).

By *developmental patterns* I refer to the more complex, diachronic forms which Simmel treats frequently enough to justify a separate heading. These include:

From *Über sociale Differenzierung:*

The differential progress of related forms;
The emergence of groups of individuals with similar interests who come from dissimilar backgrounds;
Social differentiation and its consequences;
Similarity of forms in the first and last stages of any development;
The pattern: Group G splits into factions g^1 and g^2, which are able to reunite into G again by relegating their doctrinal differences to the realm of individual preference.

From *Philosophie des Geldes:*

The tendency to develop a distinction between form and content and then come to value the form;
Lengthening means-ends chains to attain what is close at hand;
The tendency for things public to become more public, things private to become more private;
The differentiation of a unified state of things into one part which bears characteristics of the original whole and other contrasting parts;
The differentiation of an "immediate unity" into separate elements, which are later unified in a more intellectual and comprehensive synthesis.

From *Soziologie:*

Two modes of seeking social progress: [a] abolishing extant forms, [b] improving within extant forms;
Development from a local to a functional basis of social organization;
Development of functional organization from being based on "external, mechanical" criteria to being governed by rational criteria;
Development from inherently meaningful patterns of behavior to those, intrinsically mechanical and meaningless, which attain meaning by being organized in behalf of some higher purpose;
As group size increases, features common to its members which serve to fuse them into a social unit decrease, and demands regarding the behavior of its members come to be of a more prohibitive, rather than positive, nature;
Internal development, and a rhythm of peace and conflict, are essential to the persistence of a group;
Individuality of being and behavior among individuals increases in direct proportion to the expansion of the social group.

STRATEGIC PROBLEMS IN SIMMEL

The following problems were selected with an eye to securing questions which are prominent in Simmel's work and which represent relatively unfamiliar writings to the English-reading audience. They include fashion (recurrent social process), the aristocrat (social type), social differentiation (developmental pattern), and his overriding ideological consideration: freedom.

Fashion. As he so often does, Simmel begins the essay on ·fashion by speculating about some aspect of life in general in order to establish a point from which he may run a line of thought more or less directly to his topic. This characteristic of Simmel's style has earned it the epithet of "an oblique approach." In this case, it is the dualistic condition of life with which he begins—a dualism that cannot be directly apprehended, but can only be felt in the individual contrasts that mark our existence.

A series of such individual contrasts is then reviewed, from the physiological needs for movement/rest through the metaphysical conceptions of pluralism/monism to the political contrast of individualism/socialism. The history of society is seen as an interplay between the opposed tendencies: [that] for the individual to fuse himself with the group [versus that] to place himself outside the group. Imitation is a process which serves the former tendency; individualization is a medium for the latter.

Fashion is a form which combines both imitation and individualization. Fashion satisfies the individual's need to be different by the variety of contents it successively adopts, and by marking the domain of a particular class. In this latter respect, fashion is similar to honor, another form which imparts a common character to the members of a particular group and at the same time distinguishes them from those who stand outside the group.

That this purely formal social motive underlies the phenomenon of fashion is shown by the fact that fashions are often adopted for no objective, aesthetic, or other purposeful grounds whatsoever. Judging from the repugnant things that are sometimes in vogue, it would seem as though fashion desired to exhibit its power by getting us to adopt the most atrocious things for its sake alone. That both imitation and differentiation are indispensable components of fashion is shown by the following cases. In isolated, homogeneous, primitive societies there is little interest in differentiation, and so no show of fashions. Similarly, fashion was not present among the Venetian nobles, who wore black in order not to draw attention to their small numbers, and so could express no need to differentiate themselves in public. On the other hand, it is said that there was no ruling fashion in male attire in Florence toward the end of the trecento, in that everyone adopted a style of his own. Fashion was not present because the disposition to fuse with the collectivity was absent.

The upper class, most eager of all strata to maintain its inner solidarity and at the same time to distinguish itself from all other strata, originates the new fashions. Upward-mobile persons find in fashion an ideal means for imitating and identifying with the upper class. When a fashion is adopted outside the class that originates it, that class develops new fashions. This process repeats itself *within* the strata of the upper class. With the lowering of class barriers and the increase of wealth in a population, the process becomes progressively more frantic.

The dude is the leader of style—who is led by the new vogue. The enemy of fashion represents the same form, under a negative sign. The fashionable individual derives the satisfaction of knowing that he represents something special and striking, while he feels inwardly supported by a set of persons who are striving for the same thing. He is envied as an individual, approved of as a member of a group. Fashion is thus an ideal field for individuals who are dependent, yet who demand a certain prominence.

As any vogue becomes widely accepted within a collectivity, it begins to die out as a fashion. Much of the charm of fashion is owing to this character of being at once novel and transitory, of being a "boundary" between being and not-being. At its apex, a fashion imparts a peculiarly strong sense of the present, an emphasis which also accentuates the sensation of change. Another reason for the hold of fashion on the modern mind is that the great, permanent, unquestionable convictions are continually losing strength, with the result that the transitory elements of life acquire more room for their activity. Fashion has thus gained increasing influence over taste, over theoretical convictions, even over the moral foundations of life.

Women are generally the staunchest adherents of fashion, for it provides a medium by which they can attain a certain individuation otherwise denied by their normally suppressed condition, and a status denied them by not having a calling or profession.

There are other needs which the form of fashion is especially suited to satisfy. Because its place in the individual is at the periphery of personality, it serves as a mask for refined and singular persons. Blind obedience to the standards of the general public becomes for them a means of reserving to themselves all manifestations of their feelings and tastes. Again, weak and retiring natures, vulnerable to mortification or shame at any exposure of themselves, seize on fashion as a kind of collective behavior in which feelings of shame have no place. Finally, because fashion affects only the externals of life, it gives the individual an easy way to express his solidarity with his time and society, and thereby enables him to devote the freedom given one in life to inner, more essential matters.

Fashion as an interpersonal phenomenon has a certain parallel within the personality. Tendencies both toward equalizing unification and individual demarcation can be found within an individual when he creates a personal style, a mode of conduct for himself which shows the pattern—rise, sway, and decline—of social fashion. One might say that personal fashion forms a limiting case of social fashion. Between the two phenomena is the case where pet terms are applied indiscriminately to all the objects within one's purview, usually by the members of a narrow circle. By so subjecting everything under a certain category, people gain a feeling of power—a feeling whose superficiality is betrayed by the rapidity with which such expressions pass by.

The total rhythm in which individuals and groups move

has an important bearing on their relation to fashion. The lower classes are generally hard to move and slow to develop, while the upper classes are consciously conservative, often archaistic. Neither offers fertile ground for the vicissitudes of fashion. Fashion is, rather, the province of the middle classes, with their variable and restless rhythms. For this reason, the ascendance of the *tiers état* diffused and innervated the process of fashion; but this was also because frequent changes of fashion, implying as they do a huge subjugation of the individual, are a necessary complement of social and political freedom: "Man requires an ephemeral tyrant as soon as he has rid himself of the permanent and absolute one."

Despite the transiency of particular fashions, the fashionable objects of the moment seem to promise a certain permanency. This is because fashion itself, as a social form, is immortal; some fashion or other is always with us. This becomes more than symbolic in the many instances when items once fashionable have been restored to fashion after lying forgotten for a while.

Although the power of fashion is great, it cannot exploit all objects with equal success. Some things are likely to become fashionable, just as some natural objects lend themselves readily to becoming material for art; others offer resistance. Everything "classical" is relatively far removed from fashion and alien to its spirit. By contrast, everything baroque and extreme seems to be drawn to fashion. Though fashion as a form is natural to man, the utterly unnatural fares well in the form of fashion.

The aristocrat. The problem of the nature of aristocracy not only indicates the sort of thing Simmel has to say about a social type, it also represents a theme recurrent in his thinking. Like few sociologists, . . . Simmel expresses great interest in differences of quality among people and experiences. He often speaks about *finer natures, more sensitive individuals, decisive personalities.* Such interest in the human elite is not unrelated to an interest in the social elite. In the **"Exkurs über den Adel,"** Simmel seeks to define the formal position of the latter, particularly as found in monarchies.

The form of the aristocracy depends in the first instance on its character as an intermediate structure (*Zwischengebilde*). This is so in two senses: horizontally, it is midway between the individual and the widest social circle; vertically, it is midway between the ruling power and the broad mass of political and social groups. It differs from the bourgeoisie, which it resembles in these respects, by being closed above and below. Entry into the ranks of the nobility is typically difficult. Departure from those ranks is, likewise, not easy but—once it is called for—it is complete and absolute. This sharp social demarcation of the aristocracy is reflected in two stipulations: the aristocrat may do what others may not, and he may not do things which are permitted to others.

It is clear that this formal character follows from the conditions of interaction in aristocracies. The same structure appears in the greatest variety of groups—in ancient Rome, under the Normans, in the *ancien régime,* and in the "aristocracies" of such smaller collectivities as labor

groups, large family circles, and the clergy. This homogeneity of formal-sociological position is highlighted by the tendency of members of aristocracies of different lands to intermarry, in spite of the traditional localism of aristocratic groups; and by instances when connections among the nobility have provided some sort of community in nations otherwise unconsolidated.

Carrying the analysis further, we find that the sociological form distinctive of aristocracies derives from a unique relation between the general social content of the group and the individual existence of its members. Each member of an aristocracy participates in and avails himself of whatever is most valuable in all the members of the group. It is as though a substance of lasting value runs through the blood of the various members of an aristocracy, generation after generation. Aristocracies have historically been in opposition to political centralization as representing a principle opposed to their own hereditary basis. Where access to high honors on a hereditary basis is proscribed, as in Russia before Czar Feodor, the formation of an aristocratic class is prevented. To assure the continuity of their "valuable substance," equality of birth is insisted on in marriage. This in turn confirms that closed-off, self-contained character of aristocracies which, above and beyond the cultivated bodies and manners of their members, is responsible for much of the aesthetic attraction which aristocracies have always exerted.

The importance of the family tree for aristocracy lies in its indication that the substance which forms the individual concerned is indeed the same substance which has passed through the whole line of noble stock. This preoccupation with maintaining oneself intact may explain the aristocrat's aversion toward work, which, after all, demands a submergence of the self in behalf of an object. Characteristic aristocratic activities, such as war and hunting, involve the predominance of the subjective factor. The work of the artist, which seeks to articulate the inner motion of a subject, bears the closest analogy to aristocratic activity; but it is an individuality, not a common substance handed down by family and class, which comes to expression.

The motive of superiority and social exclusiveness inclines aristocratic groups toward the use of secrecy, a device for heightening the wall against outsiders. At the political level, one notes that secrecy has always been among the requisites of political aristocracies—just as, conversely, the democratic principle is associated with the principle of publicity. Acting as an individual, however, the aristocratic personality despises concealment, because his inner certainty renders him indifferent to the regard of others.

The most crucial thing about aristocracy, however, is that the whole constellation of accumulated and traditional values which confront the noble-born does not have an objective, superindividual significance. These values come to their own, rather, only in the self-reliant, self-contained existence of individual aristocrats. Aristocracy thus represents a peculiar synthesis of two extreme conditions—when the individual is swallowed up by his group, and when he stands, independent, in opposition to it. The weight of tradition the aristocrat must bear calls for strength and independence, as well as responsibility. When the personalities involved are too weak, the mere execution of traditional forms results in decadence. In sum:

> By strictness of the aristocratic style of life, which creates the widest area of contact among its members; by the demand of equal rank in marriage, which effects a physiological guarantee of the qualitative and historical unity of the class; by the technique of its tradition, which accumulates the values and achievements of the family and class without loss—by these sociological means the aristocracy fuses its members to an otherwise unattainable degree into the collectivity. But this superindividual formation, so created, finds (more than any other collective structure) its meaning and purpose in the existence of individuals, in their might and meaning, in the freedom and self-sufficiency of their lives.

Social differentiation. Differentiation as a state of social organization, as the division of labor in any of its forms, has—like conflict or fashion—the status of a recurrent process. Viewed diachronically, however, as the emergence of a more differentiated condition from a more homogeneous and unified one, it refers to a developmental pattern. In this sense, social differentiation constitutes the dominant developmental pattern in Simmel's thought (as well as perhaps the most prominent theme in the literature of social science).

At the most abstract level, Simmel is fond of showing how some commonly accepted dualism has emerged from an originally undifferentiated state (*Indifferenzzustand*). Cognition, for example, begins in children and among primitive peoples purely as awareness of impressions and ideas. The differentiation into a knowing subject and a known object comes about as a later development from this original unity. Similarly, in the realm of volition, the distinction between a desiring subject and a valued object follows, logically and psychologically, the unitary experience of pure enjoying.

There are two main contexts in which Simmel applies this sort of analysis to society. They appear in the two chapters, **"Die Ausdehnung der Gruppe und die Ausbildung der Individualität,"** and **"Über die Kreuzung socialer Kreise,"** which he included both in *Über sociale Differenzierung* and in *Soziologie*. The central proposition of the former essay is that as the size of a group increases, its members become more unlike one another. The latter essay traces much the same pattern from a different viewpoint: the movement from propinquity to interest as a basis for association. The one chapter treats the small homogeneous group as an *Indifferenzzustand* from which the large group and differentiated individuals have emerged. The other chapter stresses the fusion of individual and group when kinship and locale are the principles of social organization, and how this condition becomes differentiated into a condition wherein individuals participate in a variety of more specific associations with only certain parts of their personalities. These two aspects of social differentiation are treated as separate developmental patterns;

Simmel nowhere combines them in a single systematic analysis.

The correlation of individual differentiation with sociological expansion appears in the most diverse contents of social life. The powerful extended family is replaced by wider political groupings on the one hand, by individuals and their nuclear families on the other. Corporate guilt and the blood feud are succeeded by justice in the name of the larger society and individual responsibility. Unspecialized production for small markets gives way to production for large markets by means of considerable specialization on the part of producers.

The narrower group constitutes a sort of mean between the expanded group and individuality, i.e., these latter categories offer the same formal possibilities of social life that are combined in the first. A balance between individual and social tendencies is maintained in either case. The narrower the group, the less individuality its members have, but the more distinct the group itself is; in larger groups, the individuals have more room to differentiate themselves, but the groups as wholes tend to resemble one another. Individual uniqueness is attained at the cost of social uniqueness.

This correlation (which obtains synchronically, and in alternation, as well as in linear developmental patterns) is illustrated in antebellum American political life. The New England states were composed of small townships which absorbed and regulated much of the individual's life. The southern states, on the other hand, were populated mostly by adventurous individuals with no inclination for local self-government. They formed large, colorless counties as administrative units, and their real political unity lay in the state. The independent, almost anarchistic temperament of the southerners was complemented by this abstract (state) political structure, while the more strictly controlled citizens of New England created strongly individualized and autonomous local communities.

The realms of custom, law, and morality are seen as appropriate, respectively, to the narrower group, the larger group, and the individual. Honor, formally similar to custom, is the technique of control par excellence for the small group.

Simmel's chapter on **"Die Kreuzung socialer Kreise"** sees the development of human relations as analogous to the development of thought. To the primitive mind, any coexistence of objects in time and space is enough to bring about an association between the ideas of these objects. For our conception of an object to free itself from associations with attributes that are only accidental to it, we must become aware of it in many different connections. In this way irrelevant associations get displaced by associations based on the content of what is perceived.

Similarly, in society individuals at first associate with whoever moves in their immediate environment, without regard to one another's particular attributes. As society develops, individuals come to establish contacts with persons outside these primary groups who are related to them by actual similarity of talents, interests, and activities. Just as a general concept binds together what a number of different perceptual complexes have in common, so do practical considerations bind together like-minded individuals who stem from quite alien groups.

This pattern is illustrated in the early history of universities: from unions of nationals to organization by faculties. Similarly, English trade unions tended at first toward purely local organization, which was later replaced by a uniform organization of trades on a nationwide basis. An intermediate stage in this transition is represented by medieval group formation, in which the individual came to have affiliations beyond those of his local community. These were reached not through the individual but through the corporate group—gild, monastery, or town. The modern situation in which the individual himself chooses from a vast number of associations on the basis of his various interests results in a more complex social structure, more differentiated and hence more determinate personalities, and greater social freedom.

Freedom. If one may speak about a dominant *Problematik* in Simmel's social thought, it would surely be the complex of questions dealing with individualism and freedom. Extensive discussions of these matters appear in each of his four sociological books. The crowning achievement of his life work was to have been a comprehensive treatment of the concept of freedom, including an interpretation of the significance of this concept for the actuality and the understanding of historical life. One can but deeply regret that a scant thirty pages of notes are all that were completed at the time of his death.

Of the many aspects or kinds of freedom which Simmel mentions, three are of special sociological relevance. There is freedom in the sense of liberation from ties to things and others; freedom in the sense of the development of personality exclusively according to the laws of one's nature; and freedom in the sense of power to express one's will. Because the adoption of a money economy increases freedom in all three senses, Simmel devotes one sixth of **Philosophie des Geldes** to a study of the relation between money and freedom.

Widespread enjoyment of freedom in the first sense results above all from the numerical expansion of the group. . . . The small group is narrow in its restrictive control of the individual as well as in numbers. Expansion of the circles of social relationship increasingly frees the individual from the guardianship of community and church, from the demands of class and economic groups. Liberation from such connections is the great ideal of eighteenth century individualism.

Money advances this ideal in a number of ways. By providing a means whereby economic values can be condensed and mobilized, money extends the effective range of economic intercourse—and larger markets are larger circles. As a possession, money frees the individual from the responsibilities which usually attend possession of less mobile objects. Furthermore, money frees the subordinate from extensive duty to his lord by permitting him to discharge his obligations by handing over an object which may be acquired in any way he chooses: "Personal freedom can grow no greater, before the abolition of all rights of the landowner over subordinates, than when the obligation of the latter is turned into a money payment which the lord *must* accept." Finally, as the perfect medium for impersonal relations among people, money helps to create a situation in which the individual is dependent on a host of other people for their services, but free and independent of them as particular persons. Any extension of objectivity in social life involves a corresponding increase in individuality.

Freedom as the unhampered development of personality according to one's nature is especially favored by the development of organization on a basis of interest rather than on the basis of propinquity. In a society that contains a large number of "interest" groups, the individual may find a collectivity within which to realize each of his several aspirations and at the same time enjoy the advantages of group membership. Despite the amount of association this implies, his individuality is assured by virtue of the unique constellation of groups to which he belongs. This idea of individualism—that the individual should realize what is unique in himself and thereby distinguish himself from all others—is that expressed in the nineteenth century, in theory by the Romantic Movement, in practice by the division of labor.

This situation is encouraged by money, for money promotes the formation of groups on a purely purposeful basis. But money furthers differentiation within the individual directly, not only as a by-product of differentiation in society. It does this by providing an effective means for distinguishing between the subjective center and the objective achievement of a person. The individual's performance may be paid for, while his person remains outside the transaction; or else the person as such may be supported (by contributions from many individuals), while his specific performances remain free from financial considerations. Freedom to live according to one's nature is advanced as the different qualities and powers of an individual unfold autonomously.

Money also plays an important role in increasing freedom in the sense of extending the individual's power over things. Of all objects, money offers the least resistance to an agent. It is the most "possessible" of all things, and hence completely submissive to the will of an ego. It can be come by in countless ways. Its possession can be indefinitely increased. Its uses are without number.

The increase of freedom is not the only direction taken by social developments, however, nor is freedom the only value to be realized in society. Human beings require a certain balance of freedom and constraint in order to live well. Just as, for example, the widespread diffusion of secret societies usually indicates a condition of regimentation and political oppression, i.e., it is a reaction stemming from the need for freedom; so, conversely, does ritual regulation within secret societies reflect their relative freedom from the larger society, i.e., it provides a condition in which human nature is kept in equilibrium through the establishment of norms that counterpart the norms of the larger society which have been rejected.

Rudolph Heberle (essay date 1948)

SOURCE: "The Sociology of Georg Simmel: The Forms of Social Interaction," in *An Introduction to the History of Sociology,* edited by Harry Elmer Barnes, The University of Chicago Press, 1970, pp. 249-70.

[*In the following essay, originally published in 1948, Heberle finds that Simmel's works are more valuable for exemplifying his methods as a thinker than for any substantive contribution to the field of sociology.*]

I. SIMMEL'S LIFE AND CHIEF WRITINGS

Georg Simmel belongs to the generation of European scholars who, at the end of the nineteenth century, broke with the "classical tradition" in sociology and originated a renaissance of sociological theory and research. Born in Berlin of Jewish parentage, he became a lecturer in philosophy (*Privatdozent*) at the age of twenty-seven at the University of Berlin, in which position he remained until 1914, when he was called to Strassburg as a professor of philosophy. He taught there under the adverse conditions of wartime until he died in the fall of 1918.

Simmel was primarily a philosopher, whose interests were not at all confined to the problems of society; in fact, his sociological essays form only part of his lifework. He had a strong interest in history, in the fine arts, and in literature. Perhaps the most adequate characterization of his work as a whole would be to say that it represents a philosophy of contemporary culture. It is in this context that his sociological work has to be appraised—as *one* among several approaches. Simmel rose soon to international reputation as a sociologist; several of his studies were published almost simultaneously in German, English, and French. This accessibility of his sociological work is partly responsible for the fact that he was probably better known in his time in the United States than most of the other leading German sociologists of his generation.

II. SIMMEL'S CONCEPTION OF THE SCOPE AND METHOD OF SOCIOLOGY

To represent within the framework of a single chapter the sociological work of Georg Simmel involves some difficulty which arises from the peculiarity of his work. Simmel himself admits that he did not develop a system. His sociological work consists of a series of essays on subjects not systematically related but selected because of their importance for the study of forms of social interaction. This was the aspect of social life which Simmel considered to be the specifically sociological problem. His essays, therefore, represent a highly personal choice of subjects, and, moreover, their content is the highly personal work of a brilliant, analytical mind. Their attractiveness and their value is largely conditioned by the form of presentation; the mere skeleton of basic ideas and concepts would be a very dry and unimaginative affair if deprived of the brilliancy of illustration, the striking analogies and differentiations, and the often surprising indication of structural similarities between apparently very disparate phenomena. Even in Spykman's able condensation of Simmel's essays, much of their intellectual and aesthetic qualities is lost. Therefore, no attempt will be made here to present in a comprehensive summary the contents of Simmel's writings. For this purpose the reader may be referred to Spykman's book and to the numerous papers by Simmel which are available in English translations. Instead, this chapter deals, rather, with the methodological principles of Simmel's sociological work. Only by way of illustration will some of the main theorems be discussed. This procedure is, in fact, congenial to Simmel's own style of work.

Simmel is generally considered to be the founder of the so-called "formal school" in sociology. This is certainly an adequate designation of his main contribution to the development of sociology. How far this was an original idea is problematic. The essence of Simmel's position is that sociology, in the strict sense, or "pure" sociology, in distinction from the other social sciences which deal with special fields of human social life, has, as its specific object of cognition, the forms of social interaction that occur in all those spheres of social life and really constitute the essence of society.

Such phenomena as superordination and subordination, the specialization of functions, the phenomena of conflict and competition, the formation of parties, and the like can be studied as such, irrespective, in principle, of the fields (economic, political, religious, etc.) which form the "content" of the action of those groups in which they occur; for—and this is the empirical justification for this concept of form—the same pattern of interaction occurs in connection with quite different aims or purposes, while, on the other hand, the same aims or purposes can be realized through quite different forms of social interaction. This circumstance permits the isolation by abstraction of the various forms of interaction of the different kinds of combinations of men as such, for the purpose of analytic and comparative inquiry. In these "forms" of association and dissociation we have the phenomenon of society as such, in pure essence, separated theoretically from all its particular contents.

When Simmel first presented his ideas, he found that sociology was widely conceived of as a comprehensive study of all social facts and that, since everything in human life has a social relevance, sociology would be "the science of everything human"—except for those subjects reserved for the sciences of external nature. This position would, according to Simmel, mean merely a dumping of all existing sciences dealing with social phenomena "into one great pot," or it would reduce sociology to a mere method of investigation, a directive principle which can be applied in the most varied and diverse fields of science, without itself constituting a science.

This concept of sociology lacks a definite object of cognition (*Erkenntnisobjekt*). In a similar way psychology has been considered as a solution of the problems of all the sciences; and yet psychology, as a science, is concerned solely "with the functions of the mind as such" and is separated from "the special sciences which from particular points of view investigate the particular contents of perceptive knowledge." "Just as psychology as a science does not deal with everything conditioned by consciousness, so sociology does not necessarily include everything that belongs in a society or that is conditioned by its existence."

New sciences, Simmel points out, arise if the inquisitive mind is focused on certain aspects of the chaos of existence which can be isolated by a process of abstraction. Thus mathematics deals with the formal and numerical aspects of physical bodies, while chemistry and physics deal with the qualitative aspects of substances of those bodies. Since economics, politics, law, and the "cultural sciences" deal with the contents or the substance of society, sociology, it appears, would deal with the social as such, that is, with society in its essence. Hence the conception of the isolability of the "forms" of social interaction furnishes the basis for the abstraction of a new object of cognition. Pure sociology thus becomes a sort of geometry of social interaction.

Before entering on a further discussion of this position, some of Simmel's arguments in its defense have to be presented. One objection to the very notion of a science of society is that society is an abstraction, that only the individuals are real. Simmel, however, points out that the concept of the "individual" is also an abstraction. "Society" or human groups appear just as real, if one looks at human existence from a perspective where the single individual disappears. What is really decisive is the cognitive intention (*Erkenntnisabsicht*): "the special ends of cognition determine whether immediately manifest or experienced reality shall be inquired into with regard to a personal or a collective object."

> Any science selects from the totality of immediately experienced phenomena one series or one aspect under guidance of a certain concept; sociology thus is justified in dissecting the individual "Existenzen" and bringing them together again according to its own concept by thus asking: according to what "laws" do human beings move, in so far as they form, by interaction, groups, and in so far as they are determined by this existence in groups?

Although the primary motivation for this construction of the object of cognition of pure sociology is epistemological, Simmel is, of course, aware that a living science could develop only around significant problems. He considers, however, the systematic study of the pure forms of society as of fundamental importance. In a critical comment on historical materialism he suggests that the "real substance of the historical process" might be found in the change of sociological forms, as such, with the economic system being merely one of several "superstructures" conditioned by the basic interrelations of human beings.

While Simmel limits the field of sociology proper in this way, he does not want to see sociology restricted to the organized and "permanent" interrelations only. Besides the state, the family, the guilds and classes, and other "permanent" associations, there exists an indefinite variety of seemingly less important forms of relations and types of interaction which "by filling in the spaces between those, so to speak, official formations bring really into existence the society that we know."

Simmel's new concept of pure sociology is also directed against the identification, quite common at his time, of sociology with philosophy of history. In contrast to the latter, which always involves metaphysical, aesthetic, or religious interpretations of history, sociology "restricts itself entirely to the realm of phenomena and their immediate psychological explanation." On the other hand, he thought that sociology, by separating out the phenomena of socialization, might lead to the discovery of "historical laws" within one special field, whereas the nonspecialized historical studies had failed to reveal such laws for the historical processes as a whole. Two other concepts of sociology have to be distinguished from this concept of pure sociology:

1. In so far as economic, political, or other cultural phenomena and historical processes can be studied as phenomena of group life, as results of interaction between individuals, that is, under application of the sociological *method,* such studies might be labeled "sociology," though in a vague and inaccurate sense. However, by way of abstraction, a complex of problems can be lifted from such studies which Simmel considers as sociological in a rather specific sense. These problems are all related to the elaboration of those *general* characteristics of the realities of life which result from the fact that life occurs within the framework of social groups. The attempt to discern a general, socially conditioned "law" of historical evolution, such as Tönnies', Durkheim's or Comte's, would belong here. And so would the inquiry into the conditions of the power and value of groups and of collective action, as contrasted to power and value of individuals and their action. Simmel refers to these problems as "general sociology."

2. Any empirical science is framed by two philosophical disciplines: its epistemology and its metaphysics. Sociology, in so far as it deals with fundamental categories of social life, serves as an epistemological foundation for the special social sciences. On the other hand, there are other questions which go beyond the scope of these necessarily fragmentary special sciences. All those questions of the significance and meaning of economic, political, etc., phenomena and processes and the final question of whether the meaning and purpose of human existence are embodied in the individual or in the association—these are questions of interpretation, which cannot be solved by empirical studies. Nor is the discussion of such questions independent of personal value-judgments. Simmel suggests that this discipline be called "philosophical sociology." His main work, however, is devoted to "pure sociology."

When Simmel in his *Grundfragen* wanted to exemplify his idea of pure sociology, he included a paper originally read at the first congress of the German Sociological Society in 1910, entitled **"The Sociology of Social Entertainment."** It may, therefore, be summarized here for the same purpose, namely, that of conveying an idea of Simmel's approach and procedure and the kind of insights at which he arrives.

"Social gatherings" or sociables—or *Geselligkeit*—are a manifestation of the social urge as such. Since such social gatherings, in their true form, are not motivated by any special concrete purpose, as are all other types of associations, they represent, in a playful way, the essence of all social life. Their relation to the concreteness of society resembles the relation existing between a work of art and reality.

The relations of the individuals in social gatherings are regulated by a peculiarly ambiguous principle of a quasi-ethical nature: on the one hand, everything referring to, or reminiscent of, the roles played by the participants in their working-day life (e.g., their rank and occupation) has to be ignored; on the other hand, the most intimate and personal qualities of the individuals are also barred from entering into the relations. Every participant will use restraint in expression of his personality and of his impulses and will avoid engaging in too personal and intimate psychic relations. The participants come together "merely as human beings," and yet they refrain from letting the whole of their personality enter into the interaction process. This polarity of the behavior pattern is the essence of "tact." Furthermore, social gatherings are the artistic stylization or play-form of real society: sociable "games" and other forms of entertainment imitate societal processes of competition, conflict, and co-operation. "Flirting" is the play-form of erotics, and "conversation" becomes an end in itself, whereas, in "real society," talking serves the purpose of conveying certain "contents"—here, in social gatherings, one talks for entertainment; and, while the conversation is the better, the more interesting and significant its subject, the subject matter does not constitute its purpose. It can, therefore, be changed quickly and will never be taken seriously. Finally, social entertainment also symbolizes the ethical forces of society. The integration of the individual into the social whole, on the one side, and the enrichment of the individual by the pleasure, prestige, and other compensations received, which is the very essence of the ethical function of society, on the other side, are also found in *Geselligkeit*—in abstract form, free from all concrete ends or purposes.

However, "all *Geselligkeit* is merely a *symbol* of life, as it is reflected in the flow of an easygoing happiness-bestowing game or play, and yet it is a symbol of *life;* the picture of life is modified only as far as the distance requires, just like the most subjective and phantastic art, that renounces all copying of reality, is still nourished by a profound and faithful relation to reality—otherwise, its effect will be empty and insincere. Thus, if conviviality severs all ties connecting it with the realities of life, it changes from a play to a vain playing with meaningless forms." This phenomenon of decadence can be observed in the autumn of the *ancien régime* and similar periods.

Social entertainment is, in its true form, a stylization of society; it is a game in which one behaves "as if " everybody was everybody else's equal and friendly companion. This is no more a deception than art and play, with their deviations from reality, can be considered lies. Only when such gatherings become mere means for the promotion of aims of other than a mere sociable quality or for the concealment of such purposes does the element of lie and deception enter and the true meaning of the forms of polite sociability become corrupted. Simmel concludes:

> These forms of entertainment would not mean relief and pleasant relaxation from the ever-present burdens of life for so many serious peo-

ple, if they were merely devices of escape, merely a momentary avoidance of life's seriousness. This may often be actually the case, but the liberation and relief which are enjoyed precisely by the more serious personalities is due to the fact that the being together and the interaction through which life in all its gravity is realized can here be enjoyed in the form of an artful play—in sublimation and dilution . . . .

III. THE LEADING CONTRIBUTIONS OF SIMMEL TO SOCIOLOGICAL THEORY

A. THE NATURE OF SOCIETY

Society is, for Simmel, essentially psychic interaction between human beings both as individuals and as group members. Society is really not a substance but a process, a happening (*Geschehen*), or "something functional," something that human beings do and experience. One should perhaps, avoid the term "society" and, instead, use the term "association" to denote the true nature of social reality. However, not all psychic interaction constitutes a process of association, e.g., not the mere exchange of glances between two individuals who pass each other on the street. Such are "border phenomena," which, by repetition and intensification, may assume the character of social processes. The criterion seems to be that in association processes the individuals become "linked together" by "mutual influence and determination." One will, therefore, have to assume that between a mere being together and a perfect association there is a continuous range of more or less intensive mutual influencing. Even the large, interindividual groups (organizations), with which the idea of society is usually identified, are to Simmel "nothing but solidifications of direct interactions between individuals." However, social relations, in the perfect sense, are not only psychic but *moral* relations.

This involves the following two main principles: (1) In the case of any kind of interaction in which one party loses all human significance for the other, any relationship in which one party considers the other merely as a means for an end which is not related to this other party, or where an attitude of complete indifference of the one party to the other is existent, such relations are not *social* relations at all, in the strict sense of the term. No association exists in such cases, just as it does not exist between the carpenter and his bench. (2) "Society can be regarded as a system of relations of morally, legally, conventionally, and in many other ways, entitled and obliged beings," or association involves reciprocity of rights and duties.

This principle is of consequence in the analysis of relations of power, domination, and authority. To speak of "compulsion" in social relations is usually incorrect, since such interaction involves in most cases a measure of voluntary decision and action on the part of the "compelled" individuals.

In the ***Philosophy of Money,*** Simmel points out that even the modern state can seldom really compel citizens, it can merely induce them into certain actions because of fear of punishment. Only in matters of taxation can the state use direct compulsion, in so far as monetary wealth can be seized by force. Simmel elaborated this idea again in **"Su-**

perordination and Subordination" and pointed out that this is one reason why despotic regimes tend to favor the substitution of money taxes for contributions in kind or in services. Consequently, any kind of domination is possible only in so far as and as long as a minimum of consent is existent among the dominated—even if such consent merely takes the form of avoidance of the greater evil of disobedience.

It should also be noted that this concept of social interaction excluded the man-object relations, as such, from the realm of sociology; they constitute objects of sociology only in so far as they involve relations between persons.

The same functionalistic approach, which dissolves all social phenomena into complexes of relationships, is apparent in the treatment of social types likes "the stranger," or "the poor."

From Simmel's point of view, processes that seem to cause dissociation are as important in the life of groups as are the associating processes. There are no completely harmonious groups; and, if such a group could be found, it would not show any life. A certain amount of conflict is, for example, an organic element in marriage relations. The attitude of opposition is often the only means by which antagonistic individuals can tolerate being together in the same association. Of course, conflict relations cannot, by themselves, result in social forms but only in connection with associating forces—both together constitute the concrete living unity of a group. However, the function and effect of conflict vary with the structure of the relationships, and it requires a casuistic analysis to understand these variations. Opposition, competition, jealousy, envy—all such conflict phenomena vary with the basis and degree of likeness and integration in the groups.

There exists a definite correlation between the structure of any social group and the amount of antagonisms permissible among its members. Here, as in many cases, Simmel shows the ambiguous nature of social constellations: "The same centripetal structure of the group makes it either more resistant against dangers arising from antagonism among its members or weakens its ability to resist— depending upon the additional conditions." Among the large groups, those that are highly organized will stand a greater degree of friction and partition than the more mechanical conglomerations. However, in so far as conflicts, in societies of the less elaborately organized type, can more easily be localized, the group as a whole will be less sensitive. On the whole, the larger group will have more reserves of uniting energies. The modern state, for example, can tolerate the strife of political parties and can even utilize these antagonisms for its very equilibrium and development, while the Greek city-states were destroyed, torn to pieces by the internal party struggles.

The same principle can be observed in the effect of intergroup conflict on the solidarity of the conflicting groups; it may compel factions to unite, or it may lead to a complete secession of minorities already discontented with the course of action pursued by the majority. Simmel seems to have been deeply impressed by this ambiguity of social situations, which is one reason why accurate prediction of social events is so difficult. He refers to it on many occasions.

B. THE STRUCTURE OF SOCIETY AND THE PROBLEMS OF SOCIAL INTERACTION

In spite of Simmel's functional concept of society, the notion of "form" is largely identical with what may be more properly called "structure." His excellent study of the determination of the character groups by the number of members shows this very clearly. Among the structural problems discussed by Simmel, that of superordination and subordination deserves special consideration because of the basic importance of the phenomenon.

Three main types of domination and authority are distinguished: (1) domination by a single person, (2) domination by a group of several persons, and (3) subordination to an impersonal objective principle. The value of the treatment lies, however, not in this classification but in the execution of a minute analysis of specific situations under each of these main types.

Simmel assumes that an inverse relation exists between the extent to which each individual enters into the group with his personality and the extent to which a single ruler can dominate the group modified by the size and homogeneity of the group. While an absolutely rigid authoritarian rule is intolerable in a family group in which every member participates with almost his entire personality, it becomes possible and tolerable in a very large group into which every individual enters only with a small "quantum" of his "personality."

Rule by a body of several persons, while it can be as "absolute" and as "hard" as monocracy, is likely to be more objective and impersonal.

One of the main cases of subordination to an objective principle is the so-called "rule of law"; the others are those forms of authority which are derived from the position of the ruling person in a kinship or household group (patriarchate, matriarchate, patrimonial rule, etc.).

Simmel assumes that the development of subordination proceeds from personal rule to impersonal authority: as in the intellectual field the trend is from subordination under society (i.e., the authority of prevailing opinion) to subordination under objective (scientific) truth. Thus in the political field the ruler himself is finally subordinated to the objective principle of a social order by which his own will is bound.

This evolutionary trend can be traced in the family, in the state, and also in the economic system. In the relations between employer and employees the same evolution occurs to the extent that both parties become subordinated to the objective principle of contract, especially if the contract is based on a collective agreement between an employers' association and a labor union.

Simmel, although he is aware of the possible advantages for the subordinated individuals of the personal elements in authority, thinks that, in general, depersonalization of authority relations makes subordination more tolerable and less humiliating. In connection with this idea he offers some observations on the alternation of superordination and subordination by limitation of terms of office and other devices, which should be interesting to the student of democratic institutions.

Simmel then discusses the selection of the best-fitted individuals for positions of authority. He points out that a perfect correspondence of personal qualifications and social position is, in principle, impossible because of the always existing surplus of qualified individuals. The development of a bureaucracy with elaborate specialization of positions and the detailing of functions of authority to experts tend to minimize the required personality standards for most positions of authority. On the other hand, the highest offices in the modern states would require extraordinary personal qualifications if the officeholder were chosen strictly on account of his relative personal ability, as compared with those of other minor functionaries. The difficulty arising from the scarcity of such highly qualified individuals is often mitigated by the adaptability of men to new and larger tasks; in other cases the device of conveying an objective dignity of office, which is not based on personal qualification, is resorted to.

Since the questions "What contributes to the integration or disintegration of groups?" and "What keeps groups together over a long period of time?" may be considered as the central theme in all society, Simmel's discussion of the *self-preservation of groups* may be regarded as a testing ground of his contributions to theoretical sociology. Simmel refers here to those groupings which ordinarily last much longer than the life-span of their individual members and therefore assume, from the point of view of the individual, a relative permanence of existence.

The first problem which arises is that of the continued identity of the group, in spite of change in its membership composition. The continuity of the group as an identical unit is effected, in the first place, by the persistence of the locality or territory in which it exists, in so far as in many—though not in all—groups the sentiments and intellectual contents are definitely related to a certain special unit, to the domestic "soil" or the "fatherland."

In this connection Simmel presents a most important principle, that "the sociological characters of relationships otherwise perfectly alike, will be significantly differentiated on account of the notions of their different duration that are effective in them."

The second condition of group persistence is the physiological connection of the generations and the web of kinship relations in general. The connection of the generations is of such great importance for the preservation of the larger groups, because the replacement of one generation by the next does not occur all at once, but step by step, so that at any moment those who have already belonged to the group for some time will always be in the overwhelming majority. This permits the conservation and transmission of the objective culture which has been developed and is characteristic of the group.

The same process of gradual replacement of membership occurs in other organized groups, even where no biological relation exists between the generations, e.g., in the Roman Catholic clergy. The gradualness of the change in membership composition serves to preserve the identity of the group, even where, after a long period, the entire culture of the group has changed.

Sometimes a group, originally not based on kinship, will resort to closing its ranks against persons not related to the present members in order to preserve its existence, e.g., the guilds in their late stages or the Russian clergy, who, by contrast to the Roman Catholic clergy, developed into an inbred caste.

Simmel points out that the transmission of the objective spirit of a group through "ordination" and co-optation is superior to the system of heredity of social positions. Gradualness and slowness in the turnover of membership is, thus, a condition of the immortality of groups. Therefore, it is necessary to provide special precautions in such groups whose existence is essentially dependent on the life of a single leading or ruling individual. The main device used in such cases is the objectification of the ruler's position, that is, the development of the idea that the individual ruler is merely the personification of a supra-personal spirit or principle attached to the "office," together with the hereditariness of the ruler's position.

Most essential, however, for the continuity of any group is organization. All associations exist "originally" in immediate interaction between individuals, in their roles as group members through organization; the functions which affect the unity of the group are transferred to officials or functionaries; the direct interaction between members is replaced by interaction between members and these organs. The interrelation of individuals, which, in nonorganized groups, is purely functional, acquires through organization a separate objective existence. Originally merely interaction, the group is now represented by a particular structure.

In addition, there are the well-known technical reasons which make an organized group more resistant to dangers from without or within than an unorganized group. On the whole, this discussion may be taken as a strong plea in favor of the rational forms of association. Nevertheless, Simmel makes the interesting remark that a group which in a crisis can fall back on the unorganized interaction of the rank and file of its members has a better chance to survive than a group that cannot dispose of the functions of specialized organs or offices.

This leads to the further observation that, in some cases, a variability of structure is desirable for the preservation of the group, as evidenced by the history of the Jews. This, however, presupposes a high degree of homogeneity. In groups consisting of heterogeneous elements in latent or open conflict, greater stability of structure and conservatism with respect to changes in institutions and regulations are advisable, for in such situations any change is likely to arouse opposition in some quarters.

It is, therefore, understandable that ruling groups which are on the defensive avoid progressive changes; if they agree to reforms, they do so not because they want the change but because they want, by minor concessions, to preserve their own essential traits—a policy especially noticeable in decaying aristocracies.

Conservatism is, however, also characteristic of groups that are determined in their structure not by a dominating minority but by the broadest social stratum. This is most conspicuously the case in agrarian societies composed of freeholders. The farmer wants security more than change. Where, however, the urban middle class determines the structure, there will be change, for the continuity of such society depends on the chances for individuals to rise to higher social positions. Thus the form or structure of societies is determined by the nature of the social interests. Again, the ambiguity of social situations is apparent—stability and elasticity can both contribute to the chances of group preservation, depending on several other variables, both of structural and of substantial nature.

While the main discussion is kept within the framework of structure analysis, the psychic factors involved are dealt with in a long note on loyalty and gratitude. The structural phenomenon of group persistence after disappearance of the original purposes or motivations is one of the essential principles of sociology. Loyalty is that psychic disposition which produces this phenomenon. It is obvious that "without this phenomenon of loyalty society could not in the actually observed way exist over any length of time."

Gratitude is another essential psychic factor, since all social interaction rests on the scheme of gift-receiving and equivalent giving. The latter can be obtained by compulsion in only certain cases. Gratitude, therefore, is an indispensable complementary element in the maintenance of social interaction.

Every individual belongs as a social being to a variety of social circles which are partly overlapping and, from a different point of view, can be thought of as concentrically arranged. The narrower the circle, the less the individuality for the individual; the circle itself, however, will be something individual, sharply distinct from other circles. If the circle within which one acts expands, the margin for individuality development increases, but the circle itself, as a social whole, will show less individuality.

Simmel explains that this theorem is not meant as a sociological law but merely as an attempt to summarize by a "phenomenological formula," without any reference to causality, the uniform effects of what may be very heterogeneous "causes" in each case. If he offers a psychological explanation, he does so merely as a "heuristic principle."

It seems as though the individual was dominated by a dual urge: to differentiate himself from the social circle to which he belongs and at the same time to differentiate himself as a member of this circle from those who do not belong to it. The more the urge for differentiation from the fellow group members is satisfied, the less will the group itself be differentiated.

Certain kinds of groups assume under this aspect an intermediate position. It seems that the most unreserved emotional attachment is directed only to the most narrow and to the largest circles, not to the intermediate ones. One is willing to sacrifice one's self for one's country and for one's family, but not for the township in which one lives. While this is primarily a static principle, it lends itself obviously to application with regard to social evolution.

C. THE SOCIAL IMPLICATIONS OF A MONEY ECONOMY

Although Simmel's *Soziologie* is chiefly concerned with logicosystematical inquiry into structure elements of society in general, it also contains rather definite ideas on the main social changes in contemporary Western society. Moreover, the *Philosophy of Money* represents in the second, synthetic part, in a more organized form, his ideas on this matter. Simmel accepts here the basic notions of historical materialism or, as he suggests it should be called, "historical sensualism." His position is, however, that this theory has to be modified, in so far as the concrete economic forms are, in their turn, conditioned by profounder evaluations and by psychological, as well as metaphysical, "currents," which, again, are conditioned by profounder economic factors and so on. The main changes resulting from money as an all-pervading institution in modern society can be summarized as follows:

1. An increase of freedom of the partners in any kind of social relations: landlord and peasant, employer and employee. When contractual social relations become possible on a basis of compensation in money rather than in services and kind, they can become depersonalized, in the sense that every moral consideration or interaction process extraneous to the specific kind of relation tends to be eliminated. This gives a freer choice of action to all persons concerned, especially so far as the choice of partners is concerned and also with regard to the place of residence of each partner. There can be no doubt that the general tendency is to make man, on the one side, dependent on the services of more and more people, but, on the other hand, to make him more and more independent of the serving personalities as such.

2. The ensuing separation of objects possessed from the person of the owner permits combinations of ownership between otherwise unrelated individuals. The institution of money makes it possible for the individual to associate himself with others for a common purpose, merely by contributing money, without getting involved and bound with his entire personality—as was characteristic of the medieval corporation.

3. This depersonalization of social relations makes possible associations for limited purposes of individuals not personally attached to one another: the purely purposive voluntary association.

Consequently, the entire *style of life* is changed under the impact of money as one of the main economic institutions. The trend toward rationalistic attitudes is increased through the development, alleviated by money use, of the habit of calculation—a habit that is spreading into all spheres of life. Even time assumes a money value in Western society with the full unfolding of money economy—an idea which, later on, was elaborated by Oswald Spengler. The trend of social change is thus toward greater rationalization and depersonalization of all human relations, that is, toward a form of society in which the individuals, highly specialized in their social functions (divisions of labor), as personally free atoms tend to be related merely by purposive relations in which, again, the kind of interrelation effected by combinations of monetary wealth or by monetary compensation of services tend to become prevalent.

IV. CRITICISM AND EVALUATION

It is clear from these examples that Simmel actually intended more than a mere systematization of social forms. He made it clear enough that the conceptual distinction between "form" and "content" of society was "really nothing but an analogy," that both are "in reality inseparable elements of any social existence and process." In his sociological papers he refers repeatedly to the "meaning" of social "forms." The two questions—"What do the individuals mean by behaving in a certain way?" and "What is the objective meaning of the described action patterns in their lives?"—are constantly suggested, if not expressly put, to the reader.

As already pointed out, the search for the objective meaning leads beyond sociology, in the strict sense, into metaphysical interpretation. The inquiry into the subjective meaning requires the application of psychological knowledge and methods; yet, in its final intention, it does not aim at the regularities (laws) of psychic processes in the individual but at the causal understanding of the social interaction patterns by which individuals are united into groups.

The objects of sociology are psychic processes which can be conceived by psychological categories. These are indispensable for the description of the facts, but they do not enter into the sociological intention which aims at the association process as such—like the intention of a drama, which, although it can be understood only psychologically, is not directed at psychological insights but at those syntheses which the psychic processes form under the points of view of the tragic or of style or symbols of life.

The problems of social psychology are, according to Simmel, merely special problems of individual psychology. Therefore, these arguments also apply to the objection that Simmel's sociology is not clearly distinguished from social psychology.

The nonpsychological character of Simmel's pure sociology can be exemplified by the principle of correlation between individuality and the expansion of the social circle. The principle, as such, does not contain any psychological theorem; it merely states an observable relationship between two elements of group structure.

Here, however, one weakness of Simmel's approach is revealed. Some of the phenomena could be made intelligible, even as evidence of structural principles, only by careful inquiry into psychic attitudes and processes. Simmel, instead, merely applies a rather general psychological hypothesis as "heuristic principle." The result is often mere conjecture rather than a real insight and secure knowledge. Furthermore, one can scarcely escape the impression that Simmel views society as an interplay of structural factors, in which the human beings appear as passive objects rather than as live and willing actors. Frequently, he refers to the inherent regularities of form principles as if these were the real moving forces in social life. Nowhere do we find a systematic analysis of the will-currents, the antagonisms and harmonies of interest and will which determine the course of individual and collective action and on which the very existence of associations depends.

However, the precise determination of the nature of social forms and the skilful application of the idea in Simmel's essays have opened a new angle of perception—a new outlook on social phenomena—which proves very fruitful in the analysis of concrete social situations—if applied with the necessary discretion. Simmel's procedure of staking off a field of investigation by abstracting a certain aspect (the "form" of social interaction) from the chaos of experienced reality, is not unique, not peculiar to sociology; rather, it is the principle on which *all* specialization of the actual sciences has developed. Simmel applied this principle to a field (sociology) in which, hitherto, the notion had prevailed that its specific object of cognition was not a new abstraction but, rather, a synthesis of the insights into social life gained by the existing specialized social sciences.

Among the critical objections to this idea of pure sociology, those offered by Hans Freyer deserve special attention because they raise a question of fundamental importance. Freyer points out that the conception of pure sociology as a sort of geometry of social phenomena may prove fatal, since it leads sociological thought off on a wrong track; phenomena that ought to be conceived as historical processes, imbedded in the context of the more or less unique situation in the flow of time, become fixed as static structures. Simmel, according to Freyer's criticism, tried to establish sociology as a *Logos-Wissenschaft,* which Freyer believes to be foreign to the very nature of its subject. Freyer, however, emphasizes the fact that, in spite of this fundamental error, Simmel's essays contain "excellent sociology," because, with a fine scientific tact, Simmel applied his approach only to such subjects as lend themselves to this kind of treatment, since they are, indeed, "timeless."

The "formal," or, as one might better say, the "structural" or morphological approach, applied even to the apparently most fluid social unions or groupings, is so widely different from the layman's point of view that it becomes immensely stimulating and challenging. The student who is habitually inclined to think in compartments or fixed "contentional" categories is suddenly forced to draw comparisons between phenomena that seem to be distant in time or space and unrelated in quality, focusing his attention on the strictly social, that is, interactional, aspects. This, in itself, would be valuable in a propaedeutical sense. In addition, this approach is carried out with a meticulous casuistry in analysis. Never is Simmel content with general notions of social types; always he insists on defining the specific situations in which the phenomenon arises; always he forms, from general concepts, specific type concepts of well-defined "cases" of the general phenomenon studied. In this respect, he is perhaps surpassed among his contemporaries only by Max Weber. Among the generation of his followers, Max Graf zu Solms and Leopold von Wiese have carried on this work of classification of forms of social interaction.

While this method would finally result in a fruitless play of the mind—and, in fact, this danger zone is often touched in Simmel's essays—Simmel succeeds in making it a meaningful endeavor. This is accomplished by the introduction, into the "form" analysis, of psychological interpretations, often of a very subtle character. Spykman points out that Simmel agreed that pure sociology alone cannot convey a full understanding of society, that it needs supplementing by psychological and "factual" inquiries. As an illustration we may note his observation that conflicts between individuals intimately related by kinship or other close personal ties tend to be more bitter than those between comparatively strange and loosely related individuals. This is in itself a rather common-sense observation. The real value of Simmel's analysis lies in the fine distinctions between various typical constellations and in the sociopsychological explanations or interpretations. The same manifestations of conflict may be due to a wide variation of motivations and may, therefore, be of quite different meaning for the life of the social groups in which they occur. Furthermore, violent conflicts, such as occur in intimate relations (e.g., in marriage), just because of a profound community of values among the partners, without endangering the relation as such, would definitely destroy any relation of less intimate character. Incidentally, these subtle differentiations of configurations (or "forms") and motivations in social relations suggest the necessity of careful theoretical preparation and utmost caution in any quantitative inquiry into social attitudes and processes.

Simmel's interpretation of the trends of social change in contemporary Western society can hardly be said to be original. It is essentially a synthesis of the ideas developed previously by Marx, Tönnies, Durkheim, and others.

On the whole, his sociological interpretations, although extremely intelligent and subtle, do not betray a great deal of firsthand experience and contact with the great social movements and important societal events of his time. This may partly explain the lack of new original insights into the great social questions of the period.

It seems that Simmel's interest in sociology originated not from an immediate concern with the social problems of contemporary society but rather from a philosophic endeavor to clarify its position in a system of sciences. Obviously, Simmel's occupation with problems of ethics and morals (*Moralphilosophie*) also led him into a discussion of norms and values in their relation to social life.

These reservations have to be made in order to arrive at a fair appreciation of Simmel's work. Its real and lasting value lies not so much in the new knowledge of society it conveys as in the contribution to the classification of the purpose and procedure of sociology.

Even his most severe critics acknowledge the significance of Simmel's idea of sociology as a systematic analysis of social forms. "The influence of Simmel's concepts of 'social form' is present in contemporary sociology, even where the idea of Pure Sociology in Simmel's sense is rejected." It is Simmel's method and procedure of analysis rather than the content of his findings which constitute his unique and lasting contribution to the advancement of sociology. Thus we are confronted with the paradox that the philosopher who started out to redefine the subject matter of sociology gained his place among sociologists rather because of his methodological ideas.

K. Peter Etzkorn   (essay date 1964)

SOURCE: "Georg Simmel and the Sociology of Music," in *Social Forces,* Vol. 43, No. 1, October, 1964, pp. 101-7.

[*In the following essay, Etzkorn looks at Simmel's first published study as it relates to the modern sociological study of music.*]

Articles in sociological journals and books contain many references to the manifold aspects of Georg Simmel's work. Indeed the recent centenary of his birth (1858) occasioned several reappraisals of his various contributions to sociology in the light of contemporary scholarship. One significant aspect of his work, though, has to our knowledge been neglected. It is of sufficient merit to be brought to the attention of contemporary scholars, especially since there seems to be a growing interest in the sociology of artistic life. This is Simmel's extensive early work in what today might be called the sociology of music or ethnomusicology.

In his later life Simmel's discourse on artistic and aesthetic subjects tends to pursue more philosophical interests while it nevertheless still contains passages that reveal his sociological interests. However, more directly sociological and relevant to the traditional concerns of the social sciences is his 1882 paper **"Psychologische und Ethnologische Studien über Musik"** which he published in Lazarus and Steinthal's *Zeitschrift für Völkerpsychologie.* This study was published three years prior to the well known Alexander Ellis paper "On the Musical Scales of Various Nations," which is frequently considered the earliest important landmark in the history of ethnomusicology. Ellis' paper is concerned with the analysis of structural aspects of the tonal materials of different culture areas and with developing devices for their description and measurement. In many ways Ellis' approach is analogous to traditional anthropological concerns with the study of culture traits.

It may be idle to speculate why Simmel's study apparently did not arouse comparable attention in his own day and why it should have fallen into such neglect that even his professional colleague and personal acquaintance Max Weber ignores it in the fragment of his study of the rational bases of tonal systems. Weber's preoccupation with tonal systems as the building material of music is indicative of the trend of scholarship in this field which followed Ellis' model. Perhaps Simmel's reluctant attitude towards behavioristic psychology averted the early German ethnomusicologists from taking serious issue with his work since their professional affiliation and training was largely in this area. Perhaps these scholars felt more at ease with Ellis' "Cent System" for the objective measuring of tone intervals than with Simmel's insistence that there was an important relationship between ethnic folk music and the psychology of the social group practicing it. In this context one may be reminded that it also took several generations of sociologists before the French conception of *conscience collective* entered into the working vocabulary of British social-anthropology and American sociology. And yet it is interesting to note that the only reference to Simmel's study which we found in English appeared in 1909 in W. I. Thomas, *Source Book for Social Origins.*

In this paper we wish to address ourselves more specifically to some of our reasons for resuscitating Simmel's study rather than to paying general homage to one of the fathers of the sociological discipline. This decision does not imply that there would be no legitimate grounds for, say, searching for a sociological explanation of the neglect of this aspect of Simmel's work by sociologists, especially since several outstanding scholars later arrived independently at related and even similar positions. Nor would it be less significant to examine the variety of methodological implications that are raised by Simmel's differing epistemological positions in the treatment of the arts during the course of his scholarly life. Here, however, we wish to restrict ourselves to an exploration of this early study of Simmel in which he treats music as an aspect of social relationships by which individuals communicate among one another and which in turn, maintain, structure and restructure these relations.

In his later analytical distinctions between the various modes of sociological inquiry and related Kantian arguments, he relegated music to the sphere of *Kultur. Kultur* was to be treated aesthetically and philosophically. The early Simmel in general, therefore, might perhaps be most relevant to modern sociological appraisals of art and music. In order to make the content of the Simmel paper more accessible to contemporary readers, we first wish to provide an extensive summary of Simmel's study before we relate it to aspects of his later writings and point to its present relevance.

SIMMEL ON MUSIC

In Simmel's paper we have an example of truly 19th century scholarship. Simmel combines classical erudition (and ample quotes in Latin and Greek) with philosophical focus and the search for corroborating evidence in collections of ethnographic museums and the journals of world travellers. He opens his paper with a critical analysis of Darwin's theory of the origin of music. According to Darwin the human species developed vocal music before developing rhythm and speech. Herbert Spencer had held a related view that "all the leading vocal phenomena . . . have a physiological basis . . . " and that "the expressiveness of the various modifications of voice is . . . therefore innate."

While Simmel does not deny that vocal phenomena have physiological bases—which would be untenable from any scientific point of view—he proceeds to refute the claim of the genetic priority of musical vocal behavior over language behavior. In the course of this stimulating argument, Simmel develops his conception of music which is of interest here. He views music as an acoustic medium of communication which conveys feelings of the performer. "Just as language is related to concrete thought so is music related to feelings which are somewhat less precise. The

first [language] creates the second [thought], since the second created the first." Accepting the psychologist Steinthal's thesis—according to which the first manifestation of Man is connected with processes of thought and "human thought is derived from speech"—Simmel reasons that language could not have developed out of vocal music.

For empirical support of this argument Simmel turns to evidence contained in a number of ethnographic sources. In this fashion he presents data from a sample of societies which includes people of Rio de Janeiro, the Caribbean, the Maori, Brasilians, Australians, Caucasian soldiers, "the Tehueltschen," and classical antiquity. In addition to these data gleaned from published sources, he also reports his own experiences with a family in Berlin whose children could not sing the melodies of folksongs without also singing their words. Simmel seems to be convinced by this combined evidence that vocal music came chronologically after the development of speech in the history of communication. Thus the role of music is only to provide special emphases to existing linguistic communication patterns rather than to form the very origin of human communication.

Having established this point, he proceeds to supply further ethnographic illustrations. From this evidence he then concludes that occasions for the employment of musical emphases on speech communication occur whenever, in the view of the respective social groups, some of the human emotions are not adequately represented by speech. Anger, happiness, and joy are such occasions which are characterized in primitive and civilized discourse by variations in the voice pitch and modulations of the speech melody. Von Humboldt is quoted as having shown that the expression of sexual desire in the courting situation also leads to pitch variations in speech patterns. Another example of human emotions which find expression in music is the complex of mystic-religious phenomena.

Simmel's refutation of Darwin's hypothesis could be treated as an example of an elementary functional approach to the sociology of music. His search for the origins of music proceeds from relatively contemporary social consequences of music to the hypothetical reconstruction of its very origin. This is the identical process by which 19th century ethnography was shown to illustrate "incipient functionalism" by Evans-Pritchard. For Simmel, the definition of *vocal music* is "speech which is exaggerated by rhythm and modulation." Thus, rhythmic patterns have to be superimposed on the variation of pitch, which is the outgrowth of emotional vocal expression, before modulated speech becomes vocal music.

The structure of Simmel's argument for explaining the origin of *instrumental music* is similar. From his subsequent analysis of additional ethnological reports he infers that instrumental music is generally a further elaboration of the already practiced performance of vocal music. The use of ideophones seems to be predominantly associated with dance activities or other functions which are rhythmically patterned, such as tribal preparations for warfare. His designation of European military music as *Lärm und Blas-*

musik may suggest that he conceives of military activities as primitive, especially since he stresses that wind instruments are more characteristic of primitive society than string instruments. Instrumental music thus represents to Simmel a more elaborated mode of expressing human emotions than can be gained through vocal music alone.

Once instrumental music has been developed in the history of mankind, it can be divorced from its accompanying function for vocal music and come to stand by itself. To Simmel, vocal music expresses referential emotions in their natural state, while instrumental music can more easily approach objectivity—which is for Simmel "the ideal of art." In instrumental music "feelings do not disappear, . . . they still stimulate the production of music and are still stimulated by it." However, instrumental music and its performance are not the immediate expression of these emotions. Rather instrumental music turns out to be "an image of them which is reflected through the mirror of beauty."

Instrumental music, thus, is also shown to be related to the basic communicative function of vocal music. But it is much less direct in expressing human emotions. It is more of an imitation of the original emotions and is, therefore, not as constrained in the use of musical idioms and expressive musical symbolism as is vocal music. By being less precise in expression, instrumental music is more inclusive than vocal music. Music as an art form, according to Simmel's views in his early period, communicates feelings less precisely than vocal folkmusic. Nevertheless it creates "typical reactions which include fully the more individually specific responses which are produced by verbal communication."

MUSIC IN SIMMEL'S SOCIOLOGY

From this summary of the "forgotten" Simmel paper it may already become clear why it might be of relevance to the contemporary student of the relations between art and social structure. Simmel not only provides us with a suggestive explanation of the role of music in social life and an elementary (though theoretically based) taxonomy of types of music, but he also demonstrates that a proper sociological assessment of the social context of art requires both an understanding of the technical aspects of the musical art medium *and* an awareness of the social processes which surround it. His example suggests that it is important to study *how* the musical properties are acquired by social actors, how they become socially defined as something special and how this special status is related to the variety of special social adjustments which influence the social system and may in turn have repercussions on the musical mode of expressions. These are some of the concerns which are implied in the early Simmel, but are not as explicitly explored in his later sociological writing where he seems to be more concerned with the impact of already given art forms on selected forms of social interaction. In his *Grundfragen der Soziologie* (1917), for example, he treats art as having laws all of its own. "Fully established, art is wholly separated from life. It takes from it only what it can use, thus creating, as it were, a second time. . . . From the realities of life they [art and play] take only what they can adapt to their own nature, what

they can absorb in their autonomous existence." Even though he speaks here metaphorically, as if art by acting anthropomorphically could produce social consequences independently of human actors, he seems to employ this ambiguity in order to introduce philosophical and aesthetic ideals concerning what the ideal role of art should be. While I do not mean to suggest that one could not study sociologically the relations between some relatively autonomous properties in social life and those social action patterns which are typically influenced by them, the limitation to this approach on aesthetic (or philosophical) grounds would seem to be an unjustified truncation of other promising modes of scientific inquiry. By itself, such an approach would also tend to overlook the dynamic qualities of social life which demand that every aspect has to be given social significance anew—even though, of course, this process of continuous validation is seemingly automatic and ordinarily escapes our everyday attention. Nevertheless, J. S. Bach's music had to be composed first in its peculiar style and then had to acquire social significance in each succeeding generation of admirers of Bach. This is so even though his music represents the aesthetic perfection of the art of a period and serves as a model for the evaluation of other composers of the same period. While it is a legitimate sociological question to ask how Bach's music affects social groupings under varying circumstances, it is also a legitimate *and* fruitful approach to ask how certain social groupings today happen to appreciate Bach (and not Teleman) and what musically speaking, they come to appreciate *in* Bach and how these acquired musical insights affect other significant aspects, say, in the lives of Bach disciples. It is these latter types of questions which the early Simmel raises and which the later Simmel does not seem to entertain.

In the early Simmel analysis of music, all types of musical expressions are, as we have seen, examined in terms of their communication function in social life. A given piece of music may communicate both absolutistic and referentialistic meanings. While not ruling out the former, it is the latter meanings with which the early Simmel is principally concerned. These refer in some way to concepts, actions, and emotions of the extramusical world in which the composer and musicians (and their audiences) live. They would seem to be related to the socially mediated choice of the particular musical activity and its content. The later Simmel is more concerned with absolutistic meanings which are provided by the context of the musical composition itself. Frequently (if not exclusively) they concern formal relationships between musical elements which make up the structure of the compositions. Since music in general is defined as a vehicle for the communication of emotions and instrumental music as the vehicle for the communication of diffuse emotions, Simmel raises theoretical questions as to the basic structure of social communication.

Part of his argument is, we recall, that in instrumental music the communicative content is not as precise as in vocal music. Yet we know that the degree of communicative precision depends on a variety of social responses to the vehicle of communication. These responses, of course, are learned responses and subject to variations by changes in the learning situation. Musical themes, thus, may call forth specific emotional (or other) responses among properly prepared listeners. For example, composers of film music frequently capitalize on this phenomenon when they accompany love scenes with the sounds of soft violins. By employing systematically selected musical clichés, composers of film music have succeeded in preparing the audiences of moving pictures to expect certain happenings on the screen or to have an appropriate emotional set for the happenings. As long as the listener has learned how to convert the abstract musical tone sequences into anticipations of socially significant consequences, it is not necessary to employ Simmel's referentially more precise vocal music. Instrumental music will do the same if a sufficiently consensual group has learned to associate similar responses with appropriate musical stimuli.

Even though it might be desirable to discuss undeveloped and weak points in the Simmel paper and to comment at length on Simmel's questionable ethnographic evidence, this would not substantially contribute to what would seem to me to be the more essential contribution of the study to contemporary scholarship. That is, for him sound patterns per se are devoid of meaning unless they are perceived as conveying learned emotive content. While Simmel demonstrates that the learned emotive content and the form of expression may vary, he concludes from this examination of the descriptive materials that "apparently [the style of] music is characteristic for the character of a people." Variations in the appreciation of different musical styles might therefore be associated with social group differences. More specifically, Simmel stipulates that in order to become great art, music must embody national or social group characteristics. Only thereby will it have meaning for the members of the nation. He cautions, though, that this observation "is not to be construed to mean that they [the arts] have to be patriotic [in subject matter]. On the contrary, history shows that art could produce the most beautiful blossoms in politically most disorganized states—in analogy to flowers which grow on heaps of rubbish. What I mean is simply this, whatever great and well-formed talents an individual may bring into his life, living within his society will only transform him into what he is. It will impress his character on him. From it he will receive his goals and means. Precisely, the greater are his talents, the more will he accept from his national heritage." In order to achieve greatness, the artist has to work within an artistic tradition, parts of which he must accept *and* refine.

This train of reasoning will hardly sound revolutionary to the contemporary social scientist, even though it might have had such a flavor in the outgoing 19th century romantic era. Simmel's early conception of artistic greatness is thus based to a large extent on technical artistic dimensions, such as how an individual makes use of the artistic tools which are provided for him by his tradition. Moreover, it would seem to me that it may contain the beginnings of a theory of taste groups. In suggesting that the artist is great who refines the artistic style of his national heritage, Simmel opens the question as to (a) the social processes which differentiate between the access that individuals have to the sources of artistic traditions—e.g.,

Bach spent most of his life in Northern Germany while Händel (another North German) lived and worked in the major musical centers of the 18th century; (b) there are obvious differences in the processes of acquisition of the technical skills needed for the refining of musical traditions—e.g., Mozart's extensive and protected early studies vs. Beethoven's hardships in Bonn; and (c) there are differences in the conditions for the demonstration of acquired skills in various social circumstances—e.g., the captive audience of official court composers and the available facilities for musical performance vs. the contemporary freelance composer. What, in other words, are the social conditions that favor or tend to retard artistic greatness and the formation of taste?

The current practice of defining taste groups as acceptance groups has thus been anticipated by Simmel in his view that the artist works within the taste patterns of his artistic heritage. But Simmel did not confuse the issue of popularity with that of greatness of art (as is sometimes done today) since for him greatness in art is a matter which can be established and validated only through technical intra-artistic analysis. Success of an artist, on the other hand, may be the consequence of the size of his group of following. Russel Lynes "highbrows" would not necessarily be cultivating any greater art for Simmel than the "lowbrows." These groups would be examples of different consensual groups in which, perhaps, different meanings would be accorded to objectively identical artistic stimuli. Thus the Van Cliburn recording of the Tschaikowsky piano concerto might be played for different reasons by high and low-brows and correspondingly communicate different emotional meanings to these listeners. Nor would Simmel likely conclude from the contemporary increase in statistics of classical LP record sales that good music is becoming more widely appreciated and that the cultural level of the society is rising. Rather, in keeping with his argument, he would probably demand additional data on the social circumstances of the utilization of the records, the types of listening situations, the musical educational preparation of the listeners, the emotional impact of the music or, in short, the communicated musical meaning, before he would conclude that an increase in consumption corresponds with an increase in appreciation of classical music.

CONCLUSION

Simmel's foremost contribution to the sociology of music as contained in his early study consists, we would think, in having shown that empirical work in this area is possible and can have fruitful theoretical implications. He does not provide us with a systematic program of what the sociology of music ought to be concerned with. Thus he differs from contributors who make up the major proportion of the literature in this field which is noted for its scarcity of empirical work. Rather his focus on empirical problems and his search for empirical answers would seem to us to be an example worth emulating in the building of this branch of social science. Perhaps he might be criticized for not going far enough in his search for answers, since not having an explicit system (or explicit frame of reference) may have prevented him from asking systematic questions. To this it might be replied that there is no agreement likely to come about as to what would constitute the final boundary of asking questions or systematizing answers in science. It would seem to us to be eminently more in the interest of science to ask the kind of questions that can be answered in the light of the data and can produce new insights than to be overly concerned with the neatness of systems of analysis. While Simmel did not construct a systematic program for the sociology of music, his study makes it clear that he did not conceive of it as *Bindestrich Sociology* (special subfield) but saw it within the major sociological context of human communications and social relations.

In summing up, Simmel's early study on the ethnological and psychological foundations of music, in addition to providing stimulating suggestions for further research, touches on at least two major concerns of the contemporary sociologist dealing with artists and art. (1) His elementary taxonomy of types of music relates to the complex of questions concerning the social meaning which is represented in music. (2) His discussion of what I have here called "taste groups" relates to the general area of questions concerning the position and function of music in society. It contributes a clearer diagnosis of the relationships between different groups within the social structure and representative items of artistic production by suggesting the importance of studying the social relationship structures which are typically associated with the socialization of artists and audiences.

Everett C. Hughes (essay date 1965)

SOURCE: "A Note on Georg Simmel," in *Social Problems,* Vol. 13, No. 2, Fall, 1965, pp. 117-18.

[*In the following essay, Hughes credits Simmel with making the study of sociological phenomena accessible to a general readership.*]

Simmel was, in the original sense of the word, a dilettante, an *amateur passioné.* He appears to have written about human society, art, philosophy, religion and money because he took delight in doing so. It was characteristic of nineteenth century English that it should have given the term dilettante the pejorative connotation of smatterer, a person of shallow and passing interests. Simmel was by no means a dilettante in that sense, but neither was he devoted to any particular practical problem or reform of his day. He was committed to the study of society itself, rather than to any of its particular troubles.

Thus it is that Simmel is seldom referred to for his analysis of substantive aspects of society, such as the Protestant ethic, the relations among ethnic groups, and the like. As [R.E.] Park and [E.W.] Burgess note, Gumplowicz and Simmel saw interaction of forces as the basic concept in analysis of human society, as in all scientific analysis. Gumplowicz used the concept mainly in accounting for the general structure of society and the origin of the state. Simmel played his games of analysis of interaction on a great variety of substantive situations and problems, large and small; but it is always a game. He seems to be different from most other students of society of his time—and

ours—in somewhat the same way that the theoretical physicist is different from the laboratory man, or even the engineer. At the first meeting of the German Sociological Society in 1910, Max Weber proposed a program of study of two current phenomena—voluntary associations and the newspaper. Simmel gave a gala opening address on the apparently frivolous topic of the **"Sociology of Sociability,"** taking as one of his illustrations décolleté dress which has the double function of exciting men to playful mood while keeping them at a distance. Weber was speaking as secretary at a business session; Simmel was introducing sociology to the élite of intellectual Frankfurt. Each was perfectly cast.

Simmel took any social matter as material for his game. If he is talking of the effects of spatial dispersion as against concentration on the solidarity of a group, he picks minorities as a pertinent case. Morals, honor, and law are for him forms of social control to be distinguished in quite abstract terms, almost mathematical. He distinguishes the great universal (Catholic) church from the small sect not so much by the content of doctrine, as by the fact that the great church is slow to reject the sinner, equally slow to take him back; while the sect is quick to eject, and likewise quick to take back the back-slider. Simmel treats of many social phenomena in this way, covering the range of topics a very urbane and learned European of his time would discuss over wine and cigars. If there is a set of values implicit in his treatment of them, it is that of that same kind of man; but the values of a man both extraordinarily humane and extraordinarily detached, a complete liberal intellectual. I am always a bit astonished that he was not Viennese, for Vienna, where most people were of some minority or other, was the home of free-sweeping, detached but passionate intellectual play.

The title, **"The Poor,"** and the length of the chapter bearing it, might lead one to think that Simmel had for once departed from his usual way of playing the sociological game. Not so. This is no social survey, such as Charles Booth's, which describes in detail the condition of the poor and tries to determine the "poverty line." This is no effort, as of the American muckrakers of that period, to bring about reform by exposing the horrors of life in the slum. It is simply the longest and most thorough analysis Simmel made of a particular problem in his *Soziologie;* he undertakes it in his usual way. One doubts whether Simmel ever visited Alexanderplatz. Lewis Coser, however, shows us the uses to which Simmel's style of work can be put by a sociologist who joins delight in sociological analysis with concern for social action.

In the course of playing his game with The Poor, Simmel does—as one would expect—give us some important theoretical observations. Sociologists generally deal with deviation as departure from norms in but one direction. In fact, it is common for deviations in either direction to be disapproved of. A person—although Simmel does not say so in this connection—may work too much, be too good, or too modest. The saints—who practice the ordinary virtues in heroic degree—are often stoned before they are canonized. It is just such adding of another, unexpected dimension to analysis that makes Simmel so intriguing. I read Simmel not so much for what he may say about religion, law, or poverty—although that may be very rewarding—as for these ideas, these additional dimensions which make the study of all aspects of society one enterprise, both useful and intellectually delightful.

K. Peter Etzkorn　(essay date 1968)

SOURCE: "Georg Simmel: An Introduction," in *Georg Simmel: The Conflict in Modern Culture and Other Essays,* translated by K. Peter Etzkorn, Teachers College Press, 1968, pp. 1-8.

[*In the following essay, Etzkorn provides an overview of Simmel's work.*]

One test of the importance of ideas and contributions of eminent men is undoubtedly whether they are considered relevant by future generations. Georg Simmel's work, although it was produced over fifty years ago, is still considered of major relevance to sociological and philosophical inquiry. . . .

Simmel lived during a period of significant social and political change in Central Europe. The impact of technological developments made possible by the Industrial Revolution was increasingly changing the major modes of social life. Institutional structures were confronted with problems of adaptation. Frequent challenges were made to established modes of thought and novel ideas in response to social change. New and rapid modes of communication aided in the diffusion of ideas and made possible the emergence and sustenance of new forms of social life. To such topics much of Simmel's work is addressed and many of these topics have not lost their immediacy in spite of some substantive changes in technology and social life since then. We too are confronted with puzzles of urban growth, the "megalopolis," with technological change and political adaptation, and with the problem of the individual's integration into a largely impersonal society and the meaning of life, its values, and its cultivation and culture. Perhaps because of his having entered the discussion of these topics "earlier," before some of these issues became conventionally appropriated by emerging academic disciplines, he had the chance to develop an analytic attitude that in his hands promised to be highly productive. He could address himself to the issues of social life more directly than is possible within the restrictions of already established and frequently narrowly defined academic departments. Thus he fashioned his own sociological method for the study of social life in terms of what he conceived as the demands of the subject matter: the unending dialectic of human existence.

For Simmel, the continuity of the processes of life clashes necessarily with the acts of personal individuation, which are also the creative acts in which social institutions are established. These, in turn, gain a reality of their own which transcends their immediate *raison d'être*. Frequently in this process, what originally were considered as means come to be regarded as ends. In Simmel's dialectic, man is always in danger of being slain by those objects of his own creation which have lost their original human co-efficient. This process, however, always occurs for Simmel

within the framework of social relations regardless of specific historical periods. The dialectic is neither characteristic of capitalism, nor of socialism, nor of liberal democracy; it is much more. For Simmel, this dialectic between life and more-than-life represents the very nature of human existence, the very destiny of civilization, and thus it becomes the core of his scholarly inquiry. In his sociological studies, Simmel addresses himself most directly to the study of the forms of human interaction. Human interaction, in this instance, represents another expression of the overriding dialectic of life, because man and fellow man are simultaneously dependent and independent of one another. When studying forms of interaction, Simmel is interested in the patterning of relationships between man and man—especially in those interaction dimensions that transcend any individual's attributes. As Friedrich H. Tenbruck has observed, by studying forms of interaction Simmel wishes to ascertain the extent to which the range of individual human conduct is restrained in keeping with the individual's cognizance of his diversified relationships with other individuals. These persons, in turn, react and interact with him through concrete social relationships that at once restrain and stimulate him. These individuals, of course, are also constrained by his very own activities. Every individual who is in contact with another aids in the process of creating mutual expectations for what constitutes norms of appropriate conduct—modern sociologists would call this "normative role performance." Yet these emerging rules may soon grow so powerful in guiding any participant's choice of actions that they tend to rule him. The individual sees himself confronted with rules of his own making which have outgrown him. His initiative becomes juxtaposed to the requirements of his being part of a larger social whole. This basic dynamic of social life is explored by Simmel in its intriguing variations, whether they are manifested in man's relationships to phenomena of culture or to fellow man.

Georg Simmel, the youngest of seven children, was born in Berlin in 1858. In this capital he pursued all of his formal academic training, attending the gymnasium, completing university studies in history, philosophy, and Italian language and culture, obtaining his doctor's degree with a dissertation on Kant's *Physikalische Monadologie* (1881), and obtaining his first teaching position at the University of Berlin in 1885. He was to remain at this university until 1914, when, four years before his death, he was called to Strasbourg as full professor. He was highly respected by his students and enjoyed the satisfaction of frequently having to teach in the largest available lecture hall. That his style of delivery must have been extremely stimulating can be inferred from the many reminiscences of former students that are collected in Kurt Gassen's *Buch des Dankes an Georg Simmel.* Over many years, he offered courses on history, social psychology, sociology, and on various subfields of philosophy, such as the philosophy of religion and of art.

Simmel's intense involvement in the different ways in which the drama of life unfolds is, perhaps, better suggested by glancing at his varied publications than at his university course offerings. In order to gain a full appreciation, one really needs to peruse the long bibliography of his works in Gassen's book. . . . For further perspective, we also mention the translated titles of several of his major works: *Social Differentiation* (1890), *Problems of the Philosophy of History* (1892), *Introduction to the Philosophy of Morals* (1892-93), *The Philosophy of Money* (1900), *Sociology* (1908), *Goethe* (1913), *Rembrandt* (1916), *Major Problems of Philosophy* (1910), *The War and Spiritual Decisions* (1917), and *Perspectives on Life: Four Chapters in Metaphysics* (1918).

Whether he is dealing with the subjects of ethics and religion, with the biographies of creative men, or with the problems of artistic production, he seems always to be wrestling with the methodological implications of his basic dialectic position. He attempts to catch the subject in the net of his analytical dissection without thereby depriving it of its exciting quality, and he proceeds in this endeavor with great skill. Following him requires the close attention of the reader.

[*The Conflict in Modern Culture and Other Essays*] represents only a small fragment of Simmel's total work in this form. They are selected because of their topical concern with the question of man's relation to culture. In these essays, Simmel examines various implications the social life has for the status and development of culture in its impact on individuals and on social groups. He conceives of culture as the medium through which the basic dialectic of life is expressed. While it would be important to annotate some of the essays if they were to be regarded as definitive scientific statements, the primary goal was to make them available in English to the modern reader and to let Simmel speak as directly as possible through the medium of a translation. Nevertheless, a few introductory comments seem called for, to assist the modern reader in placing these essays in the context of the history of ideas.

Unfortunately, very little is known about the circumstances of their composition. As early as 1919, it was necessary for Köhler, in his sensitive appraisal of Simmel's work, to observe that it was not possible to learn from the essays when they were written, nor what influenced Simmel to write them, nor whether Simmel pursued any particular objective in furthering the cause of science or in attacking certain theoretical positions. Köhler wrote: "They are self-contained, as it were, timeless creations. They are enclosed by an invisible frame which guards their 'right of distance' in all directions." These words were only too prophetic. A portion of Simmel's personal notes was lost in a train compartment after his death, and the major portion confiscated by the Nazi Gestapo in Hamburg harbor when Simmel's son, having been released from Dachau concentration camp, was allowed to emigrate with his family to the United States of America.

The first essay, **"The Conflict of Modern Culture,"** was a lecture not published until 1918, the last year of Simmel's life. It may well be one of his last statements concerning the broad issues of the dynamics of culture, aesthetics, and social life. We find Simmel analyzing the peculiar characteristics of the modern era in the revolt against the rule of forms in the realm of ideas, arts, and philosophy. He provides us with an explanation for the rise of these new phenomena, which later writers came to call Mass Culture.

There are central themes reflecting social and cultural life in all epochs of human history, and it is these emerging themes in modern culture that need to be sought out, according to Simmel, if we wish to understand the movements in our own time.

In **"The Concept and Tragedy of Culture,"** first published in 1911, Simmel develops the notion of the duality between the cultural meaning of objects, on the one hand, and their substantive meaning, on the other. This duality, however, always seems to demand a synthesis of subjective developments with the appropriate objectively spiritual values. Thus he views cultural phenomena as being in a precarious balance between having meaning by gaining social and individual recognition and merely existing without recognition and value for human life. Through the use of numerous examples, Simmel helps the reader to approximate his position concerning the imperfect dimensions of this basic tragedy of culture, which to him reflects the general dialectic of life. In the process of becoming part of the culture, the individual is also being subjected to two independent and usually conflicting demands: the potentials of his human nature and the requirements of the social order.

On the basis of this discussion, Simmel then turns to an analysis of some of the major problems of culture in modern life such as the problems of the fetishism of commodities, of alienation, and of a largely refined division of labor and bureaucracy.

In **"A Chapter in the Philosophy of Value,"** published in 1900, Simmel explores the variety of social conditions under which social values are created and become attached to cultural objects. This essay is perhaps more direct in its approach than its philosophical title indicates. It offers a critical examination of a variety of explanations offered by previous writers on the subject of human values. Simmel proceeds to develop his own explanations of how objects come to attain valued positions in social behavior. Basic interpersonal relations, instead of quantitative measures, are presented as crucial elements in the process of value attribution. The exposition deals more with the economic than the cultural realm, but is equally applicable to both. An examination of particular social structures and their relationships to the valuation process concludes this essay.

The same topic is explored in the earlier essay, **"Sociological Aesthetics,"** published in 1896. Here, the beauty value of objects is held not to reside in the objects themselves, but rather in the reciprocity between the individual beholder and the object. Depending on how deeply individuals involve themselves in social relationships that result in the social objectification of their individual preoccupations with the aesthetic stimulus of symmetry, the outcome will be of greater or less aesthetic value. This preoccupation is not necessarily restricted to what are traditionally considered areas of aesthetic concern. For Simmel even such developments as the politics of socialism or certain forms of social organization such as bureaucracy are partially explained by an aesthetic drive towards symmetry. It appears that certain forms of social organization and works of art seem to attain value for the same reasons;

they may represent or express objective dimensions of the same subjective desires.

This point is further explored in Simmel's talk in 1903 to a gathering of psychologists, **"Concerning Aesthetic Quantities."** He argues that even such physiological sensations as those, for example, that result from varying the spatial dimensions of representations in painting, are perceived and mentally interpreted according to expectations identical with those that govern interpersonal relationships: "Man (as a *social* being) is the measure of all things also with respect to visual perspective."

In a later essay, **"On the Third Dimension in Art"** (1906), aesthetic problems of painting and their societal manifestations become the focus of Simmel's analysis. He argues that our perceptions are influenced by the categories under which we organize sense impressions. An analysis of the social conventions relating to the perception of a third dimension in painting serves as the starting point for a discussion which then leads to a consideration of the artistic meaning of tactile values and to an excursion into general aesthetics.

Similarly in **"The Dramatic Actor and Reality"** (1912), Simmel addresses himself to the special aesthetic questions of the legitimate theater and to the social implications of one person playing the role of another. The conditions under which a play is "more than life"—that is, art—are worked out. The artistic actor is the creator of a new world and not the imitator of an old reality. Thus, to Simmel dramatic art is genuinely rooted both in the aesthetic unity of the poetic work and in the social realities of the playwright, actor, and audience.

In . . . Simmel's first published essay, **"Psychological and Ethnological Studies on Music,"** we cannot help noting the fact that, from his earliest publications on, his work consistently revolved around the question of the place of the individual in the realm of culture. This is so even though this early study is more under the influence of the academic conventions of the late nineteenth century—such as the interest in evolutionary thought—than are his later, perhaps more personal, essays. In this lengthy study, Simmel questions a variety of evolutionary hypotheses concerning the origin of music as an art form in human society. He does this by mentally "testing" these propositions in the light of ethnographic evidence concerning musical practice in a variety of cultures. Then he proceeds with his own explanations, which establish music as a communication medium of highly diffuse information. In examining the implications of this position, he explores the dialectic relationship between the cultural product of music and the society and conditions under which music becomes meaningful. Musical values, just like other artistic and general aesthetic or simply human values can best be understood if viewed in interdependence with the specific social groups formed or somehow affected by them and affecting them in turn. Here, as in his later writing, it is the interdependence between the social actors and the results of the interactions that holds his fascination and comes to form the central subject of his inquiry.

If one considers Simmel's basic concerns and their obvious relationship to the body of traditional subjects of the various contemporary social sciences, one may wonder why more of his extensive work has not yet been made available in English translation to facilitate access to his ideas. . . . Simmel, in his perceptive analysis of **"The Dramatic Actor and Reality,"** antecedes Ralph Linton's discussion of role and status by many years. Only Lewis A. Coser, to my knowledge, has pointed this out, in an aside in his introduction to a collection of essays evaluating Simmel's sociological contributions. **"The Dramatic Actor and Reality"** also contains notions on role distance that remind us of Erving Goffman's later studies in the sociology of interaction. To give another example, a number of ideas in Simmel's **"Sociological Aesthetics"** throw light on the long standing debate within sociology between sociological nominalists and realists. To this day, however, the solution offered by Simmel, as outlined in his essay **"On the Conflict and Tragedy of Culture"** and in his other more specifically sociological writings, has not been accepted universally. There are still scholars who view society as the composite of many individuals or others who view it as some super-organism. Simmel suggested that the more appropriate conception is to view all life as being structured in various forms of mutual interaction among individuals who are structured in various relationships.

There may be many reasons why Simmel's impact has been relatively limited, even in Germany. In Germany, for example, he is perhaps more nearly identified as a philosopher, while in the United States, he belongs among the "fathers" of sociology. It would seem that in either country his influence has come not from the recognition of the total conception of his work, but only from the recognition of some selected aspect of it. We may speculate on the reasons for this partial appreciation and recognition, either of which fails to do justice to him, if only because for him the analysis of social life could not truly be compartmentalized.

The limited appeal of Simmel's work may have been related to his consistent insistence on social interaction (*Wechselwirkung*), on the mutual interdependence between culture and individual, and between individual and fellow man. Concerning his method, Raymond Aron observes that Simmel's approach has found many admirers but few disciples. There can be no doubt that becoming a disciple of Simmel's would demand a great deal of dedication, often only because of the difficulty and complexity of his arguments. A more significant reason, I believe, has been offered by Nicholas Spykman, who also can be credited with having provided the first major presentation of Simmel's epistemology in the United States. He points out that Simmel's perspective on substantive topics is always couched as a function of several variables rather than as a function of one. Since the latter, more traditional, mode of conceptualizing scientific problems had been accepted during Simmel's lifetime and had been demonstrated, more so than his own approach, to produce pragmatic results, his mode of approach was probably extremely difficult to translate into systematic methods for the study of scientific topics. Moreover, this difficulty was probably increased by the fact that he himself did not offer systematic expositions of the methodological implications of his position for the study of social dynamics.

Beginning during the latter part of Simmel's life, but primarily since his death, scientific models for the study of social phenomena that relate several variables simultaneously to one another have gained some acceptance. Perhaps Simmel was too advanced in scientific vision for his own age and may now be more easily understood in the intellectual climate of the present. There is some indication that this is so. The 1950's brought a number of new translations of Simmel's work in sociology as well as the reprinting of earlier translations in anthologies. On the centennial of his birthday (1958), commemorative volumes were prepared in German and English, with the English volume providing additional translations. Attention to Simmel's work continued in the 1960's with Rudolph H. Weingartner's study and Lewis A. Coser's book of essays. Frequent reference to Simmel's work in contemporary studies of small-group dynamics and of certain other work in social psychology suggests his usefulness to students of these subjects.

Donald N. Levine   (essay date 1970)

SOURCE: Review of *The Conflict in Modern Culture and Other Essays,* in *American Anthropologist,* Vol. 72, No. 1, February, 1970, pp. 109-11.

[*In the following essay, Levine examines Simmel's contributions not only to theories of social relationships but also to culture in general.*]

It is ironic that George Simmel is known to American anthropologists solely as a student of social relations when in fact his devotion to the study of culture was equally constant and nearly as fruitful. Simmel himself is largely to blame for this. He not only drew a sharp boundary between cultural "contents" and social structural "forms"—for which he was roundly rebuked by Durkheim—but also tried to keep inquiry into the two domains segregated. Only the latter domain, he argued, provides a proper subject matter for the discipline of sociology. Inasmuch as Simmel's ideas were imported into American social science by sociologists who followed his focus on social forms, his work on culture remained perforce unnoticed—all the more since it was usually carried out under a rubric to which American sociologists have long been allergic, that of philosophy.

Simmel came to the study of culture as a student of two eminent ethnographers, Adolf Bastian and Moritz Lazarus, and as a revisionist of Kantian and Hegelian ideas about mind. In effect, the effort to ground the latter in the evolutionary anthropology of the former was one of his abiding enterprises. It begins with the doctoral essay **"Psychological and Ethnological Studies on Music,"** published in Lazarus and Steinthal's *Zeitschrift für Völkerpsychologie* in 1882, and culminates with two essays published in his last year, 1918. One of these, **"The Conflict in Modern Culture,"** and the study on music comprise two of the seven new translations in [*The Conflict in Modern Culture and Other Essays*]. The others date from various periods in between and deal mostly with aesthetic culture.

Like his sociological writings, Simmel's essays on culture hardly commend themselves for empirical rigor, systematic exposition, universal erudition, or painstaking continuity with a scholarly tradition; their forte, rather, lies in originality of conception and fecundity of thought. The pivotal concept, here too, is that of "form," though in this context culture is now seen in terms of forms as contrasted with the unshaped contents of experience. What Simmel seeks to determine is (1) the origins and properties of various kinds of cultural forms, (2) the different ways in which individuals relate to these forms, and (3) the chief conflicts to which the forms are subjected.

The first of these questions is addressed in the essay on music. Appealing to a small sample of ethnographic fragments and personal observations, Simmel seeks to refute the Darwinian notion that vocal music preceded the development of language. He argues for the reverse order: vocal music arises when existing linguistic patterns are felt inadequate to express certain powerful emotions, like anger, joy, and mystical-religious feelings, which overflow straight language to produce rhythmic embellishments and finally melodic variations. Comparable arguments stressing the functions of music in human communication explain the origins of instrumental music, refrain singing, and folk song. Then,

> during the course of its development music rejects its natural characteristics more and more. . . . Through this process it approaches objectivity, which is the highest honor for the (performing) artist. This does not mean that all feelings disappear from music. . . . It means only that music and its manner of presentation should not be the immediate result of these emotions, as it was originally; but instead, that it should become an image of them.

At this point, the making of music is properly referred to as "playing," for play is an essential condition of art.

This two-step account of the origins of music is paradigmatic for Simmel's conception of the development of culture generally. All forms of culture begin as protoforms related to the practical exigencies of the "real world." At a certain point they become liberated from mundane teleology: they become autonomous forms, developed and enjoyed for their own sake in a spirit of play, a state that Simmel elsewhere refers to as "freedom." This is the realm of "objective culture."

It is characteristic of Simmel that he never attempts a systematic survey of the various spheres of culture, let alone a coherent analysis of how the diverse spheres are interrelated. His dogmatic relativism led him to hold that each great formative category—art, science, religion, ethics, etc.—is capable of organizing the totality of experience into a "world" that is fundamentally incommensurable with each of the others.

Certain questions, however, can be put to any of these cultural phenomena, such as, what conditions are related to involvement with them. This question is among those taken up in the brief chapters on aesthetics. Thus, there are certain "thresholds" for becoming aware of phenomena qua religious, ethical, or aesthetic. In the case of graphic art, "each artistically usable element seems to be composed of two thresholds of size. There is a certain quantity for their representation through which aesthetic reactions in the final analysis are produced, and there is one through which they disappear again." On the subjective side, "strength of emotion also has an upper and a lower aesthetic threshold. Beyond the one there is apathy; beyond the other there is realistic participation."

The individual's relation to cultural forms, however, is often conflictful and inherently problematic. This is because the same life forces that give rise to cultural forms press on inexorably against the constraints of those forms once they have attained an autonomous existence. This produces a perennial search for new forms to overturn old ones, a problem discussed in the title essay. In the contemporary (1914) scene, moreover, there are many instances of a principled rejection of forms altogether: religiosity seeking to do without religious forms, aesthetic impulses seeking to do away with all form in art. These instances may simply reflect a long transitional period, a protraction of the normal cultural process of obsolescence and reconstruction. Or perhaps a more radical alternative awaits us: "perhaps this formlessness is itself the appropriate form for contemporary life"—an alternative recently described by John Gagnon with the phrase "anomie as nomos."

In **"The Nature and Tragedy of Culture."** a different type of conflict is examined. Here Simmel considers the assimilation of objective culture by the individual so that he becomes a cultured person—the phenomenon of subjective culture. Another endemic conflict of modern life is that the autonomous development of objective culture proceeds at such a pace that it is virtually impossible for subjective culture to keep abreast, with the tragic consequence that human beings become increasingly alienated from their finest cultural products.

These few remarks scarcely circumscribe the richness of thought contained in this slim volume (and in many still untranslated essays by Simmel on culture). For example. despite Simmel's aversion to linking culture with social structure or cultural systems with one another, there are times, as in **"Sociological Aesthetics,"** when he does so with delightful results.

Murray S. Davis   (essay date 1973)

SOURCE: "Georg Simmel and the Aesthetics of Social Reality," in *Social Forces,* Vol. 51, No. 3, March, 1973, pp. 320-29.

[*In the following essay, Davis demonstrates how the aesthetic basis of Simmel's sociology supports an argument that Simmel's are theories more unified than commentators generally consider them to be.*]

Arthur Salz once said he learned from his teacher Georg Simmel, the following about society: "[Simmel] conceives of sociology as the study of the forms of sociation. But whoever speaks of forms moves in the field of aesthetics. Society, in the last analysis, is a work of art."

Society is a work of art? The comparison is an intriguing one. In this article I will try to show that it constitutes

Simmel's central vision, and that around this aesthetic model the overwhelming profusion of Simmel's sociological insights—that on first reading appear in such chaotic dissociation from one another—actually cohere. Of course, not all of Simmel's sociology can be reduced to his aesthetics, but I think it will greatly aid our comprehension of the unity of Simmel's work if we consider the ways in which much of it can.

There are three aspects of Simmel's aesthetics which underlie his sociology: (1) his particular conception of the *artistic modality;* (2) his particular conception of the *artistic product;* and (3) his particular conception of the *artistic method.* Let us proceed to discover the way in which Simmel conceives each of these components of his aesthetics, and to trace the way in which each of these aesthetic motifs runs through his treatment of social reality.

THE ARTISTIC MODALITY: VISUAL

Simmel's conception of society is based not on all the sensory modalities in different aesthetic genres, but only on art that is essentially visual. In fact, he states explicitly that ". . . in art, there is absolutely no other point of reference besides purely optical processes." This visual bias of his model has several repercussions on his thinking.

First, it means that Simmel does not see the fundamental elements of art and of society as developing through time, as he would have done had he drawn his model from the audile arts, whose tonalities and rhythms immediately draw the listener into the future or remind him of the past. Instead, Simmel conceptualizes the fundamental elements of art and society as atemporal configurations in space, as his critics point out: ". . . if Bergson repeatedly asks that we admit the importance of time, Simmel is just as insistent in stressing the significance of *space.* If Bergson is concerned with passage and duration, with the movement and change of the object observed, Simmel is preoccupied with the object's *stability*" (Lipman; emphasis mine).

Being preoccupied with stable elements and forms leads Simmel to be ". . . more concerned with a *taxonomic analysis* of these forms than with a search for the causes that permit specific men to mobilize and to direct the energies of others. His formalism diverts him from causal questions . . . " (Walter; emphasis mine) and [according to Lipman] from developmental questions:

> [Simmel's] reliance upon a spatial (or pseudospatial) frame of interpretation tends to emphasize the *static* and extended aspect of the self [and to] neglect those more dynamic aspects, less readily visualized, which are also essential to a just conception of individuality: only cursorily or obliquely does Simmel confront such problems as power, integrity, productivity, and growth (Lipman; emphasis mine).

Second, while the contrast between the visual arts and the audile arts can show us a reason for Simmel's ahistorical perspective on society, the contrast between the visual arts and the tactile ones can help us clarify his ambivalent view of human nature. In Simmel's time, the objects of the tactile arts, such as a sculpture or a building, implied, phenomenologically, the hand of their creator. The tactile arts were seen as revealing man as a forger of the forms of the world, where as the visual arts (like painting) were seen as portraying man as a contemplator of a world already formed. (Considering the recent "active" paintings of Jackson Pollack and "passive" sculptures of Henry Moore, this kind of contrast between the visual and the tactile arts no longer has the same force.) Throughout Simmel's thinking runs an ambiguous—sometimes tragically ambiguous—conception of the human predicament: at times Simmel sees man as the creator of the forms of culture and of society—forms man creates in order to satisfy his needs and serve his purposes; at other times Simmel sees man as having to endure those forms which he had previously made—forms which now neither serve nor satisfy, but which now master him. In the previous generation, Marx and Nietzsche could limit this latter view—man as passive suffer—to the present and, hence, could hope for a better future. But Simmel, like his contemporary Freud, finds the conflict between man and his social and cultural creations to be eternal, and to be a struggle which man is continually losing. Except for the brief moment of creation, man must suffer his own creations, endure his past organizations of his cultural and social worlds. If he is to master them at all, he can do so only internally, only through contemplation. To view, to point, to name, to symbolize, to describe, and thus, by this damming off, to hold back and to direct momentarily a channel of the ongoing stream of life, is the very best man can hope to achieve. But, even so, almost immediately the very tools and concepts by which he separated part of life from its source unite with what they have cut off: from this conjugation there springs a new hybrid creature which, following its own logic, its own pattern of development, grows out of man's control and hence augments still further that objective environment (that environment of cultural objects) which determines and delimits him. In point of illustration, how Simmel would have sighed to see the progeny of his few pages on dyads and triads: those hundreds of recent articles on small-group research which fill the sociology journals and which provide the corpus of an already recognized field of specialization within sociology, complete with its own ground rules and requirements.

Notice how similar this position is to Weber's notion of the "routinization of charisma." Weber shows how charismatic leaders (embodiments of the life force) are continually bursting through the old forms of social organization and creating new ones, though these new ones slowly become routinized through traditionalization or bureaucratization until the next charismatic leader comes along. On this point both Weber and Simmel are attempting to reconcile their dual heritage of Nietzsche (life) and the neo-Kantians (form). The difference between Weber and Simmel is one of emphasis. The former stresses social processes that are predominantly external to man; the latter stresses cultural processes that are predominantly internal to him. Both focus on historical periods when social energy was declining as it becomes entrapped and dissipated in elaborate cultural forms and social organizations, but Simmel (at least until the last period of his life) pays even less attention than Weber to historical periods of "negative entropy" when available social energy was increasing.

It is not clear what caused Simmel to see man as more reactive than active. Perhaps it was the helpless position of German intellectuals during his lifetime. Perhaps it was the fact that both society and culture in neo-rococo, *fin-de-siècle* Germany were composed of an enormous number of outworn institutions and lifeless values. Certainly it was also affected by Simmel's inability to swim easily through the gelatin of German academic life. In any case, the fact remains that Simmel, like Burckhardt before him, saw man as no longer a Cesare Borgia, consciously forging the state and the institutions of society as the artist creates a work of art. At best, now, man's creations are limited to small new forms in the interstices and margins of a social world already given: his imagination can guide only his sociable relations during coffee breaks in the alcoves of great institutions, grace notes to a social symphony whose main themes already have been scored.

The final implication of the fact that for Simmel art is essentially a visual phenomenon concerns geometry, the mathematics on which visual aesthetics, and hence much of Simmel's sociology, is based. (Geometry became the foundation of painting, sculpture, and architecture—Simmel's three main aesthetic interests—during the Classical period and its Renaissance revival.) Simmel sometimes considers aesthetic and sociological topics in terms of their *quantitative* rather than *geometric* properties, but usually he analyzes both aesthetic and sociological phenomena from the point of view of Euclid, not Pythagoras.

Geometry, as a visual mathematics, has two essential features: it abstracts geometric forms from the empirical world, and it systematizes these forms it abstracts. Simmel thinks sociology—like geometry—is also able to abstract its own subject matter (social forms) from one object in the empirical world and to apply (generalize) the results of this abstraction to other empirical objects:

> Sociology, the discipline that deals with the purely social aspects of man . . . , is related to the other social sciences in the same way geometry is related to the physical sciences. Geometry studies the forms through which any material becomes an empirical phenomenon—though these forms, like social forms, themselves exist only in abstraction. Both geometry and sociology leave to other (physical and social) sciences the investigation of the contents which the forms make real (i.e., which the forms turn into empirical phenomena). . . . Just as geometry discovers forms of spatial relationship which hold for all objects, so sociology discovers forms of social relationship which hold for all men (even though their contents, materials, and interests differ) (Simmel quoted by Walter, author's translation).

However, Simmel believes sociology—unlike geometry—is not yet able to organize its own forms systematically, especially because it is more difficult to isolate social forms as completely as geometric forms and more difficult to apply the few social forms already isolated to as wide a range of empirical objects as geometric forms. Nevertheless, Simmel tries to develop his sociology as a science of the social world in direct parallel to geometry as a science of the physical world.

Simmel's use of the visual science of geometry as a model for his sociology reinforced several of the important tendencies of his thinking which were mentioned above. For one thing, his sociology was deflected away from historical analysis inasmuch as geometric forms have no temporal dimension. For another, his sociology became concerned less with changing the world than with contemplating it inasmuch as geometry was concerned more with merely gazing at the forms it abstracted from empirical phenomena than with the processes by which empirical phenomena came to be organized by these particular forms and not others. Thus, insofar as Simmel viewed the social world geometrically—or, more generally visually and aesthetically—he saw it from the static perspective of the passive observer rather than from the dynamic perspective of the active creator.

THE ARTISTIC PRODUCT: A NEW INTEGRATED WORLD SEPARATED FROM LIFE

The second characteristic of art upon which Simmel bases his sociology is the assumption that the productions of art are "wholly separated from life". More specifically,

> . . . the essence of a work of art is, after all, that it cuts out a piece of the endlessly continuous sequence of perceived experience, detaching it from all connections with one side or the other. . . . the real object interacts with everything that surges or hovers around it, but the content of a work of art cuts off these threads, fusing only its own elements into a self-sufficient unity. Hence, the work of art leads its life beyond reality.

The common thesis that art is a reality independent of life places Simmel with the late nineteenth- and early twentieth-century French and English "art for art's sake" schools. The struggle for the autonomy of art is the best known instance of the general movement toward the autonomy of all cultural forms which was flourishing at the turn of the century. One of Simmel's most important contributions to social thought is his discovery of the growing autonomy of all social forms as well. In effect, Simmel here is generalizing Karl Marx's assertion of the growing autonomy of economic processes, to all social and cultural processes. The "fetishism" which Marx assigned to economic commodities represents only a special case of this general fate of the contents of culture.

Much of Simmel's analysis of specific social phenomena consists of his attempt to show that this theme of "separation from life" runs through such diverse social forms (among many others) as "faithfulness," "sociability," and the "adventure."

> A part of existence, interwoven with the uninterruptedness of that existence, yet nevertheless felt as a whole, as an integrated unit—this is the form common to both the work of art and the adventure. . . . the work of art exists entirely beyond life as a reality; the adventure, entirely beyond life as an uninterrupted course which intelligibly connects every element with its neighbors?

(Simmel has even claimed that life itself may be detached from some more cosmic process, and, hence, can itself be seen as an adventure.)

From this theorem that art and certain social processes become separated from the life which created them, Simmel draws the corollary that each of these separated processes has a place outside itself, in life, from which to draw materials that it can reshape with its own forms in its own medium.

> What may be called the art drive, extracts out of the totality of phenomena their mere form, in order to shape it into specific structures that correspond with this drive. In a similar fashion, out of the realities of social life, the "sociability drive" extracts the pure process of sociation as a cherished value. . . . As a sociological category, I thus designate sociability as the play form of sociation. Its relation to content-determined, concrete sociation is similar to that of the work of art to reality.

Just as life produces the forms of art which in turn draw their content from life again, so sociation produces the social form of sociability which likewise then draws its content from social life. This process of "selection from life" as a characteristic of both artistic and social modes is well illustrated by the "art of coquetry":

> . . . eroticism has elaborated a form of play: coquetry. . . . If the erotic question between the sexes turns about consent or denial . . . coquetry [plays] hinted consent and hinted denial against each other to draw the man on without letting matters come to a decision. . . . And this freedom from all the weight of firm content and residual reality gives coquetry that character of vacillation, of distance, of the ideal, which allows one to speak with some right of the "art"—not of the "[artifice]"—of coquetry.

This new sphere not only separates itself from life and selects its materials from life, it also organizes and forms these materials into a new unity. Again the model is art: ". . . art . . . cuts out a piece of the endless continuous sequences of perceived experience . . . giving it a self-sufficient form as though defined and held together by an inner core." This tendency toward organization may be seen on the level of the individual:

> Culture . . . is a process whereby the individual interiorizes the objects he finds everywhere about him. . . . They become his objects in that they are the objects of a unified personality; they are integrated into the course of his life. . . . Cultivation means treating one's own life as an object which must be continually shaped.

And on the level of society: "The essence of societal formation . . . [is] that out of closed units—such as human personalities more or less are—a new unit emerges."

Lewis Coser has suggested that Simmel is a functionalist thinker in that he "considers the individual's social actions not in themselves, but in relation to those of other individuals and to particular structures and processes." I would make the further suggestion that, for Simmel, functionalism is not only a methodological principle, but also an ontological feature of his subject matter. Whatever Simmel deals with seems to be trying to organize the materials in its environment into a unity around itself according to its own principles. This is true of the core of Simmel's Kantian world, the mind: "The essential accomplishment of the mind may be said to be its transformation of the multiplicity of the elements of the world into a series of unities. In the mind, things separated in space and time converge in the unity of a picture, a concept, a sentence". But in Simmel's world, as opposed to Kant's, the mind is not the only thing which organizes. We have already seen organizations by the work of art, by the adventure, by the individual, and by the society. Simmel's world possesses many such centers of organization, and, hence, looks more like Leibniz's *Weltanschauung* of self actualizing monads or, even, the primitives' animistic world-view than Kant's.

This world composed of multiple conflicting centers of organization affects both the sociologist who observes it and the individual who has to live in it. Since each area of life is trying to organize the same materials around its own principles, the sociological observer, freezing the movement at any point of time, can choose from among several centers the one around which he may say the material is being organized, for, like an optical illusion, the whole picture changes with every slight adjustment of focus. As for the individual living in this world, he finds himself continually fluctuating between the existential ecstasy of being able to draw each of these centers into his own life and the existential agony of being pulled apart by them into theirs.

> From the moment that man began to say "I" to himself, . . . from the same moment in which the contents of the soul were formed together into a center point, . . . everything connected with the center point [had to form] a unit, self-contained and self-sufficient. But the contents with which the "I" must organize itself into its own unified world do not belong to it alone. [Insofar as these contents are integrated into various outside worlds] they do not wish to dissolve into . . . the "I." [In fact,] through these contents the exterior worlds grasp the "I" and seek to draw *it* into *them*. They aim to break up the centralization of cultural contents around the "I" and reconstitute [these cultural contents] according to *their* demands.

Simmel describes the essential feature of the organization of the newly created aesthetic and social worlds with the terms "symmetry," "balance," and "equilibrium" to contrast them with the spontaneous, impulsive, disorganization of their source in life: "The origin of all aesthetic themes is found in symmetry. . . . It is possible to discover through an analysis of the role of symmetry in social life how apparently purely aesthetic interests are called forth by materialistic purposes, and how . . . aesthetic motives affect forms which seem to obey only functional purposes." (At those rare times when Simmel discusses life as balanced, he always does so in order to show the instability of its equilibrium; for instance, when he deals with architecture, which he defines as the balance between the striving of the spirit and the necessities of nature, he does so in the context of "the ruin.")

Simmel then uses these concepts of "order" as the criterion of the extent to which these aesthetic and social organizations have separated from life:

> Wherever we perceive aesthetically, we demand that the contradictory forces of existence be somehow in equilibrium, that the struggle between [spirit] and [nature] come to a standstill. . . . If [sociation] is interaction at all, it appears in its purest and most stylized form among equals, just as symmetry and balance are the most notable forms of artistic stylizing.

A society organized according to socialist principles would be the most symmetrical, most harmonious, and hence most aesthetic of all conceivable societies:

> Without any doubt, certain ideas of socialism are based on aesthetic values. That society as a whole should become a work of art in which every single element attains its meaning by virtue of its contribution to the whole; that a unified plan should rationally determine all of production, instead of the present rhapsodic haphazardness by which the efforts of individuals benefit or harm society; that the wasteful competition and the fight of individuals against individuals should be replaced by the absolute harmony of work—all these ideas of socialism no doubt meet aesthetic interest. Whatever else one may have against it, these ideas at any rate refute the popular opinion that socialism both begins and ends exclusively in the needs of the stomach.

But this most symmetrical, most harmonious, most aesthetic of all conceivable societies would also be, Simmel implies, the most separated from the pulsating forces of life.

Though Simmel sometimes compares, in static distinction, these newly formed aesthetic and social worlds with the ground out of which they evolved, more often he is concerned with describing the dynamic processes by which aesthetic and social worlds separate from, and contrast with, their ground. Matthew Lipman speaks of this "figure-ground motif" as being one of Simmel's most common analytic techniques:

> Certainly the figure-ground opposition is an important conceptual instrument for Simmel, for he often speaks of individuality as a pattern whose pronouncedness must be seen against the background of what it is not—of what contrasts with, or even contradicts it. (This chiaroscuro technique makes quite plausible his interest in Rembrandt—especially since Rembrandt used that technique for the purpose of intense individuation.)

Simmel rarely deals with anything in itself; instead, he nearly always relates it spatially to whatever is around it. For example, he contrasts the building with the surrounding countryside, the parts of the face with the whole, and the stranger with the group. He makes these comparisons in order to bring out the point that different objects are necessary to each other because they reciprocally define each other. Furthermore, he often connects the individual object not to any objects in its spatial environment, but, more specifically, to those things around it from which it arose or was differentiated. This he does both in his aesthetics (the handle against the bowl) and in his sociology (the individual against the group). Occasionally, this contrast of figure and ground actually shows the individual actively emerging from his ordinary background (as Michaelangelo's statues seem to struggle out from their stone). Lipman continues:

> The individual stands over against the common or the general; the individualized experience contrasts with the ordinary, commonplace experience. We prize the individual in this sense, not because of its intrinsic value, but because it occurs in a context of triviality, monotony, mediocrity. . . . The greater the routinization of the world, the more the genuine individual stands boldly in relief against it.

But more often Simmel considers the ground (a group, for example) to be constantly hovering, constantly oppressing the emerged individual, constantly threatening to swallow him up again.

Along with how artistic products and social processes relate externally to their ground, Simmel also deals with how their elements relate internally to one another. Simmel treats these internal relations of aesthetic and social phenomena under the concept of "distance." With the exception of Simmel's discussion of the relation between intimacy and discretion in terms of distance, Donald Levine has pointed out most of the important social phenomena which Simmel examines in the light of this concept throughout his writings:

> Simmel wrote a pioneering and penetrating account of the influence of physical distance on human relations. Furthermore, nearly all of the social processes and social types treated by Simmel may readily be understood in terms of *social distance*. . . . Conflict is considered a kind of social interaction because the individuals concerned are, despite their antagonism, relatively close. . . . Domination and subordination, the aristocrat, and the bourgeois, have to do with relations defined in terms of "above" and "below." Secrecy, arbitration, the poor man, and the stranger are some of the topics related to the inside-outside dimension (emphasis mine).

Finally, Simmel analyzes, in terms of distance, not only the generation and inner relation of objects, but also their separation from the observer. It is the observer's varying "distance" from these objects which distinguishes the various modes by which he experiences them. Not only do aesthetic and sociological modes of experience involve a different distance between the observer and his objects, but so do practical, scientific, historical, religious, and metaphysical modes.

This concern with "distance" is an especially distinctive feature of modern times, Simmel wrote in 1896. The degree to which the observer is trying to increase his distance from his objects may be seen in recent developments in painting and social relations, as well as in literature and science. The cause of this increasing desire for distance in modern culture and society? Simmel blames "the steadily deeper penetration of a money economy":

> Money is placed between man and man, between man and product, as a mediator. . . . Money, by the enlargement of its role, has placed us at a wider and more basic distance from the object. . . . Our contact with [things] becomes interrupted, and we sense them only through intermediaries, which can never fully express their genuine, unique and immediate being. Thus the most diverse features of modern art and culture seem to have in common . . . a tendency to increase the distance between man and his objects, which finds its most distinct form in the area of aesthetics.

THE ARTISTIC METHOD: UNIVERSALIZATION THROUGH PARTICULARIZATION

Simmel defines aesthetic comprehension, and hence the sociological comprehension (and, ultimately, all the modes of comprehending experience) modeled on it, as revealing the immediate relation between the individual and the universal. Unlike inductive logic which ascends from the individual to the universal slowly through intermediate steps, aesthetic comprehension bridges this gap immediately, by a sudden leap: "The essence of aesthetic contemplation and interpretation for us consists in the following: What is unique emphasizes what is typical, what is accidental appears as normal, and the superficial and fleeting stands for what is essential and basic." So too our sociological comprehension of social relations gives us the intuitive insight that, in order for the human individual to relate at all to his surrounding society, he must somehow carry within him the social universal.

Another of Simmel's major contributions to social theory is his shift in the locus and magnitude of the units which embody these social universals. Simmel claims that these social universals should be sought for not in the large, outstanding, and famous instances or individuals where Hegel and Nietzsche looked for them, but rather in the apparently low, mean, and trivial particulars of social life. Just as each of the smallest details in classical art reproduces the essential form of the work as a whole, so mere sociable conversation, seemingly about trivia, can reveal the essential processes of society, and even life itself:

> In all art, in all the symbolism of religious life, even in the complex formulations of science, we depend on a certain faith or feeling that phenomena which seem merely fragmented or superficial are in fact connected to the deepest and most comprehensive aspects of reality and therefore of life itself. . . . Art perhaps reveals the secret of life: the fact that we cannot be relieved of the real pressures of life merely by looking away from them, but only by reshaping and reexperiencing them in the unreal world of play. . . . The more serious a person, the more he finds relief and freedom in sociability. In sociability he enjoys, as in a dramatic production, a concentration and transformation of effort that simultaneously dilutes and sublimates all the tasks and seriousness of life so that its heavy burdens are

felt only faintly, their weight reduced to mere stimulation (author's translation).

It seems appropriate to end this inquiry into the unity of Simmel's thought by considering how well Simmel's own procedure in treating his various subject matters agrees with those ontological features of his world which we have noted. Though it is commonly agreed that Simmel's greatness lies in his imaginative thoughts, I would add that the logical consistency by which he combines those insights should not be overlooked in any assessment of his stature, for Simmel's methodology harmonizes completely with his metaphysics. Simmel does not merely postulate the fact that any particular subject matter embodies universal principles, he actually discusses each object of his interest "in an ever expanding context, until the context comes to include the whole of existence."

Consider Simmel's definition of "aesthetic pantheism": "Every point contains within itself the potential of being redeemed to absolute aesthetic importance. To the adequately trained eye, the totality of beauty, the complete meaning of the world as a whole, radiates from every single point." Might we not say then that what Simmel has produced—in all his writings on the human condition taken together—is a true Aesthetics of Social Reality?

CONCLUSIONS

We have seen how Simmel's views on society and sociology are derived from his aesthetics, specifically from his conception of the artistic modality, the artistic product, and the artistic method. Simmel's tendency to look at social phenomena visually led him to conceive of man as merely the contemplator of the ahistorical social forms he once created but now can no longer control. But while man is predominantly passive, his social products are not. These social products, having become autonomous from the organic processes which engendered them, are now active agents in their own right, organizing the materials of social life around themselves in an orderly—sometimes even symmetrical—manner. It is the sacred task of the sociologist—standing between relatively weak mankind on the one side and mankind's relatively strong social creations on the other—to reconcile the two. Through the method of suddenly grasping for the social universals in the most trivial particulars of human existence, the sociologist hopes to comprehend coherently for men their otherwise overwhelming social reality.

Simmel attempted to establish a sociology that had its foundation in aesthetics. He thus created a discipline whose orientation is quite different from that of Marx, who grounded his sociology in economics and political science—from that of Durkheim, who grounded his sociology in biology and statistics—and from that of Weber, who grounded his sociology in history and anthropology. These other sorts of sociologies have had their day. Perhaps the time has come to give Simmel's its due.

Charles David Axelrod   (essay date 1979)

SOURCE: "Simmel," in *Studies in Intellectual Break-*

through, University of Massachusetts Press, 1979, pp. 35-49.

[*In the following excerpt, Axelrod examines how Simmel perceived the tension between the individual and society and analyzes Simmel's writing style as reflecting his intellectual strengths and limitations.*]

[Thomas] Kuhn characterizes scientific paradigms as achievements which provide new orientations to one or many areas of scientific work, and which isolate limited sets of problems to be investigated and limited ways of formulating those problems. When a sector of the scientific community accepts the authority of a paradigm, says Kuhn, members' attention is directed solely toward that set of problems that the paradigm defines. At the same time, that particular sector rules as illegitimate or uninteresting all work that does not proceed from the paradigm. Thus while the scientific community awakens certain possibilities among its members, it also restricts—even hides—other possibilities. . . .

Kuhn shows how occasionally a scientist experiences the violence of these restrictions in the course of his work and begins to reconsider the grounds of the accepted paradigm. He finds it necessary to violate the paradigm's authority if he is to proceed with the work in which he is involved. . . . [Breakthrough], for Kuhn, not only involves overcoming restrictions imposed by the accepted paradigm, but also involves formulating a new paradigm and its acceptance within a sector of the scientific community. Thus from Kuhn we derive the notion—commonly held with reference to the scientific, philosophical, and artistic communities—that without a new paradigm there can be no breakthrough. This particular notion, however, can restrict our ability to deal with what is most relevant in the phenomenon of breakthrough. . . .

[If the career and writings of Georg Simmel, the German sociologist-philosopher,] were to be measured in terms of his power to attract followers to a new paradigm, he must be considered a virtual failure. Not only did he not attract a wide following to a new paradigm, but Simmel's audience was not convinced that he worked within a paradigm at all. With Kuhn's particular requirement of breakthrough, it is a mystery why Simmel's work is even included among the monuments of sociological thought. Yet, I have chosen to discuss Simmel precisely in order to question Kuhn's notion of breakthrough. . . . Can we formulate Simmel's work as having achieved scientific breakthrough, and can breakthrough emerge independent of the struggle for supremacy within a community?

This formulation will begin by presenting and analyzing the criticisms leveled at Simmel by his colleagues with respect to his non-paradigmatic orientation; then it will show how Simmel's major contribution to sociological-scientific thought may be seen in terms of his having anticipated these criticisms, and in terms of his having radically reinterpreted their source of authority. In doing this he tacitly formulates a new version of scientific membership and forces us to reconsider Kuhn's conception of breakthrough.

I

Simmel's writings were, and still are, received by the scientific community with a noticeable degree of ambivalence. In one respect, his work was clearly interesting or fascinating—perhaps even brilliant, for Simmel provided a rich source of new formulations and stimulating observations. Yet somehow his work was often seen as contemptible. To Emile Durkheim, the father of scientific sociology and Simmel's contemporary, it displayed no clear system of orientation. It was fragmented, with "no connection" from one piece to the next. Pitirim Sorokin writes that Simmel's work "results in a series of logical inconsistencies, and in a vagueness of theoretical constructions." Yet even those who greatly admired and were clearly influenced by Simmel's work could not overlook its fragmentary character, its apparent lack of any clear system. Max Weber, who in one comment calls Simmel's writings "simply brilliant" and says "nearly every one of his works abounds in important new theoretical ideas and most subtle observations," cannot hide his antagonism toward the fragmentary character of the work. He labels the methodology "unacceptable" and the manner of presentation "strange" and "uncongenial." Leopold von Wiese, who may be considered a formal disciple of Simmel, also takes issue with this one unacceptable trait. He refers to the "lack of transition from one [thought] to another" as a "disadvantage intimately linked with the essence of his thought." Thus for those who like Simmel's work as well as for those who do not, the criticism remains the same. The work is unbounded, fragmented, unsystematic.

Yet, what is most curious about this criticism is that Simmel's critics feel no obligation to formulate the standard by which they criticize his work. They recognize fragmentation or disunity as such negative characteristics in scientific work that no further explanation is required. In other words, since objectively visible unification is considered a fundamental necessity of scientific work, fragmentation is by its very nature a failure. However, let us try to understand the sense in which the critics consider fragmentation synonymous with failure. This will help us understand more fully the grounds upon which normal science rests, the grounds of the community upon which Simmel participates as an author. More important, it may begin to uncover the manner in which Simmel does participate. This has always been a mystery to his audience.

Lewis Coser, who edited a book of commentary on Simmel, conceives of fragmentation in the following manner: "Simmel was never tempted by the esprit de systeme. Whether from impatience or from sheer inability to concentrate for any length of time on a particular problem, he moved from one topic to the next, from one line of reasoning to another." Here Coser characterizes the failure of fragmented writing in psychological terms, as indicative of a certain negative character trait. Since Simmel lacks the necessary patience to perform the kind of strictly disciplined work that science demands, he is not fit to be a scientist. This particular criticism is traditional in the social science community. Durkheim, for example, in his effort to initiate a scientific paradigm for sociology, formulates this same notion in the preface to *The Rules of Sociological Method:* "if there is to be a social science, we shall expect it not merely to paraphrase the traditional prejudices of the common man but to give us a new and different view of them. . . . The reader must bear in mind that the ways of thinking to which he is most inclined are adverse, rather than favorable, to the scientific study of social phenomena; and he must consequently be on his guard against his first impressions." Here Durkheim provides for a distinct separation of scientific thinking from everyday thinking on the basis of a difference in quality. Scientific thinking is more trustworthy than ordinary thinking due to its meticulous processing. In contrast, ordinary thinking is not mediated by a thorough processing of the contents of thought. In fact, ordinary thinking, which Durkheim points out is inclined toward "first impressions," is hardly processed at all. It is lazy thinking. Thus for Durkheim as well as for Coser, Simmel's work fails. Science is formulated as a standard of excellence, and fragmentation, which they find in Simmel's work, becomes a metaphor for laziness.

Durkheim provides a further rationale behind authorizing science as a standard of excellence. Only within a "methodically disciplined" attitude, he says, can the science of sociology materialize as a collective intellectual activity. In an article on Simmel, Durkheim writes that "we must accurately isolate social facts and must show what it is that forms their unity in order to avoid reducing sociology to nothing but a conventional label applied to an incoherent agglomeration of disparate disciplines." And further, "while pretending that it defines research, . . . [Simmel's work] actually leaves it to the fancy of the individual." We see then that for Durkheim, if scientists were not "methodically disciplined," the doing of sociology would not lead to the formation of a unified discipline. Sociology would refer concretely to some scattered individuals who have nothing at all to do with one another. Thus the unity that Durkheim attempts to form in isolating social facts is not simply the unity of social facts, but also the unification of sociologists. The isolation of social facts becomes the mutual activity of practicing sociologists and thus the unifying mechanism within the sociological community. For Durkheim, all sociologists must work within a single, disciplined framework; without such a framework, their speech would be indistinguishable from ordinary, everyday speech. Durkheim judges Simmel's work on the basis of its inability to unify sociology. For Durkheim, then, science means living according to a community-sponsored paradigm.

But what is the purpose of this unified collective and why can we not "leave things to the fancy of the individual"? Durkheim's intention in overruling the natural diversity of practitioners is to secure a oneness, a uniformity for the fruits of sociological investigation. Given the same orientation to the acquisition of knowledge, he hopes that some agreement will be reached in explanations of the social world. Thus Durkheim organizes sociological work independently of individual fancies in order to negotiate a corpus of secure, trustworthy, and objective knowledge. The disciplined unification of sociologists provides a ground for the structural unification of sociological knowledge. Practitioners must agree once and for all to embrace this model of sociological work; but implicit here is an agreement no longer to expend energy questioning and debating its underlying, achieved character. Although discourse may transpire within the confines of this newly structured paradigm, members are encouraged not to address the grounds of the paradigm itself.

Simmel, as an outsider, a stranger to this "methodically disciplined" framework, recalls other possibilities for inquiry. As such he reminds members of the achieved character of the unified collective and threatens the euphony of the Durkheimian enterprise. The fragmentary, unsystematic character of his work makes reference to Simmel's reluctance to fit into this or any objectively disciplined framework. In this context, Simmel is seen as the enemy of concerted inquiry, and fragmentation becomes a metaphor for nihilism and intellectual anarchy.

Von Wicsc, in his critique of Simmel, supports this idea, but not for the purpose of strengthening the Durkheimian project. Rather, he attempts to reformulate Simmel's corpus into a concretely unified paradigm of its own: "But it seems to me that this science of the forms of association is in need of certain guiding ideas—of a unified goal—if it is to proceed from repeated analyses to the attainment of a concluding synthesis. This is especially true of Simmel's work: as far as I can tell, his investigations run the danger of ending in scattered fragments." For von Wiese, a work requires underlying, guiding statements, but not simply in order to produce a necessary outline for others to follow—which is what Durkheim would argue—but to ensure the concrete survival of the work. Guiding principles make the work easily tangible. A work that is reducible and then concretely reproduced in one rather neat package cannot be easily misplaced. Simmel's work fails, argues von Wiese, in its refusal to lend to reduction, with the result that some or even many of Simmel's valuable insights could easily be lost, or end in "scattered fragments." For von Wiese, fragmentation shows the work's groundlessness and lack of endurance, and is the sign of the work's probable mortality.

Thus among the various comments and criticisms regarding Simmel's work, a certain rationality emerges. It expresses an attitude that "true" scientific activity occurs only through the consolidation of a unified paradigm within the scientific community. This rationality shows itself concretely in the continuous concern for systematization and reduction to primary guiding statements. Given this expressed concern, scientific work is judged adequate only in terms of its correspondence to the achieved direction of the scientific community. Simmel does not fully share this attitude; his work contributes neither to the achievement of a unified collectivity nor to its concrete preservation over time. As such, he is judged as having failed to meet the "high standards" of membership in the scientific community.

Yet, is science necessarily synonymous with this version of the scientific community? Does doing science in this way respond fully to the essential nature of science? Is the source of this particular version of science fully integrated with the source of science? And is a scientific community of strict concrete grounding and unidirectional expression the only arena in which science can manifest itself? How would Simmel respond to these concerns?

II

Prominent among the various themes discussed by Simmel is the distinction between the concepts of "individual" and "group member." He distinguishes these two concepts in that the individual must undergo a transformation of sorts in the course of group participation. Simmel says that group members relate to one another on the basis of what is communally intelligible. What is not communally intelligible, yet what may constitute an element of an individual's personality, must be withheld or denied by him during his participation within the group. The group encourages its members to participate in the life of the group (in its ideals and aspirations) to the extent that in their life as members they may become the microcosmic embodiment of the group's personality. The member is encouraged to display for the group only those personality elements that are relevant to group life. In this way, a member's personality emerges as distinct from the individual's personality. We may interpret this as the price of membership: the group member sacrifices all that is not communally intelligible. But this is not to say that the group member necessarily participates halfheartedly. Simmel does not intend here to characterize the attitude that an individual carries into group life. In fact, a member's attitude may be totally absorbed with feelings of identification. Whether he participates wholeheartedly or halfheartedly does not negate the fact that *only a fragment of his whole self participates*. Group membership is made possible, says Simmel, by the capacity of the individual to "decompose" his personality into fragments. The group member is always a fragment of the individual.

Consider this formulation with reference to the scientific community represented above by Durkheim, von Wiese, Coser, and Weber—some of its most respected members. In this community the achievement of collective life is a more careful procedure than in most groups. During the many years that constitute an adequate scientific training, a radical transformation of the individual is called for. The individual must develop a carefully refined fragment of his personality and learn to express only that fragment, which purposely coincides with the foundation and direction of the concrete scientific community. Fragmentation of personality is the requirement of membership in any group, but in the scientific community in which Simmel participates, it is accomplished with a certain efficiency and precision. While the decision to join this community may enable a member to perfect and articulate a certain fragment of his personality, it also restricts his ability to express the remainder of his personality.

Simmel's formulation of the process of participation within groups enables him to introduce a curious tension into the notion of fragmentation. We recall that his work was judged fragmentary for its failure to provide a systematic unity believed necessary among scientists. But Simmel argues that this achievement of an objectively visible collective unity (the achievement of a unified paradigm) is only possible given the fragmentary participation of members. With this tension, a dialogue concerning priorities emerges between Simmel and representatives of the scientific community. Simmel takes the concept "individual" as a unity of its own in order to label the participation of scientists as fragmentary, while the scientific community takes its achieved unity as the standard by which to judge Simmel's work as fragmentary. The argument over priorities is concerned with which vantage point represents the highest ideal. Simmel argues that science has perfected one segment of personality at the expense of the others, while representatives of the scientific community argue that Simmel submitted too easily to every individualistic whim of his personality, and as a result, perfected very little. It is in the context of this argument that Simmel discusses the relative values of both the fragment that is visible within the collectivity and the fragment that remains the private property of the individual.

According to Simmel, elements of personality that are communally intelligible are necessarily those which are most diffuse. Moreover, in that those elements are the possessions of many, it must be easier to possess them. Thus, they must be elements which are intellectually inferior. Conversely, qualities that are intellectually superior are possessed by a few or perhaps by only one individual, and as such, do not emerge within the collectivity. The collectivity calls out to the lower elements of its members, since this is what most humans share, while it denies the higher ones. Thus Simmel locates the grounds of the highest intellectual achievement as the unique unity of the individual. In other words, the individual is the source of the highest intellectual standard.

This identical theme finds a voice in the work of Nietzsche, although in a tone that expresses the tremendous anger of this lonely philosopher. For example in a portion of *Thus Spoke Zarathustra,* sarcastically entitled "On the New Idol," Nietzsche writes of the "state, where the slow suicide of all is called 'life'. . . . Where the state ends— look there." Only in the spaces between, where the state does not intervene or interfere, does Nietzsche find the rare moments of human intellectual achievement. For Nietzsche as well as for Simmel, the collectivity does not constitute the fulfillment of the higher human qualities, but of the lower.

III

Simmel discusses the positive side of fragmentation in his article, **"The Adventure."** We speak of an adventure, says Simmel, as an experience of special quality quite distinct from our other experiences and thus separated from the continuity of our lives. The adventure is an extracted fragment, tied to our lives with "fewer threads" than are ordinary experiences. While portions of our lives are formed and recognized by what went before and what comes after and thus automatically fit into the flowing continuity of befores and afters, the adventure does not. Its beginning and end are functions of its own character. The contents of the adventure alone determine where the adventure begins and where it ends. The very character of this fragment is dependent on its being isolated.

Since the adventure is dependent on its isolation, it exists with little reference to what lies outside of it. It thus can count on minute support from the rest of life. The structure and continuity of everyday life are weakened and the

individual is left without a stable orientation. Why? Because the adventure originates precisely out of an inability to experience something "in the same old way." Whether out of a change in contents or out of some feeling of necessity or both, we sacrifice the comfort of a continuous and uninterrupted life. This may be conceived of as a negative quality of the fragmented experience (perhaps in the same sense that von Wiese spoke about "ending in scattered fragments"), or it may be considered a positive quality depending on the adventure's outcome. Still, during the adventure, the outcome (the coming out) is of little relevance, so its positive and negative characteristics are not experienced in themselves. What is experienced is the excitement of chance. Chance, which constitutes the unity of positive and negative, becomes a feature of the adventure's teleological framework. It comes to be sought for its own sake, regardless of outcome. Within the excitement of the adventure, this unity of positive and negative, as chance, comes to take on a totally positive character. Thus, adventure is characterized by its integration with chance, danger, and risk, and these are precisely what constitute its excitement.

While adventure holds the possibility of failure and destruction, it also holds the possibility of the "highest gain." Gain, in this sense, comes not only from the passion that centers within the experience, but also from experiencing the contents of the adventure in their naked form, uninhibited and unaltered by the motives of everyday life.

This direct experience of contents is intimately linked with another feature of the adventure. When Simmel writes that the adventure is attached to everyday life with "fewer threads than are ordinary experiences," he is defining more than the adventure's relationship to its surroundings. He is also referring to an important element of the adventure's form: its wholeness. Recall that the contents alone determine where the adventure begins and ends, and that much of the structure, motive, and continuity of surrounding life are suspended. Yet, if the structure does not come from outside, it must be manufactured from within as an integral commitment of the experience itself. In other words, the adventure molds its own structure. In the sense of this commitment, self-sufficiency can emerge in a fragment. This is not to say that a fragment is necessarily self-sufficient (recall von Wiese's warning about "ending in scattered fragments"). Certainly a fragment can remain without a meaning or a center that will give it substance. In the adventure, however, this need not be the case. For while it separates itself from the center of life and appears to exist "entirely beyond life," somehow, "if by a long and unfamiliar detour" it reorients itself to that center. Says Simmel, "Indeed, it is an attribute of this form to make us feel that in . . . the adventure the whole of life is somehow comprehended and consummated." The notion of the "adventure" expresses a special commitment to unity, for in this fragment lies the experience of unity itself.

Given the notion that the adventure forms its own unity, we may say that each adventure constitutes a beginning in the sense that beginnings are the product and the achievement of a new experienced unity. In *The Scientific Intellectual,* Lewis Feuer suggests that this same phenomenon characterizes the beginning of modern science. Feuer shows how the adventurous ethic was an integral feature of modern science, when in its beginning it first captured its independence and structure (unity) and surfaced concretely. We may inquire, however, whether this adventurous ethic has been neglected within the scientific community as a direct consequence of paradigmatic unity. Surely the scientific community displays a certain unity, but does it ever experience this unity? Or are the requirements of this unity merely passively and thoughtlessly met? In other words, does science suppress adventure as the result of the risk involved? In the adventure, characterized by its willingness to risk the loss of unity, unity is reconsidered, violated, and perhaps recaptured.

When Simmel discusses the professional adventurer as a human being to be admired, he does not want us to conceive of this individual only as one who swims long distances or climbs mountains. The career adventurer may also be the adventurous scientist who, relying on his own strength, violates the support of the community paradigm and makes an adventure of each scientific experience. It is characteristic that even after this individual captures unity, he must leave it in order to relocate it elsewhere. For him, unity is only authenticated when it is experienced. To hold onto the same unity and attempt to preserve it concretely would only mean that he would be present to witness its decay. It is not as important for him that each fragment of his work be the extension of the concreteness of a paradigm and that all of his work be intelligible in terms of this paradigm; it is more important that each fragment be an adventurous occasion that reconsiders its foundations and struggles toward the source from which unity arises.

IV

All the topics that Simmel concerns himself with are related in some manner to the dialectical tension between the individual and the group, that is, the dimensions of the human struggle for individuality. Whether the topic is subordination, the poor, the character of eighteenth-century thought, or the adventure, Simmel almost always expresses some concern for this theme. It should not surprise us then that this theme constitutes Simmel's personal orientation to inquiry, that his writing becomes the medium through which he experiences the tension between himself and his community, and the medium through which he struggles for his individuality.

By uncovering the potentially positive nature of fragmentation in the character of the adventurer, Simmel offers us the key to the stylistic import of the Simmelian corpus. Fragmentation does not necessarily imply failure, although it may; nor is it merely a stylistic quirk with little relation to the contents of the work. In the case of Simmel's writings, and by virtue of his topical concern with the theme of fragmentation, it points us toward a particular conception of theorizing that is characteristic of Simmel's intellectual commitment. He not only presents a concrete formulation of the dialectical tension between the individual and the group; he shows this tension to be alive in his writing. Thus Simmel's fragmentary style may suggest that he experienced each occasion of writing as synonymous with the struggle to be free from any one particular structure or foundation. Kurt Wolff writes, in his introduction to *The Sociology of Georg Simmel,* "Simmel often appears as though in the midst of writing he were overwhelmed by an idea, by an avalanche of ideas, and as if he incorporated them without interrupting himself, digesting and assimilating only to the extent granted him by the onrush." For Simmel, no paradigm is more compelling than the theorist's receptivity toward the experience of theorizing. For him, the community's paradigm often operates as a severe constraint. If Simmel's work is fragmented, it is as a consequence of his relationship with the contents of thought. In *Soziologie* he formulates this same notion as follows:

> If I myself stress the wholly fragmentary, incomplete character of this book, I do not do so in order to protect myself, in a cheap manner, against objections to this character. For when measured by the ideal of objective perfection, the selection of the particular problems and examples contained in this work doubtless presents a haphazard character. Yet if this character should strike one as a defect, this would only go to prove that I have not been able to clarify the fundamental idea of the present volume. For according to this idea, nothing more can be attempted than to establish the beginning and the direction of an infinitely long road—the pretension of any systematic and definitive completeness would be, at least, a self-illusion. Perfection can here be obtained by the individual student only in the subjective sense that he communicates everything he has been able to see.

It is in this sense that Simmel's work achieves its dialectical character. His theme of the dialectic between the individual and the group cannot emerge (cannot make its presence felt) simply by Simmel's writing about it concretely within the corpus. Talking about the dialectic is not tantamount to producing it. The dialectic can only surface when its tension also surfaces as an integral feature of the speech. In this way, Simmel's adventuring nature and thus his resulting fragmented style become the grammar of his dialectic. Moreover, with the adventurous spirit as itself an occasion of the dialectic's tension, we can suggest that Simmel provides the grounds by which we can conceptualize a work's authenticity. We can distinguish between true and false speech on the basis of whether or not the speech is contained in the life of the speaker. That is, the speech can be seen as being tested in the character and actions of the speaker. The initial question to ask is not so much whether or not we agree with Simmel's content, but whether or not Simmel should be the one presenting it. Thus what surfaces here concretely as style is really a conception of authentic speech as speech that is spoken honestly. Only in this manner is the dialectical character of the speech achieved—when the speech (theory) and the life of the speaker (practice) share an intimate relationship.

In the introduction to his commentary, *Georg Simmel,* Coser discusses Simmel's "dialectic of social life." He characterizes the dialectic in terms of the "ambivalence" of social life and the unity of "harmony and disharmony" in social relations. Yet Coser fails to grasp the essential nature of dialectical thought. At one point in the introduction, in speaking about Simmel's final work *Lebensanschuung: Vier metaphysische Kapitel,* Coser writes, "It was not granted to Simmel to solve the tensions and contradictions with which he grappled throughout his life." What Coser does not realize is that dialectical thinking is precisely an attitude in which "tensions and contradictions" are not "solved" per se. Rather, contradictions mark the complexity of human life, and the tension between the individual and the group characterizes the life experience of the dialectical thinker. Thus Coser sees *Lebensanschuung* as a failure for precisely the same reasons we may see it as a success: that it keeps open and alive the fundamental contradictions and tensions of human life and of Simmel's life as a theorist. Like Kuhn, Coser holds Simmel to the requirement of a reifiable solution—a paradigm—and fails to see Simmel's negation of the need for such a solution as the essential requirement of scientific activity.

Coser appreciates the "dialectic of social life" merely as a topic to be spoken about. Yet he cannot condone the dialectic's emergence in the character of Simmel's work. Thus Coser collapses the dialectic in order to keep it at a distance, as an abstract concept. He separates theory and practice and refuses to allow Simmel to live in the society that Simmel authored. Coser's criticism of Simmel's fragmented style, discussed earlier in this [essay], emerges as merely another example of this short-sightedness regarding the essence of the dialectic.

V

While fragmentation displays Simmel's manner of involvement with the contents of his writings, it cannot be formalized as method within a community of scientists. For Simmel, fragmentation becomes his stylistic manner in connection with, and as a consequence and symbol of, his experience of theorizing. Without this intimate link, fragmentation would lack any positive character and would rightly be subject to the criticisms leveled at Simmel. We can draw a partial comparison here with Franz Schubert's "Unfinished Symphony." The unfinishedness of the symphony becomes one of its analytic features inasmuch as the uniqueness of the piece unfolds partially through the unfinishedness. Yet unfinishedness cannot then become a formal method for composing further symphonies. That is, another composer could not reproduce the essence of Schubert's "Unfinished Symphony" simply by beginning to write a symphony and not finishing it. The core of Schubert's symphony is not determined by a particular structural method imposed beforehand. Rather, the character of unfinishedness emerges as a consequence of the symphony's composition.

For Simmel, his style as method cannot be divorced from his experience of theorizing. Instead, by virtue of his topical preoccupation with the theme of individuality, it produces a conception of method as a consequence of the individuality achieved in theorizing. For Simmel, any method imposed on a member by the scientific community binds that member and restricts his ability to articulate his individuality. Method imposed by the community is precisely what the individual must attempt to transcend, even as he is participating in the life of the group. In contrast, an individual's method (his own style, structure, and foundation) must surface as a consequence and symbol of his experience of theorizing. In other words, for Simmel, method is the responsibility of individuals. Simmel does not supply others with method (other than encourage adventure which in itself is not method), nor does he attempt to perfect and consolidate a strong paradigm designed to subject other scientists (which is incidentally what Freud did once he first captured his individuality). There can be no paradigm for individuality. Remaining faithful to this theme, Simmel must attempt to live as a nonparadigmatic author. While a paradigm may be extracted from his writings (as von Wiese and Weingartner have done) and introduced into the scientific community as foundation and method, such a paradigm misses the deeper spirit of Simmel's authorship.

Simmel does not attempt to transform his struggle for individuality into a struggle for supremacy within the scientific community. In his concern for individuality he makes no attempt to violate the individuality of his audience. Through his writing Simmel can only become the exemplar of individuality within his scientific community. His commitment to the scientific community is not directed toward the concrete preservation of its paradigm, but to the individuals who as members of that community have not seen the possibility of a life of struggle for independence from the accepted community paradigm. In this sense Simmel's breaking through is not conceivable in terms of Kuhn's notion of a paradigm shift, or in terms of the solely concrete concern that he must have attracted a wide and unified following. Rather, breakthrough, for Simmel, may be formulated in terms of his having provided a precedent and thus support for the achievement of individuality. In this sense, while his work will never be fully integrated within the scientific community's structure and ideology, it will greatly influence individuals within that community. Simmel has provoked many authors (Martin Buber, Robert Park, and Max Weber are only a few examples), but they have not been restricted as a result of their relationship with him. His success is synonymous with his refusal to manage their procedure and direction. In one comment, Simmel formulates this notion as follows: "I know that I shall die without intellectual heirs, and that is as it should be. My legacy will be like cash, distributed to many heirs, each transforming his part into use according to his nature—a use which will no longer reveal its indebtedness to this heritage."

David Frisby (essay date 1984)

SOURCE: "The Foundation of Sociology," in *Georg Simmel,* Ellis Horwood Limited and Tavistock Publications, 1984, pp. 45-64.

[*In the following excerpt, Frisby highlights Simmel's consideration of a broad range of human interactions as the reason for the wide scope of his sociological thought.*]

A NEW CONCEPT OF SOCIOLOGY: FIRST ATTEMPT

In his review of Simmel's *Sociology,* Alfred Vierkandt makes the following ambitious claim:

> If sociology succeeds in developing itself into an autonomous individual science, then its future historian will have to celebrate Simmel as its founder, and even if this process is not completed, his work remains an outstanding, penetrating achievement. He has indeed demarcated an autonomous group of problems for the study of society and thereby demonstrated the possibility and urgent need for a new discipline. His distinction between the form and content of social life elevates him above the encyclopaedic interpretation of sociology. In the same way, he distinguishes himself from those who allow sociology to be identified with the tasks of historical, cultural or social philosophy. For its specific problem is always the interactions and relationships between the individual elements of a group.

If we leave aside for the moment a judgement upon this claim, then we should at least investigate how Simmel arrived at what he himself conceived of as 'a new concept of sociology'. In order to do this it is necessary to return to his early writings so that we may reconstruct systematically and historically Simmel's progress towards this goal.

As Friedrich Tenbruck has pointed out in this connection, any attempt at a realistic assessment of Simmel's contribution to sociology must examine carefully the historical location of his interest in sociology. Simmel's

> sociological period, announced by the themes of several articles in the 1880s, commences with the study *On Social Differentiation* (1890) and reaches its real high point and fulfilment in *The Philosophy of Money* (1900). Between these dates lie a large number of articles which in changed or enlarged forms, in the original formulation or translated, improved, merged with one another, are reworked and finally presented in the collection: *Sociology.*

If we accept this assessment—and it would have to be qualified by some of the articles published after 1900 which make up the *Sociology*—then we should accept Tenbruck's inference that 'Simmel's sociological work is thus confined to a single decade. Hence, he is specifically and in the strict sense not a contemporary of Max Weber. As the latter commenced sociological work, the former had already taken his leave of it'. What is true is that within that decade Simmel had established the basic framework for his sociology. After 1898 he ceased to preface his articles on various aspects of sociology with a justification of the grounds for such a discipline.

If the subtitle of his *On Social Differentiation*—'Sociological and Psychological Investigations'—indicates an ambiguity as to the content of this work, then this same uncertainty is reflected in the title of its first chapter: 'On the Epistemology of Social Science'. It does not yet indicate a clear commitment to sociology. Nonetheless, it does represent Simmel's first attempt to demarcate sociology as an independent discipline. But before moving on to an analysis of its central arguments, we should briefly consider the context within which Simmel was seeking to establish his particular conception of sociology.

Any attempt to ground sociology anew in the late 1880s in Germany would have to confront the positivist conception of sociology developed by Comte and its extension in Herbert Spencer's evolutionary theory. In Germany, Darwin's evolutionism had already made a major impact on social theory in the biologically and organicist orientated conceptions of sociology such as those of Schäffle and Lilienfeld. Under the influence of developments in statistics, attempts were also made to develop a 'social physics'. But these directions in social theory did not go unchallenged. In his writings of the 1870s and 1880s, Wilhelm Dilthey (also in Berlin University) had already attacked the positivism of Comte and Mill and a Comtean and Spencerian conception of sociology as a 'gigantic dream concept'. In 1883 Dilthey was already speaking of society as the 'play of interactions' or 'the summation of interactions' and, in a passage very close to Simmel's conception of society (though Simmel never acknowledged Dilthey's influence), Dilthey maintained that 'the individual . . . is an element in the interactions [*Wechselwirkungen*] of society, a point of intersection of the diverse systems of these interactions who reacts with conscious intention and action upon their effects'. Similarly, Gumplowicz in his *Grundriss der Soziologie* (1885) attacked the overarching concept of society as a fundamental concept of sociology and sought to substitute the study of social groups as its object domain.

In other related areas of social science, attempts were also being made to secure firm foundations for particular disciplines. Since Simmel was attending some of the historical economist Gustáv Schmoller's seminars and in the light of the content of his 'On the Psychology of Money' (1889) he was probably acquainted with the methodological dispute, the *Methodenstreit,* in economics from the early 1880s onwards between the historical and theoretical schools of economics. More importantly, Simmel was already schooled in the *Völkerpsychologie* of his teachers Lazarus and Steinthal, as well as the work of Gustav Fechner in the field of psychology and philosophy. A recent study suggests that Fechner's doctrine of logical atomism enabled Simmel to develop a conception of society that did not move either towards 'the hypostatization of a Volksseele' as in much early *Völkerpsychologie* or towards a 'substantive anthropology' as in Spencer's work. Rather, Simmel was able to conceive of society as the interaction of its elements (individuals) rather than as a substance. Similarly, Simmel adopted Fechner's conception of the interaction of elements rather than the operation of forces in one direction, thereby producing a conception of reality whose complexity prevented the development of laws in the positivist sense. This recent study of Simmel's early work concludes that Fechner's simple atomism 'enabled Simmel to move from *Völkerpsychologie* into a sociology that no longer justified its object by a distinctive substance, but rather wished merely to describe the formal relationship of complex elements in a functional constellation'. The other conclusion which may be drawn is that in seeking to establish sociology as an independent discipline, Simmel would necessarily be confronted with the problem of the demarcation of sociology from psychology.

It is within this context that Simmel first sets out to clarify the nature of sociology. 'A newly emergent science' such as sociology seems to be 'an eclectic discipline insofar as the products of other sciences constitute its subject matter'. Seen in this light, sociology provides 'merely a new standpoint for the observation of already known facts'. Hence, sociology cannot be defined in terms of its object of study since 'in the last instance, there is no science whose content emerges out of mere objective facts, but rather always entails their interpretation and ordering according to categories and norms that exist *a priori* for the relevant science'. In other words, there can be no naive positivist grounding of a science of sociology in facts. However, Simmel goes on to argue that sociology cannot merely be grounded in conceptualizations either. Although sociology might ask 'What is a society? What is an individual? How are reciprocal effects of individuals upon each other possible?', it cannot do so on the basis of fixed *a priori* conceptions. Otherwise it 'will fall into the error of the older psychology: one must first have defined the nature of the psyche before one can scientifically recognise psychological phenomena'.

One major reason why *a priori* conceptualizations are inappropriate is that the subject-matter to which they refer, both in psychology and in sociology, is extremely complex. The diversity of 'latent and effective forces' within individuals and society and the 'reciprocal effects' [*gegenseitige Wirkungen*] of individuals and groups upon one another are so great as to make their possible combinations almost infinite and immeasurable. From this Simmel infers that

> if it is the task of sociology to describe the forms of human communal existence and to find the rules according to which he or she is the member of a group, and groups relate to one another, then the complexity of this object has a consequence for our science which places it in an epistemological relationship—which I must extensively ground—to metaphysics and psychology.

The two latter disciplines are characterized by the fact that both produce contrary propositions which have the same plausibility, probability and verifiability. For instance, in psychology the general concepts of psychological functions are so general and the 'wealth of nuances' in each psychological function so great that to subsume a complex phenomenon under the same single concept usually leads to a failure to distinguish why different causes produce the same effect. This means, Simmel argues, that 'the establishment of a causal connection between simple psychological concepts . . . is always completely one-sided'. In the same way, the sheer complexity of psychological phenomena prevents psychology from arriving at 'any laws in the natural scientific sense . . . it is never possible to establish with complete certainty what in fact is indeed the cause of a given effect or the effect of a given cause'.

Similarly, sociology too faces the same problem of the complexity of its object which 'completely prevents its separation into simple parts and its basic forces and relationships'. This also prevents sociology from generating 'laws of social development. Undoubtedly, each element

of a society moves according to natural laws. Yet for the whole there exists no law; as in nature, so equally here, there is no higher law above the laws that govern the movement of the smallest parts'. Here we see Simmel attempting to move away from his early Spencerian and Darwinian conception of social reality.

This line of argument also pushes Simmel in the direction of a critique of those conceptions of sociology that take as their starting point an all-embracing concept of society. For Simmel the only genuine reality is the activities of individuals who constitute society:

> If society is merely a . . . constellation of individuals who are the actual realities, then the latter and their behaviour also constitutes the real object of science and the concept of society evaporates . . . What palpably exists is indeed only individual human beings and their circumstances and activities: therefore, the task can only be to understand them, whereas the essence of society, that emerges purely through an ideal synthesis and is never to be grasped, should not form the object of reflection that is directed towards the investigation of reality.

Simmel here seeks to guard against both a conception of society as an autonomous entity and a thorough-going individualist foundation for sociology that reduces social reality to isolated atoms.

In order to secure sociology from this latter danger, Simmel has to indicate some object of study that is not merely individuals as such. And here we move towards the core of Simmel's early foundation of sociology. Simmel commences from 'a regulative world principle that everything interacts in some way with everything else, that between every point in the world and every other force permanently moving relationships exist'. Following on from the earlier argument about the complexity of reality, Simmel maintains that we cannot extract a single element out of this ceaseless interaction and say that it is the decisive one. Rather, we must assert that what unites individual elements in some objective form is interaction: 'there exists only one basic factor which provides at least a relative objectivity of unification: the interaction [*Wechselwirkung*] of the parts. We characterise any object as unified to the extent to which its parts stand in a reciprocal dynamic relationship'. Is this how Simmel conceives of society?

Sociology is concerned with 'empirical atoms, with conceptions, individuals and groups that function as unities'. It is concerned with social interactions. Sociology does not therefore take as its starting point the concept of society since it is

> only the name for the sum of these interactions . . . It is therefore not a unified, fixed concept but rather a gradual one . . . according to the greater number and cohesion of the existing interactions that exist between the given persons. In this manner, the concept of society completely loses its mystical facet that individualistic realism wished to see in it.

Society is thus composed of the ceaseless interaction of its individual elements—groups as well as individuals—

which impels Simmel's sociology towards a concern for social *relationships,* i.e. towards the study of social interaction.

In his early attempt to ground sociology as an independent discipline, Simmel first established the regulative principle of the interaction and inter-relatedness of all phenomena. For sociology this implied the study not of society as substance but as interaction of its elements. The more abstract grounding for his regulative principle was already present in his doctoral dissertation (1881) which criticized Kant's conception of matter:

> If matter emerges out of energies or forces [*Kraften*], then one should no longer treat them as purely possible substances upon which other energies can exercise their undisturbed interplay; for the product of these energies is no finished product, but a continuous process . . . an emergent entity . . . There exists amongst the energies no difference in their status.

Simmel was later to extend this concept of matter to society itself. Sociology was to examine the interplay of interactions without necessarily giving any of them any logical or societal priority.

THE PROBLEM OF SOCIOLOGY

What lies between Simmel's first attempt to ground sociology in 1890 and his important essay **'The Problems of Sociology'** (1894) is not merely his two-volume *Introduction to Moral Philosophy* (1892/93) but also his *Problems of the Philosophy of History* (1892). As Simmel himself subsequently reflected, he had started out from epistemological and Kantian studies together with historical and social scientific interests:

> The initial result of this was the basic insight (set out in *The Problems of the Philosophy of History*) that "history" signifies the formation [*Formung*] of the events that are objects of immediate experience by means of the *a priori* categories of the scientific intellect just as "nature" signifies the formation of sensually given materials by means of the categories of the understanding.

> This separation of the form and content of the historical image, that emerged for me purely epistemologically, was then pursued by me in a methodological principle within a particular discipline. I secured a new concept of sociology in which I separated the forms of sociation [*die Formen der Vergesellschaftung*] from the contents, i.e. the drives, purposes and material content which, only by being taken up by the interactions between individuals, become societal.

This 'new concept of sociology' is outlined in Simmel's essay of 1894 which he himself saw as being so important (1894 was the first year in which he taught a course simply entitled 'Sociology') and which, he wrote, 'contains my work programme'. Indeed, Simmel wrote in 1895: 'I take the small article to be the most fruitful one that I have written'. It is therefore worthy of detailed treatment, especially since, in revised and extended form, it later constituted the first chapter of Simmel's *Sociology*. Some of its content and developments from it also reappear either at

the beginning or end of almost every sociological essay Simmel wrote between 1894 and 1898.

Simmel starts out from 'the most significant and momentous progress' in historical and human studies in recent times, namely 'the overthrow of the individualistic perspective'. The replacement of 'individual fates' by 'social forces' and 'collective movements'—the 'real and determining' factors—has ensured that 'the science of human beings has become the science of human society'. However, this tendency can only establish 'a regulative principle for all human sciences'; it cannot be the basis for a 'specific, autonomous science' such as sociology. Rather, it is merely 'a comprehensive name' for the human sciences. Hence,

> Sociology as the history of society and all its contents, i.e. in the sense of an explanation of all events by means of social forces and configurations, is no more a specific science than, for instance, induction. Like the latter—though not in the same formal sense—it is a method of acquiring knowledge, a heuristic principle.

If sociology is to be anything more than 'a mere research tendency that is falsely hypostatized into a science of sociology' it must have a more restricted significance.

What is this more restricted sense of sociology that secures its existence as an independent discipline? Simmel provides an answer by drawing an analogy with psychology to the effect that,

> Just as the differentiation of the specifically psychological from objective matter produces psychology as a science, so a genuine sociology can only deal with what is specifically societal, the form and forms of sociation [*Vergesellschaftung*] as such, as distinct from the particular interests and contents in and through which sociation is realised.

Such interests and contents form the subject matter of other specialized sciences.

Having circumscribed the task of sociology, Simmel is obliged to outline, on the basis of this sociology, what he means by society. In the light of his earlier attempt to ground sociology, his answer is not surprising: 'Society in the broadest sense is indeed to be found wherever several individuals enter into interaction'. Therefore, 'one must recognise sociation of the most diverse levels and types' from the simplest to the most complex. The particular causes and purposes without which no sociation would occur constitute 'the body, the material of the social process'. However,

> The fact that the result of these causes, the pursuance of these goals does in fact call forth an interaction, a sociation amongst its agents, this is the *form* in which this content clothes itself. And the whole existence of a specific science of *society* rests upon the demarcation of the latter by means of scientific abstraction.

These forms of sociation are less diverse than their content since 'the same form, the same type of sociation can enter into the most diverse material'. The constitution of sociology as a discipline thus rests upon

> a realm legitimated by abstraction: that of sociation as such and its forms. These forms develop out of the contact of individuals, relatively independently of the reasons for this contact, and their sum total constitutes, concretely, that entity which is designated by the abstraction: society.

This is what distinguishes Simmel's concept of sociology from earlier theories of society which, on the basis of this abstract concept of society, were able to include within the realm of sociology, for instance, 'any ethnological or prehistorical investigation'. Without denying the value of such research, Simmel maintains that to subsume such studies under the rubric of sociology 'rests upon the faulty distinction between that "society" which is only a collective name arising out of the inability to treat separately individual phenomena and that society which determines the phenomena through specifically social forces'. In other words, there is a failure to distinguish between 'what takes place merely *within* society as a framework and that which really takes place *through* society'. Only the latter constitutes the subject matter of sociology.

Of course, this subject matter presents itself to us in social reality as a fusion of form and content. But, like other sciences, sociology proceeds on the basis of abstraction, in this case the abstraction of the form from the content of social reality. Sociology 'extracts the purely social element from the totality of human history—i.e. what occurs *in* society—for special attention, or, expressed with somewhat paradoxical brevity, it investigates that which in society is "society" '. What does the study of "society" in this second sense consist of ? It comprises 'the investigation of the forces, forms and developments of sociation, of the cooperation, association and co-existence of individuals'. This 'should be the sole object of a sociology conceived as a special science'.

If this is the legitimate object of sociology, how should it be investigated? In the light of Simmel's desire to provide the foundations for a strictly demarcated sociological discipline, his answer to this question is surprising:

> The methods according to which the problems of sociation are to be investigated are the same as in all comparative psychological sciences. As a foundation there lie certain psychological presuppositions that belong to them without which no historical science can exist: the phenomena of seeking and giving help, of love and hate, of avarice and the sense of satisfaction in communal existence, the self preservation of individuals . . . and a series of other primary psychological processes must be presupposed in order that one can at all understand how sociation, group formations, relations of individuals to a whole entity, etc., come about.

Certainly these and other psychological phenomena are dealt with by Simmel in his sociological writings. But it also makes all the more important the task of demarcating sociology from psychology, even though sociology in this period was not the only discipline to be grounded in psy-

chological presuppositions as the history of economics demonstrates. Sociology, for Simmel, does not remain content with these psychological presuppositions but through a process of 'abstraction and combination' separates the content and form of social events. It 'treats these forms by means of inductive abstraction from the collective phenomena . . . It is the only science which really seeks to know only society, *sensu strictissimo*'. And in a **'Supplementary Note'** to the English translation of 1895, Simmel argues that rather than being a narrow discipline 'as it appeared to a number of my critics' it actually deals with a whole range of forms of sociation from the most general to the most particular.

Simmel also conceives of the possibility at least of this new mode of sociological analysis providing a comprehensive understanding of society. In the opening passage to his article on **'Superiority and Subordination'** (1896) Simmel argues that 'if we could exhibit the totality of possible forms of social relationship in their gradations and variations we should have in such [an] exhibit complete knowledge of "society" as such'. But again Simmel guards against a reduction or even 'an approximate reduction' of our knowledge of society to a few simple propositions on the grounds that

> Social phenomena are too immeasurably complicated, and the methods of analysis are too incomplete. The consequence is that if sociological forms and names are used with precision they apply only within a relatively contracted circle of manifestations. Long and patient labour will be necessary before we can understand the concrete historical forms of socialisation [sociation, D.F.] as the actual compounds of a few simple fundamental forms of human association.

And even if we are able to discover the 'laws, forms and developments' of sociation then we must also recognise that they determine social reality 'only together with other functions and forces'. This implies that Simmel is not guilty of that form of sociologism that became so common in social theory. But, once more, it raises the necessity of demarcating sociology from the study of these 'other functions and forces', especially where—with considerable ambiguity—Simmel declares sociology's task to be the 'description and determination of *the historico-psychological origin* of those forms in which interactions take place between human beings'. It is to Simmel's demarcation of sociology from psychology and from history that we must now turn.

THE DEMARCATION OF SOCIOLOGY

From psychology

As someone who had started out from *Völkerpsychologie* before coming to sociology, Simmel was well aware that 'the attempt has been made to reduce all sciences to psychology'—a reference perhaps to Wilhelm Wundt (amongst others). The grounds for this reduction are that the sciences are all the product of the human mind. Simmel rejects this argument as a failure to distinguish between the science of psychology and the functions of the mind.

But as we have seen, Simmel's real demarcation problem arises out of his own inclusion of psychological presuppositions into his foundation of sociology. Certain specific structures within the socio-historical complex must be related back not only to social interactions but also 'psychological states'. Sociology confines itself to the 'immediate psychological significance' of a course of events. But sociology must go beyond this on the basis of its own abstractions. This is necessary since 'if society is to be an autonomous object of an independent science, then it can only be so through the fact that, out of the sum of individual elements that constitute it, a new entity emerges; otherwise all problems of social science would only be those of individual psychology'.

There is another reason why the demarcation of sociology from psychology is necessary for Simmel. The more he concentrated upon small-scale face-to-face interactions, upon 'microscopic-molecular processes within human material' that 'exhibit society, as it were, *statu nascendi* ', the more Simmel recognized that 'the delicate, invisible threads that are woven between one person and another' are 'only accessible through psychological microscopy'. Insofar as Simmel also maintains that explanation of the smallest interactions is necessary in order to explain the major constellations of society, he thereby traces his sociological thematic back to psychological variables.

Simmel was conscious of this problem in the first chapter of his *Sociology* in which he admits that such a focus 'seems to make the investigations planned here to be nothing other than chapters of psychology, at best social psychology'. Indeed, he concedes that 'all societal processes and instincts have their seat in minds and that sociation is, as a consequence, a psychical phenomenon'. Further, we should recognize 'psychic motivations—feelings, thoughts, and needs— . . . not merely as bearers of . . . external relations but also as their essence, as what really and solely interest us', and which 'we reconstruct by means of an instinctive or methodical psychology'.

Simmel's attempt to separate sociology and psychology does not rest upon a strong argument. He maintains that 'the scientific treatment of psychic data is not thereby automatically psychological' since the 'one reality' of social scientific study can be considered 'from a number of different viewpoints'. Hence, although 'the givens of sociology are psychological processes whose immediate reality presents itself first of all under psychological categories . . . [they] remain outside the purposes of sociological investigation. It is to this end that we direct our study to the objective reality of sociation'.

In defending Simmel against the charge of establishing a psychologistic foundation for sociology, one recent commentator has suggested with regard to the study of the regularities of human behaviour that

> Whilst statistical figures, interpreted social psychologically, bring out qualities of individuals, viewed sociologically they bring out features of interaction, qualities of systems. With this demarcation Simmel sought once more to establish the possibility of an independent sociology, although he knew that in any particular concrete

individual study the boundaries between social psychological and sociological analysis are always fluid. He therefore never seriously concerned himself with avoiding social psychological statements in his sociological investigations.

Such arguments did not, of course, prevent some of Simmel's contemporaries from arguing that he provided a psychologistic foundation for sociology. Othmar Spann, for instance, maintained that Simmel's 'psychologistic concept of society' was based on his 'definition of societal interaction as the interaction of *psychological* entities'. Against this, Spann argued that a 'specifically *social* criterion for interaction' could only be derived from an adequate conception of society not grounded in or reduced to psychological entities. Similarly, Max Weber referred to Spann's 'perceptive criticism' of Simmel's sociology prior to the publication of his *Sociology* but qualified this judgement by stating that 'in relation to the earlier work which Spann criticised, Simmel's recently published *Sociology* shows some notable, but not *fundamental,* modifications'. Viewed from a very different perspective, however, the grounding of sociology in some psychological categories may be one reason why Simmel's sociology has proved attractive not merely to the interactionist tradition but also to social psychology.

From history

In a brief notice of 1895, Simmel suggests that 'sociology might . . . unify the advantages of naturalism and idealism because its object possesses the quality of being accessible to us just as much from the inside—psychologically, through our essential identity with everything human—as from the outside—through statistical, empirical, historical observation'. Having shown that Simmel's sociology has very close connections with psychology, is this equally true for sociology's relationship to history?

As we have seen, Simmel rejects the notion of sociology as 'the history of society' as an inadequate foundation for sociology as a distinctive discipline. It is, however, 'a method of acquiring knowledge, a heuristic principle'. But insofar as sociology is the study of not merely the forces and forms of sociation but also the *'developments* of sociation' it must have a historical component. This historical dimension is a restricted one. As Dahme has argued, this historical dimension does not lead us to a 'historical' sociology:

> Since, according to Simmel, social reality is always to be grasped as a "historical reality", so similarly the actors in social life are to be viewed as historical entities. Simmel draws the unequivocal conclusion from this that a sociology cannot ignore historical developments. Simmel himself always attends to this insight in his sociological investigations, insofar as he seeks to take account of and to analyse historical developments as bringing about the modification of modes of behavior and changes in social forms. But, in *taking account of historical elements* it is still not necessary for Simmel to *practise sociology as a historical sociology.*

What this implies is that in his particular studies, on fashion for instance, Simmel shows how social formations change over time. In his *The Philosophy of Money* it is possible to trace historical variations in forms of exchange and their consequences for social relationships. What is missing, however, is a historical sociology of money relationships. This is an important distinction between the sociologies of Simmel and Max Weber. Simmel's students detected the absence of a systematic historical sociological approach. Karl Mannheim, with reference to Simmel's analysis of the money economy, suggests that though he 'has characterised in many ways the empirically changing objects of the world that are associated with money forms . . . yet in so doing he has abstracted, in a completely unhistorical manner, the capitalistic money form from its capitalistic background and imputed the characteristic structural change to "money as such" '. Simmel is aware of historical variations in forms of sociation but he seldom ever subjects them to a systematic historical analysis. As a result, the reader is often left with the impression that his works are filled with historical instances and examples. As Siegfried Kracauer said of Simmel's analyses of forms of sociation, 'none of them live in historical time'.

But perhaps there is a reason for this retreat from systematic historical analysis that relates to Simmel's attempt to establish sociology as a distinctive science. Simmel consistently seeks to guard against the reduction of sociology to a philosophy of history and any assertion of the existence of historical laws. Sociology conceived as a philosophy of history was being propagated in Germany by such theorists as Paul Barth. The existence of historical laws was asserted by various groups within German Marxism. Simmel insists that sociology must be strictly demarcated from the philosophy of history which seeks 'to subsume historical facts in their totality, both external and psychological, under "general concepts" ' whereas sociology should continue itself 'completely within the course of events and their immediate psychological significance'. And in the same context, Simmel adds—on the basis of his own arguments in *The Problems of the Philosophy of History*—that 'there is certainly no longer any doubt today that "laws of history" are not to be found; for history is, on the one hand, such a hugely complex structure, on the other, such an uncertain and subjectively demarcated section extracted from cosmic events, that no unified formula for its development as a totality can be given'. In rejecting sociology as a philosophy of history and historical laws (as also laws of society), Simmel maintains that sociology may itself provide a further contribution to the 'separation of the totality of historical events' insofar as it 'extracts the function of sociation and its countless forms and developments as a special field'.

Thus, despite Simmel's protestation that 'if one attempts to understand . . . aspects of the present time, this can be achieved only through history, i.e. by knowing and understanding the past', Simmel's sociology does not move in the direction of a historical sociology. History is one of those perspectives from which the totality of reality can be viewed but never fully grasped.

THE QUESTION OF METHOD

It should be evident that Simmel's attempt to ground sociology as an independent science does not rest upon the discovery of a new object for sociological investigation. Rather, 'Simmel's sociology is . . . based on no *new material object* but on a *formal object,* a new "mode of observation", a "standpoint", an "abstraction" '. But since Simmel, unlike Durkheim or Weber, wrote no treatise on this 'method' and regarded preoccupation with methodological issues as a form of fetishism, Becher's judgement is more appropriate, namely that 'expressions such as "mode of observation", "viewpoint", "standpoint", "research tendency" would be more accurate here. This would also correspond with Simmel's perspectivism. The concept of "method", taken in its strict sense, is false'. Bearing in mind this important qualification, it is nonetheless possible to outline the basic elements of Simmel's attempt to provide 'a new and sharply demarcated complex of specific tasks' for sociology.

As we have seen, Simmel starts out in 1890 from 'a regulative world principle that everything interacts in some way with everything else'. This implies that relationships between things are in permanent flux; 'between every point in the world and every other force permanently moving relationships exist'. Indeed, transferring this principle to the study of social reality, Kracauer detected in Simmel's work a 'core principle' of 'the fundamental interrelatedness [*Wesenszusammengehörigkeit*] of the most diverse phenomena'. In his sociological work, this enabled Simmel to start out from any point within the totality of social life and arrive at any other. But it is worth nothing here that this first regulative principle itself rests upon a 'general tendency of modern thought, with its dissolving of substances into functions, the fixed and permanent in the flux of restless development—an intellectual tendency that certainly stands in interaction with the practical movements', of the period. Its substantive foundation therefore rests in social reality itself and in his *The Philosophy of Money* we can see its social origins. In terms of Simmel's approach to sociology, however, what is important is that this first principle already points to a feature of the world that preoccupies Simmel, namely the relationships that exist between the most diverse and seemingly unconnected phenomena. We might add a further corollary here to the effect that Simmel's key concepts that define his sociology are all relational concepts: interaction [*Wechselwirkung*] and sociation [*Vergesellschaftung*]. Even the notion of form too can only be seen in relation to content.

There is a second 'regulative principle for all the human sciences' (1894) that does not yet indicate the role of sociology but which it must nonetheless presuppose. This is that 'social forces, collective movements' are 'the real and determining' factors in social life rather than individual fates. There are also two further assumptions which Simmel makes in his early writings that are significant for his delineation of sociology. The first, to which he often refers, is that the world—including the social world and the individuals in it—is an extremely complex and differentiated phenomenon. Simmel always returns to this premise as an argument against historical laws or laws of social development that seeks to encompass their particular object in its totality. And, to anticipate Simmel's conception of sociology proper, there is a second important premise that sociology in its concern with the social interactions of individuals must take account of a whole range of 'psychological presuppositions' upon which its own generalizations in part rest.

In his first attempt to ground sociology, Simmel applies the concept of interaction or reciprocal effect to social life and indicates that its basis lies in the interaction or reciprocal relationship between its elements. These elements are conscious individuals or groups of individuals who interact with one another for a variety of motives, purposes and interests. This is the source of the psychological propositions which Simmel acknowledges in his social theory.

However, in order to discover and elucidate the general features of human interaction, Simmel maintains that the investigator must proceed, as in all other sciences, on the basis of a methodical abstraction. For Simmel this constitutes the separation of the form from the content of social interactions, the forms by which individuals and groups of individuals come to be members of society. Sociology's task is therefore the investigation of the forms of being part of society, namely the forms of sociation [*Vergesellschaftung*]. Hence, as Becher has argued, 'Simmel does *not* start out from the isolated individual, *not* from society and also not from the opposition between individual and society, although this opposition greatly interested him'. In starting out from social interactions, Simmel also removes the content of that interaction by a process of abstraction. His problem is therefore that of locating 'the sociality of interaction in the *consciousness* of those interacting' without at the same time hypostatizing or psychologizing the concept of social interaction. Participants in social interaction consciously interact with one another, though Simmel recognizes that interaction also takes place between, say, individuals and supra-personal social forms such as the state and that interactions can be institutionalized in rules. In other words, there is

> no interaction in itself, in its abstract conception . . . rather always a whole wealth of diverse types and forms of interactions. This is what Simmel implies by the concept of form. Sociation is interaction. Interaction always presents itself in a particular form. Hence, society is always a formed society or it does not exist.

Society exists 'where a number of people enter into interaction and form a temporary or permanent unity'.

As Tenbruck has argued, Simmel decisively goes beyond Dilthey's use of the concept of interaction 'in that he defines the *forms* of interaction as the object of sociology'. This 'formed nature of social action does not lie uppermost in individual actions and their comparison but in the stable structure of relationships'. Even though the sociologist must abstract the forms of sociation from social reality, this does not imply that Simmel was pleading 'for the establishment of categories of a high degree of abstractedness'. Nor is the distinction between form and content, essential to the abstraction of forms of sociation, a 'pure abstraction, insofar as—just like his concept of society—it possesses a *fundamentum in re*'. All this should suggest that Simmel is not concerned to develop either an abstract classification of social forms or an endless typification and taxonomy of social interactions as formal sociology has so

often been identified with. Simmel's sociology is not grounded in a deductive procedure. As he himself often insists, in the study of human sociation 'we will . . . recognise *the forms and laws of sociation* in such a way that we combine social phenomena of the most diverse contents and in fact, *explore inductively* what is nonetheless common to all of them'. Thus, on the basis of this inductive procedure, we abstract these forms of sociation from a variety of social phenomena. Such forms, as Tenbruck suggests, 'represent a specific "layer" of reality. Although they cannot—and are not meant to—account for interaction itself, they are operative in it; they account for its patterns'. Interaction itself for Simmel has its origins in individual motives, interests, etc. This is also where the 'psychological presuppositions' of the analysis of interaction are relevant.

But Simmel is not merely interested in the forms of simple individual interactions. The study of 'sociation of the most diverse levels and types' must include not merely face-to-face interactions but also the investigation of those social relations that have become crystalized in supra-individual forms. These 'objective structures present themselves in the most diverse types of phenomena: as specific organs of the division of labour, as cohesive symbols, as timelessly valid norms'. Such processes often 'appear as products and functions of an impersonal structure' and 'confront the individual as something objective, split off from the conditions of personal life'. But when we speak of such processes as if they were autonomous entities, we ignore the fact that they are 'merely the complex of infinite mechanical interactions of the smallest parts of organic bodies'. In other words, we ignore the fact that 'the interaction between individuals is the starting point of all social formations'. Ultimately then, Simmel assumes that more complex social formations are extensions of simpler interactions between individuals.

It should follow from this that those who see in Simmel's work a formal sociology that is increasingly divorced and abstracted from social reality ignore the increasing refinement of his foundation of sociology as his work progressed. As Dahme has argued, Simmel—at least from 1894 onwards—perhaps unwittingly anticipated this charge insofar as, and in contrast to the form-content division, he increasingly

> places more emphasis upon the *interactional and reciprocal character of social relationships*. The interaction that is typical of social life is now characterised by him as sociation. Social interactions are now no longer conceived merely as abstract determinations of form and function, but rather are made more precise so that they are bound up with concrete agents of the process of sociation. Processes of sociation can only be dealt with in terms of individuals, groups or social structures.

The object of sociology, lying in social agents of sociation, thus becomes empirically accessible.

Since Simmel's guidelines to empirical sociological research are never systematically presented and are few and far between, it seems reasonable to examine his procedure within the context of his substantive works. However, some brief indication of the direction of Simmel's work can be given here.

In his essay of 1894 on **'The Problem of Sociology'**, Simmel does intimate two directions which sociological research can take. One is to follow 'the longitudinal direction of individual development' in such a way that the development of a social institution is rendered sociological 'insofar as social forms—super- and subordination, the formation of an objective community compared with the mere sum of individuals, the growth of subdivisions, the modification of the social form by quantitative changes in the group—appear in complex phenomena and are extractable from them'. A second direction is 'to draw a cross-section through individual developments' in order to extract what is common to all of them: inductively derived 'social constellations as such'. They might comprise 'those most general relationships and their transformations which are called forth by constant individual similarities and differences of individuals in the formation of any association, or . . . the special forms of association that are to be found in the sociations either within a specific sphere—economic, religious, domestic, social, political—or within a specific period'. In indicating the content of longitudinal and cross-sectional analysis, Simmel was also intimating some of the areas which his own sociological research had either already taken up or was about to embark upon.

In an important essay on **'Sociological Aesthetics'** (1896), Simmel also hints that his sociological project is no orthodox empirical sociology. There he announces that,

> For us the essence of aesthetic observation and interpretation lies in the fact that the typical is to be found in what is unique, the law-like in what is fortuitous, the essence and significance of things in the superficial and transitory . . . Every point conceals the possibility of being released into absolute aesthetic significance. To the adequately trained eye, the *total* beauty, the *total* meaning of the world as a whole radiates from every single point.

Translated into Simmel's sociology, this implies that his sociological investigations will not merely be confined to 'structures of a higher order' but also to 'the delicate, invisible threads' that bind individuals together, to the 'fortuitous fragment of social reality' whose investigation produces a 'deeper and more accurate' understanding of society than does 'the mere treatment of major, completely supra-individual total structures'. Simmel's sociology is therefore also concerned with human interaction at mealtimes, in public transport, in written communications etc. Even the monumental *Philosophy of Money* is held together, Simmel announces, by 'the possibility . . . of finding in each of life's details the totality of its meaning'. In order to indicate the breadth of Simmel's sociological project we must therefore turn to his substantive works.

Arthur A. Molitierno   (essay date 1989)

SOURCE: "Georg Simmel's Cultural Narcissism: A Non-Ideological Approach," in *The Midwest Quarterly*, Vol. XXX, No. 3, Spring, 1989, pp. 308-23.

[*In the following essay, Molitierno compares the central ideas of Christopher Lasch's* The Culture of Narcissism *with Simmel's concept of the "tragedy of culture."*]

In a comprehensive statement about the concept of instrumentality in Georg Simmel's sociological analysis of modern culture, Guy Oakes aptly refers to the concept of narcissism. Although Simmel does not refer to narcissism *per se*, his views on the problems of modernity surely encompass this concept:

> According to Simmel, the instrumentalization of culture is responsible for the belief that life has become meaningless. This perception of the pointlessness or absurdity of life is the source of the qualities of personal life that typify advanced cultures: banality, decadence, narcissism, aestheticism, solipsism, skepticism, relativism, and nihilism.

Equally true, the alienation which Marx had criticized as part of capitalism's very structure foreshadows not only Simmel's view of the problematic nature of money in advanced societies but also the current emphasis by the Left (i.e. socialist critics) on the contradictions within capitalism. The alleged crisis of modern capitalist culture has become a major ideological issue which recently has been transported to the realm of psychoanalysis by Christopher Lasch in *The Culture of Narcissism*.

Two cultural theorists could not be more removed from each other than Simmel and Lasch. Yet their analyses of the problems inherent in modern culture have parallels which cannot be ignored if social analysis is to progress beyond the realm of particular ideological approaches. On a theoretical level Simmel and Lasch have confronted the issues of anomie, relativism, nihilism, banality, and aestheticism. Lasch's approach has been systematic (to apply the same system to different facets of modern culture) while Simmel's explanation has ignored system in favor of confronting each issue as a separate question demanding a separate explanation. Lasch's theoretical investigation, based on the well-known Freudian and Marxist models, has been easier to follow and thus perhaps more easily accessible to a generation which has become accustomed to the language and metaphors of these two influential explanatory systems of thought. Since Simmel relies on no prefabricated system, his work has not been as easily accessible to the current generation; moreover, his very style makes him, unlike Lasch, a very un-"popular" writer. Both theorists have, however, confronted the same essential problem: the location, function, and dissolution of the self in modern society.

This paper suggests that a Simmelian approach to the culture of narcissism should aid us in formulating a more general perspective on narcissism in culture than Lasch's construction. In order to show how Simmel's thinking may be applied to the analysis of the problem of cultural narcissism, as identified by Lasch, I shall first present a general overview of Lasch's concept as he develops it in *The Culture of Narcissism* and then proceed to an exposition of Simmel's major cultural essays in a fairly chronological order: *The Philosophy of Money,* (1900), **"The Metropolis and Mental Life"** (1902-03), **"On the Concept and Tragedy of Culture"** (1911). Other essays by Simmel (**"Subjective Culture"** [1908], **"The Future of Our Culture"** [1909], **"The Crisis of Culture"** [1917], and **"The Conflict in Modern Culture"** [1918]) generally follow the theses of the essays under consideration.

One may ask why Lasch has received so much attention and recognition and Simmel so little if their views run parallel. Lasch's approach has to date received so much interest (approximately 80 reviews) that the issues surrounding the problematic nature of modern culture have been lost in the argument over the means and orientation of his investigation, using psychoanalysis to divulge cultural pathology rather than the psychic distress of the individual. In fact, in terms of the content of the theories themselves, Simmel's approach to the analysis of the malaise of contemporary western culture is, in many ways, superior to Lasch's analysis. Simmel's manner of investigation is to ignore totally the individual pathology in favor of the more general consideration of "forms" throughout culture. Moreover, although Lasch generally builds his case on a socialist attack of American capitalism, he ignores the question of the function of money beyond its meaning solely in capitalist terms. Simmel treats money conceptually with a deftness that goes beyond ideology or political cause and reaches the very heart of all advanced cultures. Lasch, on the other hand, is more or less limited through his analysis to the singular problems of American culture.

The answer to Simmel's lack of reception resides partly in his unwillingness to postulate rigid laws or to use structural forms of analysis, as in the psychoanalytic id, ego, superego construct. Additionally, while the "scientific community awakens certain possibilities among its members, it also restricts—even hides—other possibilities" (Axelrod). Yet we have much to gain by applying Simmel's unsystematic though theoretical approach to the investigation of cultural narcissism. To date his work has not been applied to the consideration of *The Culture of Narcissism* as text or concept. The substitution of Simmel's exegesis of money and metropolitan mind for Lasch's concept of cultural narcissism is appropriate and necessary because Simmel's approach is not allied to a decided political motive and because Lasch's Freudian-Marxist approach has a rigidity that would preclude further formulation of the problems and paradoxes confronting modern culture. The very structure of psychoanalytic criticism dispenses with the "fragmentation" and "disunity" necessary to intellectual breakthroughs (Axelrod). Throughout his career Simmel retained a philosophic distance which allowed him to see beyond any immediate ideological considerations.

Simmel avoided ideological or paradigmatic approaches because he built his analysis on the dialectical tension within all questions. Questions become adventures wherein the wholeness of "the contents alone determine where the adventure begins and ends. . . ." For him the central question of the relation of the individual to the group cannot be answered by a structure supplied from "outside" but must emerge from "within as an integral commitment

of the experience itself " (Axelrod). Thus he avoided positing psychological laws. As we know, this unsystematic analysis is not without its own problems since it does not attempt to create paradigms for others to follow. Yet, to consider alienation in modern culture solely within the framework of psychic evolution from developmental stages (oral, anal, phallic, Oedipal, narcissistic, etc.) may create more problems and limitations than even an unsystematic socio-philosophical attempt.

Originally published in 1978, *The Culture of Narcissism* was given a "Foreword" in 1980 to delineate the major argument which Lasch thought had been misread by a large number of "superficial, uncomprehending, and sometimes downright malicious reviews." Freely adapting Philip Rieff's *The Triumph of the Therapeutic* and Russell Jacoby's work, Lasch argues that humanism and religion have become "increasingly irrelevant to an understanding of our social life." Psychoanalysis alone stands as the principle intellectual tool for the study of cultural questions.

The present state of advanced capitalism has promoted the type of personality that best meets the demands for protection and performance: the narcissist. The concept of narcissism devolves to Lasch from Richard Sennett's reminder that this psychoanalytic idea has "more in common with self-hatred than with self-admiration." A narcissistic personality and its culture derive from "quite specific changes in our society—from bureaucracy, the proliferation of images, the cult of consumption, and in the last analysis from changes in family life and from changing patterns of sociation."

These forces impel the individual to be victimized by "pseudo-insight, calculating seductions, nervous self-deprecating humor." Such behavior leads to the formation of a psyche which experiences the rejection of love and turns inward upon itself in self-absorption and self-hatred. Unlike selfishness, this turning inward results in "impotent rage and 'feelings of defeat by external forces'." Thus the distinction is drawn between mere egotism or selfishness and narcissism. The narcissist is self-absorbed but at the same time attempts to gain validation and self-esteem through the approval of others. Consequently, the person is paradoxically successful in "bureaucratic institutions, which put a premium on the manipulation of interpersonal relations, [and] discourage the formation of deep personal attachments". Advanced capitalism, which is solely responsible for this mega-psychic phenomenon, results in an "overorganized society" which fosters the emergence of "narcissistic traits that are present, in varying degrees, in everyone." As a result of the "prevailing social conditions," the most intimate of relations become dominated by "envy and exploitation." As the individual is transformed by the society, so is the family, "which in turn shapes the underlying structure of personality."

Although modern man is ill, he is still functional in complying with the incessant demands of capitalism for competition and the production of engineered needs to fulfill engineered desires. At the cultural level we experience a national "malaise," and thus our own "political crisis of capitalism reflects a general crisis of western culture." The end of such decadence is the "dead end of a narcissistic preoccupation with the self " which haunts us with "anxiety instead of guilt." Cultured to meet the demands of continual immediate self-gratification, the narcissists remain in "a state of restless, perpetually unsatisfied desire." Since capitalism represents a pathological state, Lasch argues that only psychoanalysis is capable of diagnosing the complexities of the sickness because it alone can "uncover patterns, both cultural and psychological, that remain far from obvious and largely inaccessible to common sense."

Although Simmel, like Marx, analyzed the alienation fostered by a money economy, there is little indication that he had read Freud or was at least acquainted with the development of psychoanalysis. Yet Simmel was well aware of the concept of the ego. Time and again he referred to the rise of the individual historically and the individual's place of importance in cultural theory.

Moreover, his analyses stress the effect of major cultural influences not only on the general realm of the history of ideas but also the impact they have on the individual in society. As opposed to developing a particular theory of personality, however, he preferred to concentrate on the major classifications within all cultures, the objective and the subjective elements of culture. These can easily be understood as the very foundation for all his cultural theory. That is, Simmel refers to the concept of objective culture in pointing to all those aspects of the culture which are beyond the immediate control of individuals and which exist apart from them as a totality. The subjective culture is that portion of the total cultural objects which individuals may incorporate into their selves. To the extent that the individual can fully assimilate the cultural objects into the psyche, the person is cultured. To the extent that the individual cannot fully assimilate these objects into the self, the person remains uncultured or partially cultured. The crisis of modern culture, then, is that it is so diverse and productive that it is increasingly impossible for any one individual to fully assimilate the totality of objects into the psyche. This is what he refers to as the "tragedy of modern culture." Unlike Lasch's criticism, Simmel's approach would be relevant to all production-oriented modern states, regardless of their ideological positions. The sheer excess of cultural objects, Simmel argues, is at the root of modernity's psychic and cultural dilemma.

The tragedy begins with the development of natural economies (of barter, for instance) into money economies. Simmel's **Philosophy of Money** addresses cultural questions from a metaphysical viewpoint which traces "the relations of money to all the phenomena of social and cultural life and interprets modern civilization in terms of money as its functional category and symbol" (Spykman). In advanced cultures, money creates both liberty and problems for the personality. Through wages the laborer is not forced to comply with every demand of those employing him or her (as would be the case with slaves or serfs). Since one can spend wages on whatever maximizes "subjective enjoyment," money liberates the personality to forms of free expression. As money becomes the primary exchange medium, however, it reduces all values to an exchange rate. Individuals become more and more impersonally involved in their work as their lives become centered around

a "circle of objective economic functions." The paradoxes of modern culture multiply rapidly through the development of a money economy. As more and more goods are produced, less and less personal contact is made with the end-product, and the end-product is valued less and less, yet the demand for more and more production increases.

The paradoxes inherent in the development of a money economy essentially parallel the developments in our mental life. With the development of the expanding money economy there is a consequent "objectivation and depersonalization of the economic world" which in turn diminishes individuality. Since money economies create production which is impersonal, they also create the atmosphere in which human relationships and mental structures may become like the very medium of exchange of the entire culture. Money, Simmel argues, "requires no specific qualities" to possess it. To possess a cultural artifact, for example, would require some understanding of the importance of the object. Yet possessing money allows the free access to practically any object within the culture. The paradox of money, however, becomes evident when we fully realize how it is "more for us than any other object because it belongs to us without reservation, and it is less for us than any other object because it lacks any content which can be actually possessed apart from the mere form of possession as such. We possess it more completely than any other object, but we possess in it less than in any other object." Paradoxically, it also allows for the expansion of the ego in creating greater liberty, freedom, and individuality.

Money, however, also destroys sentiment and feeling because of its teleological function. The immediacy of the handicrafts of the Middle Ages is replaced by the teleological series of purposes designed well into the future and "beyond the sphere of the individual's vision." As money is injected into the economy, it requires further impersonal intellectual activity whereas formerly there were emotional attachments to things. All items become degraded and disassociated from our attachments to them. "Relativistic and objective," money and intellect lack character in excluding "personal reactions and subjective responses." The resulting combination of money and intellect in their characterless functional aspects form the "basis of economic individualism and the grossest egoism."

The bottom line reduces everything and everybody to mathematical relationships. As qualities become rationalized and depersonalized, our relationships evolve toward functions, and people become means and objects. As economies expand, arithmetic valuation (or devaluation) and depersonalized production increase. The individual's "personal culture" is overrun by the "objective culture" as fewer and fewer of the ever-expanding cultural products can be incorporated or fully assimilated into the individual's personal life or culture. Moreover, the objective culture proceeds at its own pace and follows a logic and dynamic which is inherent to its own demands. Finally, this problem and "tension in the cultural subject-object relationship may or may not lead to a rupture, but it is the fundamental tragedy of all culture that it bears within itself the element of self-destruction. If that rupture takes place, the objective forms lose their cultural significance and become mere technique, mere civilization."

The division of labor causes the greatest degree of rupture since it ultimately destroys "self-expression" in creating cultural objects. A rationalized division of labor causes individuals to produce only economic objects and not cultural objects. As individuals grow estranged from the end results of production, they experience an inability to assimilate the products of the culture into their personal lives.

While the foregoing account may seem pessimistic, Simmel also notes how a money economy still may protect the individual's "personal life from the immediate contacts with objects and thereby" allow "personal energies to grow unchanged." Yet growing individualism brings with itself its own problems. Self-sufficiency within a money economy may also remove one from the very bonds of the family. Impersonal rational relationships grow at the expense of the family and personal relationships. Money, itself functioning relativistically, encourages an overall relativism in the individual which "seems to express or rather to be the present form of intellectual adaptation" and has its complete realization in "social and subjective life."

With **"The Metropolis and Mental Life,"** (1902-03), Simmel applied his considerations of the money economy and its increased division of labor to the effects on the metropolis and the mental life of the individual. Whereas his previous consideration had argued that the individual was allowed more freedom in a money economy than in a natural economy, he now stresses the inherent psychic difficulties brought about by increased individualism: "The deepest problems of modern life derive from the claim of the individual to preserve the autonomy and individuality of his existence in the face of overwhelming social forces, of historical change, of external culture, and of the technique of life" (Wolff). The major historical change affecting the individual is the development in the 19th century of specialization in the division of labor. The modern symbol for the exacting demands of the division of labor is the metropolis, the seat of the money economy and the seat of the cultural production. Simmel argues that by studying how the individual adjusts to the city we may ascertain how the individual's personality is formed and influenced by external forces.

Since the metropolis abounds in external forces and feverish activities, the individual is brought to an *"intensification of nervous stimulation."* The sheer magnitude and multiplicity of life creates the psychological conditions which will cause the metropolitan man to further develop his mind against encroaching stimuli. Metropolitan people use their intellects to create a barrier to others and to personal relationships because it is impossible to experience truly personal relationships with everyone. Thus we may understand Simmel's metropolitan mind turning inward as a defense mechanism (not necessarily as narcissistic self-indulgence) against "nervous stimulation." Such a defense against the weight of continually increasing cultural diversity, production, and anonymity Lasch labels as pathological narcissism induced by the waning of capital-

ism and the diminishing returns of a culture bankrupt of ideals.

Furthermore, Simmel links the function of money to the mental life of the city dweller: "Money economy and the dominance of the intellect are intrinsically connected. They share a matter-of-fact attitude in dealing with men and with things; and, in this attitude a formal justice is often coupled with an inconsiderate hardness." Since money reduces all things, even social relationships, to number, it rationalizes all existence. Mutual relations in turn become regulated, impersonal, punctual, and purely mechanical. Simmel suggests this mechanization reaches into the very "depth of the psyche." And this aspect of modern culture is what Lasch refers to as the narcissist's ability to function well within a bureaucratic framework.

Overstimulation and nervous exhaustion of the psyche cause a blasé attitude. The individual becomes incapacitated, psychically exhausted, unable to discriminate, and dulled as things become "experienced as insubstantial." (In psychoanalytic terms, a person loses the sense of boundaries.) People and their relationships assume an "evenly flat and gray tone". Since money is colorless and indifferent, the individuals devoted to its economy are reduced to "the common denominator. . . . All things float with equal specific gravity. . . . "

The individual beset by these forces comes to experience a devaluation of the personality. To preserve a sense of self or worth, the individual develops a "negative behavior," the "reserve" which is necessary because there are simply too many daily contacts in the city, as opposed to the country, and partly as the need to express the "right to distrust" those whom we do not know personally. Reserve can lead to "indifference" necessarily since aversion and distance are required to maintain some sense of individuality. Paradoxically, what "appears in the metropolis style of life directly as dissociation is in reality only one of its elemental forms of socialization." The price of freedom is measured in the cost to the psyche and the loneliness and indifference of unknown persons in crowds, the picture of anonymity and congestion in the modern metropolis.

To stand out in this lonely crowd, the individual must attempt to attract attention, what in psychoanalytic terms is viewed as the narcissist's attempts to become the center of everyone's circle. The result of such *acting out* is the "specifically metropolitan extravagance of mannerism, caprice, and preciousness." As recompense for the impersonality of the city, the individual attempts to demonstrate unique qualities in an effort to exaggerate every aspect of the personality if only for his or her own benefit. This phenomenon Lasch generally refers to as the preoccupation with the self which leads to total self-absorption. Some psychologists may simply refer to such behavior as the histrionic component of the narcissistic personality.

In **"On the Concept and Tragedy of Culture"** (1911) Simmel argues from the principle of transcendence that everyone experiences the need for transcendence and that this spirit is ultimately tied to the question of culture. Since humanism is dead for Lasch, such transcendence is impossible, no matter what psychological benefits might be ascribed to such wish fulfillment. For Simmel, to be cultured requires a synthesis, a moving beyond any specializations within the culture to an incorporation of the objects of the culture into the personality. Such psychic and cultural integration becomes increasingly impossible in the modern world because of the variety of objects and the dialectical nature of their production. One is surrounded by "an innumerable number of cultural elements which are neither meaningless . . . nor, in the final analysis, meaningful" (Etzkorn).

For Simmel, then, all cultures from the moment of their inception carry with them the inherent tragedy of denying the individual his full realization. The spirit and the psyche pay the bills in culture because culture proceeds with a logic and dynamic of its own, beyond the wishes and desires of those who have helped to create it, beyond any paradigm's ability to incorporate all the dynamic variables. In all advanced cultures the same condition will inevitably exist: ". . . the contents of culture [will be eventually removed] from its essential meaning and value."

To Simmel the present question of the culture of narcissism is not only relevant but merely a sub-category of the general movement of all advanced cultures, capitalistic or socialistic. Specialization leads to technology, not to culture. Man becomes increasingly affected with the technique of means and not with the ends of existence. Money as the cornerstone of the modern world further separates people from the very substance which they create. Individuals in the modern world become less spontaneous, more reserved, and less able to strive toward the perfection of life which Simmel would see as the end of existence. Simmel would have few reservations against Lasch's view on the destruction of the individual psyche in a capitalistic economy. He would, however, indicate that any form of money economy will ultimately produce the same results. It does no good to attack capitalism as a system. It indeed has teleological consequences that are as positive as negative. For example, we need to provide for the future. (Family economies, for instance, do not direct the development of the culture at large.)

Within Lasch's critique there is the decided sense that the producers of objects in the culture have control over the items and the culture produced. Capitalistic culture is notorious, however, for its very lack of control of planning in the economic if not cultural sense. To Lasch, capitalism and those who direct the corporate enterprise are manipulating the structure of the economy to require the continual production of goods which are not necessary to lead the good life. The malaise which is the watermark of the modern capitalist society is pictured in almost totally psychoanalytic terms whose underpinning is a Laschian variety of Marxian socialism. (See, for example, his "cultural manifesto" in *The World of Nations,* 1973.) But it was quite clear to Simmel that the end of capitalism is not the end of money. There is little chance that modern culture can ever progress backwards to the natural economy with its emphasis on inherent value as opposed to arithmetic value.

Simmel had no panacea for the ills of advanced culture. And the few lines by Lasch on creating democratic social-ist communities of competence suggest that he, too, has few suggestions on how to change the nature of modern culture. Our present inability to propose avenues of change in itself reflects the extent of the dilemma of modern culture; its very formlessness *and* complex production allows us few alternatives. To Simmel, this is our tragedy. Whether we are sympathetic to our condition or not, the historic formation of the causes of our present tragedy of culture "entirely transcend the sphere for which the judge's attitude is appropriate" (Wolff). Since the culture, like the city and life itself, grows by its own unregulated organic logic, our response should be not to "accuse or to pardon, but only to understand." This is Simmel's conclusion. It should be our starting point.

FURTHER READING

Criticism

Bogardus, Emory S. *The Development of Social Thought,* pp. 462-76. New York: Longmans, Green and Co., 1940.
> Overview of what Bogardus considers Simmel's fundamental contribution to sociology: the idea of socialization, or the "social process."

Coser, Lewis A. "Georg Simmel's Style of Work: A Contribution to the Sociology of the Sociologist." *The American Journal of Sociology* LXIII, No. 6 (May 1958): pp. 635-41.
> Examines the effect of the German academic system on Simmel's thought.

Donahue, Neil H. "Fear and Fascination in the Big City: Rilke's Use of Georg Simmel in *The Notebooks of Malte Laurids Brigge.*" *Studies in Twentieth-Century Literature* 16, No. 2 (Summer 1992): 197-219.
> Assesses the influence of Simmel's writings on the German poet and novelist Rainer Maria Rilke.

Frisby, David. *Sociological Impressionism: A Reassessment of Georg Simmel's Social Theory.* London: Heinemann, 1981, 190 p.
> Study that "attempts to reconstruct some of the central themes in Simmel's work largely through the original texts themselves as well as contemporary commentary."

Green, Bryan S. *Literary Methods and Sociological Theory: Case Studies of Simmel and Weber.* Chicago: The University of Chicago Press, 1988, 303 p.
> A linguistic analysis of Simmel's writing style, followed by a semiotic analysis of *The Philosophy of Money.*

Hawthorn, H. B. "A Test of Simmel on the Secret Society: the Doukhobors of British Columbia." *The American Journal of Sociology* LXII, No. 1 (July 1956): 1-7.
> Contends that the collapse of the religious community of the Doukhobors shows that some of Simmel's sociological hypotheses must be incorrect, specifically his theory concerning the threshold for contradictive beliefs.

Lawrence, P. A. "Introduction to the Life and Work of Georg Simmel." In *Georg Simmel: Sociologist and European,* by Georg Simmel, pp. 3-53. New York: Barnes & Noble Books, 1976.

Detailed introduction to Simmel's life and work, followed by selected writings by Simmel.

Liebersohn, Harry. "Georg Simmel: From Society to Utopia." In his *Fate and Utopia in German Sociology, 1870-1923,* pp. 126-58. Cambridge, Massachusetts: The MIT Press, 1988.

Looks at the ways in which modern life—especially the modern city—shaped Simmel's thought.

Naegele, Kaspar D. "Attachment and Alienation: Complementary Aspects of the Work of Durkheim and Simmel." *The American Journal of Sociology* LXIII, No. 6 (May 1958): 580-89.

Concludes that from the writings of Simmel and Emile Durkheim "emerges a view of social arrangements as involving coherence, differentiation, involvement, and alienation. Durkheim can serve as a direct model for further work. Simmel cannot be directly continued, but he reminds us of what there is to see."

Oakes, Guy, ed. Introduction to *Essays on Interpretation in Social Science,* by Georg Simmel, pp. 3-92. Totowa, N.J.: Rowman and Littlefield, 1980.

Outlines the major themes in Simmel's writings on the philosophy of history.

———. Introduction to *On Women, Sexuality and Love,* by

Georg Simmel, pp. 3-62. New Haven: Yale University Press, 1980.

Examines Simmel's views on feminism and the relations between the sexes.

Spykman, Nicholas J. *The Social Theory of Georg Simmel.* New York: Russell & Russell, 1964, 297 p.

A discussion of problems of sociological methodology, using Simmel's work as a point of orientation.

Theory, Culture and Society 8, No. 3 (August 1991): 241 p.

Special issue devoted to Simmel that includes essays by Mike Featherstone, David Frisby, and Donald N. Levine; a bibliographical note on Simmel in translation; and three translations of essays by Simmel.

Wolff, Kurt H. Introduction to *The Sociology of Georg Simmel,* by Georg Simmel, pp. xvii-lxiv. Edited and translated by Kurt H. Wolff. New York: The Free Press, 1950.

Overview of Simmel's life and work.

———, ed. *Essays on Sociology, Philosophy, and Aesthetics.* New York: Harper & Row, 1959, 392 p.

Collection of essays on various aspects of Simmel's writings, with a selection of essays by Simmel and primary and secondary bibliographies.

Twentieth-Century
Literary Criticism

Cumulative Indexes
Volumes 1-64

How to Use This Index

The main references

Calvino, Italo
1923-1985.....CLC 5, 8, 11, 22, 33, 39,
73; SSC 3

list all author entries in the following Gale Literary Criticism series:

BLC = *Black Literature Criticism*
CLC = *Contemporary Literary Criticism*
CLR = *Children's Literature Review*
CMLC = *Classical and Medieval Literature Criticism*
DA = *DISCovering Authors*
DC = *Drama Criticism*
HLC = *Hispanic Literature Criticism*
LC = *Literature Criticism from 1400 to 1800*
NCLC = *Nineteenth-Century Literature Criticism*
PC = *Poetry Criticism*
SSC = *Short Story Criticism*
TCLC = *Twentieth-Century Literary Criticism*
WLC = *World Literature Criticism, 1500 to the Present*

The cross-references

See also CANR 23; CA 85-88;
obituary CA 116

list all author entries in the following Gale biographical and literary sources:

AAYA = *Authors & Artists for Young Adults*
AITN = *Authors in the News*
BEST = *Bestsellers*
BW = *Black Writers*
CA = *Contemporary Authors*
CAAS = *Contemporary Authors Autobiography Series*
CABS = *Contemporary Authors Bibliographical Series*
CANR = *Contemporary Authors New Revision Series*
CAP = *Contemporary Authors Permanent Series*
CDALB = *Concise Dictionary of American Literary Biography*
CDBLB = *Concise Dictionary of British Literary Biography*
DLB = *Dictionary of Literary Biography*
DLBD = *Dictionary of Literary Biography Documentary Series*
DLBY = *Dictionary of Literary Biography Yearbook*
HW = *Hispanic Writers*
JRDA = *Junior DISCovering Authors*
MAICYA = *Major Authors and Illustrators for Children and Young Adults*
MTCW = *Major 20th-Century Writers*
NNAL = *Native North American Literature*
SAAS = *Something about the Author Autobiography Series*
SATA = *Something about the Author*
YABC = *Yesterday's Authors of Books for Children*

A. E. .... TCLC **3, 10**
See also Russell, George William

Abasiyanik, Sait Faik 1906-1954
See Sait Faik
See also CA 123

Abbey, Edward 1927-1989 ...... CLC **36, 59**
See also CA 45-48; 128; CANR 2, 41

Abbott, Lee K(ittredge) 1947- ...... CLC **48**
See also CA 124; CANR 51; DLB 130

Abe, Kobo 1924-1993 ..... CLC **8, 22, 53, 81**
See also CA 65-68; 140; CANR 24;
DAM NOV; MTCW

Abelard, Peter c. 1079-c. 1142 ... CMLC **11**
See also DLB 115

Abell, Kjeld 1901-1961............ CLC **15**
See also CA 111

Abish, Walter 1931-.............. CLC **22**
See also CA 101; CANR 37; DLB 130

Abrahams, Peter (Henry) 1919- ..... CLC **4**
See also BW 1; CA 57-60; CANR 26;
DLB 117; MTCW

Abrams, M(eyer) H(oward) 1912-... CLC **24**
See also CA 57-60; CANR 13, 33; DLB 67

Abse, Dannie 1923-....... CLC **7, 29; DAB**
See also CA 53-56; CAAS 1; CANR 4, 46;
DAM POET; DLB 27

Achebe, (Albert) Chinua(lumogu)
1930- ..... CLC **1, 3, 5, 7, 11, 26, 51, 75;**
BLC; DA; DAB; DAC; WLC
See also AAYA 15; BW 2; CA 1-4R;
CANR 6, 26, 47; CLR 20; DAM MST,
MULT, NOV; DLB 117; MAICYA;
MTCW; SATA 40; SATA-Brief 38

Acker, Kathy 1948- .... CLC **45**
See also CA 117; 122

Ackroyd, Peter 1949-.......... CLC **34, 52**
See also CA 123; 127; CANR 51; DLB 155;
INT 127

Acorn, Milton 1923-........ CLC **15; DAC**
See also CA 103; DLB 53; INT 103

Adamov, Arthur 1908-1970 ...... CLC **4, 25**
See also CA 17-18; 25-28R; CAP 2;
DAM DRAM; MTCW

Adams, Alice (Boyd)
1926- .... CLC **6, 13, 46; SSC 23**
See also CA 81-84; CANR 26; DLBY 86;
INT CANR-26; MTCW

Adams, Andy 1859-1935.......... TCLC **56**
See also YABC 1

Adams, Douglas (Noel) 1952- ... CLC **27, 60**
See also AAYA 4; BEST 89:3; CA 106;
CANR 34; DAM POP; DLBY 83; JRDA

Adams, Francis 1862-1893....... NCLC **33**

Adams, Henry (Brooks)
1838-1918 ...... TCLC **4, 52; DA; DAB;**
DAC
See also CA 104; 133; DAM MST; DLB 12,
47

Adams, Richard (George)
1920- .... CLC **4, 5, 18**
See also AAYA 16; AITN 1, 2; CA 49-52;
CANR 3, 35; CLR 20; DAM NOV;
JRDA; MAICYA; MTCW; SATA 7, 69

Adamson, Joy(-Friederike Victoria)
1910-1980 .... CLC **17**
See also CA 69-72; 93-96; CANR 22;
MTCW; SATA 11; SATA-Obit 22

Adcock, Fleur 1934-.............. CLC **41**
See also CA 25-28R; CAAS 23; CANR 11,
34; DLB 40

Addams, Charles (Samuel)
1912-1988 .... CLC **30**
See also CA 61-64; 126; CANR 12

Addison, Joseph 1672-1719 .... LC **18**
See also CDBLB 1660-1789; DLB 101

Adler, Alfred (F.) 1870-1937 ...... TCLC **61**
See also CA 119

Adler, C(arole) S(chwerdtfeger)
1932- .... CLC **35**
See also AAYA 4; CA 89-92; CANR 19,
40; JRDA; MAICYA; SAAS 15;
SATA 26, 63

Adler, Renata 1938-............. CLC **8, 31**
See also CA 49-52; CANR 5, 22; MTCW

Ady, Endre 1877-1919 .... TCLC **11**
See also CA 107

Aeschylus
525B.C.-456B.C....... CMLC **11; DA;**
DAB; DAC
See also DAM DRAM, MST

Afton, Effie
See Harper, Frances Ellen Watkins

Agapida, Fray Antonio
See Irving, Washington

Agee, James (Rufus)
1909-1955 .... TCLC **1, 19**
See also AITN 1; CA 108; 148;
CDALB 1941-1968; DAM NOV; DLB 2,
26, 152

Aghill, Gordon
See Silverberg, Robert

Agnon, S(hmuel) Y(osef Halevi)
1888-1970 .... CLC **4, 8, 14**
See also CA 17-18; 25-28R; CAP 2; MTCW

Agrippa von Nettesheim, Henry Cornelius
1486-1535 .... LC **27**

Aherne, Owen
See Cassill, R(onald) V(erlin)

Ai 1947-................... CLC **4, 14, 69**
See also CA 85-88; CAAS 13; DLB 120

Aickman, Robert (Fordyce)
1914-1981 .... CLC **57**
See also CA 5-8R; CANR 3

Aiken, Conrad (Potter)
1889-1973 ... CLC **1, 3, 5, 10, 52; SSC 9**
See also CA 5-8R; 45-48; CANR 4;
CDALB 1929-1941; DAM NOV, POET;
DLB 9, 45, 102; MTCW; SATA 3, 30

Aiken, Joan (Delano) 1924-........ CLC **35**
See also AAYA 1; CA 9-12R; CANR 4, 23,
34; CLR 1, 19; DLB 161; JRDA;
MAICYA; MTCW; SAAS 1; SATA 2,
30, 73

Ainsworth, William Harrison
1805-1882 .... NCLC **13**
See also DLB 21; SATA 24

Aitmatov, Chingiz (Torekulovich)
1928- .... CLC **71**
See also CA 103; CANR 38; MTCW;
SATA 56

Akers, Floyd
See Baum, L(yman) Frank

Akhmadulina, Bella Akhatovna
1937- .... CLC **53**
See also CA 65-68; DAM POET

Akhmatova, Anna
1888-1966 .... CLC **11, 25, 64; PC 2**
See also CA 19-20; 25-28R; CANR 35;
CAP 1; DAM POET; MTCW

Aksakov, Sergei Timofeyvich
1791-1859 .... NCLC **2**

Aksenov, Vassily
See Aksyonov, Vassily (Pavlovich)

Aksyonov, Vassily (Pavlovich)
1932- .... CLC **22, 37**
See also CA 53-56; CANR 12, 48

Akutagawa Ryunosuke
1892-1927 .... TCLC **16**
See also CA 117

Alain 1868-1951 .... TCLC **41**

Alain-Fournier.................... TCLC 6
See also Fournier, Henri Alban
See also DLB 65

Alarcon, Pedro Antonio de
1833-1891 .... NCLC **1**

Alas (y Urena), Leopoldo (Enrique Garcia)
1852-1901 .... TCLC **29**
See also CA 113; 131; HW

Albee, Edward (Franklin III)
1928- ...... CLC **1, 2, 3, 5, 9, 11, 13, 25,**
53, 86; DA; DAB; DAC; WLC
See also AITN 1; CA 5-8R; CABS 3;
CANR 8; CDALB 1941-1968;
DAM DRAM, MST; DLB 7;
INT CANR-8; MTCW

Alberti, Rafael 1902- .... CLC **7**
See also CA 85-88; DLB 108

Albert the Great   1200(?)-1280.... **CMLC 16**
See also DLB 115

Alcala-Galiano, Juan Valera y
See Valera y Alcala-Galiano, Juan

Alcott, Amos Bronson   1799-1888 .. **NCLC 1**
See also DLB 1

Alcott, Louisa May
1832-1888 .... **NCLC 6; DA; DAB;
DAC; WLC**
See also CDALB 1865-1917; CLR 1, 38;
DAM MST, NOV; DLB 1, 42, 79; JRDA;
MAICYA; YABC 1

Aldanov, M. A.
See Aldanov, Mark (Alexandrovich)

Aldanov, Mark (Alexandrovich)
1886(?)-1957 .... **TCLC 23**
See also CA 118

Aldington, Richard   1892-1962...... **CLC 49**
See also CA 85-88; CANR 45; DLB 20, 36,
100, 149

Aldiss, Brian W(ilson)
1925- .... **CLC 5, 14, 40**
See also CA 5-8R; CAAS 2; CANR 5, 28;
DAM NOV; DLB 14; MTCW; SATA 34

Alegria, Claribel   1924-............ **CLC 75**
See also CA 131; CAAS 15; DAM MULT;
DLB 145; HW

Alegria, Fernando   1918-........... **CLC 57**
See also CA 9-12R; CANR 5, 32; HW

Aleichem, Sholom .... **TCLC 1, 35**
See also Rabinovitch, Sholem

Aleixandre, Vicente
1898-1984 .... **CLC 9, 36; PC 15**
See also CA 85-88; 114; CANR 26;
DAM POET; DLB 108; HW; MTCW

Alepoudelis, Odysseus
See Elytis, Odysseus

Aleshkovsky, Joseph   1929-
See Aleshkovsky, Yuz
See also CA 121; 128

Aleshkovsky, Yuz .... **CLC 44**
See also Aleshkovsky, Joseph

Alexander, Lloyd (Chudley)   1924- .. **CLC 35**
See also AAYA 1; CA 1-4R; CANR 1, 24,
38; CLR 1, 5; DLB 52; JRDA; MAICYA;
MTCW; SAAS 19; SATA 3, 49, 81

Alfau, Felipe   1902-............... **CLC 66**
See also CA 137

Alger, Horatio, Jr.   1832-1899..... **NCLC 8**
See also DLB 42; SATA 16

Algren, Nelson   1909-1981 .... **CLC 4, 10, 33**
See also CA 13-16R; 103; CANR 20;
CDALB 1941-1968; DLB 9; DLBY 81,
82; MTCW

Ali, Ahmed   1910- .... **CLC 69**
See also CA 25-28R; CANR 15, 34

Alighieri, Dante   1265-1321 .... **CMLC 3, 18**

Allan, John B.
See Westlake, Donald E(dwin)

Allen, Edward   1948-.............. **CLC 59**

Allen, Paula Gunn   1939-......... **CLC 84**
See also CA 112; 143; DAM MULT;
NNAL

Allen, Roland
See Ayckbourn, Alan

Allen, Sarah A.
See Hopkins, Pauline Elizabeth

Allen, Woody   1935-........... **CLC 16, 52**
See also AAYA 10; CA 33-36R; CANR 27,
38; DAM POP; DLB 44; MTCW

Allende, Isabel   1942- .... **CLC 39, 57; HLC**
See also CA 125; 130; CANR 51;
DAM MULT, NOV; DLB 145; HW;
INT 130; MTCW

Alleyn, Ellen
See Rossetti, Christina (Georgina)

Allingham, Margery (Louise)
1904-1966 .... **CLC 19**
See also CA 5-8R; 25-28R; CANR 4;
DLB 77, MTCW

Allingham, William   1824-1889 ... **NCLC 25**
See also DLB 35

Allison, Dorothy E.   1949- .... **CLC 78**
See also CA 140

Allston, Washington   1779-1843.... **NCLC 2**
See also DLB 1

Almedingen, E. M. .... **CLC 12**
See also Almedingen, Martha Edith von
See also SATA 3

Almedingen, Martha Edith von   1898-1971
See Almedingen, E. M.
See also CA 1-4R; CANR 1

Almqvist, Carl Jonas Love
1793-1866 .... **NCLC 42**

Alonso, Damaso   1898-1990 .... **CLC 14**
See also CA 110; 131; 130; DLB 108; HW

Alov
See Gogol, Nikolai (Vasilyevich)

Alta   1942-..................... **CLC 19**
See also CA 57-60

Alter, Robert B(ernard)   1935-..... **CLC 34**
See also CA 49-52; CANR 1, 47

Alther, Lisa   1944-.............. **CLC 7, 41**
See also CA 65-68; CANR 12, 30, 51;
MTCW

Altman, Robert   1925-............ **CLC 16**
See also CA 73-76; CANR 43

Alvarez, A(lfred)   1929-.......... **CLC 5, 13**
See also CA 1-4R; CANR 3, 33; DLB 14,
40

Alvarez, Alejandro Rodriguez   1903-1965
See Casona, Alejandro
See also CA 131; 93-96; HW

Alvarez, Julia   1950-.............. **CLC 93**
See also CA 147

Alvaro, Corrado   1896-1956 ...... **TCLC 60**

Amado, Jorge   1912-..... **CLC 13, 40; HLC**
See also CA 77-80; CANR 35;
DAM MULT, NOV; DLB 113; MTCW

Ambler, Eric   1909-............ **CLC 4, 6, 9**
See also CA 9-12R; CANR 7, 38; DLB 77;
MTCW

Amichai, Yehuda   1924- ...... **CLC 9, 22, 57**
See also CA 85-88; CANR 46; MTCW

Amiel, Henri Frederic   1821-1881 .. **NCLC 4**

Amis, Kingsley (William)
1922-1995 ..... **CLC 1, 2, 3, 5, 8, 13, 40,
44; DA; DAB; DAC**
See also AITN 2; CA 9-12R; 150; CANR 8,
28; CDBLB 1945-1960; DAM MST,
NOV; DLB 15, 27, 100, 139;
INT CANR-8; MTCW

Amis, Martin (Louis)
1949- .... **CLC 4, 9, 38, 62**
See also BEST 90:3; CA 65-68; CANR 8,
27; DLB 14; INT CANR-27

Ammons, A(rchie) R(andolph)
1926- .... **CLC 2, 3, 5, 8, 9, 25, 57**
See also AITN 1; CA 9-12R; CANR 6, 36,
51; DAM POET; DLB 5, 165; MTCW

Amo, Tauraatua i
See Adams, Henry (Brooks)

Anand, Mulk Raj   1905-........ **CLC 23, 93**
See also CA 65-68; CANR 32; DAM NOV;
MTCW

Anatol
See Schnitzler, Arthur

Anaya, Rudolfo A(lfonso)
1937- .... **CLC 23; HLC**
See also CA 45-48; CAAS 4; CANR 1, 32,
51; DAM MULT, NOV; DLB 82; HW 1;
MTCW

Andersen, Hans Christian
1805-1875 .... **NCLC 7; DA; DAB;
DAC; SSC 6; WLC**
See also CLR 6; DAM MST, POP;
MAICYA; YABC 1

Anderson, C. Farley
See Mencken, H(enry) L(ouis); Nathan,
George Jean

Anderson, Jessica (Margaret) Queale
.... **CLC 37**
See also CA 9-12R; CANR 4

Anderson, Jon (Victor)   1940- .... **CLC 9**
See also CA 25-28R; CANR 20;
DAM POET

Anderson, Lindsay (Gordon)
1923-1994 .... **CLC 20**
See also CA 125; 128; 146

Anderson, Maxwell   1888-1959 ..... **TCLC 2**
See also CA 105; DAM DRAM; DLB 7

Anderson, Poul (William)   1926- .... **CLC 15**
See also AAYA 5; CA 1-4R; CAAS 2;
CANR 2, 15, 34; DLB 8; INT CANR-15;
MTCW; SATA-Brief 39

Anderson, Robert (Woodruff)
1917- .... **CLC 23**
See also AITN 1; CA 21-24R; CANR 32;
DAM DRAM; DLB 7

Anderson, Sherwood
1876-1941 .... **TCLC 1, 10, 24; DA;
DAB; DAC; SSC 1; WLC**
See also CA 104; 121; CDALB 1917-1929;
DAM MST, NOV; DLB 4, 9, 86;
DLBD 1; MTCW

Andier, Pierre
See Desnos, Robert

Andouard
See Giraudoux, (Hippolyte) Jean

Andrade, Carlos Drummond de ...... **CLC 18**
See also Drummond de Andrade, Carlos

Andrade, Mario de 1893-1945..... **TCLC 43**

Andreae, Johann V(alentin)
 1586-1654 .... **LC 32**
 See also DLB 164

Andreas-Salome, Lou 1861-1937... **TCLC 56**
 See also DLB 66

Andrewes, Lancelot 1555-1626 .... **LC 5**
 See also DLB 151

Andrews, Cicily Fairfield
 See West, Rebecca

Andrews, Elton V.
 See Pohl, Frederik

Andreyev, Leonid (Nikolaevich)
 1871-1919 .... **TCLC 3**
 See also CA 104

Andric, Ivo 1892-1975 .... **CLC 8**
 See also CA 81-84; 57-60; CANR 43;
 DLB 147; MTCW

Angelique, Pierre
 See Bataille, Georges

Angell, Roger 1920- .... **CLC 26**
 See also CA 57-60; CANR 13, 44

Angelou, Maya
 1928- .... **CLC 12, 35, 64, 77; BLC; DA;**
                                       DAB; DAC
 See also AAYA 7; BW 2; CA 65-68;
 CANR 19, 42; DAM MST, MULT,
 POET, POP; DLB 38; MTCW; SATA 49

Annensky, Innokenty Fyodorovich
 1856-1909 .... **TCLC 14**
 See also CA 110

Anon, Charles Robert
 See Pessoa, Fernando (Antonio Nogueira)

Anouilh, Jean (Marie Lucien Pierre)
 1910-1987 ...... **CLC 1, 3, 8, 13, 40, 50**
 See also CA 17-20R; 123; CANR 32;
 DAM DRAM; MTCW

Anthony, Florence
 See Ai

Anthony, John
 See Ciardi, John (Anthony)

Anthony, Peter
 See Shaffer, Anthony (Joshua); Shaffer,
 Peter (Levin)

Anthony, Piers 1934- .... **CLC 35**
 See also AAYA 11; CA 21-24R; CANR 28;
 DAM POP; DLB 8; MTCW; SAAS 22;
 SATA 84

Antoine, Marc
 See Proust, (Valentin-Louis-George-Eugene-)
 Marcel

Antoninus, Brother
 See Everson, William (Oliver)

Antonioni, Michelangelo 1912- .:... **CLC 20**
 See also CA 73-76; CANR 45

Antschel, Paul 1920-1970
 See Celan, Paul
 See also CA 85-88; CANR 33; MTCW

Anwar, Chairil 1922-1949 .... **TCLC 22**
 See also CA 121

Apollinaire, Guillaume .. **TCLC 3, 8, 51; PC 7**
 See also Kostrowitzki, Wilhelm Apollinaris
 de
 See also DAM POET

Appelfeld, Aharon 1932- .... **CLC 23, 47**
 See also CA 112; 133

Apple, Max (Isaac) 1941-....... **CLC 9, 33**
 See also CA 81-84; CANR 19; DLB 130

Appleman, Philip (Dean) 1926- ..... **CLC 51**
 See also CA 13-16R; CAAS 18; CANR 6,
 29

Appleton, Lawrence
 See Lovecraft, H(oward) P(hillips)

Apteryx
 See Eliot, T(homas) S(tearns)

Apuleius, (Lucius Madaurensis)
 125(?)-175(?) .... **CMLC 1**

Aquin, Hubert 1929-1977......... **CLC 15**
 See also CA 105; DLB 53

Aragon, Louis 1897-1982........ **CLC 3, 22**
 See also CA 69-72; 108; CANR 28;
 DAM NOV, POET; DLB 72; MTCW

Arany, Janos 1817-1882........ **NCLC 34**

Arbuthnot, John 1667-1735 .... **LC 1**
 See also DLB 101

Archer, Herbert Winslow
 See Mencken, H(enry) L(ouis)

Archer, Jeffrey (Howard) 1940- .... **CLC 28**
 See also AAYA 16; BEST 89:3; CA 77-80;
 CANR 22; DAM POP; INT CANR-22

Archer, Jules 1915- .... **CLC 12**
 See also CA 9-12R; CANR 6; SAAS 5;
 SATA 4, 85

Archer, Lee
 See Ellison, Harlan (Jay)

Arden, John 1930- .... **CLC 6, 13, 15**
 See also CA 13-16R; CAAS 4; CANR 31;
 DAM DRAM; DLB 13; MTCW

Arenas, Reinaldo
 1943-1990 .... **CLC 41; HLC**
 See also CA 124; 128; 133; DAM MULT;
 DLB 145; HW

Arendt, Hannah 1906-1975 .... **CLC 66**
 See also CA 17-20R; 61-64; CANR 26;
 MTCW

Aretino, Pietro 1492-1556 .... **LC 12**

Arghezi, Tudor.................... **CLC 80**
 See also Theodorescu, Ion N.

Arguedas, Jose Maria
 1911-1969 .... **CLC 10, 18**
 See also CA 89-92; DLB 113; HW

Argueta, Manlio 1936-............ **CLC 31**
 See also CA 131; DLB 145; HW

Ariosto, Ludovico 1474-1533........ **LC 6**

Aristides
 See Epstein, Joseph

Aristophanes
 450B.C.-385B.C......... **CMLC 4; DA;**
                                       DAB; DAC; DC 2
 See also DAM DRAM, MST

Arlt, Roberto (Godofredo Christophersen)
 1900-1942 .... **TCLC 29; HLC**
 See also CA 123; 131; DAM MULT; HW

Armah, Ayi Kwei 1939-.... **CLC 5, 33; BLC**
 See also BW 1; CA 61-64; CANR 21;
 DAM MULT, POET; DLB 117; MTCW

Armatrading, Joan 1950-.......... **CLC 17**
 See also CA 114

Arnette, Robert
 See Silverberg, Robert

Arnim, Achim von (Ludwig Joachim von
 Arnim) 1781-1831 .... **NCLC 5**
 See also DLB 90

Arnim, Bettina von 1785-1859.... **NCLC 38**
 See also DLB 90

Arnold, Matthew
 1822-1888 ..... **NCLC 6, 29; DA; DAB;**
                                       DAC; PC 5; WLC
 See also CDBLB 1832-1890; DAM MST,
 POET; DLB 32, 57

Arnold, Thomas 1795-1842 ...... **NCLC 18**
 See also DLB 55

Arnow, Harriette (Louisa) Simpson
 1908-1986 .... **CLC 2, 7, 18**
 See also CA 9-12R; 118; CANR 14; DLB 6;
 MTCW; SATA 42; SATA-Obit 47

Arp, Hans
 See Arp, Jean

Arp, Jean 1887-1966.............. **CLC 5**
 See also CA 81-84; 25-28R; CANR 42

Arrabal
 See Arrabal, Fernando

Arrabal, Fernando 1932- ... **CLC 2, 9, 18, 58**
 See also CA 9-12R; CANR 15

Arrick, Fran..................... **CLC 30**
 See also Gaberman, Judie Angell

Artaud, Antonin (Marie Joseph)
 1896-1948 .... **TCLC 3, 36**
 See also CA 104; 149; DAM DRAM

Arthur, Ruth M(abel) 1905-1979.... **CLC 12**
 See also CA 9-12R; 85-88; CANR 4;
 SATA 7, 26

Artsybashev, Mikhail (Petrovich)
 1878-1927 .... **TCLC 31**

Arundel, Honor (Morfydd)
 1919-1973 .... **CLC 17**
 See also CA 21-22; 41-44R; CAP 2;
 CLR 35; SATA 4; SATA-Obit 24

Asch, Sholem 1880-1957 .... **TCLC 3**
 See also CA 105

Ash, Shalom
 See Asch, Sholem

Ashbery, John (Lawrence)
 1927- ...... **CLC 2, 3, 4, 6, 9, 13, 15, 25,**
                                       41, 77
 See also CA 5-8R; CANR 9, 37;
 DAM POET; DLB 5, 165; DLBY 81;
 INT CANR-9; MTCW

Ashdown, Clifford
 See Freeman, R(ichard) Austin

Ashe, Gordon
 See Creasey, John

Ashton-Warner, Sylvia (Constance)
 1908-1984 .... **CLC 19**
 See also CA 69-72; 112; CANR 29; MTCW

Asimov, Isaac
 1920-1992 ... **CLC 1, 3, 9, 19, 26, 76, 92**
 See also AAYA 13; BEST 90:2; CA 1-4R;
 137; CANR 2, 19, 36; CLR 12;
 DAM POP; DLB 8; DLBY 92;
 INT CANR-19; JRDA; MAICYA;
 MTCW; SATA 1, 26, 74

Astley, Thea (Beatrice May)
1925- .... **CLC 41**
See also CA 65-68; CANR 11, 43

Aston, James
See White, T(erence) H(anbury)

Asturias, Miguel Angel
1899-1974 .... **CLC 3, 8, 13; HLC**
See also CA 25-28; 49-52; CANR 32;
CAP 2; DAM MULT, NOV; DLB 113;
HW; MTCW

Atares, Carlos Saura
See Saura (Atares), Carlos

Atheling, William
See Pound, Ezra (Weston Loomis)

Atheling, William, Jr.
See Blish, James (Benjamin)

Atherton, Gertrude (Franklin Horn)
1857-1948 .... **TCLC 2**
See also CA 104; DLB 9, 78

Atherton, Lucius
See Masters, Edgar Lee

Atkins, Jack
See Harris, Mark

Attaway, William (Alexander)
1911-1986 .... **CLC 92; BLC**
See also BW 2; CA 143; DAM MULT;
DLB 76

Atticus
See Fleming, Ian (Lancaster)

Atwood, Margaret (Eleanor)
1939- ..... **CLC 2, 3, 4, 8, 13, 15, 25, 44,
84; DA; DAB; DAC; PC 8; SSC 2; WLC**
See also AAYA 12; BEST 89:2; CA 49-52;
CANR 3, 24, 33; DAM MST, NOV,
POET; DLB 53; INT CANR-24; MTCW;
SATA 50

Aubigny, Pierre d'
See Mencken, H(enry) L(ouis)

Aubin, Penelope 1685-1731(?) .... **LC 9**
See also DLB 39

Auchincloss, Louis (Stanton)
1917- ...... **CLC 4, 6, 9, 18, 45; SSC 22**
See also CA 1-4R; CANR 6, 29;
DAM NOV; DLB 2; DLBY 80;
INT CANR-29; MTCW

Auden, W(ystan) H(ugh)
1907-1973 ...... **CLC 1, 2, 3, 4, 6, 9, 11,
14, 43; DA; DAB; DAC; PC 1; WLC**
See also CA 9-12R; 45-48; CANR 5;
CDBLB 1914-1945; DAM DRAM, MST,
POET; DLB 10, 20; MTCW

Audiberti, Jacques 1900-1965 ...... **CLC 38**
See also CA 25-28R; DAM DRAM

Audubon, John James
1785-1851 .... **NCLC 47**

Auel, Jean M(arie) 1936- .... **CLC 31**
See also AAYA 7; BEST 90:4; CA 103;
CANR 21; DAM POP; INT CANR-21

Auerbach, Erich 1892-1957 .... **TCLC 43**
See also CA 118

Augier, Emile 1820-1889 .... **NCLC 31**

August, John
See De Voto, Bernard (Augustine)

Augustine, St. 354-430 ...... **CMLC 6; DAB**

Aurelius
See Bourne, Randolph S(illiman)

Aurobindo, Sri 1872-1950 .... **TCLC 63**

Austen, Jane
1775-1817 ..... **NCLC 1, 13, 19, 33, 51;
DA; DAB; DAC; WLC**
See also CDBLB 1789-1832; DAM MST,
NOV; DLB 116

Auster, Paul 1947- .... **CLC 47**
See also CA 69-72; CANR 23, 51

Austin, Frank
See Faust, Frederick (Schiller)

Austin, Mary (Hunter)
1868-1934 .... **TCLC 25**
See also CA 109; DLB 9, 78

Autran Dourado, Waldomiro
See Dourado, (Waldomiro Freitas) Autran

Averroes 1126-1198 .... **CMLC 7**
See also DLB 115

Avicenna 980-1037 .... **CMLC 16**
See also DLB 115

Avison, Margaret 1918- .... **CLC 2, 4; DAC**
See also CA 17-20R; DAM POET; DLB 53;
MTCW

Axton, David
See Koontz, Dean R(ay)

Ayckbourn, Alan
1939- .... **CLC 5, 8, 18, 33, 74; DAB**
See also CA 21-24R; CANR 31;
DAM DRAM; DLB 13; MTCW

Aydy, Catherine
See Tennant, Emma (Christina)

Ayme, Marcel (Andre) 1902-1967... **CLC 11**
See also CA 89-92; CLR 25; DLB 72

Ayrton, Michael 1921-1975 .... **CLC 7**
See also CA 5-8R; 61-64; CANR 9, 21

Azorin .... **CLC 11**
See also Martinez Ruiz, Jose

Azuela, Mariano
1873-1952 .... **TCLC 3; HLC**
See also CA 104; 131; DAM MULT; HW;
MTCW

Baastad, Babbis Friis
See Friis-Baastad, Babbis Ellinor

Bab
See Gilbert, W(illiam) S(chwenck)

Babbis, Eleanor
See Friis-Baastad, Babbis Ellinor

Babel, Isaak (Emmanuilovich)
1894-1941(?) ...... **TCLC 2, 13; SSC 16**
See also CA 104

Babits, Mihaly 1883-1941 .... **TCLC 14**
See also CA 114

Babur 1483-1530 .... **LC 18**

Bacchelli, Riccardo 1891-1985 ..... **CLC 19**
See also CA 29-32R; 117

Bach, Richard (David) 1936- .... **CLC 14**
See also AITN 1; BEST 89:2; CA 9-12R;
CANR 18; DAM NOV, POP; MTCW;
SATA 13

Bachman, Richard
See King, Stephen (Edwin)

Bachmann, Ingeborg 1926-1973..... **CLC 69**
See also CA 93-96; 45-48; DLB 85

Bacon, Francis 1561-1626 .... **LC 18, 32**
See also CDBLB Before 1660; DLB 151

Bacon, Roger 1214(?)-1292 ...... **CMLC 14**
See also DLB 115

Bacovia, George .... **TCLC 24**
See also Vasiliu, Gheorghe

Badanes, Jerome 1937- .... **CLC 59**

Bagehot, Walter 1826-1877 ...... **NCLC 10**
See also DLB 55

Bagnold, Enid 1889-1981 .... **CLC 25**
See also CA 5-8R; 103; CANR 5, 40;
DAM DRAM; DLB 13, 160; MAICYA;
SATA 1, 25

Bagritsky, Eduard 1895-1934 ..... **TCLC 60**

Bagrjana, Elisaveta
See Belcheva, Elisaveta

Bagryana, Elisaveta. .... **CLC 10**
See also Belcheva, Elisaveta
See also DLB 147

Bailey, Paul 1937- .... **CLC 45**
See also CA 21-24R; CANR 16; DLB 14

Baillie, Joanna 1762-1851 .... **NCLC 2**
See also DLB 93

Bainbridge, Beryl (Margaret)
1933- .... **CLC 4, 5, 8, 10, 14, 18, 22, 62**
See also CA 21-24R; CANR 24;
DAM NOV; DLB 14; MTCW

Baker, Elliott 1922- .... **CLC 8**
See also CA 45-48; CANR 2

Baker, Nicholson 1957- .... **CLC 61**
See also CA 135; DAM POP

Baker, Ray Stannard 1870-1946... **TCLC 47**
See also CA 118

Baker, Russell (Wayne) 1925- ...... **CLC 31**
See also BEST 89:4; CA 57-60; CANR 11,
41; MTCW

Bakhtin, M.
See Bakhtin, Mikhail Mikhailovich

Bakhtin, M. M.
See Bakhtin, Mikhail Mikhailovich

Bakhtin, Mikhail
See Bakhtin, Mikhail Mikhailovich

Bakhtin, Mikhail Mikhailovich
1895-1975 .... **CLC 83**
See also CA 128; 113

Bakshi, Ralph 1938(?)-............. **CLC 26**
See also CA 112; 138

Bakunin, Mikhail (Alexandrovich)
1814-1876 .... **NCLC 25**

Baldwin, James (Arthur)
1924-1987 ...... **CLC 1, 2, 3, 4, 5, 8, 13,
15, 17, 42, 50, 67, 90; BLC; DA; DAB;
DAC; DC 1; SSC 10; WLC**
See also AAYA 4; BW 1; CA 1-4R; 124;
CABS 1; CANR 3, 24;
CDALB 1941-1968; DAM MST, MULT,
NOV, POP; DLB 2, 7, 33; DLBY 87;
MTCW; SATA 9; SATA-Obit 54

Ballard, J(ames) G(raham)
1930- .... **CLC 3, 6, 14, 36; SSC 1**
See also AAYA 3; CA 5-8R; CANR 15, 39;
DAM NOV, POP; DLB 14; MTCW

Balmont, Konstantin (Dmitriyevich)
    1867-1943 .... TCLC **11**
    See also CA 109

Balzac, Honore de
    1799-1850 .... NCLC **5, 35, 53**; DA;
                DAB; DAC; SSC **5**; WLC
    See also DAM MST, NOV; DLB 119

Bambara, Toni Cade
    1939-1995 ...... CLC **19, 88**; BLC; DA;
                                                        DAC
    See also AAYA 5; BW 2; CA 29-32R; 150;
    CANR 24, 49; DAM MST, MULT;
    DLB 38; MTCW

Bamdad, A.
    See Shamlu, Ahmad

Banat, D. R.
    See Bradbury, Ray (Douglas)

Bancroft, Laura
    See Baum, L(yman) Frank

Banim, John 1798-1842 .... NCLC **13**
    See also DLB 116, 158, 159

Banim, Michael 1796-1874 ...... NCLC **13**
    See also DLB 158, 159

Banks, Iain
    See Banks, Iain M(enzies)

Banks, Iain M(enzies) 1954- .... CLC **34**
    See also CA 123; 128; INT 128

Banks, Lynne Reid .... CLC **23**
    See also Reid Banks, Lynne
    See also AAYA 6

Banks, Russell 1940- .... CLC **37, 72**
    See also CA 65-68; CAAS 15; CANR 19;
    DLB 130

Banville, John 1945- .... CLC **46**
    See also CA 117; 128; DLB 14; INT 128

Banville, Theodore (Faullain) de
    1832-1891 .... NCLC **9**

Baraka, Amiri
    1934- .... CLC **1, 2, 3, 5, 10, 14, 33**;
                BLC; DA; DAC; DC **6**; PC **4**
    See also Jones, LeRoi
    See also BW 2; CA 21-24R; CABS 3;
    CANR 27, 38; CDALB 1941-1968;
    DAM MST, MULT, POET, POP;
    DLB 5, 7, 16, 38; DLBD 8; MTCW

Barbauld, Anna Laetitia
    1743-1825 .... NCLC **50**
    See also DLB 107, 109, 142, 158

Barbellion, W. N. P. .... TCLC **24**
    See also Cummings, Bruce F(rederick)

Barbera, Jack (Vincent) 1945-...... CLC **44**
    See also CA 110; CANR 45

Barbey d'Aurevilly, Jules Amedee
    1808-1889 .... NCLC **1**; SSC **17**
    See also DLB 119

Barbusse, Henri 1873-1935 .... TCLC **5**
    See also CA 105; DLB 65

Barclay, Bill
    See Moorcock, Michael (John)

Barclay, William Ewert
    See Moorcock, Michael (John)

Barea, Arturo 1897-1957 .... TCLC **14**
    See also CA 111

Barfoot, Joan 1946- .... CLC **18**
    See also CA 105

Baring, Maurice 1874-1945 .... TCLC **8**
    See also CA 105; DLB 34

Barker, Clive 1952- .... CLC **52**
    See also AAYA 10; BEST 90:3; CA 121;
    129; DAM POP; INT 129; MTCW

Barker, George Granville
    1913-1991 .... CLC **8, 48**
    See also CA 9-12R; 135; CANR 7, 38;
    DAM POET; DLB 20; MTCW

Barker, Harley Granville
    See Granville-Barker, Harley
    See also DLB 10

Barker, Howard 1946- .... CLC **37**
    See also CA 102; DLB 13

Barker, Pat(ricia) 1943-........ CLC **32, 94**
    See also CA 117; 122; CANR 50; INT 122

Barlow, Joel 1754-1812 .... NCLC **23**
    See also DLB 37

Barnard, Mary (Ethel) 1909-....... CLC **48**
    See also CA 21-22; CAP 2

Barnes, Djuna
    1892-1982 ... CLC **3, 4, 8, 11, 29**; SSC **3**
    See also CA 9-12R; 107; CANR 16; DLB 4,
    9, 45; MTCW

Barnes, Julian 1946-........ CLC **42**; DAB
    See also CA 102; CANR 19; DLBY 93

Barnes, Peter 1931- .... CLC **5, 56**
    See also CA 65-68; CAAS 12; CANR 33,
    34; DLB 13; MTCW

Baroja (y Nessi), Pio
    1872-1956 .... TCLC **8**; HLC
    See also CA 104

Baron, David
    See Pinter, Harold

Baron Corvo
    See Rolfe, Frederick (William Serafino
    Austin Lewis Mary)

Barondess, Sue K(aufman)
    1926-1977 .... CLC **8**
    See also Kaufman, Sue
    See also CA 1-4R; 69-72; CANR 1

Baron de Teive
    See Pessoa, Fernando (Antonio Nogueira)

Barres, Maurice 1862-1923 .... TCLC **47**
    See also DLB 123

Barreto, Afonso Henrique de Lima
    See Lima Barreto, Afonso Henrique de

Barrett, (Roger) Syd 1946- .... CLC **35**

Barrett, William (Christopher)
    1913-1992 .... CLC **27**
    See also CA 13-16R; 139; CANR 11;
    INT CANR-11

Barrie, J(ames) M(atthew)
    1860-1937 .... TCLC **2**; DAB
    See also CA 104; 136; CDBLB 1890-1914;
    CLR 16; DAM DRAM; DLB 10, 141,
    156; MAICYA; YABC 1

Barrington, Michael
    See Moorcock, Michael (John)

Barrol, Grady
    See Bograd, Larry

Barry, Mike
    See Malzberg, Barry N(athaniel)

Barry, Philip 1896-1949.......... TCLC **11**
    See also CA 109; DLB 7

Bart, Andre Schwarz
    See Schwarz-Bart, Andre

Barth, John (Simmons)
    1930- ...... CLC **1, 2, 3, 5, 7, 9, 10, 14,
                                27, 51, 89**; SSC **10**
    See also AITN 1, 2; CA 1-4R; CABS 1;
    CANR 5, 23, 49; DAM NOV; DLB 2;
    MTCW

Barthelme, Donald
    1931-1989 ...... CLC **1, 2, 3, 5, 6, 8, 13,
                                23, 46, 59**; SSC **2**
    See also CA 21-24R; 129; CANR 20;
    DAM NOV; DLB 2; DLBY 80, 89;
    MTCW; SATA 7; SATA-Obit 62

Barthelme, Frederick 1943-........ CLC **36**
    See also CA 114; 122; DLBY 85; INT 122

Barthes, Roland (Gerard)
    1915-1980 .... CLC **24, 83**
    See also CA 130; 97-100; MTCW

Barzun, Jacques (Martin) 1907- .... CLC **51**
    See also CA 61-64; CANR 22

Bashevis, Isaac
    See Singer, Isaac Bashevis

Bashkirtseff, Marie 1859-1884 ... NCLC **27**

Basho
    See Matsuo Basho

Bass, Kingsley B., Jr.
    See Bullins, Ed

Bass, Rick 1958-.................. CLC **79**
    See also CA 126

Bassani, Giorgio 1916-............. CLC **9**
    See also CA 65-68; CANR 33; DLB 128;
    MTCW

Bastos, Augusto (Antonio) Roa
    See Roa Bastos, Augusto (Antonio)

Bataille, Georges 1897-1962 .... CLC **29**
    See also CA 101; 89-92

Bates, H(erbert) E(rnest)
    1905-1974 ...... CLC **46**; DAB; SSC **10**
    See also CA 93-96; 45-48; CANR 34;
    DAM POP; DLB 162; MTCW

Bauchart
    See Camus, Albert

Baudelaire, Charles
    1821-1867 .... NCLC **6, 29, 55**; DA;
                DAB; DAC; PC **1**; SSC **18**; WLC
    See also DAM MST, POET

Baudrillard, Jean 1929-........... CLC **60**

Baum, L(yman) Frank 1856-1919 ... TCLC **7**
    See also CA 108; 133; CLR 15; DLB 22;
    JRDA; MAICYA; MTCW; SATA 18

Baum, Louis F.
    See Baum, L(yman) Frank

Baumbach, Jonathan 1933- ...... CLC **6, 23**
    See also CA 13-16R; CAAS 5; CANR 12;
    DLBY 80; INT CANR-12; MTCW

Bausch, Richard (Carl) 1945- ...... CLC **51**
    See also CA 101; CAAS 14; CANR 43;
    DLB 130

Baxter, Charles 1947-........... CLC **45, 78**
    See also CA 57-60; CANR 40; DAM POP;
    DLB 130

Baxter, George Owen
See Faust, Frederick (Schiller)

Baxter, James K(eir) 1926-1972 .... **CLC 14**
See also CA 77-80

Baxter, John
See Hunt, E(verette) Howard, (Jr.)

Bayer, Sylvia
See Glassco, John

Baynton, Barbara 1857-1929 ..... **TCLC 57**

Beagle, Peter S(oyer) 1939- .... **CLC 7**
See also CA 9-12R; CANR 4, 51;
    DLBY 80; INT CANR-4; SATA 60

Bean, Normal
See Burroughs, Edgar Rice

Beard, Charles A(ustin)
    1874-1948 .... **TCLC 15**
See also CA 115; DLB 17; SATA 18

Beardsley, Aubrey 1872-1898 ..... **NCLC 6**

Beattie, Ann
    1947- .... **CLC 8, 13, 18, 40, 63; SSC 11**
See also BEST 90:2; CA 81-84; DAM NOV,
    POP; DLBY 82; MTCW

Beattie, James 1735-1803 .... **NCLC 25**
See also DLB 109

Beauchamp, Kathleen Mansfield 1888-1923
See Mansfield, Katherine
See also CA 104; 134; DA; DAC;
    DAM MST

Beaumarchais, Pierre-Augustin Caron de
    1732-1799 .... **DC 4**
See also DAM DRAM

Beaumont, Francis
    1584(?)-1616 .... **LC 33; DC 6**
See also CDBLB Before 1660; DLB 58, 121

**Beauvoir, Simone (Lucie Ernestine Marie
    Bertrand) de**
    1908-1986 .... **CLC 1, 2, 4, 8, 14, 31, 44,
        50, 71; DA; DAB; DAC; WLC**
See also CA 9-12R; 118; CANR 28;
    DAM MST, NOV; DLB 72; DLBY 86;
    MTCW

Becker, Carl 1873-1945 .... **TCLC 63:**
See also DLB 17

Becker, Jurek 1937-............ **CLC 7, 19**
See also CA 85-88; DLB 75

Becker, Walter 1950-............ **CLC 26**

Beckett, Samuel (Barclay)
    1906-1989 ...... **CLC 1, 2, 3, 4, 6, 9, 10,
        11, 14, 18, 29, 57, 59, 83; DA; DAB;
        DAC; SSC 16; WLC**
See also CA 5-8R; 130; CANR 33;
    CDBLB 1945-1960; DAM DRAM, MST,
    NOV; DLB 13, 15; DLBY 90; MTCW

Beckford, William 1760-1844 .... **NCLC 16**
See also DLB 39

Beckman, Gunnel 1910- .... **CLC 26**
See also CA 33-36R; CANR 15; CLR 25;
    MAICYA; SAAS 9; SATA 6

Becque, Henri 1837-1899........ **NCLC 3**

Beddoes, Thomas Lovell
    1803-1849 .... **NCLC 3**
See also DLB 96

Bedford, Donald F.
See Fearing, Kenneth (Flexner)

Beecher, Catharine Esther
    1800-1878 .... **NCLC 30**
See also DLB 1

Beecher, John 1904-1980.......... **CLC 6**
See also AITN 1; CA 5-8R; 105; CANR 8

Beer, Johann 1655-1700............ **LC 5**

Beer, Patricia 1924-.............. **CLC 58**
See also CA 61-64; CANR 13, 46; DLB 40

Beerbohm, Henry Maximilian
    1872-1956 .... **TCLC 1, 24**
See also CA 104; DLB 34, 100

Beerbohm, Max
See Beerbohm, Henry Maximilian

Beer-Hofmann, Richard
    1866-1945 .... **TCLC 60**
See also DLB 81

Begiebing, Robert J(ohn) 1946-..... **CLC 70**
See also CA 122; CANR 40

Behan, Brendan
    1923-1964 .... **CLC 1, 8, 11, 15, 79**
See also CA 73-76; CANR 33;
    CDBLB 1945-1960; DAM DRAM;
    DLB 13; MTCW

Behn, Aphra
    1640(?)-1689 ...... **LC 1, 30; DA; DAB;
        DAC; DC 4; PC 13; WLC**
See also DAM DRAM, MST, NOV, POET;
    DLB 39, 80, 131

Behrman, S(amuel) N(athaniel)
    1893-1973 .... **CLC 40**
See also CA 13-16; 45-48; CAP 1; DLB 7,
    44

Belasco, David 1853-1931 .... **TCLC 3**
See also CA 104; DLB 7

Belcheva, Elisaveta 1893- .... **CLC 10**
See also Bagryana, Elisaveta

Beldone, Phil "Cheech"
See Ellison, Harlan (Jay)

Beleno
See Azuela, Mariano

Belinski, Vissarion Grigoryevich
    1811-1848 .... **NCLC 5**

Belitt, Ben 1911-................. **CLC 22**
See also CA 13-16R; CAAS 4; CANR 7;
    DLB 5

Bell, James Madison
    1826-1902 .... **TCLC 43; BLC**
See also BW 1; CA 122; 124; DAM MULT;
    DLB 50

Bell, Madison (Smartt) 1957- ...... **CLC 41**
See also CA 111; CANR 28

Bell, Marvin (Hartley) 1937-..... **CLC 8, 31**
See also CA 21-24R; CAAS 14;
    DAM POET; DLB 5; MTCW

Bell, W. L. D.
See Mencken, H(enry) L(ouis)

Bellamy, Atwood C.
See Mencken, H(enry) L(ouis)

Bellamy, Edward 1850-1898 ...... **NCLC 4**
See also DLB 12

Bellin, Edward J.
See Kuttner, Henry

Belloc, (Joseph) Hilaire (Pierre)
    1870-1953 .... **TCLC 7, 18**
See also CA 106; DAM POET; DLB 19,
    100, 141; YABC 1

Belloc, Joseph Peter Rene Hilaire
See Belloc, (Joseph) Hilaire (Pierre)

Belloc, Joseph Pierre Hilaire
See Belloc, (Joseph) Hilaire (Pierre)

Belloc, M. A.
See Lowndes, Marie Adelaide (Belloc)

Bellow, Saul
    1915- ...... **CLC 1, 2, 3, 6, 8, 10, 13, 15,
        25, 33, 34, 63, 79; DA; DAB; DAC;
        SSC 14; WLC**
See also AITN 2; BEST 89:3; CA 5-8R;
    CABS 1; CANR 29; CDALB 1941-1968;
    DAM MST, NOV, POP; DLB 2, 28;
    DLBD 3; DLBY 82; MTCW

Belser, Reimond Karel Maria de
See Ruyslinck, Ward

Bely, Andrey .... **TCLC 7; PC 11**
See also Bugayev, Boris Nikolayevich

Benary, Margot
See Benary-Isbert, Margot

Benary-Isbert, Margot 1889-1979... **CLC 12**
See also CA 5-8R; 89-92; CANR 4;
    CLR 12; MAICYA; SATA 2;
    SATA-Obit 21

Benavente (y Martinez), Jacinto
    1866-1954 .... **TCLC 3**
See also CA 106; 131; DAM DRAM,
    MULT; HW; MTCW

Benchley, Peter (Bradford)
    1940- .... **CLC 4, 8**
See also AAYA 14; AITN 2; CA 17-20R;
    CANR 12, 35; DAM NOV, POP;
    MTCW; SATA 3

Benchley, Robert (Charles)
    1889-1945 .... **TCLC 1, 55**
See also CA 105; DLB 11

Benda, Julien 1867-1956 .... **TCLC 60**
See also CA 120

Benedict, Ruth 1887-1948 .... **TCLC 60**

Benedikt, Michael 1935- .... **CLC 4, 14**
See also CA 13-16R; CANR 7; DLB 5

Benet, Juan 1927-................ **CLC 28**
See also CA 143

Benet, Stephen Vincent
    1898-1943 .... **TCLC 7; SSC 10**
See also CA 104; DAM POET; DLB 4, 48,
    102; YABC 1

Benet, William Rose 1886-1950 ... **TCLC 28**
See also CA 118; DAM POET; DLB 45

Benford, Gregory (Albert) 1941-.... **CLC 52**
See also CA 69-72; CANR 12, 24, 49;
    DLBY 82

Bengtsson, Frans (Gunnar)
    1894-1954 .... **TCLC 48**

Benjamin, David
See Slavitt, David R(ytman)

Benjamin, Lois
See Gould, Lois

Benjamin, Walter 1892-1940 ..... **TCLC 39**

Benn, Gottfried 1886-1956........ **TCLC 3**
See also CA 106; DLB 56

Bennett, Alan   1934- . . . . .   **CLC 45, 77; DAB**
See also CA 103; CANR 35; **DAM MST;**
MTCW

Bennett, (Enoch) Arnold
1867-1931 . . . . **TCLC 5, 20**
See also CA 106; CDBLB 1890-1914;
DLB 10, 34, 98, 135

Bennett, Elizabeth
See Mitchell, Margaret (Munnerlyn)

Bennett, George Harold   1930-
See Bennett, Hal
See also BW 1; CA 97-100

Bennett, Hal . . . . **CLC 5**
See also Bennett, George Harold
See also DLB 33

Bennett, Jay   1912- . . . . **CLC 35**
See also AAYA 10; CA 69-72; CANR 11,
42; JRDA; SAAS 4; SATA 41, 87;
SATA-Brief 27

Bennett, Louise (Simone)
1919- . . . . **CLC 28; BLC**
See also BW 2; CA 151; **DAM MULT;**
DLB 117

Benson, E(dward) F(rederic)
1867-1940 . . . . **TCLC 27**
See also CA 114; DLB 135, 153

Benson, Jackson J.   1930- . . . . **CLC 34**
See also CA 25-28R; DLB 111

Benson, Sally   1900-1972 . . . . **CLC 17**
See also CA 19-20; 37-40R; CAP 1;
SATA 1, 35; SATA-Obit 27

Benson, Stella   1892-1933 . . . . **TCLC 17**
See also CA 117; DLB 36, 162

Bentham, Jeremy   1748-1832 . . . . . **NCLC 38**
See also DLB 107, 158

Bentley, E(dmund) C(lerihew)
1875-1956 . . . . **TCLC 12**
See also CA 108; DLB 70

Bentley, Eric (Russell)   1916- . . . . **CLC 24**
See also CA 5-8R; CANR 6; INT CANR-6

Beranger, Pierre Jean de
1780-1857 . . . . **NCLC 34**

Berendt, John (Lawrence)   1939- . . . . **CLC 86**
See also CA 146

Berger, Colonel
See Malraux, (Georges-)Andre

Berger, John (Peter)   1926- . . . . . . **CLC 2, 19**
See also CA 81-84; CANR 51; DLB 14

Berger, Melvin H.   1927- . . . . **CLC 12**
See also CA 5-8R; CANR 4; CLR 32;
SAAS 2; SATA 5

Berger, Thomas (Louis)
1924- . . . . **CLC 3, 5, 8, 11, 18, 38**
See also CA 1-4R; CANR 5, 28, 51;
DAM NOV; DLB 2; DLBY 80;
INT CANR-28; MTCW

Bergman, (Ernst) Ingmar
1918- . . . . **CLC 16, 72**
See also CA 81-84; CANR 33

Bergson, Henri   1859-1941 . . . . **TCLC 32**

Bergstein, Eleanor   1938- . . . . **CLC 4**
See also CA 53-56; CANR 5

Berkoff, Steven   1937- . . . . **CLC 56**
See also CA 104

Bermant, Chaim (Icyk)   1929- . . . . . . **CLC 40**
See also CA 57-60; CANR 6, 31

Bern, Victoria
See Fisher, M(ary) F(rances) K(ennedy)

Bernanos, (Paul Louis) Georges
1888-1948 . . . . **TCLC 3**
See also CA 104; 130; DLB 72

Bernard, April   1956- . . . . **CLC 59**
See also CA 131

Berne, Victoria
See Fisher, M(ary) F(rances) K(ennedy)

Bernhard, Thomas
1931-1989 . . . . **CLC 3, 32, 61**
See also CA 85-88; 127; CANR 32;
DLB 85, 124; MTCW

Berriault, Gina   1926- . . . . **CLC 54**
See also CA 116; 129; DLB 130

Berrigan, Daniel   1921- . . . . **CLC 4**
See also CA 33-36R; CAAS 1; CANR 11,
43; DLB 5

Berrigan, Edmund Joseph Michael, Jr.
1934-1983
See Berrigan, Ted
See also CA 61-64; 110; CANR 14

Berrigan, Ted . . . . **CLC 37**
See also Berrigan, Edmund Joseph Michael,
Jr.
See also DLB 5

Berry, Charles Edward Anderson   1931-
See Berry, Chuck
See also CA 115

Berry, Chuck . . . . **CLC 17**
See also Berry, Charles Edward Anderson

Berry, Jonas
See Ashbery, John (Lawrence)

Berry, Wendell (Erdman)
1934- . . . . **CLC 4, 6, 8, 27, 46**
See also AITN 1; CA 73-76; CANR 50;
DAM POET; DLB 5, 6

Berryman, John
1914-1972 . . . . . . **CLC 1, 2, 3, 4, 6, 8, 10,**
13, 25, 62
See also CA 13-16; 33-36R; CABS 2;
CANR 35; CAP 1; CDALB 1941-1968;
DAM POET; DLB 48; MTCW

Bertolucci, Bernardo   1940- . . . . **CLC 16**
See also CA 106

Bertrand, Aloysius   1807-1841 . . . . **NCLC 31**

Bertran de Born   c. 1140-1215 . . . . . **CMLC 5**

Besant, Annie (Wood)   1847-1933 . . . **TCLC 9**
See also CA 105

Bessie, Alvah   1904-1985 . . . . **CLC 23**
See also CA 5-8R; 116; CANR 2; DLB 26

Bethlen, T. D.
See Silverberg, Robert

Beti, Mongo . . . . **CLC 27; BLC**
See also Biyidi, Alexandre
See also **DAM MULT**

Betjeman, John
1906-1984 . . . **CLC 2, 6, 10, 34, 43; DAB**
See also CA 9-12R; 112; CANR 33;
CDBLB 1945-1960; **DAM MST, POET;**
DLB 20; DLBY 84; MTCW

Bettelheim, Bruno   1903-1990 . . . . . . **CLC 79**
See also CA 81-84; 131; CANR 23; MTCW

Betti, Ugo   1892-1953 . . . . **TCLC 5**
See also CA 104

Betts, Doris (Waugh)   1932- . . . . **CLC 3, 6, 28**
See also CA 13-16R; CANR 9; DLBY 82;
INT CANR-9

Bevan, Alistair
See Roberts, Keith (John Kingston)

Bialik, Chaim Nachman
1873-1934 . . . . **TCLC 25**

Bickerstaff, Isaac
See Swift, Jonathan

Bidart, Frank   1939- . . . . **CLC 33**
See also CA 140

Bienek, Horst   1930- . . . . **CLC 7, 11**
See also CA 73-76; DLB 75

Bierce, Ambrose (Gwinett)
1842-1914(?) . . . . **TCLC 1, 7, 44; DA;**
DAC; SSC 9; WLC
See also CA 104; 139; CDALB 1865-1917;
DAM MST; DLB 11, 12, 23, 71, 74

Biggers, Earl Derr   1884-1933 . . . . . **TCLC 65**
See also CA 108

Billings, Josh
See Shaw, Henry Wheeler

Billington, (Lady) Rachel (Mary)
1942- . . . . **CLC 43**
See also AITN 2; CA 33-36R; CANR 44

Binyon, T(imothy) J(ohn)   1936- . . . . **CLC 34**
See also CA 111; CANR 28

Bioy Casares, Adolfo
1914- . . . **CLC 4, 8, 13, 88; HLC; SSC 17**
See also CA 29-32R; CANR 19, 43;
DAM MULT; DLB 113; HW; MTCW

Bird, Cordwainer
See Ellison, Harlan (Jay)

Bird, Robert Montgomery
1806-1854 . . . . **NCLC 1**

Birney, (Alfred) Earle
1904- . . . . **CLC 1, 4, 6, 11; DAC**
See also CA 1-4R; CANR 5, 20;
DAM MST, POET; DLB 88; MTCW

Bishop, Elizabeth
1911-1979 . . . . . . **CLC 1, 4, 9, 13, 15, 32;**
DA; DAC; PC 3
See also CA 5-8R; 89-92; CABS 2;
CANR 26; CDALB 1968-1988;
DAM MST, POET; DLB 5; MTCW;
SATA-Obit 24

Bishop, John   1935- . . . . **CLC 10**
See also CA 105

Bissett, Bill   1939- . . . . **CLC 18; PC 14**
See also CA 69-72; CAAS 19; CANR 15;
DLB 53; MTCW

Bitov, Andrei (Georgievich)   1937- . . . **CLC 57**
See also CA 142

Biyidi, Alexandre   1932-
See Beti, Mongo
See also BW 1; CA 114; 124; MTCW

Bjarme, Brynjolf
See Ibsen, Henrik (Johan)

Bjornson, Bjornstjerne (Martinius)
1832-1910 . . . . **TCLC 7, 37**
See also CA 104

Black, Robert
See Holdstock, Robert P.

Blackburn, Paul 1926-1971 . . . . . . **CLC 9, 43**
See also CA 81-84; 33-36R; CANR 34;
DLB 16; DLBY 81

Black Elk 1863-1950 . . . . **TCLC 33**
See also CA 144; DAM MULT; NNAL

Black Hobart
See Sanders, (James) Ed(ward)

Blacklin, Malcolm
See Chambers, Aidan

Blackmore, R(ichard) D(oddridge)
1825-1900 . . . . **TCLC 27**
See also CA 120; DLB 18

Blackmur, R(ichard) P(almer)
1904-1965 . . . . **CLC 2, 24**
See also CA 11-12; 25-28R; CAP 1; DLB 63

Black Tarantula, The
See Acker, Kathy

Blackwood, Algernon (Henry)
1869-1951 . . . . **TCLC 5**
See also CA 105; 150; DLB 153, 156

Blackwood, Caroline 1931-1996 . . . **CLC 6, 9**
See also CA 85-88; 151; CANR 32;
DLB 14; MTCW

Blade, Alexander
See Hamilton, Edmond; Silverberg, Robert

Blaga, Lucian 1895-1961 . . . . **CLC 75**

Blair, Eric (Arthur) 1903-1950
See Orwell, George
See also CA 104; 132; DA; DAB; DAC;
DAM MST, NOV; MTCW; SATA 29

Blais, Marie-Claire
1939- . . . . **CLC 2, 4, 6, 13, 22; DAC**
See also CA 21-24R; CAAS 4; CANR 38;
DAM MST; DLB 53; MTCW

Blaise, Clark 1940- . . . . **CLC 29**
See also AITN 2; CA 53-56; CAAS 3;
CANR 5; DLB 53

Blake, Nicholas
See Day Lewis, C(ecil)
See also DLB 77

Blake, William
1757-1827 . . . . **NCLC 13, 37, 57; DA;**
DAB; DAC; PC 12; WLC
See also CDBLB 1789-1832; DAM MST,
POET; DLB 93, 163; MAICYA;
SATA 30

Blake, William J(ames) 1894-1969 . . . **PC 12**
See also CA 5-8R; 25-28R

Blasco Ibanez, Vicente
1867-1928 . . . . **TCLC 12**
See also CA 110; 131; DAM NOV; HW;
MTCW

Blatty, William Peter 1928- . . . . **CLC 2**
See also CA 5-8R; CANR 9; DAM POP

Bleeck, Oliver
See Thomas, Ross (Elmore)

Blessing, Lee 1949- . . . . **CLC 54**

Blish, James (Benjamin)
1921-1975 . . . . **CLC 14**
See also CA 1-4R; 57-60; CANR 3; DLB 8;
MTCW; SATA 66

Bliss, Reginald
See Wells, H(erbert) G(eorge)

Blixen, Karen (Christentze Dinesen)
1885-1962
See Dinesen, Isak
See also CA 25-28; CANR 22, 50; CAP 2;
MTCW; SATA 44

Bloch, Robert (Albert) 1917-1994 . . . **CLC 33**
See also CA 5-8R; 146; CAAS 20; CANR 5;
DLB 44; INT CANR-5; SATA 12;
SATA-Obit 82

Blok, Alexander (Alexandrovich)
1880-1921 . . . . **TCLC 5**
See also CA 104

Blom, Jan
See Breytenbach, Breyten

Bloom, Harold 1930- . . . . **CLC 24**
See also CA 13-16R; CANR 39; DLB 67

Bloomfield, Aurelius
See Bourne, Randolph S(illiman)

Blount, Roy (Alton), Jr. 1941- . . . . . **CLC 38**
See also CA 53-56; CANR 10, 28;
INT CANR-28; MTCW

Bloy, Leon 1846-1917 . . . . **TCLC 22**
See also CA 121; DLB 123

Blume, Judy (Sussman) 1938- . . . **CLC 12, 30**
See also AAYA 3; CA 29-32R; CANR 13,
37; CLR 2, 15; DAM NOV, POP;
DLB 52; JRDA; MAICYA; MTCW;
SATA 2, 31, 79

Blunden, Edmund (Charles)
1896-1974 . . . . **CLC 2, 56**
See also CA 17-18; 45-48; CAP 2; DLB 20,
100, 155; MTCW

Bly, Robert (Elwood)
1926- . . . . **CLC 1, 2, 5, 10, 15, 38**
See also CA 5-8R; CANR 41; DAM POET;
DLB 5; MTCW

Boas, Franz 1858-1942 . . . . **TCLC 56**
See also CA 115

Bobette
See Simenon, Georges (Jacques Christian)

Boccaccio, Giovanni
1313-1375 . . . . **CMLC 13; SSC 10**

Bochco, Steven 1943- . . . . **CLC 35**
See also AAYA 11; CA 124; 138

Bodenheim, Maxwell 1892-1954 . . . **TCLC 44**
See also CA 110; DLB 9, 45

Bodker, Cecil 1927- . . . . **CLC 21**
See also CA 73-76; CANR 13, 44; CLR 23;
MAICYA; SATA 14

Boell, Heinrich (Theodor)
1917-1985 . . . . **CLC 2, 3, 6, 9, 11, 15, 27,**
32, 72; DA; DAB; DAC; SSC 23; WLC
See also CA 21-24R; 116; CANR 24;
DAM MST, NOV; DLB 69; DLBY 85;
MTCW

Boerne, Alfred
See Doeblin, Alfred

Boethius 480(?)-524(?) . . . . **CMLC 15**
See also DLB 115

Bogan, Louise
1897-1970 . . . . **CLC 4, 39, 46, 93; PC 12**
See also CA 73-76; 25-28R; CANR 33;
DAM POET; DLB 45; MTCW

Bogarde, Dirk . . . . **CLC 19**
See also Van Den Bogarde, Derek Jules
Gaspard Ulric Niven
See also DLB 14

Bogosian, Eric 1953- . . . . **CLC 45**
See also CA 138

Bograd, Larry 1953- . . . . **CLC 35**
See also CA 93-96; SAAS 21; SATA 33

Boiardo, Matteo Maria 1441-1494 . . . . **LC 6**

Boileau-Despreaux, Nicolas
1636-1711 . . . . **LC 3**

Bojer, Johan 1872-1959 . . . . **TCLC 64**

Boland, Eavan (Aisling) 1944-... **CLC 40, 67**
See also CA 143; DAM POET; DLB 40

Bolt, Lee
See Faust, Frederick (Schiller)

Bolt, Robert (Oxton) 1924-1995 . . . . **CLC 14**
See also CA 17-20R; 147; CANR 35;
DAM DRAM; DLB 13; MTCW

Bombet, Louis-Alexandre-Cesar
See Stendhal

Bomkauf
See Kaufman, Bob (Garnell)

Bonaventura . . . . **NCLC 35**
See also DLB 90

Bond, Edward 1934- . . . . **CLC 4, 6, 13, 23**
See also CA 25-28R; CANR 38;
DAM DRAM; DLB 13; MTCW

Bonham, Frank 1914-1989 . . . . **CLC 12**
See also AAYA 1; CA 9-12R; CANR 4, 36;
JRDA; MAICYA; SAAS 3; SATA 1, 49;
SATA-Obit 62

Bonnefoy, Yves 1923- . . . . **CLC 9, 15, 58**
See also CA 85-88; CANR 33; DAM MST,
POET; MTCW

Bontemps, Arna(ud Wendell)
1902-1973 . . . . **CLC 1, 18; BLC**
See also BW 1; CA 1-4R; 41-44R; CANR 4,
35; CLR 6; DAM MULT, NOV, POET;
DLB 48, 51; JRDA; MAICYA; MTCW;
SATA 2, 44; SATA-Obit 24

Booth, Martin 1944- . . . . **CLC 13**
See also CA 93-96; CAAS 2

Booth, Philip 1925- . . . . **CLC 23**
See also CA 5-8R; CANR 5; DLBY 82

Booth, Wayne C(layson) 1921- . . . . . **CLC 24**
See also CA 1-4R; CAAS 5; CANR 3, 43;
DLB 67

Borchert, Wolfgang 1921-1947 . . . . . **TCLC 5**
See also CA 104; DLB 69, 124

Borel, Petrus 1809-1859 . . . . **NCLC 41**

Borges, Jorge Luis
1899-1986 . . . **CLC 1, 2, 3, 4, 6, 8, 9, 10,**
13, 19, 44, 48, 83; DA; DAB; DAC;
HLC; SSC 4; WLC
See also CA 21-24R; CANR 19, 33;
DAM MST, MULT; DLB 113; DLBY 86;
HW; MTCW

Borowski, Tadeusz 1922-1951 . . . . . . **TCLC 9**
See also CA 106

Borrow, George (Henry)
1803-1881 . . . . **NCLC 9**
See also DLB 21, 55

Bosman, Herman Charles
　　1905-1951 . . . . **TCLC 49**

Bosschere, Jean de　1878(?)-1953. . . **TCLC 19**
　　See also CA 115

Boswell, James
　　1740-1795 . . . . . . **LC 4; DA; DAB; DAC;**
　　　　　　　　　　　　　　　　　　　　WLC
　　See also CDBLB 1660-1789; DAM MST;
　　DLB 104, 142

Bottoms, David　1949- . . . . **CLC 53**
　　See also CA 105; CANR 22; DLB 120;
　　DLBY 83

Boucicault, Dion　1820-1890. . . . . . **NCLC 41**

Boucolon, Maryse　1937-
　　See Conde, Maryse
　　See also CA 110; CANR 30

Bourget, Paul (Charles Joseph)
　　1852-1935 . . . . **TCLC 12**
　　See also CA 107; DLB 123

Bourjaily, Vance (Nye)　1922- . . . . **CLC 8, 62**
　　See also CA 1-4R; CAAS 1; CANR 2;
　　DLB 2, 143

Bourne, Randolph S(illiman)
　　1886-1918 . . . . **TCLC 16**
　　See also CA 117; DLB 63

Bova, Ben(jamin William)　1932- . . . . **CLC 45**
　　See also AAYA 16; CA 5-8R; CAAS 18;
　　CANR 11; CLR 3; DLBY 81;
　　INT CANR-11; MAICYA; MTCW;
　　SATA 6, 68

Bowen, Elizabeth (Dorothea Cole)
　　1899-1973 . . . . . . **CLC 1, 3, 6, 11, 15, 22;**
　　　　　　　　　　　　　　　　　　　　SSC 3
　　See also CA 17-18; 41-44R; CANR 35;
　　CAP 2; CDBLB 1945-1960; DAM NOV;
　　DLB 15, 162; MTCW

Bowering, George　1935- . . . . **CLC 15, 47**
　　See also CA 21-24R; CAAS 16; CANR 10;
　　DLB 53

Bowering, Marilyn R(uthe)　1949- . . . **CLC 32**
　　See also CA 101; CANR 49

Bowers, Edgar　1924- . . . . **CLC 9**
　　See also CA 5-8R; CANR 24; DLB 5

Bowie, David . . . . **CLC 17**
　　See also Jones, David Robert

Bowles, Jane (Sydney)
　　1917-1973 . . . . **CLC 3, 68**
　　See also CA 19-20; 41-44R; CAP 2

Bowles, Paul (Frederick)
　　1910- . . . . **CLC 1, 2, 19, 53; SSC 3**
　　See also CA 1-4R; CAAS 1; CANR 1, 19,
　　50; DLB 5, 6; MTCW

Box, Edgar
　　See Vidal, Gore

Boyd, Nancy
　　See Millay, Edna St. Vincent

Boyd, William　1952- . . . . **CLC 28, 53, 70**
　　See also CA 114; 120; CANR 51

Boyle, Kay
　　1902-1992 . . . . . **CLC 1, 5, 19, 58; SSC 5**
　　See also CA 13-16R; 140; CAAS 1;
　　CANR 29; DLB 4, 9, 48, 86; DLBY 93;
　　MTCW

Boyle, Mark
　　See Kienzle, William X(avier)

Boyle, Patrick　1905-1982. . . . . **CLC 19**
　　See also CA 127

Boyle, T. C.　1948-
　　See Boyle, T(homas) Coraghessan

Boyle, T(homas) Coraghessan
　　1948- . . . . **CLC 36, 55, 90; SSC 16**
　　See also BEST 90:4; CA 120; CANR 44;
　　DAM POP; DLB 86

Boz
　　See Dickens, Charles (John Huffam)

Brackenridge, Hugh Henry
　　1748-1816 . . . . **NCLC 7**
　　See also DLB 11, 37

Bradbury, Edward P.
　　See Moorcock, Michael (John)

Bradbury, Malcolm (Stanley)
　　1932- . . . . **CLC 32, 61**
　　Scc also CA 1-4R; CANR 1, 33;
　　DAM NOV; DLB 14; MTCW

Bradbury, Ray (Douglas)
　　1920- . . . . **CLC 1, 3, 10, 15, 42; DA;**
　　　　　　　　　　　　　　DAB; DAC; WLC
　　See also AAYA 15; AITN 1, 2; CA 1-4R;
　　CANR 2, 30; CDALB 1968-1988;
　　DAM MST, NOV, POP; DLB 2, 8;
　　INT CANR-30; MTCW; SATA 11, 64

Bradford, Gamaliel　1863-1932. . . . . **TCLC 36**
　　See also DLB 17

Bradley, David (Henry, Jr.)
　　1950- . . . . **CLC 23; BLC**
　　See also BW 1; CA 104; CANR 26;
　　DAM MULT; DLB 33

Bradley, John Ed(mund, Jr.)
　　1958- . . . . **CLC 55**
　　See also CA 139

Bradley, Marion Zimmer　1930-. . . . . **CLC 30**
　　See also AAYA 9; CA 57-60; CAAS 10;
　　CANR 7, 31, 51; DAM POP; DLB 8;
　　MTCW

Bradstreet, Anne
　　1612(?)-1672 . . . . . . **LC 4, 30; DA; DAC;**
　　　　　　　　　　　　　　　　　　　　PC 10
　　See also CDALB 1640-1865; DAM MST,
　　POET; DLB 24

Brady, Joan　1939- . . . . **CLC 86**
　　See also CA 141

Bragg, Melvyn　1939- . . . . **CLC 10**
　　See also BEST 89:3; CA 57-60; CANR 10,
　　48; DLB 14

Braine, John (Gerard)
　　1922-1986 . . . . **CLC 1, 3, 41**
　　See also CA 1-4R; 120; CANR 1, 33;
　　CDBLB 1945-1960; DLB 15; DLBY 86;
　　MTCW

Brammer, William　1930(?)-1978 . . . . **CLC 31**
　　See also CA 77-80

Brancati, Vitaliano　1907-1954. . . . . **TCLC 12**
　　See also CA 109

Brancato, Robin F(idler)　1936- . . . . . **CLC 35**
　　See also AAYA 9; CA 69-72; CANR 11,
　　45; CLR 32; JRDA; SAAS 9; SATA 23

Brand, Max
　　See Faust, Frederick (Schiller)

Brand, Millen　1906-1980. . . . . **CLC 7**
　　See also CA 21-24R; 97-100

Branden, Barbara . . . . **CLC 44**
　　See also CA 148

Brandes, Georg (Morris Cohen)
　　1842-1927 . . . . **TCLC 10**
　　See also CA 105

Brandys, Kazimierz　1916- . . . . **CLC 62**

Branley, Franklyn M(ansfield)
　　1915- . . . . **CLC 21**
　　See also CA 33-36R; CANR 14, 39;
　　CLR 13; MAICYA; SAAS 16; SATA 4,
　　68

Brathwaite, Edward Kamau　1930-. . . **CLC 11**
　　See also BW 2; CA 25-28R; CANR 11, 26,
　　47; DAM POET; DLB 125

Brautigan, Richard (Gary)
　　1935-1984 . . . . **CLC 1, 3, 5, 9, 12, 34, 42**
　　See also CA 53-56; 113; CANR 34;
　　DAM NOV; DLB 2, 5; DLBY 80, 84;
　　MTCW; SATA 56

Brave Bird, Mary　1953-
　　See Crow Dog, Mary
　　See also NNAL

Braverman, Kate　1950- . . . . **CLC 67**
　　See also CA 89-92

Brecht, Bertolt
　　1898-1956 . . . . . . **TCLC 1, 6, 13, 35; DA;**
　　　　　　　　　　　　　　DAB; DAC; DC 3; WLC
　　See also CA 104; 133; DAM DRAM, MST;
　　DLB 56, 124; MTCW

Brecht, Eugen Berthold Friedrich
　　See Brecht, Bertolt

Bremer, Fredrika　1801-1865 . . . . . **NCLC 11**

Brennan, Christopher John
　　1870-1932 . . . . **TCLC 17**
　　See also CA 117

Brennan, Maeve　1917- . . . . **CLC 5**
　　See also CA 81-84

Brentano, Clemens (Maria)
　　1778-1842 . . . . **NCLC 1**
　　See also DLB 90

Brent of Bin Bin
　　See Franklin, (Stella Maraia Sarah) Miles

Brenton, Howard　1942- . . . . **CLC 31**
　　See also CA 69-72; CANR 33; DLB 13;
　　MTCW

Breslin, James　1930-
　　See Breslin, Jimmy
　　See also CA 73-76; CANR 31; DAM NOV;
　　MTCW

Breslin, Jimmy . . . . **CLC 4, 43**
　　See also Breslin, James
　　See also AITN 1

Bresson, Robert　1901- . . . . **CLC 16**
　　See also CA 110; CANR 49

Breton, Andre
　　1896-1966 . . . . . **CLC 2, 9, 15, 54; PC 15**
　　See also CA 19-20; 25-28R; CANR 40;
　　CAP 2; DLB 65; MTCW

Breytenbach, Breyten　1939(?)- . . **CLC 23, 37**
　　See also CA 113; 129; DAM POET

Bridgers, Sue Ellen　1942- . . . . **CLC 26**
　　See also AAYA 8; CA 65-68; CANR 11,
　　36; CLR 18; DLB 52; JRDA; MAICYA;
　　SAAS 1; SATA 22

Bridges, Robert (Seymour)
  1844-1930 .... **TCLC 1**
  See also CA 104; CDBLB 1890-1914;
  DAM POET; DLB 19, 98

Bridie, James .... **TCLC 3**
  See also Mavor, Osborne Henry
  See also DLB 10

Brin, David 1950- .... **CLC 34**
  See also CA 102; CANR 24;
  INT CANR-24; SATA 65

Brink, Andre (Philippus)
  1935- .... **CLC 18, 36**
  See also CA 104; CANR 39; INT 103;
  MTCW

Brinsmead, H(esba) F(ay) 1922- .... **CLC 21**
  See also CA 21-24R; CANR 10; MAICYA;
  SAAS 5; SATA 18, 78

Brittain, Vera (Mary)
  1893(?)-1970 .... **CLC 23**
  See also CA 13-16; 25-28R; CAP 1; MTCW

Broch, Hermann 1886-1951 ...... **TCLC 20**
  See also CA 117; DLB 85, 124

Brock, Rose
  See Hansen, Joseph

Brodkey, Harold (Roy) 1930-1996 .. **CLC 56**
  See also CA 111; 151; DLB 130

Brodsky, Iosif Alexandrovich 1940-1996
  See Brodsky, Joseph
  See also AITN 1; CA 41-44R; 151;
  CANR 37; DAM POET; MTCW

Brodsky, Joseph .. **CLC 4, 6, 13, 36, 50; PC 9**
  See also Brodsky, Iosif Alexandrovich

Brodsky, Michael Mark 1948- ..... **CLC 19**
  See also CA 102; CANR 18, 41

Bromell, Henry 1947- .... **CLC 5**
  See also CA 53-56; CANR 9

Bromfield, Louis (Brucker)
  1896-1956 .... **TCLC 11**
  See also CA 107; DLB 4, 9, 86

Broner, E(sther) M(asserman)
  1930- .... **CLC 19**
  See also CA 17-20R; CANR 8, 25; DLB 28

Bronk, William 1918- .... **CLC 10**
  See also CA 89-92; CANR 23; DLB 165

Bronstein, Lev Davidovich
  See Trotsky, Leon

Bronte, Anne 1820-1849 .... **NCLC 4**
  See also DLB 21

Bronte, Charlotte
  1816-1855 .... **NCLC 3, 8, 33; DA;
                              DAB; DAC; WLC**
  See also AAYA 17; CDBLB 1832-1890;
  DAM MST, NOV; DLB 21, 159

Bronte, Emily (Jane)
  1818-1848 .... **NCLC 16, 35; DA; DAB;
                              DAC; PC 8; WLC**
  See also AAYA 17; CDBLB 1832-1890;
  DAM MST, NOV, POET; DLB 21, 32

Brooke, Frances 1724-1789 .... **LC 6**
  See also DLB 39, 99

Brooke, Henry 1703(?)-1783 .... **LC 1**
  See also DLB 39

Brooke, Rupert (Chawner)
  1887-1915 ...... **TCLC 2, 7; DA; DAB;
                              DAC; WLC**
  See also CA 104; 132; CDBLB 1914-1945;
  DAM MST, POET; DLB 19; MTCW

Brooke-Haven, P.
  See Wodehouse, P(elham) G(renville)

Brooke-Rose, Christine 1926- ...... **CLC 40**
  See also CA 13-16R; DLB 14

Brookner, Anita
  1928- .... **CLC 32, 34, 51; DAB**
  See also CA 114; 120; CANR 37;
  DAM POP; DLBY 87; MTCW

Brooks, Cleanth 1906-1994 ..... **CLC 24, 86**
  See also CA 17-20R; 145; CANR 33, 35;
  DLB 63; DLBY 94; INT CANR-35;
  MTCW

Brooks, George
  See Baum, L(yman) Frank

Brooks, Gwendolyn
  1917- ...... **CLC 1, 2, 4, 5, 15, 49; BLC;
                              DA; DAC; PC 7; WLC**
  See also AITN 1; BW 2; CA 1-4R;
  CANR 1, 27; CDALB 1941-1968;
  CLR 27; DAM MST, MULT, POET;
  DLB 5, 76, 165; MTCW; SATA 6

Brooks, Mel .... **CLC 12**
  See also Kaminsky, Melvin
  See also AAYA 13; DLB 26

Brooks, Peter 1938- .... **CLC 34**
  See also CA 45-48; CANR 1

Brooks, Van Wyck 1886-1963 ...... **CLC 29**
  See also CA 1-4R; CANR 6; DLB 45, 63,
  103

Brophy, Brigid (Antonia)
  1929-1995 .... **CLC 6, 11, 29**
  See also CA 5-8R; 149; CAAS 4; CANR 25;
  DLB 14; MTCW

Brosman, Catharine Savage 1934- .... **CLC 9**
  See also CA 61-64; CANR 21, 46

Brother Antoninus
  See Everson, William (Oliver)

Broughton, T(homas) Alan 1936- ... **CLC 19**
  See also CA 45-48; CANR 2, 23, 48

Broumas, Olga 1949- .... **CLC 10, 73**
  See also CA 85-88; CANR 20

Brown, Charles Brockden
  1771-1810 .... **NCLC 22**
  See also CDALB 1640-1865; DLB 37, 59,
  73

Brown, Christy 1932-1981 .... **CLC 63**
  See also CA 105; 104; DLB 14

Brown, Claude 1937- .... **CLC 30; BLC**
  See also AAYA 7; BW 1; CA 73-76;
  DAM MULT

Brown, Dee (Alexander) 1908- .. **CLC 18, 47**
  See also CA 13-16R; CAAS 6; CANR 11,
  45; DAM POP; DLBY 80; MTCW;
  SATA 5

Brown, George
  See Wertmueller, Lina

Brown, George Douglas
  1869-1902 .... **TCLC 28**

Brown, George Mackay
  1921-1996 .... **CLC 5, 48**
  See also CA 21-24R; 151; CAAS 6;
  CANR 12, 37; DLB 14, 27, 139; MTCW;
  SATA 35

Brown, (William) Larry 1951- ...... **CLC 73**
  See also CA 130; 134; INT 133

Brown, Moses
  See Barrett, William (Christopher)

Brown, Rita Mae 1944- ..... **CLC 18, 43, 79**
  See also CA 45-48; CANR 2, 11, 35;
  DAM NOV, POP; INT CANR-11;
  MTCW

Brown, Roderick (Langmere) Haig-
  See Haig-Brown, Roderick (Langmere)

Brown, Rosellen 1939- .... **CLC 32**
  See also CA 77-80; CAAS 10; CANR 14, 44

Brown, Sterling Allen
  1901-1989 .... **CLC 1, 23, 59; BLC**
  See also BW 1; CA 85-88; 127; CANR 26;
  DAM MULT, POET; DLB 48, 51, 63;
  MTCW

Brown, Will
  See Ainsworth, William Harrison

Brown, William Wells
  1813-1884 ...... **NCLC 2; BLC; DC 1**
  See also DAM MULT; DLB 3, 50

Browne, (Clyde) Jackson 1948(?)- ... **CLC 21**
  See also CA 120

Browning, Elizabeth Barrett
  1806-1861 ..... **NCLC 1, 16; DA; DAB;
                              DAC; PC 6; WLC**
  See also CDBLB 1832-1890; DAM MST,
  POET; DLB 32

Browning, Robert
  1812-1889 .... **NCLC 19; DA; DAB;
                              DAC; PC 2**
  See also CDBLB 1832-1890; DAM MST,
  POET; DLB 32, 163; YABC 1

Browning, Tod 1882-1962 .... **CLC 16**
  See also CA 141; 117

Brownson, Orestes (Augustus)
  1803-1876 .... **NCLC 50**

Bruccoli, Matthew J(oseph) 1931- .. **CLC 34**
  See also CA 9-12R; CANR 7; DLB 103

Bruce, Lenny .... **CLC 21**
  See also Schneider, Leonard Alfred

Bruin, John
  See Brutus, Dennis

Brulard, Henri
  See Stendhal

Brulls, Christian
  See Simenon, Georges (Jacques Christian)

Brunner, John (Kilian Houston)
  1934-1995 .... **CLC 8, 10**
  See also CA 1-4R; 149; CAAS 8; CANR 2,
  37; DAM POP; MTCW

Bruno, Giordano 1548-1600 .... **LC 27**

Brutus, Dennis 1924- .... **CLC 43; BLC**
  See also BW 2; CA 49-52; CAAS 14;
  CANR 2, 27, 42; DAM MULT, POET;
  DLB 117

Bryan, C(ourtlandt) D(ixon) B(arnes)
1936- . . . . **CLC 29**
See also CA 73-76; CANR 13;
INT CANR-13

Bryan, Michael
See Moore, Brian

Bryant, William Cullen
1794-1878 . . . . . **NCLC 6, 46; DA; DAB;**
DAC
See also CDALB 1640-1865; DAM MST,
POET; DLB 3, 43, 59

Bryusov, Valery Yakovlevich
1873-1924 . . . . **TCLC 10**
See also CA 107

Buchan, John 1875-1940 . . . **TCLC 41; DAB**
See also CA 108; 145; DAM POP; DLB 34,
70, 156; YABC 2

Buchanan, George 1506-1582 . . . . **LC 4**

Buchheim, Lothar-Guenther 1918- . . . **CLC 6**
See also CA 85-88

Buchner, (Karl) Georg
1813-1837 . . . . **NCLC 26**

Buchwald, Art(hur) 1925- . . . . **CLC 33**
See also AITN 1; CA 5-8R; CANR 21;
MTCW; SATA 10

Buck, Pearl S(ydenstricker)
1892-1973 . . . . **CLC 7, 11, 18; DA; DAB;**
DAC
See also AITN 1; CA 1-4R; 41-44R;
CANR 1, 34; DAM MST, NOV; DLB 9,
102; MTCW; SATA 1, 25

Buckler, Ernest 1908-1984 . . . . **CLC 13; DAC**
See also CA 11-12; 114; CAP 1;
DAM MST; DLB 68; SATA 47

Buckley, Vincent (Thomas)
1925-1988 . . . . **CLC 57**
See also CA 101

Buckley, William F(rank), Jr.
1925- . . . . **CLC 7, 18, 37**
See also AITN 1; CA 1-4R; CANR 1, 24;
DAM POP; DLB 137; DLBY 80;
INT CANR-24; MTCW

Buechner, (Carl) Frederick
1926- . . . . **CLC 2, 4, 6, 9**
See also CA 13-16R; CANR 11, 39;
DAM NOV; DLBY 80; INT CANR-11;
MTCW

Buell, John (Edward) 1927- . . . . **CLC 10**
See also CA 1-4R; DLB 53

Buero Vallejo, Antonio 1916- . . . **CLC 15, 46**
See also CA 106; CANR 24, 49; HW;
MTCW

Bufalino, Gesualdo 1920(?)- . . . . **CLC 74**

Bugayev, Boris Nikolayevich 1880-1934
See Bely, Andrey
See also CA 104

Bukowski, Charles
1920-1994 . . . . **CLC 2, 5, 9, 41, 82**
See also CA 17-20R; 144; CANR 40;
DAM NOV, POET; DLB 5, 130; MTCW

Bulgakov, Mikhail (Afanas'evich)
1891-1940 . . . . **TCLC 2, 16; SSC 18**
See also CA 105; DAM DRAM, NOV

Bulgya, Alexander Alexandrovich
1901-1956 . . . . **TCLC 53**
See also Fadeyev, Alexander
See also CA 117

Bullins, Ed 1935- . . **CLC 1, 5, 7; BLC; DC 6**
See also BW 2; CA 49-52; CAAS 16;
CANR 24, 46; DAM DRAM, MULT;
DLB 7, 38; MTCW

Bulwer-Lytton, Edward (George Earle Lytton)
1803-1873 . . . . **NCLC 1, 45**
See also DLB 21

Bunin, Ivan Alexeyevich
1870-1953 . . . . **TCLC 6; SSC 5**
See also CA 104

Bunting, Basil 1900-1985 . . . . **CLC 10, 39, 47**
See also CA 53-56; 115; CANR 7;
DAM POET; DLB 20

Bunuel, Luis 1900-1983 . . **CLC 16, 80; HLC**
See also CA 101; 110; CANR 32;
DAM MULT; HW

Bunyan, John
1628-1688 . . . . . . **LC 4; DA; DAB; DAC;**
WLC
See also CDBLB 1660-1789; DAM MST;
DLB 39

Burckhardt, Jacob (Christoph)
1818-1897 . . . . **NCLC 49**

Burford, Eleanor
See Hibbert, Eleanor Alice Burford

Burgess, Anthony
. **CLC 1, 2, 4, 5, 8, 10, 13, 15, 22, 40, 62,**
81, 94; DAB
See also Wilson, John (Anthony) Burgess
See also AITN 1; CDBLB 1960 to Present;
DLB 14

Burke, Edmund
1729(?)-1797 . . . . **LC 7; DA; DAB; DAC;**
WLC
See also DAM MST; DLB 104

Burke, Kenneth (Duva)
1897-1993 . . . . **CLC 2, 24**
See also CA 5-8R; 143; CANR 39; DLB 45,
63; MTCW

Burke, Leda
See Garnett, David

Burke, Ralph
See Silverberg, Robert

Burke, Thomas 1886-1945 . . . . **TCLC 63**
See also CA 113

Burney, Fanny 1752-1840 . . . . **NCLC 12, 54**
See also DLB 39

Burns, Robert 1759-1796 . . . . **PC 6**
See also CDBLB 1789-1832; DA; DAB;
DAC; DAM MST, POET; DLB 109;
WLC

Burns, Tex
See L'Amour, Louis (Dearborn)

Burnshaw, Stanley 1906- . . . . . **CLC 3, 13, 44**
See also CA 9-12R; DLB 48

Burr, Anne 1937- . . . . **CLC 6**
See also CA 25-28R

Burroughs, Edgar Rice
1875-1950 . . . . **TCLC 2, 32**
See also AAYA 11; CA 104; 132;
DAM NOV; DLB 8; MTCW; SATA 41

Burroughs, William S(eward)
1914- . . . . . . **CLC 1, 2, 5, 15, 22, 42, 75;**
DA; DAB; DAC; WLC
See also AITN 2; CA 9-12R; CANR 20;
DAM MST, NOV, POP; DLB 2, 8, 16,
152; DLBY 81; MTCW

Burton, Richard F. 1821-1890 . . . . **NCLC 42**
See also DLB 55

Busch, Frederick 1941- . . . **CLC 7, 10, 18, 47**
See also CA 33-36R; CAAS 1; CANR 45;
DLB 6

Bush, Ronald 1946- . . . . **CLC 34**
See also CA 136

Bustos, F(rancisco)
See Borges, Jorge Luis

Bustos Domecq, H(onorio)
See Bioy Casares, Adolfo; Borges, Jorge
Luis

Butler, Octavia E(stelle) 1947- . . . . . **CLC 38**
See also BW 2; CA 73-76; CANR 12, 24,
38; DAM MULT, POP; DLB 33;
MTCW; SATA 84

Butler, Robert Olen (Jr.) 1945- . . . . . **CLC 81**
See also CA 112; DAM POP; INT 112

Butler, Samuel 1612-1680 . . . . **LC 16**
See also DLB 101, 126

Butler, Samuel
1835-1902 . . . . . . **TCLC 1, 33; DA; DAB;**
DAC; WLC
See also CA 143; CDBLB 1890-1914;
DAM MST, NOV; DLB 18, 57

Butler, Walter C.
See Faust, Frederick (Schiller)

Butor, Michel (Marie Francois)
1926- . . . . **CLC 1, 3, 8, 11, 15**
See also CA 9-12R; CANR 33; DLB 83;
MTCW

Buzo, Alexander (John) 1944- . . . . . . **CLC 61**
See also CA 97-100; CANR 17, 39

Buzzati, Dino 1906-1972 . . . . **CLC 36**
See also CA 33-36R

Byars, Betsy (Cromer) 1928- . . . . **CLC 35**
See also CA 33-36R; CANR 18, 36; CLR 1,
16; DLB 52; INT CANR-18; JRDA;
MAICYA; MTCW; SAAS 1; SATA 4,
46, 80

Byatt, A(ntonia) S(usan Drabble)
1936- . . . . **CLC 19, 65**
See also CA 13-16R; CANR 13, 33, 50;
DAM NOV, POP; DLB 14; MTCW

Byrne, David 1952- . . . . **CLC 26**
See also CA 127

Byrne, John Keyes 1926-
See Leonard, Hugh
See also CA 102; INT 102

Byron, George Gordon (Noel)
1788-1824 . . . . . **NCLC 2, 12; DA; DAB;**
DAC; WLC
See also CDBLB 1789-1832; DAM MST,
POET; DLB 96, 110

C. 3. 3.
See Wilde, Oscar (Fingal O'Flahertie Wills)

Caballero, Fernan 1796-1877 . . . . . **NCLC 10**

Cabell, James Branch 1879-1958 . . . **TCLC 6**
See also CA 105; DLB 9, 78

Carroll, Paul Vincent 1900-1968.... **CLC 10**
    See also CA 9-12R; 25-28R; DLB 10

Carruth, Hayden
    1921- ...... **CLC 4, 7, 10, 18, 84; PC 10**
    See also CA 9-12R; CANR 4, 38; DLB 5,
    165; INT CANR-4; MTCW; SATA 47

Carson, Rachel Louise 1907-1964... **CLC 71**
    See also CA 77-80; CANR 35; DAM POP;
    MTCW; SATA 23

Carter, Angela (Olive)
    1940-1992 ...... **CLC 5, 41, 76; SSC 13**
    See also CA 53-56; 136; CANR 12, 36;
    DLB 14; MTCW; SATA 66;
    SATA-Obit 70

Carter, Nick
    See Smith, Martin Cruz

Carver, Raymond
    1938-1988 ... **CLC 22, 36, 53, 55; SSC 8**
    See also CA 33-36R; 126; CANR 17, 34;
    DAM NOV; DLB 130; DLBY 84, 88;
    MTCW

Cary, Elizabeth, Lady Falkland
    1585-1639 .... **LC 30**

Cary, (Arthur) Joyce (Lunel)
    1888-1957 .... **TCLC 1, 29**
    See also CA 104; CDBLB 1914-1945;
    DLB 15, 100

Casanova de Seingalt, Giovanni Jacopo
    1725-1798 .... **LC 13**

Casares, Adolfo Bioy
    See Bioy Casares, Adolfo

Casely-Hayford, J(oseph) E(phraim)
    1866-1930 .... **TCLC 24; BLC**
    See also BW 2; CA 123; DAM MULT

Casey, John (Dudley) 1939-........ **CLC 59**
    See also BEST 90:2; CA 69-72; CANR 23

Casey, Michael 1947-............. **CLC 2**
    See also CA 65-68; DLB 5

Casey, Patrick
    See Thurman, Wallace (Henry)

Casey, Warren (Peter) 1935-1988... **CLC 12**
    See also CA 101; 127; INT 101

Casona, Alejandro................. **CLC 49**
    See also Alvarez, Alejandro Rodriguez

Cassavetes, John 1929-1989........ **CLC 20**
    See also CA 85-88; 127

Cassill, R(onald) V(erlin) 1919-... **CLC 4, 23**
    See also CA 9-12R; CAAS 1; CANR 7, 45;
    DLB 6

Cassirer, Ernst 1874-1945 .... **TCLC 61**

Cassity, (Allen) Turner 1929- .... **CLC 6, 42**
    See also CA 17-20R; CAAS 8; CANR 11;
    DLB 105

Castaneda, Carlos 1931(?)-........ **CLC 12**
    See also CA 25-28R; CANR 32; HW;
    MTCW

Castedo, Elena 1937- .... **CLC 65**
    See also CA 132

Castedo-Ellerman, Elena
    See Castedo, Elena

Castellanos, Rosario
    1925-1974 .... **CLC 66; HLC**
    See also CA 131; 53-56; DAM MULT;
    DLB 113; HW

Castelvetro, Lodovico 1505-1571..... **LC 12**

Castiglione, Baldassare 1478-1529 ... **LC 12**

Castle, Robert
    See Hamilton, Edmond

Castro, Guillen de 1569-1631........ **LC 19**

Castro, Rosalia de 1837-1885 ..... **NCLC 3**
    See also DAM MULT

Cather, Willa
    See Cather, Willa Sibert

Cather, Willa Sibert
    1873-1947 .... **TCLC 1, 11, 31; DA;**
                       DAB; DAC; SSC 2; WLC
    See also CA 104; 128; CDALB 1865-1917;
    DAM MST, NOV; DLB 9, 54, 78;
    DLBD 1; MTCW; SATA 30

Catton, (Charles) Bruce
    1899-1978 .... **CLC 35**
    See also AITN 1; CA 5-8R; 81-84;
    CANR 7; DLB 17; SATA 2;
    SATA-Obit 24

Catullus c. 84B.C.-c. 54B.C. ..... **CMLC 18**

Cauldwell, Frank
    See King, Francis (Henry)

Caunitz, William J. 1933-......... **CLC 34**
    See also BEST 89:3; CA 125; 130; INT 130

Causley, Charles (Stanley) 1917-..... **CLC 7**
    See also CA 9-12R; CANR 5, 35; CLR 30;
    DLB 27; MTCW; SATA 3, 66

Caute, David 1936-............... **CLC 29**
    See also CA 1-4R; CAAS 4; CANR 1, 33;
    DAM NOV; DLB 14

Cavafy, C(onstantine) P(eter)
    1863-1933 .... **TCLC 2, 7**
    See also Kavafis, Konstantinos Petrou
    See also CA 148; DAM POET

Cavallo, Evelyn
    See Spark, Muriel (Sarah)

Cavanna, Betty .... **CLC 12**
    See also Harrison, Elizabeth Cavanna
    See also JRDA; MAICYA; SAAS 4;
    SATA 1, 30

Cavendish, Margaret Lucas
    1623-1673 .... **LC 30**
    See also DLB 131

Caxton, William 1421(?)-1491(?)..... **LC 17**

Cayrol, Jean 1911-............... **CLC 11**
    See also CA 89-92; DLB 83

Cela, Camilo Jose
    1916- .... **CLC 4, 13, 59; HLC**
    See also BEST 90:2; CA 21-24R; CAAS 10;
    CANR 21, 32; DAM MULT; DLBY 89;
    HW; MTCW

Celan, Paul ...... **CLC 10, 19, 53, 82; PC 10**
    See also Antschel, Paul
    See also DLB 69

Celine, Louis-Ferdinand
    .... **CLC 1, 3, 4, 7, 9, 15, 47**
    See also Destouches, Louis-Ferdinand
    See also DLB 72

Cellini, Benvenuto 1500-1571 .... **LC 7**

Cendrars, Blaise .... **CLC 18**
    See also Sauser-Hall, Frederic

Cernuda (y Bidon), Luis
    1902-1963 .... **CLC 54**
    See also CA 131; 89-92; DAM POET;
    DLB 134; HW

Cervantes (Saavedra), Miguel de
    1547-1616 .... **LC 6, 23; DA; DAB;**
                       DAC; SSC 12; WLC
    See also DAM MST, NOV

Cesaire, Aime (Fernand)
    1913- .... **CLC 19, 32; BLC**
    See also BW 2; CA 65-68; CANR 24, 43;
    DAM MULT, POET; MTCW

Chabon, Michael 1965(?)- .... **CLC 55**
    See also CA 139

Chabrol, Claude 1930- .... **CLC 16**
    See also CA 110

Challans, Mary 1905-1983
    See Renault, Mary
    See also CA 81-84; 111; SATA 23;
    SATA-Obit 36

Challis, George
    See Faust, Frederick (Schiller)

Chambers, Aidan 1934- .... **CLC 35**
    See also CA 25-28R; CANR 12, 31; JRDA;
    MAICYA; SAAS 12; SATA 1, 69

Chambers, James 1948-
    See Cliff, Jimmy
    See also CA 124

Chambers, Jessie
    See Lawrence, D(avid) H(erbert Richards)

Chambers, Robert W. 1865-1933... **TCLC 41**

Chandler, Raymond (Thornton)
    1888-1959 .... **TCLC 1, 7; SSC 23**
    See also CA 104; 129; CDALB 1929-1941;
    DLBD 6; MTCW

Chang, Jung 1952-............... **CLC 71**
    See also CA 142

Channing, William Ellery
    1780-1842 .... **NCLC 17**
    See also DLB 1, 59

Chaplin, Charles Spencer
    1889-1977 .... **CLC 16**
    See also Chaplin, Charlie
    See also CA 81-84; 73-76

Chaplin, Charlie
    See Chaplin, Charles Spencer
    See also DLB 44

Chapman, George 1559(?)-1634...... **LC 22**
    See also DAM DRAM; DLB 62, 121

Chapman, Graham 1941-1989 ...... **CLC 21**
    See also Monty Python
    See also CA 116; 129; CANR 35

Chapman, John Jay 1862-1933 ..... **TCLC 7**
    See also CA 104

Chapman, Walker
    See Silverberg, Robert

Chappell, Fred (Davis) 1936-.... **CLC 40, 78**
    See also CA 5-8R; CAAS 4; CANR 8, 33;
    DLB 6, 105

Char, Rene(-Emile)
    1907-1988 .... **CLC 9, 11, 14, 55**
    See also CA 13-16R; 124; CANR 32;
    DAM POET; MTCW

Charby, Jay
    See Ellison, Harlan (Jay)

Chardin, Pierre Teilhard de
See Teilhard de Chardin, (Marie Joseph) Pierre

Charles I 1600-1649 .... **LC 13**

Charyn, Jerome 1937- .... **CLC 5, 8, 18**
See also CA 5-8R; CAAS 1; CANR 7; DLBY 83; MTCW

Chase, Mary (Coyle) 1907-1981 ...... **DC 1**
See also CA 77-80; 105; SATA 17; SATA-Obit 29

Chase, Mary Ellen 1887-1973 .... **CLC 2**
See also CA 13-16; 41-44R; CAP 1; SATA 10

Chase, Nicholas
See Hyde, Anthony

Chateaubriand, Francois Rene de
1768-1848 .... **NCLC 3**
See also DLB 119

Chatterje, Sarat Chandra 1876-1936(?)
See Chatterji, Saratchandra
See also CA 109

Chatterji, Bankim Chandra
1838-1894 .... **NCLC 19**

Chatterji, Saratchandra .... **TCLC 13**
See also Chatterje, Sarat Chandra

Chatterton, Thomas 1752-1770 ...... **LC 3**
See also DAM POET; DLB 109

Chatwin, (Charles) Bruce
1940-1989 .... **CLC 28, 57, 59**
See also AAYA 4; BEST 90:1; CA 85-88; 127; DAM POP

Chaucer, Daniel
See Ford, Ford Madox

Chaucer, Geoffrey
1340(?)-1400 ... **LC 17; DA; DAB; DAC**
See also CDBLB Before 1660; DAM MST, POET; DLB 146

Chaviaras, Strates 1935-
See Haviaras, Stratis
See also CA 105

Chayefsky, Paddy .... **CLC 23**
See also Chayefsky, Sidney
See also DLB 7, 44; DLBY 81

Chayefsky, Sidney 1923-1981
See Chayefsky, Paddy
See also CA 9-12R; 104; CANR 18; DAM DRAM

Chedid, Andree 1920- .... **CLC 47**
See also CA 145

Cheever, John
1912-1982 ...... **CLC 3, 7, 8, 11, 15, 25, 64; DA; DAB; DAC; SSC 1; WLC**
See also CA 5-8R; 106; CABS 1; CANR 5, 27; CDALB 1941-1968; DAM MST, NOV, POP; DLB 2, 102; DLBY 80, 82; INT CANR-5; MTCW

Cheever, Susan 1943- .... **CLC 18, 48**
See also CA 103; CANR 27, 51; DLBY 82; INT CANR-27

Chekhonte, Antosha
See Chekhov, Anton (Pavlovich)

Chekhov, Anton (Pavlovich)
1860-1904 ..... **TCLC 3, 10, 31, 55; DA; DAB; DAC; SSC 2; WLC**
See also CA 104; 124; DAM DRAM, MST

Chernyshevsky, Nikolay Gavrilovich
1828-1889 .... **NCLC 1**

Cherry, Carolyn Janice 1942-
See Cherryh, C. J.
See also CA 65-68; CANR 10

Cherryh, C. J. .... **CLC 35**
See also Cherry, Carolyn Janice
See also DLBY 80

Chesnutt, Charles W(addell)
1858-1932 .... **TCLC 5, 39; BLC; SSC 7**
See also BW 1; CA 106; 125; DAM MULT; DLB 12, 50, 78; MTCW

Chester, Alfred 1929(?)-1971 .... **CLC 49**
See also CA 33-36R; DLB 130

Chesterton, G(ilbert) K(eith)
1874-1936 .... **TCLC 1, 6, 64; SSC 1**
See also CA 104; 132; CDBLB 1914-1945; DAM NOV, POET; DLB 10, 19, 34, 70, 98, 149; MTCW; SATA 27

Chiang Pin-chin 1904-1986
See Ding Ling
See also CA 118

Ch'ien Chung-shu 1910- .... **CLC 22**
See also CA 130; MTCW

Child, L. Maria
See Child, Lydia Maria

Child, Lydia Maria 1802-1880 .... **NCLC 6**
See also DLB 1, 74; SATA 67

Child, Mrs.
See Child, Lydia Maria

Child, Philip 1898-1978 .... **CLC 19, 68**
See also CA 13-14; CAP 1; SATA 47

Childers, (Robert) Erskine
1870-1922 .... **TCLC 65**
See also CA 113; DLB 70

Childress, Alice
1920-1994 .. **CLC 12, 15, 86; BLC; DC 4**
See also AAYA 8; BW 2; CA 45-48; 146; CANR 3, 27, 50; CLR 14; DAM DRAM, MULT, NOV; DLB 7, 38; JRDA; MAICYA; MTCW; SATA 7, 48, 81

Chislett, (Margaret) Anne 1943- .... **CLC 34**
See also CA 151

Chitty, Thomas Willes 1926- .... **CLC 11**
See also Hinde, Thomas
See also CA 5-8R

Chivers, Thomas Holley
1809-1858 .... **NCLC 49**
See also DLB 3

Chomette, Rene Lucien 1898-1981
See Clair, Rene
See also CA 103

Chopin, Kate
.... **TCLC 5, 14; DA; DAB; SSC 8**
See also Chopin, Katherine
See also CDALB 1865-1917; DLB 12, 78

Chopin, Katherine 1851-1904
See Chopin, Kate
See also CA 104; 122; DAC; DAM MST, NOV

Chretien de Troyes
c. 12th cent. - .... **CMLC 10**

Christie
See Ichikawa, Kon

Christie, Agatha (Mary Clarissa)
1890-1976 ...... **CLC 1, 6, 8, 12, 39, 48; DAB; DAC**
See also AAYA 9; AITN 1, 2; CA 17-20R; 61-64; CANR 10, 37; CDBLB 1914-1945; DAM NOV; DLB 13, 77; MTCW; SATA 36

Christie, (Ann) Philippa
See Pearce, Philippa
See also CA 5-8R; CANR 4

Christine de Pizan 1365(?)-1431(?) .... **LC 9**

Chubb, Elmer
See Masters, Edgar Lee

Chulkov, Mikhail Dmitrievich
1743-1792 .... **LC 2**
See also DLB 150

Churchill, Caryl 1938- ... **CLC 31, 55; DC 5**
See also CA 102; CANR 22, 46; DLB 13; MTCW

Churchill, Charles 1731-1764 .... **LC 3**
See also DLB 109

Chute, Carolyn 1947- .... **CLC 39**
See also CA 123

Ciardi, John (Anthony)
1916-1986 .... **CLC 10, 40, 44**
See also CA 5-8R; 118; CAAS 2; CANR 5, 33; CLR 19; DAM POET; DLB 5; DLBY 86; INT CANR-5; MAICYA; MTCW; SATA 1, 65; SATA-Obit 46

Cicero, Marcus Tullius
106B.C.-43B.C. .... **CMLC 3**

Cimino, Michael 1943- .... **CLC 16**
See also CA 105

Cioran, E(mil) M. 1911-1995 .... **CLC 64**
See also CA 25-28R; 149

Cisneros, Sandra 1954- ...... **CLC 69; HLC**
See also AAYA 9; CA 131; DAM MULT; DLB 122, 152; HW

Cixous, Helene 1937- .... **CLC 92**
See also CA 126; DLB 83; MTCW

Clair, Rene .... **CLC 20**
See also Chomette, Rene Lucien

Clampitt, Amy 1920-1994 .... **CLC 32**
See also CA 110; 146; CANR 29; DLB 105

Clancy, Thomas L., Jr. 1947-
See Clancy, Tom
See also CA 125; 131; INT 131; MTCW

Clancy, Tom .... **CLC 45**
See also Clancy, Thomas L., Jr.
See also AAYA 9; BEST 89:1, 90:1; DAM NOV, POP

Clare, John 1793-1864 ...... **NCLC 9; DAB**
See also DAM POET; DLB 55, 96

Clarin
See Alas (y Urena), Leopoldo (Enrique Garcia)

Clark, Al C.
See Goines, Donald

Clark, (Robert) Brian 1932- .... **CLC 29**
See also CA 41-44R

Clark, Curt
See Westlake, Donald E(dwin)

Clark, Eleanor 1913-1996 .... **CLC 5, 19**
See also CA 9-12R; 151; CANR 41; DLB 6

Craddock, Charles Egbert
See Murfree, Mary Noailles

Craig, A. A.
See Anderson, Poul (William)

Craik, Dinah Maria (Mulock)
1826-1887 . . . . NCLC 38
See also DLB 35, 163; MAICYA; SATA 34

Cram, Ralph Adams   1863-1942. . . . TCLC 45

Crane, (Harold) Hart
1899-1932 . . . . TCLC 2, 5; DA; DAB;
DAC; PC 3; WLC
See also CA 104; 127; CDALB 1917-1929;
DAM MST, POET; DLB 4, 48; MTCW

Crane, R(onald) S(almon)
1886-1967 . . . . CLC 27
See also CA 85-88; DLB 63

Crane, Stephen (Townley)
1871-1900 . . . . TCLC 11, 17, 32; DA;
DAB; DAC; SSC 7; WLC
See also CA 109; 140; CDALB 1865-1917;
DAM MST, NOV, POET; DLB 12, 54,
78; YABC 2

Crase, Douglas   1944- . . . . CLC 58
See also CA 106

Crashaw, Richard   1612(?)-1649 . . . . . . LC 24
See also DLB 126

Craven, Margaret
1901-1980 . . . . CLC 17; DAC
See also CA 103

Crawford, F(rancis) Marion
1854-1909 . . . . TCLC 10
See also CA 107; DLB 71

Crawford, Isabella Valancy
1850-1887 . . . . NCLC 12
See also DLB 92

Crayon, Geoffrey
See Irving, Washington

Creasey, John   1908-1973 . . . . CLC 11
See also CA 5-8R; 41-44R; CANR 8;
DLB 77; MTCW

Crebillon, Claude Prosper Jolyot de (fils)
1707-1777 . . . . LC 28

Credo
See Creasey, John

Creeley, Robert (White)
1926- . . . . . CLC 1, 2, 4, 8, 11, 15, 36, 78
See also CA 1-4R; CAAS 10; CANR 23, 43;
DAM POET; DLB 5, 16; MTCW

Crews, Harry (Eugene)
1935- . . . . CLC 6, 23, 49
See also AITN 1; CA 25-28R; CANR 20;
DLB 6, 143; MTCW

Crichton, (John) Michael
1942- . . . . CLC 2, 6, 54, 90
See also AAYA 10; AITN 2; CA 25-28R;
CANR 13, 40; DAM NOV, POP;
DLBY 81; INT CANR-13; JRDA;
MTCW; SATA 9

Crispin, Edmund . . . . CLC 22
See also Montgomery, (Robert) Bruce
See also DLB 87

Cristofer, Michael   1945(?)- . . . . CLC 28
See also CA 110; DAM DRAM; DLB 7

Croce, Benedetto   1866-1952 . . . . . . TCLC 37
See also CA 120

Crockett, David   1786-1836 . . . . NCLC 8
See also DLB 3, 11

Crockett, Davy
See Crockett, David

Crofts, Freeman Wills
1879-1957 . . . . TCLC 55
See also CA 115; DLB 77

Croker, John Wilson   1780-1857 . . NCLC 10
See also DLB 110

Crommelynck, Fernand   1885-1970 . . CLC 75
See also CA 89-92

Cronin, A(rchibald) J(oseph)
1896-1981 . . . . CLC 32
See also CA 1-4R; 102; CANR 5; SATA 47;
SATA-Obit 25

Cross, Amanda
See Heilbrun, Carolyn G(old)

Crothers, Rachel   1878(?)-1958 . . . . . TCLC 19
See also CA 113; DLB 7

Croves, Hal
See Traven, B.

Crow Dog, Mary . . . . CLC 93
See also Brave Bird, Mary

Crowfield, Christopher
See Stowe, Harriet (Elizabeth) Beecher

Crowley, Aleister . . . . TCLC 7
See also Crowley, Edward Alexander

Crowley, Edward Alexander   1875-1947
See Crowley, Aleister
See also CA 104

Crowley, John   1942- . . . . CLC 57
See also CA 61-64; CANR 43; DLBY 82;
SATA 65

Crud
See Crumb, R(obert)

Crumarums
See Crumb, R(obert)

Crumb, R(obert)   1943- . . . . CLC 17
See also CA 106

Crumbum
See Crumb, R(obert)

Crumski
See Crumb, R(obert)

Crum the Bum
See Crumb, R(obert)

Crunk
See Crumb, R(obert)

Crustt
See Crumb, R(obert)

Cryer, Gretchen (Kiger)   1935- . . . . . . CLC 21
See also CA 114; 123

Csath, Geza   1887-1919 . . . . TCLC 13
See also CA 111

Cudlip, David   1933- . . . . CLC 34

Cullen, Countee
1903-1946 . . . . . . TCLC 4, 37; BLC; DA;
DAC
See also BW 1; CA 108; 124;
CDALB 1917-1929; DAM MST, MULT,
POET; DLB 4, 48, 51; MTCW; SATA 18

Cum, R.
See Crumb, R(obert)

Cummings, Bruce F(rederick)   1889-1919
See Barbellion, W. N. P.
See also CA 123

Cummings, E(dward) E(stlin)
1894-1962 . . . . . . CLC 1, 3, 8, 12, 15, 68;
DA; DAB; DAC; PC 5; WLC 2
See also CA 73-76; CANR 31;
CDALB 1929-1941; DAM MST, POET;
DLB 4, 48; MTCW

Cunha, Euclides (Rodrigues Pimenta) da
1866-1909 . . . . TCLC 24
See also CA 123

Cunningham, E. V.
See Fast, Howard (Melvin)

Cunningham, J(ames) V(incent)
1911-1985 . . . . CLC 3, 31
See also CA 1-4R; 115; CANR 1; DLB 5

Cunningham, Julia (Woolfolk)
1916- . . . . CLC 12
See also CA 9-12R; CANR 4, 19, 36;
JRDA; MAICYA; SAAS 2; SATA 1, 26

Cunningham, Michael   1952- . . . . CLC 34
See also CA 136

Cunninghame Graham, R(obert) B(ontine)
1852-1936 . . . . TCLC 19
See also Graham, R(obert) B(ontine)
Cunninghame
See also CA 119; DLB 98

Currie, Ellen   19(?)- . . . . CLC 44

Curtin, Philip
See Lowndes, Marie Adelaide (Belloc)

Curtis, Price
See Ellison, Harlan (Jay)

Cutrate, Joe
See Spiegelman, Art

Czaczkes, Shmuel Yosef
See Agnon, S(hmuel) Y(osef Halevi)

Dabrowska, Maria (Szumska)
1889-1965 . . . . CLC 15
See also CA 106

Dabydeen, David   1955- . . . . CLC 34
See also BW 1; CA 125

Dacey, Philip   1939- . . . . CLC 51
See also CA 37-40R; CAAS 17; CANR 14,
32; DLB 105

Dagerman, Stig (Halvard)
1923-1954 . . . . TCLC 17
See also CA 117

Dahl, Roald
1916-1990 . . . . . . CLC 1, 6, 18, 79; DAB;
DAC
See also AAYA 15; CA 1-4R; 133;
CANR 6, 32, 37; CLR 1, 7; DAM MST,
NOV, POP; DLB 139; JRDA; MAICYA;
MTCW; SATA 1, 26, 73; SATA-Obit 65

Dahlberg, Edward   1900-1977 . . . CLC 1, 7, 14
See also CA 9-12R; 69-72; CANR 31;
DLB 48; MTCW

Dale, Colin . . . . TCLC 18
See also Lawrence, T(homas) E(dward)

Dale, George E.
See Asimov, Isaac

Daly, Elizabeth   1878-1967 . . . . CLC 52
See also CA 23-24; 25-28R; CAP 2

de la Roche, Mazo 1879-1961 . . . . . . **CLC 14**
See also CA 85-88; CANR 30; DLB 68;
SATA 64

Delbanco, Nicholas (Franklin)
1942- . . . . **CLC 6, 13**
See also CA 17-20R; CAAS 2; CANR 29;
DLB 6

del Castillo, Michel 1933- . . . . **CLC 38**
See also CA 109

Deledda, Grazia (Cosima)
1875(?)-1936 . . . . **TCLC 23**
See also CA 123

Delibes, Miguel . . . . **CLC 8, 18**
See also Delibes Setien, Miguel

Delibes Setien, Miguel 1920-
See Delibes, Miguel
See also CA 45-48; CANR 1, 32; HW;
MTCW

DeLillo, Don
1936- . . . . . **CLC 8, 10, 13, 27, 39, 54, 76**
See also BEST 89:1; CA 81-84; CANR 21;
DAM NOV, POP; DLB 6; MTCW

de Lisser, H. G.
See De Lisser, Herbert George
See also DLB 117

De Lisser, Herbert George
1878-1944 . . . . **TCLC 12**
See also de Lisser, H. G.
See also BW 2; CA 109

Deloria, Vine (Victor), Jr. 1933- . . . . **CLC 21**
See also CA 53-56; CANR 5, 20, 48;
DAM MULT; MTCW; NNAL; SATA 21

Del Vecchio, John M(ichael)
1947- . . . . **CLC 29**
See also CA 110; DLBD 9

de Man, Paul (Adolph Michel)
1919-1983 . . . . **CLC 55**
See also CA 128; 111; DLB 67; MTCW

De Marinis, Rick 1934- . . . . **CLC 54**
See also CA 57-60; CANR 9, 25, 50

Dembry, R. Emmet
See Murfree, Mary Noailles

Demby, William 1922- . . . . **CLC 53; BLC**
See also BW 1; CA 81-84; DAM MULT;
DLB 33

Demijohn, Thom
See Disch, Thomas M(ichael)

de Montherlant, Henry (Milon)
See Montherlant, Henry (Milon) de

Demosthenes 384B.C.-322B.C. . . . . **CMLC 13**

de Natale, Francine
See Malzberg, Barry N(athaniel)

Denby, Edwin (Orr) 1903-1983 . . . . . **CLC 48**
See also CA 138; 110

Denis, Julio
See Cortazar, Julio

Denmark, Harrison
See Zelazny, Roger (Joseph)

Dennis, John 1658-1734 . . . . **LC 11**
See also DLB 101

Dennis, Nigel (Forbes) 1912-1989 . . . . **CLC 8**
See also CA 25-28R; 129; DLB 13, 15;
MTCW

De Palma, Brian (Russell) 1940- . . . . **CLC 20**
See also CA 109

De Quincey, Thomas 1785-1859 . . . **NCLC 4**
See also CDBLB 1789-1832; DLB 110; 144

Deren, Eleanora 1908(?)-1961
See Deren, Maya
See also CA 111

Deren, Maya . . . . **CLC 16**
See also Deren, Eleanora

Derleth, August (William)
1909-1971 . . . . **CLC 31**
See also CA 1-4R; 29-32R; CANR 4;
DLB 9; SATA 5

Der Nister 1884-1950 . . . . **TCLC 56**

de Routisie, Albert
See Aragon, Louis

Derrida, Jacques 1930- . . . . **CLC 24, 87**
See also CA 124; 127

Derry Down Derry
See Lear, Edward

Dersonnes, Jacques
See Simenon, Georges (Jacques Christian)

Desai, Anita 1937- . . . . . . **CLC 19, 37; DAB**
See also CA 81-84; CANR 33; DAM NOV;
MTCW; SATA 63

de Saint-Luc, Jean
See Glassco, John

de Saint Roman, Arnaud
See Aragon, Louis

Descartes, Rene 1596-1650 . . . . **LC 20**

De Sica, Vittorio 1901(?)-1974 . . . . . **CLC 20**
See also CA 117

Desnos, Robert 1900-1945 . . . . **TCLC 22**
See also CA 121; 151

Destouches, Louis-Ferdinand
1894-1961 . . . . **CLC 9, 15**
See also Celine, Louis-Ferdinand
See also CA 85-88; CANR 28; MTCW

Deutsch, Babette 1895-1982 . . . . **CLC 18**
See also CA 1-4R; 108; CANR 4; DLB 45;
SATA 1; SATA-Obit 33

Devenant, William 1606-1649 . . . . . . **LC 13**

Devkota, Laxmiprasad
1909-1959 . . . . **TCLC 23**
See also CA 123

De Voto, Bernard (Augustine)
1897-1955 . . . . **TCLC 29**
See also CA 113; DLB 9

De Vries, Peter
1910-1993 . . . . **CLC 1, 2, 3, 7, 10, 28, 46**
See also CA 17-20R; 142; CANR 41;
DAM NOV; DLB 6; DLBY 82; MTCW

Dexter, Martin
See Faust, Frederick (Schiller)

Dexter, Pete 1943- . . . . **CLC 34, 55**
See also BEST 89:2; CA 127; 131;
DAM POP; INT 131; MTCW

Diamano, Silmang
See Senghor, Leopold Sedar

Diamond, Neil 1941- . . . . **CLC 30**
See also CA 108

Diaz del Castillo, Bernal 1496-1584 . . **LC 31**

di Bassetto, Corno
See Shaw, George Bernard

Dick, Philip K(indred)
1928-1982 . . . . **CLC 10, 30, 72**
See also CA 49-52; 106; CANR 2, 16;
DAM NOV, POP; DLB 8; MTCW

Dickens, Charles (John Huffam)
1812-1870 . . . . . . **NCLC 3, 8, 18, 26, 37,
50; DA; DAB; DAC; SSC 17; WLC**
See also CDBLB 1832-1890; DAM MST,
NOV; DLB 21, 55, 70, 159; JRDA;
MAICYA; SATA 15

Dickey, James (Lafayette)
1923- . . . . **CLC 1, 2, 4, 7, 10, 15, 47**
See also AITN 1, 2; CA 9-12R; CABS 2;
CANR 10, 48; CDALB 1968-1988;
DAM NOV, POET, POP; DLB 5;
DLBD 7; DLBY 82, 93; INT CANR-10;
MTCW

Dickey, William 1928-1994 . . . . . . **CLC 3, 28**
See also CA 9-12R; 145; CANR 24; DLB 5

Dickinson, Charles 1951- . . . . **CLC 49**
See also CA 128

Dickinson, Emily (Elizabeth)
1830-1886 . . . . **NCLC 21; DA; DAB;
DAC; PC 1; WLC**
See also CDALB 1865-1917; DAM MST,
POET; DLB 1; SATA 29

Dickinson, Peter (Malcolm)
1927- . . . . **CLC 12, 35**
See also AAYA 9; CA 41-44R; CANR 31;
CLR 29; DLB 87, 161; JRDA; MAICYA;
SATA 5, 62

Dickson, Carr
See Carr, John Dickson

Dickson, Carter
See Carr, John Dickson

Diderot, Denis 1713-1784 . . . . **LC 26**

Didion, Joan 1934- . . . . . **CLC 1, 3, 8, 14, 32**
See also AITN 1; CA 5-8R; CANR 14;
CDALB 1968-1988; DAM NOV; DLB 2;
DLBY 81, 86; MTCW

Dietrich, Robert
See Hunt, E(verette) Howard, (Jr.)

Dillard, Annie 1945- . . . . **CLC 9, 60**
See also AAYA 6; CA 49-52; CANR 3, 43;
DAM NOV; DLBY 80; MTCW;
SATA 10

Dillard, R(ichard) H(enry) W(ilde)
1937- . . . . **CLC 5**
See also CA 21-24R; CAAS 7; CANR 10;
DLB 5

Dillon, Eilis 1920-1994 . . . . **CLC 17**
See also CA 9-12R; 147; CAAS 3; CANR 4,
38; CLR 26; MAICYA; SATA 2, 74;
SATA-Obit 83

Dimont, Penelope
See Mortimer, Penelope (Ruth)

Dinesen, Isak . . . . **CLC 10, 29; SSC 7**
See also Blixen, Karen (Christentze
Dinesen)

Ding Ling . . . . **CLC 68**
See also Chiang Pin-chin

Disch, Thomas M(ichael) 1940-... **CLC 7, 36**
See also AAYA 17; CA 21-24R; CAAS 4;
CANR 17, 36; CLR 18; DLB 8;
MAICYA; MTCW; SAAS 15; SATA 54

Disch, Tom
See Disch, Thomas M(ichael)

d'Isly, Georges
See Simenon, Georges (Jacques Christian)

Disraeli, Benjamin 1804-1881 .. **NCLC 2, 39**
See also DLB 21, 55

Ditcum, Steve
See Crumb, R(obert)

Dixon, Paige
See Corcoran, Barbara

Dixon, Stephen 1936 ..... **CLC 52; SSC 16**
See also CA 89-92; CANR 17, 40; DLB 130

Dobell, Sydney Thompson
1824-1874 .... **NCLC 43**
See also DLB 32

Doblin, Alfred .... **TCLC 13**
See also Doeblin, Alfred

Dobrolyubov, Nikolai Alexandrovich
1836-1861 .... **NCLC 5**

Dobyns, Stephen 1941-............ **CLC 37**
See also CA 45-48; CANR 2, 18

Doctorow, E(dgar) L(aurence)
1931- ..... **CLC 6, 11, 15, 18, 37, 44, 65**
See also AITN 2; BEST 89:3; CA 45-48;
CANR 2, 33, 51; CDALB 1968-1988;
DAM NOV, POP; DLB 2, 28; DLBY 80;
MTCW

Dodgson, Charles Lutwidge 1832-1898
See Carroll, Lewis
See also CLR 2; DA; DAB; DAC;
DAM MST, NOV, POET; MAICYA;
YABC 2

Dodson, Owen (Vincent)
1914-1983 .... **CLC 79; BLC**
See also BW 1; CA 65-68; 110; CANR 24;
DAM MULT; DLB 76

Doeblin, Alfred 1878-1957....... **TCLC 13**
See also Doblin, Alfred
See also CA 110; 141; DLB 66

Doerr, Harriet 1910- .... **CLC 34**
See also CA 117; 122; CANR 47; INT 122

Domecq, H(onorio) Bustos
See Bioy Casares, Adolfo; Borges, Jorge
Luis

Domini, Rey
See Lorde, Audre (Geraldine)

Dominique
See Proust, (Valentin-Louis-George-Eugene-)
Marcel

Don, A
See Stephen, Leslie

Donaldson, Stephen R. 1947-....... **CLC 46**
See also CA 89-92; CANR 13; DAM POP;
INT CANR-13

Donleavy, J(ames) P(atrick)
1926- .... **CLC 1, 4, 6, 10, 45**
See also AITN 2; CA 9-12R; CANR 24, 49;
DLB 6; INT CANR-24; MTCW

Donne, John
1572-1631 ...... **LC 10, 24; DA; DAB;**
                              DAC; PC 1
See also CDBLB Before 1660; DAM MST,
POET; DLB 121, 151

Donnell, David 1939(?)-........... **CLC 34**

Donoghue, P. S.
See Hunt, E(verette) Howard, (Jr.)

Donoso (Yanez), Jose
1924- .... **CLC 4, 8, 11, 32; HLC**
See also CA 81-84; CANR 32;
DAM MULT; DLB 113; HW; MTCW

Donovan, John 1928-1992 .... **CLC 35**
See also CA 97-100; 137; CLR 3;
MAICYA; SATA 72; SATA-Brief 29

Don Roberto
See Cunninghame Graham, R(obert)
B(ontine)

Doolittle, Hilda
1886-1961 ..... **CLC 3, 8, 14, 31, 34, 73;**
                              DA; DAC; PC 5; WLC
See also H. D.
See also CA 97-100; CANR 35; DAM MST,
POET; DLB 4, 45; MTCW

Dorfman, Ariel 1942-.... **CLC 48, 77; HLC**
See also CA 124; 130; DAM MULT; HW;
INT 130

Dorn, Edward (Merton) 1929-... **CLC 10, 18**
See also CA 93-96; CANR 42; DLB 5;
INT 93-96

Dorsan, Luc
See Simenon, Georges (Jacques Christian)

Dorsange, Jean
See Simenon, Georges (Jacques Christian)

Dos Passos, John (Roderigo)
1896-1970 ...... **CLC 1, 4, 8, 11, 15, 25,**
                              34, 82; DA; DAB; DAC; WLC
See also CA 1-4R; 29-32R; CANR 3;
CDALB 1929-1941; DAM MST, NOV;
DLB 4, 9; DLBD 1; MTCW

Dossage, Jean
See Simenon, Georges (Jacques Christian)

Dostoevsky, Fedor Mikhailovich
1821-1881 ...... **NCLC 2, 7, 21, 33, 43;**
                              DA; DAB; DAC; SSC 2; WLC
See also DAM MST, NOV

Doughty, Charles M(ontagu)
1843-1926 .... **TCLC 27**
See also CA 115; DLB 19, 57

Douglas, Ellen .... **CLC 73**
See also Haxton, Josephine Ayres;
Williamson, Ellen Douglas

Douglas, Gavin 1475(?)-1522....... **LC 20**

Douglas, Keith 1920-1944 .... **TCLC 40**
See also DLB 27

Douglas, Leonard
See Bradbury, Ray (Douglas)

Douglas, Michael
See Crichton, (John) Michael

Douglass, Frederick
1817(?)-1895 .... **NCLC 7, 55; BLC; DA;**
                              DAC; WLC
See also CDALB 1640-1865; DAM MST,
MULT; DLB 1, 43, 50, 79; SATA 29

Dourado, (Waldomiro Freitas) Autran
1926- .... **CLC 23, 60**
See also CA 25-28R; CANR 34

Dourado, Waldomiro Autran
See Dourado, (Waldomiro Freitas) Autran

Dove, Rita (Frances)
1952- .... **CLC 50, 81; PC 6**
See also BW 2; CA 109; CAAS 19;
CANR 27, 42; DAM MULT, POET;
DLB 120

Dowell, Coleman 1925-1985........ **CLC 60**
See also CA 25-28R; 117; CANR 10;
DLB 130

Dowson, Ernest (Christopher)
1867-1900 .... **TCLC 4**
See also CA 105; 150; DLB 19, 135

Doyle, A. Conan
See Doyle, Arthur Conan

Doyle, Arthur Conan
1859-1930 .... **TCLC 7; DA; DAB;**
                              DAC; SSC 12; WLC
See also AAYA 14; CA 104; 122;
CDBLB 1890-1914; DAM MST, NOV;
DLB 18, 70, 156; MTCW; SATA 24

Doyle, Conan
See Doyle, Arthur Conan

Doyle, John
See Graves, Robert (von Ranke)

Doyle, Roddy 1958(?)-............ **CLC 81**
See also AAYA 14; CA 143

Doyle, Sir A. Conan
See Doyle, Arthur Conan

Doyle, Sir Arthur Conan
See Doyle, Arthur Conan

Dr. A
See Asimov, Isaac; Silverstein, Alvin

Drabble, Margaret
1939- .... **CLC 2, 3, 5, 8, 10, 22, 53;**
                              DAB; DAC
See also CA 13-16R; CANR 18, 35;
CDBLB 1960 to Present; DAM MST,
NOV, POP; DLB 14, 155; MTCW;
SATA 48

Drapier, M. B.
See Swift, Jonathan

Drayham, James
See Mencken, H(enry) L(ouis)

Drayton, Michael 1563-1631........ **LC 8**

Dreadstone, Carl
See Campbell, (John) Ramsey

Dreiser, Theodore (Herman Albert)
1871-1945 .... **TCLC 10, 18, 35; DA;**
                              DAC; WLC
See also CA 106; 132; CDALB 1865-1917;
DAM MST, NOV; DLB 9, 12, 102, 137;
DLBD 1; MTCW

Drexler, Rosalyn 1926- .... **CLC 2, 6**
See also CA 81-84

Dreyer, Carl Theodor 1889-1968.... **CLC 16**
See also CA 116

Drieu la Rochelle, Pierre(-Eugene)
1893-1945 .... **TCLC 21**
See also CA 117; DLB 72

Drinkwater, John 1882-1937...... **TCLC 57**
See also CA 109; 149; DLB 10, 19, 149

Drop Shot
See Cable, George Washington

Droste-Hulshoff, Annette Freiin von
1797-1848 .... NCLC **3**
See also DLB 133

Drummond, Walter
See Silverberg, Robert

Drummond, William Henry
1854-1907 .... TCLC **25**
See also DLB 92

Drummond de Andrade, Carlos
1902-1987 .... CLC **18**
See also Andrade, Carlos Drummond de
See also CA 132; 123

Drury, Allen (Stuart) 1918- .... CLC **37**
See also CA 57-60; CANR 18;
INT CANR-18

Dryden, John
1631-1700 .... **LC 3, 21; DA; DAB;**
DAC; DC 3; WLC
See also CDBLB 1660-1789; DAM DRAM,
MST, POET; DLB 80, 101, 131

Duberman, Martin 1930- .... CLC **8**
See also CA 1-4R; CANR 2

Dubie, Norman (Evans) 1945- ...... CLC **36**
See also CA 69-72; CANR 12; DLB 120

Du Bois, W(illiam) E(dward) B(urghardt)
1868-1963 ...... **CLC 1, 2, 13, 64; BLC;**
DA; DAC; WLC
See also BW 1; CA 85-88; CANR 34;
CDALB 1865-1917; DAM MST, MULT,
NOV; DLB 47, 50, 91; MTCW; SATA 42

Dubus, Andre 1936- ... CLC **13, 36; SSC 15**
See also CA 21-24R; CANR 17; DLB 130;
INT CANR-17

Duca Minimo
See D'Annunzio, Gabriele

Ducharme, Rejean 1941- .... CLC **74**
See also DLB 60

Duclos, Charles Pinot 1704-1772 ..... LC **1**

Dudek, Louis 1918- .... CLC **11, 19**
See also CA 45-48; CAAS 14; CANR 1;
DLB 88

Duerrenmatt, Friedrich
1921-1990 ...... **CLC 1, 4, 8, 11, 15, 43**
See also CA 17-20R; CANR 33;
DAM DRAM; DLB 69, 124; MTCW

Duffy, Bruce (?)- .... CLC **50**

Duffy, Maureen 1933- .... CLC **37**
See also CA 25-28R; CANR 33; DLB 14;
MTCW

Dugan, Alan 1923- .... CLC **2, 6**
See also CA 81-84; DLB 5

du Gard, Roger Martin
See Martin du Gard, Roger

Duhamel, Georges 1884-1966 .... CLC **8**
See also CA 81-84; 25-28R; CANR 35;
DLB 65; MTCW

Dujardin, Edouard (Emile Louis)
1861-1949 .... TCLC **13**
See also CA 109; DLB 123

Dumas, Alexandre (Davy de la Pailleterie)
1802-1870 ...... NCLC **11; DA; DAB;**
DAC; WLC
See also DAM MST, NOV; DLB 119;
SATA 18

Dumas, Alexandre
1824-1895 .... NCLC **9; DC 1**

Dumas, Claudine
See Malzberg, Barry N(athaniel)

Dumas, Henry L. 1934-1968 ..... CLC **6, 62**
See also BW 1; CA 85-88; DLB 41

du Maurier, Daphne
1907-1989 .... CLC **6, 11, 59; DAB;**
DAC; SSC 18
See also CA 5-8R; 128; CANR 6;
DAM MST, POP; MTCW; SATA 27;
SATA-Obit 60

Dunbar, Paul Laurence
1872-1906 ...... **TCLC 2, 12; BLC; DA;**
DAC; PC 5; SSC 8; WLC
See also BW 1; CA 104; 124;
CDALB 1865-1917; DAM MST, MULT,
POET; DLB 50, 54, 78; SATA 34

Dunbar, William 1460(?)-1530(?) .... LC **20**
See also DLB 132, 146

Duncan, Lois 1934- .... CLC **26**
See also AAYA 4; CA 1-4R; CANR 2, 23,
36; CLR 29; JRDA; MAICYA; SAAS 2;
SATA 1, 36, 75

Duncan, Robert (Edward)
1919-1988 .... CLC **1, 2, 4, 7, 15, 41, 55;**
PC 2
See also CA 9-12R; 124; CANR 28;
DAM POET; DLB 5, 16; MTCW

Duncan, Sara Jeannette
1861-1922 .... TCLC **60**
See also DLB 92

Dunlap, William 1766-1839 .... NCLC **2**
See also DLB 30, 37, 59

Dunn, Douglas (Eaglesham)
1942- .... CLC **6, 40**
See also CA 45-48; CANR 2, 33; DLB 40;
MTCW

Dunn, Katherine (Karen) 1945- ..... CLC **71**
See also CA 33-36R

Dunn, Stephen 1939- .... CLC **36**
See also CA 33-36R; CANR 12, 48;
DLB 105

Dunne, Finley Peter 1867-1936.... TCLC **28**
See also CA 108; DLB 11, 23

Dunne, John Gregory 1932- .... CLC **28**
See also CA 25-28R; CANR 14, 50;
DLBY 80

Dunsany, Edward John Moreton Drax
Plunkett 1878-1957
See Dunsany, Lord
See also CA 104; 148; DLB 10

Dunsany, Lord................. TCLC **2, 59**
See also Dunsany, Edward John Moreton
Drax Plunkett
See also DLB 77, 153, 156

du Perry, Jean
See Simenon, Georges (Jacques Christian)

Durang, Christopher (Ferdinand)
1949- .... CLC **27, 38**
See also CA 105; CANR 50

Duras, Marguerite
1914-1996 .. CLC **3, 6, 11, 20, 34, 40, 68**
See also CA 25-28R; 151; CANR 50;
DLB 83; MTCW

Durban, (Rosa) Pam 1947-........ CLC **39**
See also CA 123

Durcan, Paul 1944-............ CLC **43, 70**
See also CA 134; DAM POET

Durkheim, Emile 1858-1917 ...... TCLC **55**

Durrell, Lawrence (George)
1912-1990 .... CLC **1, 4, 6, 8, 13, 27, 41**
See also CA 9-12R; 132; CANR 40;
CDBLB 1945-1960; DAM NOV; DLB 15,
27; DLBY 90; MTCW

Durrenmatt, Friedrich
See Duerrenmatt, Friedrich

Dutt, Toru 1856-1877........... NCLC **29**

Dwight, Timothy 1752-1817...... NCLC **13**
See also DLB 37

Dworkin, Andrea 1946- .... CLC **43**
See also CA 77-80; CAAS 21; CANR 16,
39; INT CANR-16; MTCW

Dwyer, Deanna
See Koontz, Dean R(ay)

Dwyer, K. R.
See Koontz, Dean R(ay)

Dylan, Bob 1941- ...... CLC **3, 4, 6, 12, 77**
See also CA 41-44R; DLB 16

Eagleton, Terence (Francis) 1943-
See Eagleton, Terry
See also CA 57-60; CANR 7, 23; MTCW

Eagleton, Terry .... CLC **63**
See also Eagleton, Terence (Francis)

Early, Jack
See Scoppettone, Sandra

East, Michael
See West, Morris L(anglo)

Eastaway, Edward
See Thomas, (Philip) Edward

Eastlake, William (Derry) 1917-..... CLC **8**
See also CA 5-8R; CAAS 1; CANR 5;
DLB 6; INT CANR-5

Eastman, Charles A(lexander)
1858-1939 .... TCLC **55**
See also DAM MULT; NNAL; YABC 1

Eberhart, Richard (Ghormley)
1904- .... CLC **3, 11, 19, 56**
See also CA 1-4R; CANR 2;
CDALB 1941-1968; DAM POET;
DLB 48; MTCW

Eberstadt, Fernanda 1960-........ CLC **39**
See also CA 136

Echegaray (y Eizaguirre), Jose (Maria Waldo)
1832-1916 .... TCLC **4**
See also CA 104; CANR 32; HW; MTCW

Echeverria, (Jose) Esteban (Antonino)
1805-1851 .... NCLC **18**

Echo
See Proust, (Valentin-Louis-George-Eugene-)
Marcel

Eckert, Allan W. 1931- .... CLC **17**
See also CA 13-16R; CANR 14, 45;
INT CANR-14; SAAS 21; SATA 29;
SATA-Brief 27

Eckhart, Meister   1260(?)-1328(?) . . CMLC 9
See also DLB 115

Eckmar, F. R.
See de Hartog, Jan

Eco, Umberto   1932- . . . . CLC 28, 60
See also BEST 90:1; CA 77-80; CANR 12,
33; DAM NOV, POP; MTCW

Eddison, E(ric) R(ucker)
1882-1945 . . . . TCLC 15
See also CA 109

Edel, (Joseph) Leon   1907- . . . . . . CLC 29, 34
See also CA 1-4R; CANR 1, 22; DLB 103;
INT CANR-22

Eden, Emily   1797-1869 . . . . NCLC 10

Edgar, David   1948- . . . . CLC 42
See also CA 57-60, CANR 12;
DAM DRAM; DLB 13; MTCW

Edgerton, Clyde (Carlyle)   1944- . . . . CLC 39
See also AAYA 17; CA 118; 134; INT 134

Edgeworth, Maria   1768-1849. . . NCLC 1, 51
See also DLB 116, 159, 163; SATA 21

Edmonds, Paul
See Kuttner, Henry

Edmonds, Walter D(umaux)   1903- . . CLC 35
See also CA 5-8R; CANR 2; DLB 9;
MAICYA; SAAS 4; SATA 1, 27

Edmondson, Wallace
See Ellison, Harlan (Jay)

Edson, Russell . . . . CLC 13
See also CA 33-36R

Edwards, Bronwen Elizabeth
See Rose, Wendy

Edwards, G(erald) B(asil)
1899-1976 . . . . CLC 25
See also CA 110

Edwards, Gus   1939- . . . . CLC 43
See also CA 108; INT 108

Edwards, Jonathan
1703-1758 . . . . LC 7; DA; DAC
See also DAM MST; DLB 24

Efron, Marina Ivanovna Tsvetaeva
See Tsvetaeva (Efron), Marina (Ivanovna)

Ehle, John (Marsden, Jr.)   1925- . . . . CLC 27
See also CA 9-12R

Ehrenbourg, Ilya (Grigoryevich)
See Ehrenburg, Ilya (Grigoryevich)

Ehrenburg, Ilya (Grigoryevich)
1891-1967 . . . . CLC 18, 34, 62
See also CA 102; 25-28R

Ehrenburg, Ilyo (Grigoryevich)
See Ehrenburg, Ilya (Grigoryevich)

Eich, Guenter   1907-1972 . . . . CLC 15
See also CA 111; 93-96; DLB 69, 124

Eichendorff, Joseph Freiherr von
1788-1857 . . . . NCLC 8
See also DLB 90

Eigner, Larry . . . . CLC 9
See also Eigner, Laurence (Joel)
See also CAAS 23; DLB 5

Eigner, Laurence (Joel)   1927-1996
See Eigner, Larry
See also CA 9-12R; 151; CANR 6

Einstein, Albert   1879-1955 . . . . TCLC 65
See also CA 121; 133; MTCW

Eiseley, Loren Corey   1907-1977 . . . . . CLC 7
See also AAYA 5; CA 1-4R; 73-76;
CANR 6

Eisenstadt, Jill   1963- . . . . CLC 50
See also CA 140

Eisenstein, Sergei (Mikhailovich)
1898-1948 . . . . TCLC 57
See also CA 114; 149

Eisner, Simon
See Kornbluth, C(yril) M.

Ekeloef, (Bengt) Gunnar
1907-1968 . . . . CLC 27
See also CA 123; 25-28R; DAM POET

Ekelof, (Bengt) Gunnar
See Ekeloef, (Bengt) Gunnar

Ekwensi, C. O. D.
See Ekwensi, Cyprian (Odiatu Duaka)

Ekwensi, Cyprian (Odiatu Duaka)
1921- . . . . CLC 4; BLC
See also BW 2; CA 29-32R; CANR 18, 42;
DAM MULT; DLB 117; MTCW;
SATA 66

Elaine . . . . TCLC 18
See also Leverson, Ada

El Crummo
See Crumb, R(obert)

Elia
See Lamb, Charles

Eliade, Mircea   1907-1986 . . . . CLC 19
See also CA 65-68; 119; CANR 30; MTCW

Eliot, A. D.
See Jewett, (Theodora) Sarah Orne

Eliot, Alice
See Jewett, (Theodora) Sarah Orne

Eliot, Dan
See Silverberg, Robert

Eliot, George
1819-1880 . . . . . NCLC 4, 13, 23, 41, 49;
DA; DAB; DAC; WLC
See also CDBLB 1832-1890; DAM MST,
NOV; DLB 21, 35, 55

Eliot, John   1604-1690 . . . . LC 5
See also DLB 24

Eliot, T(homas) S(tearns)
1888-1965 . . . . . CLC 1, 2, 3, 6, 9, 10, 13,
15, 24, 34, 41, 55, 57; DA; DAB; DAC;
PC 5; WLC 2
See also CA 5-8R; 25-28R; CANR 41;
CDALB 1929-1941; DAM DRAM, MST,
POET; DLB 7, 10, 45, 63; DLBY 88;
MTCW

Elizabeth   1866-1941 . . . . TCLC 41

Elkin, Stanley L(awrence)
1930-1995 . . . . . . CLC 4, 6, 9, 14, 27, 51,
91; SSC 12
See also CA 9-12R; 148; CANR 8, 46;
DAM NOV, POP; DLB 2, 28; DLBY 80;
INT CANR-8; MTCW

Elledge, Scott . . . . CLC 34

Elliott, Don
See Silverberg, Robert

Elliott, George P(aul)   1918-1980 . . . . . CLC 2
See also CA 1-4R; 97-100; CANR 2

Elliott, Janice   1931- . . . . CLC 47
See also CA 13-16R; CANR 8, 29; DLB 14

Elliott, Sumner Locke   1917-1991 . . . CLC 38
See also CA 5-8R; 134; CANR 2, 21

Elliott, William
See Bradbury, Ray (Douglas)

Ellis, A. E. . . . . CLC 7

Ellis, Alice Thomas . . . . CLC 40
See also Haycraft, Anna

Ellis, Bret Easton   1964- . . . . CLC 39, 71
See also AAYA 2; CA 118; 123; CANR 51;
DAM POP; INT 123

Ellis, (Henry) Havelock
1859-1939 . . . . TCLC 14
See also CA 109

Ellis, Landon
See Ellison, Harlan (Jay)

Ellis, Trey   1962- . . . . CLC 55
See also CA 146

Ellison, Harlan (Jay)
1934- . . . . CLC 1, 13, 42; SSC 14
See also CA 5-8R; CANR 5, 46;
DAM POP; DLB 8; INT CANR-5;
MTCW

Ellison, Ralph (Waldo)
1914-1994 . . . . CLC 1, 3, 11, 54, 86;
BLC; DA; DAB; DAC; WLC
See also BW 1; CA 9-12R; 145; CANR 24;
CDALB 1941-1968; DAM MST, MULT,
NOV; DLB 2, 76; DLBY 94; MTCW

Ellmann, Lucy (Elizabeth)   1956- . . . . CLC 61
See also CA 128

Ellmann, Richard (David)
1918-1987 . . . . CLC 50
See also BEST 89:2; CA 1-4R; 122;
CANR 2, 28; DLB 103; DLBY 87;
MTCW

Elman, Richard   1934- . . . . CLC 19
See also CA 17-20R; CAAS 3; CANR 47

Elron
See Hubbard, L(afayette) Ron(ald)

Eluard, Paul . . . . TCLC 7, 41
See also Grindel, Eugene

Elyot, Sir Thomas   1490(?)-1546 . . . . . LC 11

Elytis, Odysseus   1911-1996 . . . . . CLC 15, 49
See also CA 102; 151; DAM POET; MTCW

Emecheta, (Florence Onye) Buchi
1944- . . . . CLC 14, 48; BLC
See also BW 2; CA 81-84; CANR 27;
DAM MULT; DLB 117; MTCW;
SATA 66

Emerson, Ralph Waldo
1803-1882 . . . . . NCLC 1, 38; DA; DAB;
DAC; WLC
See also CDALB 1640-1865; DAM MST,
POET; DLB 1, 59, 73

Eminescu, Mihail   1850-1889 . . . . . NCLC 33

Empson, William
1906-1984 . . . . CLC 3, 8, 19, 33, 34
See also CA 17-20R; 112; CANR 31;
DLB 20; MTCW

Enchi Fumiko (Ueda)   1905-1986 . . . . CLC 31
See also CA 129; 121

Ende, Michael (Andreas Helmuth)
    1929-1995 .... **CLC 31**
    See also CA 118; 124; 149; CANR 36;
    CLR 14; DLB 75; MAICYA; SATA 61;
    SATA-Brief 42; SATA-Obit 86

Endo, Shusaku 1923- ..... **CLC 7, 14, 19, 54**
    See also CA 29-32R; CANR 21;
    DAM NOV; MTCW

Engel, Marian 1933-1985 .... **CLC 36**
    See also CA 25-28R; CANR 12; DLB 53;
    INT CANR-12

Engelhardt, Frederick
    See Hubbard, L(afayette) Ron(ald)

Enright, D(ennis) J(oseph)
    1920- .... **CLC 4, 8, 31**
    See also CA 1-4R; CANR 1, 42; DLB 27;
    SATA 25

Enzensberger, Hans Magnus
    1929- .... **CLC 43**
    See also CA 116; 119

Ephron, Nora 1941- .... **CLC 17, 31**
    See also AITN 2; CA 65-68; CANR 12, 39

Epsilon
    See Betjeman, John

Epstein, Daniel Mark 1948- .... **CLC 7**
    See also CA 49-52; CANR 2

Epstein, Jacob 1956- .... **CLC 19**
    See also CA 114

Epstein, Joseph 1937- .... **CLC 39**
    See also CA 112; 119; CANR 50

Epstein, Leslie 1938- .... **CLC 27**
    See also CA 73-76; CAAS 12; CANR 23

Equiano, Olaudah
    1745(?)-1797 .... **LC 16; BLC**
    See also DAM MULT; DLB 37, 50

Erasmus, Desiderius 1469(?)-1536.... **LC 16**

Erdman, Paul E(mil) 1932- .... **CLC 25**
    See also AITN 1; CA 61-64; CANR 13, 43

Erdrich, Louise 1954- .... **CLC 39, 54**
    See also AAYA 10; BEST 89:1; CA 114;
    CANR 41; DAM MULT, NOV, POP;
    DLB 152; MTCW; NNAL

Erenburg, Ilya (Grigoryevich)
    See Ehrenburg, Ilya (Grigoryevich)

Erickson, Stephen Michael 1950-
    See Erickson, Steve
    See also CA 129

Erickson, Steve .... **CLC 64**
    See also Erickson, Stephen Michael

Ericson, Walter
    See Fast, Howard (Melvin)

Eriksson, Buntel
    See Bergman, (Ernst) Ingmar

Ernaux, Annie 1940- .... **CLC 88**
    See also CA 147

Eschenbach, Wolfram von
    See Wolfram von Eschenbach

Eseki, Bruno
    See Mphahlele, Ezekiel

Esenin, Sergei (Alexandrovich)
    1895-1925 .... **TCLC 4**
    See also CA 104

Eshleman, Clayton 1935- .... **CLC 7**
    See also CA 33-36R; CAAS 6; DLB 5

Espriella, Don Manuel Alvarez
    See Southey, Robert

Espriu, Salvador 1913-1985........ **CLC 9**
    See also CA 115; DLB 134

Espronceda, Jose de 1808-1842... **NCLC 39**

Esse, James
    See Stephens, James

Esterbrook, Tom
    See Hubbard, L(afayette) Ron(ald)

Estleman, Loren D. 1952- .... **CLC 48**
    See also CA 85-88; CANR 27; DAM NOV,
    POP; INT CANR-27; MTCW

Eugenides, Jeffrey 1960(?)- .... **CLC 81**
    See also CA 144

Euripides c. 485B.C.-406B.C. .... **DC 4**
    See also DA; DAB; DAC; DAM DRAM,
    MST

Evan, Evin
    See Faust, Frederick (Schiller)

Evans, Evan
    See Faust, Frederick (Schiller)

Evans, Marian
    See Eliot, George

Evans, Mary Ann
    See Eliot, George

Evarts, Esther
    See Benson, Sally

Everett, Percival L. 1956- .... **CLC 57**
    See also BW 2; CA 129

Everson, R(onald) G(ilmour)
    1903- .... **CLC 27**
    See also CA 17-20R; DLB 88

Everson, William (Oliver)
    1912-1994 .... **CLC 1, 5, 14**
    See also CA 9-12R; 145; CANR 20; DLB 5,
    16; MTCW

Evtushenko, Evgenii Aleksandrovich
    See Yevtushenko, Yevgeny (Alexandrovich)

Ewart, Gavin (Buchanan)
    1916-1995 .... **CLC 13, 46**
    See also CA 89-92; 150; CANR 17, 46;
    DLB 40; MTCW

Ewers, Hanns Heinz 1871-1943 ... **TCLC 12**
    See also CA 109; 149

Ewing, Frederick R.
    See Sturgeon, Theodore (Hamilton)

Exley, Frederick (Earl)
    1929-1992 .... **CLC 6, 11**
    See also AITN 2; CA 81-84; 138; DLB 143;
    DLBY 81

Eynhardt, Guillermo
    See Quiroga, Horacio (Sylvestre)

Ezekiel, Nissim 1924- .... **CLC 61**
    See also CA 61-64

Ezekiel, Tish O'Dowd 1943- .... **CLC 34**
    See also CA 129

Fadeyev, A.
    See Bulgya, Alexander Alexandrovich

Fadeyev, Alexander.............. TCLC 53
    See also Bulgya, Alexander Alexandrovich

Fagen, Donald 1948- .... **CLC 26**

Fainzilberg, Ilya Arnoldovich 1897-1937
    See Ilf, Ilya
    See also CA 120

Fair, Ronald L. 1932-............. **CLC 18**
    See also BW 1; CA 69-72; CANR 25;
    DLB 33

Fairbairns, Zoe (Ann) 1948- .... **CLC 32**
    See also CA 103; CANR 21

Falco, Gian
    See Papini, Giovanni

Falconer, James
    See Kirkup, James

Falconer, Kenneth
    See Kornbluth, C(yril) M.

Falkland, Samuel
    See Heijermans, Herman

Fallaci, Oriana 1930-............. **CLC 11**
    See also CA 77-80; CANR 15; MTCW

Faludy, George 1913-............. **CLC 42**
    See also CA 21-24R

Faludy, Gyoergy
    See Faludy, George

Fanon, Frantz 1925-1961..... **CLC 74; BLC**
    See also BW 1; CA 116; 89-92;
    DAM MULT

Fanshawe, Ann 1625-1680 .... **LC 11**

Fante, John (Thomas) 1911-1983 ... **CLC 60**
    See also CA 69-72; 109; CANR 23;
    DLB 130; DLBY 83

Farah, Nuruddin 1945-....... **CLC 53; BLC**
    See also BW 2; CA 106; DAM MULT;
    DLB 125

Fargue, Leon-Paul 1876(?)-1947 ... **TCLC 11**
    See also CA 109

Farigoule, Louis
    See Romains, Jules

Farina, Richard 1936(?)-1966 .... **CLC 9**
    See also CA 81-84; 25-28R

Farley, Walter (Lorimer)
    1915-1989 .... **CLC 17**
    See also CA 17-20R; CANR 8, 29; DLB 22;
    JRDA; MAICYA; SATA 2, 43

Farmer, Philip Jose 1918-....... **CLC 1, 19**
    See also CA 1-4R; CANR 4, 35; DLB 8;
    MTCW

Farquhar, George 1677-1707 .... **LC 21**
    See also DAM DRAM; DLB 84

Farrell, J(ames) G(ordon)
    1935-1979 .... **CLC 6**
    See also CA 73-76; 89-92; CANR 36;
    DLB 14; MTCW

Farrell, James T(homas)
    1904-1979 .... **CLC 1, 4, 8, 11, 66**
    See also CA 5-8R; 89-92; CANR 9; DLB 4,
    9, 86; DLBD 2; MTCW

Farren, Richard J.
    See Betjeman, John

Farren, Richard M.
    See Betjeman, John

Fassbinder, Rainer Werner
    1946-1982 .... **CLC 20**
    See also CA 93-96; 106; CANR 31

Fast, Howard (Melvin) 1914- ...... **CLC 23**
See also AAYA 16; CA 1-4R; CAAS 18;
CANR 1, 33; DAM NOV; DLB 9;
INT CANR-33; SATA 7

Faulcon, Robert
See Holdstock, Robert P.

Faulkner, William (Cuthbert)
1897-1962 ..... **CLC 1, 3, 6, 8, 9, 11, 14,
18, 28, 52, 68; DA; DAB; DAC; SSC 1;
WLC**
See also AAYA 7; CA 81-84; CANR 33;
CDALB 1929-1941; DAM MST, NOV;
DLB 9, 11, 44, 102; DLBD 2; DLBY 86;
MTCW

Fauset, Jessie Redmon
1884(?)-1961 .... **CLC 19, 54; BLC**
See also BW 1; CA 109; DAM MULT;
DLB 51

Faust, Frederick (Schiller)
1892-1944(?) .... **TCLC 49**
See also CA 108; DAM POP

Faust, Irvin 1924- .... **CLC 8**
See also CA 33-36R; CANR 28; DLB 2, 28;
DLBY 80

Fawkes, Guy
See Benchley, Robert (Charles)

Fearing, Kenneth (Flexner)
1902-1961 .... **CLC 51**
See also CA 93-96; DLB 9

Fecamps, Elise
See Creasey, John

Federman, Raymond 1928- ...... **CLC 6, 47**
See also CA 17-20R; CAAS 8; CANR 10,
43; DLBY 80

Federspiel, J(uerg) F. 1931- .... **CLC 42**
See also CA 146

Feiffer, Jules (Ralph) 1929- .... **CLC 2, 8, 64**
See also AAYA 3; CA 17-20R; CANR 30;
DAM DRAM; DLB 7, 44;
INT CANR-30; MTCW; SATA 8, 61

Feige, Hermann Albert Otto Maximilian
See Traven, B.

Feinberg, David B. 1956-1994 ..... **CLC 59**
See also CA 135; 147

Feinstein, Elaine 1930- .... **CLC 36**
See also CA 69-72; CAAS 1; CANR 31;
DLB 14, 40; MTCW

Feldman, Irving (Mordecai) 1928- .... **CLC 7**
See also CA 1-4R; CANR 1

Fellini, Federico 1920-1993 ..... **CLC 16, 85**
See also CA 65-68; 143; CANR 33

Felsen, Henry Gregor 1916- .... **CLC 17**
See also CA 1-4R; CANR 1; SAAS 2;
SATA 1

Fenton, James Martin 1949- .... **CLC 32**
See also CA 102; DLB 40

Ferber, Edna 1887-1968 .... **CLC 18, 93**
See also AITN 1; CA 5-8R; 25-28R; DLB 9,
28, 86; MTCW; SATA 7

Ferguson, Helen
See Kavan, Anna

Ferguson, Samuel 1810-1886 ..... **NCLC 33**
See also DLB 32

Fergusson, Robert 1750-1774 .... **LC 29**
See also DLB 109

Ferling, Lawrence
See Ferlinghetti, Lawrence (Monsanto)

Ferlinghetti, Lawrence (Monsanto)
1919(?)- .... **CLC 2, 6, 10, 27; PC 1**
See also CA 5-8R; CANR 3, 41;
CDALB 1941-1968; DAM POET; DLB 5,
16; MTCW

Fernandez, Vicente Garcia Huidobro
See Huidobro Fernandez, Vicente Garcia

Ferrer, Gabriel (Francisco Victor) Miro
See Miro (Ferrer), Gabriel (Francisco
Victor)

Ferrier, Susan (Edmonstone)
1782-1854 .... **NCLC 8**
See also DLB 116

Ferrigno, Robert 1948(?)- .... **CLC 65**
See also CA 140

Ferron, Jacques 1921-1985 ... **CLC 94; DAC**
See also CA 117; 129; DLB 60

Feuchtwanger, Lion 1884-1958 ..... **TCLC 3**
See also CA 104; DLB 66

Feuillet, Octave 1821-1890 ...... **NCLC 45**

Feydeau, Georges (Leon Jules Marie)
1862-1921 .... **TCLC 22**
See also CA 113; DAM DRAM

Ficino, Marsilio 1433-1499 .... **LC 12**

Fiedeler, Hans
See Doeblin, Alfred

Fiedler, Leslie A(aron)
1917- .... **CLC 4, 13, 24**
See also CA 9-12R; CANR 7; DLB 28, 67;
MTCW

Field, Andrew 1938- .... **CLC 44**
See also CA 97-100; CANR 25

Field, Eugene 1850-1895 .... **NCLC 3**
See also DLB 23, 42, 140; DLBD 13;
MAICYA; SATA 16

Field, Gans T.
See Wellman, Manly Wade

Field, Michael .... **TCLC 43**

Field, Peter
See Hobson, Laura Z(ametkin)

Fielding, Henry
1707-1754 ...... **LC 1; DA; DAB; DAC;
WLC**
See also CDBLB 1660-1789; DAM DRAM,
MST, NOV; DLB 39, 84, 101

Fielding, Sarah 1710-1768 .... **LC 1**
See also DLB 39

Fierstein, Harvey (Forbes) 1954- ... **CLC 33**
See also CA 123; 129; DAM DRAM, POP

Figes, Eva 1932- .... **CLC 31**
See also CA 53-56; CANR 4, 44; DLB 14

Finch, Robert (Duer Claydon)
1900- .... **CLC 18**
See also CA 57-60; CANR 9, 24, 49;
DLB 88

Findley, Timothy 1930- ...... **CLC 27; DAC**
See also CA 25-28R; CANR 12, 42;
DAM MST; DLB 53

Fink, William
See Mencken, H(enry) L(ouis)

Firbank, Louis 1942-
See Reed, Lou
See also CA 117

Firbank, (Arthur Annesley) Ronald
1886-1926 .... **TCLC 1**
See also CA 104; DLB 36

Fisher, M(ary) F(rances) K(ennedy)
1908-1992 .... **CLC 76, 87**
See also CA 77-80; 138; CANR 44

Fisher, Roy 1930- .... **CLC 25**
See also CA 81-84; CAAS 10; CANR 16;
DLB 40

Fisher, Rudolph
1897-1934 .... **TCLC 11; BLC**
See also BW 1; CA 107; 124; DAM MULT;
DLB 51, 102

Fisher, Vardis (Alvero) 1895-1968 .... **CLC 7**
See also CA 5-8R; 25-28R; DLB 9

Fiske, Tarleton
See Bloch, Robert (Albert)

Fitch, Clarke
See Sinclair, Upton (Beall)

Fitch, John IV
See Cormier, Robert (Edmund)

Fitzgerald, Captain Hugh
See Baum, L(yman) Frank

FitzGerald, Edward 1809-1883 .... **NCLC 9**
See also DLB 32

Fitzgerald, F(rancis) Scott (Key)
1896-1940 .... **TCLC 1, 6, 14, 28, 55;
DA; DAB; DAC; SSC 6; WLC**
See also AITN 1; CA 110; 123;
CDALB 1917-1929; DAM MST, NOV;
DLB 4, 9, 86; DLBD 1; DLBY 81;
MTCW

Fitzgerald, Penelope 1916- ... **CLC 19, 51, 61**
See also CA 85-88; CAAS 10; DLB 14

Fitzgerald, Robert (Stuart)
1910-1985 .... **CLC 39**
See also CA 1-4R; 114; CANR 1; DLBY 80

FitzGerald, Robert D(avid)
1902-1987 .... **CLC 19**
See also CA 17-20R

Fitzgerald, Zelda (Sayre)
1900-1948 .... **TCLC 52**
See also CA 117; 126; DLBY 84

Flanagan, Thomas (James Bonner)
1923- .... **CLC 25, 52**
See also CA 108; DLBY 80; INT 108;
MTCW

Flaubert, Gustave
1821-1880 .... **NCLC 2, 10, 19; DA;
DAB; DAC; SSC 11; WLC**
See also DAM MST, NOV; DLB 119

Flecker, Herman Elroy
See Flecker, (Herman) James Elroy

Flecker, (Herman) James Elroy
1884-1915 .... **TCLC 43**
See also CA 109; 150; DLB 10, 19

Fleming, Ian (Lancaster)
1908-1964 .... **CLC 3, 30**
See also CA 5-8R; CDBLB 1945-1960;
DAM POP; DLB 87; MTCW; SATA 9

Fleming, Thomas (James) 1927- . . . . **CLC 37**
  See also CA 5-8R; CANR 10;
  INT CANR-10; SATA 8

Fletcher, John 1579-1625. . . . . **LC 33; DC 6**
  See also CDBLB Before 1660; DLB 58

Fletcher, John Gould 1886-1950 . . . **TCLC 35**
  See also CA 107; DLB 4, 45

Fleur, Paul
  See Pohl, Frederik

Flooglebuckle, Al
  See Spiegelman, Art

Flying Officer X
  See Bates, H(erbert) E(rnest)

Fo, Dario 1926- . . . . **CLC 32**
  See also CA 116; 128; DAM DRAM;
  MTCW

Fogarty, Jonathan Titulescu Esq.
  See Farrell, James T(homas)

Folke, Will
  See Bloch, Robert (Albert)

Follett, Ken(neth Martin) 1949- . . . . **CLC 18**
  See also AAYA 6; BEST 89:4; CA 81-84;
  CANR 13, 33; DAM NOV, POP;
  DLB 87; DLBY 81; INT CANR-33;
  MTCW

Fontane, Theodor 1819-1898 . . . . . **NCLC 26**
  See also DLB 129

Foote, Horton 1916- . . . . **CLC 51, 91**
  See also CA 73-76; CANR 34, 51;
  DAM DRAM; DLB 26; INT CANR-34

Foote, Shelby 1916- . . . . **CLC 75**
  See also CA 5-8R; CANR 3, 45;
  DAM NOV, POP; DLB 2, 17

Forbes, Esther 1891-1967. . . . . **CLC 12**
  See also AAYA 17; CA 13-14; 25-28R;
  CAP 1; CLR 27; DLB 22; JRDA;
  MAICYA; SATA 2

Forche, Carolyn (Louise)
  1950- . . . . **CLC 25, 83, 86; PC 10**
  See also CA 109; 117; CANR 50;
  DAM POET; DLB 5; INT 117

Ford, Elbur
  See Hibbert, Eleanor Alice Burford

Ford, Ford Madox
  1873-1939 . . . . **TCLC 1, 15, 39, 57**
  See also CA 104; 132; CDBLB 1914-1945;
  DAM NOV; DLB 162; MTCW

Ford, John 1895-1973. . . . . **CLC 16**
  See also CA 45-48

Ford, Richard 1944- . . . . **CLC 46**
  See also CA 69-72; CANR 11, 47

Ford, Webster
  See Masters, Edgar Lee

Foreman, Richard 1937- . . . . **CLC 50**
  See also CA 65-68; CANR 32

Forester, C(ecil) S(cott)
  1899-1966 . . . . **CLC 35**
  See also CA 73-76; 25-28R; SATA 13

Forez
  See Mauriac, Francois (Charles)

Forman, James Douglas 1932- . . . . . . **CLC 21**
  See also AAYA 17; CA 9-12R; CANR 4,
  19, 42; JRDA; MAICYA; SATA 8, 70

Fornes, Maria Irene 1930- . . . . . . **CLC 39, 61**
  See also CA 25-28R; CANR 28; DLB 7;
  HW; INT CANR-28; MTCW

Forrest, Leon 1937- . . . . **CLC 4**
  See also BW 2; CA 89-92; CAAS 7;
  CANR 25; DLB 33

Forster, E(dward) M(organ)
  1879-1970 . . . . . **CLC 1, 2, 3, 4, 9, 10, 13,
  15, 22, 45, 77; DA; DAB; DAC; WLC**
  See also AAYA 2; CA 13-14; 25-28R;
  CANR 45; CAP 1; CDBLB 1914-1945;
  DAM MST, NOV; DLB 34, 98, 162;
  DLBD 10; MTCW; SATA 57

Forster, John 1812-1876 . . . . **NCLC 11**
  See also DLB 144

Forsyth, Frederick 1938- . . . . . . **CLC 2, 5, 36**
  See also BEST 89:4; CA 85-88; CANR 38;
  DAM NOV, POP; DLB 87; MTCW

Forten, Charlotte L. . . . . **TCLC 16; BLC**
  See also Grimke, Charlotte L(ottie) Forten
  See also DLB 50

Foscolo, Ugo 1778-1827. . . . . **NCLC 8**

Fosse, Bob . . . . **CLC 20**
  See also Fosse, Robert Louis

Fosse, Robert Louis 1927-1987
  See Fosse, Bob
  See also CA 110; 123

Foster, Stephen Collins
  1826-1864 . . . . **NCLC 26**

Foucault, Michel
  1926-1984 . . . . **CLC 31, 34, 69**
  See also CA 105; 113; CANR 34; MTCW

Fouque, Friedrich (Heinrich Karl) de la Motte
  1777-1843 . . . . **NCLC 2**
  See also DLB 90

Fourier, Charles 1772-1837 . . . . . . **NCLC 51**

Fournier, Henri Alban 1886-1914
  See Alain-Fournier
  See also CA 104

Fournier, Pierre 1916- . . . . **CLC 11**
  See also Gascar, Pierre
  See also CA 89-92; CANR 16, 40

Fowles, John
  1926- . . . . . . **CLC 1, 2, 3, 4, 6, 9, 10, 15,
  33, 87; DAB; DAC**
  See also CA 5-8R; CANR 25; CDBLB 1960
  to Present; DAM MST; DLB 14, 139;
  MTCW; SATA 22

Fox, Paula 1923-. . . . . **CLC 2, 8**
  See also AAYA 3; CA 73-76; CANR 20,
  36; CLR 1; DLB 52; JRDA; MAICYA;
  MTCW; SATA 17, 60

Fox, William Price (Jr.) 1926- . . . . . **CLC 22**
  See also CA 17-20R; CAAS 19; CANR 11;
  DLB 2; DLBY 81

Foxe, John 1516(?)-1587 . . . . **LC 14**

Frame, Janet . . . . **CLC 2, 3, 6, 22, 66**
  See also Clutha, Janet Paterson Frame

France, Anatole. . . . . **TCLC 9**
  See also Thibault, Jacques Anatole Francois
  See also DLB 123

Francis, Claude 19(?)- . . . . **CLC 50**

Francis, Dick 1920- . . . . **CLC 2, 22, 42**
  See also AAYA 5; BEST 89:3; CA 5-8R;
  CANR 9, 42; CDBLB 1960 to Present;
  DAM POP; DLB 87; INT CANR-9;
  MTCW

Francis, Robert (Churchill)
  1901-1987 . . . . **CLC 15**
  See also CA 1-4R; 123; CANR 1

Frank, Anne(lies Marie)
  1929-1945 . . . . **TCLC 17; DA; DAB;
  DAC; WLC**
  See also AAYA 12; CA 113; 133;
  DAM MST; MTCW; SATA 87;
  SATA-Brief 42

Frank, Elizabeth 1945-. . . . . **CLC 39**
  See also CA 121; 126; INT 126

Frankl, Viktor E(mil) 1905-. . . . . **CLC 93**
  See also CA 65-68

Franklin, Benjamin
  See Hasek, Jaroslav (Matej Frantisek)

Franklin, Benjamin
  1706-1790 . . . . . **LC 25; DA; DAB; DAC**
  See also CDALB 1640-1865; DAM MST;
  DLB 24, 43, 73

Franklin, (Stella Maraia Sarah) Miles
  1879-1954 . . . . **TCLC 7**
  See also CA 104

Fraser, (Lady) Antonia (Pakenham)
  1932- . . . . **CLC 32**
  See also CA 85-88; CANR 44; MTCW;
  SATA-Brief 32

Fraser, George MacDonald 1925-. . . . **CLC 7**
  See also CA 45-48; CANR 2, 48

Fraser, Sylvia 1935- . . . . **CLC 64**
  See also CA 45-48; CANR 1, 16

Frayn, Michael 1933- . . . . . . **CLC 3, 7, 31, 47**
  See also CA 5-8R; CANR 30;
  DAM DRAM, NOV; DLB 13, 14;
  MTCW

Fraze, Candida (Merrill) 1945- . . . . . **CLC 50**
  See also CA 126

Frazer, J(ames) G(eorge)
  1854-1941 . . . . **TCLC 32**
  See also CA 118

Frazer, Robert Caine
  See Creasey, John

Frazer, Sir James George
  See Frazer, J(ames) G(eorge)

Frazier, Ian 1951-. . . . . **CLC 46**
  See also CA 130

Frederic, Harold 1856-1898. . . . . . **NCLC 10**
  See also DLB 12, 23; DLBD 13

Frederick, John
  See Faust, Frederick (Schiller)

Frederick the Great 1712-1786 . . . . . . **LC 14**

Fredro, Aleksander 1793-1876. . . . . **NCLC 8**

Freeling, Nicolas 1927- . . . . **CLC 38**
  See also CA 49-52; CAAS 12; CANR 1, 17,
  50; DLB 87

Freeman, Douglas Southall
  1886-1953 . . . . **TCLC 11**
  See also CA 109; DLB 17

Freeman, Judith 1946-. . . . . **CLC 55**
  See also CA 148

Freeman, Mary Eleanor Wilkins
1852-1930 . . . . **TCLC 9; SSC 1**
See also CA 106; DLB 12, 78

Freeman, R(ichard) Austin
1862-1943 . . . . **TCLC 21**
See also CA 113; DLB 70

French, Albert 1943- . . . . **CLC 86**

French, Marilyn 1929- . . . . . . **CLC 10, 18, 60**
See also CA 69-72; CANR 3, 31;
DAM DRAM, NOV, POP;
INT CANR-31; MTCW

French, Paul
See Asimov, Isaac

Freneau, Philip Morin 1752-1832 . . **NCLC 1**
See also DLB 37, 43

Freud, Sigmund 1856-1939 . . . . **TCLC 52**
See also CA 115; 133; MTCW

Friedan, Betty (Naomi) 1921- . . . . . . **CLC 74**
See also CA 65-68; CANR 18, 45; MTCW

Friedlander, Saul 1932- . . . . **CLC 90**
See also CA 117; 130

Friedman, B(ernard) H(arper)
1926- . . . . **CLC 7**
See also CA 1-4R; CANR 3, 48

Friedman, Bruce Jay 1930- . . . . **CLC 3, 5, 56**
See also CA 9-12R; CANR 25; DLB 2, 28;
INT CANR-25

Friel, Brian 1929- . . . . **CLC 5, 42, 59**
See also CA 21-24R; CANR 33; DLB 13;
MTCW

Friis-Baastad, Babbis Ellinor
1921-1970 . . . . **CLC 12**
See also CA 17-20R; 134; SATA 7

Frisch, Max (Rudolf)
1911-1991 . . . . . **CLC 3, 9, 14, 18, 32, 44**
See also CA 85-88; 134; CANR 32;
DAM DRAM, NOV; DLB 69, 124;
MTCW

Fromentin, Eugene (Samuel Auguste)
1820-1876 . . . . **NCLC 10**
See also DLB 123

Frost, Frederick
See Faust, Frederick (Schiller)

Frost, Robert (Lee)
1874-1963 . . . . **CLC 1, 3, 4, 9, 10, 13, 15,**
26, 34, 44; DA; DAB; DAC; PC 1; WLC
See also CA 89-92; CANR 33;
CDALB 1917-1929; DAM MST, POET;
DLB 54; DLBD 7; MTCW; SATA 14

Froude, James Anthony
1818-1894 . . . . **NCLC 43**
See also DLB 18, 57, 144

Froy, Herald
See Waterhouse, Keith (Spencer)

Fry, Christopher 1907- . . . . **CLC 2, 10, 14**
See also CA 17-20R; CAAS 23; CANR 9,
30; DAM DRAM; DLB 13; MTCW;
SATA 66

Frye, (Herman) Northrop
1912-1991 . . . . **CLC 24, 70**
See also CA 5-8R; 133; CANR 8, 37;
DLB 67, 68; MTCW

Fuchs, Daniel 1909-1993 . . . . **CLC 8, 22**
See also CA 81-84; 142; CAAS 5;
CANR 40; DLB 9, 26, 28; DLBY 93

Fuchs, Daniel 1934- . . . . **CLC 34**
See also CA 37-40R; CANR 14, 48

Fuentes, Carlos
1928- . . . . . . **CLC 3, 8, 10, 13, 22, 41, 60;**
DA; DAB; DAC; HLC; WLC
See also AAYA 4; AITN 2; CA 69-72;
CANR 10, 32; DAM MST, MULT,
NOV; DLB 113; HW; MTCW

Fuentes, Gregorio Lopez y
See Lopez y Fuentes, Gregorio

Fugard, (Harold) Athol
1932- . . . . **CLC 5, 9, 14, 25, 40, 80; DC 3**
See also AAYA 17; CA 85-88; CANR 32;
DAM DRAM; MTCW

Fugard, Sheila 1932- . . . . **CLC 48**
See also CA 125

Fuller, Charles (H., Jr.)
1939- . . . . **CLC 25; BLC; DC 1**
See also BW 2; CA 108; 112;
DAM DRAM, MULT; DLB 38;
INT 112; MTCW

Fuller, John (Leopold) 1937- . . . . **CLC 62**
See also CA 21-24R; CANR 9, 44; DLB 40

Fuller, Margaret . . . . **NCLC 5, 50**
See also Ossoli, Sarah Margaret (Fuller
marchesa d')

Fuller, Roy (Broadbent)
1912-1991 . . . . **CLC 4, 28**
See also CA 5-8R; 135; CAAS 10; DLB 15,
20; SATA 87

Fulton, Alice 1952- . . . . **CLC 52**
See also CA 116

Furphy, Joseph 1843-1912 . . . . **TCLC 25**

Fussell, Paul 1924- . . . . **CLC 74**
See also BEST 90:1; CA 17-20R; CANR 8,
21, 35; INT CANR-21; MTCW

Futabatei, Shimei 1864-1909 . . . . . . **TCLC 44**

Futrelle, Jacques 1875-1912 . . . . . . **TCLC 19**
See also CA 113

Gaboriau, Emile 1835-1873 . . . . . . **NCLC 14**

Gadda, Carlo Emilio 1893-1973 . . . . **CLC 11**
See also CA 89-92

Gaddis, William
1922- . . . . . **CLC 1, 3, 6, 8, 10, 19, 43, 86**
See also CA 17-20R; CANR 21, 48; DLB 2;
MTCW

Gaines, Ernest J(ames)
1933- . . . . **CLC 3, 11, 18, 86; BLC**
See also AITN 1; BW 2; CA 9-12R;
CANR 6, 24, 42; CDALB 1968-1988;
DAM MULT; DLB 2, 33, 152; DLBY 80;
MTCW; SATA 86

Gaitskill, Mary 1954- . . . . **CLC 69**
See also CA 128

Galdos, Benito Perez
See Perez Galdos, Benito

Gale, Zona 1874-1938 . . . . **TCLC 7**
See also CA 105; DAM DRAM; DLB 9, 78

Galeano, Eduardo (Hughes) 1940- . . . **CLC 72**
See also CA 29-32R; CANR 13, 32; HW

Galiano, Juan Valera y Alcala
See Valera y Alcala-Galiano, Juan

Gallagher, Tess 1943- . . . . **CLC 18, 63; PC 9**
See also CA 106; DAM POET; DLB 120

Gallant, Mavis
1922- . . . . . . **CLC 7, 18, 38; DAC; SSC 5**
See also CA 69-72; CANR 29; DAM MST;
DLB 53; MTCW

Gallant, Roy A(rthur) 1924- . . . . **CLC 17**
See also CA 5-8R; CANR 4, 29; CLR 30;
MAICYA; SATA 4, 68

Gallico, Paul (William) 1897-1976 . . . **CLC 2**
See also AITN 1; CA 5-8R; 69-72;
CANR 23; DLB 9; MAICYA; SATA 13

Gallois, Lucien
See Desnos, Robert

Gallup, Ralph
See Whitemore, Hugh (John)

Galsworthy, John
1867-1933 . . . . . . **TCLC 1, 45; DA; DAB;**
DAC; SSC 22; WLC 2
See also CA 104; 141; CDBLB 1890-1914;
DAM DRAM, MST, NOV; DLB 10, 34,
98, 162

Galt, John 1779-1839 . . . . **NCLC 1**
See also DLB 99, 116, 159

Galvin, James 1951- . . . . **CLC 38**
See also CA 108; CANR 26

Gamboa, Federico 1864-1939 . . . . . . **TCLC 36**

Gandhi, M. K.
See Gandhi, Mohandas Karamchand

Gandhi, Mahatma
See Gandhi, Mohandas Karamchand

Gandhi, Mohandas Karamchand
1869-1948 . . . . **TCLC 59**
See also CA 121; 132; DAM MULT;
MTCW

Gann, Ernest Kellogg 1910-1991 . . . . **CLC 23**
See also AITN 1; CA 1-4R; 136; CANR 1

Garcia, Cristina 1958- . . . . **CLC 76**
See also CA 141

Garcia Lorca, Federico
1898-1936 . . . **TCLC 1, 7, 49; DA; DAB;**
DAC; DC 2; HLC; PC 3; WLC
See also CA 104; 131; DAM DRAM, MST,
MULT, POET; DLB 108; HW; MTCW

Garcia Marquez, Gabriel (Jose)
1928- . . . . **CLC 2, 3, 8, 10, 15, 27, 47, 55,**
68; DA; DAB; DAC; HLC; SSC 8; WLC
See also AAYA 3; BEST 89:1, 90:4;
CA 33-36R; CANR 10, 28, 50;
DAM MST, MULT, NOV, POP;
DLB 113; HW; MTCW

Gard, Janice
See Latham, Jean Lee

Gard, Roger Martin du
See Martin du Gard, Roger

Gardam, Jane 1928- . . . . **CLC 43**
See also CA 49-52; CANR 2, 18, 33;
CLR 12; DLB 14, 161; MAICYA;
MTCW; SAAS 9; SATA 39, 76;
SATA-Brief 28

Gardner, Herb(ert) 1934- . . . . **CLC 44**
See also CA 149

Gardner, John (Champlin), Jr.
1933-1982 ..... **CLC 2, 3, 5, 7, 8, 10, 18,**
28, 34; SSC 7
See also AITN 1; CA 65-68; 107;
CANR 33; DAM NOV, POP; DLB 2;
DLBY 82; MTCW; SATA 40;
SATA-Obit 31

Gardner, John (Edmund) 1926- ..... **CLC 30**
See also CA 103; CANR 15; DAM POP;
MTCW

Gardner, Noel
See Kuttner, Henry

Gardons, S. S.
See Snodgrass, W(illiam) D(e Witt)

Garfield, Leon 1921- .... **CLC 12**
See also AAYA 8; CA 17-20R; CANR 38,
41; CLR 21; DLB 161; JRDA; MAICYA;
SATA 1, 32, 76

Garland, (Hannibal) Hamlin
1860-1940 .... **TCLC 3; SSC 18**
See also CA 104; DLB 12, 71, 78

Garneau, (Hector de) Saint-Denys
1912-1943 .... **TCLC 13**
See also CA 111; DLB 88

Garner, Alan 1934- .... **CLC 17; DAB**
See also CA 73-76; CANR 15; CLR 20;
DAM POP; DLB 161; MAICYA;
MTCW; SATA 18, 69

Garner, Hugh 1913-1979 .... **CLC 13**
See also CA 69-72; CANR 31; DLB 68

Garnett, David 1892-1981 .... **CLC 3**
See also CA 5-8R; 103; CANR 17; DLB 34

Garos, Stephanie
See Katz, Steve

Garrett, George (Palmer)
1929- .... **CLC 3, 11, 51**
See also CA 1-4R; CAAS 5; CANR 1, 42;
DLB 2, 5, 130, 152; DLBY 83

Garrick, David 1717-1779 .... **LC 15**
See also DAM DRAM; DLB 84

Garrigue, Jean 1914-1972 .... **CLC 2, 8**
See also CA 5-8R; 37-40R; CANR 20

Garrison, Frederick
See Sinclair, Upton (Beall)

Garth, Will
See Hamilton, Edmond; Kuttner, Henry

Garvey, Marcus (Moziah, Jr.)
1887-1940 .... **TCLC 41; BLC**
See also BW 1; CA 120; 124; DAM MULT

Gary, Romain .... **CLC 25**
See also Kacew, Romain
See also DLB 83

Gascar, Pierre .... **CLC 11**
See also Fournier, Pierre

Gascoyne, David (Emery) 1916- .... **CLC 45**
See also CA 65-68; CANR 10, 28; DLB 20;
MTCW

Gaskell, Elizabeth Cleghorn
1810-1865 .... **NCLC 5; DAB**
See also CDBLB 1832-1890; DAM MST;
DLB 21, 144, 159

Gass, William H(oward)
1924- ... **CLC 1, 2, 8, 11, 15, 39; SSC 12**
See also CA 17-20R; CANR 30; DLB 2;
MTCW

Gasset, Jose Ortega y
See Ortega y Gasset, Jose

Gates, Henry Louis, Jr. 1950- ...... **CLC 65**
See also BW 2; CA 109; CANR 25;
DAM MULT; DLB 67

Gautier, Theophile
1811-1872 .... **NCLC 1; SSC 20**
See also DAM POET; DLB 119

Gawsworth, John
See Bates, H(erbert) E(rnest)

Gay, Oliver
See Gogarty, Oliver St. John

Gaye, Marvin (Penze) 1939-1984 ... **CLC 26**
See also CA 112

Gebler, Carlo (Ernest) 1954- .... **CLC 39**
See also CA 119; 133

Gee, Maggie (Mary) 1948- .... **CLC 57**
See also CA 130

Gee, Maurice (Gough) 1931- .... **CLC 29**
See also CA 97-100; SATA 46

Gelbart, Larry (Simon) 1923- ... **CLC 21, 61**
See also CA 73-76; CANR 45

Gelber, Jack 1932- .... **CLC 1, 6, 14, 79**
See also CA 1-4R; CANR 2; DLB 7

Gellhorn, Martha (Ellis) 1908- .. **CLC 14, 60**
See also CA 77-80; CANR 44; DLBY 82

Genet, Jean
1910-1986 ... **CLC 1, 2, 5, 10, 14, 44, 46**
See also CA 13-16R; CANR 18;
DAM DRAM; DLB 72; DLBY 86;
MTCW

Gent, Peter 1942- .... **CLC 29**
See also AITN 1; CA 89-92; DLBY 82

Gentlewoman in New England, A
See Bradstreet, Anne

Gentlewoman in Those Parts, A
See Bradstreet, Anne

George, Jean Craighead 1919- ...... **CLC 35**
See also AAYA 8; CA 5-8R; CANR 25;
CLR 1; DLB 52; JRDA; MAICYA;
SATA 2, 68

George, Stefan (Anton)
1868-1933 .... **TCLC 2, 14**
See also CA 104

Georges, Georges Martin
See Simenon, Georges (Jacques Christian)

Gerhardi, William Alexander
See Gerhardie, William Alexander

Gerhardie, William Alexander
1895-1977 .... **CLC 5**
See also CA 25-28R; 73-76; CANR 18;
DLB 36

Gerstler, Amy 1956- .... **CLC 70**
See also CA 146

Gertler, T. .... **CLC 34**
See also CA 116; 121; INT 121

Ghalib........................ **NCLC 39**
See also Ghalib, Hsadullah Khan

Ghalib, Hsadullah Khan 1797-1869
See Ghalib
See also DAM POET

Ghelderode, Michel de
1898-1962 .... **CLC 6, 11**
See also CA 85-88; CANR 40;
DAM DRAM

Ghiselin, Brewster 1903- .... **CLC 23**
See also CA 13-16R; CAAS 10; CANR 13

Ghose, Zulfikar 1935- .... **CLC 42**
See also CA 65-68

Ghosh, Amitav 1956- .... **CLC 44**
See also CA 147

Giacosa, Giuseppe 1847-1906 ...... **TCLC 7**
See also CA 104

Gibb, Lee
See Waterhouse, Keith (Spencer)

Gibbon, Lewis Grassic .... **TCLC 4**
See also Mitchell, James Leslie

Gibbons, Kaye 1960- .... **CLC 50, 88**
See also CA 151; DAM POP

Gibran, Kahlil
1883-1931 .... **TCLC 1, 9; PC 9**
See also CA 104; 150; DAM POET, POP

Gibran, Khalil
See Gibran, Kahlil

Gibson, William
1914- .... **CLC 23; DA; DAB; DAC**
See also CA 9-12R; CANR 9, 42;
DAM DRAM, MST; DLB 7; SATA 66

Gibson, William (Ford) 1948- ... **CLC 39, 63**
See also AAYA 12; CA 126; 133;
DAM POP

Gide, Andre (Paul Guillaume)
1869-1951 .... **TCLC 5, 12, 36; DA;**
DAB; DAC; SSC 13; WLC
See also CA 104; 124; DAM MST, NOV;
DLB 65; MTCW

Gifford, Barry (Colby) 1946- .... **CLC 34**
See also CA 65-68; CANR 9, 30, 40

Gilbert, W(illiam) S(chwenck)
1836-1911 .... **TCLC 3**
See also CA 104; DAM DRAM, POET;
SATA 36

Gilbreth, Frank B., Jr. 1911- .... **CLC 17**
See also CA 9-12R; SATA 2

Gilchrist, Ellen 1935- .. **CLC 34, 48; SSC 14**
See also CA 113; 116; CANR 41;
DAM POP; DLB 130; MTCW

Giles, Molly 1942- .... **CLC 39**
See also CA 126

Gill, Patrick
See Creasey, John

Gilliam, Terry (Vance) 1940- .... **CLC 21**
See also Monty Python
See also CA 108; 113; CANR 35; INT 113

Gillian, Jerry
See Gilliam, Terry (Vance)

Gilliatt, Penelope (Ann Douglass)
1932-1993 .... **CLC 2, 10, 13, 53**
See also AITN 2; CA 13-16R; 141;
CANR 49; DLB 14

Gilman, Charlotte (Anna) Perkins (Stetson)
1860-1935 .... **TCLC 9, 37; SSC 13**
See also CA 106; 150

Gilmour, David 1949- .... **CLC 35**
See also CA 138, 147

Haley, Alex(ander Murray Palmer)
1921-1992 .... **CLC 8, 12, 76; BLC; DA;**
DAB; DAC
See also BW 2; CA 77-80; 136; DAM MST,
MULT, POP; DLB 38; MTCW

Haliburton, Thomas Chandler
1796-1865 .... **NCLC 15**
See also DLB 11, 99

Hall, Donald (Andrew, Jr.)
1928- .... **CLC 1, 13, 37, 59**
See also CA 5-8R; CAAS 7; CANR 2, 44;
DAM POET; DLB 5; SATA 23

Hall, Frederic Sauser
See Sauser-Hall, Frederic

Hall, James
See Kuttner, Henry

Hall, James Norman 1887-1951 ... **TCLC 23**
See also CA 123; SATA 21

Hall, (Marguerite) Radclyffe
1886-1943 .... **TCLC 12**
See also CA 110; 150

Hall, Rodney 1935- .... **CLC 51**
See also CA 109

Halleck, Fitz-Greene 1790-1867 .. **NCLC 47**
See also DLB 3

Halliday, Michael
See Creasey, John

Halpern, Daniel 1945- .... **CLC 14**
See also CA 33-36R

Hamburger, Michael (Peter Leopold)
1924- .... **CLC 5, 14**
See also CA 5-8R; CAAS 4; CANR 2, 47;
DLB 27

Hamill, Pete 1935- .... **CLC 10**
See also CA 25-28R; CANR 18

Hamilton, Alexander
1755(?)-1804 .... **NCLC 49**
See also DLB 37

Hamilton, Clive
See Lewis, C(live) S(taples)

Hamilton, Edmond 1904-1977 .... **CLC 1**
See also CA 1-4R; CANR 3; DLB 8

Hamilton, Eugene (Jacob) Lee
See Lee-Hamilton, Eugene (Jacob)

Hamilton, Franklin
See Silverberg, Robert

Hamilton, Gail
See Corcoran, Barbara

Hamilton, Mollie
See Kaye, M(ary) M(argaret)

Hamilton, (Anthony Walter) Patrick
1904-1962 .... **CLC 51**
See also CA 113; DLB 10

Hamilton, Virginia 1936- .... **CLC 26**
See also AAYA 2; BW 2; CA 25-28R;
CANR 20, 37; CLR 1, 11, 40;
DAM MULT; DLB 33, 52;
INT CANR-20; JRDA; MAICYA;
MTCW; SATA 4, 56, 79

Hammett, (Samuel) Dashiell
1894-1961 .... **CLC 3, 5, 10, 19, 47;**
SSC 17
See also AITN 1; CA 81-84; CANR 42;
CDALB 1929-1941; DLBD 6; MTCW

Hammon, Jupiter
1711(?)-1800(?) .... **NCLC 5; BLC**
See also DAM MULT, POET; DLB 31, 50

Hammond, Keith
See Kuttner, Henry

Hamner, Earl (Henry), Jr. 1923- ... **CLC 12**
See also AITN 2; CA 73-76; DLB 6

Hampton, Christopher (James)
1946- .... **CLC 4**
See also CA 25-28R; DLB 13; MTCW

Hamsun, Knut .... **TCLC 2, 14, 49**
See also Pedersen, Knut

Handke, Peter 1942- .. **CLC 5, 8, 10, 15, 38**
See also CA 77-80; CANR 33;
DAM DRAM, NOV; DLB 85, 124;
MTCW

Hanley, James 1901-1985 ... **CLC 3, 5, 8, 13**
See also CA 73-76; 117; CANR 36; MTCW

Hannah, Barry 1942- .... **CLC 23, 38, 90**
See also CA 108; 110; CANR 43; DLB 6;
INT 110; MTCW

Hannon, Ezra
See Hunter, Evan

Hansberry, Lorraine (Vivian)
1930-1965 ...... **CLC 17, 62; BLC; DA;**
DAB; DAC; DC 2
See also BW 1; CA 109; 25-28R; CABS 3;
CDALB 1941-1968; DAM DRAM, MST,
MULT; DLB 7, 38; MTCW

Hansen, Joseph 1923-............. **CLC 38**
See also CA 29-32R; CAAS 17; CANR 16,
44; INT CANR-16

Hansen, Martin A. 1909-1955..... **TCLC 32**

Hanson, Kenneth O(stlin) 1922- .... **CLC 13**
See also CA 53-56; CANR 7

Hardwick, Elizabeth 1916- .... **CLC 13**
See also CA 5-8R; CANR 3, 32;
DAM NOV; DLB 6; MTCW

Hardy, Thomas
1840-1928 ...... **TCLC 4, 10, 18, 32, 48,**
53; DA; DAB; DAC; PC 8; SSC 2; WLC
See also CA 104; 123; CDBLB 1890-1914;
DAM MST, NOV, POET; DLB 18, 19,
135; MTCW

Hare, David 1947- .... **CLC 29, 58**
See also CA 97-100; CANR 39; DLB 13;
MTCW

Harford, Henry
See Hudson, W(illiam) H(enry)

Hargrave, Leonie
See Disch, Thomas M(ichael)

Harjo, Joy 1951- .... **CLC 83**
See also CA 114; CANR 35; DAM MULT;
DLB 120; NNAL

Harlan, Louis R(udolph) 1922- ..... **CLC 34**
See also CA 21-24R; CANR 25

Harling, Robert 1951(?)- .... **CLC 53**
See also CA 147

Harmon, William (Ruth) 1938-..... **CLC 38**
See also CA 33-36R; CANR 14, 32, 35;
SATA 65

Harper, F. E. W.
See Harper, Frances Ellen Watkins

Harper, Frances E. W.
See Harper, Frances Ellen Watkins

Harper, Frances E. Watkins
See Harper, Frances Ellen Watkins

Harper, Frances Ellen
See Harper, Frances Ellen Watkins

Harper, Frances Ellen Watkins
1825-1911 .... **TCLC 14; BLC**
See also BW 1; CA 111; 125; DAM MULT,
POET; DLB 50

Harper, Michael S(teven) 1938- .. **CLC 7, 22**
See also BW 1; CA 33-36R; CANR 24;
DLB 41

Harper, Mrs. F. E. W.
See Harper, Frances Ellen Watkins

Harris, Christie (Lucy) Irwin
1907- .... **CLC 12**
See also CA 5-8R; CANR 6; DLB 88;
JRDA; MAICYA; SAAS 10; SATA 6, 74

Harris, Frank 1856-1931........ **TCLC 24**
See also CA 109; 150; DLB 156

Harris, George Washington
1814-1869 .... **NCLC 23**
See also DLB 3, 11

Harris, Joel Chandler
1848-1908 .... **TCLC 2; SSC 19**
See also CA 104; 137; DLB 11, 23, 42, 78,
91; MAICYA; YABC 1

Harris, John (Wyndham Parkes Lucas)
Beynon 1903-1969
See Wyndham, John
See also CA 102; 89-92

Harris, MacDonald................. CLC 9
See also Heiney, Donald (William)

Harris, Mark 1922- .... **CLC 19**
See also CA 5-8R; CAAS 3; CANR 2;
DLB 2; DLBY 80

Harris, (Theodore) Wilson 1921-.... **CLC 25**
See also BW 2; CA 65-68; CAAS 16;
CANR 11, 27; DLB 117; MTCW

Harrison, Elizabeth Cavanna 1909-
See Cavanna, Betty
See also CA 9-12R; CANR 6, 27

Harrison, Harry (Max) 1925-...... **CLC 42**
See also CA 1-4R; CANR 5, 21; DLB 8;
SATA 4

Harrison, James (Thomas)
1937- .... **CLC 6, 14, 33, 66; SSC 19**
See also CA 13-16R; CANR 8, 51;
DLBY 82; INT CANR-8

Harrison, Jim
See Harrison, James (Thomas)

Harrison, Kathryn 1961-......... **CLC 70**
See also CA 144

Harrison, Tony 1937-............. **CLC 43**
See also CA 65-68; CANR 44; DLB 40;
MTCW

Harriss, Will(ard Irvin) 1922-...... **CLC 34**
See also CA 111

Harson, Sley
See Ellison, Harlan (Jay)

Hart, Ellis
See Ellison, Harlan (Jay)

Hart, Josephine 1942(?)-.......... **CLC 70**
See also CA 138; DAM POP

Hempel, Amy 1951- . . . . CLC 39
See also CA 118; 137

Henderson, F. C.
See Mencken, H(enry) L(ouis)

Henderson, Sylvia
See Ashton-Warner, Sylvia (Constance)

Henley, Beth . . . . CLC 23; DC 6
See also Henley, Elizabeth Becker
See also CABS 3; DLBY 86

Henley, Elizabeth Becker 1952-
See Henley, Beth
See also CA 107; CANR 32; DAM DRAM,
MST; MTCW

Henley, William Ernest
1849-1903 . . . . TCLC 8
See also CA 105; DLB 19

Hennissart, Martha
See Lathen, Emma
See also CA 85-88

Henry, O. . . . . TCLC 1, 19; SSC 5; WLC
See also Porter, William Sydney

Henry, Patrick 1736-1799 . . . . LC 25

Henryson, Robert 1430(?)-1506(?) . . . . LC 20
See also DLB 146

Henry VIII 1491-1547 . . . . LC 10

Henschke, Alfred
See Klabund

Hentoff, Nat(han Irving) 1925- . . . . . CLC 26
See also AAYA 4; CA 1-4R; CAAS 6;
CANR 5, 25; CLR 1; INT CANR-25;
JRDA; MAICYA; SATA 42, 69;
SATA-Brief 27

Heppenstall, (John) Rayner
1911-1981 . . . . CLC 10
See also CA 1-4R; 103; CANR 29

Herbert, Frank (Patrick)
1920-1986 . . . . . . CLC 12, 23, 35, 44, 85
See also CA 53-56; 118; CANR 5, 43;
DAM POP; DLB 8; INT CANR-5;
MTCW; SATA 9, 37; SATA-Obit 47

Herbert, George
1593-1633 . . . . LC 24; DAB; PC 4
See also CDBLB Before 1660; DAM POET;
DLB 126

Herbert, Zbigniew 1924- . . . . CLC 9, 43
See also CA 89-92; CANR 36;
DAM POET; MTCW

Herbst, Josephine (Frey)
1897-1969 . . . . CLC 34
See also CA 5-8R; 25-28R; DLB 9

Hergesheimer, Joseph
1880-1954 . . . . TCLC 11
See also CA 109; DLB 102, 9

Herlihy, James Leo 1927-1993 . . . . . . CLC 6
See also CA 1-4R; 143; CANR 2

Hermogenes fl. c. 175- . . . . CMLC 6

Hernandez, Jose 1834-1886 . . . . . . NCLC 17

Herodotus c. 484B.C.-429B.C. . . . . CMLC 17

Herrick, Robert
1591-1674 . . . . . LC 13; DA; DAB; DAC;
PC 9
See also DAM MST, POP; DLB 126

Herring, Guilles
See Somerville, Edith

Herriot, James 1916-1995 . . . . CLC 12
See also Wight, James Alfred
See also AAYA 1; CA 148; CANR 40;
DAM POP; SATA 86

Herrmann, Dorothy 1941- . . . . CLC 44
See also CA 107

Herrmann, Taffy
See Herrmann, Dorothy

Hersey, John (Richard)
1914-1993 . . . . . . CLC 1, 2, 7, 9, 40, 81
See also CA 17-20R; 140; CANR 33;
DAM POP; DLB 6; MTCW; SATA 25;
SATA-Obit 76

Herzen, Aleksandr Ivanovich
1812-1870 . . . . NCLC 10

Herzl, Theodor 1860-1904 . . . . TCLC 36

Herzog, Werner 1942- . . . . CLC 16
See also CA 89-92

Hesiod c. 8th cent. B.C.- . . . . CMLC 5

Hesse, Hermann
1877-1962 . . . . CLC 1, 2, 3, 6, 11, 17, 25,
69; DA; DAB; DAC; SSC 9; WLC
See also CA 17-18; CAP 2; DAM MST,
NOV; DLB 66; MTCW; SATA 50

Hewes, Cady
See De Voto, Bernard (Augustine)

Heyen, William 1940- . . . . CLC 13, 18
See also CA 33-36R; CAAS 9; DLB 5

Heyerdahl, Thor 1914- . . . . CLC 26
See also CA 5-8R; CANR 5, 22; MTCW;
SATA 2, 52

Heym, Georg (Theodor Franz Arthur)
1887-1912 . . . . TCLC 9
See also CA 106

Heym, Stefan 1913- . . . . CLC 41
See also CA 9-12R; CANR 4; DLB 69

Heyse, Paul (Johann Ludwig von)
1830-1914 . . . . TCLC 8
See also CA 104; DLB 129

Heyward, (Edwin) DuBose
1885-1940 . . . . TCLC 59
See also CA 108; DLB 7, 9, 45; SATA 21

Hibbert, Eleanor Alice Burford
1906-1993 . . . . CLC 7
See also BEST 90:4; CA 17-20R; 140;
CANR 9, 28; DAM POP; SATA 2;
SATA-Obit 74

Hichens, Robert S. 1864-1950 . . . . . TCLC 64
See also DLB 153

Higgins, George V(incent)
1939- . . . . CLC 4, 7, 10, 18
See also CA 77-80; CAAS 5; CANR 17, 51;
DLB 2; DLBY 81; INT CANR-17;
MTCW

Higginson, Thomas Wentworth
1823-1911 . . . . TCLC 36
See also DLB 1, 64

Highet, Helen
See MacInnes, Helen (Clark)

Highsmith, (Mary) Patricia
1921-1995 . . . . CLC 2, 4, 14, 42
See also CA 1-4R; 147; CANR 1, 20, 48;
DAM NOV, POP; MTCW

Highwater, Jamake (Mamake)
1942(?)- . . . . CLC 12
See also AAYA 7; CA 65-68; CAAS 7;
CANR 10, 34; CLR 17; DLB 52;
DLBY 85; JRDA; MAICYA; SATA 32,
69; SATA-Brief 30

Highway, Tomson 1951- . . . . . CLC 92; DAC
See also CA 151; DAM MULT; NNAL

Higuchi, Ichiyo 1872-1896 . . . . . . NCLC 49

Hijuelos, Oscar 1951- . . . . . . CLC 65; HLC
See also BEST 90:1; CA 123; CANR 50;
DAM MULT, POP; DLB 145; HW

Hikmet, Nazim 1902(?)-1963 . . . . . . CLC 40
See also CA 141; 93-96

Hildesheimer, Wolfgang
1916-1991 . . . . CLC 49
See also CA 101; 135; DLB 69, 124

Hill, Geoffrey (William)
1932- . . . . CLC 5, 8, 18, 45
See also CA 81-84; CANR 21;
CDBLB 1960 to Present; DAM POET;
DLB 40; MTCW

Hill, George Roy 1921- . . . . CLC 26
See also CA 110; 122

Hill, John
See Koontz, Dean R(ay)

Hill, Susan (Elizabeth)
1942- . . . . CLC 4; DAB
See also CA 33-36R; CANR 29;
DAM MST, NOV; DLB 14, 139; MTCW

Hillerman, Tony 1925- . . . . CLC 62
See also AAYA 6; BEST 89:1; CA 29-32R;
CANR 21, 42; DAM POP; SATA 6

Hillesum, Etty 1914-1943 . . . . TCLC 49
See also CA 137

Hilliard, Noel (Harvey) 1929- . . . . . . CLC 15
See also CA 9-12R; CANR 7

Hillis, Rick 1956- . . . . CLC 66
See also CA 134

Hilton, James 1900-1954 . . . . TCLC 21
See also CA 108; DLB 34, 77; SATA 34

Himes, Chester (Bomar)
1909-1984 . . . . CLC 2, 4, 7, 18, 58; BLC
See also BW 2; CA 25-28R; 114; CANR 22;
DAM MULT; DLB 2, 76, 143; MTCW

Hinde, Thomas . . . . CLC 6, 11
See also Chitty, Thomas Willes

Hindin, Nathan
See Bloch, Robert (Albert)

Hine, (William) Daryl 1936- . . . . CLC 15
See also CA 1-4R; CAAS 15; CANR 1, 20;
DLB 60

Hinkson, Katharine Tynan
See Tynan, Katharine

Hinton, S(usan) E(loise)
1950- . . . . CLC 30; DA; DAB; DAC
See also AAYA 2; CA 81-84; CANR 32;
CLR 3, 23; DAM MST, NOV; JRDA;
MAICYA; MTCW; SATA 19, 58

Hippius, Zinaida . . . . TCLC 9
See also Gippius, Zinaida (Nikolayevna)

Hiraoka, Kimitake 1925-1970
See Mishima, Yukio
See also CA 97-100; 29-32R; DAM DRAM;
MTCW

Hirsch, E(ric) D(onald), Jr. 1928-... **CLC 79**
See also CA 25-28R; CANR 27, 51;
DLB 67; INT CANR-27; MTCW

Hirsch, Edward 1950- .... **CLC 31, 50**
See also CA 104; CANR 20, 42; DLB 120

Hitchcock, Alfred (Joseph)
1899-1980 .... **CLC 16**
See also CA 97-100; SATA 27;
SATA-Obit 24

Hitler, Adolf 1889-1945......... **TCLC 53**
See also CA 117; 147

Hoagland, Edward 1932- .... **CLC 28**
See also CA 1-4R; CANR 2, 31; DLB 6;
SATA 51

Hoban, Russell (Conwell) 1925- .. **CLC 7, 25**
See also CA 5-8R; CANR 23, 37; CLR 3;
DAM NOV; DLB 52; MAICYA;
MTCW; SATA 1, 40, 78

Hobbs, Perry
See Blackmur, R(ichard) P(almer)

Hobson, Laura Z(ametkin)
1900-1986 .... **CLC 7, 25**
See also CA 17-20R; 118; DLB 28;
SATA 52

Hochhuth, Rolf 1931-........ **CLC 4, 11, 18**
See also CA 5-8R; CANR 33;
DAM DRAM; DLB 124; MTCW

Hochman, Sandra 1936-......... **CLC 3, 8**
See also CA 5-8R; DLB 5

Hochwaelder, Fritz 1911-1986...... **CLC 36**
See also CA 29-32R; 120; CANR 42;
DAM DRAM; MTCW

Hochwalder, Fritz
See Hochwaelder, Fritz

Hocking, Mary (Eunice) 1921- ..... **CLC 13**
See also CA 101; CANR 18, 40

Hodgins, Jack 1938-............. **CLC 23**
See also CA 93-96; DLB 60

Hodgson, William Hope
1877(?)-1918 .... **TCLC 13**
See also CA 111; DLB 70, 153, 156

Hoffman, Alice 1952-............ **CLC 51**
See also CA 77-80; CANR 34; DAM NOV;
MTCW

Hoffman, Daniel (Gerard)
1923- .... **CLC 6, 13, 23**
See also CA 1-4R; CANR 4; DLB 5

Hoffman, Stanley 1944-............ **CLC 5**
See also CA 77-80

Hoffman, William M(oses) 1939- ... **CLC 40**
See also CA 57-60; CANR 11

Hoffmann, E(rnst) T(heodor) A(madeus)
1776-1822 .... **NCLC 2; SSC 13**
See also DLB 90; SATA 27

Hofmann, Gert 1931-............. **CLC 54**
See also CA 128

Hofmannsthal, Hugo von
1874-1929 .... **TCLC 11; DC 4**
See also CA 106; DAM DRAM; DLB 81,
118

Hogan, Linda 1947-............. **CLC 73**
See also CA 120; CANR 45; DAM MULT;
NNAL

Hogarth, Charles
See Creasey, John

Hogarth, Emmett
See Polonsky, Abraham (Lincoln)

Hogg, James 1770-1835.......... **NCLC 4**
See also DLB 93, 116, 159

Holbach, Paul Henri Thiry Baron
1723-1789 .... **LC 14**

Holberg, Ludvig 1684-1754.......... **LC 6**

Holden, Ursula 1921-............. **CLC 18**
See also CA 101; CAAS 8; CANR 22

Holderlin, (Johann Christian) Friedrich
1770-1843 .... **NCLC 16; PC 4**

Holdstock, Robert
See Holdstock, Robert P.

Holdstock, Robert P. 1948-........ **CLC 39**
See also CA 131

Holland, Isabelle 1920- .... **CLC 21**
See also AAYA 11; CA 21-24R; CANR 10,
25, 47; JRDA; MAICYA; SATA 8, 70

Holland, Marcus
See Caldwell, (Janet Miriam) Taylor
(Holland)

Hollander, John 1929-...... **CLC 2, 5, 8, 14**
See also CA 1-4R; CANR 1; DLB 5;
SATA 13

Hollander, Paul
See Silverberg, Robert

Holleran, Andrew 1943(?)-......... **CLC 38**
See also CA 144

Hollinghurst, Alan 1954-....... **CLC 55, 91**
See also CA 114

Hollis, Jim
See Summers, Hollis (Spurgeon, Jr.)

Holmes, John
See Souster, (Holmes) Raymond

Holmes, John Clellon 1926-1988.... **CLC 56**
See also CA 9-12R; 125; CANR 4; DLB 16

Holmes, Oliver Wendell
1809-1894 .... **NCLC 14**
See also CDALB 1640-1865; DLB 1;
SATA 34

Holmes, Raymond
See Souster, (Holmes) Raymond

Holt, Victoria
See Hibbert, Eleanor Alice Burford

Holub, Miroslav 1923-............. **CLC 4**
See also CA 21-24R; CANR 10

Homer
c. 8th cent. B.C.-..... **CMLC 1, 16; DA;
DAB; DAC**
See also DAM MST, POET

Honig, Edwin 1919-.............. **CLC 33**
See also CA 5-8R; CAAS 8; CANR 4, 45;
DLB 5

Hood, Hugh (John Blagdon)
1928- .... **CLC 15, 28**
See also CA 49-52; CAAS 17; CANR 1, 33;
DLB 53

Hood, Thomas 1799-1845........ **NCLC 16**
See also DLB 96

Hooker, (Peter) Jeremy 1941-...... **CLC 43**
See also CA 77-80; CANR 22; DLB 40

hooks, bell .... **CLC 94**
See also Watkins, Gloria

Hope, A(lec) D(erwent) 1907- .... **CLC 3, 51**
See also CA 21-24R; CANR 33; MTCW

Hope, Brian
See Creasey, John

Hope, Christopher (David Tully)
1944-...................... **CLC 52**
See also CA 106; CANR 47; SATA 62

Hopkins, Gerard Manley
1844-1889 .... **NCLC 17; DA; DAB;
DAC; PC 15; WLC**
See also CDBLB 1890-1914; DAM MST,
POET; DLB 35, 57

Hopkins, John (Richard) 1931-...... **CLC 4**
See also CA 85-88

Hopkins, Pauline Elizabeth
1859-1930 .... **TCLC 28; BLC**
See also BW 2; CA 141; DAM MULT;
DLB 50

Hopkinson, Francis 1737-1791 ...... **LC 25**
See also DLB 31

Hopley-Woolrich, Cornell George 1903-1968
See Woolrich, Cornell
See also CA 13-14; CAP 1

Horatio
See Proust, (Valentin-Louis-George-Eugene-)
Marcel

Horgan, Paul (George Vincent O'Shaughnessy)
1903-1995 .... **CLC 9, 53**
See also CA 13-16R; 147; CANR 9, 35;
DAM NOV; DLB 102; DLBY 85;
INT CANR-9; MTCW; SATA 13;
SATA-Obit 84

Horn, Peter
See Kuttner, Henry

Hornem, Horace Esq.
See Byron, George Gordon (Noel)

Hornung, E(rnest) W(illiam)
1866-1921 .... **TCLC 59**
See also CA 108; DLB 70

Horovitz, Israel (Arthur) 1939-..... **CLC 56**
See also CA 33-36R; CANR 46;
DAM DRAM; DLB 7

Horvath, Odon von
See Horvath, Oedoen von
See also DLB 85, 124

Horvath, Oedoen von 1901-1938... **TCLC 45**
See also Horvath, Odon von
See also CA 118

Horwitz, Julius 1920-1986........ **CLC 14**
See also CA 9-12R; 119; CANR 12

Hospital, Janette Turner 1942-..... **CLC 42**
See also CA 108; CANR 48

Hostos, E. M. de
See Hostos (y Bonilla), Eugenio Maria de

Hostos, Eugenio M. de
See Hostos (y Bonilla), Eugenio Maria de

Hostos, Eugenio Maria
See Hostos (y Bonilla), Eugenio Maria de

Hostos (y Bonilla), Eugenio Maria de
1839-1903 .... **TCLC 24**
See also CA 123; 131; HW

Houdini
See Lovecraft, H(oward) P(hillips)

Hougan, Carolyn 1943- .... **CLC 34**
See also CA 139

Household, Geoffrey (Edward West)
1900-1988 . . . . **CLC 11**
See also CA 77-80; 126; DLB 87; SATA 14;
SATA-Obit 59

Housman, A(lfred) E(dward)
1859-1936 . . . . . . **TCLC 1, 10; DA; DAB;
DAC; PC 2**
See also CA 104; 125; DAM MST, POET;
DLB 19; MTCW

Housman, Laurence 1865-1959 . . . . . **TCLC 7**
See also CA 106; DLB 10; SATA 25

Howard, Elizabeth Jane 1923- . . . **CLC 7, 29**
See also CA 5-8R; CANR 8

Howard, Maureen 1930- . . . . . **CLC 5, 14, 46**
See also CA 53-56; CANR 31; DLBY 83;
INT CANR-31; MTCW

Howard, Richard 1929- . . . . . . **CLC 7, 10, 47**
See also AITN 1; CA 85-88; CANR 25;
DLB 5; INT CANR-25

Howard, Robert Ervin 1906-1936 . . . **TCLC 8**
See also CA 105

Howard, Warren F.
See Pohl, Frederik

Howe, Fanny 1940- . . . . **CLC 47**
See also CA 117; SATA-Brief 52

Howe, Irving 1920-1993 . . . . **CLC 85**
See also CA 9-12R; 141; CANR 21, 50;
DLB 67; MTCW

Howe, Julia Ward 1819-1910 . . . . . **TCLC 21**
See also CA 117; DLB 1

Howe, Susan 1937- . . . . **CLC 72**
See also DLB 120

Howe, Tina 1937- . . . . **CLC 48**
See also CA 109

Howell, James 1594(?)-1666 . . . . **LC 13**
See also DLB 151

Howells, W. D.
See Howells, William Dean

Howells, William D.
See Howells, William Dean

Howells, William Dean
1837-1920 . . . . **TCLC 7, 17, 41**
See also CA 104; 134; CDALB 1865-1917;
DLB 12, 64, 74, 79

Howes, Barbara 1914-1996 . . . . **CLC 15**
See also CA 9-12R; 151; CAAS 3; SATA 5

Hrabal, Bohumil 1914- . . . . **CLC 13, 67**
See also CA 106; CAAS 12

Hsun, Lu
See Lu Hsun

Hubbard, L(afayette) Ron(ald)
1911-1986 . . . . **CLC 43**
See also CA 77-80; 118; CANR 22;
DAM POP

Huch, Ricarda (Octavia)
1864-1947 . . . . **TCLC 13**
See also CA 111; DLB 66

Huddle, David 1942- . . . . **CLC 49**
See also CA 57-60; CAAS 20; DLB 130

Hudson, Jeffrey
See Crichton, (John) Michael

Hudson, W(illiam) H(enry)
1841-1922 . . . . **TCLC 29**
See also CA 115; DLB 98, 153; SATA 35

Hueffer, Ford Madox
See Ford, Ford Madox

Hughart, Barry 1934- . . . . **CLC 39**
See also CA 137

Hughes, Colin
See Creasey, John

Hughes, David (John) 1930- . . . . **CLC 48**
See also CA 116; 129; DLB 14

Hughes, Edward James
See Hughes, Ted
See also DAM MST, POET

Hughes, (James) Langston
1902-1967 . . . . . **CLC 1, 5, 10, 15, 35, 44;
BLC; DA; DAB; DAC; DC 3; PC 1;
SSC 6; WLC**
See also AAYA 12; BW 1; CA 1-4R;
25-28R; CANR 1, 34; CDALB 1929-1941;
CLR 17; DAM DRAM, MST, MULT,
POET; DLB 4, 7, 48, 51, 86; JRDA;
MAICYA; MTCW; SATA 4, 33

Hughes, Richard (Arthur Warren)
1900-1976 . . . . **CLC 1, 11**
See also CA 5-8R; 65-68; CANR 4;
DAM NOV; DLB 15, 161; MTCW;
SATA 8; SATA-Obit 25

Hughes, Ted
1930- . . . . **CLC 2, 4, 9, 14, 37; DAB;
DAC; PC 7**
See also Hughes, Edward James
See also CA 1-4R; CANR 1, 33; CLR 3;
DLB 40, 161; MAICYA; MTCW;
SATA 49; SATA-Brief 27

Hugo, Richard F(ranklin)
1923-1982 . . . . **CLC 6, 18, 32**
See also CA 49-52; 108; CANR 3;
DAM POET; DLB 5

Hugo, Victor (Marie)
1802-1885 . . . . **NCLC 3, 10, 21; DA;
DAB; DAC; WLC**
See also DAM DRAM, MST, NOV, POET;
DLB 119; SATA 47

Huidobro, Vicente
See Huidobro Fernandez, Vicente Garcia

Huidobro Fernandez, Vicente Garcia
1893-1948 . . . . **TCLC 31**
See also CA 131; HW

Hulme, Keri 1947- . . . . **CLC 39**
See also CA 125; INT 125

Hulme, T(homas) E(rnest)
1883-1917 . . . . **TCLC 21**
See also CA 117; DLB 19

Hume, David 1711-1776 . . . . **LC 7**
See also DLB 104

Humphrey, William 1924- . . . . **CLC 45**
See also CA 77-80; DLB 6

Humphreys, Emyr Owen 1919- . . . . . **CLC 47**
See also CA 5-8R; CANR 3, 24; DLB 15

Humphreys, Josephine 1945- . . . . **CLC 34, 57**
See also CA 121; 127; INT 127

Huneker, James Gibbons
1857-1921 . . . . **TCLC 65**
See also DLB 71

Hungerford, Pixie
See Brinsmead, H(esba) F(ay)

Hunt, E(verette) Howard, (Jr.)
1918- . . . . **CLC 3**
See also AITN 1; CA 45-48; CANR 2, 47

Hunt, Kyle
See Creasey, John

Hunt, (James Henry) Leigh
1784-1859 . . . . **NCLC 1**
See also DAM POET

Hunt, Marsha 1946- . . . . **CLC 70**
See also BW 2; CA 143

Hunt, Violet 1866-1942 . . . . **TCLC 53**
See also DLB 162

Hunter, E. Waldo
See Sturgeon, Theodore (Hamilton)

Hunter, Evan 1926- . . . . **CLC 11, 31**
See also CA 5-8R; CANR 5, 38;
DAM POP; DLBY 82; INT CANR-5;
MTCW; SATA 25

Hunter, Kristin (Eggleston) 1931- . . . **CLC 35**
See also AITN 1; BW 1; CA 13-16R;
CANR 13; CLR 3; DLB 33;
INT CANR-13; MAICYA; SAAS 10;
SATA 12

Hunter, Mollie 1922- . . . . **CLC 21**
See also McIlwraith, Maureen Mollie
Hunter
See also AAYA 13; CANR 37; CLR 25;
DLB 161; JRDA; MAICYA; SAAS 7;
SATA 54

Hunter, Robert (?)-1734 . . . . **LC 7**

Hurston, Zora Neale
1903-1960 . . . . . **CLC 7, 30, 61; BLC; DA;
DAC; SSC 4**
See also AAYA 15; BW 1; CA 85-88;
DAM MST, MULT, NOV; DLB 51, 86;
MTCW

Huston, John (Marcellus)
1906-1987 . . . . **CLC 20**
See also CA 73-76; 123; CANR 34; DLB 26

Hustvedt, Siri 1955- . . . . **CLC 76**
See also CA 137

Hutten, Ulrich von 1488-1523 . . . . **LC 16**

Huxley, Aldous (Leonard)
1894-1963 . . . . . **CLC 1, 3, 4, 5, 8, 11, 18,
35, 79; DA; DAB; DAC; WLC**
See also AAYA 11; CA 85-88; CANR 44;
CDBLB 1914-1945; DAM MST, NOV;
DLB 36, 100, 162; MTCW; SATA 63

Huysmans, Charles Marie Georges
1848-1907
See Huysmans, Joris-Karl
See also CA 104

Huysmans, Joris-Karl . . . . **TCLC 7**
See also Huysmans, Charles Marie Georges
See also DLB 123

Hwang, David Henry
1957- . . . . **CLC 55; DC 4**
See also CA 127; 132; DAM DRAM;
INT 132

Hyde, Anthony 1946- . . . . **CLC 42**
See also CA 136

Hyde, Margaret O(ldroyd) 1917- . . . **CLC 21**
See also CA 1-4R; CANR 1, 36; CLR 23;
JRDA; MAICYA; SAAS 8; SATA 1, 42,
76

Hynes, James 1956(?)- . . . . **CLC 65**

Ian, Janis 1951- .... **CLC 21**
See also CA 105

Ibanez, Vicente Blasco
See Blasco Ibanez, Vicente

Ibarguengoitia, Jorge 1928-1983 .... **CLC 37**
See also CA 124; 113; HW

Ibsen, Henrik (Johan)
1828-1906 ...... **TCLC 2, 8, 16, 37, 52;**
DA; DAB; DAC; DC 2; WLC
See also CA 104; 141; DAM DRAM, MST

Ibuse Masuji 1898-1993 .... **CLC 22**
See also CA 127; 141

Ichikawa, Kon 1915- .... **CLC 20**
See also CA 121

Idle, Eric 1943- .... **CLC 21**
See also Monty Python
See also CA 116; CANR 35

Ignatow, David 1914- ...... **CLC 4, 7, 14, 40**
See also CA 9-12R; CAAS 3; CANR 31;
DLB 5

Ihimaera, Witi 1944- .... **CLC 46**
See also CA 77-80

Ilf, Ilya .... **TCLC 21**
See also Fainzilberg, Ilya Arnoldovich

Immermann, Karl (Lebrecht)
1796-1840 .... **NCLC 4, 49**
See also DLB 133

Inclan, Ramon (Maria) del Valle
See Valle-Inclan, Ramon (Maria) del

Infante, G(uillermo) Cabrera
See Cabrera Infante, G(uillermo)

Ingalls, Rachel (Holmes) 1940- ..... **CLC 42**
See also CA 123; 127

Ingamells, Rex 1913-1955 .... **TCLC 35**

Inge, William Motter
1913-1973 .... **CLC 1, 8, 19**
See also CA 9-12R; CDALB 1941-1968;
DAM DRAM; DLB 7; MTCW

Ingelow, Jean 1820-1897 .... **NCLC 39**
See also DLB 35, 163; SATA 33

Ingram, Willis J.
See Harris, Mark

Innaurato, Albert (F.) 1948(?)- .. **CLC 21, 60**
See also CA 115; 122; INT 122

Innes, Michael
See Stewart, J(ohn) I(nnes) M(ackintosh)

Ionesco, Eugene
1909-1994 .... **CLC 1, 4, 6, 9, 11, 15, 41,**
86; DA; DAB; DAC; WLC
See also CA 9-12R; 144; DAM DRAM,
MST; MTCW; SATA 7; SATA-Obit 79

Iqbal, Muhammad 1873-1938 ..... **TCLC 28**

Ireland, Patrick
See O'Doherty, Brian

Iron, Ralph
See Schreiner, Olive (Emilie Albertina)

Irving, John (Winslow)
1942- .... **CLC 13, 23, 38**
See also AAYA 8; BEST 89:3; CA 25-28R;
CANR 28; DAM NOV, POP; DLB 6;
DLBY 82; MTCW

Irving, Washington
1783-1859 ..... **NCLC 2, 19; DA; DAB;**
SSC 2; WLC
See also CDALB 1640-1865; DAM MST;
DLB 3, 11, 30, 59, 73, 74; YABC 2

Irwin, P. K.
See Page, P(atricia) K(athleen)

Isaacs, Susan 1943- .... **CLC 32**
See also BEST 89:1; CA 89-92; CANR 20,
41; DAM POP; INT CANR-20; MTCW

Isherwood, Christopher (William Bradshaw)
1904-1986 .... **CLC 1, 9, 11, 14, 44**
See also CA 13-16R; 117; CANR 35;
DAM DRAM, NOV; DLB 15; DLBY 86;
MTCW

Ishiguro, Kazuo 1954- ...... **CLC 27, 56, 59**
See also BEST 90:2; CA 120; CANR 49;
DAM NOV; MTCW

Ishikawa, Takuboku
1886(?)-1912 .... **TCLC 15; PC 10**
See also CA 113; DAM POET

Iskander, Fazil 1929- .... **CLC 47**
See also CA 102

Isler, Alan .... **CLC 91**

Ivan IV 1530-1584 .... **LC 17**

Ivanov, Vyacheslav Ivanovich
1866-1949 .... **TCLC 33**
See also CA 122

Ivask, Ivar Vidrik 1927-1992 .... **CLC 14**
See also CA 37-40R; 139; CANR 24

J. R. S.
See Gogarty, Oliver St. John

Jabran, Kahlil
See Gibran, Kahlil

Jabran, Khalil
See Gibran, Kahlil

Jackson, Daniel
See Wingrove, David (John)

Jackson, Jesse 1908-1983 .... **CLC 12**
See also BW 1; CA 25-28R; 109; CANR 27;
CLR 28; MAICYA; SATA 2, 29;
SATA-Obit 48

Jackson, Laura (Riding) 1901-1991
See Riding, Laura
See also CA 65-68; 135; CANR 28; DLB 48

Jackson, Sam
See Trumbo, Dalton

Jackson, Sara
See Wingrove, David (John)

Jackson, Shirley
1919-1965 .... **CLC 11, 60, 87; DA;**
DAC; SSC 9; WLC
See also AAYA 9; CA 1-4R; 25-28R;
CANR 4; CDALB 1941-1968;
DAM MST; DLB 6; SATA 2

Jacob, (Cyprien-)Max 1876-1944 ... **TCLC 6**
See also CA 104

Jacobs, Jim 1942- .... **CLC 12**
See also CA 97-100; INT 97-100

Jacobs, W(illiam) W(ymark)
1863-1943 .... **TCLC 22**
See also CA 121; DLB 135

Jacobsen, Jens Peter 1847-1885 .. **NCLC 34**

Jacobsen, Josephine 1908- .... **CLC 48**
See also CA 33-36R; CAAS 18; CANR 23,
48

Jacobson, Dan 1929- .... **CLC 4, 14**
See also CA 1-4R; CANR 2, 25; DLB 14;
MTCW

Jacqueline
See Carpentier (y Valmont), Alejo

Jagger, Mick 1944- .... **CLC 17**

Jakes, John (William) 1932- .... **CLC 29**
See also BEST 89:4; CA 57-60; CANR 10,
43; DAM NOV, POP; DLBY 83;
INT CANR-10; MTCW; SATA 62

James, Andrew
See Kirkup, James

James, C(yril) L(ionel) R(obert)
1901-1989 .... **CLC 33**
See also BW 2; CA 117; 125; 128; DLB 125;
MTCW

James, Daniel (Lewis) 1911-1988
See Santiago, Danny
See also CA 125

James, Dynely
See Mayne, William (James Carter)

James, Henry Sr. 1811-1882 ..... **NCLC 53**

James, Henry
1843-1916 ...... **TCLC 2, 11, 24, 40, 47,**
64; DA; DAB; DAC; SSC 8; WLC
See also CA 104; 132; CDALB 1865-1917;
DAM MST, NOV; DLB 12, 71, 74;
DLBD 13; MTCW

James, M. R.
See James, Montague (Rhodes)
See also DLB 156

James, Montague (Rhodes)
1862-1936 .... **TCLC 6; SSC 16**
See also CA 104

James, P. D. .... **CLC 18, 46**
See also White, Phyllis Dorothy James
See also BEST 90:2; CDBLB 1960 to
Present; DLB 87

James, Philip
See Moorcock, Michael (John)

James, William 1842-1910 ..... **TCLC 15, 32**
See also CA 109

James I 1394-1437 .... **LC 20**

Jameson, Anna 1794-1860 .... **NCLC 43**
See also DLB 99

Jami, Nur al-Din 'Abd al-Rahman
1414-1492 .... **LC 9**

Jandl, Ernst 1925- .... **CLC 34**

Janowitz, Tama 1957- .... **CLC 43**
See also CA 106; DAM POP

Japrisot, Sebastien 1931- .... **CLC 90**

Jarrell, Randall
1914-1965 .... **CLC 1, 2, 6, 9, 13, 49**
See also CA 5-8R; 25-28R; CABS 2;
CANR 6, 34; CDALB 1941-1968; CLR 6;
DAM POET; DLB 48, 52; MAICYA;
MTCW; SATA 7

Jarry, Alfred
1873-1907 .... **TCLC 2, 14; SSC 20**
See also CA 104; DAM DRAM

Jarvis, E. K.
See Bloch, Robert (Albert); Ellison, Harlan (Jay); Silverberg, Robert

Jeake, Samuel, Jr.
See Aiken, Conrad (Potter)

Jean Paul 1763-1825 . . . . **NCLC 7**

Jefferies, (John) Richard
1848-1887 . . . . **NCLC 47**
See also DLB 98, 141; SATA 16

Jeffers, (John) Robinson
1887-1962 . . . . **CLC 2, 3, 11, 15, 54; DA;**
DAC; WLC
See also CA 85-88; CANR 35;
CDALB 1917-1929; DAM MST, POET;
DLB 45; MTCW

Jefferson, Janet
See Mencken, H(enry) L(ouis)

Jefferson, Thomas 1743-1826 . . . . **NCLC 11**
See also CDALB 1640-1865; DLB 31

Jeffrey, Francis 1773-1850 . . . . **NCLC 33**
See also DLB 107

Jelakowitch, Ivan
See Heijermans, Herman

Jellicoe, (Patricia) Ann 1927- . . . . . . **CLC 27**
See also CA 85-88; DLB 13

Jen, Gish . . . . **CLC 70**
See also Jen, Lillian

Jen, Lillian 1956(?)-
See Jen, Gish
See also CA 135

Jenkins, (John) Robin 1912- . . . . **CLC 52**
See also CA 1-4R; CANR 1; DLB 14

Jennings, Elizabeth (Joan)
1926- . . . . **CLC 5, 14**
See also CA 61-64; CAAS 5; CANR 8, 39;
DLB 27; MTCW; SATA 66

Jennings, Waylon 1937- . . . . **CLC 21**

Jensen, Johannes V. 1873-1950 . . . . **TCLC 41**

Jensen, Laura (Linnea) 1948- . . . . . . **CLC 37**
See also CA 103

Jerome, Jerome K(lapka)
1859-1927 . . . . **TCLC 23**
See also CA 119; DLB 10, 34, 135

Jerrold, Douglas William
1803-1857 . . . . **NCLC 2**
See also DLB 158, 159

Jewett, (Theodora) Sarah Orne
1849-1909 . . . . **TCLC 1, 22; SSC 6**
See also CA 108; 127; DLB 12, 74;
SATA 15

Jewsbury, Geraldine (Endsor)
1812-1880 . . . . **NCLC 22**
See also DLB 21

Jhabvala, Ruth Prawer
1927- . . . . **CLC 4, 8, 29, 94; DAB**
See also CA 1-4R; CANR 2, 29, 51;
DAM NOV; DLB 139; INT CANR-29;
MTCW

Jibran, Kahlil
See Gibran, Kahlil

Jibran, Khalil
See Gibran, Kahlil

Jiles, Paulette 1943- . . . . **CLC 13, 58**
See also CA 101

Jimenez (Mantecon), Juan Ramon
1881-1958 . . . . **TCLC 4; HLC; PC 7**
See also CA 104; 131; DAM MULT,
POET; DLB 134; HW; MTCW

Jimenez, Ramon
See Jimenez (Mantecon), Juan Ramon

Jimenez Mantecon, Juan
See Jimenez (Mantecon), Juan Ramon

Joel, Billy . . . . **CLC 26**
See also Joel, William Martin

Joel, William Martin 1949-
See Joel, Billy
See also CA 108

John of the Cross, St. 1542-1591 . . . . **LC 18**

Johnson, B(ryan) S(tanley William)
1933-1973 . . . . **CLC 6, 9**
See also CA 9-12R; 53-56; CANR 9;
DLB 14, 40

Johnson, Benj. F. of Boo
See Riley, James Whitcomb

Johnson, Benjamin F. of Boo
See Riley, James Whitcomb

Johnson, Charles (Richard)
1948- . . . . **CLC 7, 51, 65; BLC**
See also BW 2; CA 116; CAAS 18;
CANR 42; DAM MULT; DLB 33

Johnson, Denis 1949- . . . . **CLC 52**
See also CA 117; 121; DLB 120

Johnson, Diane 1934- . . . . **CLC 5, 13, 48**
See also CA 41-44R; CANR 17, 40;
DLBY 80; INT CANR-17; MTCW

Johnson, Eyvind (Olof Verner)
1900-1976 . . . . **CLC 14**
See also CA 73-76; 69-72; CANR 34

Johnson, J. R.
See James, C(yril) L(ionel) R(obert)

Johnson, James Weldon
1871-1938 . . . . **TCLC 3, 19; BLC**
See also BW 1; CA 104; 125;
CDALB 1917-1929; CLR 32;
DAM MULT, POET; DLB 51; MTCW;
SATA 31

Johnson, Joyce 1935- . . . . **CLC 58**
See also CA 125; 129

Johnson, Lionel (Pigot)
1867-1902 . . . . **TCLC 19**
See also CA 117; DLB 19

Johnson, Mel
See Malzberg, Barry N(athaniel)

Johnson, Pamela Hansford
1912-1981 . . . . **CLC 1, 7, 27**
See also CA 1-4R; 104; CANR 2, 28;
DLB 15; MTCW

Johnson, Samuel
1709-1784 . . . . . **LC 15; DA; DAB; DAC;**
WLC
See also CDBLB 1660-1789; DAM MST;
DLB 39, 95, 104, 142

Johnson, Uwe
1934-1984 . . . . **CLC 5, 10, 15, 40**
See also CA 1-4R; 112; CANR 1, 39;
DLB 75; MTCW

Johnston, George (Benson) 1913- . . . **CLC 51**
See also CA 1-4R; CANR 5, 20; DLB 88

Johnston, Jennifer 1930- . . . . **CLC 7**
See also CA 85-88; DLB 14

Jolley, (Monica) Elizabeth
1923- . . . . **CLC 46; SSC 19**
See also CA 127; CAAS 13

Jones, Arthur Llewellyn 1863-1947
See Machen, Arthur
See also CA 104

Jones, D(ouglas) G(ordon) 1929- . . . . **CLC 10**
See also CA 29-32R; CANR 13; DLB 53

Jones, David (Michael)
1895-1974 . . . . **CLC 2, 4, 7, 13, 42**
See also CA 9-12R; 53-56; CANR 28;
CDBLB 1945-1960; DLB 20, 100; MTCW

Jones, David Robert 1947-
See Bowie, David
See also CA 103

Jones, Diana Wynne 1934- . . . . **CLC 26**
See also AAYA 12; CA 49-52; CANR 4,
26; CLR 23; DLB 161; JRDA; MAICYA;
SAAS 7; SATA 9, 70

Jones, Edward P. 1950- . . . . **CLC 76**
See also BW 2; CA 142

Jones, Gayl 1949- . . . . **CLC 6, 9; BLC**
See also BW 2; CA 77-80; CANR 27;
DAM MULT; DLB 33; MTCW

Jones, James 1921-1977 . . . . **CLC 1, 3, 10, 39**
See also AITN 1, 2; CA 1-4R; 69-72;
CANR 6; DLB 2, 143; MTCW

Jones, John J.
See Lovecraft, H(oward) P(hillips)

Jones, LeRoi . . . . **CLC 1, 2, 3, 5, 10, 14**
See also Baraka, Amiri

Jones, Louis B. . . . . **CLC 65**
See also CA 141

Jones, Madison (Percy, Jr.) 1925- . . . **CLC 4**
See also CA 13-16R; CAAS 11; CANR 7;
DLB 152

Jones, Mervyn 1922- . . . . **CLC 10, 52**
See also CA 45-48; CAAS 5; CANR 1;
MTCW

Jones, Mick 1956(?)- . . . . **CLC 30**

Jones, Nettie (Pearl) 1941- . . . . **CLC 34**
See also BW 2; CA 137; CAAS 20

Jones, Preston 1936-1979 . . . . **CLC 10**
See also CA 73-76; 89-92; DLB 7

Jones, Robert F(rancis) 1934- . . . . . . **CLC 7**
See also CA 49-52; CANR 2

Jones, Rod 1953- . . . . **CLC 50**
See also CA 128

Jones, Terence Graham Parry
1942- . . . . **CLC 21**
See also Jones, Terry; Monty Python
See also CA 112; 116; CANR 35; INT 116

Jones, Terry
See Jones, Terence Graham Parry
See also SATA 67; SATA-Brief 51

Jones, Thom 1945(?)- . . . . **CLC 81**

Jong, Erica 1942- . . . . . . **CLC 4, 6, 8, 18, 83**
See also AITN 1; BEST 90:2; CA 73-76;
CANR 26; DAM NOV, POP; DLB 2, 5,
28, 152; INT CANR-26; MTCW

Kelley, William Melvin 1937- ...... **CLC 22**
　See also BW 1; CA 77-80; CANR 27;
　DLB 33

Kellogg, Marjorie 1922- .... **CLC 2**
　See also CA 81-84

Kellow, Kathleen
　See Hibbert, Eleanor Alice Burford

Kelly, M(ilton) T(erry) 1947- .... **CLC 55**
　See also CA 97-100; CAAS 22; CANR 19,
　43

Kelman, James 1946- .... **CLC 58, 86**
　See also CA 148

Kemal, Yashar 1923- .... **CLC 14, 29**
　See also CA 89-92; CANR 44

Kemble, Fanny 1809-1893 .... **NCLC 18**
　See also DLB 32

Kemelman, Harry 1908- .... **CLC 2**
　See also AITN 1; CA 9-12R; CANR 6;
　DLB 28

Kempe, Margery 1373(?)-1440(?) ..... **LC 6**
　See also DLB 146

Kempis, Thomas a 1380-1471 .... **LC 11**

Kendall, Henry 1839-1882 .... **NCLC 12**

Keneally, Thomas (Michael)
　1935- ...... **CLC 5, 8, 10, 14, 19, 27, 43**
　See also CA 85-88; CANR 10, 50;
　DAM NOV; MTCW

Kennedy, Adrienne (Lita)
　1931- .... **CLC 66; BLC; DC 5**
　See also BW 2; CA 103; CAAS 20; CABS 3;
　CANR 26; DAM MULT; DLB 38

Kennedy, John Pendleton
　1795-1870 .... **NCLC 2**
　See also DLB 3

Kennedy, Joseph Charles 1929-
　See Kennedy, X. J.
　See also CA 1-4R; CANR 4, 30, 40;
　SATA 14, 86

Kennedy, William 1928- ... **CLC 6, 28, 34, 53**
　See also AAYA 1; CA 85-88; CANR 14,
　31; DAM NOV; DLB 143; DLBY 85;
　INT CANR-31; MTCW; SATA 57

Kennedy, X. J. .... **CLC 8, 42**
　See also Kennedy, Joseph Charles
　See also CAAS 9; CLR 27; DLB 5;
　SAAS 22

Kenny, Maurice (Francis) 1929- .... **CLC 87**
　See also CA 144; CAAS 22; DAM MULT;
　NNAL

Kent, Kelvin
　See Kuttner, Henry

Kenton, Maxwell
　See Southern, Terry

Kenyon, Robert O.
　See Kuttner, Henry

Kerouac, Jack ..... **CLC 1, 2, 3, 5, 14, 29, 61**
　See also Kerouac, Jean-Louis Lebris de
　See also CDALB 1941-1968; DLB 2, 16;
　DLBD 3; DLBY 95

Kerouac, Jean-Louis Lebris de 1922-1969
　See Kerouac, Jack
　See also AITN 1; CA 5-8R; 25-28R;
　CANR 26; DA; DAB; DAC; DAM MST,
　NOV, POET, POP; MTCW; WLC

Kerr, Jean 1923- .... **CLC 22**
　See also CA 5-8R; CANR 7; INT CANR-7

Kerr, M. E. .... **CLC 12, 35**
　See also Meaker, Marijane (Agnes)
　See also AAYA 2; CLR 29; SAAS 1

Kerr, Robert .... **CLC 55**

Kerrigan, (Thomas) Anthony
　1918- .... **CLC 4, 6**
　See also CA 49-52; CAAS 11; CANR 4

Kerry, Lois
　See Duncan, Lois

Kesey, Ken (Elton)
　1935- ...... **CLC 1, 3, 6, 11, 46, 64; DA;**
　　　　　　　　DAB; DAC; WLC
　See also CA 1-4R; CANR 22, 38;
　CDALB 1968-1988; DAM MST, NOV,
　POP; DLB 2, 16; MTCW; SATA 66

Kesselring, Joseph (Otto)
　1902-1967 .... **CLC 45**
　See also CA 150; DAM DRAM, MST

Kessler, Jascha (Frederick) 1929- .... **CLC 4**
　See also CA 17-20R; CANR 8, 48

Kettelkamp, Larry (Dale) 1933- .... **CLC 12**
　See also CA 29-32R; CANR 16; SAAS 3;
　SATA 2

Keyber, Conny
　See Fielding, Henry

Keyes, Daniel 1927- .... **CLC 80; DA; DAC**
　See also CA 17-20R; CANR 10, 26;
　DAM MST, NOV; SATA 37

Keynes, John Maynard
　1883-1946 .... **TCLC 64**
　See also CA 114; DLBD 10

Khanshendel, Chiron
　See Rose, Wendy

Khayyam, Omar
　1048-1131 .... **CMLC 11; PC 8**
　See also DAM POET

Kherdian, David 1931- .... **CLC 6, 9**
　See also CA 21-24R; CAAS 2; CANR 39;
　CLR 24; JRDA; MAICYA; SATA 16, 74

Khlebnikov, Velimir .... **TCLC 20**
　See also Khlebnikov, Viktor Vladimirovich

Khlebnikov, Viktor Vladimirovich 1885-1922
　See Khlebnikov, Velimir
　See also CA 117

Khodasevich, Vladislav (Felitsianovich)
　1886-1939 .... **TCLC 15**
　See also CA 115

Kielland, Alexander Lange
　1849-1906 .... **TCLC 5**
　See also CA 104

Kiely, Benedict 1919- .... **CLC 23, 43**
　See also CA 1-4R; CANR 2; DLB 15

Kienzle, William X(avier) 1928- .... **CLC 25**
　See also CA 93-96; CAAS 1; CANR 9, 31;
　DAM POP; INT CANR-31; MTCW

Kierkegaard, Soren 1813-1855 .... **NCLC 34**

Killens, John Oliver 1916-1987 ..... **CLC 10**
　See also BW 2; CA 77-80; 123; CAAS 2;
　CANR 26; DLB 33

Killigrew, Anne 1660-1685 .... **LC 4**
　See also DLB 131

Kim
　See Simenon, Georges (Jacques Christian)

Kincaid, Jamaica 1949- ... **CLC 43, 68; BLC**
　See also AAYA 13; BW 2; CA 125;
　CANR 47; DAM MULT, NOV;
　DLB 157

King, Francis (Henry) 1923- ..... **CLC 8, 53**
　See also CA 1-4R; CANR 1, 33;
　DAM NOV; DLB 15, 139; MTCW

King, Martin Luther, Jr.
　1929-1968 .... **CLC 83; BLC; DA; DAB;**
　　　　　　　　　　　　　　　　DAC
　See also BW 2; CA 25-28; CANR 27, 44;
　CAP 2; DAM MST, MULT; MTCW;
　SATA 14

King, Stephen (Edwin)
　1947- ...... **CLC 12, 26, 37, 61; SSC 17**
　See also AAYA 1, 17; BEST 90:1;
　CA 61-64; CANR 1, 30; DAM NOV,
　POP; DLB 143; DLBY 80; JRDA;
　MTCW; SATA 9, 55

King, Steve
　See King, Stephen (Edwin)

King, Thomas 1943- .... **CLC 89; DAC**
　See also CA 144; DAM MULT; NNAL

Kingman, Lee .... **CLC 17**
　See also Natti, (Mary) Lee
　See also SAAS 3; SATA 1, 67

Kingsley, Charles 1819-1875 ..... **NCLC 35**
　See also DLB 21, 32, 163; YABC 2

Kingsley, Sidney 1906-1995 .... **CLC 44**
　See also CA 85-88; 147; DLB 7

Kingsolver, Barbara 1955- ...... **CLC 55, 81**
　See also AAYA 15; CA 129; 134;
　DAM POP; INT 134

Kingston, Maxine (Ting Ting) Hong
　1940- .... **CLC 12, 19, 58**
　See also AAYA 8; CA 69-72; CANR 13,
　38; DAM MULT, NOV; DLBY 80;
　INT CANR-13; MTCW; SATA 53

Kinnell, Galway
　1927- .... **CLC 1, 2, 3, 5, 13, 29**
　See also CA 9-12R; CANR 10, 34; DLB 5;
　DLBY 87; INT CANR-34; MTCW

Kinsella, Thomas 1928- .... **CLC 4, 19**
　See also CA 17-20R; CANR 15; DLB 27;
　MTCW

Kinsella, W(illiam) P(atrick)
　1935- .... **CLC 27, 43; DAC**
　See also AAYA 7; CA 97-100; CAAS 7;
　CANR 21, 35; DAM NOV, POP;
　INT CANR-21; MTCW

Kipling, (Joseph) Rudyard
　1865-1936 ...... **TCLC 8, 17; DA; DAB;**
　　　　　　　　DAC; PC 3; SSC 5; WLC
　See also CA 105; 120; CANR 33;
　CDBLB 1890-1914; CLR 39; DAM MST,
　POET; DLB 19, 34, 141, 156; MAICYA;
　MTCW; YABC 2

Kirkup, James 1918- .... **CLC 1**
　See also CA 1-4R; CAAS 4; CANR 2;
　DLB 27; SATA 12

Kirkwood, James 1930(?)-1989 ...... **CLC 9**
　See also AITN 2; CA 1-4R; 128; CANR 6,
　40

Kirshner, Sidney
  See Kingsley, Sidney

Kis, Danilo 1935-1989 . . . . **CLC 57**
  See also CA 109; 118; 129; MTCW

Kivi, Aleksis 1834-1872 . . . . **NCLC 30**

Kizer, Carolyn (Ashley)
  1925- . . . . **CLC 15, 39, 80**
  See also CA 65-68; CAAS 5; CANR 24;
  DAM POET; DLB 5

Klabund 1890-1928 . . . . **TCLC 44**
  See also DLB 66

Klappert, Peter 1942- . . . . **CLC 57**
  See also CA 33-36R; DLB 5

Klein, A(braham) M(oses)
  1909-1972 . . . . **CLC 19; DAB; DAC**
  See also CA 101; 37-40R; DAM MST;
  DLB 68

Klein, Norma 1938-1989 . . . . **CLC 30**
  See also AAYA 2; CA 41-44R; 128;
  CANR 15, 37; CLR 2, 19;
  INT CANR-15; JRDA; MAICYA;
  SAAS 1; SATA 7, 57

Klein, T(heodore) E(ibon) D(onald)
  1947- . . . . **CLC 34**
  See also CA 119; CANR 44

Kleist, Heinrich von
  1777-1811 . . . . **NCLC 2, 37; SSC 22**
  See also DAM DRAM; DLB 90

Klima, Ivan 1931- . . . . **CLC 56**
  See also CA 25-28R; CANR 17, 50;
  DAM NOV

Klimentov, Andrei Platonovich 1899-1951
  See Platonov, Andrei
  See also CA 108

Klinger, Friedrich Maximilian von
  1752-1831 . . . . **NCLC 1**
  See also DLB 94

Klopstock, Friedrich Gottlieb
  1724-1803 . . . . **NCLC 11**
  See also DLB 97

Knebel, Fletcher 1911-1993 . . . . **CLC 14**
  See also AITN 1; CA 1-4R; 140; CAAS 3;
  CANR 1, 36; SATA 36; SATA-Obit 75

Knickerbocker, Diedrich
  See Irving, Washington

Knight, Etheridge
  1931-1991 . . . . . . **CLC 40; BLC; PC 14**
  See also BW 1; CA 21-24R; 133; CANR 23;
  DAM POET; DLB 41

Knight, Sarah Kemble 1666-1727 . . . . . **LC 7**
  See also DLB 24

Knister, Raymond 1899-1932 . . . . . . **TCLC 56**
  See also DLB 68

Knowles, John
  1926- . . . . . . **CLC 1, 4, 10, 26; DA; DAC**
  See also AAYA 10; CA 17-20R; CANR 40;
  CDALB 1968-1988; DAM MST, NOV;
  DLB 6; MTCW; SATA 8

Knox, Calvin M.
  See Silverberg, Robert

Knye, Cassandra
  See Disch, Thomas M(ichael)

Koch, C(hristopher) J(ohn) 1932- . . . **CLC 42**
  See also CA 127

Koch, Christopher
  See Koch, C(hristopher) J(ohn)

Koch, Kenneth 1925- . . . . **CLC 5, 8, 44**
  See also CA 1-4R; CANR 6, 36;
  DAM POET; DLB 5; INT CANR-36;
  SATA 65

Kochanowski, Jan 1530-1584 . . . . **LC 10**

Kock, Charles Paul de
  1794-1871 . . . . **NCLC 16**

Koda Shigeyuki 1867-1947
  See Rohan, Koda
  See also CA 121

Koestler, Arthur
  1905-1983 . . . . **CLC 1, 3, 6, 8, 15, 33**
  See also CA 1-4R; 109; CANR 1, 33;
  CDBLB 1945-1960; DLBY 83; MTCW

Kogawa, Joy Nozomi 1935- . . . **CLC 78; DAC**
  See also CA 101; CANR 19; DAM MST,
  MULT

Kohout, Pavel 1928- . . . . **CLC 13**
  See also CA 45-48; CANR 3

Koizumi, Yakumo
  See Hearn, (Patricio) Lafcadio (Tessima
  Carlos)

Kolmar, Gertrud 1894-1943 . . . . . . **TCLC 40**

Komunyakaa, Yusef 1947- . . . . . . **CLC 86, 94**
  See also CA 147; DLB 120

Konrad, George
  See Konrad, Gyoergy

Konrad, Gyoergy 1933- . . . . . . **CLC 4, 10, 73**
  See also CA 85-88

Konwicki, Tadeusz 1926- . . . . . **CLC 8, 28, 54**
  See also CA 101; CAAS 9; CANR 39;
  MTCW

Koontz, Dean R(ay) 1945- . . . . **CLC 78**
  See also AAYA 9; BEST 89:3, 90:2;
  CA 108; CANR 19, 36; DAM NOV,
  POP; MTCW

Kopit, Arthur (Lee) 1937- . . . . **CLC 1, 18, 33**
  See also AITN 1; CA 81-84; CABS 3;
  DAM DRAM; DLB 7; MTCW

Kops, Bernard 1926- . . . . **CLC 4**
  See also CA 5-8R; DLB 13

Kornbluth, C(yril) M. 1923-1958 . . . . **TCLC 8**
  See also CA 105; DLB 8

Korolenko, V. G.
  See Korolenko, Vladimir Galaktionovich

Korolenko, Vladimir
  See Korolenko, Vladimir Galaktionovich

Korolenko, Vladimir G.
  See Korolenko, Vladimir Galaktionovich

Korolenko, Vladimir Galaktionovich
  1853-1921 . . . . **TCLC 22**
  See also CA 121

Korzybski, Alfred (Habdank Skarbek)
  1879-1950 . . . . **TCLC 61**
  See also CA 123

Kosinski, Jerzy (Nikodem)
  1933-1991 . . . . **CLC 1, 2, 3, 6, 10, 15, 53, 70**
  See also CA 17-20R; 134; CANR 9, 46;
  DAM NOV; DLB 2; DLBY 82; MTCW

Kostelanetz, Richard (Cory) 1940- . . **CLC 28**
  See also CA 13-16R; CAAS 8; CANR 38

Kostrowitzki, Wilhelm Apollinaris de
  1880-1918
  See Apollinaire, Guillaume
  See also CA 104

Kotlowitz, Robert 1924- . . . . **CLC 4**
  See also CA 33-36R; CANR 36

Kotzebue, August (Friedrich Ferdinand) von
  1761-1819 . . . . **NCLC 25**
  See also DLB 94

Kotzwinkle, William 1938- . . . **CLC 5, 14, 35**
  See also CA 45-48; CANR 3, 44; CLR 6;
  MAICYA; SATA 24, 70

Kozol, Jonathan 1936- . . . . **CLC 17**
  See also CA 61-64; CANR 16, 45

Kozoll, Michael 1940(?)- . . . . **CLC 35**

Kramer, Kathryn 19(?)- . . . . **CLC 34**

Kramer, Larry 1935- . . . . **CLC 42**
  See also CA 124; 126; DAM POP

Krasicki, Ignacy 1735-1801 . . . . **NCLC 8**

Krasinski, Zygmunt 1812-1859 . . . . **NCLC 4**

Kraus, Karl 1874-1936 . . . . **TCLC 5**
  See also CA 104; DLB 118

Kreve (Mickevicius), Vincas
  1882-1954 . . . . **TCLC 27**

Kristeva, Julia 1941- . . . . **CLC 77**

Kristofferson, Kris 1936- . . . . **CLC 26**
  See also CA 104

Krizanc, John 1956- . . . . **CLC 57**

Krleza, Miroslav 1893-1981 . . . . **CLC 8**
  See also CA 97-100; 105; CANR 50;
  DLB 147

Kroetsch, Robert
  1927- . . . . **CLC 5, 23, 57; DAC**
  See also CA 17-20R; CANR 8, 38;
  DAM POET; DLB 53; MTCW

Kroetz, Franz
  See Kroetz, Franz Xaver

Kroetz, Franz Xaver 1946- . . . . **CLC 41**
  See also CA 130

Kroker, Arthur 1945- . . . . **CLC 77**

Kropotkin, Peter (Aleksieevich)
  1842-1921 . . . . **TCLC 36**
  See also CA 119

Krotkov, Yuri 1917- . . . . **CLC 19**
  See also CA 102

Krumb
  See Crumb, R(obert)

Krumgold, Joseph (Quincy)
  1908-1980 . . . . **CLC 12**
  See also CA 9-12R; 101; CANR 7;
  MAICYA; SATA 1, 48; SATA-Obit 23

Krumwitz
  See Crumb, R(obert)

Krutch, Joseph Wood 1893-1970 . . . . **CLC 24**
  See also CA 1-4R; 25-28R; CANR 4;
  DLB 63

Krutzch, Gus
  See Eliot, T(homas) S(tearns)

Krylov, Ivan Andreevich
  1768(?)-1844 . . . . **NCLC 1**
  See also DLB 150

Kubin, Alfred (Leopold Isidor)
1877-1959 .... **TCLC 23**
See also CA 112; 149; DLB 81

Kubrick, Stanley 1928- .... **CLC 16**
See also CA 81-84; CANR 33; DLB 26

Kumin, Maxine (Winokur)
1925- .... **CLC 5, 13, 28; PC 15**
See also AITN 2; CA 1-4R; CAAS 8;
CANR 1, 21; DAM POET; DLB 5;
MTCW; SATA 12

Kundera, Milan
1929- .... **CLC 4, 9, 19, 32, 68**
See also AAYA 2; CA 85-88; CANR 19;
DAM NOV; MTCW

Kunene, Mazisi (Raymond) 1930- ... **CLC 85**
See also BW 1; CA 125; DLB 117

Kunitz, Stanley (Jasspon)
1905- .... **CLC 6, 11, 14**
See also CA 41-44R; CANR 26; DLB 48;
INT CANR-26; MTCW

Kunze, Reiner 1933- .... **CLC 10**
See also CA 93-96; DLB 75

Kuprin, Aleksandr Ivanovich
1870-1938 .... **TCLC 5**
See also CA 104

Kureishi, Hanif 1954(?)- .... **CLC 64**
See also CA 139

Kurosawa, Akira 1910- .... **CLC 16**
See also AAYA 11; CA 101; CANR 46;
DAM MULT

Kushner, Tony 1957(?)- .... **CLC 81**
See also CA 144; DAM DRAM

Kuttner, Henry 1915-1958 .... **TCLC 10**
See also CA 107; DLB 8

Kuzma, Greg 1944- .... **CLC 7**
See also CA 33-36R

Kuzmin, Mikhail 1872(?)-1936 .... **TCLC 40**

Kyd, Thomas 1558-1594 ...... **LC 22; DC 3**
See also DAM DRAM; DLB 62

Kyprianos, Iossif
See Samarakis, Antonis

La Bruyere, Jean de 1645-1696 ...... **LC 17**

Lacan, Jacques (Marie Emile)
1901-1981 .... **CLC 75**
See also CA 121; 104

**Laclos, Pierre Ambroise Francois Choderlos
de** 1741-1803 .... **NCLC 4**

Lacolere, Francois
See Aragon, Louis

La Colere, Francois
See Aragon, Louis

La Deshabilleuse
See Simenon, Georges (Jacques Christian)

Lady Gregory
See Gregory, Isabella Augusta (Persse)

Lady of Quality, A
See Bagnold, Enid

**La Fayette, Marie (Madelaine Pioche de la
Vergne Comtes** 1634-1693 .... **LC 2**

Lafayette, Rene
See Hubbard, L(afayette) Ron(ald)

Laforgue, Jules
1860-1887 .... **NCLC 5, 53; PC 14;
SSC 20**

Lagerkvist, Paer (Fabian)
1891-1974 .... **CLC 7, 10, 13, 54**
See also Lagerkvist, Par
See also CA 85-88; 49-52; DAM DRAM,
NOV; MTCW

Lagerkvist, Par .... **SSC 12**
See also Lagerkvist, Paer (Fabian)

Lagerloef, Selma (Ottiliana Lovisa)
1858-1940 .... **TCLC 4, 36**
See also Lagerlof, Selma (Ottiliana Lovisa)
See also CA 108; SATA 15

Lagerlof, Selma (Ottiliana Lovisa)
See Lagerloef, Selma (Ottiliana Lovisa)
See also CLR 7; SATA 15

La Guma, (Justin) Alex(ander)
1925-1985 .... **CLC 19**
See also BW 1; CA 49-52; 118; CANR 25;
DAM NOV; DLB 117; MTCW

Laidlaw, A. K.
See Grieve, C(hristopher) M(urray)

Lainez, Manuel Mujica
See Mujica Lainez, Manuel
See also HW

Lamartine, Alphonse (Marie Louis Prat) de
1790-1869 .... **NCLC 11**
See also DAM POET

Lamb, Charles
1775-1834 .... **NCLC 10; DA; DAB;
DAC; WLC**
See also CDBLB 1789-1832; DAM MST;
DLB 93, 107, 163; SATA 17

Lamb, Lady Caroline 1785-1828 .. **NCLC 38**
See also DLB 116

Lamming, George (William)
1927- .... **CLC 2, 4, 66; BLC**
See also BW 2; CA 85-88; CANR 26;
DAM MULT; DLB 125; MTCW

L'Amour, Louis (Dearborn)
1908-1988 .... **CLC 25, 55**
See also AAYA 16; AITN 2; BEST 89:2;
CA 1-4R; 125; CANR 3, 25, 40;
DAM NOV, POP; DLBY 80; MTCW

Lampedusa, Giuseppe (Tomasi) di ... **TCLC 13**
See also Tomasi di Lampedusa, Giuseppe

Lampman, Archibald 1861-1899 .. **NCLC 25**
See also DLB 92

Lancaster, Bruce 1896-1963 .... **CLC 36**
See also CA 9-10; CAP 1; SATA 9

Landau, Mark Alexandrovich
See Aldanov, Mark (Alexandrovich)

Landau-Aldanov, Mark Alexandrovich
See Aldanov, Mark (Alexandrovich)

Landis, John 1950- .... **CLC 26**
See also CA 112; 122

Landolfi, Tommaso 1908-1979 ... **CLC 11, 49**
See also CA 127; 117

Landon, Letitia Elizabeth
1802-1838 .... **NCLC 15**
See also DLB 96

Landor, Walter Savage
1775-1864 .... **NCLC 14**
See also DLB 93, 107

Landwirth, Heinz 1927-
See Lind, Jakov
See also CA 9-12R; CANR 7

Lane, Patrick 1939- .... **CLC 25**
See also CA 97-100; DAM POET; DLB 53;
INT 97-100

Lang, Andrew 1844-1912 .... **TCLC 16**
See also CA 114; 137; DLB 98, 141;
MAICYA; SATA 16

Lang, Fritz 1890-1976 .... **CLC 20**
See also CA 77-80; 69-72; CANR 30

Lange, John
See Crichton, (John) Michael

Langer, Elinor 1939- .... **CLC 34**
See also CA 121

Langland, William
1330(?)-1400(?) ...... **LC 19; DA; DAB;
DAC**
See also DAM MST, POET; DLB 146

Langstaff, Launcelot
See Irving, Washington

Lanier, Sidney 1842-1881 .... **NCLC 6**
See also DAM POET; DLB 64; DLBD 13;
MAICYA; SATA 18

Lanyer, Aemilia 1569-1645 ...... **LC 10, 30**
See also DLB 121

Lao Tzu .... **CMLC 7**

Lapine, James (Elliot) 1949- .... **CLC 39**
See also CA 123; 130; INT 130

Larbaud, Valery (Nicolas)
1881-1957 .... **TCLC 9**
See also CA 106

Lardner, Ring
See Lardner, Ring(gold) W(ilmer)

Lardner, Ring W., Jr.
See Lardner, Ring(gold) W(ilmer)

Lardner, Ring(gold) W(ilmer)
1885-1933 .... **TCLC 2, 14**
See also CA 104; 131; CDALB 1917-1929;
DLB 11, 25, 86; MTCW

Laredo, Betty
See Codrescu, Andrei

Larkin, Maia
See Wojciechowska, Maia (Teresa)

Larkin, Philip (Arthur)
1922-1985 .... **CLC 3, 5, 8, 9, 13, 18, 33,
39, 64; DAB**
See also CA 5-8R; 117; CANR 24;
CDBLB 1960 to Present; DAM MST,
POET; DLB 27; MTCW

Larra (y Sanchez de Castro), Mariano Jose de
1809-1837 .... **NCLC 17**

Larsen, Eric 1941- .... **CLC 55**
See also CA 132

Larsen, Nella 1891-1964 ..... **CLC 37; BLC**
See also BW 1; CA 125; DAM MULT;
DLB 51

Larson, Charles R(aymond) 1938- ... **CLC 31**
See also CA 53-56; CANR 4

Las Casas, Bartolome de 1474-1566 .. **LC 31**

Lasker-Schueler, Else 1869-1945 .. **TCLC 57**
See also DLB 66, 124

Latham, Jean Lee 1902- .... **CLC 12**
See also AITN 1; CA 5-8R; CANR 7;
MAICYA; SATA 2, 68

Latham, Mavis
See Clark, Mavis Thorpe

Leino, Eino . . . . TCLC **24**
See also Loennbohm, Armas Eino Leopold

Leiris, Michel (Julien) 1901-1990 . . . CLC **61**
See also CA 119; 128; 132

Leithauser, Brad 1953- . . . . CLC **27**
See also CA 107; CANR 27; DLB 120

Lelchuk, Alan 1938- . . . . CLC **5**
See also CA 45-48; CAAS 20; CANR 1

Lem, Stanislaw 1921- . . . . CLC **8, 15, 40**
See also CA 105; CAAS 1; CANR 32;
MTCW

Lemann, Nancy 1956- . . . . CLC **39**
See also CA 118; 136

Lemonnier, (Antoine Louis) Camille
1844-1913 . . . . TCLC **22**
See also CA 121

Lenau, Nikolaus 1802-1850 . . . . . . NCLC **16**

L'Engle, Madeleine (Camp Franklin)
1918- . . . . CLC **12**
See also AAYA 1; AITN 2; CA 1-4R;
CANR 3, 21, 39; CLR 1, 14; DAM POP;
DLB 52; JRDA; MAICYA; MTCW;
SAAS 15; SATA 1, 27, 75

Lengyel, Jozsef 1896-1975 . . . . CLC **7**
See also CA 85-88; 57-60

Lennon, John (Ono)
1940-1980 . . . . CLC **12, 35**
See also CA 102

Lennox, Charlotte Ramsay
1729(?)-1804 . . . . NCLC **23**
See also DLB 39

Lentricchia, Frank (Jr.) 1940- . . . . . . CLC **34**
See also CA 25-28R; CANR 19

Lenz, Siegfried 1926- . . . . CLC **27**
See also CA 89-92; DLB 75

Leonard, Elmore (John, Jr.)
1925- . . . . CLC **28, 34, 71**
See also AITN 1; BEST 89:1, 90:4;
CA 81-84; CANR 12, 28; DAM POP;
INT CANR-28; MTCW

Leonard, Hugh . . . . CLC **19**
See also Byrne, John Keyes
See also DLB 13

Leonov, Leonid (Maximovich)
1899-1994 . . . . CLC **92**
See also CA 129; DAM NOV; MTCW

Leopardi, (Conte) Giacomo
1798-1837 . . . . NCLC **22**

Le Reveler
See Artaud, Antonin (Marie Joseph)

Lerman, Eleanor 1952- . . . . CLC **9**
See also CA 85-88

Lerman, Rhoda 1936- . . . . CLC **56**
See also CA 49-52

Lermontov, Mikhail Yuryevich
1814-1841 . . . . NCLC **47**

Leroux, Gaston 1868-1927 . . . . TCLC **25**
See also CA 108; 136; SATA 65

Lesage, Alain-Rene 1668-1747 . . . . . . LC **28**

Leskov, Nikolai (Semyonovich)
1831-1895 . . . . NCLC **25**

Lessing, Doris (May)
1919- . . . . . CLC **1, 2, 3, 6, 10, 15, 22, 40,
94; DA; DAB; DAC; SSC 6**
See also CA 9-12R; CAAS 14; CANR 33;
CDBLB 1960 to Present; DAM MST,
NOV; DLB 15, 139; DLBY 85; MTCW

Lessing, Gotthold Ephraim
1729-1781 . . . . LC **8**
See also DLB 97

Lester, Richard 1932- . . . . CLC **20**

Lever, Charles (James)
1806-1872 . . . . NCLC **23**
See also DLB 21

Leverson, Ada 1865(?)-1936(?) . . . . TCLC **18**
See also Elaine
See also CA 117; DLB 153

Levertov, Denise
1923- . . . . . . CLC **1, 2, 3, 5, 8, 15, 28, 66;
PC 11**
See also CA 1-4R; CAAS 19; CANR 3, 29,
50; DAM POET; DLB 5, 165;
INT CANR-29; MTCW

Levi, Jonathan . . . . CLC **76**

Levi, Peter (Chad Tigar) 1931- . . . . . CLC **41**
See also CA 5-8R; CANR 34; DLB 40

Levi, Primo
1919-1987 . . . . CLC **37, 50; SSC 12**
See also CA 13-16R; 122; CANR 12, 33;
MTCW

Levin, Ira 1929- . . . . CLC **3, 6**
See also CA 21-24R; CANR 17, 44;
DAM POP; MTCW; SATA 66

Levin, Meyer 1905-1981 . . . . CLC **7**
See also AITN 1; CA 9-12R; 104;
CANR 15; DAM POP; DLB 9, 28;
DLBY 81; SATA 21; SATA-Obit 27

Levine, Norman 1924- . . . . CLC **54**
See also CA 73-76; CAAS 23; CANR 14;
DLB 88

Levine, Philip 1928- . . CLC **2, 4, 5, 9, 14, 33**
See also CA 9-12R; CANR 9, 37;
DAM POET; DLB 5

Levinson, Deirdre 1931- . . . . CLC **49**
See also CA 73-76

Levi-Strauss, Claude 1908- . . . . CLC **38**
See also CA 1-4R; CANR 6, 32; MTCW

Levitin, Sonia (Wolff) 1934- . . . . CLC **17**
See also AAYA 13; CA 29-32R; CANR 14,
32; JRDA; MAICYA; SAAS 2; SATA 4,
68

Levon, O. U.
See Kesey, Ken (Elton)

Lewes, George Henry
1817-1878 . . . . NCLC **25**
See also DLB 55, 144

Lewis, Alun 1915-1944 . . . . TCLC **3**
See also CA 104; DLB 20, 162

Lewis, C. Day
See Day Lewis, C(ecil)

Lewis, C(live) S(taples)
1898-1963 . . . . . CLC **1, 3, 6, 14, 27; DA;
DAB; DAC; WLC**
See also AAYA 3; CA 81-84; CANR 33;
CDBLB 1945-1960; CLR 3, 27;
DAM MST, NOV, POP; DLB 15, 100,
160; JRDA; MAICYA; MTCW;
SATA 13

Lewis, Janet 1899- . . . . CLC **41**
See also Winters, Janet Lewis
See also CA 9-12R; CANR 29; CAP 1;
DLBY 87

Lewis, Matthew Gregory
1775-1818 . . . . NCLC **11**
See also DLB 39, 158

Lewis, (Harry) Sinclair
1885-1951 . . . . . TCLC **4, 13, 23, 39; DA;
DAB; DAC; WLC**
See also CA 104; 133; CDALB 1917-1929;
DAM MST, NOV; DLB 9, 102; DLBD 1;
MTCW

Lewis, (Percy) Wyndham
1884(?)-1957 . . . . TCLC **2, 9**
See also CA 104; DLB 15

Lewisohn, Ludwig 1883-1955 . . . . . . TCLC **19**
See also CA 107; DLB 4, 9, 28, 102

Leyner, Mark 1956- . . . . CLC **92**
See also CA 110; CANR 28

Lezama Lima, Jose 1910-1976 . . . CLC **4, 10**
See also CA 77-80; DAM MULT;
DLB 113; HW

L'Heureux, John (Clarke) 1934- . . . . CLC **52**
See also CA 13-16R; CANR 23, 45

Liddell, C. H.
See Kuttner, Henry

Lie, Jonas (Lauritz Idemil)
1833-1908(?) . . . . TCLC **5**
See also CA 115

Lieber, Joel 1937-1971 . . . . CLC **6**
See also CA 73-76; 29-32R

Lieber, Stanley Martin
See Lee, Stan

Lieberman, Laurence (James)
1935- . . . . CLC **4, 36**
See also CA 17-20R; CANR 8, 36

Lieksman, Anders
See Haavikko, Paavo Juhani

Li Fei-kan 1904-
See Pa Chin
See also CA 105

Lifton, Robert Jay 1926- . . . . CLC **67**
See also CA 17-20R; CANR 27;
INT CANR-27; SATA 66

Lightfoot, Gordon 1938- . . . . CLC **26**
See also CA 109

Lightman, Alan P. 1948- . . . . CLC **81**
See also CA 141

Ligotti, Thomas (Robert)
1953- . . . . CLC **44; SSC 16**
See also CA 123; CANR 49

Li Ho 791-817 . . . . PC **13**

Liliencron, (Friedrich Adolf Axel) Detlev von
1844-1909 . . . . TCLC **18**
See also CA 117

Lilly, William 1602-1681 . . . . LC **27**

Lowell, Robert (Traill Spence, Jr.)
1917-1977 ... **CLC 1, 2, 3, 4, 5, 8, 9, 11,
15, 37; DA; DAB; DAC; PC 3; WLC**
See also CA 9-12R; 73-76; CABS 2;
CANR 26; DAM MST, NOV; DLB 5;
MTCW

Lowndes, Marie Adelaide (Belloc)
1868-1947 .... **TCLC 12**
See also CA 107; DLB 70

Lowry, (Clarence) Malcolm
1909-1957 .... **TCLC 6, 40**
See also CA 105; 131; CDBLB 1945-1960;
DLB 15; MTCW

Lowry, Mina Gertrude 1882-1966
See Loy, Mina
See also CA 113

Loxsmith, John
See Brunner, John (Kilian Houston)

Loy, Mina .... **CLC 28**
See also Lowry, Mina Gertrude
See also DAM POET; DLB 4, 54

Loyson-Bridet
See Schwob, (Mayer Andre) Marcel

Lucas, Craig 1951- .... **CLC 64**
See also CA 137

Lucas, George 1944- .... **CLC 16**
See also AAYA 1; CA 77-80; CANR 30;
SATA 56

Lucas, Hans
See Godard, Jean-Luc

Lucas, Victoria
See Plath, Sylvia

Ludlam, Charles 1943-1987 ..... **CLC 46, 50**
See also CA 85-88; 122

Ludlum, Robert 1927- .... **CLC 22, 43**
See also AAYA 10; BEST 89:1, 90:3;
CA 33-36R; CANR 25, 41; DAM NOV,
POP; DLBY 82; MTCW

Ludwig, Ken .... **CLC 60**

Ludwig, Otto 1813-1865 .... **NCLC 4**
See also DLB 129

Lugones, Leopoldo 1874-1938 ..... **TCLC 15**
See also CA 116; 131; HW

Lu Hsun 1881-1936 ...... **TCLC 3; SSC 20**
See also Shu-Jen, Chou

Lukacs, George .... **CLC 24**
See also Lukacs, Gyorgy (Szegeny von)

Lukacs, Gyorgy (Szegeny von) 1885-1971
See Lukacs, George
See also CA 101; 29-32R

Luke, Peter (Ambrose Cyprian)
1919-1995 .... **CLC 38**
See also CA 81-84; 147; DLB 13

Lunar, Dennis
See Mungo, Raymond

Lurie, Alison 1926- .... **CLC 4, 5, 18, 39**
See also CA 1-4R; CANR 2, 17, 50; DLB 2;
MTCW; SATA 46

Lustig, Arnost 1926- .... **CLC 56**
See also AAYA 3; CA 69-72; CANR 47;
SATA 56

Luther, Martin 1483-1546 .... **LC 9**

Luxemburg, Rosa 1870(?)-1919 .... **TCLC 63**
See also CA 118

Luzi, Mario 1914- .... **CLC 13**
See also CA 61-64; CANR 9; DLB 128

L'Ymagier
See Gourmont, Remy (-Marie-Charles) de

Lynch, B. Suarez
See Bioy Casares, Adolfo; Borges, Jorge
Luis

Lynch, David (K.) 1946- .... **CLC 66**
See also CA 124; 129

Lynch, James
See Andreyev, Leonid (Nikolaevich)

Lynch Davis, B.
See Bioy Casares, Adolfo; Borges, Jorge
Luis

Lyndsay, Sir David 1490-1555 ...... **LC 20**

Lynn, Kenneth S(chuyler) 1923- .... **CLC 50**
See also CA 1-4R; CANR 3, 27

Lynx
See West, Rebecca

Lyons, Marcus
See Blish, James (Benjamin)

Lyre, Pinchbeck
See Sassoon, Siegfried (Lorraine)

Lytle, Andrew (Nelson) 1902-1995 .. **CLC 22**
See also CA 9-12R; 150; DLB 6; DLBY 95

Lyttelton, George 1709-1773 .... **LC 10**

Maas, Peter 1929- .... **CLC 29**
See also CA 93-96; INT 93-96

Macaulay, Rose 1881-1958 ..... **TCLC 7, 44**
See also CA 104; DLB 36

Macaulay, Thomas Babington
1800-1859 .... **NCLC 42**
See also CDBLB 1832-1890; DLB 32, 55

MacBeth, George (Mann)
1932-1992 .... **CLC 2, 5, 9**
See also CA 25-28R; 136; DLB 40; MTCW;
SATA 4; SATA-Obit 70

MacCaig, Norman (Alexander)
1910- .... **CLC 36; DAB**
See also CA 9-12R; CANR 3, 34;
DAM POET; DLB 27

MacCarthy, (Sir Charles Otto) Desmond
1877-1952 .... **TCLC 36**

MacDiarmid, Hugh
.... **CLC 2, 4, 11, 19, 63; PC 9**
See also Grieve, C(hristopher) M(urray)
See also CDBLB 1945-1960; DLB 20

MacDonald, Anson
See Heinlein, Robert A(nson)

Macdonald, Cynthia 1928- ...... **CLC 13, 19**
See also CA 49-52; CANR 4, 44; DLB 105

MacDonald, George 1824-1905 ..... **TCLC 9**
See also CA 106; 137; DLB 18, 163;
MAICYA; SATA 33

Macdonald, John
See Millar, Kenneth

MacDonald, John D(ann)
1916-1986 .... **CLC 3, 27, 44**
See also CA 1-4R; 121; CANR 1, 19;
DAM NOV, POP; DLB 8; DLBY 86;
MTCW

Macdonald, John Ross
See Millar, Kenneth

Macdonald, Ross ..... **CLC 1, 2, 3, 14, 34, 41**
See also Millar, Kenneth
See also DLBD 6

MacDougal, John
See Blish, James (Benjamin)

MacEwen, Gwendolyn (Margaret)
1941-1987 .... **CLC 13, 55**
See also CA 9-12R; 124; CANR 7, 22;
DLB 53; SATA 50; SATA-Obit 55

Macha, Karel Hynek 1810-1846 .. **NCLC 46**

Machado (y Ruiz), Antonio
1875-1939 .... **TCLC 3**
See also CA 104; DLB 108

Machado de Assis, Joaquim Maria
1839-1908 .... **TCLC 10; BLC**
See also CA 107

Machen, Arthur .... **TCLC 4; SSC 20**
See also Jones, Arthur Llewellyn
See also DLB 36, 156

Machiavelli, Niccolo
1469-1527 ...... **LC 8; DA; DAB; DAC**
See also DAM MST

MacInnes, Colin 1914-1976 ...... **CLC 4, 23**
See also CA 69-72; 65-68; CANR 21;
DLB 14; MTCW

MacInnes, Helen (Clark)
1907-1985 .... **CLC 27, 39**
See also CA 1-4R; 117; CANR 1, 28;
DAM POP; DLB 87; MTCW; SATA 22;
SATA-Obit 44

Mackay, Mary 1855-1924
See Corelli, Marie
See also CA 118

Mackenzie, Compton (Edward Montague)
1883-1972 .... **CLC 18**
See also CA 21-22; 37-40R; CAP 2;
DLB 34, 100

Mackenzie, Henry 1745-1831 .... **NCLC 41**
See also DLB 39

Mackintosh, Elizabeth 1896(?)-1952
See Tey, Josephine
See also CA 110

MacLaren, James
See Grieve, C(hristopher) M(urray)

Mac Laverty, Bernard 1942- .... **CLC 31**
See also CA 116; 118; CANR 43; INT 118

MacLean, Alistair (Stuart)
1922-1987 .... **CLC 3, 13, 50, 63**
See also CA 57-60; 121; CANR 28;
DAM POP; MTCW; SATA 23;
SATA-Obit 50

Maclean, Norman (Fitzroy)
1902-1990 .... **CLC 78; SSC 13**
See also CA 102; 132; CANR 49;
DAM POP

MacLeish, Archibald
1892-1982 .... **CLC 3, 8, 14, 68**
See also CA 9-12R; 106; CANR 33;
DAM POET; DLB 4, 7, 45; DLBY 82;
MTCW

MacLennan, (John) Hugh
1907-1990 .... **CLC 2, 14, 92; DAC**
See also CA 5-8R; 142; CANR 33;
DAM MST; DLB 68; MTCW

MacLeod, Alistair 1936- ..... **CLC 56; DAC**
See also CA 123; DAM MST; DLB 60

McNickle, (William) D'Arcy
1904-1977 . . . . **CLC 89**
See also CA 9-12R; 85-88; CANR 5, 45;
DAM MULT; NNAL; SATA-Obit 22

McPhee, John (Angus) 1931- . . . . . . **CLC 36**
See also BEST 90:1; CA 65-68; CANR 20,
46; MTCW

McPherson, James Alan
1943- . . . . **CLC 19, 77**
See also BW 1; CA 25-28R; CAAS 17;
CANR 24; DLB 38; MTCW

McPherson, William (Alexander)
1933- . . . . **CLC 34**
See also CA 69-72; CANR 28;
INT CANR-28

Mead, Margaret 1901-1978 . . . . **CLC 37**
See also AITN 1; CA 1-4R; 81-84;
CANR 4; MTCW; SATA-Obit 20

Meaker, Marijane (Agnes) 1927-
See Kerr, M. E.
See also CA 107; CANR 37; INT 107;
JRDA; MAICYA; MTCW; SATA 20, 61

Medoff, Mark (Howard) 1940- . . . **CLC 6, 23**
See also AITN 1; CA 53-56; CANR 5;
DAM DRAM; DLB 7; INT CANR-5

Medvedev, P. N.
See Bakhtin, Mikhail Mikhailovich

Meged, Aharon
See Megged, Aharon

Meged, Aron
See Megged, Aharon

Megged, Aharon 1920- . . . . **CLC 9**
See also CA 49-52; CAAS 13; CANR 1

Mehta, Ved (Parkash) 1934- . . . . **CLC 37**
See also CA 1-4R; CANR 2, 23; MTCW

Melanter
See Blackmore, R(ichard) D(oddridge)

Melikow, Loris
See Hofmannsthal, Hugo von

Melmoth, Sebastian
See Wilde, Oscar (Fingal O'Flahertie Wills)

Meltzer, Milton 1915- . . . . **CLC 26**
See also AAYA 8; CA 13-16R; CANR 38;
CLR 13; DLB 61; JRDA; MAICYA;
SAAS 1; SATA 1, 50, 80

Melville, Herman
1819-1891 . . . . . **NCLC 3, 12, 29, 45, 49;**
DA; DAB; DAC; SSC 1, 17; WLC
See also CDALB 1640-1865; DAM MST,
NOV; DLB 3, 74; SATA 59

Menander
c. 342B.C.-c. 292B.C. . . . . **CMLC 9; DC 3**
See also DAM DRAM

Mencken, H(enry) L(ouis)
1880-1956 . . . . **TCLC 13**
See also CA 105; 125; CDALB 1917-1929;
DLB 11, 29, 63, 137; MTCW

Mercer, David 1928-1980 . . . . **CLC 5**
See also CA 9-12R; 102; CANR 23;
DAM DRAM; DLB 13; MTCW

Merchant, Paul
See Ellison, Harlan (Jay)

Meredith, George 1828-1909 . . . **TCLC 17, 43**
See also CA 117; CDBLB 1832-1890;
DAM POET; DLB 18, 35, 57, 159

Meredith, William (Morris)
1919- . . . . **CLC 4, 13, 22, 55**
See also CA 9-12R; CAAS 14; CANR 6, 40;
DAM POET; DLB 5

Merezhkovsky, Dmitry Sergeyevich
1865-1941 . . . . **TCLC 29**

Merimee, Prosper
1803-1870 . . . . **NCLC 6; SSC 7**
See also DLB 119

Merkin, Daphne 1954- . . . . **CLC 44**
See also CA 123

Merlin, Arthur
See Blish, James (Benjamin)

Merrill, James (Ingram)
1926-1995 . . . . **CLC 2, 3, 6, 8, 13, 18, 34,**
91
See also CA 13-16R; 147; CANR 10, 49;
DAM POET; DLB 5, 165; DLBY 85;
INT CANR-10; MTCW

Merriman, Alex
See Silverberg, Robert

Merritt, E. B.
See Waddington, Miriam

Merton, Thomas
1915-1968 . . **CLC 1, 3, 11, 34, 83; PC 10**
See also CA 5-8R; 25-28R; CANR 22;
DLB 48; DLBY 81; MTCW

Merwin, W(illiam) S(tanley)
1927- . . . **CLC 1, 2, 3, 5, 8, 13, 18, 45, 88**
See also CA 13-16R; CANR 15, 51;
DAM POET; DLB 5; INT CANR-15;
MTCW

Metcalf, John 1938- . . . . **CLC 37**
See also CA 113; DLB 60

Metcalf, Suzanne
See Baum, L(yman) Frank

Mew, Charlotte (Mary)
1870-1928 . . . . **TCLC 8**
See also CA 105; DLB 19, 135

Mewshaw, Michael 1943- . . . . **CLC 9**
See also CA 53-56; CANR 7, 47; DLBY 80

Meyer, June
See Jordan, June

Meyer, Lynn
See Slavitt, David R(ytman)

Meyer-Meyrink, Gustav 1868-1932
See Meyrink, Gustav
See also CA 117

Meyers, Jeffrey 1939- . . . . **CLC 39**
See also CA 73-76; DLB 111

Meynell, Alice (Christina Gertrude Thompson)
1847-1922 . . . . **TCLC 6**
See also CA 104; DLB 19, 98

Meyrink, Gustav . . . . **TCLC 21**
See also Meyer-Meyrink, Gustav
See also DLB 81

Michaels, Leonard
1933- . . . . **CLC 6, 25; SSC 16**
See also CA 61-64; CANR 21; DLB 130;
MTCW

Michaux, Henri 1899-1984 . . . . . . **CLC 8, 19**
See also CA 85-88; 114

Michelangelo 1475-1564 . . . . **LC 12**

Michelet, Jules 1798-1874 . . . . **NCLC 31**

Michener, James A(lbert)
1907(?)- . . . . **CLC 1, 5, 11, 29, 60**
See also AITN 1; BEST 90:1; CA 5-8R;
CANR 21, 45; DAM NOV, POP; DLB 6;
MTCW

Mickiewicz, Adam 1798-1855 . . . . . **NCLC 3**

Middleton, Christopher 1926- . . . . . . **CLC 13**
See also CA 13-16R; CANR 29; DLB 40

Middleton, Richard (Barham)
1882-1911 . . . . **TCLC 56**
See also DLB 156

Middleton, Stanley 1919- . . . . **CLC 7, 38**
See also CA 25-28R; CAAS 23; CANR 21,
46; DLB 14

Middleton, Thomas
1580-1627 . . . . **LC 33; DC 5**
See also DAM DRAM, MST; DLB 58

Migueis, Jose Rodrigues 1901- . . . . . **CLC 10**

Mikszath, Kalman 1847-1910 . . . . . **TCLC 31**

Miles, Josephine
1911-1985 . . . . **CLC 1, 2, 14, 34, 39**
See also CA 1-4R; 116; CANR 2;
DAM POET; DLB 48

Militant
See Sandburg, Carl (August)

Mill, John Stuart 1806-1873 . . . . . **NCLC 11**
See also CDBLB 1832-1890; DLB 55

Millar, Kenneth 1915-1983 . . . . **CLC 14**
See also Macdonald, Ross
See also CA 9-12R; 110; CANR 16;
DAM POP; DLB 2; DLBD 6; DLBY 83;
MTCW

Millay, E. Vincent
See Millay, Edna St. Vincent

Millay, Edna St. Vincent
1892-1950 . . . . . . **TCLC 4, 49; DA; DAB;**
DAC; PC 6
See also CA 104; 130; CDALB 1917-1929;
DAM MST, POET; DLB 45; MTCW

Miller, Arthur
1915- . . . . **CLC 1, 2, 6, 10, 15, 26, 47, 78;**
DA; DAB; DAC; DC 1; WLC
See also AAYA 15; AITN 1; CA 1-4R;
CABS 3; CANR 2, 30;
CDALB 1941-1968; DAM DRAM, MST;
DLB 7; MTCW

Miller, Henry (Valentine)
1891-1980 . . . . **CLC 1, 2, 4, 9, 14, 43, 84;**
DA; DAB; DAC; WLC
See also CA 9-12R; 97-100; CANR 33;
CDALB 1929-1941; DAM MST, NOV;
DLB 4, 9; DLBY 80; MTCW

Miller, Jason 1939(?)- . . . . **CLC 2**
See also AITN 1; CA 73-76; DLB 7

Miller, Sue 1943- . . . . **CLC 44**
See also BEST 90:3; CA 139; DAM POP;
DLB 143

Miller, Walter M(ichael), Jr.
1923- . . . . **CLC 4, 30**
See also CA 85-88; DLB 8

Millett, Kate 1934- . . . . **CLC 67**
See also AITN 1; CA 73-76; CANR 32;
MTCW

Millhauser, Steven 1943- . . . . **CLC 21, 54**
See also CA 110; 111; DLB 2; INT 111

Millin, Sarah Gertrude 1889-1968 . . **CLC 49**
See also CA 102; 93-96

Milne, A(lan) A(lexander)
1882-1956 . . . . **TCLC 6; DAB; DAC**
See also CA 104; 133; CLR 1, 26;
DAM MST; DLB 10, 77, 100, 160;
MAICYA; MTCW; YABC 1

Milner, Ron(ald) 1938- . . . . . . **CLC 56; BLC**
See also AITN 1; BW 1; CA 73-76;
CANR 24; DAM MULT; DLB 38;
MTCW

Milosz, Czeslaw
1911- . . . **CLC 5, 11, 22, 31, 56, 82; PC 8**
See also CA 81-84; CANR 23, 51;
DAM MST, POET; MTCW

Milton, John
1608-1674 . . . . . . **LC 9; DA; DAB; DAC;**
WLC
See also CDBLB 1660-1789; DAM MST,
POET; DLB 131, 151

Min, Anchee 1957- . . . . **CLC 86**
See also CA 146

Minehaha, Cornelius
See Wedekind, (Benjamin) Frank(lin)

Miner, Valerie 1947- . . . . **CLC 40**
See also CA 97-100

Minimo, Duca
See D'Annunzio, Gabriele

Minot, Susan 1956- . . . . **CLC 44**
See also CA 134

Minus, Ed 1938- . . . . **CLC 39**

Miranda, Javier
See Bioy Casares, Adolfo

Mirbeau, Octave 1848-1917 . . . . **TCLC 55**
See also DLB 123

Miro (Ferrer), Gabriel (Francisco Victor)
1879-1930 . . . . **TCLC 5**
See also CA 104

Mishima, Yukio
. . . . . . **CLC 2, 4, 6, 9, 27; DC 1; SSC 4**
See also Hiraoka, Kimitake

Mistral, Frederic 1830-1914 . . . . . . **TCLC 51**
See also CA 122

Mistral, Gabriela . . . . **TCLC 2; HLC**
See also Godoy Alcayaga, Lucila

Mistry, Rohinton 1952- . . . . . . **CLC 71; DAC**
See also CA 141

Mitchell, Clyde
See Ellison, Harlan (Jay); Silverberg, Robert

Mitchell, James Leslie 1901-1935
See Gibbon, Lewis Grassic
See also CA 104; DLB 15

Mitchell, Joni 1943- . . . . **CLC 12**
See also CA 112

Mitchell, Margaret (Munnerlyn)
1900-1949 . . . . **TCLC 11**
See also CA 109; 125; DAM NOV, POP;
DLB 9; MTCW

Mitchell, Peggy
See Mitchell, Margaret (Munnerlyn)

Mitchell, S(ilas) Weir 1829-1914 . . **TCLC 36**

Mitchell, W(illiam) O(rmond)
1914- . . . . **CLC 25; DAC**
See also CA 77-80; CANR 15, 43;
DAM MST; DLB 88

Mitford, Mary Russell 1787-1855 . . **NCLC 4**
See also DLB 110, 116

Mitford, Nancy 1904-1973 . . . . **CLC 44**
See also CA 9-12R

Miyamoto, Yuriko 1899-1951 . . . . . **TCLC 37**

Mo, Timothy (Peter) 1950(?)- . . . . . . **CLC 46**
See also CA 117; MTCW

Modarressi, Taghi (M.) 1931- . . . . . . **CLC 44**
See also CA 121; 134; INT 134

Modiano, Patrick (Jean) 1945- . . . . . **CLC 18**
See also CA 85-88; CANR 17, 40; DLB 83

Moerck, Paal
See Roelvaag, O(le) E(dvart)

Mofolo, Thomas (Mokopu)
1875(?)-1948 . . . . **TCLC 22; BLC**
See also CA 121; DAM MULT

Mohr, Nicholasa 1935- . . . . . . **CLC 12; HLC**
See also AAYA 8; CA 49-52; CANR 1, 32;
CLR 22; DAM MULT; DLB 145; HW;
JRDA; SAAS 8; SATA 8

Mojtabai, A(nn) G(race)
1938- . . . . **CLC 5, 9, 15, 29**
See also CA 85-88

Moliere
1622-1673 . . . . . **LC 28; DA; DAB; DAC;**
WLC
See also DAM DRAM, MST

Molin, Charles
See Mayne, William (James Carter)

Molnar, Ferenc 1878-1952 . . . . **TCLC 20**
See also CA 109; DAM DRAM

Momaday, N(avarre) Scott
1934- . . . **CLC 2, 19, 85; DA; DAB; DAC**
See also AAYA 11; CA 25-28R; CANR 14,
34; DAM MST, MULT, NOV, POP;
DLB 143; INT CANR-14; MTCW;
NNAL; SATA 48; SATA-Brief 30

Monette, Paul 1945-1995 . . . . **CLC 82**
See also CA 139; 147

Monroe, Harriet 1860-1936 . . . . **TCLC 12**
See also CA 109; DLB 54, 91

Monroe, Lyle
See Heinlein, Robert A(nson)

Montagu, Elizabeth 1917- . . . . **NCLC 7**
See also CA 9-12R

Montagu, Mary (Pierrepont) Wortley
1689-1762 . . . . **LC 9**
See also DLB 95, 101

Montagu, W. H.
See Coleridge, Samuel Taylor

Montague, John (Patrick)
1929- . . . . **CLC 13, 46**
See also CA 9-12R; CANR 9; DLB 40;
MTCW

Montaigne, Michel (Eyquem) de
1533-1592 . . . . . . **LC 8; DA; DAB; DAC;**
WLC
See also DAM MST

Montale, Eugenio
1896-1981 . . . . **CLC 7, 9, 18; PC 13**
See also CA 17-20R; 104; CANR 30;
DLB 114; MTCW

Montesquieu, Charles-Louis de Secondat
1689-1755 . . . . **LC 7**

Montgomery, (Robert) Bruce 1921-1978
See Crispin, Edmund
See also CA 104

Montgomery, L(ucy) M(aud)
1874-1942 . . . . **TCLC 51; DAC**
See also AAYA 12; CA 108; 137; CLR 8;
DAM MST; DLB 92; JRDA; MAICYA;
YABC 1

Montgomery, Marion H., Jr. 1925- . . **CLC 7**
See also AITN 1; CA 1-4R; CANR 3, 48;
DLB 6

Montgomery, Max
See Davenport, Guy (Mattison, Jr.)

Montherlant, Henry (Milon) de
1896-1972 . . . . **CLC 8, 19**
See also CA 85-88; 37-40R; DAM DRAM;
DLB 72; MTCW

Monty Python
See Chapman, Graham; Cleese, John
(Marwood); Gilliam, Terry (Vance); Idle,
Eric; Jones, Terence Graham Parry; Palin,
Michael (Edward)
See also AAYA 7

Moodie, Susanna (Strickland)
1803-1885 . . . . **NCLC 14**
See also DLB 99

Mooney, Edward 1951-
See Mooney, Ted
See also CA 130

Mooney, Ted . . . . **CLC 25**
See also Mooney, Edward

Moorcock, Michael (John)
1939- . . . . **CLC 5, 27, 58**
See also CA 45-48; CAAS 5; CANR 2, 17,
38; DLB 14; MTCW

Moore, Brian
1921- . . . . . . **CLC 1, 3, 5, 7, 8, 19, 32, 90;**
DAB; DAC
See also CA 1-4R; CANR 1, 25, 42;
DAM MST; MTCW

Moore, Edward
See Muir, Edwin

Moore, George Augustus
1852-1933 . . . . **TCLC 7; SSC 19**
See also CA 104; DLB 10, 18, 57, 135

Moore, Lorrie . . . . **CLC 39, 45, 68**
See also Moore, Marie Lorena

Moore, Marianne (Craig)
1887-1972 . . . . **CLC 1, 2, 4, 8, 10, 13, 19,**
47; DA; DAB; DAC; PC 4
See also CA 1-4R; 33-36R; CANR 3;
CDALB 1929-1941; DAM MST, POET;
DLB 45; DLBD 7; MTCW; SATA 20

Moore, Marie Lorena 1957-
See Moore, Lorrie
See also CA 116; CANR 39

Moore, Thomas 1779-1852 . . . . **NCLC 6**
See also DLB 96, 144

Morand, Paul 1888-1976 . . **CLC 41; SSC 22**
See also CA 69-72; DLB 65

Morante, Elsa 1918-1985 . . . . **CLC 8, 47**
See also CA 85-88; 117; CANR 35; MTCW

Moravia, Alberto . . . . . . **CLC 2, 7, 11, 27, 46**
See also Pincherle, Alberto

More, Hannah 1745-1833 . . . . **NCLC 27**
See also DLB 107, 109, 116, 158

More, Henry 1614-1687 . . . . **LC 9**
See also DLB 126

More, Sir Thomas 1478-1535 . . . . **LC 10, 32**

Moreas, Jean . . . . **TCLC 18**
See also Papadiamantopoulos, Johannes

Morgan, Berry 1919- . . . . **CLC 6**
See also CA 49-52; DLB 6

Morgan, Claire
See Highsmith, (Mary) Patricia

Morgan, Edwin (George) 1920- . . . . . **CLC 31**
See also CA 5-8R; CANR 3, 43; DLB 27

Morgan, (George) Frederick
1922- . . . . **CLC 23**
See also CA 17-20R; CANR 21

Morgan, Harriet
See Mencken, H(enry) L(ouis)

Morgan, Jane
See Cooper, James Fenimore

Morgan, Janet 1945- . . . . **CLC 39**
See also CA 65-68

Morgan, Lady 1776(?)-1859 . . . . . . **NCLC 29**
See also DLB 116, 158

Morgan, Robin 1941- . . . . **CLC 2**
See also CA 69-72; CANR 29; MTCW;
SATA 80

Morgan, Scott
See Kuttner, Henry

Morgan, Seth 1949(?)-1990 . . . . **CLC 65**
See also CA 132

Morgenstern, Christian
1871-1914 . . . . **TCLC 8**
See also CA 105

Morgenstern, S.
See Goldman, William (W.)

Moricz, Zsigmond 1879-1942 . . . . . **TCLC 33**

Morike, Eduard (Friedrich)
1804-1875 . . . . **NCLC 10**
See also DLB 133

Mori Ogai . . . . **TCLC 14**
See also Mori Rintaro

Mori Rintaro 1862-1922
See Mori Ogai
See also CA 110

Moritz, Karl Philipp 1756-1793 . . . . . . **LC 2**
See also DLB 94

Morland, Peter Henry
See Faust, Frederick (Schiller)

Morren, Theophil
See Hofmannsthal, Hugo von

Morris, Bill 1952- . . . . **CLC 76**

Morris, Julian
See West, Morris L(anglo)

Morris, Steveland Judkins 1950(?)-
See Wonder, Stevie
See also CA 111

Morris, William 1834-1896 . . . . **NCLC 4**
See also CDBLB 1832-1890; DLB 18, 35,
57, 156

Morris, Wright 1910- . . . **CLC 1, 3, 7, 18, 37**
See also CA 9-12R; CANR 21; DLB 2;
DLBY 81; MTCW

Morrison, Chloe Anthony Wofford
See Morrison, Toni

Morrison, James Douglas 1943-1971
See Morrison, Jim
See also CA 73-76; CANR 40

Morrison, Jim . . . . **CLC 17**
See also Morrison, James Douglas

Morrison, Toni
1931- . . . . **CLC 4, 10, 22, 55, 81, 87;**
BLC; DA; DAB; DAC
See also AAYA 1; BW 2; CA 29-32R;
CANR 27, 42; CDALB 1968-1988;
DAM MST, MULT, NOV, POP; DLB 6,
33, 143; DLBY 81; MTCW; SATA 57

Morrison, Van 1945- . . . . **CLC 21**
See also CA 116

Mortimer, John (Clifford)
1923- . . . . **CLC 28, 43**
See also CA 13-16R; CANR 21;
CDBLB 1960 to Present; DAM DRAM,
POP; DLB 13; INT CANR-21; MTCW

Mortimer, Penelope (Ruth) 1918- . . . . **CLC 5**
See also CA 57-60; CANR 45

Morton, Anthony
See Creasey, John

Mosher, Howard Frank 1943- . . . . . . **CLC 62**
See also CA 139

Mosley, Nicholas 1923- . . . . **CLC 43, 70**
See also CA 69-72; CANR 41; DLB 14

Moss, Howard
1922-1987 . . . . **CLC 7, 14, 45, 50**
See also CA 1-4R; 123; CANR 1, 44;
DAM POET; DLB 5

Mossgiel, Rab
See Burns, Robert

Motion, Andrew (Peter) 1952- . . . . . . **CLC 47**
See also CA 146, DLB 40

Motley, Willard (Francis)
1909-1965 . . . . **CLC 18**
See also BW 1; CA 117; 106; DLB 76, 143

Motoori, Norinaga 1730-1801 . . . . **NCLC 45**

Mott, Michael (Charles Alston)
1930- . . . . **CLC 15, 34**
See also CA 5-8R; CAAS 7; CANR 7, 29

Mountain Wolf Woman
1884-1960 . . . . **CLC 92**
See also CA 144; NNAL

Moure, Erin 1955- . . . . **CLC 88**
See also CA 113; DLB 60

Mowat, Farley (McGill)
1921- . . . . **CLC 26; DAC**
See also AAYA 1; CA 1-4R; CANR 4, 24,
42; CLR 20; DAM MST; DLB 68;
INT CANAR-24; JRDA; MAICYA;
MTCW; SATA 3, 55

Moyers, Bill 1934- . . . . **CLC 74**
See also AITN 2; CA 61-64; CANR 31

Mphahlele, Es'kia
See Mphahlele, Ezekiel
See also DLB 125

Mphahlele, Ezekiel 1919- . . . . . **CLC 25; BLC**
See also Mphahlele, Es'kia
See also BW 2; CA 81-84; CANR 26;
DAM MULT

Mqhayi, S(amuel) E(dward) K(rune Loliwe)
1875-1945 . . . . **TCLC 25; BLC**
See also DAM MULT

Mr. Martin
See Burroughs, William S(eward)

Mrozek, Slawomir 1930- . . . . **CLC 3, 13**
See also CA 13-16R; CAAS 10; CANR 29;
MTCW

Mrs. Belloc-Lowndes
See Lowndes, Marie Adelaide (Belloc)

Mtwa, Percy (?) . . . . **CLC 47**

Mueller, Lisel 1924- . . . . **CLC 13, 51**
See also CA 93-96; DLB 105

Muir, Edwin 1887-1959 . . . . **TCLC 2**
See also CA 104; DLB 20, 100

Muir, John 1838-1914 . . . . **TCLC 28**

Mujica Lainez, Manuel
1910-1984 . . . . **CLC 31**
See also Lainez, Manuel Mujica
See also CA 81-84; 112; CANR 32; HW

Mukherjee, Bharati 1940- . . . . **CLC 53**
See also BEST 89:2; CA 107; CANR 45;
DAM NOV; DLB 60; MTCW

Muldoon, Paul 1951- . . . . **CLC 32, 72**
See also CA 113; 129; DAM POET;
DLB 40; INT 129

Mulisch, Harry 1927- . . . . **CLC 42**
See also CA 9-12R; CANR 6, 26

Mull, Martin 1943- . . . . **CLC 17**
See also CA 105

Mulock, Dinah Maria
See Craik, Dinah Maria (Mulock)

Munford, Robert 1737(?)-1783 . . . . **LC 5**
See also DLB 31

Mungo, Raymond 1946- . . . . **CLC 72**
See also CA 49-52; CANR 2

Munro, Alice
1931- . . . **CLC 6, 10, 19, 50; DAC; SSC 3**
See also AITN 2; CA 33-36R; CANR 33;
DAM MST, NOV; DLB 53; MTCW;
SATA 29

Munro, H(ector) H(ugh) 1870-1916
See Saki
See also CA 104; 130; CDBLB 1890-1914;
DA; DAB; DAC; DAM MST, NOV;
DLB 34, 162; MTCW; WLC

Murasaki, Lady . . . . **CMLC 1**

Murdoch, (Jean) Iris
1919- . . . . . . **CLC 1, 2, 3, 4, 6, 8, 11, 15,**
22, 31, 51; DAB; DAC
See also CA 13-16R; CANR 8, 43;
CDBLB 1960 to Present; DAM MST,
NOV; DLB 14; INT CANR-8; MTCW

Murfree, Mary Noailles
1850-1922 . . . . **SSC 22**
See also CA 122; DLB 12, 74

Murnau, Friedrich Wilhelm
See Plumpe, Friedrich Wilhelm

Nik. T. O.
See Annensky, Innokenty Fyodorovich

Nin, Anais
1903-1977 ..... **CLC 1, 4, 8, 11, 14, 60;
SSC 10**
See also AITN 2; CA 13-16R; 69-72;
CANR 22; DAM NOV, POP; DLB 2, 4,
152; MTCW

Nishiwaki, Junzaburo 1894-1982 .... **PC 15**
See also CA 107

Nissenson, Hugh 1933- .... **CLC 4, 9**
See also CA 17-20R; CANR 27; DLB 28

Niven, Larry .... **CLC 8**
See also Niven, Laurence Van Cott
See also DLB 8

Niven, Laurence Van Cott 1938-
See Niven, Larry
See also CA 21-24R; CAAS 12; CANR 14,
44; DAM POP; MTCW

Nixon, Agnes Eckhardt 1927- ...... **CLC 21**
See also CA 110

Nizan, Paul 1905-1940 .... **TCLC 40**
See also DLB 72

Nkosi, Lewis 1936- .... **CLC 45; BLC**
See also BW 1; CA 65-68; CANR 27;
DAM MULT; DLB 157

Nodier, (Jean) Charles (Emmanuel)
1780-1844 .... **NCLC 19**
See also DLB 119

Nolan, Christopher 1965- .... **CLC 58**
See also CA 111

Noon, Jeff 1957- .... **CLC 91**
See also CA 148

Norden, Charles
See Durrell, Lawrence (George)

Nordhoff, Charles (Bernard)
1887-1947 .... **TCLC 23**
See also CA 108; DLB 9; SATA 23

Norfolk, Lawrence 1963- .... **CLC 76**
See also CA 144

Norman, Marsha 1947- .... **CLC 28**
See also CA 105; CABS 3; CANR 41;
DAM DRAM; DLBY 84

Norris, Benjamin Franklin, Jr.
1870-1902 .... **TCLC 24**
See also Norris, Frank
See also CA 110

Norris, Frank
See Norris, Benjamin Franklin, Jr.
See also CDALB 1865-1917; DLB 12, 71

Norris, Leslie 1921- .... **CLC 14**
See also CA 11-12; CANR 14; CAP 1;
DLB 27

North, Andrew
See Norton, Andre

North, Anthony
See Koontz, Dean R(ay)

North, Captain George
See Stevenson, Robert Louis (Balfour)

North, Milou
See Erdrich, Louise

Northrup, B. A.
See Hubbard, L(afayette) Ron(ald)

North Staffs
See Hulme, T(homas) E(rnest)

Norton, Alice Mary
See Norton, Andre
See also MAICYA; SATA 1, 43

Norton, Andre 1912- .... **CLC 12**
See also Norton, Alice Mary
See also AAYA 14; CA 1-4R; CANR 2, 31;
DLB 8, 52; JRDA; MTCW

Norton, Caroline 1808-1877 ...... **NCLC 47**
See also DLB 21, 159

Norway, Nevil Shute 1899-1960
See Shute, Nevil
See also CA 102; 93-96

Norwid, Cyprian Kamil
1821-1883 .... **NCLC 17**

Nosille, Nabrah
See Ellison, Harlan (Jay)

Nossack, Hans Erich 1901-1978 ..... **CLC 6**
See also CA 93-96; 85-88; DLB 69

Nostradamus 1503-1566 .... **LC 27**

Nosu, Chuji
See Ozu, Yasujiro

Notenburg, Eleanora (Genrikhovna) von
See Guro, Elena

Nova, Craig 1945- .... **CLC 7, 31**
See also CA 45-48; CANR 2

Novak, Joseph
See Kosinski, Jerzy (Nikodem)

Novalis 1772-1801 .... **NCLC 13**
See also DLB 90

Nowlan, Alden (Albert)
1933-1983 .... **CLC 15; DAC**
See also CA 9-12R; CANR 5; DAM MST;
DLB 53

Noyes, Alfred 1880-1958 .... **TCLC 7**
See also CA 104; DLB 20

Nunn, Kem 19(?)- .... **CLC 34**

Nye, Robert 1939- .... **CLC 13, 42**
See also CA 33-36R; CANR 29;
DAM NOV; DLB 14; MTCW; SATA 6

Nyro, Laura 1947- .... **CLC 17**

Oates, Joyce Carol
1938- ...... **CLC 1, 2, 3, 6, 9, 11, 15, 19,
33, 52; DA; DAB; DAC; SSC 6; WLC**
See also AAYA 15; AITN 1; BEST 89:2;
CA 5-8R; CANR 25, 45;
CDALB 1968-1988; DAM MST, NOV,
POP; DLB 2, 5, 130; DLBY 81;
INT CANR-25; MTCW

O'Brien, Darcy 1939- .... **CLC 11**
See also CA 21-24R; CANR 8

O'Brien, E. G.
See Clarke, Arthur C(harles)

O'Brien, Edna
1936- ... **CLC 3, 5, 8, 13, 36, 65; SSC 10**
See also CA 1-4R; CANR 6, 41;
CDBLB 1960 to Present; DAM NOV;
DLB 14; MTCW

O'Brien, Fitz-James 1828-1862... **NCLC 21**
See also DLB 74

O'Brien, Flann .... **CLC 1, 4, 5, 7, 10, 47**
See also O Nuallain, Brian

O'Brien, Richard 1942- .... **CLC 17**
See also CA 124

O'Brien, Tim 1946- .... **CLC 7, 19, 40**
See also AAYA 16; CA 85-88; CANR 40;
DAM POP; DLB 152; DLBD 9;
DLBY 80

Obstfelder, Sigbjoern 1866-1900... **TCLC 23**
See also CA 123

O'Casey, Sean
1880-1964 ...... **CLC 1, 5, 9, 11, 15, 88;
DAB; DAC**
See also CA 89-92; CDBLB 1914-1945;
DAM DRAM, MST; DLB 10; MTCW

O'Cathasaigh, Sean
See O'Casey, Sean

Ochs, Phil 1940-1976 .... **CLC 17**
See also CA 65-68

O'Connor, Edwin (Greene)
1918-1968 .... **CLC 14**
See also CA 93-96; 25-28R

O'Connor, (Mary) Flannery
1925-1964 .... **CLC 1, 2, 3, 6, 10, 13, 15,
21, 66; DA; DAB; DAC; SSC 1, 23; WLC**
See also AAYA 7; CA 1-4R; CANR 3, 41;
CDALB 1941-1968; DAM MST, NOV;
DLB 2, 152; DLBD 12; DLBY 80;
MTCW

O'Connor, Frank .... **CLC 23; SSC 5**
See also O'Donovan, Michael John
See also DLB 162

O'Dell, Scott 1898-1989 .... **CLC 30**
See also AAYA 3; CA 61-64; 129;
CANR 12, 30; CLR 1, 16; DLB 52;
JRDA; MAICYA; SATA 12, 60

Odets, Clifford
1906-1963 .... **CLC 2, 28; DC 6**
See also CA 85-88; DAM DRAM; DLB 7,
26; MTCW

O'Doherty, Brian 1934- .... **CLC 76**
See also CA 105

O'Donnell, K. M.
See Malzberg, Barry N(athaniel)

O'Donnell, Lawrence
See Kuttner, Henry

O'Donovan, Michael John
1903-1966 .... **CLC 14**
See also O'Connor, Frank
See also CA 93-96

Oe, Kenzaburo
1935- .... **CLC 10, 36, 86; SSC 20**
See also CA 97-100; CANR 36, 50;
DAM NOV; DLBY 94; MTCW

O'Faolain, Julia 1932- .... **CLC 6, 19, 47**
See also CA 81-84; CAAS 2; CANR 12;
DLB 14; MTCW

O'Faolain, Sean
1900-1991 .... **CLC 1, 7, 14, 32, 70;
SSC 13**
See also CA 61-64; 134; CANR 12;
DLB 15, 162; MTCW

O'Flaherty, Liam
1896-1984 .... **CLC 5, 34; SSC 6**
See also CA 101; 113; CANR 35; DLB 36,
162; DLBY 84; MTCW

Ogilvy, Gavin
See Barrie, J(ames) M(atthew)

Palazzeschi, Aldo 1885-1974 . . . . **CLC 11**
See also CA 89-92; 53-56; DLB 114

Paley, Grace 1922- . . . . **CLC 4, 6, 37; SSC 8**
See also CA 25-28R; CANR 13, 46;
DAM POP; DLB 28; INT CANR-13;
MTCW

Palin, Michael (Edward) 1943- . . . . . **CLC 21**
See also Monty Python
See also CA 107; CANR 35; SATA 67

Palliser, Charles 1947- . . . . **CLC 65**
See also CA 136

Palma, Ricardo 1833-1919 . . . . **TCLC 29**

Pancake, Breece Dexter 1952-1979
See Pancake, Breece D'J
See also CA 123; 109

Pancake, Breece D'J . . . . **CLC 29**
See also Pancake, Breece Dexter
See also DLB 130

Panko, Rudy
See Gogol, Nikolai (Vasilyevich)

Papadiamantis, Alexandros
1851-1911 . . . . **TCLC 29**

Papadiamantopoulos, Johannes 1856-1910
See Moreas, Jean
See also CA 117

Papini, Giovanni 1881-1956 . . . . **TCLC 22**
See also CA 121

Paracelsus 1493-1541 . . . . **LC 14**

Parasol, Peter
See Stevens, Wallace

Parfenie, Maria
See Codrescu, Andrei

Parini, Jay (Lee) 1948- . . . . **CLC 54**
See also CA 97-100; CAAS 16; CANR 32

Park, Jordan
See Kornbluth, C(yril) M.; Pohl, Frederik

Parker, Bert
See Ellison, Harlan (Jay)

Parker, Dorothy (Rothschild)
1893-1967 . . . . **CLC 15, 68; SSC 2**
See also CA 19-20; 25-28R; CAP 2;
DAM POET; DLB 11, 45, 86; MTCW

Parker, Robert B(rown) 1932- . . . . . . **CLC 27**
See also BEST 89:4; CA 49-52; CANR 1,
26; DAM NOV, POP; INT CANR-26;
MTCW

Parkin, Frank 1940- . . . . **CLC 43**
See also CA 147

Parkman, Francis, Jr.
1823-1893 . . . . **NCLC 12**
See also DLB 1, 30

Parks, Gordon (Alexander Buchanan)
1912- . . . . **CLC 1, 16; BLC**
See also AITN 2; BW 2; CA 41-44R;
CANR 26; DAM MULT; DLB 33;
SATA 8

Parnell, Thomas 1679-1718 . . . . **LC 3**
See also DLB 94

Parra, Nicanor 1914- . . . . **CLC 2; HLC**
See also CA 85-88; CANR 32;
DAM MULT; HW; MTCW

Parrish, Mary Frances
See Fisher, M(ary) F(rances) K(ennedy)

Parson
See Coleridge, Samuel Taylor

Parson Lot
See Kingsley, Charles

Partridge, Anthony
See Oppenheim, E(dward) Phillips

Pascoli, Giovanni 1855-1912 . . . . . . **TCLC 45**

Pasolini, Pier Paolo
1922-1975 . . . . **CLC 20, 37**
See also CA 93-96; 61-64; DLB 128;
MTCW

Pasquini
See Silone, Ignazio

Pastan, Linda (Olenik) 1932- . . . . . . **CLC 27**
See also CA 61-64; CANR 18, 40;
DAM POET; DLB 5

Pasternak, Boris (Leonidovich)
1890-1960 . . . . . . **CLC 7, 10, 18, 63; DA;**
DAB; DAC; PC 6; WLC
See also CA 127; 116; DAM MST, NOV,
POET; MTCW

Patchen, Kenneth 1911-1972 . . . **CLC 1, 2, 18**
See also CA 1-4R; 33-36R; CANR 3, 35;
DAM POET; DLB 16, 48; MTCW

Pater, Walter (Horatio)
1839-1894 . . . . **NCLC 7**
See also CDBLB 1832-1890; DLB 57, 156

Paterson, A(ndrew) B(arton)
1864-1941 . . . . **TCLC 32**

Paterson, Katherine (Womeldorf)
1932- . . . . **CLC 12, 30**
See also AAYA 1; CA 21-24R; CANR 28;
CLR 7; DLB 52; JRDA; MAICYA;
MTCW; SATA 13, 53

Patmore, Coventry Kersey Dighton
1823-1896 . . . . **NCLC 9**
See also DLB 35, 98

Paton, Alan (Stewart)
1903-1988 . . . . . . **CLC 4, 10, 25, 55; DA;**
DAB; DAC; WLC
See also CA 13-16; 125; CANR 22; CAP 1;
DAM MST, NOV; MTCW; SATA 11;
SATA-Obit 56

Paton Walsh, Gillian 1937-
See Walsh, Jill Paton
See also CANR 38; JRDA; MAICYA;
SAAS 3; SATA 4, 72

Paulding, James Kirke 1778-1860 . . **NCLC 2**
See also DLB 3, 59, 74

Paulin, Thomas Neilson 1949-
See Paulin, Tom
See also CA 123; 128

Paulin, Tom . . . . **CLC 37**
See also Paulin, Thomas Neilson
See also DLB 40

Paustovsky, Konstantin (Georgievich)
1892-1968 . . . . **CLC 40**
See also CA 93-96; 25-28R

Pavese, Cesare
1908-1950 . . . . . **TCLC 3; PC 13; SSC 19**
See also CA 104; DLB 128

Pavic, Milorad 1929- . . . . **CLC 60**
See also CA 136

Payne, Alan
See Jakes, John (William)

Paz, Gil
See Lugones, Leopoldo

Paz, Octavio
1914- . . . . **CLC 3, 4, 6, 10, 19, 51, 65;**
DA; DAB; DAC; HLC; PC 1; WLC
See also CA 73-76; CANR 32; DAM MST,
MULT, POET; DLBY 90; HW; MTCW

Peacock, Molly 1947- . . . . **CLC 60**
See also CA 103; CAAS 21; DLB 120

Peacock, Thomas Love
1785-1866 . . . . **NCLC 22**
See also DLB 96, 116

Peake, Mervyn 1911-1968 . . . . **CLC 7, 54**
See also CA 5-8R; 25-28R; CANR 3;
DLB 15, 160; MTCW; SATA 23

Pearce, Philippa . . . . **CLC 21**
See also Christie, (Ann) Philippa
See also CLR 9; DLB 161, MAICYA;
SATA 1, 67

Pearl, Eric
See Elman, Richard

Pearson, T(homas) R(eid) 1956- . . . . **CLC 39**
See also CA 120; 130; INT 130

Peck, Dale 1967- . . . . **CLC 81**
See also CA 146

Peck, John 1941- . . . . **CLC 3**
See also CA 49-52; CANR 3

Peck, Richard (Wayne) 1934- . . . . **CLC 21**
See also AAYA 1; CA 85-88; CANR 19,
38; CLR 15; INT CANR-19; JRDA;
MAICYA; SAAS 2; SATA 18, 55

Peck, Robert Newton
1928- . . . . **CLC 17; DA; DAC**
See also AAYA 3; CA 81-84; CANR 31;
DAM MST; JRDA; MAICYA; SAAS 1;
SATA 21, 62

Peckinpah, (David) Sam(uel)
1925-1984 . . . . **CLC 20**
See also CA 109; 114

Pedersen, Knut 1859-1952
See Hamsun, Knut
See also CA 104; 119; MTCW

Peeslake, Gaffer
See Durrell, Lawrence (George)

Peguy, Charles Pierre
1873-1914 . . . . **TCLC 10**
See also CA 107

Pena, Ramon del Valle y
See Valle-Inclan, Ramon (Maria) del

Pendennis, Arthur Esquir
See Thackeray, William Makepeace

Penn, William 1644-1718 . . . . **LC 25**
See also DLB 24

Pepys, Samuel
1633-1703 . . . . . **LC 11; DA; DAB; DAC;**
WLC
See also CDBLB 1660-1789; DAM MST;
DLB 101

Percy, Walker
1916-1990 . . . . **CLC 2, 3, 6, 8, 14, 18, 47,**
65
See also CA 1-4R; 131; CANR 1, 23;
DAM NOV, POP; DLB 2; DLBY 80, 90;
MTCW

Perec, Georges 1936-1982 . . . . **CLC 56**
See also CA 141; DLB 83

Pereda (y Sanchez de Porrua), Jose Maria de
1833-1906 . . . . **TCLC 16**
See also CA 117

Pereda y Porrua, Jose Maria de
See Pereda (y Sanchez de Porrua), Jose
Maria de

Peregoy, George Weems
See Mencken, H(enry) L(ouis)

Perelman, S(idney) J(oseph)
1904-1979 . . . **CLC 3, 5, 9, 15, 23, 44, 49**
See also AITN 1, 2; CA 73-76; 89-92;
CANR 18; DAM DRAM; DLB 11, 44;
MTCW

Perct, Benjamin 1899-1959 . . . . . . **TCLC 20**
See also CA 117

Peretz, Isaac Loeb 1851(?)-1915 . . . **TCLC 16**
See also CA 109

Peretz, Yitzhok Leibush
See Peretz, Isaac Loeb

Perez Galdos, Benito 1843-1920 . . . **TCLC 27**
See also CA 125; HW

Perrault, Charles 1628-1703 . . . . **LC 2**
See also MAICYA; SATA 25

Perry, Brighton
See Sherwood, Robert E(mmet)

Perse, St.-John . . . . **CLC 4, 11, 46**
See also Leger, (Marie-Rene Auguste) Alexis
Saint-Leger

Perutz, Leo 1882-1957 . . . . **TCLC 60**
See also DLB 81

Peseenz, Tulio F.
See Lopez y Fuentes, Gregorio

Pesetsky, Bette 1932- . . . . **CLC 28**
See also CA 133; DLB 130

Peshkov, Alexei Maximovich 1868-1936
See Gorky, Maxim
See also CA 105; 141; DA; DAC;
DAM DRAM, MST, NOV

Pessoa, Fernando (Antonio Nogueira)
1888-1935 . . . . **TCLC 27; HLC**
See also CA 125

Peterkin, Julia Mood 1880-1961 . . . . **CLC 31**
See also CA 102; DLB 9

Peters, Joan K. 1945- . . . . **CLC 39**

Peters, Robert L(ouis) 1924- . . . . **CLC 7**
See also CA 13-16R; CAAS 8; DLB 105

Petofi, Sandor 1823-1849 . . . . **NCLC 21**

Petrakis, Harry Mark 1923- . . . . **CLC 3**
See also CA 9-12R; CANR 4, 30

Petrarch 1304-1374 . . . . **PC 8**
See also DAM POET

Petrov, Evgeny . . . . **TCLC 21**
See also Kataev, Evgeny Petrovich

Petry, Ann (Lane) 1908- . . . . . . **CLC 1, 7, 18**
See also BW 1; CA 5-8R; CAAS 6;
CANR 4, 46; CLR 12; DLB 76; JRDA;
MAICYA; MTCW; SATA 5

Petursson, Halligrimur 1614-1674 . . . . **LC 8**

Philips, Katherine 1632-1664 . . . . **LC 30**
See also DLB 131

Philipson, Morris H. 1926- . . . . **CLC 53**
See also CA 1-4R; CANR 4

Phillips, David Graham
1867-1911 . . . . **TCLC 44**
See also CA 108; DLB 9, 12

Phillips, Jack
See Sandburg, Carl (August)

Phillips, Jayne Anne
1952- . . . . **CLC 15, 33; SSC 16**
See also CA 101; CANR 24, 50; DLBY 80;
INT CANR-24; MTCW

Phillips, Richard
See Dick, Philip K(indred)

Phillips, Robert (Schaeffer) 1938- . . . **CLC 28**
See also CA 17-20R; CAAS 13; CANR 8;
DLB 105

Phillips, Ward
See Lovecraft, H(oward) P(hillips)

Piccolo, Lucio 1901-1969 . . . . **CLC 13**
See also CA 97-100; DLB 114

Pickthall, Marjorie L(owry) C(hristie)
1883-1922 . . . . **TCLC 21**
See also CA 107; DLB 92

Pico della Mirandola, Giovanni
1463-1494 . . . . **LC 15**

Piercy, Marge
1936- . . . . **CLC 3, 6, 14, 18, 27, 62**
See also CA 21-24R; CAAS 1; CANR 13,
43; DLB 120; MTCW

Piers, Robert
See Anthony, Piers

Pieyre de Mandiargues, Andre 1909-1991
See Mandiargues, Andre Pieyre de
See also CA 103; 136; CANR 22

Pilnyak, Boris . . . . **TCLC 23**
See also Vogau, Boris Andreyevich

Pincherle, Alberto 1907-1990 . . . **CLC 11, 18**
See also Moravia, Alberto
See also CA 25-28R; 132; CANR 33;
DAM NOV; MTCW

Pinckney, Darryl 1953- . . . . **CLC 76**
See also BW 2; CA 143

Pindar 518B.C.-446B.C. . . . . **CMLC 12**

Pineda, Cecile 1942- . . . . **CLC 39**
See also CA 118

Pinero, Arthur Wing 1855-1934 . . . **TCLC 32**
See also CA 110; DAM DRAM; DLB 10

Pinero, Miguel (Antonio Gomez)
1946-1988 . . . . **CLC 4, 55**
See also CA 61-64; 125; CANR 29; HW

Pinget, Robert 1919- . . . . **CLC 7, 13, 37**
See also CA 85-88; DLB 83

Pink Floyd
See Barrett, (Roger) Syd; Gilmour, David;
Mason, Nick; Waters, Roger; Wright,
Rick

Pinkney, Edward 1802-1828 . . . . . **NCLC 31**

Pinkwater, Daniel Manus 1941- . . . . **CLC 35**
See also Pinkwater, Manus
See also AAYA 1; CA 29-32R; CANR 12,
38; CLR 4; JRDA; MAICYA; SAAS 3;
SATA 46, 76

Pinkwater, Manus
See Pinkwater, Daniel Manus
See also SATA 8

Pinsky, Robert 1940- . . . . . **CLC 9, 19, 38, 94**
See also CA 29-32R; CAAS 4;
DAM POET; DLBY 82

Pinta, Harold
See Pinter, Harold

Pinter, Harold
1930- . . . . . **CLC 1, 3, 6, 9, 11, 15, 27, 58,
73; DA; DAB; DAC; WLC**
See also CA 5-8R; CANR 33; CDBLB 1960
to Present; DAM DRAM, MST; DLB 13;
MTCW

Piozzi, Hester Lynch (Thrale)
1741-1821 . . . . **NCLC 57**
See also DLB 104, 142

Pirandello, Luigi
1867-1936 . . . . . . **TCLC 4, 29; DA; DAB;
DAC; DC 5; SSC 22; WLC**
See also CA 104; DAM DRAM, MST

Pirsig, Robert M(aynard)
1928- . . . . **CLC 4, 6, 73**
See also CA 53-56; CANR 42; DAM POP;
MTCW; SATA 39

Pisarev, Dmitry Ivanovich
1840-1868 . . . . **NCLC 25**

Pix, Mary (Griffith) 1666-1709 . . . . . . **LC 8**
See also DLB 80

Pixerecourt, Guilbert de
1773-1844 . . . . **NCLC 39**

Plaidy, Jean
See Hibbert, Eleanor Alice Burford

Planche, James Robinson
1796-1880 . . . . **NCLC 42**

Plant, Robert 1948- . . . . **CLC 12**

Plante, David (Robert)
1940- . . . . **CLC 7, 23, 38**
See also CA 37-40R; CANR 12, 36;
DAM NOV; DLBY 83; INT CANR-12;
MTCW

Plath, Sylvia
1932-1963 . . . . . **CLC 1, 2, 3, 5, 9, 11, 14,
17, 50, 51, 62; DA; DAB; DAC; PC 1;
WLC**
See also AAYA 13; CA 19-20; CANR 34;
CAP 2; CDALB 1941-1968; DAM MST,
POET; DLB 5, 6, 152; MTCW

Plato
428(?)B.C.-348(?)B.C. . . . . . **CMLC 8; DA;
DAB; DAC**
See also DAM MST

Platonov, Andrei . . . . **TCLC 14**
See also Klimentov, Andrei Platonovich

Platt, Kin 1911- . . . . **CLC 26**
See also AAYA 11; CA 17-20R; CANR 11;
JRDA; SAAS 17; SATA 21, 86

Plautus c. 251B.C.-184B.C. . . . . **DC 6**

Plick et Plock
See Simenon, Georges (Jacques Christian)

Plimpton, George (Ames) 1927- . . . . . **CLC 36**
See also AITN 1; CA 21-24R; CANR 32;
MTCW; SATA 10

Rolland, Romain 1866-1944...... **TCLC 23**
See also CA 118; DLB 65

Rolvaag, O(le) E(dvart)
See Roelvaag, O(le) E(dvart)

Romain Arnaud, Saint
See Aragon, Louis

Romains, Jules 1885-1972.......... **CLC 7**
See also CA 85-88; CANR 34; DLB 65;
MTCW

Romero, Jose Ruben 1890-1952 ... **TCLC 14**
See also CA 114; 131; HW

Ronsard, Pierre de
1524-1585 .... **LC 6; PC 11**

Rooke, Leon 1934-........... **CLC 25, 34**
See also CA 25-28R; CANR 23; DAM POP

Roper, William 1498-1578.......... **LC 10**

Roquelaure, A. N.
See Rice, Anne

Rosa, Joao Guimaraes 1908-1967 ... **CLC 23**
See also CA 89-92; DLB 113

Rose, Wendy 1948-......... **CLC 85; PC 13**
See also CA 53-56; CANR 5, 51;
DAM MULT; NNAL; SATA 12

Rosen, Richard (Dean) 1949-....... **CLC 39**
See also CA 77-80; INT CANR-30

Rosenberg, Isaac 1890-1918....... **TCLC 12**
See also CA 107; DLB 20

Rosenblatt, Joe .... **CLC 15**
See also Rosenblatt, Joseph

Rosenblatt, Joseph 1933-
See Rosenblatt, Joe
See also CA 89-92; INT 89-92

Rosenfeld, Samuel 1896-1963
See Tzara, Tristan
See also CA 89-92

Rosenthal, M(acha) L(ouis) 1917-... **CLC 28**
See also CA 1-4R; CAAS 6; CANR 4, 51;
DLB 5; SATA 59

Ross, Barnaby
See Dannay, Frederic

Ross, Bernard L.
See Follett, Ken(neth Martin)

Ross, J. H.
See Lawrence, T(homas) E(dward)

Ross, Martin
See Martin, Violet Florence
See also DLB 135

Ross, (James) Sinclair
1908- .... **CLC 13; DAC**
See also CA 73-76; DAM MST; DLB 88

Rossetti, Christina (Georgina)
1830-1894 ..... **NCLC 2, 50; DA; DAB;**
DAC; PC 7; WLC
See also DAM MST, POET; DLB 35, 163;
MAICYA; SATA 20

Rossetti, Dante Gabriel
1828-1882 .... **NCLC 4; DA; DAB;**
DAC; WLC
See also CDBLB 1832-1890; DAM MST,
POET; DLB 35

Rossner, Judith (Perelman)
1935- .... **CLC 6, 9, 29**
See also AITN 2; BEST 90:3; CA 17-20R;
CANR 18, 51; DLB 6; INT CANR-18;
MTCW

Rostand, Edmond (Eugene Alexis)
1868-1918 ...... **TCLC 6, 37; DA; DAB;**
DAC
See also CA 104; 126; DAM DRAM, MST;
MTCW

Roth, Henry 1906-1995 .... **CLC 2, 6, 11**
See also CA 11-12; 149; CANR 38; CAP 1;
DLB 28; MTCW

Roth, Joseph 1894-1939 .... **TCLC 33**
See also DLB 85

Roth, Philip (Milton)
1933- ...... **CLC 1, 2, 3, 4, 6, 9, 15, 22,**
31, 47, 66, 86; DA; DAB; DAC; WLC
See also BEST 90:3; CA 1-4R; CANR 1, 22,
36; CDALB 1968-1988; DAM MST,
NOV, POP; DLB 2, 28; DLBY 82;
MTCW

Rothenberg, Jerome 1931-....... **CLC 6, 57**
See also CA 45-48; CANR 1; DLB 5

Roumain, Jacques (Jean Baptiste)
1907-1944 .... **TCLC 19; BLC**
See also BW 1; CA 117; 125; DAM MULT

Rourke, Constance (Mayfield)
1885-1941 .... **TCLC 12**
See also CA 107; YABC 1

Rousseau, Jean-Baptiste 1671-1741 ... **LC 9**

Rousseau, Jean-Jacques
1712-1778 ..... **LC 14; DA; DAB; DAC;**
WLC
See also DAM MST

Roussel, Raymond 1877-1933 ..... **TCLC 20**
See also CA 117

Rovit, Earl (Herbert) 1927-......... **CLC 7**
See also CA 5-8R; CANR 12

Rowe, Nicholas 1674-1718........... **LC 8**
See also DLB 84

Rowley, Ames Dorrance
See Lovecraft, H(oward) P(hillips)

Rowson, Susanna Haswell
1762(?)-1824 .... **NCLC 5**
See also DLB 37

Roy, Gabrielle
1909-1983 ..... **CLC 10, 14; DAB; DAC**
See also CA 53-56; 110; CANR 5;
DAM MST; DLB 68; MTCW

Rozewicz, Tadeusz 1921-........ **CLC 9, 23**
See also CA 108; CANR 36; DAM POET;
MTCW

Ruark, Gibbons 1941- .... **CLC 3**
See also CA 33-36R; CAAS 23; CANR 14,
31; DLB 120

Rubens, Bernice (Ruth) 1923-... **CLC 19, 31**
See also CA 25-28R; CANR 33; DLB 14;
MTCW

Rudkin, (James) David 1936- ...... **CLC 14**
See also CA 89-92; DLB 13

Rudnik, Raphael 1933-............. **CLC 7**
See also CA 29-32R

Ruffian, M.
See Hasek, Jaroslav (Matej Frantisek)

Ruiz, Jose Martinez .... **CLC 11**
See also Martinez Ruiz, Jose

Rukeyser, Muriel
1913-1980 .... **CLC 6, 10, 15, 27; PC 12**
See also CA 5-8R; 93-96; CANR 26;
DAM POET; DLB 48; MTCW;
SATA-Obit 22

Rule, Jane (Vance) 1931-.......... **CLC 27**
See also CA 25-28R; CAAS 18; CANR 12;
DLB 60

Rulfo, Juan 1918-1986.... **CLC 8, 80; HLC**
See also CA 85-88; 118; CANR 26;
DAM MULT; DLB 113; HW; MTCW

Runeberg, Johan 1804-1877...... **NCLC 41**

Runyon, (Alfred) Damon
1884(?)-1946 .... **TCLC 10**
See also CA 107; DLB 11, 86

Rush, Norman 1933-.............. **CLC 44**
See also CA 121; 126; INT 126

Rushdie, (Ahmed) Salman
1947- ...... **CLC 23, 31, 55; DAB; DAC**
See also BEST 89:3; CA 108; 111;
CANR 33; DAM MST, NOV, POP;
INT 111; MTCW

Rushforth, Peter (Scott) 1945- ..... **CLC 19**
See also CA 101

Ruskin, John 1819-1900......... **TCLC 63**
See also CA 114; 129; CDBLB 1832-1890;
DLB 55, 163; SATA 24

Russ, Joanna 1937-.............. **CLC 15**
See also CA 25-28R; CANR 11, 31; DLB 8;
MTCW

Russell, George William 1867-1935
See A. E.
See also CA 104; CDBLB 1890-1914;
DAM POET

Russell, (Henry) Ken(neth Alfred)
1927- .... **CLC 16**
See also CA 105

Russell, Willy 1947-.............. **CLC 60**

Rutherford, Mark .... **TCLC 25**
See also White, William Hale
See also DLB 18

Ruyslinck, Ward 1929-............ **CLC 14**
See also Belser, Reimond Karel Maria de

Ryan, Cornelius (John) 1920-1974 ... **CLC 7**
See also CA 69-72; 53-56; CANR 38

Ryan, Michael 1946- .... **CLC 65**
See also CA 49-52; DLBY 82

Rybakov, Anatoli (Naumovich)
1911- .... **CLC 23, 53**
See also CA 126; 135; SATA 79

Ryder, Jonathan
See Ludlum, Robert

Ryga, George 1932-1987 ..... **CLC 14; DAC**
See also CA 101; 124; CANR 43;
DAM MST; DLB 60

S. S.
See Sassoon, Siegfried (Lorraine)

Saba, Umberto 1883-1957 .... **TCLC 33**
See also CA 144; DLB 114

Sabatini, Rafael 1875-1950 .... **TCLC 47**

Sabato, Ernesto (R.)
1911- .... **CLC 10, 23; HLC**
See also CA 97-100; CANR 32;
DAM MULT; DLB 145; HW; MTCW

Sacastru, Martin
See Bioy Casares, Adolfo

Sacher-Masoch, Leopold von
1836(?)-1895 .... **NCLC 31**

Sachs, Marilyn (Stickle) 1927- ..... **CLC 35**
See also AAYA 2; CA 17-20R; CANR 13,
47; CLR 2; JRDA; MAICYA; SAAS 2;
SATA 3, 68

Sachs, Nelly 1891-1970 .... **CLC 14**
See also CA 17-18; 25-28R; CAP 2

Sackler, Howard (Oliver)
1929-1982 .... **CLC 14**
See also CA 61-64; 108; CANR 30; DLB 7

Sacks, Oliver (Wolf) 1933- .... **CLC 67**
See also CA 53-56; CANR 28, 50;
INT CANR-28; MTCW

Sade, Donatien Alphonse Francois Comte
1740-1814 .... **NCLC 47**

Sadoff, Ira 1945-................. **CLC 9**
See also CA 53-56; CANR 5, 21; DLB 120

Saetone
See Camus, Albert

Safire, William 1929-............. **CLC 10**
See also CA 17-20R; CANR 31

Sagan, Carl (Edward) 1934-........ **CLC 30**
See also AAYA 2; CA 25-28R; CANR 11,
36; MTCW; SATA 58

Sagan, Francoise .... **CLC 3, 6, 9, 17, 36**
See also Quoirez, Francoise
See also DLB 83

Sahgal, Nayantara (Pandit) 1927-... **CLC 41**
See also CA 9-12R; CANR 11

Saint, H(arry) F. 1941- .... **CLC 50**
See also CA 127

St. Aubin de Teran, Lisa 1953-
See Teran, Lisa St. Aubin de
See also CA 118; 126; INT 126

Sainte-Beuve, Charles Augustin
1804-1869 .... **NCLC 5**

Saint-Exupery, Antoine (Jean Baptiste Marie
Roger) de
1900-1944 .... **TCLC 2, 56; WLC**
See also CA 108; 132; CLR 10; DAM NOV;
DLB 72; MAICYA; MTCW; SATA 20

St. John, David
See Hunt, E(verette) Howard, (Jr.)

Saint-John Perse
See Leger, (Marie-Rene Auguste) Alexis
Saint-Leger

Saintsbury, George (Edward Bateman)
1845-1933 .... **TCLC 31**
See also DLB 57, 149

Sait Faik .... **TCLC 23**
See also Abasiyanik, Sait Faik

Saki .... **TCLC 3; SSC 12**
See also Munro, H(ector) H(ugh)

Sala, George Augustus .... **NCLC 46**

Salama, Hannu 1936-............. **CLC 18**

Salamanca, J(ack) R(ichard)
1922-.................... **CLC 4, 15**
See also CA 25-28R

Sale, J. Kirkpatrick
See Sale, Kirkpatrick

Sale, Kirkpatrick 1937-........... **CLC 68**
See also CA 13-16R; CANR 10

Salinas, Luis Omar 1937- ... **CLC 90; HLC**
See also CA 131; DAM MULT; DLB 82;
HW

Salinas (y Serrano), Pedro
1891(?)-1951 .... **TCLC 17**
See also CA 117; DLB 134

Salinger, J(erome) D(avid)
1919- ...... **CLC 1, 3, 8, 12, 55, 56; DA;
DAB; DAC; SSC 2; WLC**
See also AAYA 2; CA 5-8R; CANR 39;
CDALB 1941-1968; CLR 18; DAM MST,
NOV, POP; DLB 2, 102; MAICYA;
MTCW; SATA 67

Salisbury, John
See Caute, David

Salter, James 1925- .... **CLC 7, 52, 59**
See also CA 73-76; DLB 130

Saltus, Edgar (Everton)
1855-1921 .... **TCLC 8**
See also CA 105

Saltykov, Mikhail Evgrafovich
1826-1889 .... **NCLC 16**

Samarakis, Antonis 1919- .... **CLC 5**
See also CA 25-28R; CAAS 16; CANR 36

Sanchez, Florencio 1875-1910 ..... **TCLC 37**
See also HW

Sanchez, Luis Rafael 1936-........ **CLC 23**
See also CA 128; DLB 145; HW

Sanchez, Sonia 1934- ... **CLC 5; BLC; PC 9**
See also BW 2; CA 33-36R; CANR 24, 49;
CLR 18; DAM MULT; DLB 41;
DLBD 8; MAICYA; MTCW; SATA 22

Sand, George
1804-1876 .... **NCLC 2, 42, 57; DA;
DAB; DAC; WLC**
See also DAM MST, NOV; DLB 119

Sandburg, Carl (August)
1878-1967 .... **CLC 1, 4, 10, 15, 35; DA;
DAB; DAC; PC 2; WLC**
See also CA 5-8R; 25-28R; CANR 35;
CDALB 1865-1917; DAM MST, POET;
DLB 17, 54; MAICYA; MTCW; SATA 8

Sandburg, Charles
See Sandburg, Carl (August)

Sandburg, Charles A.
See Sandburg, Carl (August)

Sanders, (James) Ed(ward) 1939- ... **CLC 53**
See also CA 13-16R; CAAS 21; CANR 13,
44; DLB 16

Sanders, Lawrence 1920-.......... **CLC 41**
See also BEST 89:4; CA 81-84; CANR 33;
DAM POP; MTCW

Sanders, Noah
See Blount, Roy (Alton), Jr.

Sanders, Winston P.
See Anderson, Poul (William)

Sandoz, Mari(e Susette)
1896-1966 .... **CLC 28**
See also CA 1-4R; 25-28R; CANR 17;
DLB 9; MTCW; SATA 5

Saner, Reg(inald Anthony) 1931- .... **CLC 9**
See also CA 65-68

Sannazaro, Jacopo 1456(?)-1530...... **LC 8**

Sansom, William
1912-1976 .... **CLC 2, 6; SSC 21**
See also CA 5-8R; 65-68; CANR 42;
DAM NOV; DLB 139; MTCW

Santayana, George 1863-1952..... **TCLC 40**
See also CA 115; DLB 54, 71; DLBD 13

Santiago, Danny .... **CLC 33**
See also James, Daniel (Lewis)
See also DLB 122

Santmyer, Helen Hoover
1895-1986 .... **CLC 33**
See also CA 1-4R; 118; CANR 15, 33;
DLBY 84; MTCW

Santos, Bienvenido N(uqui)
1911-1996 .... **CLC 22**
See also CA 101; 151; CANR 19, 46;
DAM MULT

Sapper .... **TCLC 44**
See also McNeile, Herman Cyril

Sappho fl. 6th cent. B.C.-.... **CMLC 3; PC 5**
See also DAM POET

Sarduy, Severo 1937-1993.......... **CLC 6**
See also CA 89-92; 142; DLB 113; HW

Sargeson, Frank 1903-1982 .... **CLC 31**
See also CA 25-28R; 106; CANR 38

Sarmiento, Felix Ruben Garcia
See Dario, Ruben

Saroyan, William
1908-1981 ..... **CLC 1, 8, 10, 29, 34, 56;
DA; DAB; DAC; SSC 21; WLC**
See also CA 5-8R; 103; CANR 30;
DAM DRAM, MST, NOV; DLB 7, 9, 86;
DLBY 81; MTCW; SATA 23;
SATA-Obit 24

Sarraute, Nathalie
1900- .... **CLC 1, 2, 4, 8, 10, 31, 80**
See also CA 9-12R; CANR 23; DLB 83;
MTCW

Sarton, (Eleanor) May
1912-1995 .... **CLC 4, 14, 49, 91**
See also CA 1-4R; 149; CANR 1, 34;
DAM POET; DLB 48; DLBY 81;
INT CANR-34; MTCW; SATA 36;
SATA-Obit 86

Sartre, Jean-Paul
1905-1980 .... **CLC 1, 4, 7, 9, 13, 18, 24,
44, 50, 52; DA; DAB; DAC; DC 3; WLC**
See also CA 9-12R; 97-100; CANR 21;
DAM DRAM, MST, NOV; DLB 72;
MTCW

Sassoon, Siegfried (Lorraine)
1886-1967 .... **CLC 36; DAB; PC 12**
See also CA 104; 25-28R; CANR 36;
DAM MST, NOV, POET; DLB 20;
MTCW

Satterfield, Charles
See Pohl, Frederik

Saul, John (W. III) 1942- . . . . **CLC 46**
See also AAYA 10; BEST 90:4; CA 81-84;
CANR 16, 40; DAM NOV, POP

Saunders, Caleb
See Heinlein, Robert A(nson)

Saura (Atares), Carlos 1932- . . . . **CLC 20**
See also CA 114; 131; HW

Sauser-Hall, Frederic 1887-1961. . . . **CLC 18**
See also Cendrars, Blaise
See also CA 102; 93-96; CANR 36; MTCW

Saussure, Ferdinand de
1857-1913 . . . . **TCLC 49**

Savage, Catharine
See Brosman, Catharine Savage

Savage, Thomas 1915- . . . . **CLC 40**
See also CA 126; 132; CAAS 15; INT 132

Savan, Glenn 19(?)- . . . . **CLC 50**

Sayers, Dorothy L(eigh)
1893-1957 . . . . **TCLC 2, 15**
See also CA 104; 119; CDBLB 1914-1945;
DAM POP; DLB 10, 36, 77, 100; MTCW

Sayers, Valerie 1952- . . . . **CLC 50**
See also CA 134

Sayles, John (Thomas)
1950- . . . . **CLC 7, 10, 14**
See also CA 57-60; CANR 41; DLB 44

Scammell, Michael . . . . **CLC 34**

Scannell, Vernon 1922- . . . . **CLC 49**
See also CA 5-8R; CANR 8, 24; DLB 27;
SATA 59

Scarlett, Susan
See Streatfeild, (Mary) Noel

Schaeffer, Susan Fromberg
1941- . . . . **CLC 6, 11, 22**
See also CA 49-52; CANR 18; DLB 28;
MTCW; SATA 22

Schary, Jill
See Robinson, Jill

Schell, Jonathan 1943- . . . . **CLC 35**
See also CA 73-76; CANR 12

Schelling, Friedrich Wilhelm Joseph von
1775-1854 . . . . **NCLC 30**
See also DLB 90

Schendel, Arthur van 1874-1946 . . . **TCLC 56**

Scherer, Jean-Marie Maurice 1920-
See Rohmer, Eric
See also CA 110

Schevill, James (Erwin) 1920- . . . . . . **CLC 7**
See also CA 5-8R; CAAS 12

Schiller, Friedrich 1759-1805 . . . . **NCLC 39**
See also DAM DRAM; DLB 94

Schisgal, Murray (Joseph) 1926- . . . . . **CLC 6**
See also CA 21-24R; CANR 48

Schlee, Ann 1934- . . . . **CLC 35**
See also CA 101; CANR 29; SATA 44;
SATA-Brief 36

Schlegel, August Wilhelm von
1767-1845 . . . . **NCLC 15**
See also DLB 94

Schlegel, Friedrich 1772-1829 . . . . **NCLC 45**
See also DLB 90

Schlegel, Johann Elias (von)
1719(?)-1749 . . . . **LC 5**

Schlesinger, Arthur M(eier), Jr.
1917- . . . . **CLC 84**
See also AITN 1; CA 1-4R; CANR 1, 28;
DLB 17; INT CANR-28; MTCW;
SATA 61

Schmidt, Arno (Otto) 1914-1979. . . . **CLC 56**
See also CA 128; 109; DLB 69

Schmitz, Aron Hector 1861-1928
See Svevo, Italo
See also CA 104; 122; MTCW

Schnackenberg, Gjertrud 1953- . . . . . **CLC 40**
See also CA 116; DLB 120

Schneider, Leonard Alfred 1925-1966
See Bruce, Lenny
See also CA 89-92

Schnitzler, Arthur
1862-1931 . . . . **TCLC 4; SSC 15**
See also CA 104; DLB 81, 118

Schopenhauer, Arthur
1788-1860 . . . . **NCLC 51**
See also DLB 90

Schor, Sandra (M.) 1932(?)-1990 . . . **CLC 65**
See also CA 132

Schorer, Mark 1908-1977 . . . . **CLC 9**
See also CA 5-8R; 73-76; CANR 7;
DLB 103

Schrader, Paul (Joseph) 1946- . . . . . . **CLC 26**
See also CA 37-40R; CANR 41; DLB 44

Schreiner, Olive (Emilie Albertina)
1855-1920 . . . . **TCLC 9**
See also CA 105; DLB 18, 156

Schulberg, Budd (Wilson)
1914- . . . . **CLC 7, 48**
See also CA 25-28R; CANR 19; DLB 6, 26,
28; DLBY 81

Schulz, Bruno
1892-1942 . . . . **TCLC 5, 51; SSC 13**
See also CA 115; 123

Schulz, Charles M(onroe) 1922- . . . . **CLC 12**
See also CA 9-12R; CANR 6;
INT CANR-6; SATA 10

Schumacher, E(rnst) F(riedrich)
1911-1977 . . . . **CLC 80**
See also CA 81-84; 73-76; CANR 34

Schuyler, James Marcus
1923-1991 . . . . **CLC 5, 23**
See also CA 101; 134; DAM POET; DLB 5;
INT 101

Schwartz, Delmore (David)
1913-1966 . . . **CLC 2, 4, 10, 45, 87; PC 8**
See also CA 17-18; 25-28R; CANR 35;
CAP 2; DLB 28, 48; MTCW

Schwartz, Ernst
See Ozu, Yasujiro

Schwartz, John Burnham 1965- . . . . **CLC 59**
See also CA 132

Schwartz, Lynne Sharon 1939- . . . . . **CLC 31**
See also CA 103; CANR 44

Schwartz, Muriel A.
See Eliot, T(homas) S(tearns)

Schwarz-Bart, Andre 1928- . . . . **CLC 2, 4**
See also CA 89-92

Schwarz-Bart, Simone 1938- . . . . **CLC 7**
See also BW 2; CA 97-100

Schwob, (Mayer Andre) Marcel
1867-1905 . . . . **TCLC 20**
See also CA 117; DLB 123

Sciascia, Leonardo
1921-1989 . . . . **CLC 8, 9, 41**
See also CA 85-88; 130; CANR 35; MTCW

Scoppettone, Sandra 1936- . . . . **CLC 26**
See also AAYA 11; CA 5-8R; CANR 41;
SATA 9

Scorsese, Martin 1942- . . . . **CLC 20, 89**
See also CA 110; 114; CANR 46

Scotland, Jay
See Jakes, John (William)

Scott, Duncan Campbell
1862-1947 . . . . **TCLC 6; DAC**
See also CA 104; DLB 92

Scott, Evelyn 1893-1963. . . . . **CLC 43**
See also CA 104; 112; DLB 9, 48

Scott, F(rancis) R(eginald)
1899-1985 . . . . **CLC 22**
See also CA 101; 114; DLB 88; INT 101

Scott, Frank
See Scott, F(rancis) R(eginald)

Scott, Joanna 1960- . . . . **CLC 50**
See also CA 126

Scott, Paul (Mark) 1920-1978. . . . **CLC 9, 60**
See also CA 81-84; 77-80; CANR 33;
DLB 14; MTCW

Scott, Walter
1771-1832 . . . . **NCLC 15; DA; DAB;
DAC; PC 13; WLC**
See also CDBLB 1789-1832; DAM MST,
NOV, POET; DLB 93, 107, 116, 144, 159;
YABC 2

Scribe, (Augustin) Eugene
1791-1861 . . . . **NCLC 16; DC 5**
See also DAM DRAM

Scrum, R.
See Crumb, R(obert)

Scudery, Madeleine de 1607-1701. . . . . **LC 2**

Scum
See Crumb, R(obert)

Scumbag, Little Bobby
See Crumb, R(obert)

Seabrook, John
See Hubbard, L(afayette) Ron(ald)

Sealy, I. Allan 1951- . . . . **CLC 55**

Search, Alexander
See Pessoa, Fernando (Antonio Nogueira)

Sebastian, Lee
See Silverberg, Robert

Sebastian Owl
See Thompson, Hunter S(tockton)

Sebestyen, Ouida 1924- . . . . **CLC 30**
See also AAYA 8; CA 107; CANR 40;
CLR 17; JRDA; MAICYA; SAAS 10;
SATA 39

Secundus, H. Scriblerus
See Fielding, Henry

Sedges, John
See Buck, Pearl S(ydenstricker)

Sedgwick, Catharine Maria
1789-1867 . . . . **NCLC 19**
See also DLB 1, 74

Sherburne, Zoa (Morin) 1912-...... **CLC 30**
See also AAYA 13; CA 1-4R; CANR 3, 37;
MAICYA; SAAS 18; SATA 3

Sheridan, Frances 1724-1766........ **LC 7**
See also DLB 39, 84

Sheridan, Richard Brinsley
1751-1816 .... **NCLC 5; DA; DAB;
DAC; DC 1; WLC**
See also CDBLB 1660-1789; DAM DRAM,
MST; DLB 89

Sherman, Jonathan Marc.......... **CLC 55**

Sherman, Martin 1941(?)-........ **CLC 19**
See also CA 116; 123

Sherwin, Judith Johnson 1936-... **CLC 7, 15**
See also CA 25-28R; CANR 34

Sherwood, Frances 1940-......... **CLC 81**
See also CA 146

Sherwood, Robert E(mmet)
1896-1955 .... **TCLC 3**
See also CA 104; DAM DRAM; DLB 7, 26

Shestov, Lev 1866-1938......... **TCLC 56**

Shevchenko, Taras 1814-1861.... **NCLC 54**

Shiel, M(atthew) P(hipps)
1865-1947 .... **TCLC 8**
See also CA 106; DLB 153

Shields, Carol 1935-........ **CLC 91; DAC**
See also CA 81-84; CANR 51

Shiga, Naoya 1883-1971... **CLC 33; SSC 23**
See also CA 101; 33-36R

Shilts, Randy 1951-1994 .... **CLC 85**
See also CA 115; 127; 144; CANR 45;
INT 127

Shimazaki, Haruki 1872-1943
See Shimazaki Toson
See also CA 105; 134

Shimazaki Toson.................. **TCLC 5**
See also Shimazaki, Haruki

Sholokhov, Mikhail (Aleksandrovich)
1905-1984 .... **CLC 7, 15**
See also CA 101; 112; MTCW;
SATA-Obit 36

Shone, Patric
See Hanley, James

Shreve, Susan Richards 1939-...... **CLC 23**
See also CA 49-52; CAAS 5; CANR 5, 38;
MAICYA; SATA 46; SATA-Brief 41

Shue, Larry 1946-1985............ **CLC 52**
See also CA 145; 117; DAM DRAM

Shu-Jen, Chou 1881-1936
See Lu Hsun
See also CA 104

Shulman, Alix Kates 1932-...... **CLC 2, 10**
See also CA 29-32R; CANR 43; SATA 7

Shuster, Joe 1914-............... **CLC 21**

Shute, Nevil..................... **CLC 30**
See also Norway, Nevil Shute

Shuttle, Penelope (Diane) 1947-..... **CLC 7**
See also CA 93-96; CANR 39; DLB 14, 40

Sidney, Mary 1561-1621 .... **LC 19**

Sidney, Sir Philip
1554-1586 ..... **LC 19; DA; DAB; DAC**
See also CDBLB Before 1660; DAM MST,
POET

Siegel, Jerome 1914-1996 .... **CLC 21**
See also CA 116; 151

Siegel, Jerry
See Siegel, Jerome

Sienkiewicz, Henryk (Adam Alexander Pius)
1846-1916 .... **TCLC 3**
See also CA 104; 134

Sierra, Gregorio Martinez
See Martinez Sierra, Gregorio

Sierra, Maria (de la O'LeJarraga) Martinez
See Martinez Sierra, Maria (de la
O'LeJarraga)

Sigal, Clancy 1926-............... **CLC 7**
See also CA 1-4R

Sigourney, Lydia Howard (Huntley)
1791-1865 .... **NCLC 21**
See also DLB 1, 42, 73

Siguenza y Gongora, Carlos de
1645-1700 .... **LC 8**

Sigurjonsson, Johann 1880-1919... **TCLC 27**

Sikelianos, Angelos 1884-1951 .... **TCLC 39**

Silkin, Jon 1930- .... **CLC 2, 6, 43**
See also CA 5-8R; CAAS 5; DLB 27

Silko, Leslie (Marmon)
1948- .... **CLC 23, 74; DA; DAC**
See also AAYA 14; CA 115; 122;
CANR 45; DAM MST, MULT, POP;
DLB 143; NNAL

Sillanpaa, Frans Eemil 1888-1964... **CLC 19**
See also CA 129; 93-96; MTCW

Sillitoe, Alan
1928- .... **CLC 1, 3, 6, 10, 19, 57**
See also AITN 1; CA 9-12R; CAAS 2;
CANR 8, 26; CDBLB 1960 to Present;
DLB 14, 139; MTCW; SATA 61

Silone, Ignazio 1900-1978 .... **CLC 4**
See also CA 25-28; 81-84; CANR 34;
CAP 2; MTCW

Silver, Joan Micklin 1935- .... **CLC 20**
See also CA 114; 121; INT 121

Silver, Nicholas
See Faust, Frederick (Schiller)

Silverberg, Robert 1935- .... **CLC 7**
See also CA 1-4R; CAAS 3; CANR 1, 20,
36; DAM POP; DLB 8; INT CANR-20;
MAICYA; MTCW; SATA 13

Silverstein, Alvin 1933- .... **CLC 17**
See also CA 49-52; CANR 2; CLR 25;
JRDA; MAICYA; SATA 8, 69

Silverstein, Virginia B(arbara Opshelor)
1937- .... **CLC 17**
See also CA 49-52; CANR 2; CLR 25;
JRDA; MAICYA; SATA 8, 69

Sim, Georges
See Simenon, Georges (Jacques Christian)

Simak, Clifford D(onald)
1904-1988 .... **CLC 1, 55**
See also CA 1-4R; 125; CANR 1, 35;
DLB 8; MTCW; SATA-Obit 56

Simenon, Georges (Jacques Christian)
1903-1989 .... **CLC 1, 2, 3, 8, 18, 47**
See also CA 85-88; 129; CANR 35;
DAM POP; DLB 72; DLBY 89; MTCW

Simic, Charles 1938-... **CLC 6, 9, 22, 49, 68**
See also CA 29-32R; CAAS 4; CANR 12,
33; DAM POET; DLB 105

Simmel, Georg 1858-1918 .... **TCLC 64**

Simmons, Charles (Paul) 1924-..... **CLC 57**
See also CA 89-92; INT 89-92

Simmons, Dan 1948-.............. **CLC 44**
See also AAYA 16; CA 138; DAM POP

Simmons, James (Stewart Alexander)
1933-..................... **CLC 43**
See also CA 105; CAAS 21; DLB 40

Simms, William Gilmore
1806-1870 .... **NCLC 3**
See also DLB 3, 30, 59, 73

Simon, Carly 1945-............... **CLC 26**
See also CA 105

Simon, Claude 1913-....... **CLC 4, 9, 15, 39**
See also CA 89-92; CANR 33; DAM NOV;
DLB 83; MTCW

Simon, (Marvin) Neil
1927-........... **CLC 6, 11, 31, 39, 70**
See also AITN 1; CA 21-24R; CANR 26;
DAM DRAM; DLB 7; MTCW

Simon, Paul 1942(?)- .... **CLC 17**
See also CA 116

Simonon, Paul 1956(?)- .... **CLC 30**

Simpson, Harriette
See Arnow, Harriette (Louisa) Simpson

Simpson, Louis (Aston Marantz)
1923- .... **CLC 4, 7, 9, 32**
See also CA 1-4R; CAAS 4; CANR 1;
DAM POET; DLB 5; MTCW

Simpson, Mona (Elizabeth) 1957-... **CLC 44**
See also CA 122; 135

Simpson, N(orman) F(rederick)
1919- .... **CLC 29**
See also CA 13-16R; DLB 13

Sinclair, Andrew (Annandale)
1935- .... **CLC 2, 14**
See also CA 9-12R; CAAS 5; CANR 14, 38;
DLB 14; MTCW

Sinclair, Emil
See Hesse, Hermann

Sinclair, Iain 1943-.............. **CLC 76**
See also CA 132

Sinclair, Iain MacGregor
See Sinclair, Iain

Sinclair, Mary Amelia St. Clair 1865(?)-1946
See Sinclair, May
See also CA 104

Sinclair, May.................. **TCLC 3, 11**
See also Sinclair, Mary Amelia St. Clair
See also DLB 36, 135

Sinclair, Upton (Beall)
1878-1968 ...... **CLC 1, 11, 15, 63; DA;
DAB; DAC; WLC**
See also CA 5-8R; 25-28R; CANR 7;
CDALB 1929-1941; DAM MST, NOV;
DLB 9; INT CANR-7; MTCW; SATA 9

Singer, Isaac
See Singer, Isaac Bashevis

Sontag, Susan 1933-... **CLC 1, 2, 10, 13, 31**
See also CA 17-20R; CANR 25, 51;
DAM POP; DLB 2, 67; MTCW

Sophocles
496(?)B.C.-406(?)B.C.... **CMLC 2; DA;**
DAB; DAC; DC 1
See also DAM DRAM, MST

Sordello 1189-1269............ **CMLC 15**

Sorel, Julia
See Drexler, Rosalyn

Sorrentino, Gilbert
1929-............ **CLC 3, 7, 14, 22, 40**
See also CA 77-80; CANR 14, 33; DLB 5;
DLBY 80; INT CANR-14

Soto, Gary 1952-....... **CLC 32, 80; HLC**
See also AAYA 10; CA 119; 125;
CANR 50; CLR 38; DAM MULT;
DLB 82; HW; INT 125; JRDA; SATA 80

Soupault, Philippe 1897-1990 ...... **CLC 68**
See also CA 116; 147; 131

Souster, (Holmes) Raymond
1921-.............. **CLC 5, 14; DAC**
See also CA 13-16R; CAAS 14; CANR 13,
29; DAM POET; DLB 88; SATA 63

Southern, Terry 1924(?)-1995 .... **CLC 7**
See also CA 1-4R; 150; CANR 1; DLB 2

Southey, Robert 1774-1843 .... **NCLC 8**
See also DLB 93, 107, 142; SATA 54

Southworth, Emma Dorothy Eliza Nevitte
1819-1899 .... **NCLC 26**

Souza, Ernest
See Scott, Evelyn

Soyinka, Wole
1934-....... **CLC 3, 5, 14, 36, 44; BLC;**
DA; DAB; DAC; DC 2; WLC
See also BW 2; CA 13-16R; CANR 27, 39;
DAM DRAM, MST, MULT; DLB 125;
MTCW

Spackman, W(illiam) M(ode)
1905-1990 .... **CLC 46**
See also CA 81-84; 132

Spacks, Barry 1931-.............. **CLC 14**
See also CA 29-32R; CANR 33; DLB 105

Spanidou, Irini 1946-............. **CLC 44**

Spark, Muriel (Sarah)
1918-..... **CLC 2, 3, 5, 8, 13, 18, 40, 94;**
DAB; DAC; SSC 10
See also CA 5-8R; CANR 12, 36;
CDBLB 1945-1960; DAM MST, NOV;
DLB 15, 139; INT CANR-12; MTCW

Spaulding, Douglas
See Bradbury, Ray (Douglas)

Spaulding, Leonard
See Bradbury, Ray (Douglas)

Spence, J. A. D.
See Eliot, T(homas) S(tearns)

Spencer, Elizabeth 1921-.......... **CLC 22**
See also CA 13-16R; CANR 32; DLB 6;
MTCW; SATA 14

Spencer, Leonard G.
See Silverberg, Robert

Spencer, Scott 1945-.............. **CLC 30**
See also CA 113; CANR 51; DLBY 86

Spender, Stephen (Harold)
1909-1995 ...... **CLC 1, 2, 5, 10, 41, 91**
See also CA 9-12R; 149; CANR 31;
CDBLB 1945-1960; DAM POET;
DLB 20; MTCW

Spengler, Oswald (Arnold Gottfried)
1880-1936 .... **TCLC 25**
See also CA 118

Spenser, Edmund
1552(?)-1599 .... **LC 5; DA; DAB; DAC;**
PC 8; WLC
See also CDBLB Before 1660; DAM MST,
POET

Spicer, Jack 1925-1965 ...... **CLC 8, 18, 72**
See also CA 85-88; DAM POET; DLB 5, 16

Spiegelman, Art 1948-............. **CLC 76**
See also AAYA 10; CA 125; CANR 41

Spielberg, Peter 1929-............. **CLC 6**
See also CA 5-8R; CANR 4, 48; DLBY 81

Spielberg, Steven 1947-........... **CLC 20**
See also AAYA 8; CA 77-80; CANR 32;
SATA 32

Spillane, Frank Morrison 1918-
See Spillane, Mickey
See also CA 25-28R; CANR 28; MTCW;
SATA 66

Spillane, Mickey .... **CLC 3, 13**
See also Spillane, Frank Morrison

Spinoza, Benedictus de 1632-1677 .... **LC 9**

Spinrad, Norman (Richard) 1940-... **CLC 46**
See also CA 37-40R; CAAS 19; CANR 20;
DLB 8; INT CANR-20

Spitteler, Carl (Friedrich Georg)
1845-1924 .... **TCLC 12**
See also CA 109; DLB 129

Spivack, Kathleen (Romola Drucker)
1938-....................... **CLC 6**
See also CA 49-52

Spoto, Donald 1941-.............. **CLC 39**
See also CA 65-68; CANR 11

Springsteen, Bruce (F.) 1949- ...... **CLC 17**
See also CA 111

Spurling, Hilary 1940-............ **CLC 34**
See also CA 104; CANR 25

Spyker, John Howland
See Elman, Richard

Squires, (James) Radcliffe
1917-1993 .... **CLC 51**
See also CA 1-4R; 140; CANR 6, 21

Srivastava, Dhanpat Rai 1880(?)-1936
See Premchand
See also CA 118

Stacy, Donald
See Pohl, Frederik

Stael, Germaine de
See Stael-Holstein, Anne Louise Germaine
Necker Baronn
See also DLB 119

Stael-Holstein, Anne Louise Germaine Necker
Baronn 1766-1817 .... **NCLC 3**
See also Stael, Germaine de

Stafford, Jean 1915-1979... **CLC 4, 7, 19, 68**
See also CA 1-4R; 85-88; CANR 3; DLB 2;
MTCW; SATA-Obit 22

Stafford, William (Edgar)
1914-1993 .... **CLC 4, 7, 29**
See also CA 5-8R; 142; CAAS 3; CANR 5,
22; DAM POET; DLB 5; INT CANR-22

Staines, Trevor
See Brunner, John (Kilian Houston)

Stairs, Gordon
See Austin, Mary (Hunter)

Stannard, Martin 1947-........... **CLC 44**
See also CA 142; DLB 155

Stanton, Maura 1946- .... **CLC 9**
See also CA 89-92; CANR 15; DLB 120

Stanton, Schuyler
See Baum, L(yman) Frank

Stapledon, (William) Olaf
1886-1950 .... **TCLC 22**
See also CA 111; DLB 15

Starbuck, George (Edwin) 1931-.... **CLC 53**
See also CA 21-24R; CANR 23;
DAM POET

Stark, Richard
See Westlake, Donald E(dwin)

Staunton, Schuyler
See Baum, L(yman) Frank

Stead, Christina (Ellen)
1902-1983 .... **CLC 2, 5, 8, 32, 80**
See also CA 13-16R; 109; CANR 33, 40;
MTCW

Stead, William Thomas
1849-1912 .... **TCLC 48**

Steele, Richard 1672-1729.......... **LC 18**
See also CDBLB 1660-1789; DLB 84, 101

Steele, Timothy (Reid) 1948-....... **CLC 45**
See also CA 93-96; CANR 16, 50; DLB 120

Steffens, (Joseph) Lincoln
1866-1936 .... **TCLC 20**
See also CA 117

Stegner, Wallace (Earle)
1909-1993 .... **CLC 9, 49, 81**
See also AITN 1; BEST 90:3; CA 1-4R;
141; CAAS 9; CANR 1, 21, 46;
DAM NOV; DLB 9; DLBY 93; MTCW

Stein, Gertrude
1874-1946 ...... **TCLC 1, 6, 28, 48; DA;**
DAB; DAC; WLC
See also CA 104; 132; CDALB 1917-1929;
DAM MST, NOV, POET; DLB 4, 54, 86;
MTCW

Steinbeck, John (Ernst)
1902-1968 ...... **CLC 1, 5, 9, 13, 21, 34,**
45, 75; DA; DAB; DAC; SSC 11; WLC
See also AAYA 12; CA 1-4R; 25-28R;
CANR 1, 35; CDALB 1929-1941;
DAM DRAM, MST, NOV; DLB 7, 9;
DLBD 2; MTCW; SATA 9

Steinem, Gloria 1934-............. **CLC 63**
See also CA 53-56; CANR 28, 51; MTCW

Steiner, George 1929-............. **CLC 24**
See also CA 73-76; CANR 31; DAM NOV;
DLB 67; MTCW; SATA 62

Steiner, K. Leslie
See Delany, Samuel R(ay, Jr.)

Steiner, Rudolf 1861-1925....... **TCLC 13**
See also CA 107

Stendhal
1783-1842 .... NCLC 23, 46; DA; DAB;
DAC; WLC
See also DAM MST, NOV; DLB 119

Stephen, Leslie 1832-1904 .... TCLC 23
See also CA 123; DLB 57, 144

Stephen, Sir Leslie
See Stephen, Leslie

Stephen, Virginia
See Woolf, (Adeline) Virginia

Stephens, James 1882(?)-1950 ...... TCLC 4
See also CA 104; DLB 19, 153, 162

Stephens, Reed
See Donaldson, Stephen R.

Steptoe, Lydia
See Barnes, Djuna

Sterchi, Beat 1949- .... CLC 65

Sterling, Brett
See Bradbury, Ray (Douglas); Hamilton,
Edmond

Sterling, Bruce 1954- .... CLC 72
See also CA 119; CANR 44

Sterling, George 1869-1926 .... TCLC 20
See also CA 117; DLB 54

Stern, Gerald 1925- .... CLC 40
See also CA 81-84; CANR 28; DLB 105

Stern, Richard (Gustave) 1928-... CLC 4, 39
See also CA 1-4R; CANR 1, 25; DLBY 87;
INT CANR-25

Sternberg, Josef von 1894-1969 ..... CLC 20
See also CA 81-84

Sterne, Laurence
1713-1768 ...... LC 2; DA; DAB; DAC;
WLC
See also CDBLB 1660-1789; DAM MST,
NOV; DLB 39

Sternheim, (William Adolf) Carl
1878-1942 .... TCLC 8
See also CA 105; DLB 56, 118

Stevens, Mark 1951- .... CLC 34
See also CA 122

Stevens, Wallace
1879-1955 .... TCLC 3, 12, 45; DA;
DAB; DAC; PC 6; WLC
See also CA 104; 124; CDALB 1929-1941;
DAM MST, POET; DLB 54; MTCW

Stevenson, Anne (Katharine)
1933- .... CLC 7, 33
See also CA 17-20R; CAAS 9; CANR 9, 33;
DLB 40; MTCW

Stevenson, Robert Louis (Balfour)
1850-1894 ..... NCLC 5, 14; DA; DAB;
DAC; SSC 11; WLC
See also CDBLB 1890-1914; CLR 10, 11;
DAM MST, NOV; DLB 18, 57, 141, 156;
DLBD 13; JRDA; MAICYA; YABC 2

Stewart, J(ohn) I(nnes) M(ackintosh)
1906-1994 .... CLC 7, 14, 32
See also CA 85-88; 147; CAAS 3;
CANR 47; MTCW

Stewart, Mary (Florence Elinor)
1916- .... CLC 7, 35; DAB
See also CA 1-4R; CANR 1; SATA 12

Stewart, Mary Rainbow
See Stewart, Mary (Florence Elinor)

Stifle, June
See Campbell, Maria

Stifter, Adalbert 1805-1868 ...... NCLC 41
See also DLB 133

Still, James 1906- .... CLC 49
See also CA 65-68; CAAS 17; CANR 10,
26; DLB 9; SATA 29

Sting
See Sumner, Gordon Matthew

Stirling, Arthur
See Sinclair, Upton (Beall)

Stitt, Milan 1941- .... CLC 29
See also CA 69-72

Stockton, Francis Richard 1834-1902
See Stockton, Frank R.
See also CA 108; 137; MAICYA; SATA 44

Stockton, Frank R. .... TCLC 47
See also Stockton, Francis Richard
See also DLB 42, 74; DLBD 13;
SATA-Brief 32

Stoddard, Charles
See Kuttner, Henry

Stoker, Abraham 1847-1912
See Stoker, Bram
See also CA 105; DA; DAC; DAM MST,
NOV; SATA 29

Stoker, Bram
1847-1912 .... TCLC 8; DAB; WLC
See also Stoker, Abraham
See also CA 150; CDBLB 1890-1914;
DLB 36, 70

Stolz, Mary (Slattery) 1920- .... CLC 12
See also AAYA 8; AITN 1; CA 5-8R;
CANR 13, 41; JRDA; MAICYA;
SAAS 3; SATA 10, 71

Stone, Irving 1903-1989 .... CLC 7
See also AITN 1; CA 1-4R; 129; CAAS 3;
CANR 1, 23; DAM POP;
INT CANR-23; MTCW; SATA 3;
SATA-Obit 64

Stone, Oliver 1946- .... CLC 73
See also AAYA 15; CA 110

Stone, Robert (Anthony)
1937- .... CLC 5, 23, 42
See also CA 85-88; CANR 23; DLB 152;
INT CANR-23; MTCW

Stone, Zachary
See Follett, Ken(neth Martin)

Stoppard, Tom
1937- ...... CLC 1, 3, 4, 5, 8, 15, 29, 34,
63, 91; DA; DAB; DAC; DC 6; WLC
See also CA 81-84; CANR 39;
CDBLB 1960 to Present; DAM DRAM,
MST; DLB 13; DLBY 85; MTCW

Storey, David (Malcolm)
1933- .... CLC 2, 4, 5, 8
See also CA 81-84; CANR 36;
DAM DRAM; DLB 13, 14; MTCW

Storm, Hyemeyohsts 1935- .... CLC 3
See also CA 81-84; CANR 45;
DAM MULT; NNAL

Storm, (Hans) Theodor (Woldsen)
1817-1888 .... NCLC 1

Storni, Alfonsina
1892-1938 .... TCLC 5; HLC
See also CA 104; 131; DAM MULT; HW

Stout, Rex (Todhunter) 1886-1975 ... CLC 3
See also AITN 2; CA 61-64

Stow, (Julian) Randolph 1935- .. CLC 23, 48
See also CA 13-16R; CANR 33; MTCW

Stowe, Harriet (Elizabeth) Beecher
1811-1896 ..... NCLC 3, 50; DA; DAB;
DAC; WLC
See also CDALB 1865-1917; DAM MST,
NOV; DLB 1, 12, 42, 74; JRDA;
MAICYA; YABC 1

Strachey, (Giles) Lytton
1880-1932 .... TCLC 12
See also CA 110; DLB 149; DLBD 10

Strand, Mark 1934- ...... CLC 6, 18, 41, 71
See also CA 21-24R; CANR 40;
DAM POET; DLB 5; SATA 41

Straub, Peter (Francis) 1943- ...... CLC 28
See also BEST 89:1; CA 85-88; CANR 28;
DAM POP; DLBY 84; MTCW

Strauss, Botho 1944- .... CLC 22
See also DLB 124

Streatfeild, (Mary) Noel
1895(?)-1986 .... CLC 21
See also CA 81-84; 120; CANR 31;
CLR 17; DLB 160; MAICYA; SATA 20;
SATA-Obit 48

Stribling, T(homas) S(igismund)
1881-1965 .... CLC 23
See also CA 107; DLB 9

Strindberg, (Johan) August
1849-1912 ...... TCLC 1, 8, 21, 47; DA;
DAB; DAC; WLC
See also CA 104; 135; DAM DRAM, MST

Stringer, Arthur 1874-1950 .... TCLC 37
See also DLB 92

Stringer, David
See Roberts, Keith (John Kingston)

Strugatskii, Arkadii (Natanovich)
1925-1991 .... CLC 27
See also CA 106; 135

Strugatskii, Boris (Natanovich)
1933- .... CLC 27
See also CA 106

Strummer, Joe 1953(?)- .... CLC 30

Stuart, Don A.
See Campbell, John W(ood, Jr.)

Stuart, Ian
See MacLean, Alistair (Stuart)

Stuart, Jesse (Hilton)
1906-1984 ...... CLC 1, 8, 11, 14, 34
See also CA 5-8R; 112; CANR 31; DLB 9,
48, 102; DLBY 84; SATA 2;
SATA-Obit 36

Sturgeon, Theodore (Hamilton)
1918-1985 .... CLC 22, 39
See also Queen, Ellery
See also CA 81-84; 116; CANR 32; DLB 8;
DLBY 85; MTCW

Sturges, Preston 1898-1959 .... TCLC 48
See also CA 114; 149; DLB 26

Styron, William
1925- .... CLC 1, 3, 5, 11, 15, 60
See also BEST 90:4; CA 5-8R; CANR 6, 33;
CDALB 1968-1988; DAM NOV, POP;
DLB 2, 143; DLBY 80; INT CANR-6;
MTCW

Suarez Lynch, B.
See Bioy Casares, Adolfo; Borges, Jorge
Luis

Su Chien 1884-1918
See Su Man-shu
See also CA 123

Suckow, Ruth 1892-1960 . . . . **SSC 18**
See also CA 113; DLB 9, 102

Sudermann, Hermann 1857-1928 . . **TCLC 15**
See also CA 107; DLB 118

Sue, Eugene 1804-1857 . . . . **NCLC 1**
See also DLB 119

Sueskind, Patrick 1949- . . . . **CLC 44**
See also Suskind, Patrick

Sukenick, Ronald 1932- . . . . . **CLC 3, 4, 6, 48**
See also CA 25-28R; CAAS 8; CANR 32;
DLBY 81

Suknaski, Andrew 1942- . . . . **CLC 19**
See also CA 101; DLB 53

Sullivan, Vernon
See Vian, Boris

Sully Prudhomme 1839-1907 . . . . . . **TCLC 31**

Su Man-shu . . . . **TCLC 24**
See also Su Chien

Summerforest, Ivy B.
See Kirkup, James

Summers, Andrew James 1942- . . . . . **CLC 26**

Summers, Andy
See Summers, Andrew James

Summers, Hollis (Spurgeon, Jr.)
1916- . . . . **CLC 10**
See also CA 5-8R; CANR 3; DLB 6

Summers, (Alphonsus Joseph-Mary Augustus)
Montague 1880-1948 . . . . **TCLC 16**
See also CA 118

Sumner, Gordon Matthew 1951- . . . . **CLC 26**

Surtees, Robert Smith
1803-1864 . . . . **NCLC 14**
See also DLB 21

Susann, Jacqueline 1921-1974 . . . . **CLC 3**
See also AITN 1; CA 65-68; 53-56; MTCW

Su Shih 1036-1101 . . . . **CMLC 15**

Suskind, Patrick
See Sueskind, Patrick
See also CA 145

Sutcliff, Rosemary
1920-1992 . . . . **CLC 26; DAB; DAC**
See also AAYA 10; CA 5-8R; 139;
CANR 37; CLR 1, 37; DAM MST, POP;
JRDA; MAICYA; SATA 6, 44, 78;
SATA-Obit 73

Sutro, Alfred 1863-1933 . . . . **TCLC 6**
See also CA 105; DLB 10

Sutton, Henry
See Slavitt, David R(ytman)

Svevo, Italo . . . . **TCLC 2, 35**
See also Schmitz, Aron Hector

Swados, Elizabeth (A.) 1951- . . . . **CLC 12**
See also CA 97-100; CANR 49; INT 97-100

Swados, Harvey 1920-1972 . . . . **CLC 5**
See also CA 5-8R; 37-40R; CANR 6;
DLB 2

Swan, Gladys 1934- . . . . **CLC 69**
See also CA 101; CANR 17, 39

Swarthout, Glendon (Fred)
1918-1992 . . . . **CLC 35**
See also CA 1-4R; 139; CANR 1, 47;
SATA 26

Sweet, Sarah C.
See Jewett, (Theodora) Sarah Orne

Swenson, May
1919-1989 . . . . **CLC 4, 14, 61; DA; DAB;**
DAC; PC 14
See also CA 5-8R; 130; CANR 36;
DAM MST, POET; DLB 5; MTCW;
SATA 15

Swift, Augustus
See Lovecraft, H(oward) P(hillips)

Swift, Graham (Colin) 1949- . . . . **CLC 41, 88**
See also CA 117; 122; CANR 46

Swift, Jonathan
1667-1745 . . . . . . **LC 1; DA; DAB; DAC;**
PC 9; WLC
See also CDBLB 1660-1789; DAM MST,
NOV, POET; DLB 39, 95, 101; SATA 19

Swinburne, Algernon Charles
1837-1909 . . . . . . **TCLC 8, 36; DA; DAB;**
DAC; WLC
See also CA 105; 140; CDBLB 1832-1890;
DAM MST, POET; DLB 35, 57

Swinfen, Ann . . . . **CLC 34**

Swinnerton, Frank Arthur
1884-1982 . . . . **CLC 31**
See also CA 108; DLB 34

Swithen, John
See King, Stephen (Edwin)

Sylvia
See Ashton-Warner, Sylvia (Constance)

Symmes, Robert Edward
See Duncan, Robert (Edward)

Symonds, John Addington
1840-1893 . . . . **NCLC 34**
See also DLB 57, 144

Symons, Arthur 1865-1945 . . . . **TCLC 11**
See also CA 107; DLB 19, 57, 149

Symons, Julian (Gustave)
1912-1994 . . . . **CLC 2, 14, 32**
See also CA 49-52; 147; CAAS 3; CANR 3,
33; DLB 87, 155; DLBY 92; MTCW

Synge, (Edmund) J(ohn) M(illington)
1871-1909 . . . . **TCLC 6, 37; DC 2**
See also CA 104; 141; CDBLB 1890-1914;
DAM DRAM; DLB 10, 19

Syruc, J.
See Milosz, Czeslaw

Szirtes, George 1948- . . . . **CLC 46**
See also CA 109; CANR 27

Tabori, George 1914- . . . . **CLC 19**
See also CA 49-52; CANR 4

Tagore, Rabindranath
1861-1941 . . . . **TCLC 3, 53; PC 8**
See also CA 104; 120; DAM DRAM,
POET; MTCW

Taine, Hippolyte Adolphe
1828-1893 . . . . **NCLC 15**

Talese, Gay 1932- . . . . **CLC 37**
See also AITN 1; CA 1-4R; CANR 9;
INT CANR-9; MTCW

Tallent, Elizabeth (Ann) 1954- . . . . . **CLC 45**
See also CA 117; DLB 130

Tally, Ted 1952- . . . . **CLC 42**
See also CA 120; 124; INT 124

Tamayo y Baus, Manuel
1829-1898 . . . . **NCLC 1**

Tammsaare, A(nton) H(ansen)
1878-1940 . . . . **TCLC 27**

Tan, Amy 1952- . . . . **CLC 59**
See also AAYA 9; BEST 89:3; CA 136;
DAM MULT, NOV, POP; SATA 75

Tandem, Felix
See Spitteler, Carl (Friedrich Georg)

Tanizaki, Jun'ichiro
1886-1965 . . . . . . **CLC 8, 14, 28; SSC 21**
See also CA 93-96; 25-28R

Tanner, William
See Amis, Kingsley (William)

Tao Lao
See Storni, Alfonsina

Tarassoff, Lev
See Troyat, Henri

Tarbell, Ida M(inerva)
1857-1944 . . . . **TCLC 40**
See also CA 122; DLB 47

Tarkington, (Newton) Booth
1869-1946 . . . . **TCLC 9**
See also CA 110; 143; DLB 9, 102;
SATA 17

Tarkovsky, Andrei (Arsenyevich)
1932-1986 . . . . **CLC 75**
See also CA 127

Tartt, Donna 1964(?)- . . . . **CLC 76**
See also CA 142

Tasso, Torquato 1544-1595 . . . . **LC 5**

Tate, (John Orley) Allen
1899-1979 . . . . **CLC 2, 4, 6, 9, 11, 14, 24**
See also CA 5-8R; 85-88; CANR 32;
DLB 4, 45, 63; MTCW

Tate, Ellalice
See Hibbert, Eleanor Alice Burford

Tate, James (Vincent) 1943- . . . **CLC 2, 6, 25**
See also CA 21-24R; CANR 29; DLB 5

Tavel, Ronald 1940- . . . . **CLC 6**
See also CA 21-24R; CANR 33

Taylor, C(ecil) P(hilip) 1929-1981 . . . **CLC 27**
See also CA 25-28R; 105; CANR 47

Taylor, Edward
1642(?)-1729 . . . **LC 11; DA; DAB; DAC**
See also DAM MST, POET; DLB 24

Taylor, Eleanor Ross 1920- . . . . **CLC 5**
See also CA 81-84

Taylor, Elizabeth 1912-1975 . . . **CLC 2, 4, 29**
See also CA 13-16R; CANR 9; DLB 139;
MTCW; SATA 13

Taylor, Henry (Splawn) 1942- . . . . . . **CLC 44**
See also CA 33-36R; CAAS 7; CANR 31;
DLB 5

Taylor, Kamala (Purnaiya) 1924-
See Markandaya, Kamala
See also CA 77-80

Tolkien, J(ohn) R(onald) R(euel)
    1892-1973 ...... **CLC 1, 2, 3, 8, 12, 38;**
                DA; DAB; DAC; WLC
    See also AAYA 10; AITN 1; CA 17-18;
    45-48; CANR 36; CAP 2;
    CDBLB 1914-1945; DAM MST, NOV,
    POP; DLB 15, 160; JRDA; MAICYA;
    MTCW; SATA 2, 32; SATA-Obit 24

Toller, Ernst   1893-1939 .... **TCLC 10**
    See also CA 107; DLB 124

Tolson, M. B.
    See Tolson, Melvin B(eaunorus)

Tolson, Melvin B(eaunorus)
    1898(?)-1966 .... **CLC 36; BLC**
    See also BW 1; CA 124; 89-92;
    DAM MULT, POET; DLB 48, 76

Tolstoi, Aleksei Nikolaevich
    See Tolstoy, Alexey Nikolaevich

Tolstoy, Alcxcy Nikolaevich
    1882-1945 .... **TCLC 18**
    See also CA 107

Tolstoy, Count Leo
    See Tolstoy, Leo (Nikolaevich)

Tolstoy, Leo (Nikolaevich)
    1828-1910 ...... **TCLC 4, 11, 17, 28, 44;**
                DA; DAB; DAC; SSC 9; WLC
    See also CA 104; 123; DAM MST, NOV;
    SATA 26

Tomasi di Lampedusa, Giuseppe   1896-1957
    See Lampedusa, Giuseppe (Tomasi) di
    See also CA 111

Tomlin, Lily .... **CLC 17**
    See also Tomlin, Mary Jean

Tomlin, Mary Jean   1939(?)-
    See Tomlin, Lily
    See also CA 117

Tomlinson, (Alfred) Charles
    1927- .... **CLC 2, 4, 6, 13, 45**
    See also CA 5-8R; CANR 33; DAM POET;
    DLB 40

Tonson, Jacob
    See Bennett, (Enoch) Arnold

Toole, John Kennedy
    1937-1969 .... **CLC 19, 64**
    See also CA 104; DLBY 81

Toomer, Jean
    1894-1967 ...... **CLC 1, 4, 13, 22; BLC;**
                PC 7; SSC 1
    See also BW 1; CA 85-88;
    CDALB 1917-1929; DAM MULT;
    DLB 45, 51; MTCW

Torley, Luke
    See Blish, James (Benjamin)

Tornimparte, Alessandra
    See Ginzburg, Natalia

Torre, Raoul della
    See Mencken, H(enry) L(ouis)

Torrey, E(dwin) Fuller   1937- .... **CLC 34**
    See also CA 119

Torsvan, Ben Traven
    See Traven, B.

Torsvan, Benno Traven
    See Traven, B.

Torsvan, Berick Traven
    See Traven, B.

Torsvan, Berwick Traven
    See Traven, B.

Torsvan, Bruno Traven
    See Traven, B.

Torsvan, Traven
    See Traven, B.

Tournier, Michel (Edouard)
    1924- .... **CLC 6, 23, 36**
    See also CA 49-52; CANR 3, 36; DLB 83;
    MTCW; SATA 23

Tournimparte, Alessandra
    See Ginzburg, Natalia

Towers, Ivar
    See Kornbluth, C(yril) M.

Towne, Robert (Burton)   1936(?)- .... **CLC 87**
    See also CA 108; DLB 44

Townsend, Sue   1946- .. **CLC 61; DAB; DAC**
    See also CA 119; 127; INT 127; MTCW;
    SATA 55; SATA-Brief 48

Townshend, Peter (Dennis Blandford)
    1945- .... **CLC 17, 42**
    See also CA 107

Tozzi, Federigo   1883-1920 .... **TCLC 31**

Traill, Catharine Parr
    1802-1899 .... **NCLC 31**
    See also DLB 99

Trakl, Georg   1887-1914 .... **TCLC 5**
    See also CA 104

Transtroemer, Tomas (Goesta)
    1931- .... **CLC 52, 65**
    See also CA 117; 129; CAAS 17;
    DAM POET

Transtromer, Tomas Gosta
    See Transtroemer, Tomas (Goesta)

Traven, B.   (?)-1969 .... **CLC 8, 11**
    See also CA 19-20; 25-28R; CAP 2; DLB 9,
    56; MTCW

Treitel, Jonathan   1959- .... **CLC 70**

Tremain, Rose   1943- .... **CLC 42**
    See also CA 97-100; CANR 44; DLB 14

Tremblay, Michel   1942- ...... **CLC 29; DAC**
    See also CA 116; 128; DAM MST; DLB 60;
    MTCW

Trevanian .... **CLC 29**
    See also Whitaker, Rod(ney)

Trevor, Glen
    See Hilton, James

Trevor, William
    1928- ..... **CLC 7, 9, 14, 25, 71; SSC 21**
    See also Cox, William Trevor
    See also DLB 14, 139

Trifonov, Yuri (Valentinovich)
    1925-1981 .... **CLC 45**
    See also CA 126; 103; MTCW

Trilling, Lionel   1905-1975 .... **CLC 9, 11, 24**
    See also CA 9-12R; 61-64; CANR 10;
    DLB 28, 63; INT CANR-10; MTCW

Trimball, W. H.
    See Mencken, H(enry) L(ouis)

Tristan
    See Gomez de la Serna, Ramon

Tristram
    See Housman, A(lfred) E(dward)

Trogdon, William (Lewis)   1939-
    See Heat-Moon, William Least
    See also CA 115; 119; CANR 47; INT 119

Trollope, Anthony
    1815-1882 ..... **NCLC 6, 33; DA; DAB;**
                DAC; WLC
    See also CDBLB 1832-1890; DAM MST,
    NOV; DLB 21, 57, 159; SATA 22

Trollope, Frances   1779-1863 ..... **NCLC 30**
    See also DLB 21

Trotsky, Leon   1879-1940 .... **TCLC 22**
    See also CA 118

Trotter (Cockburn), Catharine
    1679-1749 .... **LC 8**
    See also DLB 84

Trout, Kilgore
    See Farmer, Philip Jose

Trow, George W. S.   1943- .... **CLC 52**
    See also CA 126

Troyat, Henri   1911- .... **CLC 23**
    See also CA 45-48; CANR 2, 33; MTCW

Trudeau, G(arretson) B(eekman)   1948-
    See Trudeau, Garry B.
    See also CA 81-84; CANR 31; SATA 35

Trudeau, Garry B. .... **CLC 12**
    See also Trudeau, G(arretson) B(eekman)
    See also AAYA 10; AITN 2

Truffaut, Francois   1932-1984 .... **CLC 20**
    See also CA 81-84; 113; CANR 34

Trumbo, Dalton   1905-1976 .... **CLC 19**
    See also CA 21-24R; 69-72; CANR 10;
    DLB 26

Trumbull, John   1750-1831 .... **NCLC 30**
    See also DLB 31

Trundlett, Helen B.
    See Eliot, T(homas) S(tearns)

Tryon, Thomas   1926-1991 .... **CLC 3, 11**
    See also AITN 1; CA 29-32R; 135;
    CANR 32; DAM POP; MTCW

Tryon, Tom
    See Tryon, Thomas

Ts'ao Hsueh-ch'in   1715(?)-1763 .... **LC 1**

Tsushima, Shuji   1909-1948
    See Dazai, Osamu
    See also CA 107

Tsvetaeva (Efron), Marina (Ivanovna)
    1892-1941 .... **TCLC 7, 35; PC 14**
    See also CA 104; 128; MTCW

Tuck, Lily   1938- .... **CLC 70**
    See also CA 139

Tu Fu   712-770 .... **PC 9**
    See also DAM MULT

Tunis, John R(oberts)   1889-1975 ... **CLC 12**
    See also CA 61-64; DLB 22; JRDA;
    MAICYA; SATA 37; SATA-Brief 30

Tuohy, Frank .... **CLC 37**
    See also Tuohy, John Francis
    See also DLB 14, 139

Tuohy, John Francis   1925-
    See Tuohy, Frank
    See also CA 5-8R; CANR 3, 47

Turco, Lewis (Putnam)   1934- ... **CLC 11, 63**
    See also CA 13-16R; CAAS 22; CANR 24,
    51; DLBY 84

Walker, Alice (Malsenior)
1944- . . . . . . **CLC 5, 6, 9, 19, 27, 46, 58;
BLC; DA; DAB; DAC; SSC 5**
See also AAYA 3; BEST 89:4; BW 2;
CA 37-40R; CANR 9, 27, 49;
CDALB 1968-1988; DAM MST, MULT,
NOV, POET, POP; DLB 6, 33, 143;
INT CANR-27; MTCW; SATA 31

Walker, David Harry 1911-1992. . . . **CLC 14**
See also CA 1-4R; 137; CANR 1; SATA 8;
SATA-Obit 71

Walker, Edward Joseph 1934-
See Walker, Ted
See also CA 21-24R; CANR 12, 28

Walker, George F.
1947- . . . . **CLC 44, 61; DAB; DAC**
See also CA 103; CANR 21, 43;
DAM MST; DLB 60

Walker, Joseph A. 1935- . . . . **CLC 19**
See also BW 1; CA 89-92; CANR 26;
DAM DRAM, MST; DLB 38

Walker, Margaret (Abigail)
1915- . . . . **CLC 1, 6; BLC**
See also BW 2; CA 73-76; CANR 26;
DAM MULT; DLB 76, 152; MTCW

Walker, Ted . . . . **CLC 13**
See also Walker, Edward Joseph
See also DLB 40

Wallace, David Foster 1962- . . . . **CLC 50**
See also CA 132

Wallace, Dexter
See Masters, Edgar Lee

Wallace, (Richard Horatio) Edgar
1875-1932 . . . . **TCLC 57**
See also CA 115; DLB 70

Wallace, Irving 1916-1990 . . . . . . **CLC 7, 13**
See also AITN 1; CA 1-4R; 132; CAAS 1;
CANR 1, 27; DAM NOV, POP;
INT CANR-27; MTCW

Wallant, Edward Lewis
1926-1962 . . . . **CLC 5, 10**
See also CA 1-4R; CANR 22; DLB 2, 28,
143; MTCW

Walley, Byron
See Card, Orson Scott

Walpole, Horace 1717-1797 . . . . **LC 2**
See also DLB 39, 104

Walpole, Hugh (Seymour)
1884-1941 . . . . **TCLC 5**
See also CA 104; DLB 34

Walser, Martin 1927- . . . . **CLC 27**
See also CA 57-60; CANR 8, 46; DLB 75,
124

Walser, Robert
1878-1956 . . . . **TCLC 18; SSC 20**
See also CA 118; DLB 66

Walsh, Jill Paton . . . . **CLC 35**
See also Paton Walsh, Gillian
See also AAYA 11; CLR 2; DLB 161;
SAAS 3

Walter, Villiam Christian
See Andersen, Hans Christian

Wambaugh, Joseph (Aloysius, Jr.)
1937- . . . . **CLC 3, 18**
See also AITN 1; BEST 89:3; CA 33-36R;
CANR 42; DAM NOV, POP; DLB 6;
DLBY 83; MTCW

Ward, Arthur Henry Sarsfield 1883-1959
See Rohmer, Sax
See also CA 108

Ward, Douglas Turner 1930- . . . . **CLC 19**
See also BW 1; CA 81-84; CANR 27;
DLB 7, 38

Ward, Mary Augusta
See Ward, Mrs. Humphry

Ward, Mrs. Humphry
1851-1920 . . . . **TCLC 55**
See also DLB 18

Ward, Peter
See Faust, Frederick (Schiller)

Warhol, Andy 1928(?)-1987 . . . . **CLC 20**
See also AAYA 12; BEST 89:4; CA 89-92;
121; CANR 34

Warner, Francis (Robert le Plastrier)
1937- . . . . **CLC 14**
See also CA 53-56; CANR 11

Warner, Marina 1946- . . . . **CLC 59**
See also CA 65-68; CANR 21

Warner, Rex (Ernest) 1905-1986. . . . **CLC 45**
See also CA 89-92; 119; DLB 15

Warner, Susan (Bogert)
1819-1885 . . . . **NCLC 31**
See also DLB 3, 42

Warner, Sylvia (Constance) Ashton
See Ashton-Warner, Sylvia (Constance)

Warner, Sylvia Townsend
1893-1978 . . . . **CLC 7, 19; SSC 23**
See also CA 61-64; 77-80; CANR 16;
DLB 34, 139; MTCW

Warren, Mercy Otis 1728-1814. . . **NCLC 13**
See also DLB 31

Warren, Robert Penn
1905-1989 . . . . **CLC 1, 4, 6, 8, 10, 13, 18,
39, 53, 59; DA; DAB; DAC; SSC 4; WLC**
See also AITN 1; CA 13-16R; 129;
CANR 10, 47; CDALB 1968-1988;
DAM MST, NOV, POET; DLB 2, 48,
152; DLBY 80, 89; INT CANR-10;
MTCW; SATA 46; SATA-Obit 63

Warshofsky, Isaac
See Singer, Isaac Bashevis

Warton, Thomas 1728-1790 . . . . **LC 15**
See also DAM POET; DLB 104, 109

Waruk, Kona
See Harris, (Theodore) Wilson

Warung, Price 1855-1911. . . . . **TCLC 45**

Warwick, Jarvis
See Garner, Hugh

Washington, Alex
See Harris, Mark

Washington, Booker T(aliaferro)
1856-1915 . . . . **TCLC 10; BLC**
See also BW 1; CA 114; 125; DAM MULT;
SATA 28

Washington, George 1732-1799 . . . . . . **LC 25**
See also DLB 31

Wassermann, (Karl) Jakob
1873-1934 . . . . **TCLC 6**
See also CA 104; DLB 66

Wasserstein, Wendy
1950- . . . . **CLC 32, 59, 90; DC 4**
See also CA 121; 129; CABS 3;
DAM DRAM; INT 129

Waterhouse, Keith (Spencer)
1929- . . . . **CLC 47**
See also CA 5-8R; CANR 38; DLB 13, 15;
MTCW

Waters, Frank (Joseph)
1902-1995 . . . . **CLC 88**
See also CA 5-8R; 149; CAAS 13; CANR 3,
18; DLBY 86

Waters, Roger 1944- . . . . **CLC 35**

Watkins, Frances Ellen
See Harper, Frances Ellen Watkins

Watkins, Gerrold
See Malzberg, Barry N(athaniel)

Watkins, Gloria 1955(?)-
See hooks, bell
See also BW 2; CA 143

Watkins, Paul 1964- . . . . **CLC 55**
See also CA 132

Watkins, Vernon Phillips
1906-1967 . . . . **CLC 43**
See also CA 9-10; 25-28R; CAP 1; DLB 20

Watson, Irving S.
See Mencken, H(enry) L(ouis)

Watson, John H.
See Farmer, Philip Jose

Watson, Richard F.
See Silverberg, Robert

Waugh, Auberon (Alexander) 1939- . . **CLC 7**
See also CA 45-48; CANR 6, 22; DLB 14

Waugh, Evelyn (Arthur St. John)
1903-1966 . . . . . . **CLC 1, 3, 8, 13, 19, 27,
44; DA; DAB; DAC; WLC**
See also CA 85-88; 25-28R; CANR 22;
CDBLB 1914-1945; DAM MST, NOV,
POP; DLB 15, 162; MTCW

Waugh, Harriet 1944- . . . . **CLC 6**
See also CA 85-88; CANR 22

Ways, C. R.
See Blount, Roy (Alton), Jr.

Waystaff, Simon
See Swift, Jonathan

Webb, (Martha) Beatrice (Potter)
1858-1943 . . . . **TCLC 22**
See also Potter, Beatrice
See also CA 117

Webb, Charles (Richard) 1939- . . . . . . **CLC 7**
See also CA 25-28R

Webb, James H(enry), Jr. 1946- . . . . **CLC 22**
See also CA 81-84

Webb, Mary (Gladys Meredith)
1881-1927 . . . . **TCLC 24**
See also CA 123; DLB 34

Webb, Mrs. Sidney
See Webb, (Martha) Beatrice (Potter)

Webb, Phyllis 1927- . . . . **CLC 18**
See also CA 104; CANR 23; DLB 53

Webb, Sidney (James)
1859-1947 .... **TCLC 22**
See also CA 117

Webber, Andrew Lloyd .... **CLC 21**
See also Lloyd Webber, Andrew

Weber, Lenora Mattingly
1895-1971 .... **CLC 12**
See also CA 19-20; 29-32R; CAP 1;
SATA 2; SATA-Obit 26

Webster, John
1579(?)-1634(?) ...... **LC 33; DA; DAB;
DAC; DC 2; WLC**
See also CDBLB Before 1660;
DAM DRAM, MST; DLB 58

Webster, Noah   1758-1843 .... **NCLC 30**

Wedekind, (Benjamin) Frank(lin)
1864-1918 .... **TCLC 7**
See also CA 104; DAM DRAM; DLB 118

Weidman, Jerome   1913- .... **CLC 7**
See also AITN 2; CA 1-4R; CANR 1;
DLB 28

Weil, Simone (Adolphine)
1909-1943 .... **TCLC 23**
See also CA 117

Weinstein, Nathan
See West, Nathanael

Weinstein, Nathan von Wallenstein
See West, Nathanael

Weir, Peter (Lindsay)   1944- .... **CLC 20**
See also CA 113; 123

Weiss, Peter (Ulrich)
1916-1982 .... **CLC 3, 15, 51**
See also CA 45-48; 106; CANR 3;
DAM DRAM; DLB 69, 124

Weiss, Theodore (Russell)
1916- .... **CLC 3, 8, 14**
See also CA 9-12R; CAAS 2; CANR 46;
DLB 5

Welch, (Maurice) Denton
1915-1948 .... **TCLC 22**
See also CA 121; 148

Welch, James   1940- .... **CLC 6, 14, 52**
See also CA 85-88; CANR 42;
DAM MULT, POP; NNAL

Weldon, Fay
1933- .... **CLC 6, 9, 11, 19, 36, 59**
See also CA 21-24R; CANR 16, 46;
CDBLB 1960 to Present; DAM POP;
DLB 14; INT CANR-16; MTCW

Wellek, Rene   1903-1995 .... **CLC 28**
See also CA 5-8R; 150; CAAS 7; CANR 8;
DLB 63; INT CANR-8

Weller, Michael   1942- .... **CLC 10, 53**
See also CA 85-88

Weller, Paul   1958- .... **CLC 26**

Wellershoff, Dieter   1925- .... **CLC 46**
See also CA 89-92; CANR 16, 37

Welles, (George) Orson
1915-1985 .... **CLC 20, 80**
See also CA 93-96; 117

Wellman, Mac   1945- .... **CLC 65**

Wellman, Manly Wade   1903-1986 .. **CLC 49**
See also CA 1-4R; 118; CANR 6, 16, 44;
SATA 6; SATA-Obit 47

Wells, Carolyn   1869(?)-1942 ...... **TCLC 35**
See also CA 113; DLB 11

Wells, H(erbert) G(eorge)
1866-1946 .... **TCLC 6, 12, 19; DA;
DAB; DAC; SSC 6; WLC**
See also CA 110; 121; CDBLB 1914-1945;
DAM MST, NOV; DLB 34, 70, 156;
MTCW; SATA 20

Wells, Rosemary   1943- .... **CLC 12**
See also AAYA 13; CA 85-88; CANR 48;
CLR 16; MAICYA; SAAS 1; SATA 18,
69

Welty, Eudora
1909- ...... **CLC 1, 2, 5, 14, 22, 33; DA;
DAB; DAC; SSC 1; WLC**
See also CA 9-12R; CABS 1; CANR 32;
CDALB 1941-1968; DAM MST, NOV;
DLB 2, 102, 143; DLBD 12; DLBY 87;
MTCW

Wen I-to   1899-1946 .... **TCLC 28**

Wentworth, Robert
See Hamilton, Edmond

Werfel, Franz (V.)   1890-1945 ...... **TCLC 8**
See also CA 104; DLB 81, 124

Wergeland, Henrik Arnold
1808-1845 .... **NCLC 5**

Wersba, Barbara   1932- .... **CLC 30**
See also AAYA 2; CA 29-32R; CANR 16,
38; CLR 3; DLB 52; JRDA; MAICYA;
SAAS 2; SATA 1, 58

Wertmueller, Lina   1928- .... **CLC 16**
See also CA 97-100; CANR 39

Wescott, Glenway   1901-1987 .... **CLC 13**
See also CA 13-16R; 121; CANR 23;
DLB 4, 9, 102

Wesker, Arnold   1932- .. **CLC 3, 5, 42; DAB**
See also CA 1-4R; CAAS 7; CANR 1, 33;
CDBLB 1960 to Present; DAM DRAM;
DLB 13; MTCW

Wesley, Richard (Errol)   1945- .... **CLC 7**
See also BW 1; CA 57-60; CANR 27;
DLB 38

Wessel, Johan Herman   1742-1785 .... **LC 7**

West, Anthony (Panther)
1914-1987 .... **CLC 50**
See also CA 45-48; 124; CANR 3, 19;
DLB 15

West, C. P.
See Wodehouse, P(elham) G(renville)

West, (Mary) Jessamyn
1902-1984 .... **CLC 7, 17**
See also CA 9-12R; 112; CANR 27; DLB 6;
DLBY 84; MTCW; SATA-Obit 37

West, Morris L(anglo)   1916- ..... **CLC 6, 33**
See also CA 5-8R; CANR 24, 49; MTCW

West, Nathanael
1903-1940 ..... **TCLC 1, 14, 44; SSC 16**
See also CA 104; 125; CDALB 1929-1941;
DLB 4, 9, 28; MTCW

West, Owen
See Koontz, Dean R(ay)

West, Paul   1930- .... **CLC 7, 14**
See also CA 13-16R; CAAS 7; CANR 22;
DLB 14; INT CANR-22

West, Rebecca   1892-1983 .. **CLC 7, 9, 31, 50**
See also CA 5-8R; 109; CANR 19; DLB 36;
DLBY 83; MTCW

Westall, Robert (Atkinson)
1929-1993 .... **CLC 17**
See also AAYA 12; CA 69-72; 141;
CANR 18; CLR 13; JRDA; MAICYA;
SAAS 2; SATA 23, 69; SATA-Obit 75

Westlake, Donald E(dwin)
1933- .... **CLC 7, 33**
See also CA 17-20R; CAAS 13; CANR 16,
44; DAM POP; INT CANR-16

Westmacott, Mary
See Christie, Agatha (Mary Clarissa)

Weston, Allen
See Norton, Andre

Wetcheek, J. L.
See Feuchtwanger, Lion

Wetering, Janwillem van de
See van de Wetering, Janwillem

Wetherell, Elizabeth
See Warner, Susan (Bogert)

Whale, James   1889-1957 .... **TCLC 63**

Whalen, Philip   1923- .... **CLC 6, 29**
See also CA 9-12R; CANR 5, 39; DLB 16

Wharton, Edith (Newbold Jones)
1862-1937 ...... **TCLC 3, 9, 27, 53; DA;
DAB; DAC; SSC 6; WLC**
See also CA 104; 132; CDALB 1865-1917;
DAM MST, NOV; DLB 4, 9, 12, 78;
DLBD 13; MTCW

Wharton, James
See Mencken, H(enry) L(ouis)

Wharton, William (a pseudonym)
.... **CLC 18, 37**
See also CA 93-96; DLBY 80; INT 93-96

Wheatley (Peters), Phillis
1754(?)-1784 .... **LC 3; BLC; DA; DAC;
PC 3; WLC**
See also CDALB 1640-1865; DAM MST,
MULT, POET; DLB 31, 50

Wheelock, John Hall   1886-1978 .... **CLC 14**
See also CA 13-16R; 77-80; CANR 14;
DLB 45

White, E(lwyn) B(rooks)
1899-1985 .... **CLC 10, 34, 39**
See also AITN 2; CA 13-16R; 116;
CANR 16, 37; CLR 1, 21; DAM POP;
DLB 11, 22; MAICYA; MTCW;
SATA 2, 29; SATA-Obit 44

White, Edmund (Valentine III)
1940- .... **CLC 27**
See also AAYA 7; CA 45-48; CANR 3, 19,
36; DAM POP; MTCW

White, Patrick (Victor Martindale)
1912-1990 .. **CLC 3, 4, 5, 7, 9, 18, 65, 69**
See also CA 81-84; 132; CANR 43; MTCW

White, Phyllis Dorothy James   1920-
See James, P. D.
See also CA 21-24R; CANR 17, 43;
DAM POP; MTCW

White, T(erence) H(anbury)
1906-1964 .... **CLC 30**
See also CA 73-76; CANR 37; DLB 160;
JRDA; MAICYA; SATA 12

White, Terence de Vere
1912-1994 . . . . **CLC 49**
See also CA 49-52; 145; CANR 3

White, Walter F(rancis)
1893-1955 . . . . **TCLC 15**
See also White, Walter
See also BW 1; CA 115; 124; DLB 51

White, William Hale 1831-1913
See Rutherford, Mark
See also CA 121

Whitehead, E(dward) A(nthony)
1933- . . . . **CLC 5**
See also CA 65-68

Whitemore, Hugh (John) 1936- . . . . . **CLC 37**
See also CA 132; INT 132

Whitman, Sarah Helen (Power)
1803-1878 . . . . **NCLC 19**
See also DLB 1

Whitman, Walt(er)
1819-1892 . . . . . **NCLC 4, 31; DA; DAB;
DAC; PC 3; WLC**
See also CDALB 1640-1865; DAM MST,
POET; DLB 3, 64; SATA 20

Whitney, Phyllis A(yame) 1903- . . . . **CLC 42**
See also AITN 2; BEST 90:3; CA 1-4R;
CANR 3, 25, 38; DAM POP; JRDA;
MAICYA; SATA 1, 30

Whittemore, (Edward) Reed (Jr.)
1919- . . . . **CLC 4**
See also CA 9-12R; CAAS 8; CANR 4;
DLB 5

Whittier, John Greenleaf
1807-1892 . . . . **NCLC 8, 57**
See also CDALB 1640-1865; DAM POET;
DLB 1

Whittlebot, Hernia
See Coward, Noel (Peirce)

Wicker, Thomas Grey 1926-
See Wicker, Tom
See also CA 65-68; CANR 21, 46

Wicker, Tom . . . . **CLC 7**
See also Wicker, Thomas Grey

Wideman, John Edgar
1941- . . . . **CLC 5, 34, 36, 67; BLC**
See also BW 2; CA 85-88; CANR 14, 42;
DAM MULT; DLB 33, 143

Wiebe, Rudy (Henry)
1934- . . . . **CLC 6, 11, 14; DAC**
See also CA 37-40R; CANR 42;
DAM MST; DLB 60

Wieland, Christoph Martin
1733-1813 . . . . **NCLC 17**
See also DLB 97

Wiene, Robert 1881-1938 . . . . **TCLC 56**

Wieners, John 1934- . . . . **CLC 7**
See also CA 13-16R; DLB 16

Wiesel, Elie(zer)
1928- . . . . . . **CLC 3, 5, 11, 37; DA; DAB;
DAC**
See also AAYA 7; AITN 1; CA 5-8R;
CAAS 4; CANR 8, 40; DAM MST,
NOV; DLB 83; DLBY 87; INT CANR-8;
MTCW; SATA 56

Wiggins, Marianne 1947- . . . . **CLC 57**
See also BEST 89:3; CA 130

Wight, James Alfred 1916-
See Herriot, James
See also CA 77-80; SATA 55;
SATA-Brief 44

Wilbur, Richard (Purdy)
1921- . . . **CLC 3, 6, 9, 14, 53; DA; DAB;
DAC**
See also CA 1-4R; CABS 2; CANR 2, 29;
DAM MST, POET; DLB 5;
INT CANR-29; MTCW; SATA 9

Wild, Peter 1940- . . . . **CLC 14**
See also CA 37-40R; DLB 5

Wilde, Oscar (Fingal O'Flahertie Wills)
1854(?)-1900 . . . . **TCLC 1, 8, 23, 41; DA;
DAB; DAC; SSC 11; WLC**
See also CA 104; 119; CDBLB 1890-1914;
DAM DRAM, MST, NOV; DLB 10, 19,
34, 57, 141, 156; SATA 24

Wilder, Billy . . . . **CLC 20**
See also Wilder, Samuel
See also DLB 26

Wilder, Samuel 1906-
See Wilder, Billy
See also CA 89-92

Wilder, Thornton (Niven)
1897-1975 . . . . . . **CLC 1, 5, 6, 10, 15, 35,
82; DA; DAB; DAC; DC 1; WLC**
See also AITN 2; CA 13-16R; 61-64;
CANR 40; DAM DRAM, MST, NOV;
DLB 4, 7, 9; MTCW

Wilding, Michael 1942- . . . . **CLC 73**
See also CA 104; CANR 24, 49

Wiley, Richard 1944- . . . . **CLC 44**
See also CA 121; 129

Wilhelm, Kate . . . . **CLC 7**
See also Wilhelm, Katie Gertrude
See also CAAS 5; DLB 8; INT CANR-17

Wilhelm, Katie Gertrude 1928-
See Wilhelm, Kate
See also CA 37-40R; CANR 17, 36; MTCW

Wilkins, Mary
See Freeman, Mary Eleanor Wilkins

Willard, Nancy 1936- . . . . **CLC 7, 37**
See also CA 89-92; CANR 10, 39; CLR 5;
DLB 5, 52; MAICYA; MTCW;
SATA 37, 71; SATA-Brief 30

Williams, C(harles) K(enneth)
1936- . . . . **CLC 33, 56**
See also CA 37-40R; DAM POET; DLB 5

Williams, Charles
See Collier, James L(incoln)

Williams, Charles (Walter Stansby)
1886-1945 . . . . **TCLC 1, 11**
See also CA 104; DLB 100, 153

Williams, (George) Emlyn
1905-1987 . . . . **CLC 15**
See also CA 104; 123; CANR 36;
DAM DRAM; DLB 10, 77; MTCW

Williams, Hugo 1942- . . . . **CLC 42**
See also CA 17-20R; CANR 45; DLB 40

Williams, J. Walker
See Wodehouse, P(elham) G(renville)

Williams, John A(lfred)
1925- . . . . **CLC 5, 13; BLC**
See also BW 2; CA 53-56; CAAS 3;
CANR 6, 26, 51; DAM MULT; DLB 2,
33; INT CANR-6

Williams, Jonathan (Chamberlain)
1929- . . . . **CLC 13**
See also CA 9-12R; CAAS 12; CANR 8;
DLB 5

Williams, Joy 1944- . . . . **CLC 31**
See also CA 41-44R; CANR 22, 48

Williams, Norman 1952- . . . . **CLC 39**
See also CA 118

Williams, Sherley Anne
1944- . . . . **CLC 89; BLC**
See also BW 2; CA 73-76; CANR 25,
DAM MULT, POET; DLB 41;
INT CANR-25; SATA 78

Williams, Shirley
See Williams, Sherley Anne

Williams, Tennessee
1911-1983 . . . . . **CLC 1, 2, 5, 7, 8, 11, 15,
19, 30, 39, 45, 71; DA; DAB; DAC;
DC 4; WLC**
See also AITN 1, 2; CA 5-8R; 108;
CABS 3; CANR 31; CDALB 1941-1968;
DAM DRAM, MST; DLB 7; DLBD 4;
DLBY 83; MTCW

Williams, Thomas (Alonzo)
1926-1990 . . . . **CLC 14**
See also CA 1-4R; 132; CANR 2

Williams, William C.
See Williams, William Carlos

Williams, William Carlos
1883-1963 . . . . **CLC 1, 2, 5, 9, 13, 22, 42,
67; DA; DAB; DAC; PC 7**
See also CA 89-92; CANR 34;
CDALB 1917-1929; DAM MST, POET;
DLB 4, 16, 54, 86; MTCW

Williamson, David (Keith) 1942- . . . . **CLC 56**
See also CA 103; CANR 41

Williamson, Ellen Douglas 1905-1984
See Douglas, Ellen
See also CA 17-20R; 114; CANR 39

Williamson, Jack . . . . **CLC 29**
See also Williamson, John Stewart
See also CAAS 8; DLB 8

Williamson, John Stewart 1908-
See Williamson, Jack
See also CA 17-20R; CANR 23

Willie, Frederick
See Lovecraft, H(oward) P(hillips)

Willingham, Calder (Baynard, Jr.)
1922-1995 . . . . **CLC 5, 51**
See also CA 5-8R; 147; CANR 3; DLB 2,
44; MTCW

Willis, Charles
See Clarke, Arthur C(harles)

Willy
See Colette, (Sidonie-Gabrielle)

Willy, Colette
See Colette, (Sidonie-Gabrielle)

Wilson, A(ndrew) N(orman) 1950- . . **CLC 33**
See also CA 112; 122; DLB 14, 155

Wilson, Angus (Frank Johnstone)
  1913-1991 .. **CLC 2, 3, 5, 25, 34; SSC 21**
  See also CA 5-8R; 134; CANR 21; DLB 15,
  139, 155; MTCW

Wilson, August
  1945- .... **CLC 39, 50, 63; BLC; DA;**
                              DAB; DAC; DC 2
  See also AAYA 16; BW 2; CA 115; 122;
  CANR 42; DAM DRAM, MST, MULT;
  MTCW

Wilson, Brian 1942- .... **CLC 12**

Wilson, Colin 1931- .... **CLC 3, 14**
  See also CA 1-4R; CAAS 5; CANR 1, 22,
  33; DLB 14; MTCW

Wilson, Dirk
  See Pohl, Frederik

Wilson, Edmund
  1895-1972 .... **CLC 1, 2, 3, 8, 24**
  See also CA 1-4R; 37-40R; CANR 1, 46;
  DLB 63; MTCW

Wilson, Ethel Davis (Bryant)
  1888(?)-1980 .... **CLC 13; DAC**
  See also CA 102; DAM POET; DLB 68;
  MTCW

Wilson, John 1785-1854......... **NCLC 5**

Wilson, John (Anthony) Burgess 1917-1993
  See Burgess, Anthony
  See also CA 1-4R; 143; CANR 2, 46; DAC;
  DAM NOV; MTCW

Wilson, Lanford 1937- .... **CLC 7, 14, 36**
  See also CA 17-20R; CABS 3; CANR 45;
  DAM DRAM; DLB 7

Wilson, Robert M. 1944- .... **CLC 7, 9**
  See also CA 49-52; CANR 2, 41; MTCW

Wilson, Robert McLiam 1964- ..... **CLC 59**
  See also CA 132

Wilson, Sloan 1920- .... **CLC 32**
  See also CA 1-4R; CANR 1, 44

Wilson, Snoo 1948-............... **CLC 33**
  See also CA 69-72

Wilson, William S(mith) 1932- ..... **CLC 49**
  See also CA 81-84

Winchilsea, Anne (Kingsmill) Finch Counte
  1661-1720 .... **LC 3**

Windham, Basil
  See Wodehouse, P(elham) G(renville)

Wingrove, David (John) 1954-...... **CLC 68**
  See also CA 133

Winters, Janet Lewis .... **CLC 41**
  See also Lewis, Janet
  See also DLBY 87

Winters, (Arthur) Yvor
  1900-1968 .... **CLC 4, 8, 32**
  See also CA 11-12; 25-28R; CAP 1;
  DLB 48; MTCW

Winterson, Jeanette 1959-......... **CLC 64**
  See also CA 136; DAM POP

Winthrop, John 1588-1649.......... **LC 31**
  See also DLB 24, 30

Wiseman, Frederick 1930-......... **CLC 20**

Wister, Owen 1860-1938 .... **TCLC 21**
  See also CA 108; DLB 9, 78; SATA 62

Witkacy
  See Witkiewicz, Stanislaw Ignacy

Witkiewicz, Stanislaw Ignacy
  1885-1939 .... **TCLC 8**
  See also CA 105

Wittgenstein, Ludwig (Josef Johann)
  1889-1951 .... **TCLC 59**
  See also CA 113

Wittig, Monique 1935(?)-.......... **CLC 22**
  See also CA 116; 135; DLB 83

Wittlin, Jozef 1896-1976 .... **CLC 25**
  See also CA 49-52; 65-68; CANR 3

Wodehouse, P(elham) G(renville)
  1881-1975 ... **CLC 1, 2, 5, 10, 22; DAB;**
                              DAC; SSC 2
  See also AITN 2; CA 45-48; 57-60;
  CANR 3, 33; CDBLB 1914-1945;
  DAM NOV; DLB 34, 162; MTCW;
  SATA 22

Woiwode, L.
  See Woiwode, Larry (Alfred)

Woiwode, Larry (Alfred) 1941-... **CLC 6, 10**
  See also CA 73-76; CANR 16; DLB 6;
  INT CANR-16

Wojciechowska, Maia (Teresa)
  1927- .... **CLC 26**
  See also AAYA 8; CA 9-12R; CANR 4, 41;
  CLR 1; JRDA; MAICYA; SAAS 1;
  SATA 1, 28, 83

Wolf, Christa 1929- .... **CLC 14, 29, 58**
  See also CA 85-88; CANR 45; DLB 75;
  MTCW

Wolfe, Gene (Rodman) 1931-....... **CLC 25**
  See also CA 57-60; CAAS 9; CANR 6, 32;
  DAM POP; DLB 8

Wolfe, George C. 1954-........... **CLC 49**
  See also CA 149

Wolfe, Thomas (Clayton)
  1900-1938 ..... **TCLC 4, 13, 29, 61; DA;**
                              DAB; DAC; WLC
  See also CA 104; 132; CDALB 1929-1941;
  DAM MST, NOV; DLB 9, 102; DLBD 2;
  DLBY 85; MTCW

Wolfe, Thomas Kennerly, Jr. 1931-
  See Wolfe, Tom
  See also CA 13-16R; CANR 9, 33;
  DAM POP; INT CANR-9; MTCW

Wolfe, Tom .... **CLC 1, 2, 9, 15, 35, 51**
  See also Wolfe, Thomas Kennerly, Jr.
  See also AAYA 8; AITN 2; BEST 89:1;
  DLB 152

Wolff, Geoffrey (Ansell) 1937- ..... **CLC 41**
  See also CA 29-32R; CANR 29, 43

Wolff, Sonia
  See Levitin, Sonia (Wolff)

Wolff, Tobias (Jonathan Ansell)
  1945-.................... **CLC 39, 64**
  See also AAYA 16; BEST 90:2; CA 114;
  117; CAAS 22; DLB 130; INT 117

Wolfram von Eschenbach
  c. 1170-c. 1220 .... **CMLC 5**
  See also DLB 138

Wolitzer, Hilma 1930-............ **CLC 17**
  See also CA 65-68; CANR 18, 40;
  INT CANR-18; SATA 31

Wollstonecraft, Mary 1759-1797...... **LC 5**
  See also CDBLB 1789-1832; DLB 39, 104,
  158

Wonder, Stevie .... **CLC 12**
  See also Morris, Steveland Judkins

Wong, Jade Snow 1922-........... **CLC 17**
  See also CA 109

Woodcott, Keith
  See Brunner, John (Kilian Houston)

Woodruff, Robert W.
  See Mencken, H(enry) L(ouis)

Woolf, (Adeline) Virginia
  1882-1941 ...... **TCLC 1, 5, 20, 43, 56;**
                      DA; DAB; DAC; SSC 7; WLC
  See also CA 104; 130; CDBLB 1914-1945;
  DAM MST, NOV; DLB 36, 100, 162;
  DLBD 10; MTCW

Woollcott, Alexander (Humphreys)
  1887-1943 .... **TCLC 5**
  See also CA 105; DLB 29

Woolrich, Cornell 1903-1968....... **CLC 77**
  See also Hopley-Woolrich, Cornell George

Wordsworth, Dorothy
  1771-1855 .... **NCLC 25**
  See also DLB 107

Wordsworth, William
  1770-1850 .... **NCLC 12, 38; DA; DAB;**
                              DAC; PC 4; WLC
  See also CDBLB 1789-1832; DAM MST,
  POET; DLB 93, 107

Wouk, Herman 1915-......... **CLC 1, 9, 38**
  See also CA 5-8R; CANR 6, 33;
  DAM NOV, POP; DLBY 82;
  INT CANR-6; MTCW

Wright, Charles (Penzel, Jr.)
  1935- .... **CLC 6, 13, 28**
  See also CA 29-32R; CAAS 7; CANR 23,
  36; DLB 165; DLBY 82; MTCW

Wright, Charles Stevenson
  1932- .... **CLC 49; BLC 3**
  See also BW 1; CA 9-12R; CANR 26;
  DAM MULT, POET; DLB 33

Wright, Jack R.
  See Harris, Mark

Wright, James (Arlington)
  1927-1980 .... **CLC 3, 5, 10, 28**
  See also AITN 2; CA 49-52; 97-100;
  CANR 4, 34; DAM POET; DLB 5;
  MTCW

Wright, Judith (Arandell)
  1915- .... **CLC 11, 53; PC 14**
  See also CA 13-16R; CANR 31; MTCW;
  SATA 14

Wright, L(aurali) R. 1939-........ **CLC 44**
  See also CA 138

Wright, Richard (Nathaniel)
  1908-1960 .... **CLC 1, 3, 4, 9, 14, 21, 48,**
             74; BLC; DA; DAB; DAC; SSC 2; WLC
  See also AAYA 5; BW 1; CA 108;
  CDALB 1929-1941; DAM MST, MULT,
  NOV; DLB 76, 102; DLBD 2; MTCW

Wright, Richard B(ruce) 1937- ...... **CLC 6**
  See also CA 85-88; DLB 53

Wright, Rick 1945-............... **CLC 35**

Wright, Rowland
  See Wells, Carolyn

Wright, Stephen Caldwell 1946- .... **CLC 33**
  See also BW 2

Literary Criticism Series
Cumulative Topic Index

This index lists all topic entries in Gale's *Classical and Medieval Literature Criticism, Contemporary Literary Criticism, Literature Criticism from 1400 to 1800, Nineteenth-Century Literature Criticism,* and *Twentieth-Century Literary Criticism.*

Topic Index

Topic Index

Topic Index

TCLC Cumulative Nationality Index

Nationality Index

TCLC 64 Title Index

Title Index